IRELAND'S AVIATOR HEROES OF WORLD WAR II

By John C. Hewitt

Published by John Cecil Hewitt

This is the first edition, printed in 2003.

Printed by The Northern Whig Limited

Published by John Cecil Hewitt

ISBN No. 0-9545965-0-1

DEDICATION

In August 1945, the Second World War, in which tens of millions of people had died worldwide, ended.

I would like to dedicate this book to the memory of all of the brave Irishmen and women who served in the Royal Air Force, 1,352 of whom gave their lives for their country during the Second World War.

Their bravery is legendary; their courage is unsurpassed and will be remembered as long as history is recorded. My own personal admiration and respect for them is timeless.

I would also like to dedicate this collection of stories to those who made it home from the war and have made their last flight over the past 56 years. Many of them I have had the honour and pleasure to know personally.

In conclusion, I would like to dedicate it to all those who still now survive.

Sir Winston Churchill paid these two tributes to the people of Northern Ireland at the end of the Second World War:

"Never in the Field of human conflict was so much owed by so many to so few."

"But for the Loyalty of Northern Ireland and its devotion to what has now become the cause of thirty Governments or nations, we should now have been confronted with slavery and death and the light which now shines so strongly throughout the world would have been quenched."

These biographies tell their own stories.

This book is the product of 22 years work, and all the proceeds that I receive for it will be donated to the Royal Air Force Association.

John C. Hewitt

TABLE OF CONTENTS

ACKNOWLEDGEMENTS

Firstly I would like to thank my devoted wife Pat, for her help and encouragement when it was most needed, and who for years has suffered my isolation and never once complained. My daughter Jennifer and husband Phillip, granddaughters Sophie and Eve. My son Johnathan and his wife Suzanne.

I would also extend my sincere thanks to the families of Air Crew, both past and present, who have very kindly withstood my numerous interviews and never ending questions for hours on end. I remain indebted.

The names of those who have helped me with this publication over the past 22 years would fill a book, but I feel that I must make a special mention of a few of them. **A very special thanks to Mr Jim Burgess without whose help this book would not have been published**. Air Vice Marshall AJ Stables, CBE FRAeS. Group Captain JMM Ponsonby, OBE ADC, RAF. Wing Commander KW MacKenzie, DFC AFC AE, for writing the Foreword. Squadron Leader NH Corry, DFC AE, for the beautiful poem he wrote in memory of his friends in the RAFVR. Squadron Leader Peter Brown, AFC. Mr Jack Graham, Pittsburgh Institute of Aeronautics (second Foreword).

Mrs Josephine Henshaw. Alderman Billy Ashe, Carrickfergus Borough Council Community Relations Unit. Mr John Davies, Director (RAFANI). Mrs ME Sloan. Mr RA Sterling. Mr RS Sterling. Mr Jack Woods. Sir Robert Porter. Mr John Simpson. The Ballymena, Larne, Omagh, Lisburn, Republic of Ireland Branches of the Royal Air Forces Association. The Comber, Finaghy & District, Magherafelt, Enniskillen and Newry Branches of the Royal British Legion. The 31 Group Royal Observer Corps.

My grateful thanks to Damien Maddalena (graphic designer) who brought this published work together; it would not have been possible without his dedication and professionalism.

In addition, I would like to thank Andrew Castles (web page), Anthony Bourke (IT advisor), Rhonda McMullan (proofreader), Mr George Carvell (Sales Executive, The Northern Whig), Mr Noel Lynch, Mr Geoffrey Salisbury, Mr Wally Carter, Mr Ron Marshall, Mr Roger Corry, Mr Harry Clarke, Mr Ron Shimmons, Mr RD Babington, DSC QC, Mrs Valerie Gorman, Mr Doug Cooper, Miss DG Wright, Mr Colin McCadden, Mrs Barbara Castle, WH Wright, Mr WJ Lawson, Mrs G Black, Alan and Sharon Caldwell, Ms Carol McMullan, Mrs Katie McLean.

"No biographer could have asked for better assistants."

'THE LADY IN WHITE'

There is one very special person whom I must mention in this book and that is Perla Siedle Gibson, better known to millions of Naval, Army and Air Force personnel as 'The Lady in White'.

Many of the people who I have met remember her with great admiration and affection. Perla Gibson was one of those very special people who gave up a lot of her time just to sing to the troopships, which sailed into Durban harbour in South Africa.

Perla was born in 1889 and had a son who was killed serving with the Black Watch Regiment in Italy 1944 and even though grief stricken on hearing the news of her only son, she met a ship coming into Durban harbour and sang, "We'll Meet Again". It is recorded that at least 400 convoys carrying six million serving personnel sailed into Durban between 1940 and 1971, and that Perla sang to at least half of them.

It is now known that she had 'inside' information, which came from the British Consulate in Durban, about when a convoy was coming into and when it would leave Durban Harbour. Some of the songs that she sang as she stood at the end of the harbour holding her megaphone were, "Land Of Hope And Glory", Jeannie With The Light Brown Hair", "I'll Walk Beside You", Will Ye No Come Back Again", "Its A Long Way To Tipperary", "Pack Up Your Troubles In Your Old Kit Bag". On one particular day she sang over 280 tunes.

She often went home with a permanent 'crick' in her neck from looking up at the ships, and would carry on singing until the ship was out of sight, just in case someone was still listening. Everyone who saw or heard Perla took courage from her. She is the only known civilian woman in naval history to whom the Ensign is lowered in salute by so many ships. In 1946 she came to England and was awarded a Certificate on Commendation by King George VI, and received many other awards from other Commonwealth countries worldwide. Perla is one of the few singers in history, who in their lifetime has achieved so universal a fame and is described so affectionately in more servicemens magazines than any other individual in World War II.

FOREWORD

By Wing Commander Kenneth William MacKenzie, DFC AFC AE FIMgt

Aviation in Ireland dates back to when Harry Ferguson of Austin Car and Ferguson Tractor fame; designed, built and finally flew his first aeroplane from Hillsborough County Down on 31st December 1909. Since then, followed by World War I in 1918 Irishmen have been 'air minded' in one way or another, Service or Civilian. In May 1925 No 502 Squadron was formed at Aldergrove as a Special Reserve Squadron manned by Irish Volunteers and Regular personnel. Initially equipped with the Vickers Vimy, Hyderabad and later Vickers Virginia night bombers for ten years. It then became a Day Squadron on Westland Wallace and Hawker Hinds. In 1937 it became a fully fledged Auxiliary Squadron, locally manned and assigned to Coastal Command on Avro Ansons, Armstrong Whitworth Whitleys and Handley Page Halifaxes. Operating long-range anti-submarine patrols being it credited with four destroyed and three damaged in World War II.

During these years air minded Irishmen had formed the Ulster Flying Club at Newtownards Airfield in County Down. Run by Airwork Limited the club was encouraged and sponsored by Lord Londonderry, Secretary of State for Air and local landowner. His daughter, Lady Mari Stewart became an enthusiastic initial pupil pilot and I was fortunate to obtain my Private Pilots Licence around the same time.

In 1938, with the threat of war looming ever nearer the Royal Air Force had to plan a rapid expansion. In Ulster No 502 Squadron was expanded and the Volunteer Reserve (VR) Pilot and Navigator rapid expansion scheme was initiated to meet the threat. Recognising the spirit of Ulster No 24 Elementary and Reserve Flying School was established at Sydenham Airport near Belfast and adjacent to the Short and Harland shipbuilding and aircraft factories. The school was equipped with Tiger Moth and Hawker variant aircraft and was commanded by Wing Commander Gauntlet with Flight Lieutenant Sloan as Chief Instructor. Staffed by Regular and Reserve personnel and Short & Harland engineers. This VR Unit rapidly grew to over 100 pupil Pilots and Navigators and became a well integrated and enthusiastic team of like-minded volunteers, I was proud to be one of them. From the outbreak of World War II, 3rd September 1939 all of us were absorbed into flying units in the RAF to be followed during the war by a continuous flow of volunteers, there being no conscription in Ulster. The Army and Navy benefited from various similar units in there before and throughout the war.

The contribution of all those concerned, Service and Civilian has never been fully recognised, or chronicled. This book, by John Hewitt, goes a long way to acknowledge the heroism, sacrifice and devotion to duty by the people of Ireland, which contributed to the final victory in World War II. It is hoped that more will follow so that those involved and those who gave their lives will never be forgotten. Their deeds have been painstakingly researched and recorded by John Hewitt as a fitting tribute to the freedom, which they gave us. I am honoured to have been asked to write this foreword and to have been one of them.

Wing Commander KW MacKenzie,
DFC AFC AE FIMgt

FOREWORD

By Mr Jack Graham, Chairman of the Pittsburgh Institute of Aeronautics.

What better way to pay homage to those who gave (in) immeasurable ways to protect and defend their country's precious freedoms than between (the) two covers of this book. Memories of the sacrifices attributable to the thousands of military aviators from the British Isles during World War II as well as World War I have begun to fade in recent generations. It is incumbent upon all who have personal memories and memorabilia from the war years to preserve and pass on to the present and future generations these historical treasures from what has been called "The Greatest Generation".

My father and grandfather contributed to the war effort by providing pilot training to hundreds of young British and Irishmen in the United States. A concept that seems to be known by only those who were students and those who were instructors. My Grandfather, Jock Graham was born in Bangor, County Down, Northern Ireland. He was a plumber by trade, but bad times forced Jock, his two brothers and sister, to immigrate to the United States in search of work. He settled in Pittsburgh, Pennsylvania where my father, Wm J (Bill) was born in 1903. After completing his education at Carnegie Institute of Technology, he joined his father in the Plumbing business in 1928.

Unfortunately, the depression began in 1929, which forced young Bill to look for supplementary income outside the plumbing business. He earned his license as a Flight Instructor in 1934 and in 1936 borrowed money in order to purchase a flying school just north of Pittsburgh. He named it Graham Aviation and set about the task of acquiring every aeronautical rating offered to a school by the then Civil Aeronautics Authority. When World War II began in Europe in 1939, the skies over Great Britain were less suitable for pilot training than in previous times due to enemy air activity.

Responding to the problem USAAF General 'Hap' Arnold instituted a civilian pilot training program under contract to the US Government which would provide primary pilot training to pilots from the United Kingdom prior to the US entry into the war. Graham Aviation was the first civilian contractor chosen from the scores of other contractors who could eventually establish USAAF primary flying schools in nearly every state in the country. The Graham Aviation Flag flew over the base headquarters at Southern Field in Americus, Georgia, where between the years of 1939 through 1942 nearly 1,800 young men from both England and Ireland learned their primary flying skills in the PT-17 Stearman bi-plane.

For his contribution to the war effort, Bill Graham was given the King's Medal for Service, awarded by King George VI in 1948. The award occupies a conspicuous space in my office and in my heart.

Jack Graham

'THE RAF VOLUNTEER RESERVE'

Young Men, little more than school boys,
Jousting with the Luftwaffe in the sky
To determine whose turn it is to die today.

If it's mine, I'll not have seen the wily one
That came at me from out of the sun
And set my world alight.

And then, how shall I fare?
I trust that you, so very far below,
Will never get to know the way of it.

Poem written by
Squadron Leader Noel Henry Corry, DFC AE RAF
(Retired)
Ex No 25 (F) and No 12 (HB) Squadrons

WARRANT OFFICER
RALPH HAROLD GIBSON ABERNETHY, DFC
ROYAL AIR FORCE NO. 1140272
WIRELESS OPERATOR/AIR GUNNER
NO. 44 AND 97 PATHFINDER FORCE SQUADRON

Harold Abernethy was born in Stewartstown in County Tyrone on the 16th June 1914 and was educated at Gortnagrig Primary School. On leaving school he was employed at the Moygashel Textile Factory, Messrs. Stevenson and Sons Ltd., in Dungannon as Quality Controller. He left the Moygashel factory and enlisted into the Royal Air Force on the 20th August 1941 as a wireless Operator/Air Gunner. His pay was just nine shillings per day (40p).

After completing his basic training in September 1942 he was posted to No2 Signals School (Air Operation Section). On the 9th September 1942 at 1405hrs he boarded a Dominie 5925 to start his wireless operator training. The aircraft was piloted by Wing Commander Greal and the exercise lasted for 1hr.30mins. On the 7th October he had his first flight in a Percival Proctor. His wireless operator training consisted of RX tuning and reception, DF loop, BK tuning, DF bearings and HC approaches. He successfully passed the course on the 16th October having accumulated 14hrs.20mins flying.

On the 1st November 1942 he was posted to No1 Air Gunnery School at Pembrey in South Wales were he completed the gunnery course on the Bristol Blenheim Revolving Browning Turret. He finished the course on the 2nd December with a quite acceptable 66% pass and the school's chief instructor added into his logbook that he was 'steady and reliable. His flying time at the course on Blenheims was 6hrs.25mins.

Early January 1943 saw Harold posted to No 29 OTU at Bruntingthorpe to start his operational training on Wellingtons and where he was to meet his new crew. His pilot was Squadron Leader Lynch who he was to remain with until the 24th January 1944. His first flight in a Wellington was on the 20th January with Pilot Officer Sharp as the Captain. They took off at 1120hrs in the morning along with Squadron Leader Lynch on a 40 minute familiarisation flight. Training continued at Bruntingthorpe until the 1st February when it moved to Woolfox Lodge near Leicester and made a second move

to North Luffenham, which was nearby. The course finished on March 31st.

His next and final move before joining an operational squadron was to 1654 Conversion Unit. where he converted from the twin engine unto the four engine aircraft.

Their first flight at the OTU was not in a Lancaster as they had thought, but in a Manchester. They took off at 1205hrs on the 7th May in Manchester 'H' that was captained by Squadron Leader Whamond and Squadron Leader Lynch as his second pilot. The air experience flight lasted for 2hrs.10mins. The Manchester training continued for two days

On the 9th June they had their first air experience flight in the mighty four engined Lancaster that was under the command of Pilot Officer Meaghel with Squadron Leader Lynch as his Second Pilot. Harold was in the Wireless Operators seat for the duration of the exercise. Squadron Leader Lynch took over the reins of the aircraft on the 11th May and continued to do so until the conversion course was completed by the end of May 1943.

Warrant Officer Abernethy had now completed a total of 133hrs.50mins flying training time.

Having now completed all the training that was required of them Squadron Leader Lynch and his crew were posted to No 44 (Rhodesia) Squadron which was based at Dunholme Lodge near Scampton in Lincolnshire and was equipped with Lancaster B.1s and 111s. No 44 Squadron RFC was formed at Hainault Farm in Essex on the 24th July 1917 as a Home Defence Squadron and gained the fame of pioneering the use of the Sopwith Camel for night operations. One of its early commanding officers was none other than (then) Major A.T. Harris, later to become Marshal of the Royal Air Force Sir Arthur Harris.

At the outbreak of the Second World War another famous airman Wing Commander J.N. Boothman, winner of the famous Schneider Trophy, commanded the squadron. The squadron also enjoyed the distinction of having on its strength, two recipients of the supreme award for valour, the Victoria Cross. Wing Commander R.A.B. Learoyd and Wing Commander J.D. Nettleton. Both became Commanding Officers of 44 Squadron.

Wing Commander Nettleton VC was awarded the honour on the 17th April 1942 when he carried out a roof top attack on Augsburg. Harold actually flew with Wing Commander Nettleton on an 'air test' on the 20th June 1943.

Squadron Leader Lynch took over command of 'A' Flight and their first operation was to Bochum on the 12th June 1943. They carried out a further sixteen operations with 44 Squadron to Cologne, Krefeld, Elderfeld, Gelsen Kirken, Turin, Nuremburg, Milan, Berlin (3), Munchen Gladbach, Hanover, Kassel and Modane.

Their last operation with the squadron was to Berlin on the 18th November 1943.

After completing 17 Operations with 44 Squadron, Harold and the crew were posted to 97 Squadron in January 1944. The squadron was based at Bourn in Cambridgeshire at that time but moved to Coningsby in Lincolnshire to join No 8 Pathfinder Force Group and soon became a 'Marker' squadron. Their first operation with the squadron was on the 27th January 1944 to bomb Berlin. They took off in Lancaster 'D' at 1110hrs. The return trip took 7hrs.50mins. They bombed Berlin the following night and again on the 30th.

In all Warrant Officer Harold Abernethy carried out 55 high risk operations with Squadron Leader Lynch marking important targets.

I have listed some of these high-risk targets: Stuttgart (Bosh Works & Daimler Benz Motor Works), Frankfurt (general), Berlin (Waffen SS barracks), Aachen (general), La Chapelle (Railway), Brunswick (general), and Munich.

June 5th 1944: St Pierre Du Mont (coastal batteries), Argentan (railways), Etampes (bBridge), Poiters (railways), Gelsenkirchen (Nordstern Synthetic Oil Plant), Creil, Caument, Givors, Stuttgart, Bremerhaven, Munster (aqueduct), Bergen (U-boat pens), Karls Ruhr, Dortmund Emms Canal, Harburg (Rhenania - Ossag Oil Refinery), Graaven Horst, Trondheim (U-boat pens), Oslo Fiord (To bomb German Cruiser 'Koln'), Seigen PBM (railway station), Rositz (oil refinery), Horton (U-boat base on Oslo Ford), and Bohlen (synthetic oil plant).

Warrant Officer Abernethy's last Operation of the war was on the 7th April 1945 when his aircraft Lancaster 'P' took off to bomb the Benzol Plant at Molbis (near Leipzig).

Warrant Officer Harold Abernethy was awarded his Pathfinder badge in May 1945 by the officer commanding Pathfinder Force. He had now completed a total of 72 operations over enemy territory 17 with 44 Squadron and 55 with 97 Pathfinder Squadron.

On the 17th November 1945, Warrant Officer Ralph Harold Gibson Abernethy was awarded the Distinguished Flying Cross and the citation reads:

> Warrant Officer Abernethy has completed a large number of operational sorties, the majority of which have been flown with a Pathfinder Force. He has attacked many of the most heavily defended targets, including Berlin. Cologne, Gelsen Kirchen, Munich, Brunswick and Bremen. He took part in many of the pre-invasion attacks against transports in France and the Low Countries. As wireless operator his expert knowledge has been invaluable. On one occasion during an attack against Hamburg, some of the equipment failed as the aircraft was running up to the target. With great presence of mind this Warrant Officer effected repairs in time to enable a successful attack to be completed. Warrant Officer Abernethy has always shown, courage, high technical skill, and presence of mind in the face of the enemy.

Like many more before him, and many after him he received his award by post with a letter inside signed by the King, which reads:

> I greatly regret that I am unable to give you personally the award, which you so well earned. I now send it to you with my congratulations and my best wishes for your future happiness.
>
> Signed
> George R.I.

The reason so many of these awards were posted out to their recipients was, by the end of the war the King had personally presented more than 44,000 decorations and still had to confer over 55,000 decorations.

The King's desire was to present these personally, but it was impossible to do so. Most were posted out but he did continue to hand medals awarded to those who fell in action before they could receive them.

With the war almost over Warrant Officer Abernethy was taken off operational duties and was posted to 1381 Transport Conversion Unit. Here he was to convert onto the Douglas DC3 (Dakota) which paved the way for him to join transport command. The course lasted for two months. On completion of the conversion course he was posted to 271 Squadron at Broadwell, which was sited between Swindon and Oxford. 271 Squadron had a distinguished career during the war with coastal and ferry commands. It flew many Entertainments National Service Association (ENSA) shows around the country and it began airborne glider towing and paratroop dropping in 1944 and later flew Operation Tonga which was dropping 165 men of the third Para into France. On D - Day itself fifteen Dakotas from 217 Squadron towed Horsa Gliders to Landing Zone 'N' (LZ-N) and overnight supplied the troops with much needed supplies. At the end of the war in Europe 271 Squadron began flying to open new air-routes in Europe.

Harold flew with the squadron locally from the 10th January until the 15th February 1946, mostly carrying out training and air testing aircraft.

He left 271 Squadron in March to join 525 Squadron at Membury as a wireless operator. By this time the squadron was now operating mail and newspaper flights to and from the Continent between Membury, Buckenburg, Schleswig and Brussels. His last flight with the RAF as a wireless operator was on the 31st March 1946 when he flew a one hour flight to Lyneham with Flight Lieutenant Forteith in Dakota Code 234. At the end of April Harold was informed that he was to be released from the RAF.

An internal return and receipt form which I had on loan from his daughter Trudy showed that he returned his equipment to the station stores at Membury. On May 1st 1946 Warrant Officer Harold Gibson Abernethy proceeded to No 104 Personnel Despatch Centre (PDC) at Henesford where he was given 56 days leave that would take him up to his actual release date from the RAF which was the 26th June 1946.

He arrived back in Belfast on the 1st Anniversary of D-Day and said, "There was a great feeling of rejoicing in the city as most people expected that at this stage. I met up with some friends and that night I took part in some street parties that were being held all over the City. The next day I came home to Cookstown to meet my family and attend a function, everyone was delighted that the war in Europe had finally ended."

He was immediately reinstated at the Moygashel Factory in Dungannon and on the 15th August he was married. He left the Moygashel Factory to join the Northern Ireland Civil Service in Dungannon and Omagh and he very soon worked his way up the ladder and became head of the Ministry of Labour (Local Office) at Netherly House in Belfast. On his retirement from the Civil Service (and as he was not one for sitting around), he was employed by Menary's of Dungannon and Cookstown, hanging and fitting curtains right up until he was almost 80 years of age and I have no doubt he would have continued on only for his doctor telling him it was time to stop.

Harold Abernethy also did sterling work with the British Legion as secretary of the welfare committee in Omagh and Cookstown. He holds the Gold Badge for Meritous Service. He was also Welfare Officer of the Royal Air Force Association for 20 years and holds the Gold Badge for Meritous Service and was also Wings Appeal Officer for the Cookstown area and gave up a lot of his time to the Poppy Day appeal. He was the Northern Ireland Civil Defence representative at the Remembrance Day parade at the Cenotaph in Whitehall in London. He had joined the Civil Defence in 1958 as a Signals Officer and instructor for three of the organisations divisions, Signals, Operations and Intelligence.

Sadly Warrant Officer Harold Ralph Gibson Abernethy DFC died in October 1997. A funeral service was held for him at Derryloran Parish Church on Saturday 18th October 1997. The Service was conducted by the Reverend Robert Boyd.

SERGEANT
SINGLETON WILSON ADAIR
ROYAL AIR FORCE NO. 749453
WIRELESS OPERATOR/AIR GUNNER
NO. 82 SQUADRON

KILLED IN ACTION 20TH MARCH 1941

Wilson Adair was born in Dublin on the 6th May 1918. On leaving school he became a trainee apprentice at the Jenny Mount Mill in Dublin.

Wilson joined the Royal Air Force on the 3rd March 1940 at the Clifton Street recruiting office in Belfast where he was selected as aircrew and became a Wireless Operator/Air Gunner. He was posted to the Padgate Receiving Centre near Liverpool in April were he was issued with his RAF uniform and then posted to an initial training wing where he carried out his basic training. On completion of his basic training he was then posted to the No 1 Signals School to start his wireless training. His first training flight was in a Westland Wallace (Code K3603) on the 30th September 1940.

The flight lasted for 50 minutes, and on the 1st October 1940 he flew a cross-country exercise in a Harvard (AT-6) (Code N7100) for 25 minutes. He successfully completed the wireless course on the 2nd October 1940. On the 7th October 1940 Wilson was posted to the No 1 Air Armament School at Manby where he completed his air gunnery training in Fairey Battles, Hawker Demons and Bristol Blenheims. His instructors were Polish and their names are: Leading Aircraftman Skrzypczak, Pilot Officer Sczodrowski, Flight Lieutenant Kolodynski and Flying Officer Syszkowski.

Wilson completed the air gunnery course on the 9th November 1940 with a pass mark of 84%. His total flying time was 15hrs.40mins. On successfully completing both his wireless and air gunners course, Wilson was awarded his Wireless Operator/Air Gunners Brevet and promoted to the rank of Sergeant.

Wilson's next posting was to the No 17 Operational Training Unit at Upwood near Peterborough where he was to meet his pilot, Sergeant Kelly, an Australian. They both joined the Unit's 'B' Flight and started their operational training. Wilson's Log Book shows that he completed an advanced wireless course at Upwood in an Avro Anson (Code L9570) before starting his operational training.

His operational training commenced on the 17th January 1941 in Bristol Blenheim (Code 5390) and was completed on the 23rd February 1941. Wilson's total flying hours were now 68hrs.05mins. On completion of their operational training, Wilson and Sergeant Kelly were posted to No 82 Squadron at Watton near Norfolk in early March 1941.

No 82 Squadron was formed at Doncaster in Yorkshire in January 1917, and from November 1917 until the end of the war, served as an Army CO-OP Unit. It was disbanded in 1919 and reformed as a Bomber Unit in 1937, and during the early part of the war was equipped with the Bristol Blenheim MK 1s, and played a prominent part in No Groups offensive against German shipping in the English Channel, North Sea and fringe targets on the Continent. On two occasions during the summer of 1940 the squadron was almost wiped out, but thanks to the exceptional determination of the squadrons commanding officer, Wing Commander 'The Earl of Brandon', it was reformed within 48 hours, and ready to fight again. The squadron moved to India in May 1942 where it was equipped with the American Vultee Vengeance dive bombers (The first RAF Squadron to be equipped with the Vengeance) to operate against the Japanese in Burma. In 1944 the squadron was re-equipped with the Mosquito F.B. to attack the Japanese, and in 1946 the squadron returned to RAF Benson. Sergeant Kelly and Wilson's first flight with 82 Squadron was on the 18th March 1941 when they took of in Blenheim (Code 5818) at 19.55 hours on a 'night' cross country exercise. Their flying time was 1hr.55mins. The next day, 19th March they took off at 1510hrs on a low flying exercise in Blenheim (Code 3604).

Wilson's third and last flight which took place on the 20th March 1941 is not entered in his flying log, but I can tell you what happened on that fatal day.

On the night of the 20th March 1941, Sergeant J.H. Kelly (Pilot, RAAF), Sergeant G.R. Wilson (Navigator, RNZAF) and Sergeant S.W. Adair (Air Gunner) took off from RAF Bodney at 1109hrs in Blenheim (Code R3604) UX-R. Their mission was to fly low and attack German shipping near the Dutch coast. While attacking shipping they were shot down by Minenraumboot 64 (Mine Sweeper 64) and crashed into the sea off the Dutch coast. Wilson's body was never found, and has no known grave, his colleagues Sergeant Kelly and Sergeant Wilson are both buried in Bergen op Zoom War Cemetery in Holland. Sergeant Singleton Wilson Adair is remembered on the Runnymede Memorial.

FLIGHT LIEUTENANT
JAMES BOUCHER AGNEW, AE
RAFVR NO. 133806
NO. 112 SQUADRON

Flight Lieutenant James Boucher Agnew was born in Belfast on the 2nd March 1920. He was educated at The Belfast College of Technology. On leaving school, he was employed by the Belfast Corporation Transport as a time keeper.

James always had a great desire to learn how to fly, so on the 24th February 1939 he decided to join the Royal Air Force Volunteer Reserve and became their 13th volunteer since forming.

Thirteen was an unlucky number for some, but proved very lucky for James during the war years to come. James started his RAF career at No 24 Elementary and Reserve Flying Training School that was based at Sydenham and was equipped with Tiger Moths and Hawker Harts.

His first 25-minute air experience flight was on the 26th February 1939 in Tiger Moth N6462 under the instruction of Flight Lieutenant Lindsay. On the 4th March Flight Lieutenant David Sloan, the schools chief flying instructor (CFI) took James up for a 30-minute flight to explain the effect of controls. James continued his training with Flight Lieutenant Sloan and Sergeant Lake through March and April. In the afternoon of 24th April James had his first solo check with Flight Lieutenant Sloan. They landed back at the airfield at 1620hrs and were given the 'thumbs up' by the CFI and off he went on his own for the first time landing back at the airfield 10 minutes later.

With war looming ever closer, James was called to full time service with the Royal Air Force, and he knew that his 44 hours flying training with the VR would stand him in good steed. Although James was called to full time service in September 1939, he had to wait until December until his posting came through for his initial training that took him to Hastings on the South Coast of England. They were also taken a short distance along the coast to St Lenards-on-Sea for different forms of training. His initial training finished at Hastings and St Lenards in May 1941. In the middle of May 1940 James was posted to No 8 Elementary & Reserve Flying Training School at Reading to start his flying training in Miles Magisters. His first

flight in the Magister was on the 27th May under the instruction of Sergeant Thompson and lasted 35 minutes.

On the 31st May the Schools chief flying instructor Squadron Leader Moir took James for a 30-minute instructional flight and on the 3rd June after receiving his first solo test with Flight Lieutenant Hooper flew Magister N3798 solo for 30 minutes. James continued training in the Magister until July 20th when he did his final test with the schools examining officer, Flying Officer Dale, and on the 21st July had his last flight at the school in Magister R1893. His flying time on Magisters was 80hrs.45mins the course finished on the 23rd July and he was assessed by the CFI as an 'average' pilot

In July 1940 Jim was posted to No 12 FTS that was based at Grantham, the school was equipped with Fairey Battles. Jim's first air experience flight in a Fairey Battle was on the 29th July and his instructor was Sergeant Chinnery. The flight lasted one hour. On the morning of the 31st July he was given his first solo test by Flight Lieutenant Butcher and after landing was given the go ahead to fly the aircraft solo. On August 1st while flying the Fairey Battle under the instruction of Sergeant Chinnery, Jim had his first 'lucky' prang when he had to make a forced landing due to engine failure.

During his training at Grantham and flying with another Ulsterman Lockington 'Lockie' Lilburn their wingtips touched, causing a large dent in Jim's aircraft. On landing Jim had to report this accident to the chief flying instructor Flight Lieutenant Butcher, he was not amused by this and gave both pilots a 'right rollicking'. His training continued through August, and on September 6th was awarded his Flying Wings. Jim had done exceptionally well at Grantham, his last flight with the school was on the 10th October and on the 12th the schools commanding officer gave him an 'above the average' assessment.

In October 1940 Jim was posted to No 6 OTU that was based at Sutton Bridge and was equipped with Hawker Hurricanes. He was very excited by the prospect of flying the Hurricane but was to be slightly disappointed when he was told he would be flying a Miles Master for a few days. His instructors were Squadron Leader Kelly and Flight Lieutenant Sing. Jim flew the Master on the 16th and on the 19th flew it solo.

October 20th, the day he had been waiting for had arrived. He climbed into the cockpit of Hawker Hurricane 2052 and flew it for 1hr.05mins. Sutton Bridge was covered with man made canals, making the area very good for low level training. One of his 'hairy' moments flying the Hurricane up one of these canals 'below ground level' when suddenly in front of him, he spotted high-tension cables. As he was 'motoring' along the canal he realised there was not time to pull up and fly over the cables, so he just flew under them. (I bet he did not report that one.)

Jim continued his operational training on Hurricanes until the 5th December when he was posted to his first operational squadron that was No 3 Squadron. His stay with this squadron was to be only for one week when he was posted to 260 Squadron at Skitten on the 13th December. No 260 Squadron was formed from a coastal reconnaissance flight at Westward Ho in August 1918, and served in this role until the 22nd February 1919, when it was disbanded. 260 was reformed as a Fighter Squadron at Castletown in Scotland on 22nd November 1940, primarily for the defence of Scapa Flow. The squadron did not receive its Hurricanes until the following month. Jim had the distinction of being the first pilot posted to the newly reformed squadron. His first flight was on the 15th December in Hurricane V.7158 being used to his new surroundings. Jim flew with the squadron every day, sometimes four times on the same day trying to get it up to scratch to become operational.

On the 22nd December 1940, Jim had his second 'lucky' escape when he had to force land P.3168 due to engine failure. Jim's logbook shows that he carried out his first operation with the squadron when he was 'scrambled' on the 4th January and again on the 6th, 9th, 12th, 20th, and 27th. Their task was dawn to dusk patrols protecting convoys.

February was quieter than January as he carried out just two operations, one on February 9th and the second on the 10th. On the 3rd March 1941 the squadron was moved to Drem for the purpose of protecting the city of Edinburgh. He was again operational on March 6th, 9th, 12th, 22nd, 30th, and on the 31st he led a flight of six Hurricanes fitted with long-range tanks on an 'anti-submarine patrol'. April was a very quiet month for the squadron flying only a few 'practice dogfights' and some 'formation flying'.

At the end of April the squadron was informed that it was being posted overseas and to make ready for the journey. On the 17th May the squadron that consisted of twelve Hurricanes was transported to Scapa Flow where they were hoisted aboard the aircraft carrier HMS Victorious, which was bound for Malta. Victorious arrived in Gibraltar early June, where HMS Ark Royal was waiting to transfer the cargo of Hurricanes onto her deck. As the Hurricanes could not land on the deck of an aircraft carrier, someone devised an ingenious method of transferring them to the Ark Royal. The flight decks of both carriers were positioned 'nose to nose' allowing the aircraft to be pushed from one deck to the other.

The Ark Royal sailed from Gibraltar with two squadrons of Hurricanes on board, arriving off Malta on the 14th June. The Hurricanes were refuelled and fitted with long-range tanks, although only three out of the six machine guns were armed because of the take off weight factor. Before taking off from the carrier, all the pilots had been briefed that if any emergency arose once they were airborne, they could not return to the carrier but were to ditch near a destroyer. Jim said that this was a really hairy exercise as it was the first time that Hurricanes had taken off from an aircraft carrier. He lined up his Hurricane Z4374 behind the squadron commanding officer, Squadron Leader CJ Mount, DFC and watched him take off, and disappear momentarily under the bow of the great carrier only to reappear again. All the aircraft got off the Ark Royal safely.

After take off they rendezvoused with a Lockheed Hudson that was to navigate the four hour flight to Halfar in Malta. During the trip they had to pass close to the island of Pantelleria that was occupied by the Italians, and were told to expect some sort of attack, but this did not materialise. On the morning of the 15th June, Jim and the squadron had taken off from Malta and set course for Mersa Matruh in Palestine.

The Hurricanes again were fitted with the long range tanks as the flight time from Malta to Mersa Matruh was to a long six hours. On their safe arrival at Mersa Matruh the Hurricane was refuelled and immediately took off for Abu Sueir in Egypt, this was a much shorter flight of 1hr.30mins. The squadron were rested here for two days and on the 18th June they took off again and headed for Haifa. On arrival at Haifa 260 Squadron was amalgamated with 450 Squadron where they flew ground-attack sorties in the Syrian campaign.

Jims first operation with the squadron from Haifa on the 20th June 1941 and was a recon flight to Damascus and Beyruth. The flight lasted 1hr.20mins.

On June 23rd Jim had his first "kill" while strafing an Italian Airfield.

His Log Book shows:

June 23rd   Hurricane Z7013
                Ground Strafing Italian Airfield 'Destroyed
                1 Potez'. Damaged two other aircraft

Jim carried out a further four dawn offensive patrols that took him to June 30th when the squadron was moved to Amman. On July 3rd while flying from Amman to Damascus to ground strafe an enemy airfield at Hamma Jim destroyed another Potez and damaged two twin-engined aircraft. On July 9th while ground strafing Aleppo airfield Jim destroyed one GR and damaged two aircraft. Jim explained to me that it was very difficult and dangerous to fly low in this type of terrain, so much so, they were all issued with 'Gouly Chits' in case of capture by the Jebel Druz. (I am sure most of the readers know why they were called Gouly Chits). On August 1st 260 Squadron was moved to Syria, its task was to protect Beyrouth, an Army Co-op Unit. It also took the offensive by attacking enemy armour, strafing enemy positions, and bomber escorts.

On the 12th August Jim was scrambled to intercept an unidentified aircraft, which turned out to be a Bristol Bombay transport aircraft. During the month of August things were quiet and this time was used to carry out some training with the Army Co-op Units, some practice scrambles and ground strafing technique were also carried out. The Royal Navy controlled all of 260 Squadrons operations and training.

By the end of September Jim had completed 36 operations with 260 Squadron that was more than one complete tour; it was now time for a rest.

On the 24th September 1941 Jim was posted to 71 MU, which was based at El-Basa in Palestine to become a test pilot. His duties with the MU were flight-testing aircraft that had just completed minor and major overhaul. The types of aircraft, which Jim tested, were Hawker Hurricane, Mohawk, Tomahawk, Harvard, and Gloster Gladiators. On the 14th November 1941 71 MU moved to Gordons Tree in Khartoum, Sudan. Here Jim's duties were very similar to thosewhich he had carried out at El-Basa. During his flight testing at Khartoum his aircraft was involved in three forced landings, two of which were due to engine failure. The third however nearly killed him. He was flight-testing a Tomahawk at 6,000ft when the aircraft suddenly without warning and for no apparent reason plunged nose down, with no response from the controls.

Jim struggled with the controls as the aircraft plummeted earthwards, and at zero feet the Tomahawk pulled out of its dive scraping along some camel thorns.

On the 1st May 1941 Jim was asked if he would like to fly a Lysander with Sergeant Woolfries from Gordons Tree to Adbara and then on to Carthago and back to base. He readily agreed and said it was a beautiful aircraft to fly. His last flight with 71 MU was on the 5th May when he flew alone to the summit of Carthago and back to base. He completed 247 hours test flying various types of aircraft with 71 MU. When you consider that each test flight varied from fifteen minutes to one hour. That constituted a hell of a lot of testing. Jim's log book entry for the 5th shows that the officer commanding 71(ME) OTU, RAF Wing Commander Ellis, gave Jim an assessment of 'above the average' as a test pilot.

112 Squadron Gambut, 2nd Operational Tour

May 1942 to March 1943. Towards the end of May 1942 Jim was posted to 112 (F) Squadron, which was based at Gambut and was equipped with Curtiss Mk1 Kittyhawks. This was to be the start of his second tour. The Squadron was commanded by a Squadron Leader B. Drake, DSO DFC & Bar.

Short history of 112 (F) Squadron

The Squadron was formed at Throwley on 30th July 1917, and was a home defence squadron during the First World War. It was equipped with Sopwith Pups, Camels, and towards the end of the conflict was re-equipped with Snipes. The squadron was disbanded 13th June 1919 and was reformed as a Fighter Squadron for service in the Middle East in May 1939. The squadron at that time was based at Helwan and was equipped with Gloster Gladiators and Gloster Gauntlets and in June 1941 was re-equipped with the Curtiss Tomahawk. Between June 1942 and the end of the war 112 squadron was equipped with Mk1a, 111, 1V, Kittyhawks and Mk 111, and 1V Mustangs. Jim started his 2nd operational tour with the 112 in May 1942 and his first flight with the squadron was on 29th May in Kittyhawk AL170 escorting 53 Repair and Salvage Unit to Sidi-Henish. Most of the operations that were carried out by Jim and the squadron were fighter bomber sorties. The Curtiss Kittyhawk could be equipped with 250lb bombs and it was soon found that the pilots could drop these bombs accurately on the enemy. When Rommel attempted an offensive at the end of May the squadron was very busy both carrying out interception and strafing raids on the Afrika Corps.

On the 28th June while returning from a fighter patrol Jim spotted a lone Wellington in the desert not to far from his base. He told a friend Flight Lieutenant Garton about this and they decided to investigate. Jim borrowed a couple of 'bods' who drove them out to where the Wellington was located and on close inspection of the bomber she looked intact and ready to fly. Jim and Flight Lieutenant Garton decided to fly the Wellington to LG 91 that was a code name for an airfield called Amriya.

On the 1st July 1942, Jim was flying Kittyhawk ET910 and was escorting a flight of Bostons when he was jumped by three Me109's. His starboard rudder control was shot away, the electrical system for his airscrew was U/S and his starboard wing and tail plane was severely damaged. Most serious of all was when a cannon shell exploded directly behind his seat causing him great pain right up until his death in 1997.

Yet, inspite of all this damage Jim managed to bring the aircraft back safely by hand pumping the undercarriage down. Unfortunately with his rudder control shot away his aircraft veered of the runway on landing.

On the 8th July 1942 Jim's logbook entry shows that he was flying Kittyhawk ET1024 on a bombing raid when he damaged a Me109 in a head on attack (this was confirmed by Pilot Officer Gardiner). On 31st July while leading six aircraft he attacked and bombed the German Panzer Headquarters.

On November 1st his log book entry shows that he was leading six aircraft on an Armed Recco, he attacked and destroyed 1 Junkers 87, two probably destroyed and one damaged. On the way back to base he was shot up by an Me109 forcing him to crash land just south of El-Alamein in a mine field.

Jim had to remain in his aircraft until the Army arrived to escort him safely out of the Mine Field. Once out of danger, he was driven back to base complete with parachute. On the 2nd November Jim was again leading six aircraft hoping for a breakthrough to El Alamein. His logbook entry for the 4th November 1942 shows that while returning from a bombing raid on Galal and Fuka, he attacked and damaged a Me109. This aircraft we now know after much research is none other than our own Black Six 'Gustav'.

Jim was now promoted as a Flight Commander with 112 Squadron.

His logbook shows that on December 10th 1942 he flew a captured Ju87d twice, his passengers were Flying Officer Eberle, and Pilot Officer Rhooes.

January 1943 through to March the squadron was kept fairly busy, a lot of Jim's time was taken up training new pilots. Jim's logbook shows that on the 1st and 2nd March he flew a captured Italian Savoia Macchetti with Squadron Leader Garton and Flight Sergeant Brown as his passengers. On March 2nd he flew the aircraft From El-Assa to Castel Benito and then on to Marble Arch.

On March 10th 1943, 112 Squadron celebrated its 200th victory, but during the same operations six of its gallant pilots failed to return. On the 29th March while on a bombing and strafing operation he attacked and damaged three enemy transports. Jim's last flight with 112 Squadron was on the 30th March 1943 flying Kittyhawk FR440-K. Ironically his log book entry reads "Show cancelled". Between May 1942 and March 1943 Jim had carried out an amazing 100 operations with the Squadron. He was credited with destroying 4 enemy aircraft; two probables destroyed, and 12 damaged. On the 31st March 1943 Jim's flying assessment by the then officer commanding 112 Squadron, Squadron Leader G.W. Garton was 'above the average' as a Fighter Pilot.

Having completed two tours of operations Jim was posted as officer commanding 239 Wing Training Flight that was based in Italy until January 1944.

In February 1944 Jim was posted back to the UK to take part in a special low-level attack instructors course, which was held at the Fighter Leader School at Milfield. The course lasted for a month. On April 6th Jim flew to Belfast to join 290 Squadron AACU. This unit was attached to the Radar Direction and Ranging Unit that

was run by the Naval Co-operation Unit. However this was to be an extremely short posting home for Jim, on the 9th April he was informed that he was being attached to 1606 Anti-Aircraft Co-op Unit which was based at Bodorgan in Anglesey. His duties there were towing a Drogue behind a Martinet so the anti-aircraft units could practice firing at it. On June 3rd his attachment ended and he was posted back to 290 Squadron target towing and practicing low-level bombing.

The target towing was carried out in Martinets, and the low-level bombing in Hawker Hurricanes Some of the local stations Jim visited were Sydenham, Long Kesh, and Bishops Court.

In January 1945 Jim was posted to No 2 Flying Instructors School at Montrose where he was to teach pilots advanced flying in Harvards and Oxfords. In April 1945 he was posted home again to Bishops Court in Northern Ireland where he was to become the Gas and Salvage Officer and was eventually demobbed from the Royal Air Force at the end of 1945. Jim returned to his employer the Belfast City Transport and became their chief engineering officer. He could not settle with the BCT so in 1946 he decided to become a teacher and was the very first student to enrol at the Larkfield Training College and eventually qualified as a teacher in art and crafts. Jim rejoined the Royal Air Force in 1950 and was soon posted to Fighter Control Station at Trimly Heath that was near to Felixstowe. His next posting was to Royal Air Force Station at Bawdsey were he took charge of 3502 Fighter Control Unit.

Jim transferred with 3502 Fighter Control Unit when it was moved to Bishops Court in Northern Ireland eventually finishing his Royal Air Force career at Edenmore that was the headquarters of Royal Air Force Northern Ireland. During his distinguished career Jim flew many different types of aircraft, Tiger Moth, Miles Magister, Fairey Battle, Miles Master, Hawker Hurricane, Hawker Hart, North American Harvard, Tomahawk, Mohawk, Kittyhawk, Gloster Gladiator Mk11, Lysander, Junkers JU88 (Stuka), Warhawk, Savoia-Marchetti, and Spitfire MVB. His total flying hours with the Royal Air Force was 1112 hrs.05mins. Jim left the Royal Air Force in 1957 and returned to teaching at Ashfield Boys High school on the Holywood Road in Belfast. He later joined the College of Art where he soon qualified to teach art at junior level. Last but not least he was appointed chief education officer with the Borstal and Northern Ireland Prison Service at Dundonald House, eventually retiring in 1982.

Jim was a member of the Aircrew Association Northern Ireland Branch. Sadly he died on the 29th July 1997 and is buried at Roselawn Cemetery.

FLIGHT LIEUTENANT
NORMAN GEOFFREY ALDERDICE, DFC
ROYAL AIR FORCE NO. 170402
PILOT
NO. 229, 94, 123 & 335 SQUADRONS

Norman Geoffrey Alderdice was born on 28th July 1919 in Drumaleen, Aldergrove, Newry and was the son of Mr & Mrs G. Walter Alderdice. He was educated at the Mourne Grange Prep School and entered Campbell College in Belfast in July 1936. He became a college prefect in 1937 and was a member of the College's 1st X1 (Cricket) 1937; 1st X1 (Hockey) 1938. He graduated to Queens University, where he studied medicine for two years. His heart was not in medicine but rather in flying, so he volunteered to join the Royal Air Force as a Pilot.

Norman Geoffrey Alderdice joined the RAF on the 30th September 1940 and was posted to No 6 Initial Training Wing at Aberystwyth on the west coast of Wales.

On completion of his initial training he went to 'A' Flight, No 7 EFTS at Desford near Leicester to start his elementary flying in DH-82s (Tiger Moths). His first air experience flight in the DH-82 was on the 16th December 1940 in N.9514, his instructor was a Flight Lieutenant Hyland. The flight lasted for 35 minutes.

He continued with his instructor carrying out medium turns, taking off into wind, power approaches, gliding approaches etc until the 1st January 1941 when he flew his first 10 minute solo in DH-82 (G-AECI) after nine hours tuition.

His second solo was on January 5th when he practiced some medium turns, take off into wind, powered approaches and landings and gliding approaches and landings.

He finished the course on 28th February 1941 and was assessed as 'average' as a pilot.

On the 16th March he was posted to No 17 EFTS at North Luffenham for one month and then on to No 15 Service Flying Training School at Kidlington for his link training.

On the 8th May Geoffrey was posted north to Scotland where he joined No 8 SFTS at Montrose to start training in the Miles Magister. His first flight in the 'Maggie' was on the 9th when he took to the air in T.8881 'R' carrying out one through to eight flying exercises.

He soloed on the type two days later. The 'Maggie' training was of course preparing him for the Hawker Hurricane Fighter. Training continued flying in the Magister practically every day until the afternoon of the 8th July when he climbed into the seat of Hurricane P2914 'U' and flew it for half an hour. He flew the Hurricane again on the 9th, 11th, 12th, 13th, 17th and 20th. The course finished on the 22nd July when he was posted to No55 OTU at Usworth.

Geoffrey arrived at Usworth on the 27th July and commenced his OTU training on the 2nd August starting with a test flight in a Magister with a Flight Lieutenant Royce. He flew a second test flight the next day with a Flight Lieutenant Slewwacki and from then on it was strictly flying Hurricane Mk1s.

His logbook shows that he flew a few sector reconnaissance flights in a Dominie and Master during the course. His OTU training consisted of low level aerobatics, formation flying, section attacks on sector, camera air, ground, air-to-air camera, aerobatics at 20,000ft, and cross country exercises.

He successfully completed the course on the 8th September 1941 when he was assessed by Wing Commander Ken Gough as 'average' as a fighter pilot. His total flying hours was now 183hrs.50mins.

Geoffrey's logbook shows that on the 15th September 1941 he was posted across to Northern Ireland where he joined 504 (F) Squadron at Ballyhalbert in County Down. Here he gained one week's experience on the squadrons Mk11b Hurricanes.

I suspect the reason for him being here was that he was given some home leave on finishing his OTU training and as his next posting was overseas to a Hurricane Mk11 squadron, it suited everyone to let him obtain some experience on the type here.

On his arrival back in the UK his overseas posting had just come through which informed him that he was to join No 229 (F) Squadron which at that time was based at Sidi Haneish on the north coast of Egypt.

No 229 Squadron was first formed at Great Yarmouth in August 1918 where it flew Short 184s on coastal defence duties and was disbanded on 31st December 1919. It reformed again at Digby in October 1939 and was equipped with the Bristol Blenheim Fighter carrying out 'Kipper' patrols over the North Sea. In May 1941 the squadron was posted overseas and set sail on board HMS Furious. The squadron left the carrier at Malta and flew on to Egypt arriving there in September 1941.

It began operating as a night defence squadron and soon moved up to form the Mersa Matruh defence unit and stop Rommel. In March 1942 it moved to Malta where it saw a lot of action over Sicily. During the Sicily landings the squadron was heavily involved with other units and in April 1944 flew a detachment to Catania in Sicily. In April 1944 the squadron moved back to the UK operating from Detling and on D-Day 6th June it operated shipping escorts and waves of gliders being towed across to Europe. On January 10th 1945 it was disbanded at Coltishall and renumbered 603 Squadron.

His logbook shows that he left the UK shores on board His Majesty's Troop Ship 'Narkunda'. On the same day he boarded another of His Majesties Troop Ships the 'Royal Ulsterman' (that must have made him a little homesick) arriving three days later at Takoradi on the Gold Coast. On the 24th he boarded a Bristol Bombay aircraft (L5828), which took him to Lagos in Nigeria. The flying time for that trip was 3 hours. On the 25th he flew on the same aircraft to Kano in Nigeria and then on to Maidugri on the 26th. They took off again and landed at El Geneina 5hrs.30mins later. From El Genina he flew to El Fasher and then on to Khartoum.

The next day 28th October he boarded a Lockheed aircraft (G-AGCT) that was captained by a Captain Garland and headed north for Wadi Halfa, the flight took 2hrs.45mins. He took off on the last part of the journey with Captain Garland on the 29th landing at Cairo 3hrs 20 mins later.

The trip from the Uk to Cairo took 30 days, 30 hours of which were spent in the air.

Geoffrey arrived at 229 Squadron on the 1st November 1942. The squadron at that time was based at Sidi Haneish and was equipped with the Hurricane Mk 11c.

Between the 1st November 1941 when Geoffrey joined the squadron and until he left in June 1942, he operated from thirteen different airfields, namely:

1941

1st November	Sidi Haneish	(Egypt)
23rd November	Fort Maddalena	(Libya)
13th December	Bu Amud	(Libya)
19th December	El Mechili	(Libya)
28th December	Fort Msos	(Libya)

1942

10th January	Antelat	(Libya)
24th January	Gazala	(Libya)
4th February	Ismailia	(Egypt)
26th March	Gambut	(Libya)
3rd April	Wadi Matrun	(Egypt)
9th April	Ballah	(Egypt)
19th April	Halfar	(Malta)
31st June	Aboukir	(Egypt)

His logbook shows that his first flight with the squadron was in a Mk 1 Hurricane code Z4255 and the task was a 'sector recco' and the next day he flew a Hurricane Mk 11 on formation flying.

Flight Sergeant Geoffrey Alderdice had completed 255 operations with 299 Squadron and I have listed some of the more interesting ones below.

His first operational patrol was on the 24th November 1941 In Hurricane 11 code HB-F.

These operations that he carried out were 'offensive sweeps' and 'bomber escorts'.

Log Book Entries

November 24th 1941: Pilot Officer Stideford and Pilot Officer Raun missing after Squadron intercepted formation of Ju88s with Me109s. Several of these were shot down.

November 26th 1941: Saw 6 Me109s, no interception. Warrant Officer Hoare missing while returning from BL 9.

November 27th 1941: Saw 2 Me109s, M.T. bombed west of El Adam, 1 Blenheim shot down.

November 28th 1941: Pilot Officer Raun returned after an exciting time with our Tanks.

November 29th 1941: Landed in desert about 25 miles south of LG 76, and walked all night to get there. Missing for 4 days.

December 11th 1941: Tobruk, Gazala, El Adem area. Several 110s dropped bombs and disappeared into cloud. Several 109s also landed at Tobruk to refuel.

December 16th 1941: Gazala area. Pilot Officer Mailand killed while flying up from B.L.G.

December 17th 1941: Hurricane bombers dropped bombs near Mecluli. Me109s tried to attack, one shot down by Sgt Carson. Sgt Burns and F/O Allcock missing.

December 31st 1941: Top cover to 6 Blenheims of 14 Squadron. MT bombed at Agedabra. Medium Ack Ack, 2 Lt Jones shot down but baled out.

January 2nd 1942: Sgt Case missing after squadron met some Me109s, F/Lt Johns damaged one.

January 3rd 1942: Met some Me109s, but did not get close enough. Saw one go into cloud after attacking P/O Rain, but could not get my sights on him.

January 7th 1942: Sgt Case returned after getting a probable Me109 and being shot down himself 'ground-strafed'. 2 Lt Jones reported safe but POW.

January 13th 1942: 3 Me109s over aerodrome. Chased one but could not get within range.

January 17th 1942: 208 Squadron's Wing Commander shot down and killed.

January 24th 1942: Antelat area, chased a G.50, but no one got within range.

January 26th 1942: Landed Derma. Section chased a 110, P/O Russel & Roy fired.

January 27th 1942: 200 MT (German) saw in Wadi N. of Msus. Landed Mecluli Main.

February: Two operations carried out on the 1st and two on the 2nd.

March 1st: He carried out three cannon tests.

March 2nd: Five cannon tests.

March 3rd: Seven cannon tests.

Squadron moved to Luqa, Malta

Flight Sergeant Alderdice's logbook shows that the squadron moved to help in the defence Malta in early April 1942.

April 1st: Force landed at Gambut 2, (burst oil pipe)

April 6th: On his way to Malta but had to turn back due to a burst oil pipe

On the 15th April 1942: King George sent a message to the Islands governor, Lieutenant-General Sir William Dobbie, and it read, "To honour her brave people I award the George Cross to the Island of Malta, to bear witness to a heroism and devotion that will long be famous in history".

May 6th 1942: Gambut (Libya) to Halfar (Malta), Met 2 Ju88s half way over. No attack. Landed during raid.

May 9th 1942: Cover for delivery of Spitfires, Landed Takali, Lots of 109s but no trouble.

May 10th 1942: Cover for Launch rescuing Spitfire pilot.

May 14th 1942: 40+ Ju88s, Me 109s. Saw a 109 but to far away to fire.

May 14th 1942: JU88s, Me109s and Macchi 202s. over Grand Harbour.

May 17th 1942: Carson, Pailey and self strafed an Italian E-Boat (destroyed). Later Me109s returned and set it on fire, to prevent us capturing it.

The Squadron was disbanded at Halfar in Malta on 31st May 1942 and Geoffrey was posted to 94 Squadron at El Gamil , Port Said in Egypt.

When Geoffrey left 229 Squadron he had carried out 78 operations and had now accumulated 311hrs.05mins flying experience.

No 94 was sometimes affectionately known as the 'MacRoberts' Squadron and I am sure many readers are already familiar with this story. But for those who are unaware of Lady MacRobert and the wonderful gift that she donated in memory of her sons I shall do my best to tell you about it. In 1942 Lady MacRobert very generously donated £25,000 to the Secretary of State for Air for him to carry on the work of her three sons who had been killed while flying, two with the Royal Air Force during the Second World war.

The Secretary of Sate for Air purchased four Hawker Hurricane Mk 11bs and one Short Stirling Mk1.

Three of the Hurricanes were named after her three sons, 'Sir Iain', 'Sir Roderic' and 'Sir Alasdair', the fourth was named 'The MacRobert Salute to Russia - The Lady' after Lady MacRoberts. All four Hurricanes were donated to No 94 Squadron as her second son Sir Roderic had been killed while serving with the squadron in Libya in May 1941.

When Air Vice Marshal McClaughey Air Officer Commanding Egypt, presented the aircraft to the squadron at Port Said in September 1942 he brought with him a message from Lady MacRoberts:

> "The name MacRobert returns to the Squadron on these aircraft. My boys names they bear were fighters. Their spirit lives on. They inspire confidence and would never let you down. I shall be proud when you pilot the MacRoberts Fighters. My heart and thoughts will be with you. I am confident that you will strike hard for victory. May yours be the 'Spirit of the Few'. God bless you all."

When the AVM had finished reading out this message he said:

> "When we have mothers like this one, there is little fear that the British people will fail through no matter what difficulties. How many can claim to have Spirit and Courage like hers which willingly gives all and then only regrets that she cannot do more in the service of her country."

The four Hurricane Mk11bs

Sir Alasdair HL.844 GO-C was named in memory of Lady MacRoberts eldest son and flown by Norman Geoffrey Alderdice, DFC. from Newry.

MacRoberts Salute to Russia - The Lady BP. 536 was flown by, described on the back of his Mae West as 'a hostile type', Royal New Zealand Air Force.

Sir Roderic was flown by a 25 year old ex-brick layer who later became a director of a Building Contractor.

Sir Ian was flown by a 24 year old Flight Sergeant who was an accountant from Wolverhampton (he worked in an aircraft factory).

The Short Stirling Mk1

Lady Mac Roberts also purchased a Short Stirling Mk1, which was presented to No 15 Squadron.

The Stirling LS-F, WG6085 was named 'The MacRoberts Reply'. The Squadron Commander read out a message from Lady MacRobert to its new crew:

> "Let it be used where it is most needed, may good fortune go with it. I have no more sons to wear the

badge or carry into fight. You are the crew who have been chosen to fly this Stirling and to carry the MacRoberts Crest."

The MacRoberts Reply was used by 15 Squadron during the period October 1941 and January 1942. It carried out 12 Operations. The first one on the 12th/13th October 1941 and the last one on 29th January 1942. It had attempted to bomb the 'Tirpitz' in Trondheim Fjord and failed. It was subsequently damaged in an accident at Lossiemouth and went to No 101 Conversion Flight and then to No 1651 Conversion Unit where it was written off in early 1943 and burned. It was decided to replace this Stirling so a second one was allocated to 15 Squadron and named MacRobert Revenge. Sadly it failed to return from an operation in 1942.

Lady MacRoberts wrote a personal letter to all the pilots' parents and I am honoured to have a copy of the letter, which she sent to Geoffrey's father, and I would like to share with you:

> Douneside
> Tarland
> Aberdeenshire
> 5th October 1942.
>
> Dear Mr Alderdice,
>
> I have just heard that your son, Sergeant Pilot N. Geoffrey Alderdice has been selected in the Middle East to fly one of my four Hurricane Fighters, called the 'MacRobert Fighters'. I don't know if you have heard from him. The aircraft he is piloting is called after my eldest son Sir Alasdair. The presentation ceremony, performed by Air Vice Marshall McClaughey, Air Officer Commanding Egypt, seems to have been very impressive. He made a fine address to the squadron and met all the boys who are to fly my fighters, and no doubt you will be hearing of it.
>
> Meantime, I am very happy to think that such a jolly, capable boy has been selected. I have a photograph of him with the aircraft. I believe the filming of the ceremony will soon reach this country, and will in due course reach Ireland. So you should look out for it and you will see your boy.
>
> The best of luck to your son, and I hope he will be spared you many years.
>
> Truly Yours,
> (signed) **Rachel MacRoberts**.
>
> P.S. I have sent your son an airgraph letter.

This was taken from a newspaper cutting and found in Geoffrey's photograph album.

> **He services the "MacRoberts" aircraft.**
> Twenty four year old Aircraftman Robert Ferguson sent a five page letter to his father in Belfast from a base in the Middle East a few days ago, it was a chatty letter but silent about his job. The next post brought a letter from Lady MacRobert telling his father that his son was doing "a fine job" in servicing the 'MacRobert' Hurricane Fighters which she has given to the nation in memory of her gallant sons. The letter, written from

> Lady MacRobert's home, Douneside, Aberdeenshire, said: "I have heard from H.Q. that your boy in Egypt is one of the crew on the ground who look after the 'The MacRoberts Fighters'. He is doing a fine job. I just want to send you these few lines of greetings and my thanks. Let us pray he will have the best of luck and will be brought safely home to you again.

This also was taken from a newspaper cutting and found in Geoffrey's photograph album.

> Lady MacRobert, whose indomitable spirit, shown in the gift of aircraft to avenge the death of her three sons, will be remembered in history, has befriended serving officers. A gift of £1,000 has made possible the early opening of the Lady MacRobert Club in Aberdeen for Officers of all three Services.

What a wonderful Lady and mother.

Going by Flight Sergeant Alderdice's logbook he in fact flew Hurricane BP.536 The Lady before he flew his own Sir Alasdair. Geoffrey joined 94 Squadron at Port Said on the 22nd June 1942 and his first flight was on the 26th when he was scrambled on a sea patrol. Most of the sorties being carried out by the squadron at this time were convoy patrols and intercepting lone bandits.

Between 22nd June 1944 and 13th March 1943 he carried out one hundred and seventy six sorties, some of which I have listed below:

June 29th	Scramble to 24,000ft. Bandit in Damietta area.
July 1st	Scramble to 20,000ft. Bandit 100 miles West of Damietta.
July 17th	Scramble to 7,000ft. Patrol Suez. Nothing seen.
July 19th	Scramble to 10,000ft. Ju88 over Suez got within 10 miles.
July 23rd	Scramble to 20,000ft. Bandit very close, but no interception.
Aug 24th	Scramble to 40,000ft. Chased Ju86 for 20 minutes. Had two 'Squirts', landed Shandur.
Sept 2nd	Patrol over Suez. Intercepted Ju88 at 26,000ft West of Suez. Destroyed by self and 'Blondie Walker'.
Sept 15th	**Presentation of the MacRobert Hurricanes by AOC Egypt.**
Sept 16th	First flight in 'The Lady' BP.536. Heliopolis to Port Said.
Sept 19th	First flight in 'Sir Alasdair' GO-C HL844. Fly-Past for AOC.
Sept 20th	First sortie in 'The Lady' Shipping Patrol.
Sept 23rd	Flying 'Sir Alasdair' in Formation for photographs.

On September 28th his logbook shows that he joined No 27 Course at No 1 Middle East Advanced Flying Training School at Ballah. He returned to his squadron on 10th October 1942.

Operations commenced again on the 12th October when he flew from Port Said to Shandur. Flight Sergeant Alderdice flew Sir Roderic on November 14th, 16th and 17th.

Nov 16th   Patrol over rescue launch (Ju88) shot
             down by George Imme)

The squadron moved to Martuba in Libya on 1st January 1943.

Sortie number 243 saw Geoffrey on a Patrol over a captured U-boat. His logbook shows that on the 17th February, 'U-boat depth charged and captured by HMS Paladin.'

The submarine was in fact U205 a type V11C that was launched on 20th March 1941 and commissioned on 3rd May 1941 and was commanded by Oberleutnant zur See Friedrich Burgel (he survived). U205s location was in the Mediterranean, North West of Derna. It was attacked with depth charges and gunfire from the Destroyer HMS Paladin. Eight German sailors were killed, three officers, 17 Senior Ratings and 22 Junior Ratings survived. According to Geoffrey's logbook the captured U-boat was beached near Derna.

Flight Sergeant Alderdice flew the Sir Alasdair for the last time on March 16th 1943. This was on a shipping patrol and had been his 250th sortie. Sortie number 255 was to be his last with 94 Squadron. This was on March 28th 1943 when he flew on patrol between Sidi Barrani and Aboukir. He had now carried out 255 sorties and had accumulated 563hrs.35mins flying time. It was time for a rest from operations. On the 15th April he was posted to No 119 MU at Shaibah in Iraq where he was to become a test pilot for 6 months. His journey to Shaibah started on the 13th April when he boarded a Lockheed Lodestar (EW993) of 173 Squadron, which took him form Heliopolis (Cairo) to Lydda in Palestine. From Lydda he flew on the same day arriving at Habbaniya in Iraq. He took off the next morning in a USAAF Boston and set course for Abadan. The morning of the 15th he boarded a Bristol Blenheim Mk 1V that was piloted by a Sergeant Stacey arriving a short time later in Shaibah.

His duty at Shaibah as a test pilot was to flight test Spitfires and Hurricanes. A few extremely interesting entries that appears in his log for April and May will interest some of you Spitfire buffs as it shows that he test flew Spitfire MkV, EP 497, EP498, EP788, EP797 and AD301. These five Spitfires were destined for Russia. On June 13th his log shows that he flew from Habbaniya to Basra in the Empire Flying Boat 'Cambria' (G-ADUV) and returned to Abadan on June 16th in a Hurricane Mk11 (HV784).

From then until the 6th October 1943 it was strictly Hurricane flight testing. The types of tests he carried out were air test, gun test, rigging test, hydraulic test, engine and assembly test.

By now Geoffrey had had enough of 'flight testing' and requested to join another operational squadron. His request was granted and he was given two weeks leave in Heliopolis (Cairo) before joining 123 (East India Squadron) that was based at Bu Amud in Libya.

Short History of No 123 Squadron

No 123 Squadron was formed at Upper Heyford on 20th January 1918 and consisted of Canadian personnel. It was disbanded on 5th February 1920 and reformed on 10th May 1941 at RAF Turnhouse near Edinburgh in Scotland and was equipped with Spitfire Mk1s. For the most of 1941 it served as an OTU receiving pilots who were trained on Spitfires and transferring them to squadrons in the south once they had gained some operational experience. In June 1942 the squadron moved to Egypt where it flew a number of Gloster Gladiators for a few weeks until its Hurricanes arrived. The squadron then moved to India in November 1943 and was first engaged in flying escort to Vultee Vengeance Bombers. It was now engaging the Japanese with ferocity and in September the squadron was re-equipped with Republican Thunderbolts. By March 1944 its duties were 'Cab-Rank' operations with the Army and this continued until June 1945 when the squadron was renumbered No 81 Squadron.

Soon after his arrival at Bu Amud he was informed that the squadron was to move Fenni in India. Their journey to Fenni started on the 1st November and finished on November 23rd. It took them via Mersa Matruh (Egypt), Quassassim (Egypt), Lydda (Palestine), Habbaniya (Iraq), Shaibah (Iraq), Bahrain (Arabia), Sharjah (Arabia), Jiwani (Pakistan), Mauripur (India), Jodphur (India), Delhi (India), Allahabad (India), Calcutta (India) and finally Fenni.

His first sortie with the squadron (No 256) was a scramble on the 26th December 1943 in Hurricane XE-A. logbook records: 'Patrolled Chittagong at 27,000ft. Nothing seen, Spits got 5 Japs out of 50+'.

He was scrambled again on the 28th: '3+ Bogies, Intercepted'.

I have decided to include some of the many operations that Flight Sergeant Alderdice carried out between 1st January 1944 and 4th April 1945 that I know will be of interest.

Jan 19th   While escorting dive bombers:
             Vengeances dived bombed Jap camp at
             Kindat. Strafed by us later.

Flight Sergeant Alderdice received his commission and was promoted to Pilot Officer.

February 21st Lawngkawng Village.
             Made two attacks, strikes on 3 Bashas,
             believed to be HQ of JIFS.
March 25th   Cover for supply dropping.
             DC3s dropped supplies to troops South
             of Ukral.

April 7th   Strafe Mawlaik-Auktaung.
No targets on river so beat up a Basha.

April 17th   Escort to DC.3s.
Supply dropping to Wingate's forces south of Indaw.

April 23rd   Bomber escort.
Top cover to 15 Vengeance dive-bombers

May 8th   Bomber escort.
Escorted 36 Vengeances to Kalewa, Japanese camp dive-bombed.

May 8th   Bomber escort.
40 Bombers, Wellingtons, Liberators and Mitchells on Jap concentrations in the Imphal Valley. Bombing appeared excellent.

On May 15th the Squadron moved to St Thomas Mount (Madras).

Only one operation was carried out in June, which was a sector recco on 9th June. The rest of the month and all of July the squadron carried out flight formation, liberator co-op, air tests, ack-ack co-op, Beaufighter affiliation and Aerodrome defence exercises.

In August two scrambles were carried out, one on the 3rd and the second on the 6th.

On the 19th September the squadron moved to Yelahanka and was re-equipped with the Republican P-47 Thunderbolt Mk1 and 11s.

Pilot Officer Alderdice had his first experience flight on the P-47 on October 3rd 1944. The whole squadron continued training on the P-47 through October and November carrying out battle formations, low level bombing and low level cross-country exercises and it wasn't until December that the squadron was ready for operations again.

Most of the operations the squadron carried out were escorting Dakotas on supply dropping runs and in between times it would carry out bombing raids and 'rhubarbs' on the Japanese.

Pilot Officer Alderdice's first operation in the P-47 was on 27th December 1944 when he was cover for 14 Dakotas supplying the 81st (West African) Division.

Below is a selection of some of his operations carried out between January 1945 and April 1945 in the P-47 Thunderbolt. By January the squadron was carrying out on average 1,000 hours per month.

January 2nd   Dive bombed 'Shrine Hill'.
Bombed Japanese Supply dump with 2X 500lb bombs

January 16th   Patrol: Myebon Peninsula.
Covering Army and Navy who had landed at Myebon on 12th January.

January 21st   Patrol invasion beaches.
25th Division landed this morning on Ramree Island.

January 21st   Patrol Ramree beaches.
Battleship Queen Elizabeth and carrier present.

January 29th   Escort B-24s Rangoon Area.
Close escort to 12 B-24s who destroyed bridges 71 and 41 on Burma-Siam Railway. Also bombed Mokpalin Rail Yards. Bombing excellent. 4 'Oscars' around, but not very enterprising.

February 1st   Dive bomb and strafe Jap position NW of Kangaw. 1,100 Japanese counted at Kangaw Myebou. Written off by Army and RAF.

February 11th   Dive bomb and strafe Jap occupied village. Bombs on target, which was strafed by 5 Squadron and us. One good fire with smoke to 3,000ft. 'V' report says 150 Japanese killed.

February 25th   Dive bomb railway bridge at Toungoo. Six direct hits including mine on bridge, which blew up 50ft of it.

March 2nd   Dive bomb stores dump at Payangazu. All bombs except two in target area. Own troops shelling Meikteila that was on fire.

March 5th   Dive bomb Japanese HQ at Pyinmana. Bombs undershot. Spike got a petrol dump, which went up in flames.

March 15th   'Cab-rank' over Meikteila. Dive bombed Kalaywa. One hit, one hang-up. One fore going after strafing run. (Army reported strike successful).

March 20th   'Cab-rank' over Meikteila. Dive bombed 2,000 Japanese in slit trenches etc., Made many strafing runs in conjunction with Artillery barrage.

March 22nd   'Cab-rank' over Meikteila. Dive bombed and strafed 2 pagodas at Meikteila Lake. Near misses.

March 30th   'Cab-Rank' over Meikteila. All bombs on target, and eight strafing runs. Village left in flames. Return fire from Bofors or 20mm guns.

Pilot Officer Alderdice carried out his last operation with the 123 Squadron on April 4th. He had by now accumulated 415hrs.55minoperational flying hours, 183hrs.25mins of which were in India and his total operational hours with 123 Squadron were 330hrs. 25mins. Between 25th October 1944 and 10th April 1945, 123 Squadron was based at Cholavrum, Trichinopoly, Nazir, and Cox's Bazaar and back to Nazir. On the 6th April Pilot Officer Alderdice was informed that he was being posted back to the UK for a well-earned rest. On the 10th April 1945 he left Nazir and headed overland for Worli in Bombay arriving there on the 16th. On the 29th April he boarded MV 'Winchester Castle' and arrived back in the UK almost a month later on the 24th May. His logbook shows that on the 26th April he went to

Head Quarters Fighter Command at Bentley Priory for three days.

Flying Officer Norman Geoffrey was awarded the Distinguished Flying Cross on 19th October 1945. He was to be presented with the award by the King at Buckingham Palace. Unfortunately the King was ill at that time and like so many he received the award by post. The Citation for his DFC reads:

> Flying Officer Alderdice has completed two operational Tours in the Middle East, Malta and South East Asia. Since his arrival in South East Asia he has completed numerous Sorties ranging between escort missions, supply dropping sorties, reconnaissance patrols and dive-bombing attacks. During one mission he scored two hits, which destroyed 50 feet of Railway Bridge at Toungoo. His devotion to duty throughout his operational career has been outstanding.

His next posting was to RAF Castle Bromwich near Birmingham on the 9th July 1945 and he remained there until 8th October 1946. (I dont know what his duties were at Castle Bromwich).

His logbook shows that his total flying for 1946 were:

June 29th	Dakota KN433, Flt/Lt Harris, Self Hendon to Long Kesh.
July 9th	Beaufighter, Flt/Lt Garland, Self Long Kesh to Honiley.
Aug 20th	Dakota, Flt/Lt Harris, Self Long Kesh to Prestwick.
Aug 23rd	Anson, G/Capt Vickers, Self Honiley to Bishops Court.
Aug 24th	Anson, G/Capt Vickers, Self Bishops Court to Honily.
Nov 10th	Oxford, Flt/Lt Collin-Jones, Self Castle Bromwich-Bury St Edmunds - West Raynham.

228 Operational Conversion Unit, Leeming

On the 8th October 1946 his next posting was to 228 OCU at RAF Leeming where he remained until November 1948. His logbook shows that his total flying for 1947 were:

April 20th	Oxford, Flt/Lt Smyth, Self Leeming to Middleton St George
April 20th	Oxford, Flt/Lt Smyth. Self Middleton to Leeming.
May 26th	Martinet, G/Capt Ryan, Self Leeming to Middleton.
May 26th	Martinet, G/Capt Ryan, Self Middleton to Leeming.
May 30th	Mosquito, Flt/Lt Hill, Self Night Flying Training.
Aug 3rd	Oxford, Flt/Lt Smyth, Self Leeming to Sydenham.
Aug 22nd	Master 11, Flt/Lt Roberts, Self Circuits and Bumps.

(I would hazard a guess and say that his flight on August 3rd was hitching a lift home for some leave.)

In November 1948 he was posted back onto flying with 631 Squadron at Llanbedr in Wales flying Harvards, Martinets and Spitfire XV1s. 631 Squadron was disbanded at Llanbedr on 11th February 1949 and became 20 Squadron Army Co-Operation Development Unit (AACU) in March 1949.

On the 3rd November 1949 the logbook shows that he was assessed as being 'above the average' as a Fighter Pilot. His logbook also shows that on June 17th 1949 he had his first and only taste of Jet Power when he flew solo in a Vampire. The squadron moved to RAF Valley in July 1949 and he remained here until 6th November 1950. On 6th November 1949 he was posted to RAF Station at Linton-on-Ouse where he attended a six week course on Beaufighters, Mosquito Mk111s and Hornets.

During the first week in January he was promoted to Flight Lieutenant and was informed that he was returning to an operational squadron. His new posting was to 33 Squadron that was based at RAF Butterworth in Malaya. The squadron had stayed in Germany after the war was over where it remained part of the British Air Forces of Occupation (Germany) BAFO (G) until 1949 when it was sent to the Far East to reinforce the Far East Air Force in its anti-terrorist operations. 33 Squadron was equipped with the Rocket firing Tempest F.2s and later the Hornet F.3s.

On January 11th 1951 Geoffrey took off from RAF Lyneham in a Hastings that was to take him to RAF Butterworth in Malaya. The flight was to take nine days, via Malta, Habbaniya, Mauripur, Negombo, Changi, Kualalumpur, arriving in Butterworth on January 19th. On January 23rd he had a local flight in a Harvard with Flight Lieutenant Evans and on the 24th and 25th he had four conversion flights in an Anson. On the 29th January he had his first flight in a Hawker Tempest Mk 11 and on the 4th of February he carried out his operation in Tempest SR-X, which was a strike west of Sungakai.

Between January 29th 1951 and June 6th he had carried out 52 operations in Malaya flying the Tempest. In early June the squadron was re-equipped with the DH Hornet F.3. His first flight in the Hornet with the squadron was a 're-familiarisation' exercise on June 12th. He continued flying training on this type through to August 7th when he took part in a strike east of Rengam (this was his 53rd operation).

Flight Lieutenant Alderdice took part in a total of 152 strike sorties and 231 strike hours with 33 Squadron, the last one was carried out on April 25th 1953. His flying logbook records that on 1st February 1953 he was assessed by the squadron commanding officer as 'above the average' as a Fighter Pilot, 'above the average' as a Pilot Navigator, 'average' in bombing and 'above the average' as an Air Gunner.

During his operational tour with 33 Squadron he also found time to carry out other more enjoyable flying duties, such as, Singapore air day formation, farewell fly-past for the AOC, fly-past for the Queens Birthday, Battle of Britain fly-past and his last duty with the squadron was taking part in a fly-past over HMS Unicorn on April 26th 1953. His logbook also shows that on March 26th 1952 while flying Hornet SR-F he carried out a napalm demonstration at Bahau. He left RAF Butterworth on May 28th and returned to the UK. By this time he must have accumulated a lot of home leave as his record of service shows a space between May 28th and September 3rd when he was posted to the No 11 School of RT at RAF Hednesford as an instructor. His next flight is recorded on January 27th 1954 when he flew a Chipmunk with a Flight Lieutenant Laidlay. In March and April he carried an instrument rating course at RAF Debden on Oxfords returning to Hednesford at the end of April.

August 9th to the 12th he gave air experience flights to air training corps cadets in a Chipmunk at 229 Operational Conversion Unit at RAF Chivenor. On the 26th September 1955 Geoffrey was promoted to Squadron Leader and posted to RAF Filton near Bristol. Here he became an instructor on Chipmunk, Meteor V11 and Vampire V until August 26th 1957.

On the 3rd November 1957 he was posted to Headquarters No 18 Group flying VIPs around the country and on 24th April 1961 he was posted to 4 School of Technical Training where he flew air training corps cadets and boy entrants on air experience flights on Chipmunks. His last flight with the RAF was at No 4 School of Technical Training on November 28th in Chipmunk code 569.

Squadron Leader Norman Geoffrey Alderdice DFC retired from the Royal Air Force in 1963. He returned to Northern Ireland and took up residence in Lisburn, County Antrim. He joined the firm of Securicor and became it's first Northern Ireland employee. He soon became the company's area manager firstly in Great Victoria Street and then at Stranmillis. He moved to England in 1977 where he joined Securicor's Head Office in London, finally retiring in 1984 and sadly he died two years later. When Squadron Leader Alderdice retired from the Royal Air Force he had been awarded the Distinguished Flying Cross, entitled to wear the Africa Star and Rosette, he had carried out 525 operational strike sorties, accumulated 1940 flying hours, visited over 120 aerodromes world-wide and had flown at least 25 different types of military aircraft including Tiger Moth, Airspeed Oxford, Miles Master MK 1&2, Hurricane MK 1 and 2, Spitfire MK VB & XV1, Harvard Mk 2, Thunderbolt MK 1&2, Martinet 1, Vampire 1,5 & 9, Mosquito Mk3, Hornet Mk3 & 4, Anson, Hawker Tempest Mk2, Chipmunk, Oxford, Meteor Mk 7, Handley Page Hastings, and Bristol Bombay.

FLIGHT SERGEANT
GEORGE REX BLACOE ARMSTRONG
FLIGHT ENGINEER
NO. 195 SQUADRON.

George Rex Blacoe Armstrong was born in the Ardoyne Fire Station in Belfast on the 20th March 1925. He was educated at Donaghadee Public Elementary School and later in the town's Technical College. On completion of his education, he was employed at Short and Harlands for a brief period, and later began to serve his engineering apprenticeship with the Belfast County Down Railway.

Rex was member of the No 1195 Squadron, Air Training Corps in Donaghadee before joining the Royal Air Force at the Clifton Street recruiting office in 1943. He applied for an aircrew position and on passing the aircrew selection board on the Antrim Road, he was offered the job of flight engineer, which he accepted.

He then went to London where he had to complete some trade exams, and was then posted to an ITW at Newquay in Cornwall for six weeks basic training. On completion of this training he was transferred to RAF Locking in Weston-Super-Mare to start his flight engineers course. He completed the course at RAF St Athans in Wales where he passed out as a fully qualified flight engineer, and was awarded his 'FE' Brevet. From St Athans he went up to Winthorpe in Nottingham where he was 'crewed up' with his new crew, and then started a three-week intensive course on the Avro Lancaster. On completion of his Lancaster training he joined 195 Squadron at Wratting Common in Cambridgeshire.

195 Squadron was formed at Duxford in November 1942 as an army support squadron and was equipped with the Hawker Typhoon. It was disbanded in February 1944, but was re-formed at Witchford as a heavy bomber squadron, equipped with the Avro Lancaster. In 1944 the squadron moved to Wratting Common where it was finally disbanded in August 1945. Rex carried out 26 operations with the squadron, four of which he says modestly, do not count as they were dropping supplies to the starving in Holland. Most of his operations were carried out over the Ruhr, Cologne and Dresden.

He especially remembers the Dresden raid as they were told at the briefing, just before they took off, that the target was to be a residential area. This had been the first time that he had heard this, as the targets were usually military. Rex told me, "The Americans bombed Dresden by day and we bombed it at night, the city was like hell, an inferno". On another raid, the flak was extremely heavy over the target. He and the bomb aimer were dropping 'window' through the Lancaster's floor, when suddenly there was a loud bang and a large piece on anti-aircraft shrapnel exploded through the floor close to his feet. A little panic had now set in, so he grabbed for his parachute to clip it on just in case. In doing so he unfortunately grabbed it by the 'D' ring (release handle) and it burst open into the aircraft. Luckily, they got back to base without any further problems. When he returned the parachute to the stores he was fined two shillings for 'opening a parachute when it wasn't necessary'.

On another occasion when returning from an operation, and coming into land, a red light indicated to him that one of the Lancaster's main under-carriage legs was not locked down properly. He went back to have a look but could not see anything obviously wrong. So he tried operating the under-carriage down manually, but still this did not get rid of the red light. Because of this his pilot decided to land his aircraft at RAF Manston as it had an extra long and wide runway that was designed and built for such emergencies. Twice enemy night fighters had attacked his aircraft during his 26 operations; luckily no damage or casualties resulted from either attack.

On leaving the Royal Air Force after the war he returned to the County Down Railway where he finished his apprenticeship. It was policy of the railway at that time, when you finished your apprenticeship you would be automatically paid off, and asked to re-apply in a years time. Rex worked in various jobs for while until he joined the International Computer Company in Belfast. After a year he was promoted to assistant foreman, and rose through the company's ranks to become a superintendent. He was employed with the company from the day it opened until the day it closed. In 1999

Rex decided to try and find his pilot, Mr George Scolley. He wrote to local newspapers in England and contacted various aviation associations. This soon paid off and they met after nearly sixty years, and have remained in close contact ever since. Rex is a member of the Royal Air Force Association and the Aircrew Association (N. Ireland Branch).

EDWARD WILSON ARMSTRONG
ENGINE MECHANIC
NO. 502 (ULSTER) SPECIAL RESERVE SQUADRON

Rex's father, Edward Wilson Armstrong (Senior), served in the Royal Flying Corps during the Great War and in 1926 joined 502 Ulster Special Reserve Squadron at RAF Aldergrove in 1926, where he served for three years as an engine mechanic.

He like his son Rex was also born in a fire station in Chichester Street, Belfast in 1889. He was educated at a school on the Grosvenor Road in Belfast, and when he left school he was employed with the firm of Victor H. Robb as a motor mechanic and later became one of their best sales representatives selling cars all over Northern Ireland.

When the Second World War came it put a stop to the car sales and he found himself out of a job. He applied for, and was offered a post in the production office at Short and Harlands, where he was put in charge of the local works home guard company. During the war Shorts had its own company of part-time and full-time home guard. This was because the company played a very important role in the war effort, designing and building many different types of aircraft for the Royal Air Force.

Edward Wilson Armstrong's father, Mr J. Armstrong had formed the Donaghadee Auxiliary Fire Service in the early 1900's. Every member of his family, which included his grandfather, father, two sons, and a daughter, had served in the service at one time or another. In those days the fire wagon was pulled by hand.

One of Edward's brothers had been the engineering officer on board the mail ship Princess Victoria when it sank on the morning of the 31st January 1953. The ship had left Stranraer in Scotland in a gale with winds in access of 120mph. She nose dived and sank in appallingly stormy seas, four miles off the Copeland Islands, with the loss of 128 souls. Edward's brother had helped in the rescue of thirty of the passengers.

Edward Wilson Armstrong (Senior) died on the 1st November 1985 aged 86 years of age.

WARRANT OFFICER
EDWARD WILSON ARMSTRONG
ROYAL AIR FORCE NO. 1079926
FLIGHT ENGINEER
NO. 90 AND 617 SQUADRONS

Edward Wilson Armstrong, named after his father, was born in Belfast on the 5th November 1922. He was the older brother of George Rex Blacoe Armstrong. The family moved from Belfast to Donaghadee when they were all very young. He was educated in Donaghadee Public Elementary School and on completing his education was employed with the firm of Short Brothers and Harlands, as an apprentice airframe fitter from June 16th 1938 and was part of a team that built the four-engined Short Stirling Bomber.

Edward applied to join the Royal Air Force in December 1940 and was accepted as aircrew and became a flight engineer.

After he had completed his basic training and flight engineers course he was posted to the 1651 Conversion Unit at Water Beach in Cambridge, where he converted onto the Short Sterling, (possibly one of the ones that he had helped to build earlier). The conversion course started on the 13th April 1943, and he had his first flight in the Stirling with his new crew on the 15th April. The Stirling's code letters were 'N-N' and its pilots were Pilot Officer Watson and Sergeant Wood. The training was very intense and continued day and night until the end of April.

On the 3rd May1943 Edward and his crew were posted to 90 Squadron at Ridgewell in Essex. 90 Squadron was formed originally at Shawbury in Shropshire in October 1917, and was equipped with Sopwith Dolphins for use in France. The squadron was disbanded in August 1918, and was reformed in March 1937 with the Short Nosed Blenheim. In April 1940 it was absorbed into No 17 OTU, and reformed again in May 1941. It had been selected as the RAF squadron that was to receive the first Boeing B-17s, and its role was now high altitude day-bombing. The squadron flew its first operation with the B-17 on the 8th July 1941 to Wilhelmshaven and attacked the target from 30,000ft. The squadron was again disbanded in February 1942, but reformed as a heavy bomber squadron in November 1942, equipped with the Short Sterling four-engined bomber, and later with the Avro Lancaster.

Edward started training exercises with Sergeant Wood and the crew on the 4th June 1943. Their first operation with the squadron was to Dusseldorf on the 25th May in Stirling (EF334). They carried out a total of 24 operations with the Squadron to Wuppertal, Mulheim, Gelsenkirchin, Cologne, Hamburg, Essen, Remscheid, Peenemunde, Berlin, Nurnburg, Munchen Gladbach, Mannheim, Bologne, Kassel, Bremen, and several 'gardening' operations.

The raid to Peenemunde is of particular interest as approximately forty-five aircraft from various squadrons were shot down that night. Most of the casualties were from the last wave of attackers. It is noted that some of the twin engined Me110s that found the bomber stream were fitted with cockpit mounted cannons, which were angled to fire upwards thus allowing the night fighter crews to align themselves under and slightly behind the wing of the unsuspecting bombers. This allowed the Germans to stalk their prey in virtual certainty they would not be sighted. These weapons were known as 'Schrage Musik' (Organ Music) and caused great carnage amongst the bomber crews who were blissfully ignorant of their existence. 596 aircraft took part in the Pennemunde raid which bomber command was ordered to carry out against the German Research Establishment on the Baltic Coast where the V-2 Rockets were being built and tested.

Edward's last operation with the squadron was on the 18th November 1943 when he and his crew bombed the city of Mannheim. Having completed a gruelling tour of operations Edward was taken off operations and posted to No 1661 Conversion Unit at Winthorpe where he became an engineering instructor until the 28th October 1944. Edward wrote a letter to the officer commanding the unit on the 11th August 1944 requesting to be allowed back on to operations. It reads:

> To O/C 1661 Conversion Unit,Winthorpe.
> From Flight Sergeant Armstrong 1079926.
> Flight Engineer.
>
> Date 11th August 1944.
>
> Sir,
>
> I have the honour to request that I be posted to an Operational Squadron to commence a Second Tour of Operations. My First Tour was completed in November 1943 on Stirling Aircraft.
>
> I have the Honour to be, Sir
> Your Obedient Servant
> E.W. Armstrong.

His request was turned down by the commanding officer who wrote in blue pencil at the bottom of his letter, "Good show, but sorry". Edward requested back onto operations again on in November 1944, and this time he was successful, and was informed that he was being transferred to the now famous 617 (Dam Buster) Squadron at Woodhall Spa. But first he had to attend No 5 Lancaster Finishing School at Syerston for one month. No 617 Squadron was formed on the 21st March 1943 at Scampton near Lincoln, under the command of Wing Commander Guy Penrose Gibson, and it occupies a unique place in the annals of the Royal Air Force. It was the only squadron formed to undertake a specific operation, which was the breaching of the Ruhr Dams in Germany. It is also the youngest squadron to have been awarded a Squadron Standard.

Edward joined the Squadron on the 25th May 1944 as a flight engineer. His first flight with the squadron was on the 29th November 194 with Squadron Leader Bill Iveson, and Flight Lieutenant Horsley who was to be his pilot until the end of his tour. Squadron Leader Iveson was officer commanding 'A' Flight. Edward completed fourteen operations with 617 Squadron, the first one being to Rotterdam on the 29th December 1944 with Flight Lieutenant Flatman.

The following Operations have been taken from Edward's Flying Log Book

30th Dec 1944   Lanc YZ-'G' PD233 Take off 14.57.
Operations to Imuiden
13 Lancasters of 617 Squadron took off to bomb the U-boat Pens at Ijmuiden, but was abandoned because of bad weather. One 'Tallboy' bomb returned.

31st Dec 1944   Lanc YZ-'G' PD233
Operation to Oslo Fjord
To attack German Cruisers in Fjord but no hits were scored. It was a bit murky and we couldn't see well enough to bomb. The ship was taking violent evasive action. One 'Tallboy' bomb returned. Flying time 7hrs.50mins.

3rd Feb 1945   Lanc YZ-'F'
Operations to Midget U-boat Pens at PoortersHaven
Attacked Poortershaven with one 'Tallboy' 12,000lb bombs. It was believed that these pens, in that part of Holland were still occupied by Germans, were sheltering Midget Submarines. The 'gaggle' formation was good. Our bomb disappeared into cloud of smoke over the target. The weather was clear and hits were claimed on the target. Flying time 3hrs.10mins. Height 13,100ft.

22nd Mar 1945   Lanc YZ-'H'
Operations to Neinburg Bridge
20 Aircraft from 617 Squadron destroyed the bridge. One 'Tallboy' bomb. Flying time 5hrs.15mins. Height 10,000ft.

23rd Mar 1945   Lanc YZ-'H'
Operations to Railway Bridge at Bremen
Bridge destroyed. Our bomb was a hit on the south-east side of the bridge. Three bombs burst about the same time and all appeared to be direct hits, a fourth fell shortly afterwards. One 'Tallboy' bomb. Flying time 4hrs.50mins. Height 16,450ft.

6th April 1945   Lanc YZ-'E'
Operations to Ijmuiden
Raid had to be abandoned due to bad weather. One 'Tallboy' bomb returned. Flying time 2hrs.55mins.

7th April 1945   Lanc YZ-'E'
Operations to Ijmuiden
Accurate attack carried out on ships at Ijmuiden. Two bombs seen to burst between the ship and the Quay and another was a slight undershoot to the east. Ship appeared to be still afloat after the attack. One 'Tallboy' bomb. Height 13,600ft. Flying time 3hrs.15mins.

9th April 1945   Lanc YZ- 'E'
**Operations to Hamburg
U-boat Pens**
Attacked the U-boat Pens at
Hamburg with 'Tallboy' (12,000lb)
and 'Grandslam' (22,000lb) bombs.
Height 16,400ft. Flying time 7hrs.

13th April 1945   Lanc YZ- 'E'
Operations to Swinemunde
Operation to bomb the Prince
Eugen and Lutzow. Raid had to
be abandoned. Bad weather.
One 'Tallboy' bomb. Flying
time 7hrs.15mins.

15th April 1945   Lanc YZ- 'E'
Operations to Swinemunde
As above. Raid had to be
abandoned. Bad weather. One
'Tallboy' bomb returned.

16th April 1945   Lanc YZ- 'O'
**Operations to Lutzow,
Swinemunde.**
18 Lancasters from 617 Squadron
flew to Swinemindu to attack the
Pocket Battleship Lutzow. The force
flew through intense flak. One
Lancaster was shot down, (617
Squadrons last loss of the war), and
all but two of its aircraft were
damaged. Fifteen aircraft managed to
bomb the Lutzow with 'Tallboy'
bombs or 1,000 pounders. The
effects of one near miss with a
'Tallboy' tore a large hole in the
bottom of the Lutzow and she sank
in shallow water at her moorings.
Our own 'Tallboy' bomb was
an overshoot by 100 yards.
Height 13,500ft. Flying time
7hrs.10mins.

18th April 1945   Lanc YZ- 'D'
Operations to Heligoland
The Naval Base, and the Airfield
was bombed. Flying time
4hrs.40mins.

25th April 1945   Lanc YZ- 'F'
**Operations to bomb
the Berchtesgaden**
We made one run and could not
identify the primary Target, so we
asked for permission to bomb a
bridge at Salzburg, we received this
permission from Control and did so,
our 'Tallboy' bomb was seen to
strike the side of the bridge near the
river bank. Height 15,000ft. Flying
time 8hrs.15mins.

This raid was against Hitler's 'Eagles Nest' chalet and the local S.S. Guard Barracks. This operation could not be considered as a success for the squadron by reason of several things beyond their control: (1) The Met office had got things wrong; (2) The marking left something to be desired. 617 Squadron was only part of a large force attacking this target.

Today the target is a tourist attraction with most of the wartime workings remaining untouched. 'Tallboys' could not move mountains. This was the **last** time that 617 Squadron dropped their 'Tallboys' in anger.

On the 16th June 1945, Lanc YZ- 'G', Flight Lieutenant Horsley (Pilot) took some of the 617 Squadron personnel on a 'Continental Cross Country' or 'Cooks' tour. They took off from Base and set a course for Germany, flying low over Heligoland, Desermunde, Hamburg, Dortmund Ems, Bielefield, Cologne, Dusseldorf, Essen, Wesel, Ijmuiden, and returned to Base.

On the 1st and 2nd of September 1945, Edwards logbook also shows that he carried out two Operation 'Spasm's'. This was bringing prisoners of war back to the UK from Germany. His pilot for both trips was Squadron Leader Saxelby.

He also carried out four 'Dodge' operations to Bari and Pomegiliano in Italy on the 4th, 7th, 27th, 29th of September, and two on the 6th and 9th of October 1945. These operations were again to repatriate Prisoners of War.

On the 13th November 1945 after taking off in Lancaster KC-'Z', the starboard outer engine cut on take off, and 'Z' was written off due to a 'wheels up' to stop. Edward's last trip with 617 Squadron was on the 20th December 1945 as a flight engineer when he ferried Lancaster YZ- 'E' to Lindholme with his skipper, Flying Officer Hall, and returned to base the same day in YZ- 'N' as a passenger. His flying hours when he left 617 Squadron were 569hrs.20mins by day and 324hrs.35mins by night. Total hours. 893hrs. 55mins.

AV Roe, Langer, Nottinghamshire

Edward was sent to the 104 Personnel Dispatch Centre in January 1946 and was then de-mobbed from the RAF. It was back to Civvy Street, but not for long. Eight months after leaving the RAF he applied to join the Ranks of AV Roe at Langer and was accepted as a flight engineer, assisting Mr Fields Richards who was AV Roe's chief test pilot. Edward was involved in the flight testing, assessing and acceptance checks on the Avro Lincoln, Avro York, Avro Lancastrian, Avro Shackelton Mk 1,2,3 and 4s and Gloster Meteor Mk 7,12 and 14s.

"Squadron Leader Peter Fields Richards was the chief wartime test pilot for AV Roe at Langer, and he was awarded his pilots licence in 1929. It is said of him that he had a tongue as abrasive as the harshest sand paper and an icy glare which would spot a fool at one hundred paces, but the fairest of men".

In November 1947, Edward was part of the AV Roe team who trained a number of Argentine pilots to fly the Avro Lincoln. When the training program had finished, he received a letter from Mr CL Hatton telling him that the Managing Director of AV Roe Limited , Sir Roy Dobson, had agreed to pay him and ex-gratia payment of £25 in recognition of his excellent work acting as flight engineer during the training of the Argentinean pilots. CL Hatton went on to say, "I would like to add my own personal congratulations on a job of work excellently carried out. It is an undoubted fact that you inspired confidence in the pilots under training and in doing so, considerably helped the training program.

A few interesting Logbook entries

28th November 1946: Air testing Field Marshal Jan Christian Smuts Aircraft. (This was a new Avro York Code **MW107**).

16th June 1947; Air testing Avro York (G-AFHI) 'Skyways Aircraft'

23rd June 1947: Air display at Rearsby in Avro York (MW 146).

23rd June 1947: Air display at Langer in Avro York (MW 171).

25th September 1947: Air test for Argentine Aircraft. Avro Lincoln (B-006).

3rd November 1947: Argentine Pupils, Avro Lincoln (B-010).

23rd November 1947: Circuits & landings in Avro Lincoln (B-008) BSAA Pilots.

5th July 1948: Avro Lancaster B-040. Hydraulic pipe burst. Cockpit and crew covered in oil. Landed at Waddington ('well oiled').

28th August 1948: Avro Lincoln RE 292. Langer to Farnborough to attend the Society of British Aircraft Constructor (SBAC) Display. Stayed five days displaying aircraft.

15th December 1948: Avro Lancaster B-036. 'Mid Upper Gunner'.

13th May 1949: Avro Lincoln (RE) Test. Both outboard engines 'Bristol Theseus', Emergency air used to lower undercarriage. Flaps U/S, flapless landing.

18th September 1949: BSSA Avro York G-AHFE Acceptance Test.

6th February 1950: Avro Lincoln RF339. Test. Both Outboard engines, 'Bristol Theseus' prop jets.

7th June 1950: Avro Lancaster. Royal Egyptian Air Force (1801) test & re-test.

22nd June 1950: Avro Lancaster (80001) Delivery to Air Service Training.

July 4th, 7th, 13th & 24th: Air testing Avro Lancasters (1802-1803-1804-1805) for delivery to the Royal Egyptian Air Force).

September 14th, 15th: Air testing Avro Lancaster (1806) for delivery to the REAF.

October 3rd, 4th: Air testing Avro Lancaster (1807) for delivery to the REAF.

October 26th: Air testing Avro Lancaster (1808) for delivery to the REAF.

November 17th: Air testing Avro Lancaster (1809) for delivery to the REAF.

March 11th 1952: Avro Lancaster (WU-17) Pilot, Captain 'De Louche'. Acceptance test for the French National Air Force.

November 3rd: Avro Lancaster (WU- 51) Pilot Captain 'Jermine'. Acceptance tTest for the French National Air Force.

May 2nd 1953. Avro Lincoln (E-21) (Argentine Pilot) Acceptance check.

August 20th. Avro Shackelton (VP-254) Langar - Woodford - Langar.

31st December 1953: Gloster Meteor Mk14 Captain, Squadron Leader Walton. 'Passenger'.

Argentinean Pilot training

The training of the Argentineans started on the 4th November 1947 and finished on the 9th January 1948 with Lieutenant Neitardt making the last training flight. The types of training exercises, which they carried out, were Circuits & Landings, Overshoots, Three engine Overshoots, Solo Landings, Flight Engineer Instruction, Three engine landings, and Flapless Landings.

The names of the Argentinean Aircrew were Captain Gonzalez, Lt Siri, Lt Solas, Lt Rosi, Lt Mendiorez, Lt Naveiro, Lt Cochello, Lt Goette, Lt Neithart, Lt Stagnaro, and Lt Gondolfo.

The Argentine Aircraft codes were B-005, B-006, B-007, B-008.

On the 6th January 1948 Edwards log book shows that he had just completed 1000 flying hours.

Edward joined the No 664 (Operational) Squadron Royal Auxiliary Air Force at Hucknall in Nottinghamshire on the 1st July 1956 as an airframe fitter, and was given the rank of sergeant. Unfortunately the Unit was disbanded in March the following year. Edward continued working for AV Roe's until the 31st May 1968, although his flying logbook shows that he last flew with the company as an observer in a Mk 2 Shackelton (LR960) on the 26th November 1965. When he left the company he had completed over 1300 flying hours. He left AV Roe in 1968; to take up employment with Airworks Services Ltd in Dhahran in Saudi Arabia, and in June 1972 became the company's deputy chief engineer. Edward departed Air works Services in April 1977 and was employed with BAC (Military Division) in Riyadh as their chief engineer, working on the English Electric Lightnings. Sometime between 1980 and when he retired he also worked for the Fokker Aircraft Company in Holland as their chief engineer.

A final tribute to an airman

When Edward died in July 1994 his son Edward (Junior) now 48 and living in Grantham contacted the Battle of Britain Memorial Flight at Conningsby in

Lincolnshire to ask if it would be possible to have his father's last wish carried out, and that was to have his ashes scattered over Langer Airfield from the Lancaster. The RAF at Conningsby wrote back to Edward and told him that it would be an honour to carry out his father's last request.

In July 1994 Edward's son Geoffrey boarded the Avro Lancaster, carrying his fathers ashes on their final journey to Langer Airfield. Looking on were his Widow Dorothy who he married in 1946 and standing beside her were Dorothy's six other sons, daughter, and 22 grandchildren. Around 300 people, friends and work colleagues had turned up to watch the memorial ceremony. Parachutists gracefully floated towards the ground from every corner of the sky. The Battle of Britain's Memorial Flights Hurricane, Lancaster and Spitfire roared low the airfield, scattering the ashes of Warrant Officer Edward Wilson Armstrong.

But one very special person who was there that day believed Edward was already there in 'Spirit'. His widow Dorothy said, "We say he would have loved it. But I think he was here already."

FLIGHT LIEUTENANT
CECIL WILLIAM STEAD AUSTIN
IE NO. 69486
ROYAL AIR FORCE FIGHTER COMMAND

Cecil William Stead Austin, son of Glover and Mary (Molly) Austin, was born in Londonderry on the 17th January 1920. He was educated at the Foyle College, Londonderry and later at Queens University, Belfast, in 1938, where he studied Dentistry. Cecil enjoyed rowing for the Queens University first eight and he also was a very keen rugby player. Unfortunately, his rugby days were brought to an abrupt halt after he fell out of tree, breaking an arm and a leg.

His father's brother was killed fighting in the Boar War in South Africa and his father survived the trenches of the 1914-1918 conflict. During the Second World War he donned the uniform once more and became Commanding Officer of the Londonderry branch of the Air Training Corps. Cecil had three brothers, Campbell, Stanley and Claude, all of whom were in the services during the Second World War.

Flying Officer Stanley M. Austin.
RAF No 113412.

Stanley applied to join the Royal Air Force one week after Cecil in June 1940. He was a very keen all round sports enthusiast, rowing for the Foyle College and becoming the Irish Universities featherweight boxing champion. On joining the Royal Air Force he became part of their boxing team, having six fights he won them all with a knock out. When he was posted out to America to commence his flying training in Phoenix Arizona, he fought against the American Golden Gloves champion and beat him. Sadly Stanley was killed in action on the 3rd February 1943 while flying his Spitfire with 243 Squadron at Souk-el-Khemis (Algeria) He is buried in Tunisia.

Claude Austin

Claude Austin joined the Royal Air Force after Stanley and after training was posted out to Rhodesia where he became an instructor on Boeing Stearmans completing two tours. He also took command of a communication Flight of Avro Ansons in between instructional duties and just as the war ended he was posted to a Spitfire squadron. He returned home to Londonderry after the war where he was needed in the family business of Austin and Co. Claude was very keen and proficient sailor, and tragically lost his life while sailing his yacht 'Granuaile' (Irish Sea Princess) in 1972 on his way from Hoathe to take part in the Fastness Race.

Major Campbell Austin

Campbell was the oldest of the four Austin brothers. He too decided to join one of His Majesties Services, favouring the Royal Enniskillen Fusiliers and was already a Second Lieutenant in the Regiment when war broke out. Campbell was seconded to the Seiks in India and served on horseback on the northwest frontier. Later on moving over to Burma where he had a lucky escape when the jeep that he was travelling in blew up when it hit a land mine.

Cecil had joined the Londonderry Unit of the Territorial Army and when war broke out on the 3rd September 1939, they were shipped out to France extremely quickly, leaving Cecil behind. Not sure of what to do he returned to Queens University in Belfast to await his call-up.

Nothing seemed to be happening so he decided to have a word with the commanding officer of Queens University Officer Training Corps (OTC) of which he was member. He informed the CO of his predicament and told him that he would now like to join the Royal Air Force and become a pilot but was not sure if he could under the circumstances. The CO made a few enquiries and advised Cecil to go ahead with his plans, as he did not think that there would be any repercussions. On the 10th

June 1940 Cecil went along to the Clifton Street recruiting centre and volunteered his services for the Royal Air Force. He did not have long to wait as AC2 CWS Austin was informed that he was being posted to Padgate Receiving Centre in August.

After spending three weeks being kitted out, square bashing, medicals etc., he was off to the Royal Air Force Station at Sealand for a period, eventually reaching Babicombe, Newquay in Cornwall where he attended a navigation, gunnery and airmanship course which lasted 3 months. In January 1941 he was posted to No 4 Elementary Flying Training school at Brough where on the 9th he had his first air experience flight in a Tiger Moth Coded 5539 His instructor was a Flying Officer Fourth and who was to remain his instructor until he went solo on the 4th February 1941. When the EFTS course ended on the 9th March, Cecil was assessed as 'above the average', which was an excellent grade for a trainee pupil.

Cecil was posted to No 17 EFTS at North Luffan in Rutland for a few weeks filling in time while awaiting a place at No 15 Service Flying Training School at Kiddington to start his training on Multi-Engined aircraft. No 17 EFTS was equipped with Oxfords and Cecil had his first trip in one on the 18th April 1941 under the instruction of a Flying Officer Oldacre, soloing on the type five days later. At the end of the course Cecil was awarded his 'Wings' and had been selected for fighter command.

After successfully completing his SFTS training he was posted to No 56 Operational Training Unit that was based at Sutton Bridge and was equipped with Hawker Hurricane Fighters. His first flight at the OTU was in a Miles Master on the 3rd July and on the 4th he had his first taste of the Hurricane. He continued training on the type until the course ended around the end of July. On completion of his operational training Cecil was posted to 504 (County of Nottingham) Squadron based at Swansea and was equipped with Hurricane 11Bs. Unfortunately when he arrived to take up his new post he was informed that the squadron had moved to Chilbolton, just outside Andover in Hampshire. He soon caught up with the Squadron and on his arrival was sent for by the squadron adjutant who informed him that they were moving to Ballyhalbert in Northern Ireland and that he had been selected to take charge of the 'advance party'.

Cecil arrived at Ballyhalbert on the 27th August 1941 (it was 59 years to the day after that I interviewed him).

He arrived a week or so early setting up the squadron headquarters, administration system and generally getting things ready for the arrival of the squadron aircraft and personnel. The day the squadron did arrive at Ballyhalbert it was blowing a gale and the main runway into the wind was out of action. As the Hurricane 11Bs came into land the gusting winds caught the aircraft tails and overturned quite a few of them. Miraculously no one was seriously hurt although twelve of the squadron's Hurricanes were destroyed or damaged. Cecil's first flight

from Ballyhalbert was in Hurricane 11B, TM-Z Code 23986. This MK of Hurricane was equipped with the more powerful Rolls Royce engine and armed with eight .303 machine guns.

On the 4th September Cecil took off from Ballyhalbert in a Miles Mentor to fly to Carlisle - Dishforth, eventually landing at Brough where he spent the night. He departed the following morning with his passenger and flew across to RAF Cranwell for a private visit and then on to RAF Baggington near Birmingham where he and his passenger picked up two of the squadrons new MK11B Hurricanes. These were to help replace the twelve that had been put out of action when landing at Ballyhalbert. They flew on to Squires Gate the same day only to find themselves fog bound for a few days, eventually arriving back in Ballyhalbert on the 16th September. It was decided to re-equip 504 squadron with Spitfire 11As and train a band of new pilots including Pilot Officer Prince Galitzine, a Russian, naturalised Britain, who had fought with the Finns against the Communists. Free French, Royal Australian and New Zealand Air Force pilots swelled the ranks of 504 Squadron. Squadron Leader PT Parsons who had joined its ranks as a junior officer now assumed command. Cecil said he was a terrific commanding officer, and sadly had to watch him crash to his death in a Mosquito coming onto land at RAF Colerne. "The Mosquito just veered off the runway after landing and crashed into a hangar and blew up killing both crew."

504 Squadron's routine was mainly carrying out convoy patrols, air sea rescue flights and were frequently scrambled to try and catch intruders that were high flying Luftwaffe Reconnaissance aircraft that would visit Northern Ireland from time to time. These were pursued to the limit of the Spitfires fuel, some being shot down into the sea with a few making 'neutral Eire'.

Spitfire Mk 11A 'County Down' P7823

One of the Spitfires that Cecil flew during his tour with 504 Squadron at Ballyhalbert was named 'County Down'. This was one of fifteen Mk 11A Spitfires that had been purchased for the war effort by the people of Ulster. P7823 survived until the 7th January 1942 when it was being flown by Pilot Officer WB McManus, RCAF, was involved in an accident, the cause of which is to this day is still a mystery. He was considerably overdue flying Spitfire 11A P7823 back from St Angelo and subsequently it was reported that an aircraft had crashed and burned out at Roughlan near Lurgan in County Armagh. On the 8th January 1942 it was established beyond doubt that the body in the crashed aircraft was that of Pilot Officer McManus, although very few traces remained of him or his aircraft.

Shot in the leg

This accident happened when Cecil was out practising clay pigeon shooting with some of his fellow pilots on

Ballyhalbert airfield. Clay pigeon shooting was part of an ongoing training to help with deflection shooting. A Sergeant Francis was standing behind Cecil with a loaded shot gun, which was touching his flying boot with its muzzle. Suddenly and without warning the gun went off shooting Cecil in the back of the leg and causing him a horrific injury. The shot went in through the back of his leg and out the front. What saved him was, his thick leather flying boot and the fact that the barrel of the gun was so close to his leg. Had it been a few inches back it would have taken his leg clean off. Cecil was admitted to the Bangor Hospital where he remained for a few days and then transferred to an RAF Hospital in England. This unfortunate accident put paid to his flying career for the next nine months.

After his leg had fully recovered and he was passed medically fit, he was informed that he could not fly operationally again. He was posted to 286 which was an Army Co-op Squadron based at ZEAL, flying Masters, Defiants, Oxfords and managing to fly the odd Hurricane from time to time (just keeping his hand in).

His job was to carry out Army Co-op flights by day allowing the Army to calibrate their guns and their search lights by night. On the night of the 9th August 1944 he was returning to base from a searchlight exercise when he ran into thick fog. The operations room advised him to get down as quick as possible. As he descended through the fog to land one of the Oxfords engines cut, Cecil's immediate reaction was to open up the other one. The increase in power made little or no difference to the Oxford, she just kept sinking. As he approached the runway he could see through the fog the Red and Green lights in front of him, first two greens then a green and red followed by two reds. Cecil knew that he was not going to make the runway, he managed to miss a clump of trees and crash landed upside down in a field, thankfully he walked away unhurt.

He was posted to Long Kesh Airfield which was just outside Lisburn in Northern Ireland where he joined 289 and 290 Army Co-op Squadrons flying Martinets, target towing for the Royal Navy around Garron Point and Islandmagee for the Merchant Navy. After that he came back to join 587 Squadron now at Western Zoyland near Bridgewater in England flying the Vultee Vengeance Dive Bombers.

Another hairy moment for Cecil that I should mention was when he was stationed with 286 Squadron at Colerne, where he had another very lucky escape. He had just landed in his Hurricane and while slowing down to turn off the main runway he felt a terrific thump behind him and suddenly noticed that his aircraft was speeding up. A Spitfire had landed on top of his Hurricane. The Spitfire was being flown by an RAF 'Test Pilot' *who shall remain nameless*. The propeller of the spitfire had stopped just behind Cecil's seat.

After a short spell with 587 he re-joined 286 Squadron and applied for permanent commission. Cecil was sent up to London to sit a medical board who turned him down for a higher category of flying. Because of this decision Cecil decided to leave the Royal Air Force and returned to Queens University where he finished he degree in dentistry. On doing so he became a dentist and practised for the next 50 years finally retiring in 1991. Cecil's total flying hours is in and around 800. The aircraft types that he flew are, Tiger Moth, Hawker Hurricane, Oxford, Miles Master, Miles Mentor, Miles Magister, Spitfire, Defiant, Piper Cub, Vultee Vengeance, Harvard, Martlet and Cygnet. Cecil's daughter Wendy started her career with the Larne Times, later joining Downtown Radio as a newsreader and is currently with the British Broadcasting Company where she hosts the 'Good Morning Ulster' programme.

Cecil now lives in retirement with his wife in their Bungalow on the Upper Lisburn Road and is a keen member of the Aircrew Association Northern Ireland Branch.

LIEUTENANT
'A' ROBERT JOHN BABINGTON, DSC QC
ROYAL NAVY VOLUNTEER RESERVE
OBSERVER
FLEET AIR ARM
NO. 806, 815, 826, 784 AND 746 SQUADRONS

Robert John Babington was born in Dublin on the 9th April 1920 and was educated at St Columba's College, Rathfarnham, for four years and then entered Trinity College in Dublin, where he studied Philosophy for one year, before deciding to switch to History. He completed his first year at Trinity in 1937. He is the son of Major DLJ Babington, who served with the Royal Army Service Corps in France during the First World War and who was twice mentioned in Despatches.

At the outbreak of the Second World War he volunteered his services again and re-joined the RASC as a Major and was based at Barnetts Park. He was always very proud of the fact that he was in charge of a mixed Company, both men and women.

His mother who came from Carndona in County Donegal joined the First Aid Nursing Yeomanry (FANY) and drove an ambulance in France during the First World War.

It was while he was studying at Trinity that he answered an advertisement for recruitment into the FAA and a short time later was summoned to the Royal Naval Establishment in Liverpool to sit in front of a Board. The Board was headed by a senior Admiral who asked Robert what would he like to do in the Fleet Air Arm. Robert told him that he would like to become a pilot. The Admiral responded by telling him that he had quite a lot of pilots at the moment and would he consider becoming an Observer. The Admiral painted a very nice picture for Robert of the Observer 'running' the show and the Pilot only being the driver. On completion of the interview Robert was accepted into the Fleet Air Arm as an observer. He returned to Dublin to inform his parents and awaited the information on his 'call up' and during this period war had been declared.

Naval Airman 2nd Class Babington was soon sent for and his first posting was to Gosport where he joined HMS Daedalus, where he completed four weeks initial training. Robert explained to me that, "The instructors taking the course couldn't be less interested in aircraft. We received lectures on the history of the Royal Navy which included how Nelson won the Battle of Trafalgar but nothing on aviation". After completing the course he emerged as a Acting Leading Naval Airman and now was familiar with the art of boat work, signalling, ships routines, the history of the navy, knots and splices, ship and aircraft recognition, elementary navigation, and not forgetting good old square bashing. He was also 'encouraged' to climb the mast, which was quite an ordeal if you did not like heights. He was then transferred to the Air Observers School in Arbroath, Scotland, to commence his Observers Training in Percival Proctors. His training here was, signalling and wireless telegraphy, navigation and reconnaissance techniques. While he was there he also had a chance to fly in the Supermarine Walrus. He liked this particular aircraft as the fuselage was enclosed and you were allowed to smoke in it. Robert told me that during his course at Hatson, he once watched as a Walrus actually flew backwards in a howling gale.

After successfully completing the observers course he was promoted to Acting Sub-Lieutenant (A) RNVR and transferred to the Royal Navy College at Greenwich where he attended a two week officer training course. The Navy's idea was that these new airmen needed a taste of veneer and polish. They ate in the Painted Hall, using silver service and linen napkins and the waiters always wore white gloves. "They educated me in how to eat, behave properly and become an officer and a gentleman". While he was training in London, he went along to the naval tailor Messrs Geeves of Piccadilly where he purchased his new officers uniform that consisted of two sets of 'browns' and two sets of 'whites' long and short and to his amazement was issued with a Topee which came complete with its own tin box. (The Topee stayed with him for much of his tour of the Middle East Campaign, until it was stolen by one of the Arab servants.)

At this time, Robert was a little naive about money matters and had frittered all his uniform allowance away on 'other things'. He decided to visit his grandfather to see if he could borrow the money from him, but failed utterly. His grandfather told him, "Don't worry Robert just you make an allotment to the tailor". Robert thought he was going to be sacked from the Fleet Air Arm before he even got started. At the end of his officer training he was given some leave and was then directed to join the SS Warwick Castle which was berthed on the Clyde in Scotland. The Admiralty had now taken over the ship (complete with its crew), which in peace time had sailed back and forward between England and South Africa. All of the officers, no matter how junior had first class accommodation.

The SS Warwick Castle was part of an enormous convoy, hundreds of ships of all sizes filled to capacity with troops and supplies heading for the Middle East. Robert remembered wakening up early one morning during the long journey and decided to go for a walk on deck. He discovered that HMS Nelson, one of the Royal Navy's capital ships had joined the convoy during the night and had positioned herself right in the middle of the convoy next to the Warwick Castle. "It was a magnificent sight", Robert said, as she shouldered her course through a south Atlantic swell. The Nelson was over 700 ft long, and part of her armament was 9-16 inch, 12-6 inch and 6-4.7 inch guns. Her sister ship was the Rodney, both were launched 1925 and both were broken up in 1948. Two formidable warriors.

The convoy eventually reached Durban in South Africa and when it docked, Robert managed to get some shore leave and play a round of golf at a place called Umbogatwini. He met some very hospitable people during his short stay who looked after him extremely well. When they eventually set sail, as was the tradition at that time, the ships company was met by the sound of the beautiful voice of the 'The Lady in White', singing, 'Wish me luck as you wave me goodbye'. This remarkable lady met every troop ship that sailed in and out of Durban harbour and knew the exact time they would arrive and depart by way of a code that was given to her by the authorities.

Robert celebrated his 21st birthday just as the Warwick Castle crossed over the equator and of course was initiated by Father Neptune. As this was a special birthday his friends gave him a terrific party and needless to say it carried on into the wee small hours. A birthday that he will remember in more ways than one as this was to be the first time he came across an angry senior naval officer. The Commodore of the convoy was staying on board the Warwick Castle and was a stickler for discipline and he insisted on giving the junior officers lectures every morning and expected them all to be present. The subject matter of the Commodores lectures was 'British Israelism' which maintained that the British were a Jewish lost tribe. The morning after Robert's 21st birthday, he had woken up with a dreadful hangover and went back to sleep, hoping that he would not be missed at the lecture. Unfortunately the Commodore being the man that he was did miss Robert and he was furious. So much so that he sent for the Master at Arms and told him to bring Lieutenant Babington to him. He gave Robert a right dressing down, and ordered the Master of Arms to take him up on deck and give him a few hours arms drill. This was not too bad until Robert appeared up on deck with his rifle and kit and discovered that there were thousands of troops sunbathing just below him (I dare say there was a bit of banter). Robert remarked, "It certainly taught me that senior naval officers had to be obeyed."

The convoy was now moving up the coast of Africa into the Red Sea and sailed into the Suez Canal. When they reached the end of the canal they met another equally large convoy with thousands of Australian and New Zealand troops on board. These were the reinforcements to assist the British Army in Egypt. Robert then went by train to Alexandria and a few days later in May 1941 was posted to the Naval Air Station at Dekailia where he joined 806 Squadron which was equipped with Fairey Fulmars. He and the squadron were then immediately ordered to board HMS Formidable.

HMS Formidable was built in Belfast, her keel was laid down on the 17th June 1937, launched on the 17th August 1939 and completed on 24th November 1940 and after a very distinguished war record was broken up in 1953.

The evacuation of Crete

Formidable set sail right away, her job was to help with the evacuation of troops from the island of Crete in the Mediterranean, which the Germans were in the process of capturing. It was here that Robert had his first introduction to war, enemy air attacks and to be under fire. He had never seen a Fulmar, let alone fly one until he boarded the Formidable, and so was not allowed to take part in any flying operations. While on action stations he was given the job of standing on the bridge beside a designated telephone, and if it rang he would answer it. He said laughingly, "That was my contribution to the battle." He also told me that he considered that he was very lucky, as it was a fascinating experience just being there and watching what went on during this air attack. "The Admiral was stalking up and down smoking his pipe, paying little or no attention to the Captain who was shouting orders, fighting for his ship, and you could see the distinctive role that each had during the action, even when the bombs where bursting on the Carrier." Bombs from Stukas hit the Formidable at least three times, fortunately causing little damage. On one occasion Robert remembers that a bomb had severed the main mast over the bridge, causing it to fly through the air, ending up embedding itself right in the middle of the flight deck. He also recalls watching the commanding officer of 805 Squadron a Lieutenant Commander Evans who had a very prominent long red beard taking off to engage the Stuka dive-bombers and watching his beard blowing backwards in the slipstream.

The evacuation of Crete started on the 28th May 1941 under the cover of darkness where thousands of exhausted Anzac, British, Greek and Cretan troops had gathered on the beaches of Heraklion.

The German Stuka dive-bombers had already sunk two British Destroyers with 1,000lb bombs on the 23rd May off Crete, HMS Kashmir and HMS Kelly. Lord Louis Mountbatten captained HMS Kelly and although she had been damaged just above the engine room, her crew kept firing at the enemy and refused to abandon their ship until ordered to do so by their captain.

The evacuation ended on the 1st June 1941, exactly one year since Dunkirk.

British and Commonwealth losses amounted to 1,742 dead and 1737 wounded and the Germans by no means had it all their own way. Their losses amounted to 3,985 dead and 2,131 wounded and the Germans lost 220 aircraft to the RAF's 46. The Royal Navy also took a terrible pounding, 3 Cruisers and 6 Destroyers were sunk and 17 ships crippled with the loss of 2,011 lives.

By the time the Royal Navy had taken the last soldier from the Heraklion beach they had rescued 18,000 men, leaving 12,000 behind to be taken prisoner. After the evacuation of Crete was completed Robert returned with HMS Formidable to Egypt where he joined 815 (TBR) Squadron, which was equipped with the Fairey Swordfish and were fitted with the air-to-surface vessel (ASV) type radar. The squadron's commanding officer was a Lieutenant Commander Gick. 815 Squadron was subsequently joined by 826 and 821 Squadron to become part of the Desert Air Force under the command of 201 Group.

HMS Formidable was ordered down the Suez Canal and after that to America to be repaired. That left the Eastern Mediterranean without any carriers and her aircraft squadrons became shore based. The reason for sending a fighter squadron to Gaza was to provide a fighter squadron to provide fighter cover for ships taking part in the invasion of Syria, which the Allies next undertook. The invasion went well and the only brush the squadron had was with the French on the first day of the invasion. While Robert and his crew were on patrol in a Fairey Fulmar they saw two French De Woiteen fighter aircraft flying around the ships just off Haifa. They dived to attack, and when they reached them they opened fire and the De Woiteen's fired back, after that they made off and they were never seen again. It was just as well because one De Woiteen could have easily handled the Fulmar. The squadron specialised in anti-shipping strikes and in particular hunting for U-boats using ASV radar. Their night patrols were very long

sometimes taking up to six hours. In nine months the squadron had attacked over 30 U-boats, badly damaging three of them.

On the 2nd June 1942 a Swordfish (Code 'L' V7407) which was operating from L.G. 121 in North Africa and, was crewed by Lieutenant Bates (Captain), Lieutenant A.W. Lawrie (Observer) and Air Gunner A.K. Kims attacked and damaged U-652 with Depth Charges in the Mediterranean, off Sollum. The U-boat was unable to submerge and was sinking slowly after the attack. It's Captain, Kapitanleutnant George Werner Fraatz decided to Scuttle it and he contacted another U-boat (U-81), which was close by and asked its captain, (Kapitanleutnant Friedrich Guggenberger) to come to his assistance. On U-81s arrival, Kapitan Fraatz transferred his crew and, told Kapitan Guggenberger to sink his submarine. He allowed Fraatz the privilege of firing one torpedo at the stricken U-boat, which hit her amidships, sinking her immediately.

After a week or two the squadron was ordered to Ramat David, a kibbutz that was almost exactly halfway between Haifa and Jerusalem, a very beautiful place with easy access to the nightlife on Mount Carmel in Haifa. The kibbutz, which was run on communist lines, seemed to be largely composed of university graduates from Europe. There were also a number of very beautiful girls who worked in the fields and who were very scantily clad, however armed guards always accompanied them, which frustrated the sailors. The graduates were of course Jewish and were refugees from central Europe. After a time the squadron was ordered back to Dhekelia and Robert was posted to 815 Squadron that was equipped with Swordfish. At this time he met his pilot, Sub Lt 'Doc' Stewart, who came from Ballymoney in Northern Ireland. They were together for the rest of the time that Robert was in the Middle East. The squadron was commanded by Lt Gick, RN, who later became an Admiral. The squadron's role was to carry out anti-submarine patrols from the North African coast and also to attack any enemy shipping such as U-boats, E-boats and cargo boats.

This also included attacking the harbours occupied by the enemy and such inland targets as the Army wished .

For patrols at sea the Swordfish was equipped with an early form of radar called ASV (air to surface vessels). This required the observer to sit with a cathode ray tube between his legs and into which he had to gaze for the duration of the patrol. The patrols were always at night because it was then that the submarines came to the surface to charge their batteries. The cathode ray screen, when lit, had a most soporific effect and Doc on one occasion had to violently waggle his wings to wake Robert up. A rumour circulated to the effect that the cathode ray tube, because of the position in which it was operated, caused the operator to become impotent. The Swordfish also carried two large depth charges; the object was to straddle the submarine before it dived.

Two days and nights in a dinghy

On another occasion Robert was sent out on a night patrol with his Pilot Doc Stuart and his Gunner Linley to try and find a U-boat that had been sighted. The distance involved in finding this submarine was almost beyond the aircraft's endurance but nevertheless they pushed on to their target. Unfortunately a very heavy gale blew up from the South, which was quite unusual for those parts. Pilot Doc Stuart now realised that they would not have enough fuel to get back to base and made the decision to put the Swordfish down onto the sea. The weather and visibility by now was terrible and the sea was very turbulent. Using all his skill Doc managed to put the aircraft down safely. The dinghy had deployed automatically but unfortunately the few implements i.e., paddles and fresh water that should have been in the survival kit were missing. All three managed to scramble into the dinghy and shortly afterwards they watched as the Swordfish sank. Robert had a pretty good idea where they were as he had spotted land on his radar just before they put down into the sea. The wind and the tide were very strong and they were now concerned that they might be heading towards the Germans. They sat in the dinghy for two days not being able to see anything as the storm had blown the desert sand up into the air and out to sea. Then suddenly the wind dropped and they could see that they were very close to land. They managed to paddle, push and swim and eventually came ashore 10 miles from their base. Doc Stuart, had somehow managed to loose all his clothes and was completely naked, and the air gunner Linley had lost the power of his legs. The place was deserted, so Robert and his pilot decided to look around the area. Within a short space of time they came upon an Arab with a herd of donkeys and Robert remembered that he still had some Arab currency, although a little wet in his pocket. He offered this to the Arab in return for one of his donkeys which he eagerly took and Doc also managed to acquire a set of Arab clothes from him.

They returned to where they left the air gunner Linley and put him on the donkey and then set off looking for a railway line. In due course they found it and Robert now knew exactly where they were. They turned right and kept walking until they reached a railway station where they telephoned the commanding officer who came and picked them up . The desert life was for the crews not always easy. It was mostly hard work, flying long hours in a cold cockpit. As observer, Robert's job could be particularly arduous as he had sometimes not only to do his own job as radar operator and navigator, but also had to assist as gunner and telegraphist. The food was not as it should be at times, shortage of water from time to time, and very little in the way of transport.

Robert was asked to report to his squadron commander, Lieutenant Commander Gick who informed him that he had been awarded the Distinguished Service Cross and was to be posted back to England for a rest from operations. He was in due course summoned to attend an Investiture at Buckingham Palace where the Queen presented him with the award, as the King was on a visit to North Africa at that time.

The DSC Citation reads:

"The Distinguished Service Cross has been awarded to Sub-Lieutenant (A) Babington for his skill, bravery and sustained resolution in many air attacks against enemy submarines and E-boats in the Mediterranean."

Home to the UK

Robert told me that his journey home was quite an amazing one, as he flew right across the middle of Africa in short hops in various types of aircraft, mainly in Sabena Airways aircraft. He set off from Cairo in Egypt in October 1942 and flew to Khartoum and then on through the Congo to Stanleyville and then into French Equatorial Africa, finishing up in Lagos, Nigeria. He had to stay in Lagos for six weeks waiting on another aircraft to pick him up, and while he was there he stayed in the officers mess, sunbathing and swimming. He eventually managed to hitch a lift in a Catalina to Lisbon in 'neutral' Portugal where he spent a few days in the British Embassy. He had to remove all badges of rank from his uniform and was warned not to pick a fight with the Germans who were staying in the hotel next door. He took off again in the Catalina and landed a few hours later in Poole on the south coast of England. Here Robert's memory becomes a little bit hazy although he does remember joining a Swordfish squadron (possibly at Yeovilton) and remembers carrying out two low level mining sorties with the squadron, one to Le Havre and the other to Cherbourg Harbour. The Cherbourg sortie must have been exciting, as his pilot came in at zero feet, under the cover of darkness and hopped over the harbour wall, dropped his mines and made a hasty retreat.

HMS Dasher, 816 Squadron, Hatson in the Orkneys

In December 1942 Robert was posted to 816 Squadron that was equipped with Fairy Fulmars and was stationed on board HMS Dasher at Hatson in the Orkneys, Scotland. While at Hatson he met King George V when he was carrying out a Royal Inspection of the Air Station. The Dasher sailed from Scapa Flow to Iceland to act as part of a covering force for a large convoy that was heading for Russia. The weather en-route to Iceland was atrocious and visibility very poor. Nevertheless the squadron had two planes ready to take off at a moments notice. They ploughed on in a northerly direction while the weather grew steadily worse. The ship seemed to make heavy weather of the rough seas, and Robert remembers on one occasion when he was on deck she seemed to get across wind which caused her to list right over and suggested to him she might turn turtle. The creaks and the groans of the ships structure were awful to listen to. Flying in those conditions was impossible but they still kept to a state of readiness. It was impossible to stand on the flight deck and Robert remembers being told by someone that the anemometer had jammed at a record wind speed of 120 knots.

The weather was so bad on board, that it had damaged the Dasher below the water line, necessitating her captain to make the decision to put into one of the sheltered fjords in Iceland to carry out some temporary repairs. Robert said, "The scenery was wonderful with no signs of life whatsoever to be seen. The ship had to be careened over on her side to allow welders to go down and repair a large split that had opened up below her waterline". Once the temporary repairs had been carried the Dasher returned to the Clyde where permanent repairs could be carried out. While waiting for the Dasher to be repaired the squadron moved to Drem where it carried out interception exercises.

Robert remarked, "I think remembering all this now that we were rejoining Dasher after the repair had been completed when the explosion occurred."

27th March 1943, that fateful day

The Squadron returned to the Dasher on the 27th March 1943.

The next few paragraphs are a personal account by Lieutenant RJ Babington of what happened on the 27th March 1943.

"Before I deal with the events of the 27th March 1943 I must explain some of the things that have happened to me since because I believe they have permanently affected my memory. I attended a Court of Inquiry that was held a few days after the sinking and I was called to give evidence. Presumably what evidence I gave is to be found in the records of the inquiry. What I remember now most vividly is the constant demands and orders of the senior officers that we must tell no one anything about the sinking or what had happened. In pursuance of these orders I told no-one anything and sought to put all the details out of my mind.

This was made easy for me as my next posting was to an RAF Station at Ford in Sussex where there was a Naval Night Fighter unit.

The unit there was full of interest as I was flying in quite different aircraft that I was used to, namely Beau fighters and Mosquitoes, which were fitted with experimental radar devices. We operated over London and tried to shoot down German bombers and Doodle Bugs (V1s), a different type of activity to what I had undertaken before. I never mentioned Dasher incident to a soul, and nor did anyone mention it to me. To my family I merely said that I had been sunk in the Western Approaches and gave no details whatsoever. The result of all this restraint is that I have little recollection of the details of the affair. I cannot now recall the number of the squadron, nor the name of the pilot with whom I flew that day. I do not know now what sort of exercise we had been doing or why I was airborne at all [Robert's

flying log book with records up to March 1943 were lost on the Dasher]. However since I have started writing this I believe I have recalled the name of the commanding officer of my squadron, namely Lieutenant Commander Penoyer.

"We landed on HMS Dasher on the afternoon of the 27th March 1943. The time was 4.45pm and I am sure that our aircraft was the last to land on board before she blew up as I and my pilot had just enough time to get out of the aircraft and see it being pushed back to where the lift was as the aircraft were always refuelled before being sent below. I also remember seeing no other aircrew entering or going towards the office.

"The ship was situated in the Clyde and when I saw her before the explosion was heading straight towards the Isle of Arran. The weather was good and fine. After we landed my pilot and myself got out of the aircraft and went into the commander of flying's office situated in the 'Island' on the starboard side of the ship. We were in the process of reporting to him when the explosion occurred. I felt a terrible crunch coming from below and almost immediately the ship lurched and went down at the stern, rather more on the port side. I went out of the office and back on the flight deck when the ship began to settle quite slowly by the stern. I don't remember seeing anyone else although there must have been some. I crossed the flight deck to the port side and went along the walkway just below the flight deck on the port side. I remember as I stood there that something very large hurtled down the deck past me and into the sea at the stern, this was because of the ever increasing inclination of the flight deck. I looked to my left as I was standing on the walkway and found that I could see far below in the entrails of the ship a large fire was raging. Again I don't remember seeing any other people near me at this stage. It is obvious to me that the ship was sinking. I was clothed in my flying suit and May West. I jumped feet first into the sea and struck out vigorously away from the sinking ship. I had heard that when a large ship went down one should get away as far as possible otherwise one would be sucked down with it. I was very glad to have my May West on but it does hamper speed through the water. I looked back towards the ship and by this time she was practically vertical in the water, the bow now pointing towards the sky.

"Inside I could hear the awful bangs, explosions and screams. She slowly slid down and disappeared. At this time I began to notice other men in the water and some Carley Floats with people in and near them. I swam towards a float which was quite near but decided I would leave it to others as I had the May West.

"I remember seeing one man with his head split open. Just then there was a boiling sound in the water and flames that shot high in the air as the surface of the sea caught fire. I turned and swam away from the flames and managed to escape from the fire but a number of men were caught and burned to death. I was fortunate in that the wind was blowing the flames away from me. The next thing I remember was a ship arriving. It had put down scrambling nets and a rope ladder, I went up the rope ladder to be met on deck by a number of young Indian Ratings of the Royal Indian Navy. They supplied me with tea and dried my clothes. I cannot remember the name of this ship and was taken back to Glasgow in it.

"About the time of the explosion, 'Shore Leave' had been piped on board and this meant most of the ships company would have been below in the changing rooms or showers. My commanding officer Lieutenant Commander Penoyer was drowned in the incident but as to the fate of my pilot I am unsure."

The Dasher Memorials

To this day it is not entirely clear what caused the explosion on board HMS Dasher, some say an electrical spark caused it from a faulty light switch and others say it was someone smoking. After this incident the American designed aviation gasoline system used to refuel the aircraft on this type of vessel was modified on all other carriers. It is known that 379 men died that day and it was one of the Royal Navy's biggest catastrophes in home waters.

On the 27th March 1993 the 50th anniversary of the sinking the Royal Naval Association undertook to place a permanent memorial of pink granite stone at the Sunken Garden in Ardrossan. The memorial reads:

"This Memorial is dedicated to the Officers and men who perished when HMS Dasher, an Arch Class Aircraft Carrier."

On June 28th 2000, a team of divers in Scapa Flow dived down to the deck of the Dasher and laid a brass memorial plaque on her deck which reads:

"Dedicated in memory of the 379 men who perished when HMS Dasher blew up and sank on 27th March 1943. RIP."

On his arrival back in Glasgow Robert was given a thorough check by a naval doctor and then sent home on leave. He arrived in Belfast and decided to stop off and meet his cousin, Lord Justice Babington, who was just about to go the Assize. He insisted that Robert should go with him to the County Antrim Grand Jury lunch and get a taste of a very different life, which he did, and it was then, that he decided he wanted to become a barrister. Robert continued on down to Dublin where he spent a few days with his parents.

After the war his cousin invited Robert to come and stay with him while he was studying at Queens University and introduced him to some of his friends. On his return from Shore Leave in April 1943, Robert was posted to 784 Squadron, which was based at Drem in Scotland. This was a Naval Night Fighter School and was equipped with Percival Proctor, Avro Anson and Fairey Fulmars and later in the war Wildcats and Harvards. The course started on

the 24th April 1943 when he flew a 40-minute air experience in a Proctor around Drem with his instructor Lieutenant Kneale. On the 26th April he started his Night Fighter training in Avro Ansons and Fairey Fulmars. On the 24th May 1943 he carried out his first night AI training and his logbook shows for that trip, "Weapon Bent. Carried on as Target". The day and night AI training continued until 18th June when he successfully completed the course and was given an 'average' assessment by the squadron commanding officer, Lieutenant Commander Humphrey's.

On completion of this course Robert's total flying time was now:

Day	431hrs.35mins
Night	282hrs.45mins
Total	714hrs.20mins

At the beginning of July 1943 he then joined 746 (Night Fighter) Squadron at Ford in Sussex, which was under the command of Major 'Skeets' Harris, DSC, Royal Marines. Major Harris trained as a night fighter pilot in 1942 and became the first in the Fleet Air Arm in June 1942. He formed 784 Squadron, which was the first Naval Night Night Fighter Training Squadron and then later established a Night Fighter School at Drem near Edinburgh in Scotland. In December 1942 he moved to Ford, near Little Hampton in Sussex where he set up the first Naval Night Fighter Squadron, which was 746 (NF) Squadron. He also was the first pilot to land a radar fitted night fighter on the deck of an aircraft carrier at sea on HMS Illustrious.

Robert told me that this was a very interesting and fascinating job as he was involved with new experimental AI Radar equipment. He helped to develop and evaluate what a night fighter required in the way of radar and how much the scientific 'boffins' at various establishments could produce and his job was to test it. This was really the pioneering days of radar when night fighting was developing radar techniques such as being able to direct a fighter onto their targets by 'lock on radar' and 'head up cockpit windscreen display.

The Naval Unit also worked very closely with the Radar Experimental Department at Boscombe Down and the Royal Air Force in developing AI (Aircraft Interception), ASV (Air to Surface) and PPI (Plan Position and Tail Defence) and H2S radar systems, and who from time to time would 'allow' the navy to fly some of their aircraft including Beaufighters and Mosquitoes on operations to try out new radar systems. Robert's first flight with 746 Squadron was on the 5th July in a Beaufighter (8319) with his pilot Lieutenant Holme. He flew on operations in the RAF's Mosquito on a number of occasions as well as his own squadron aircraft Fairey Fulmars and Fireflys and became the squadrons senior observer. He also flew as observer, on one flight in a Boston Havoc on the afternoon of the 16th July 1943 with his pilot Sub Lieutenant Twiss. He continued flying on operations and helping with the development of various radar systems until the end of the war. The end came on VJ Day sometime after the squadron joined HMS Ocean in the Irish Sea.

Time to leave

With the war now over Robert was keen to leave and get back to studying law, so he went along to his Flight commander and explained the situation to him and stated that he wanted to leave the Fleet Air Arm and return to Trinity College in Dublin. To his surprise he was allowed to go. He was sent to a personnel dispatch centre at RAF Wittering near Leicester where he handed in his uniform and flying equipment. When it came to his watch that had been issued to him in 1940, the clerk said, "No sir, keep the watch as we don't have any forms for that". When he left the Fleet Air Arm, Robert had accumulated a total of 1051hrs.04mins, 378 of which was at night and had flown in Percival Proctor, Fairey Shark, Supermarine Walrus, Fairey Albacore, Fairey Fulmar, JU52, Consolidated PBY Catalina, DH Tiger Moth, Bristol Blenheim, Bristol Beaufighter, Fairey Swordfish, DH Mosquito, Havoc, and Avro Anson.

He returned to Dublin and joined Trinity again where he studied for his BA Degree and travelled north once a week where he studied Law at Queens University. When he had completed his studies he was eventually called to the Bar and joined the family firm of Solicitors in Belfast He also became a Member of Parliament for South Down in 1969 for four years and subsequently became Chief Crown Prosecutor in Belfast and later, a County Court Judge in Fermanagh and Tyrone He officially retired in 1982 but carried on in a temporary basis. His son Phillip has carried on the family tradition and became a Solicitor and is now a senior partner in the firm of Babington & Croasdaile (Solicitors) in Londonderry.

Robert J Babington is a past Chairman of the Aircrew Association Northern Ireland Branch and still a keen golfer.

WING COMMANDER
JOHN VINCENT CLARENCE BADGER, DFC
ROYAL AIR FORCE NO. 33046
COMMANDING OFFICER
NO. 43 (F) SQUADRON

John Vincent Clarence Badger was born in London on 31st May 1911. His father was a Sergeant Major in the British Army and was stationed at Wellington Barracks near Bird Cage Walk. His mother happened to be over visiting when young Badger decided to come into the world.

When his father left the army he came back to the family home at Leverogue near Lisburn in County Antrim to take up the post of Superintendant at Queens University in Belfast. John Vincent Clarence Badger wasn't particularly keen on being called by any of his Christian names and preferred to be called 'Mac' by his friends.

Mac was educated at the Fountainville Public Elementary School on the Lisburn Road and the Royal Belfast Academical Institute from 1925 to 1928. He did well at school, and played for the 1st Fifteen Rugby Team. He also was a very keen Scout leader so much so that he was selected to take the 'Ulster Patrol' of the Boy Scouts as Patrol Leader to attend the very first ever International Boy Scouts Jamboree, which was held at Chingford, Essex in 1924.

The beginning of his aviation career

While studying at the RBAI he decided to pursue a career in the Royal Air Force, so his school Principal applied on his behalf in September 1927 to the Air Ministry at Gwydyr House in Whitehall to see if he could be accepted for an aircraft apprenticeship examination.

On the 20th September 1927 the Principal received the following reply from the Director of Training:

Air Ministry
Weedier House
Whitehall
London, SW1

20th Sept 1927

Aircraft Apprentices; examination of candidates recommended by education authorities - acknowledgement of nomination forms.

Sir,

I am directed to acknowledge receipt of your communication of the 15th. and enclose a nomination form for the above mentioned examination, and to inform you that it has been accepted.

The centre indicated by you has been noted and the necessary question papers and instructions with regard to the conduct of the examination will be forwarded in due course, but I am to remind you that the responsibility of informing candidates as to the time and place of the examination Devolves upon nominating authorities.

I am, Sir

Your obedient Servant
AH Rolison
For Air Commodore
Director of Training.

Mac sat the apprenticeship exam on the 1st November 1927, which he passed with flying colours and the letter below was sent to his school Principal.

Air Ministry
London WC2

29th December 1927

Sir,

In reply to your letter of the 20th instant, I am directed to inform you that it has been decided to call up JVC Badger with the August 1928 Entry of Aircraft Apprentices.

I am therefore to request that you will be good enough to arrange for the railway warrant and calling up instructions now in his possession to be returned to the Inspector of Training at Gwydyr House in Whitehall.

I am, Sir

Your Obedient Servant
Squadron Leader AS Bond
For Deputy Director of Training

Mac finished his education at the Royal Belfast Academical Institution on the 26th June 1928 and in September was off to No 1 School of Technical Training (Apprentices) Halton to commence his aircraft apprenticeship. This course was the 18th entry where he was given his Royal Air Force Number 562677. Mac settled in well to the course and got his head down, and did brilliantly at Halton finishing his apprenticeship third in order of merit with an 88% pass mark. He qualified as a Fitter Aero Engines with the rank Leading Aircraftsman (LAC). The total number of apprentices on the course was 574.

During my research into Mac's career, I had a very interesting letter from one of his Halton chums a Squadron Leader LA Bailey, RAF (Retired) who was on the same course as Mac. He said in his letter that he was very friendly with Mac and in fact helped him with his maths which was one of his weak subjects, "I did not serve with him after Halton, but did meet him briefly on the tarmac at Hawkinge when he flew in on one occasion during 1935. Mac was a bright lad and was going to go far in the Royal Air Force2 and having passed out of Halton with such a high pass mark, this was rewarded with a Flying Scholarship at the Royal Air Force College Cranwell. The Deputy Director of Training at the Air Ministry sent a letter to the Principal of RBAI on the 25th August 1931 and it read:

Sir,

I am commanded by the Air Council to inform you that Mr. J.V.C. Badger, formerly a scholar of the Royal Belfast Academical Institution, who was nominated by the governing body of the Royal Belfast Academical Institution for the examination held in November, 1927, for entry into the Royal Air Force as an aircraft apprentice under the regulations contained in AM Pamphlet 15, a copy of which is enclosed for information, has been selected for entry into the Royal Air Force College Cranwell, in September 1931, as a result of the passing out examination held in July 1931, at No 1 School of Technical Training (Apprentices) Halton. This aircraft apprentice was selected with five others out of an original entry of some 575 boys.

As explained in paragraph 20 of these accompanying regulations Mr Badger will be excused payment of the uniform deposit of £100 and also of the tuition fees usually payable amounting to £150 for the two years course. On passing out successfully from the College in July 1933, he will be gazetted to a permanent commission as a Pilot Officer.

The Council have much pleasure in thus bringing to the notice of your Committee the very real ability and industry displayed by Mr Badger in competition with the other boys of his course.

I am, Sir,

Your Obedient Servant
JS ROSS

Mac joined Halton College on the 3rd September 1931 and on the 7th he was promoted to Cadet Corporal and was to start his elementary flying training on Avro 504 N, Avro Tutor, Siskin 3 A, and Atlas type aircraft. On the course previous to his 1928 to 1930 two very famous aviators passed out, one was Sir Frank Whittle who was the inventor of the jet engine, and the other was none other than Sir Douglas Bader who unfortunately lost both his legs in a tragic flying accident flying a Bristol Bulldog at Kenley on the 14th December 1931. He also like Mac had won his cadetship through examination. Cranwell was like a public school; it was a tough regime, rooted in naval traditions the site near Sleaford in Lincolnshire, had been a Royal Naval Air Station. It was a regime designed to create officers in Humanities, Engineering, Administration, Service subjects as well as flying. The young officers who were produced by Cranwell were of the highest calibre.

I would like to point out to that Wing Commander Badger's first flying logbook has unfortunately been lost through the ravages of time. I have a copy of his second logbook, which was kindly loaned to me by Mac's brother Lt Colonel DC Badger that starts October 27th 1937. By the time Mac had finished his flying training he would in all probability have clocked up 150 hours on these types. At Cranwell Mac excelled himself, working very hard with every subject. He especially enjoyed the sports, playing for the college football and hockey teams. On the 15th January 1932 he was promoted to the rank of Cadet Sergeant and Flight Cadet Under Officer on 13th January 1933.

On the 14th July 1933 Mac passed out from RAF Cranwell as the best all round Cadet and was awarded the coveted college prize 'The Sword of Honour' which was presented to him by Air Marshal Brooke-Popham and with it came promotion to Pilot Officer. The Commandant of the college, Air Vice Marshal WGS Mitchell commented, that since the formation of the College 646 Flight Cadets had graduated.

He also mentioned that during this term one Cadet had been withdrawn because of inability to become a safe pilot, and two others were withdrawn owing to 'incurable air sickness'.

A flight Cadet, John William Gard from the College was killed on the 16th June in an accident at Ruskington Sleaford. He was flying an Atlas aircraft, which crashed on landing in a field. The aircraft caught fire and before anyone could reach him he had burned to death.

In 1933 the cost of training a Cadet for the three years was £539.

43 (F) Fighter 'Fighting Cocks' Squadron Tangmere 15.7.33 to 6.7.34.

On passing out from Cranwell Pilot Officer Badger was posted to 43 (F) Squadron on the 15th July 1933. The squadron was commanded by Squadron Leader RH Hammer, MC and was equipped with Hawker Furys. Mac Finished his tour with 43 (F) Squadron on the 6th July 1934 and on the 10th July went to RAF Base at Leuchars for 2 months and then down to RAF Base at Calshot.

I have no record of Macs flying at Leuchars or Calshot.

On the 15th September 1934 he was posted to the RAF Base at Gosport for 1 month, then on the 11th October he was posted to the School of Naval Cooperation at Lee-on-Solent for three months.

On the 4th January 1935 Mac seconded into the Fleet Air Arm as a test Pilot and joined 821 Torpedo Spotter Reconnaissance (TSR) Fleet Air Arm Squadron at their shore base at Eastleigh and at sea onboard the aircraft carrier HMS Courageous. I do know that he did sail with Courageous and was involved in the Abyssinian campaign; unfortunately I do not know what his involvement was there. HMS Courageous was sunk on the 17th September 1939, hit by two torpedoes from the German U-boat U-29.

Mac was promoted to the rank of Flying Officer on the 15th January 1935 and Flight Lieutenant on the 15th January 1937. He left HMS Courageous on the 25th October 1937 to join the Marine Aircraft Experimental Establishment at Felixstowe as a seaplane test pilot for eighteen months.

It is at this point that his second flying logbook starts which shows to date he had flown 1115hrs.05mins in the following types: Avro 504N, Avro Tutor, Siskin 111, Atlas, Hawker Fury, Hawker Hart, Tiger Moth and Nimrod.

The aircraft types, which he flew as a test pilot at the MAEE, were all float planes: Seal, Fairey 111, Shark, Swordfish, Seafox, Queen Wasp, Hawker Osprey, Scapa, Walrus, Stranraer, and London.

Some interesting extracts from his log with MAEE

Jan 17th	Swordfish, Self, A.C.Graves Calshot to HMS Birmingham (Crusier)
Mar 4th	Seafox, Self, AC Graves Rear Gun Mounting Trial.

Parachute Ripping Carried out 2/3/37.

April 25th	Scapa, F/Lt Ryley, Self Anchor Trials.
May 5th	Walrus, Self, Lt/Cdr Ronald Catapult Launch and rough weather landings from 'Pegasus'. (The aircraft Carrier Ark Royal was renamed Pegasus on 21st December 1934. She was used mostly as a depot ship, but a catapult was fitted in 1938.)

May 28th	Warrus, Self, AC Kelling Empire Air day.

In June 1937 Mac was assessed as a Sea Plane Test Pilot as 'above the average' and promoted to Flight Lieutenant.

Parachute ripping carried out 16/6/38.

June 14th	Walrus, Self, LAC Freeman Flare Dropping
June 16th	Walrus, Self, AC Peach. Dropping Smoke Floats.
June 21st	Sunderland, S/Ldr Collins, F/Lt Ryley, Self, S/Ldr Bardon.
July 6th	Queen Wasp, Self Tests with Autopilot.
Aug 18th	Walrus, Self, Cpl Wood Test on new chassis.
Aug 27th	Scapa, S/Ldr Ryley, Self Anchor Trial.
Sept 10th	Walrus, Self, AC Barham Embarking HMS Albatross. (Albatross was laid down for the Royal Australian Navy on the 5th May 1926 and completed in January 1929. She was later transferred to Britain and commissioned in the Royal Navy on 29th September 1938. The hangar forward could accommodate nine aircraft, though initially six single engine Seagull amphibian flying boats were carried, and later six to nine Walrus.)

1939

Feb 14th	Seafox, Self, LAC Wiseman Air test on reasssembly.
Feb 18th	Shark, Self Target for gunners.
Mar 4th	Seal, Self, Cpl Gilbert Photography Cabot jettison.

In June 1938 Mac was again assessed as a Seaplane Pilot as 'above the average'.

Mac Left the Marine Aircraft Experimental Establishment in Felixstowe on the 20th April 1939 and was transferred back to the Royal Air Force where he joined 13 (F) Fighter Group Head Quarters at Hucknal, as a staff officer. At this point in time I am not sure what his duties were, perhaps he was involved on the staff helping to set up and locate this new fighter group which had to be up and running at Newcastle by September 1939 for the protection of the North of England. Mac had a great love for animals and had his own dog, which was a beautiful German Shepherd whose name was 'Linty'.

His logbook shows him visiting Usworth, Acklington, Hucknall, Leconfield and Turnhouse in a Magister between May 1939 and December 1939, all these stations came under the umbrella of 13 (F) Group HQ at Newcastle. His log book also shows an entry for the 10th July 1939 when he took his brother Lieutenant Dennis Badger for a 30 minute flying practice flight. This was probably the last time they saw each other until after the Fall of France in May 1940. Lt Badger was one of the thousands lucky enough to be evacuated of the Dunkirk beaches. On The 28th October 1939 RAF fighters East of Dalkeith in South East Scotland shot down a Heinkel 111. This was the first German aircraft to be shot down over British soil, two of the four-man crew survived. There is a photograph on the front page of The War Illustrated Volume 1, No 10 of this crash and standing on the wing looking into the fuselage is Mac probably visiting the downed aircraft in his official capacity as a Staff Officer for 13 (F) Fighter Group H.Q.

On the 18th January 1940 Mac was posted as a Staff Officer to join the 14 Group Headquarters to join the British Expeditionary Force at ARRAS in France.

His logbook shows his first flight with 14 Group was on the 24th February when he flew with Squadron Leader Morris in a Tiger Moth from Arras to Le Touget on the French coast and returned to Arras the same day. On March the 2nd he flew again in the Tiger Moth and this time with Flying Officer MacCarthy from Glissay to Arras and return, and again on the 7th from Arras to Seclin and return.

On the 17th he flew Flight Lieutenant Domville from Arras to Seclin and return and the 18th he flew him to Glissay and return. His last flight in March was on the 26th when he flew with Leading Aircraft Man (LAC) Batte to Glissay and return.

On April 7th he flew with fellow Ulsterman Flying Officer Bickerton to Le Touquet and return and again to Arras on the 19th.

On the 20th April he flew Wing Commander Harvey from Arras to Glissay and on to Le Touqet and on the 21st flew him again from Le Touqet to Abbeyville and back to Headquarters at Arras.

On the 23rd he flew Wing Commander Harvey from Arras to Merville and back to Arras and on the 24th met up with Flying Officer Bickerton and flew him to from Arras to Vitry, returning himself to Arras later that day. May 2nd, 5th, 7th and 8th was spent flying with Flying Officer MacCarthy between Arras, Seclin, Merville, Abbeyville and his last trip in the Tiger Moth was to Le Touquet and return with Flying Officer MacCarthy.

This story, which I am about to tell, takes place between the 10th and 22nd May 1940.

When the invasion of Belgium began Flying Officer Bickerton and Mac 'commandeered' a car, I know this because I have a letter, which was sent by Flying Officer Bickerton to the Badger family when he was killed.

Flying Officer Bickerton writes:

"Mac and I drove together from Achicourt near Arras where our Headquarters was, to Lille. We had to leave there hurriedly and Mac had just told me the reason why. I went with him onto Norrent Fontes and we decided to go onto Boulogne and see what was happening there. It was a long and slow journey; the roads were chocked with refugees. We hadn't had a meal for a considerable time

but we had some rations and a bottle of champagne in the car. So we rested up there and discussed what we were going to do if we were cut off and could not get out of France. In Boulogne bombs were dropping, and the house, which we tried to get food in, was badly hit when we were about 200 yards from it. We decided to return to Norrent Fontes and we slept in the car. The next day was a bit of a strain and eventually an aircraft was sent for us from England and we took off later that evening."

Mac's Flying logbook indeed shows that a Bristol Bombay did in Norrent Fontes on the 20th May and took himself Wing Commander Boret, Flying Officer Bickerton, AC Fullard, himself and others back to Hendon. During those ten days when Mac and Flying Officer Bickerton were trying to get out of France, the Germans had invaded Belgium, attacking The Hague, and the Belgium Fortress of Eben Email, Maastrict and Leige. Allied troops began crossing into Belgium under the command of Major General Montgomery, the Germans had invaded Holland, and France had braced itself invasion. The Royal Air Force had lost 70 aircraft on attacks on bridges across the Meuse including five Fairey Battles, which were shot down attacking the bridges over the Albert Canal. Germany had occupied Brussels, Louvaine, Malines, and Namur, Antwerp and Bolougne surrendered and the bulk of the British Expeditionary Force were forced back to the Channel and trapped at Dunkirk. Calais and Belgium had surrendered and by the 4th June 1940 a total of 338,226 Allied troops were taken off the Dunkirk beaches, leaving 40,000 behind.

Mac's logbook shows that on June 8th he returned to France in a De Havilland Dominee with Pilot Officer Ledley, he flew firstly to Everux and then on to Orleans, returning the next day to Jersey in the Channel Islands. Why you might ask, did Mac return to France at that time, I don't know, except to say it must have been for something extremely important? The last log entry before he joined 43 (F) Squadron was on the 11th June when he flew the Dominee back to Hendon.

After a spell of well-earned leave Mac was told that he was being posted to join 43 (F) Fighter Squadron, which was based at Tangmere as Supernumerary for Flying Duties on the 22nd June 1940.

43 (F) Fighter Squadron's Motto is 'Gloria Finis', 'Glory for all'

The squadron badge is a Game Cock which commemorates the first post war designed fighter with which the Squadron was equipped in 1926. 43 Squadron was formed at Stirling on the 15th April 1916, and moved to Netheravon in August. It was posted overseas to France in January '917, equipped with Sopwith Strutters in the scout role. The squadron was re-equipped with Sopwith Camels in September 1917, and the record score in air combat for numbers of aircraft destroyed in one day had been secured by a 43 Squadron pilot, Captain JL Trollope on the 24th March when he destroyed six German aircraft and on the 12th April this was equalised by another 43 Squadron pilot Captain Captain HW Wollet. The squadron was disbanded at Spittlegate on the 31st December 1919 and was reformed at Henlow on the 1st July 1925, equipped with the Gloster Gamecock which formed the foundation for 43 Squadron's aerobatic prowess which came to its height in the 30's with Hawker Furys.

In December 1926 the Squadron moved to Tangmere where it remained until World War II. In November 1938 the squadron was equipped with Hurricane 1s and moved up to Newcastle where it flew mostly convoy patrols. The squadron's first victory came on the 20th January when Flight Lieutenant Hull and Sergeant Carey shot down a He111 while on convoy patrol. On the 1st June 1940, 43 Squadron returned to Tangmere and went straight into patrols covering the Dunkirk Beaches,

The squadron was heavily involved fighting the Luftwaffe during the Battle of Britain, during that period loosing three of its commanding officers, ten pilots were also killed and ten others were wounded (two of them twice). During the Battle 43 Squadron destroyed sixty enemy aircraft, thirteen more probables and twenty five damaged.

Squadron Leader CG Lott, DSO

Squadron Leader Lott, Pilot Officer Carey and Sergeant Mills met six Me110s head on. Squadron Leader Lott was wounded when a cannon shell exploded on his armoured windscreen. Blinded in one eye and suffering intense pain and with his aircraft on fire he attempted to return to base, but three miles short of Tangmere increasing flames forced him to abandon his Hurricane at 700 feet. His aircraft crashed on Fontwell Race course and was completely burnt out, only the tail wheel was recognisable.

Squadron Leader Lotts removal from the squadron was devastating both for him and its personnel.

Squadron Leader Caesar B Hull

Squadron Leader Caesar Hull, Rhodesian by birth, South African by upbringing came to 43 Squadron on 8th August 1936 as a Pilot Officer and by 1939 he commanded 'A' Flight. There was no man better fitted to take over 43 Squadron and to revive the spirit which was sagging from the loss of Acting Wing Commander JVC Badger, DFC when he was so grievously wounded on the 30th August 1940. For 43 Squadron Caesar Hull seemed more than a man could be, and already he was a living legend to a battle weary, sadly tired squadron. Caesar merely by his presence brought a new source of vitality to the squadron. Caesar Hull was outstanding as a man, he was a star that shone brighter and higher than his fellows, and in the reflection of his twinkling light 43 was a better and stronger squadron because of it. Pilots found a confidence when flying with him that was wholly lacking otherwise and no one could throw a

Hurricane around the sky the way he could. Nobody ever heard him say a nasty unkind word about anyone and because of him, 43 Squadron prospered so much. Sadly, one week after he took over the command of the Squadron he too was dead.

At 1635 hrs on the 7th September 1940, nine aircraft from 43 Squadron were scrambled and ordered to fly on varying vectors. They finally sighted a formation of 25 Dornier 17s crossing the coast near Folkstone at 18,000 feet with a ring of fighters circling 500 feet above, and following some miles behind were two similar groups of escorted Dorniers. Squadron Leader Caesar Hull led his nine Hurricanes towards the front group, climbing until he was 1500 feet above the enemy bombers. He peeled of to the left and dived down, "We heard his throaty chuckle as he told us to sail in and 'smash 'em', those were the last words anybody ever heard from him." At 1750 hrs when the pilots returned from this bitter battle, Flight Lieutenant Kilmartin took off his flying helmet and said just two words to Flight Sergeant Parker "My God", turned and went into the dispersal hut.

Caesar Hull and Dick Reynell had been killed, Dick Reynell had bailed out seconds before his Hurricane blew up in mid air over Black Heath but something had gone wrong with his parachute and he died on hitting the ground. Squadron Leader Hull was found ten miles away from his comrade at Purley still in his aircraft, itself so badly damaged by fire that it was identified only by the serial numbers on its guns. Squadron Leader Hull's death shattered the squadron for a long time there after.

I would like to add this story, which I borrowed from Hector Bolitho's book, Combat Report.

In the first year of the war, 43 Squadron lost thirty-six pilots for the reward of ninety-seven German aircraft. 'Tubby Badger', who had been with 43 in the early days came back as its third commanding officer since the war began. He was shot down on August 30th and was unable to fly again. Caesar Hull took over command on September 1st, a fulfilment to his career, which meant more to him than all his victories. He didn't live long enough to have the third stripe sewn on his sleeve. He led 43 through a succession of combats for only seven days. On the 8th September he was found dead, beside his aircraft in a field in Kent and had been killed by a bullet during the battle of the London Docks.

The Huns had come over in continuous waves all day and Caesar had led the squadron in to attack a formation of Dornier Bombers and was never seen alive again.

All the key men fighting with 43 were shot down or killed within eight days, Squadron Leader Badger was shot down on August 30th. Tony Woods-Scawen was shot down and killed when his aircraft crashed near an aircraft of 85 Squadron, which also had been shot down in the same battle. His brother flew unknown to Tony Woods-Scawen, the aircraft. They were killed within a few minutes of each other and fell side by side.

Acting Wing Commander JVC Badger, DFC

Squadron Leader JVC Badger was no stranger to 43 Squadron, for their flight order book of 1932 shows that Pilot Officer Badger had been authorised to fly their chequered Furies. Now he had returned, in days of greater moment to lead the camouflaged successors to those Furies around the self same Sussex sky.

In June 1940, Mac was posted to 43 Squadron as a Supernumerary Squadron Leader to gain operational and administration duties.

His flying logbook shows that his first flight with the squadron was on the 24th June in Hurricane 1836 and was an hours air experience flight.

Log book entries for June.

June 24th	Hurricane 1836, self Experience on type. 1hr.
June 24th	Hurricane 3531, self Experience on type. 1 hour.15mins
June 25th	Hurricane 1727, self Experience on type. 50mins.
June 25th	Hurricane 1936, self Experience on type. 1hr.
June 26th	Hurricane 3466, self Witnessing, FC Attacks. 55mins.
June 28th	Hurricane 1739, self Formation Practice. 55mins
June 28th	Hurricane 1836, self Fixing Guns in sea. 1 hr.
June 29th	Hurricane 1836, self No 1 Attacks & Form, Drill. 50mins.

JULY 1940

On the 4th July Mac flew his first operation with the squadron and on the 9th July he took command of the squadron due to Squadron Leader Lott's forced retirement after enemy action.

On the 12th July flying Hurricane P3531 Mac intercepted and shot down his first enemy aircraft, which was a Heinkel 111. On the 21st July while on a convoy patrol Mac shot down two Dornier 17s flying Hurricane P3971. (P3971 became Mac's personal steed during the battle). During the combat with Hauptmann Gerlitz of 111/ JG27, ten miles south of the 'Needles' his starboard aileron jammed by damage caused by an exploding 20mm cannon shell. Mac managed to return to base and the aircraft was repairable.

This extract for the 21st July was taken from AB Austin's book Fighter Command.

On the afternoon of July 21st, six Hurricanes of 43 Squadron went up on patrol over the English Channel. A quarter of an hour later five of them landed again at their aerodrome, one was missing. Squadron Leader Badger, commanding 43 Squadron, had come back with a dent in one wing where a Messerschmitt cannon shell exploded. "How many did you meet?" asked the Intelligence Officer. "Oh, about forty Dornier 17s and the same number of Messerschmitt 109s and 110s, they said, "Yes, must have been about eighty in all".

The six Hurricane pilots were flying at 11,000 feet over the sea when they saw, 2000 feet above them, the massed formation of German bombers and fighters, tightly packed for safety, circling over a convoy. The Hurricanes were flying in two sections of three one above each other and Badger was leading the lower and Flight Lieutenant Morgan the upper. As they flew across the bows of the convoy, Badger looked up quickly, and heard two words on the radiotelephone. "Huns ahead," Morgan had spoken. The six pilots, looking up into the sun, saw the enemy rising in tiers as far as the eyes could see. From a fighting point of view, everything was wrong. They were greatly outnumbered. They were below the enemy, and would have to manoeuvre for a better position. The Messerschmitt pilots, high above, were perfectly placed for a dive out of the sun on to an enemy whom they could see plainly, but who could not expect to have a clear view of them unless he did something about it quickly. Badger ordered his section of three into line astern. "The situation", as he said, "looked pretty grim", but he hoped to be able to "upset them a bit." There was, however, one possibility. The enemy bombers looked as if they were preparing to dive on the convoy. If they did, the Hurricanes might hope to catch some of them at a disadvantage, Badger flew to a point where he judged they would begin their shallow dive for bomb dropping.

They followed each other very closely to the attack on the convoy, Badger firing, a short burst at one of them and had to pull away quickly, because he found himself in close line abreast with the following Dornier. He swung back to attack another Dornier, and had just opened fire when tracer bullets began to whip past him. Though he dodged at once, his Hurricane was hit, his starboard aileron had jammed, making his aircraft difficult to control, and useless for the kind of dogfight into which he might expect to be flung at any moment. There was nothing for it but to return to base.

On the 22nd July 1940 Mac received a letter from the then Secretary of State for Air, and it read.

Acting Wing Commander JVC Badger
Royal Air Force
Was mentioned in a despatch from Air Marshal Sir Arthur S Barratt, KCB CMG MC
Dated 22nd July 1940
For gallant and distinguished services.
I have it in command from the King to record His Majesty's high appreciation of the services rendered.

Archibald Sinclair
Secretary of State for Air

By the end of July 1940 Mac had completed 31 operations with the squadron.

August 1940

On the 8th August 1940 flying his Hurricane P3971 Mac claimed a BF 109E as a 'probable' and on the 13th August, which was 'Adler Tag' Eagle day, Mac engaged and damaged two Ju88s.

Extract from Mac's combat report for 13th August 'Adler Tag':

"I was leading No 43 Squadron as Green 1, when we were ordered to patrol at 10,000 feet and contact 'Red' Section who was already in the air. After rendezvous we were ordered to 18,000 feet and warned of a large formation of bandits approaching from the South. At 13,000 feet approx 'Red' 1 gave 'Tally Ho' and bandits were seen approaching our starboard beam. They were in two large formations of approx. 25 each. I climbed squadron up sun of nearer formation and turned south to meet them. When 1,000 feet above I turned in to attack with sections in line astern. I went in behind one JU88 and gave him two steady bursts of five seconds. I could see I was hitting but the target did not seem distressed except for the emission of black smoke, which I believe was due to full throttle opening. I then noticed tracer passing me from the port quarter so broke away and gave alarm that Me110s were attacking us. I returned to attack a straggler in the other formation and gave him two bursts to finish my ammunition but enemy aircraft did not go down.

"Return fire was pretty intense and appeared to be controlled as it was withheld until I was about 400 yards astern. The Me110s did one dive and then climbed out of reach showing no willingness to fight. I saw one enemy aircraft crash just west of Arundel and one parachute descending North of Littlehampton.

"For the third time in succession that my squadron has been ordered to intercept enemy aircraft I have heard German being clearly spoken on our wavelength. Squadron Leader JVC Badger, Green 1."

On the 14th he intercepted and destroyed two more Junkers 88s.

On the 15th he destroyed another Junkers 88, his Hurricane was hit in the glycol system by return fire from the Ju88 of 4/LG1, which he had engaged over Emsworth. Mac returned to base with engine and cockpit hood damaged at 1730 hrs. He was unhurt and his aircraft was repairable.

The 16th of August was a busy day for Mac and P3971 when they engaged and destroyed three Junkers 87s and on the 26th he destroyed a Heinkel 111 and claimed a half share on a second.

For some unknown reason Mac has written an entry in his logbook between the 25th and 26th August.

August 12th   Hurricane 3971, self
              'X' Raid.

Sadly, while flying Hurricane V6548 on the 30th August, his aircraft was attacked by BF109s. He baled out at 22,000 feet over Woodchurch and came down in a copse of trees at 'Townland Farm' impaling himself on a branch, splitting his spine.

Mrs Mary Manton (I think this is how her name was spelt) who owned Townland Farm rushed to Mac's aid, but there was little she could do for him due to the seriousness of his injuries. She went on to say, that Mac's courage at the time was absolutely unswaying and she will never forget it. She visited Mac a few times at Ashford Hospital and though he was so gravely ill, he was always brave and smiling.

Wing Commander John Vincent Clarence Badger was awarded the Distinguished Flying Cross on the 9th September 1940, and the Citation reads:

> This Officer assumed command of a squadron in July 1940, and it is through his personal leadership that the squadron has achieved so many successes since the intensive air operation began.
>
> He has been instrumental in destroying six enemy aircraft inspite of the fact that on three occasions he has returned with his aircraft very badly damaged through enemy cannon fire.
>
> He has immediately taken off in another aircraft to lead the squadron on patrol.
>
> Squadron Leader Badger has displayed great courage and resolution.

Through the months Mac spent in Ashford hospital with his horrific injuries, he was always smiling, joking and keeping everyone else's spirits up. Mac bravely bore much agony for almost a year, when on the 30th August 1941 he finally succumbed to his great suffering, eleven months to the day from he was shot down.

Wing Commander JVC Badger is buried in the Churchyard of St Michael and All Angels Church at Halton in Buckinghamshire. He was 29 years old. Quite fittingly Mac's final resting place is only half a mile away from were he started his Royal Air Force Career thirteen years earlier.

Mac had carried out almost one hundred sorties with 43 Squadron between July and August 1940, sometimes flying five sorties in one day. Many tributes were sent to the Badger family, some of which I would like to share with you. Personal Tribute to Squadron Leader JVC Badger, DFC from a correspondent of the London Times 5th August 1941. All of his friends, particularly those on Fighter Command, learnt with grief of the death of Squadron Leader JVC Badger, DFC who died in hospital after a long and painful illness. He had had the great misfortune to be twice wounded in the course of a descent by parachute, and although he put up a stiff fight and was bravely attempting to meet his friends again his injuries were too severe.

Those who served with him at Cranwell between 1931 and 1933, as well as many others will think with pleasure and regret of his quiet efficiency and his most attractive ways.

London Times, 5th August 1941

The second was sent to his father from one of Mac's close school friends Lieutenant Commander Sayers:

> Upper War Room
>
> July 3, 1941
>
> Dear Mr Badger:
>
> I was grieved to read today of Mac's death. I knew him when he was at Inst and I at Methody and on my first RNVR training was lovely to meet him again and to fly with him.
>
> It was easy to see on board what a leader he was. Since that time I have heard many RAF speak of him with admiration and I know that the war proved all his powers. We can ill afford to lose men as fearless and skilled as he. May I offer to Mrs Badger and yourself my deep respect and sympathy?
>
> Yours Sincerely,
> John E Sayers

Lt Commander Sayers was on the Staff of Churchill's Map Room, and was also a survivor of the sinking of the Courageous in 1939, a ship which Mac was no stranger to.

Thirdly a moving tribute from Squadron Leader TFD Morgan who took Command of 43 Squadron in September 1941.

> No. 43 Squadron,
> RAF Station,
> Drem, East Lothian.
>
> 2nd July 1941
>
> Dear Mr Badger,
>
> It was with very great regret that I heard today of Tubby's death. I was one of his Flight Commanders when 43 Squadron were in the thick of things last July and August, and his leadership and outstanding personality were a marvellous inspiration not only to myself but also to the other members of the squadron.
>
> I had hoped that by now he would have started to recover, but I knew from inquiries I made from time to time at the hospitals he was in that his injuries were very severe. All of us who were privileged to know him have deeply regretted that he should have suffered so much during the last months.
>
> With my sincere sympathies.
>
> Yours Sincerely,
> Tom Morgan
> Squadron Leader,
> No 43 Squadron, RAF

Mac's name is also on the Royal Belfast Academical Institute War Memorial to the memory of those Instonians who gave their lives in World war 1939-1945.

Wing Commander John Vincent Clarence Badger, DFC

Although one of 'Churchill's Few', he considered himself as one of the 'Many' who did what was expected of him, and also one of the 'Many' who suffered a similar fate.

On the 30th August Mac had flown 1373hrs. 50mins in 23 different types of RAF and FAA aircraft. The types were:

Avro 504 N Atlas	Avro Tutor
Siskin 111A	Hawker Hart
Hawker Fury	Nimrod
Tiger Moth	Fairey 111F
Seal	Fairey Swordfish
Shark	Queen Wasp
Seafox	Scapa
Hawker Osprey	Stranraer
Walrus	Magister
London	Hawker Hurricane
Harvard	Moth

I had the pleasure to meet Mac's brother, Mr Dennis Badger, OBE a few years ago and when I told him about my book he had no hesitation in supplying me with Mac's flying logbook, photographs and all the relevant information, which I needed. He also made me custodian of Mac's Cranwell Sword of Honour, which was on permanent loan to 43 (F) Squadron. The squadron at the time of writing was based at Royal Air Force Leuchars. It is in the safe keeping of 43 Squadrons Commanding Officer Wing Commander Simon Bryant.

When I suggested to Wing Commander Bryant that the Squadron might like to have the sword for the 60th Anniversary of the Battle of Britain, he kindly invited me over to Leuchars to attend a 43 Squadron dinner and present the Sword to him. I was asked to make a speech during the dinner, which I duly did, mentioning Mac's career, when I had finished there wasn't a dry eye in the room. A very moved and young Italian Air Force Officer approached me, and with tears coming from his eyes, he said, "Sir, tonight has been a very special night for me, one I shall never forget, thank you."

That was an evening I shall never forget.

Mr Dennis Badger joined 502 Ulster squadron in the 1930's and was awarded his Wings when he was a student at Queens University Belfast. On applying for a permanent commission after his Graduation he unfortunately failed his medical and was grounded. So he decided there and then that if he could not fly there was no point in remaining in the Royal Air Force, so he volunteered for the army. He joined the Royal Electrical & Mechanical Engineers and finished the war as Lieutenant Colonel and was mentioned in Despatches. Sadly he to has passed away.

SERGEANT
WILLIAM JOHN BARRISKILL
ROYAL AIR FORCE NO. 1126133.
AIR GUNNER
NO. 104 SQUADRON
MIDDLE EAST FORCES

KILLED IN ACTION 7TH AUGUST 1943

William John Barriskill, son of Mr David Barriskill, was born in Ballyoran, in the Parish of Mullavilly, Portadown, County of Armagh on the 12th September 1915. He was educated at Mullavilly Primary School and his further education was completed at the Portadown Technical College. On leaving the college he was employed as a greengrocer with the Co-op group in Portadown.

John applied to join the RAF at the recruiting office in Clifton Street in early October 1940 and was accepted as aircrew. Leading Aircraftsman Barriskill was then posted to No 3 Receiving Centre at Padgate on 26th October, and then on 11th January 1941 was sent to No 9 Receiving Wing at Stratford where he received his uniform and medical.

On the 15th March 1941 John's next posting was to No 6 Initial Training Wing at Aberystwyth, near Cardington Bay in Wales. His training here consisted of square bashing, how to make a bed properly, and most important of all, how to salute etc. On completion of his initial training, John was posted to No 9 EFTS at RAF Ansty, near Coventry on 31st May 1941 to start his pilots training. On 2nd June 1941 he made his first flight in a Tiger Moth and went solo on 1st July 1940. Unfortunately during his first Solo flight and while coming into land, John stalled the aircraft causing it to hit the runway. There was some minor damage to the aircraft's undercarriage, and as a result of this, John was turned down for aircrew.

His next posting was to No 30 MU on 12th August 1941 as a clerk, and then on to RAF Station St Andreas in the Isle of Man where he was put in charge of provisions and accounts, arriving there on 7th October 1941. John hated administration work, and after sticking it for six months, he decided to re-apply for aircrew duties. On 29th March 1942 he was sent to the No 3 Air Gunnery School were he completed an air gunnery course. John's

record of service shows that he then went in front of an air crew selection board in Edinburgh on 1st October 1942, and then on 5th October 1942 trained down to RAF Abbey Lodge Air Crew Reception Centre where he sat a selection board. On completion of the selection board John was delighted to hear that he had been accepted as an air gunner.

On the 10th October 1942 he was posted to No 14 Initial Training Wing for one month and on 14th November posted to No 4 Air Gunnery School, no doubt to complete another air gunnery course. On 19th January 1943, John was posted to No 21 Operational Training Unit at Morton-on-the-Marsh to start his operational training on the Vickers Wellington. On successfully completing the course on 27th March 1943 he was informed that he would be joining 104 Squadron, which was attached to Middle East command. John's record of service also shows that he joined 104 Squadron at Hani West in Tunisia on 6th June 1943. On the 7th August 1943 he took off on operations along with his crew on a night raid to bomb Sicily. His aircraft failed to return, feared shot down close to the Straits of Messina. All onboard were lost.

John's total Service with the RAF was two years and 287 days. He is remembered by his sister Nan, and brother who to this very day never forgets to put a memorial notice to John in the Belfast Telegraph every year, on the eve of his death.

SERGEANT
EDMUND BEATTIE BECKETT
ROYAL AIR FORCE NO. 1795992
PILOT

Edmund was born in Belfast on the 21st June 1924 and was educated at Sullivan Upper School in Holywood County Down. Edmund was the youngest of the family of four brothers, all of who served in the Royal Air Force. Edmund completed his 'senior certificate' in June 1942 and in October 1942 was accepted into the Queens University Air Squadron where he completed a short course.

He joined the Royal Air Force on the 23rd April 1943 and was posted to the Aircrew Reception Centre at St Johns Wood in London. Shortly afterwards he was posted to the No 11 Initial Training Wing (ITW) at Scarborough and completed the course on the 14th August 1943.

Edmund was then posted to No 4 Elementary Flying Training School at Brough for grading flying in DH 82 As (Tiger Moths). Here he flew solo and completed 11hrs.50mins in the air. His next posting was to the Aircrew Dispatch Centre (ACDC) at Heaton Park in Manchester, where under the pilot, navigator, bomber scheme (PNBS he was graded as pilot.

On the 31st October 1943 he boarded the liner 'Andes', arriving in New York in early November. From there he transferred by train to No 31 Personnel Despatch Centre (PDC) at Moncton in Nova Scotia Canada, arriving there on the 10th November 1943.

On the 17th December he transferred to No 32 Elementary Flying Training School (EFTS) at Bowden in Alberta to commence flying training in Cornell 11s. His first flight, under the instruction of Pilot Officer Pilbrow, was on January 29th and lasted for one hour. The tuition consisted of cockpit drill, flight preparation, air experience, effect of controls, and taxing etc, etc. He flew 'Solo' in the Cornell after 6hrs.30mins tuition and he continued his flying training at Bowden until the 21st April when he transferred to No 34 Service Flying Training School (SFTS) at 'Medicine Hat' for CFI and IF tuition. His total flying time on the Cornell was now 71 hours. His first assessment was 'average' as a Pilot.

Shortly after this Edmund was posted to No 17 Service Flying Training School at Souris, Manitoba, to complete his flying training on the twin engined Avro Anson. His first

flight in the Anson was on the 5th September 1944 under the instruction of Flying Officer Breakenridge who remained his principal instructor until he flew solo on the type on the 13th September. Edmund successfully completed the course on the 16th February 1945 and was awarded his 'Wings'. He then returned to the No 31 Personnel Despatch Centre at Moncton and boarded the Queen Elizabeth, arriving back in the UK on the 1st March 1945. He was given a weeks leave and on the 1st April he was posted the No 7 Personnel Reception Centre at Harrogate where he remained until the middle of May 1945.

On the 17th May he was posted to No 15 Elementary Flying Training School (EFTS) at Carlisle flying Tiger Moths. On the 6th June 1945, he entered the No 4 School of Technical Training at St Athan in Wales where he studied engineering for six months. He successfully passed the course on the 10th August 1945. On the 11th January 1946 he was posted to the No 1668 Heavy Conversion Unit at Cottesmore were he flew as flight engineer on a number of flights in Lancasters. On the 21st March he was transferred to No 1653 Heavy Conversion Unit at RAF Luffenham once again as a flight engineer on Lancasters. On the 20th June 1946 he was posted to No 7 personnel Reception Centre at Market Harboro were he was demobbed on the 26th October 1946. Edmunds total flying time was 238 hours.

He returned home to Northern Ireland and rejoined Queens University where he completed a BA Degree and a Post Graduate Diploma in Education. He eventually became Principal of Glastry High School in Ballyhalbert, County Down, and finally retired in 1988. Edmund is an enthusiastic member of the Aircrew Association (Northern Ireland Branch).

FLIGHT LIEUTENANT
SAMUEL BECKETT
ROYAL AIR FORCE NO. 106061
PILOT
NO. 298 SQUADRON

Samuel Beckett was born in Belfast on the 1st April 1921 (twin brother of Joseph Beckett). He was one of four brothers in the family who joined the Royal Air Force, each one qualifying as a Pilot. Samuel was educated at Sullivan Upper School in Holywood, County Down and after completing his education, moved to London were he joined the Imperial Civil Service.

He joined the Royal Air Force in early 1941 and after passing aircrew board (ACRC) and initial training, he was posted to No 24 Elementary Flying Training School (EFTS) at Luton in 1941 to start his elementary flying in Miles Magisters. He finished the course in June 1941 and was posted to No 12 Service Flying Training School (SFTS) at Grantham where he trained on the twin engined Oxford. He successfully passed the course in September 1941 and was awarded his 'Wings. His next posting was to No 15 Operational Training Unit (OTU) at Harwell were he commenced training on Wellingtons. On completing the course in December, Samuel and his crew accompanied by two other Wellingtons were detached to deliver the aircraft to the Middle East, the route being via Gibraltar, Malta and Cairo.

After leaving Gibraltar in late December 1941 the aircraft encountered severe weather conditions and they found themselves well off course over the Italian coast. His aircraft was hit by lightning and they eventually they ran out of fuel and crash-landed on the north coast of Sicily. The two other Wellingtons were lost. Samuel and his crew managed to set fire to the Wellington, destroying all the equipment before being taken prisoner by the Italians. They were interrogated in the Central Railway Station in Rome and ended up in POW camp near Bologna.

When Mussolini and his government surrendered in September 1943, all the POWs escaped but most were quickly recaptured by the Germans. Samuel along with two other RAF Officers 'Packers' and 'George' managed to evade the Germans for 10 months living off the land and avoiding German troops and Italian collaborators. They could not have achieved this without the help of

many Italian families who hid and fed them in their homes. On the 4th June 1944 at 2100 hrs while hiding in the village of Montiocco, they encountered the first of the British troops. Samuel asked, "Where are you going"? The troops replied, "Looking for Jerries, seen any about"?. Samuel told them, "They were here until about 8 o'clock but they are retreating through the Paglio Gap." One of the troops shouted, "Thanks, You speak very good English". Samuel replied, "We ought to, we are English."

He heard one of the troops muttering as he marched on up the road, "What! Well for....."

When Samuel was eventual liberated, during his rehabilitation period which followed he wrote a diary of his times on the 'run', which is a story on its own. It is quite astonishing how he evaded capture during his journey through Italy, often by rail, and often in the company of German troops. He was sent to the Middle East for recuperation and rehabilitation before returning to the UK.

On his safe return to the UK Samuel was posted to No 17 Service Flying Training School at Caistor to start a refresher course on Airspeed Oxfords. It was nearly three years since he had been flying but within a few hours tuition he was flying solo once again. He successfully completed the course on the 9th October with an assessment of "Average" as a Pilot/Navigator. On the 11th October 1944 he was posted to No 1545 Beam Approach Training (BAT) at Halfpenny Green to train in the use of the Lorenz Beam Approach system. The training was carried out in Oxfords and included Beam Approach procedure and IF code, (Link Test), receiver operation, instrument flying, cloud flying, night flying and application of Beam Approach (BA) flying. He completed the course on the 15th October.

On the 6th November Samuel was posted to No 19 Operational Training Unit at Lossiemouth in Scotland to start operational re-training on Wellington Mk X. He started his training in the Wellington on the 18th November 1944 almost three years since he crashed in Italy. He completed the course on the 11th January 1945 with an assessment of 'above the average' as a medium bomber, Pilot/Navigator. On the 23rd March 1945 he was posted to No 1663 Heavy Conversion Unit (HCU) at Rufforth to convert to Halifax 111s. He completed the course on the 16th May and transferred to No 15 Operational Refresher Training Unit (ORTU) for advanced training in Halifax aircraft. This advanced training included X-country exercises, container drops, Rebecca runs, and glider towing.

On the 6th June 1945 Samuel joined 298 Squadron at Tarrant Rushton. During the war 298 was one of the 'specialist' squadrons taking part in the Normandy landings, Arnhem, Rhine crossings and dropping SAS and SOE agents behind enemy lines. Although the war was now over the squadron continued extensive training with glider towing, gun and jeep dropping, mass lift of gliders and Rebecca runs all of which Samuel took part in.

On the 23rd June 1945 Samuel moved with the squadron to Raipur in India were he became flight commander of 'B' Flight and on arrival started route schedules including the 'hump' route to China. The also maintained an airborne support role for the Indian Army and in March 1946 the squadron spent one month with the 2nd Indian Airborne Division at Meiktela, flying Operation Hunger 11 in which they dropped one thousand tons of rice to the starving population. He also was involved in the return of troops and equipment after the Japanese surrender. The journey to India took a total of 27hrs.35mins via High Ercall, Castel Benito, Cairo West Shaibah and Karachi. By this time Samuel had accumulated a total of 787hrs.5mins flying time. During his tour in India Samuel had the opportunity to visit many of India's beautiful cities, among which were, Raipur, Digri, Dum Dum, Santa Cruz, Mauripur, Bilaspur, Karachi, Chaklala and Delhi.

His tour ended with 298 Squadron in March 1946 and on his return to the UK, he was posted to No 1 Reserve Flying School at Panshanger as an instructor on Tiger Moths and then two years instructing on Tiger Moths and Prentices at No 9 Reserve Flying Training School at Doncaster (Aug 1950-Aug 1952).

In 1946 Samuel returned to 'civvy street' and resumed his civil service career, this time in the Air Ministry in London and was posted out to Malta for a number of years to help wind up the RAF there. Samuel was the only one of the family to carry on flying with the RAFVR. This included being seconded to No 202 Squadron at RAF Aldergrove on the first of two annual continuous training - fifteen day detachments, training on Hastings aircraft. The squadron carried out long range meteorological flights over the Atlantic code named 'Bismouth'. Their job was carried out in all weathers making temperature, pressure and humidity recordings on a set pattern and at varying heights.

Samuels last flight was with the Royal Air Force was in fact with 202 Squadron at Aldergrove on the 26th August 1952.

His total flying hours were now:

Single Engine aircraft: 171hrs.30mins day, 8hrs.10mins night. Total 179hrs.40mins.

Twin Engine aircraft: 621hrs.65mins day, 153hrs.80mins night. Total 955hrs.25mins.

He had flown in the following aircraft types: Tiger Moth, Miles Magister, Airspeed Oxford, Wellington Mk 1C & X, Halifax Mk 111 & V11, Percival Prentice and Handley Page Hastings.

Sadly Flight Lieutenant Samuel Beckett died in November 1995.

WING COMMANDER
CHARLES ROBERTSON MacDONALD,
DSO DFC AE

Wing Commander (Chuck as he liked to be called) MacDonald, DSO DFC, the eldest brother of four was born in South Africa on the 31st December 1916 to Ulster parents. He returned to live in Northern Ireland when he was very young. He was educated at the Royal Belfast Academical Institution (Inst) between 1929 and 1934 and, on completing his education joined the Northern Ireland Civil Service.

Chuck joined the Royal Air Force Volunteer Reserve in Belfast in August 1939 and on the outbreak of war was called to full time service with the RAF. He had three brothers, Joseph, Samuel and Edmund all of who joined the RAF and qualified as pilots. Chuck served with great distinction in Bomber Command, being awarded the DSO and DFC. His outstanding leadership, courage and skill (as one citation reported) made him one of the top RAF bomber aces along with Gibson, Cheshire, Tait and Cunningham.

Chuck's Royal Air Force career

On the 2nd October Sergeant Charles Robertson MacDonald was posted to No 3 Initial Training Wing (ITW) at Hastings on the south coast of England to commence his basic training. He completed the course successfully on the 11th April 1940 and transferred to No 13 Elementary Flying Training School (EFTS) at Whitewaltham (The De Havilland School of Flying) training in Tiger Moths.

His first air experience flight was on the 13th April 1940 in a civilian registered (G-AEMF) Tiger Moth and, after 8 hours tuition he went solo on the 2nd May. An entry in his logbook shows a 'pass' signed by the commanding officer entitling him to fly cross-country without a Pilots licence in accordance with an Act of 1926. He successfully completed the course on the 2nd June, being assessed as 'average' by the chief flying instructor and had a total of 53 hours flying time. On the 8th June 1940 he was transferred to No 8 Service Flying Training School (SFTS) at Shawbury to start training in twin engine Oxfords. His first flight on this type was on the 11th June and after just three hours tuition went

'solo' on the 13th June. He successfully completed the course on the 5th September 1940 and was awarded his Wings and assessed as 'average'. His total flying time was now 155hrs.20mins. On the 7th September 1940 he moved on to No 19 Operational training Unit (OTU) at RAF Kinloss in Scotland to start his operational training in Whitley aircraft. His first instructional flight in the Whitley was on the 22nd September (K9019) under the command of Pilot Officer Flower. His instructors for the course were Pilot Officer Flower, Pilot Officer Painter and Sergeant Pocock. Chuck successfully completed the OTU course on the 1st November 1940. His total flying time was now 249hrs.50mins.

On the 7th November 1940 Sergeant Pilot MacDonald reported to No 10 Squadron at RAF Leeming where he joined 'A' Flight. His first operation as 2nd Pilot was on the 26th November to Antwerp, but this operation was aborted due to technical difficulties. He completed 12 operations with No 10 Squadron, four of which where as 2nd Pilot. They were to Le Havre (docks bombed), Brest (Hipper class cruiser bombed), Dunkirk (Calais bombed), Hanover (fire blitz), Duisberg, Rotterdam, Kiel (docks bombed), Lorient, Dusseldorf and Kiel. On the 9th April Chuck made his first flight to Berlin. This was quite an achievement in a Whitley as the flying time there and back was 8 hours. (Mac wrote in his logbook "Fires visible over Kiel 80 miles from target.")

In early April he was transferred to No 76 Squadron at Linton-on-Ouse and converted to the Halifax aircraft. Chuck's first flight with the squadron was on the 13th April in a Halifax piloted by Squadron Leader Willie Tait (later to become Group Captain, DSO*** DFC AFC). From

August 1942 until April 1943 Group Captain Cheshire, VC DSO and DFC, commanded the squadron. On the night of the 10th/11th April 1942 the squadron made history by dropping bomber command's first 8,000 lb bomb on Essen. On the 28th June 1941 the squadron moved to Middleton-St-George and on the 16th June Mac carried out his first operation in a Halifax, the target being Cologne. During this operation a Me109 attacked him and he was later highly commended for his evasive action. On his second operation to Kiel on the 23rd June his aircraft was caught in a flak barrage and received shrapnel damage. On the 2nd of July 1941 Chuck was transferred to No 90 Squadron at RAF Polebrook. In May 1941 the squadron had been selected to receive the first Boeing B-17 Flying Fortress aircraft from America. Its role was high altitude day bombing and its first operational mission, was carried out on the 8th July 1941, when it bombed Wilhelmshaven from 30,000ft. Chuck first flew the B-17C (AN523) on the 4th July 1941, his instructor being Captain Connelly.

The squadron flew a total of 51 sorties in the B-17s, of which 25 were completely abandoned due to frozen guns, turbo and super charger failures and severe oil loss through the breathers causing engine failures. Another problem was the Sperry bombsight, which was not effective above 30,000ft. The Americans had a more efficient bombsight called the Norden, which they refused to release to Britain *(it was still a secret)*. The squadron had to endure severe losses, largely of air gunners, who were attacked by fighters on the long ascent and decent of the Fortress. The number of aborted missions due to technical troubles caused the RAF to conclude the Fortress was not yet suitable for bomber command. The remaining aircraft were transferred to coastal command where they carried out long range maritime reconnaissance duties.

Chuck carried out 7 operations with the squadron in the B-17, the first one on the 12th August in AN532 to Cologne. Chuck records in his logbook that they bombed from 35,000ft; the outside air temperature was -34 degrees C, "No flak and no fighters".

Log extracts for the B-17.

Aug 16th	Fortress AN532, with P/Off Wayman. Bombed Docks at Brest from 35,000ft **Temp -38 degrees. Port inner U/S**
Aug 19th	Fortress AN532, with P/Off Wayman. Dusseldorf. Returned with bombs due heavy vapour trails.
Aug 21st	Fortress AN532, with P/Off Wayman. Dusseldorf. Two inner engines U/S Jettisoned bombs and returned.
Aug 29th	Fortress AN536, with P/Off Wayman. Dusseldorf. 10/10 cloud returned with bombs.
Aug 31st	Fortress AN532, with P/Off Wayman. Kiel. Turbo failed on No 2 engine. Returned with bombs.

Sept 15th	Fortress AN536, with P/Off Wayman. Cologne. Turned back at Dutch Coast Heavy vapour trails.

On the 15th September 1941 Mac received his commission and was promoted to the rank of Pilot Officer. On the 23rd September he and Pilot Officer Wayman were seconded to the No 2 School of Air Navigation at Cranage were they completed a 2 week advanced navigational course, returning to the squadron on the 7th October. (Logbook entry for the 22nd September shows that Chuck and P/Off Wayman hitched a lift on board a Blenheim to Cranage, which was captained by Wing Commander Webster.)

During the course they flew one flight in an Anson (K8718) when they carried out a wind finding and map reading exercise.

On the 3rd November 1941 he was seconded to No1 blind approach training (BAT) course at Horsham flying in Blenheims and Fortresses, returning to 90 Squadron on the 13th February 1942 as a qualified instructor on B-17s. When he had completed the BAT course he was assessed by the unit's commanding officer as being 'above the average'. By this time he had accumulated 534hrs.5mins flying time. On the 14th February 1942 he was transferred to No 1653 Conversion Unit at Polebrook where he became an instructor on B-17.s, Liberators and Blenheims.

Around this time Richard Green, (the star Robin Hood), was making a movie called 'Flying Fortress'. Chuck and his crew were picked to do the flying sequences in the film and in one sequence at the end of the film they were allowed to appear in a minute speaking scene with a little dog jumping into Mac's arms.

In late February 1942 Chuck was selected by the Air Ministry to travel to America and evaluate the B-17 and Liberator Bombers and explain the problems that our pilots were experiencing with these two aircraft. On the 25th February 1942 he travelled to Liverpool and boarded the M.V. Glenstrae, arriving in New York on St Patricks day 17th March. After spending a few days sight seeing in New York he was trained down to the No 66 Bombardment Group at Barksdale Field in Louisiana arriving there on the 26th March. On April 8th/11th/16th/21st, Chuck flew one of the Squadrons B-24 Ds on an air firing exercise in the Gulf of Mexico, and, on a low flying trip along the Mississippi River. He also had the opportunity to pass on information regarding the operational problems that he had had flying the B-17 and as well made a few appearances as a 'veteran' of the air war against Germany to publicise the bond between the two English speaking nations for whom the wars against Japan and Germany were not going well at that time.

On the 16th May 1942 he was posted to Ferry Command at Dorval in Canada and on the 21st May he carried out a ferry command check on Liberator 11124. On the 23rd May he ferried the aircraft, along with F/Off Purceval (Captain), P/Off Sutton, P/Off Danby, Sgt Shadwell, Sgt Hugill, F/Sgt Street and Sgt Willis to Gander and after refuelling set a course for Prestwick in Scotland.

On his return from Canada he was posted to 1653 Conversion Unit at Burn as an instructor on Liberators and Blenheims. On one occasion he flew to Aldergrove, and took the opportunity of flying low over the schoolmaster's residence in Hillsborough. The schoolmaster was his father-in-law. Unfortunately someone had complained about this low flying and he received a reprimand from his CO on his return to base. He remained at the conversion unit until the 5th November 1942 and received the following assessments, 'above the average' as a heavy bomber Pilot and 'above the average' as a Pilot Navigator/Navigator. His total flying hours were now 688 hours and during this period he was promoted to Flying Officer.

Chuck's next posting was to 1652 Conversion Unit at Marston Moor, arriving there on the 9th November 1942 as an instructor on Halifaxes. He remained at Marston Moor until the 14th March 1943 when he was posted to 1663 Conversion Unit at RAF Rufforth for three months again instructing on Halifaxes. During this period he was promoted to Flight Lieutenant and again assessed as 'above the average' as a heavy bomber Pilot. Chuck was posted back onto operations on the 1st July 1943 and joined 78 Squadron at Breighton on the 1st July 1943 as officer commanding 'A' Flight and promoted to Squadron Leader. Among the highlights of the squadron's war record was participation in the first 1000 Bomber Raid on Cologne and the epic raid on the V2 Rocket site at Peenemunde on August 1943. 78 Squadron is recorded as having flown the most sorties in 4 Group, and to have suffered the most losses and the highest percentage losses in any Halifax squadron, and the third largest heaviest losses overall in bomber command.

Chuck completed a total of 41 operations with 78 Squadron the first being on the 3rd July to Cologne. His crew were Sergeant Jackson, Rogers, Middlemiss, Veale, Jackson and Torppa. He carried out five operations during July to Gelsenkirchen, Aachen, Montgeliard and the last one was to Hamburg. The raid on Peugeot Motor Factor at Montgeliard was unsuccessful as the pathfinder Halifaxes were inaccurate; consequently the vast majority of 4 Groups bombs fell on the town of Sochaux. The Peugeot factory only suffered minor damage and production was not effected. Chuck also carried out seven raids on Berlin. On the 1st July 1943 Chuck and his crew took in Halifax (HR874) and set a course for the city of Cologne. This was the first of four major raids on the city in the space of ten nights and, the first time that 'Window' had been used. A force of 791 Aircraft had carried it out and a total of 2,284 tons of bombs were dropped within 50 minutes. Approximately 1,500 people died in that first raid.

Among his 41 operations with 78 Squadron some of which I have listed below, were raids on Mannheim, Milan, Berlin, Munchen Gladbach, Hannover, Dusseldorf, Ludwigshaven, Keil Bay, Schweinfurt and Trappes.

Chuck was awarded the Distinguished Flying Cross in September 1943.

His superiors as well as his peers regarded him as an outstanding pilot and leader. Flight magazine includes him along with Cheshire, Cunningham, Malan, Johnston and three others under the title of 'Aces All'.

On the 28th March he was taken off operations once more and posted 1663 Heavy Conversion Unit at Rufforth as an instructor on Halifaxes. On completion of this posting on the 30th October 1944, he was awarded the Distinguished Service Order. In May 1945 Chuck received his DSO from King George VI in Buckingham Palace at the first public investiture of the war. 'Picture Post' featured it in their magazine and, in two photographs, his mother and wife appear. By coincidence Jimmy Stark received his DFC at the same investiture, and his wife is seated near to Chuck's mother. His other three brothers Joseph, Samuel and Edmund were also able to attend.

The Citation for the DSO is as follows:

Squadron Leader CR MacDonald, DFC

This officer has completed a very large number of sorties and has successfully bombed some of the most heavily defended targets in Germany. He has set the highest example of bravery and devotion to duty, which together with great skill, have inspired all. His record is worthy of the greatest praise.

Chuck's total flying hours now was 1282hrs.30mins.

On the 1st November 1941 he was promoted to Wing Commander and seconded to BOAC as a pilot where he was involved with the evaluation and development of world air routes for the company flying in Dakota aircraft. Before he took to the air with BOAC he attended a 10-day course at the No 1 Beam Approach School at Watchfield on the 4th January 1945. He flew the first route flight to Lisbon with BOAC on the 23rd January 1945 in Dakota (G-AGHN). The flight took him from Croydon to Madrid, Lisbon, Madrid and St Morgan.

Other new routes that he helped to inaugurated were: Croydon to Istres, Castel Benito, Cairo, Abadan, Basra and Cairo; Cairo to Nicisia and Cairo; Cairo to Kasfareet, Lydda and Cairo; Cairo to Luxor and Khartoum; Lagos to Accra, Takoradi, Freetown, Bathurst, Sal, Port Etienne, Gibralter and Lisbon; Hurn to Istres, Castel Benito, El Adem, Almaza Castel Benito, Istres and Hurn; and Hurn to Istres, Luqa, Almaza, Bagdad, Sharjah, Mauripur, Cairo, El Adem, Luqa, Istres and Hurn.

Chuck's last flight with BOAC was in Dakota FL630, on the 3rd November 1945, when he flew from Elma to Hurn. His total flying time was now 1846hours. 15minutes. On leaving the Royal Air Force in November 1945 he returned to Norrthern Ireland and rejoined the civil service. His obvious abilities resulted in his promotion to a senior rank. In 1950 he was introduced to the Baha'i faith, which soon became the dominant force in his life. He gave distinguished service at local and national levels and in 1970 was elected as secretary of the National Spiritual Assembly of the faith in the UK. This being a full time post, he sacrificed his promising career in the civil service and moved to London with his wife and family. He retired from the post in 1987 and from the assembly in 1991, because of illness. Sadly his retirement was cut short as he died in September 1991.

FLIGHT LIEUTENANT
JOSEPH BECKETT, DFC
ROYAL AIR FORCE NO. 161408
PILOT
NO. 115 AND 102 SQUADRONS
BOMBER COMMAND

Flight Lieutenant Joseph Beckett, DFC was born in Belfast on the 1st April 1921 (twin brother of Flight Lieutenant Samuel Beckett). He was educated at the Royal Belfast Academical Institution (Inst). On completing his education he moved to London and joined the Imperial Civil Service.

His RAF career started a few weeks after his twin brother Samuel. He had some difficulty in joining the Royal Air Force, because he had volunteered as a part-time member of the AFS in London, and they were reluctant to release him. He enlisted in the Royal Air Force on the 3rd July 1940 and was posted to Padgate Receiving Centre were he remained until the 7th August. He transferred to the Initial Training Wing at Blackpool on the 3rd July for basic training, which lasted for two weeks and then to a holding centre at Shoreham. On the 29th September Joseph transferred to Aberystwyth to complete his initial training, which he successfully completed in mid-December 1940. He was then posted down to Wilmslow for three days awaiting orders. At Liverpool he boarded His Majesties Troopship in Leopoldville on the 18th December and arrived in Toronto, Canada on the 31st December 1940.

On the 11th January 1941 he transferred by train and arrived at No 1 Elementary Flying Training School (EFTS) at Maltby a few hours later. He commenced his pilot training on the 13th January in a 'fleet' aircraft and went solo on the 23rd January after a total of 8hrs.40mins tuition. He successfully completed the course on the 21st February 1941 and transferred to the Royal Canadian Air Force Station at Picton for twelve days classroom training.

His next posting was to the No 5 Service Flying Training School at the Royal Canadian Air Force Station at Brentwood flying the twin engine Avro Anson. His first flight in the Anson was on the 10th March and he went solo on the type after 3hrs.15mins tuition. He completed the course successfully, and on the 17th May 1941 was awarded his Wings, promoted to Sergeant, and was assessed as 'above the average' as a Pilot. His total flying hours had accumulated to 160hrs.10mins. Joseph then transferred by train to Nova Scotia and boarded the armed

merchant cruiser HMS Derbyshire on the 30th June 1941, which took him to Helgafell in Iceland. He had to remain there for eight days before boarding the Royal Ulsterman, which arrived back in the UK on the 28th June 1941.

He was then trained to a Holding Centre in Bournemouth and on the 12th July 1941 he was posted to No 12 Operational Training Unit at RAF Benson to commence heavy bomber training. The OTU was equipped with the Vickers Wellington and his first flight in a Wimpy was on the 4th August. He flew the aircraft solo on the same day. Joseph completed the course successfully on the 24th October 1941 and again was assessed as 'above the average' as a heavy bomber Pilot. He had now accumulated a total of 250hrs.5mins flying time. His next posting was to 115 squadron at Marham in Norfolk, where he joined 'B' Flight arriving there on the 29th October 1941. Two days later he went on his first operational trip to Bremen. His aircraft was damaged by flak over the target. The first 1000 bomber raid was to Cologne on the 30th May and Joseph was one of the 1000. The original target had been Hamburg but persistent bad weather caused a switch to Cologne. The raid was a complete success but 41 aircraft were lost. He also participated in the other two 1,000 bomber raids on Essen and Bremen.

Sergeant Joseph Beckett went on to complete 36 operations in three months with 115 Squadron, visiting some of the most heavily defended targets in Europe. On June 1st he was promoted to Flight Sergeant. It is known that Joseph's aircraft was holed by shrapnel at least six times and he was frequently 'coned' by searchlights. Particularly noticeable was the number of passes he made over a target to ensure a successful dropping of his bombs. One attack on a Hipper Class Cruiser involved six passes and on a number of occasions his aircraft is recorded as being over the target for 20 minutes.

Some of his other targets were:

Bremen (three times), Brest (three times), Cologne (four times), Essen (eight times), Wilhelmshaven, Munster, Le Havre, Hamburg, Dortmund, Emden, Gennevillers, La Rochelle, Stuttgart, WarneMunde, Heligoland, Mannheim and Borkum.

Having completed his first operational tour, Joseph was posted to No 20 Operational Training Unit at Lossiemouth in Scotland as an instructor in Avro Ansons and Oxfords and an occasional flight in a Wimpy. He instructed at Lossiemouth for two months and was then seconded to No 3 Flying Instructors School (FIS) at Castle Combe for a flying instructors course. When the course finished three weeks later Joseph was assessed as 'above the average' as a Pilot and 'above the average' as a Pilot Instructor, with a special endorsement written in his logbook by the officer commanding, "An extremely useful instructor, recommended for a long course." On his return to Lossiemouth on the 3rd November, he began instructing on Wellingtons. On the 4th January 1943 he was seconded to No 1501 Blind Approach Training (BAT) at Abbingdon. He successfully completed the course on the 11th January and returned to Lossiemouth where he remained as an instructor until the 31st July 1943.

Joseph was posted the Bogs 'O' Mayne, (Satellite of 20 OTU Lossiemouth) where he continued instructing aircrew on Wellingtons. In early September he was seconded to the No 1 Engine Control Demonstration Unit (ECDU) at Westcott for a weeks training. He remained at Elgin until the 22nd October 1944 and had now accumulated a total of 1471hrs.15mins flying time.

(Prior to joining the HCU at Rufforth he was sent to Marston Moor Engine Control Development Unit for two weeks training and then to Acaster Malbis for one month's ground training, finishing at the Engine Handling Unit Henlease in Bristol.)

Joseph felt that he had now done his share of instructing and requested back onto operations. His request was granted and on the 8th November 1944 he was posted to No 1663 Heavy Conversion Unit (HCU) at Rufforth to commence training to Halifaxes. (His brother Charles was a flight commander on the squadron and they met and chatted many times during the twelve week course.) Joseph's first flight in the Halifax was on the 8th November 1944 under the instruction of a Flying Officer Moore. He had a further five flights with Moore and went solo on the 23rd and successfully completed the course on the 31st December 1944. He was then posted to No 102 Squadron at Pocklington. The squadron will always be remembered by the name of Group Captain GL Cheshire, VC, when on the night of the 12th/13th November 1940, the then Pilot Officer was captain of Whitley V P005 'N' - Nuts. While over the target his aircraft was rocked by a number of violent explosions, allowing the cockpit to be filled with thick black smoke and fumes, resulting in Pilot Officer Cheshire loosing control of his aircraft. The Whitley dropped 2,000ft, but in the meantime he had gained control and the fires had been extinguished. For this he was awarded an immediate DSO and later added a DFC to this while flying operations with 102 Squadron.

Flying Officer Joseph Beckett arrived at No 102 Squadron on the 1st January 1945. The squadron was equipped with Halifax 111s, and after two weeks training with his new crew, they carried out their first operation to Gilsenkirchen on the 22nd January 1945 and went on to complete a further 18 operations with 102 Squadron.

Operations were prevented between January 23rd and January 28th due to severe winter weather.

Some of the other targets he visited:

Stuttgart, Kamen, Chemnitz, Mainz, Wanne Eickel, Goch, Kamen, Barmen, Homburg, Witten, Dulmen, Sterkrade, Flensburg, Heligoland and Wangerooge (these were mostly oil and transport targets).

Joseph's last flight with the squadron was on the 9th June 1945 when he took his crew on a 'Cooks Tour' of Europe, visiting Emden, Bremen, Hamburg, Kiel and Heligoland. On completion of his second tour of operations he was promoted to Flight Lieutenant and posted to No 1516 BAT Flight at Odiham as an instructor on Oxfords. The Flight moved to Snaith on the 1st September 1945 for 11 days and then to Prestwick for one week returning to Snaith on the 21st. He continued to instruct at the BAT Flight until the 14th April and made his last flight in the RAF on the 11th April 1946 flying in an Oxford with Flying Officer Gregory.

Joseph was awarded the Distinguished Flying Cross on the 26th October 1945. His citation refers to his high qualities of Airmanship and Captaincy, his consistent skill and courage maintained over a long period and his unremitting determination to assail the enemy. He then was transferred to the 104 Personnel Despatch Centre at Hednesford where he was demobbed on the 15th April 1946. His total flying time was now 1962 hours.

The last entry on his Record of Service page reads, "TTFN" 15.4.46. 'Civvy St'.

TTFN meant 'Ta Ta for now', a catch phrase from Tommy Handleys radio show 'ITMA', 'Its that man again').

When he ended his career with the RAF he had flown a total of 54 operations over enemy occupied territory and, had flown in all 1,000 bomber raids (he was No into Cologne) accumulating 1962 flying hours. He had flown in 10 different types of aircraft including the Fleet Finch, Avro Anson, Wellington Mk 1,1A, 1C, 111 and X, Bristol Blenheim Mk1V, Tiger Moth, Miles Master 11, Airspeed Oxford 1, Handley Page Halifax Mk 11,V.111 and V1.

Flight Lieutenant Joseph Beckett, DFC rejoined the Imperial Civil Service in 1946 and finally retired in 1980.

FLIGHT LIEUTENANT
JOHN THOMAS BOAL
ROYAL AIR FORCE NO. 175987
AIR GUNNER
NO. 40 SQUADRON

John Thomas Boal, the son of Mr John Boal, was born on the 21st June 1918 in a house on the Ballymaconnell Road, Bangor, in the County of Down. He was educated at the Primacy School in Bangor and his higher education was carried out in Bangor Commercial College in Main Street. John had two sisters, Ella and Mary, and three brothers, one of whom, Henry, had served throughout the war in the Royal Navy on mine sweepers.

John unfortunately was one of those lads who 'refused' or couldn't walk or talk until he was nearly five years old. Some people thought he had 'rickets', (a disease in children which effected the bones through insufficient vitamins). His mother, Agnes, took him to see many doctors and specialists, one of whom told her to take John home and look after him as he would not live for very much longer. Finally as a last resort she took him to a lady in Ballymena who put a 'charm' on him. She told Johns mother to take him home and to get warm cows milk every morning and bathe his legs with it. John's mother also had a charm of her own, and that was, every morning she would go down to the shore and fill a bucket with salt seawater and seaweed. She would return home with the bucket and its contents, boil it up on the cooker and bathe John's legs with it. Then one morning just before his fifth birthday and completely out of the blue, he pulled himself up from the floor and walked across the room. He immediately started talking to his mother and father as if nothing had been wrong.

John's sister Ella told me that the night before he was going off to join the RAF, she asked her mother, "Are you not worried about him going of the war?" she replied, "No, because he won't pass the medical." Before joining the RAF John was employed in the office of the Antrim Iron Ore and Coal Company in High Street, Bangor.

John began his RAF career as an air gunner on the 25th November 1942 at the No 2 Air Gunnery School in Dalcross in Scotland. The school was equipped with the Boulton Paul Defiants. The Defiant Mk 1 and 11s had a Frazer-Nash hydraulically operated turret, and each turret had four 0.303-inch (7.7mm) mounted in it. When production ended in 1943 1,065 Defiants had been built. His first training flight in the Defiant was on the 7th November 1942 with his pilot instructor Sergeant Walczak. John successfully completed the course on the 11th December 1942, with a pass mark of 72.1%. His total flying hours were now 8hrs.20 mins.

The following information is of aviation research interest

Bolton Paul Defiant codes at Dalcross: 38/N1729; 52/V1119; 3/N3498; 10/V1174; 80/N1793; 94/N1557; TT/N1339; 8/T4067; 20/N3329; 31/T4101; 87/N3437; and 66/N1555.

Other Instructors at Dalcross were Sergeant Romatakis, Pilot Officer Wiltshire, Sergeant Slon, Sergeant Dawson, Pilot Officer Hammond, Sergeant King, Flight Sergeant Walker, Pilot Officer Taylor, Sergeant Tanobranski and Sergeant Langford. The school's Chief Instructor remarks in John's Log Book reads, "John has worked very hard with enthusiasm during the course and should do well."

John next posting was to No 26 Operational Training Unit where he joined 'B' Flight, which was equipped with Wellingtons. John had his first flight in the Wimpy on the 16th January 1942 with his pilot Squadron Leader Todd. They carried out circuits and bumps for forty minutes. The OTU training continued until the 26th April 1942, when John was assessed as 'above the average' as an Air Gunner by the units commanding officer.

John had now completed 72hrs.45mins day flying and 34hrs.45minutes night flying.

Having completed his training John was given some leave, and on his return was informed that he was being posted overseas to the Middle East where he would join No 40 Squadron at Hani West in Tunisia. On the 9th August 1943 John boarded a Wellington (LN303) at Harwell, which was to take him to Kairouan in Tunisia. This was to be the start of his operational career as he was the aircraft's official gunner for this flight. The captain of the aircraft was Sergeant Hamilton, and the journey took them via, Hurn, Ras el Ma and Kairouan. The first leg of the journey was from Harwell to Hurn on the 9th August. This was a short hop of 25 minutes, probably to fill up with fuel and take on as many spares as they could. The second leg began two days later on the 11th August when they took off from Hurn and set course for Ras el Ma in Saudi Arabia. The flying time from Hurn to Ras el Ma was nine hours. John's logbook shows that he stayed in Ras el Ma until the 28th August. He then flew on to Kairoun, and the flying time from Ras el Mas to Kairouan was 5hrs.20mins.

John joined 40 Squadron at Hani in Tunisia at the beginning of September 1943.

Brief wartime history of No 40 Squadron

No 40 Squadron was formed initially at Gosport in Hampshire during February 1916 as a Fighter Squadron. During its service in the First World War it was credited with the destruction of 130 German aircraft and 30 kite balloons. The squadron was disbanded in 1919 and was reformed as a bomber squadron in 1931 at Upper Heyford, equipped with Fairey Gordons. In 1935 it was re-equipped with Hawker Harts, and in 1936 changed again to Hawker Hinds. In 1938 the squadron received its first Fairey Battles, and moved to Betheniville in France and just after the outbreak of war was re-equipped with the Bristol Blenheim Mk 1V. In November 1940 the squadron received its first Vickers Wellington Mk I Cs, and in October 1941 sixteen of its aircraft and crews were posted out to Malta. In August 1942 the squadron moved lock stock and barrel to Kabrit in Egypt. It was based at various airfields in the Middle East and Italy during the war, bombing targets in North Africa, Sicily, Sardinia, Rhodes, Crete, Greece, Pantellaria, Lampedusa and Italy. The squadron ended the war flying Liberators and Lancasters and brought back liberated troops back to the UK. No 40 Squadron was disbanded at Shallufa in Egypt on the 1st April 1947.

John joined No 40 Squadron at Hani at the beginning of September 1943. His logbook shows that he carried out 40 operations with the squadron between the 5th September 1943 and the end of April 1944. The biggest percentage of his operations were carried out with his skipper and good friend Warrant Officer Hamilton. He also flew on ops with Sergeant Costin, Flying Officer Cheek, Flying Officer Huggler, and two ops with the Squadron Commander, Wing Commander Kirwan, DFC. John also flew as Air Gunner on a ferry Flight from Kairovan to Blida with Group Captain Harris. When the squadron moved to Italy in December 1943, they were billeted in Mussolini's house.

The following are some of the targets visited by John and his crew during their tour: Villa Literno (aerodrome); Veterbo (aerodrome); Grosseto (marshalling yards); Castel Nuovo (X roads); Battipaglia (X roads); Ceruteri (aerodrome); Bastia (docks, harbour shipping and troops in town); Leghorn (docks disembarkation port for German troops from Corscia); Formia (X roads); Mareigliani (aerodrome North of Rome); Guilianova (X roads, *first time east coast of Italy*); Grosseto (marshalling yards); Perugia (aerodrome); Spezia (nickel raid); Prato, north west of Florence (marshalling yards); Turin (ball bearing factory); Pontassieue (marshalling yards); Salonika harbour in Greece (bombed shipping); Pisa (marshalling yards with 4,000lb bomb); Leghorn (railway line); Maribor (aircraft factory in Yugoslavia), Arezio (marshalling yards in Italy); Verona; and Giulanova (railway lines).

On the 12th and 14th December 1944 John's logbook shows that he was on operations during the Anzio Beach Head, bombing the Herman Goering Division.

San Stefano Port (German Shipping for Anzio Beach Head), Steyr, Ploudiv (Bulgaria), Vicenza (Marshalling Yards in North Italy, his port engine was hit by flak), Milan (marshalling yards, his aircraft was attacked by two Ju88 Night Fighters), Fano (Railway Bridge, East Coast of Italy, 4,000lb bomb dropped from 700ft with eleven second delay), Porto Sanstefano (Docks and Harbour, flak hit front turret and tail fin badly damaged), Varese (aircraft factory near the Swiss Border, undercarriage collapsed on landing), Turnul Severen (marshalling yards, aircraft attacked by JU88), Piombino (docks).

John's last operation with the squadron was on the 28th April when they attacked the docks and shipping in Leghorn.

His total operational hours was now 101hrs.25 mins.

The officer commanding No 40 Squadron wrote in John's logbook on the 26th April, "A very keen and efficient gunner who has worked hard during his tour and has been an excellent example to other gunners." He also assessed John as 'above the average' as an air gunner.

It was now time for a rest from operations for John and he was posted back to the UK in June 1944. In July 1944 he attended an instructors course at a bombing and gunnery school, training in Baltimores, and at the end of the course he became a gunnery leader and received a well earned commission and promotion to Pilot Officer. He then was posted to No 76 Operational Training Unit at the beginning of October 1944 for a month instructing on Wellingtons. He first flight as an instructor was on the morning of the 9th November 1944 in Wellington (Code No 27). John's logbook shows that he left No 76 OTU on the 20th November 1944. The chief gunnery officer for the unit, Flight Lieutenant CA Evans, DFC DFM gave him an 'above the average' assessment and added that, "Although this officer has only been here a short while, he has proved himself to be very capable and reliable, and definitely fulfils his job as gunnery leader."

I am not sure what happened to John during the next seven months as the next entry in his logbook starts on the 9th June 1945 when he was flying as air gunner on a return trip from Abbingdon to Church Bronton in a Wellington Coded C.9407. The skipper of the aircraft was Flight Lieutenant Stockdale. He flew again on the 11th June on a Cine Camera (G4) exercise with Flying Officer Trevitt, and again on the 13th and 14th June on a night flying solo cross country bombing exercise.

His logbook also shows that on the 8th July he flew his last flight with the Royal Air Force with his skipper Flying Officer Trevitt in Wellington coded 'A' on a 3hour 50 minute night time solo cross country exercise. At the end of his air gunners career, John had flown a total of 430 hours day and night, (247 of which where operational hours) in Boulton Paul Defiants, Vickers Wellingtons, and Baltimores.

John left the RAF on the 8th October 1946 and returned home to Northern Ireland and immediately took up his old job of working for the Antrim Iron Ore and Coal Company in Bangor. A few years later he opened up his own greengrocer's shop in High Street, Bangor, but sadly John died in 1966 at the very young age of forty-eight. He was one of the Founder Members of the Ex Service Mens Club in Bangor. Two of his closest friends who were also in the RAF during the war would come up from Dublin for nights out in the club, and when it came time to sing the National Anthem, they would stand to attention and sing loudly, "God Save Your Gracious Queen".

FLIGHT SERGEANT
RICHARD BOLITHO
ROYAL AIR FORCE NUMBER 1211045
NO. 617 DAMBUSTER SQUADRON

KILLED 17TH MAY 1943

Flight Sergeant Richard Bolitho was born in Portrush, County Antrim, on the 19th January 1920, shortly afterwards his parents William and Jane Bolitho moved to Barrow-in-Furness in England. Richard was educated at Church Hill School in Nottingham and when he was eight years old they moved again to Kimberly in Nottinghamshire, where he joined the Kimberly Church School and later Heanor Grammar School, Heanor, Derbyshire.

Richard's father owned a private hotel in Nottingham. Richard later went to live with his aunt, who kept a fruit and vegetable shop in Kimberly, but after she died, his father sold the hotel and took over the shop. Richard left school to join the firm of Ericcsons Telephones in Beeston Derbyshire (a telephone Company). He left Ericcsons and joined the Royal Air Force on 25th November 1940 as an Air Gunner.

He went No 2 Recruit Centre on 25/11/40 and then to No 4 Recruit Centre on 9/12/40. He was then posted to: RAF Calshot on 10/1/41; No 1 Recruit Wing on 26/4/41; No 7 ITW on 10/5/41; No 51 Group Pool on 28/6/41; Aircrew Reception Centre on 5/8/41; and No 14 ITW on 10/1/42. When he had finished his initial training he was posted to No 9 Air Gunnery School at Kinloss in Scotland on the 5th June 1942 where his gunnery training was carried out in Whitleys and then on to No 19 Operational Training Unit on 27/8/42. He was then posted to No 1654 Conversion Unit (CU) at Wigsbey to convert onto the Lancaster Bomber. Richard was posted to his first operation squadron on 23rd December 1942, this was No 9 Squadron based at Waddington and equipped with the four-engined Avro Lancaster. He was only with the squadron for one month as he was posted to No 57 Squadron at Scampton.

On the 25th March 1943, four days after it was formed Richard was posted to 617 Dambuster Squadron, which was based at Scampton under the command of Wing Commander Guy Gibson. As we all now know 617 Squadron occupies a unique place in the history of the Royal Air Force. It was the only squadron formed to undertake a specific operation - the breaching of the Ruhr Dams in Germany. Richard was promoted to Sergeant on the 16th May 1943.

Wing Commander Gibson who had distinguished himself as an outstanding bomber and night fighter pilot was granted the unprecedented privilege of selecting crews from other squadrons of bomber command to fly in this special operation. One of those he picked was Flight Sergeant Richard Bolitho from Portrush.

Details of Involvement in Operation Chastise

This story is about one of the crews that were posted missing during the operation. On the night of the 16th May 1943 nineteen specially modified Avro Lancasters took off from RAF Scampton in Lincolnshire in three groups. The first group to take off consisted off five aircraft led by Flight Lieutenant RNG Barlow, DFC, Royal Australian Air Force who was first away at 2128 hrs. The second group consisted of nine aircraft and were led by the commanding officer Wing Commander Guy Gibson, DSO* DFC* and took off at 2139 hrs leading a 'V' formation of three aircraft. The next three aircraft were led by Squadron Leader HM Young, DFC* and took off at 2147 hrs. also in a 'V' formation. The last three aircraft in the group were led by Squadron Leader HE Maudslay, DFC, and they took off at 2159 hrs.

Flight Lieutenant William Astell, DFC was part of this group and his rear gunner was Flight Sergeant Richard Bolitho. Sergeant Richard Bolitho flew as rear gunner to Flight Lieutenant Astell in Lancaster ED864 (AJ-B). They took off from Scampton at 2159 hrs as part of the main wave, bound for the Mohne Dam. Soon the group headed out over the friendly shores of England and for many of the aircrew this would be the last time they would see it. They soon passed over the Dutch coast line and the air gunners in particular were told to keep a look out for enemy activity. At the turning point near Rees on the Rhine, and Dulmen, Flight Lieutenant Astell seemed a little uncertain of his position and hesitated to turn with the other two aircraft in his formation, putting himself some way behind when he eventually did. At 0015 hrs, the aircraft was hit by flak positioned on the ground, they continued to fly on however, about eight miles north west of Dorsten, they were about two miles behind the formation, the aircraft became engulfed in flames and flew straight into some overhead high tension power lines and crashed into a field close to a farm in the village of Marbeck. All the crew of Lancaster AJ-B sadly died in the inferno including Sergeant Richard Bolitho. This was the first of the squadrons several casualties.

The Crew

Flight Lieutenant Bill Astell was born in Peover about 15 miles from Manchester and joined the RAF in June 1939. His DFC was awarded for flying with 148 Squadron in the Middle East. His Flight Engineer was Scottish born Sergeant John Kinnear who joined the RAF a few months earlier than to Astell. The Navigator was Pilot Officer Alwin Wile Royal Canadian Air Force who came from Nova Scotia in Canada.

The Wireless Operator was Sergeant Abram Garshowitz Royal Canadian Air Force who came from Ontario Canada. The Bomb Aimer was Flying Officer Donald Hopkinson who came from Oldham in Lancashire. The Air Gunners were Sergeant Francis Anthony Garbas Royal Canadian Air Force from Ontario Canada, and the other Air Gunner was our very own Flight Sergeant Richard Bolitho from Portrush.

A local farmer who lived very close to the crash site said, "It was about 2300 hrs when I was awoken by the sound of aircraft which were flying so low that it seemed that they would tear down the roof of my farm house. I rushed out into the garden and saw that one of the planes had struck a high-tension cable pylon and had come down into the field. The top section of the pylon was broken off and lying in the meadow of my neighbour Mr Thesing. There was a loud explosion and the Lancaster burst into flames and the machine guns began to fire. As I watched the burning wreckage I saw a fiery red ball rolling away from the front of the aircraft.

It travelled for about 150 metres and then blew up. This was no doubt the Dams Mine. It was half an hour before we could approach the site because of the exploding ammunition. When we did eventually get to the aircraft we saw in front a man on his hands and knees, stiff and totally burned, a ghastly sight. We then went to the crater caused by the bomb, which was about 12 meters wide and unbelievably deep, and I found round the edge, three or four more young fliers, dead, but with no visible external injuries. On the edge of the crater, I found a statue of St Joseph undamaged, but for a distance of three kilometres, roofs were torn off, and windows and doors smashed in.

We realised there was nothing we could do for the crew and to this day our local farmers are still ploughing up pieces of the Lancaster. The bodies were eventually recovered from the crash site and were buried in the city cemetery in Borken, (Plot 2, Grave 7), which is about fivemiles from, where the Lancaster crashed."

On February 5th 1947 a team from No33 Grave Registration Unit under the command of a Captain H. Butcher exhumed their bodies for formal identification and reburial in the Reichswald Forest War Cemetery, Cleve, Germany (Plot 21, Row E, Grave 1). There was little to aid this due to the length of time the bodies were buried and the effects of the crash, but on a shirt collar was written 'SM1045', the last four digits in Richard's service number confirming the identity of the body.

The forest as its name implies is situated in the centre of the Reichswald Forest and is 2 miles from the German-Dutch Border. Richard and his crew were one of the first to join 617 Squadron, and also made the first squadron flight, in Lancaster 'B' W4940, a nine-hour trip on March 27th 1943, to photograph some reservoirs.

They flew Lancaster 'B' W4940 practically every day and night carrying out low-level, cross-country exercises until the 1st May 1943 when Flight Lieutenant Astell took possession of their 'special' Lancaster, ED 864. which was to take part in the Dams Raid.

They practiced low level cross-country exercises in ED 864 on the 6th, 7th, 9th, 11th, 13th and 14th of May.

On his last leave, Richard took with him three of his crew, Pilot Officer Floyd Wile his navigator and Warrant Officer Albert Garshowitz the wireless operator. (both Canadians), as well as John Kinnear, his Scots flight engineer. They spent a happy time in Kimberly, before returning to Scampton.

Sergeant Bolitho had completed 147hrs.40mins flying by day and 138hrs.45mins by night.

THE BRADY BROTHERS

JOHN BRADY
AIRCRAFT ENGINEER

John Brady, the oldest of four brothers, all of whom served as ground crew in the Royal Air Force during the Second World War, joined in 1938. He became a Ground Engineer working on all types of aircraft. He was based in England and later posted out to work in South Africa. When he returned to the UK he was stationed at Doncaster where he lived with his wife. He retired from the RAF in the 1960's.

DENNIS BRADY
WIRELESS OPERATOR MECHANIC

Dennis, the second oldest of the Brady brothers joined the Royal Air Force in 1937 and became a Wireless Operator Mechanic (WOM). He was posted out to Burma to help fight the Japanese and during his time there he contacted Malaria. When he was demobbed he returned home to Northern Ireland and went to College where he completed a wireless engineering course. He was employed with the Company Standard Telephones and Cables for a time and eventually joined the Harbour Police from which he finally retired.

AC2
JAMES GERARD BRADY
DRIVER

James Gerard Brady was born at Prospect in Woodburn, Carrickfergus, on the 28th October 1924 and was educated at St Nicholas Public Elementary School. On leaving school he was employed at Taylors Mill and later at Joymount Dye Works in Carrickfergus. James joined the Royal Air Force in 1944 at the Clifton Street Recruiting Centre and was immediately posted to the Long Kesh Airfield outside Lisburn to start his basic training. On completion of this he reported the Padgate Receiving Centre in England where he was selected to become a driver. He was then posted to a maintenance unit in Cambridgeshire for one year where he completed his driver training and was then posted overseas with the unit to Egypt. The trip took him by ship from Liverpool to Dieppe in France, then by train overland to Toulouse where he boarded another ship, which took him on to Port Said. He was stationed in the canal zone with another maintenance unit, carrying out various duties that included, driving heavy vehicles, guard duty and working in the unit's stores. He remained in Egypt until 1948 until he was posted back to the UK and demobbed at Padgate. He returned home to Carrickfergus where he was employed at a factory at Woodburn that made Churchill Tanks during the war, but was now used for storing large calibre (3.7" diameter anti-aircraft) guns. He was then transferred to Kinnegar Army Camp in County Down where he was employed for ten years. He left Kinnegar and later joined the Feldon House Training Works and Apprentice Training School near Whitehouse, however had to retire from Feldon House in 1981 on medical grounds.

CORPORAL
DONALD BRADY
CLERK

Corporal Donald Brady was the youngest of the Brady brothers and was a very keen member of the Carrickfergus Air Training Corps where he excelled at morse code. He joined the Royal Air Force in 1942 as a clerk and was posted to various RAF Stations in England and overseas (Karachi) during the war. He finished his RAF Career at Aldergrove as a clerk in 1950 and was later employed with the Post Office until he retired.

WING COMMANDER
JOHN KENNETH BREW
ROYAL AIR FORCE NO. 28244
PILOT
NO. 502 (ULSTER) SQUADRON

Wing Commander John Kenneth Brew was born in Portadown, County Armagh, on the 17th January 1909 and was educated at the Coleraine Academical Institution, and later at Ruthin College in North Wales. Before joining the Royal Air Force, he was employed in the family firm of James Clow & Co. (Millars).

Kenneth Brew joined 502 (Ulster) Bombing Squadron in January 1929 and made his first flight in an aircraft on 16th January 1929, when he took off in an Avro Lynx 504N (J 8702) with his instructor Flight Lieutenant Sugden. This exercise was to let him feel the 'effect on controls' and 'flying straight'. His logbook shows that he was flying at a height of 2,000ft for 20 minutes. He flew solo after an hours instruction at 1530 hours on 5th February 1929, taking off in Avro Lynx (J 8702), flying at a height of 1,000 ft for 15 minutes. In the afternoon of 8th March 1929 he had an hours flight in a Hyderabad, which was captained by Squadron Leader King, himself, Pilot Officer Reid and four other crewmembers. They flew at a height of 6,000 for 1 hour. He continued training in the Avro Lynx, carrying out, forced landings, gliding turns, take offs, cross-country weather tests, and side slips and formation exercises until the 28th March 1929. On the 2nd April he started flying the Handley Page Hyderabad and went solo on the 5th April in (H-H 7742). His logbook shows that the exercises where carried out from Aldergrove to Lurgan and Portadown, around Lough Neagh, Aldergrove to Randleslstown, Ballymena, Kells and Lisburn, Aldergrove to Lurgan, Portadown, Newry and Newtownhamilton and usually at a height of between 1,000 and 3,000ft. On the 12th, 13th and 17th March they flew to Belfast, Holywood, Craigavad, Carrickfergus, Ballymena, Portadown, Lurgan, Dungannon, Cookstown, Randalstown, Toome, Kells Ballymena and Antrim.

On the 2nd June 1929, Flight Lieutenant Hargroves (1st Pilot) and Pilot Officer Brew (2nd Pilot) flew their Hyderabad (H-H 7742) on a cross-country exercise from Aldergrove to Blackhead, Catterick, Digby, Northweald, Bigginhill, Kenley, Northolt, Henlow, Wittering, Digby,

Catterick, Blackhead and Aldergrove. They made four re-fuelling stops that day. Pilot Officer Brew attended a short flying course at RAF Calshot from the 27th June 1929 until 9th July 1929 flying as navigator on a Southampton Flying Boat, completing 12 hours on the type. He was awarded his Wing on 8th July 1929 and his first squadron assessment on the 9th July shows that he was 'above the average' as a Pilot and his total flying hours in Avro Lynx, Hyderabad and Southampton were 197hrs.50mins. On his return to 502 Squadron Pilot Officer Brew continued flying training in the Avro Lynx and Hyderabads. On the 24th August 1929, Pilot Officer Britton (1st Pilot) and Pilot Officer Brew (2nd Pilot) took off from Aldergrove in Hyderabad (H-H 8811) along with two other aircraft on a long cross-country exercise to Manston and Sealand. The exercise took four days to complete and over ten hours flying time. Unfortunately on the return trip from Sealand Pilot Officer Brews aircraft had to force land at Groomsport owing to low cloud over the Belfast hills.

The following story has been taken from the County Down Spectator newspaper dated Saturday August 1929.

"Giant Bombing Machine Crashes", "Crews Miraculous Escape"

"Seven members of No 502 (Ulster) Bombing Squadron, RAF, Special Reserve, three officers and four aircraftsmen, had a narrow escape from death on Tuesday when a machine in which they were travelling crashed at Groomsport, County Down. The machine, a Handley Page Hyderabad night bomber was returning to Aldergrove with two others after a practice flight to the South of England when the visibility became bad and two of the pilots decided to land. One of the machines alighted safely in a field, which has been used as an aerodrome by a private company for some time, but the other on landing ran into a clump of trees. So great was the impact that one of the wings and starboard engine were ripped off the machine, which fell over on its side. The tanks contained about a ton of petrol at the time, but fortunately an explosion did not follow the crash. There were three officers and four aircraftsmen in the aeroplane, which was returning, with two other machines, from a successful long distance flight to the south coast of England. As far as can be ascertained, the visibility over Ulster was so bad that it became almost impossible to identify landmarks, even a prominent town. The machines were flying in arrowhead formation and the one forming the right 'barb' of the arrow lost touch with the others and eventually reached Aldergrove Aerodrome."

The Descent

The pilots of the machines decided to land, and seeing an aeroplane and an aerial wind gauge in a field concluded it was a recognised landing ground and began to descend. This ground is used by a private aviation company. One of the bombers landed successfully in a field nearby, and the other choose the ground already mentioned. It came down wind and the landing wheels first touched ground at the foot of a gentle slope. The pilot, Squadron Leader King, taxied his machine up the incline at the normal speed and unfortunately went straight into a clump of half a dozen fir trees on the crest of the slope. With remarkable prescience of mind he managed to steer the nose of the machine clear of a tree, but the wings were caught by the other trees, and inside a second or two the great bomber lay on its side, a mass of wreckage. In the forward machine gun cockpit was Flying Officer Bashford (an Ulsterman) who 'sat tight' when the crash came and by doing so escaped injury. The pilot held on to the 'steering wheel', and although thrown violently against the side of the plane was unhurt. Immediately behind him, in the second pilot's cockpit, was Flying Officer Stevens. As the machine tore through the tiny thicket, he ducked his head and this action saved him from a terrible fate, for the part of the machine, which he occupied, bore against a tree, which would otherwise have struck him on the head. The remainder of the crew, Leading Aircraftsman Jones, Hill, and Buckler (Belfast) and Aircraftsman Wallace were in the navigation cabin, and as one of them put it, "We didn't know what had happened until we crawled out. I felt a terrific jolt and heard most awful sounds, which must have been the wings being ripped off. The bus turned on her side and we were flung all of a heap."

One of the crew when asked about the crash, refused to say anything, but significantly patted a toy rabbit, which was carried as a mascot. An examination of the grounds brought home to a large crowd, which collected around the wrecked aeroplane how near the airmen were to a terrible death. The place was strewn with wreckage. One of the wings, shorn off as by a gigantic razor stroke,

was suspended between two trees. Part of another wing hung by a thread to the fuselage. The starboard engine was ripped off and flung clear of the machine and seemed to be badly damaged. The port engine was intact and remained attached to a portion of the wing, which remained on the port side. two of the landing wheels were buckled and lay some distance away. Part of the tail was bent, and that part of the undercarriage, which contains the bomb carrier, was stove in. The propellers were smashed to matchwood. There was over a ton weight of petrol on board, and luckily only a small quantity escaped on to the ground. Spectators were forbidden to smoke within fifty yards of the wreckage, and numerous souvenir hunters were sternly commanded to "clear off". At least one tree was uprooted, "cut down like a blade of grass," said one eyewitness of the smash. "I was in my house," he said, "and heard the terrific roar of engines. I knew the sound was much greater that of the small aeroplanes which have been 'stunting' at Groomsport, and I rushed out in time to see a machine crash into the trees. I was the first on the scene, and did not expect to see a soul alive. You can imagine my surprise when I saw the crew standing beside the wrecked machine calmly as if they were looking into a shop window." Further inquiries established the fact that the three machines, Handley Page Hyderabad Night Bombers, left Aldergrove on Saturday last on a practice long-distance flight.

They flew over the Mull of Kintyre and then southward down the Thames to Margate. They left Margate at 0900 hrs on Tuesday morning and landed at Sealand Aerodrome, near Liverpool at mid-day. Leaving there at 1330 hrs, they flew towards Scotland and finally headed towards Ulster. "We couldn't see the ground until we flew quite low," said one member of the expedition, "and it was impossible to pick out a town which would give us our position. We decided to come down, halt for the night and move on to Aldergrove in the morning." The machine, which made the successful landing, took off at 5.30pm with Squadron Leader King onboard. The crew of the wrecked bomber were taken by car to Aldergrove, and a guard, and a breakdown gang took charge of the damaged machine. On 4th January 1930 Pilot Officer Brew was posted to No 99 (B) Squadron at Upper Heyford in Oxon. The squadron was equipped with the Handley Page Hinaidis a large twin engined Bomber. His first flight in the Hinaida (9301) as Second Pilot was on 4th January 1930 and his captain was Flying Officer Johnston. They carried out a one hour photography exercise to Abingdon at 4,000ft.

During his posting with 99 Squadron he completed a parachute course at Hendon. An interesting log entry for that period shows that he took off at 1400 hrs on 29th April in a Vickers Vimy (J9704) with his Captain Flying Officer Maclean 'drop testing' eight dummies from a height of 1,000ft, flying time 10 minutes.

The first two weeks in September 1930 where spent at RAF Practice Camp at Catfoss, where he carried out a bombing and gunnery course, and in December 1930 he was then posted to the No 22 Air Pilotage School at Calshot on a navigation course flying as 1st, 2nd and third navigator in the Short Southampton Flying Boat. The types of air exercises that he was carrying out where, practical navigation, swinging compass by transit bearings.

He returned to 99 Squadron in early January 1931 and commenced flying again in Hinaidas on the 16th carrying out, forced landing practice, test on drift sights, practical aiming points, map reading, camera gun and wind speed, night flying and direction finding. In February 1932 Pilot Officer Brew was posted to the Central Flying School at Wittering where he joined the 37th Flying Instructors Course. The School was equipped with the Avro Lynx (505N), Atlas, Fairey 111Fs and Fairey Siskins. He successfully completed the course on 16th April 1932 with a pass mark of 79.2%. On 15th April his logbook shows that he was assessed by the Chief Flying Instructor as 'average' and 'above the average' as an Instrument Pilot.

Pilot Officer Brew then rejoined 99 Squadron where he remained until the 10th December 1932 when he was posted back to Northern Ireland to re-join 502 Squadron. Just before he left he was assessed as 'above the average' in all four categories by the commanding officer. He started flying again with 502 Squadron on the 17th December 1932, by now the squadron was also equipped with Vickers Virginias. Some of the names, who he flew as passengers, some you may remember or have heard of: Pilot Officer Badger, MR; TM Bulloch (later to become Squadron Leader, DSO*, DFC*); Pilot Officer RT Corry; Pilot Officer Brian Corry; Pilot Officer Stanley; Pilot Officer Stanley; Pilot Officer Robinson; Pilot Officer Newton; Flying Officer Lindsay; Pilot Officer Gardiner; Flight Lieutenant Sender; Pilot Officer Raphael; Flight Lieutenant Taylor; and Flight Lieutenant Nash.

On 27th November 1933 Pilot Officer Brew was posted back to the Central Flying School at Wittering for a five week instructors refresher course on Avro Tutor and Avro 504Ns. He was assessed at the end of the course as 'above the average' as a Pilot and returned to 502 Squadron on 15th December 1930. On the 13th February 1934 Pilot Officer Brew had accumulated 835 hours on fifteen different types of aircraft and again assessed as 'above the average'.

On the 19th February 1934 Pilot Officer Brew was posted to the RAF College at Cranwell as an instructor on Avro Tutors for one month and then went on to No 5 Flying Training School at Sealand instructing on Avro Tutors until the 1st June 1934.

Flying Officer Brew's logbook shows that he had been suffering from acute appendicitis, and had been certified as medically unfit for flying for the period from 5th May 1934 until 30th November 1934. His logbook then shows that he was sent to the RAF Depot at Uxbridge (possibly for a Medical Examination).

On 29th November 1934 he was promoted to Flight Lieutenant and transferred to the Headquarters Air Defence of Great Britain at Northolt, where he returned to flying again, instructing on Tom-Tits, Hawker Harts, Hawker Hinds, DH Moths, Tiger Moths, Westland Wapitis, Gloster Gauntlets and Avro 504.Ns. His log book shows that he returned some life jackets to Hendon on 21st May 1935 in Moth (K 1850) flying at a height of 1,000ft and on August 12th flew from Northolt to Tangmere to Umpire 604 Squadrons Esher Trophy air navigation test. He also flew a Comper Swift (G-ACGL) from Northolt to Castlebromwich on 11th July 1936 at a height of 1,000ft, flying time 20 minutes. His last flight with the HQ ADGB was on 13th July 1936.

His next posting was to the Anti-Aircraft School at Eastchurch where he was given a desk job until the 23rd October 1936.

His logbook shows that he did not fly between July and December 1936 as he had been preparing for his posting to Iraq in the Middle East by ship.

In early January 1937 Flight Lieutenant Brew arrived in Hinaida near Iraq where he joined the No 1 Armoured car Company which was equipped with Hardys, Vickers Valentias and Avro Tutors. His first flight with the Company was on 11th January 1937 in Hardy (K 5914). He took off at 0920 hrs with Squadron Leader Stevens on a local flying practice at 2,000ft (logbook shows for that flight, "first landing on Mutti"). I am not sure what the armoured car companies role was at that time in Iraq or what Flight Lieutenants Brew role was.

His logbook shows that he flew, cross-country, aircraft acceptance tests, ferrying aircraft, flying practice, collecting stores, inspecting service police and IACC quarters and aerial inspections of proposed HC training grounds, conveying works directorate to landing grounds, inspections of new airway beacons, and policing duties. These duties took him to Dhibban, Rutbah, Amman, Heliopolis, Habbaniya Aboukir, Ismalia and Hinaida. On 11th June 1937 he flew Colonel Merry from Hinaida to Dhibban to visit the ADF Mess. In early September 1938 Flight Lieutenant Brew was advised that he was being posted back to the UK. On 17th October 1938 he boarded a Vickers Valentia in Habbaniya along with 12 other passengers, which would take them to Basra Airport (flying time 3hrs.30mins). His logbook again shows that he did not fly between November 1938 and April 1939.

On his return to the UK he was promoted to Squadron Leader and posted to Aldergrove in Northern Ireland where he became the commanding officer of No 3 AOS from June 1939 until February 1940. The school was equipped with Avro Tutors, Miles Ministers, Handley Page Hayforks, Avro Ansons and Fairey Battles.

A selection of Squadron Leader log entries for 1939

11th May 1939	Tutor (K3399). Self & P/O Nicholls Flying practice.
22nd June 1939	Magister (P2402). Self & P/O Falkus. Target for camera gun.
29th June 1939	Anson (N5239). Self & F/Lt Thomas- Ferrand Flying practice.
4th July 1939	Heyford (K5192). Self & F/Lt Carnac Flying practice.
3rd Aug 1939	Hanford (K6876). Self & F/Lt Lee Dual.

Two weeks after the outbreak of war

22nd Sept 1939	Magister. (P2402) Self & Pilot Officer Bennett. Height 3000ft. Inspection of anti-aircraft guns.
29th Sept 1939	Magister. (P2402) Self & Pilot Officer Bennett. Height 1000ft. Clearing fishing boats out of danger area.
18th Dec 1939	Heyford (K6864) Self & Flying Office Siminuteson. Height 1000ft. Night flying exercise.

Squadron Leader Brew flew three flights in January 1940 in a Miles Magister (L5957) Instructing Pilot Officer Maclean, Flight Sergeant Harvey and Sergeant Ball.

His logbook records his last flight with the Royal Air Force as:

25th Feb 1940	Heyford (K5182) Self & F/Lt Coventry & F/Sgt Harvey. Height 4,000ft. Take off 2015 hrs. Aldergrove, Belfast, Bangor, Lisburn.

Survey of black-out of Belfast area

The log page also records, "OC ATS No 3 B&G School. 4/3/40."

At the end of his flying career, Squadron Leader Brew had flown a total of 1026hrs.45mins, in the following aircraft types: Avro Lynx 504N; Handley Page Hyderabad; Hinaida; Atlas; Bristol Bulldog; Siskin 111A; Siskin Dual; Fairey 111 (F); Short Southampton Flying Boat; Vickers Vimy and Virginia; Tiger Moth; Gloster Gauntlet; Hawker Hart and Hind; Vickers Experimental Night Bomber; Fairey Monoplane; Hawker Tom-Tit; Fairey Battle; Avro Anson; Westland Wapiti; Miles Magister; Handley Page Heyford; Avro Tutor; Hardy; and Gordon.

As well as being an expert Pilot, Wing Commander Brew had an expert administrative brain, and this had not gone unnoticed. In March 1940 he was posted to the Air Ministry in London (German Section) and his duties were to collect intelligence from reliable sources in Germany and their newspapers. Anthony Wedgewood Benn's father was his junior at the Air Ministry.

Wing Commander Brew's record of service shows that he was discharged from the RAF in 1940 but was recalled a few months later.

He was severely injured by a German bomb, sometime during 1941 and was sent to a hospital in Torquay to convalesce from blood poisoning. In 1941 he was then posted to Headquarters in Reading and put in charge of purchasing all airfields and locating sites for new ones and fixing prices for the land. Sometime during 1943, Wing Commander Brew was posted to Edinburgh where he was placed in Charge of Pilot assessment. He was released from the Royal Air Force in 1945, and returned to Northern Ireland and joined the family business of Hutchinson and Haddow (motor trade).

In 1975 Wing Commander John Kenneth Brew was set upon by some thugs close to his home and was found later lying unconscious on the ground with a head wound. He never fully recovered from this encounter and died in 1987.

FLIGHT LIEUTENANT
ALEXANDER GARDINER BURGESS, DFC
NAVIGATOR
ROYAL AIR FORCE NO. 125033

Flight Lieutenant Alex Burgess was born in Belfast on 26th July 1915 and was educated at the Belfast College of Technology. On leaving school in 1931, he was employed as an office clerk with the firm of solicitors James A Culbert for nine years.

In September 1940 he applied at the Clifton Street Recruiting Office to join the Royal Navy, only to be told that there were no vacancies at that time and was advised to apply to the Royal Air Force Volunteer Reserve. This he did and was accepted. After a few weeks he was posted to the Padgate Receiving Centre in Lancashire where he was kitted out with his uniform and received the necessary inoculations. In November 1940 Alex was posted to Royal Air Force Station St Eval in Cornwall for his initial training as a defence gunner. St Eval was a new station and was still under construction. The station had suffered a lot at the hands of the Luftwaffe, so much so it had to be evacuated at night. On one particular night when the station was under attack by the Luftwaffe, Alex's billet suffered a direct hit from a German land mine, and out of 25 Service Men, 24 were killed. Alex was the only survivor and had to be dug out of the rubble.

In early 1941 he was posted to the Aircrew Selection Centre at Torquay, where he spent two weeks undergoing various exams and procedures to see if he would be suitable for aircrew. He was then sent back to St Eval and within a few weeks was informed that he had been selected to become a Navigator/Air Gunner. Towards the end of June 1941 Alex was posted to No 6 Air Observers School at Millom in Cumberland, to begin a career in navigation. This was to be the last air observers course within the RAF as it was decided to replace the Observer Brevet with the Navigator Brevet in 1942. The 'O' Badge originates back to the late 19th Century and the era of the Royal Engineer Balloon Companies, however, the more commonly accepted version was introduced in September 1915 with the Royal Flying Corps.

The course was a very intensive one that lasted five months, taking in subjects such as, 'dead reckoning navigation', 'compasses', 'meteorology', 'maps and charts',
'instruments', 'reconnaissance', 'photography', 'wireless', 'pyrotechnics', 'bomb aiming', and 'air gunnery'.

The flying training part of the course was completed in Blackburn Botha and Avro Ansons. Alex had his first flight in a Botha on the 1st July 1941, this was a 1hr.45mins map reading exercise under the instruction of Flight Sergeant Green. By the time the course ended five months later he had accumulated 72 hours on both types of aircraft and was awarded his 'O' Brevet. Having successfully completed the air observers course, Alex was posted to No 2 Air Navigation School at Cranage at the beginning of November to begin a five-week advanced navigators instructors course.

Alex was soon on the move again to Flying Training Command at Bournemouth in January 1942 as an instructor. His duty there was to undertake the training of overseas aircrew in the art of navigation, and this training was carried out entirely in the classroom. He remained at training command for one year, leaving at the end of October 1942, when he was attached to 102 Squadron at Pocklington in Yorkshire where he took part in some operational training. During this training Alex was sent on an operation to Genoa on the night of the 7/8th November in Halifax J-Johnny. The aircraft was piloted by another Ulsterman, Flight Lieutenant Sidney Hamilton who resided on the Lisburn Road, Belfast.

These remarks were taken from his flying log regarding this Operation:

"Did first operation with 102 Squadron at Pocklington in Yorkshire. Sidney Hamilton was Flight Commander; I went as 2nd Navigator. Very long trip at 20,000ft over the Alps. Bombed at that height, saw direct hits on railway station. Descended slowly on return journey to conserve fuel. Took evasive action to avoid searchlights over France. Petrol gauges reading zero on crossing Channel. Landed at

Manson - tanks almost empty. Flew back to Pockington next day on 8.11.42."

PS Hamilton was from the Lisburn Road where his mother had an antique shop above Tates Avenue.

He was later awarded the DFC. Shortly after this short spell of training, Alex found himself back at the reception centre in Bournemouth again as an instructor.

Towards the end of August he was posted to RAF Bishopscourt near Downpatrick in Northern Ireland as an instructor for six months. This was a handy posting for him as he could be home in one hour. By this time Alex had been commissioned and promoted to Flying Officer and posted to No 13 Operational Training Unit at Bicester Near Oxford where he was teamed up with Wing Commander Boult, AFC. This again was to be a very concentrated course that lasted for six weeks, flying practically every day. Their training was carried out in Avro Anson, Mosquito and B 25 Mitchell Bombers. 13 OTU moved to RAF Finmere on the 25th June where Alex and Wing Commander Boult were teamed up with their two air gunners. Their course finished on the 28th June 1944, with Alex being promoted to Flight Lieutenant.

No 180 Squadron, Dunsfold, Surrey

Wing Commander Boult, Alex, and their two air gunners were posted to 180 Squadron that was based at Dunsfold. 180 Squadron was formed at West Raynam on 13th September 1942 as a light bomber squadron, equipped with North American (B25) Mitchell Bombers. In early October it moved to Foulsham in Norfolk and it was from there on the 22nd January 1943 it flew its first mission to Terneuzen in Belgium to bomb an oil refinery. In mid August the squadron was on the move again, this time to Dunsfold in Surrey and subsequently took part in the pre-invasion attacks on northern France and the 'Noball' sites in the Pas-de-Calais. After D-Day it operated in close support of the advancing Allied Armies, and from October onwards was based on the Continent.

Alex's first flight with the squadron was on the 11th July, along with Wing Commander Boult and the crew in Mitchell P.133, they did a spot of local flying and formation practice for one hour.

Their first operation came the next day 12th July, they took off at 1705 hrs in Boston 'U' FL 679. and were designated No 3 in a leading box of three aircraft, their target was the oil refinery at Chatre. They encountered light but inaccurate flak over the target, their results were not observed owing to cloud over the target. The operation took 2hrs.50mins.

They took off on their second operation from Dunsfold at 2000 hrs on the 15th July in Mitchell 'O' code FW 190 and headed for the Caen Area in support of the advancing Armies. They had to abandon the operation due to cloud over the French coast. On the 16th and 17th July they bombed the fuel dumps at Chartres and Alencon, again results not observed due to

cloud over the targets. On the 19th July they were again in action bombing the fuel depot at Orleans. Hits were observed over the target area. This operation was the deepest penetration by B25 Mitchel Bombers in enemy territory so far. On the 20th July they had to abandon their operation to bomb the fuel dumps at Argentan due to cloud and icing half way across the Channel. On the 23rd July they took off at 15.05 in 'V' code FW.125, their target was the railway junction near Mont Ford. Results not observed due to cloud over the target area.

The next day 24th July 1944 they took off at 1940hrs to bomb the Steelworks at 'Caen'. When over the target, tragedy struck. This is an extract from Alex's logbook of what happened next.

"Pinpoint bombing steelworks, massive defence 600 guns - box barrage, hit often, Squadron Leader Griffiths (2nd Pilot) killed, self wounded in left knee, Wing Commander Boult injured in left arm, lost right eye, Hydraulics gone. Front and starboard wheels gone. Successful hits smack on aircraft. Crashed landing at Tangmere Hospital. (Boult and self awarded the Distinguished Flying Cross (Field). The target was protected by a Box Barrage of some 600 - 88 millimetre anti-aircraft guns. These guns were all synchronised and could change height - direction in a matter of seconds." (Indeed the Germans boasted that if any enemy aircraft entered the Barrage, it would be shot down)

They were now on their third run into the target and their aircraft was hit many times.

Directly over the target, heavy flak scored a direct hit in Wing Commander Boults cockpit, killing Squadron Leader Griffiths (2nd Pilot) and severely wounding Wing Commander Boult (lost his right eye and was wounded in left arm) and Alex. Despite their wounds, their hydraulics gone, nose and main wheels shot away, they managed to guide their crippled aircraft back to Tangmere for a belly landing. Wing Commander Boult never flew operationally again, Alex was in hospital nursing his injuries for four months and later spent a short time at Loughborough rehabilitation centre. When Alex had fully recovered from his ordeal, he was posted to No 2 Ground Support Unit (GSU) at Swanton Morley in the middle of November 1944. His task there was to ferry crews in Avro Ansons to France to support different squadrons who were moving across to Europe. No 2 GSU eventually moved across the Channel to Melsbroek in Belgium.

Meanwhile a Wing Commander Paul Marriott who was a very close friend of Wing Commander Boult had approached him and asked if he could recommend a good Navigator as he had lost his own. Without hesitating, he gave him Alex's name. Wing Commander Marriott, a Canadian pilot, arrived at Melsbroek in Belgium with 320 Squadron, where he contacted Alex and explained that he was looking for a Navigator to fly with him. Alex was only too happy to oblige and get back on operations.

320 Squadron was equipped with North American Mitchell (B25) Bombers Mk 11s and 111s. It was formed mostly from personnel of the Royal Dutch Naval Service who had escaped to England after the invasion of Holland. The squadron supported the Allied advance across Europe including the Rhine Crossing, and the support of the Ardennes break through, right up to VE Day, its final war mission being flown from Achmer airfield in Germany, where it was disbanded on the 2nd August 1945. Alex joined 320 Squadron at the beginning of February 1945 and immediately teamed up with Wing Commander Marriott.

On the 25th February Alex and Wing Commander Marriott's first operation was to Udem to bomb the cross roads and communication centre.

Between the 25th February 1944 and 26th April 1945 Alex carried out 26 operations with 320 Squadron, including some of its final Missions of the war from Achmer airfield in Germany in May 1945.

The 26 Operations

25th Feb 1945	Operation to U" (crossroads and communication centre)
27th Feb 1945	Operation to Sonsbeck (communication centre)
28th Feb 1945	Operation to Geldern (railway crossing)
28th Feb 1945	Operation to Rheinberg (communication centre)
1st Mar 1945	Operation to Xanten (communication centre)
2nd Mar 1945	Operation to Dunkirk (food store)
3rd Mar 1945	Operation to The Hague (V2 site)
3rd Mar 1945	Operation to Wezel (rail bridge over Rhine)
5th Mar 1945	Operation to Wezel (rail bridge over Rhine)
9th Mar 1945	Operation to Dorstan (marshalling yards)
9th Mar 1945	Operation to Haltern (marshalling yards)
10th Mar 1945	Operation to Burgsteinfurt (marshalling yards)
12th Mar 1945	Operation to Dorstan (South marshalling yards)
14th Mar 1945	Operation to Haltern (marshalling yards)
15th Mar 1945	Operation to Dorstan (marshalling yards)
15th Mar 1945	Operation to Dulmen (railway crossing)
18th Mar 1945	Operation to Borken (marshalling yards)
18th Mar 1945	Operation to Bocholt (marshalling yards)
20th Mar 1945	Operation to Bocholt (marshalling yards)
21st Mar 1945	Operation to Bocholt (marshalling yards)
22nd Mar 1945	Operation to Drevevack (enemy billets)
25th Mar 1945	Operation to Mechelen (enemy heavy gun positions) (supporting the Rhine crossing)
28th Mar 1945	Operation to Engelskirchen (marshalling yards) (supporting American Army)
23rd Apl 1945	Operation to Bremen (enemy strong point)
23rd Apl 1945	Operation to Bremen (enemy strong point)
26th Apl 1945	Operation to Potrau-Buchen (railway junction) (marshalling yards)

Most of May was spent ferrying VIPs to Copenhagen to re-start the Belgium Government and administration after the German occupation, and returning RAF prisoners of war to England for repatriation.

When Alex completed his last flight with 320 Squadron on 9th June, he was recommended for the Dutch Distinguished Flying Cross (not awarded). Just before he was given some well-earned leave he was offered the position of Squadron Adjutant, as the squadron was moving to Japan. After careful consideration he decided to decline the offer. When he returned from leave, Alex was posted to Watchfield on the 25th August 1945 for a three week Ground Controller course and offered a permanent commission. On the 17th September he was posted from Charterhall to Nutts Corner in Northern Ireland as Ground Controller.

Alex was eventually demobbed at Long Kesh in 1946, and after his release from the RAF, he applied for a position with the firm of Maginess who were solicitors in Lisburn and was employed as a book keeper.

Through a very good friend Blair Maine he made application to Lord Chief Justice Andrews for exemption from having to complete a University Degree, based on his training in the Royal Air Force. This request was eventually granted, and it is only fair to point out that this was the only time that this has been permitted. In the early 1950s Alex was employed by the firm of Neilson and Park as a apprentice manager clerk. He studied hard at night and finally qualified as a solicitor in 1952. He soon set up his own practice as solicitor in Waring Street and Custom House Square in Belfast, and finally retired in 1992 after working for 61 years.

Alex's elder son has followed in his father's footsteps and became a solicitor, he was appointed President of the Northern Ireland Law Society in 1987, and in 1992 was appointed a County Court Judge. (This is the first time a Solicitor had been appointed to that position as it is normally appointed from the Bar.)

His younger son Jim is a chartered surveyor.

Flight Lieutenant Alex Gardiner Burgess DFC

Total flying hours: 303.65 day and 13.25 night.

Total No of Operations: 180 Squadron   9
                              320 Squadron 26
                              Total   35

Aircraft types flown in:
Avro Anson
Blackburn Botha
Handley Page Halifax
De Havilland Mosquito
North American (B25) Mitchell

SQUADRON LEADER
T M BULLOCH, DSO* DFC*
ROYAL AIR FORCE NO. 39373
PILOT
NO. 206 & 120 SQUADRONS

Terrence Malcolm Bulloch was born in Malone Park, Belfast, on the 19 February 1916 and was educated at Mourne Grange Preparatory School, which stood in splendid grounds at the foot of the famous Mourne Mountains. Mourne Grange prided itself on its high standards of scholarship, games, sport and school plays. The school prepared boys for the better-known public schools in Northern Ireland.

Terry was an ardent cricketer and in his last year at the school took 32 wickets in the school matches. Although I think it is true to say golf is his first love, which he still plays to this day. After Mourne Grange he went to Campbell College, which was close to Stormont Castle, the seat of government in Northern Ireland. Campbell College like all public schools of that time was largely controlled by prefects and strict discipline. Terry became a member of the Officer Training Corps at Campbell as he enjoyed the parades. The long marches allowed him to prove to people how tough he was and the level of his endurance. He also became pipe major in the Corps Band.

A lecture was given at the college by a visiting Squadron Leader from Ulster's own Auxiliary Squadron and after the lecture a few of the pupils were selected and given a flight. Terry was one of the lucky ones and remembers well the flight in old bi-plane and this had left an indelible mark on him. Terry was mad about flying and the decision to put all of his considerable energies toward a career in the RAF stemmed from that visit and flight.

With his love for fitness Terry took up rugger like a duck to water. At rugger he was in the First XV for two years. He also took up boxing and earned school colours at this.

At the age of 18 Terry applied to join the RAF and sat the extremely stiff entrance exam for RAF College Cranwell, The Officers Training College.

Although he found the maths exam extremely difficult he managed to pass it anyway and all he had to do was to pass his medical. Terry being an extremely fit boy thought he would have no problem passing it but it was not to be as the medical board found a swollen gland on his neck and turned him down. Terry was shattered to say the least. This had been a bitter disappointment to his father, as he knew only to well of his son's love for flying. His father contacted the family doctor who came to examine Terry and in due course with treatment the swelling disappeared. After a time the medical board agreed to examine Terry again. He passed without difficulty. However owing to the lapsed time between the two medical examinations. Terry found himself too old to join Cranwell.

Terry managed to get himself employment at Newtownards Flying Club. The club at that time belonged to Lord Londonderry. Terry did all sorts of odd jobs at Newtownards just to be near Aircraft. While at Newtownards his enthusiasm and knowledge for aviation gained him respect from some of the pilots and some began taking him with them on local flights and showing him the 'ropes' as it were. Fate however was to give Terry a second chance at joining the RAF as Mussolini in Italy and Hitler in Germany were sabre-rattling and threatening Europe and Britain. Thanks to this, Winston Churchill and others to decide to increase the size of the RAF. One means of achieving this was to launch a new pilot training scheme and under this scheme young aviators would be offered four short service commissions. The Graduates would never achieve the promotion prospects that Cranwell offered but it was the next best thing.

Terry jumped at the second chance and applied again to join the RAF. He had no bother passing all the necessary written and medical tests and was duly accepted. Subject only to the usual proviso that he showed sufficient aptitude for flying. Terry now an acting

Pilot Officer was posted to Scottish Aviation in Prestwick for flying training in November 1936 at the age of 20. This was a civilian flying training sschool, which held the RAF contract. Terry found himself assigned to F/Off capper and he had his first flight in a Tiger Moth on the 16th November and after less than six hours was allowed to go solo.

The chief flying instructor was Sq/Ldr David McIntyre and he had earned the nickname 'All Weather Mac' because of his aridity to fly in all weathers. As was the schools custom every new pupil was personally tested by All Weather Mac before being sent off on their own. More advanced instruction followed a few weeks before his 21st birthday Terry passed all necessary tests which were laid down by the EFTS and was assessed as average by Scottish Aviation. He was now ready to fly the bigger RAF planes. Terry was next posted to No 6 Flying Training School at Nether Avon in Wiltshire. This was his first RAF Station here he would be taught to fly the much bigger and faster bi-plane the Hawker Hart. The Hart was a beautiful aircraft to fly; it was fast and handled like a dream. Terry commenced night flying in Hawker Audaxs, which had the same engine as the Hart, a Rolls Royce Kestrel Engine. He also learned aerobatics and began to put into practice navigation methods, which he was taught at ground school.

In May 1937 Terry was officially commissioned into the RAF and by now he had become a proficient pilot. He passed out from Nether Avon assessed as 'above the average' and this was to be the lowest rating that Terry henceforth was to receive. The only higher which was rarely given was exceptional. Terry now had to make a choice between bomber and coastal command. History was Terry's best subject at school and he new that the fate of the British Isles in war depended upon its ability to maintain maritime invincibility.

He wanted to be a permanent part of the RAF so he thought the new coastal command would offer quick promotion and security. He excelled in the art of navigation and this would stand him great steed in long range flying. So coastal it was! In 1937 coastal command consisted of a few squadrons of obsolete bi-plane torpedo bombers and several squadrons of Ansons.

Having made the decision to join coastal command, Terry was posted to 220 Squadron, which was based at the new RAF station Bireham Newton. It was situated in Norfolk and build beside the sea. To be in a good position to be able to send aircraft out to look for German ships that would try and break out into the Atlantic.

220 Squadron was equipped with 'Faithful Anne' the Avro Anson and Terry needed only the briefest of instruction to fly it. For the next eight months Terry settled down to enjoy squadron life. Hitler was getting bolder and Mussolini more truculent. The unwillingness of either Britain or France to take decisive action had encouraged them. Italy had invaded Abyssinia and proclaimed it as part of the new Italian Empire. Hitler

was slowly devouring Europe bit by bit and Austria was overrun without a shot having been fired. In the middle of 1938 Terry was sent to attend a three month long nav. course with the school of General Reconnaissance at Thorney Island to be taught the finer points of navigation. It was a food course but Terry did not enjoy the flying classrooms. Europe wad drifting closer to war and by October 1938 Terry was back with his squadron. 220 Squadron was preparing for war and might even have to bomb the enemy with its quiver of light bombs. A diversion from their normal duties came on the 21st March when the squadron was ordered to provide an escort across the channel to the plane carrying the French President, Monsieur Lebrun to London on a formal visit. Fifteen Ansons carried out this escort and repeated the performance a few days later when he returned. In dropping bombs he earned the nickname 'Dead Eye Dick'. As the Anson carried no bombsight bombs had to be dropped by the pilot simply by eye. Terry was regarded as a first class navigator, and had passed his CR course and was recognised as one of the squadrons best pilots.

Terry however did make a few blunders and one in particular that almost resulted in his dismissal from the service. He was sent out on an exercise to locate a Battleship Force headed by HMS Nelson. At that time the most powerful battleship in the Navy. Terry found his target and to emphasise the point came diving out of the clouds and planted an aluminium marker right on the fore deck of the Nelson. However the Navy did not appreciate this move and Terry was officially reprimanded for some unknown reason he was promoted to Flying Officer.

The Bullocks of the world are not always appreciated especially during sleeping years of peace. But they certainly came into their own during war and when the chips are down. The RAF was expanding and coastal command now had 16 squadrons nearly all equipped with Ansons. Eyes were now turning to the USA for new aircraft namely the Lockheed Hudson. It was to be the saviour of coastal command. Terry flew across England on various exercises and had learnt his way around all the major RAF Stations on the east coast. The exercise had also taught him to recognise the coast line of England, Belgium and Holland. In classrooms he was taught ship recognition both British and our enemy. Aerial photography was another skill when the squadron practised looking for the backbone of the German Navy. The two battle cruisers Scharnhorst and Gneisenau.

Terry had flown over 700 hours now and at 11.oclock on the 3rd September Terry Bulloch was at war with Nazi Germany.

In Terry's logbook are written the words in large red letters WAR DECLARED AGAINST GERMANY 1 00 HRS 3/9/39.

For the next three days he didn't put a foot inside an aircraft and when he did it was just an exercise. A new exercise, anti-submarine. The enemy had developed a new form of mine one which blew up when a ship passed by, known as the magnetic mine. These were spread all over the North Sea by U-boats and other craft. They caused heavy casualties amongst ships that sailed the east coast. Fortunately the Navy were quick to remedy this awful threat and this was to demagnetise all ships. Terry and a senior officer from the Station HQ answered a call to send another Anson on an extra North Sea patrol. Terry and Tim Vickers who was 2nd Pilot took off and were cursing the Dutch coast when they were attacked by a passing German HE 115. It fired at them as it flew past (luckily no hits) the Anson was no match in speed for the Heinkel. However the war was soon to give Terry a severe blow as his brother Larmor who also had joined the RAF and was a bomber pilot had been killed on a raid on a Heligoland Bight.

Terry could not believe the news and to make matters worse Larmor had married shortly before the war and Terry had not had the opportunity to meet her.

Terry was shattered by news so much so it instilled in him a burning hatred of the Germans. The day Terry flew back to Bircham Newton he was a changed man, a man with a mission to kill Germans.

On the 5th April Terry was sent to Boscombe Down, which was the RAF's main experimental station to learn beam and blind flying. He passed the course without difficulty. Terry was posted from 220 to 226 nothing really changed as both squadrons were based at Bircham Newton. With Denmark fallen and Norway over run. Terry and his new squadron stepped up the numbers of North Sea patrols. This was the only type of work that the Anson could do. Fortunately 206 Squadron was re-equipped with the new Lockheed Hudson and it was like switching from an Austin 7 to a Ferrari. Among the new devices fitted to the Hudson was the top secret ASU Mark 1. This was the first form of radar fitted to an RAF aircraft.

On the 28th August while patrolling the enemy coast Terry spotted a Heinkel 115 and brought his Hudson into a position for a stern attack. The Heinkel seemed to be unaware of Terry's presence so he opened up with his front guns. The Heinkels rear gunner returned fire. Terry blasted the Hun again hitting the rear gunner. By this time both aircraft were over Ijmuiden Harbour, which was ringed with guns. Terry decided that the Heinkel crew were either killed or wounded so he decided to return to patrolling the enemy coast line. But it was a good start one Heinkel out of action. On August 30th, rather to his surprise. Terry was ordered to take his Hudson T 9331 loaded with station personnel to Aldergrove. This was close to Belfast and Terry's home. Aldergrove a detachment from 206 joined other coastal command units carrying out Atlantic convoy escort duties. The Hudson could reach convoys 3 to 400 miles into the Atlantic, was capable of sinking a U-boat and could also chase the Focke-Wulf Condors, which were as big a menace as the U-boats. On September 6th the squadron

was ordered back to Bircham Newton and on the same day Terry carried out a dusk sweep of an area in the North Sea to look for surface raiders sneaking their way into the North Sea. Flying about 500 about 90 miles NE of Cromer Terry spotted another Heinkel. He knew the aircraft's outline well and manoeuvred his Hudson for a stern attack and fired his front guns until all his ammo was spent. The return fire from the Heinkel's rear gunner hit Terry's aircraft with a loud explosion but the Heinkel dived and splashed into the sea. Terry dropped down low and his turret gunner Sergeant Coldbert plastered the Heinkel. The Heinkel was still floating so Terry decided to plaster it with two his 250 lb bombs. After the second flypast the Heinkel disappeared. 206 Squadron pilots had been operational for the best part of six months and were given long overdue leave. Terry was one of them.

On this return from leave Terry was awarded the DFC (22/11/1940) and was one of the first pilots in the squadron to receive this distinction. Terry was also due for an operational rest. He was recognised as an exceptional pilot. He had never damaged an aircraft and was above average as a navigator and one who took his job seriously and tackled all tasks given to him with coolness and courage. He was so determined to get even with the enemy that he once swept low in his Hudson over Holland and shot a German whom he had sighted cycling down a street in Ijmuiden.

Altantic ferry pilot

Terry had now been promoted to FLT/LT and the work he was about to undertake would make him a very valuable pilot to the RAF. He had been selected to take part in a vital experiment to fly American aircraft across the Atlantic to Britain. Terry and a few other pilots were ordered to report to coastal command HQ at Uxbridge for briefing. After the briefing they caught the night train from Euston to Glasgow and another train to Greenock. They boarded the troopship Leopold Ville that was at anchor in the Clyde. Which was to take them to Canada. Terry could not understand why there were so many RAF personnel on board the ship but was soon made aware that they were all off to No 2 School of ground recon. This was moving all to the safety of Canada for training. The Leopold Ville sailed just before exams 1940 and arrived in Halifax Nova Scotia on the 28th December. They spent two weeks in Halifax before Terry was told to proceed to Los Angeles and after an interesting train journey of four days they were met and taken by bus to the small town of Riverside. Terry had a co-pilot assigned to him a young New Zealander F/Off Ian Patterson and each day they would be picked up and taken to March Field which was a US Army Air Corps base. They were attached to the 30th Air Bombardment Squadron this was the top squadron which operated the four engine B-17 Flying Fortress. It soon became clear to Terry that he and another experienced pilot Donald Ross had been selected to bring the first Two B-17s across to Britain.

As America was not at war the USA could not be seen to be helping Britain train bomber crews so Terry and the other RAF crews had been given passports declaring that they were civil test pilots and were over in America to purchase American aircraft.

During the rest of January and into March Terry and D Ross were taught to fly and handle the huge B-17. Flights were made to San Francisco, Tucson and Texas. Bombing practices were carried out and they were even taught to use the Nordin bombsight.

By mid March Terry and Ian went to the giant Boeing plant in Seattle to pick up a B-17 the particular A/C had certain RAF mods carried out on it. Terry and the 30th Bombardment CO Colonel Walter R. Peck flew the B-17 code AN 534 to Portland Oregon and on the 19th March Terry flew it to Boise in Idaho from there to Salt Lake City and on to Kansas.

The Fortress was about to fly the Atlantic and only a handful of pilots in peacetime had ever flown across. At Dayton, Ohio the B-17 of Terry and Donald Ross was repainted in RAF camouflage while at Wright Field they were fitted with armour plate and RAF roundels. On the 15th March the two B-17s took off from Dayton Ohio and headed for Montreal in Canada. In Montreal Terry met a former 206 Squadron pilot F/Off Willie Watson who had been attending a course and was keen to get back to the UK so Terry signed him on as an extra Navigator. Terry and Willie were later to become post war captains with BOAC pioneering the trans-Atlantic route in 1946/7. From Montreal they flew to Gander in New Foundland to be made ready for its trip across the Atlantic and the UK. Terry's plan was to take off towards dusk and fly through the night and arrive in the U.K. at daylight. The B-17 was filled to the gunnels with fuel last checks were made and spares loaded on board. The four Wright cyclones engines each capable of 1,200 hp roared into life and the great A/C taxied out. Suddenly as it made the final turn onto the main runway Terry felt a severe bump and realised that they had burst a tyre and it wasn't until the next evening that it could be changed. The A/C eventually took off for the UK on April 13th and climbed to 15,000 and on to 30,000 for the journey of 2110 miles to Prestwick on the Ayrshire Coast. The flight was swift an uneventful however at this time Prestwick was being rebuilt with huge ultra wide runways so they had to fly to an airfield in Ayr called Heathfield which was a few miles South of Prestwick. On arrival at Heathfield the A/C was checked and refuelled for its flight the same day to Squires Gate in Blackpool.

Soon after Terry's flight across the Atlantic he found himself posted to 120 Squadron, which was being reformed at Nutts Corner in Northern Ireland. He had enjoyed his rest from op flying but was glad to get back in the thick of it. 102 Squadron had been earmarked to receive a completely new type of American A/C about which no details were known. Nutts Corner in Northern Ireland was to the west of Belfast and had the longest

runways in coastal command. The new airfield had a strange name (Nutts Corner). It was built beside a main road, along which ran a bus route. A bus stop was at the corner near a farm, which belonged to a family called Nutt so, the bus stop and the airfield became known as Nutts Corner. The aircraft for which Nutts Corner was built was the long range American B-24 (Liberator). Like the US built B-17, which it was designed to replace it was capable of operating at heights up to 30,000 ft and was powered by four P & Whitney Radial engines each one producing 1200 H.R. with its twin rudders and deep stubby fuselage and its revolutionary nose wheel landing gear. It looked like no other aircraft. The B-24 had twice the range of any other aircraft flying at that time and would prove to be of the utmost value to coastal command.

Before Terry joined 120 at Nutts Corner he became an Atlantic ferry pilot. He ferried Liberators, B17s, Lockheed Hudsons from America and Canada to the UK.

Terry joined 120 Squadron at Nutts Corner at the beginning of August 1941 and made his first flight with the squadron in Lib AM 911 on the 13th August 1941. He went up with his flight commander FLT/LT Harrison; always known as Harry John. Terry himself acted as an instructor passing on the knowledge, which he gained from his Atlantic flights. The squadron was now working itself up for the job, which it was reformed to do sinking U-boats. Terry had by now been assigned a crew and started 'licking them into shape' for operational standards. The war had been in progress for two years by the time Terry joined 120 Squadron and sinking by U-boats had reached alarming proportions.

In September 1941 a new commanding officer arrived at Nutts Corner and he was Wing Commander VHA McBratney an Ulsterman who was educated at BRAI (Inst). W/Co McBratney was a strict disciplinarian and did not suffer fools lightly. He did not like what he saw and so started getting the squadron into shape.

At that time the DFC was a relatively rare decoration in coastal command and the ribbon on Terry's tunic made him stand out among his fellow pilots.

During September 1941 Terry began anti sub patrols over the Atlantic. His crew included Pilot Off. Dear who was second pilot Sgt. McColl (Flight Eng) P/Off Mitchell (Navigator) and Sgt 'Ginger' Turner (WOP/AG). Ginger Turner was one of the few of his trade who seemed to grasp how to get the best out of the ASU Radar. Sgt McColl was to become a key man in Terry's crew not only with 120 Squadron but also for years afterwards. On the 22nd Oct 1941 while doing a sweep of the Atlantic Terry caught sight of his first U-boat. Terry had been sent to find and protect Convoy SC 89 and when he did he discovered that a Fouke Wolf 200 (Condor) was shadowing the convoy. Like the Lockheed Hudson the Condor was a wartime conversion of a civil aircraft and was extremely efficient at its job. In April 1941, German aircraft sank 323,000 tons of shipping while U-boats sank 249,000 tons. The Condors main role was to find shadow and report the position of the convoys.

The Liberator which were originally delivered to 120 Squadron had been fitted with four 20 mm cannons fixed to fire forward in the aircrafts nose.

Although Terry did attack and get in one burst at the Condor no visible effects could be seen. Over the next few hours Terry spotted the Condor at least three more times shooting at it on each occasion. The Condor sometimes returning fire. Terry's lib AM 926 appeared to be unscathed but hours later on the ground he discovered that one engine had been hit and that a bullet from the Condor had passed clean through a propeller. An hour after joining the convoy Terry sighted a U-boat with its conning tower awash three miles away on the port bow. Terry had sharp eyesight, so good was it, that he usually was the first on board to detect the enemy below. He dived his Lib steeply from 1,500 and dropped three depth charges across the path of the fast disappearing U-boat. The third depth charge was estimated a hit. The under water explosion caused a considerable disturbance to the surface. This occurred at the end of the U-boats track and as usual that was all that the crew circling above could see. Was the U-boat sunk, damaged or missed? It was impossible to tell and all that Terry could claim was that the depth charges were dropped bang on as he had dropped three depth charges but had seen four explosions. It had been quite an eventful day for the crew and the legend of Terry Bulloch with 120 Squadron had begun.

15th Dec. when Terry, in Lib AM 928 was detailed to fly all the way from Ballykelly to find and dive bomb a ship near Biarritz off the French Atlantic coast the ship was believed to be carrying iron ore from Spain to a French port. The vessel was small, only about 1000 tons and it most have been inconceivable that the tonnage of iron ore, which it carried, could have affected the mighty war efforts of Nazi Germany.

Finding the ship was no problem to Terry. It was flying the German flag and was escorted by a heavily armed flak ship of the kind, which was normally used to protect U-boats. Terry was no stranger to attacking ships. His Lib carried no low level bombsight so the attack had to be made by eye from mast height. His bombs had been fitted with an eleven second delay other wise a hit on the ship so close to the water would have destroyed his A/C as well as the ship. In the event his bombs near missed but he hit one with his cannons both the ore carrying ship and the flak ship returned a hail of accurate fire. Terry's Lib suffered damage and the Conner Sgt Hollis, was severely wounded in head and face. The port rudder was damaged so Terry set course for St Eval, Sgt Hollis lost an eye. But the question remains why was one of coastal commands few Liberators used in this manner for such a trivial target? As it was coastal command came within weeks of loosing not only a hare to replace A/C but also the most successful U-boat hunter of all times.

On one of his few days off Terry paid his first visit to Buckingham Palace to receive from the hands of King George VI the DFC that he so richly earned with 206 Squadron. For a second time, Terry was ordered on the 19th December to take his Lib down to the Bay of Biscay. This time the target he had to search for was a more worthwhile one. The heavy cruiser Prinz Eugen was in Brest with Scharn Horst and Gneisenau and everyone was ever VGL in case they should break out into the Atlantic.

The crew hunted for the enemy cruiser for 14 Hrs and found nothing and Terry landed back at St Eval since to do so extended his search by a few hours. Terry had already found methods of extending the duration of their trips by careful fuel management. Three days later on the 22nd Terry, while guarding convoy HG 76 far into the Atlantic, sighted not just one U-boat positioning itself for attack, but three.

All spotted him and submerged before he could bring his A/C into an attacking position. Terry had managed to keep the A/C in the air for 16 hrs but because of this had to land back at Limavady as it reduced the return flight by 100 miles. 120 Squadron was finding U-boats faster than any other squadron in the command. Its total was four and all four to the same pilot (Terry).

Although the 'Bull' was still widely used as his nickname and one which suited him so well that it incorporated his name and his aggressive look; many now referred to him as 'Hawkeye's' as he alone seemed to be able to detect the insignificant difference between a half submerged sub's wake and the white caps that so frequently blew off the Atlantic waves. ASU was not finding U-boats the way the experts had thought it would. U-boats and convoys were not all that Hawkeyes was finding in the Atlantic. On 2nd January 1942 in AM 925 he located a tanker, which had been torpedoed and abandoned. During the same month he was ordered to go on a photo recon sortie to try and find the mighty German battleship Tirpitz that was thought to be lurking in Trondhiem Fjord in the North of Norway. Already there were signs that Terry thought things out for himself and landed back where he thought was right. The loner was becoming a law onto himself. But no pilot was fighting the war with greater determination than he.

The squadron commanding officer, Group Capt McBratney relates, "He is a supreme Liberator Captain, and a first class Navigator. And inspiring crew Capt and one who new the value of meteorology and who made a point of mastering this science as well as a Pilot he was, of course 'exceptional'."

January and February 1942 were very wet months. March was also wet, and Terry when taking a Lib to Prestwick skidded off the wet grass into a shallow trench, which had been dug in connection with the ever extending of that important receiving base for trans Atlantic flights. The U/C collapsed and Terry was not pleased with this blemish on his excellent flying record. He was even more displeased when the report of the accident threw part of the blame on him and not the chaotic state of the airfield at the time. Terry being the out spoken individual that he was made no secret of his dislike for senior officers who wore two pilots" wings but sat on their 'fannies' and who never came near operational airfields; they were labeled as 'windy buggers' or 'useless bastards'.

But he held a very high opinion of G Capt McBratney the squadron CO and did not mind how tough he was. Although coming from different parts of Northern Ireland they were both used to speaking their minds and getting on with the business. Terry had little time for those who didn't share his enthusiasm for hunting down the enemy. McBratney was also quick to appreciate that Terry did not mind how hard he worked and used him when not operating his own flights and other pilots as well as a flight instructors to teach the steady stream of new converts to the squadron how to fly the B-24. In April 1942 a detachment from 120 moved to Iceland leaving the bulk of the A/C behind at Nutts Corner Terry and the detachment headed for Reykjavik. On April 24th Hawkeyes did it again he gained surprise over a U-boat and was able to drop a 'stick' of depth charges; six in all which straddled his target in theory, at least this should have been the end of the U-boat. However theory and practice do not always match. These U-boats were superbly built and could withstand pressures up to 14 tons per square inch. This meant that a 250lb depth charge had to dropped with almost incredible accuracy for the welding and riveted hull to be ruptured. In the few months that 120 Squadron had become operational Terry had detected no less than five U-boats.

Within 10 days five had become six while defending convoy HAG. 82 on 3rd May Hawkeye's sighted and attacked another U-boat, again catching it on the surface in the act of crash diving he dropped eight depth charges and it was impossible to tell what their effect had been on the retreating enemy. Post war research and records show that coastal command sank more U-boats that it claimed.

May and June passed without Terry sighting a U-boat but he earned his bread in other ways. On 9th June he located a missing tanker and on the 17th June found a lifeboat with 42 survivors in it and guided HMS Orissa to the spot. In June Terry flew over 100 hours. His annual assessment was due and to no ones surprise Terry was officially rated 'exceptional' both as a Pilot and Navigator. Having by May 1942 attacked more U-boats from the air than any other pilot Terry had evolved his own firm notion of how the attacks should be made and by the wars end his tactics had become the recognised ones.

By July Terry had been promoted to the rank of Sqd/Ldr and that month he had flown over 120 hours and used airfields as far apart as Iceland and Cornwall and Northern Ireland and several others in England. He was enduring long hours and fruitless searching fighting fatigues and cold being perpetually bumped about as he skirted the low clouds, which hung around the Atlantic causing severe back pain, which he still has to this day. On average coastal command crews flew for over a year before sighting a single U-boat and the majority of anti U-boat crews never saw one. On the 10th August Terry sighted his seventh U-boat but it was able to submerge before he could get at it.

Two days later he was out over the Atlantic searching for the survivors of the SS Letitia his flight time was 11hrs.40mins. The flight was cut short much to Terry's annoyance by a fuel leak. He flew again on the 16th 17th in AM 917 from Ballykelly protecting convoy 0537 this gave him the opportunity to sight his eighth U-boat and for once he caught it on the surface and attacked dropping a stick of six depth charges and straddling the U-boat with its conning tower still awash. After the attack wood wreckage was seen floating on the surface. Terry reported, "I certainly gave it a good shaking" and landed at Predannick at Cornwall. After a good rest he took off again on the 18th to protect another convoy SL 118 while circling the convoy he spotted another U-boat. He again dropped six depth charges close to the U-boat track this time he knew for sure that his aim was good. The U-boat abandoned all attempts to dive. This gave Terry a chance to blast the stationary sub with his 20mm cannon. As he swept in he also dropped the two anti sub bombs. After about ten minutes on the surface while Terry fumed inwardly that he lacked the weapon to finish the U-boat off the U-boat gingerly submerged again it had been saved by the ability to absorb a close hit. Oil was leaking from it and it was in no fit state to continue with the war. It is now known that this was U-653 and it did manage to limp back to port for major repair, which took three months to complete.

Terry and his crew were delighted, as they knew they had caused serious damage to the U-boat. The Bulls reputation in the squadron had grown to enormous size. It was puzzling to others how was it that he and he alone seemed to find U-boats with such frequency. He had by then far exceeded the numbers found by any other whole squadron and he was fast becoming a living legend. In Iceland he was entirely his own boss and could fly as often as he wanted and largely let the office work look after itself.

Where flying was involved Terry took his command of the Iceland flight seriously and when a fellow captain, probably the next most senior and one whom Terry had known for many years took a short cut over a corner of Iceland and in Terry's estimation, risked flying into rising ground, Terry promptly sent him back to Nutts Corner. In operational matters he was only concerned with 100% efficiency and was quick to blast anything less. Terry had also acquired a 'dislike' for MR. In his eyes they were a bunch of able-bodied men who should have been doing something more useful to help win the war. On the odd occasion Terry liked to get 'jugged' up with the boys and on one occasion was part of a noisy crowd in a smart hotel the locals resented being invaded by Britain and

America so the manager sent for the MPs who arrived in due course to read the riot act. Now this was like waving a 'red flag to a bull' there were never any half measures about Terry if he wanted to get 'jugged' up he would do the thing properly. So the SQ Officer ended up in the hotels lake dumped there personally by Terry. No action was taken against Terry for as long as he was able to find U-boats he could probable get away with murder.

On the 12th October Hawkeye, ace U-boat hunter was sent to cover convoy ON5136 in almost mid-Atlantic. He soon spotted a U-boat on the surface and dropped all ninedepth charges after the attack wreckage and oil could be seen on surface and during the attack a crewmember saw a large metal object being blown into the air. U-597 had been hit and sunk with the loss of all on board this was the first U-boat attacked and sunk by 120 Squadron. Terry had done it again first in coastal to attack one first to damage one, and first to sink one. Four days later he spotted another U-boat while escorting convoy SC 104. The weather was bad with fog down to the dock. This one was picked up by ASU. Terry attacked and by his own admission according to his logbook he writes. 'Low visibility and unsatisfactory attack.' The sinking of U 597 was not the only success Terry had at Iceland. Before the month was out while escorting convoy HX 212 on 28th October he broke up a wolf pack by diving upon three separate ones. On 5th November Terry was assisting convoy 107 well south of Iceland in the area 58-59N-32-33W – sighting a U-boat he swung into the attack. The U-boat was well and truly caught while on the surface. Using his own, by now well proved method of attack Terry dropped six depth charges along the track of the boat from stern to stern. Even by his own standards he felt obliged to record in his logbook "Excellent attack". The bomb aiming was by eye alone as expected he had destroyed the U-boat U-132 had gone down never to surface again. Another U-boat destroyed with all hands lost.

Within less than one month Terry had sent 90 German sailors to a watery grave in circumstances that must have been sheer terror and mindful of the agony and grief that he had so poignantly had to witness from the brother's widow. He was recently asked if he felt any compassion then or later, for the loved ones of the enemy dozens of whom must have had young wives. There was no hesitation in the terse and forthright reply, "they started this thing not us." As usual he didn't mince his words.

The sinking of U-132 was not the end of the days work. Later he spotted another U-boat this was to be his 18th detection. Terry received a bar to his DFC. Well earned on 27th November 1942 it was not until the 11th December after he had sunk two U-boats did he receive the considerably higher award of the DSO.

In normal circumstances at that time a confirmed kill was so rare that the successful pilot almost always received a DSO. In Terry's case he had to sink two per hour again. He was moving too fast for the system; to an impartial observer, there seems to have been almost a

reluctance to pin medals on a great U-boat hunter. The powers that be must have had a logistical problem of how to decorate a pilot who month after month out performed whole squadrons with personal feats which merited decoration. November 1942 was an exceptionally bad month, foul weather visibility near zero strong winds swept the airfields. The rain and snow lashed down. Runways were covered in slush and the AC with ice and the U-boats made the most of it. News reached the German high command that two massive convoys were being assembled at Halifax. The one sure ice-free port in Canada at that time of year. He had plenty of U-boats at sea. The weather was grounding the Liberators. He could have field day in them in the 'Happy Hunting Ground' better know as 'The Notorious Gap'. The convoys sailed they were picked up and shadowed almost at once and while Down L25 patrol were in position awaiting them U-boats were summoned from near and far both convoys were heading for the Gap. The omens for the killers were good but in war, the unexpected so often seems to upset the best laid plans. Up in Iceland Terry Bulloch and the squadron were cooling their heels but within a week would be a part a vital part of 'a day to remember'.

After a day to remember Terry Bulloch was made an officer and was advised that if he attended a lengthy admin course at Cranwell he could return to 120 Squadron as it CO and this would mean promotion to W/CO. Terry being Terry turned the offer down flat, as he never had much time for those who sat in offices and ordered others into action. He knew well that a W/CO never had a regular crew. He decided that with the outcome of the battle of the Atlantic poised very much in the balance the offer was not for him. The decision certainly did not impress his seniors at CCHQ and the offer was not repeated for the next three years, he was to remain SQ/LDR while others men, junior to him and with far less impressive records were promoted above him. Terry was a patently honest man and when asked recently if he would have wanted to stay in the RAF after the war he replied that he would have liked to have done so. "But they never asked me to stay on." They seemed anxious to get rid of me in spite of which they buggered me up by keeping me busy on transport work with the result I missed my rightful de-mob date and lost my seniority getting into BOAC.

Posted to Ferry Command

Terry was awarded the Bar to his DSO on the 12th January 1943. He now faced the press and gave talks on the radio much as he had done earlier in the USA. This lasted for a whole month and the only time during the war that Terry never flew an A/C. Then on the 10th January he found himself in a VIP A/C as a passenger side by side with Prince Bernhard of The Netherlands who was moving to Canada. They flew the Atlantic in Lib AL512 as far as Montreal then in a Hudson for the final leg to Otiana, which only had a small airport. Terry had been selected to give lectures all around Canada on the finer points of coastal command. The campaign took him in various A/C types all of which he tried to fly, whether or not he was familiar with them. Places like Moncton, Dartmouth, Sydney, Cawder, Torbay and up to Goose Bay in Labrador. It wasn't Terry's idea of war but if a pilot of his fame had to be rested (which the powers that be decided what to next with him) it made sense to use him in this way. By the end of February 1943, Terry had had more than enough of his role as a propagandist which was not really his forte. Pleasant as it was he was therefore delighted when he was told that his request for more action had been granted and he was to deliver a Lib to the UK and stay there! The A/C was Lib.I FL981 Terry had great faith in the Liberator and had dispensed with the usual test flight and at Gander merely re-fuelled and carried straight on as he seems to be eager to get back into the war.

Terry was back but what to do with him. This was coastal command's problem his rank and experience merited him being given a position as a flight commander this was a stepping stone to taking over a squadron. But he had turned that down. So Terry was appointed chief instructor of a Lib HQ at Beaulieu and made an exceptionally good instructor (respected by all). He could fly as much as he wanted i.e. every day and several times a day. Compared with U-boat hunting it seemed a little tame. "All right but not active enough" were his words.

He also managed to get involved in the testing of some 'secret equipment' and also enjoyed the experimental work. This was ASV Mark III a vastly improved version of the earlier equipment and for the first time a really effective radar device for CC. It operated in a frequency range that the Germans couldn't even credit as possible. Because they had not yet conceived the magnetron value. Terry was on a night detail with some pupils when a rare alert was sounded a few FW 190s Fighter Bombers were bombing near by Bournemouth. The order went out to all A/C to switch off all their lights. Terry didn't like such an order it smacked of cowardice to hide away for fear of being attacked. Terry did douse his lights and decided to go back to land. The airfield at Beaulieu was 100% blacked out. This gave Terry a problem as he needed lights to get down but he had the solution on board. The Lib he was flying was one of those that had been fitted with the 2,000,000 candle power Leigh light which was powerful in the extreme as it not only illuminated Beaulieu in full but half the countryside as well. Terry defied orders or, "Defying Germans more like it". He admitted with his characteristic smile, "I had ceased to be CFI by the next day." He had become very interested in experimental work and was sent to Boscombe Down the RAF main experimental airfield. At Boscombe Down Terry began perfecting the new ASV III. He also contacted W/Co Leigh, the inventor of the Leigh Light

to determine where best to add this device to the Lib on several occasions W/Co Leigh flew with Terry and they worked very closely.

Other trials he was involved with were: the fitting of a new forward firing gun turret and something that he had never needed but which was greatly demanded elsewhere."A simple but effective low level bomb sight." One of Terry's complaints while hunting subs had been the relative ineffectiveness of the depth charges carried on board the Lib. If he had been armed with a more deadly weapon he would have sunk a dozen or more U-boats not just three. Boscombe Down was again coming up with the answers this unit with Terry taking part was in process of adding two new killers to the Liberators arsenal. One device was a homing torpedo to be dropped immediately after a U-boat had won the race for safety and submerged. The second killer developed by the boffins was RP5 Rocket Projectiles. In Terry's eyes these were just what he wanted; the rockets were so small the Lib could carry a dozen or so. They were blazed off of 1,000mph. They contained no explosives just a solid head that would literally go through anything they hit. They could be dropped low without the risk of damaging the plane. Terry and his experimental crew managed to wangle a temp posting to 224 Squadron. They were not exactly welcomed by 224 because like other squadrons 224 had a balanced compliment. A Wing CO as CO and two Sqd/Ldrs as flight commanders and a full quota of A/C. The arrival of Terry with far more decorations on his tunic than seen in CC rather upset 224's applecart. This was the start of the quip. One of the smart Asses remarked "We've got Terry Bulloch BOAC with us". BOAC? Why BOAC? "Bullock's own Air Force Corporation".

No 224 Squadron was based at St Eval along with nearly a dozen other squadrons (mainly Liberators) their job was to bottle up U-boats as flying non stop patrols across the Bay of Biscay one A/C being relieved by the next etc. Never one to waste time Terry put himself on extra patrol within a couple of days of arriving at St Eval and again two days later. For this second op he armed his Lib with the full quota of twelve RPs. A bomb Bay of eight depth charges and a 'Wandering-Willie' Mark 24 mine, the secret homing torpedo. The patrol was to the southern end of the Bay of Biscay. After about 5hrs Terry with his wonderful sight again sighted a U-boat. The drill that Terry had worked out was to fire two RPs from each side in a dive at eight. Another Salvo of four at 600 and the two final pairs at 500, after which he would start to trim the adjustable tail-plane to get the big A/C level again. The A/C would be at less than 100 of the sea at the end of the delicate maneuvre. The attack went well just as Terry had hoped several 01 RP. had struck home and no sub built could possiblly survive this treatment, as one good strike was all that was needed. Terry Bulloch was never one to let an enemy escape if it at all possible. To make absolutely sure Terry now turned on his other weapons "No point having them on board and not use them, is there?"

First he levelled off at 500. The prescribed height for the release of Wandering Willie this floated down on a parachute to ensure it struck the water gently and not damage its sensitive homing mechanism. To mark the spot Terry also dropped a smoke flare to burn on the water. He saw the torpedo circling aimlessly in a circle of about 30-40 DA. It was the torpedo searching in vain for a clue as to which direction to head. This could also have been the sub damaged.

To counter this possibility Terry made another run and this time dropped all eight depth charges. These fell slap into the middle of the wandering objects swirl and were followed by a colossal explosion. The ace killer had done it again. The admiralties were able to confirm the kill almost at once. This was no ordinary kill U-514 was a type lXC built at Hamburg. The larger U-boats were prized kills. They had an operational range of 11,000 miles Terry had sent another 50 men to the bottom. In many respects this was the single most outstanding anti-U-boat attack by a pilot of CC during the entire war. Terry and his crew received absolutely nothing for this attack. Terry should have had a third bar to his DSO and an AFC for his great work at Boscombe Down. When the subject was raised all Terry would say was, "They might have given me, or perhaps my crew something". "Anyhow, I wasn't doing it for the medals." A decision was made that Liberators would not be equipped with RPs and those units which were already so equipped would have to remove them. This made Terry hopping mad. He became in fact just another frustrated CC Pilot forever searching but never finding. Bad luck also dogged his flying when taking off in his overloaded Lib Terry had the misfortune to run into a flock of seagulls. By skill and keeping his head he struggled to get the damaged aircraft back safely on the runway several tons over its allowable max weight. All aboard could so easily have joined the 14 seagulls later found on the runway.

After his second spell at Boscombe Down (proving RP could be carried inside the Lib without the flying qualities being adversely effected Terry who's time in Lib B 2501 took himself to Ballykelly in N. Ireland and was attached to 59 Squadron N. Ireland had been a previous happy hunting ground so perhaps BOAC could operate successfully from there. Not only did he not sight any U-boats during his brief spell with 59 Squadron he suffered the indignity of damaging an A/C for the first time since Prestwick. On a flight to show off what his own brand of RP could do and should be doing. He pulled up the A/C a fraction too quickly with the result that the big A/C collapsed on it belly and slid to the end of the runway. On board was a number of officers from HQ they were not impressed. The Command decided to rub Terry's nose in the mess he had created. The affixed a red endorsement in his logbook which was a supreme insult to their most experienced and most successful U-boat

hunter. Terry would have none of this and by skilful use of a kettle wasted on time in promptly removing the insult if the Bull decided to do something he does it properly. The A/C was not seriously damaged and was operational again within a week or so. Finding no pickings with 59 Squadron Terry took BOAC to Iceland. By then he appeared to have been fighting a purely personal war. Taking himself to wherever he fancied and taking with him a personal A/C.

By June 1944, almost exactly on D-Day during the weeks that followed when CC achieved their greatest triumph of the war. Terry with 86 Squadron was nearly 1000 miles away in the tip of N. Scotland. 86 Squadron had helped to train in order to hunt for U-boats, which were lurking in wait for Artic convoys. He therefore missed Coastal's wonderful period when in June 1944 they with massive Naval help successfully bottled up the U-boats, which had been assembled in large numbers at the adjacent French Ports. In order to prevent the Allies landing in France. Not a single ship out of the many thousands involved in D-Day was hit by a submarine, or for weeks after. Terry was detailed to carry out a search in an area up to the Artic Circle in latitude, 72 degrees North in poor visibility with a sea fog. A strange thing was that Terry was being compelled to fly a Lib that lacked most of the main advantages it had not even been fitted with the ASI MK III. The earlier Mk II was on board. The MK II ASU was useless, as it actually warned a U-boat if an aircraft was searching it for.

Terry's Lib was detected first by the noise of its engines, and then visually by U-636. By 1944 U-boats had been armed to the teeth and were equipped with a number of Anti Aircraft guns mounted in pairs. When Terry's Lib was almost on top of the U-boat it opened up with accurate fire and hit both starboard engines and the starboard rudder. The plane was 900 miles from friendly shores and beneath was icy waters. Terry knew he was in trouble. The Lib had shuddered and rattled upon being hit and almost at once the STB engine ran down without delay Terry and his engineer Jock McColl stopped and feathered the engine, before the hydraulic oil of the sophisticated feathering system drained out.

If it couldn't be feathered the wind milliner prop would add a lot of drag to the A/C using up precious fuel.

Terry had other problems. The A/C was not responding normally to its flying controls with No 4 eng. stopped and feathered. The A/C had much more power on one side than the other. To counteract this Terry and his 2nd Pilot P/Off Lord were shoving hard with their left feet to apply max. Rudder but it was the rudder that was not responding properly. Jock McColl (Eng) added to Terry's problems by telling him that No. 3 Engine was also damaged and that in his view should be stopped and its prop. feathered. Terry was trying to gain height by using the good engines. Height meant safety. The increased power made the big A/C slew sideward. The tail gunner had a good view of both rudders and informed Terry that a large part of the stern rudder was missing and bits were falling off the stern engines. Terry told Jock do not feather No 3 but to reduce power on it and see if he could get something useful out of it to help his situation. Next decision would they send an SOS or MAYDAY on the wireless. At their height they were now operation and at the distance from base it was doubtful if 'any' message would be received and it was also important to report the U-boat position. The two pilots by exerting all their strength on the rudder bard-gradually brought the A/C around onto a home course. Terry said, "OK we've got some height now so I will feather No. 3 now in case it catches fire." No 1 and 2 were at full power and if they overheated and either gave up all would be lost. The bomb doors were opened and over a ton of depth charges were dumped into the sea. Guns and Ammo followed. The Lib responded almost at once so Terry could throttle back on No 1 and 2 and decrease the engines temperature. Terry and Lord were also able to relax their feet pressures as their legs by now really hurt. For five long hours they battled and nursed the Lib home on two engines and a damaged rudder. It was a feat of physical endurance. With the problems of the flights largely solved and base only minutes away. Terry found that his track would take him over the Naval base at Scapa Flow. It was of course a prohibited flying area marked by a great splodge of Red on all RAF Maps. Terry decided to fly straight through it (Good for you, Terry).

Although the time Terry spent here were probably the most disappointing of his wartime career, especially those when posted to 59 and 86 Squadrons. There were a few enjoyable moments. One came at Tain, his most unhappy station. Terry for once decided to let his hair down and arranged to meet his crew for a booze up. He borrowed a set of bagpipes marched up and down the streets of Tain playing Irish Eyes with his crew marching behind him. This proved too much however for the inhabitants of Tain, to be awakened from their sleep in the middle of the night by someone playing Irish Tunes in their Scottish High Street. The local bobby was summoned. The defender of the law fortunately took a tolerant view with the boys in blue and by that and persuasion managed to persuade the inebriated crew to wobble homewards as best they could.

This incident may be behind a photo, which the CO of the Squadron W/Co C Drapper has preserved which is re-produced in his book. It shows Terry and him enjoying a beer with Terry's arm in a sling when asked about the photo Terry would say "Oh That. I fell off my bicycle while playing bagpipes." Terry was also a demon potter at snooker.

A transport Squadron had been formed at Lyneham to operate one of the transport versions of the Lib now being produced. This version was known as the C 87c. It flew mail, urgently wanted freight and VIPs to almost anywhere – Russia, Cairo, India, West Africa. The UMT also flew Avro Yorks. Its Liberators were known as the Liberator Express Aircraft. Terry joined the unit on 29th August 1949 and without further ado promptly settled down to the next task along with Jock McColl. His first flight was to Gibraltar. And then to RaBat normally when not on Ops. Or training, the crew separated into their respective Messes and saw little of each other but the camaraderie was always there and at suitable opportunities both sides willingly and eagerly removed the official barriers that separated them. Intelligent Commanders were prepared to close their eyes to such fraternization. They knew it was good for crew moral and for the Squadron spirit. Flights to other places followed to the Azores, Karachi, Malta, Calcutta, Allahabad, Tobruk, and Naples etc and between flights Terry also found time to attend a radio Nav. Course at Prestwick. Terry 'never' pretended that he knew it all and if meteorology radio aid or Navigation courses were around he would somehow attend them and usually passed any course with honours towards flying his attitude was 100% professional. The C 87 Liberators he was flying have been described as the worst B-24s ever built. Tons overweight and reluctant to leave the ground and wallowed laboriously until as fuel was consumed it became more manageable. Terry had been flying over loaded Liberators for years and didn't notice anything much different. It caused him no problems.

By 1945 it was obvious to all, except perhaps Adolph Hitler that the war in Europe could only end one way. Pilots with Terry's love for flying were looking around to see how they could equip themselves for a career in post war aviation. Terry had acquired vast experience already but he saw a chance to obtain even more. Somehow he got to know about a Squadron, which almost no one in Britain had ever heard about either then or since. At the time he was based in Montreal with 45 Group. He got himself posted there from Lyneham. For one thing it was offering an advanced Radio-Range (Beam) Navigation course. He had previously passed the one at Prestwick but realised that the North American way of flying the Beam was more advanced. He duly passed this course with a rating of 'up to good airline standards'. This was a real feather in his cap. It was 45 Group and Montreal, which had arranged the early Trans Atlantic flights and the return ferry service of the Real BOAC. Terry had mastered all that Montreal could offer and thanks to his spell at Lyneham the routes to Europe Africa and India.

As soon as he heard about 231 Squadron he reckoned that this was 'right up his alley'. This almost unknown RAF unit was based in San Diego, Southern California and flew a transport version of the Lib all the way to Auckland, New Zealand by way of Hawaii, Canton Islands and Fiji and although the war in Europe had ceased. The fight was still raging with fury in that area. By some unique method Terry got himself posted to this 'one-off' RAF Station Squadron, based within sight of Mexico. It satisfied a number of his wants. It gave him a chance to fly and navigate across an ocean that he had not mastered. It enabled him, ever active, to get closer to where the only remaining action of war was taking place and it enabled him always stagnantly British to be 'showing the flag' in a theatre of war almost entirely dominated by the Americans. The aircraft used by 231 Squadron were the Lib RY-3s-IT was a version originally ordered by the US Navy and was the only version to be fitted with a huge single tail. All the others had the familiar twin rudders, which looked like a pair of dustbins. The RY-3s carried up to 20 passengers but had plenty of room for urgent freight as well. It was strictly a VIP run. The flight time to Sydney was about 38 hours with the longest leg of the journey - San Diego to Hawaii. Which took about 12 hours. It was a tiring schedule but Terry never seemed to tire in the air. It also had a reliable engine the ever-present F/Off Jock McColl. Jock had come along way since being discovered in the hangers at Nutts Corner when a Fitter 2 (e). All along that route he had sat only inches away from the same Ulster Skipper.

By then Terry was ready and waiting for the years of peace, which stretched ahead. In all, he had passed with distinction. These advanced radio navigation courses of the kind, which benefit a civil pilot. He had flown literally all over the world and spanned its oceans and while a part of him still wanted to serve the RAF, "his boyhood dream", he was realistic to acknowledge that he and they didn't quite fit.

Terry by 1945 was aged thirty and an unconfirmed offer of a career which would see him 'turned out to grass' at aged 40 was hardly attractive. The civil aviation field beckoned. The sheer statistics of his qualifications were formidable.

Total flying hours	4,568
Hours on liberators	1,721
OP trips	0,350
OP hours	2,059

His hours flown with the RAF alone were probably unique. His decorations were also formidable but in civil aviation they count for nothing. The hours would speak louder as would the Navigation courses this would separate him form the other aces in the RAF. Terry naturally set his sights on BOAC. He had worked for them on and off for years and had crossed the Atlantic with BOAC as crewmen several times. He knew them and more importantly they knew him at his best.

Terry had problems getting himself de mobilised being so far away from Britain. His papers were delayed he had to spend many a month cooling his heels awaiting release. While he was waiting to be released Terry passed another Navigation course to add to he impressive list of qualifications. The RAF navigation warrant. Although he was 'late' in joining BOAC and lost out some valuable places in seniority he was taken on direct as a Captain. If BOAC had not taken Terry on, then almost every other airline would have done. So

ended the wartime career of CC most celebrated, most decorated, most successful anti sub pilot and for the last three years he hardly if ever sighted the enemy but by then he had done more than enough.

He had shown the way to others in the Command that followed by wars end the Lib was the top U-boat killer in the Command with the reformed 120 Squadron at Nuts Corner and heading the list with 16 kills (now 17) four by Squadron Leader TM Bulloch Britain would be a poorer place without the Terry Bullochs of this world. Britain might never exist at all. As both sides found out 1939/45, when the Bull set his sights on a target, he is a mighty hard man to stop. Terry Bulloch's career as a civil pilot was all that was expected of him. He flew as much or more than any other pilot and never had difficulty in mastering any of the aircraft he had to handle. He would never have anything to do with positions of authority, which his seniority opened up for him and his smooth accident free flying record was punctuated by the occasional provocative quirk. Terry always had a short fuse especially where inefficiency in the air was concerned. His blasting of an inefficient officer could be withering but such outburst was short lived. Terry was privileged right from the out set, to join BOACs prestigious Trans-Atlantic route. Not only was this BOAC's premier route and one which at the time, only the pre-war civil pilots operated (the so called Atlantic Barons) but for the first few years after the war. It meant being based in Montreal away from all the privations of Britain and receiving extra pay and allowances. BOAC knew about Terry and he knew about them. It was the right and obvious spot for him and he at once settled down among the elite holding his own by his usual hard work. He soon passed the top Navigation Exam and became a first class Navigator. A master pilots certificate followed there was no higher qualification. From crudely converted Liberators BOAC rapidly progressed to a handful of early constellations then on to Double Decker Boeing Stratocruisers. Pan Am and BOAC ruled the Atlantic in these comfortable, but difficult A/C to handle. Eventually these give way to the DC 7Cs and then to big Boeing jets. Terry took all these in his stride. The Atlantic division was given to deliver them to the UK. He was not alone regarding Boeing as the supreme civil aircraft manufacturer. They built in extra strength of their aircraft impressed his as a pilot. Jock McColl followed Terry into BOAC as an Flt/Eng and in no time was flying in his accustomed position. At times a few inches away from Terry over the ocean they had got to know so well in wartime. As I said before in this story Terry was a person who didn't suffer fools lightly.

On one occasion they were late starting from New York due to an US ground starter truck, and during the long taxi to take off. Sir Miles Thomas (chairman of BOAC) who happened to be on board sent the Chief steward up with a note to Terry suggesting that the passengers might like to know the reason for the late departure. Terry didn't want to hear the request. The steward retreated without so much a hint of a reply only to re-appear a few moments later to repeat the request. Terry turned on the unsuspecting steward and yelled, "You get back and tell Sir Miles with my compliments that I'm in charge of this bloody A/C and not him and to mind his own business"

"In those exact words, Sir?"

"Yes."

On another occasion

When BOAC became British Airways, Terry went on flying just the same and when an early retirement scheme came along he ignored it. When the Jumbo Jet (747) arrived he converted onto it and went on crossing the Atlantic as diligently as before.

Eventually he reached the age when BA were compelled to retire him by then he had flown over 6 million miles and post war had crossed the Atlantic 1,113 times probably more often than any other British Pilot and always without cause or alarm for his tens of thousands of passengers were unaware that they were in the hands of the most outstanding of all Coastal Command Teams.

After retiring from BA Terry joined the Portuguese Airline TAR and promptly took command of a 707. When he finally retired from flying for good he worked hard at his golf as he had done at flying and aged 83 now is no mean performer. In 1983 he won the RAF Golf Societies Veterans Trophy. Terry has found happiness with his Canadian born wife Linda (He calls her the colonial) He keeps himself wonderfully fit and still plays 18 holes almost daily. A wonderful find gentle understanding man. It has indeed been an honour to know and meet him.

W/Co McBratney, his CO when together they put 120 Squadron on the map and the U-boats to rout. He described Terry as, "A living Legend."

Few have ever said it better.

Another day in the life of 'Hawkeye' to remember

Convoy HX 217 Departed from Halifax Nova Scotia on almost the last day of November 1942. Its ships were loaded with food and war supplies for Britain, which alone was struggling to protect herself. The slightly slower convoy SC111 had departed a day or so earlier its cargo was equally valuable to the allies. Both convoys were heading for Britain and both had to run the U-boat gauntlet. In total the two convoys comprised of over 70 ships. By 1st December the two convoys were running - barely 25 miles apart each occupied several square miles of sea. It was then that they were sighted by on of Admiral Donitiz's U-boats. To the U-boat commander the whole ocean must have seemed full of ships. He made no attempt to attack his job was to report and shadow. Because the convoy had been sighted so early in the passage. There would be ample time for the 'Wolves' to surround the convoys and tear them apart. Not for

nothing were these flotillas called 'Wolf Packs'. A second U-boat joined the original shadower the two convoys and their respective tracks were noted and plotted. The slower on was taking a more Southerly track. Faster ships usually carried more valuable cargo.

On December 2nd one of the shadowers was spotted by a Canadian A/C and forced to dive. This meant both sides now knew what to expect. Both could even predict where and when the attack would most likely take place: - in Mid Atlantic - in the so-called Dreaded Gap. The notorious Gap was far away from allied airfields. Donitz was rerouting 22 U-boats from their various Atlantic patrols and was informed by the shadower of every change of speed and course of the convoy when all the U-boats were in position the attacks would begin. The report of the sighting by the Canadian A/C prepared the contestants German sailors, tired and weary from days and weeks at sea would perk up crash dive drills would be practiced Navigators with compasses and divers would be plotting fresh tracks. The British sailors could guess what was happening and were powerless to stop the U-boat attack. The Senior Naval Officer (5 No) responsible for guarding each convoy had a bare half dozen ships under his command. He could not spare them to search for the U-boats as a skilled U-boat Captain could keep the convoy under surveillance from Astern. Even in daylight, hunting for a U-boat was like looking for a needle in a haystack. The convoy could do little but wait. Sudden alterations of course as night fell were on tactic at times brought success.

By December 7th convoy HX 217 was almost within range of 120 Squadron on detachment to Reykjavik and two A/C were sent to locate it and give it what protection they could. Only on managed to find the convoy this was not too surprising as the convoy was still 800 miles from Reykjavik. Terry had been clicking his heels at Nutts Corner for days and when the order came he had no hesitation in assigning himself the important task ahead - Convoy HX 217 was in grave danger. He picked his most skilful pilot Sq/Ldr Desmond Istead for the second A/C Istead was commonly know as 'Wizz' he too had acquired a reputation for finding U-boats in the featureless waters of the North Atlantic. True to form Terry and his crew located HX 217 it was still dark with the dawn light beginning to spread over the Eastern Horizon. Hawkeyes Bulloch knew precisely what the convoys Senior Naval Officer would require of him. His job for the next two hours would be to hunt around the edges of the convoy and try to locate and attack the shadowers that both he and the SNO knew would be there. The convoy was now in its most venerable position, as U-boats from far and wide would have been summoned for the massacre, which would take place that night.

The stage was set for the kill. The nearest Airfield being 700 miles away and the night of 8th December could be the night of the lone knives. Terry began his search a dozen or so miles from the flanks of the convoy all his crew kept their eyes peeled ceaselessly scanning the horizon.

Terry's A/C was being buffeted about the sky and he and his crew had already been up most of the night. It was cold and draughty but Terry and his crew were well used to these hostile conditions. All the crew wore fur lined boots, padded Sid cot Suits, inner and outer gloves, scarves, helmets and as many sweaters as they could get into underneath. One advantage of the Lib was the Auto pilot (for the period) was more reliable than most. This meant that the pilots were relatively free of the weary task of manually controlling the A/C keeping it level and heading correctly. However while searching for a convoy, courses had constantly to be altered and each had to be meticulously plotted by the Navigator. On the charts that crowded the small desk. Terry's judgment was soon proved to be correct. Just before 1130 hrs astern of the convoy his exceptional eyesight once again brought results. Amidst the ever-changing pattern of waves he had spotted the fractionally firmer wake of a U-boat traveling on the surface. Not only had he spotted his 20th U-boat but also this time he had managed to do so in a hailstorm. The U-boat was traveling fast and heading for HX 217. He shouted, "Action stations", his crew knew exactly what to do Terry cut out ('George') autopilot and now was in complete control of the A/C.

Terry decided to attack the U-boat along its track and as usual a race against time. Somehow he had to reach the U-boat before it could escape under the waves. Without having to be told, the W/OP/A/G manning the wireless set would immediately begin to tap out in Morse code the standard U-boat flash which was relayed to base. Command had to be advised that an attack was taking place in case anything happened the A/C. It was rare for a U-boat to fight it out with a diving plane. But in the latter years of the war some U-boats would as they were armed to the teeth with AA Guns. The bomb doors were now opened and now started his attack 'too late' the U-boat had spotted him and commenced its crash dive and it was tilting steeply as the Lib swept overhead. The attack was almost a copybook one all six depth charge were seen by the W/OP/AC in the tail gun position. To explode one after the other in the prescribed manner and to explode around the U-boat as it dived. No 3 and 4 fell right along side the fast disappearing grey hull as it slid under the waves with its stern protruding at an angle of 30 degrees. The explosions rose to a height of around 50' the crew spotted dark brown oil on the surface and yellow planking float to the surface and if from no where a large flock of seagulls appeared wheeling around excitedly and diving down to feast upon something edible below. The big clumsy RAF hand held camera was put to use. Jock McColl had made it his business to use this whenever possible as photographic evidence was useful in helping to sway the hard nosed critics back at base of a kill as the command was rightly distrustful of claims of aircrew. All the attacks might look good, but it was commands job to get to the truth.

It was usual for a skipper to steer an escorting Naval ship to the scene of the attack which would pick up an oil sample from the sea some wreckage and one or two bodies. It would use its flash lamp to send a message to the circling A/C above Y.O.U.KILL.E.D.H.I.M. The middle of the Atlantic as it was possible to be Terry had sank U-254. Barely had the details been duly logged when Terry shouted, "Action stations", once again the Bull had spied another U-boat. The tell tale signs in the water told him that this time he had picked up two U-boats traveling together about 300 yards apart at a distance of about 20 miles from the convoy and going like mad to catch up with the convoy. The U-boats were on the A/C port bow. The nearer had been quick to spot the Lib and was hastily crash diving the other which appeared to be trailing oil was less alert but managed to submerge as the Bull came roaring overhead. It had only submerged for about 15 seconds. This meant to Terry that there was still a chance to inflict damage or scoring a second kill.

The crew knew their drills. The Bulls wrath would be blistering if a false move had been made. He could be as unmerciful of inefficiency with his crew as he could. He could be with his sworn enemy he neither asked nor gave quarter. His two depth charges were dropped from about 200! Ahead of the swirl left behind by the diving U-boat. Both were seen to explode just above were the conning tower would have been. After the spray subsided there was a further upheaval about 50. A head of the earlier explosion it rose to about 30' – solid water not just spray in the Rear Gunner's estimation. It was considerably larger than any air bubble rising to the surface as a result of a U-boat blowing its tanks to achieve stability under the water. This indicated damage below. It was now 1245 hrs barely 75 minutes after the first attack and this was turning out to be quite a day for the Ulster man and his crew.

The crew were in their more customary position of doubt, had they sent another U-boat to the bottom? How could they tell? It was maddening not to know.

Although Terry and his crew obtained little satisfaction from the inconclusive attack the effect below was considerable. Even if undamaged a U-boat that was forced to crash dive had problems and once below it was as blind as a mole. The longer it stayed out of sight the safer the convoy would be and also made it much harder for the U-boat to regain contact with the convoy. Although the attack had been inconclusive, all aboard knew they had made history. Most crews flew for months or years before sighting a U-boat yet although they had been only around the convoy for less than two hours. They had sighted three and attacked two. They also knew that their Captain Hawkeyes had now sighted 22 U-boats and attacked 12, which was far more than most Squadrons had, or ever did through out five years of war over the Atlantic.

Terry and his crew still faced many hours of cold, bumpiness and watchfulness before they could turn for home, which was some 70 miles away. Their ability to stay in the air so long was partially due to Jock McCalls skilful manipulation of the aircrafts fuel supply. Meaning that a 15 hour sortie could be turned into a 17 hour one. This became of considerable significance in those instances. Such as all convoy protection flights when several hours had to spend getting to and returning from the area were U-boats were most likely to be located vigilance at the fuel panel was almost as important as vigilance at the look out stations. The fact that Terry's Lib now had no depth charges did not alter the role that it had to play. The U-boat commander could not possibly know that an A/C diving at him had no means of sinking him.

One asset of operating out of Iceland was that food there was not rationed as it was in the UK Terry had arranged to get hold of some steaks and found a way of serving them hot on board. Terry as usual ate with his plate on his lap never more than a second or two would he take his eyes away from the grey waters below. "Action Stations" he bellowed again. He had spotted another U-boat. Plates of food went crashing to the floor as the crew jumped to their assigned positions. He swung his A/C into a tight turn and dived down. No need to dive with care this time his Lib had been fitted with 4 x 20 mm cannons fixed to fire forwards in the nose. The hull of a U-boat was under attack and 20mm cannons could not penetrate this. Only if a U-boat fought it out on the surface could the cannon play a decisive role blowing a few heads off in a crowded conning tower. True to expectations, U-boat No 4 of this patrol began to crash dive. The cannons were fed from clips each held 15 rounds 60 rounds in all. There was no means of aiming other than point the nose of the A/C at the target. All 60 rounds were fired in one furious burst and several hit around the Conning tower. After such an attack a man was sent below to rearm the cannons with replacement clips. Terry could not claim even minor damage to the U-boat but he had done his best. The most positive evidence of damage was the remains of the steak and chips littering the A/Cs floor Terry commented later "Our lunch was ruined but that sub didn't get within torpedo range of the convoy."

Scarcely had the guns been reloaded. The incident duly logged timed at 1426 hrs when another U-boat was sighted. The sea was full of them: As indeed it was subs kept bobbing up all over the place remarked Terry later at an interview. Doenitz had summoned them from near and far. This was a prize convoy given luck with the weather. He had hoped to wipe it out completely. Recently over twenty ships had been lost from one convoy and November 1942 had been a record month for tonnage sunk – over three quarters of a million. He hoped Britain would be starved into submission or at least rendered impotent. This must have seemed a very real possibility. Again Terry sent his Lib into a flat dive and attacked the U-boat. The odds against U-boat No5 again catching up with Hx217 were grim. Terry spotted No 6 at 1524 hrs while his crew were warming themselves with mugs of hot tea from their thermos flasks

and his cannons had been again reloaded and were again fired as the U-boat dived. Like the others its commander was probably astonished to be attacked from the air in a 'plane free' area. Almost every hour on the hour the crew heard Terry call, "Action stations". It was becoming a routine and down would go the Lib into a dive with guns blazing Terry had only four more clips of ammunition left. Terry and his crew had now broken all possible records. They had put down six U-boats recording one for each hour spent protecting the convoys flank. It was also heartening for the Merchant Seamen below. 55 minutes later Terry spotted No 7 once again he dived at the U-boat firing 15 rounds from each cannon around the disappearing enemy. Before half an hour had passed No 8 was sighted. The flight Engineer had luckily found another clip of ammo. Once more Terry sent the big Lib hurling seawards. The U-boat was slow to respond and so the plane passed over it the tail gunner was able to blast it with 100 rounds of 303 from his machine gun. It really agonised Terry that he had no depth charges to drop as this time he had achieved almost total surprise and the U-boat was on the surface just asking to be sunk.

Back at base he laminated "It was a sitter, if I'd have any depth charges left. It would have been a dead duck." Some would have been satisfied with what he had already accomplished but not the Bull. He had good reason to hate the Germans and would have gladly slaughtered the lot. As had been planned. 'Wizz' Isted duly arrived to take over from Terry by the time that he departed from Iceland the convoy had moved closer to that island with less mileage to cover. Terry and Wizz between them had forced no less than 13 U-boats to dive and to lose contact with the convoy. They had broken up what otherwise would in all probability have been the most damaging attack of the war.

Never before had Doenitz managed to get 22 U-boats into attacking positions against a single convoy and he passed up the opportunity to attack the slow SC111 to do so. Perhaps most damaging of all was the effect of these attacks on the moral of his U-boat crews. Most were new to the game. His three great aces, commanders Kretschmer, Prien and Schepke. Each a German hero known to every boy in the fatherland, were by 1942 all gone. Never after the 8th December could the U-boat commanders feel safe in the 'Gap' By the time Terry landed his Lib safely back in Iceland he and his crew had been in the air for nearly 17 hours including eight spent protecting Hx217. In all they had been on duty for the best part of 24 hours. The real proof of their accomplishments came that night in the Gap. Conditions were right for the U-boats to attack. However the attackers had been thrown into disarray as their positions had been revealed.

Terry had been awarded a DSO only five days before setting out to protect convoy Hx217 and to the surprise of none he was awarded a bar to his DSO for the outstanding work. Michael Layton was also awarded a

DSO, one of the few Navigators to earn the exceptional award. Such was his known skill that earlier, he had been detailed to navigate the Lib in which Churchill had first flown to Moscow. It was a quite remarkable achievement for Terry to have been awarded two DSOs within a week of each other. The C-in-C of Coastal Command ACM Sip Philip, Jeo Bert De La Fertr' summed it up in his signal of 9th December to A.O.C. Iceland:

> Please convey my warmest congratulations to the Captain and aircrew of B120 for their magnificent days work on December 8th in support of convoy Hx217. They showed the greatest skill and determination in making depth charge and cannon attacks and in their efforts were crowned by the destruction of a U-boat which was confirmed by surface craft. While all share the success, I wish you to convey my special congratulations to Squadron Leader Bulloch and his navigator Flying Officer Layton.

Similar signals were also sent to Terry and his crew by AOC Iceland, the C/O of 120 Squadron back at Nutts Corner and most generously by the Admiralty which freely acknowledged the part played by him and his crew. All stressed that the efforts of Terry and his crew (backed by those of Isted and his crew) had saved the convoy. The nation was in a mood for heroes and the press had been given a new one in Terry. They made the most of it because of its secret equipment Coastal Command rarely gave the press any news. It preferred to work quietly and keep the enemy guessing. This time however, they revealed practically all. Every paper in the land welcomed the unexpected bonanza with open arms. "The Bull gets a U-boat" was one headline. "Ulster Man's success, RAF Terrors Decorated", "Atlantic Convoy gets through", "Belfast ace sinks two U-boats", "Atlantic convoy fights off 35 U-boats", "U-boats packs routed in Atlantic battle", "One bomber hits 7 Subs".

Terry was long overdue an operational rest, so the command grounded him and used him to tell his own tale over the radio. His BBC account was typical of the man. Terse, modest and much to the point. December 8th 1942 was a memorable day. Its like would never be repeated. A further 615 U-boats would be commissioned and built before the war finally drew to a close and Doenitz never wavered from the belief, well founded, that he had stated in January 1942. "Whatever the course of, and end of, the Russian campaign may be. The war against Anglo Saxon power will be decided at sea. It is only the U-boat arm that we can take the offensive." One of our own war leaders took the same view when he said, "It is on the sea and only on the sea that we can lose this war". History has confirmed both statements Doenitz's U-boats arm was being twisted as the war progressed. One of the principal twisters was squadron leader Terence Malcolm Bulloch, DSO DFC. "The Bull with the Hawkeyes." The Ulsterman to whom flying was his life: To whom revenge was sweet and to whom the war meant kill or be killed and whose only desire was to be in the thick of it and leading from the front.

FLIGHT LIEUTENANT
GEORGE CALWELL, AE
ROYAL AIR FORCE VOLUNTEER RESERVE NO. 745250
NAVIGATOR
NO. 99 SQUADRON

George Calwell was born in Whitehead, County Antrim, on the 20th June 1918 and was educated at the Royal Belfast Academical Institution. On leaving school, he was employed with the Belfast Steamship Company as a Shipping Clerk.

He joined the Royal Air Force Volunteer Reserve in Belfast in May 1939 and commenced his flying training at 24 Elementary and Reserve Flying Training School at Sydenham in Tiger Moths. When war was declared in September 1939 he was called to full-time service and in October he was posted to an Initial Training Wing at Hastings on the South Coast of England. Here he completed six weeks of basic training (square bashing etc.). In early February he finished his basic training and was posted to No 1 Air Navigation and Observers School (ANOS) at Prestwick on the 11th February to start his Navigation Training. He completed his Navigation Training and was then posted to No 4 Bomber and Gunnery School at West Freugh where he carried out a four-week course in Bombing and Gunnery practice in Avro Ansons and Fairey Battles.

It was now July 1940 and George had just been awarded his 'N' Brevet and was posted to an Operational Training Unit at Harwell where he met his new crew and started training immediately on Wellington 1cs. Once George and his new crew had completed their Operational Training they were posted to 99 (Madras Presidency) Squadron on the 4th October 1940. The Squadron was based at Newmarket Race Course in Cambridgeshire and was equipped with Vickers Wellington Mk 1s.

Brief wartime history of 99 Squadron

In 1939/40 the squadron was engaged for a while on armed searches for German Naval Units in the North Sea and also 'Nickel' (leaflet dropping) raids. In 1941 the squadron attacked the Scharnhorst and Gneisenau. In 1942 the Squadron moved to India and in November began Operations against the Japanese in Burma. In 1944 the squadron recorded its 1,000 bombing operation of the

Second World War. During the siege of Imphal the squadron took on an emergency assignment that was to use its Wellingtons to ferry 250 lb bombs to the Hurri-bomber squadrons operating against the Tiddim-Imphal road. In the latter part of the war the squadron converted to Liberators and attacked a wide variety of targets, some operations taking up to 16 hours or more. One of its notorious hot spots was the Siam-Burma railway that supplied the Japanese army. It also dropped much needed supplies to the POWs inside Changi jail. The squadron was disbanded in November 1945. The aircraft did actually use the Newmarket racecourse for take-off and landings, this I can vouch for having seen photographs of them doing so.

George made his first operation from Newmarket on the 9th October 1940, their target was to Brebengroitch. Other targets that they visited were Eindhoven, Keil, Buer, Emden, Leunan, Berlin, Wilhelmshaven, and Lorient (U-boat base).

On returning from an operation one night and while taxiing slowly to a dispersal point, their aircraft ran into an unfilled bomb crater. The aircraft was badly damaged but none of the crew was injured. Around the middle of December 1940 George spotted a notice on the Operations board requesting for volunteers to go to Malta with 148 Squadron. George very quickly volunteered for this, as he always wanted to see a bit of the world. He joined 148 Squadron at Stradishall on the 28th December 1940 and it was not long before he and the squadron were off to Malta via France and the North African Coast.

The flight took a long 10 hours and he was quite pleased with his navigation on such a long trip and this did his ego a world of good. His first Operation with the squadron was to Tarranto in Italy on the 30th December

1940 in a Wellington. He also visited the enemy held port of Tripoli and Catania and altogether carried out 12 Operations with the squadron.

On the 8th February 1941 George was transferred to 37 squadron that was based at Abisweir in Egypt. On his arrival he was informed that he was to fly on the Shaloufa.

Tragedy was to befall George at 37 Squadron, while on a flight from Shaloufa to Athens the Wellington in which he was navigating developed engine problems. The aircraft's starboard propeller came off and the engine caught fire, which led to it crashing in flames at Athens. On board the Wellington were both air and ground crews, only three survived.

George was later posted home from Greece on board a ship. The ship left on the 24th March 1941 and its route back to the UK was via Durban Capetown and on to Halifax Nova Scotia (long way home).

Greece. Durban.Capetown. Canada. While he was on the ship he developed a severe fever and very nearly died as the ship's doctor mistakenly gave him the wrong medicine. The trip from Athens to Canada took over two months. Canada, Greenock and 99 Squadron, Bombay, India. After a short spell in a Canadian hospital George boarded a troop ship that was bound for Iceland and then on to Greenock in Scotland. On his arrival at Greenock he found that all his kit had either been lost or stolen. He was then given some home leave and on his return was posted to an Operational Training Unit at Harwell. Here he met his crew and commenced Operational Training for a second time.

On completion of their Operational Training George and the crew were informed that they were being posted to Bombay in India to start their second tour. On their arrival in Bombay they were told to proceed to No 3 Refresher Flying Unit (RFU) at Poona were they were to undertake some jungle surviving training.

On completion of this training George and the crew were sent by troopship in June 1944 to No 1673 Heavy Conversion Unit at Kolar in Southern India arriving there on the 18th and to begin a conversion course onto Liberators. He completed the course on the 10th August 1944. He was pleasantly surprised when he was told that he would be re-joining 99 Squadron at Dhubalia in India. They were to attack a wide variety of targets, some of the sorties were to last 16 hours or more and particular emphasis was put on the notorious Siam - Burma railway, which was a vital Japanese supply line. It was not long until George and his crew were off on their first raid that was on the 1st January 1945 to attack the Siam-Burma Railway. Altogether George completed 35 Operations with the Squadron visiting targets: Siam-Burma Railway; Bangkok; Chenghai Railway; Zayatkwin Airfield; Amarapura bomb dumps; Mahlaing bomb dumps; Myinsyan; Martaban.... Nanoi; Istmus of Kra; Pauk; Salbani;. Kaeng; Koi (Thailand); and Rangoon.

In early July 1945 George was advised that he was being posted to No 1675 HCU in Egypt where he was to become an Instructor. He was very disappointed with this move, as he would have preferred to stay with the Squadron. He left India in a Short Sunderland and the journey took him via Sharjah, Bahrain, Basra and finally landed on the Nile on the 22nd July 1945. When he arrived at the Unit he was informed that the war was almost over and that he was not needed and was posted back to the UK.

He was released from the Royal Air Force in December 1945 and during his six years in the RAF he had accumulated 1,500 flying hours, completed 60 operations and had flown in Tiger Moths, Fairey Battle, Wellington 1cs and 10s, Dominie and Liberator V1s. On his return to Northern Ireland he re-joined the Belfast Steamship Company where he remained until he retired in 1980.

FLIGHT LIEUTENANT
MATTHEW CAMERON
BATTLE OF BRITAIN
PILOT
NO. 66, 198 & 609 SQUADRONS

Matt Cameron, son of Mr & Mrs James Cameron, was born on May 22nd 1916 in a farmhouse opposite Ballinrees National School, not far from Coleraine. He was the fourth son in a family of five boys and one girl. Matt joined Ballinrees National School at the early age of three, and as he said, "Mother either wanted rid of me for a few hours, or to keep the school numbers up, as there was a danger of the school numbers dropping below that required for a two teacher school."

Matt progressed very well at primary school, especially in maths, algebra and geometry and found this ability helped him greatly in later years in the RAF with the computation of setting courses to fly, allowing for wind speed and direction and setting compass deflection. At the age of twelve Matt left Balinrees National School to further his education at the Model School in Collaring and at the age of fourteen, sat the School Leaving Certificate examination and gained a scholarship to Royal Belfast Academical Institution (Inst). Due to the great distance, and having to get up at an unearthly hour that would have been required for him to attend Inst, it was decided that Matt should attend the Coleraine Technical College and Hughes Civil Service Academy in Ballymena where he made excellent progress. Matt at that time had his sights turned to a service career in the Royal Air Force as an apprentice at Halton or Cranwell, as the elite tradesmen came from these two schools. On leaving Hughes Academy, Matt took up employment as a butcher, driving a delivery van for the firm of TK Usher and later a horse drawn cart for the local Co-op store until he was nearly eighteen and could join the RAF Men's Branch as an Airman 2nd Class. His pay was twelve shillings a week (60p), uniform and three meals a day.

It was the end of February 1935 when a young Matt Cameron said goodbye to his parents at Coleraine Railway Station. The train took him to Belfast where he boarded the Liverpool Boat, next stop, England. When the boat docked at Liverpool he then caught a train to London, arriving on the morning of the 4th July with £1 in his pocket, shaving gear and a comb. On his arrival at the recruitment office Matt was informed that if he were accepted for recruitment all his civilian clothes would be sent home. An exception to this rule, were citizens of the Irish Republic who were not allowed to wear RAF uniform when on leave, and therefore were permitted to travel in civvies. After being sworn in at the recruitment centre, Matt had to sign a form renouncing his right to vote in elections. Now an Airman 2nd Class he was then taken to a holding centre at West Drayton where he remained for three days. Here he had his first taste of RAF food and living in a dormitory with twelve beds down either side. His three days at West Drayton were spent learning basics such as how to make a bed properly and to polish a floor etc.

He then proceeded to the training centre at Uxbridge where he was required to complete six months 'square bashing', physical exercises, rifle shooting and guard duties and was kitted out with his new uniform. That is to say he was taken to the equipment section and issued with everything that he would require for life in the RAF, that included a Drill .303 Lee Enfield rifle, complete with bayonet, a haversack, which when in use, held in the bottom portion, a great coat, and the top portion a small kit, consisting of shaving gear, mug, knife fork and spoon, long johns and had a draw string at the top.

In the Mess there was no choice of food, you took what was offered or went hungry.

Each intake of twenty-four men carried out guard duties for a period of 24 hours, (two hours on and four hours off), and your home for this period was the guard house. Matt's six months passed slowly at Uxbridge and after the Passing Out Parade he was posted to the No 5 Flying Training School at Sealand as a 2nd Class Airman and was immediately put on to duties as an untrained policeman. These duties included the raising and lowering of the flag at morning parade and evening bugle call. Matt could not say anything derogatory about the RAF Police, only that it was not his 'cup of tea'. He could not understand why having a button undone should constitute a chargeable offence, warranting an award of three days confinement to camp with all the extra fatigues, which the award entailed. Other offences which warranted the same punishment were cap badge not polished at the back or just dumb insolence which Matt defines as 'breaking wind' loudly when the NCO in charge was not looking (did he want to hear it) but within hearing distance.

Matt's first flight at Sealand was in a Bristol Bulldog Trainer and he remembers quite well that his knees were shaking like a leaf and he was in a cold sweat. After the trip he found out that the Pilot was an aerobatic ace and that his Fitter and Rigger gratefully allowed anyone to fly on a 'test flight' with him.

I am sure if Matt had known what had been in store for him, he would have said, "Thank you very much and goodbye." However had he not had that first experience, perhaps he would never have caught the flying bug and his life would have followed an entirely different path. After this 'traumatic' experience, which he never forgot, Matt decided then and there that he was going to be a Pilot no matter what it cost.

After his flight Matt went off to the 'orderly room' and enquired of the NCO in charge whether he could help him with information regarding how to become a Pilot. The orderly was extremely helpful, but in his opinion Matt might be better trying for a Wireless Operator or Air Gunner's course. Matt decided to apply for the Armourer's course and on completion of the application form he was told that there were no vacancies. So he had to be satisfied with the Wireless Operator's course. Soon after he was accepted Matt was posted to the No 1 School of Technical Training at RAF Cranwell at the end of June 1936. He thoroughly enjoyed his time at Cranwell where he learned the Morse code and achieving 25 words a minute, sending and receiving. He was also trained in the art of battery charging and wiring, stripping and assembling wireless sets and faultfinding. Part of this training also meant going up in an aircraft, dropping a trailing aerial, tuning into the ground station, and when this was completed winding in the aerial and returning to base. Semaphore was also taught but no great emphasis was put on it. The working routine at the Electrical and Wireless school was Monday, Tuesday, Thursday and Friday, 9.00am to 4.30pm. Wednesday 9.00am to 1.00pm as Wednesday afternoons were reserved for sports. (Matt, who is now 77 years old, is quite proud of the fact that he can still, from memory, repeat the Morse code.) Christmas came and he had successfully completed the course and was granted

two weeks leave. A railway warrant was issued to him from the nearest railway station to wherever the leave was to be spent. So Matt headed home on his first leave to meet his family and friends and the next two weeks seemed like days. Time just flew in, and he was back at Cranwell.

Matt's Passing Out examinations started in early June and were completed in about a week. He waited anxiously for the results, as he knew that he would need 80% to pass. He needn't have worried as he had attained a pass with 79%. His marks were the highest in the class and he was posted to No 7 Squadron at Finningley with a special recommendation that he be permitted to sit the first available re-sit examination for promotion. No 7 Squadron had been a pre-war night flying squadron and was equipped with the Handley Page Heyford twin-engined bomber. Matt's pay at that time as an Airman 1st Class Wireless Operator was 28 shillings per week. He felt like a millionaire. His stay with No 7 Squadron was of short duration, about two months and during that time he acted as wireless operator on seven or eight flights. The aircraft to which he was attached had a Sergeant as its Captain, the Second Pilot was also a Sergeant Pilot and he acted as Navigator. When I asked Matt to describe a Heyford he told me, "It was clapped out 'string bag' with a cruising speed of 115 mph and a bomb load of 500 lbs." The duration of a flight was two hours. Once airborne Matt's duties were to lower the trailing aerial, its length was about fifty feet and then he connected the aerial plug to the transmitter and receiver set. Using Morse he called the ground controller and tuned in the receiver and transmitted messages given to him by the two Pilots. Mostly such messages referred to weather conditions and the position of the aircraft relative to the ground.

In 1936 there had been trouble in Palestine and when Matt was notified that he was to be posted overseas and he assumed it would be Palestine. He was given several health injections and four weeks leave which he spent home in Ballinrees. During his leave Matt received notification to attend the medical centre at RAF Aldergrove and here he was to receive the dreaded Yellow Fever injection. By this time Matt had been given an armful of injections, but this one was the daddy of them all. Because he had been given the Yellow Fever injection Matt thought he might now be going to West Africa. Matt returned to No 7 Squadron still in the dark as to where his eventual destination would be. He packed his kit bag, which contained all his overseas kit, and proceeded to the orderly room where he collected a railway warrant for Southampton. Eventually Matt arrived at Southampton and to his amazement met several other Wireless Operators' from his class at Cranwell. They were travelling not in a troop ship but a civilian boat and were given births, four men to each one, and were not allowed to mix in anyway with the civilian passengers.

No one knew his or her destination but Palestine was the general consensus of opinion. They passed through the Bay of Biscay and called at Gibraltar and after two days, out in the Mediterranean Matt was informed that his final destination was Malta.

The others were proceeding on to various stations. This was in the days of the Great British Empire where there were manned outposts in various countries all the way to Singapore. On the fifth day from Southampton the ship anchored in the Grand Harbour of Malta. Matt disembarked in an RAF Pinnacle and arrived at Valletta with a short walk to his Billet in Floriana, which was to be his home for the next five years. The wireless section was located in Valletta and it was the nerve centre of the RAF in Malta. There were only a few Wireless Operators, Mechanics and an Air Sea Rescue contingent in Matt's billet. Messages from the Air Ministry in London, sometimes in plain language and sometimes in code were taken down at 25 words per minute. He often had to re-transmit messages from land out to far off stations including Australia. The Army, Navy and Air Force used the only transport on the island. There were no civilian cars or buses, normal working hours on the island were 0700 hrs to 1100 hrs, lunch was at mid-day and from then until 1600 hrs it was siesta time as it was to humid between these hours for anyone to work. Matt managed to get a one month secondment as Wireless Operator on an Air Sea Rescue launch and his duties consisted of making contact with Air Sea Rescue Control morning and evening and keeping a listening watch. It was a pleasant period and enjoyable but all too soon he was back on normal work at Headquarter Signals. In the middle of August 1937, Matt was told that there would be an examination held to determine promotions to Leading Aircraftsman and as he was the only airman in Malta he entered for the exam. He was successful and was promoted to Leading Aircraftsman with a pay rise to £1.15 Shillings per week, and of much more importance to him was the fact that he was on target to achieve his goal of becoming a pilot. The next day he completed the necessary application form for Pilot Training and it wasn't long before he was sent to complete a medical examination and interviews after which he was finally accepted for Pilot Training. So four days before Christmas 1937 Matt set sail onboard a troopship bound for England.

The journey back to the UK was not a very comfortable one, Matt's bed was a hammock, which he did not like very much, and to make things worse it blew up a gale on Christmas Day as the ship entered the Bay of Biscay. Christmas dinner onboard ship was under cooked turkey and a raw potato. The journey took a long eight days to Southampton. Having survived the troopship journey Matt headed back to Uxbridge where he met other airmen who had also been successful in their pilot training ambition. However the course of 24 was mostly officer cadets. Matt and the other trainees were given an immediate four weeks leave, travel passes, four weeks pay, and ration money in lieu of food. He

headed home to Ballinrees once more and during that time he got engaged to Jean. The four weeks passed quickly and he returned to West Camp at Uxbridge to start his flying career. On the first March 1937 he was posted along with the other cadets to Hamble. His first dual flight was in an Avro Cadet on 8th March 1937 with his instructor Flight Sergeant Newton. This was an air experience flight and lasted for 35 minutes. The cadet trainer was not unlike the Tiger Moth and made of a wooden construction. He flew solo in the Avro Cadet on the 20th March after ten hours instruction and completed the basic flying course on the 7th May 1937 with an assessment of 'average'. He was then posted to the No 2 Flying Training School at Brize Norton on the 21st May 1937. His first day at the FTS started at 0630 hrs with thirty minutes of physical training and at 0730 hrs, was dismissed for a quick shower and shave, buttons and shoes polished to a brilliant shine, all spic and span and he presented himself to the dining hall for breakfast. At 0900 hrs he was required to attend lectures in the appropriate classroom where he spent the next four days learning the petrol, oil and brake systems of the Hawker Hart and Audax Trainers.

His first flight at the school was on the 25th May 1937 in a Hawker Hart with his instructor Flight Lieutenant Simms. This was an air experience and test exercise and lasted for 40 minutes. The Hawker Hart and Audax, which were used during the course, were the most advanced fighters that the RAF had at that time. Matt's logbook shows that although he soloed on the Hart, he more often flew in the Audax Trainer. Matt successfully completed the intermediate course on 12th August 1938 and was assessed again as 'average' and on 13th August was awarded his Wings. Although he was not considered fully trained and had to complete a further advanced training course before he became a service pilot and took the name Fighter Pilot. The final course started on 6th September and was comparatively uneventful, and he finished it on 2nd December with an assessment by the commanding officer as 'average' and 'needs constant practice'. Matt's goal of becoming a fully-fledged Fighter Pilot had now been achieved with a total flying experience of 223hrs.20mins. Although he still had a long way to go.

Passing Out Parade was on the afternoon of 12th December where they were all presented with their coveted Wings. After the parade Matt dashed off with the other newly promoted NCOs to the clothing store to collect their sergeant stripes for their various uniforms and great coat. The evening of 12th December saw Matt in the sergeant's mess with the rest of his friends enjoying the waiter served evening meal and a pint of beer to follow. There would be no more queuing for meals and he was not required to book in or out of camp. He was also not required to have a late pass to stay out after 2359 hrs and above all his pay was now £4.15 shillings per week, a princely sum in those days. On the 17th

December 1938 Matt was posted to No 66 (F) Squadron that was based at Duxford. He had always been used to flying biplanes but when he arrived at his new squadron he found it was equipped with Gloster Gauntlets but was in the process of being re-equipped with the new Mk1 Supermarine Spitfires. On the 18th January he flew two air experience flights in a Miles Magister (L5359) with Pilot Officer Graafstra and on the 20th and 24th he flew a further two air experience flights with flaps in Magister (L5953) solo getting him ready for his first flight in a Spitfire.

Matt's first 45 minute flight in an Mk1 Spitfire (K9803) took place on the 27th January 1939 and he remembers it as if it was yesterday. With some trepidation he donned his parachute and climbed into the Pilot's seat and strapped himself into the cockpit. The forward take-off and landing view was poor in the Spitfire and the aircraft had a tendency to overheat if there was any waiting time. The Rolls Royce Merlin was capable of producing speeds over 310mph and the armament was four 303 machineguns. The Mk 1 could operate up to a height of 28,000ft and because its role in air fighting was usually against enemy fighters, this might have been the reason for the certain mystique that it held in the public view. The mighty Merlin roared into life and Matt carefully taxied out to the take-off point to carry out his pre-flight checks. Petrol on, flaps up, and various gauges all correct and the aircraft positioned at right angles to the wind direction. Still no concrete runways, just a grass field. Matt requested permission from Control to take off. The coolant temperature was increasing, so he turned the Spitfires' nose into wind, gently opened the throttle, the aircraft started to move forward, control column moved forward to raise the tail and he felt as though he had been kicked in the back. The power generated by the Merlin was terrific at full throttle, and before he knew what had happened, Matt was airborne and by the time he collected his thoughts he was at 8,000ft. The slightest movement of the controls was sufficient to control the aircraft. After thirty minutes Matt had sorted things out and was reasonably sure that he could make a successful landing. He climbed the aircraft to 10,000ft testing the capabilities of the Spitfire. He then received a compass course from Control to return to base, a few minutes later he sighted the airfield, made a successful approach and landed having spent 45 minutes on his first solo flight in a Spitfire.

Matt continued intensive training in the Spitfire right through June 1939, carrying out sector recco, cross country, formation practice, pin pointing practice, target for attack, battle flight climb, formation attacks, endurance test, battle formation attacks, tactical exercises, night flying test, ceiling climbs to 28,000ft, and range finding practice. On the 16th June 1939, Matt's Commanding Officer, Squadron Leader JLF Fuller-Good, wrote in his log book, "Completed training in fighter duties day and night." Although no one voiced an opinion at that time, Matt and his colleagues were all aware of the 'sword rattling' in Germany and on September 3rd 1939 while listening to the radio at 1100 hrs, he heard the immortal words from the Prime Minister Neville Chamberlain, "We are at war with Germany." Matt told me that it is hard to put into words how he felt that morning, and what went through his mind after listening to the news. They were well aware that the life of a Fighter Pilot in the 1914-18 war was just three weeks. (Matt married Jean on 30th October 1939 and at the time of writing this story he was married 54 years.)

66 Squadron's role at that time was the defence of Britain and after the Phoney War; Matt was engaged mainly in the defence of sea convoys against the hit-and-run raiders and air strikes over Rotterdam. Then in early May 1940 he was engaged in providing air cover for the withdrawal of the BEF from France. The action was brisk until June, and then came the Battle of Britain. At this time there was a requirement for Pilots to fly Spitfires, camouflaged in Duck Egg Blue on the Photographic Reconnaissance Units at a height of 36,000ft. Several of the more experienced NCO Pilots volunteered for this type of flying.

Two of Matt's friends who were chosen for this type of operation, were subsequently lost, the reason is not known. It could have been due to interception by enemy fighters, although this was a remote possibility or perhaps a failure in the oxygen supply as they used additional oxygen above 10,000ft. More likely the losses were due to fuel shortage, a sudden change of wind direction. The change from a tailwind to a head wind could add a lot of time to a long flight and the subsequent use of fuel not allowed for in computing the fuel needed according to the weather forecast.

Matt's first operation of the war was on 4th September 1939, the day after war was declared on Germany. He took off in Spitfire K9944 on a 'home defence patrol'; his flight time was 1hr.05mins. For himself and two other Sergeant Pilots the first call to fighting was on 11th January 1940, when he was flying (N3029). The squadron was flying from a forward base when Matt and the two other Sergeant Pilots from 'A' Flight formed a section detailed to patrol a North Sea convoy. They were flying in echelon formation at 3,000ft and Matt was in No 2 position, as he approached the convoy, he realised that a Heinkel 111 bomber was attacking it. It had just dropped it's bombs and was strafing the ships from low-level. The section leader gave the order to attack and led them down to the target. There did not appear to be any defensive armament on the ships, as Matt did not see any attempt by them to engage the enemy aircraft. Once the Heinkel saw the three Spitfires it turned and flew due east at low-level. The No 1 went into the attack and closed up to about 100ft and continued to fire bursts until his ammunition was finished. The No 1 broke off, and Matt followed into attack the Heinkel and after three or four bursts from his eight machine-guns, he saw pieces fly off its starboard engine and the propeller stopped. Matt then heard a loud bang in his cockpit and noticed a hole in his windshield on the left hand side. He then concentrated all his effort on the Heinkel's port engine, but without visible result and with all his ammo gone he broke off the attack. When Matt returned to base he saw that the bullet, which had come through his windscreen, had cut a furrow out of his left shoulder strap and lodged in the radio casing behind his seat. His No 1 informed him next day that the Heinkel was forced to land in Holland and the crew were taken prisoner. Matt's first engagement with the enemy almost ended in disaster. This was a narrow escape from death and a warning of the dangers that lay ahead.

Matt's squadron consisted of two flights of six aircraft. 'A' Flight was commanded by a Flight Lieutenant and sub-divided into two sections. 'Red' and 'Blue' sections. 'B' Flight was also under the Command of a Flight Lieutenant and sub-divided into two sections 'Green' and 'Yellow'. When flying in battle formation the overall command of the squadron was of Squadron Leader rank. The Squadron Leader was in overall control of the complete air and ground staff of the squadron. In battle formation the Squadron Leader led Red Section, in line astern was Blue Section normally led by 'A' Flight Commander Green Section by 'B' Flight Commander and Yellow Section (known as 'Tail End Charlie' section, because they were usually the section to be jumped by enemy fighters), was usually led by the next most experienced Pilot, not necessarily of commissioned rank. Sections flew about ten feet below each other and the distance of an aircraft behind the section in front. Yellow three was usually required to fly above the squadron and kept a very sharp look out for enemy fighters.

66 Squadron moved from Duxford to Coltishal in May 1940 and remained there until September when it moved to Kenly and Gravesend.

It would be fair to say that section leaders in the absence of the Flight Commanders and also if flying as a single section carrying out convoy patrols would have the most experienced Pilot as leader. This might well be a non-commissioned officer with one or perhaps two commissioned officers as his no 2 and no 3 and completely under his command; experience was the operative word. Matt's next combat came on 13th May 1940 flying an 'offensive patrol' in (N3029) with 'A' Flight of his squadron. Six aircraft took part along with six Boulton Paul Defiants from another squadron. They rendezvoused at the nearest base on British soil to Rotterdam, and on the evening of 12th May all aircraft were refuelled and rearmed.

At early dawn on the 13th the section took off on patrol and it wasn't long until they met a 'shoal' of enemy Ju87 (Stuka) Dive Bombers and a horde of ME109 fighters. Several dog fights ensued; Matt attacked two ME109s and was then attacked himself, but was successful in shaking his attackers off his tail. He had a go

at a second Ju87 with a second burst and followed the bomber down and saw him crash close to a large building on the outskirts of Rotterdam. His ten minutes were up so he set course for home. This was a sad day for the squadron as only five aircraft out of the twelve that set off that morning returned.

After landing his aircraft was refuelled and rearmed, his fitter informed him that it took 84 gallons to fill the Spits tanks (This was the maximum amount of fuel a Spitfire could hold). It had been a successful patrol in Matt's case but not for everyone. Matt's next big push was covering the evacuation of Dunkirk and his first offensive patrol in that area was on May 31st when he took off in (N3033). He would patrol at 26,000 to 28,000ft and every subsequent patrol saw him engaged in action against enemy fighters. It was so normal an occurrence that his logbook simply records, "Offensive patrol - Dunkirk." On his last patrol over Dunkirk in (N3033) on 31st May 1940 he engaged an enemy fighter and followed him down firing all the time with some degree of success. At about 16,000ft he pulled out looking for another target when there was a horrible noise from his engine and suddenly the propeller would only 'windmill' around giving no power. He had been hit either by another aircraft or anti-aircraft fire. He decided to glide towards the French coast in a southerly direction as he knew he was somewhere north of Dunkirk when the fighting started. Thankfully there was no sign of fire coming from the engine and Matt did not fancy bailing out from his stricken aircraft. Preferring to trust his flying ability to get him down and make a 'wheels up' landing. He glided through patchy cloud at about 4,000ft and having covered a considerable distance, he saw what he had hoped for, a small number of boats close to shore and a much larger one further out. He decided to make a wheels up landing near the waters edge and with flaps down, wheels up he made contact with the ground. N3033 ploughed along the shore for at least 220 yards and stopped. Matt undid his harness and jumped out of the Spitfire and pressed the button, which would detonate a very small charge, sufficient to destroy the VHF radio. As he made his way quickly towards the boat, suddenly a few Tommies appeared from around a hillock, he could smell safety in the air. He scrambled on board one of the small boats back to England and rejoined his squadron. Twenty-four hours later he was flying again in defence of his country.

Two interesting log entries for June 1940

June 1st Spitfire (N3032)
Offensive Patrol Over Dunkerque. 27,000ft. No result.

June 2nd Spitfire (N3032)
Offensive Patrol Dunkerque. 29,000ft. Intercepted five Ju88s & a No of Me109s at 6,000ft. Windscreen Froze during descent. No attack made. Experienced Considerable AA fire. Forced landed in a field Stoke By Clare due to lack of fuel. Landed successfully No damage. Flight time 2hrs.30mins.

June 6th Spitfire (N3029)

Patrol Sector N & S. 10 Miles from Coast. Considerable searchlight activity No interception. Returned to base. 'Duxford'.

July was spent mainly spent covering 'Convoy Patrols'

The 19th August 1940 was a low cloud day over the airfield, with ten/tenths cloud at 1,000ft. This type of weather was ideal for sneak raiders and on that particular day a Dornier 17 enemy bomber suddenly came out of a cloud and dropped a stick of bombs on the airfield, leaving a few craters but no great damage.

Matt's log entry for 19th (P9316): Aerodrome bombed by Do17, Out of cloud. "No interception" Flying time 40 mins.

A few hours later on the same day while flying with 'A' Flight in Spitfire (P9316) Matt spotted a Heinkel 111 of Winterton flying low at sea level. This time he made no mistakes and shot it down.

August 20th 'A' Flight and six other aircraft were ordered to patrol the same sector as on the 19th. On this occasion they were in two sections, flying line abreast and about 500ft apart when they intercepted three Me110s at 2,000ft heading out to sea. The enemy dived to get near ground level as quick as possible. Matt pressed home his attack on a Me110 and it blew apart. The enemy formation had now disintegrated.

Matt's Flight was frequently on patrol between 20th August and 1st September as they were now part of 12 Group responsible for the defence of Britain. 66 Squadron was ordered to Kenley, an airfield adjacent to Bigging Hill on 2nd September as a replacement squadron and were now in the thick of the Battle of Britain.

Matt's logbook shows that he and "A" Flight were on interception patrols practically every day and sometimes two or three times on the same day. His flying position continued to be between 20,000 to 28,000ft and was always in battle with enemy fighters, with a prominence against Me109s.

Some of Matt's log entries from 1st September & October 1940

Sept 1st   Spitfire (3121)
                Squadron reinforcement.

Sept 2nd   Spitfire (4052)
                Formation & calling Sgt Smith off leave.

Sept 5th   Spitfire (3121)
                Intercepted FW 190s.

Sept 6th   Spitfire (3121)
                Intercepted large formation of bombers
                & Me109s No claim.

Sept 6th   Spitfire (4322)
                Intercepted Me109s.

Sept 7th   Spitfire (4326)
                Intercepted Me 109s and FW 190s.

Sept 9th   Spitfire (4326)
                Intercepted large formation of He111 and
                Me109s, attacked Me109 (Probable).
                Attacked Me109 (Damaged). Broke off
                on being attacked myself.

Sept 11th   Spitfire (4326)
                Hawking to Calais, Escort to Anson.
                on. Spotting. R. Exp. Accurate AA Fire at
                10,000ft over Calais.

Matt told me that this had been his most dangerous Operation. "I was based at Gravesend at the time. The squadron Commanding Officer requested two of his most experienced Pilots to act as escort to an Anson to Calais and return. The Anson's task was to take photographs of Calais for reasons, which I was not made aware. The flight was to require some thought as the Anson would be flying at a speed of around 120mph and my Spitfire's minimum speed was 190mph. I decided to fly one Spitfire just above the Anson doing 'S' turns to keep in close contact and the other Spitfire was to fly 500ft higher to widen the range of sight. The formation proved successful and we arrived over Calais with the Anson, which was just completing its first run over the target. Suddenly all hell let loose when the ports anti-aircraft guns opened up on them. I decided that I would be of more help to the Anson Pilot if I flew underneath it, hopefully drawing the enemy fire onto myself. The mission was successful and neither aircraft were damaged. Shortly after arriving back at Gravesend, the Anson crew rang the Station Commander, thanking us for the way in which we had carried out the operation."

Sept 11th   Spitfire (4326)
                Matt carried out further six sectors that
                day. Interceptions on the 11th. Me109s
                and Fw190s. No claims.

Sept 23rd   Spitfire (4020)
                Two Sectors that day. Intercepting
                Me109s. No claims.

Sept 27th   Spitfire (3121)
                Four Sectors that day. Matt Intercepted a
                large formation of Ju88s Ju21s and
                Me109s. Shot one Ju88 down in flames.

Sept 28th   Spitfire (6800 & 3121)
                Two Sectors that day Intercepted
                FW190s Me109s. Not engaged.

Sept 30th.   Spitfire (3043)
                Three Sectors that day. 11 aircraft told to
                land. Mix-up with 109s

Oct 2nd   Spitfire (N3121)
Three Sectors that day. Saw number of
Me109s above. Not in position po pttack.

Oct 8th   Spitfire (R6927)
Two Sectors that day. Four of us attacked
nine Me109s at 33,000ft. Fired at long
range with no apparent result. Couldn't
get among them at height.

Oct 8th   Spitfire (R6927)
Jumped by Me109s at 16,000ft. Sgt
Ward shot down. He didn't have a
chance to retaliate.

Oct 10th   Spitfire (R6800)
Three Sectors that day.

Oct 11th   Spitfire (R6800)
Four Sectors that day. Jumped by Me109s
while still gaining height. P/O Pickering
and P/O Allen in hospital (32,000ft)
Patrol. We jumped 32 Me109s. Shambles
followed. "Only six of us."

Oct 12th   Spitfire (X4421)
Three Sectors that day. Attacked
Me109s At 30,000ft. Me109s at
30,000ft Slightly above us. Could
not get into position for attack.

Oct 13th   Spitfire (X4421)
Three Sectors that day. Intercepted 30
Me109s below us. Shambles followed.
I got one probable. Squadron got
five probables.

The Battle of Britain was drawing to a close and there were no interceptions between October 24th and November 27th 1940. Matt was now a Flight Sergeant having been promoted prior to his deployment to the Battle of Britain and a Section Leader. The squadron had lost a lot of its Pilots for various reasons, killed, wounded, and posted to other duties, having endured all they could take. Matt's Flight Commander and himself were the only two left from the original peacetime squadron still alive.

Matt's last action with the enemy during those hectic months

It took place on November 14th when he was flying (P7520) on an interception patrol over Dover. Matt was 'Red Leader' and the squadron was ordered to patrol Dover at 20,000ft. They were in full battle formation over Dover when they saw approximately 40 Ju87 dive bombers at 15,000ft, being protected by a large number of Me109s who were at 18,000ft. This time the Me109s fled for home and they were able to attack the JU87s unhindered. Matt took his section in echelon port formation into a dive and turning to port, he came in

behind to attack the bombers. It was an epic air battle as they chased them down to sea level. Matt attacked two Ju87s and claimed one was probably destroyed, having seen many pieces flying off one wing. He saw hits on the second one but no disintegration. Matt and the 'Few' like him had won the Battle of Britain and thanks to them there would be no invasion. The Luftwaffe was by no means defeated and still a fighting force, but its leaders had now realised that they could not achieve air superiority over South East England, and so withdrew from the battle.

The 12th of December 1940 heralded a change in Matt's fortunes, as this was to be his last flight in a Spitfire as a Section Leader. He took off in Spitfire 'N' to patrol Maidstone at 15,000ft. The patrol lasted for 1hr.45mins. He had completed countless numbers of sorties between 3rd September 1939 and the 12th December 1940 and had accumulated 350hrs.10mins day flying and 20hrs.55mins night flying, making a total of 391hours.05mins.

Matt was approached by his commanding officer Squadron Leader AS Forbes, DFC, (his second during the battle) and asked if he would like a 'change', as he had been asked to send an experienced Pilot to undergo a flying instructors course. Matt felt that he had had enough, and agreed to the move. His commanding officer gave him an 'exceptional' assessment on flying Spitfires and recommended him for a commission in the Regular Air Force. At the same time he was promoted to Warrant Officer.

Matt had shot down eight enemy aircraft, three of which had been confirmed and five probables.

Why the hell didn't this man get a DFM?

On the 16th December 1940 Matt said goodbye to his friends at 66 Squadron and joined the No 7 (War Instructors) course at Upavon the next day. The school was equipped with Miles Masters, Avro Tutors and the course lasted for four weeks. Matt completed the course on 17th January 1941 and was given an 'average' assessment by the officer commanding and he also added that, "He should improve and be a very useful instructor." On completion of his instructors course Matt was posted to No 5 Service Flying Training School (No 1 Intermediate Training Squadron) at Ternhill on 17th January 1941. The school was equipped with Miles Masters. Matt was allocated four pupils, each of whom had already gone solo on an initial training course. If they completed this course they would be posted direct to a squadron or to an Officers Training Unit where they would fly fighters.

February 2nd 1941 saw him airborne in Master N7875 with his first pupil (LAC Allward) in the front seat. The exercise lasted for 55 minutes. In March 1941 Matt received his commission and was promoted to the rank of Pilot Officer, and the next day to Flying Officer. *Apparently there was an arrangement that airmen in the*

Regular Air Force would be promoted to Flying Officers because of their service experience. On 2nd April 1942 Matt was posted to No 5 (P) Advanced Flying Unit for a ten week advanced instructors course and on the 9th April his log book records that he flew Hawker Hurricane (L1653) on a test flight for 40 minutes and again on the 16th and 18th. On 9th June 1942 his logbook also records that he was a passenger onboard a Wellington (XL224) to Limavady in Northern Ireland (perhaps hitching a lift home). At the end of the course Matt was assessed as 'above the average' as a Pilot Instructor and posted to No 3 Flying Instructors School. Matt was getting fed up being a flying instructor, and when he was informed that he was being posted as an instructor to the Central Flying School in August 1942 he liked it even less. The school's commanding officer met Matt and informed him that he would be instructing on Oxfords. Matt explained to him as politely as he could, that there had been a mistake as he was a single engine pilot. "Not now," replied the commanding officer, "You're on twins." Matt then told him, "In that case I will need a course of instruction onto twins".

"No problem," he said, "your logbook records that you have had 3hrs.15mins dual on Oxfords and 1hr.50mins solo, consider yourself fully trained on twins". Matt was by now pulling his hair out and somehow I don't think he and the CO saw eye-to-eye. He thought long and hard, he made the decision, and applied to be posted back onto operations. Matt told me, "A continual drip will wear away a stone." He instructed at the CFS from 6th August 1942 until 30th November 1942 when a present from heaven arrived for him. His application had been accepted and was being posted back onto Operational Flying.

No 55 Operational Training Unit...

He was posted immediately to No 55 OTU, which was equipped with Hawker Hurricanes. His first flights with the unit were on the morning of 26th November when he flew Oxford 8621 on two local solo trips that lasted for one hour and that afternoon he was back in the seat of a Fighter. His log shows that on 30th November he flew a Beaufort by himself on an 'experience on type' exercise. He then continued his training on Hurricanes until the course ended on 22nd January 1943.

At the end of the course the OTU's commanding office gave him an assessment of:

"As a Fighter, 'above the average'."

"As a Pilot/Nav., 'above the average'."

"In Air Gunnery, 'above the average'."

Matt was back

Matt was told to report to the Wing Commander's office to await word of his posting, and he was convinced that his previous Spitfire experience would

ensure him a posting to a Spitfire Squadron. He was extremely disappointed when he was informed that he was being posted to a Typhoon Squadron. On the 28th January 1943 Matt was posted to 609 Squadron at Manston and his logbook records that his first of two flights with the squadron was on 29th January 1943 in a Hawker Hurricane; the second flight was, "to shoot down a balloon." His first flight in a Typhoon was on 30th January 1943 when he flew 'PR-X' on an air test.

No 609 Squadron was formed at Yeadon in February 1936, flying Hart and Hind variants and it wasn't until the outbreak of war was it equipped with Spitfire Mk1s. The squadron took part in the Battle of Britain and moved to Bigging Hill in September 1942. It began converting to Typhoons in April 1942 and carried out mainly 'sweeps'. It moved to Manston in November where it started to carry out 'intruder' and 'roadstead' (protection of troops on roads) operations. It also attacked the 'Noball' (V1 & V2) sites in Northern France. The squadron's commanding officer was shot down at the end of December by P-47s, one of the few squadron losses at that time. For some time the squadron had a compliment of Belgian Pilots and in June one of them, Squadron Leader LEJ Geerts, became the CO.

In July 1944 the squadron moved to France where it harassed the enemy whilst the army advanced into Belgium and Germany. The squadron remained on the continent until September 1945 when it was disbanded. The Hawker Typhoon was an extremely fast machine with a top speed in excess of 450mph. It was equipped the Napier Sabre 2,180-hp engine and its armament was four 20mm cannon in wings, or up to eight 60lb rocket projectiles or two 1,000lb bombs on underwing racks. To enable Matt to get used to this new element of the flying experience, he asked to be permitted to carry out a lone cross-country flight to Ahgadowey in Northern Ireland. He received the authorisation and once again combined 'business with pleasure'. He duly arrived at Aghadowey and decided to 'beat up' the airfield with a few climb and turns and finished with a high-speed flypast past the control tower. He parked his aircraft and went home to spend the evening with his wife Jean and family. Several years later when Matt farmed at Seacon near Ballymoney, his wife Jean was having a few of her children's friends around for a birthday party. When the parents arrived to take their offspring home, one of them looked at Matt and said, "It's the mad Squadron Leader." He had been the Aerodrome's Control Officer at Aghadowey when Matt gave the high-speed flypast.

Matt's first operation with the squadron was on 4th February 1943 when he carried out a patrol around Dungeness and intercepted four FW 190s and six Me109s. He chased one of the raiders and got in behind him and gave it several 'squirts' of cannon, but did not manage to shoot him down. Flying Officer Nankivell destroyed one of the FW190s.

A selection of Matt's operations with 609 Squadron taken from his flying logbook

March 7th   Typhoon 'U'
Sweep, Somme to Boulogne. Accurate AA fire 1/2 mile off Boulogne. Nothing seen.

March 20th   Typhoon 'S'
Rhubarb, Somme Area. Attacked train no cloud. Much flak. Returned. Weather U/S.

April 4th   Typhoon 'C'
Escort to Whirlwinds. To Abbeyville Yards. Slight flak. Six of us detailed to attack E & R Boats off Friz. Result, two Destroyed and six damaged.

April 6th   Typhoon 'S'
Bombphoon. Escort. Bombphoons attacked ST Omer. 7,000ft. Little flak and no opposition.

April 22nd   Typhoon 'S'
Rhubarb. 160 rounds. Area. Ghent-Coutrai. One Barge. Cat 111. Ace flak.

April 25th   Typhoon 'S'
Rhubarb, Ghent-Coutrai. One locomotive. Cat11. Much flak.

"Score April: Half an 'R' Boat, one barge, one locomotive."

198 Squadron, Manston

Matt was promoted to Flight Lieutenant on 1st May 1943 and posted to 198 Squadron as 'A' Flight Commander carrying out the same types of operations as he did with 609 Squadron.

July 7th   Typhoon 'B'
Rhubarb. Two barges Cat 11 on Canal Ghent-Neuzen. Much flak.

July 11th   Typhoon 'N'
Rhubarb. Squirted gun going in. One barge Cat111. Two Barges Cat11. Short two seconds burst at Me109, no result. Told No 2 to get into cloud. Apparently He was doing so anyway. Me109 not in position to shoot. Went into cloud myself. Pilot Officer Mouat 'missing' in area of Neuzen Canal. Little flak.

Matt had now completed 1,544hrs.15mins flying time.

At the end of August 1943 Matt was taken off Typhoon operations and posted to 275 (Air Sea Rescue) Squadron, which had a detached Flight at Eglinton in Northern Ireland. (For what reason this posting took place I do not know, perhaps he wanted to be closer to his family. Matt was a very quiet and private person, so I did not press him on this). He arrived at the squadron sometime nearing the end of August 1943 to take up his Air Sea Rescue duties and made his first flight with the squadron in Anson (E9538) with a Flight Lieutenant Calvert for experience on the type. His duties entailed flying Ansons out over the Atlantic and around the western coast of Donegal, "Outside territorial waters," of course, with a full crew that entailed Pilots, Navigator and Top-Gunner who also acted as Wireless Operator. The Anson carried a number of small dinghies, which they would drop to anyone who was unfortunate enough to be in the sea and requiring assistance. Later in the year he was posted with the squadron to the Isle of Man where he patrolled the Irish Sea as required and was occasionally able to direct Air Sea Rescue boats to pick up aircrew who had been forced down in the sea. It was now April 1944 and it was obvious that a massive build up was underway for the invasion of Europe. America had entered the war, men and materials were flooding into the UK and it was now not a case of would we invade Europe, but rather, when will we invade.

On April 29th 1944, Matt was ordered to fly to the South of England and on his arrival he found that he was to be in charge of a 'special flight of Spitfires' (six aircraft). The Spitfires were attached to 275 Squadron and were to be used to protect the Air Sea Rescue aircraft, (Walrus) and the Air Sea Rescue boats when they were rescuing aircrew that had ditched in the sea, anywhere between the French Coast and the English Coast. This was right up Matt's street.

On June 6th, D-Day, Matt and his flight carried out three patrols over the Cherbourg Peninsula and noticed that one of the convoys was apparently steering the wrong course. He decided to fly his Spitfire over the lead ship and flash his downward recognition light for it to steer a new course of 60 degrees. He flew over the ship several times flashing this message before it answered with the green letter 'R', by aldis lamp, meaning message received.

His last flight in a Spitfire was with 275 Squadron on 28th July 1944 in Spitfire MkVb (846), (local flight).

On 5th September 1944 Matt was assessed by 275 Squadrons commanding officer, Squadron Leader EW Seabourne as 'above the average'.

Matt was then posted to No 12 Air Gunnery School at Bishops Court in Northern Ireland as a Flight Commander in charge of a 'Drogue Training' Unit. The unit was equipped with Martinets, Masters and Ansons, which were used for towing targets. On the 11th January 1945 Matt had a 30 minute flight as Captain of a Wellington. His last flight with the RAF was on 14th February 1945 when he flew Martinet 'T' on a target towing exercise. On 28th February 1945 he was assessed by Squadron Leader BS Smallman, officer commanding flying Bishops Court as 'above the average' as a Staff Pilot.

The war was by now in its final stages and the air gunnery courses had been discontinued. Matt was given some ground duties until his demobilisation when he said goodbye to the service. He had on the 28th February 1945 accumulated 1645hrs.15mins flying hours and had flown in Avro Cadets, Hawker Harts, Audax and Furys. Miles Magisters, Masters, Spitfire Mk1, 11, Avro Tutors, Fairey Battles, Vickers Wellingtons, Avro Ansons, Hawker Hurricanes, Typhoons and Oxfords. Matt told me that if he was asked what he remembered most of his service career, it would not be of the fighting and death, or of Battles won and lost. His thoughts would be to those who nursed the wounded, who devoted their lives to healing. Those whom he had seen carrying out their tragic duties in hospitals, giving help to the injured and disfigured.

Matt recited a poem to me that he had learned in his youth and feels it is very appropriate to the above paragraph.

Then as she mounted the stairs to the corridors,
Cooled by the east wind.
Distant and soft on her ears,
Fell the sound of the belfry of Christchurch chimes.
Something within her said,
At length thy trials are ended.
And with light on her looks, she entered,
The chamber of darkness.
Noiselessly moved about, assiduous,
Carefully attending.
Moistening the feverish lips and the aching brow.

And in silence, closing the sightless eyes,
Of the dead and concealing their faces.
Where on their pallets lay,
Like drifts of snow by the roadside.
Many a languid head upraised as Evangeline entered.
Turned on their pillow of pain to gaze
While she passed, for her presence.
Fell on their hearts like the rays of the sun
On the walls of a prison.
Motionless, senseless, dying they lay
And their spirit exhausted,
Seemed to be sinking down through
Infinite depth into darkness
Darkness of slumber and sleep
Forever sinking and sinking.

He told me, "A Fighter Pilot is by training a 'loner'. In a Fighter you are completely dependant on your own ability. There is no crew as there is in a Bomber aircraft".

Matt spent the rest of his life working the 'Carneybaun' farm at Seacon, near Ballymoney, which had been left to him by his father's brother. Matt later took over the office of Secretary of the Northern Ireland Branch of the Ulster Farmers Union, which he held for twenty years. He was also a member of the Battle of Britain Fighter Association.

Sadly Flight Lieutenant Matt Cameron died on 16th September 1995, his wife Jean, two daughters and two sons survive him.

FLIGHT LIEUTENANT
THOMAS McCARTNEY
ROYAL AIR FORCE NO. 1494950
WIRELESS OPERATOR/AIR GUNNER
NO. 10 SQUADRON

Thomas McCartney was born in Carrickfergus on the 30th December 1913 and was educated at Sullatober Primary School and Joymount in Carrickfergus. He came from a farming family who lived at Ballynure, near Larne in County Antrim.

Thomas joined the RAF at the Clifton Street Recruiting Office in January 1943 and was posted to Blackpool to start his basic training. Here he was kitted out with his uniform and learned the art of drill (good old square bashing). On completion of his basic training he was then transferred to No 1441 Flight at Dundonald in Scotland were he was to commence his basic wireless training in Avro Ansons. His first training flight in the Anson was on the morning of the 19th February 1943 in Anson (DG903). He was then posted to the No 4 Radio School at Madley on the 21st April and then on to the No 8 Gunnery School at Evanton, which was equipped with the Blackburn Bothas for his gunnery course. His first flight in the Botha (W5110) was on the 7th July, and was captained by Pilot Officer Robinson.

He was then transferred to No 2 (O) Advanced Flying Unit at RAF Millom and then on the 28th September 1943 he went to No 10 Operational Training Unit at Abbingdon to start his operational training on Whitleys. The operational training started on the 16th October and lasted for 14 weeks and finished in the middle of January 1944. From Abbingdon he went on to the 1652 Conversion Unit at Marston Moor where he was to convert to the Handley Page Halifax and meet his new crewmembers. His captain was Pilot Officer Peacock, who he was to fly with throughout his operational career. His first flight in the Halifax ("A" DT768) was on the 20th March 1944. Having successfully completed his training he was posted to his first operational squadron, which was No.10 Squadron and based at Melbourne in Yorkshire and was equipped with the Halifax Mk B111s. Thomas and his crew joined 'B' Flight on the 2nd May 1944 and made their first flight with the squadron on the 3rd May (Halifax LD909K) and their first operational flight on the 19th May to Boulogne in France dropping leaflets.

Brief History of No 10 Squadron

No 10 Squadron, Royal Flying Corps was formed at Farnborough in January 1915 and went to France in July the same year and was equipped with BE2cs. Its role was Army Co-op duties and served on the Western Front until the Armistice. The squadron was re-equipped with Armstrong Whitworth FK 8s in July 1917. The squadron returned to England in February 1919 and was disbanded in December 1919. It was re-formed in January 1928 as a heavy bomber squadron equipped with the Handley Page Hyderabads, Hinaidis and Heyfords. At the outbreak of war in 1939 the squadron was equipped with Whitleys and made a leaflet raid on Berlin on the 2nd October 1939. This was the first RAF squadron to visit the German capital in wartime. The squadron attacked a German battleship in Fotten Fjord in Norway on the 27th April 1942, the Squadron Commander, Wing Commander DCT Bennett, who later was to form the Pathfinder Force was shot down. He managed to escape through Sweden and was back in command of his station within five weeks. The squadron's wartime awards were nine DSO, 333 DFC, 173 DFM.

In May 1945 the squadron was transferred to Transport Command and was posted to India equipped with the Douglas Dakota and was disbanded in December 1947.

Thomas and his crew went on to complete 39 operations with 10 Squadron, visiting some of the most heavily defended targets: Quend Plage; Bourg-Leopold;, Furne Durville; Mont Fleurs; St Lo, Juvisy; Laval Aerodrome; Amiens Railway Yards; Rennes Marshalling Yards; Domleger; Laon Railway Yards; Nouvelle-en-Chausse; Montorguer; Thiverny; Nacourt; Bottrop; Kiel; Stuttgart; Ferfay; Foret; Le Nieppe; Prouville; Bois De Cassan; Caen; Divon; Soumont; St Squntin; Tirlemont;

Brest; Sterkrade; Soesterberg; LeHavre; and Munster. Their last operation was to bomb the railway yards at Munster on the 12th September 1944 in Halifax 'P' MZ413. The flight time to the target and back was 4hrs.05mins.

His total flying hours were now 168hrs.35mins.

Thomas was now screened of operations and was posted to No 16 Service Flying Training School at Newton in January 1945 and then in February 1945 was transferred to No 16 Heavy Glider Conversion Unit (HGCU) at Keevil near Bath as Wireless Operator. This was a specialised unit set up to train pilots how to tow heavy gliders (Airspeed Horsa and Waco) using Albemarles. He was also attached to HGCU units at Blakehill Farm (near Swindon), Snaith and Fairford between February 1945 and March 1946. On the 2nd March 1946 he was posted to No 1665 Heavy Transport Conversion Unit (HCTU) at Linton-on-Ouse in Yorkshire and six months later to 1322 Heavy Conversion Unit at Dishforth were he became a Wireless Instructor.(both units were equipped with Halifaxes). In October 1946 Thomas was posted to the No 5 Parachute

Training School at Upper Heyford where he became a Wireless Operator on Dakotas for two weeks and then on to Syerston in October where he joined a transport support conversion unit, again as a Wireless Operator. The unit was equipped with Halifaxes and its job was to carry out container dropping, parachute dropping and glider towing training. Then in December it was back to 47 Squadron at Fairford on training flights in Halifaxes and then to Schleswig in Germany on the 19th April 1948. His last flight with the RAF before he was de-mobbed at Fairford was on the 5th May 1948 in Halifax 'W' with Flight Lieutenant Fell.

When his RAF career finished in May 1948, Thomas had accumulated 969hrs.50mins flying time. He had flown in 12 different types of aircraft, which included: Avro Anson; Domine; Percival Proctor; Blackburn Botha; Armstrong Whitworth Whitley; Handley Page Halifax Mk 11-111 and 111A; Miles Master; Airspeed Oxford; Douglas Dakota; Horsa; and Waco Gliders. He returned to home to Ballynure where he took up pig farming and never really retired. His hobbies are making model aircraft.

GROUP CAPTAIN
PETER REGINALD CASEMENT, DSO DFC* AFC
ROYAL AIR FORCE NO. 44188
PILOT
NO. 61, 210 & 120 SQUADRONS

Group Captain Peter Casement was born in Ballycastle, County Antrim, on the 22nd May 1921 and was educated at Marlborough Public School in England. His parents were living in India where his father was a senior executive in the Indian State Railways.

He joined the Royal Air Force straight from school in October 1939. He was due to enter Cranwell in September 1939, but as war was declared on the 3rd September, his entry was put off. Rather he was posted to No 9 Elementary Flying Training School at Ansty in Coventry on the 10th October 1939 where he was taught to fly Tiger Moths. His first flight was at the end of October and he went solo in early November after 11hrs.30mins tuition. Later in early 1940 he went on to complete a twin engined course at RAF Cranwell on Oxfords and Ansons. His first flight in the Oxford was on the 12th April 1940; he went on to complete the course in July 1940 and received his commission. Group Captain Casement told me, "I was lucky at this stage, because most of the better 'natural' pilots were creamed off and became Fighter Pilots, just in time for the Battle of Britain with inevitable consequences. Meanwhile the 'heavier' footed lot were sent elsewhere. It was all Biggles stuff at the time, but in retrospect, it was an unfortunate period which I am quite happy to leave."

After attending some short courses at The School of Air Navigation at RAF St Athan and the Hampden Crew Training School at RAF Finningley) he had his first flight in a Hampden on the 13th October 1940 at 14 Operational Training Unit at RAF Cottesmore.

He then joined No 61 Squadron on the 1st January 1941, when it was stationed at Helmswell in Lincolnshire, and later that year he moved with the squadron to North Luffenham in 5 Group. Despite it being maligned, he found the Hampden to be an excellent aeroplane and it worked extremely well for him. He had completed his first tour by the end of September 1941 and was awarded the Distinguished Flying Cross on the 24th October 1941.

The squadron was initially formed at Rochford in Essex, on the 2nd August 1917. It was one of the first three single seater fighter squadrons of the London Air Defence area and was first equipped with Sopwith Pups and then in 1918 was re-equipped with SE5s and later Sopwith Camels. It was disbanded in 1919 and reformed in 1937 as a Bomber Squadron with 5 Group. It took part in the first bombing of Hornum, and the first large bombing raid on the German mainland Munchen-Gladbach. It also took part in the first raid on Berlin, and attacked some of Germany's most heavily defended targets, i.e. Le Creusot, Peenemunde, Dortmund Ems and Mitteland Canals.

Flight Lieutenant Casement began operations in Hampdens with 61 Squadron on the 9th February 1941. He then converted onto the Avro Manchester on 2nd May 1942. The squadron was re-equipped with the Avro Lancaster in which he had his first flight on 13th May 1942. On the 17th July 1942 an aircraft that was captained by Flight Lieutenant PR Casement, Lancaster R5724 became the first bomber command crew to bring back irrefutable evidence that they had sunk a U-Boat. On the 14th December Flight Lieutenant Bill Reid (161 Squadron) was awarded the Victoria Cross. In September 1941 Flight Lieutenant Casement was screened off operations and was transferred to the Central Flying School at RAF Upavon where he attended a short instructor's course, and in October 1941 he then joined the staff of No 16 Operational Training Unit at Upper Heyford. He spent the first two weeks of April with 144 Squadron at North Luffenham and then at the end of April he rejoined 61 Squadron at Woolfox Lodge and Syerston where he went on to complete his second tour of operations on Avro Manchesters and Lancasters.

It was during his second tour with the squadron that he attacked and sunk U-751 on the 17th July 1942.

The sinking of U 751, 17th July 1942

U-751 was a type V11C class Submarine and was launched on 16th November 1940. It had just left on it's seventh war cruise from St Nazaire on the 14th July 1942 and had already sunk five ships. The U-Boat's Captain, Korvettenkapitan Gerhard Bigalk had just been awarded the Knights Cross.

U-751 had already been attacked with two 100lb anti-submarine bombs from a Whitley of 502 Squadron. After nearly an hour the U-Boat was seen to sink stern first. Lancaster 'F' R5724, piloted by Flight Lieutenant Casement on patrol from St Eval, spotted the oil slick on the surface of the sea, which had seeped from the damaged submarine and had now located it on the surface North West of Cape Ortegal, about a mile away. He made two attacks, the first with depth charges and the second with anti-submarine bombs. His air gunner's shot several of the U-Boats crew who were trying to man the guns. The U-Boat then slid stern first under the water and its crew were seen swimming in the water.

Group Captain Casement himself explained to me, "Attacking the submarine was very straight forward, and I had no great problem in attacking what, later turned out to be a 'sitting duck', because at that time I was totally unaware that 502 Squadron had already attacked and damaged the submarine. There was some anxiety from my crew as the U-Boats gunner's were firing at us, and we did sustain damage to one propeller spinner. I have to say that no skill or daring was required, and I felt no sense of satisfaction, in fact I felt sick."

Flight Lieutenant Casement was again screened off operations and, on the 1st September 1942 added a bar to his DFC.

In October 1942 he was posted to Headquarters No 5 Group at Grantham where he spent the next year on the air staff learning the elements of staff work. He was awarded the Distinguished Service Order on the 29th December 1942. In July 1943, and at his own request, he was transferred to Coastal Command Headquarters, where he hoped to become a Sunderland pilot. This was not to be as the maritime version of the Liberator (B24) was now arriving in numbers. He was steered to a Liberator Conversion Unit, firstly to Beaulieu near Southampton in August and then to RAF Aldergrove in September. His first flight in a Liberator was on the 8th July 1943 (FL924). This proved very convenient for him as Aldergrove was quite close to home in Ballycastle. Unfortunately this posting did not last very long as he was posted to 120 Squadron which at that time was stationed at Meeks Field in Reykjavik, Iceland. On his arrival he was appointed Flight Commander and made his first flight with the squadron on 8th October 1943 and his first operational flight was on 19th October 1943. In late 1943, he returned to Ballykelly where he collected a new Liberator (fitted with a Leigh Light) and returned with it to Reykjavik. The squadron spent an exciting Icelandic winter at Reykjavik, flying long-range patrols over the Atlantic, against the U-Boats, and learning to use the new Leigh Lights, which were very effective.

Group Captain Casement told me, "Coastal Command was quite different, although less dangerous. Operations were almost always specifically aimed at U-Boats. Either destroying them or denying them their objective. The Leigh Light was a useful device and I was first introduced to it at Reykjavik in November 1943. On one occasion I saw a U-Boat conning tower in the light but the weather was stormy and seas were high and I think I did not allow sufficiently for drift and did not attack. Plenty of practice and experience in its use would have been valuable but time probably did not allow."

In the spring of 1944 the squadron returned to Ballykelly, where he stayed until September 1944, covering the Normandy Landings with anti-U-Boat patrols. In those days, Flight Commanders were issued with motorcycles and, as he had one, the road from Ballykelly to Ballycastle became very familiar, as did the Alexander Arms in Limavady. He finished his tour with 120 Squadron in September 1944 having completed a further 27 operations. He then spent the next two years at the Royal Air Force College at Cranwell, learning to be an RAF Officer, learning to fly Oxfords and Hawker Harts, getting married and completing a tour at the Headquarters of Technical Training Command.

His next posting was to the Middle East in May 1946 where he joined RAF Amman in Trans Jordan until November 1947, as an instructor of administration, he then joined the Staff Air Headquarters at Levant in Jerusalem. At that time they were withdrawing from Palestine and the Israeli Terrorists were much in evidence. He even suffered the indignity of being bombed one night at Amman, by Israelis flying an old DH Dominee. The only casualty was the Station Warrant Officer who had his bedroom door blown in onto his recumbent form. He returned to the UK in October 1948 and did a lot of refresher flying at RAF Finningley and at 201 Advanced Flying School at Swinderby (Wellingtons). In February 1949 he was posted to the Lancaster Conversion Unit at RAF Kinloss in Scotland where he converted onto Lancasters.

The die were cast by this time as most Commands, apart from Coastal were being equipped with Jet aircraft, as he was getting typecast on anti-submarine work he returned to Coastal Command and in April 1949 became the Commanding Officer of 210 Squadron at St Eval. The squadron was equipped with Avro Lancaster GR2s. This was an active tour, despite the war being over. The inter-squadron competition was very intense. During his tour with 210 Squadron he had several interesting detachments to Gibraltar, Malta, Singapore where he carried out anti-submarine and fleet exercises and of course Ballykelly.

Like Group Captain Casement, 210 Squadron had a very distinguished war record. At the outbreak of war it was equipped with the Short Sunderland carrying out anti-submarine patrols. It was one of 210 Squadrons aircraft that spotted the Bismark on 26th May, and by the summer of 1944 had accounted for the sinking of seven U-Boats. Flying Officer Cruickshank despite having 72 different wounds went on to attack and sink U-347 on the 17th July 1944. For his gallant effort was awarded the Victoria Cross.

He left 210 Squadron in June 1951 and joined the air staff at the Air Ministry in London for three years. During the latter months of 1954 he completed a Meteor conversion course and a Shackelton conversion course at RAF Kinloss. In November 1954 it was back home to Northern Ireland, where he became Officer Commanding Flying at RAF Aldergrove, in charge of flying operations for six months. He spent many a happy hour here with 502 (Ulster) Squadron flying in their Mosquito and Vampires. On the 16th April 1955, Wing Commander Casement became Commanding Officer of 120 Squadron at Aldergrove. 120 squadron was still an anti-submarine squadron and was now equipped with search and rescue exercises. Taking part in maritime exercises with national and NATO navies, mail drops to weather ships and overseas detachments to Malta and Gibraltar etc. In 1956 it's Shackletons were used as emergency transports flying troops out to Cyprus during the Suez Crisis.

In February 1957 he completed a four week course at the Joint Services Staff College

In March 1957 he was given a non-flying appointment in Cyprus where he spent the next three years as Secretary to the Commanders-in-Chief Committee which he enjoyed tremendously and which kept him extremely busy drawing up plans for probable and possible 'operational activities' jointly with the other services.

He returned home to the UK in February 1960 where he attended a Meteor refresher course at Manby and in April 1960 spent the next six months completing a course at the Flying College. He had flown Meteors from time to time since 1954 but was never an operational Jet or fighter pilot. After this he was posted once again to Northern Ireland were he was appointed Director of the Joint Anti-Submarine School at RAF Station Ballykelly in County Londonderry for three years. The Joint Anti-Submarine School was established as a joint service organisation, directed (jointly) by a Royal Navy Captain and a RAF Group Captain. The job involved mainly arranging large-scale exercises at sea with Royal Navy vessels (Frigates, etc.), helicopters and RAF Squadrons. The school also ran courses for senior officers, and studied anti-submarine tactics for development. While at Ballykelly he decided to buy a Caravan and he and his wife spent many happy hours at Port Salon, enjoying sailing from Buncrana and many other places.

By now he was well versed in the art of submarine warfare and in October 1963, spent the next two years at headquarters 19 Group at Mountbatton, as Senior Air Staff Officer i.e., chief of staff to the air officer commanding. His duties were mainly related to anti-submarine warfare squadrons. Mountbatton had been an old flying boat base in Plymouth. Then in August 1966 he went to RAF Topcliffe as the Station Commander until May 1968 where he retired voluntarily in 1968.

On his retirement from the Royal Air Force Group Captain Casement had flown a total of 3,800 hours in 27 different types of service aircraft, which included:

Initial Training - Tiger Moth, Airspeed Oxford and Avro Anson.

Operationally - Handley Page Hampden, Avro Lancaster, Liberator (B-24) and Avro Shackleton.

Others - Vickers-Armstrong Wellington, Avro Manchester, DH Mosquito, Westland Lysander, Harvard, Varsity, Handley Page Hastings, Lockheed VP-26 USN Neptune, Jet Provost, Gloster Meteor, Hawker Hunter, DH Vampire, English Electric Canberra, Chipmunk, Miles Magister and master, Auster, Fairchild Argus, Dominie and Westland Walrus.

On retiring from the RAF he became self-employed in the travel trade and is life member of the Royal Air Force Association and was deeply involved helping the RAF Benevolent Fund (just retired). He has no specific hobbies but does enjoy the outdoors.

WARRANT OFFICER
WILLIAM CHRISTIE, DFM MBE
ROYAL AIR FORCE NUMBER 1672387
FLIGHT ENGINEER
NO. 57, 578 AND 356 SQUADRONS

William Christie was born on the 7th January 1924 in the Town Land of Bellemont near Coleraine in County Londonderry and was educated at Dundooan Primary School and at Coleraine Technical College.

On leaving college he was employed as a Shop Assistant in the local Chemist in Portstewart, which was owned by a Mr WM Reville.

Bill was keen member of the Portrush Air Training Corps 815 Squadron and remembers well his first flight in Lockheed Hudson from the Coastal Command Station at Analoo near Limavady in County Londonderry.

He applied to join the RAFVR in July 1942 and was accepted for initial training at Blackpool in England where he was kitted out and learned how to march, etc.

From Blackpool he was posted to RAF Cosford where he successfully completed his Flight Engineers (Engine) course. From Cosford he went to St Athan in South Wales were he completed a Flight Engineer course. He said, "The highlight of the course for me being invited to spend a week at the Rootes Factory at Speke in Liverpool where the Handley Page Halifax Bomber was being assembled."

During his stay in Liverpool Bill was billeted with a civilian family, which made a pleasant change from the usual service routine.

Having passed out at St Athan as a fully-fledged Flight Engineer he received his 'E' Brevet and was immediately posted to 1658 Heavy Conversion Unit (HCU) at Riccal in Yorkshire where he was promoted to Sergeant.

Bill arrived at the HCU in July 1943 and it was not long before he met his new crew who were:

Flight Lieutenant A.Harte-Lovelace, Skipper.
Sergeant D.Entwistle, Navigator
Pilot Officer P. Coryton, Bomb Aimer
Sergeant J.L. Sidley, Wireless Operator
Sergeant A. McLachlan, Mid Upper Gunner
Flight Lieutenant A.McMullan (DFM), Rear Gunner
Sergeant William Christie, Flight Engineer

Bill had his first flight with his new crew on the afternoon of the 4th August 1943. They took off in a Halifax at 1320 hrs to carry out some circuits and landings. Their conversion training on Halifaxes consisted of air test, X-country, air-to-sea firing (Filey Bay) and a 'Bullseye', which was cancelled. They completed the course at the end of September and were posted to an operational squadron.

Having completed their conversion course they were posted to 51 Squadron at Snaithe, near Goole in Yorkshire. The squadron was equipped with the Handley Page Halifax B.11s.

51 Squadron was formed at Thetford in Norfolk in May 1916 and its role was a home defence squadron and was equipped with BE2c and BE12 aircraft. It was disbanded in 1919 and reformed again in 1937 as a night bomber squadron and when war broke out it was equipped with Whitleys, with the Yorkshire based No 4 Group. On the very night of the war it carried out the 1st 'Nickel' raid over Germany. One of the squadron's claims to fame was when its aircraft carried Operation Biting when a raiding party that was led by Wing Commander Pickard captured a complete 'Wurzburg' radar installation at Bruneval, near Le Havre.

(Wing Commander Pickard who was then Commanding Officer of 51 Squadron was already well known as he was the pilot of the Wellington 'F' for Freddie in the documentary film Target for Tonight.)

Another serious incident occurred on the 13th/14th January 1945 when one of the squadron's aircraft collided with another Halifax over Saarbrucken. It lost at least nine feet from its nose (neither the Navigator nor the Bomb Aimer were wearing their parachutes at the time of the collision and were lost overboard). The aircraft had dived 1,500ft with the Captain struggling to keep control of the damaged aircraft. He managed to regain control and brought the aircraft back home safely at 7,000ft.

At the end of the war the squadron was transferred to transport command and re-equipped with Stirlings and Avro Yorks replacing them in 1946. The squadron played a very important role during the Berlin Airlift and was disbanded in 1950.

They arrived at 51 Squadron then spent a few days settling in and had their first flight on the 23rd September. They took off at 1940 hrs in Halifax 'C' and carried out a four hour night cross-country exercise.

Tragedy hit Bill's crew when the Navigator Sergeant Entwistle and the Bomb Aimer Pilot Officer Coryton were lost when flying as 'spare bods' (flying as stand in for sick crewmembers of other aircraft).

Twice during his career Bill had to fly as 'spare bod' to Berlin and Frankfurt. Luckily he was not with them on later dates when both the crews that he had been flying with had been shot down. He learnt after the war that one of the crews had survived.

Their new Navigator was Pilot Officer Phillips and the Bomb Aimer was Flight Sergeant J Collins.

Bills first operation with the Squadron was on the 27th September, They took off at 1935 hrs in Halifax MH-C and set course for Hannover and returned safely to base 5hrs.20 mins later.

Other targets they visited

Bochum, Kassel (railway system and Henschel Aircraft Factories), Cannes (railway workshops), Ludwigshafen (factory), Leverkausen, Frankfurt, Leipzig, Lisset, Schweinfort (ball bearing factories), Stuttgart, Essen, Nuremburg, Teagnier (railway yards), Dusseldorf, Karlsruhe, Orleans (railway repair workshops) Aachen (railway yards), Boerg-Leopold (military camp), Trappes (railway yards), Haringzelles, Boulogne (gun positions), Mont Eleury (6th June 1944 D-Day "Der Tag".), Douismont (flying bomb sites target obliterated), Mimoyecques (V-weapon site), Villers Bocage (German Panzer Divisions), St Matin L'Hortier (flying bomb sites), Croix Dalles (V-weapon sites), Cattelliers (flying bomb sites), Nucourt (flying bomb supply dump), Bois De La Haie (flying bomb sites), Vaires (marshalling yards), Kiel (U-Boat yards and Naval facilities), Foret De Nieppe (flying bomb supply sites), Ander Belck, Foret De Mormal (flying bomb sites), Tirlemont (Luftwaffe night fighter stations), Brest (shipping), and Homberg (oil plant 'Happy Valley').

Bill's logbook shows that the raid to Hamburg on the 27th August 1944 was his 39th Raid. He entered in his logbook below the entry, "First Tour Completed".

In January 1944 the 'Top Brass' of Bomber Command decided that they would form a new squadron from the nucleus of 'C' Flight of 51 Squadron. This new squadron would be No 578 Squadron and would be based at Burn not far from Selby.

The new squadron was to be commanded by Group Captain David Marwood-Elton, DFC and not knowing that within three months he would be shot down and taken prisoner by the Germans.

Many years later when the only surviving Wellington Bomber was fished out of Loch Ness it was revealed that this Group Captain who a few years earlier in 1942 when of a lower rank had ditched the Wimpy there.

When Bill and the crew completed their 39th operation his skipper was promoted to Squadron Leader and made a Flight Commander of the new squadron.

After a well-earned rest Bill was posted to India where he spent some time training in Calcutta School where he was instructed on the workings of the B24 (Liberator).

Soon after this he was posted to No 355 Squadron, which was based at Salbani near Calcutta and was equipped with the B24.

355 Squadron was formed at Salbani in India in August 1943 as a heavy bomber unit and was equipped with Liberators. It played a very creditable part in the air offensive against the Japanese in Burma. Its operations included attacks on land communications far behind the enemy lines that included the notorious Burma railway, airfields, harbours and shipping and some of its round trips involved flying more than 2,000 miles. During one of its long-range operations on the 2nd May 1945, Wing Commander JB Nicolson, VC (the first Fighter Command VC of the war) lost his life when flying as a passenger in one of the squadron's Liberators when it crashed into the sea. After the Japanese surrender in 1945 it carried out transport duties (dropping supplies to POWs in Burma and French Indo-China. The squadron was finally disbanded in May 1946).

Bill's first operation with the squadron was on the 16th June 1945 when he attacked Japanese troop concentrations. The aircraft was Liberator 'T' KG 884 and it was captained by a Wing Commander Gilmore.

He carried out three more operations with the squadron which were to Mokpalin, Kanchanaburi and on the last operation to Rajburi on the 10th July 1945 his Liberator 'X' KG 844 crash landed at Hmawbi when one of the main undercarriage legs would not come down and the other retracted. The Liberator suffered extensive damage but the crew were all unhurt.

The Atom Bomb was dropped on Hiroshima on the 6th August and Nagasaki was flattened by a second on the 9th August. On the 14th August Japan surrendered.

The remainder of Bill's time in India was spent ferrying freight and passengers between Burma and India with 1354 DDT Flight and 355 Squadron.

His last flight with the squadron before returning to the UK was on the 15th January 1946 in Liberator KP. 136 on a night 'x' country exercise with Flight Sergeant PR Jones.

Bill had completed 39 operations over enemy territory and had accumulated a total of 397hrs.52mins flying time in Lockheed Hudson, Handley Page Halifax, B24 Liberator, Flying Fortress and Douglas Dakota (DC3).

On his return to the UK he was de-mobbed from the RAF on the 19th May 1946. Bill returned home to Northern Ireland where he worked for a time as a Salesman with Inglis & Co and later joined GEC in Larne where he remained for the next 28 years until ill health forced him to retire.

Although Bill is retired from full time employment he still maintains a very active roll in the Air Crew Association, Royal Air Force Association where he has been an active member since 1948 and has been Treasurer and Welfare Officer for many years.

He is also Vice President of the Northern Ireland Committee and Standard Bearer of the Larne Branch of RAFA and also is a member of the Royal British Legion in which he plays an active part.

Bill was awarded the MBE by Queen Elizabeth II at Buckingham Palace on the 31st December 1996 (New Years Honour List) for all his devoted work as Welfare Officer in the Larne Branch of the Royal Air Force Association.

FLIGHT LIEUTENANT
HAROLD REGINALD CLARKE, AE
ROYAL AIR FORCE VOLUNTEER RESERVE N0. 754383
ROYAL AIR FORCE COMMISSION NO. 102587
BATTLE OF BRITAIN
FIGHTER PILOT
NO. 74, 66 AND 610 SQUADRONS

Harold Reginald Clarke was born in Belfast on the 23rd August 1917 and his primary education commenced at Dale Holme Private School on the Ballygomartin Road and the Belfast Technical College. He applied to join the Royal Air Force Volunteer Reserve in Belfast in July 1939 and was accepted. He then went to 24 Elementary and Reserve Flying Training School at Sydenham where he had his first flight in a Tiger Moth on July 13th and soloed on the type on the 1st August 1939.

With the war only a month away he was called to full time Service on the 2nd September 1939 and was posted to No 3 Initial Training Wing at St Lenards on Sea on the south coast of England for basic training. He remembers well marching up and down the sea front day after day. On December 18th he was posted to No 4 EFTS at Brough to commence his flying training in Blackburn B2s. Having completed his elementary training he was posted to 14 FTS at Kinloss in Scotland on the 10th April 1940. The school was equipped with Harvards.

With his training completed he went to No 7 OTU at Hawarden on the 10th August 1940 and it was from here on the 11th August that he had his first flight in a Spitfire Mk1. When he completed his Operational Training he had flown the Spitfire for 28 hours. He received his Wings and was promoted to Sergeant Pilot.

Harry joined 74 Squadron at Kirton-in-Lindsey in Yorkshire on the 26th August but stayed only a few days before going onto 66 Squadron at Coltishall. He arrived at Coltishall on the 29th/30th August and again it was a short stay as he was posted to 610 Squadron at Acklington on the 11th September 1940.

Saved by a strap

It was here with 610 Squadron that Pilot Officer HR Clarke had an incredible escape from death in his Spitfire DW-'D'. On Monday 30th September he was giving some combat instruction to another 610 squadron pilot, Flying Officer CH Bacon, when they had a head on collision. Harry told me that their wings hit and his

propeller had sliced into the other Spitfire as his engine started to run 'very rough'. He decided to throttle back and bale out as quickly as he could; he trimmed the nose of Spitfire down, opened the hood, undid his Sutton Harness and baled out.

When he baled out he hit the tail of his aircraft and was knocked unconscious. When he came to he found himself hanging upside down and suspended by one strap of the Sutton harness that was fastened very insecurely around one leg. He managed to pull himself up and got hold of the rest of the harness and wrapped it around his arm moments before passing out again and hitting the ground. Flying Officer Bacon's aircraft dived straight into the beach at Alnmouth from 14,000ft and he was killed. Harry's aircraft also crashed onto the same beach.

His aircraft DW-'D' was excavated from the beach in 1997 and he was later presented with its gun sight by Group Captain Brian Freeman who at that time was the Senior Royal Air Force Officer for Northern Ireland. *(I had the honour of making the little mahogany base for the sight to sit on.)*

After the accident Harry found it extremely difficult to come to terms with flying the Spitfire and although he did fly it for a short time when he was transferred to 602 Squadron at Prestwick in Scotland in December and for one week at 266 Squadron at Wittering

Harry decided to ask for a transfer to a squadron with a different type. This request was granted and he was posted to 255 Squadron at Kirton-on-Lindsey on the 3rd January 1941 initially flying Boulton Paul Defiants and later the Bristol Beaufighter. Harry received his

Commission in August 1941 and promoted to Pilot Officer. He moved with the Squadron to Coltishall in September 1941 and then to High Ercol in March 1942 and finally Honiley in June 1942. In August 1942 he was promoted to Flying Officer. The squadron had by now been equipped with the Beaufighter V1f and left for North Africa on the 13th November 1942. The Squadron was stationed at Maison Blanche and Harry was sent with a detachment to Souk-el-Arba.

He returned to the UK in January 1943 and was sent for by the Air Ministry where he was offered a Test Pilot's position back home at RAF Aldergrove with 23 Maintenance Unit. He was delighted with this offer a quickly accepted. He moved to 23 MU at Aldergrove on the 18th April 1943 was promoted to Flight Lieutenant and remained there Flight Testing numerous types of Aircraft until he left the RAF in June 1947.

His last flight with the RAF was on the 18th August 1947 in an Avro Anson Code N502H. Harry's RAF career spanned from July 1939 until August 1947 and during that time he had accumulated 1716 hours in Tiger Moth, Blackburn B2, Harvard, Miles Master and Magister, Supermarine Spitfire, Hawker Hurricane, Boulton Paul Defiant, Bristol Blenheim and Beaufighter, Oxford, Avro Anson, Blackurn Botha, Handley Page Hampden, Vickers Wellington, Warwick, Short Stirling, Corsair, and Whitleys.

He returned to civilian life soon after to take up his responsibility in the family business of Joseph Braddell and Son Ltd Gunsmiths Belfast.

FLIGHT LIEUTENANT
HARRY D CONNOLLY
ROYAL AIR FORCE NO. 100653
FIGHTER PILOT
NO. 32 SQUADRON

KILLED IN ACTION 19TH AUGUST 1942
AGE 26

Harry D Connolly was born near the Holywood Arches on 25th September 1916. He was the son of Mr William James Connolly and Mrs Jane Connolly. He had two sisters, Gretta and Elsie. His parents decided to move Lisburn in the same year, where they established the family business of WJ Connolly Newsagents in Castle Street and took up residence at No 6 Conway Street, Wallace Avenue.

Harry was educated at Market Square Primary School and later at Lisburn Intermediate School (now Wallace High School). He excelled in many sports, and proved to be a useful Rugby player in the schools 1st Fifteen in 1933/34 seasons. He also played cricket for Lisburn and was a member of the team that beat RBAI in 1927 and was a member of the first Boys XI to win the Graham Schoolboys Cup in 1930, and was on the team when they won the Northern Cricket Union Senior League in 1937. *A memento of the 1930 Graham Cup still remains with the Connolly family. The very cricket ball that was used in the final against Armagh all those years ago.* His father was also an influential figure in the Lisburn Cricket Club in the early 1900's and umpired many of its games. Harry also played centre half for South Antrim hockey eleven and captained the Ulster Schoolboys inter-provincial side.

But it was at golf Harry found his particular forte; he was a born natural. A member of the Lisburn, Knock, Balmoral and Belvoir Park clubs, and held the record at all four. He played for Belvoir in the Irish Senior Cup and Barton Shield, and was never beaten. On the 24th May 1939 Harry was playing at Belvoir in the Captains Prize, and set a new Course record of 68. (The record still remains unbeaten to this day.) His scorecard for the competition was framed by the clubs committee in 1944 and still hangs in the dining room of the Belvoir Park Golf Club. At the age of 16 he took part in the British Boys Championship at Royal Lytham St Anne's in 1932, and was second in the qualifiers in the Ulster Scratch Singles at Portrush. He participated in the Boy's Amateur Golf Championship at Carnoustie in Scotland, which he was tipped to win. Although this prophecy was not entirely

fulfilled, he was the only Irish competitor to reach the third round.

He was a former officer of the Lisburn Cathedral Company of the church Boys Brigade, and a popular member of the Lisburn Newsroom. Friends advised him that the best way to further his interest in golf was to join the Metropolitan Police in London, which he duly did, entering the training college in 1938 before joining the regular force. But the cost of playing on courses there proved prohibitive and he returned home to Lisburn to work in the family newsagents in No 3 Castle Street.

RAF Career

It was now January 1940; the war was just four months old. Harry decided to join the Royal Air Force and went to the recruiting office in Clifton Street, Belfast where he offered his services to King and Country. He was sent home and was told that he would be sent for as soon as there was a course available for him. On the 1st June 1940 he received word from the recruiting officer that he was to report to the Receiving Centre at Padgate near Liverpool on the 25th July. He spent the next five days at Padgate being kitted out with his uniform etc. On the 31st July AC 2 Harold D Connolly was posted to an Initial Training Wing at Blackpool to commence his basic training (good old square bashing, rifle drill and learning how to salute Officer, etc.).

His record shows that on the 26th August 1940 he was transferred to Brize Norton in Oxon, Oxfordshire for five days, and from the 3rd September until the 15th September he was stationed at the Babbacombe Hotel in Torquay. He then went to No 2 Initial Training Wing, No 5 Flight (B) Squadron Trinity Hall in Cambridge where he spent the next six weeks. Having successfully passed all his exams and being selected for Aircrew Duties he was posted to No 11 Elementary Flying Training School at Perth in Scotland. The aerodrome was known locally as Scone and has been associated with pilot training for nearly 50 years. The school was established in January 1937 and was initially equipped with Avro Tutors, Hawker Harts and Fairey Battles, but with the outbreak of war it was re-equipped with Tiger Moths.

Harry joined the school on the 14th November 1940, so it is safe to say he had his first flight in a Tiger Moth soon after that. On the 10th January Harry was informed that he had passed the course, and promoted to Leading Aircrafts Man. He was then in formed that he was being posted out to Canada on the Empire training scheme where he would continue his flying training in earnest. He soon boarded a ship, which was to take him and other trainee pilots to Canada. When they docked they were surprised to be surrounded by newsreel men, and a roaring mass of cheering people. They very quickly boarded a train which would take them on a long three day (3,000 mile) journey via Quebec, Montreal, Ottawa, along the north shore of Lake Superior, Port Arthur and Winnipeg. The train stopped twice each day for exercise, and on all occasions the hospitality of the local people was tremendous.

On their arrival at Winnipeg, they were given a civic reception. They were marched from the station to a huge hall, and all they there they were followed by a seething mass of cheering, clapping people, whose only ambition seemed to be the shaking of everyone's hand. When they arrived in the hall they each received fruit, cigarettes, chocolate and magazines. Some of the local people who had immigrated to Canada earlier tried to find airmen from their own hometowns. Harry was lucky, he found a lady called Mrs JP Edgar of Ellice Avenue, Winnipeg who was an Aughey, and had a sister married to an Aughey of Lisburn. He arrived at No 37 Service Flying Training School in Calgary, Canada in early 1941 to start flying training on Tiger Moths. From Calgary he then went to No 33 Service Flying Training School at Carberry in Manitoba where he completed his flying training on Harvards. On the 1st June 1941 Harry successfully completed his training, and was awarded his Wings. He received an immediate commission, and promoted to Pilot Officer, and on the 10th June he returned to the UK. Pilot Officer Connolly was posted to No 1 Squadron at Tangmere in Sussex on the 5th April 1942 to start his operational flying in Hurricane Mk IIcs.

Sometime during April, while on patrol, Harry's aircraft was hit by enemy fire and he had to bale out into the English Channel. On the 18th April while home on leave Harry was invited by the Commanding Officer of 817 Air Training Corps Squadron (Lisburn Schools) to give the cadets a talk on his career in the RAF. This he did, and also gave a graphic account of how he baled out of his Hurricane fighter over the English Channel one morning.

"I was 12 miles out to sea at about 5,000ft when my aircraft developed engine trouble. Despite my efforts, I continued to loose altitude and when I reached 2,000ft I decided to bale out. When I got out of my aircraft, I immediately pulled the ripcord, and inflated my Mae West life jacket. On reaching the water I discarded my parachute, inflated the dinghy and was soon safely afloat on the sea. I spent the next fourteen hours waiting to be rescued and eventually was picked up by a Trawler. I was taken off the Trawler the next morning by an RAF Rescue Launch, and returned safely to my squadron."

Because Harry had to bale out of his damaged aircraft, when it had been hit by enemy fire, he automatically became a member of that elite bunch of aviators the 'Caterpillar Club', and was presented with the coveted golden Caterpillar brooch.

On the 1st/2nd June he was tasked for an 'intruder' operation into France and Belgium. While near St Trond he attacked and damaged a JU 88.

The following information has been taken from his official Combat Report.

Intruder Operation - Tangmere Sector

Pilot Officer Connolly - No 1 Squadron. The date was 1st/2nd June 1942. The aircraft was a Hawker Hurricane Mk IIc (Long Range). The time the attack was delivered was 0145 hrs. The place of the attack was near St Trond. The weather was clear over the Channel and ground haze over the land. At 0050 hrs on the 2nd June 1942, Pilot Officer Connolly took off from RAF Station Manston in a long range Hurricane MkIIc, Coded JX-H on an 'Intruder' operation to St Troud in Belgium.

The Belgium coast was crossed at 6,000ft at Nieuport, after which Pilot Officer Connolly came down to 1,5000ft, and flew direct to the target. Just before reaching St Troud, a Ju88 was seen at the same height against the moon. Pilot Officer Connolly made an astern attack from 100yds range, firing one short burst and observing strikes. The port guns jammed and the Hurricane sideslipped while manoeuvring back into position; a twin-engined aircraft believed to be another Ju88 was seen behind. The enemy aircraft opened fire, and the two aircraft circled, trying to get on each other's tail, but after a few minutes contact was lost. Pilot Officer Connolly then flew south to River Dambre and between 0215 hrs and 0230 hrs saw some air firing south of Brussels and one aircraft going down in flames.

The coast was re-crossed at Cayeux, and the Channel was crossed at 9,000ft. Pilot Officer Connolly landed at Tangmere at 0415 hrs on the 2nd June, and claimed one Ju88 damaged.

Signed: Flying Officer CS Flick, Intelligence Officer, No 1 Squadron.

Flight Lieutenant Karel Miroslav Kuttelwasher, DFC & Bar

While at No 1 Squadron Harry made friends with some of its Czech pilots, one of them was Flight Lieutenant KM

Kuttelvasher, DFC & Bar. Flight Lieutenant Kuttlevasher asked Harry to be his best man when he was married. Kuttelvasher was born in Svaty Kriz in Czechoslovakia in 1916, and in 1934 he joined the Czech Air Force, qualifying for his wings in 1937. He joined the RAF in early 1940 and went on to destroy 18 German Aircraft. Harry also befriended another Czech pilot who he brought home to Lisburn to meet his parents. This particular pilot told Harry that if he was killed he was to give his Pilot's Wings to one of his sisters. Sadly the pilot was killed and Harry's sister still has the Czech Wings.

Also in No 1 Squadron was Squadron Leader McLoughlin - The one armed pilot.

Harry's cricketing skills came in handy as he was picked to represent the RAF at Lords, and played a few rounds of golf with Wing Commander Laddie Lucas.

In early June Harry was promoted to the rank of Flight Lieutenant and posted to No 32 Squadron at West Malling in Kent. On the 1st July 1942 the squadron moved to RAF Friston, which was on the south coast of England, and the nearest airfield to France.

Brief wartime history of 32 Squadron

No 32 Squadron was formed at Netheravon in January 1916, and in May that year went to France. The squadron was equipped with the DH 2 Pusher Fighter. On the first day of the Somme battle the commanding officer Major LWB Rees spotted a formation of ten German aircraft. He decided to attack and although he was badly wounded, he managed to shoot down two of the enemy aircraft, for this he was awarded the Victoria Cross. In May 1917 the squadron was re-equipped with the DH5 and in January 1918 SE5as. The squadron returned to England and was disbanded at the end of December 1919.

The squadron entered the Second World War with Gloster Gauntlets and Hawker Hurricanes. By the end of January the squadron had destroyed at least 16 enemy aircraft and damaged six others. The squadron took the full weight of the Luftwaffe attacks over London during the Battle of Britain, and in early 1941 took over the roll of flying convoy patrols. On the 19th August it took part in the Dieppe raid, flying from 0445 hrs until 1850 hrs. It took part in the North African landings in December 1942 moving to Phillippeville and Maison Blanche. In May 1943 the squadron was re-equipped with Spitfire Mk Vcs and Mk1Xs in June 1943. The squadron was also involved in the Italian Front and bombing targets in Yugoslavia. In September it moved to Greece with detachments sent to Metokhi and Araxos, covering the Salonika landings. It then moved to Palestine where it remained until 1947.

'Operation Jubilee', the Dieppe raid, 19th August 1942

Harry had carried out many sorties during his short time with 32 Squadron. Sadly while taking part in the infamous 'Operation Jubilee' on 19th August 1942, Flight Lieutenant Harry Connolly, on his third sortie of the day, collided with his No 2 as they were attacking the German heavy gun positions on the cliffs at Puys (code named Blue Beach) from low level. His Hurricane (HL860) was seen to crash in flames, and he was killed. His No 2 lost three feet from his port wing but managed to make it back to base.

Harry is buried in Hatut-Sur-Mer-Cemetery, which is just outside Dieppe

Squadron Leader Thorn led No 32 Squadron through the operation. He was awarded the Distinguished Flying Cross for his leadership at Dieppe. The RAF's first casualty of Operation Jubilee was when a Blenheim Mk IV, Code LV, Serial No V5380 from No 13 Squadron crashed killing all of its crew. Pilot Officer Cecil Woodland (Pilot), Sergeant Henry Neville (Air Gunner) RAAF, and Sergeant AS Boyd (Observer) from Belfast Aged 32 are buried in a common grave in a Cemetery in France.

Many words have been written about the RAF's 2,000 sorties and sixteen hour involvement in Operation Jubilee. It has been regarded by many, both British and German to be the greatest air battle of the Second World War. Operation Jubilee was the code name for the harbour town of Dieppe. This was an attack against an enemy occupied territory. The purpose was to capture, by assault, and occupy the town of Dieppe for at least twelve hours, and then withdraw with German prisoners. The RAF's primary job was to provide fighter cover and general protection throughout the hours of daylight for the troops on the ground, and cover for their withdrawal. They were also tasked to destroy local defences, power stations, aerodromes, German invasion barges and any other enemy targets that were in the harbour at that time.

History has now informed us of Operation Jubilee, and can be summed up in four words, "**It was a slaughter.**" Out of a total of 6,100 brave men, over 1,000 were killed, (tragically 907 of those were Canadians), 600 plus were wounded, and 1,950 were taken prisoner. Not a single tank and only a handful of men managed to get to the town. It was one of the darkest days of World War II.

Lord Louis Mountbatten summed the battle up by saying, "The Duke of Wellington said that the Battle of Waterloo was won on the playing fields of Eton, and I say that the battle of Normandy was won on the beaches of Dieppe."

SQUADRON LEADER
HDH COOPER, DFC
ROYAL AIR FORCE No. 39499
PRISONER OF WAR No. 3795
No. 110 (HYDERABAD) SQUADRON & 21 SQUADRON

Herbert Douglas Haig Cooper was born in the town of Strabane, County Tyrone, in 1917 and was educated at a mixed school called PNAU, which was a type of Kindergarden. After Kindergarden he went to Prior School, which was just across the Border in Lifford. This move involved crossing the Border twice a day just to go to school.

He remembered very well, that when crossing the railway line to get to school, the boys discovered that if they laid a halfpenny (old money) on the steel track and waited for a train to pass over it, he could get a penny worth of sweets for it. The Prior School building is still standing in Lifford but has now been taken over by the Eire Army, and the modern day Prior School is now in the town of Raphoe and is now known as the Prior and Raphoe Royal School.

In 1934 he left Prior and went as a Boarder to Portora Royal in Enniskillen where he spent two years. When Douglas left school his father wanted him to have a career in banking like his older brother, but he didn't really want this because as a small boy of five years he enjoyed making model aircraft out of balsa wood and had always had his heart set in joining the Royal Air Force and becoming a pilot. To please his father he decided to sit the banking exam, and in his own words, "I made an excellent job of failing it on purpose." When Douglas' mother was alive she would never have had considered him joining the Royal Air Force as she thought it was too dangerous. When she died very early in life his father realised that nothing else was going to suit him so he finally gave his consent for Douglas to join the Royal Air Force.

It was now 1936 and unfortunately meant that Douglas was too old for a Cranwell Entry and had to settle for a Short Service Commission, so in December 1936 he started what was to become an eventful and memorable career in the RAF.

After passing a medical test and interview at AD Astral House, Douglas was posted to commence his initial training at a civilian flying school at Brough, which was also the home to the Blackburn Aircraft Establishment.

Douglas remembers well traveling on the train from Hull to Brough where he met up with a tall 'gangly'

character and who was going in the same direction and destination as him. This gangly person turned out to be a New Zealander called Edward James 'Cobber Cain', who in June 1940 was the Royal Air Force's top scorer with 14 kills to his credit. Yet who, to celebrate yet another kill in a fit of bravado, fatally flick rolled his Hurricane into a crash at Echmines and was killed, just at the end of the Battle of France.

Douglas and Cobber became good friends on the train and decided to share a room; he remembers that Cobber had already attained his equivalent of the 'A' license in New Zealand before the war. Although Cobber had a little more experience in flying than the rest, he hadn't trained on aircraft that had no brakes and on one occasion after landing his B 2 (which was an all metal biplane with side by side seating) and taxiing in a gust of wind caught his aircraft and blew him into a hangar. The aircraft ended up with a broken propeller that hung over the door of their room until the end of the course.

Douglas first flight at Brough was on the 21st December 1936 in a B 2 type aircraft G-ACBK with his instructor Flight Lieutenant Snelling for 25 minutes. His training continued through December into January 1937 with Flight Lieutenant Snelling and on January 21st after 10hrs.45mins instruction he flew solo in G-ACZH. The course ended on the 6th March and his logbook shows that he was assessed by the schools chief flying instructor Flight Lieutenant Loton as having completed 60hrs.05mins and was 'above the average' as a Pilot.

On the 20th March 1937 Douglas was posted to No 5 Flying Training School (FTS) at Sealand to join the 33rd Course which was equipped with Hawker Hart, Audax, and Furys. He said he had a wonderful time at Sealand being with a really crazy bunch of blokes who were so 'cocky' they thought they were the cream of the Royal Air Force, so cocky in fact that they had their own course tie made with the "33rd Course" emblazoned on it. On the 24th March Douglas took to the sky for the first time in a Hawker Hart (T), his Instructor was a Flight Lieutenant Ridge who was suitably impressed enough to let him fly solo the next day. On one occasion he nearly came to grief in a Hawker Hart while taking part in an air firing exercises that were carried out at Pethelly on the west coast. He explained what happened, "I took off in my Hart using the gravity feed tank and once airborne I was supposed to change over to the main tank, this of course I completely forgot about. The inevitable happened, my engine started to splutter and cough and finally petered out due to being starved of fuel." Douglas and the aircraft were making a rapid decent towards the sea when he suddenly remembered, "God I'm not on the main tank." Quickly he turn the cock over and the Kestrel V spluttered back into life. This was a lesson he never forgot.

Douglas also remembers the 31st May very well as that was the first time he ever flew at night, and said it was a wonderful experience flying over Liverpool in his Hawker Hart on a beautiful moonlit night. The stars were so bright in the sky and you seem to have the whole world to your self. "A most exhilarating experience."

He told me another story about one of the 'lads' taking off from Sealand in a slightly intoxicated state, and when returning to land mistook the lights of a local swimming pool for the flare path, he emerged sodden, and quite sober but otherwise unscathed.

Douglas had now started some advanced flying in the other Hawker variants, Audax and Furys at No 5 FTS and said they all were a joy to fly. He was awarded his Wings on the 25th June 1937 and on the 30th he was assessed by the schools commanding officer Group Captain AH Gallihawk as 'above the average' as a Pilot with no special faults. The course at Sealand finished on the 23rd October 1937 and his total hours flying B2s and the Hawker Variants were now 158hrs. He was again assessed as 'above the average' by Group Captain AH Hallihawk.

Having completed his flying training Douglas was posted to his first operational squadron, which was 110 (Hyderabad) Squadron at RAF Station Waddington in Lincolnshire. The squadron was equipped with Hawker Hinds until January 1938 when it was re-equipped with the new Bristol Blenheim Short Nosed Bomber aircraft.

Short history of 110 Squadron

No 110 Squadron Royal Flying Corps was formed at Rendcombe in Gloucestershire on 1st November 1917 and crossed to France in late August 1918. The squadron was tasked with carrying out long distance day bombing with DH 9As. 110 Squadron was the very first squadron to be equipped with the DH 9A and its original batch of this type was a gift of his Serene

Highness the Nizam of Hyderabad. Each aircraft bore an inscription to that effect and that is how the unit became known as the Hyderabad Squadron. It was disbanded in 1919 and reformed again in May 1937 as a bomber squadron at Waddington and was equipped with the Hawker Hinds. With the outbreak of war in 1939 the Nizam contributed again towards the cost of three new squadrons, one of which was 110 and once again its aircraft proudly bore the name Hyderabad. On the 4th September 1939 110 Squadron was led by Flight Lieutenant KC Doran on the very first raid of the war, when five Blenheims flew from the Civil Airport at Ipswich to make an attack on German warships at Wilhelmshaven. Only one of the squadron's aircraft failed to return, it was shot down over the target area. The aircraft was Blenheim N6199 VE-? and was captained by Flying Officer Ebden there were no survivors and they are buried in Sage War Cemetery, in Oldenburg. For his part in the operation Flight Lieutenant Doran was awarded one of the first Distinguished Flying Crosses of the war. The squadron moved to India in early 1942 and in March 1943 began to operate with Vengeance dive bombers against the Japanese in Burma. In March 1945 the squadron was re-equipped with Mosquitos, and claimed that an attack made by eight of its aircraft on some Japanese troops in the Tikeda area on the 20th August 1945 (six days after the unconditional surrender of the Japanese) was the Royal Air Force's last offensive action against the Japanese.

On the 2nd November 1937 Douglas took to the air in a Hawker Hind with 110 Squadron, he was accompanied by Sergeant Storran and his second flight of the day in K6816 with Aircraftman Cahoon must a been quite eventful as his log book shows, "Crashed on landing." Douglas continued flying the Hind until the squadron was re-equipped with the new Short Nosed Blenheim in January 1938. His first flight in the Blenheim was on January 18th under the instruction of Pilot Officer McKenzie. The squadron's commanding officer Squadron Leader Cameron took him up on the 26th and 27th January to check him out and on the 27th he flew the Blenheim solo for 20 minutes.

The squadron continued flying training with the squadron through 1938 and in May 1939 moved to the RAF station at Wattisham. A log entry in Douglas' flying logbook shows that he flew to Aldergrove on the 12th July with Pilot Officer Wright and Pilot Officer Arderne.

With the threat of war getting ever closer 110 Squadron started to intensify its training during June, July and August. His log shows that on the 6th, 8th, 10th and 11th August he was carrying out home defense operations and on the 14th the squadron carried out some live bombing at Larkhill range.

September 3rd 1939 Great Britain and France are again at war with Germany, and on that day Douglas had been deputised to take a flight of Blenheims to the Middle East. All the crews had gone to the uniform stores six days previous and drawn Tropical Kit. Only to be told late on the sixth that the duty had been canceled and to make matters worse they had missed the first operation of the war against Germany. September thru December Douglas was in the air practically every day helping to train new crews in the art of air fighting tactics, formation flying, air firing and low level bombing.

Douglas explained to me one of the design faults of the Blenheim was the position of the flying controls, the Blenheim had two spade-type grips that were side by side and one just in front of the other. One of these grips raised and lowered the undercarriage while the other did them same to the flaps. After landing a Blenheim and before taxiing in, the pilot was supposed to raise the flaps so as to avoid stone damage and foreign object damage (FOD), which could be caused by thrown up by the draught from the powerful Bristol Mercury engines. "One had to be extremely careful and make sure you pulled the right grip," as many a Blenheim came to grief when the undercarriage was retracted in error.

It wasn't until January 10th 1940 when Douglas saw his first shots fired in anger. He was flying Blenheim P4858 with Sergeant Robertson and Aircraftsman Street on a North Sea sweep when they were attacked by six ME110s that were led by Oberst IG Wolfgang Falck, (who in later years was to become great friends with Douglas). After the Me110 attacks on the 10th January two of 110 Squadrons aircraft were badly shot up but managed to make it back to base, while the third was shot down and exploded on impact hitting the sea. Then when the Germans invaded the Low Countries the squadron was in the thick of things trying to destroy their advanced airfields and fighting vehicles. Douglas explained to me that the Germans were an extremely efficient fighting force and deadly accurate with their 88mm anti-aircraft guns.

The Finland Operation February 23rd 1940

In February 1940 the Ministry of Defense asked for Volunteers to fly twelve Bristol Blenheim Mk1s to Finland that were to be used to attack the Russians. This was to be a highly secret operation and Douglas Cooper was one of those volunteers, this is his story.

The operation from the very start was exciting as the Blenheim Mk1s which were to be used for this task would be drawn from the stocks of No 2 group squadrons stationed at Bicester and Upwood. The transfer was formally made through the Bristol Aircraft Company as Great Britain elected not to be a direct supporter of the Finnish Armed Forces for political reasons (mainly due to Soviet criticism.) The Blenheims would require thirty six crewmembers, made up of Pilots, Observers, and Radio Operators for each aircraft. Douglas' crew was made up of himself, Sergeant Robertson and Leading Aircraftsman Swallow. Douglas by this time had flown Blenheims for two years and was sufficiently experienced to carry out this long ferry flight of 1020 Miles. All of the crews were

provided with winter flying gear, civilian clothes, passport, life vest and raft, suitable rations, overcoat, suitcase, and a minimum of £5 in sterling and all pilots received £50 for emergency use only. Their aircraft was similarly supplied with signal equipment for British Admiralty codes for crossing the North Sea. For flights over the British Isles civilian register G-EZAA (2) to G-EZAA (13) codes were provided for radio communication. It was ordered that use of the radio be kept at a minimum and ground station calls were prohibited by station names rather using only a code, otherwise Fighter Command would send up their own fighters to intercept. This was the main reason the Blenheims were given Finnish Civil codes (unarmed weapons were disassembled and stored in the aircraft). Douglas' aircraft took off from Bicester on 23rd February at 1940 hrs and headed for RAF Dyce in Scotland. All flying was carried out at 5,000ft using IFR procedures and all the aircraft reached Dyce without any problems, the flight took almost 3hrs.30mins in perfect flying conditions. The crew's night ended at Dyce and after a good breakfast the next morning they took off using Aberdeen as there turning point over the sea and using Perth radio beacons to give necessary bearings. As they approached the coast of Norway, Stavanger radio frequencies were tuned into the Sola beacon, all the aircraft arrived safely and the flight was made without any problems taking just 2hrs.50mins again in perfect weather. The crews were all put up in the Hotel Hummmeren in Tananger for the night.

The next leg of the journey planned to fly in a straight line to Finland, when they arrived over the airfield at Vasteras in Sweden they circled for two hours waiting for recognition, which didn't come, with the Blenheims becoming low on fuel it was decided to land all twelve aircraft anyway. The crews were night stopped once more and on the morning of the 26th February they were joined by three Finnish Pilots who would assist as Navigators for the final leg into Finland. The names of the Finnish crews were Captain Armas Eskola, Lieutenants Onni-Pesola and Jouko Wartiovaara and who would also be flying the new Blenheims against the Russians.

The twelve Blenheims took off early on the 26th from Vasturas and set their heading for the operational base at Juka Jarva that was near Mikkeli, arriving safely 2hr.35mins later. This was a unique experience for the British crews as they never had to land on a frozen lake before and as their Blenheims weighed almost seven Metric Tons, I am sure they felt a little bit uneasy. All twelve Blenheims landed safely and the crews were accommodated in various houses that were dotted around the lake and the next day they were brought to Helsinki and were given VIP treatment. After a few days each crewmember was presented with a traditional Finnish fur hat and knife, both of which Douglas still cherishes to this day. They were also given fifty cigarettes each, which were like gold dust to the Finns as the Russians had just blown up their last cigarette Factory. Douglas and the crews visited various places of interest in Helsinki, one of which was a Military Museum; they were shown shelves upon shelves of Russian helmets and each one having a bullet hole in it. They all enjoyed the kind hospitality of the Finns but it was now time to return to the UK. On the 28th February they were picked up at their Hotel and taken by bus to Helsinki airport where they boarded a Finnish Airline Junkers JU52, which flew them to Stockholm in Sweden. On their arrival at Stockholm they were taken to the British Embassy and informed that they would have to wait until the 6th March when an aircraft would arrive to fly them back to the UK. They had quite an enjoyable stay at the Embassy; while they were there they met some British Nurses who were waiting for their ambulances to arrive which would take them to the Finnish Front. Douglas commented to me, "They were all top bracket stuff," and were under the charge of a right 'Old Battle Axe' called Lady Runciman who kept them like Nuns.

Douglas and the lads approached Lady Runciman one evening and politely asked if they could take the girls out for the evening while they were in Stockholm and to their surprise she agreed.

Lady Runston was heard to remark, "They must be nice boys, we met them at the Embassy."

Douglas gave me a great laugh and said, "Little did she know."

On the 6th March 1940 a Junkers JU52 code G-AERX arrived to pick Douglas and the rest of the Blenheim crews and fly them back to Perth in Scotland via Oslo and Stavanger. When the got onboard the aircraft they found that all the seats had been taken out and the windows painted black, which meant they had to sit on the floor for the duration of the flight. It was not until 1992 that the Finnish Embassy in London officially notified Douglas that he was to be awarded the Finnish Medal of Winter War for his efforts in 1940. The award was also given to two other crewmembers, RR Trew and J Fancy. The Award ceremony took place at the Finnish Embassy in London on 4th June 1992.

The twelve Blenheims that were delivered to the Finnish Air Force during February 1940 suffered different fates.

BL-144 was destroyed in the Winter War 1940; the other ten were destroyed between 1941 and 1944.

BL-142 was damaged by straffing from Soviet fighters but was repaired, and on January 20th 1942 the crew abandoned BL-142 when its skis broke loose which would prevent a safe landing.

The pilot-less aircraft circled around nicely by itself, and the three man crew descending by parachute witnessed a beautiful landing by the aircraft below them that carefully avoided all buildings and obstacles.

BL-142 was dubbed the 'Lucky' one after that and went on to survive the war until she made her last flight on 9th September 1946 and was eventually scrapped in September 1952.

When Douglas and the crews returned to Bicester they were given a few days leave. His Logbook shows that he carried two further operations before the end of March one of which was reconnaissance flight to the important German Luftwaffe Seaplane Base at Sylt on the 22nd March.

Douglas arrived over the target in N-6214 at 8,000ft only to find it obscured by cloud, so Douglas informed his crew that he was going to dive down and hopefully break through the cloud at 1,000ft. He put the Blenheim into a steep dive and down they went passing, 5,000ft, 4,000ft, 3,000ft, 2,000ft, 1,000ft, 500ft and still no sign of breaking through the cloud, Douglas thought it was time to pull out of this dive which he very quickly did. A nervous voice soon crackled in his earpiece, it was his observer Sergeant Robertson, "Hey Skipper, our tail has just touched the sea." At the end of March 1940 Douglas was given two weeks leave, returning on the 15th April to take part in some W/T practice. He carried out one operation in April and that was on the 25th to bomb shipping in Hardanger Fiord.

110 Squadron lost one aircraft that day L8750 VE-that was piloted by Sergeant Priestly who was tasked to attack shipping in Gransvin Fiord. The other members of the crew were Sergeant WT Howells and Leading Aircraftsman RA Roberts. Sergeant Howells is buried in Sondre Nissum Churchyard Denmark; his two companions have no known Grave.

Maastrict bridges May 1940

At that particular time it was extremely difficult to get an accurate picture of what was happening at Maastrict, there was undoubtedly a very serious threat from the Germans and air support was urgently needed. British Air Forces in France (BAFF) had repeatedly asked for air strikes from Bomber Command. 110 Squadron was put on full alert and suitably briefed.

On 11th May at 1450 hrs took off in Blenheim L9217 with his observer Sergeant Robertson and air gunner Leading Aircraftsman Simpson. Douglas was the leader of 12 Blenheims and their objective was to bomb the German controlled bridges at Maastrict. If the bridges could be destroyed it would stop or slow down the German advance. The twelve Blenheims crossed the North Sea and then turned towards the Belgium countryside, flying at 3,000ft. Just before they reached Recklein, Douglas noticed black puffs of smoke in the sky in front of him; he said laughingly, "They looked quite harmless." (This was the first but not the last time that he had encountered flak.) When they arrived over Maastrict, they were met with an intense barrage of anti-aircraft fire and came under attack from enemy fighters, only one of the Blenheims managed to get back undamaged. Douglas was awarded the Distinguished Flying Cross for his part in the attack and his Observer was awarded the Distinguished Flying Medal for the valuable photographs that he took during the attack. His

Gunner Leading Aircraftsman Simpson was promoted soon after to Sergeant.

The quiet and modest Douglas remarked to me, "I thought the chaps who came behind me should have got the 'Gongs' as my aircraft was the only one without a bullet hole in it." On May 22nd and 24th Douglas attacked the German columns advancing on Boulogne, on returning to base on the 24th he had to belly land his Blenheim due to a large hole in his wing caused by flak that damaged his hydraulics and left him without undercarriage or flaps. On the 26th, 28th 30th and 31st May he attacked enemy positions at St Pols, Hesdin Wood, Eperculques Forest, St Omer, and Nieuport. All these operations were in support of the Allied troops who had fallen back to Dunkirk. Between these hectic days the 22nd to the 31st May 110 Squadron lost one aircraft which was shot down by flak near Abbeyville killing its crew, a second returned to base with its undercarriage shot away.

In June 1940 he carried out similar operations at St Andeleys and June 3rd saw the end of the Dunkirk evacuation. He also successfully bombed Schipol and Merville airfields that were now in enemy hands.

I would like to point out just how hectic things were at that time, between the 7th and 13th June 1940 Blenheims of 2 Group attacked German targets in Northern France every day, 355 sorties were flown with the loss of 23 Blenheims.

Flight Lieutenant Douglas Cooper and his crew had now completed 30 operations with 110 Squadron and were subsequently given a well-earned rest.

Douglas was posted to No 13 Operational Training Unit at Bicester on the 24th June where he was to become an instructor on Blenheims. On the 26th, 27th, 28th, June he started his 'short' conversion course at Bicester to become an instructor under the guidance of Flight Lieutenant Redgrave, Sergeant Williams, Pilot Officer Yarrow and the Chief Flying Instructor (CFI) a Wing Commander Knight.

He told me that being an instructor in those days was a somewhat hazardous occupation, mainly because trainees kept forgetting to put their undercarriage down. Douglas started Instructing on Blenheims at Bicester in early July 1940 and continued until the 20th February 1941, save for being attached to a Fairey Battle flight at Squires Gate for two weeks in September 1940 to train gunners in the art of air firing.

Experienced Pilots found the Blenheim Mk1V a delight to fly but it was quite a handful for someone who only had under 50 hours total flying time and with no night experience whatever. Douglas had clocked up over 100 hours Instructing at the OTU before he was recalled back into operational flying with 21 Squadron with immediate effect 20th February 1941.

So on the 21st February 1941 Douglas was posted back onto operations again with 21 Squadron at Watton in Norfolk, and was immediately paired up with his 110 Squadron crewmembers Sergeant Robertson and Sergeant Simpson.

Brief history of 21 Squadron

21 Squadron was formed at Netheravon in Wiltshire on 23rd July 1915 and went to France in January 1916 and was equipped with RE7 aircraft. In February/March 1917 was re-equipped with the RE8. In 1918 the squadron was personally congratulated by the then General Trenchard for the best artillery spotting squadron in France. The squadron was disbanded in October 1918 and was reformed as a bomber squadron at Bircham Newton in December 1935 and was equipped with the Hawker Hind two seater aircraft. By the time war had broken out the squadron had moved to Watton in Norfolk. During the early part of the war, 21 Squadron was equipped with Blenheim 1Vs and it played a prominent role in No 2 Groups offensive against shipping in the English Channel and North Sea. The squadron moved to Malta in December 1941 and in late 1942 was flying Lockheed Venturas. In September 1943 the squadron was to be equipped with Mosquitos and took part in the raid against the Gestapo Headquarters in Aarhus in Denmark and later the Gestapo Headquarters in Copenhagen. It also carried out a very successful raid against the V-Weapon sites at Bois Coquerie, and at the end of the war operated as a courier service between Furth Airfield in Nurenburg and Blackbushe during the period of the Nazi war criminal trials.

When Douglas joined 21 Squadron in February 1941 he was delighted to find out that its commanding officer was another Irish man, a Wing Commander Miles Villiers Delap who actually lived just across the Irish Border from Douglas in Ramelton County Donegal. Wing Commander Delap was credited with the sinking of the first German U-Boat (U-31) by the Royal Air Force (bomber command) [another story].

Douglas' first flight with the squadron was on the 21st February; he took off with his crew Sergeant Robertson and Sergeant Simpson to take part in some flying training just to get into the way of things and to become a formidable team once more.

In March they started night raids.

Log entries for March

March 2nd	Bombed	Rotterdam (oil tanks)
March 12th	Bombed	Hamburg (Blohm & Voss shipyard)
March 13th	Bombed	Bremen (Focke-Wulf aircraft factory)
March 21st	Bombed	Lorient (U-Boat base)
March 31st	Bombed	Terschelling

In April they started to attack shipping which Douglas said was really 'suicidal stuff', on April 8th they were carrying out a fringe attack on Nordency when they were attacked by two Me110s, his Gunner (who had been promoted) Flight Sergeant Simpson managed to shoot down one of the attackers while the other one escaped.

Log entries for April

April 4th Sweep of Lorient (attacked and hit Trawler 400 Tons)

April 6th Sweep of Hague (bombs dropped on a wreck)

April 8th Fringe attack on Nordency (attacked by two Me110s destroyed one (and one escaped)

April 10th Sweep on Lorient (near miss with 4 x 250lb bombs on trawler)

April 13th Attack on Flushing (bombs dropped on docks)

April 14th Attack on Haarlem (low level attack on power house)

April 24th Sweep on LeHarve (no bombs dropped)

In May they carried out six operations, during one of these operations; while attacking a Convoy of Heligoland, they themselves were attacked by two Me 109s. During the attack one of the 109s shot down a 21 squadron that crashed into the sea. There were no survivors.

Log entries for May

May 6th 4 x 250lb bombs dropped on 5,000 ton ship

May 8th Bombed Bremerhaven

May 13th Sweep of Holland (no bombs dropped)

May 15th Attacked a convoy of Heligoland (attacked by two Me109s one A/C missing)

May 21st High level attack on oil refinery with fighter escort (all bombs dropped on target area)

May 24th Hits gained on 2,500 ton ship

Log entries for June

June 7th Returned to base (weather U/S)

June 19th Day ops with fighter escort

June 23rd Day ops with fighter escort

June 26th Day ops with fighter escort

June 27th Bombed power station

That Fateful Day July 1st 1941.

Last Log Entry.

July 1st Attack on the Keil Canal (failed to return)

On the 1st July 1941 Douglas and his crew Flight Sergeant Robertson and Flight Sergeant Simpson were briefed in the Operations Room at Watton.

Douglas was to lead a formation of three aircraft from 21 Squadron, as Tail End Section of another Squadron to bomb and sink shipping in the Kiel Canal and block it. At the briefing they were told by the Met Officer that there would be cloud cover over the target, and if there was not they were to turn back. At 0830 hrs on the morning of the 1st July Douglas and the other two Blenheims from 21 Squadron taxied out for take off, Douglas took off first, but the other two aircraft went U/S and he was on his own.

Shortly after take off he located and joined another squadron that was going to the same target and it wasn't long before he spotted them tagged on as tail end Charlie. On their way to the target they were informed by the Met people that they would not get cloud cover before arriving at point 'X'. However before they got to point 'X' the squadron in front of him turned around for home. Douglas did not have great faith in the Met people, so he talked it over with his crew and decided to continue on to the target and see if the Met people were right. "For once they were right," there was cloud cover. He could not find a ship to sink, but spotted a bridge over the canal and decided to bomb it instead. He attacked the bridge from 1,000ft and made the mistake of coming around to see if his bombs had hit the target. The Germans had spotted him and opened up with their 88s. One of the Flak Batteries that was on the bridge hit Douglas' aircraft, shooting the hell out of his flying controls and wounding him in the leg. He admits himself that he should have known that every bridge in Germany would by now have its own Flak Battery.

With his flying controls gone, Douglas gave the order to his crew to bale out, Douglas himself managed to get out okay but Sergeant Robertson's parachute must have opened prematurely and became entangled in the tail of the Blenheim. Flight Sergeant Simpson was killed by the Flak.

Flight Sergeant Robertson, DFM and Flight Sergeant Simpson are buried in Hamburg.

Douglas was quite low when he exited the aircraft; his parachute had just opened when he landed on the bank of the canal. The Germans had watched his decent and were waiting for him; he released his parachute harness and tried to stand up but collapsed due to his severe leg wound.

The Germans tried to help him to his feet, but Douglas was having none of this and said, "Bugger you," and shook them off, in doing so he collapsed again in pain. He finally gave in and let the Germans carry him to the gun emplacement that had just shot him down and laid him on a table to await medical assistance. He searched his pockets for a cigarette and his Dunhill lighter; he found his packet of cigarettes but no lighter, so he thought it must have fallen out of his pocket when he hit the ground. Douglas could not speak a word of German, but fortunately one of the Guards could speak French, so he somehow was able to explain to him what had happened to his lighter, that it could be lying somewhere near to where he landed on the bank. The Germans sent out a search party to look for it, and they did eventually find the lighter and returned it to him. However the next place he was moved to the Dunhill lighter was taken from him and he never saw it again. While he was waiting for medical assistance to come the

Germans offered him some food that consisted of German sausage and sour kraut. This he refused, but as he said himself, "If it had have been offered to me one week later, I would have scoffed the lot without hesitation." When medical assistance eventually came he was taken to a hospital in Hamburg where he was treated very well. The ward was crammed full of French occupants, one of whom was like a skeleton offered Douglas with a razor and shaving brush. The French man showed Douglas a photograph of himself that had been taken a few months earlier it showed him fit and healthy and said his weight loss was due to forced labour on the German roads. When he was fit to leave the Hamburg hospital he was taken to Dulag Luft at Oberusel that was a reception centre for Prisoners of War, and put into another hospital along with several other prisoners who had been badly hurt.

One of the badly injured was a young Fighter Pilot who had his face badly burned, Douglas said it was a terrible sight and felt very sorry for him. Another chap had a severe case DTs (alcoholic) and he was in a very bad way, so much so he ripped a hand basin from the wall and flung it out the window. Douglas said there were some terrible cases in that ward.

From there he was taken to Lubeck on the Baltic and put into a Prisoner of War (POW) camp sick quarters. There he said food was very short and everyone was starving, he had his eye on an old stray cat that he hoped to 'knock off' and eat, but someone else from another hut beat him to it. The liquid they were given to drink was mint tea, "terrible stuff." Every now and again Red Cross parcels would be delivered to the sick quarters but at first the Germans refused to issue them to the sick, but eventually did so. When Douglas received his first Red Cross parcel and opened it he found inside a tin of sardines and found that the empty tin made quite a good frying pan. In the bed next to Douglas was an army chap who had been watching him attentively and said, "Christ now that was clever."

Oflag V1B Kassel

POW camp near Frankfurt. Here he met a lot of army bods who had been taken prisoner at Dunkirk and who had been in the camp for some time. There were between 500 and 600 Air Force prisoners in the camp, one of whom was the intrepid Wing Commander Douglas Bader, whom we knew about very well now and who gave the Germans a hell of a time. Douglas told me that the POWs got up to some of the craziest things; he explained that there had been drainage ditches dug all around the camp and when it rained they would become raging torrents senior officers would come and race little paper boats down these just to relieve the boredom and place bets on who would win.

The tunnel that never was

The tunnel that never was, was the brainchild of Flight Lieutenant Robert James McConnell, another Ulsterman from Omagh (sadly Flight Lieutenant McConnell died in

July 1992). Douglas' hut was bang in the middle of the camp, where there was always lots of 'industrial' noise to be heard, sawing, hammering, banging, shouting was going on all the time making bits and pieces that the Germans were well aware of. Tunnels were being dug everywhere; the place was like a rabbit warren. So Bobby McConnell, Douglas and the rest of their hut decided to construct a tunnel that started right under Douglas' bed. They dug a vertical shaft down about ten feet that was made into a bell shaped chamber, they then dug a horizontal shaft that sloped slightly uphill going towards the perimeter fence wire that was about 100 yards away. The horizontal shaft was about 25ft long and when they came to the end of it they dug down vertically three feet and started digging the main tunnel horizontally again towards the perimeter fence. There was a team of about seventy blokes working on the tunnel and they theory was that if the Germans did find out about the tunnel they would only see about 25ft it and a dead end. The team had made up a little trolley on wheels that was pulled up and down the tunnel bringing the soil from the tunnel face that was then distributed under the floor of the hut via another railway line. These chaps were very well organised, they had electric light the whole way down the tunnel and when they eventually ran out of wire, they had an ingenious way of obtaining some more. There was a Tannoy system that went all around the camp, so what the team did was to position a bod at each pole and at dusk one evening they cut the wire from each pole. Had this tunnel gone to plan Douglas reckons that half the camp would have escaped; unfortunately during July and August torrential rain poured down on the camp the ground was flooded and began to sink. The blokes tried to disguise the great hollow by cutting sods and using them as sun beds, but alas, it was no use as the tunnel was discovered by a German officer who brought along some soldiers with probes.

When they eventually found the tunnel entrance under Douglas' bed they shone a torch down it and there was Squadron Leader Armitage standing stark naked with water up to his chest. Someone said politely, "Don't you think you had better come up Mr Armitage?" "Yes," came the reply, "I think I better had." When Mr Armitage had vacated the tunnel the Germans went down to inspect it, and of course all they saw was a dead end and remarked, "Crazy bloody Englishmen." What the Germans would do if they found a tunnel was to bring the 'Honey Bucket' round and dump its contents into the tunnel. Now during one of these dumpings, some wag had written in chalk on the side of it "Deutches Culture". A short time later a high ranking German officer had arrived to inspect the camp; he spotted the writing on the Honey Wagon and took an extremely dim view of this. He came along to where Douglas and the lads were sunbathing stark naked and started to blow his top, ordering them to stand up, but they refused until guns were drawn as a bunch of naked guys stood smartly to attention, Douglas said you never saw a funnier sight in your life.

Shubin Oflag XX1B, Poland

They eventually left Kassel and were taken to a POW camp in Poland where they stayed for a short time. (The Germans kept moving them about.) Shubin had been originally a girl's school that was a big improvement to Kassel; tomatoes were growing everywhere, beautiful gardens, etc.

It was at Shubin they met the Gestapo for the first time, and the reason for them being there was because there had been a daring and brilliant escape by some Czechs and Poles wearing gas masks who had jumped into a Honey Wagon just before it rolled through the camp gates. There were at least eight other Ulstermen at Shubin, Pilot Officer McConnell from Omagh, Flight Lieutenant KW MacKenzie DFC from Enniskillen, Pilot Officer Brown from Belfast, Pilot Officer Thallan from Holywood, Pilot Officer R.S. Ayton DFM* from Londonderry, Pilot Officer Buckley and Pilot Officer Hanna both from Belfast.

Stalag Luft 111, Sagan

From Shubin Douglas was sent to Stalag Luft 111 that was just outside the town of Sagan. Stalag Luft 111 was purpose built by the Germans for Air Force personnel only and usually held around 3,000 POWs.

Douglas was billeted in the East Compound of the Camp where the famous 'Wooden Horse' was built. He was personally involved with this project helping to make the tools, saws were made out of gramophone springs, bolts taken from the hut windows made very fine chisels, and lots of other bits and pieces were adapted for various uses.

Authors Note

I think most of you reading this book will know most of the stories that have come from Stalag Luft 111, some are fascinating like the Wooden Horse some are horrific when after The Great Escape the Germans murdered 50 of its inmates just to prove a point. I am not going elaborate on these except to give you a brief account of Douglas Cooper's experiences but I would suggest if you are interested in the Stalag Luft 111 story, then read "The Stolen Journey" by Oliver Philpot. I asked Douglas how they managed to find the wood to shore up these escape tunnels as I had heard different stories as to how it was done. He explained to me, "We slept in a three tier bunk with a straw filled mattress, each tier had about ten or twelve boards across. Now and again there would be a demand for a few bed boards for the tunnels, so everyone coughed up two or three each. One would end up sleeping in a 'wave' type structure. Some of the blokes came up with some very ingenious ideas to supplement the missing boards by saving the string from their Red Cross parcels, knitting it into a net to fill the spaces in the bunks. The Germans were not stupid and would

come round every now and again and catch this on."

It was not until a few days after the Wooden Horse that the Germans found out that anyone had escaped, as the blokes had devised a brilliant way of fooling them at Roll Call. When they did eventually find out, they were hopping mad, especially when they did not know who was missing. The senior British officer (SBO) was sent for and was ordered to get everyone out of their huts and on parade at 1400 hrs. He refused and told everyone to stay put. One hour later there was still no one on the parade ground. At exactly one minute to 1400 hrs it seemed as if half the German Army converged into the camp complete with tin hat and tommy gun. They surrounded every hut and fired a short burst into each one, when two of the POWs had the audacity to come out, sit down and started to play a game of chess. A highly annoyed German officer walked towards them and removed his gun from its Holster, by now he was frothing at the mouth, at about this time in the adjacent compound a lot of the American blokes were sitting on the roofs of their huts cheering the guys on. Douglas to this day does now know how the German officer restrained himself from shooting the two chess players, because Douglas had no doubt in his mind, that if he had fired one shot, the rest of the Germans being so wound up would have opened fire and there may have been a slaughter. Instead the two chess players were escorted to the 'Cooler' for a few days and the Americans who were sitting on the roof egging things on had a burst of machine gun bullets fired over their heads. They came down a lot quicker than they went up. The senior British officer, who wasn't too bright, told the blokes afterwards, "You know of course, that those were only 'blanks' that the Germans were firing." So some of the lads picked the 'blanks' out of the hut walls and presented them to him. This day was marked by calling it "Tommy Gun Saturday".

One or two stories on the lighter side of things

Douglas' compound did not have its own doctor, so when they needed medical assistance they had to go across to the north compound under escort that was about a half mile walk. He had a cyst on his cheek, which had been removed by an Air Force medical officer but had come back again. So he thought that he would take the opportunity to go and see the north compound and have it removed. He told me that some of the guys had all sorts of mad ideas to relieve the boredom, some would go and have themselves circumcised, some would have their heads shaved, etc. Anyway the day came for Douglas to visit the camp doctor to have his cyst removed; he joined some blokes who had decided to have themselves circumcised. On the way back (you have to remember that some of these blokes had not seen a female for a very long time) they happened to meet a rather young and beautiful blond German Fraulien. Well, you can guess what happened next, their testosterone level rose by about 100% and they all 'limped' back to camp in pure agony.

The lighter side of things

Word got about one day that a very high ranking German officer was about to arrive for an inspection of the camp. So everyone had gathered to watch this. He arrived in typical German style in his Mercedes staff car and drove right into one of the compounds, got out and proceeded with his inspection, leaving his driver in charge of the car. The lads were dying to see what was in the car, so they all moved towards it only to be told by the driver to, "clear off." Their idea now was to somehow get the driver out of the car, what happened next was that some of the blokes gathered up a lot of old newspapers placing them behind one of the compound huts and setting them alight. When the papers were well alight great shouts of "Fire, fire," went up from everywhere, and of course the driver of the staff car got out to see what all the commotion was about. The car was stripped in seconds of every single document that was in it. Now the blokes knew quite well what was going to happen when the officer returned to his car and found these things missing. Sure enough when he returned to his car and saw what had happened, he was furious, and issued an ultimatum that all his documents were not returned within half an hour, "Everyone would suffer the consequences." Eventually all the documents were returned to the officer but not before they were copied and over stamped with the words "Censured by Churchill" by the camp's experts.

This had been a staggering success for the camp and also meant because the documents having been over stamped with Churchill's name the German Officer could never report what happened.

The winter march

In early 1945 all the POWs were marched out of the camp at short notice and were told that were going to Lubeck. The reason for the quick evacuation was Field Marshal Montgomery's army was getting close. It was the middle of winter, the snow was thick on the ground and the conditions could not have been any worse. However, as Douglas said, "Their sense of humour during this arduous and tiring march never faltered." The first day out, they were herded into an old school house in a small village and were made to lay nose to tail with each other and squashed like sardines. A young adventurous Canadian lad decided to nip out past the guards and went down to the village to see if he could scrounge any food. He returned about two hours later with a large continental bread roll over his shoulder and said, "Boys, I have just had a terrific time down in the village, I met a beautiful wee local girl and gave her a bar of chocolate and this is the change." They were marched eastwards for a week and on the way some of the POWs made sleighs to help carry the sick and injured. Unfortunately when the snow melted they had to change the sleighs skis to wheels. Things were pretty grim

for the blokes; they had to scrounge food and water all along the route from the locals and even traded cigarettes for a horse and cart along the way.

Eventually the reached a place called Marlag Nor that had been a naval prison camp, the conditions there were absolutely appalling, and the worst they had come across yet. They were all put into damp, empty concrete floored rooms; their morale by now was very low. Thankfully they did not have to stay at Marlag for very long and were soon marching east again towards Lubeck. By now it was spring of 1945 and the weather was getting a lot warmer, things were so relaxed now, the POWs even carried the guards' guns for them when they got tired. Food was much more plentiful now as they were able to scrounge eggs, butter, and chickens along the route from the locals. Things were at last getting better. The guards knew that Germany was beaten, so they all decided not to go any further, and settled down in an attractive spot in a huge farm area and wait for Montgomery to find them. They were able to listen to the BBC News every day and knew that help was not to far away.

Douglas' repatriation is now a bit vague, but he does remember spending VE Day in Brussels, and to this very day still has no clue how he got there. He also remembers that the troops who did repatriate him had passed through some of the Nazi concentration camps making them very bloody-minded and giving the Germans a very hard time. Douglas was flown back from Germany to RAF Station Cardington around the end of June, beginning of July 1945. As the RAF did not seem interested in retaining anyone who was an ex-POW, except possibly for administration jobs, Douglas decided he did not want to stay under those circumstances so he opted to be de-mobbed. He was issued with his de-mob kit, which consisted of a pinstripe suit, hat, gloves, shoes and money that was owed to him while he was a POW in Germany.

When Douglas was taken prisoner in July 1941 all his personal effects were taken away from him including a pair of solid gold cuff-links that he cherished as they were given to him by a very close friend. When he arrived back a letter was waiting for him, which was addressed and sent via the Red Cross:

From HQ AEF Paris to WD Liverpool
S/Ldr HDH Cooper 39499
Safe at home in Ireland
No 21 Sqdn Watton. Norfolk.
Blenheim 1V V 6399
3601 9/41
1.7.41.

Also on the front of this letter were two Nazi postmarks. Inside the envelope was a German receipt for his gold cuff links that was dated, Lubeck September 1941 and signed by Douglas. I am sure you readers are dying to know; yes the gold cuff links were still inside.

He returned to the family home in Strabane, where his father who was a brilliant photographer and owned the local Cinema called the 'Commodore' had decided to retire and hand over the reins to Douglas. His father was also a director of three cinemas in Belfast, The Troxy, Lido, and the Duncairn. When his father died, Douglas left his entire collection of 40,000 photographs to the Public Records Office in Belfast.

Douglas himself is now retired and living life to the full, he was a keen golfer until recently and enjoys working in his very large garden and is also a member of the Aircrew Association Northern Ireland Branch

Oberst Wolfgang Falck

I mentioned in an earlier paragraph that Douglas had met Wolfgang Falck in combat on the 10th January 1940 and that they would meet again under happier circumstances. But first let me give you a brief resume on the man himself. Wolfgang Falck was born in Berlin in 1910, and joined the army in 1931. In 1932 he transferred to the Luftwaffe as a Fighter Pilot and was trained in Lipezk in Russia for six months and then a further two years as an instructor in a flying school. He was then posted to Jagdgeshwader Richthofen as Adjutant, later becoming Staffelkapitan of 8. /JG 132. He flew with this Unit during the Polish Campaign. He was later responsible for 'inventing' the night fighter system and soon after Field Marshal Goring made him the youngest Group Commander in the Luftwaffe. In July 1943 he worked on the Staff of the Luftflotte Reich where he was responsible for a number of tasks, one was the setting up of the Auxiliary Night Fighter Units on the Eastern Front and the setting up of the defence of the Romanian oil fields. In the autumn of 1944 he

became the officer in charge of night fighter operations and was Colonel on the General Staff and made responsible for the Air Defence of Germany. In the winter of 1944 he became head of staff for flying training. After the war he joined the ranks of North American Aviation as their Aviation Consultant for Germany, and after working for them for six years he changed to McDonnell Douglas as their Consultant for Germany and Australia where he stayed until he was 75 and a half years old. On the 8th February 1993 Wolfgang wrote a letter to Douglas introducing himself to him by way of, "We met 53 years ago when I tried to shoot you down on the 10th January 1940," and that he was delighted to have obtained his address, as he would like to meet Douglas in person.

Douglas was delighted to receive Wolfgang's letter and of course could not believe that this old advisory would take the time to contact him. He wrote back immediately saying that he would very much like to meet him. So later in 1993 Douglas and his wife Betty travelled to St Ulrich in Austria to meet Wolfgang and his partner Gisela where they had a wonderful time. In 1997 Douglas invited Wolfgang and his wife to visit them in Strabane, and during their visit they were both invited to meet Group Captain Brian Freeman (Senior RAF Officer Northern Ireland) at Royal Air Force Station Aldergrove. A visit I know they both thoroughly enjoyed.

Douglas and Betty returned to visit Wolfgang in October 1998 and while he was there he was honoured when he was asked to lay a wreath jointly with Wolfgang at the International Flyers Memorial in Strasburg.

WING COMMANDER
BRIAN GEORGE CORRY, OBE DFC

ROYAL AIR FORCE NO. 90003
PILOT
NO. 502 (ULSTER) AUXILIARY AIR FORCE SQUADRON

Wing Commander BG Corry, OBE DFC, was born in 1909 and was educated at Campbell College on the Belmont Road in Belfast.

He was an extremely keen all-round sportsman and excelled himself in Sailing, golf (he was a member of the winning team of the Belfast and District Cup Match that was held in Holywood County Down in 1935). He was also a very proficient motorcyclist, winning the Ulster Grand Prix 350cc handicap race at a speed of 72.65mph on a Velocette. He was also winner of the Knock Motor Cycle Club speed championship in 1928 in Minerstown, County Down on a Matchless and in 1930 won the Temple 60 on his 350cc Velocette reaching speeds of 59.1mph. On leaving College he became an apprentice with the firm of McLaughlin and Harvey and in 1933 joined the 502 (Ulster) Special Reserve Squadron at Aldergrove. He had his first flight in 1933 in an Avro 504N, the Captain of the aircraft was a Wing Commander Brew. In 1937 he was involved in a serious crash in his Hawker Hind at Aldergrove when it clipped the top of a radio mast and crashed within feet of his own quarters, so close in fact that the fuel from it ran down into his room. He made a miraculous escape sustaining a fractured skull, serious pelvis and facial injuries. His air gunner was not so fortunate and regrettably was killed in the crash. One of Wing Commander Corry's shoes which his son still has to this day were badly mangled and crumpled in the crash, yet he had no injuries what so ever to his foot.

At the outbreak of war, Wing Commander Corry insisted on returning to active service and transferred to the Royal Auxiliary Air Force. On the 1st February 1940 he was posted the Central Flying School at Upavon for flying training and given a ground reconnaissance and war course, which he completed by the 17th May 1940. He returned to 502 Squadron (at that time based at Limavady) at the end of May and his duties there were primarily anti-submarine patrols in Ansons.

His flying log book shows that on the 21st August 1940 he was flying in Anson 5216 with Aircraftsman Cornish, Flying Officer Worthington and Sergeant

Robertson on an anti-submarine patrol when they spotted and flew over an enemy submarine dropping parachute flares onto it. In August 1940 he was posted to Abbingdon where he completed a conversion course onto Whitleys and then on to Prestwick for one month as an instructor on Whitleys.

Some interesting Logbook entries for 1940 and 1941

8th October in Anson 5008 with Pilot Officer Longhurst and crew, "Search for Whitley of 102 Squadron."

29th October 1940 in Whitley 5052 with Pilot Officer Parke and crew, "Attacked and destroyed" a submarine with 4 x 250lb bombs on its stern *(this was one of the first U-Boats sank by Coastal Command since the out break of war)*.

15th November 1940 in Whitley 5049 with Flight Lieutenant Rees and crew. While on an, "Anti-submarine patrol." their aircraft was hit by a shell from an American Destroyer.

28th March 1941 in Whitley E6553 with Pilot Officer Howard Jones, while on an anti-submarine sweep attacked suspicious oil streak with two 500lb bombs with no result.

29th March 1941 in Whitley E6553 with Pilot Officer Howard Jones, while on anti-submarine sweep they had engine failure and some of the crew had to bale out at 500ft "All safe."

On this occasion Wing Commander Corry and his crew were on an anti-submarine patrol some 300 miles off the west coast of Ireland when one of its engines failed in gale force winds. The aircraft lost height to the extent that the sea spray was licking its belly.

Wing Commander Corry managed to regain enough height to reach the Irish Coast, just as the remaining engine caught fire. He ordered the crew to bale out and landed the Whitley safely in 'neutral' Eire on the shores of

Lough Melvin. By some incredible coincidence, just as he and his crew made their way across the Moors, he stumbled on a lonely farm house which was the home of a lady who had served as a maid in the Corry house hold and who he remembered very well from his childhood. The lady also remembered him; she warmed and fed them before they made their 'escape' over the Border into County Fermanagh. Only then did the Wing Commander remember the special 'secret' equipment that had been left behind in the cockpit of the Whitley and in a 'neutral' country, which was riddled with spies. He managed to 'borrow' some civilian clothes and returned alone to the stricken aircraft and destroyed the secret equipment before returning to the North for a second time.

On the 1st July Wing Commander Corry was awarded the Distinguished Flying Cross.

On the 15th August 1941 Wing Commander Corry's logbook shows that he had been assessed as 'above the average'. On the 7th August 1941 he was posted to the Royal Air Force College at Cranwell No 3 Operational Training Unit where he became the Chief Flying Instructor on Oxford, Whitley and Wellingtons, instructing pilots who would later join 502, 612 and 221 Squadrons. On the 15th April 1942 Wing Commander Corry was appointed Controller of No 16 Group visiting various stations in a Tiger Moth. His log book shows that on the 22nd June when he was flying from Cranwell to Cromer he had to make an emergency landing in a field as he was out of petrol. He remained as Controller of 16 Group until the 29th February 1943 when he posted to RAF Silloth to complete a five day conversion course onto Lockheed Hudsons.

On the 20th January 1943 Wing Commander Corry took command of 279 Squadron at Bircham Newton and was equipped with the Lockheed Hudson Mk 111, V and V1. 279 Squadron was formed at Bircham Newton on the 16th November 1941 as an Air Sea Rescue Squadron and its task was to drop specialised boats and equipment to crews who were unlucky enough to be downed in the sea. It was the first ASR Squadron to be fitted with the airborne lifeboats. Some of this specialised equipment was called the Lindholme Gear, this was an elaborate system of life rafts that could be dropped to survivors providing a wide range of necessities.

Some interesting log book entries

On the 8th March in a Lockheed Ventura conducted an ASR search for a Hudson.

On the 15th arch in a Lockheed Hudson carried out a test of 'Walter' in dinghy.

On the 22nd March carried out a demonstration of a Lifeboat at Cranwell OTU.

On the 26th July in Hudson he dropped an airborne boat to a Fortress 40 miles off Cromer Coast. "All rescued." *(This was the first airborne boat to be dropped in operations made to a stricken crew.)*

On the 27th July in Hudson he located a Danish trawler with an Airborne boat on deck and, "Completed rescue."

On the 31st August in a Hudson he completed an Air Sea Rescue search for Danish Trawlers. "Nine found by search."

Wing Commander Corry went on to carry out many air sea rescues with 279 Squadron and with his crew was undoubtedly responsible for saving hundreds of lives. As well his ASR duties he was responsible for testing and demonstrating many various types of lifeboats and crafts. On the 1st March 1944 he became Senior Controller of No 16 Group and part of his duty there was to take part in the testing of new cannons, which were being fitted to Beaufighters and Mosquitos.

Awards and decorations

Wing Commander Corry was awarded the Distinguished Flying Cross on the 1st July 1941. The Order of the British Empire (OBE) by King George V1 on the cessation of hostilities and was twice Mentioned in Despatches.

He flew over 1,500 hours in 40 different types of aircraft during his flying career that included: Avro 504N; Vickers Virginia; Westland Wallace; Hawker Hart; Hawker Hind; Avro Anson; Harvard; Fairey Battle; Bristol Blenheim; Hawker Hurricane; Blackburn Botha; Tiger Moth; Moth Minor; Supermarine Spitfire; Lockheed Hudson; Lockheed Ventura; Boeing Fortress (B-17); Westland Wapiti; Avro Tutor; Whitley; DH 84. Bristol Blenheim; Lysander; Miles Magister; Hend Heck; Handley Page Hampden; Me108 (captured); Tomahawk; Whitney Strait; Wellington; Oxford; Monospar; P & P Hector; Avro Lancaster; Warwick; Percival Proctor; Miles Martinet; De Havilland Mosquito; Bristol Beaufighter; Miles Mentor; and Domine.

He flew both Fighters and Bombers, which included a captured Messerschmitt 108 (he was one of the few British pilots to fly the captured 108). After leaving the Royal Air Force in 1945 he spent five years with the engineering firm of AW Hamilton & Co in Belfast and in 1951 joined the family business of JB Corry & Co on the Springfield Road as its Managing Director. Wing Commander Brian George Corry, OBE DFC died in July 1973 and is survived by his two sons Roger and Clive Corry who I am indebted to for all the help with there father Royal Air Force career.

GROUP CAPTAIN
ROBERT TERENCE CORRY, OBE
PILOT
ROYAL AIR FORCE
NO. 502 (ULSTER) AUXILIARY AIR FORCE SQUADRON

Robert Terence Corry the older brother of Wing Commander BG Corry was born in 1911 and was educated at Campbell College on the Belmont Road in Belfast.

He was an outstanding all round sportsman, extremely good rugby player and was on the team for the Schools 1st Fifteen for Ulster. In addition to Rugby he excelled as a heavyweight boxer and boxed for the Ulster Amateur Championships and was a member of the Northern Ireland Cricket and Football team where he achieved fame by winning the All Ireland Bateman Cup. He was also a keen yachtsman and tennis player. On leaving college he joined the family business of JB Corry and Co, which was situated on the Springfield Road on the outskirts of Belfast.

In 1933 like his brother he joined 502 (Ulster) Special Reserve Squadron at RAF Aldergrove and four days before the outbreak of war he was granted a permanent Commission by King George V1 and promoted to Squadron Leader. In early 1940 he opened up the new Limavady Coastal Command Station in County Londonderry. The runways of the new airfield where first used by Whitleys of 'A' Flight 502 (Ulster) Squadron on December 4th 1940. The squadron was equipped with the new long range ASV Radar. The airfield had a range of hills in its circuit, the highest being Binevenagh at 1,260ft. It was not surprising that the crews referred to the heights as 'Ben Twitch'.

In early 1944 he was promoted to Wing Commander and posted to join the Banff Strike Wing in Scotland, which was under the Command of Group Captain Max Aitken. At one time his six Squadron Commanders were made up of an Englishman, an Australian, a New Zealander, a Norwegian, a Frenchman and an Irishman (Wing Commander Corry). Wing Commander Corry's Squadron took part in the famous "Dallachy Shipping Strike" on the 5th April 1945 when 24 Beaufighters accompanied by 14 Mustangs from Dallachy made an almost impossible attack on shipping in a Norwegian Fjord. The enemy ships were anchored tight against the cliff face at either end of the Fjord necessitating a steep dive to hit the ships.

In 1944 one of his aircraft crashed on landing with a live torpedo onboard; the aircraft burst into flames and in attempting to save the Pilot, Wing Commander Corry was severely burned and rushed to hospital.

He was promoted to the rank of Group Captain at the age of thirty-two which made him the youngest to hold that rank at Coastal Command. Group Captain Corry was 'Mentioned in Despatches' five times and awarded the Order of the British Empire (OBE). On leaving the Royal Air Force he returned to the family company where he became Chairman. His service to the Company started in 1928 and had only been broken by the war years.

He was elected to the Belfast Harbour Commissioners in 1960 and was Vice Chairman of the Territorial Army Volunteer Reserve. He was also a past member and Chairman of the works committee of the Royal Victoria Hospital and was made Deputy Lieutenant for the City of Belfast.

FLYING OFFICER
ALBERT CRAIG
ROYAL AIR FORCE NO. 1796326
AIR GUNNER
No. 77 SQUADRON

Flying Officer Albert 'Paddy' Craig was born in Dunmurry on the 24th January 1922 and was educated at Fane Street Primary School and Methody College on the Lisburn Road Belfast. On leaving college, Albert was employed for seven years at Hewitt's of Sandy Row in Belfast (no relation). On the 17th March 1943 (St Patrick's Day) he decided to join the Royal Air Force and became an Air Gunner.

He was posted to the Air Crew Reception Centre in London a few weeks later to await selection that was to take about two weeks. He was then posted to Initial Training Wing (ITW) at Bridlington to commence his six weeks basic training and to be kitted out. On completion of his initial training he was posted to No 4 Air Gunnery School at Morpeth which is near Newcastle-upon-Tyne. The gunnery training at the school was very interesting and consisted of instruction on all types of power assisted turrets both .303 and .5 Browning. He was also trained on the use of Pyrotechnics. He had his first air experience flight in a Martinet on the 14th June 1943 and on the 5th July his gunnery training started on Blackburn Bothas.

Having successfully completed the gunnery course in July 1943 Albert was awarded his Sergeants stripes and Air Gunner's Brevet. His logbook remarks show that he was 'average' in his theory and 'average' in his air firing. The chief instructor Squadron Leader Simpson added, "A keen worker should do well with more experience."

On the 20th July 1943 He was posted to 'D' Flight, No 20 OTU at Elgin in Scotland to begin his operational training and meet his new crew (minus the engineer). Elgin was a satellite airfield to Lossiemouth and was sometimes referred to as 'Bogs' O'Mayne. His operational training started on the 6th August when he took to the air in Wellington Xl-Q that was under the Command of a Sergeant Dury who would be his Skipper until they completed their first operational tour in September 1944. Operational training continued for the next seven weeks and consisted of X-country, live bombing, air to sea firing and good old circuits and bumps. On the 5th November they left Scotland and came south to 1663 Heavy Conversion

Unit at Rufforth in Yorkshire to start a conversion course onto Halifaxes and met the Flight Engineer.

One 'mishap' that happened during his training was on the 22nd November when he and the crew were taking part in a x-country exercise when the aircraft's port outer engine seized causing its propeller to come adrift hitting the port inner and went right through into the Halifaxes fuselage leaving a very large hole. The skipper gave the order immediately to bale out which they did leaving him at the controls. He managed to nurse and keep control of his Halifax and landed it later safely back at Elgin. Albert and the rest of the crew landed safely near the little town of Beatock, 17 miles North West of Dumfries in Scotland. During his descent Albert lost one of his flying boots, this was later returned to him by an honest farmer.

Albert and the crew arrived at 77 Squadron in Elvington on Boxing Day 1943 and soon became familiar with the running of the station. 77 Squadron was initially formed in Edinburgh on the 1st October 1916 and its role was to defend Britain against attacking enemy airships. It was disbanded in 1919 and reformed at Finningley in Yorkshire as a bomber unit and at the outbreak of war was equipped with Whitleys dropping leaflets over enemy occupied Europe. Its first operation of the war was on the 19th/20th March when it took part in the first attack on an enemy target that was Hornum on the Isle of Sylt and the first attack on the German mainland to bomb Munchen Gladbach and also took part on the first attack on Italy to bomb the Fiat Works in Turin. Their first flight with the squadron was on the 9th January 1944 when they carried out some local flying. Their first operational flight was on the 21st January to bomb the city of

Magdeburg. This was the first major raid on the city and the operation consisted of 684 aircraft, made up of Lancasters, Halifaxes and Mosquitos. Their next raid was to Berlin on the 28th January 1944.

In all Albert and his crew carried out 37 operations with 77 Squadron that included, Magdeburg, Berlin, Lumbries, Le Harve, Stuttgart, Keil, Amiens, Trappses, Le mans, Meulan, Tergnier, Caen, Chappelle, Notre Dam, Denmark, Russellsheim, Vaires, Laon, Lille, Aulnoye, Tergnier, Lens, Cherbourg (Sortosville Radar Station). Noyelle and Courtrai (Belgium). They attacked the V1 flying bomb sites at St Mortin L Hortier, Domleger, Marquise and Mimoyecques, St Leu d'Esserent, Chapel Notre Dam and Lumbries.

On returning from a raid on Courtrai in Belgium in the early hours of the 27th March 1944 the Engineer had an embarrassing moment when the Halifax did a belly landing due to him not pulling up the 'Uplocks' for landing. No one was hurt unlike the Engineer's pride. During May 1944 the squadron moved to Full Sutton near Yorkshire and from here they carried out raids on the German radar installations around Cherbourg. They carried out a lot of day and night raids over France around D-Day 'softening' up targets and attacking troop concentrations for the Allied landings. On the 10th September 1944 Albert carried out his final operation as rear gunner with his skipper, now Flying Officer Jury. The operation was to bomb German positions in and around Le Havre that were still holding out after being bypassed by the Allied advance.

With his first tour now completed he was screened off operations and on the 4th December 1945 he received his commission and promoted to Flying Officer. He was posted to No 28 Air Crew Officer's Training School at Hereford for one month where he trained on how to become an officer. He was then posted to Carnaby near Bridlington. This was a 'crash' aerodrome and his duties there were to pick up crashed aircrews (those who survived) and look after their needs, i.e., making them tea, giving them a cigarette and making arrangements for their safe return to their home base.

During one of those nights at Carnaby and while helping a crashed crew, a German Focke Wulf 190 attacked them on the ground luckily no one was hurt.

In February 1945 Albert was posted to No 12 AGS at Bishops Court in Northern Ireland where he became a gunnery instructor on Wellingtons. He spent three and a half months at Bishops Court as an instructor and while he was there one of his pupils was Sir Richard Attenborough (who I am reliably informed was always air sick). Flying Officer Albert Craig had his last flight with the RAF from Bishops Court on the 28th May 1945 in a Wellington; the skipper was a Flight Lieutenant Johnston.

He finished his flying career with 230hrs.25mins day flying and 200hrs.50mins night flying and the aircraft types, which he flew in were Martinet, Blackburn Botha, Vickers Wellington and Handley Page Halifax

Albert was then posted to an Air Crew Holding Unit at Brackla in Scotland where he spent the next two months. After that he was posted to another holding unit in Wales for a further two months. During this period of waiting he spent more time at home on leave than he did work. Albert was beginning to wonder what his vocation was going to be in the RAF when he was offered a variety of jobs. He decided that he would like to try his hand at photography but like many strange things that happened in the RAF at that time he was sent on an Equipment Course. He hated this right from the word go and put up with it for one day. He decided to return to the Holding Unit and complained bitterly to the commanding officer to whom he explained that he joined the RAF as aircrew and not a store man. It wasn't long before he was offered the thirteen-week photography course at Farnborough. On completion of the course he was posted to Bomber Command Head Quarters at Swinderby in Lincolnshire. From there he went No 1 Group Headquarters at Bawtry Hall where he remained until 1947. His duties were to visit all the UK RAF Stations making sure that their Photography Sections were kept up to scratch and had adequate materials for their darkrooms, etc. In February 1947 Flying Officer Albert Craig was demobbed from the RAF and he returned to Northern Ireland taking employment in the textile industry and then Securicor, finally retiring in January 1987.

He is a Life Member of the Royal Air Force Association and a member of the Northern Ireland Branch of the Air Crew association.

FLIGHT LIEUTENANT
WILLIAM JOHN CROZIER, AFC
PILOT
NO. 159 & 355 SQUADRONS

William John (Bill) Crozier was born in Trillick County Tyrone on the 23rd March 1917 and was educated at the Model Elementary School in Enniskillen.

Bill joined the Royal Air Force at the Clifton Street Recruiting Office in Belfast in February 1941 and after completing his medical was sent to the Receiving Centre at Padgate in Lancashire. He must have been sent home to await his call-up, as his next posting was not until February 1942 when he was told to report to the Aircrew Reception Centre at Lord's Cricket Ground for selection. Bill was accepted for pilot training and posted to No 10 Initial Training Wing (ITW) at Scarborough for basic training. After basic training he was then posted to Canada where he joined an Elementary Flying School to start his elementary flying. He was awarded his wings on the 9th October 1942 and received his commission. After graduating he attended an advanced instructor's course at the No 1 Flying Instructors School (FIS) at Trenton in Ontario. The School was equipped with Fawn, Finch, Tiger Moth, Harvard, Cornell, Crane and Avro Ansons. He successfully completed the course and was then posted to the No 33 Service Flying Training School at Carberry in Manitoba on 1st January 1943. The SFTS at Carberry was equipped with the Avro Anson and Crane aircraft.

During his posting at Trenton Bill met up with his brother George, who was in the Royal Canadian Air Force and was completing a QF instructor's course. This coincidence was discovered when they saw mail for each other.

At Carberry he became an instructor on Avro Ansons until August 1943 and was then posted to Pennfield Bridge in Newhampshire, instructing on Ventura Aircraft.

In March 1944 he was then posted to No 5 Operational Training Unit at Boundary Bay where he crewed up for operational flying in Mitchell B-25s and Liberator B-24s. On completion of his OTU training Bill went by train to Lachine in Quebec, where he and his crew waited for two weeks before boarding a ship, which would take them to England. On arrival at Liverpool, Bill

and his crew proceeded to Harrogate where they spent two weeks being equipped for the Far East. He eventually boarded a ship, which was to take him to Bombay in India stopping off at Port Said for one day. This was the first convoy to sail through the Mediterranean. He spent two weeks in Bombay before boarding a train, which was to take him to Mysore where he and his crew carried out a three-week refresher course. He then went by truck to 159 Squadron at Digri in West Calcutta. The squadron was equipped with the Consolidated Liberator Mk11s. On their arrival they were met by a Squadron Leader Gauntlet who casually asked them if they would like to take part in an operation the following morning.

Brief history of 159 Squadron

159 Squadron had been formed at Molesworth in Huntingdonshire in January 1942 as a Heavy-Bomber squadron for possible transfer to the Middle East. The squadron moved to Salbani in India where it operated against enemy targets in North Africa, Sicily Southern Greece and eventually against the Japanese in Burma right up until VJ Day. After the Japanese surrender the squadron was employed on transport duties, dropping supplies to ex-prisoners of war in Burma, Siam and French Indo-China. It also took part in 'Operation Hunger'; this was dropping rice by the ton to the starving inhabitants of Southern Burma. The squadron dropped over one and a half million pounds of rice in 486 operations. It also carried out an Aerial Survey of Bengal for the Bengal Government and was then disbanded in April 1946.

Bill and his navigator went with another experienced crew for the next four operations, before operating independently as a crew. Initially they operated in the Liberators with an 11-man crew, but seldom operated with less that seven or eight. This would have included, Bill, himself as Pilot, Navigator, Bomb Aimer, Wireless

Operator, and Rear Gunner and occasionally with a Front Gunner. As a crew they carried out 28 operations over targets in Burma, Thailand and Malaysia, the shortest trip being 8hrs.55mins, and the longest being 18hrs.25mins. The type of operations, which they carried out where, bridge attacks on Bangkok, Moulmein main railway lines; mine lying in harbours from 400ft, bombing supply dumps and marshalling yards. On completion of their tour, Bill and his crew were transferred to 355 Squadron where they carried out a further four operations. His total operational tour amounted to 300 hours officially, but with going to 355 Squadron it was well over 300 hours. Bill was promoted to Flight Lieutenant while in India, and war with Japan was not yet ended. He was interviewed by a senior RAF officer and asked if he would return to England and go round and visit RAF Stations where crews were destined for the Far East and advise them what to expect when they arrived.

He returned from Bombay by ship to England and was on disembarkation leave when the war with Japan ended. When his leave finished he was posted to No 1653 Heavy Conversion Unit on Lancasters as an instructor until April 1945 when he was de-mobbed. He returned to civilian life for just over a year and decided to rejoin the RAF on a Short Service Commission. He became an instructor on Lancasters at 230 Operational Conversion Unit at Lindholme in Yorkshire. Later on, post war aircrews had to take training for occupations other than flying. Bill chose Air Traffic Control and, after training was posted to the Air Traffic Control Centre at Hanover in Germany. When he completed his tour at Hanover he returned to take up ATC duties at Anglesey in North Wales. He remained on ATC duties in different parts of the world, until his retirement in June 1966. Bill was awarded the Air Force Cross in the Queens Birthday Honours list in 1952. He and his wife attended the Investiture at Buckingham Palace.

After Bill retired from the Royal Air Force, he and his family immigrated to Winnipeg in Canada where he still lives today. During his service career he was stationed in England, Canada, India, Germany, Nairobi, Libya and El Adam.

FLIGHT LIEUTENANT
WILLIAM RICHARD CUFFE SMITH, DFC CDG
ROYAL AIR FORCE NO. 1126986
PILOT
NO. 613 & 21 SQUADRONS

William Richard Cuffe Smith was born in Dublin in the South of Ireland in 1922 and was completing a course in civil engineering at the outbreak of war. On reaching the age of eighteen, he travelled to Belfast and joined the RAF. Two of Cuffe's uncles had served in the Royal Flying Corps and unfortunately one of them was killed one week before the cessation of hostilities. The other uncle attained the rank of Air Vice Marshall and went to Canada to help in the formation with the Royal Canadian Air Force.

A few days after his eighteenth birthday Cuffe was sent to Padgate near Warrington to complete the necessary forms and medicals to enlist in the Royal Air Force as a pilot. Unfortunately at this time the Air Force could not train the number of volunteers so Cuffe was sent home in deferred service. During this time he continued his education in civil engineering at Manchester University. He eventually received his Call Up papers and after completing his introduction at the Air Crew Receiving Centre and Initial Training Wing he was transferred to complete his Grading Course at an Elementary Flying Training School near Peterborough in North Hants flying in Tiger Moths. He had his first Air Experience flight in a Tiger Moth (T5807) with his instructor a Pilot Officer Tatam on January 9th and during the next ten days he accumulated a total of 4hrs.10mins flying time, he completed the course on the 29th January 1942.

Training in the USA

He then transferred to the USA under the Arnold Scheme and started his primary training on Course 42J on 30th April 1942 at the Army Air Forces Training Detachment in Albany Georgia which he completed on 4th July 1942. His primary training was carried out in Boeing Stearmans (PT17s) and his instructor was Mr JG Rabbe. Cuffe's first flight in a PT17 was on 3rd May 1942 and he flew solo on 20th May after a total of 10hrs.57mins. By the 29th June he had completed the course and now had a total of 30hrs.55mins dual and 29 hrs.10mins solo. In July 1942, Cuffe was transferred to Cochran Field Basic Flying School in Macon to start his

basic flying training in BT13s. His first flight in this type was on 6th July and his instructor, Lt Szold let him fly solo on 31st August and on completion of the course he was presented with a book on the history of Cochran Field by Captain WM Van Sickle.

On the 10th September 1942 he transferred to Napier Field in Alabama where he completed the advanced flying course, which lasted until 10th November. The type of aircraft at the advanced school were At.6s (Harvards) and after a total of five hours, Cuffe made his solo trip. Having successfully completing this advanced flying course he was awarded his American Wings by the commanding officer of Napier Field Colonel James L Daniel (Junior) US Air Corps and received an assessment of 'above average'. In December 1943 he returned to the UK by ship via Moncton, Ontario, Canada and on his arrival back was posted to No 15 Elementary Flying Training School in Kingston, Carlisle training in Tiger Moths. In January 1943 he was then posted to No 5 (Pilot) Advanced Flying Unit at Tern Hill flying in Master 111 aircraft. This course was completed on 14th March 1943 and he was assessed as 'average'.

He then went to Calvely in Cheshire on 9th March for Night Flying Training again on Master 111s and completed the course on 16th March when he was posted to Weston Zoyland just south of Bristol flying in Martinets and Henleys, target towing (this he hated). He was very unsettled here and on the 26th March transferred to No 1614 Flight Anti-Aircraft Co-operation at Cark in Lancashire flying in Tiger Moths

Anson and Martinets carrying out anti-aircraft gun co-operation training with the army until the 19th July when he was assessed as 'above the average'. On the 21st July 1943 Cuffe was posted to No 41 Operational Training Unit at Hawarden and Poulton to start his operational training on Harvards and Mustangs. His first flight at the OTU was on July 26th in a Harvard and his instructor was a Flight Lieutenant Plumbridge. His solo flight in the P51 Mustang was on the 23rd August 1943 and he completed the course at the end of September.

Cuffe was then posted to No 613 Squadron at Howarden on 6th October 1943 where he completed two operations in Mosquito Mk 1Vs. His first flight in a Mosquito was on the 25th November 1943 with his instructor a Flying Officer Chin. The two operational flights that he carried out were photographic and shipping reconnaissance and were briefed **not** to engage enemy aircraft.

On the second operation three aircraft were on patrol flying in formation, suddenly the leader shouted over the intercom, "Bandits," so it was full throttle and back home. In fact the three bandits turned out to be Mustangs. Neither patrol had been briefed about the other. Cuffe recalls the report for the patrol, "Six pairs of underpants to the laundry and six engines over cooked." Cuffe was then transferred to a Holding Centre, which was full of pilots all waiting and hoping for a posting to an operational squadron. There was a long delay and one night in the mess, Cuffe happened to be overheard saying, "I am browned off hanging around here, I think I will go back home and stay there." His remarks were reported to the commanding officer of the Holding Unit and he was hauled in front of him. The CO asked Cuffe, "What do you mean Paddy?" Cuffe said that he was only joking because he was absolutely fed up waiting for a posting. The CO said, "I know what I will do with you, one of your countrymen is Air Vice Marshal Embry and he will be arriving in a few days and I will arrange for you to meet him." The AVM met Cuffe and listened to his moans and informed him that he was going to post him to his 'pet' Squadron, No 21. Cuffe asked, "Sir, What do they fly?" and the reply was Mosquitos.

On 13th December 1943 Cuffe was posted to No 21 Squadron, which was based at Scunthorpe in Norfolk. On the 24th December he was given a couple of lessons in the Mossie by Flight Lieutenant Wickham and much to Cuffe's surprise was instructed to go off on his own, Cuffe's reply was, "But sir, I'll kill myself," he carried out his solo successfully. His first operation with the squadron was on the 26th January 1944 to bomb military constructions at Les Escarpes and on the 26th January bombed the military constructions at St Pierre and had to land at West Malling on his return due to flak damage on his tail.

A selection of the operations carried out by Cuffe, taken from his logbook

Jan 30th	Mosquito 'H' Nav F/Sgt Spooner. Low-level ops to military construction Beaumont area. (One 303 through fuse, near tail. Flight time 1hr.45mins.
Feb 3rd	Mosquito 'Z' Nav F/Sgt Spooner. Low-level ops to military construction one .303 hole in port tyre landed OK.

For this particular landing Cuffe received a 'Green' endorsement in his logbook: *Flying Officer Smith returning from an operation on 3rd February 1944 with a damaged aircraft, succeeded by quick and skilful use of the controls in landing the aircraft without further damage. Signed: Group Captain Pickard OC 140 Wing.*

Cuffe had used brake and engine power to control the Mossie, some pilots who had tried this previously had wiped the undercarriage off. 18th February 1944 was the date on which 21, 464 and 487 Squadrons carried out the famous raid on Amiens Prison. Group Captain Pickard, DSO** DFC with his Navigator Flight Lieutenant Broadley, DSO DFC DFM were lost downed by a FW 190 when they may have stayed too long over target taking photos. Air Vice Marshal Basil Embry, DSO** DFC* was also on this raid, an officer of this rank was not allowed to fly over enemy territory, so he flew using the alias Wing Commander Smith.

Feb 29th	Mosquito 'F' Nav F/Sgt Spooner. Ops as detailed. BBB. Snow over target "Offler lost." Flying time 1hr.50mins.
Mar 3rd	Mosquito 'V' & 'F' He flew two raids that day with F/Sgt Spooner on military construction sites.
Mar 15th	Mosquito 'B' Nav F/O Bulmer. Night Intruder to Gilzel Rijen Aerodro Near Breda.
Apl 11th	Mosquito 'H' Nav F/Sgt Spooner. Night Intruder to Vechta Germany.

Authors note: The next two entries mention 'HighBall'. Highball mentioned above was an invention of Barnes Wallace *(another story).*

Apl 30th	Mosquito 'W' Nav F/Sgt Spooner. Highball railway junction near Abancourt O/K.
May 7th	Mosquito 'A' Nav F/Sgt Spooner. Highball railway junction near Serquex. Could not find Black Chief.
May 23rd	Mosquito 'D' Nav F/Sgt Spooner Operation to bomb Gee Station at Lamuer, (Cherbourg Area)
June 6th	**D-Day.** Mosy 'H' Nav F/Sgt Spooner Patrolled road between Caen and Boisney. Bombed O/K.

June 7th	Mosquito 'H' Nav F/Sgt Spooner. Road patrol South of Lisieux.
June 14th	Mosquito 'H' Nav F/Sgt Spooner. Road patrol South of Caen.
June 22nd	Mosquito 'H' Nav F/Sgt Spooner. Road patrol, Bombed O/K. and shot up lights on road.
June 24th	Mosquito 'H' Nav F/Sgt Spooner. Area patrol bombed road and rail junction, lit up by Mitchell Flares.
June 29th	Mosquito 'H' Nav F/Sgt Spooner Bombed Thury Harcourt South of Caen in support of Army.
July 4th	Mosquito 'H' Nav Sgt Hill. Patrolled South of Loire & Bombed a bridge over same & railway a lot of flak South of Angers.

"Old 'H' Belly-Landed by Buck Taylor after 51 Operations.... Received our new 'H' on 9th July 1944.

July 18th	Mosquito. 'H' Nav F/O McKee. Bombed railway at St Pierre Sur

On the 18th July 1944 Cuffe had completed his first tour of thirty operational trips and his logbook shows that he was granted an extension of 20 trips.

July 19th	Mosquito. 'H' Nav F/O McKee. Bombed road, river & railway nr Cunde Sur. N. Strafed Pontoon. Bridge over Orne.
July 28th	Mosquito. 'H' Nav F/O McKee. 'Zombie' train hunting strafed truck nr Poix, strafed & bombed fire on railway.
July 29th	Mosquito. 'H' Nav F/O McKee. Patrol of bridges over Seine, coned by searchlights, bags of flak from Elbeuf. Bombed bridge at same & shot up Rly Station Nt of Gourney.
July 30th	Mosquito. 'H' Nav F/O McKee. Patrolled railways, N & South of Loire, flak from searchlights from Rly junction East of Tours. Bombed and strafed wood of Chinon (full of troops).
Aug 1st	Mosquito. 'H' Nav F/O McKee. Low level on military barracks on East of Poitiers. Flak on way back, lost Mussett. One Bird in Wing.
Aug 8th	Mosquito. 'H' NavF/O McKee. Patrolled Seine crossings, bombed jetties at Quille Boehf, Strafed lights in wood.
Aug 12th	Mosquito. 'H' Nav F/O McKee. Detailed retreat reported East. Shot up Sven Tucks on Road, near Thiberval, bombed road East of Lisieux.

Aug 16th & 17th	Patrolled Seine crossings bombed Ducclair, and Bombed railway bridge over River Risle under Mitchell Flares. Shot up one motor transport.
Aug 18th	Mosquito. 'H' Nav F/O McKee. Found bags of transport at Orbec acted as Controller for 1hr.20mins. 'Wizard' pile up.
Aug 28th	Mosquito. 'H' Nav F/O McKee. Bombed Duclair Crossing. Strafed gun position and transporter near Amiens.
Aug30th	Mosquito. 'H' Nav F/O McKee. Patrolled Somme Crossings bombed South of Abbeyville.

On the 30th August Cuffe had completed his second tour and Wing Commander Dale his commanding officer arranged for Cuffe to go on three weeks leave. During this period the squadron moved frequently from Hawarden to Gravesend, Thorney Island and then to Rosieres-en-Santeere in France in February 1945, and on to Brussels/Melsbroek in April.

During his third Tour of Operations he had attacked the following targets: Factories at Enschede; Paderborn Aerodrome; trains; marshalling yards; troops; motor transports; Bonn; Siegen; Kassel; Allendorf; Remagen; Koln; Krefield; Dorssten; Geldern; Wesel; Minden; Gutersloh; Venlo; Bullingen; Osnabruik; Hanover; Siegburg; Cologne; Iserlohn; Marburg; Khehztal; Bocholt; Dulmen; Ostrich; Ludenscheid; Ronkhsn; Northeim; Eisleben; Weimar; Eisenach; Erfurt; Nordhausen; Aschersleben; Halbersatdt; Wegeleben; Brunswick; Magdeburg; Hildesheim; Meppen; Leer; Oldenburg; Quaken; Essen; Ulzen; Stendal; Berlin; Schenbeck; Rotenburg; Bockel; and Bremen.

Cuffe went on to complete 78 operations with 21 Squadron, the last one being on the 26th April 1945 when he attacked the Army Headquarters at Ostereis-Tedt (he was hit in the elevator by flak). His total flying hours was now 860.

On the 5th May 1945 his log book shows that after completing 18 months with 21 Squadron the commanding officer had assessed Cuffe:

As a Fighter Bomber Pilot	**Above the average**
As Pilot-Navigator/Navigator.	**Above the average**
In Bombing.	**Above the average**
In Air Gunnery.	**Above the average**

When the squadron moved to Gutersloh in Germany, which was the first Luftwaffe Aerodrome to be captured in Germany, the Adjutant called Cuffe into his office and said, "Paddy, you have had it." He handed Cuffe a letter and asked him to read it. It was a signal from the Air Ministry to 140 Wing and it stated the Flight Lieutenant William Richard Cuffe Smith was to be taken off operations immediately as they could not understand how he had been still on operations with 21 Squadron for over two years and he was to be grounded. This was only one week and ten days before the end of the war and he was posted to Catfoss, north of Hull on a Wing Gunnery course. His pals in 21 Squadron put Cuffe into a Mosquito and flew him there instead of having to go by road. As he was leaving the station and saying cheerio to all his friends, the CO approached him and asked, "Paddy, How would you like to come back again?" Cuffe replied, "Sir, this is no time for leg pulling." The CO told him, "I will see what I can do."

Cuffe told me that looking back, this was another incident, which made him suspicious of the guiding hand of AVM Embry.

AVM Embry and Cuffe Smith

Cuffe told me that AVM Embry used to slip in at night when 'specials' were taking place (AVM Embry was on the Amiens and Shell House Gestapo HQ Raids) although he was told not to fly he did so on a number of occasions and was known as Wing Commander Smith. Cuffe found out later that if AVM Embry was on an operation with 21 Squadron, Cuffe would not be! Cuffe was never allowed to take part in an operation that AVM Embrey was on, and he often wondered was the AVM using his name.

The gunnery course at the Catfoss Central Gunnery School lasted for six weeks and was carried out in Mosquitos and Beaufighters. At the end of the course Cuffe was assessed as 'above the average' as a marksman, air to ground, on drogue, rocket projectile and as marksman in twin engine fighter combat aircraft.

Looking back, this was another incident, which made Cuffe suspicious of the guiding hand of AVM Embry. On completion of his Gunnery course, everyone was posted except Cuffe. On making enquiries his CO said, "I don't know Smith, and the Air Ministry don't seem to know much about you either." Some time later after the next course had started the CO informed him that he was being posted to 140 Wing as Gunnery Officer and that a Mossie from 21 Squadron would collect him the next day. Sure enough the next morning a Mossie arrived at Blackbushe to take him back to join the Squadron in Berlin. His job as Gunnery Officer was to organise air to air-and-air to ground firing for 487, 464 and 21 Squadrons. 464 were RAAF and 487 were RNZAF and 21 were a bit of a mixture. He continued flying as Gunnery Officer with the squadrons until his last flight with them on February 24th 1944.

During one of his earlier leaves in Dublin, and walking down O'Connell Street, he noticed an advertisement for staff at Aer Lingus, he decided to apply for a position as a pilot and on entering the office was greeted with a voice saying, "Hi ya Bill." It was Harry Williams, a friend that Cuffe who he used to play rugby with.

Later Cuffe received a Telegram from Aer Lingus while he was stationed at Gutersloh asking him if he could come for an interview. He told his CO about this and he immediately told Cuffe to take a Mossie to Blackbushe and make your own way to Dublin from there.

He informed the airline that he was not due for demobilisation for another seven months, but they wanted him tomorrow as they were hoping to get Dakotas and start training right away. On his return to the squadron, he talked to the CO about it, and he said he would see what he could to help. Three or four days later Cuffe and Group Captain Embry were chatting in the Bar and he asked him what Aer Lingus was flying these days. He told the Group Captain I think its 86s but I know they are getting Dakotas. Two days later he sent for Cuffe and handed him a letter and said, "Off you go to Bigging Hill in your Mosquito, a friend of mine has three squadrons there, give him this letter and he will organise some flying for you in Dakotas." Cuff arrived at Bigging Hill at the end of February 1946 and went straight to the CO's office and handed him the letter. He told Cuffe he would do this on one condition, "I can have your Mosquito while you have my Dak." Cuffe spent the next 12 days training at Oxford on Dakotas with Flight Lieutenant Dean, Flight Lieutenant Mather and Flying Officer Keogh. One month later a telegram arrived for Cuffe to report immediately to Aer Lingus, and the unseen hand was again behind him as he was demobbed on 27th March 1946 and joined Aer Lingus the following day. Cuffe was in no doubt that the casual remark that he was fed up awaiting a posting to an operational squadron two years earlier, and his subsequent meeting with a fellow Irishman, namely Air Vice Marshal Embry, had a considerable influence in his Royal Air Force Career.

Cuffe was now fully aware that every time the AVM flew on operations as Wing Commander Smith he was using his surname, and Cuffe was never allowed to fly himself during these operations by the AVM.

Cuffe was awarded his Distinguished Flying Cross while at 21 Squadron, this was presented to him by his squadron commander, and at a later date was informed that he had been awarded a further honour of a Bar to the DFC or a Croix De Guerre, he chose the latter.

During this time Cuffe decided to go into Hull to find a shop that supplied Medal Ribbons. He asked, "Do you have any Croix De Guerre medal ribbon?" The answer was yes and he purchased some. The next morning Cuffe was having breakfast in the mess when a friend came up to him and asked what age he was. The reason I ask is the ribbon that you are wearing is 1914/18 Croix de Guerre Ribbon. On the 18th March 1946 Flight Lieutenant William Richard Cuffe Smith was assessed as 'above the average' as a Fighter Bomber Pilot by the commanding officer of 140 Wing British Air Forces of Occupation (Germany).

He made his last flight with the RAF on 26th March 1946 when he flew his Mosquito back from Gutersloh to Blackbushe. His total flying hours were now 1030hrs.25 mins.

Cuffe added some notes in his logbook regarding his last flight. *(First, by mistake of D/F landed at Farnborough. Due snow took off again and landed Blackbushe, trouble with weather flying to Blackbushe, as CO Farnborough had phoned, OK he was Irish, laid on a jeep to take me to Uxbridge for demob, caught train to Holyhead and boat home).*

A funny RAF story from Cuffe

On one particular raid the Mosquitos operated in pairs; one-carried candles (flares) to light up the target and the second aircraft carried bombs. Someone broke radio silence and asked if anyone had any candles left, "Yes," came the reply in a broad Aussie accent, "and we will stick them up your arse," was the reply.

His flying career with Aer Lingus started on April 1st when he flew as 2nd Pilot to Captain Wells in a DC3 on a familiarisation flight. He also flew in Vikings, Wayfarers, Viscounts, Boeing 707, F27, Heralds, Electra, B170, Boeing 720, V808, Constellation and Boeing 747s. He joined as Captain in 1946 and in 1960 was made a Senior Captain. His last flight as a commercial pilot was on 1st November 1977. By this time he had accumulated a total of 17,981hrs.35mins. During his period as Senior Captain with Aer Lingus he was seconded to Air Siam, responsible for training their pilots. On one occasion whilst taking off from Hawaii with a full load of fuel and passengers he felt some bumps as he lifted off. Neither the second or third pilot were not aware of anything, and shortly afterwards Hawaii control informed Cuffe that he had left a lot of 'garbage' on the runway. The Control Tower also informed him that one of his undercarriage doors and the remains of two wheels and tyres were on the runway. By this time the aircraft had reached altitude height and the Third Pilot informed Cuffe that the aircraft was not maintaining cabin pressure and it was possible that there was a hole in the fuselage. Cuffe had decided to continue the flight to Tokyo where he would be able to get all the spares that would be required to repair the aircraft. These would not have been available at Hawaii. With the aid of an extra turbo, cabin pressure was maintained and Cuffe informed Tokyo of the circumstances. He sent for the chief of the stewardesses and informed her of the position and said that he would inform the remainder of the crew and passengers prior to landing. On arriving at Tokyo he did a low level pass over the airfield and was told that his outer starboard truck was missing. Cuffe lined up the huge aircraft with the runway and carried out what he described as a 'light landing' holding the aircraft away from the damaged side. Once the damaged truck came in contact with the runway it dug in and had the same effects as full brakes on. To counteract this he had to apply full brake on the opposite side to keep the aircraft on the runway. The aircraft ended up with a stub and left a deep groove on the runway from the point of impact.

After completing a full report of the incident he went to his hotel and switched on the television and watched the landing in the local news every hour on the hour. From this he observed that the minute the undercarriage stub came in contact with the runway there was a sheet of flame. Cuffe thinks that initially on take off, the first bump was the tyre bursting, the second was the brake unit disintegrating and bursting the tyres behind it, and when the undercarriage was retracted a hole was punched in the undercarriage bay causing the drop in cabin pressure.

Cuffe joined Howth Yacht Club as a Junior Member on 11th June 1937 and was Commodore from 1980 to 1983 and also served as Chairman for a period. His wife and daughters were also members of the club and like their father were keen yachts people. His daughters Lee and Margaret won the International Junior Regatta Premier Trophy in 1967. Cuffe sailed some 5,000 miles to Rio de Janeiro in 1983 and his total sailing mileage was in excess of 25,000 miles. He also played a major role in the building of Howth Yacht Club and Harbour, which started in 1985 and was completed in March 1987.

Sadly Cuffe died in 2000.

PILOT OFFICER
VIVIEN LESTER CURRIE
ROYAL AIR FORCE NO. 106035
PILOT
NO. 263 SQUADRON

KILLED IN ACTION 23RD JULY 1942

Vivien Lester Currie was born in Newhaven on the 17th July 1920 and was the son of Commander Samuel Currie of Ballyshannon County Donegal. Commander Currie was a Navigating Officer in the Mercantile Marine in July 1920.

Lester was educated at Methody College in Belfast and was a consistently good student throughout his eight years at the College, and his aptitude for maths and science were extremely good. He passed his Junior Certificate in 1936 with two distinctions in arithmetic and geometry, plus three credits in English, French and algebra. For his Senior Certificate in 1938 he passed with two credits in higher mathematics, elementary maths and a distinction in physics. In Upper V1 he continued to excel in higher maths, physics and chemistry.

Lester was a College Prefect for the period 1938/1939 where he showed vigilance, initiative and command in football. He played for the schools 1st XV 1938/1939 and rowed for the Rowing Club. He was the schools Boxing Champion and captained his House Athletic Team in 1938 and was also a member of the 13th Boy Scout Troop for four years.

When war was declared in September 1939 Lester went to the Recruiting Office in Clifton Street Belfast and joined the RAF. He was immediately selected for Air Crew and posted off via Padgate to start his flying training. After completing his flying training Lester was posted to 236 Squadron at RAF Filton.

The month of July was not a good one for the squadron as it lost two of its pilots on the 23rd while on a 'Rhubarb' operation, (ground strafing raid). This operation involved twelve of the squadron's

Whirlwinds, which were escorted by No 234 Squadron Spitfires. The squadron rendezvoused with the Spitfires at the Lizard and then dropped to zero feet, still at this height when crossing the coast of France to avoid radar. Attacks had been made on the railway lines and stations. One Whirlwind belonging to Pilot Officer Walker was attacked by two Me109s and, before anyone could help, it had gone into the sea. The squadron was returning home, and just as they were ten minutes from the English coast a second Whirlwind belonging to Pilot Officer Lester Currie was attacked by three Me109s, which again went down into the sea. Lester's body was never found and he is remembered on the Runnymede Memorial.

It has been mentioned to me by his nephew, Mr Alan Caldwell that a pilot from the squadron who was on the same raid as Pilot Officer Currie remembers Lester's aircraft being attacked. He also remembers that after the attack, Lester was able to climb back up and rejoin his squadron. The Flight Commander asked him was he all right, and he replied that he had lost one engine but should be able to make it back to base. Just as he said that, his aircraft nose-dived and crashed into the sea. This may have been caused by two factors, one being that he was critically wounded and didn't realise it, or, second that his aircraft had a catastrophic control failure which may have been caused by the ensuing dog-fight.

FLIGHT LIEUTENANT
JOHN TERENCE CUTHBERTSON, AE
ROYAL AIR FORCE VOLUNTEER RESERVE NO. 751832
NAVIGATOR

NO. 38 AND 211 SQUADRONS

John Terence Cuthbertson was born in Bangor, County Down in 1920. His parents moved to Belfast when he was still very young. Terry, as he likes to be called, attended Inchmarlo for the early part of his education and then continued his higher education at the Belfast Royal Academical Institution.

He enjoyed sports very much and played for the schools rugby, hockey, and cricket teams. After leaving school he gained employment with the firm of Shaw and McMullan (Tea Merchants) Victoria Street, Belfast.

On the 20th June 1939 Terry joined the Royal Air Force Volunteer Reserve and was called to full time service with the outbreak of war. In November 1939 he was posted to the No1 Air Observers Navigation School, (AONS) in Prestwick where he successfully passed his air observers course. In February 1940 he was transferred to the No 7 Bombery and Gunnery School at Stormy Down where he completed his Air Gunner's course. In April 1940 he was posted to No 211 Squadron at El Daba in the Western Desert. The squadron was equipped with the Short Nose Bristol Blenheim MK1s. Terry had a lucky escape one dark night at El Daba when another Blenheim crashed into his on take off. Luckily neither of the crews was seriously hurt; although he did tell me that he tripped over one of the Blenheims bombs that was lying around after the collision. In 1941 he was transferred to No 38 Squadron, which was equipped with the Vickers Wellington Mk1s and based at Shallufa, Egypt. He carried out operations on the Suez Canal, Western Desert, North Africa, and Greece. He returned to the UK in late 1942 where he became a Flying Control Officer at several stations in Scotland and England. In 1945 he was posted out to India as a Flying Control Officer and on his return to the UK in 1946 he was released from the Royal Air Force.

In 1946 he joined the Ministry of Civil Aviation, (now named the Civil Aviation Authority) as an Air Traffic Control Officer, stationed at Belfast (Sydenham, Nutts Corner, Preston, Wick and Prestwick. He finally hung up the headset in 1980 and made his home in Prestwick along with his wife. He is a life member of the RAFA, joining in 1946 in Belfast and a member of the CAA Retired Staff Association, and a member of the Probus Club.

FLIGHT LIEUTENANT
MATTHEW WHITE DALE
ROYAL AIR FORCE NO. 1076213
FLIGHT ENGINEER
NO. 428 (GHOST) SQUADRON RCAF & 460 SQUADRON

Matthew White Dale was born in Drumadreen near Limavady on the 14th December 1919 and was educated at Limavady High School. He enlisted into the RAF on the 10th October 1940 as an AC2 and eventually qualified as a Flight Engineer.

His flying career started in October 1943 at the 1664 Heavy Conversion Unit on Halifaxes. On the morning of the 25th October he had his first familiarisation flight in the type with his Pilot Officer Barker. During the course he carried out three and two engine exercises, air to air firing, and cross-country training. During the conversion course he was transferred No 1666 Heavy Conversion Unit where he took part in a five day cross-country bombing course. On the 3rd December 1943 Matthew was posted to No 428 Squadron at Middleton St George in County Durham where he would commence operational flying. 428 Squadron was formed at Dalton in Yorkshire in November 1942 as part of No 4 Group. In January 1943 it transferred to No 6. RCAF Group. The squadron earned its nickname 'Ghost' because of the many hours it spent carrying out nighttime bombing. By the end of the war the squadron had won over 200 decorations, and in June 1945 it flew its Lancasters home to Canada, and was disbanded at Yarmouth in Nova Scotia. 'Ghost' name, the number and in June 1954 was revived with the formation of CF-100 All-Weather Fighter Squadron at Uplands in Ontario. The squadron served as a unit of Air Defence Command for seven years, and was finally disbanded in May 1961.

Matthew's first operation of the war was successfully carried out in Halifax 'M'. The Target was Berlin. His skipper for the operation was a Flying Officer Woolverton, the flying time to Berlin and back was 8hrs.30mins. He again visited Berlin on the 20th January 1944, and went on to complete 85 operations in the RAF.

Other targets he visited during his operational career

The Baltic, Keil Bay, Le Havre, St Malo, St Nazaire, Heligoland, Lorient, Dunkirk, Girond River, Meulan, marshalling yards at Trappe, Le Mans, Amiens, Leon, Aulnoye, Courtrai, Ghent, Villeneuve, Friesian Isles, Brest Harbour, Trouville, Coutances, St Pol. Boulogne (daylight), Duisburg, St Martin, Le Hortier (robot works), Ardovual (Robot Flying Bomb Site), Acquet, Wesseling (Cologne), Ruhr, and LeHaye (flying bomb site).

In June 1944 he was promoted to Pilot Officer and converted onto Lancasters, and on June 27th had completed his first tour with 428 Squadron. On the 8th August he was transferred to an Air Gunnery School at RAF Dalton where he completed a six-month instructor's course on Martinets and Oxfords. On the 28th January 1945 he was transferred to No 1665 Heavy Conversion Unit for a refresher course on Lancasters and in early February 1945 joined No 460 Squadron RAAF at RAF Binbrook in Lincolnshire.

He started operations again on the 10th February 1945 and completed his second tour on 2nd June 1945.

No 460 Squadron was formed at Molesworth in Huntingdonshire in November 1941 and was equipped with the Vickers Wellington. It began operations on the 12th March 1942, and was re-equipped with Halifaxes and later Lancasters. The squadron took part in many epic raids during the war including the attack on Peenemunde. The squadron was finally disbanded in October 1945. One of its Lancasters Serial No W4783, also known as 'G' for George, carried out over 90 operations with the squadron, was presented to the Australian war Museum. At the end of June 1945 Matthew left 460 Squadron and was posted to No 12 Squadron at Wickonby as a flight engineer instructor until December, when he was posted to No 100 Squadron. Here he completed two trips with his pilot Flight Sergeant Syloski. In January 1946 he was transferred to No 300 (Masovian) Polish Squadron, bringing back troops from Italy. No 300 Squadron was the first Polish Bomber Squadron in the Royal Air Force, and served with distinction through out the war years and won more than 100 decorations. At the end of hostilities the squadron took part in Operation Manna, dropping over 152 tons of food to the starving Dutch people. It also repatriated ex-prisoners of war back to Britain, and carried Red Cross supplies for liberated Poles in German concentration camps. The squadron was disbanded in October 1946. Matthew's final flight in a Lancaster was on the 3rd April 1946. He was promoted to Flight Lieutenant on the 20th March, and after completing a total of 311hrs.40mins on Halifaxes. Lancasters. Martinets, Oxfords and Dakotas he was finally de-mobbed from the RAF on July 9th 1946. Flight Lieutenant Dale returned home to Northern Ireland where he was employed as an Inspector with the Ministry of Agriculture. He had to retire at the age of forty-eight due to ill health, which was attributed to his intense operational career during the war years in the Royal Air Force.

WARRANT OFFICER
AUSTIN DESMOND DALTON, DFC
(DUTCH)
WIRELESS OPERATOR/AIR GUNNER
295 SQUADRON

Austin Desmond Dalton was born in Bloomfield, Belfast on the 2nd March 1922 and was educated at the Belfast Mercantile College (now Belfast High School) in Glenravel Street. On leaving school Desmond was employed as an apprentice compositor with the Belfast Telegraph. However before he completed the apprenticeship he decided to join the Royal Air Force as aircrew.

His RAF career started in October 1941 when he signed up at Clifton Street Recruiting Office. From Clifton Street he joined Queens University Air Squadron were he completed No 2 Course. Not long after he was posted to Padgate Receiving Centre and then trained down to the Aircrew Reception centre at Blackpool where he was selected to become a Wireless Operator/Air Gunner. His rank was LAC at this time. From ACRC he went to No 2 Radio School at Yatesbury where he embarked on his first Radio Course. On passing the course he was sent to Station Headquarters at Wick in Scotland. From SHQ at Wick he was posted to the No 1 Radio School at RAF Cranwell where he began his advanced wireless training on Dominie and Proctors. The course consisted of calibration and gyros, D/F loops, Q-code and frequency changes, homing and fixes. He successfully passed the course on the 9th April with 21hrs flying completed and posted to the No 10 Signals School at Madley and then it was time for his Air Gunnery course. On the 16th June 1943 Desmond was posted to the No 10 Air Gunnery School at Barrow where he embarked on his air gunnery training. The training was carried out on Avro Ansons and when the course was finished he was assessed as 'above the average in theory and practical'.

No 11 Radio School, Hooton Park

In early July Desmond was promoted to the rank of Sergeant and posted to No 11 Radio School at Hooton Park where he carried out an ASV course (Special Equipment Training). The 'specialised' training was carried out on Blackburn Bothas and Avro Ansons. The

course was completed by the end of August. His total flying hours was now 29hrs.35mins.

Around the beginning of September Desmond was sent to the Dispersal centre at Blackpool to await his posting to an Operational Training Unit. On the 30th September he received his posting, which took him to No 7 Operational Training Unit, which was at Limavady in Northern Ireland. This was a bonus for Desmond as it was only an hour away from his home. The operational training was carried out in Wellingtons and Ansons and consisted X-County and local navigational exercises, air to air firing, low level bombing, and splash firing. The course finished on the 4th December 1943. Total flying hours was now 116hrs.30mins (day) and 17hrs.55mins (night).

On the 1st January Desmond was posted to a Maintenance Conversion Unit at Tiree in Scotland where he joined No 4 Course, which was a conversion course onto Halifaxes and to familiarise himself with the aircrafts radio and armament. On the 19th January he carried out his first operation in a Halifax code named 'Mercer' with Flying Officer Brown and crew. When the course was completed by the end of February 1944 Desmond was promoted to the rank Of Warrant Officer. Warrant Officer Dalton having completed his operational training was posted to No 295 Squadron that was based at Harwell and equipped with the Armstrong-Whitworth Albemarle 1. The Squadron had been formed at Netheravon in August 1942 and immediately began training in dropping paratroops with Whitleys. In October it began a ferry service to Northern Ireland, towing Hotspur gliders to Nutts

Corner. Its main task from 1943 to 1945 was towing gliders and troops to France, dropping SAS and SOE personnel into occupied territory and dropping supplies and food to the resistance forces in Holland. Desmond joined the squadron on the 1st April 1944 and had his first flight on the 4th in an Albemarle coded V1750. The Pilot was a Squadron Leader Potter. This had been a test flight that lasted for 1hr.45mins. On the 8th May 1944 he met his new crew the pilot being a Pilot Officer Jolliffe and they immediately started glider towing exercises, which continued non-stop right through until the 1st June 1944.

On the 5th June 1944 at 2200 hrs his aircraft Albemarle V1436 took off from Harwell with twenty-two other aircraft. Eleven of them had paratroops on board and twelve towing Horsa gliders. This was Operation Tonga, the beginning of the invasion of Europe. Apart from a few gliders all forces reached their dropping zones and landing zones successfully.

On the 6th June 'D-Day', Desmond and the crew carried out a second Operation Tonga. This time they were dropping SOE and SAS soldiers behind enemy lines to disrupt enemy communications.

Other code names that were used for these type of glider towing, SAS and SOE operations were: Hugh; Giles; Hart; John; Glover; Pistol; and Ditcher.

On the 8th August 1944 Desmond was posted to No 1665 Heavy Conversion Unit at Tilstock where he was to convert unto the Short Sterling Bomber. The course finished on the 11th August 1944.

On the 31st August Desmond's aircraft was part of Operation Ditcher; this was to drop SOE personnel into Southern France and allow them to arm the French Maquis who would stop the Germans escaping.

That month 295 Squadron achieved 87.5% successful drops; this was the highest in 38 Group.

September found the squadron extremely busy with the start of Operation Market Garden. His first Market Garden was on the 17th September 1944. They took off from Harwell at 1300 hrs along with 22 other aircraft towing gliders to Arnheim. On the 19th they took off again phase three with 17 other Stirlings towing Gliders to Arnheim. The German flak was very accurate and heavy so much so all 17 aircraft were hit including Desmonds, some had to turn back and one was shot down. They took off again on the 21st and 23rd (phase five and six) re-supplying the Allied forces on the ground and were again hit by the murderous flak.

In October 1944 the squadron moved to RAF Rivenhall, Desmond and the crew only had three flights that month all non-operational. In early November 1945 Desmond was informed that he was being posted to 570 Squadron for three days, which was also based at Rivenhall and was equipped with the Short Stirling (I am not sure why he was seconded to 570 Squadron). Desmond returned to 295 Squadron on the 16th November and returned to operations on the 3rd

February 1945. The operation was code named Operation Fibian; his log shows that they dropped five containers and two pans. The next operation was on the 7th February bombing the city of Weeze.

On the 24th February they carried out Operation Dudley this was dropping 24 containers, one SIS and seven Pkts. From the 1st March until the 18th March they carried out an almost daily practice of glider towing across country. This was getting ready for Operation Market Garden, the crossing of the Rhine.

Operation Varsity

570 Squadrons part was to tow thirty Horsas successfully across without loss to the gliders or tugs. Desmond and his crew took off from Rivenhall at 0700 hrs in Stirling LJ662 complete with their Horsa clinging on behind and headed for the Rhine. This was to be the final phase of the land war, with the amphibious crossing of the Rhine on the Wesel sector and the airborne landings among the enemy defences a few hours later. On the 21st April Desmond and the crew delivered a 'load of petrol' into Germany.

On the 3rd of June 1945 they started the first of their Operations Ambea and Useful, these operations were to ferry POWs home to England. In all Desmond and the crew carried out twelve of these operation Usefuls bringing POWs home from Brussels, Hamburg, Stavanger and Schleswig. Desmond's last one was on the 12th August from Prague. During the last weeks of the war, Desmond and his crew took part in Operation Necking. This was to supply the starving Dutch people with food from very low level. For these heroic deeds Prince Bernhardt of Holland presented the Dutch Distinguished Flying Cross to him in January 1947 (Desmond is the only Ulsterman to hold this award).

The citation reads, "Awarded for gallantry and leadership displayed during the Operations for the liberation of the Netherlands enemy occupied territory in 1945. While in charge, as a member of 38 Group Royal Air Force of supplying Allied Troops and the Dutch Underground Forces from the air. Signed: Wilhelmina, The Minister of Foreign Affairs W Van Doetzelaer and the Minister of War, AHJL Fievez."

In October 1945, Desmond was posted to No 14 radio School at St Athan were he completed an instructors course. He returned to No 295 Squadron on the 1st December 1945. With the war now over, Desmond and his crew began 'Milk' operations to and from Brussels and in July regular runs were flown to Hamburg, Aldergrove, Oslo and Copenhagen. These runs were extended to Castel Benito, Lydda, Shiabah, Mmauripur, and Alhallabad and continued through to the 13th January 1946 when the squadron was disbanded at Rivenhall. On the 12th March 1946 Desmond was posted to a Transport Command Development Unit at Brize Norton were he flew in Halifaxes carrying out experimental work dropping containers. His last flight with the RAF was in a Dakota of TDCU on the 27th May 1946. By the time of his de-mob from the RAF on the 4th June 1946 he had accumulated at total of 518 hours flying. The aircraft types that he flew in were, Dominie, Proctor, Anson, Botha, Wellington, Halifax, Albemarle, Stirling and Dakota.

Warrant Officer Dalton returned home to Northern Ireland and was married on the second anniversary of D-Day. He rejoined the Belfast telegraph where he finished his apprenticeship as a Computer Operator. He remained with the Company for the next 45 years. Desmond is a member of the RAFA, the British Legion, and the Stirling Association.

WARRANT OFFICER
ALEXANDER WILLIAM DANN
WIRELESS OPERATOR/AIR GUNNER
NO. 45 SQUADRON

Alexander William Dann was born in Dublin in 1921, and a short time later his parents moved up to live in Belfast. Lex, as he likes to be called, was educated at the Connells Institute and later at Belfast Royal Academy. When he had finished his education, Lex joined the Royal Air Force on the 11th September 1939 at the Clifton Street Recruiting Office in Belfast and was selected to become a Wireless Operator/Air Gunner.

At the end of September he was posted over to the Padgate Receiving Centre near Liverpool where he was issued with his uniform and kit. He then went to an Initial Training Wing for basic training, and on completion of this he was posted to the No 2 Electrical & Wireless School at Yatesbury where he carried out his Wireless Operator's training. The course lasted for six months.

On passing his wireless exam Lex was transferred to the No 9 Bomber and Gunnery School at Penhros in Wales where he completed his air gunner's course in Hawker Demons. He then went to the No 1 Air Observers Navigational School in Prestwick, Scotland where he carried out his navigation course. This particular course was very advanced and consisted of learning how to read maps, the art of dead reckoning navigation, compasses, meteorology charts, instrument flying, reconnaissance, direction finding, photography, and how to navigate. The course training was carried out in the Avro Anson. Lex passed all his navigation exams and was awarded his Wireless Operator/Air Gunner's Brevet and promoted to Sergeant.

It was now January 1941, and Lex was told that he was going overseas where he was to join the No 70 Operational Training Unit at Ismalia in Egypt. The OTU was equipped with the Bristol Blenheim Bomber Mk 1 & 4. Here Lex met his crew, which consisted of Sergeant Naldrett-Jays (Pilot), Doc Proctor (Observer) and Lex (Wireless Operator). Once the formalities were over they started their operational training in the Blenheims. The training exercises consisted of formation flying, cross-country, circuits & bumps, beam attacks, air to Air & air to ground firing. When Lex finished the course he had accumulated 15hrs.40mins instructional training by day and 2hrs.40mins by night.

"The record of the heavy night bombing campaign by bomber command against Europe during the Second World War is very well known, However, less well known is the fact that the RAF had a substantial night bomber force based in the Mediterranean who's campaign over Central and South Eastern Europe was as effective as the bomber command one and had a considerable effect on the outcome of the war."

Having now completed their operational training, Lex and his crew were given a few days leave which they spent in the town of Ismalia, and on their return they were told that they were to report to No 45 Squadron which was based at Helwan near Cairo, and then would be taken on to it's satellite airfield at Fuka. 45 Squadron was equipped with Blenheim Mk 1s and 4s. No 45 Squadron was originally formed in Gosport in Hampshire in March 1916 as a fighter reconnaissance unit. It then moved to France and at the end of 1917 moved to Italy. While serving in France and Italy the squadron shot down no less than 164 enemy aircraft all with Sopwith Camels. The squadron was disbanded on the last day of 1919, but was reformed at Helwan in Egypt in 1921 flying the Vickers Vernon. From 1927 until the outbreak of the Second World War the squadron had been equipped with the De Havilland 9A, Fairey 111Fs, Hawker Hart, Vickers Vincent, Fairey Gordon and Vickers Wellesley. In 1939 it was equipped with the Bristol Blenheim Mk 1s up until 1942 when it received the Mk 1's. In December 1942 it was re-equipped with the Vultee Vengeance, and finally the De Havilland Mosquito F.B VIs in February 1944.

On his first operation with the squadron Lex's Blenheim crashed 24 miles from El Alamein, injuring his Pilot and the Observer whose leg had been broken in two places. Lex started to walk the 24 miles to El Alamein to get help. Luckily he managed to get a lift when a lorry stopped which was full of Argyle and Sutherland soldiers. Being curious to what they were doing he inquired from one them and was told that they were looking for good sites that would be of use for burying fuel and ammunition for any forthcoming battles. In August 1941 the squadron was moved to Habbaniya in Iraq where it spent the next month dropping leaflets on the towns of Kashan, Burujird and Gulpaigan. It returned to Fuka at the end of September. Lex remained with the squadron until the end of October 1941 when he was posted on detachment to the No 21 South African Air Force Conversion Unit where he was to convert onto the Martin Marylands and Baltimores.

After his conversion training was completed he was posted to No 1437 Strategically Reconnaissance Flight, which was equipped with nine Marylands and Baltimores. Lex flew 40 reconnaissance flights with the unit to Medur, Hasan, Derna, Ras-el-Milai, Laalmuda and Ezzeiat to name but a few. On the 21st November 1942 Lex had completed his first tour of operations and was given some well-earned leave. He returned from leave in early January 1943, and on the 26th he was posted to No 72 Operational Training Unit in Nanyuki, Kenya as a Wireless Operator/Air Gunner Instructor. He remained here instructing until the 12th May 1943 when the unit was moved to Alexandria in Egypt.

In June 1943 he successfully applied to get back onto an operational squadron and was posted to No 178 Squadron at Benghazi. The squadron was formed at Shandur on the Great Bitter Lakes in Egypt on the 15th January 1943 from the aircrew of No 160 Squadron's Middle East Detachment, some of the ground crews of the 159/160 Squadron (Middle East Detachment) and No 147 Squadron. It was commanded by Wing Commander JJ McRay, DSO, and was equipped with the Liberator Mk11 heavy bomber as part of No 205 Group.

The squadron played an important part in the North African and Italian campaigns. It bombed targets in North Africa, Sicily, Greece, Crete, the Aegean Islands, Italy and the Balkans (including the famous raid on the Ploesti Oil Refinery).

Lex's first operational flight with the squadron took place at the beginning of July 1943 in Liberator (AL525), which was piloted by Flight Lieutenant Whyard. Their Target was to bomb Messina in Italy, with a bomb load of 8 X 4,000lb and 2 X 500lb bombs.

Other targets visited by Lex and his crew

Reggio Aerodrome, Reggio Harbour, San Giovanni Harbour, Crotone marshalling yards, Grottaglie Aerodrome (all in Italy). Potenza, Maritza and Calato aerodromes. (Rhodes). Larrias aerodrome, mine laying in Salamis. (Greece). Mine laying in Candia Harbour, Suda Bay and Piraeus Harbour. (Crete).

Shortly after the Allied landings in February 1944 the squadron was moved from Benghazi to Celone Airfield in Southern Italy where it commenced operations against the marshalling yards at Sofia, Padua, and Milan, and the submarine workshops at Manfalcone. The war in Europe was almost over. Lex was posted back to the UK and was given six weeks leave which he spent home with his family in Northern Ireland. On his return from leave he was transferred to a Holding Unit in Nairn, Scotland. After a short spell there doing absolutely nothing he was told that he was being transferred to the No 1 Electrical and Wireless School at the RAF College at Cranwell, where he was to attend a Wireless Operator and Radar course. On successfully completing the course he was promoted to Warrant Officer and posted to No 2 Squadron which was a Coastal Command Station, equipped with Liberators at Oakes Field in the Bahamas.

It was now August 1945; the War with Japan was over. Lex found himself being returned to the UK once more, where he was finally demobbed from the Royal Air Force in January 1946 after completing 110 operations against the enemy. During his career in the RAF Lex had been mentioned in Despatches. On leaving the RAF, he returned home, where he was employed with the BBC as a Technical Assistant until 1948. He left the BBC to take up employment with the Electricity Board Northern Ireland until 1954. He then joined the Northern Ireland Civil Service, finally retiring from there in 1984. Lex was a very active member of the Aircrew Association, and was a true and dedicated member of Action Cancer, giving up many hours every week to help those in their suffering. Sadly Lex died a year after writing these words.

FLYING OFFICER
TOM DAVISON
ROYAL AIR FORCE NO. 1543555
NAVIGATOR
NO. 44 (RHODESIA) SQUADRON

Flying Officer Tom Davison was born in Belfast on the 26th June 1918 and was educated at Mount Collier Public Elementary School that was located on the Limestone Road. Tom's father had been a Pattern maker in the employ of Harland and Wolf and who was a member of the Irish Labour Party.

Tom wanted to be an electrician but had found it impossible to get that type of work anywhere due to the low employment rate at that time. He eventually became a 'Page Boy' in the Royal Cinema in Arthur Square in Belfast where he spent two years. His father through various contacts managed to obtain employment for Tom with the Ormeau Bakery as an Apprentice Baker. He remained at the Bakery until 1941 when he applied to join the Royal Air Force at Clifton Street Recruiting Office and was eventually called up in early 1942. Tom was posted to St John's Wood ACRC in London, where he was selected to become a Pilot, but failed the test at the end of the training and was offered a navigational course, which he accepted.

From the ACRC he was posted to No 3 Initial Training Wing at Painton in Devonshire, for the usual square bashing, PT, etc. He was later trained up to a transit camp in Manchester to await transport and posting.

In September 1942 Tom boarded a ship that would take him to Regina in Canada where he would start his navigational training. He arrived at No 3 Air Observers School around the end of October 1942 and after some classroom work he took to the air in an Avro Anson. His first flight was on the 29th November and by the first week in February he had completed and passed the course.

Story about No 3 AOS

It was the 2nd February 1942. The time was 1900 hrs when Tom and his pilot a Mr Draper took off from Regina airfield for a night flying exercise. The Pilot who had been flying all the previous day and night suddenly decided to take a nap during the course of the night. He woke up with a start and ordered Tom to bale out as he

had lost control of the aircraft. The Pilot was the first person out, then Tom, then the Air Gunner. On his way down to earth by parachute the high winds tore his flying boots off. The prairies were covered in freezing snow and on his way down he managed to get a glimpse of light in the distance, and after landing safely he made his way to glow in dark. He eventually came across a house, which he approached from the back, by now his feet were completely frozen and as he walked up the wooded steps of the house he thought he was wearing clogs. When he entered the house he found the pilot Mr Draper close to the warm log fire. The owners who had by now contacted the Royal Canadian Mounted Police gave him a hot drink and made him as comfortable as they could until help arrived form the camp. Tom ended up in hospital for five months with severe frostbite to both feet and very lucky not to have lost them.

It was now June and Tom had fully recovered from his ordeal he was posted to No 2 AOS at Edmonton where he finished his navigational training. He passed the course on the 17th September with 171 hours completed on Ansons. He then went to No 3 Advanced Flying Unit, which was equipped with Ansons for some advanced navigation exercises. He completed the advanced course by the 18th January and was then posted No 17 Operational Training Unit at Turkeston, Silverstone. No 17 OTU at Silverstone was equipped with the Vickers Wellington, which Tom had his first flight in on the 15th February 1944. The training here consisted of mostly high-level bombing, formation and instrument flying, cine gun exercise, and circuits and landings.

Around the middle of March 1944 Tom was posted back to the UK and on his arrival was assigned to 1660 Heavy Conversion Unit at Swinderby where he met his new crew. The Unit was equipped with the four-engine Short Stirling and Avro Lancasters. Tom had 18 flights on the Stirling before going onto the Lancaster.

Tom was posted to No 44 (Rhodesia) Squadron that was based at Dunholme Lodge in Lincolnshire at the end of July 1944.

A brief history of 44 Squadron

No 44 (Rhodesia) Squadron was formed at Hainault in Essex on the 24th July 1917 as a Home Defence Squadron. It was the first squadron to use the Sopwith Camel and one of the squadron's early commanding officers was none other than Sir Arthur (Bomber) Harris. The Squadron was disbanded in 1919 and reformed at Wyton in March 1937 as a Bomber Squadron, equipped with Hawker Hinds and later Bristol Blenheims and Hampdens. Wing Commander JN Boothman of the Schneider Trophy fame commanded the squadron at the outbreak of war. 44 Squadron was also the first to be equipped with the Avro Lancaster. The squadron added two Victoria Crosses to its Battle Honours when Wing Commander Learoyd and Squadron Leader Nettleton won the distinction. The squadron played its share in bombing the German U-Boat pens and also the Peenemunde Experimental Rocket Station, the V1 Rocket Sites in the Pas-de-Calais.

44 Squadrons last operation of the war was to bomb the SS Barracks at Berchtesgaden.

Tom's first operation with his new squadron and crew was on the 2nd August. They took off in Lancaster U 222; the Captain was Flying Officer Richardson. The Target was the flying bomb stores at Trossy. They visited Trossy again the next day and on the 5th August attacked the flying bomb stores at Criel. On the 31st August 1944 they attacked and bombed the flying bomb stores at Auchy-les-Hesdin in the Pas-de-Calais. They bombed shipping in Brest Harbour, airfields in Deeland Holland, V2 launching sites at Handorf, railway yards at Siegen, the Dykes at Walcheren in Holland, U-Boat pens at Bergen, the Ruhr Valley and the Urft Dam on the 10th and 11th January 1945.

They also bombed the Dortmund Ems canal at Ladbergen, the oil plants at Bohlen and Harburg and Hamburg. Tom's last operation with Flight Lieutenant Richardson and the crew was in Lancaster PA256 to bomb Pilsen. They took off at 2230 hrs and returned safely 8hrs.30mins later.

With his operational tour of duty now completed it was time for a rest. Tom was posted to 1661 Heavy Conversion Unit at Winthorpe on the 7th May 1945 until the 4th August 1945. His duties there were to carry out air tests, ferrying and cooks tours on Lancasters. Tom left the Heavy Conversion Unit at the end of September and joined No 16 Communication Flight that was based at Castle Donnington where he carried out two weeks training (mostly circuits and bumps) on Dakotas. His pilot was Flying Officer Quick.

Around the end of October 1945 both Tom and Flying Officer Quick were posted to 1382 Conversion Unit, based at Wymeswold. Again they were training on Dakotas mostly cross country exercises. After completing all this conversion training Tom was posted to a Metropolitan Communication Squadron at RAF Hendon (without F/O Quick). The squadron was equipped with Dominies and his duties were to ferry VIPs around Europe, visiting Rennes, Bordeaux, Le Bourget and Paris. Tom's last flight with the unit and the Royal Air Force was on the 24th May 1946. He had accumulated 444hrs.05mins flying hours by day and 318hrs.50mins by night. The aircraft types that he flew in were Avro Anson, Dominie Wellington, Short Stirling, Avro Lancaster and Dakotas.

Tom was finally demobbed from the Royal Air Force in June 1946. He applied and was accepted for a two year Degree course at a Bakery College in London and while there he lodged in the Elephant and Castle. He returned home to Northern Ireland in 1948 and rejoined the Ormeau Bakery in Belfast working his way up to Manager. The Management then decided in 1974 that the Company needed restructuring, unfortunately during that restructuring Tom was made redundant. He decided to buy his own Bakery on the Antrim Road where he worked for almost nine years finally retiring in 1980. Tom is a very ardent member of the Air Crew Association (Northern Ireland Branch) and his hobby is making sundials.

SERGEANT
THOMAS DICK
ROYAL AIR FORCE NO. 1798176
AIR GUNNER
NO. 12 SQUADRON

KILLED IN ACTION 30TH AUGUST 1944

Thomas Dick was born in No. 13, Irish Quarter in Carrickfergus, County Antrim on the 2nd March 1924 and was educated at the Church of Ireland School in Carrickfergus. On leaving school, he gained employment as a Porter in the LMS Railway in York Street, Belfast. A Memorial still stands in the station in remembrance of him.

Thomas joined the Royal Air Force on the 3rd June 1943 and was posted to the Padgate Receiving Centre in England. He was accepted as aircrew, and volunteered for the position of Air Gunner. He was then posted back to Bishops Court in Northern Ireland where he attended a Gunnery School. On successfully completing his Air Gunner's course he was awarded his A/G Brevet, and posted to No 12 squadron, which was based at Wickenby. There is no record of how many operations he carried out before his death. On the 29th August 1944 Lancaster Serial No. PD273, Code PH-K took off from Wickonby at 2048 hrs. The navigator Flying Officer Cordner set a course for Stettin in Poland. During its run into the Target, PH-K was badly damaged by flak and crashed, killing Sergeant Thomas Dick (rear gunner) and Sergeant TB Dufty (Mid-Upper Gunner).

The rest of the crew survived and were taken prisoner, they were:

Flying Officer JH Spurs, Captain.
Sergeant A Madelaine, Flight Engineer.
Flying Officer J Cordner, Navigator.
Pilot Officer KJ Chambers, Bombardier.
Flying Officer PLA Richardson (RAAF), Wireless Operator.

Sergeant Thomas Dick and Sergeant TB Dufty are both buried in Pozan Old Garrison Cemetery in Poland.

Flight Lieutenant Thomas, the pilot of Lancaster PD207 and who was also on the Stettin raid made the following report.

"Our height into the target was 12,000ft. The target was well lit by Newhaven marking and TIs were concentrated. Target was easily identified visually through a gap in the cloud. Basement figure of 12,000ft was given by M/B (Master Bomber). Bombing was concentrated and several large fires were observed. It appeared as if streets were ablaze. No fighters were seen. Slight flak was experienced over target. Layers of stratus cloud en-route, which in my opinion afforded good cover, as owing to the state of the moon it was very bright. Route chosen was definitely very good."

That night 402 Lancasters and one Mosquito took part on the raid to Stettin, 23 Lancasters failed to return. 12 Squadron despatched 12 Lancasters that night, PD273 failed to return. For you Lancaster researchers, Lancaster PD273 was one of a batch of 200 Lancaster Mk1s built by Metropolitan Vickers at Trafford Park Manchester between June and December 1944.

SQUADRON LEADER
GEORGE MILLAR DONALDSON, MID
ROYAL AIR FORCE NO. 49277
NO. 113/112/501 SQUADRONS

Squadron Leader 'Paddy' Donaldson was born in Belfast on the 8th July 1911 and was educated at Duncairn Primary School and Belfast Technical College. On leaving the College, he was employed for several years in an office in Belfast.

He joined the Royal Air Force in September 1936 and went to Austy Air Service Training for two months. At the beginning of November he was posted to Uxbridge forthree weeks and on the 15th November started his flying career at Number 7 Flying Training School (FTS) Peterborough in Avro Cadets.

(His first logbook, which covers the period 1936 to 1941, was left behind in his hasty retreat from Crete in April 1941.)

After successfully completing his flying training he was awarded his Wings on the 31st July 1937. He was promoted to Sergeant and posted to 113 Squadron. On August 1st 1937 he joined 113 Squadron, which had just been reformed at Upper Heyford in Oxon and went with the squadron when it moved to Egypt in May. In September 1938 he was transferred to 6 (AC) Army Co-operation Squadron, which was based in Palestine and was equipped with Hawker Harts. Sergeant Donaldson did see action against dissidents in Palestine, being involved in fierce peacetime fighting on the Arab-Jewish Border and many of the squadron's aircraft were either damaged or shot down by ground fire. In May 1940 Sergeant Donaldson was transferred to 112 (F) Fighter Squadron, which was based at Helwan in Egypt. In June 1940 the squadron moved to the Sudan, equipped with its new Gloster Gladiator fighters for action against the Italians in Central Africa. In November 1940 Sergeant Donaldson flying his Gladiator shot down his first enemy aircraft which was an Italian CR.42 and on the 28th February 1941 claimed his second kill which was an Italian G.50 over the Tepeline Coast and was also credited with a probable G.50 on the same day. On the 28th February 1941 the squadron destroyed ten Italian aircraft and three damaged.

On March 4th he claimed his second probable G.50 in the Valona-Himara area and on the 9th March destroyed two Italian CR42s and on the 14th March another two CR42s over the Kelcyre-Tepeline area.

Total: Six destroyed and two probables. The squadron itself was still involved in Wavell's Advance in the Desert, patrolling and escorting the bombing raids.

In January 1942 the squadron moved to Greece and in March the enemy offensive began to become extremely dangerous. The squadron was now involved in providing escorts for the retreating Greek Armies and had itself to be withdrawn to the coast and four days later was ordered off Crete. It was here during his hasty retreat that Sergeant Donaldson lost his first log book. However his log book number two starts April 22nd, this will give you readers an insight regarding the type of operations he was involved in until the 30th April when the Squadron had to hastily evacuated Crete.

An interesting selection of his log book entries

April 22nd	Gladiator N5776 Self
	Hussani to Elevsis 1hr.45mins.
April 22nd	Gladiator N5776 Self
	Elevsis to Candia in Crete. 1hr.10mins.
	(Aerodrome on fire and evacuated).
April 23rd	Gladiator N5753 Self
	Protective Patrol Candia Harbour.
	1hr.40mins
April 23rd	Gladiator N5753 Self
	Protective patrol Candia Harbour.
	1hr.40mins.
April 24th	Gladiator N5754 Self
	Protective patrol Candia Harbour.
	1hr.10mins.
April 24th	Gladiator N5754 Self
	Protective patrol Candia Harbour.
	1hr.10mins

April 25th	Gladiator N5832 Self	
	Scramble, two bandits chased. 20mins.	
April 25th	Gladiator N5832 Self	
	Scramble, aborted. 55mins.	
April 27th	Gladiator N5832 Self	
	Interception patrol. 30mins.	
April 27th	Gladiator N5832 Self	
	Safety patrol for Lockheeds. 1hr.00mins.	
April 28th	Gladiator N5832 Self	
	Escort fleet (low cloud). 1hr.30mins	
	(One ship on fire and seven Ju87'	
	engaged.) (Nil results).	
April 30th	Loadstar Self	
	As passenger Crete to Baguish 1hr.50mins	

This indicates that Sergeant Donaldson did in fact attack the Invasion Force. His total flying hours on the 30th April 1942 were 1076hrs.50mins.

When 112 Squadron left Crete the personnel were so dispersed that it was unable to be of any effect. Sergeant Donaldson ended up at Matti Baguish. Back in the safety of Egypt he was promoted to Warrant Officer and in June he was posted to 102 Maintenance Unit as a test pilot. His job was to test and evaluate many different types of both fighter and bomber aircraft including Hurricane, Blenheim, Tomahawk, Magister, Bombay, Valencia and Loadstars.

On August 21st he moved to 107 Maintenance Unit where he served for almost a year for test and delivery duties for mainly American types being delivered to the Western Desert Air Force (WDAF) and again the types flown included both fighter and bombers and these included Tomahawk, Maryland, Lysander, Hurricane, Oxford, Harvard, Gladiator, Grumman Widgeon, Kittyhawk, Hawker Hart, Boston, Baltimore and Fairchild. From he first started testing and delivering aircraft for 102 and 107 MUs in June 1941 until his last delivery flight in a Boston on the 15th July 1942 Warrant Officer Donaldson had flown in 20 different types and had accumulated almost 700hrs test flying. Most of his test flights averaged 30mins. His last flight with 107 MU was on 15th July 1942 when he was posted back to the UK.

Before he left 107 MU the chief test pilot Squadron Leader WB Price-Owen wrote the following assessment in his logbook. "The flying ability as a pilot of Warrant Officer Donaldson is 'exceptional', he has shown himself to be a very round and capable type and as will be seen from the number of Aircraft types in his logbook a very versatile pilot. Signed WB Price-Owen, Chief Test Pilot, 107 MU, Middle East."

The Chief Technical Officer of 107 MU also wrote in his log, "Warrant Officer Donaldson has given the most satisfactory service during his tour of duty as a Test Pilot at this unit. Nothing has been too much trouble for him and his energy and zeal has been most commendable. The many times he has flown bad 'belly landed' aircraft which could not have otherwise saved are many."

It is regrettable that he lost his logbook in Greece but it is certified that he has completed 220hrs Operational flying with 150 Sorties.

Warrant Officer Donaldson was commissioned on his arrival home to the UK in July 1942 and in October he was posted to 501 Squadron, which was based at Ballyhalbert in County Down, Northern Ireland.

501 Squadron had been sent to Northern Ireland for a rest in October 1942 and to be equipped with new aircraft and pilots which had been lost during the previous years operations. Pilot Officer Donaldson was not the only Ulsterman to serve with 501 Squadron; Sergeant SA Fenemore who was from Belfast was shot down and killed by a BF109 over Redhill on the 15th October 1940. Wing Commander KW Mackenzie, DFC AFC AE, also from Belfast, Flight Lieutenant WF Polley from Lisburn County Down and Flight Lieutenant Cecil Austin from Belfast also served with 501. Pilot Officer Donaldson was quite at home being posted to Ballyhalbert, as it was a short drive to his parent's house in Belfast. He started flying Spitfire Mk1s with the squadron on the 29th October carrying out convoy patrols and local fighter tactical exercises. On the 25th January 1942 and the 2nd February 1943 his logbook shows, "Beat up off Derry gun ports." How things have changed. He also carried out searches for crashed aircraft, gun testing and air to ground firing.

On the 17th November he was attached to the Central Gunnery School at Sutton Bridge where he attended a Gunnery Leaders Course. At the end of the course one month later the schools Officer Commanding as assessed him:

As a Marksman, Air to Ground	Average
As a Marksman, On Drogue	Above the average
As a Marksman in Combat	Good average
As an Instructor	Average

In February 1943 he was posted back to Ballyhalbert to take up the post as Gunnery Officer with 1493 Flight and in April moved with the Flight to Eastchurch. He returned with the Flight to Ballyhalbert on the 5th June 1943 as Gunnery Officer and started target towing duties in Martinets and Lysanders with 887 and 894 Fleet Air Arm Squadrons, and 315/26/303 Royal Air Force Squadrons. In July 1944 he was promoted to Flight Lieutenant and made Sector Gunnery Officer and Officer Commanding 1494 Flight carrying mostly local flying and visiting various local airfields including the United States Air Force Base at Langford Lodge near Crumlin. In January 1945 he attended the Officers Advanced Training School at Cranwell and was then posted back to Northern Ireland as Officer Commanding the Royal Air Force Communication Flight at Sydenham and Long Kesh (which is now the notorious MAZE prison). His duties were to fly Royal Air Force personnel between Northern Ireland and the Mainland. The Flight was equipped with

Oxfords, Proctors and Martinets. On June 12th 1945 Wing Commander E Brook who was the Senior Air Staff Officer (SASO) RAFNI signed the yearly assessment in Flight Lieutenant Donaldson's Log Book as an 'exceptional' Pilot and as 'above the average' as a Pilot Navigator.

On 13th September 1945 Field Marshall Montgomery visited Northern Ireland to pay tribute to the fighting men and women of Northern Ireland who gave so much voluntarily, and one of places he visited was Long Kesh. Flight Lieutenant GM Donaldson had the honour to be his escort for the tour of the station. In January 1946 he became the Officer Commanding RAFNI Communications Flight and the Royal Naval Air Service and now added the Dominie to his list of types. On the 2nd April 1946 he was attached to 1335 Flight Meteor Conversion Course at RAF Station Molesworth and on April 3rd flew the Meteor Mk3 solo for 40 minutes and again on the 4th, 6th, 8th and 9th. The course finished on the 10th April and on the 11th he was posted to 263 Squadron at Church Fenton Flying Meteors. 263 Squadron was to remain part of Britain's defence force with Meteors for the next nine years.

On May 1st he was attached to the Central Fighter Establishment where he attended a Day Fighter Leader's Course at West Raynam for two months flying Spitfire 9s and 16s. The course finished on the 12th July 1946. His logbook shows that he carried out the following exercises: Taffu; Rover; Joe; Underlord; Busker; Holborn; Breakway; Shambles; Nissan; Reunion; Hiroshima; Interdiction; Blackgang; Roundabout; Battle; Sopley; and Liberation. He completed the course on the 12th July 1946 and returned to 263 Squadron, which had now moved to Boxted.

On September 14th 1946 he took part in the Battle of Britain Flypast over London and in November he was on attachment with the Squadron to Lubeck in Germany, returning to the UK in the Middle of December. On the 5th April 1947 he was posted to Number 19 Squadron, which was based at Church Fenton as 'A' Flight Commander. The squadron was equipped with DH Hornet F1 aircraft, and was the second unit to receive these long-range fighter versions. At that time the Hornet was the fastest piston engined aircraft in the RAF. His first solo trip in the Hornet was on the 28th April 1947 and on the 21st September flew to Manston in his Hornet 'K' PX233 to prepare for a long range exercise to EL Adem in Egypt.

The five-day trip would take him via Manston, Istres, Elmas, Castle Benito, El Adem and Fayid. The return journey was via El Adem, Castle Benito, Elmas, Istres and Manston. On October 28th he had his first flight in a Mosquito with 19 Squadron. He did however continue to fly Hornets and Mosquitos with the squadron carrying out air to ground firing, camera gun attacks and formation flying until the 5th November 1948, when he was posted to Station Headquarters at Church Fenton as

Weapons Officer. The Station Commanding Officer was Wing Commander MD 'Thunder'.

Early in 1949 Flight Lieutenant Donaldson broke his leg very badly playing rugby and because of this was hospitalised for nine months. His logbook shows that he flew a Hornet on January 27th 1950 and it was after that he unfortunately lost his flying category and was transferred to the Secretarial Branch where he attended an administration course at Bircham Newton. Although he had lost his flying category his logbook shows that he was able to get in the odd flight in a Spitfire 16 between June and October 1950.

In February 1954 he began an exchange posting to the Headquarters' United States Air Force working with the Directorate of Intelligence in the Pentagon Washington. During his time with the Directorate he managed to get a chance to fly the B-25 Mitchell when he was visiting Andrew's/Maxwell and Dallas Air Force Bases. He did pretty well on the B-25 accumulating 119hrs.05mins as a 1st and 2nd Pilot.

Before he left the Pentagon to return to the UK he was given a Commendation by Major General Lewis, United States Air Force.

Department of the Air Force
Headquarters United States Air Force
Washington 25 DC

SUBJECT: Commendation

TO: Squadron Leader GM Donaldson, RAF.

1. During your tour of duty in the Directorate of Intelligence, USAF, you have performed your duties in a commendable manner. Your mature professional competence and great range of operational experience have been of inestimable value to this Directorate.

2. Rapid and efficient liaison between the USAF Directorate of Intelligence and the British Air Ministry through your efforts has enabled a valuable exchange of information and views on highly important Intelligence matters.

3 Your wholehearted and friendly participation in the efforts of this Directorate have been above the normal obligations of an exchange liaison officer. This is apparent by the high esteem and personal amity with which your superior officers and co-workers regard you.

4. I commend you for the effectiveness, which has characterized your service with the United States Air Force, and for the congenial manner with which you have conducted your duties reflecting the true spirit of cooperation in the officer exchange program.

Signed

Millard Lewis
Major General, USAF
Director of Intelligence

He returned home to the UK on the 24th November 1956 to take up Air Ministry duties with the A13 (E), but decided to take early retirement from the Royal Air Force in March 1958. By this time Squadron Leader Donaldson had completed 22 very interesting years in the RAF, having flown a total of 3160hrs in 40 different types of aircraft.

The aircraft types, which Squadron Leader George Millar Donaldson flew during his RAF career, are:

AVRO CADET	MARYLAND
HAWKER HART (T)	BOSTON
HAWKER HART (S)	BALTIMORE
HAWKER AUDAX	FAIRCHILD AMPHIBIAN
HAWKER HARDY	SPITFIRE MK VB
HAWKER HIND	MILES MASTER 1
WESTLAND LYSANDER 1&2	TIGER MOTH
MILES MAGISTER	PERCIVAL PROCTOR
GLOSTER GAUNTLET	AVRO ANSON
GLOSTER GLADIATOR 1&2	DOMINEE
AVRO TUTOR	GLOSTER METEOR 111 & 111A
HAWKER HURRICANE	SPITFIRE MK XIV
TOMAHAWK	GLOSTER METEOR MK 1
KITTYHAWK	HORNET MK 1
OXFORD	MOSQUITO MK 111
HARVARD	HORNET MK 111
VALENCIA	SPITFIRE MK XV1
GRUMMAN HK8	CHIPMUNK
GRUMMAN WIDGEON	MITCHELL (B25).

On his retirement from the Royal Air Force Squadron Leader Donaldson joined the Midland bank in London serving until 1976 when he finally retired. He had a passion for sport and reading and sadly died in 1986. I had the honour to talk to Mrs Donaldson many times on the telephone, and nothing was too much trouble for her. She was delighted to hear of my project and helped me in every way possible, and looked forward to seeing the finished book. Sadly she to passed away a short time ago.

Squadron Leader Donaldson is survived by son Michael and daughter Diana. Both his children decided to follow in their fathers footsteps and joined the Royal Air Force, creating for themselves a career in the RAF that their parents where proud of.

Air Vice Marshall Michael Donaldson, MBE

Squadron Leader Donaldson's son Michael was educated at Alice Deal Junior High School in Washington DC, Hazlehurst and Sidcup Grammar School in Kent.

Michael learned to fly initially on Tiger Moth and Jackfruit Aircraft in 1961 as an Air Training Corps cadet whilst at school.

He joined the RAF straight from school on 29th October 1962 to fly operationally as a Pilot. He passed the Aircrew selection board at RAF Hornchurch and went on fly Jet Provosts at 3 Flying Training School (FATS) RAF Lemming were he soloed on 21st June 1963. He served as a pilot and then as an interceptor weapons instructor flying Lightnings,

first on 23 Squadron at Leuchars from 1965 to 1968, where he was also the Lightning solo aerobatic display pilot for the 1968 season and then in 1969 as a member of the interceptor weapons instructor staff on 266 Operational Conversion Unit at Coltishall. From 1970 to 1973 he served on exchange duties with the United States Air Force as an instructor and, following to Squadron Leader, as a flight commander on the Weapons School at Tyndall Air Force Florida flying F-106 Delta Darts. In 1974 he converted to the Phantom and served as the squadron weapons instructor on 29 Squadron before taking charge in 1977 of the weapons instructor staff on 288 Operational Conversion Unit, both at Coningsby. In 1978 he attended the Army Staff College at Camberly. He was then appointed as Personal Staff Officer to the Deputy Commander-in-Chief Allied Forces Central Europe (Air Chief marshal Sir John Stacey) at Brunssum in the Netherlands. In 1980 he was promoted to Wing Commander and joined the Ministry of Defence in Whitehall in the Royal Air Force Operational Requirements Branch dealing with the Tornado Air Defence Variant development project. In 1983, following refresher courses, he assumed command of 19 Squadron flying Phantoms at Wildenrath in West Germany, and in 1985 he took command of 23 Squadron at Stanley in the Falkland Islands, also flying Phantoms for four months. In January 1986 he was promoted to Group Captain and was appointed Deputy Personal Staff Officer to the Chief of the Defence Staff (Admiral of the Fleet Sir John Fieldhouse) in Whitehall, a post he held until April 1987.

Following a refresher course on Phantoms, he commanded RAF Wattisham and its Phantom Wing from June 1987 to September 1989. In 1990 he attended the Royal College of Defence Studies in London. After this in November 1990 he was promoted to Air Commodore and appointed as Senior Air Staff Officer at Headquarters 11 Group at Bentley Priory, where from December 1990 to May 1991 he was Acting Air Officer Commanding. In this appointment he converted to the Tornado F3 and continued periodically to fly the aircraft. He was promoted to Air Vice Marshal in March 1993 and then held the appointment of Commandant of the Royal Air Force College based at Bracknell from April 1993 to January 1996. He left the Royal Air Force in September 1996, and since December 1996 he has been Principal and Chief Executive of Yorkshire Coast College of Further and Higher Education based in Scarborough, North Yorkshire. Air Vice Marshal Donaldson was awarded the MBE in the Birthday Honours list in 1973. He is a fellow of the Royal Aeronautical Society and is a member of the Royal United Services Institute for Defence Studies and also of the Institute of Directors. He was appointed Life Vice-President of the Royal Air Force Squash Racket Association in September 1996. He is married to Mavis who is a school teacher and they have two children Sarah and Duncan and his interests include music (listening, history (reading), most sports, in particular squash (still playing), rugby, tennis and golf, and walking the dogs.

Flight Lieutenant Diana Elizabeth Guthrie

Squadron Leader Donaldson's daughter Diana was born in York on the 28th June 1947 (her father was stationed at Church Fenton) and began her education in 1953 at Sidcup Hill Primary School. In 1954 she attended the Lafayette School in Washington DC, USA until 1956 returning to England in 1958 where she joined Lamorley Church of England Primary School in Sidcup. She then continued her education at University Private School in Kent and in 1966 moved to Chiselhurst and Sidcup Technical High School for Girls. In 1983-1986 after leaving the Royal Air Force she attended the Lowell University in Massachusetts USA where she obtained a BA (Hons) Degree in French and Psychology and finished her education at the University of Greenwich England (1995-1996) were she was awarded a Post Graduate Certificate in Education.

Diana joined the Royal Air Force in June 1967 and started her training at the RAF Henlow's Officer Cadet Training Unit. The types of courses she attended at OCTU were: officer training, officer's administration, schools liaison and recruiting, personnel selection, ground instructional techniques, officer's management and officer's finance. All of which she successfully completed one year later and was promoted to Pilot Officer and joined the Branch of Secretarial Officer which later became Administrative Officer Branch.

Primary duties

From 1968 until 1970 she became a Personnel Assistant/Staff Officer to a One Star General commanding an operational Royal Air Force Station and in 1970/1971 was promoted to Flying Officer and became the Administrative Officer at the Apprentice Training School where her duties were, administration of: control of leave, temporary movements, promotions, decorations and compassionate leave for all ranks. In 1971 to 1973 she became the Schools Liaison and Personnel Selection Officer and from 1973 to 1976 was Flight Commander on the Directing Staff of the Officer Cadet Training Schools: teaching and assessing leadership, social, general and specialised knowledge and skills for male and female officer cadets recruited for all the professional disciplines. During this period Diana was promoted to Flight Lieutenant. From 1976 to 1977 she was Finance Administration Officer: responsible for approximately £24,000 annually, personnel management, book keeping, budgeting, cashier pay (military and local national merchants), contracts allowances, bills, recoveries and financial advice. Diana is an all round sportswomen and represented the RAF at tennis and squash and represented Command at tennis, squash, badminton, hockey and racquetball, all of which she still plays competitively. During her RAF career, Diana became the WRAF Secretary of the RAF Racquets Association, WRAF Secretary to the RAF Germany Squash Racquets Association and the WRAF RAF Lawn Tennis Association. For these three Associations she was responsible for the arranging of fixtures, coaching, competitions and overseas tours. She also enjoys Skiing and Travel. In 1977 she became the United Kingdom Financial Officer at NATO Headquarters and finally retired from the Royal Air Force in 1979.

Today, Diana is working at the Bromley College of Further and Higher Education where she is Course Director and Tutor and teaches Post Compulsory Education. She is a member of the Royal Air Force Association, Aircrew Association, The Royal British Legion, WRAF Officers Association, WRAF Squash Golden Oldies Association and WRAF Veterans Tennis Association.

FLIGHT LIEUTENANT
WILLIAM WALTER DOUGAN
ROYAL AIR FORCE NO. 567164
PILOT
NO. 159 & 160 SQUADRONS

This is one of my more remarkable stories, in as much that Walter 'Dickie' Dougan started his Royal Air Force career in 1934 and is still flying today 64 years later. The Civil Aviation Authority deemed it necessary due to medical reasons to remove his instructors licence on his 80th birthday. He feels, and quite rightly so, that he was cut off in his prime, but can still teach aerobatics at the age of 84, as his licence is still current (and he is still the captain). He said, "It is the first time in my life I cannot get paid for doing the job I love."

William Walter Dougan was born in Ballycross, Bandbridge in the County of Down on the 22nd October 1917. He was the eldest son of Mrs Jennie Dougan and his father was Mr Lockhart Dougan, JP RDC. William began his education at Mullafernaghan Primary School and later at Bandbridge Academy (where he enjoyed a good game of rugby) and Lisburn Technical College. When he left the RAF many years later he continued his education at St Lukes Teacher Training College in Exeter.

Ten years after he retired from the RAF he had the honour of opening Mullafernaghan's new Primary school.

Ever since he was ten years old Dickie had thought of nothing else only aircraft and aviation. In 1934 he joined the RAF as an apprentice fitter (Airframe and Engines) at the No 1 School of Technical Training, Halton. On completion of his apprenticeship at Halton in 1937, he almost won a cadetship to Cranwell, but failed to pass the final interview at the Air Ministry. He did however start his flying career at Halton in 1937 in Avro Tutors.

Dickie's first logbook was lost due to enemy action in Gambut, North Africa in the early stages of the war.

On leaving Halton in 1937 he was posted to No 83 Squadron at Turnhouse near Edinburgh in Scotland where several of his Seniors from Halton were already there as pilots, and who allowed him to get a lot of dual instruction in on Hawker Harts and Tigermoths. Dickie had made up his mind that he wanted to become a pilot, so in 1941 he was posted to No 2 School of Flying Training at Brize Norton were he was later awarded his Wings. Eventually

his pilot's course came through and after training on Tigermoths and Oxfords he was posted to No 15 Operational Training Unit at Harwell on Wellingtons.

On completion of his operational training he was then posted with his crew to the Middle East via Portreath, Gibraltar, eventually arriving in Malta on the 18th April 11942 in Wellington DV643 *(DV643 was completely destroyed by enemy action a few hours after landing)*. Dickie was a 'Malta Harrier' until he had to return to the UK due to shortage of pilots and aircraft. Dickie left Malta on the 21st April 1942 in Wellington HF893. After take-off, his Wellington sustained damage due to enemy action. The aircraft had a complete electrical failure, necessitating the navigator to navigate by DR to Helwan in Egypt. When they arrived over Helwan they found it covered by low stratus clouds. Almost out of fuel and about to give the order to his crew to bail out, Dickie spotted a dark area in front of which indicated the River Nile. Flying on one engine now, he descended and broke cloud at 100ft and landed at the civilian airport of Almaza just outside Cairo. Three hours later the damage to HF893 was repaired and they were able to proceed to Helwan in brilliant sunshine. On his arrival back to the UK he was posted to the Consolidated Liberator Conversion Unit at RAF Bourne.

On completion of conversion training onto Liberators, Dickie and his crew were again posted out of the Middle East where they joined 159 and 160 Squadrons which were equipped with the Mk11 Long Range Liberators at Aqir near Tel Aviv in Israel, later to Shandur on the Great

Bitter Lakes in Egypt and finally to Gambut in Lybia. Their task was to bomb, Crete, Tobruk, Sousse, Sfax, Tunisia and shipping strikes. Walter and his crew completed a full tour of operations in the Middle East on Liberators. At the end of his tour he was 'hijacked' onto a special assignment flying the personal Liberator of Air Vice Marshal Dawson who was the Chief of Supply and Engineering for the Middle East. This assignment was very interesting, but not as exciting as bombing. It entailed flying VIPs all over Africa and Europe. In his spare time he would volunteer to fly various types of aircraft around the country for 144 MU in Algeria. The time he spent over enemy territory counted as half operational time (known as 'Z' Operations). At the end of the war he flew all the War Correspondents back to the RAF Lyneham in the UK. He was then posted to 53 Squadron in Transport Command at Netheravon and later at Waterbeach flying Halifaxes and then on Dakotas. Dickie then joined the squadron at Fassberg and Lubeck in Germany at the beginning of the Berlin Airlift.

The Berlin Airlift

With the end of World War II, the west began to look hopefully to the future, but with the German struggle finishing a new conflict began between former allies. It was the Cold War. One of the early symptoms of which was the Berlin Airlift. The Berlin Airlift was an enormous airdrop of essential supplies of food and fuel flown into Berlin by the RAF and the USAAF in around the clock missions. It was launched in response to the Soviet military authorities in Berlin under the orders of Stalin. He attempted to isolate the city from the West by severing all overland communication routes in June 1948. The Allies refused to withdraw from the western zones of Berlin and continued to fly in these supplies for 11 months. Stalin was eventually forced to back down and his blockade of Berlin ended on May 12th 1949. Dickie took part in this operation from the beginning to the end and he flew over 400 of these operations into Berlin day and night, taking much needed supplies into the city which was all but closed of to the outside world. He would also fly many women and children out of Berlin who were very frightened and did not want to stay. The types of supplies, which he flew into Berlin, were coal, flour, newspaper, dehydrated vegetables, medical supplies, and anything else, which were needed. During the airlift the Royal Air Force flew a staggering 30,900,000 miles, taking more than 540,000 tons of materials into Templehof Airport. The RAF aircraft were affectionately called 'Candy Bombers' by the young Berliners.

Dickie explained

"Flying was the only way of getting anything into Berlin, and we used an International Corridor which the Russians couldn't do anything about to stop our aircraft.

We built a power station in Berlin by flying the materials in by air. It was very exciting work, but very hard work. Our main problem was, perhaps, overcrowding. Some days there could be up to 100 aircraft flying along the corridor, which made the limited space somewhat, congested. Every few minutes an aircraft flew into Berlin separated by just a few thousand yards. The aircraft were being flown daily to their limit, and we must not forget the Ground Crews who worked day and night to keep them in the air. The Dakota was an invaluable aircraft to us, a great workhorse, and I don't think there will ever be another aircraft like it. We must not forget also that the Berlin Airlift was not without its casualties as almost 40 RAF Aircrew lost their lives. We thought it was going to lead to World War Three because the Americans were standing by to attack the Russians. It was really the threat of the Atomic bomb that eventually made them give in. It seemed to be that one day we were bombing Berlin and the next thing we were taking in supplies. Things change and a soldier does what he is told and we didn't think anything of it."

A week on the Berlin Airlift at Lubeck

"**Monday** morning we would pick up our Load Sheet, F700 and slot time. At 0930 hrs we were airborne from Lucbeck en-route for Templehof. At 1045 hrs we land at Templehof and unload our supplies. 1100 hrs we are airborne again and head back to Lubeck for lunch. 1400 hrs Airborne again this time for Gatow with more supplies land and unload and return to Lubeck to eat. 1700 hrs Airborne to Templehof with supplies unload and return to Lubeck. 2115 hrs Land at Lubeck eat, drink and fall into bed exhausted.

"**Tuesday**, **Thursday** and **Sunday** were our days off and generally messed about with our boat on the Blankense or visit the town of Lubeck and 'fraternise' (illegally) with the German Frauliens (only nice ones of course).

"**Wednesday**, **Friday** and **Saturday** were the exact same as **Monday**.

"The weeks would continue like this and repeat. It sounds boring but with only one pilot and no autopilot it was hard work and at times very exciting. Russian Mig aircraft would sometimes make 'dummy attacks' on us. You could feel the bullets even if they didn't fire. Also we had to fly exact speeds and heights (130k at 5,500ft) whatever the weather at three-minute intervals. As good transport pilots we were used to avoiding icing but that option was not available to us, because of the number of aircraft above and below us in the narrow corridor there was always the danger of a mid-air collision. We would arrive in Berlin at the Froneau Beacon and let down on a heading of 180 degrees until picked up by Ground Controlled Approach (GCA) talk down and landed on Runway 26. If unable to land or hindered by anything, we had to return to base, refuel and join the next slot back to Templehof."

In 1995, Dickie was able to take control of the very same Dakota he used throughout the Berlin Airlift. In

1998 he was reunited with his aircraft as it is still flying and based in Scotland where it is used for North Sea oil spill clean up. He said, "It was fantastic, she is flying as well as ever, a really grand old lady." Dickie returned to Germany in 1998 to take part in the Berlin Airlift 50th Anniversary celebrations and was a guest of the cities Mayor. During his posting in Germany he also flew scheduled services for British European Airways between London and Warsaw. The squadron continued doing the same type of job after the airlift. In 1949 Dickie was posted to the Central Flying School at Little Risington were he became an instructor. During the next ten years he became an instructor at No 1 Flying Training School at South Cerney, Morton in Marsh, and No 6 Flying Training School at Ternhill. Then back to Transport Command were he joined a Transport Command Development Unit (TCDU) at RAF Abbingdon where he flew Avro Ansons and DH Devons. Dickie told me, "Although I had the highest category in transport, I soon learnt that I knew nothing about flying, however as I was a good boy and worked hard and after about ten years, became an A1 instructor. This was a great relief as I no longer required to be tested."

In 1955 the TDCU was disbanded and Dickie volunteered to become a flying instructor at Queen's University Air Squadron at Sydenham instructing on Chipmunks, Harvards and Provosts.

A week at Queens University Air Squadron

"Monday morning would start with our arrival before 0900 hrs for weather briefing and plan programme. Two flights were usually carried out a.m. and two p.m. We would have two basic students and two advanced students for aerobatics and instrument flying etc.

"Lunch was from 1230 to 1400 hrs at the Wardroom in the Royal Navy Air Yard. Each day was pretty much the same finishing at 1700 hrs. Sydenham had only one runway, which meant during strong crosswinds we had to fly from Newtownards airfield, courtesy of 'Tubby Dash'. Thursday night was 'ground lectures' and 'drink training' for the students at Headquarters College Gardens in Belfast. Friday was 'hangover day' and hard work as most flying was carried out on Friday, Saturday and Sunday. Monday and Tuesday was our weekend and the social life was great. Occasionally we would take the whole squadron on a formation flight to Glasgow University Air Squadron or Limavady for lunch. Life was very laid back during those wonderful days and we could always 'borrow' an aircraft to visit another station. Night flying was carried out at RAF Bishops Court or RAF Aldergrove. Aldergrove was the best, as we had to stay overnight. Although we had our own Squadron Commanders, the squadron was run very efficiently by the secretary, a very formidable lady called Maggie Russell. During my posting with the QUAS I lived with my family at Carnalea near Bangor and my local was the Crawfordsburn Inn. This was an ideal life, and I couldn't believe I was getting paid

for it." He left QUAS in 1958 and volunteered to join the RAF Mission to help form the new German Air Force at Landsberg am Leck in Bavaria, where he flew Harvards and Fougga Magisters and Dakotas, training the German pilots to Wings standard. After six years in Bavaria he was then posted to the University of Glasgow and Strathclyde Air Squadron flying from Scone in Chipmunks. He also managed to get some flying in Meteors and Vampires as he was next door to the Unit, which towed 'flags' for the anti-aircraft guns. *(Back in the firing line once more as sometimes the Army hit the aircraft and not the flag.)*

His next posting was in 1966 to RAF Exeter were he became Officer Commanding No 4 air experienced flight instructing on Chipmunks. Walter told me, "At the end of this tour, the RAF had tumbled to the fact that I had never done a ground tour in my 34 years service and on being threatened with becoming an Air Traffic Controller (they considered that I had used devious means to evade ground tours). I resigned in a fit of pique." By now Walter had obtained ground licences and was able to get a job with South West Aviation flying their Short Skyvans and Aztecs. Sadly after just a few months with the company they went bankrupt, and Walter was for the first time in his life unemployed.

He decided to form his own Flying Club at Dunkeswell near Honiton in East Devon, and eventually moved the club to Exeter where he ran it for the next few years. This did not seem like a full time job to him so he decided to enrol at St Luke's College, Exeter University where he started a Teachers Training Course. On graduating he was offered a teaching position at Dawlish College, teaching geography, technical drawing and metal work. Walter longed to get back into full-time flying, so in 1972 he left the college to become the Chief Flying Instructor at Wycombe Air Centre. Here he was offered a job with the United Nations, training East African students at the East African Flying School at Soroti in Uganda. Walter explained, "This was a great job in a wonderful country, it was a paradise except for one thing. General Idi Amin was President of Uganda, and the country was ruled by the bullet." In 1975, Walter felt that he had crossed Amin's path, and thought it was time to make a hurried exit from the country. He returned to England and joined the Dawlish College Air Training Corps Squadron and Exeter Flying Club again where he trained instructors and civil pilots for their basic commercial licence. He was also able to rejoin his old unit No 4 Air Experience Flight and fly as an RAFVR (T) Pilot. This turned out to be very convenient as he was able to take his geography class flying frequently.

During the school holidays, Walter ran instructor classes at Exeter Flying Club and examined instructors for Grant and renewal of ratings, and did the same for Mike Woodgate in Northern Ireland. He also did a lot of aerial photography and banner towing as it made more money than instructing.

When Walter retired from school teaching at 65, he then started full time flying for a living until the Civil

Aviation Authority Medical Branch cut him off in his prime. They were wrong as he still teaches aerobatics at the ripe young age of 83 to those PPLs who wants it.

A Flight to remember

On June 16th 1992 Dougies family arranged for him to fly 'Diamond Lil', a wartime B24 (Consolidated Liberator) which was visiting Dunkeswell Aerodrome. Diamond Lil was a beautifully restored wartime Mk1. Liberator that belonged to the Confederate Air Force in America and was on a tour of England at that time. This was a surprise of a life time for Dougie and as he was a veteran of over 2,000 hours on the B24. He was allowed to take over the captain's seat to fly Diamond Lil the 200 miles back to Norwich from Dunkeswell. During the flight he was told that he had been given special permission to fly over his former wartime airfield of RAF Lyneham in Wiltshire, and was allowed to fly down the same runway he had flown down many times during the war. Dougie said, "The Liberator was (a) beautiful aircraft and with Diamond Lil, one of only two still left flying in the world, I never expected ever to see one again in my lifetime. It had always been a dream of mine ever since the war to get behind the controls once more, so you can imagine how I felt being allowed to fly one once more." While home visiting his brother in Bandbridge in March 2003 Dickie met some aviation enthusiasts in a field flying Micro-Lights. He politely asked if there was any chance of a flight, and they said no problem, and off he went at the ripe young age of 86. He also very recently took the controls of a friends 'Extra' and carried out a 'few' aerobatics (unofficially of course).

His Flying Log Book entry shows for that memorable day:

June 16th. 1992.   Liberator 1. N24917. R. Krotinger (Captain). Self (Co-Pilot) Norwich to Exeter. 1hr.50mins.

Dougies son Bruce decided to follow in his father's footsteps and joined the RAF as a Radar Mechanic for 12 years. When he was 15 he joined the West Buckland School Combined Cadet Force and his father who at that time was in charge of the No 4 Air Experience Flight at Exeter gave him his very first lesson in a DH Chipmunk. Walter has completed well over 20,000 flying hours, half of which was with the RAF and half with civil flying.

The aircraft types that he has flown are (RAF types) Avro Tutor, Tiger moth, Airspeed Oxford, Vickers Wellington, Consolidated Liberators (B-24), Handley Page Halifax, Douglas Dakota, Devon and numerous other light single engine and twin engine training aircraft. (Civilian types) All types of single and multi-engine aircraft.

Promotions: Sergeant 1940, Flight Sergeant 1942, Warrant Officer 1943, Master Pilot 1947, Flying Officer 1954, Flight Lieutenant 1956.

Civil Occupation: Flying Instructor and School Master. Walter is a Member of RAFA and ACA. His hobbies are, archaeological photography (air), model engineering and travel.

WARRANT OFFICER
JOHN JOSEPH DRUMM
ROYAL AIR FORCE NO. G1799920
AIR GUNNER
NO. 630 SQUADRON

John Joseph Drumm was born on the 28th May 1923 in Tullamore, in the County of Offaly In Southern Ireland, and was educated at the Christian Brothers School in Tullamore. Sean's (as he was known by his friends) military career started in the late 1930's as an Infantryman in The Irish Army and a short time later transferred into the Irish Air Corps where he became a Rigger.

The story of what happened next has been given to me by Sean's eldest son David John Drumm. "My father was on guard duty at the camp one night, and when some of his friends failed to return at the proper time, my father took it upon himself to sign them in. When they had not returned by daybreak he knew he was in trouble and would have some explaining to do. *(His friends had deserted and came north to join the British Army)*. My father decided to contact an old Army Officer friend and ask his advice. He told him, 'If I were you, I would join my friends up North'.

"This my father did and went to the Clifton Street Recruiting Office in Belfast to join the British Army. *(This in fact made Sean Drumm a 'deserter' in the eyes of the Eire Government and it became a Court Marshall Offence. When he eventually returned to Ireland in the Seventies he wrote to the Southern Government explaining his actions during 1939 and was given a full 'Pardon' by the Authorities.)* By the time he got to Belfast he was tired and hungry and asked to see the Army recruiting Officer, only to be told that he had gone out. The RAF Recruiting Sergeant approached my father and asked him if he would like a cup of tea and a bun while he was waiting. The RAF Sergeant was so good to him, he changed his mind and joined the RAF on the 31st August 1943."

He was then sent to a Holding Unit at Newtownards in County Down where he completed some aptitude and educational tests and to await further selection. After a few weeks at the Holding Unit he was posted to the Padgate Receiving Centre where he received his uniform and basic training. Sean was eventually posted down to the Aircrew Reception Centre in London at St Johns Wood where he was selected as an Air Gunner. Sean then

returned to Northern Ireland on 12th February 1944 where he completed and passed his Air Gunner's course at No 12 Air Gunnery School Bishops Court. His first flight with the school was on the 24th February 1944 in an Avro Anson, Captained by a Sergeant Maybury. He pass mark for the course was 62.8%. The OC of the school, Wing Commander PH Agnew, added a remark in his logbook stating that he was, "Very keen to pass the course. Needs more aircraft 'Recco' Instruction."

Sean was then posted to No 17 Operational Training Unit (OTU) at Turweston to commence his operation training on Wellington Mk 111 and Xs and meet his other crewmembers. His captain who he was to remain with until the end of his tour was Flight Lieutenant GW 'Jock' Hoare, RAAF. Sean's first operational training flight was on the morning of 20th May 1944 in Wellington (209), which was under the command of Flying Officer Grimwood. His log shows that he fired off 500 rounds. Flight Sergeant Hoare, as he was then, took command of the Wellington on the 24th May and they continued training exercises,ie, air firing, high level bombing, single engine flying, instrument flying, night fighter affiliation, air combat and circuit and landings, until the 15th June 1944. No 17 OTU then moved to Silverstone on the 16th June were Sean and his fellow crewmembers started X-country, high level bombing and fighter affiliation exercises (the attack aircraft used for his Gunnery exercises were Hawker Hurricanes and Martinets). At the end of his operational training, the Chief Gunnery instructor gave Sean a pass mark off 70.1%.

On the 12th August 1944 Sean and his crew were transferred to No 1660 Heavy Conversion Unit (HCU), which was based at Swinderby, in Lincolnshire. The Unit at that time was commanded by a Wing Commander RJ Oxley, DSO DFC and was equipped with the Short Stirling Mk111 four engine Bomber. The units aircraft were coded YW/TV. Sean's first flight on the Short Stirling was on the 31st August 1944. They took off in Stirling 'L' at 1530 hours with a Flying Officer Barnett at the helm and completed a 2hr.05mins familiarisation exercise. Their next flight was on the 2nd September at 0915 hrs again with Flying Officer Barnett and an hour later, now Pilot Officer, 'Jock' Hoare took command of Stirling 'D' himself. Sean and the crew successfully finished the Stirling conversion course on the 18th September 1944.

Sean and the crew were then posted to No 5 Lancaster Finishing School at Syerston, near Nottingham where they converted onto Lancaster Mk 111s. Their first flight in a Lancaster was on the 4th October 1944 and the aircraft was under the command of Flying Officer Davis. The course was completed on the 16th October. Sean's total flying training hours were now 162. Having now completed all his training Sean and his crew were posted to their first operational squadron, which was 630 Squadron at East Kirkby, near Spilsby in Lincolnshire. The squadron was commanded by Wing Commander LM Blome-Jones, DFC and was equipped with the Avro Lancaster Mk 111s and were coded 'LE'. Sean went on to complete 32 operations with the squadron as a rear gunner including the last raid carried out by Lancaster bombers on Hitler's Retreat in Berchtesgaden. Sean's favourite Lancaster was LE - 'L' for love.

Short history of 630 Squadron

The squadron was formed on the 15th November 1943 at East Kirkby near Spilsby in Lincolnshire where it remained until it was disbanded in July 1945. Its first operation was on the 18/19th November 1943 to Berlin, and its last bombing operation was to Berchtesgaden, (Hitler's Home) in Salzburg. It also took part in each of the large raids on the German Capital, Berlin, which came to known as the Battle of Berlin. It also took part in the Ferrying home of British ex-Prisoners of War from Europe.

His first flight with his new squadron was on the 25th October 1944 in Lancaster LE-'G' PD317 when Flying Officer Hoare took them on 4hr.45mins cross country exercise. Their first operation was to bomb the U-Boat pens at Bergen in Norway on the 28th October in Lancaster LE-'X' NN703.

Targets visited

Weskapelle (gun positions, Homburg (oil plant), Dusseldorf (railways), Duren (German strong point), Trondheim (submarine bases), Munich (industrial area), Giessen (town centre & railway yards), Heinbach Dam *(They attacked the Dam on the 10th and the 11th December 1945, each time they were hit by flak and a*

German fighter), Houffalize (German Supply Point), Graavenhorst (Dortmund-Ems-Canal, A Victoria Cross was awarded posthumously to Flight Sergeant George Thompson Wireless Operator of 9 Squadron on this raid when his Lancaster was set on fire during the bombing run. He rescued both gunner's from their burning turrets, and in doing so suffered severe burns to himself and died three weeks later.

Other Targets visited, continued: Royan; (read, the Bomber Command War Diaries for the 4th & 5th January 1945) Politz; (synthetic oil plant was reduced to rubble); Brux (synthetic oil plant in Western Czechoslovakia); Dresden (industrial centre); Rossitz (synthetic oil plant): Gravenhorst (Dortmund-Ems-Canal); Ladbergen (Dortmund-Ems-Canal); Bohlen (oil plant); Essen (11th March 1945, 1,079 aircraft were sent to bomb Essen that night. This was the largest number of aircraft sent to a target so far in the war); Dortmund (railway yards); Molbis (Benzol plant), Sean's Lancaster was attacked by a Focke Wulf 190; Lutzkendorf (oil refinery); Leipzig (Englesdorf & Mockau railway yards); and Flensburg (railway yards and shipping in port area).

The last bombing raid of the war, was on 25th April 1945, to bomb the Berchtesgaden, Hitler's 'Eagles Nest' Chalet and the SS Barracks. The flying time for this operation was eight hours. Sean and his fellow crew members had now completed 32 operations with 630 Squadron attacking some of the most heavily defended targets in Europe and it was now time for a rest. His total operational hours were now 178hrs.40mins by night and 47hrs.45mins by day.

The Crew of LE-'L' for 'Love'.

Flying Officer GW Hoare (Captain)
Pilot Officer R Ireland (Bomb Aimer)
Pilot Officer MA Cavanagh (Wireless Operator)
Flight Sergeant R Findlay (Navigator)
Sergeant T Bowie (Engineer)
Flight Sergeant M Blythe (Rear Gunner)
Flight Sergeant J Drumm (Front Gunner)

On the 3rd May 1945 Sean married ACW1 (WAAF) Catherine Mary Walters in Pontypridd in the County of Glamorgan. Sean was then 'screened' off operations and was posted overseas where he saw service in Italy and Austria in the Prisoner of War Camps until 1947 when he was released from the RAF. He enjoyed his time in the RAF so much, he decided to rejoin on a five-year engagement in February 1951, and was posted to No 97 Squadron at Hemswell as an air gunner on Avro Lincolns. This engagement lasted for 20 days and his logbook does not show any flying at Hemswell.

He was then transferred to No 230 Operational Conversion Unit at Scampton on the 20th March 1951 where he became a rear gunner on Avro Lincolns. His posting here was to last for seven months. His first flight in the Lincoln was at 1315 hrs on the 20th April 1945.

This was a 'familiarisation' exercise that lasted for 1hr.55mins. Other types of exercises he carried out were, circuits & landings, IF. & ASS flying, three engine landings, air to sea firing, GCA and QGH and babbs. On the 18th May 1951 his log book shows that he carried out a high level bombing exercise and that his "Ear was U/S." this explains why he did not fly again until the 18th October when he carried out a fighter affiliation exercise. This was to be his last flight with the unit.

On the 20th October 1951, Sean was posted to No 61 Squadron at Waddington, as a rear gunner on Lincolns. On August 15th 1952 he completed a six week Gunnery course at the Central Gunnery School at Leconfield and returned to Waddington. He left 61 Squadron on the 21st October 1952 and went 207 Squadron at Marham. Sean then Joined 207 Squadron at Marham on the 22nd October 1952. The squadron at that time was equipped with the Boeing Washington (B-29). With the introduction of the B-29 into the RAF, the duties of the Air Gunner were being phased out and eventually became obsolete. He finished this engagement employed in Air Traffic Control in Pembrey and Turnberry. He rejoined the RAF again in April 1957 as a supplier and was posted to No 16 maintenance unit where he worked in the Unit's Supply Squadron and also qualified as a Parachutist at the No 1 Parachute Training School at Abingdon in April 1961. The course lasted for five weeks and the training was carried out in Hastings, Beverlys and Balloons.

On the 2nd May 1961 Sean joined No 242 Operational Conversion Unit at Dishforth were he completed a five week course on quartermaster duties and was posted to No 36 Squadron at RAF Colerne which was equipped with the Handley Page Hastings, and after a tour which included service in Cyprus, Jamaica, Honduras, Nigeria, Gibraltar, Malta, and the Congo, he returned to his unit in September 1963. A posting followed this to Malaya and later Singapore and in 1970 he returned again to his unit at Colerne and finally retired from the RAF on 8th July 1970.

On leaving the RAF he was employed with the British Aircraft Company in Saudi Arabia and, on his return to England sometime later he was employed as a bus driver with the London Transport and also in South Wales. Sean eventually became a pub landlord at the Lord Nelson in Eastgate, Stafford, where he welcomed many of his RAF friends. He returned to Ireland where he bought his own Pub, which was called Drumm's Bar. Sean was a member of the Royal Air Force Association and his hobby was golf.

Sadly Sean died peacefully after a short illness on the 16th February 1999 in St Joseph's Hospital, Clonmel, Ireland.

The Gunner's Story in memory of Warrant Officer John Joseph Drumm

The Veterans were gathered together
On a wild night to talk to the Sprogs
It was not really good flying weather
So they drank and enjoyed burning logs.

A gunner asked someone to tell all
Just what was it like over there
How does one fell on an Ops call
Let us all know the worst, fair and square.

Then spoke Sgt Drumm from his corner
As each Sprog gripped his tankard more tight
As their thoughts turned to Junkers and Dorniers
And things that go bang in the night.

Have you ever flown deep in the Rhur lads
Where cold searchlights shimmer and shake
And like pink snakes tracer up rises
And life is no helping of cake.

Where heavy flak rattles and rends you
While Messerschmitts queue for a shot
And you've only your guns to defend you
If you haven't then you've missed a lot.

It was Christmas last year I remember
Quote Drumm as he tossed back his beer
Like a pre-war fifth night on November
With flak bursting round far and near.

I was staring straight over my gun sight
And searching the sky all around
I kept hoping this would be a good night
And I'd soon be safe on the ground.

With a sudden wild horror I startled
Get weaving Skip madly I cried
As a dark aircraft after us darted
O'er moonlit clouds on port side.

Turn port, no turn starboard I shouted
As my guns rattled out their grim hail
But the fellow tuck close, no sign of leaving
And stubbornly clung to our tail.

Here Drumm paused with glass dangled slyly
For some overawed Sprog to reply
When a lean sad-eyed pilot asked dryly
Can shadows be shot from the sky.

FLYING OFFICER
ROBERT DUNLOP
ROYAL AIR FORCE VOLUNTEER RESERVE
SIGNALS OFFICER
HMS BULOLO

Robert Dunlop was born on Garvagh, County Londonderry. He was educated at the Model School in Carrickfergus, and later at the Royal Belfast Academical Institution and studied for a Degree in Engineering at Queens University in Belfast.

At the outbreak of war Robert joined the Queens University Air Squadron where he successfully completed the No 2 Course. In early 1941 he joined the Royal Air Force where he hoped to become aircrew and was sent to Ad Astra House in London for an interview and medical. It was during the medical that it was discovered he had an eye problem, which unfortunately put paid to him becoming a member of aircrew. Not one to be put off, he asked if there was any other position open to him. He was eventually offered the job of signals officer and promoted to Pilot Officer. He was then posted to RAF Oxbridge where he was to start six months of initial training, and on completion of this was transferred to 11 Group at RAF Kenley as a Technical Signals Officer, where he was to be familiarised on the tactics of fighter control.

Robert was then posted to the RAF College at Cranwell where he began a six month advanced signals course. On completion of the course he was then interviewed by a Board and asked if he would agree to be assigned to a 'special' job, to which he promptly said yes.

In January 1942 Robert was posted to the Royal Naval Office at Greenock in Scotland to begin his 'specialised' training. On completing the course he was immediately posted to HMS Bulolo where he became the assistant to the Senior Signals Officer, Squadron Leader Sarrel.

A brief history of HMS Bulolo

HMS Bulolo was the Combined Operation Headquarters ship for the Royal Navy, Army and the Royal Air Force. It was to take part in all of the wartime landings including D-Day, with the exception of those at Madagascar and Salerno. Her Captain in 1943 was a Mr CA Kershaw, and old English rugger International Scrum-half, who had taken over from its previous skipper, Captain RL Hamer, DSO.

HMS Bulolo was of 9,000 tons displacement and graceful in her lines, she was built for the Burns Philip Line of Sydney, by Barclay, Curle's and Co of Glasgow, and engined by Kincaid of Greenock. She made her maiden voyage in September 1938, and her peacetime role as a Luxury Liner was to sail from Sydney to New Guinea, New Britain, New Ireland, and many other Pacific Islands. She got the name Bulolo from a gold mining district in Australia with the same name. The ship was taken over by the Royal Navy at the outbreak of war at fitted out at Simonstown as an Armed Merchant Cruiser. Her luxury fittings, including the swimming pool and nursery were ripped out. She was armed with seven 6-inch guns and two 3-inch anti-aircraft guns, and other light weapons. From January 1940 until April 1942 she was employed on convoy escort duties in the Atlantic, escorting over 400 ships without losing one. Between 1940 and 1942 she covered over 175,000 miles in the Atlantic. In 1942 she was taken over as a combined operation ship, being the ideal size for the job. She was Rear Admiral Burrough's flagship for the North Africa Landings, and then at Algiers she took over the communications work for the Casablanca Conference at the beginning of 1943. She then went round the Cape to become Rear Admiral Troubridge's flagship before being involved in the Sicilian landings and later at Syracuse she was the flagship of his Overseas Assault Force. The Bulolo was a quite lucky ship, as she was always first to face the shore batteries. Her record of narrow escapes is a great one. Perhaps her most dramatic arrival was at Algiers, where she was near-missed as she entered harbour. Engine room communications from the Bridge were destroyed as she came in at eight knots. In her there was perfect integration of all the fighting forces, including those of the United States of America and

Canada. On the 24th June 1943 Field Marshal Montgomery came aboard Bulolo at Acaba in the Gulf of Suez to be briefed on the Sicily landings. The ship then sailed back to Port Chufick in Egypt to replenish her stores with spares and equipment for the Invasion of Sicily. Bulolo was then ordered to return to the UK and where it set sail a few days later escorting a large convoy to Freetown (Sierra-Leone), Capetown, Durban, then passing through the Suez Canal to Abadea and finally arriving in Acaba for a final rehearsal for the Invasion. Bulolo sailed out of the Suez Canal on the 5th July 1943 and docked at Alexandria where it formed up with the main Invasion Fleet on Tuesday the 6th July and while at sea the entire ships crew received its full and final briefing for the landings.

Robert's duty that day on board Bulolo was to co-ordinate all the aircraft by radar and guide them to their pre-selected targets. On the 10th July 1943 a huge armada of ships and 470,000 plus British and American troops invaded Sicily and finally Italy.

The following are a few interesting extracts taken from Robert's diary written on board HMS Bulolo:

July 9th	Sighted Mt Etna. Weather bad. Saw many Allied gliders crash into the sea.
July 10th	Bombing the coast. Syracuse in flames with air raids... Nazi radio controlled aircraft bombed hospital ship off the Coast of Syracuse. Stopped to pick up survivors.
July 11th	Raids all day by Germans. three hours sleep (100 plus air raids).
July 12th	Spitfires, Hurricanes and Beaufighters fill the sky (six hours sleep). Syracuse Harbour badly damaged. "Heard German radio mention HMS Bulolo."
July 15th	Ashore with Gun Battery (checking Nazi equipment).
July 16th	Went ashore to Syracuse.
July 17th	Left Malta. Arrived on My 21st birthday. Big air raid in Grand Harbour Malta that night.
July 18th	After the Sicily landings were completed, Bulolo set sail for Malta via Alexandria and Port Tufick.

On his arrival at Port Tufick Robert was promoted to Flight Lieutenant.

On the 10th September 1943 while at sea Bulolo struck an unknown underwater object causing some damage necessitating her to sail immediately for examination to Bombay in India, where she was put in dry dock until repairs could be carried out. When the repairs were completed, she set sail once more and started preparing for the Anzio landings. Under the cover of darkness Bulolo arrived at Anzio along with 50,000 British and American Troops to take part in Operation Shingle. A convoy of 243 ships took part and when the troops landed they found Anzio beach deserted and the road to Rome wide open. On the 17th January 1944, HMS Bulolo then sailed back to Malta en-route for Algiers where it was to commence training for the Normandy Landings.

D-Day, 6th June 1944

Sir Winston Churchill along with General Smuts and Ernest Bevin visited the ship on the eve of the D-Day landings, and wished the ships company the very best of luck before they sailed. On the 6th June 1944, HMS Bulolo was the flagship of the assault force and part of the Eastern Task Force, she arrived at 0500 hrs off the coast of France to commence operation Gold Beach. An hour later she was anchored about seven miles off the Normandy Beaches, roughly between La Riviere and Le Hamel. Bulolo had the honoured duty to direct the landing for the famous 50th Division (Northumbrian) Commanded by Major General DAH Graham, DSO MC, and later the 7th Armoured Division (the Desert Rats) and many other supporting troops including the guards. The ship was flying the pennant of Commodore CE Douglas, CBE DSC, Royal Navy Commanding the Task Force. Although Bulolo was well armed, she was not there to engage the enemy. Her mission was to carry the Navy, Army and Air Force Commanders, and through her internal organisation and channels of communication to be responsible for seeing that the storming of the beaches and the Allied air strikes were successfully carried out. Bulolo was twice attacked by German bombers during the landings and put out of action twice. Twelve out of her fifty crew were killed during these attacks. After the landings were completed, Bulolo returned to England and was de-commissioned. Robert left the ship and was instructed to report to the Combined Operation Headquarters at Richmond Terrace in London. On his arrival he learnt that he was to be posted to Headquarters 105 Wing at Danketh House near Prestwick in Scotland. Here he spent the next few weeks training at HMS Dundonald in Kilmarnock.

Robert left the Combined Operations Group and was transferred to Bigging Hill for a short time. From there he went to West Malling where he became 11 Groups Signals Officer. His next posting was to RAF Odiham again as Signals Officer and he was engaged with converting bombers to bring back troops and Prisoner of War from overseas. When this was completed he was transferred to a Transmitter Station in Prestwick in Scotland, and then to Symington Wireless Station in Ayrshire. He was finally de-mobbed on the 26th September 1946. Robert returned home to Northern Ireland where he re-joined Queens University and finished his Engineering Degree. He then joined the family Business of James Dunlop. Although Robert retired in 1984, he remains on the Board of Directors of the Company. He is a very keen golfer (living a stones throw from Greenisland Golf Club), and is a member of the Carrickfergus Branch of the Royal Air Forces Association.

SERGEANT
THOMAS NORMAN DUNLOP
ROYAL AIR FORCE NO. 1798048
FLIGHT ENGINEER
NO. 57 SQUADRON

KILLED IN ACTION 8TH MARCH 1945

Thomas Norman Dunlop, the son of Mr Willam Dunlop, was born in Newtownards, County Down, on the 17th May 1925. Norman had two brothers and a sister called Molly. His older brother (Jim) served in the Royal Navy. Norman was one of the founder members of the 1901 (Cregagh) Air Training Corp Squadron, and was an apprentice electrician before joining the Royal Air Force on 22nd June 1943 as a Flight Engineer.

Norman's career in the RAF stared on the 22nd June 1943 when he signed on at the Clifton Street Recruiting Centre. Two days later he was on the Liverpool boat bound for the No 3 Reception Centre. On the 31st July he was transferred to No 21 Initial Training Wing where he spent the next six weeks on his basic training course. On 14th September he was then posted to No 3 Initial Training Wing. Here he was selected for aircrew duties and was offered the position of flight engineer. On the 29th September 1943 Norman was posted to the No 4 School of Technical Training at Cranwell. Here he was to commence his flight engineers training. On successfully passing the course he was then posted to No 51 Base at Scampton 27th May 1944.

On completion of his Flight Engineers course, was posted to No 1654 Conversion Unit at Wigsley in Nottinghamshire to start training on the Short Stirling. His first flight with the Unit took place on the 15th June 1944. The aircraft was a Short Sterling coded JF-R and was captained by Flying Officer Ash and Flight Lieutenant Gorton. Thomas was Second Engineer. His Log Book shows that he carried out his first operation on the 7th July 1944. This was a diversionary raid to the coast of Holland. On the 15th July 1944 Norman was introduced to his new crew. His Skipper was Sergeant Baush, (later promoted to Flying Officer). Norman flew with the same crew throughout his operational service. They continued with the Conversion Course until the 11th August 1944 when they were transferred to No 5 Lancaster Finishing School at Syerston in Nottinghamshire. Their 'conversion' course onto Lancasters lasted for three days and consisted of five training flights. The first of these training flights took place

on the 28th August in Lancaster ED802, Code RC-D. They carried out a one hour familiarisation exercise, which entailed, practicing Stalls, Steep Turns, and 3 & 2 engine flying. On the 29th March in Lancaster CE-B they carried out Circuits and Landings and on the 30th and 31st they completed various exercises that included, Corkscrews, and three Engine Landings in CE-V and CE-C (ED866).

During the first week in September 1944 Norman and his crew were posted to No 57 Squadron at East Kirby in Lincolnshire to start operational flying. On the 6th September they made their first flight with the squadron in Lancaster Serial No PB382, Code DX-N. This was a cross-country training flight around Exeter, Reading and East Kirkby. They completed a few more cross-country, and bombing exercises during September, and on the 17th September carried out their first operation with the squadron to Boulogne. They took off in Lancaster Serial No PB382, Code DX-N at 0640 hrs on the 17th September with a bomb load of 12 x 1,000lb and 4 x 500lb bombs and set a course for Boulogne. They bombed the German positions around the city in preparation for an attack by allied troops. They returned to base safely four hours later.

A brief wartime history of No 57 Squadron

No 57 Squadron (RFC) was formed at Copmanthorpe in June 1916. The squadron moved to France in the same year as a Fighter Reconnaissance unit, and was equipped with FE 2ds. During 1918 the squadron suffered a lot of casualties but also had a great record of achievement. By the end of the war it had destroyed 166 enemy aircraft, dropped 290 tons of bombs, awaken 22,000 photographs and carried out almost 200 reconnaissance's. The squadron returned to England after the war and was disbanded in December 1919. It was reformed again in October 1931 at Netheravon as a day bomber squadron equipped with Hawker Harts, and in 1936 with Hawker Hinds. In 1938 it was re-equipped with the Bristol Blenheim Mk 1s. At the outbreak of war in September 1939 the squadron was sent once again to France, firstly at Amy, and then moving to Poix, and Crecy. In May 1940 the squadron returned to the UK In January 1941 the squadron received the Vickers Wellington, and joined the night bombing offensive to France and Germany. In September 1942 the Avro Lancaster replaced the Wellingtons, which were involved in the historic low-level dusk raid on the Schnieder Works at le Creusot. In 1944 it also took part in the raids against the V-1 sites, which were hidden in the caves at Caen, and many other important and heavily defended targets in Germany. The squadron took part in the very important bombing of the defences at Wessel allowing the Allied armies to cross the Rhine in the town much more easily. The squadron was disbanded in November 1945.

A summary of Sergeant Dunlop's operations

Sept 17th   Lancaster DX-N, (PB382)
Target Bremerhaven. 4hrs.40mins
Bomb load: 1 x 2000lbs & 12 J x 500lb (clusters).

Sept 19th   Lancaster DX-O, (LM114)
Target Munchen Gladbach 4hrs.40mins.
Bomb Load: 1 x 2000lbs & 12 J x 500lb (clusters) (this was the operation in which Wing Commander Guy Gibson and his navigator Squadron Leader JB Warwick were killed).

Sept 23rd   Lancaster DX-O, (LM114)
Target Munster. Bomb load: 12 x 1000lb & 4 x 500lb bombs.

Sept 26th   Lancaster DX-O, (LM114)
Target Karlsruhe.

Sept 27th   Lancaster LE-F, (LM259
Target Kaiserslautern.

Oct 3rd   Lancaster DX-O, (LM114)
Target Wilhelmshaven. 5hrs.20mins.
Bomb load:10 x 1,000lb & 4 J (clusters) - 500lbs.

Oct 6th   Lancaster DX-J, (ME626)
Target Bremen. 1hr.55mins.
Returned early due to rear turret U/S.

Oct 30th   Lancaster DX-V, (LM618)
Target Weskapelle. 2hrs.50mins. Bomb load: 14 x 1,000lb HE bombs.

Nov 1st   Lancaster DX-V, (LM678)
Target Homburg. 4hrs.35mins.
Bomb load: 11 x 1,000lb & 4 x 500lb bombs. (Attack on the Meerbeck Oil Plant.)

Nov 22nd   Lancaster DX-V, (LM678)
Target Trondheim 11hrs.40 mins.
Bomb load: 8 x 1,000lb bombs. (Attack on U-Boat Pens.)

Dec 8th   Lancaster DX-W, (PB280)
Target Henlach Dam. 4hrs.45mins.
Bomb lLoad:14 x 1,000lb bombs.

Nil Operations carried out in January 1945.

Feb 2nd   Lancaster DX-V, (PB852)
Target Karlsruhe. 7hrs.20mins. Bomb Load: 1 x 4,000lb HC & 12 x 150 x 4lb incendiaries.

Feb 7th   Lancaster DX-V, (PB852)
Target Dortmund-Ems-Canal. 6hrs.50mins. Bomb load: 12 x 1,000lb bombs. This attack was on a canal section at Ladbergen.

Feb 8th   Lancaster DX-V, (PB852)
Target Politz. 9hrs.45mins. Bomb load: 1 x 4,000lb & 9 x 500lb bombs. Severe damaged caused to Synthetic Oil Plant (this was a big setback to Germany).

Feb 13th   Lancaster DX-V, (PB853)
Target Dresden. 9hrs.35mins. Bomb Load: 1 x 2,000lb & 14 x 500lb 'N' incendiaries. The 'N' before incendiaries stands for napalm.

Feb 14th   Lancaster DX-V (PB852)
Target Rositz. 9hrs.30mins. Bomb load: 1 x 4,000lb & 9 x 500lb bombs. The target was an oil refinery (near Leipzig and Altenburg).

Mar 6th   Lancaster DX-V, (PB852)
Target Bohlan. 10hrs.05mins. Bomb load: 1 x 4,000lb & 9 x 500lb bombs. The target was a synthetic oil refinery.

Their final raid

Sergeant Dunlop and his crew took off on their 22nd operation from East Kirby at 1815 hrs on the evening of the 7th March 1945. The aircraft was Lancaster DX-V, which had brought them back safely on many previous occasions from operations. Their target was the oil installations in a small port on the Island of Rugen in the Baltic. Their bomb load for the attack was 8 x 1,000lb bombs. Somewhere close to the target, Lancaster DV-V was lost without trace. All are remembered on the Runnymede Memorial.

The crew of DX-V

Flying Officer	CW Baush
Sergeant	TN Dunlop
Flight Sergeant	N Cooper
Flight Sergeant	JE Thompson
Flight Sergeant	DS Whitehouse
Flight Sergeant	JL Stone
Warrant Officer	D Forbes

Letters of condolence where sent to Mr & Mrs Dunlop, from the commanding officer of 57 Squadron, and the adjutant, Pilot Officer Rolanson of 1901 Cregagh Air Training Squadron. Sergeant Norman Thomas had served 259 days in the Royal Air Force. The Dunlop family lived in No 30 Delaware Street in Belfast.

FLYING OFFICER
JOHN ACHESON ESLER, DFC
ROYAL AIR FORCE NO. 64903
PILOT
NO. 86 SQUADRON

KILLED IN ACTION 17TH MAY 1942

John Acheson Esler, son of Logan and Margaret Esler, was born in Ballymena on February 5th 1915 and was educated at the Ballymena Academy for two years and later completed five years (1928-1933) at Coleraine Academical Institution. He was an excellent rugby player and was Captain for the Institution's 1st Fifteen 1931-32 & 1932-33. He was also selected to play 'Out-Half' for Ulster. He then went to Queens University in 1933 to study medicine but a short time later decided to change to engineering and was awarded a Degree in Applied Science and Technology.

John joined the RAF in Belfast early in September 1939 and was selected as aircrew. He was sent to Cornwall and North Coates near Grimsby where he completed his flying training and was awarded his Wings. On completion of his training he was posted to 86 Squadron at RAF Leuchars in Scotland. The squadron at that time was equipped with the Bristol Beaufort Mk 1s. While serving with 86 Squadron, Pilot Officer John Acheson Esler was awarded the Distinguished Flying Cross on the 15th march 1942.

The Citation reads:

"Flying Officer John Acheson Esler (64903), Royal Air Force Volunteer Reserve, No 86 Squadron. (Deceased), awarded with effect from 15th March 1942. In February 1942, this officer was the pilot of an aircraft detailed to attack shipping. No shipping was observed in the area reconnoitred so Flying Officer Esler decided to attack an alternative target, near Batonne. He made a low level attacking run over the target but his bombs failed to release. With great perseverance he spent a further 20 minutes over the target area, meanwhile making several low level attempts to attack but his bombs would still not release. He therefore decided to abandon his project. On his return journey a large enemy ship was observed near the coast south of Brest. Although Flying Officer Esler had made several valiant but unsuccessful attempts to release his bombs on the target, at Bayonne, he decided to attack the ship in the hope that his bombs would fall at

the next attempt. In spite of heavy defensive fire he made two runs over the objective but his bombs again failed to release during the second run, he attempted to release them by means of a jettison toggle but they would not fall. In his efforts to release them by this method, he failed the aircraft clear of the ship and struck the mast, smashing away two feet of the port wing of his aircraft. He then flew safely back to base. Throughout, this officer showed the utmost determination to complete his allotted task. He has recently completed two valuable reconnaissance sorties in the most hazardous weather. His gallantry has set an inspiring example."

17th May 1942

After only nine months on operations Flying Officer John A Esler took off with his crew in a Beaufort from RAF Skitten in Scotland on the 17th May 1942. His mission was to attack and destroy the heavy German cruiser, Prinz Eugen which was spotted sailing off the mountainous coast of Norway. As Flying Officer Esler and his crew were making their attack on the cruiser they were shot down and killed by enemy fighters. Their bodies were recovered from the sea and buried in Mollendal Church Cemetery in Bergen, Norway.

The following is an extract from War Commentary by Group Captain W Helmore. Thursday 28th May 1942, 9.25 p.m. Home Service.

"It sounds rather banal to have to say it but this nation has yearned for heroes, not the dead heroes of the past whose deeds are always being thrown at us, but the heroes of today with whom this Empire is studded, and whose selfless idealism is one bright streak in the dark cloud of war cynicism. Excluding the aeroplanes, there are three things alone, according to the proverb, which reach out beyond the edges of the world, the light of the sun, the darkness of the night, and the long arm of God. Listen to this, and try to visualise what sort of a man must have stored instinctively in his mind to render him capable of scaling such heights of sacrifice. I don't know whether history will record the air action against the Prince Eugen as one of the occasions when fortune specially favoured us, a second or so earlier or later pressure on the torpedo release button, a few feet away on the run, and this iron prize might have been in the bag. But I am not so much concerned with the Prince Eugen, she may yet rust away at the bottom in her good time, or be turned into kettles in the post war scrappers yard, for I am interested in the thing about the action which has in it something of the mental rhythm to which many of us in our youth accompanied Sir Richard Greenville and the Revenge on their last journey against the Spanish Fleet.

"On the 17th May 1942 when they took off with four hundred miles of ocean between them and this floating fort, it was well known to everyone of the men in those fifty aircraft how the odds stood. The ship itself had the advantage of mobility and every modern armament. She was running almost within the shadow of the mountainous coast of Southern Norway. The coast itself could provide and renew at ten minutes notice, the cloud of fighters that hovered over her, and there were four destroyers. As they gazed ahead over those miles of seascape, flecked by wind and the scanting light of early evening, they had leisure to check their navigation, prepare their equipment, and prepare themselves for an ordeal which might well have made old Sir Richard spin the wheel and turn for home. Concerning the attack, which followed, I have heard several experts in mathematics wondering how a ship six hundred and fifty feet long could possibly have been missed from 1,200 yards range, and there is a strictly mathematical answer to this problem, although it has no relation to angular velocities. Of the nine Beauforts that went in on the first wave, everyone had two or more German fighters on its tail during the run up to the target, the hand that presses a torpedo release button derives its motivation from a human body, and three of those hands probably received no such impulse.

"Of the surviving six, the rear gunner's of two were shot up by cannon shell, the navigator of another was knocked out, and yet, they flew straight and eighty feet above the eater directly into the line of the Eugen's guns, with the destroyer's flak blazing almost at point blank range. It does not require any very abstruse mathematics to determine why of these six, only three

were able to watch the run of their torpedo towards the ship and claim a hit or probable hit, why as they swerved away after attack with every detail of the Eugen's deck planking in view, three of the survivors merely expressed a pious hope that their torpedo had hit. In the melee of the terrific air battle which ensued, the Eugen could well have sunk without it being specially noticed by the contestants, for it developed into a battle between airmen in which ships were only an incident, a battle in which, however, one crew found time to throw a rubber dinghy to drowning friends, in which another crew bound up their wounded gunner so that he could man his guns and fight on. It was an action against odds for a great prize, and we are left rather grimly, with the other prize so execrated the school, but so precious in war, the prize for good conduct. Don't think I'm trying to sentimentalise about these chaps, its just that I happen to know the people and their ideals and triumphs every disaster, in a way which makes me want to convey to others, who need a torch on a dark night as much as I do, something of the selfless devotion which has left nearly forty of the best type of men this race had ever bred, upon an unscarred battleground off the Norwegian coast. In the terms of that ancient proverb, they passed from the light of the sun and the darkness of the night, to within reach of that long arm and welcoming hand which stretches out beyond the dim confines of space.

"Goodnight."

On the 27th July 1943 a letter was sent to John's father from the Air Ministry in London and it reads:

Mr L Esler Esq	Air Ministry
Lisvarna	London, WC2
Broughshane Road	27th July 1943
Ballymena	
Northern Ireland	

Sir,

1. I am directed to inform you that the King has been graciously pleased to confer the Distinguished Flying Cross on your son, the late Flying Officer JA Esler (64903) with effect from the 15th march 1942, and I attach for your information details of the services for which the award was granted. The award will be notified in the London Gazette on Tuesday 27th July 1943.

2. If you should desire, arrangements will be made for you, as the recorded next of kin, to attend at Buckingham Palace to receive the decoration from His Majesty. It is not yet possible at this stage to give any indication of the date of the ceremony you would be required to attend, but reasonable notice would be given. One other person, a blood relative of the deceased officer would be allowed to attend with you.

3. If for any reason you should not wish to attend, the decoration would be forwarded to you by post.

4. Please be good enough to indicate your wishes as soon as convenient.

I am, Sir,
Your Obedient Servant,
(Signed) FE Sheppard

John's twin sister new exactly the time and the day when her brother died. She along with her mother and father did eventually go to Buckingham Palace to receive their sons well earned Distinguished Flying Cross.

SQUADRON LEADER
RA ESLER, DSO DFC & BAR AE
RAFVR NO. 748614
PATHFINDER
NO. 149 & 109 SQUADRONS
OBSERVER/NAVIGATOR

Raymond Alexander Esler was born in Belfast on the 30th April 1917, and like so many subjects in this book, was educated at the Royal Belfast Academical Institution, attending between 1930-1936. Known for his energy and infectious enthusiasm, Ray engaged in most available sports and other school activities from day one, becoming a Prefect and Kelvin House Captain in his final year.

In addition he was a member of the Scout Troop and ended as assistant Scout master, having been both a patrol and troop leader. He would also appear to have been drama minded, joining the schools Dramatic Society and taking roles as Demetrious and Mark Antony in Midsummer's Night Dream and Antony and Cleopatra respectively. Ray was known as one who sought perfection in any situation, not for purposes of self-gratification but rather for his team or side, and it was this quality, which would be most noticeable to others in the years of war ahead.

On leaving Inst, Ray took up a post on the Manager's staff at the Midland Hotel in York Street, Belfast, but as war was looming, volunteered for the Royal Air Force Volunteer Reserve on the 1st September 1939 and was called to full time service when war was declared. On the 2nd October Leading Aircraftsman RA Esler departed Belfast along with four other Ulster Reservists to report to No 1 Initial Training Wing (ITW) at Cambridge for square bashing, injections, and to be kitted out with RAF uniform, etc.

After finishing his initial training Ray's next stop was No 11 Air Observers Navigational School (AONS) at Hamble, arriving mid-March 1940. He had his first flight in an Avro Anson N9735 under the Instruction of Flying Officer Mack on the 30th, which was a 1hr.35mins air experience flight. On the 3rd April he had four map reading exercises in an Avalon G-ACRM with Sergeant Trumper. (This was the prototype Avro Anson). At No 11 AONS he achieved an 81% pass mark in normal navigation related subjects and passed out as a qualified navigator on the 29th June. Dumfries and the No 10

Bombing and Gunnery School followed with an initial flight in a Fairey Battle aircraft coded 2170, with Pilot Officer Quartermaine on the 25th July. The next three weeks were spent carrying out exercises on the bombing range, and firing the Lewis gun at drogue targets. On the 31st July Ray had two gunnery exercises flying in a Handley Page Harrow, firing 400 and 200 rounds consecutively at a drogue target. Ray passed the course with an 80% grade in bombing and 81% in gunnery, and then proceeded to his first Operational Training Unit (OTU) at Lossiemouth in Scotland in late August.

Ray arrived at Lossiemouth on the 25th August, and flew his first operational training flight on the 10th September under the guidance of Flight Lieutenant Mitchel in an Anson. At the OTU he completed a dozen flights around the Highlands and Islands, primarily he concentrated on dead-reckoning exercises, high level bombing, and bombing sea markers, all this training was carried out in Ansons, and on the 23rd September he had his first experience flight in a Wellington in which he would later fly operational. This 24-day period until the 16th October was one of constant training on navigation and bombing techniques and entailed no fewer than 31 sorties. In total at Lossiemouth, Ray added 118 flying hours to take his total to 215. In this period he also met up with Pilot Officer Grimston, who would be his Skipper on their first operational posting.

Ray's first operational squadron was 149 Squadron that was based at Mildenhall in East Anglia. The pair arrived at the station on the 19th October, making their first flight for the squadron's 'B' Flight on the 25th and, four training flights later went on their first operational duty, which was to Wilhelmshaven in Germany. On the last day of April 1941, Ray's birthday, they had completed 32 operations with 149 Squadron, the last being a 5hr.40mins raid to Keil. They had survived during this early war period that resulted in such horrendous losses amongst the crews of Bomber Command.

Some interesting extracts from Ray's flying log

On the 3rd March 1941, Pilot Officer Grimston and Ray collected Wellington W5399 from Linton-on-Ouse and returning to Mildenhall. Ray notes clearly that this was a, Merlin-engined aircraft, and it is understandable that he did so as so few Merlin-engined Wellington Mk11s were produced. On the 12th March they used this aircraft to do a 'special test' drop of a single 4,000lb bomb, which they jettisoned over Fenny Stratford. (The 4,000lb HC bomb at that time was Top Secret and this was the first time that it had been tested.) They continued to use the 4,000lb bomb operationally following the first recorded use of this weapon on the last day of March 1941.

On the 17th March 1941 (St Patrick's Day) their target was Bremen, which they bombed from 8,000ft. On the way back they were attacked by a Ju88 over the English Coast and shot it down, landing at Honington as their own Base was closed. On the 19th March 1941 while bombing Cologne from 7,500ft, they were attacked by a Me110 on three occasions while held in cone of searchlight (uncomfortable while it lasted).

Sharnhorst and Gneisenau story 4/4/41

On the 31st March 1941 Wellington T.2737 took off from Mildenhall at 1935 hrs with Pilot Officer Grimstead at the controls, and Pilot Officer Esler as his Observer. Their objective was to bomb and destroy two German cruisers, the Sharnhorst and the Gneisenau. They bombed the targets twice, once from 9,500ft and the second time from 7,000ft. Rays job was to take photographs of the ships during the attacks which he did, and succeeded in getting at least one outstanding photograph showing the Gneisenau in dock.

On the 5th April eleven aircraft were detailed to attack the two German cruisers again at Brest. Rays aircraft arrived over the target and bombed from 8,500ft and 7,500ft both times from East to West over number 1 dock. These two capital ships were Germany's finest and were heavily defended by countless Flak Batteries. Despite very heavy anti-aircraft fire they pressed home their attacks, both runs up to the target were excellent. On the first run bomb bursts could not be seen owing to search light dazzle, but on the second run their bombs could be seen to straddle the two ships. Eleven aircraft were detailed for this attack on the German Cruisers, all returned safely.

The Operations Record Book shows that Pilot Officer Esler was awarded the DFC for his part in this epic raid.

The Crew

Pilot	Pilot Officer Grimston
2nd Pilot	Sergeant Hook
Navigator/Bomb Aimer	Ray Esler
Wireless Operator/	
Air Gunner	Sergeant Leahy
2nd Wireless Operator/	
Air Gunner	Sergeant Westmacott
Rear Gunner	Sergeant Bainbridge

The Targets

Wilhelmshaven	Turin
Gelsenkerchen	Bordeaux
Cologne	Genoa
Hamburgh	Bremen
Berlin	Venice
Duisberg	Brest
Keil	
Mannheim	

And so, on the 10th May 1941 Ray had completed his time with 149 Squadron, having carried out each of the 32 raids with Pilot Officer Grimston who was posted to another squadron.

Ray was then posted to No 31 Air Navigation School at Prince Edward Island in Canada for the No 20 special navigation course, the long 'N' as he refers to it in his log. The course started in June and lasted until the 5th April 1942. Ray completed the course with an average of 80% and returned to England on the 20th May 1942, in time to be married to Ulster girl Joan de Winter.

Ray's Log notes, "No flying-grounded due to duodenal ulcer," and it is thought that this may have first developed whilst with 149 Squadron. Whether this caused any problem on the course is not known - no flying is logged for this period, which would indicate that the training was carried out indoors.

In all likelihood, he was chosen for the course, (a) because he was a first rate navigator, (b) because he was unable to fly, and (c) because he was earmarked for instructional duties as would be normal following a completed tour.

(These various complaints were quite common amongst aircrew during the war, for obvious reasons.)

Ray returned from Canada on the 20th May 1942, and was immediately posted to No 20 Operational Training Unit as Station navigation Officer arriving at Lossiemouth the next day.

On the 19th June he underwent a medical examination and was passed fit for flying, which he resumed on the 24th. The 24th was a special trip to Snaith, as he was sent there to assist with the navigation planning for the imminent 1,000 bomber raid on Bremen, this was to be the second such raid following the first on the last day of May which was to Cologne. En-route to Snaith the starboard engine failed on their

Anson and forced them to land at East Fortune near Edinburgh, and although he arrived at Snaith a few hours later, he again suffered a force landing on the return to Lossiemouth three days later in a Wellington, this time putting down into Driffield.

Buckingham Palace

On the 22nd October 1942 Ray received a letter from St James' Palace with instructions for him to attend Buckingham Palace, where he would receive his Distinguished Flying Cross:

Central Chancery of
The Orders of Knighthood
St Jame's Palace, SW1

22nd October 1942

CONFIDENTIAL.

Sir,

The King will hold an Investiture at Buckingham Palace on Tuesday, 3rd November 1942, at which your attendance is requested.

It is requested that you should be at the Palace not later than 10.15 o'clock am. Dress - Service Dress, Morning Dress, or Civil Defence Uniform.

This letter should be produced on entering the Palace, as no further card of admission will be issued. Two tickets for relations or friends to witness the Investiture may be obtained on application to this Office and you are requested to state your requirements on the form enclosed.

Please complete the enclosed form and return immediately to the Secretary, Central Chancery of the Orders of Knighthood, St. James's Palace, London, SW1.

I am, Sir,
Yours Obedient Servant
Secretary.

Squadron Leader Raymond A Esler, DFC RAF

Thereafter flying duties were not required too often as he continued instructing the navigators passing through the unit although he did make many liaison visits to various parts of the country, including a few returns to his old base at Mildenhall. Training duties continued throughout 1943, again with the occasional flights and his logbook shows flights with what would appear to be the 'resting' pilots - Wing Commander Farr, Mitchell, Martin, and Karowin, all DFCs.

On the 9th June 1943 Ray received a letter from Group Captain Melleer who was the Station Commanding and it reads as follows:

Dear Esler,

I am very pleased to be able to inform you that the King has been graciously pleased to give orders for the publication of your name as being mentioned in Despatches, by the Air Officer Commanding in Chief.

I send you my congratulations, and thanks for all the good work you have done.

Yours faithfully,

Group Captain Commanding,
RAF Station, Lossiemouth

S/Ldr RA Esler, DFC
RAF Station,
Lossiemouth.

This was the second award to Ray, and one he so richly deserved for all his hard and dedicated work at Lossiemouth.

In advance of a return to operations, Ray attended a refresher 'N' Course at the Central Navigational School at Cranage in June, now a Squadron Leader, and completed his time at Lossiemouth in late October, he was posted to RAF Upwood near Peterborough for a one week course at the Pathfinder Force, Navigation Training Unit (PFF) [NTU]. To obtain this posting to the elite Pathfinders was a measure of his ability as a Navigator. Having completed the Pathfinder Force Navigational course he was posted to No 1655 Mosquito Training Unit at RAF Marham near Kings Lynn in East Anglia where he would meet up with his new skipper and learn the ropes on the 'Oboe' equipped Mosquito.

Ray arrived at Marham on the morning of 8th November 1943, and commenced training flights on Oxfords, his first one being on the 14th with Flight Lieutenant Burley. On the 10th December he was teamed up with Flying Officer Robert 'Bob' Palmer, a Pilot already known for his tenacity and one who could be depended upon to take whatever risks were required in order to complete his mission. Ray probably little realised at this time that together they would clock up over 70 operations together.

Their first flight in a Mosquito came on the 28th December and they continued training together until the 20th January 1944, learning about each other and laying the foundations for what was to become a superb team of 'Pathfinders'.

RAF Marham 109 Squadron, Pathfinder Force

Ray and Flying Officer Palmer were posted to 109 Squadron Pathfinder Force on 21st January 1944; the squadron was based at Marham and equipped with Mosquito B.1Vs. Ray became the squadron's Flight Navigation Officer and Deputy Squadron Navigation Officer. The pair had one flight with their new unit during the day of the 3rd February before taking the same aircraft Mk1V DK558 on their first operation together to Krefeld on the same evening. This was quickly followed by flights on the 5th, 7th and the 11th, in Mk1V, Mk1X, and MkX aircraft to Hambourne, Krefeld and Aachen respectively, all with 'B' Flight, where they would remain until the end of May when they moved to 'B' Flight. On the 22nd April Ray received a letter from Air Vice Marshall Bennet who at that time was the commanding officer of the Pathfinder

Force, advising him that he was now entitled to wear the Pathfinder Force Badge, but added, you will not be entitled to wear the badge after you leave the Pathfinder Force without further written authority from me entitling you to do so. Ray went on to complete 78 operations with 109 Squadron, 72 of them with Squadron Leader Palmer.

Some interesting extracts from Ray's flying log

On the 15th February 1944 Flt/Lt Palmer and Ray took off from Marham at 2020 hrs, their target was Aachen. As they approached the target, aircraft flicked onto its back and went into a spin on opening the radiator flaps.

109 Squadron moved to Little Staughton on the 2nd April 1944.

On 5/6th June 1944, D-Day, the pair took off from Marham at 0245 hrs in Mosquito X1V Code. ML929 "Attacking heavy gun positions, Invasion Force landed on French Coast two hours after this attack."

On the 17/18th June 1944; "Attacked (rocket installation) at Quisemont Berbille."

On 12th, 15th, 17th, 20th, 23rd, July: "Attacked V1 rocket sites, at Les Hautes Boisson, Bois des Jardins, Bois de la Hail, Chappelle Notre Dame and Mont Candon."

On 28th July they took off at 1710 hrs in Mosquito XV1, "Attacked 'special target' at Forret de Nieppe, believed to be a Rocket Shell Installation."

On 25th, 27th, 28th: "Attacked V2 sites at Watten, Marquise Mimoyecques, and Oeuf en Ternois."

On 10th September 1944: "Final assault on German garrison, at Le Havre. Attack on long range gun positions at Cap Griz Nez."

On 28th September 1944. Ray and Squadron Leader Palmer would go on to complete 72 operations together, when fate provided a dramatic and terrible intervention on Ray's 105th operation. At 0840 hrs on the morning of 30th September Ray and Squadron Leader Palmer took off in Mosquito XV1 ML997, their target was to be the Ruhroel AG Synthetic Oil Plant in the Wilhem suburb of Bottrop. "Bomb load: One 4,000lb Cookie". Just after take-off the Mosquitos port engine cut, causing the aircraft to crash approximately 1.5 miles from the end of the Runway. When the aircraft impacted with the ground the 4,000lb Cookie exploded with devastating effect (I have personally viewed photographs which were very kindly loaned to me by Ray's family and taken just after this horrific crash, the biggest piece I saw was the size of a large dinner plate).

When the fire and ambulance crews arrived at the site, they found Ray alone still strapped into his navigator's seat. The seat I might add was sitting in the field with nothing else attached to it.

(The 30th of September was not a lucky date or day for the Esler family, five years later to the very day Ray's cousin Samuel Eric Esler, DFC AE was killed test flying the Avro 707).

Ray had suffered appalling injuries in this crash and was fortunate to survive at all. His back was broken, however

as worded in his later DSO citation; with praiseworthy determination he achieved a complete recovery and returned to operational flying with undiminished enthusiasm. He was taken initially to the American Hospital at Diddington before being transferred to the Royal Air Force Hospital at Ely. He lay in hospital for endless weeks determined to recover and showing all the fortitude for which he was known. Squadron Leader 'Bob' Palmer had miraculously suffered only minor injuries in the crash and was able to walk away from it.

Whilst in hospital two notable events occurred

Firstly, in December Ray was awarded a Bar to his Distinguished Flying Cross. This was just before the second event. Squadron Leader Robert Palmer, with whom he had flown 72 operations, had resumed flying following a rest period after the crash. As an Oboe trained pilot, training which was specialised and long, he was soon returned to operations. On the 23rd December 1944 he led a daylight raid a daylight formation of Lancasters on a raid to the marshalling yards at Cologne. He encountered the most savage flak but, as bombing leader, pressed home his attack, despite being on fire with two engines in flames, in order to give the following aircraft the best chance of success. He succeeded, but his aircraft was last seen spiralling down, and he was killed. He was posthumously awarded the Victoria Cross.

Ray's log notes as follows:

"Awarded Bar to DFC in December 1944 while in hospital.

"On 23rd December my Pilot, Squadron Leader Palmer led a formation raid on a marshalling yard in Cologne. Against intense flak and fighter opposition he pressed home the attack although the aircraft was badly damaged. He got a zero error and then went down in flames. He has been awarded the Victoria Cross."

The Victoria Cross Citation stated, "It was known that he could be relied on to press home his attack, whatever the opposition, and to bomb with great accuracy. He was always selected, therefore, to take part in special operations against vital Targets. Squadron Leader Palmer distained the possibility of taking avoiding action."

Taken from a subsequent newspaper

Squadron Leader RAM Palmer, VC DFC and Bar, who was reported missing when his plane was shot down in a daylight raid on Cologne on December 23rd, is now known to have lost his life. Five other members of the crew died with him.

The only survivor, the rear gunner, attended their funeral 10 miles south of Cologne, and had written to Palmer's father giving him the sad news.

Such was the calibre of the individual with whom Ray had flown on so many occasions. There is little doubt they were very alike.

Ray's recovery was such that in the new year of 1945 he flew again on the 29th January and the 9th February with

Squadron Leader Burt, both flights were 50 minute hops, possibly to get the feel again. Having already completed 104 operations the questions have to be asked about his return to operations. Why did he do so? Did the death of his pilot, Bob Palmer have any bearing on this decision?

Is it coincidence that Ray finished on 111 raids - the same as Bob when he died. Ray Esler felt that he had more reason to fight now and protect his country as he was married and his wife Joan was expecting her first child. Perhaps he just wanted to see the job finished or was avoiding a boring ground job but whatever the answer, Ray Esler did return for his 105th raid on the 4th April, his first flight since the 9th April 1945

His final seven raids were all completed with Wing Commander Cobbe, DSO and a month later Ray left 109 Squadron at Little Staughton.

The final seven raids

April 4th	Mosquito XV1 W/CO Cobbe Operations to Hamburg *(bombing oil refinery)*
April 9th	Mosquito 1X W/CO Cobbe Operations to Berlin *(Marking for LNSF)*.
April 16th	Mosquito XV1 W/CO Cobbe Operations to Schwandorf *(marshalling yards)*.
April 21st	Mosquito 1X W/CO Cobbe Operations to Eggeek Airfield *(bombing)*.
April 25th	Mosquito XV1 W/CO Cobbe Operations to Berchtesgaden 'The Eagles Nest', Hitler's Mountain Retreat.
April 29th	Mosquito XV1 W/CO Cobbe Operations to La Hague *(dropping food to Dutch)*.
May 2nd	Mosquito XV1 W/CO Cobbe Operations to Keil. *

On the 19th May 1945 Ray received a second letter from Air Vice Marshal Bennet, Air Officer Commanding, Pathfinder Force, advising him that he was now permanently awarded the Pathfinder Badge, having now completed satisfactorily the requisite conditions of operational duty in the Pathfinder Force.

Ray left 109 Squadron on the 22nd June with the best wishes of the Squadron Commanding Officer, Wing Commander Law, who completed his final Assessment as 'exceptional', the highest assessment that Aircrew can achieve. Ray's war was now over having completed 415 operational hours in 111 raids. He had two Distinguished Flying Crosses, and seemingly somewhat overdue given his outstanding record, his Distinguished Service Order would be confirmed a few months later.

Ray's next posting was to No 16 Mosquito Operational Training Unit at Upper Heyford on the 23rd

June 1945 as Station Navigation Officer, and his first flight came on the 4th July, flying with Wing Commander Elliot in and Oxford, they completed a navigation exercise to Little Staughton. His second flight must have been a little special as it saw him being flown to Farnborough by his cousin Squadron Leader Eric Esler, DFC AE, who was also an Ulsterman and a former 120 Squadron Liberator pilot who was then with the Royal Aircraft Establishment (RAE) at Farnborough. Ray flew with Eric again on four occasions in August, mostly as passenger, and again on 13th October.

On the 26th October 1945 Squadron Leader RA Esler, DFC and Bar, was awarded his long overdue Distinguished Service Order.

The Citation of his DSO award states, "Squadron Leader Ray Esler, DFC* has taken part in three tours of operational duty, during which he attacked many of the most heavily defended targets in Germany, France and Italy. In September 1944 his aircraft crashed and his back was broken, but with praiseworthy determination he achieved a complete recovery and resumed operational flying with undiminished enthusiasm. He has accomplished duties of Flight Navigation Officer and later, Deputy Squadron Navigation Officer, with outstanding ability, making a valuable contribution to his Squadron's high efficiency."

On the 21st November 1945, Ray became the 15th holder of the First Class Navigation Warrant. The Warrant was signed and authorised by Air Marshal Roderic Hill.

Squadron Leader RA Esler, DSO DFC* AE, Royal Air Force career came to an end when he was demobbed from Upper Heyford on the 1st November 1945

Ray was invited to attend an Investiture at Buckingham Palace on the 9th December 1947 to receive his Distinguished Service Order from His Majesty King George V1. I can only assume that the time lapse between when Ray was awarded his DSO and actually receiving it was because of the backlog of awards, which had accumulated over the previous months.

Returned home

On returning home to his native Ulster, Ray joined the British Broadcasting Company in December, in charge of the Outside Broadcast department, and established himself quickly as popular broadcaster of growing repute. Unfortunately his new career of such promise was not to last and he died at a Belfast Nursing Home following an operation on 11th February 1948. He was only 30 years old. He is survived by his wife Joan, daughter Pamela and his second daughter Ray Alexandra (Sandra) who was born five months after his death.

---

*   *This Operation to Keil was the 'Last Operation of the European War' as it was feared that the Germans were assembling ships at Keil to transport troops to Norway in order to carry on the war from there.*

During his short time in the broadcasting service, Ray became a familiar and popular figure all over the province. As producer of "Concert from the Country" series and dozens of similar programmes, he was known in almost every town and village. His duties as organiser of "Workers Playtime" programmes brought him into contact with industrialists and thousands of factory workers in town and country. He was also producer of the "Behind the Scenes" series, "Starlight Serenade", "Time for Melody" and variety and pantomime broadcasts and a broadcaster on various sporting events, especially rugby, motor and motorcycle racing. His charming personality and his natural gifts at the microphone marked him out as a broadcaster of great promise. One of his notable broadcasting feats was when he recorded a commentary for the BBC in a Halifax Bomber, 50 miles out over the Atlantic during a meteorological flight from Aldergrove.

Sometime after leaving the Royal Air Force, Ray applied to the Air Ministry to ask if he was entitled to hold the Air Efficiency award. He later received a letter (not dated) from the Air Ministry:

Sir,

I am directed to inform you that as a result of amendments to the Royal Warrant governing the Air Efficiency Award, you have now qualified for this award.

I have the pleasure in advising you, therefore, that your claim has been approved and a piece of the appropriate ribbon is enclosed.

The award will be promulgated in Air Ministry Orders in 'N' series in due course.

I am, Sir,
Your obedient Servant

Ray's wife Joan received this letter on the 17th August 1950 eighteen months after his death.

Air Ministry,
London, WC2

17th August, 1950

Madam,

I am directed to forward herewith the Air Efficiency Award granted to your husband, the late Squadron Leader RA Esler, DSO DFC, for service with the Royal Air Force Volunteer Reserve. It is deeply regretted that he did not live to receive it. It would be appreciated if you would kindly complete the attached receipt form and return it to this Department at your convenience.

I am, Madam.
Your obedient servant.

Shortly after Ray's death his wife Joan received a letter and Scroll from the King, It reads:

This scroll commemorates Squadron Leader RA Esler, DSO DFC* Royal Air Force held in honour as one who served King and Country in the world war of 1939-1945 and gave his life to save mankind from tyranny. May his sacrifice help to bring the peace and freedom for which he died.

The Pathfinder

Fearless, he gazes on the vaulted nights
and scans the limits of the outer skies
A world of darkness lying on his eyes
His pinions tremble radiant into flight.

Spanning the arc of space, he sees the light
of many suns unborn, and soaring, flies
into its source where slumbering hosts arise
To hail their eagle monarchs golden might.

We, in our night, behold his rising star
Enshrined in jewels of our mortal tears
and see him clasp the sceptre of the dawn.

Now, triumph- crested, from a throne afar
he smiles upon the unforgotten years.
Our memories crown, whose highest gem is gone.

Matt Graham (1931-1937)

Captain John Shaw wrote this poem in memory of Ray Esler.

This is the tale of one who died from wounds received
in battle
Months after he had been demobbed and guns had
ceased to rattle
The war had taken toll again of a hero tried and true
Who put his duty first of all, one of the all too few.

A boy he was when country called for men to fill
the breach
For King and Country needed them, to guard the home
and beach
It was his lot to guard the skies, as he so nobly did
Along with many other chaps, our skies of Huns to rid.

For six long years the fight went on, and he was in the thick
And many times in those long years this lad was very sick
He carried on against the odds, as time has surely proved
His death it was untimely, the country greatly moved.

His many pals have scattered to all parts of the world
His special friends of Air Force days with whom the
bombs he hurled
Upon the towns and cities where machines for war
were made
He was the skipper of the plane and he his crew obeyed.

His glory has not faded, his name will never die
'Twill thrill the many millions and all the men who fly
They know the funny feeling of loneliness up there
And marvel at his courage 'a cockshot from the flare.

The boys who flew with Raymond all thought a lot of him
And privileged they thought themselves when he
bestowed a grin
They would have died to save him, but then it was
so deemed

That he should die for all of us, and hard to us
it seemed.

A boy of only thirty, with honours from our King
Has blazed a trail of courage, and may his name long ring
Where heroes are debated and deeds are told again
A gentleman and hero who did not ask for fame.

His age was only thirty when he died from such a pace
That he had got to live at, it paled his open face
No man could stand it longer, the worry and the strain
Had sapped the vital organs, before our Lord did claim.

And now the war is over and our hero gone to rest
The country needed men like him to make our country best
A gentleman he lived and died, as all of us well know
A short and great life was his lot, when called he had
to go.

A fitting tribute.

SERGEANT
STANLEY ALAN FENEMORE
ROYAL AIR FORCE VOLUNTEER RESERVE NO. 745110
BATTLE OF BRITAIN PILOT
NO. 245 AND 501 SQUADRONS

KILLED IN ACTION 15TH OCTOBER 1940

Stanley Alan Fenemore, son of William Allen and Gertrude Fenemore, was born in Liverpool in 1920. He moved to Belfast and lived on the Whitewell Road in Belfast. In early 1939 he joined the RAFVR at Sydenham, and trained at 24 Elementary and Reserve Flying Training School at Sydenam, now Belfast City Airport.

After completing his flying training he was posted to 245 Squadron at Aldergrove on July 17th 1940. The squadron at that time was allocated for the Defence of Belfast and was equipped with Hawker Hurricane Mk1s for Night Fighter Patrols. The squadron was commanded by Squadron Leader JWC Simpson, DFC & Bar, who alone shot down a Dornier 17 near the Maidens in County Down on the 9th April 1941 at 0515 hrs (this was his third kill and Belfast's first raid of the war). In September 1940 he was posted to No 501 Squadron at Kenley. On October 15th while in action with a Me109, he was shot down and killed. His Hurricane V6722 crashed at Posterngate Farm, near Godstone at 0815 hrs. A memorial seat was erected in his memory close to his crash site.

Sergeant Fenemore was 20 years of age, and is buried in Allerton Cemetery in Liverpool, Section 2D, Church of England Grave 218.

FLIGHT LIEUTENANT
FRANK FERGUSON
ROYAL AIR FORCE NO. 147940
NAVIGATOR
NO. 264 SQUADRON (MOSQUITOES)

Frank Ferguson was born in the town of Doagh (Holestone), County Antrim on the 23rd June 1923 and was educated at Coleraine College. While at Coleraine, he decided to join the college Air Training Corps Squadron and had his first flight in 1936 with Cobham's Flying Circus. After finishing College he went to Queens University, where he studied for an Aeronautical degree.

He joined the Royal Air force Volunteer Reserve at the Dunlambert Recruiting Centre (now the Dunlambert High School) on the 5th October 1941 as an AC2. On the 11th December 1941 he joined Queens University Air Squadron where he finished his Aeronautical Degree. He passed out of the air squadron on the 19th June 1942 as an LAC "Under training Navigator Radio Operator". On the 8th August 1942 Frank was posted to the Aircrew Reception Centre at Lords in London and then on to the Brighton ACDW. While in Brighton he was billeted at the Grand Hotel where he attended lectures on the theory of navigation and radio.

On completion of this course Frank was posted to the RAF Bridgnorth (IEANS) for two months and then on to No 6 Advanced Flying Unit at Little Rissington. On the 1st June 1943 he moved on to No 5 Air Observers School that was based at Jurby in the Isle of Man where he commenced his navigational training on the 1st June in Avro Ansons and Bristol Blenheims. The course lasted until the 26th August, which he passed and was awarded his (N) Brevet and promoted to the rank of Sergeant

With all the training finished he was posted to No 62 OTU at Ouston on the 26th July for a five-week course on A1 radar and Gee in Ansons. On the 1st September he gained his commission and promoted to the rank of Pilot Officer.

His Log Book assessment shows:

Airwork - Good Average.
Ground Subjects - Average.

From Ouston he went straight to No 52 OTU at Cranfield for a nine-week course on advanced training on A1 radar. The training was carried out on Dominie, Beauforts and Beaufighter aircraft. On the 5th October while training in a Beaufighter, Frank and his Pilot had a narrow escape when they lost all their instruments in low cloud.

On the 7th December 1943 Frank was posted to No 551 Squadron at RAF Twinwood and it was here that he met his Pilot Squadron Leader Elwell. They carried out some training on Beaufighters that were equipped with A1 radar. Frank's log shows that on the 16th and 23rd November he returned to base with a bent weapon. This course lasted for five weeks and the officer commanding wrote in his log, "A keen type," and had "A good average" (Squadron Leader Elwell and Frank remained a team until 2nd November 1944).

On the 10th December 1943 he was on the move again being posted to No 29 Squadron that was based at RAF Ford in Sussex. He along with his pilot was billeted in Tortington Hall Girl's School (that must have been fun). 29 Squadron was equipped with the De Havilland Mosquito Mk X11. His first operation with the squadron was on the 30th December 1943 in Mosquito HK 174. This was a 'Duskies', and 'night sector affiliation' operation. Unfortunately the operation had to be cut short due to brake failure. They carried out three more ops with 29 Squadron two Ground Controlled Interceptions when they made three contacts and one 'Bull's Eye' patrol.

On the 22nd January 1944 Squadron Leader Elwell and Frank were posted to 264 Squadron at Church Fenton. When they arrived on station they were informed that they would be billeted in tents that were quite uncomfortable and very cold. In early February 1944 Frank was promoted to Flight Lieutenant and on the 2nd February carried out his first operation with the squadron that then became part of the part of the 2nd Tactical Air Force.

His log shows that on the 2nd February 1944 they were on a Bulls Eye patrol when they had "Five visuals, all Lancasters, violent evasion action taken, all killed."

In June 1944 the squadron moved to Hartford Bridge.

Frank and his Pilot Squadron Leader Elwell carried out 80 operations with 264 Squadron some of which I have entered below.

Their first kill - Me110, Me410

On the 15th February 1944 they took off at 2254 hrs in Mosquito 519. They were on patrol with Durrington over the Channel and were vectored onto a Hun flying on 030 degrees at 16,000ft. Contact was obtained and hard weaving, target was chased to 21,000ft. Visual was obtained on bright exhausts and identified as a Me110. Got off two bursts from above. No strikes were observed. On third burst enemy aircraft blew up. Starboard wing buckled up. Position 40 miles south west of Selsey Bill. Our returning Bombers reported aircraft burning in sea. Position and time coincide with our attack. *(Later Freelanced in Stream shot down and destroyed a Me410.)*

On the 26th March 1944 Frank was detached to 96 Squadron at West Malign for a week and carried out three Patrols without any 'trade' returning to Hartford Bridge on the 3rd April 1944.

D-Day

At 0345 hrs of the 5th June Frank and Squadron Leader Elwell took off from Hartford Bridge. His logbook shows "Last patrol, 'D-Day', missed the boat again. Overhead Beach-head Landings in Normandy. A big show." On the 8th, 12th, 13th and 16th June they patrolled the D-Day beaches with four Mosquitoes and four Spitfires. Again, "No trade."

Their Second kill - two Focke Wulf 190s

On the 26th April 1944 the pair took off at 2220 hrs in Mosquito 518 to go on Patrol over France. In Fighter Pool 1 at 2245 hrs they saw Flares and Flak to west of the Seine. The decided to investigate and obtained a contact which they followed until they obtained a visual contact at two miles against the Northern Sky. Five Focke Wulf 190s were sighted, two of which peeled to Port. They followed the other three onto an easterly course and closed in and fired at them. Strikes were seen on port Focke Wulf that disappeared in flames. Strikes on starboard Focke Wulf that did a flick roll and went down also in flames. The pilot looked back and saw one enemy plane on his tail; he put the aircraft over onto its back and eluded it. With no ammunition left they flew home at 'zero' feet.

On the 2nd July while patrolling over the Beachhead they sighted 4 Ju188s but eventually lost contact with them.

On the 10th July 1944, while on patrol with 'Radox' they obtained a freelance contact at four o'clock. They followed round head on and closed in very quickly on the Aircraft that they identified as a Dornier 217 doing about 140mph. Squadron Leader Elwell gave two bursts, the enemy aircraft returned fire and went down in flames and soon disappeared.

Squadron Leader Elwell was awarded a DFC for that raid (nothing for Frank).

On the 15th July, the went on their first anti-diver patrol. They made contact with a V1 (Doodle-Bug) but their cannons failed.

On the 18th July, they were sent out an air sea rescue to try and find a Martin Marauder, which crashed and sank off Little Hampton. When they arrived in the area they found two of the crew in the sea, unfortunately one had died.

On the 22nd July, they attacked another V1. Again their cannons failed.

On the 24th July Frank was given two weeks leave and managed to hitch a lift in a Dominie from Hendon to Sydenham in Belfast.

On his return from leave on the 6th August the squadron moved to RAF Hunsdon in preparation for the move to France.

They took off from Hunsdon on the 11th August 1944 at 1500 hrs arriving in St Mere Eglise 1hour and twenty minutes later. They were on patrol the same night over St Malo when the weather turned bad and they had to land back at Middle Wallop where they saw a crashed aircraft on the runway. Flying Officer Wilmott, DFC* was killed in this crash. They continued patrols around St Mere Eglise (mostly covering attacks from V1s that where heading for England and looking for enemy aircraft around Paris).

On the 4th September 1944 the squadron moved to Bayaux, then down to Caen eventually arriving at Carpiquet where they set up base and patrolled around Cherbourg, Caen, Seine, Alencon, Argentan, Rouen, Dieppe, Abbyville, and Le Harve. The squadron was ordered back to England on the 24th September 1944 arriving at Predannack mid-day. Frank was given two weeks leave and flew home to Northern Ireland in a Hudson. When he returned to Predannack he found that the officer's mess was now in the Hotels Paul Den and Palloreum. Just one operation was covered at Predannack as the squadron was ordered up to RAF Colerne (the officer's mess was in Hardwick Hall). On the 2nd November 1944 Frank carried out his last operation with Squadron Leader Elwell and was crewed with a Flight Lieutenant Trigg.

A story

On the 16th December 1944 and with the 'Christmas Turkey' situation being practically nil on mainland England Frank and a Flight Lieutenant Marshall borrowed a Mosquito and took off on an X-country exercise that just happened to take them to Long Kesh in Northern Ireland. Here with the help of two friends a Mr PJ Morgan and a Mr Davy McKee, who had managed to obtain 64 of the best Belfast Market turkeys. They flew back to Colerne two days later with the 64 Turkeys in the Mosquito's Bomb Bay via Ballyhalbert and the Isle of Man.

He was posted to RAF Odiham for two weeks to revise A1 training. Flight Lieutenant Cecil Austin (Ulsterman) was commanding officer of the station at that time.

At the end of December 1944 the squadron returned to the 2nd Tactical Air Force and prepared to move back to France (Battle of the Bulge). They arrived at Lille Venderville in a Dakota midday on the 7th January 1945 but did not start operations until the 21st January. Most of their patrols now covered the Rhine, with only the occasional combat. Patrols were carried out around Brussels, Utrecht, Nimagen, Tilburg, Gladbach, Cologne, Dusseldorf, Essen, Scheldt, Munster, Osnabruck, Bremen, Hanover and Arras. On the 15th April 1945 the Squadron moved to Gilze-Rijen in Holland covering the Rhine Crossing and Franks log entry for the 3rd May shows "Berlin has fallen". The Squadron moved up to the Rhine on the on the 6th May 1945 where it helped with the repatriation of some 400 airmen who had been walking for fifteen weeks.

Franks last flight with Flight Lieutenant Trigg and the squadron was on the 6th May 1945 when they did an X-country looking at the damage done to various cities. His last flight with the Royal Air Force was on the 12th May 1945 in an Avro Lancaster when he hitched a lift back to RAF Odiham via Rotterdam. The pilot of the Lancaster was Flying Officer McDonald. On his arrival back at Odiham he was sent down to Aircrew Reception Centre at Regents Park where he waited for one month seeing the sites.

Frank was then posted down to the Rehabilitation Unit at Catterick. Here he was told that he was being posted to Elstree Central Link Trainer School (CLTS) as assistant station adjutant and promoted to Flight Lieutenant on the 23rd August 1945 and 'Mentioned in Dispatches' *(two days after I was born)*.

On the 29th August Frank was posted to Hereford where he completed No 34 course at the School of Administration and Accountancy. From Hereford he was posted to No 11 Elementary Flying Training School where he became the station adjutant for five weeks. Finally he was posted to Woodley for two days where he received the relevant information for leaving the RAF. Frank was demobbed from the RAF at Heamsford 104 Personnel Dispatch Centre Christmas 1946. He had completed 80 operations and had a total of 479 flying hours in fourteen different types of aircraft.

He returned home to Northern Ireland and rejoined Queens University where he studied for a Degree in Architecture and Town Planning. He became a Civil Engineer in 1949 and formed the Company Frank Ferguson and Associates that is a Multi Diciple Consultancy with over forty years direct experience in environmentally orientated construction and engineering.

Frank still works today from his home at Raw Brae in Whitehead County Antrim and is a member of the Aircrew Association Northern Ireland Branch.

LEADING AIRCRAFTSMAN
JAMES LESLIE CREIGHTON GASTON
RAF NO. 617514
WIRELESS OPERATOR/AIR GUNNER
NO. 142 SQUADRON (FAIREY BATTLES)
RADIO OFFICER MERCHANT NAVY
NO. 3502 (ULSTER) FIGHTER CONTROL UNIT

LAC Gaston was born in Whitehead County Antrim on 2nd December 1915 and was educated at the Belfast Royal Academy. On completion of his education, he was employed as an audit clerk with the LMS/NCC railway.

On the 10th August 1938, Leslie visited the RAF Recruiting Office in Ann Street Belfast and volunteered as aircrew. He was informed that they had just accepted an entry for aircrew training and it could be six months before places would become available again. They then told Leslie that they were extremely short of Wireless Operator/Air Gunners, and could fit him into that position right away. Leslie quickly accepted his offer, and was told to report to RAF West Drayton where. After passing his medical he was 'sworn' in, received the Kings shilling, service number, and RAF kit. He was then given the basic rank of aircraftsman 2nd Class (AC2). On completion of all these formalities he was posted to No 2 Depot at Cardington for basic training, which lasted approximately two months. On completion of his basic training on 21st October, Leslie was posted to No 8 Electrical & Wireless School at RAF Cranwell as a Wireless Operator (under training).

This was a four months intensive course that included radio theory, Morse code, and the first stage of air operating was carried out in Vickers Virginia aircraft (at that time were known as flying class rooms). On completion of the course at Cranwell on 10th February 1939, Leslie was then posted to No 2 Electrical & Wireless School at RAF Yatesbury to complete the final part of his flying training and wireless operating.

On 22nd May 1939, Leslie was then posted to No 3 Air Observer School at RAF Aldergrove to train as an air gunner flying in Handley Page Heyfords. On successfully completing the course 14 weeks later he was promoted to Aircraftsman First Class (AC1). On 8th September 1939 he was posted to 207 Squadron at Cranfield to carry out operational training in Fairey Battles. The training consisted of air firing and cross country exercises and was completed in early November when Leslie was transferred to a holding squadron at RAF Hucknall to await posting to an operational squadron. A few days later this was confirmed as 142 Squadron flying Fairey Battles and stationed at Berry-au-Bec in France. Leslie was trained down to Southampton Docks where he boarded a troopship that would take him to Cherbourg and joined the squadron on the 26th November.

Leslie remarked, "I never flew the Channel, because of my short RAF Career, I went out in a troop ship and came back in a hospital ship."

The squadron was equipped with Fairey Battles and was part of the Advanced Air Strike Force (AASF) and gained the distinction of being the first AASF Unit to bomb the advancing German Army. On the 2nd February, Leslie was awarded his Air Gunners Badge, and had many stories to tell about his time in France.

On one occasion during a night flying exercise, they encountered a severe snowstorm. The pilot informed Leslie he was lost and when the blizzard subsided he would descend and try to ascertain were they where. There was no sign of the storm abating so the pilot decided to drop down and try to get under it and get a bearing on their position. Just as they were coming out of the storm Leslie heard an almighty bang, they had flown into some telephone wires sustaining damage to the propeller blades. They carried on flying south, eventually spotting a farmer ploughing his field. The pilot decided to land nearby and as Leslie was the only one who could speak any French was despatched map in hand and advanced towards the farmer to determine their exact position. They had in fact landed near Avigion and after consultation with the farmer who informed him that the French airfield of San Lorrient was nearby, they took off, refuelled at the French Airfield and returned to base at Berry-au-Bec.

"On one occasion the German Luftwaffe bombed the airfield and sustained a direct hit on the officer's toilets."

During his operations with 142 Squadron Leslie was unfortunate enough to be involved in three crashes. The first crash occurred on 10th May 1940 when Group Headquarters ordered an all out attack on a large German troop column advancing along the Luxembourg-Dippach Road.

Flights from No 12, 103, 105, 142, 150 and 218 Squadrons, a total of 32 Fairey Battles escorted by Hawker Hurricanes from No 1, and 73 Squadrons took part in this operation.

The German troops were units of the 16th Panzer Korps under the command of General Hopner.

Three Battles took off from 142 Squadron, and as they approached the target, their fighter escort broke off to patrol at 15,000ft over the city of Luxembourg. Leslie's flight spotted troops on motorcycles and sidecars and made a low level attack at about 40ft. *(Leslie told me he was so close to the Germans he could see their black uniforms quite clearly)* dropping their bombs and the air gunners strafing the column on their way past. There were no enemy fighters, but they encountered heavy accurate fire from 20mm cannons and heavy machine guns. As Leslie was reloading his guns the aircraft received many direct hits and lurched violently, the Pilot and Observer were badly wounded. The crippled Battle broke away and made course for home. Leslie was able to crawl forward and dress the Observer's wounds, but was unable to reach the Pilot due to the distance between them and the design of the aircraft. Just as they landed back at base the exhausted Pilot WH Corbett passed out due to the loss of blood and was awarded an immediate DFC. Their No 2 L5578 was shot down near Petange 18km SW of Luxembourg (no survivors) and the No 3 just made it back to base. On inspecting his aircraft later, Leslie found that it was like a colander; riddled with holes.

On May 10th at 1530 hrs a second attack was mounted against the German columns, a total of 32 Battles were involved in this sortie. This time no fighter escorts were provided and a squadron of Me109s attacked the bombers. A total of ten aircraft failed to return. This brought the total up to 23 Battles lost in the two raids and as many severely damaged and out of action for a considerable time.

Shortly before the dawn on the same day, No 114 Blenheim Squadron was preparing to take off from Conde Vraux airfield to attack the Meuse Bridge at Maastrict and General Hopner's 16th Panzer Korps, Dornier 17'Zs of 4. /KG2 carried out a low level attack fanning out over the airfield. In exactly 45 seconds 114 Squadron ceased to exist. By nightfall on May 15th 1940 the RAF in France had lost a total 205 aircraft, comprising of 86 Fairey Battles, 39 Blenheims, nine Lysanders, and 71 Hurricanes. No 2 group had lost a further 43 aircraft. After five weeks of fighting the RAF lost a total of 1,029 aircraft of which 299 belonged to the AASF and over 1,500 personnel were killed or missing.

Flying Officer Donald Garland and his Observer Sergeant Tom Gray were both awarded posthumously the Victoria Cross for their gallant attack on the Vroen Houen Bridge

As Leslie did not have a logbook the date of the second crash is approximate.

On the 17th/18th May 1940 they took off to bomb another German column, which was located north of Beauois, again attacking at low level (40'), unfortunately they had a hang up with one of their bombs; return fire was again intense and accurate. Their engine was hit and making strange noises, eventually catching fire compelling the pilot to make a forced landing, which he did close to a goods yard. On landing the crew quickly exited the Battle in case the hung up bomb would go off. They were immediately arrested by French soldiers who mistook them for Germans. They tried to explain who they were but the French did not understand and took them to a local police station. Eventually things were sorted out and they were sent by train to Paris where they reported to the local British Embassy. After some sightseeing in Paris and in due time they returned to their unit. By this time the German Army was only a few miles away, everyone was told to report to the Armoury to be issued with rifles and bayonets. The purpose of this exercise was that they would be taken to a wood on the outskirts of the airfield, where the petrol was stored in 'Jerry' cans. They used the bayonets to puncture them all so as the Germans could not benefit from the fuel. The airfield defence crews, (later to become the RAF Regiment) began to dig large holes all around the perimeter of the airfield and mounted machine guns in them, and even assembled some home made 'Molitov Cocktails'. Eventually the crews were ordered to fly their aircraft to Troyes and Faux-Villecerf airfields and to await further orders.

Cobber Kane, DFC

Leslie remembers very well the 6th June 1940, the day Flying Officer James Edgar 'Cobber' Kane, DFC was doing a low slow victory roll for the press, the wingtip of his Hurricane caught some trees however and he crashed to his death.

Pilot Officer Kane at that time was the RAF's top scoring pilot, having destroyed 16 enemy aircraft and one damaged.

142 Squadron was ordered to attack Rouen, which the Germans were using as a supply base for moving troops and ammunition. Again the attack was at low level, and Leslie was able to see one of his bombs hitting the bridge. They were so low their Fairey Battle (L5397) was either caught by the blast from their bomb or by return fire. They immediately set course for base, and had just reached its safety, when three specs came out of the sun, they soon realised that they were being attacked by three German 109s. The first Me109 attacked and was unsuccessful, the second one opened up just as Leslie returned fire, he was

sure he hit him. The third Me109 attack was successful; Leslie remembers a blinding flash and a loud bang, and going unconscious. His next memory is of waking up in an ambulance with severe head and leg wounds.

He also remembers being blown out of a hospital train that was being bombed by the Luftwaffe, and ending up in a field on the stretcher. He then slipped out of consciousness for quite a while as he had been heavily sedated. He eventually arrived at No 2 Field Hospital at Chateau-le-Mans, which was run by the Royal Army Medical Corps (RAMC). After a time he was moved to La Boule which is in the Bay of Biscay and then on to Quibron (a French fishing village) where he was put on a French fishing vessel, and then ferried out to the hospital ship Doretshire. He was immediately shipped home, arriving at Southampton Docks. Here he was put on a train that would take him to Plymouth, eventually arriving at Monmouthshire Hospital in Newport. The hospital was absolutely chocker block with Dunkirk casualties. Leslie remained at the hospital until he recovered in September 1940. On the 16th September 1940 he was requested to attend a medical at the RAF Hospital in St Athans, where he was classified as unfit for further flying duties. Leslie decided there and then that he could not stay on in the RAF, and was discharged on 16th September as physically unfit for air force service, although fit for employment in civilian life.

Leslie came home to Northern Ireland, but could not settle into civilian life, so he decided in June 1941 to apply to join the Merchant Navy as a Radio Officer. He was immediately sent on a 'crash course' on wireless and maintenance procedures to the Belfast Wireless College, which at that time was in North Street Arcade. Leslie had no problem gaining his certificate. On the 5th August 1941 he joined his first ship the Swift Pool, and in mid-Atlantic, five hundred miles south of the Irish coast the ship was torpedoed and sunk by a German U-boat. Leslie and one other crew member were picked up after a few hours by HMS Bluebell. They were the only survivors.

Between the 10th September 1941 and 2nd April 1945, Leslie survived in various types of Merchant Ships, including the San Adolfo (fleet oiler), Sierra Leone (iron ore carrier), Baron Forbes (cargo), Port Adelaide (refrigerator), and the Cijneros (cargo). He was finally discharged from the Merchant Navy on the 10th April 1946 and returned to Northern Ireland where he joined the civil service as a junior staff officer.

On the 25th October 1949, Leslie joined 3502 (Ulster) Fighter Control Unit as a Radar Operator. The unit was based at the Edenmore Hotel on the Shore Road and later at Greenisland House. He joined with the rank of Sergeant, and eventually reached the rank of Pilot Officer before leaving in 1960. Leslie finally retired from the civil service in 1980 and was an active member of the Aircrew Association (Northern Ireland Branch) and the Royal Air Force Association (Carrickfergus Branch). Leslie died in 1999.

FLIGHT LIEUTENANT
JACK 'PADDY' GINGLES, DFC DFM

RAF NO. 1113981
ROYAL AIR FORCE BOMBER COMMAND
NO. 9 & 617 (DAM BUSTER) SQUADRONS

John Gingles, youngest son of Thomas Hugh and Sarah Ann Gingles, was born on the 24th July 1922 in the County Antrim hamlet of Hightown near the ferry port of Larne. He had one brother and one sister. From the family home at Park View House, he attended the local Kilwaughter Primary School until 1935 when, aged 13, he continued his education at Larne Grammar School. Unconfirmed evidence, by way of oral tradition, would appear to suggest that he was obliged to leave school after a physical exchange with a teacher.

Always a bit of a lad, Jack was never one to pass up the opportunity of a good prank, and this changed little over time, leading to trouble with his superiors. Described in later years as 'exuberant and over-enthusiastic' he is probably best described at this stage as caring little for authority and having absolutely no patience with time wasters. As time passed little was to change and he would have no respect for 'self pompous' stiff shirts and could not suffer fools by the same measure.

It is probably true to say that although he graduated to become an excellent pilot. he did not feel at home until he reached the sanctity of No 617 Squadron where he was surrounded by many people he admired and vice versa. He totally worshipped, even revered Leonard Cheshire. They were two personalities who, with many within the squadron, were bonded by mutual admiration and respect. Cheshire, to those who knew him, was a naturally gifted leader of men. There is little doubt that Cheshire soon recognised the quality and finer points of Jack Gingles, and nurtured them during his period as commanding officer of the squadron.

John Gingles, also known to some as Jack but to his flying colleagues as 'Paddy', was interviewed by me at some length in February 1986 at the home of his brother Eric. Although not one known to hang back, Jack was initially reluctant to open up about his considerable experiences but with the help of Eric's sherry, he became chatty and admitted to enjoying the nostalgia evoked by the session. However it was felt that not all was being told by this superbly capable and gifted aviator and a second

in-depth meeting was requested and agreed to. Indeed Jack admitted to welcoming it, commenting that it gave him the excuse to think seriously about his former colleagues, about whom he thought so highly. Then aged 63 years, Jack had been retired from flying for almost six years and was looking forward to his continuing retirement. Sadly he was to have a heart attack and died whilst on a 'Guinea Pig' holiday in January 1988 at the age of 65, and sadly for me the follow up meeting never took place.

His story is now told using information gained at the one and only meeting, from personal surviving papers, from printed data, researchers and from meetings with those who remembered him. It is sad that fuller details are not available as it is felt that there were certain segments in his wartime flying years that were not clear from his personal papers. Indeed there is a feeling that some elements were not logged. Included with his flying log is a (personal) record of the airfields at which he was stationed and those at which he landed, plus a listing of those pilots and co-pilots flown with. In some cases these records have helped me to piece together or confirm events, and are occasionally referred to in isolation throughout the story simply to complete a period or for fullness of account. Whilst every effort has been made to piece together this fascinating tale, there are inevitably some gaps and, where there is doubt, no attempt has been made to second-guess the events. Further research will continue and, if other facts emerge, an update will be included in the next volume of this work.

What is not in doubt is that Jack Gingles was one of the finest pilots who flew with the renowned aviators of 617 Squadron. He was revered by his crews, admired by both the great Leonard Cheshire and by his successor Willie Tait. There is no doubt in mind and many others within the squadron that Paddy would have been awarded with higher honours had it not been for a combination of his wayward temperament, a refusal to suffer fools gladly, his disdain for authority and the political considerations of the time. It is known that he was twice put forward for the DSO without result, although it was of no concern to a man who did not seek personal glory, rather one who would always sing the praises of others.

His love of a good prank is undoubted and yet, whilst carrying out operations, he displayed a cool and raw courage that belied his apparent lack of discipline.

In the early summer of 1940, at the age of 17, he tried to enlist in the Royal Air Force but was told to return when he was 18 years of age. Although he would be 18 in less than two months time, he waited one week before visiting the recruiting office once again and being less that truthful about his age. This time he was accepted and did actually commence his induction before turning 18 although official RAF records showed him as being older.

In early July 1940 he left Ulster for the induction unit at Padgate and onward for basics at Ford before arriving at the Initial Training Wing at Newquay on the 11th October. Flying training commenced on the 9th of January 1941 at No 4 Elementary Flying Training School at Brough, near Hull, using the ubiquitous Tiger Moth (DH82). His Solo flight followed on his 19th flight on Wednesday 5th February when he had completed 9hrs.05mins flying and he continued training until being assessed as 'average' when the course ended in late March.

Some references would suggest him being stationed at Gilberdyke in January and also landing at Lincoln in February 1941.

His service flying training commenced at the No 14 Service Flying Training School at Cranfield, near Bedford that was equipped with the trusty Oxford. Ten flights later he went solo and continued through the entire day/night flying syllabus, being awarded his wings in late June with an 'average' rating. Jack was now posted to No 20 Operational Training Unit at Lossiemouth for two months. He started training on Wellingtons in Conversion Flight 'C' on Wednesday 16th of July, and took the controls of Wellington 1665 for the first time four days later, and completed his conversion training on Wednesday 6th August and moved the same day to 'D' Flight for operational training. By Saturday 23rd he had finished here and was posted to operations with No 9 Squadron at Honington in East Anglia.

On Sunday 7th September, he took the No 2 seat on his first operation that was to Berlin. The aircraft was Wellington 8853 and its Captain was Sergeant Clayton (later awarded the DFC, CGM & DSO). Jacks logbook shows the flying time to Berlin was 6hrs.20mins and they

were hit by flak causing them to land at Marham on the return journey. This was followed by two operations with Sergeant Roberts (later awarded two DFCs) to Turin and Frankfurt. As one of the youngest fully qualified bomber pilots in the RAF, (Jack was now six weeks past his 19th birthday), and having first flown in an aeroplane less than eighth months previously he was now days away from commanding his first operation over Germany.

He was also only 19 days away from a crash that left him badly injured and killed most of his crew.

His first operation in command was on Wednesday 17th of September to Le Harve and this was followed by one he would never forget. On Friday 26th September, after a 4hr.30mins trip to Emden, in Wellington B222 where they suffered damage from heavy flak, he remembered only too well the events of the return to base.

On a night of poor visibility the last thing they needed was a malfunctioning altimeter aboard their Wellington Mk 111, the latest version of the Wimpy which was being introduced at that time, and in which they carried out a one hour air test earlier that day. The uncertainty over their altitude necessitated dropping down to try and find their base. Unfortunately in so doing they came into land too far down the runway overshooting and ploughing into some trees, causing Jack to be thrown through the cockpit canopy and he sustained serious facial lacerations and leg injuries.

His crew were less fortunate, three of which were killed.

Jack's serious injuries necessitated a skin graft some eighteen months later at the East Grinstead Hospital and it was here that the famous Sir Archibald McIndoe restored so many badly burned and injured aircrew back to normality - later known as the 'Guinea Pigs'.

He did not fly again for over three months, when he returned to operations. It would appear he was not fit enough to regain his commanders position for almost a year and completed a further 26 operations in the No 2 seat until he left No 9 Squadron in 1942. The majority of these 26 operations being into the German heartland including seven to the dreaded Ruhr Valley as well as Hamburg, Warnemunde, Dortmund, Essen, Stuttgart, Keil and Brest.

One operation worth mentioning was on Tuesday 20th January when they bombed Schiphol airfield at low level (400ft), they destroyed one enemy aircraft and shot out the searchlights. On their return the front gunner was awarded the Distinguished Flying Medal. Of interest also during this period was the attempt on Thursday 12th of February to locate the Scharnhorst and Gneisenau during their Channel dash. In the event they were not located.

Of these 31 raids, 26 were completed as No 2 to Pilot Officer Casey, DFC. Paddy's personal details record him as being killed later. On Monday 1st June he had completed 462hrs.30mins flying, 147 of which were operational. In late June, now screened off operations, he arrived at No 22 Operational Training Unit at Wellesbourne Mountford where, using the Avro Anson, he was to instruct many crews in the period until late September, by which time the OTU was also operating from Gaydon, near Coventry. His first check trip with 'C' Flight at Wellesbourne was with Flight Lieutenant SJ Hookway, DFC, who was promoted Squadron Leader and took over as officer commanding 'C' Flight the next month. Jack notes him also as being later killed.

On Thursday July 23rd his entry notes an engine failure in Anson 501 whilst at 1,500ft on a cross-country exercise. A crash landing followed in a field near RAF Station Hemswell although no detail of injury or damage is noted. On Thursday 1st of October he joined No 3 Flying Instructors School at Hullavington. Operating out of Castle Combe he continued to give instruction in Oxfords before returning to No 22 Operational Training Unit at Wellsbourne/Gaydon in late October, where he remained until early May. His start at Castle Combe was less than auspicious when, on his second day with the unit his Oxford, ED271, crash landed at Hullavington. His pupil at the time was a Pilot Officer Wilson and it is interesting to note that, on the return from Hullavington the following day, in a different Oxford, that Jack took the No 1 seat himself. On leaving No 3 FIS in October to return to Gaydon, his commanding officer Wing Commander Gosnell, DFC and Bar, rated him as an 'average' Pilot and Instructor. Back at Gaydon he joined the Technical Training Flight and flew mainly Wellingtons in a considerable number of air firing and cine camera exercises with many different aircrew. This took him through the turn of the year and on into April.

Jack's records show a visit to RAF Brighton from mid-April to early May. This is thought to be to the RAF Disciplinary Centre, known to fliers as 'Prune's Purgatory', a persuasive penitentiary designed to curb the excesses of over enthusiastic and exuberant aircrew. It is not known why he was sent here.

From Brighton Jack was posted to No 432 Squadron, Royal Canadian Air Force that was based at Skipton-on-Swale. On the 14th May he made his first flight with the squadron in the form of an air test and air experience flight on the Wellington Mk X, which was being introduced at that time to the squadron. This was also his first flight with the crew whom he would fly with on the majority of his 16 operational flights.

His crew

Navigator	Pilot Officer Laberge
W/Op	Pilot Officer Kemp
Air Bomber	Pilot Officer Redman
Air Gunner	Flight Sergeant Bybee.

(Jack notes that Laberge and Redman as being Prisoners of war and Bybee as missing!)

On Sunday May 16th he was posted to 1835 (RCAF) Blind Approach Training (BAT) at Middleton St George for five days, the unit was equipped with Oxfords.

With Flight Lieutenant Murrell he had his obligatory operation as No 2 on Tuesday 25th May which was to Dusseldorf before taking command with his own crew for a further 15 operations between Thursday 27th May and Friday 6th August.

Targets Jack visited with 432 Squadron

Dusseldorf, Essen, Wuppertal, Krefeld, Mulheim, Elberfeld, Cologne, Brest, Aachen, Hamburg and Lorient.

Three trips worth mentioning

The first was on Saturday 3rd July when he was taking part on a raid on Cologne, his aircraft was shot up by a Lancaster's rear gunner who was heading in the same direction, and flying directly over the top of him. The Lancaster crew had obviously mistaken the Wellington for a German night-fighter, since the rear gunner opened fire and sprayed the Wimpy with bullets, knocking out one of its engines. Onboard Jacks aircraft, in the rear turret was an American, and who according to Jack was a bit of a 'Cowboy', himself, and he was anything but amused at being shot up by one of his own aircraft. "Lancaster or no Lancaster, he was for shooting back at the 'Ba----d," and it took all of Jacks persuasion to cool the Yank down.

He continued on to bomb the target on one engine and returned safely for an emergency landing at Graves End in Kent. The second was on Tuesday 3rd August when he was returning from a mine laying operation to Lorient, his record shows that, "I was hit by one dirty piece of flak." The third was on a raid to the German capital, Berlin, his aircraft was hit by heavy flak which caused a fuel leak, but undeterred, Jack carried to the target, dropping his bombs and returned safely to base. After the aircraft had landed, it was inspected, and found to have no fewer than 144 holes in the structure. Some confusion exists as to his movements between this time and his arrival at No 5 Lancaster Finishing School at Syreston near Nottingham in March 1944.

It is known that he had skin grafts carried out at the East Grinstead hospital by the famous Sir Archibald McIndoe and I think it could have been during this period that they were carried out.

On Wednesday 21st July 1943 Flight Sergeant John Gingles had been recommended for the Distinguished Flying Medal by Wing Commander WC McKay, Officer Commanding 432 (RCAF) Squadron.

His Citation reads:

This NCO has completed thirty-seven successful trips, the majority of them over heavily defended targets in the Ruhr Valley. He has proven himself an outstanding pilot, and has inspired his crew with his coolness and his dogged determination. For this fine record of achievement, his exceptional coolness and skill, and his devotion to duty, he is strongly recommended for the award of Distinguished Flying Medal.

Additional remarks by the Station Commander

Sergeant Gingles is regarded as one of the outstanding Captains in his squadron, and his example has been an important factor in elevating the general standard of efficiency of the squadron as a whole.

I strongly recommend that he be awarded the DFM.

JL Plant, Group Captain, Commanding Officer RCAF Station Leeming.

Air Vice Marshall GE Brookes, Air Officer Commanding No 6 (RCAF) Group fully supported the recommendation and Paddy was awarded the Distinguished Flying Medal on the 9th September 1943. Jack had an appointment at Buckingham Palace on the 6th June 1944 to receive his DFM from King George V1, but due to his operational commitments with 617 Squadron that day (Operation Taxable) he was unable to attend. His record shows visits to hospital during July and August and it is possible that this period gave him some time to think and make a decision to volunteer for No 617 Squadron. In any event he joined the famous Dambuster Unit immediately after his hospitalisation although it has been suggested that he was approached personally by Leonard Cheshire.

His records show him leaving No 432 Squadron at Eastmoor at the end of October 1943 and spending time with 617 Squadron at Scampton, Coningsby and Woodhall in the period to mid-March. What was done in this period is again not known, peculiarly in his records reference to his being with the squadron at Scampton on Monday 1st/Tuesday 2nd November 1943, a time when the squadron was actually based at Coningsby.

No 617 Squadron. I have no doubt that Jack was a member of 617 Squadron from Monday 1st November 1943, but had been temporarily screened off operations by reasons of convalescence. However it would appear that he volunteered for a 'special duties' Squadron that took only the best, which Jack was as attested to by the wording of his DFM Citation.

In any event he arrived first at No 5 Lancaster Finishing School at Syreston in early-mid March 1944 and completed a ten day conversion to the Lancaster before arriving at Woodhall Spa in early April to join 'A' Flight of the famous Dambusting squadron, by now teamed with the crew who would serve him faithfully in the coming months. However he did not leave Syreston without one of the pranks for which he had become well known. Unfortunately these remain largely undocumented but we know from his disciplinary record that he was not averse to taking any opportunity to have some fun.

On this occasion he was on his last flight at Syerston before departing for Woodhall spa and gave his own farewell to the station by doing a spectacular and highly accomplished 'beat up' of the airfield. It is to be hoped he thought it worthwhile as his departure to Woodhall Spa was delayed by the punishment he received - five days in a row as Duty Pilot in the Syreston Control Tower. This opinion about Jack Gingles which I received from George Riley (God bless him) is only his personal opinion but I thought it should be mentioned. "He was to grace 617 Squadron for a considerable period. He had no superior in the squadron as an operational pilot and captain at a time when 617 Squadron could boast many a superb pilot and aircrew."

Resuming with No 617 Squadron

He first flew with his new squadron on Wednesday 5th April and carried out cross country, night and dummy run exercises before his first operation on the night of the 18th April. The Target was the marshalling yards in Paris, the Crew were:

Pilot	Officer Beale
Flying Officer	Scott-Kiddie
Flying Officer	Hall
Warrant Officer	Riley
Flying Officer	Hazell
Sergeant	Gallagher

The aircraft was Lancaster 'L'.

Jack had now resumed his First Pilot responsibilities with his own crew and not, as was normal with a new unit, in the No 2 seat, and had only been undertaken following the mandatory sessions on the bombing range which had been insisted on by Cheshire, who would not permit any new crew to go operational unless they had successfully carried out three exercises on the range. In addition, all crews were required to maintain standards and to continue visiting the ranges, their records forming a league table which was kept up to date by the squadron bombing leader.

Note: With No 617 Squadron the new pilots only had one or two training flights as a No 2, if they were not up to scratch, they were posted back to their Unit. 'No second chances'.

A crews position in the league table could be used by Cheshire to determine if they went on ops or not and, later, whether they were to be entrusted with the very expensive 12,000lb (Tallboy) and 22,000lb (Grandslam) bombs.

It is very interesting to note that Jacks record of Sunday 16th April. Two days before his first operation for the squadron he flew Lancaster 'V' ED932 to Metheringham. Previously registered 'G', his log notes show this to be the aircraft used by Gibson for the famous Dams raid of May 1943.

Together with most of the squadron he spent all of May practising for the upcoming operation to provide a major diversion for the D-Day landings on Tuesday 6th June. Requiring navigational and timing skills of the highest order, 617 Squadron was tasked on the 6th June 1944 to carry out under conditions of greatest secrecy to undertake 'Operation Taxable, which would involve the aircraft dropping 'Window' (metallic foil strips that created false images of the invasion fleet) on German Radar seeking to convince the German defences that the main allied invasion fleet was aiming to land well to the north of Normandy. At the same time No 218 Squadron was undertaking Operation Glimmer, a complimentary and duplicate operation further north.

After D-Day Jack then continued to operate with his colleagues in the 'special duties' squadron in bombing, principally in daylight, the important targets on the French coast. These comprised of the submarine pens at Le Harve, Lorient, and La Pallice, the Flying Bomb and rocket installations at Pas-de-Calais, St Pol, Paris, and Wizernes. All of these targets were heavily defended but of vital strategic importance to the Allies. In the majority of these raids the new and formidable 'Tallboy', the 12,000lb bomb, was used. The weapon having been designed by Barnes Wallace of Vickers and having been first dropped by the squadron a few days after D-Day. In Jack's records from this time with 617 Squadron, it is interesting to note the weight quoted for the Tallboy bomb. The Barnes Wallis design was actually of 12,000lbs but it was so secret the exact weight was apparently not given to the aircrews initially for security reasons. Jacks log book entries up to the raid of the 7th August 1944 show the weight of the bomb as 14,000lbs and it would appear that this was the 'guide' weight given to the crews in order to calculate their take off weights, etc. Thereafter the weight is correctly stated at 12,000 pounds.

Another famous raid which Jack was involved in was the bombing of the sluice gates of the Kembs Dam, which was situated six miles north-west of Basle. The Dam governed the flow of the Rhine between the Swiss town of Strasburg. It was the intention of the German high command to destroy the dam as the American army advanced a few miles downstream causing a tidal wave and taking thousands of lives. To avoid such a catastrophe 617 Squadron were detailed to blow up the dam before the Americans crossed the Rhine. This they did on the 7th October 1944. Thirteen Lancasters from 617 Squadron, each carrying a 12,000lb Tallboy bomb, were escorted by P-51 (Mustang) aircraft to the target. The operation was split into two waves. One low (300ft) flying of six aircraft, with each Tallboy having a long delay fuzing. One high flying of seven aircraft, with each Tallboy having a intermediate delay fuzing. The losses of KC-S and KC-Q came from the lower wave, afterwards referred to as the 'Suicide Wave'.

The operation was a complete success, unfortunately and as mentioned 617 Squadron lost two of its aircraft and crews to flak,

NG180 KC-'S' and LM482 KC-'Q'. The Polish fighter escort also suffered considerable losses.

Some 20 operations were carried out leading up to the major and highly risky daylight raid against the German Battleship Tirpitz, of which Churchill had said;

'The destruction of this ship is the greatest event at sea at the present time. No other target is comparable to it. I regard the matter as of the highest urgency and importance." So began the attack on the Tirpitz.

The keel for the Tirpitz was laid down at Wilhelmshaven in 1936, launched in April 1939 by the granddaughter of Admiral von Tirpitz in the presence of Adolf Hitler and completed in 1941. She was the sister ship to the Bismarck and regarded by the Germans as the finest battleship ever designed. Her original displacement was 41,000 tons, plus length 791ft, beam 118ft, draught 26ft, speed 30knots and carried a compliment of 2,400 officers and men. Her armament consisted of eight x 15" guns, twelve x 4.9" guns, and sixteen x 4.1" guns. Her side belting armour was 15" thick, horizontal deck armour consisted of two layers: The upper layer of 2.5" armour plate and the lower layer (some 20feet below) was 3.5" thick.

The Tirpitz had been attacked on a number of occasions by the Navy, Fleet Air Arm, and the Royal Air Force, but finally succumbed to Lancasters of 617 and 9 Squadrons of the Royal Air Force on the 12th November 1944. Amongst the first air attacks, was that carried out by Halifaxes in the early months of 1942, when the Tirpitz was anchored in Trondheim Fiord in Norway. Amongst the ordnance carried on this particular operation, included a type of 'spherical mine'. It would appear that several Halifaxes carried six each of the spherical mine, while others a mixture of the 2,000lb SA weapon, as well the 1,900lb HE weapon. The RAF now realised that there was four main problems in attacking the Tirpitz, weather, smoke screen, range, and weapon. The latter was to be 617 Squadron and 9 Squadrons Tallboys that was the only weapon that could possibly penetrate the ships armour.

617 and 9 Squadrons were to attack the Battleship on three occasions; Jack participated on all three Operations.

The first attack

On Friday 15th September from Russia when the Tirpitz lay in Alten Fiord. The reason they attacked from Russia was Alten Fiord was 1,000 miles from the nearest British base. A Lancaster with a full fuel load and carrying a 12,000lb Tallboy bomb could not fly to Alten Fiord and back in one go, even using the most northerly bases in Scotland. Some aircraft carried the 'Johnny Walker Mine', which had a self-destruct mechanism, which remains a secret to this day. *(Possibly hydrostatically fused)*. No damage was done to the Tirpitz. An arrangement had been made with the Russians for the Lancasters of 617 and 9 Squadron to use the Soviet Base at Yagodnik that was some 30 miles from Archangel.

Jacks records show that he took off from the Shetlands on Monday 11th September in Lancaster 'A' and flew to Archangel in Russia via, Norway, Sweden, and Finland.

His crew were:

Flight Sergeant	Mason
Flight Sergeant	Hazell
Flight Sergeant	Johnson
Warrant Officer	Riley
Flight Sergeant	Kiddie
Flight Sergeant	Hunisette

The flight time from the Shetlands to Archangel was 10hrs.30min

Jack was the life and soul of any party and was not afraid to try anything, so much so he found himself playing a football match against the Russian X1 on the eve of the operation. The match took place at Yagodnik airfield on an island in the Dvina River, near Archangel, some 600 miles away from where the Battleship lay at Alten Fjord. Not long after the Russians had won 7-0, a band playing their national anthem after each goal, Jack was airborne and setting course for the Tirpitz. On Friday 15th September, 15 Lancasters including Jack's took off from Yagodnik, most were carrying the 12,000lb Tallboy bombs. At least five of the aircraft returned with their Tallboys because of the smoke screen around the Tirpitz. The mighty Battleships superstructure was clearly seen to the attacking Lancasters, but soon disappeared in the smoke screen. Because of the smoke around the Tirpitz the bomb aimers could only aim in the middle of it. A later reconnaissance flight found the ship still afloat and seemingly undamaged. After the raid the aircraft landed back at Yagodnik taking off again the next day for their return journey to Base in Lincolnshire, again taking the same route via Finland, Sweden, Norway and Denmark. The return trip taking 9hrs.05mins.

One of the squadron's aircraft PB416 KC-Y crashed into high ground near Nesbyen shortly after taking off from Yagodnik for their return journey back to the UK killing all nine members of aircrew aboard, who are buried in Nesbyen (Hallingdal) cemetery. PB 416 KC-Y was also carrying members of aircrew from one of the crashed Lancasters near Yagodnik that had been abandoned to the Russians.

The German records showed after the war that the battleship had been so severely damaged that it was impossible to return her back to Germany for major repairs. The German high command therefore decided that the Battleship would be used as a 'floating fortress', and was moved to Tromso Fiord under her own power.

The second attack

On Saturday 28th October 1944, 617 and 9 Squadrons moved again to the forward bases at Lossiemouth and Milltown in Scotland and took off at 0100 hrs heading for Norway and Tromso Fiord to bomb the Tirpitz.

The problem was patches of cloud were drifting over the battleship sometimes completely hiding it, except for brief glimpses of the ships guns firing at them. When the raid was completed, Tirpitz was still afloat with all guns blazing. All 617 and 9 Squadron's aircraft returned safely to Scotland with the exception of 617s NF920 KC-E which was captained by Flying Officer Carey who had made six runs over the battleship and had sustained severe flak damage. Subsequently crash landing in a bog near Porjus in Sweden.

The third and decisive attack

On Saturday 11th November 1944, both squadrons again moved to the forward bases at Lossiemouth, and it's supporting airfields, and at 0230 hrs on the morning of the 12th October the engines of Jacks Lancaster roared into life with Flight Sergeants Felton, Tirel, Johnson, and Warrant Officers Hazell and Riley on board. Take off was set for 0300 hrs. After take off he set course for Norway at a height of 1,500ft avoiding the German Radar. The squadrons rendezvous point was Akka Lake and then onto Tromso. Jack told me that when he was 15 miles from the target, he was hit by flak from her 15" guns which damaged one of his fuel tanks and it was touch and go if he would land in Sweden. Jack bombed the Tirpitz at exactly 0842 hrs. The Tirpitz was struck by three direct hits. The first just aft of the bow by Taits Air Bomber, the second amidships by Jacks Air Bomber, and a third just aft amidships by Air Bomber still under debate. Almost at the same time two Tallboys exploded very near and alongside the Tirpitz. All five bombs had been delivered in a space of 3 minutes 10 seconds. Jack's Tallboy penetrated the Teak Deck, then the light armour plate covering the centre ('A') magazine, resulting in the very large explosion observed. This explosion coupled with the explosions of the near misses alongside (Tamping Effect) caused the ship to slowly list at first. The list gathered momentum until she lay fully capsized. Technically the Tirpitz was never sunk, by reason she was in shallow water. But she was capsized forever, a total loss.

After the crews returned to base and debriefed, they were informed that Sir Archibald Sinclair (Secretary of State for Air) had ordered that they be given three days off. Air Vice Marshal Cochrane had said that it was the riskiest attack he had ever mounted. Had the German defence (especially Focke Wulf 190s) operated properly the bombers would have been completely wiped out (no mid upper turret) against cannon firing fighters. Jacks logbook shows that the flight time for the whole operation on the 12th November was 13hrs.05mins.

When I interviewed Jack, he explained to me that the success in sinking the Tirpitz was due to a new bombsight that was known as SABS (semi-automatic-bombsight) that had a very high degree of accuracy thus allowing a considerable number of direct hits on the battleship. The average bombing error for this sight was in the region of 30 to 40 yards from 17,000ft. So impressed were the Americans with its accuracy that General Spatz and Doolittle came to the base to examine it. In retrospect it would appear as unusual that although 9 squadron had operated in concert with 617 squadron with the Tallboy weapon, it was never issued with SABS having to soldier on with a standard bomb sight.

The following is an edited report of an eyewitness on the sinking of the battleship Tirpitz by Lars Thoring, who was the town clerk of Tromso.

During the last days of October 1944, the German Battleship Tirpitz was sailed from Alta to a little Island, Hakoy in the Tromso Fiord some three miles to the south west of Tromso. The Tirpitz was moored and surrounded by torpedo nets at the southern end of Hakoy, from where she controlled with her guns the approaches to Tromso from the north end to the south.

One of the most active men in the Norwegian resistance movement in Tromso, was the radio operator Egil Lindberg (1906-1952). He watched with his portable equipment the movements of the battleship and signalled London the arrival and position of the ship and anything else that was going on regarding the enemy activities. During the days after the Battleship had been berthed, there were constantly British scouting planes over Tromso, and the air alert was often sounded several times a day. The situation in Tromso those days was hectic, to say the least. This was due to the war activities on the Northern frontiers. After Russian troops having passed the Norwegian border and on the 23rd October 1944 liberated Kirkenes and part of the Pasvik valley. The retiring German Army from Finland practised the tactics of the 'scorched earth' with compulsory evacuation of the civil population as a consequence. This meant up to 10,000 refuges in Tromso per day, besides the fact that 15,000 troops of the German Finland Army were in town and its surroundings. Everybody realised that something extraordinary was impending after the arrival of the Tirpitz.

The attack on Sunday the 29th October

"I lived at that time temporarily at the Weather Office on top of the island of Tromso, from where there was a good view in the direction on the Battleship. After the occupation of Norway the Norwegian weather service was closed, the Germans having established their own weather centres for military purposes. (In 1943 my residence in the town was requisitioned by the Germans, and I got a provisional dwelling-place at the Weather Office.) It was about 9 o'clock in the morning the air alert was sounded, and some minutes later the Lancaster Bomber Squadrons in formation came sailing in above the town from the east above Tromsdaistind, the highest peak in the vicinity. I counted thirty aircraft in all. The Germans immediately struck up with all their anti-aircraft guns and there was a deafening noise. The shell fragments rained down upon the town, without, oddly enough any damage worth mentioning being caused or anybody being hurt. When the planes approached the Tirpitz she also began to shoot with her powerful anti-aircraft guns. The height of the cloud base was some 6,000 feet, and you could see the planes dive into the cloud and out of them, while the anti-aircraft shells exploded around them. When the bombs were dropped and exploded it sounded like thunder in midst of the other infernal noise. The attack lasted for about a quarter of an hour. Then the aircraft disappeared. Because of the cloud cover visibility was poor, and it turned out that the Tirpitz had only suffered minor damage, no direct hit having struck the ship. Radio reports from London confirmed this. Then exactly a fortnight passed until the next and final attack. On Sunday the 12th November the air alert was sounded again at 9 o'clock in the morning. It was an unusual day considering the time of the year. The sky was clear, it was bright, and there was not a breath of wind. The planes passed by in an altitude of some 12,000ft somewhat to the south of Romso to avoid as much as possible the German anti-aircraft on the island itself. Therefore there was not so much shooting from the anti-aircraft defences this time. In return the guns of the Tirpitz put in a veritable display of fireworks, aided by a powerful anti-aircraft on Hakoy.

"We were standing with some other Norwegians and I on the first floor of the weather office while the huge 5.5 ton bombs were dropped concentricity down to the battleship. As the bombs burst the opened windows went off their hooks and several panes were broken by the air pressure that was so strong that it was felt in the room and an effect as if the house would be lifted off its foundation. From the bombs exploding in the sea, columns of water rose several hundred feet into the air exactly like a fireworks display. The anti-aircraft fire from the Tirpitz soon became tamer. Only the aftermost guns were still shooting angrily. The battery on Hakoy also continued. This apparently irritated the RAF men, for a bomb was dropped against the battery and caused an outright earthquake on the island. As earth and stones spurted sky-high it looked as if a volcanic eruption was in progress. The battery was silenced, and some minutes later the guns of the Tirpitz also fell silent. A tremendous mass of smoke rose from the target, and we presumed that an explosion of the boilers or the ammunition magazines had occurred. In order to have a better view we ran up to the platform on the roof of the Weather Office. When the smoke had lifted and was lying like a dark thundercloud in the sky, you could see the battleship lying there stripped of masts and tower and everything on deck. She looked rather like an unfinished construction on the stocks.

"When the Battleship started to heel over, a German Officer came up and turned all of us down without further comments. In the course of a quarter of an hour the attack was over, and Hitler's last battleship had gone the same way as had the Bismarck and the Sharnhorst before her."

1,346 men went down with the Tirpitz. Only 86 were saved, more or less hurt. About one hundred bodies drifted ashore. The rest remained onboard the ship which stuck out of the water like a stranded whale. During all these deadly attacks, the ships company never once hesitated to protect her. After the war the Tirpitz was broken up bit by bit and sold as scrap.

A Memorial Plaque to the Tirpitz was unveiled in Tromso by the Veterans from Germany and Great Britain on the 29th July 1984.

This is a poem written by Flight Lieutenant John Pryor, DFC, who was a 617 Squadron Pilot from February 1944 until January 1945:

'617 Squadron and the Tirpitz'
Among those fields rich with corn
Clear on a cool summer's morn
The clustered hangars of Woodhall stand
Green walled in the trees of bomber land
Around about them airfield sweep
Lancs in dispersal fruited deep
As fair as the garden of the Lord
In the eyes of that squadron hoard
Twenty Lancs with petrol stowe
Twenty Lancs with a Tallboy load
All ready in the morning sun
But the noon day saw not one
Higher rose six one seven's men
Bowed with their early teens plus ten
Taking up that late summer's task
What of us all bomber Harris did ask
Down the track came the marauding throng
Wille Tirpitz tait leading along
Under that slouched hat far to the right
Tirpitz the target met his sight
On went the dusty blue ranks so fast
Down went the bombs - up went the blast
Shoot if you must this young grey head
But spare your country's navy he said
To humbler nature within them stirred
To life at that squadron's deed and word
Who touches a hair on Norwegian head
Dies like a dog - fly on he said.

Summer brought a move which Jack had been resisting for some time, despite some duress and under protest he reluctantly accepted a commission. This time he had no choice, for Bomber Command Headquarters had issued a directive in July that all bomber command pilots would be officers.

Many NCOs and Warrant Officers, found themselves as budding Pilot Officers, with several going on to become squadron Leaders. This directive was followed by a second, "That all aircrew *(other than pilots in the first directive)* that had completed a tour and had volunteered for a second tour, would also become officers."

Harris was hell bent on destroying the 'us and them' scenario that he hated. That is the reason why 617 Squadron had so many officers on board each aircraft as a crew.

George Riley recalls that Jack now a Pilot Officer was never happier than when an excuse arose to take him into the sergeant's mess. The chief cook in the mess, Arthur Rowell, was very friendly with Jack and often did him a favour, supplying him and his crew with unscheduled meals. To repay these favours, Jack had Arthur smuggled aboard his Lancaster in July for a raid to Wizernes. After the raid Arthur told his wife of the experience, she was understandably furious and told Jack in no uncertain terms how she considered his actions to be irresponsible. Jack being Jack was unperturbed by the tirade and simply pointed out that few sergeant cooks had had the privilege of operational flying with 617 Squadron.

In late August Jack was recommended for the Distinguished Flying Cross, this being awarded on 8th December 1944. The citation from the station commander, Group captain Philpott was as follows:

"Flying Officer Gingles has now completed a tour of operations in a Special Duties Squadron since being awarded the Distinguished Flying Medal on 9th September 1943. This Squadron has recently been employed on daylight attacks against flying bomb and rocket installations, and submarine pens, all of which have been small targets, well defended, and specially constructed to withstand bombing attacks. He has taken part in attacks against such installations as Watten, Wizernes, Siracourt, Mimoyecques, Lorient, La Pallice and Brest. On these occasions each aircraft was normally armed with a single large calibre bomb of special design. A very high standard of skill and determination has, therefore, been necessary in order to ensure effective damage from a direct hit. This officer has always shown outstanding calmness and determination during the critical bombing runs and he has virtually ignored the intense fire from the enemy ground defences. His aircraft has been frequently hit by shell splinters and so seriously that it was unserviceable for several days on three occasions. Flying Officer Gingles has nevertheless less maintained an exceptionally high standard of bombing accuracy and he has played a big part in the success of the operations. His gallantry and determination under fire have been an example to the whole Squadron and I recommend this officer for the award of the Distinguished Flying Cross."

George Riley who was Jack's wireless operator, had vivid memories of his skipper and took delight in relating them both socially and in print.

"Jacks pranks and capers were not all related to life in the RAF, I remember an international football match between England and Scotland at Maine Road in my home town of Manchester. Jack and I were staying there on leave at the time. We couldn't get tickets but thought 'what the heck!' - we'll join in with everyone else outside the ground and hope some kind soul will take pity on a pair of Warrant Officers. Time was dragging on and we were getting nowhere when a squad of Air Training Corps cadets appeared, marching smartly towards the ground. Possibly they were to sell programmes or something, but

Jack saw the opportunity. Nudging me he said, 'Come on, we'll take charge of these erks----, Right you lot, look lively, swing those arms and get those heads back. That's it, left right, and left right. Show 'em what you're made of.' I shouldn't have been surprised by Jack but I couldn't believe it, it was working like a charm and within minutes we were sitting by the touchline so close to the action I could have tripped Stanley Matthew's as he passed by!

"Another time our mutual love for football took us to Blackpool. The return train to Manchester was packed with never a chance of us getting onboard. Jack grabbed my arm, 'Let's try the driver.' With that, we nipped through the crowd and along the platform to the engine. A word from Jack to the driver and we were both on the footplate as the train pulled out of Blackpool heading for Manchester. Not content with our luck, Jack soon had the driver giving him some 'Dual' on driving the engine. Within minutes, he was in charge, at the same time directing me to take over the fireman's duties. As the driver took over for the run to Manchester, he casually observed that we had beaten all records for the stretch between Preston and Bolton. When we reached home, with our faces and uniforms still covered with coal dust, it took a lot of hot water and a pint or two to clean us up internally and externally".

Jacks brother Eric recalls George Riley telling him this story at Jacks Funeral:

One dark misty night while he and jack were returning to Woodhall Spa from a visit to a local pub, they heard a clanking noise behind them. When they stopped to look round the noise also stopped and as the started to walk the clanking noise started again. Jack and George decided to investigate, so they hid behind a tree and waited. Out of the gloom came this rather large 'billy goat' dragging its chain behind it. Now Jack being a farmer's son knew exactly what to do with the goat. He smuggled it into camp and locked it in Wing Commander Cheshire's room. When the Wing Commander returned later that night and discovered the 'intruder' he knew exactly who was responsible. He went straight to Jack and George's room and got them out of bed. He gave them a right old rollicking and told them to be on parade the next morning at 9 o'clock. They were to meet him at the rifle range, and not to forget their revolvers. When they arrived at the range the next morning Wing Commander Cheshire was already waiting. He had brought with him a large box of ammunition. Turning to face Jack and George he held up one round and informed them both that it cost sixpence (old money). He then told them that they would continue firing their revolvers for one hour or until the box was empty and they would pay the cost each round.

As a measure of the man and what his friends and comrades meant to him in 617 came when the Squadrons Memorial fund was opened years after the war. He simply asked how many names the Memorial would carry. When told, he just multiplied the total by the current cost of a pint of beer, and that was the amount of his donation - a beer with one of his departed friends.

Jacks last Operation with 617 Squadron was the successful raid on the Tirpitz and he was screened off operations following the completion of his tour with the famous Dambusters. He was then seconded to British Overseas Airways Corporation at Hurn, RAF Talbenny and Ossington, flying Lancasters for the opening period of 1945 before arriving at No 246 Squadron Transport Command at Holmesly South, near Bournemouth, in April. Here Jack began familiarising himself on the Avro York with Flight Lieutenant Dave Shannon (ex 617 and Dams Raid veteran) following a one month stint at No 1332 Heavy Conversion Unit at Riccall, he rejoined the squadron to help out with the many movements needed in the tidying up period towards and following the ending of the European hostilities. He then did the same in more distant destinations prior to VJ Day, with single flights of up to 12 hours. Some of his trips took him to Malta, Cairo, Shaibah, Karachi, Calcutta, Delhi, Palam, Castel Benito, Almazq, Mauripur, Istres, Naples, Maison Blanche, Azores, Aden, Habanniya, Ceylon, Singapore, and Aldergrove. He would appear to have had a wide reaching role at this time being involved in air tests, checking out new crews, passenger carriage and general transport.

Another one of Jacks pranks came in the summer of 1946 while air testing Avro Yorks with 246 Squadron. Whilst in the Southampton area he remembered a county cricket match was being played. Curious to know the score he dropped down to see what the score was. As can be imagined the sight of a four engined heavy transport letting down towards the 'crease' caused quite a stir and resulted in players and crowd taking cover. The incident featured on the radio and in the press under the headline, 'Four engined bomber stops county cricket match in Southampton.' *(A photograph of the aircraft appeared in the newspaper showing it's registration).* The press also reported umpire Frank Lee waving a white pullover to 'shoo' the plane away! An Air Ministry investigation team duly arrived at Holmsley South and during their deliberations heard Jacks Commanding Officer state that, "Flight Lieutenant Gingles is the squadron's test pilot and as such has a radio altimeter to test down to 100 feet.'

At around the same time another prank involved the Aircraft Carrier HMS Illustrious. Once again in a York, Jack was flying over the Solent when he spotted the vessel. Always ready for a spot of fun, he decided to see if the Navy bods were awake. Jack contacted the Illustrious and informed them that he had a problem with his aircraft and would have to make an emergency landing on the deck of the carrier. He dropped down to circuit height, lowered the flaps and undercarriage and came into short finals in the lumbering Avro. Lining up with the flight deck he made as if landing, dropping to a mere 50 feet off the water before over-shooting the carrier. He never did hear anything of the incident so perhaps sleep was the order of the day!

Jack remained in this role with 246 Squadron until Monday 30th September 1946 and was posted, as Commanding Officer 'C' Flight, with No 242 Squadron at Oakington near Cambridge. His duties here involved much testing of the Avro York that continued until his demob from the Service in March 1947. By this time he had accumulated a total flying time of 2,374 Hours in the Royal Air Force. Final leave took him to April when he left the RAF and joined BOAC, here he obtained his civilian flying licence, again on Yorks, but his stay with the Company was brief for he remained for only seven months.

It is believed that it was during this time he met his future wife, Thelma. She was a stewardess for the Company and it would appear that the initial attraction was strong, as much jigging of schedules was attempted to ensure they rotated on the same flights. Not too much is known about this period or his relationship with Thelma which Jack did not discuss. They did have one son Michael, who I had the privilege to meet and speak to me about his father. I never met Thelma but would speak to her often on the telephone, and she would tell me all about Jack and his pranks. Following his short spell with BOAC Jack moved to Flight refuelling for a period in which he flew supplies for the Berlin Airlift. Again not too much is known here although it is known from the incomplete records that he flew a Lancastrian, York and Oxford and completed some 150 flights for the German emergency. His total flying time in this period was 800 plus hours.

At the end of this Airlift period there was a slump in Civil flying in the post war era. Not wanting to be away from aviation Jack decided to rejoin the Royal Air Force and was accepted. He was posted to the Flight Refresher School at RAF Finningley on Harvards for one month. His first flight on the Harvard was on July 17th, his instructor was MP Davidson. Jack soloed the next day after two hours tuition. His next posting was to the Central navigation and Control School at RAF Shawbury flying Ansons. Here he completed his re-introduction to military flying in early November with an unsurprising 'above average' rating and joined 'A' Flight of the Wellington Squadron . Here at least he was back in a familiar aircraft given his previous 350 plus flights in the type.

When I had the pleasure of interviewing Jack he told me a story about Shawbury, regarding crew training. On one particular day, Jack and the training crew were driven out to the aircraft, he completed his outside checks and was just about to get into the aircraft. A smart arsed young Officer who Jack had been training and was one rank above him made the mistake of pulling rank on him in front of the others remarking, "I should be onboard the aircraft before you." Jack asked him to remain at the steps until everyone else was on board, and informed him that 'he' was the Captain of the aircraft. Jack boarded, lifting

the steps behind him and closed the door, started the engines and took off leaving the 'smartarse' behind (Jack did not suffer fools gladly).

Jack remained with the Wellington Squadron until October 1951 training new crews and in March found himself in another old acquaintance, the Lancaster. From then until the autumn it was both the old faithfuls until he converted onto Lincolns. During the interim period changing from Wellington to the Lincoln Squadron, Jack spent a month at the No 5 Air Navigation School at RAF Lindholme, presumably being checked out or perhaps updating. At this time, RAF Lindholme was No 1 Group Main Base for Lincoln Conversions. Lindholme also specialised in Navigation for Lincoln pilots with a number of aircraft going and coming from Woomera in Australia.

The Base also specialised in High Flying the Lincoln, some reaching 30,000ft. Lindholme also had on its strength some heavily modified Lincolns, very strange looking indeed.

Thereafter he flew mainly Lincolns on a variety of tasks world-wide until he finally left the RAF in January 1954 with, as was now the norm for Jack, an 'above average' rating.

Back to civilian life

With a total flying time of 4,564 hours to his credit Jack joined Skyways in early 1953 and remained with them until they went into liquidation in 1962. Unfortunately his records covering this period are missing and do not re-appear again until 1976. However it is known that the period with Skyways was spent on the Avro York. Following the demise of this company Jack departed these shore for Tanzania in 1962 and, for two years, flying Government Ministers around east Africa, as well as being the personal pilot for the President. He returned to the UK in 1964 and joined Airlinks later renamed Trans Globe. For some three years he flew Argonauts and Britannia aircraft before departing the country for a spell in Swiss Air again flying Britannias between Switzerland and the Far East. In 1969 it was back home again to join British Caledonian, again on Britannia aircraft. Two years later he moved to Donaldsons, continuing in the old faithful Bristol but also converting to jets for the first time in Boeing 720 and 707s. At the time of his last flight in a Britannia Jack had logged over 6,000 hours on this one type.

Donaldson's went into Liquidation in 1973 and it is not known what Jack did in the three years before joining Pakistan International Airways (known affectionately as "Perhaps it'll arrive") making his first flight on the 23rd March 1976.

Here he flew Boeing 720 and 707s for the final years of his career, flying to destinations, Instanbul, Karachi, Rawalpindi, Amsterdam, Lahore, Jeddah, Tehran, London, Muscat, Colombo, Dubai, Kuala Lumpur, Peshwar, Lyallpur, Abu Dhabi, Damascus, Ahtens, Tripoli, Cairo, Suetta, Nairobi, Baghdad, Copenhagen, Rome, Kuwait,

Rome, Bahrain, Frankfurt, Zurich, Islamabad, New York, Multan, Lyallpur, Bangkok, Zahedan, Kilimanjaro, Dar-es-Salam, Quetta, Rawalpindi, and Fablab.

Jack's flying career came to and end in 1980 when he was approaching 60 years of age. His last flight with Pakistan International Airways came on the 12th August 1980 with a 4hrs.30mins Boeing 707 leg from Frankfurt to Cairo. This final flight, his 1,014th for PIA, took his flying career hours in excess of an incredible 22,000 hours. He had carried out 73 Operations with the RAF, and had flown in 40 plus different types of aircraft and was awarded the Distinguished Flying Cross and Distinguished Flying Medal.

Jack was on holiday in the Algarve with his good friend Bob Knights (ex 617) in a 'Guinea Pig Club' villa, (provided for those who had undergone plastic surgery at the East Grinstead hospital) in 1988. Sadly he died prematurely of a heart attack.

George Riley speaking about an event after Jack's death

"Four months after the sad news, shared by many, of Jacks death, it was the 45th Anniversary of the famous Dams Raid. To mark the occasion we gathered at the Derwent Dam where years before, the boys had practised for the raid. The Lancaster of the Battle of Britain Memorial Flight was to make a commemorative fly pass over the site to mark the occasion. Thousands of people watched the fly-past and I was in a group from 617s wartime crews. As the Lanc. lumbered over the water at a couple of hundred feet one of them remembered our Skipper. "At that height," he observed, "Paddy Gingles would have been on oxygen!"

Tom Bennett another 617 Squadron Pilot and close friend of Jack's. Tom was a powerful man, and would not hesitate to defend himself, as his nose suggested. He has been described as stubborn, tenacious and fearless, amongst the most desirable assets for any member of the reverend 617 Squadron, whom he would join. Like Jack he liked a prank and little time for the authority that he saw as being inefficient, as his personal experience had shown. Also like Jack, he totally refused to suffer fools willingly and his reactions to such had produced a poor disciplinary record.

Of Jack Gingles he said, "I most of all found myself watching and approving Warrant Officer Paddy Gingles, who seemed to bestride the mess like some colossus by the sheer force of his personality."

It was not possible to be in the mess and not be aware of Paddy. He had a magnificent operational record and, on a squadron with many exceptional pilots, he still stood out. The fact that he had resisted every attempt to make him take a commission endeared him to many. Paddy's crew always seemed to be together and so very obviously idolised their skipper that it would have been a very foolish man who would utter any criticism of him.

Dave Shannon 617 Squadron recalled at Jack's Memorial Service, that he was one of the best pilots 617 had produced.

Bob Knights (617 squadron) recalls that there had been a German prisoner of war transit camp set up on the perimeter of Woodhall, where they were made to pick potatoes in the local fields. The Germans always gave the 'Hitler Salute', and 'two fingers' to the returning Lancasters and their crews. On returning from one particular raid. I was in front of Jack just about to land, when true to form there they were standing in a neat row chanting, "Seig Heil, Seig Heil," and giving the two finger salute. Now this type of behaviour did not bother me at all, but Paddy was a different kettle of fish, and he was in no mood for the 'smart arsed' Germans as his own aircraft had been damaged by heavy flak. I landed and listened as Paddy's Lancaster roared overhead at full throttle, and watched him do a circuit of the airfield, approaching the POW Transit camp so low I could see the Germans and their guards running in all directions and a cloud of dirt and soil rise into the air from the field.

Needless to say we had no more trouble.......

WARRANT OFFICER
JOHN GRACEY
ROYAL AIR FORCE VOLUNTEER RESERVE
WIRELESS OPERATOR/AIR GUNNER
NO. 201 SQUADRON

John Gracey, the son of Mr John Gracey, was born in Belfast on 16th December 1921. John and his twin brother Herbert were both educated at Methody College in Belfast during the term 1935-1938. Herbert was killed on Active Service with the RAF on 21st/22nd January 1944.

Before joining the Royal Air Force at Oxbridge in early 1940, John was employed at the Air Ministry in London as a clerical officer. John was selected for aircrew at Oxbridge, and after completing his initial training at Torquay, was posted overseas to start his flying training in Albany, Georgia.

John sailed from Greenock in Scotland on an armed Merchant Ship in May 1941, bound for Moncton in Canada. After a few days at sea the convoy was diverted into Iceland where it stayed for the next six weeks. The reason for this was, HMS Hood had been sunk on 24th May 1941 by the Bismarck and this necessitated the convoys escort ships being diverted to other duties. When the convoy eventually arrived in Moncton, John left the ship, and was trained down to New Brunswick and then on to Albany in Georgia. His basic flying training was carried out in Boeing Stearmans. John unfortunately failed his pilots training and was re-mustered for training as a Wireless Operator/Air Gunner in Jacksonville, Florida. After successfully completing the wireless and gunnery course he was awarded his WOP/AG Brevet. He then returned to the UK by sea, and on his arrival was posted to a Wellington Squadron at Davidstow-Moor in Cornwall. This particular squadron was an anti 'E' boat squadron but had to be disbanded due to the heavy losses of aircraft and personnel.

In October 1943 John was transferred to No 201 Coastal Command Squadron which was based at Castle Archdale near Irvinestown in County Fermanagh. *(It was a Catalina from 209 Squadron operating from Castle Archdale in May 1941 that sealed the fate of one Germany's Capital ships, the Bismarck.)*

The squadron's commanding officer at that time was Wing Commander REC Van der Kiste, DSO. The squadron was equipped with the Short Sunderland Mk111 Flying Boat, and the squadron's first confirmed U-boat sinking was on the 31st May 1943 when a Sunderland (ZM-R) piloted by Flight Lieutenant Hall sank U-440. John told me that from the day he joined 201 Squadron until the day he left he never saw a U-boat.

After VE Day John was re-mustered as a clerk to the Air Ministry Research Unit at Bush House in London, where he was involved mainly with the setting up of the staging posts and gathering data for the new BOAC routes that were being launched from London to Cairo and Australia. John was eventually de-mobbed in 1946 and returned to the Air Ministry in London as a civilian and successfully completed his Custom and Excise examinations. He then returned home to Northern Ireland where he became a senior customs officer at Belfast International Airport. Three years before he retired, he became a coastal protection officer in Northern Ireland, and this involved the checking of all private craft which entered Belfast Lough and any other County Antrim ports.

John finally retired in 1984 and was a member of the Air Crew Association (Northern Ireland Branch)

Sadly John died just after writing his memoirs.

His twin brother Pilot Officer Herbert Gracey, Royal Air Force Volunteer Reserve No 155208 was a Navigator with No 10 Squadron, based at Melbourne in Yorkshire. He was killed on active service on the night of 21st/22nd January 1944 when the Halifax (Code HX165, Code ZA-J he was navigating was shot down over Schoningen. Their target for that night was Magdeburg, Germany.

Pilot Officer H.Gracey is buried in Hanover War Cemetery.

SQUADRON LEADER
THOMAS DONALD GRANT, DFM AE GSM
ROYAL AIR FORCE NO. 816117
AIR GUNNER
NO. 502 (ULSTER), 51 AND 150 SQUADRONS

Thomas Donald Grant was born in Belfast on the 27th January 1921 and was educated at the Belfast Boys Model and Belfast High School in Clifton Street. He left school to seek an apprenticeship with Harland and Wolf and in September 1938 at the age of seventeen years and six months he joined 502 (Ulster) Squadron at Aldergrove as a trainee air gunner.

Tom's air gunnery training started on the squadron's Hawker Hinds that were equipped with the Vickers Twin Lewis guns. He also received some basic training as a bomb aimer on the Hawker Hinds. He reminded me that the Bomb Aimer's position the Hind was just below the Pilot and Gunners 'department'. You would lie down on your stomach in the prone position with the bomb sight and the Pilot would have to raise the Hinds radiator by a means of winding it up out of the way to give you a clear forward view.

Samuel Eric Esler, DFC AE and Jack Hutchinson, DFC AE and Tom joined 502 Squadron on a Sunday morning in September 1938. They with a few others sat down in a class room to sit an entrance exam. They were all informed soon after that they all had passed. As it was a Sunday all three were wearing their best suits and while on parade that afternoon in the 502 Squadron hangar a pigeon position himself right above Tom and yes it splatted him. Tom did not mind at all as he knew this could only be a good luck sign.

As Tom explained to me, he had had a 'safe' war. One of the incidents that we spoke about regarding his RAF career was when he was based in Marseilles Sept/Oct 1946 and was preparing to come home to the UK by train via Paris and the French coast and ferry across to the UK.

This was going to be a long and tedious trip that would take two days. The night before he left Marseille for the UK he was offered a lift home to Aldergrove in a Warwick by an old friend. The friend had a dead line to keep so Tom declined his offer as he wanted to see the Paris sights and night life. When Tom did eventually arrive back in

England and was sitting on a train for Belfast he purchased a local newspaper and on the front page was the headline, "RAF Warwick missing in Channel." Tom checked this out and indeed it was his old friend who had offered him a lift. *(The pigeon's dirt was lucky.)*

Leading Aircraftsman (LAC) Grant made his first flight with 502 squadron on the 23rd March 1939 in an Avro Anson code N5063. This was a map reading exercise that lasted for one hour. He continued with these types of exercises up until September 1939 when he was called to full time service with the declaration of war. Tom's first operation with 502 Squadron was on the 13th September 1939 with Flying Officer Garrett in Anson N5064 who was the captain of the aircraft. The operation was a reconnaissance patrol that was followed by an anti-submarine patrol on the 21st September.

On the 17th June 1940 the squadron's 'A' Flight moved to Dishforth in England where it remained until the 22nd January 1941 when it returned to Limavady in Northern Ireland. The squadron moved to Limavady on the 25th January 1941 were it carried out convoy patrols, anti submarine patrols, dusk patrol, and dawn patrols. These were the main types of operations that were carried out by the squadron during that period. Tom as posted to Castle Kennedy just outside Stranraer where he completed an eight week gunnery leader's course. The weather was terrible, he was billeted out in tents, the mess was a large marquee and it rained practically every day of the course. Everyone was covered in mud and rain sodden and getting from one place to another on 'duck boards' was a nightmare. He was glad when the course finished and returned to Aldergrove.

The commanding officer of the squadron was a Squadron Leader LR Briggs who was a Special Reserve Officer. I have entered the names of some of the crew that Tom flew with during those early days for the readers. P/O Billing, F/Lt Stanley, S/Ldr Bob Mooney, F/O Bell, F/O Stanley, F/O H McGiffin, F/O Jack Harrison, Sgt Eric Esler, Jack Hutchinson, S/Ldr Brian Corry, F/O Garret, F/O Bell, P/O Harding, P/O Barclay, P/O Henderson, F/O Foster, P/O Egerton, P/O Ward, P/O Hodgkinson, P/O Sloane, P/O Longhurst, P/O Barckey, P/O Worthington, P/O Petit, P/O Osborne, P/O McNeill, P/O Pugh, P/O Golmore, P/O Dickson and S/Ldr Stanley. I apologise if I have left anyone out.

Few people would have realised at that time when a young Pilot Officer Len Cheshire flew into Aldergrove to fly with 502 Squadron that by the end of the war he would be Group Captain and have been awarded the Victoria Cross, three Distinguished Service Orders and three Distinguished Flying Crosses.

Tom's flying logbook shows that he had carried out 80 operations with the squadron between September 1939 and June 1941.

Tom was feeling very bored with these four and eight hour flights in the Anson and Whitleys and so he decided to apply for a transfer to a bomber squadron. He was delighted when his posting came through on the 7th June 1941 for 51 Squadron that was based at Kinloss in Scotland. The squadron had been 'on loan' to No 18 Group Coastal Command and equipped with Whitleys. His first operation with 51 Squadron was on the 2nd July 1941 and was to attack Koln in Whitley Z6480. He went on to carry out a total of 23 operations with the squadron to Brest, Aachen, Texel Aerodrome, Hamburg, Hanover, Emden, Frankfurt, Bologne, Stuttgart, Nuremburg, Wilhelmshaven and Mannheim.

On the 27th/28th February 1942, the squadron was being led by the commanding officer Wing Commander PC Pickard on Operation Biting. This was when a raiding party captured a complete 'Wurzburg' radar installation at Bruneval near Le Havre. (See story below).

Wing Commander Pikard who was then also well known as being the pilot of the Wellington 'F-Freddie' in the documentary film "Target for Tonight", and he later achieved immortal fame as leader of the Mosquito raid on Amiens prison.

Operation to Texel, 7th July 1941
(Toms own words)

"Texel Aerodrome was on one of a small group of Islands of the Dutch coast and was used by the German night fighters. Our experts were very concerned the Germans were using it as an early warning means of detecting our aircraft fly over it on their way to operations.

"A scheme was devised whereby we would send one aircraft to attack Texel and disrupt things before the main force would arrive. On my second visit to Texel on the 7th July 1941, the first being the day before, our crew's task was to climb to 3,000ft over Holland and swing around down to 1,500ft across the Island. We throttled back in a slow descent, nice and quiet on a moonlit night. We put a stick of bombs across the island were the hangar and runway was and immediately opened up the throttles the same time the first bomb went down. We knew the airfields 20 and 40mm light flak guns would erupt once we had bombed. It was a real 'Guy Fawkes' night, all hell let loose below us. I was the Rear Gunner and could see the line of light flak creeping up on the aircraft. I advised the Skipper of the immediate danger and advised to weave, he replied, "I can't," because the flak was now coming up between the aircrafts engines and close to the fuselage. The engine did sustain three hits causing it to close down as they crossed the coast of the island at 11,000ft and we were loosing height now, eventually dropping down to 300ft and loosing power all the time. With only one engine serviceable, our skipper gave the order to dump everything overboard to lighten the load so the Whitley could gain some height. We reached the Yorkshire coast and Scarborough and were so low we could not fly over Scarborough Head we had to go round it and had to do a 'wheel up' landing at Drifield that had also just been bombed. What we didn't know was that the good engine on our Whitley had also been damaged and had lost all of its Glycol and just seized on landing. The Whitley was completely destroyed. A close shave."

Operation to Frankfurt, 22nd July 1941

"We had arrived over target and completing our run in at 11,000ft when a heavy flak shell burst close to our aircraft's fuselage causing the aircraft to tip up onto its back. The Skipper, skilfully as able to right the aircraft but as he did the altimeter was now showing 3,000ft."

Operation to Mannheim, 22nd October 1941

"Just after take off for Mannheim the Wireless Operator informed the Skipper that the radio had failed. The Skipper asked him if he could try and fix it and that he would press on to the coast. When they arrived at the coast the Wireless Operator had still not been able to fix the radio. The Skipper decided to fly over the enemy coast a little way and if it's not sorted out soon we will turn back.

"The radio operator did all he could but the radio was still U/S but the skipper took the decision to fly on to the target. When we arrived over the target we dropped our bombs and we received a terrific welcome from the German flak batteries. It was like Halloween, the Germans threw everything up at us, including the 'kitchen sink'. We began to wonder if every flak gun in the German army was now in Mannheim. We made course for home and received some more flak from the coastal batteries just for luck. Anyway we arrived back at our base and landed and at the debriefing were asked, "Where have you been?" Ten minutes after the had taken off the operation had been cancelled and all the aircraft had been recalled. We did not receive this message as our radio was U/S. We were just finishing of our breakfast in the mess and having a smoke when we heard the radio going in the background with the morning news being broadcast. It said, 'Last night a Force of our aircraft attacked Mannheim'."

"Tom remarked to me, 'To be honest John, in the winter of 1941 bomber command started to back off in the latter part of the winter as casualties had been so heavy the power that be in bomber command were reaching the stage that if they didn't slacken off, there might not be a bomber squadron left.' A major effort in 1941 was 200 aircraft, compare that with 11943/44 operation."

Operation to Poissy, 1st April 1942 & Wing Commander Pickard

"Poissy was on the suburbs of Paris and in Poissy there was a large factory that produced lorries for the German Army. So on the 1st April 1942 bomber command decided to have a go at it. The factory was situated in a heavily built up area and was located by the River Seine and I reckon that raid was the first attempt at 'Pathfinding'. It had been a full moonlit night, beautiful weather and my Skipper was none other than Wing Commander Pickard. The idea was to fly up the River Seine and count the bridges, I think it was three we counted then we turned right. Just as we turned right there was a large factory block and we dropped a container of incendiaries down onto it. Ten minutes later there was a 'gaggle' of Wellingtons that dropped 4,000 pounders on it. The strategy was that Wing Commander Pickard was to light up the target with the incendiaries and then the Wellingtons would blast the factory."

Operation Genoa, 12th April 1942 & Wing Commander Pickard

"I accompanied Wing Commander Pickard on a second night operation on the 12th April 1942. It was a memorable 9hrs.15mins flight. We had flown to the south of England to refuel and then took off and crossed the enemy coast over Northern France and ended up slap into a heavy German flak battery which knocked one of our engines out. I saw the cloud of Glycol coolant rushing past my rear turret and thought there is no way now that are going to be able to fly over the Alps and down to Italy. Wing Commander Pickard calmly said over the intercom, 'Oh well, I think we will just press on'. As sure as I am sitting in this chair John, we could not fly over the Alps, so we flew through them. Luckily the weather and visibility was excellent and you could see the snow on the Alps. We did fly through the Alps down to Genoa, bombed the target and headed home, meeting a few enemy aircraft on the way. This had been the first operation into Italy and we received an intelligence report later about the raid. It told of how the civilians rushed to the air raid shelters and were beaten to it by the flak crews."

Bruneval Radar Station

"My squadron had been training Paratroopers for some weeks for Operation Biting. This was a raid to capture a complete and intact Wurzburg radar installation near Bruneval. The raid was to be done at night and the paras were to be dropped at 300ft. The raid went off perfectly and there were no casualties. Now I had heard that the 'boffins' back home had wanted a special piece of 'kit' form the radar dish itself. They did not know what it was for, possibly for improving its performance. They sent a Flight Sergeant radar technician along with the paras and his job was to bring the 'special' bit back to the UK. The radar technician had a personal escort, two paras and their duty was to get the technician there in one piece and then to get him and the special bit down to the beaches. What the poor radar technician did not know was and he only discovered this himself quite recently was, that the escort were told if there was any danger of him being captured, they were to shoot him because he knew to much about our own radar."

A story about the quality and leadership of Wing Commander Pickard

"Wing Commander Pickard sent for Tom one morning and informed him that one of his gunners had been arrested in Harrogate by the Special Police (SP) for fighting and had the report of the incident in front of him. He said to Tom, 'This is rather amusing Tom,' and a stupid waste of time. The gunner had flattened a corporal SP who was coming up to the station to identify him. Tom said, 'Sir it may not have been one of our chaps,' Wing Commander Pickard answered immediately by saying, 'Well it states in this report that the gunner was from Dishforth.' The Deputy Air Provost Marshal a Flight Lieutenant ?????, was arriving that afternoon with their victim to identify the person who assaulted him. Wing Commander Pickard told Tom, 'Will you have all your gunners on parade by 1400 hrs.' Tom replied, 'Yes Sir.' Now Tom knew fine well who the culprit was. Tom saluted the Wing Commander and as he was about to walk out of the room, a voice from behind said, 'Grant, I know you know who the gunner is, make sure he is not on parade.' Now that is the sort of man you work hard for," said Tom.

At an Aircrew meeting one evening Wing Commander Pickard was addressing the crews, he started of by saying, "Your mine, you fly, you work and will do what I tell you to do. I don't give a damn how often you have to go over the target but you will hit it and I want the photographs back to prove it. You will work hard as I am not interested in anything else, when you are off camp and off duty, go and enjoy yourselves, but when you walk back in through those camp gates, your mine and nobody will touch you."

After the Brunevald raid

The King and Queen were to visit the station, when the word came through that they were coming the adjutant was running around like a 'wet hen'. Best uniforms where to be worn, everything was to be cleaned up and polished. Wing Commander Pickard heard about this 'bullshit' and sent for the adjutant and told him, "Forget the Bull, stand back and forget it and if the King wants to see a parade with 'bullshit' fine. He has the Guards depot just beside him in London where he can go and see all the 'bullshit' he wants. He is coming here to see a working squadron and that's what he will see, a normal working day. You will all wear your normal battle dress tunic and trousers and nothing will be 'bulled up'." The King and Queen arrived that morning and came to the front of the squadron parade. One aircraft flew past and dropped a 'stick' as a demonstration over the airfield. When the aircraft landed the crew rushed over and fell in on parade. The Skipper of the aircraft was a very tall ex-Welsh Guard about 6ft 2ins tall who had volunteered for the RAF. While this was going on Wing Commander Pickard was standing there in his normal battle dress talking to the King and Queen, his hand in his pockets talking away to his guests and the only thing he did not do was take out his pipe and smoke it. Tom said, "The entire station from an Lac up had the greatest respect and admiration for Wing Commander Pickard."

Tom was awarded the Distinguished Flying Medal on the 26th June 1942.

By June 1942 Tom Grant had completed 103 operations and it was time for a rest. So it was decided to post him to 19 OTU that was also based at Kinloss as a gunnery instructor. Tom did not mind the instructing but after five months he requested to be put back on operations. On the 13th October Tom was posted to 150 Squadron at Snaith in Yorkshire and was equipped with the Vickers Wellington. A week later the squadron moved to Kirmington in Lincolnshire. Tom flew 25 operations with the squadron between October 1943 and March 1943, seven of these were to Essen, St Nazaire, Stavanger, Hamburg and La Rochelle before the squadron was to Blida in Algeria.

The squadron arrived in Blida via Gibraltar on the 18th December 1942 and its first operation was carried out on Bizerta 29th November 1942. Tom carried out 25 operations with 150 Squadron that included attacks on Ferryville, Trapani, Tunis and El Maou. His last operation with the squadron was to El Maou on the 21st March 1943 and on the 26th April he was informed that he was being posted back the UK. On his arrival back in the UK he was posted to No 11 Air Gunnery School on the Isle of Man as a gunnery instructor from the 30th June 1943 until the 29th April 1944.

Tom had to finish his flying career due to a previous illness and his last flight was with No 11 AGS in an Anson on the 29th April 1944. He had completed 128 operations with the three squadrons and had accumulated over 550 hours flying in Hawker Hind, Avro Anson, Whitley and Wellingtons. In November 1944 he sent on a flying control course and after completing it he was posted home to Nutts Corner (or as the Americans called it 'Luney Bend') where he became a Air Traffic Controller. He was detached briefly down to the Azores, then across to France, Belgium, and Germany and eventually finished up in the south of France.

Tom was demobbed from the RAF in 1946 and came home where he applied for a position with the Ministry of Aviation on Ground Control Approach, GCA and Radar at Nutts Corner. He was detached for a short time to Heathrow (he was in one of the first Radar team at Heathrow), and was posted from time to time to other stations to help out with air traffic duties. When Nutts Corner closed in 1963 and moved to Aldergrove. Tom actually controlled the last aircraft out of the station and drove down the road a few miles and controlled the first civilian aircraft into Aldergrove. He retired from Aldergrove when he was fifty eight years young and became a Major in the Ulster Defence Regiment. He is a member of the Royal British Legion, The Aircrew Association (Northern Ireland Branch) and the Royal Air Force Association.

FLIGHT SERGEANT
THOMAS GRIBBEN
ROYAL AIR FORCE NO. 1333297
MID UPPER GUNNER
NO. 12 SQUADRON

KILLED IN ACTION 13TH JUNE 1944

Thomas Gribben was born in 18 Raby Street just off the Ormeau Road in Belfast in 1921 and was educated at Rossetta Public Elementary School. He joined the RAF as an Air Gunner in the summer of 1944 and successfully completed his Air Gunnery course at No 12 Air Gunnery School in Bishops Court, County Down, in Northern Ireland.

RAF Bishops Court was built quite late in the war and 12 AGS was formed there during July 1943 and was equipped with Avro Ansons and Martinet Target tugs. The AGS closed down in May 1945 having completed 47 courses of Air Gunners.

The Air Gunner's course commenced on the 14th August 1943 and on the 25th August Thomas had his first flight in an Avro Anson code MG109 on the 25th August 1943. At the end of the course he accumulated 15hrs.10mins flying time and was assessed as 'average' as an Air Gunner. In October 1943 he was posted to No 30 OTU at RAF Hixon to start his air gunnery training on Wellingtons which he successfully completed on the 14th December 1943. Early January 1944 saw him posted to No 1656 Conversion Unit where he converted onto Halifaxes. During the course he also completed an air safety course that involved him completing 16 dummy crash landings, dinghy and parachute drills. The conversion course finished on the 2nd February and three days later he went to No 1 Lancaster Finishing School completing the course on the 9th February. By this time he had reached 66 flying hours and was promoted to Flight Sergeant.

With all his training now finished Flight Sergeant Gribben was posted to No 12 Squadron that was based at Wickenby during the 2nd week in February 1944. His logbook shows that his first operational flight was on the 16th February and was to Berlin. 891 aircraft, made up of 561 Lancasters, 314 Halifaxes and 16 Mosquitoes were sent to Berlin. This was the largest force sent to Berlin and the largest non-1,000 bomber force sent to any target. This was the end of the Battle for Berlin as only one

more raid took place on the city and that was not until the next month.

Some of the other targets which Sergeant Gribben visited were: Augsburg; Stuttgart; Frankfurt; Nurnberg; Aulnoyne; Cologne; Dusseldorf; Karls Ruhe; Essen; Friedrichshafen; Maintenon; Orleans; Duisberg; Dortmund; Aachen; Tergnier; Berneval; Le Grand; Pas-De-Calais; Crisbecq; Acheres; and Evreau.

He completed of his 28th operation on D-Day the 6th June 1944 in Lancaster PS986 when they attacked the German coastal batteries at Crisbecq.

Missing

On the night of the 12th/13th June 1944 Flight Sergeant Thomas Gribben and the crew of Lancaster PA896 (PH-'D') took of from Wickenby at 2301 hrs. Their target was the Nordstern synthetic oil plant at Gelsenkirchen in Germany. They were part of a force of 303 aircraft made up of Lancasters and Mosquitoes of 1, 3 and 8 Groups. The Pathfinders did an exceptional job marking the target as 1,500 fell inside the oil plant area.

Seventeen of the Lancasters failed to return from the Raid. PA 896 was one of them, and here is a partial account of what happened to it and its crew.

PA896 was captained by Pilot Officer A Williams that night and things were comparatively uneventful going to and over the target. However on their return they were attacked by German night fighters and shot down over Holland.

PA 896 (PH-'D') was one of seventeen Lancasters lost that night and crashed in farm land at Masten Broek which is eight kilometres North West of Zwolle in the Netherlands with the loss of seven of its crew.

Pilot Officer 174529 A Williams, Captain
Flying Officer 151424 DFW Keyte, DFC, Navigator
Sergeant 1577217 RC Barber, Wireless Operator
Flight Sergeant 1333297 T Gribben, Mid-Upper Gunner
Sergeant 2209263 D Lloyd, Rear Gunner
Sergeant 1636803 J Plant, Flight Engineer
Sergeant W Wallinger, Air Bomber/Bomb Aimer

The bodies of five of the crew, Pilot, Navigator, Wireless Operator, Flight Engineer and Rear Gunner were recovered, identified and buried in the Ijsselmuiden General cemetery close to the crash site. These are the only military graves in the cemetery.

The remains of a sixth crew member (either the Bomb Aimer or the Mid Upper Gunner) were also recovered but as it could not be positively identified, was buried in an adjoining, but unnamed grave. The remains of the seventh crew member were not recovered. Subsequently the names of both Sergeant Wallace Wallinger and Sergeant Thomas Gribben were commemorated on the Panels at Runnymede memorial as having no known graves.

In 1989 the crash site of PA 986 (PH-'D') was re-excavated by a recovery unit from the Royal Netherlands Air Force and during that recovery further human remains were found. These were collectively identified as those of Flight Sergeant Thomas Gribben and another crew member. The excavation of Lancaster PA986 was due entirely to the persistence of a local young aviation enthusiast whose name was Gerrit De Reuter. During the excavation the complete remains of a crew member were recovered, still at his position in the Mid-Upper Turret position. It is now accepted beyond doubt that the unidentified remains discovered in 1944 are those of the Bomb Aimer Sergeant Wallinger and the remains discovered in 1989 are those of those of Flight Sergeant Thomas Gribben. The remains of Flight Sergeant Thomas Gribben were buried on the 8th December 1992 next to his fellow crew members in Ijsselmuiden General Cemetery with full Military Honours in the presence of a large congregation that included Flight Sergeant Gribben's sister, brother and nephew Tom Richardson. Also present were representatives of the Dutch Military and Civil Authorities, Ex-Service Associations, Lieutenant-Colonel Cook the British Military Attaché at The Hague. The Gribben and Richardson families are now comforted in the knowledge that Flight Sergeant Thomas Gribben has now a known grave that rests with the remainder of his crew in Ijsselmuiden Cemetery.

THE HAMILTONS

This is a story about a family whose four sons and a daughter gave some years of their life for God and Country. Mr William John Hamilton and Mrs Elizabeth Lavinia Hamilton were the proud parents of six sons and two daughters. Four of their sons served in the Royal Air Force during World War II and one of their daughters, Rosemary also served throughout the war as a driver in the Royal Navy.

Mr William John Hamilton had his own Upholstery and Soft Furnishing business at 338 Lisburn Road in Belfast. Mrs Elizabeth Lavinia Hamilton also had her own antique shop at 509 Lisburn Road, on the corner of Rathgar Street. Mrs Hamilton was later killed in a motor car accident while visiting her son Jack in Canada. All of her sons were educated at Fane Street Primary School, which was at the bottom of Ashley Avenue on the Lisburn Road, and their higher education was carried out at Shaftsbury House.

Their eldest son was Jack, followed by Norman, Winston, Sidney, Dennis, and the youngest was Ian. The oldest daughter is Rosemary and the youngest is Edna Patricia. There was a third daughter but sadly she died in infancy. Unfortunately many of the family documents and photographs have been lost with the ravages of time, but thankfully the youngest daughter, now Mrs Patricia Deering, allowed me into her home a talk about her family. The oldest brother Jack went to Canada when he was very young, and Norman is now ninety six years of age and living in a nursing home in Holywood, County Down.

GROUP CAPTAIN SIDNEY JAMES BROWNLEE HAMILTON
RAF NO. 62703
NO. 102 SQUADRON

Sidney James Brownlee Hamilton joined the Royal Air Force prior to the outbreak of war, and trained as a bomber pilot on Whitleys, Wellingtons and Halifaxes. He completed at least forty five operations over enemy territory with 102 Squadron. On returning from one of these operations, on 9th February 1943 he was awarded the Distinguished Flying Cross for taking daring low level photographs of an important German ammunition dump at Karls Ruhre in Germany.

Sidney had a couple of hairy moments during his war time career, one of which was when he had just taken off for an operation to Germany. His aircraft developed a problem, which necessitated him returning to the aerodrome immediately. The aircraft crash landed, complete with its full bomb load and it was thanks to Sidney's skilful flying, everyone survived. As he left the aircraft he noticed that his rear gunner was missing, he immediately returned to see where he was. As he was running towards the aircraft, shouting, "Jock, Jock, where are you?" He heard a voice with a Scottish accent behind him shouting, "Here I am Skipper, over here, I passed you a couple of minutes ago." These were the actions of a very brave man, who was prepared to return to his aircraft to save one of his fellow crew members, knowing that it's bomb load was liable to explode at any minute. On another occasion, returning from an operation on only one engine, he managed to land the stricken aircraft on a beach near Dover. His sister Patricia remembers well him telling her, "Anyone who said they were not scared flying a bomber, are liars. Many a time I was physically sick on returning from a raid."

102 Squadron also had another famous son and he was, Group Captain GL Cheshire, VC. He is remembered for bringing his badly damaged aircraft and crew safely back from a raid on the heavily defended marshalling

yards at Cologne. His Whitley (P5005) DY-'N' was rocked by a succession of violent explosions over the target and went on fire. He lost control of the aircraft for a time loosing approximately 2,000ft. He struggled with the controls and managed to bring the aircraft out of its dive. He brought the Whitley back to base with a huge gaping hole in the side of the aircraft, and was awarded an immediate Distinguished Service Order. He was later awarded the Distinguished Flying Cross for operations with 102 Squadron. 102 Squadron had a very distinguished part in the war, taking part in each of the three historic 1,000 bomber raids in May and June 1942, and later in the battles of the Ruhr, Hamburg, and Berlin. On the eve of D-Day the squadron sent 26 of its aircraft to bomb the railway communications in northern France, and the German gun batteries on the coast of Normandy. In September and October 1944, the squadron transported fuel into Belgium for the Second Army and in just over one week carried 134,250 gallons without mishap. During the closing stages of the war some of the squadron's crews carried out two round trips to Duisburg within 24 hours (1,000 bomber raids). Between 1939 and 1945 102 Squadron dropped a total of 14,118 tons of bombs and laid 1,865 mines. The squadron's personnel were awarded five DSOs, 115 DFCs, two Bars to the DFC, and 34 DFMs.

Sidney James Hamilton also became an aid to General Lee in Italy, and spent a lot of time in Egypt. He left the RAF after the war, but rejoined again and eventually retired as a Group Captain. Group Captain Sidney Hamilton died in 1987.

FLIGHT LIEUTENANT WINSTON HAMILTON

Flight Lieutenant Winston Hamilton was born on 3rd April 1907 and joined the Royal Air Force administration branch before the war. He trained in the secretarial and accountancy branch in Prince Edward Island in Canada, and saw service in Egypt and the Azores. In August 1943 the Portuguese leader Dr Salazar agreed to allow Britain to use its military bases in the Azores, and on the 12th October 1943 the British land, sea and air forces arrived on the island. The islands which were strategically placed in the middle of the Atlantic were to be used by the RAF to give aerial protection to the merchant shipping which sailed between the United States and Britain. The RAF used Catalinas to close the 'Gap', where the U-boats assembled to prey on Allied shipping. Winston was one of the first onto the island where the RAF established a new airfield. On 19th September 1946 he received his commission, and was posted to RAF Bishops Court in Northern Ireland where he became adjutant until he retired. He finally retired from the RAF on 30th May 1962, and joined the civil service where he worked in the Unemployment Department in Corporation Street Belfast. (BRU). Flight Lieutenant Hamilton died during the 1990s.

WARRANT OFFICER 1ST CLASS DENNIS HAMILTON

Warrant Officer 1st Class Dennis Hamilton also joined the Royal Air Force before the war. He was posted out to India, and then went to Burma where he helped with the evacuation of women and children before the Japanese took over. On leaving the RAF he married a County Durham girl and became a teacher in a Sunderland school. He was passed over several times as Headmaster and decided to move to London where he took up a long standing job offer in marine insurance with the Firm of Lang. Warrant Officer Dennis Hamilton died in 2000.

IAN HAMILTON

Ian Hamilton the youngest of the brothers had been studying Pharmacy for two years, and was exceptionally good at languages. In 1938 he decided to join his brothers in the RAF, and applied for and was accepted for a short service commission. He trained as a Wireless Operator/Air Gunner and at the outbreak of war was posted to a New Zealand Squadron. Possibly based at Rothshire in Scotland Feltwell in Suffolk and Norfolk.

Ian was a very quiet lad who always liked keeping to himself, and it now seems that the RAF life was not for him. On one occasion while home on leave he took ill and went to see his doctor. He examined Ian, and gave him a certificate stating that he was unfit to travel. When he eventually got back to his squadron he was given 14 days in the Glass House for returning late for duty. In 1941 he was discharged from the RAF on medical grounds.

He returned home and never worked again. His mother fought for the next ten years to get him a pension and finally succeeded.

Ian is 83 years young and is living in a residential home on the outskirts of Belfast.

ROSEMARY HAMILTON

Rosemary Hamilton is the older of the two daughters. She joined the Royal Navy during the war, and was a driver in London. She was posted back to Northern Ireland sometime during the war as a driver. Rosemary now lives in Kent not far from Canterbury.

SERGEANT
HUGH HARPER
ROYAL AIR FORCE NO. 651082
FITTER/RIGGER

JAPANESE PRISONER OF WAR

Hugh Harper was born in Whitehouse, Northern Ireland, on the 11th April 1918. He received his Primary education at Whitehouse Public Elementary School, and remained there until the age of fourteen. He immediately started his first job as a message boy with the firm of Hall Hymans of Queens Street in Belfast.

Hall Hymans was a wholesale millinery company and Hugh worked his way up with the company and soon became an Overlooker in charge of a complete section. After two years he decided he would like to serve his time as an apprentice fitter with the Firm of Jennymount Mill.

On the 20th July 1938 Hugh visited the Royal Air Force Recruiting Office in Ann Street, Belfast and enlisted as a Fitter. On completing the necessary forms, he was given the princely sum of three shillings and sixpence for his breakfast and dinner, plus another sixpence to get his haircut. He was then instructed to report to the Royal Air Force Station at West Drayton, near London, and so on the evening of the 20th July 1938 AC2 Harper said his goodbyes to his mother and father and boarded the Heysham boat to commence his Royal Air Force career.

On his arrival in Heysham the next morning he boarded a train that took him to the Padgate Receiving Centre, where he was kitted out with his uniform and commenced his basic training. The training lasted for three months and consisted of square bashing, rifle drill and physical training. He successfully completed the course on the 13th September 1938. His next posting was to Royal Air Force Station Locking, No 5 Technical Training School and he soon commenced his training as a Fitter/Flight Rigger. On completion of the course, Hugh was passed out as an aircraftsman first class (AC1) with a recommendation for further promotion to leading aircraftsman (LAC). At that time his pay was fourteen shillings per week, with two shillings deducted for credits (savings). In September 1940, war had now been declared on Germany, and Hugh was posted to No 50 Squadron that was based at Waddington. The squadron was equipped with the Handley Page Twin Engined Hampden

Bomber. Shortly after this the squadron moved to RAF Lindolme and was the first squadron to occupy the brand new airfield. It was here that Hugh had the misfortune to be put on his first charge when he tried to ride his bicycle under the wing of a Miles Magister aircraft causing slight damage. He was confined to the camp for three days. After a few weeks at Lindholme he was transferred to Royal Air Force Station at Innsworth where he completed a two week Fitter 2/Airframe course. He then reported to RAF Halton, and on the 1st December 1940 was given some home leave.

On his return from leave on the 20th December, he was informed that he was being posted overseas, no destination was given. Hugh was then told to report to the ex-Working Mens Club in Baker Street, London to wait there until he received his orders for his overseas trip. On the 5th January 1941 he was trained up to Liverpool where he boarded the Liner SS Empress of Australia, which had just returned from a good will trip to America with King George 1V and the Queen. (The Empress of Australia had been originally built for Kaiser Willhelm to tour the world after the end of the Firstst World War.)

After briefing, the officer-in-charge discovered that he had an extra ten people on board, and Hugh was one of them. Despite frantic appeals made by the OIC the ten were informed that no bunks were available and that they would have to sleep wherever they could find a space. Hugh did not mind this too much as he had made friends with a group of Newfoundland sailors who looked after him very well. He was also given permission to dine in the sergeant's mess. On leaving Liverpool the Empress lay off the coast of Anglesey for five days before heading into Belfast Lough where it joined a large convoy. While the

Liner was at anchor in Bangor Bay, small boats where shuttling back and forward. Hugh noticed a local lad passing a letter to one of the crew in the small boats. The person concerned knew very well that this was forbidden and was caught. As he was onboard ship, it was decided that his punishment would be 'runner' (gofer) until the ship arrived at its destination. (All Union Castle ships were commandeered for this convoy, which turned out to be one of the biggest of the war.)

The convoy sailed on the 12th January 1941, its first port of call being Freetown in South Africa, then sailed on to Mombassa for refuelling and taking on stores. The liner then headed north to Bombay in India where Hugh was told to disembark. He was transferred to the four-funnelled liner the Aquatania, and as the liner was at anchor out in the Bay, he had a terrible time climbing up ropes clad with his kitbag. Hugh learned sometime later that the reason he had to leave the Empress was that it was much larger than the Aquatania and was needed to evacuate the troops from Crete. Hugh had to spend the next five days onboard ship in the soaring heat, and still not knowing where his final destination would be, but he had an idea it would be either Hong Kong or Singapore (the latter being the right one). HMS Dauntless arrived to escort them on the next stage of their journey, arriving in Singapore in early March 1941. After much confusion Hugh and nine others were posted to No 100 Squadron, a Maintenance Unit based at Seletar where their work was mainly servicing Vildebeests of No 36 Squadron, and Short Singapore Flying Boats of No 205 Squadron. The Singapores were soon to be replaced with the new Short Sunderland and Catalina flying boats. Hugh was also involved assembling the Brewster F2A Buffalo fighter (186 in total). This was an entirely new way of life for Hugh, beautiful weather, no black outs, no bombs, no rationing, a five day week, camp swimming pool, and a station cinema. But unknown to him this was all about to change.

Rumours had already started about the Japanese invasion of Malaya. The battleships Prince of Wales and Repulse called to refuel and set sail. It was only when survivors were brought ashore into Singapore a few days later that servicemen stationed there realised the serious situation they were in. Three days after Pearl harbour, the Prince of Wales and the Repulse had been sunk by the Japanese aircraft on the 10th December 1941. It took 88 Japanese aircraft less than two hours to destroy the only two effective battleships left in the Pacific, 840 men died. They were now aware that the Japanese had landed at Alorstar in Northern Malaya and were rapidly advancing towards Singapore. Enemy air-raids were happening every day now over Singapore, and on the 8th December 1941, Japanese aircraft bombed 205 Squadron's, hospital and sick bay, killing one airman. Hugh and some other airmen had now been formed into a group of anti-paratroopers for their Depot.

The enemy aircraft usually came in groups of twenty-seven, three echelons of nine, and continually bombing the naval base and troops, who were trying to leave Singapore. There was no doubt in Hugh's mind that the Japanese were out to kill everyone.

As the Japanese advanced towards Singapore it was decided to evacuate both military and civilian personnel to Java. On the morning of the 13th February 1942, they received a briefing by the air officer commanding Group Captain Young, who informed them that a ship was waiting at the docks to take them to Java. They boarded the SS.Empire Star (built by Harland and Wolff of Belfast) and set sail, lying off the coast of Singapore until the next morning. The journey took almost thirty six hours and during that time the ship received two direct hits from enemy aircraft, killing many of the passengers (men, women and children) and crew. Hugh was detailed to work in the butcher's shop onboard ship and though there were no rations available for the evacuees, he did manage to feed a few of his friends. The Empire Star docked at Batavia on 15th February 1942, where Hugh and his friends were accommodated in the King William School. Escape now was impossible as the Japanese army had the island occupied and surrounded. A convoy of military and civilian cars was assembled. a civilian asked Hugh to change places with him so Hugh politely said certainly, and transferred to a military vehicle. He learned later that the civilian had been killed in an ambush.

Later on Hugh and some of his friends commandeered a water tanker which held 300 gallons of water, thinking this would be of use to them for their ongoing journey. It was of use to them as sometime later on they met up with an army lorry which was filled with rations, and was short of water, so a swap was done.

By now, the 8th March 1942 they were well aware that the Dutch troops on the island had already surrendered to the Japanese. Eventually, along with other British troops, they all assembled at a tea plantation while a British officer negotiated their surrender. They were instructed by their captors to drive to the small town of Garvet which housed the local headquarters of the Japanese Army. This was Hugh's first encounter with the ememy and he knew it would not be his last. The Japanese didn't bother too much at that time, just a few of them keeping a eye on things. Here they were allowed to camp in the outskirts of the town, and would drive in once a day for water. Two weeks later they were transferred to a captured airfield at Kalaigata where they repaired bomb damage. They established a small camp for themselves just outside the perimeter fence of the airfield and were divided up into two shifts. One worked in the morning, and one in the afternoon. Their task set them by the Japanese was to completely level the airfield and build a new one (the airfield had been so badly damaged it seemed the sensible thing to do).

The working parties had the help of a small gauge railway system, which unfortunately had been damaged during the battle for the aerodrome and was not repairable. This meant that the wagons had to be pushed by hand. The POWs were given two meals of rice a day, and this meagre ration was sometimes supplemented by duck eggs and tobacco which was smuggled to them by the locals. Roll call was held twice a day, 0500 hrs, and 2100 hrs in the evening.

The Japanese asked for five aircraft fitters to volunteer to work on damaged Dutch and British aircraft. The alternative to this was to be shipped out to work on the railways. Hugh and four others hastily volunteered and set to work repairing the damaged aircraft, which included a Hawker Hurricane fighter aircraft and a Bristol Blenheim bomber. Naturally a job which would have normally taken a few days was stretched out into weeks. Hugh recalls one occasion they were all assembled on parade for an inspection at 1200 hrs in the stifling heat for a visit by a high ranking Japanese officer. Finally at 1500 hrs, just before he arrived, a junior officer quickly turned the hands of the large camp clock back to 1200 hrs, just to impress the VIP.

Around the beginning of September 1942, Hugh was transferred to a POW camp at Wanerali where he was allocated the dreary task of grinding monkey nuts for the Japanese soldiers. As usual the meals were a bowl of rice twice a day, and occasionally they included a couple of 'dough-balls' which were horrible and were used by the POWs for playing bridge. October saw Hugh on the move again, a long march to the docks at Tanjong Priok where he boarded the ship, Yoshidalia Maru ('Maru' is Japanese for ship or boat) which was bound for Singapore. (Hugh pointed out that not all the Japanese were cruel as some of them risked severe punishment, slipping cigarettes and food when they could to the POWs.)

They left Java on October 22nd and arrived at Singapore on the 26th, and during the trip Hugh met up with three other Ulstermen. One was an Airforce chap from Newtownards and the other was Tom Finlay from Whitehouse, and the third turned out to be an old army friend whom he went to school with. On leaving the Yoshidalia Maru they were herded into a shed and told to get ready for a medical examination, which Hugh said was very embarrassing as the Japanese allowed the local female population to watch the proceedings. They were tested for dysentery (glass rod treatment) and again fumigated. They were then taken to the infamous Changi Prison where they remained for the next few days before boarding the Dianichi Maru. They were packed into the ships hold like sardines as there were a lot of Japanese soldiers going home on leave and naturally had the pick of the accommodation. The prisoners had not had any food for 24 hours, and their first meal on board consisted of rice, vegetables and soya sauce. Food then consisted of one bowl of rice a day, and the only supplies which the medical officers had were Epsom Salts. The POWs started to die of dysentery and other related diseases. Shortly after leaving harbour the ships boilers broke down and the POWs were ordered to repair them. Many volunteered for the job as they were supplied with an extra bowl of rice. The ship left Singapore on the 28th October 1942, and arrived of Saigon on the 4th November 1942. They were unable to dock because of an American air-raid, and continued the journey arriving at Takao in Formosa on 11th November. They left Takao on the same day and arrived at Shiminosaki in Japan on the 23rd November, finally disembarking the ship three days later.

Again and no doubt just to humiliate them they were given another so called medical examination in front of Japanese women. After the medical had been completed they were all marched to Shiminosaki railway station watched by hundreds of Japanese men, women and children. They were immediately put onto a train, but had to wait onboard in the terrible heat and humidity for at least four hours before leaving the station. Just before the train moved off, an unknown hand passed a very welcome packet of cigarettes through the shuttered window.

Onimichi, Hitachi Zosen ship yard

The train finally departed Shima late that night, and after a very uncomfortable journey, they were given breakfast, which consisted of a small portion of cold rice, a slice of orange, some seaweed, and one pickle called Dikon. They arrived at Onimichi which was to be their home until the end of the war. When they disembarked the train at Onimichi there were only one hundred men left. They consisted of three officers and ninety seven airmen, and of the ninety, seventy three were Sergeant Pilots and the rest were ground crew. Sadly one the airmen had died just as he got off the train. His name was Corporal Campbell and he was over six feet tall. The Japanese gave the airmen permission to make a coffin for him out of cardboard boxes, and after they held a funeral service were ushered to a local crematorium. On their arrival the old lady in charge flew into a rage, screaming that the coffin would not fit into her oven. Eventually the airmen built a bonfire and cremated the body themselves. By January 1943 deaths had reached double figures, mainly caused by dysentery and pneumonia, but no more coffins were allowed to be made. Remains were doubled up and placed in a box in a crouching position and burned. Later, the ashes were placed in a small urn and placed in the local Shinto temple.

Onimichi itself was on the mainland and every morning Hugh and the lads had to board a ferry which would take them to the island of Mukiashina where they would work repairing ships at the Hitachi Zosen shipyard. On their arrival at the shipyard they were given a pep talk by a Japanese army officer, who spoke to them via an interpreter. The interpreter's name was Nito San, who had been educated in America. The camp was to be split into twelve groups, each containing eight airmen. Each group would consist of carpenters, welders, plumbers, heavy machinists and labourers (Hugh was given the job of carpenter). Hugh and his pals were made work thirteen days out of fourteen, and had one Sunday off to clean their billet and mend clothes. Once a week they were able to have a communal bath. In the summer their working hours were form 0700 hrs to 1730 hrs and in the winter from 0700 hrs to 1630 hrs.

Daily routine was:

Reville 0530 hrs and breakfast - one bowl of rice.

Parade and roll call, 0615 hrs. Physical training for 30 minutes and everyone was made bow to the east and thank the Emperor for the days work ahead.

Lunch time was at 1200 hrs for 30 minutes. Lunch consisted of one bowl of rice.

Evening meals were at 1800 hrs and consisted of one bowl of rice and (if you were lucky and the cook was in a good mood) fish-heads or Dikons.

Roll call was at 1900 hrs, then you were dismissed and lights out 2030 hrs.

There was a makeshift dining room for the airmen, and they were not allowed to speak or communicate to the Japanese civilians at any time. It was half an hour's march from the camp to ferry and when they arrived each morning for work they were handed over to civilian workers called Honchos (Leaders). Their work clothes were made out of a hessian material, and their boots were like a pair of boxing gloves, and everyone was given his own works number. Each billet had to supply its own fire-watch crew. This consisted of each airman taking it in turn to patrol his billet for one hour. Fire was always a danger, as the wood in the huts was always tinder dry. The billet was divided up into six rooms with sixteen airmen to a room. They lay on hard wooden beds with rice paper for a mattress. No one ever managed to escape from the camp, as Japanese soldiers patrolled it twenty four hours a day. Lack of warm clothing was also a problem as the Japanese issue was a thin suit made of green material. The temperature fell well below freezing during January and February. During their first year in captivity the death toll rose to twenty four caused mainly by malnutrition and pneumonia. However with the coming of spring and the appearance of the cherry blossom helped to improve the morale. During the summer they were made to wear heavy Japanese uniforms. During his three years in captivity Hugh had worked as a carpenter, pipe lagger, fitter (changing bilge pumps) and many other non-carpentry tasks. The tools for these jobs were in a locked tool shed at the shipyard, and were picked up every morning and left back at night. In those three years Hugh only received three food parcels, and never got a whole one. Each parcel was split between three airmen. This made them last longer. (The food parcels consisted of butter, sugar, chocolate, tinned milk and salmon.)

The following are some of Hugh's personal memories

"On one very hot night the medical officer was woken up, as one of the airmen had severe pains in his lower abdomen. It was thought that he had stolen what looked like food from a locker on the boat, but this turned out be a large bandage. Once an airman managed to pinch a toaster from a boat that he had been working on and brought it back to camp. What he didn't know was that the Japanese had a hidden voltage regulator in their guardroom and knew something was going on with a surge in voltage. The billets were searched that night and the toaster found. One night at the camp the commanding officer had gone out for a 'jolly', and the camp guards were at a low profile. Four airmen decided to take advantage of this by visiting the naval stores. They found food and drink which they brought back to camp and hid under the floor boards. When the Japanese discovered the break-in they took the camp apart until they found the missing food. The four airmen concerned were caught and given seven days in the 'cooler'. The cooler was a small tin hut, so small in fact that you could not stand up in it, and too narrow to sit down in. Therefore all one could do was kneel in that position without food or water for seven days. Another type of punishment at our camp was when the Japanese made you kneel on the rungs of a ladder for five hours at a time with your back straight, if you even flinched during that time you would be beaten with a bamboo stick. The 'ladder' treatment was given to me once, when I was playing tag with some of my mates in the hut. I was being chased and decided to jump out the hut window to escape them. Little did I know there was a Japanese guard passing at that moment, and I jumped right into his arms, knocking him flying. When I explained to him what had happened, he seemed to see the funny side of it. I still got a few hours on the ladder.

"When General James H Doolittle bombed Tokyo on 18th April 1942, the Japanese Army high command issued orders to all Prisoner of War, banning whistling and singing for a period of fourteen days. Anyone caught would be severely beaten. Needless to say the whistling and singing continued and there were more people punished during that period than any other.

"When a certain Japanese ship came into our shipyard we would play the record 'I'm going to park my tank outside the Tokyo bank'.

"If we were working on a boat and found some rice or grain we would pour it into the trousers and tunic of our uniform. We soon discovered that the grain had a tendency to leak through the bottom of our trousers, so we made bags out of old hessian to fit inside them so as the rice and grain would take their body shape.

"The Japanese hated flies and would pay five cigarettes for every fifty caught. They would also pay well for sparrows as they were a delicacy to them. For three years we foxed the Japanese by stealing a newspaper from a certain house every morning while marching from camp to work. One of the RAF chaps who could speak and read Japanese would translate the papers every day for us. The Japanese would also issue an English variation of the Nippon newspaper from time to time. All our shoes came in the one size, so if yours were too big, you just had to stuff them with rags to make them fit. The Japanese would sometimes give a 'prize' of ten cigarettes and some fruit to the best workers. From time we were given Japanese Army uniforms to wear, this was to supplement our hessian clothes, but we were never allowed to wear them at work.

"During the end of 1944 and the beginning of 1945. The American air-raids became more frequent, and when an air-raid warning was sounded all of the Japanese workers would leave the shipyard and make for high ground. This gave us POWs a little time to complete a little bit of sabotage like welding the tools to the decks of the ships etc.

"Nails were always in very short supply for the civilians, so on our way from camp to the shipyard we would swap some of ours for cigarettes. Sometime during 1944 approximately one hundred Americans arrived on the island. They had been captured on the Philippines and were in a terrible state. They had not seen water or food for days and possibly weeks. The only officer in charge of them was a doctor. They were accommodated in a hastily made camp opposite us. They were forbidden to mix with us, but this was ignored, and only served to bring us closer. The Americans were able to give us all the up-to-date news about the war. Long hours in the shipyard coupled with the meagre rations, was beginning to take its toll on us. Almost everyone was showing the symptoms of 'Beri-Beri', which caused paralysis, dropsy, swollen joints, and anaemia, etc.

"Towards the end of 1944, repair work on the Japanese ships had dropped considerably as we were now made to work tunnelling air raid shelters into the surrounding hillsides in the vicinity of the shipyards. We could see the American B-29i Bombers frequently heading north, the Japanese would just stand and stare whilst the POWs headed jubilantly to the nearest air-raid shelter. American night-raids increased but thankfully no bombs fell on us.

"I remember well the 6th August 1945. The air raid sirens had sounded just before 8.00am. Our guards appeared shouting, 'Speedo. Speedo. Tenko. Tenko,' as we had to be counted before leaving the dockyard. It was beautiful clear morning, and we watched as a small group of B-29 aircraft, flying at a terrific height heading for their target. A few minutes later I felt a rumbling under my feet and at first I thought it was another earthquake or tremor. After the 'all clear' sounded we returned to work. The following morning the locals were berating the Americans about the heavy bombing the previous day. One week later we learned that an atomic bomb had been dropped on Hiroshima that morning at 0815 hrs. The shipyard was only 20 miles north on Hiroshima.

"On the 8th August 1945 we all watched as the Japanese camp guards put down their weapons in a neat pile in the middle of the camp. We were then all paraded in front of a senior Japanese officer who spoke to us in perfect English and who simply said, 'There

will be no work today, the war is over, and you must all be sorry to leave Japan after being the guest of Nippon for three years.'

"A few days later Emperor Hirohito agreed to the American terms of surrender. Everything stopped at noon on this auspicious occasion. We had a surprise visit when a downed B-29 crew were brought into the camp. From them we received the latest information on recent weeks and the atomic bombs which had been dropped on Hiroshima and Nagasaki. The downed crew told us to paint large POW letters on the roofs of our huts so that the American aircraft could pick them out. The next day the Americans sent out their aircraft to locate the POW camps. Two B-29s flew low over our camp and made an unofficial food drop, which also consisted of Camel cigarettes, sweets, toothbrushes, toothpaste and soap. There was so much food it filled one of our billets. The two B-29 aircraft came back for a second run over us, and dropped us letters which read:

> Dear Boys,
>
> This parcel is just something to help out until real aid gets here. It is unofficial of course, but you will probably be able to use it. I would like to express my admiration and respect for each and every one of you from the bottom of my heart.
> Good Luck and God Speed.
>
> Tom
> Lieutenant Thomas W Teale
> United States Naval Air Corps
>
> Dear Fellows,
>
> This is an unofficial drop, we don't exactly know what you need, so we scraped up a few things we could get our hands on. Real help no doubt is in the making, but if possible be calm and stay out of trouble.
>
> Good Luck and God Bless You All.
>
> Lieutenant (JG) Richard E Sclevendeman
> United States Airplane Driver

"The unofficial drop referred to in both messages consisted of:

> "All kinds of food.
> 1 tin of Camel cigarettes.
> 1 bar of soap.
> 1 tube of toothpaste.
> 1 handkerchief duplicated for parachute."

Hugh had a silk handkerchief made from one of the parachutes dropped by the B-29s which he kept until the day he died.

The following poem was composed and written by Peter Thorne in August 1945. He was a Royal Air Force prisoner of war at the Mukaishime Japanese Camp. Peter said, "I dedicate this poem with gratitude and admiration, from all the Royal Air Force Prisoners of War to the B-29 Crews who flew into their midst so near the end."

Peter Thorne died in the camp shortly after writing these words.

We have watched you pass above us
so near and yet so far.
Close as twenty thousand feet
yet distant as a star,
So wonder not we watched your flight
with envy in our eyes,
for us the confines of four walls
for you the boundless skies,
and here were we with nought but hope
and daily growing thinner.
While five miles up were ten free men
Who'd see no rice for dinner.

You were our single concrete sign
of how the war progressed.
So obviously the masters,
Twas evident the Nippon claims
were nought but empty boasts
and how the bitter pill disturbed
the liver of our hosts.
Thus as the sirens frequency,
through you each day increased,
so was the venom of our guards
proportionately released.

Twas then we prayed that you'd avenge
and with a salvo rock
the furthermost foundations
of that cursed and hated dock.
But now we've heard about that bomb
we breathe a grateful sigh,
and think we're mighty lucky
that you just passed us by.

And now the war is over
We know our freedom's due
to those three million and a half
whose battlefield was blue.
They may have fought by sea and land
In Battleships and Tanks,
but yours the greatest glory
To you our warmest thanks.

Hugh did not know until he got home that one of his letters which he wrote from the camp did get home to his parents. The following is a verbatim extract from the Belfast Telegraph newspaper printed on Saturday, July 1st 1944.

Missing three years, Belfast airman

Letter to his Parents

Mr William Harper, 6 Plantation Terrace, Whitehouse, Belfast, has received a letter from his son, Hugh Harper, an LAC in the Royal Air force, after three years silence. LAC Harper, who before joining the RAF at the outbreak of war, was an apprentice fitter,

was reported missing three years ago and the first word his parents got was through the Red Cross a year ago, when they reported that he was a prisoner of War in Japanese hands. This week a letter reached his parents addressed from "Zentsuji War Prison Camp Nippon". Inside the envelope neatly written on good quality foreign notepaper, was a message dated November 20, 1943, and signed "Hugh".

It began "Dearest Mum, Dad and all", and went on: "I suppose you have been informed that I am a prisoner of war. My health is excellent, and I thank God I have not had a days illness since I was interned. I am working every day as a carpenter. On our rest days in warm weather we go swimming. In winter we usually play football. My evenings are usually spent playing bridge, reading or mending my clothes. I have received three Red Cross parcels containing a lovely variety of tinned foodstuffs, including butter, sugar, chocolate, milk, salmon etc., and I am living in the high expectations of receiving another for Christmas. I sincerely hope you are all enjoying the best of health and that everything is going on as usual. On no account are you to worry about me , as I am OK. You are always in my thoughts and I am eagerly awaiting the day when, God willing, we will be reunited."

The letter closes, "Looking forward to that day, God willing, when we shall meet again."

The British Navy was the first to enter Hugh's camp, and they quickly established a list of the sick and dying so as they could organise what was required when they would come to evacuate the camp. They were later examined by a British Naval officer doctor, and a Queen Alexandria nurse whose task it was to arrange repatriation for the POWs. By mid November Hugh had said his farewells to the island, he boarded a train at Onimichi. and twenty four hours later he arrived in Yokohama. From there he was taken to Tokyo where he met a Roman Catholic priest, Arch Bishop Spellman, who arranged for Hugh to be re-clothed in an American uniform and transferred to the British Aircraft carrier HMS Ruler. Once on board the carrier, Hugh settled down for the long trip home, but it wasn't long until he met an old friend, Graham Skelton who happened to be the carrier's butcher and who lived in Barber Street in Greencastle, not far from Hugh's own home. The carrier set course in October 1945 for Sydney in Australia, and on his arrival he was billeted at Warwick's Farm near Gunning, a beautiful area in the Blue Mountains. After being there a month waiting for another ship he finally boarded the liner Dominion Monarch, whose first port of call was Freemantle in Australia, where he spent three days sightseeing. Hugh and a couple of friends went into a local pub, and the first thing he spotted on entering was a reminder of home. Nailed up on the wall behind the bar was a picture of the Belfast Celtic Football Club (small world).

They left Freemantle and sailed through the Suez Canal, calling at Port Taufiq in Egypt, where they disembarked and were issued with a RAF uniform. Hugh left Port Taufiq feeling like a new pin. The liner eventually arrived at the port of Southampton, where Hugh and his friends were taken aside to a special room, and cleared by customs (checking they did not have any Japs. in their luggage). He was then taken by truck to a railway station, where he boarded a train which took him to RAF Cosford.

On his arrival all POWs were taken to a camp of unknown origin and given a lunch fit for a king. Hugh said, "We had table cloths on the tables, with a vase of flowers in the middle and were attended had and foot by ladies of Women's Auxiliary Air Force. It had been so long since they had seen a woman or a tablecloth." After the VIP lunch they returned to RAF Cosford and were given free passes into the local cinema. Next morning, Hugh had a medical to see if he was fit to travel home and was given a clean bill of health. Hugh was immediately discharged from the station and headed straight for Wolverhampton railway station where he boarded the train which would take him to Stranraer in Scotland, and a little nearer home. He was just in time to catch the boat for Larne, Hugh finally reached home in late November 1945.His parents had not seen their son for four years and were totally surprised when he walked into the house. It was a very emotional reunion.

Hugh's sister had told Hugh that there was only one of his friends left to come home and that was Tom Finlay. Hugh had the sad task of telling her that Tom had died on the Dianichi Maru while being sent to Japan and was buried at sea. This was to be the first of Hugh's visits, when he and his minister had to go to Tom's mother and tell her of her son's death. Another one of Hugh's POW friends was Jim Shaw, although the last time he saw him was in Java, waiting in a queue for tea and sticky buns. On being de-mobbed from the Royal Air Force and returning home, he had missed the Royal Air Force so much he decided to enlist as an AC1 Fighter Plotter in the local Royal Auxiliary Air Force 3502 (Ulster) Squadron which was based at the Edenmore Hotel in Whiteabbey, and eventually reached the rank of Flight Sergeant.

The unit was disbanded in the early 1960s, and in 1966 he then joined 1134 Squadron Air Training Corps as a civilian instructor rising to the rank of Flight Lieutenant with 1919 Squadron. Hugh retired from the Royal Air Force in 1988 at the age of seventy after completing 50 years service. During his service with 3502 Squadron, Hugh became firm friends with another ex Royal Air Force man Harry McNab, who during his service with the Royal Air Force was stationed at Seletar in Singapore with 84 Squadron.

It should be noted that when Hugh Harper was finally de-mobbed, one of the many jobs he applied for was that of postman with the General Post Office in Belfast. Hugh was unsuccessful because being only five foot, tall, he was considered not tall enough to reach the knockers on the doors. (In those days the postman would knock the door knocker when he delivered the mail.)

Hugh returns to Mukaishima Prisoner of War Camp

Over the years an argument developed between Hugh and Harry McNabb over which side of the road the British War Cemetery was on in Singapore. This argument continued over a period of years so in 1979 they decide that the only way to settle this was to visit the Far East for themselves, including visits to Singapore. Bangkok, Hong Kong, and Japan returning via Hawaii San Francisco, Vancouver, Toronto and New York (the complete thirty eight day trip cost them £3,000 each).

Eventually on the 1st April 1982 they left Belfast on the first leg of their journey, arriving in London (Heathrow) the same day. The then boarded a Boeing 747 direct flight to Singapore, where they were met by one of Hugh's neighbour's sons who had kindly offered to accommodate them for the duration of their stay. The following day Hugh telephoned the high commissioner to ask if they could visit Seletar Airfield as they had worked there during the war (Seletar airfield was now the Headquarters of the Singapore Air Force). To their delight the commissioner said yes and gave them the telephone number of the commanding officer at Seletar, who arranged everything for their visit. On their arrival at the station they were met by the commanding officer who gave them a conducted tour of the airfield. Hugh was able to visit 'B' Block where he was billeted, but Harry was disappointed to discover that the small west camp Sergeants Mess was now a hairdresser's salon. However most things had not changed in forty years. Their visit was rounded off by the commanding office (Major General) taking them into the officers mess for lunch. They then travelled back to Singapore by public transport as they wanted to visit the War Graves Cemetery. On their arrival they discovered that all the British troops had been re-interred in Changi Cemetery.

During their visit to Bangkok Hugh and Harry visited the infamous 'Bridge over the River Kwai', its Prisoner of War camp, and the military cemetery at Kanibury which is lovingly looked after by Saffron Monks, dressed in orange robes. From Bangkok Hugh and Harry travelled on to Hong Kong and finally arrived at Tokyo's Haneda airport. They checked into the Grand Palace Hotel and after breakfast the next morning they travelled by bullet train to Onimichi, where they were given VIP treatment, and were met by the Mayor and representatives of the Hitachi Zosen Shipyard, as well as the local TV cameras. They arrived at the island by limousine which was by now connected to the mainland by a bridge. Hugh spent a very sad, moving few hours there, remembering all his friends who had died in the camp, a lot had changed, the company was now into heavy engineering. Wartime employees were invited to meet Hugh. However all declined except the photographer, who had taken Hugh's photograph just before he left the Island in 1945.

As a final gesture the Hitachi Zosen Company booked Hugh and Harry into a luxury hotel in Hiroshima, where they visited the peace park. The next day they left for Tokyo and after a few days rest, started the long journey home. After the war, Hugh and many other POWs were paid compensation of £72 which came from frozen Japanese assets, in instalments of £30, £30 and £12.

(All Japanese Prisoners of war or their surviving families were paid £10,000 compensation in 2001, by the British Government. Hugh, unfortunately, like many others, did not live to enjoy it.)

Hugh was a very active member of the Royal British Legion and the Royal Air Forces Association (Carrickfergus Branches), and secretary of the Belfast Branch of the Far East Prisoners of War association.

Hugh's wartime and civilian awards

1935-45: Star; The Pacific Star; The Defence Medal; The Victory Medal; Air Efficiency Medal for twelve years service in the Royal Auxiliary Air Force; and the Air Training Corps Cadet medal for twelve years service in the Royal Air Force Volunteer Reserve Training.

Sadly Hugh died on the 18th March 2000.

FLIGHT SERGEANT
FRED HEWITT
ROYAL AIR FORCE NO. 522615
SIGNALS OFFICER

Flight Sergeant Fred Hewitt was born in Belfast on the 14th July 1918 and was educated at Templemore Public Elementary School. On leaving school, he was employed by the Maypole Dairies and Thomas Kirk (Wholesale Chemist) as a traveller.

He joined the RAF on the 8th August 1935 at Ann Street Recruiting Centre as a Wireless Operator. His initial training consisted of a four week course at RAF Uxbridge and a week course at RAF Orpington. He was then posted to the No 1 Electrical Wireless School at RAF Cranwell where he passed out as a fully fledged wireless operator. Fred's first posting was to the No 4 Army-Co-op Unit which was based at Farnborough. After one year here he was posted to RAF Dishforth attached to Bomber Command as Regional Control Officer. His task was to track bomber aircraft. By now it was the middle of 1939 and war was getting closer. Fred was posted to RAF Station at Linton-on-Ouse as signals officer with No 4 Bomber Group. After a short stay at Linton-on-Ouse he went to No 4 Group Headquarters at Hesslington in York as a signals 3A officer and was put in charge of all signals, wireless telephones and 40 teleprinters.

He was also in charge of all Wireless Operators (Ground) and located 'spoof' signals from the enemy, and looked after aircraft spares. He also maintained the Defence Teleprinter Network and the organisation of aircraft codes.

In June 1945 Fred was posted to Calcutta in India where he took charge of the Signals Investigation Unit. This posting required him visiting many RAF stations in India that included Ranchi, Dum Dum and Banglelore. During his posting in India Flight Sergeant Hewitt was put in charge of a race course in Delhi for one Year. The story behind this was that the RAF had borrowed the race course that it used as a storage unit. It had in storage over 300 signals vans that had to be ready at a moments notice

for transit to Burma. The vans interiors were made into operations rooms, control rooms and signals rooms. In 1948 Fred was posted back to the UK and station at RAF Helmswell. This was a Bomber Command station where he was in charge of the Signals Unit. Shortly after his stint at Helmwell he decided re-mustered to Aircraft Wireless (Fitter) and was now responsible for the care, maintenance and installation of wireless equipment for the Avro Lincolns.

It was not long before he was bound for the Middle East on board the Empress of Australia where he found himself on an eight year posting based in Habbia in Iraq. Habbia was the headquarters for the Middle East and he was to take charge of the signals unit. The unit was responsible for the servicing of Hastings Aircraft. Back to the UK for a second time and posted to RAF Kirkum where he completed a course with the Aero Inspection Service (AIS) which was controlled by the Air Investigation Department (AID). On completing the AIS course he was posted north to Kinloss in Scotland for a time and then on to 61 Maintenance Unit at Hanworth where he was in charge of the servicing of Supermarine Swifts.

His final posting with the RAF was to Burton Wood where he was put in charge of sorting out all the American Aircraft spares which had been left behind after the war (the task he told me took three years to complete). Flight Sergeant Hewitt finally retired form the Royal Air Force in 1957 after 22 years service. He still plays an active part in the Royal Air Force Association and is a member of the Bomber Command Association.

FLIGHT LIEUTENANT
CHARLES IRELAND HICKS, DFC BSC
MSC FIME
ROYAL AIR FORCE NO. 1796424
FLIGHT ENGINEER
PATHFINDER FORCE
NO. 156 SQUADRON UPWOOD

Flight Lieutenant Charles Ireland Hicks was born in Belfast on the 2nd September 1920, and was educated at Malone Public Elementary School, which he attended from 1926 until 1930. From Malone, he graduated to the Royal Belfast Academical Institution where he spent eight years. From RBAI, he graduated to Queens University Belfast, where he attained the Honours Bsc and Msc and is also a member of the FI Mechanical Engineers in Dublin.

On completion of his education Charles decided to seek employment with the firm Harland and Wolf (Shipbuilders) Belfast as a graduate trainee engineer. He worked there for a few months and decided this was not for him and so joined the Royal Air Force at Clifton Street in 1943. He was told that he would be sent for as soon as there was a course available.

Charles soon received word to report to Padgate Receiving Centre that was near Liverpool. He boarded a ship at Belfast Docks which took him to Liverpool and then by train to Padgate. Unfortunately he got off at the wrong Station that resulted in him arriving at Padgate after the preliminaries (medical aptitude tests, kitted out, etc.) were carried out and some of the tasks that he asked to do were to carry coal and wash dishes. It was not long however until he posted down to the ACRC Reception Centre at Regents Park in London where he was selected to become a flight engineer. At the ACRC he received various inoculations and was then trained down to an Initial Training Wing at Torquay on the south coast of England for six weeks of intensive basic training that included square bashing, PT and rifle drill.

In November 1943 he was posted to the Flight Engineer Training School at St Athan in Wales where he spent the next six months. Charles was informed that those on the course who showed the best potential were usually seconded onto a manufacturer course at AV Roe where they would be instructed on the construction of the Avro York. Now here he thought they where being schooled for a cushy number like transport command, little did he know how wrong he was. He successfully completed the Flight

Engineers course and received his Flight Engineers Brevet and promoted to Sergeant.

From St Athan he was posted to the Pathfinder Force Navigational Training Unit at Warboys. The unit was equipped with Lancaster, Mosquito and Oxfords. His flying training commenced on the morning of the 9th April 1944 as 2nd Engineer in Lancaster QF-O under the command of Squadron Leader Oliver. The flight lasted for 1hr.10mins. On the 29th April Charles met his new crew, his Pilot was Wing Commander Burrough. At 1155 hrs on the same day they carried out a mock operation and practice bombing in Lancaster QF-X. This exercise lasted for four hours. They carried out a further four mock operational exercises on the 2nd, 4th, 6th and 7th June. The course finished on the 7th May and they awaited a posting to an operational squadron. Within 24 hours of completing the course at Warboys, Charles and the crew were posted to 156 Pathfinder Squadron at RAF Station Upwood in Huntingdon.

156 Squadron initially formed in October 1918 and disbanded one month later. It was reformed 24 years later in February 1942 at Alconbury in Huntingshire, as a medium bomber squadron equipped with Wellingtons. When the Pathfinder Force was formed in August 1942, 156 was one of the four squadrons selected to form the embryo of the new force. During its 38 months of war time service the squadron dropped some 16,100 tons of bombs but not without enormous cost in aircraft and personnel. 45 Wellingtons and 117 Lancasters did not return. At the end of the war the squadron marked the dropping zones at Rotterdam and The Hague for the following bombers to engage in dropping food supplies to the starving Dutch

people. It also helped with the re-partition of ex British prisoner of War from Germany and Italy. The squadron was disbanded in September 1945 and at that time the squadrons awards list consisted of 22 DSOs, one Bar to the DSO, 296 DFCs, 22 Bars to the DFCs, five CGMs (Flying), 110 DFMs, one Bar to the DFM and one BEM.

The squadron moved to RAF Station Upwood in March 1944 and that is where Charles and the crew joined it at the beginning of May 1944. Charles made his first flight with 156 squadron that was a night flying test on the 11th May 1944 in Lancaster EE 108 GT-O with a Flying Officer Wiseman. From the 12th to the 24th May he flew with his own Skipper Wing Commander Burrough on cross-country and night flying bombing exercises.

At precisely 2319 hrs on the 24th May they took off in Lancaster ND618, GT-M on their first operation that was to mark and bomb the two railway yards at Aachen and on the 28th May marked the railway yards at Angers.

Targets visited during June 1944: Rennes Airfield; Tours (railway yards); St Omer (flying bomb sites); and Middel-Straete.

July 1944: L'Hey (flying bomb sites); Gapennes (first heavy Oboe attack on flying bomb sites); Coulon Villers (flying bomb sites); Foret Du Croc (flying bomb sites); Stuttgart; Chateau Bernapre (flying bomb sites); Hamburg; and Battle Area A/P 'E' (Battle Area 'E' was one of six German positions in front of a mainly American ground attack in the Villers Bocage-Caumont area).

August 1944: Forret De Nieppe (flying bomb site); Fort D Englos (flying bomb storage site); Kiel (docks area); and Connantre (railway station and yards). The Raid to Keil on the 26th August was the last time Charles flew with Wing Commander Burrough.

September 1944: Gelsenkirchen (oil storage plants) (On the 12th September 1944 Charles took on the role of bomb aimer on a raid to Frankfurt); Moerdijk (flak position at Moerdijk airfield, two Lancasters were lost on the Moerdijk raid); Bottrop (oil storage plant); and Cap Gris Nez (German Battery positions).

October 1944: Kleve (a small town which contained German units that could pose a problem for the Allied right flank); Duisberg (support of Operation Hurricane); and Stuttgart (Bosch factory).

November 1944: Duren (to cut enemy communications). On the way back from this raid Charlie's pilot Squadron Leader Letford was informed that most of the airfields in the UK were closed owing to Fog and they were being diverted to Downham Market. This particular airfield was one of several that were equipped with Fog Intensifying Dispersal Operation (FIDO).

FIDO was a very costly and crude method that was used to clear fog and mist. It worked by pouring thousands of gallons of petrol into channels along both sides of the runway and setting light to it. The heat of the flames dispersed the fog and mist for approximately 20 minutes, long enough for the crew and aircraft to land safely. Although a crude and expensive operation, setting

fire to many thousand gallons of valuable petrol, FIDO undoubtedly saved hundreds of lives which otherwise may have been lost.

Also in November 1944: Munster; Koblenz (possibly rail bridges over the Rhine); Freiburg (railway targets); and Duisberg.

December 1944: Urft Dam (the destruction of this dam was to stop the Germans releasing large amounts of water a flooding areas through which the American troops were advancing); Karlsrhue; Soest (railway installations); Osnabruck (first raid since 1942); and Koblenz (Battle of the Ardennes).

January 1945: Nurnberg (this raid was perfect example of precision marking); Royan; Hannover; Munich; and Leuna (synthetic oil plant).

February 1945: Bohlen (synthetic oil plant); Chemnitz (Operation Thunderclap); and Worms (industrial targets).

March 1945: Cologne (RAF's 'Perfect Raid'); Chemnitz (industrial targets); Dessau (industrial and railway targets); Hamburg (shipyards now assembling the new Type XX1 U-Boats); Dortmund (1,108 aircraft bombed Dortmund, a new record which would stand to the end of the war); Homberg (to block the passage of German troops bringing stores to the front line); and Misburg (Deurag Oil Refinery).

April 1945: Lutzkendorf, Leipzig (oil refinery); and Kiel (Deutsche Werke U-Boat yard, the Admiral Scheer was sunk, the Admiral Hipper and Emden were badly damaged).

On the 10th April Charles carried out his 58th and last operation with Squadron Leader Letford that was to mark the railway yards at Plauen. They took off from Upwood at 1857 hrs in Lancaster ME377, GT-H to mark the railway yards at Plauen. Flight Lieutenant Charles Hicks was Master Bomber on that 7hr.25mins raid and it was a complete success. He was commissioned in early 1945 and was awarded a well earned Distinguished Flying Cross on the 20th July 1945 by King George V. The permanent award of the Pathfinder Force Badge.

He had completed two operational tours with 156 Pathfinder Squadron. Flew on 58 operations. Flew a total of 273 hours operationally 199hrs.10mins by night and 73hrs.50mins by night. His total flying hours including training of 394 hours.

On the 2nd June 1946 he had his last flight in the RAF when he flew in a Wellington as a passenger from Nuneaton to Aldergrove (Northern Ireland) returning to Nuneaton on the 26th June 1946. Flying time was 1hr.40mins. Charles left the Royal Air Force in 1946 and returned to Northern Ireland to take up his civilian occupation as a chartered mechanical engineer with the Sirocco Engineering Works in Belfast from October 1948 until July 1975. Then joined the Northern Ireland Electricity Service until he retired on the 1st September 1985.

Charles still keeps himself busy with his 1937 Austin Ruby Seven Saloon that he has painstakingly restored to pristine condition. His second love is his Volkswagen Caravanet.

SERGEANT
CHARLES JULIUS HOLLAND
ROYAL AIR FORCE NO. 745631
OBSERVER
NO. 107 SQUADRON

KILLED IN ACTION 23RD JULY 1940

Charles Julius Holland was born in India on 20th January 1920. His parents moved to Bangor in County Down, Northern Ireland, shortly after he was born. Julius was educated at the Bangor Grammar School and sang in the Parish Church Choir. On leaving school, he joined the Northern Ireland Civil Service and served in their Ordinance Survey Department. Julius joined the Royal Air Force Volunteer Reserve in Belfast in 1939 and commenced his flying training at the 24 Elementary & Reserve Flying Training School at Sydenam.

At the outbreak of war he was called to full-time service and posted to Moncton in Ayrshire for his basic training and then down to RAF Station Upwood on February 3rd 1940 where he was trained as a Navigator/Observer. He was awarded his 'O' Brevet on 24th June 1940. On July 3rd he was then posted to West Raynam in Norfolk where he carried out his operational training in Bristol Blenheims. On completion of his operational training Julius was posted to No 107 Squadron at RAF Wattisham in Suffolk. He had completed four operations with the squadron during July 1940, one on the 5th, two on the 7th, one the 9th and one on the 20th.

On the 23rd July 1940 he had volunteered for a 'special' duty to attack the airfield at Criel in northern France. He was killed while flying in a Blenheim Mk 1V (OM-Z) L9414 when his aircraft was shot down by a German night fighter and was seen to crash into the English Channel. Sergeant Holland's body was washed ashore at Littlehampton near Bognor Regis and taken to the RAF Station at Tangmere where he is buried. Sergeant Holland's body was the only one recovered from the crash. His colleague's names were Pilot Officer PGA Watson and the Air Gunner was Sergeant WP O'Heney.

AIR VICE MARSHAL
FREDERICK DESMOND HUGHES,
DSO DFC** AFC CBE ADC
ROYAL AIR FORCE NO. 74706
BATTLE OF BRITAIN PILOT
NO. 264, 125, 600 AND 604 SQUADRONS

Frederick Desmond Hughes was the son of a Belfast Linen Manufacturer and was born in Belfast on June 6th 1919. The family moved to the seaside town of Donaghadee where he spent most of his youth.

He was educated at Campbell College and later at Pembroke College in Cambridge where he served with the University Air Squadron. He was called to full time service at the outbreak of war and received his commission and promoted to Pilot Officer. His first posting was to No 1 Initial Training Wing at Cambridge for basic training and on January 1st 1940 went to the Flying Training School at RAF Cranwell where he attended the first war course. On completion of this course he was then posted to the School of Army Co-operation at Old Sarum. In June 1940 he was sent to No 5 Operational Training Unit at Aston Down to start his operational training on Boulton Paul Defiants. On finishing his operational training in early 1940 he was then posted to his first operational squadron. No 26 Squadron was equipped with the Westland Lysander and was sent to France where it was involved in the second Front. He stayed with the squadron for a short period. In the middle of June 1940 he was then posted to 264 Squadron which was equipped with Boulton Paul Defiant Mk1s and was based at Duxford. On August 26th while on patrol over Manston he claimed his first two victories during the Battle of Britain, both of which were Dornier 17s.

26th August 1940

He had been scrambled in good time, with escorting Spitfires above them to distract the German Me109s using high cover. Pilot Officer Hughes along with six other aircraft from 264 Squadron flying in line astern, made a converging attack on twelve Dornier 17s at 12,000ft. For a vital few seconds the concentrated fire of seven Frazer Nash turrets each with 4 x .303 machine guns raked the Dornier 17s, Pilot Officer Hughes and his gunner Sergeant F Gash claiming two of them. Two other Dornier 17s were also shot down in the same attack. The Dornier escorts, Me 109s then swooped down on the Defiants, three were lost and most of the others were damaged. 264 Squadron then switched to its new role of night fighting, this was like trying to find a 'needle in a haystack' for the Defiants as they were equipped with the very new and unreliable basic air interception radar. In October 1940 he was promoted to Flying Officer, and on October 15th/16th shot down and destroyed a JU88 over Brentwood and on 23rd/24th November, damaged a He111. On November 23rd/24th he shot down and claimed as a probable an He111 over Braintree, and on 12th/13th March 1941 destroyed another He111 over Dorking. On April 8th/9th he claimed an He111 as a probable over Bigging Hill, and on 10th/11th April shot down and destroyed a Ju88 over the Isle of Wight. All these successes were gained with the help of his outstanding Gunner, Sergeant Fred Nash, DFM. It was during his time with 264 Squadron that he was given the nick-name 'Hawkeye' Hughes.

On April 18th 1941 Flying Officer Desmond Hughes was awarded the Distinguished Flying Cross and in January 1942 was posted to 125 Squadron at RAF Colerne, as a Flight Commander. 125 squadron had been reformed as a Fighter Squadron at Colerne in June 1941 and had been equipped with Defiants, but now had the new radar equipped Beaufighters. Flying Officer Hughes was teamed up with his new radar operator, Pilot Officer Lawrence Dixon and on June 27th they destroyed a Ju88 just off Hook Head and another Ju88 on November 4th 1942, 130 miles East of Stonehaven. On 3rd November he was promoted to Flight Lieutenant.

Unauthorised Cargo

In November 1942 he was attached to Peterhead, and for the trip north he decided to take along his dog, 'Wee

Scruffy' and that the best place to hide Scruffy was inside his flying suit to keep him warm and quiet. On an earlier operation, Flight Lieutenant Hughes was about to take off over the north sea when wee Scruffy eluded the ground crew, jumped into his master's aircraft and settled down for a snooze on the floor of the fuselage. While flying some thirty miles east of Stonehaven Flight Lieutenant Hughes spotted a Ju88 moving against the grey sea, and called to his radar operator Pilot Officer Dixon, "Tally-Ho," and dived down with nearly 350mph on his air speed indicator. He closed rapidly on the enemy aircraft and attacked it with four sharp bursts of cannon. The Ju88s rear gunner had returned fire hitting the Beaufighter, and at the same time he watched as his cannon shells hit the Ju88s wing root, where its fuel began to burn. A second Beaufighter which was accompanying him set the other wing alight and the Ju88 went screaming down and exploded on impacting the sea. But what of Scruffy, as his master opened fire on the Ju88 he barked and bucked and nearly hit the ceiling before finding a hiding place near the tailwheel. After landing, Scruffy jumped out of the hatch and ran into the middle of the airfield until eventually, after about half an hour, he was persuaded to rejoin his master.

600 Squadron, North Africa

On January 19th 1943 Flight Lieutenant Hughes and his radar operator Pilot Officer Dixon were posted to join 600 Squadron at Souk el Khemis in North Africa as a Flight Commander and where they were to see much action. The squadron was equipped with the Bristol Beaufighter MkV1fs and had been earlier responsible for the night protection of the Casablanca Conference. In January 1943 it had played a major role in attacking the German armies fleeing Tunisia. Then two months later the squadron moved to Malta being prepared for the invasion of Sicily, and in January 1944 provided the air cover for the Anzio landings. On January 23rd/24th 1943 Flight Lieutenant Hughes shot down and destroyed two Ju88s near Philippeville and on 12th/13th February destroyed an Italian Cant 'Z' 1007 30 miles North of Souk el Khemis. On the 13th April 1943 he was awarded a Bar to his Distinguished Flying Cross. On 25th.26th April he attacked and shot down a Ju88 on the south east Coast of Tunis and on 12th/13th July destroyed a He111 over Augusta. On the 20th/21st July the intrepid duo destroyed a Ju88 10 miles south west of Cape Corranti, and on 11th/12th August destroyed three Ju88s over Augusta and Catania. Their last kill with 600 Squadron was on 17th/18th August when they shot down and destroyed a Ju87 110 miles North East of Syracuse. Flight Lieutenant Hughes was awarded a second Bar to his Distinguished Flying Cross on 23rd September 1943.

He was then posted back to the UK and in February 1944 was promoted to Squadron Leader and given a staff role at headquarters fighter command, Bentley Priory, and later with 85 Group, 2nd Tactical Air Force (TAF).

He then returned to operations on July 19th, and promoted to Wing Commandeer, and took Command of 604 Squadron at Hurn and led it into France in August 1944. The squadron became the first night fighter squadron to be based in France at A8 which was an airstrip close to the Arrowmanches beaches and had just celebrated its 100th victory a month before. The squadron at that time was equipped with the DH Mosquitoes MkX111 which where night fighters and equipped with the Rolls Royce 21 and 23 engines. They had four nose mounted 20-mm cannons and were also fitted with the new AI Mk V111 Centimetric radar and had increased wing fuel tankage. On 6th/7th August 1944, he and his radar operator Flight Lieutenant Dixon destroyed a JU88 over South Avraches, and on 13th/14th January he claimed his final kill which was another Ju88 destroyed three miles south of Rotterdam. On the 23rd March 1945 Wing Commander Hughes was awarded the Distinguished Service Order.

After the war he made steady progress in the Royal Air Force, and served again at Headquarters Fighter Command at Bentley Priory from 1946 until 1953. On January 1st 1954 he was awarded the Air Force Cross. He was also a member of the directing staff of the RAF College, Bracknell from 1954 to 1956, and was then Personal Staff Officer to the Chief of Air Staff from 1956 to 1958. On his promotion to Group Captain he commanded RAF Geilenkirchen in Germany from 1959 to 1961, receiving a CBE in 1961. He also held the position of Director of Staff Plans at the Ministry of Defence in London from 1962 until 1964. He was promoted to Air Commodore in 1963 and made an Aide-de-Camp (ADC) to the Queen. From 1962 until 1968 he became Air Officer Commanding Administration, Headquarters Flying Training Command, and promoted to Air Vice Marshal in July 1967. In 1968 he became Air Officer Commanding, 18 Group Coastal Command, and Air Office, Scotland and Northern Ireland until 1970, when he became Commandant of the RAF College at Cranwell. In 1972 he became Senior Air Staff Officer, Near East Air Force in Cyprus until his retirement from the service in June 1974. He became a CB in 1972 and settled in the Sleaford area of Lincolnshire, where he became Deputy Lieutenant of Lincolnshire in 1983. Although he was retired he always kept in touch with the service, and was made honorary Air Commodore of No 2503 Royal Auxiliary Air Force Regiment Squadron and Director of the Trident Trust. His hobbies were fishing, shooting and music. He married his wife Pamela in 1941, she was the daughter of Julius Harrison, composer and conductor. He was blessed with three sons, one of whom had predeceased him. On 2nd September 1990 Air Vice Marshal Frederick Desmond Hughes, CB CBE DSO DFC** AFC MA DL returned to Northern Ireland to present a Memorial Book to St Anne's Cathedral in Belfast, in which are commemorated the names of 1,352 men and women from Northern Ireland who lost their lives while serving in the Royal Air Force during the Second World

War. In January 1992 he caught a severe cold which developed suddenly into pneumonia, from which he died on 11th of the same month. Air Vice Marshall Hughes had destroyed eighteen enemy aircraft between August 1940 and January 1945, fifteen of which were destroyed at night. He had risen from the ranks to become one of the Royal Air Forces best known and liked Air Vice Marshals.

I am indebted to the Hughes family, and especially to Mrs Pamela Hughes for all her help in making this story possible.

SERGEANT
JOHN MICHAEL HUNTER
WIRELESS OPERATOR/AIR GUNNER

John Michael Hunter was born in Whitehead in 1921 and was educated at the Belfast Royal Academy. On completion of his education he was employed as a dry cleaning manager with the Glen Laundry in Newtownards.

In August 1939 he decided to join the Royal Air Force, and went along to the recruiting office in Clifton Street in Belfast. On passing the preliminary exams he requested to be posted to an air sea rescue unit, but was told that there weren't any vacancies in that section. He then requested that he would like to try aircrew, and again after passing the various medical tests was selected as a Wireless Operator/Air Gunner. He was then sent home and told that they would send for him when a suitable course became available. In December 1939 Michael was posted to the Receiving Centre at Padgate for one week. Here he was issued with his uniform and kit and signed the necessary forms to complete his entry into the RAF. From Padgate he went to an Initial Training Wing at Blackpool where he carried out his four month basic training course which consisted of square bashing, marching up and down the Promenade for hours on end, learning how to salute properly, etc. He also completed his basic wireless training, which was carried out in a local Tram Depot, the floor of which was made of cobble stones. The Depot was poorly heated and was bitterly cold as it was now the middle of January 1940 *(1940 had a particularly severe winter)*, so cold in fact that the trainee wireless operators had to wear their great-coats and thick mittens which made the feel of the Morse key difficult.

Having now acquired all the basic knowledge that was required of him, Michael was then posted to an advanced Wireless Operator's school at Compton Basset where he attended a Wireless course. This particular training course was very advanced and intensive, learning how to operate, strip down and re-build all of the transmitter and receiver types of radios that he would be required to operate, and little did he know that this training would be of great help to him in the not so distant future.

From Compton Basset he proceeded to Jurby in the Isle of Man where he completed his Gunnery course.

Michael had now completed all of his training, and was promoted to Sergeant, and was awarded his Wireless Operator/Air Gunners Brevet. He was then posted to an OTU at RAF Station Binbrook. Here he met his new crew and started training as a Rear Gunner on the Vickers Wellington twin engined bomber.

It was now the middle of summer and the Battle of Britain was at its height. During the next five months Michael completed 13 operations from Binbrook which included bombing targets in Hamburg, Aachen, Frieburg, and German shipping in Norwegian Fiords. During his last few weeks at Binbrook Michael complained of an aching tooth. The pain got so bad he decided to pay a visit to the medical officer, who referred him immediately to the hospital at Weeton House in Lancashire. After a thorough examination he was diagnosed as having Septicaemia, (blood poisoning). He became so dangerously ill, that his parents were sent for, and on their arrival they were told that there was little or no hope for Michael to survive the night. Michael was a fighter and wasn't about to give up, painfully and slowly he bravely fought back. When he had sufficiently recovered he was sent home but was still in a weakened state. It took quite a while for him to make a full recovery and when he did he was sent to an aircrew convalescence hospital in Blackpool where he spent the next few weeks. When he had sufficiently recovered he was called to appear in front of a medical board, who after examining him, passed him as 'unfit for flying duties'.

Because he was passed unfit for flying duties, his Sergeant's stripes were immediately removed (War-Substantive) and he was demoted back to Leading Aircraftsman. Michael felt terribly annoyed about this and that he had been let down, but nevertheless he decided to remain in the RAF and re-mustered to Radio Mechanic. He was then posted to No 313 Squadron at Hornchurch.

No 313 (F) Squadron was the third of the Czech fighter squadrons to be formed in the RAF. Its motto was "One Hawk Chases Away Many Crows". It was formed at Catterick in May 1941 and was equipped with the Spitfire Mk 1s. The squadron was then transferred to Portreath in Cornwall in August 1941 where its task was primarily protecting convoys. In December 1941 it was on the move again to Hornchurch where it spent most of it's time carrying out Rhubarbs and Ramrod sorties. The squadron moved to various stations during the war, and in August 1945 it finally left Manston for Czechoslovakia where it was disbanded in February 1946. Michael joined the squadron at Portreath in Cornwall in December 1941, just before it moved to Hornchurch. In June 1942 he was sent with a detachment of Spitfires to RAF Harrowbeer near Plymouth where Focke Wulf 190s were continually strafing Torquay and the surrounding area and causing a lot of casualties. (One FW190 & one Me109 were destroyed by the squadron with another 'probable' Me 109.)

He was also sent on detachment with the squadron to Bolt Head which was right on the coast line near Salcombe in Cornwall. Bolt Head was a very hastily erected airstrip. The runway was constructed out of wire-mesh and was so short that when the Spitfires took off, they dropped out of sight over the cliff to obtain airspeed. Two Spitfires sat on the runway for two hours at a time on full alert to cover the FW190 attacks on Torquay. When 313 Squadron moved to Church Stanton near Taunton in June 1942 Michael was transferred to 255 Squadron at Honiley. At this time the squadron was equipped with the Bristol Beaufighter Mk V1fs and was being prepared for overseas service in North Africa. In November 1942 the squadron's personnel were trained up to Liverpool where they boarded the troop ship Maloja which was built by Harland & Wolf in Belfast in 1923. They convoy sailed into the Atlantic Ocean where it was joined by other convoys which made up a massive force. The large convoy sailed west heading for America, and when it was two thirds of the way there it turned south to try and fox the German U-boats. Michael

commented that a lot of the ships in the convoy were sunk during the journey, four of which where very close to his own. When they approached the Straits of Gibraltar the massive convoy was joined by her sister convoy en-route from America. When they had passed safely through the Straits under the cover of darkness, the convoy split up, some continued onto Iran and Algiers. Michael's convoy continued on up the Mediterranean to the airfield at Bone on the north coast of Africa, and when they arrived they found that the French Vichy still occupied the airfield and had to fight to capture it.

255 Squadron's aircraft had been serviced in Gibraltar prior to have been flown to Bone airfield. Their journey from Gibraltar to Bone took them via Maison Blanche near Algeria, then across to Bone, and then down to Setif in Algeria where they commenced operations. The squadron operated every single night, attacking the German shipping which was supplying Rommel's Afrika Corps. Michael said, "Our airfield at Setif was continuously attacked by FW 190s and always at the same time. The Jerries seemed to know our 'meal times' when a large group would be gathered in one building."

It was during one of these attacks that Michael received a serious wound to his neck and back. He was rushed to a field hospital where he unfortunately contracted a bad infection in his wounds, which eventually turned into Osteomalacia (softening of the bones). As a result of the seriousness of his illness it was decided by his doctors that it would be best to send Michael home. He was taken onboard the hospital ship Oxfordshire, and several times during the long voyage, the sick and wounded had to be brought up on deck because of U-boat alerts. The ship eventually sailed into Bristol where three hospital trains were waiting to take them to Nottingham Hospital. On their arrival they were met by the Mayor of Nottingham and various military VIPs, and each patient was given a gift parcel as they went into their various wards. Mike remained in Nottingham Hospital for the next four months, and when he was feeling stronger he was shipped back to the Military Hospital at Palace Barracks near Holywood in Northern Ireland. The Osteomalacia had left him very weak, and as a result of this he was in and out of various hospitals for the next 30 years. Michael's wife also served in the RAF during the war as a Teleprinter Operator.

SQUADRON LEADER
THOMAS HARDY HUTTON
ROYAL AIR FORCE NO. 1108958
WIRELESS OPERATOR/AIR GUNNER
NO. 12 SQUADRON

Tommy Hutton was born in Belfast in 1912, and when he completed his education he was employed with the Ulster Transport Authority (Green Buses).

When the war clouds loomed over the UK, Tommy, like his father before him decided to join the Royal Navy. He went to the Clifton Street Recruiting Office in Belfast, but was bitterly disappointed when told, "Sorry, there will be no vacancies for the Royal Navy for at least nine months."

This did not deter Tommy one bit, so he enquired if there were any vacancies in the Royal Air Force as he was very interested in radios. The recruiting officer said yes there was, and after signing all the relevant documents, was surprised when he was told to go home and they would send for him in due course (this was quite normal for 1940). After patiently waiting for three months the letter arrived, instructing him to report to the Padgate Receiving Centre near Liverpool and enclosed with the letter was his travel documents. After completing the 'do's and don'ts' at Padgate he was then posted to an Initial Training Wing at Blackpool to start his basic training which included square bashing, physical training and learning the Morse code. By the time he had finished his training he could manage twelve words a minute on the Morse 'tapper'.

From Blackpool his next posting was to the Wireless Training School at Yatesbury where he was instructed on how to operate and maintain all of the different types of wireless transmitters and receivers that he would be required to operate. On completing the course he could now transmit and receive eighteen words a minute, and was awarded his Wireless Operators 'Brevet'. From Yatesbury he was posted to RAF Binbrook where he completed an advanced Ground Operator's Wireless course. It was now January 1941 and it was bitterly cold. On completion of this course, and for some unknown reason the whole class were sent back to Yatesbury for a refresher course. He was promoted to Sergeant and given fourteen days leave. On returning from leave Tommy was

transferred to RAF Station Ben Brae in Scotland, where he successfully completed an Air Gunners course. On completion of the course he was sent to No 13 Operational Training Unit at Bicester to convert onto Bristol Blenheims.

With all his training completed, Tommy was informed that he was being posted out to join a squadron the Middle East. Unfortunately for him he caught a severe virus which left him covered in large boils, which required him to spend some time at the RAF Hospital in Halton. His new crew were told to wait until he was better, but during their wait Tobruk had fallen and their posting had been cancelled, and were instead transferred to RAF Lindholme. In June 1942 Tommy was posted from Lindholme to RAF Finningley where he completed a conversion course onto Wellingtons. During this training his Wellington ran out of fuel and he had to bail out, and on landing broke an ankle. The Pilot of the Wellington died in the accident. Again Tommy was hospitalised this time in Rauceby's hospital waiting for his ankle to mend. Once the ankle had healed he was posted to No 25 Operational Training Unit where he met his new crew and was immediately sent to RAF Boughtry to convert onto Avro Lancasters. Once they had completed the conversion course they were sent to No 12 squadron at Wickonby, and little did Tommy know what was in store for him over the next few months and how it would change his life.

On April 16th 1943, Tommy's Lancaster W4366-'R' took off from Wickonby and set a course for Pilsen in Czechoslovakia. Their target was the Skoda armament factory which made and supplied a very large percentage of ball bearings for the Nazi war machine. On the way back from the target his Lancaster was hit by flak setting the starboard inner engine on fire. The Pilot climbed the aircraft to 10,000ft and successfully extinguished the fire, but as he was trying to feather the damaged engine the starboard outer engine blew up, about one and half miles from the French coast. The Pilot was having difficulty in controlling the stricken Lancaster and ordered his crew to bale out (an order which was disputed by the Skipper at a later date when he stated that his crew had misunderstood his order). After Tommy, Sergeant McKay (Bomb Aimer) and Sergeant Rudkin (Rear Gunner) had bailed out the Skipper was able to nurse the damaged Lancaster back to Wickonby.

For Tommy and his two fellow crew members, the trip back to Wickonby would take them a little longer.

Tommy had landed safely on top of a tree and was uninjured. He soon spotted Sergeant Rudkin who helped him down with the aid of their parachute harness, which they later buried out of sight. Sergeant McKay had fractured his hip on landing and was eventually taken prisoner by the Germans. Tommy and Sergeant Rudkin were very relieved that they hadn't been captured by the Germans, and were not sure if they were in Germany or France. They had in fact landed near the town of Arlow in Belgium. They gathered their themselves together and decided to try and find out exactly where they were. They had just started to walk down a narrow road when they heard dogs barking in the distance, and felt sure that it was a German patrol hard on their heels. It was a beautiful moonlit night, and at about 0345 hrs they decided to get away as far as possible from the crash site before dawn. They started walking again and came upon a small stream, which they jumped into, and waded a few miles to try and put the dogs of their scent. The water was bitterly cold, and their feet were getting numb but they kept on walking, and when they no longer heard the dogs barking in the distance they got out of the stream, and looked for a hiding place for the night. By this time they were both very tired, cold and hungry; and seeing an isolated house in the distance were solely tempted to knock on the door and hope for the best. As they still were unsure of what country they were in, their better judgement told them not to stop, and so they pressed on, eventually reaching a main road. At the time it seemed a good idea to lay behind a ditch, in the expectation that if someone did come along, they could listen to their conversation, thus giving them some indication which country they were in. A few cyclists passed by chatting in French, they sighed with relief and thought, "Thank God we are not in Germany."

They walked on down the main road and met a cyclist who advised them to keep to fields, which they did. They eventually came across a farmer who spoke fluent English, as he had spent eighteen years in Canada with his brother. It took a great deal of conversation, and questions, to convince the farmer that they were downed Allied airmen and not masquerading Germans in captured airmen's uniforms in the hope of contacting some of the French Resistance people. After a while the Frenchman was in no doubt that they were both genuine and said that he would help them get back to England.

The Frenchman told Tommy and Sergeant Rudkin that as most of the villagers had seen them by now, and that he had made contact them, this most certainly would mean that the Germans would pay him a visit that evening for questioning because of this threat he dare not take them to his home, he instead led them both to a wood nearby and told them to stay undercover until he could return and show them to a better and safer hiding place. At around 2100 hrs, the Frenchman, true to his word returned and took them to a small outhouse near his home where he had some food waiting. This consisted of black bread, greasy potatoes and Ersatz coffee. This was very welcome to the pair as they had not eaten anything since leaving England.

17th April 1943: The Frenchman called the next night and took them to a pre-arranged place, near Aix-s-Croix to meet another contact by the name of La Fontaine. They were taken to a house where they met some more contacts who would eventually help them escape back to the UK. One of them was called Eugene Joseph's, who was a devoted Resistance worker, as was his daughter. (Tommy met up with his daughter after the war.)

18th April 1943: La Fontaine took Tommy and Sergeant Rudkin to the nearby village of Musson, where they met the local priest, father George Goffinet, who was an outstanding man, and a fervent member of the French Resistance, and dedicated to help any allied soul who was in trouble. Tommy told me that Father Goffinet was aged about 35 years and was one of the most charming, sincere and bravest characters that he had ever met. His fierce love for France and determination was unequalled. He made Tommy and Sergeant Rudkin very welcome and greeted them with a firm handshake. Father Goffinet spoke very little English, but was able to sing a few songs in English on his piano, i.e., 'Horsey, Horsey, don't you stop', and sang the words with a beautiful French accent. Venetian blinds covered the large windows of his house, and a huge letter 'V' was superimposed on each blind, which of course stood for 'V' for 'Victory'. The Germans in their ignorance did not recognise this gesture of defiance as they probably thought it was for decoration, that is if they even considered it at all. On one particular occasion Father Goffinet had just returned to the village from a visit to Liege with an automatic pistol hidden under his cloak that he had obtained from a 'friend', and declared meaningfully that he was looking forward to using it. During his visit to Liege he had watched the German troops waiting outside the local cinema with a number of lorries, and he soon realised that the Germans were waiting to arrest young Frenchmen and women as the left the cinema to be taken to forced labour camps in Germany. Father Goffinet decided to enter the cinema and when inside he warned the manager of the Germans outside and their intentions. A message was cleverly flashed up on the cinema screen, and the young people where able to escape by the rear door.

Tommy and Sergeant Rudkin were the first airmen who Father Goffinet had helped to escape, and they were the first of many. Sadly, towards the end of the war Father Goffinet took a German priest into his confidence, who said that he was an anti-Nazi sympathiser. He asked Father Goffinet if he could join one of his escape parties as he wished to flee to England. As he was a fellow priest Father Goffinet had no reason not to trust him, and agreed to accept him for the journey. When the escape party arrived at St Jean-de-Luz, the German priest, if he ever was one, betrayed him to the Germans and he was arrested, as were many of his helpers. Father Goffinet was taken to the Buchenwald Concentration Camp in Germany, where he was tortured and imprisoned. Tommy learnt later that on one particular day in the camp, all the inmates had been herded into the main compound and told by the Germans that the Americans were only twenty four hours away, and that on their arrival they all would be liberated. Everyone clapped and cheered, but as they did so, the German guards cocked their machine guns and opened fire indiscriminately into the gathering from their watch towers. Many lay dead and dying, and one of them was Father Goffinet who later died in the arms of an American soldier.

On the 10th July 1945, Tommy's second daughter was born. He decided then that he would call her Goffinet, after his gallant friend and helper. On her 10th birthday Tommy took her to France to see Father Goffinet's Convent, and there she met some of the sisters who showed her his name heading the list on the village War memorial, and told her that the village square was also named Goffinet Place.

Back to the escape

29th April 1943: Tommy and Sergeant Rudkin had by now been given excellent false identity papers and arrived at Spiramont Railway Station in the evening of the 29th April. Here they were met by Joseph Brasseur and Arthur Defosse. Joseph Brasseur was the proprietor of the local garage and Arthur Defosse was the village postman. Once they left the railway station they were taken to the Brasseur family home where they were given some hot food and wine. Joseph Brasseur was a member of the Resistance Movement and involved with stealing food coupons from the local town hall which went to provide food for the many young people who were hiding in the woods and elsewhere to avoid arrest and deportation to forced labour camps in Germany. On their third day at Spiramont, Joseph Brasseur had arrived home very agitated, and informed Tommy that he was made aware by a friend that the Germans had suspected him of being in the Resistance. Because of this Tommy and Rudkin would have to leave his house immediately, and were taken that night to the home of Arthur Defosse and his wife Zenerine. Joseph Brasseur visited the Defosse family home daily, bringing with him fresh food, wine and cigarettes for Tommy and Sergeant Rudkin. The pair

never wanted for anything. Tommy and Sergeant Rudkin were made very welcome in the Defosse home, as indeed they were wherever they stayed. Mrs Defosse had two little daughters, Marie aged six, and Adele aged four. The children were warned never to mention to anyone the fact that the two airmen were staying at their home, and of course they never did. Arthur Defosse's income did not permit feeding two extra mouths with healthy appetites, but with their help and the Brasseurs, the two airmen never went without anything. Arthur Defosse had a cellar under his house that had a secret entrance which led to the garage. The garage had a hidden trap door, which was concealed by wood shavings scattered all around the floor. If the Resistance were having a secret meeting in the cellar and were 'disturbed', a push button was situated at the back of the front door was pushed by the heel of a foot, this operated a red light in the cellar, warning all to be quiet. Arthur Defosse survived the war and received many decorations for his Resistance activities. His wife Zenerine was also a very enthusiastic supporter of her husbands 'anti-social' actions. Early one morning the intrepid airmen were awakened by Joseph Brasseur who told them that they were about to undertake a long and arduous journey which would eventually take them back to England, and that they must build up their strength.

1st June 1943: Tommy travelled on his own to the town of Watterlos near Lille where arrangements were made for him to stay overnight in a villa that was owned by a charming couple, Henri Vandespye and his wife Cerealia. (Sergeant Rudkin was to follow later, the explanation for this was that Tommy for reasons best known to himself did not trust him, and so did not want to jeopardise the operation or the lives of his friends.)

The Vandespye's home consisted of two bedrooms, one large room and the other a quite small one. They normally would have occupied the larger of the two and their daughter Roseline had the small one. However they insisted that Tommy move into their room and that they would be quite comfortable in their daughters room. Henri was a small and insignificant looking man, but he had a large and generous heart, and at times was quite fearless and foolhardy.

On returning from a night out with Tommy to a local cafe which was owned by a member of the local underground, ("Allo, Allo," this sounds familiar), and for no apparent reason, he produced a pistol from his pocket and fired a few shots across the canal. Tommy said, "It was a stupid and dangerous action as curfew had started an hour earlier and we could have been arrested for that alone never mind the gun shot. Fortunately there were no German patrols in our vicinity or you would not be writing my memoirs." Henri was employed in the local town hall and was able to use his position to further the progress of the Resistance Movement whenever he could, and in order to fool the Germans he wore a Field Marshal Petain lapel badge on his tunic to indicate that he was a collaborator. Henri took great pleasure in taking Tommy to all the different cafes and introduced him to his most trusted friends. They would come over to Tommy's table one by one and wish him all the luck with his escape. During the entire time he was in France, Tommy was never once stopped and asked for his identification papers. Henri's wife Cerealia showed Tommy where she kept a hand grenade in an empty flower pot under the downstairs front window, where the path leading to the front door could be seen, and told him that should a German come up her path she would kill him with the grenade. She was a very brave and courageous lady and dedicated to the safety of her husband and daughter and the liberation of France.

Tommy stayed with the Vandespyes for fourteen days.

On returning one night from one of their visits to a local cafe, Cerealia informed Tommy that a Captain Mitchel who worked for British Intelligence wanted to meet him. *(Captain Mitchel was a Secret Agent working from his headquarters near Lille, and his job was to supply false identity papers, French currency, English cigarettes, tobacco, and other necessities for allied personnel escaping to England.)*

On the 17th November 1944, Captain Mitchel was betrayed by a fellow Frenchman and was executed by the Gestapo while asleep in his bed. Tommy was taken to meet with Captain Mitchel at his headquarters in Lille, and there he met up with Sergeant Rudkin again. In the same room was a Canadian Flight Sergeant whose name was Ford, and a Dutch Civilian who was wanted by the Gestapo for operating an underground press. Under the cover of darkness they left for the railway station where they said their goodbyes to Captain Mitchel, who handed them over to their guide. The guides name was Pierre who told them that they would be going by train to St Jean-de-Luz, via Paris. Tommy remembers that Pierre had a very bad limp, but learnt nothing more about him.

10th June 1943: On the 10th June the they boarded a train which was to take them to St Jean-de-Luz, and would there the next day. Pierre decided not to take any chances, and left the train at the village before St Jean-de-Luz. They walked the track in single file at a distance of 100 yards apart, and when they arrived at St Jean-de-Luz Pierre led them to a safe house in the centre of the town. This part of the journey was a particularly dangerous one as the town was crawling with Germans, however they managed to get safely through, and after a nights rest and preparations the next morning, Pierre introduced them to their Basque guide who would lead them over the Pyrenees into Spain.

12th June 1943: So, on the 12th June Tommy, Sergeant Rudkin and their companions set off on their twelve hour journey across the mountains. The journey was an exhausting one, so much so that one of the party was almost tempted to give up. They had to be physically fit for the crossing and that's why their French friends fed them so well. They all arrived safely at the end of this harrowing journey in the town of San

Sebastian where they met up with a Spanish, British sympathiser who gave them a room in his home for the next ten days. On June 24th they were taken to the British Embassy in Madrid, and then proceeded on to Gibraltar the same day.

They were to be flown home on the 24th, but were told that the aircraft was to be used to fly VIPs (President Sicowski of Poland and his family) back to England, but sadly their aircraft crashed en-route and all on board were killed, including the crew. Tommy and Sergeant Rudkin eventually arrived back in Liverpool the next day. Tommy later made a few enquiries about the people who had helped him escape and was informed that Mr Vandespye had been arrested by the Gestapo and tortured, and never fully recovered from his treatment, and died in 1959. His daughter Rosealine came to stay with Tommy when she was fourteen, but sadly she also died in a drowning accident some years later. Tommy returned to France in 1945 and again in 1955 to visit his old friends who gave so much for him. He never heard from Rudkin again after they returned to the UK. After being interrogated about his escape by MI9 Tommy was given a complete rest, and on his return to duty was told that he would be unable to go back to his old squadron. This was a legal technicality as it involved another airman who had been shot down over enemy territory twice and who had been wearing civilian clothes in an occupied land. This meant that you could be arrested as a spy and shot.

Tommy was eventually posted to RAF Bishops Court in his native Ulster as a Staff Wireless Operator and received his commission in November 1944. Pilot Officer Hutton left Bisops Court in June 1945 and was then posted to RAF Penrose in North Wales. In August he was sent home to Northern Ireland on indefinite leave, but that was short lived as he received a telegram instructing him to report back to Penrose. On his arrival there he was told that he was being transferred to 18 Group Headquarters in Inverness as equipment officer. In September 1945 he was again on the move to the Orkney Islands where he remained until February 1946 when he was posted to Skeabrae to assist with the closure of the station. Then it was back to Bishops Court as equipment officer, and between May 1946 and February 1947 he had two further postings as equipment officer, one to Aldergrove and the second to Castle Archdale in County Fermanagh. In October 1947 he was on the move again to RAF Hednesford where he trained on various types of explosives and fuels, and on completion of the course he was promoted to Flight Lieutenant.

In February 1948 Tommy was posted to 28 Maintenance Unit at Buxton as explosives officer and then in May 1949 was posted overseas to Headquarters 205 Group being responsible for the supply of ammunition and fuel at RAF Arryadd. He left Arryad in December 1951 to take up the post of Officer Responsible for Supplies at RAF Bishops Court in Northern Ireland. This posting lasted until December 1952 when he was again on the move to Headquarters 76 Group as Equipment Officer where he was responsible for all Air Training Corps (Air Cadets) equipment. In December 1957. Tommy decided to retire from the RAF in 1957, however his retirement was short lived as he was re-commissioned on November 20th 1958 and became the Admin. Officer for the Northern Ireland Wing of the Air Training Corps in the RAF Recruiting Office in Ann Street, and the Waverly Hotel in Waring Street. He spent the next 19 years at this post and finally retired from the RAF in November 1977. It was in Ann Street in Belfast that I first met Squadron Leader

Tommy Hutton, when I applied to join the ATC in 1959. I will always remember him sitting in his chair wearing his Harris Tweed sports coat complete with padded elbows and his first words to me were, "Why do you want to join the Air Training Corps?' I remained in contact with him ever since, and in later years would come to my home. Tommy was a member of the Air Crew Association and the Caterpillar Club. Sadly Squadron Leader Hutton died in 1995 and is buried in Victoria Cemetery in Carrickfergus. He is survived by his children Ruby, Thomas, Samuel, Goffinet and Adrian.

SERGEANT
SYDNEY IRELAND
ROYAL AIR FORCE NO. 745103
PILOT
NO. 610 SQUADRON

Sydney Ireland was the son Mr Robert and Mrs Sadie Ireland and was born in Belfast on the 29th July 1918. He was educated at the Belfast Royal Academical Institution (1937-1939) and was keen on all sports, being especially good at rugby and swimming.
He played Scrum Half for the schools first fifteen during the period 1937-39 and there is no doubt that he would have been picked to play for Ireland if he had not joined the RAF.

He also took part in the schools dramatic society and acted in a number of plays. Sydney also had an elder brother Harry who after the war was attached to the CID in Scotland Yard.

On leaving school Sydney was employed with the Belfast Steamship Company and later as a motor salesman with Messrs Victor H Robb Ltd, Belfast.

He joined the Royal Air Force Volunteer Reserve in Belfast in November 1938 and was trained in the art of flying on Tiger Moths at the newly formed 24 Elementary & Reserve Flying Training School at Sydenham a few miles from Belfast. He flew solo sometime in April or May 1939. Twice weekly he would attend aeronautic lectures which were being held in the headquarters of the RAFVR in the Saxone Building in Belfast's Royal Avenue. Sydney was one of those people who are always full of fun and you could just not help but like him, he was always there to lend a helping hand to anyone who needed it. He was a great personal friend of Noel Corry, George Calwell, and Herbie McGarry, they were inseparable and went everywhere together. Noel Corry said of him, "Sydney set himself a very high standard in everything he did, even down to cleaning his motorbike which was always immaculate and highly tuned. At rugby and swimming he was outstanding and would have made an exceptional pilot. Sydney, George Calwell and myself joined the RAFVR at Sydenham on the same day, we were very close friends, and we never fell out, never had a disagreement, but would maybe 'tease' each other from time to time. He would have been a good citizen, a great friend, would have had lot to contribute. He was always happy and always looked after

his friends. The last time I saw Sydney alive was at Christmas 1940 when I visited him at the SFTS in RAF Sealand where he carried out his flying training. There was a slight difference of opinion whether or not we should get involved in flying. Our first idea of flying did not come from the RAFVR but from 'China'. Chang-Ki-Chec, rumour had it, that if you volunteered to fly with his Air Force you would be paid something like £200 per week, a free house and servants. Nobody had explained that the reason you could earn this high income from Chang-Ki-Chec was that very few pilots survived more than a week. But as we now know Hitler changed all that.

"The day war was declared, Sydney, George and myself were down in the centre of Belfast. A special edition of the Belfast Telegraph had been printed and poured onto the streets. On its front page was a large picture of Hitler and on seeing this Sydney grabbed a local paper boy and took all his papers, paid him of course. He laid all the telegraphs out on the footpath of Royal Avenue, and made the public walk on the face of Adolf Hitler."

When Noel first met Sydney's parents they lived on of the Stranmillis Road in Belfast. His father Robert was the 'head cutter' in the family business of 'Ireland the Tailors' whose shop was in Chichester Street in Belfast. He was also a great modelmaker specialising in sailing ships. Sydney's mother, Sadie was a wonderful, charming lady and he loved her very much. Sometime during early 1940 his parents moved to Castle Hill in Ballywalter, County Down.

One of Sydney's hobbies was playing the guitar, which he would take along to the VR lectures and entertain his friends. There is a wonderful story attached to Sydney and 'one' of his guitars.

No ordinary guitar

The RAFVR were automatically called to full-time Service in September 1939 with the outbreak of war, but it wasn't until November 1939 that Sydney and about thirty others were sent to England for training. They all had arranged to meet at the LMS railway station in York Street where they would board a train which would take them to Larne and across on the Ferry to Stranraer and then on to their various training stations. The morning they met Sydney was asked, "Where is your guitar?" He replied, "I left it at home." Well, this was just was not on, there was no way that they were going to board the train without Sydney's guitar and a farewell sing song. So one of them decided that they would have to get Sydney a guitar to play on the journey. What happened next was, they decided that the quickest way to get a guitar was buy one from Matchettes of Wellington Place, so they all put some money into a hat. Some of the gang went to the engine driver and explained the 'crisis' and asked him if he would wait for thirty minutes. He readily agreed, so off they went to Matchettes to purchase a guitar for Sydney. They hailed a taxi outside the station and rushed off to Matchetts in Wellington Place and bought a guitar for Sydney. On their return they all boarded the train and started their sing-song. During the journey it was suggested that they all sign the guitar for posterity. They tried signing it with pencil and fountain pen but as it was made of wood it was discovered that this would rub off easily. Cecil Smylie (later to become Wing Commander Smylie, DFC American DFC DFM AE) pulled out his Boy Scout knife and they all their signatures on the back of the guitar using the spike part of the knife.

50 years later while meeting with Wing Commander Smylies son Peter, he told me that his father had mentioned the story of the guitar, and that he had that very knife. Peter asked me if I would like to have it to put along with the guitar. From time to time I am asked to display the guitar and the knife at various aviation functions which I am delighted and honoured to do. Shortly after Sydney's death his mother Sadie, gave the guitar to her son's best friend, Squadron Leader Noel Corry, who kept it safe for the next 50 years. I was very proud and honoured when squadron Leader Corry gave the guitar to me to look after for the years to come and to remember Sydney and the people who signed it.

On the back of the guitar are inscribed the names of 27 members of the RAFVR who took that journey to England, ten of whom would not return.

The names are:

Sergeant Stanley Allen Fenemore	Killed 20/02/1940
Sergeant HR Megarry	Killed 8/05/1940
Sergeant NRA Hawthorne	Killed 28/06/1940
Sergeant Sydney Ireland	Killed 12/07/1940
Sergeant S Sanderson	Killed 09/08/1940
Pilot Officer J McCausland	Killed 08/09/1940
Sergeant Victor Skillen	Killed 11/03/1941
Pilot Officer T McCann	Killed 27/07/1942
Flying Officer Victor S Neill	Killed 04/05/1943
Flying Officer WG Wood	Killed 06/11/1943

Wing Commander Gauntlet
Squadron Leader NH Corry, DFC AE
Wing Commander WW McConnell, DFC* AE
Flight Lieutenant CC Johnston, AE
Squadron Leader RR Wright, DFC AE
Wing Commander KW MacKenzie, DFC AFC AE
Wing Commander JH Simpson, DFC
Flight Lieutenant G Calwell, AE
Flight Lieutenant HJ Geary
Flight Lieutenant JL Lilburn, AE
Flight Lieutenant C Smylie, DFC DFC (USA) DFM AE
Flight Lieutenant JF Conway, AE
Squadron Leader Hugo Shannon, DFC AE
JH Campbell ?
GWA Neill ?
HM McMillan ?
A Pattison ?

The day Sydney was killed

On the morning of the 12th July 1940, Sergeant Sydney Ireland had been taking part in a dog fight practice. He was flying his Spitfire DW-Q (P9502) when it seems that he may have lost control of his aircraft diving through cloud. He crashed at Titsey Park and was killed. His aircraft was a complete write-off. Sergeant Sydney Ireland's remains were taken back to his native home and buried in Knockbreda Church of Ireland graveyard. His name is the first one that is recorded on the Roll of Honour in the Bigging Hill Chapel. The crash site of (P9502) was in later years excavated by the London Air Museum and recovered a complete Rolls Royce engine, propeller boss, with two of its blades still attached. They also recovered a .303 Browning machine gun with (P9502) stencilled on the ammunition feed mechanism, the blind flying panel, and one complete under-carriage leg.

FLIGHT LIEUTENANT
CHRISTOPHER KITCHEN JOHNSTON, DFM
ROYAL AIR FORCE NO. 625298
WIRELESS OPERATOR/AIR GUNNER
NO. 75, 214, 115 SQUADRONS

Christopher Kitchen Johnston was born in Hillsborough County Down on the 10th August 1920 and was educated at the Dr Renshaws College in Belfast. On leaving school, he was employed with the Saxone shoe Company in Royal Avenue Belfast.

He joined the Royal Air Force on the 3rd November 1938 at the North Street Recruiting Centre during the Munich Crisis, and was posted to RAF Oxbridge where he was sworn in and was then immediately sent off to Cardington Recruit Training Depot for basic training, radio and Morse code tuition. When he had completed his basic training he was posted to RAF Yatesbury for advanced Wireless Operator and Technical training where on passing out he received his Wireless Operator's badge. As a fully fledged W/Op Chris was assigned to No 75 (New Zealand) Squadron which was based at Harwell in Berks. It was the first Commonwealth Squadron to be formed within Bomber Command No 6 Group. In 1939, 75 Squadron assumed the role as an operational training unit and was equipped with Wellington Mk1s and one Avro Anson.

His first operational flight was in an Avro Anson of 148 Squadron (this squadron also became a training squadron at Harwell) on the 28th September 1939. The exercise lasted for 3hrs.15mins. He had a further four flights in the Anson before going onto the Wellingtons of 78 Squadron. On 29th November 1939 Chris was posted to 215 Squadron at Jurby on the Isle of Man where he was to complete a Gunnery course. When he had finished the course he was posted to a squadron at Feltwell, but on his arrival he found that the entire squadron had been shot to pieces and had only one operational aircraft and even it had gone U/S. As a result of this he was immediately posted to 115 Squadron.

115 Squadron was formed at Catterick in December 1917 and was disbanded in 1919. It was reformed in 1937 at Marham in Norfolk as a bomber squadron and on the 11th April 1940 had the distinction of having flown on the first international raid by bomber command on a European mainland target which was the enemy held Stavanger Airfield in Norway. (Chris was on this raid, see below).

Some of Chris's log extracts for 1940

March 28th	Sweep over the North Sea.
April 2nd	To Kinloss, Germans invade Norway (sweep over North Sea). Shot up by 110s, lost two A/C out of six, one enemy A/C shot down.
April 7th	Ops to Danish Coast, attacked by 110s (Pilot wounded).
April 10th	Ops to Christen Sands, Norway (looking for German Cruisers).
April 11th	Ops attacked Stavanger. Lost one A/C out of six (lead aircraft). Attacked by Me110s while attacking airfield A/C badly damaged. My Pilot, Flight Sergeant Powell was shot through the shoulder but managed to get the A/C back safe. *"He was awarded the first DFM of the War."*
April 26th	Night operation on Norway.
May 9th	Night operation to Rotterdam, bombing troops.
May 15th	Ops to the Ruhr and Duisberg bombing troops.
May 17th	Ops to bomb bridges at Meuse and Namur.
May 20th	Ops to bomb road and rail targets at Cambrai-Guise-Hiron and St Quentin.
May 23rd	Ops to bomb Chiminy-Leiart (road & rail targets), bombing search lights & anti-aircraft guns.
May 25th	Ops to Antwerp (bombing trains & troops).
May 28th	Ops to Roulers-Aire (Bombing road, rail, troops & bridges).

June and July operations

Aschweiler (railway yards), Abbeyville (bombed airfield), Wanne-Eickel (oil plant), Rottenburg & Oldenburg (airfields), Denhelder (airfield), Munster (airfield), Aureux (airfield), Frankfurt, Zoest (marshalling yards), Diepholtz (airfield).

Chris flew on his last operation with 115 Squadron to bomb the Marshalling Yards at Leipzig and Zoest on the 20th July 1940. On the 1st August 1940 Chris was promoted to Flight Sergeant and screened of operations. That same day, he received his posting to No 15 OTU at Harwell where he was to become a Wireless Operator Instructor until the end of February 1941. In March 1941 Chris was posted to 'D' Flight at No 21 OTU at Morton On The Marsh as a 1st Wireless Instructor. No 21 OTU had just been formed and was equipped with Ansons and Wellingtons. Having had his fill of instructing for almost two years Chris requested to be allowed back on operations. His request was granted and in April 1942 he joined 214 (Federated Malay States) Squadron.

214 Squadron was originally formed at Coudekerque which is very close to Dunkirk in July 1917. Its role was a heavy night bombing squadron and in December 1917 it became 14 Squadron RNAS and on the day the RAF was formed 200 was added to its number and it became 214 squadron RAF. The squadron was disbanded in Egypt 11920 and reformed at Boscombe Down in 1935 as a bomber squadron. For most of the Second World War the squadron was equipped with Wellingtons and in 1942 Short Stirlings. The squadron was transferred to No 100 Bomber Group in early 1944 and was re-equipped with Flying Fortresses (B-17) on radio counter-measures. Chris joined the squadron in early April 1942 and his logbook shows that his carried out his first operation with 214 in a Stirling on the 17th April. The operation was to drop leaflets on the Vichy.

His logbook shows that on the 28th June 1942 while on a raid to Emden they shot down two enemy aircraft but not before they had been badly shot up themselves. The aircraft was so severely damaged and they had to make an emergency landing at RAF Coltishall. His logbook shows the remark, "Just made it."

This happened again on the 25th June 1942 when they were badly shot up by Me110s and Me109s. Their port engine was on fire and its propeller eventually came off. The aircraft's under-carriage was wrecked, the mid-upper and rear gun turrets were also U/S. On the 7th August he was sent on a weeks Gunnery course to Marham, this was to allow him to take over a gun position in his aircraft should the need ever arise (he had in fact done this on several occasions).

Other targets visited during his second tour with 214 Squadron were: Bremen; Emden; Juist Island; Duisberg; Vegesack; Hamburg; Osnabruck; Frankfurt; Kiessel; Nuremburg; Zaarbrucken; Charlsrhue; Vegessack; Genoa; and many mine laying trips to the Baltic.

On the 4th September 1942 he was give some home leave and left the camp very early in the morning to catch the Starnraer boat. He arrived in Hillsborough the next morning and was married at 0200 hrs the same day. They happy couple spent their honeymoon in Portrush. On his arrival back at Camp he received the sad news that his crew were lost on a raid the night he left for home. As Chris had left the camp early that morning he did not know that his leave had been cancelled. His last operation with the squadron was on the 8th December 1942. This made a total of 50 operations carried out between February 1940 and December 1942 and he had carried out 519 hours flying by day and 482 hours by night.

On the 29th December 1942 Flight Sergeant Christopher Kitchen Johnston was awarded the Distinguished Flying Medal. Having now completed 50 of the most hazardous operations and 1,000 flying hours it was time for a rest. It was decided to post Chris to RAF Manby on the 25th February 1943 where he was to complete a two month Air Armament course. On completion of this course he was posted to No 3 Air Gunnery School at Angelsey as an Air Gunner Instructor on Blackburn Bothas and Avro Ansons.

Eight months later he got a posting home to Northern Ireland where he became a Gunnery Instructor with No 12 Air Gunnery School at Bishops court in County Down. On the 30th May 1945 Chris was posted to RAF Debden where he instructed on radar and radio. This posting lasted for the next five years.

On the 14th May 1950 he was posted to No 235 Operational Conversion Unit at Calshot where he carried out a conversion course onto Sunderland flying boats. The course instructed him in the art of re-fuelling, radio and radar, how to moor the Sunderland and general seamanship.

He joined 230 Squadron a short time later at Pembroke Dock. He flew with the squadron to Singapore (took ten days) and trips to Gibraltar, Malta, Fanara (Bitter Lakes in Egypt), Bahrain (Brooke Ballard), Karachi (Karangi Creek), Trinco Malee, Singapore and to Castle Archdale for Air Sea Rescue exercises. 230 Squadron still serves at RAF Aldergrove in Northern Ireland supporting The Army and RUC in a ground support role and is equipped with the Puma Helicopter. In February 1942 he was posted to 236 OCU at Kinloss as the stations Senior Signals Officer and still managed to get the odd flight in a Shackleton. His last flying trip in the RAF was in a Shackleton on the 17th November 1952. Towards the end of 1952 he was posted to RAF Shawbury were he completed an Air Traffic Controllers course. On completing the course he was posted to RAF Valley where he took up his first assignment as a fully qualified Air Traffic Controller. In 1954 he was given a three year posting out to Seletar in Singapore returning to the UK in 1957 to take up a posting at RAF Aldergrove. In 1961 he found himself being posted to Hanover and Wildenrath in Germany where he taught the Luftwaffe personnel the art of Air Sea Rescue. In 1963 he returned to Ballykelly in Northern Ireland as Air Traffic Controller, he did a spell as ATC in Tawau (Borneo) and returned to Oxbridge in 1970 where he became a Super Numery at Bishops Court in Northern Ireland and finally retired from the RAF on the 9th August 1970.

On leaving the Royal Air Force he was employed as a clerk with the Department of Education, finally retiring in 1985. He is a Life Member of the Royal Air Force Association.

WING COMMANDER
HUGH ANTHONY STEPHEN JOHNSTON, DFC* OBE CMG
ROYAL AIR FORCE NO. 88723
FIGHTER PILOT
NO. 66, 165,257, AND 611 SQUADRONS

Hugh Anthony Stephen Johnston was born in Belfast on the 7th December 1913. He was the son of an Indian Civil Servant. He was educated at Brasenose College in Oxfordshire, where he graduated in 1935. He was very keen on sports at the college and excelled at rugby. On finishing his education, he joined the ranks of the overseas civil service, and in May 1940 joined the Royal Air Force.

After completing his basic training he was posted to No 50 Operational Training Unit, and then joined No 257 Squadron at RAF Coltishall. It was here on the 9th April that he was to have his first taste of action when he claimed a half share in a BF110 near East Southwold. On the 21st August 1941 he claimed a Dornier 17, which he shot down about 25 miles East of Lowestoft.

Towards the end of the year he was posted to 133 Squadron as a flight commander. 133 Squadron was formed in late July 1941 at RAF Coltishall as the third of the Eagle Squadrons, which was formed in Fighter Command entirely from United States volunteers. The squadron was equipped initially with Hawker Hurricanes Mk11bs, however a few months later, was re-equipped with the Spitfire Mk 11. On February 5th he claimed a quarter share in a Dornier 217 near Spurnhead, flying a Spitfire MkVa. In March 1941 he was posted to Gibraltar where he flew off one of the second batches of Spitfires to fly to the defence of Malta of the deck of HMS Eagle. He then was transferred to 126 Squadron where he became a Flight Commander. 126 Squadron was formed at Ta Kali in Malta on the 28th June 1941, and was equipped initially with Hawker Hurricane Mk 11a, and 11bs. The squadron was re-equipped with the Supermarine Spitfire MkVb and Vc. During the next few weeks he was constantly in action during some of the heaviest fighting over the island. On the 23rd March 1941 he shot down a Ju88, and on the 24th he again was in action shooting down a Ju87. On the 26th March he shot down another two Ju87s one of which returned fire, damaging his Spitfire. On the 2nd April he shot down a Ju88 and on the 5th a Bf109. On the 20th April 1941, while he was

attacking a Ju88 at low level, its bombs blew up. The blast from the bombs damaged his aircraft so badly he had to bale out.

On the 24th of April he claimed a Ju88 (probable), and on the 28th claimed a Ju87 (damaged).

On the 6th May 1941 he attacked another Bf109 and damaged it. He immediately went after a second, with only one of his four cannons working. Unfortunately for him a third Bf109 was lurking close by and attacked. His aircraft shuddered with the impact of the impact of the 109s cannon shells hitting it and caught fire. With his aircraft in flames, he baled out with severe burns to his face, legs and arms. On reaching the safety of the ground he was picked up by ambulance and rushed to hospital. Acting Flight Lieutenant Hugh Anthony Johnston was awarded a well earned Distinguished Flying Cross on the 5th June 1941. When he had recovered sufficiently from his burns, he returned to the UK and was attached for a short time to 611 Squadron at Kenley as a Super-Numerary. Here he also managed to get in a few flights in a Hawker Typhoon with his old unit 257 Squadron. In August 1942 he was posted to Headquarters Fighter Command, where he remained until June 1943. He took command of 165 Squadron at Ibsley, and while with the squadron he shot down and destroyed his first Focke Wulf 190 over St Briens on the 31st December 1943. In January 1944 he was transferred to Headquarters, No 10 Group, and in March moved to the Headquarters of the 2nd Tactical Air Force. On the 28th March 1944, now Acting Squadron Leader he was awarded a well deserved bar to his Distinguished Flying Cross. On the 23rd May 1944 he took command of 66 Squadron at Tangmere, alongside No 331 and 332 Norwegian Squadrons. 331 Squadron was the first of the Norwegian squadrons to join the RAF and 332 was the second. The motto of 331 Squadron was "For Norge". On the 15th June 1944 he shot down his second Focke Wulf 190 over Evreux in northern France.

Squadron Leader Jonhston had now completed his third tour and received a non-operational posting for the rest of the war. He was released from the RAF in June 1945 and was mentioned in Despatches. On leaving the Royal Air Force he rejoined the Colonial Service in Africa. In 1954 he was awarded the OBE and an CMG in 1959. He became Deputy Governor of the northern region of Nigeria in 1960, and the following year returned to the UK and became director of the Overseas Resettlement Bureau until 1965. He then became clerk to the City Parochial Foundation, and around this time he published two books about his times in Africa. Shortly after being awarded his DFC in 1942 he wrote a book entitled "Tattered Battlements, The Diary of a Malta Fighter Pilot" which was published later in 1943. Wing Commander Hugh Anthony Stephen Johnston, DFC* OBE CMG, mentioned in Despatches, died at the very young age of 54 on the 9th December 1967 after a short illness. Wing Commander Johnston's total tally for the war was five enemy aircraft destroyed, and one shared destroyed, five probables, two and one shared damaged.

WARRANT OFFICER
CECIL WATSON ALBERT KEYS
ROYAL AIR FORCE NO. 1795285
WIRELESS OPERATOR (AIR)
NO. 624 & 61 SQUADRONS

Cecil Watson Albert Keys was born on the 12th September 1913 in Aghavilly near the city of Armagh, and was educated at the local primary school, which was half a mile from where he was born. On leaving primary school, at the age of fourteen, he continued his higher education at the Cathedral Grammar School in Armagh. Cecil was born in the family farm house, and in those days, he tells me, that the mid-wife or family doctor would arrive by bicycle or motorbike.

Cecil had three brothers who all worked on the family farm. From a very early age Cecil had always been interested in aviation, and at the age of 28 years he travelled to Belfast where he joined the RAF at the Clifton Street Recruiting Office. He knew that he could leave the farm in the capable hands of two of his brothers.

He was called up on the 20th January 1942 and was sent across to the receiving centre in Padgate via Larne and Stranraer. It was the first time in his life that he had seen such a large boat. He spent the next 20 hours travelling from Stranraer by train down to Padgate. It was the middle of winter and the snow was three to four feet deep. The train which was full of small children as well as adults eventually did get stuck in the snow near Carlisle. The children were crying, cold, thirsty and hungry. Cecil remembered that he had a 'pack lunch' in his pocket and decided to share it amongst them. The track was eventually cleared and he arrived at Padgate around 3.00 am in the early hours of the morning.

On his arrival, he was met by an RAF Policeman who asked Cecil, "Are you for Padgate?" Cecil replied, "Yes," and the policeman told him to, "Knock on that door and wait." Cecil was eventually shown to a room and told to find a bed and try a get some sleep. The room was in complete darkness, so he groped around until he found a light switch which he switched on, and was met with a barrage of verbal abuse from the room's occupants, "Put that bloody light out." He managed to find a bed and got some sleep. He was awakened the next morning at 6.00 am with a loud voice shouting, "Wakey, wakey," and it felt like he was just into bed when he had to get back out

again. After he had his breakfast Cecil was told to report to a particular room, wherein was a sergeant who kitted him out with his new uniform. The sergeant stamped Cecil's cutlery with his number and charged him two shillings and sixpence (12p). Cecil said that this guy must have made a fortune.

Cecil was then posted to the Initial Training Wing at Blackpool where he received a twelve week basic training course in square bashing, Morse code and the basics of training as a Wireless Operator. After twelve weeks training and having passed the first hurdle, and as he was the only one who had passed out as a AC1 from Blackpool and who was potential aircrew he was posted to the headquarters of the Western Approaches at Mount Wise in Plymouth were he worked as a Ground Wireless Operator.

Cecil remembers one day in particular when they were on parade in the street, when the Corporal in charge of them, *(he still remembers his name)* Corporal Ember and who had been a professional boxer in civvy street; noticed that one of the trainees had torn his new uniform trousers. The Corporal said to him, " You have torn your trousers." "Yes Corporal," came the reply. "You had better get back to your billet and put on your best 'Blues' if necessary, and I will give you just seven minutes to get back here." The billets were at least three to four blocks away from where they were. The trainee ran like the 'clappers of hell' and the Corporal kept looking at his watch, pacing up and down. Sometime later a taxi drove up alongside the Corporal, and out got the trainee wearing his best 'Blues' and joined the ranks. The Corporal who by now was fuming stepped up to the trainee and said, "That will cost you plenty." "Oh no," came the reply from the trainee, "My Aunt is married to a taxi driver." On hearing this reply, everyone present started to laugh. The little Corporal didn't find it so amusing and gave them all an extra two hours drill.

Another time when at Blackpool the trainees where taken to a shooting range at Notts Edge which was about three miles north of the town. They were marched all the way, and when the arrived at the range they were all given rifles, a type which Cecil had not seen before. They were the Canadian made P14s. Cecil had been used to the Lee Enfield in the 'B' Specials back home. The Canadian P14s were half as long again as the Lee Enfield and twice as heavy. When they had finished shooting, Cecil was informed that he had come second overall and the guy who had beat him came from Brazil in South America, and ended up with the nickname 'South American Joe'. When they came out of the shooting range all the English trainees were complaining that their feet were sore and were refusing to march. This put the corporal in charge up the walls and he threatened them with putting them all on a charge (Cecil didn't know what they were complaining about as three miles was only a 'wee dawdle' back home). In the end they didn't have to walk back to their billets as they were put on trams. While they were stationed in Blackpool, NCOs and lower ranks were billeted in lodging houses. The officers were put up in the local hotels.

Morse Code story

Every Friday morning, after the trainees had been on a certain speed of 4, 8, 10, 12 words per minute, they were given a test on each speed. They were marched in squads down the town to Burtons the tailors which had been taken over by the Air Ministry and put into a large room. There would have been approximately 200 airmen in that room, all sitting at tables wearing head-phones with a sergeant positioned at the top of the room. He did not use the Morse machine but instead used the Morse key. They were given two minutes Morse and were only allowed two mistakes (two letters wrong) otherwise you were FT'd, that is put back onto the next course. Cecil told me that you went into the room, sat down at a table and put your head-phones on all around the room there were WAAFS handing out pieces of paper. Some one would then shout, "Read." You would have in front of you, three or four pencils, just in case you broke a lead or two. You were given two minutes to read the paper and when the two minutes were up a Wireless Operator took the papers away from each airman in case they had the time to read them and make corrections.

The trainees were all billeted in guest houses in Blackpool, and that was the only way the land ladies could make a living in those days. The Ministry of Defence footed the bill. Cecil was staying in the same guest house as the Brazilian and in the same bedroom. He said, "Many a yarn we both had together." The

Brazilian was well used to horses a topic Cecil, new a lot about as there were many on his farm back home in Northern Ireland. During one of their many conversations Cecil said to him, "You are a good shot Joe," and back came the reply, "Yes Paddy, I did a lot of shooting with the P14 in Brazil." Joe had come from a very well to do family, and he had the BLAF badge on the shoulders of his tunic which stood for British Latin American Forces. He also insisted on putting on his pyjamas at night before settling down to clean his uniform buttons and polishing his shoes.

From the Headquarters Western Approaches he was posted to St Eval which at that time was a Coastal Command Station and where 502 Ulster (B) Squadron was operating with Whitley, to await his posting to a Flying Training School at Madley. On the 20th June 1943 Cecil arrived at the No 4 SFTS at Madley in Herefordshire where he was to start a long two month Advanced Radio course. Here he joined the No 4 Signals course and was immediately put in charge of the training personnel as he was the only AC1 and the others were AC2s. The course training included the use of the Morse tapper and in the use of the various transmitter/receivers that was in use at that time in the RAF. The training school time was equipped with Dominees and Proctors and were used to carry out all the wireless training Cecil's first flight was at 1030 hrs on the morning of the 20th June 1943, when he took off in Dominee (K7441) with its Pilot Flying Officer Payne. The types of exercises that were carried out in the air were, receiving. tuning and sending signals, homing in on signals, tuning by calibration, frequency check and homing. Cecil successfully completed the course on the 29th August 1943.

His next posting was to the No 9 Advanced Flying Unit at Llandurwrog in North Wales for an Advanced Flying Training and Wireless Operating course on Avro Ansons. He again passed the course and was awarded his 'S' Brevet and promoted to Sergeant. His Morse code operating speed was now eighteen words per minute. Cecil's was then transferred to No 12 Operational Training Unit at Chipping Warden and its satellite at Edgehill in Oxen. When he arrived at the front gates of the OTU, one of the other trainee aircrew remarked, "Look at that big sign on the front gate, it says 'Wimpy', I didn't think the RAF would use a slang word for Wellington and put it up there." He was duly informed by the Gate Commander, who seemed a bit miffed, that was the name of the contractor who was renovating the airfield. The unit was equipped with the Vickers Wellington and his first flight on the type was on 5th December 1943. Here he met his new crew and skipper (Flight Sergeant Soar) and had his first flight with them on 27th December 1943. Having completed all of the training that was required of him, Cecil and his new crew were posted to No 1657 Heavy Conversion Unit at RAF Stradishall where they were to convert on to the heavy four engined Short Stirling Bomber. Their first flight on the type was on the 3rd May 1943 when they took Sterling 'P' up for circuits and landings. The intensive conversion training continued for the next four weeks. Stradishall is situated near the small village of Clare and as the crews all had their own bicycles went to the local dances when not flying. Cecil said, "Getting back to base in the 'blackout' was tricky, especially after a few beers."

On one of their training flights they took off at night for Sterling in Scotland. The weather was terrible with heavy snow and icy gales buffeting the large bomber. When they got within a few miles from Sterling, the propellers started to ice up badly. The ice built itself up in thick layers and would fly off and smash against the fuselage. The Pilot immediately decided to turn back for base. Just then the Navigator arrived beside Cecil to inform him that he was 'lost'. Cecil immediately got several QDMs and got them back on course for base. On their return to Stradishall the Navigator was taken off the course and the crew got a new replacement who was a Canadian and who turned out to be a brilliant Navigator. On another night while at the conversion unit and not flying, Cecil was just about to get into bed when he glanced out of the window in his Nissan hut, and saw a large red glow in the sky. It turned out to be a Stirling which had been carrying out circuits and bumps and had been shot down by a 'sneak' enemy night fighter. These aircraft were sometimes easy targets for the enemy. Three Stirlings had been shot down on that particular night.

Next day they took off on a training flight and had an engine failure necessitating the Skipper to return to base. As they had just taken off, and had a full load of fuel still onboard which meant they had to dump most of it before they could land. This was accomplished by a length of hose pipe which was snaked along the outside of the aircraft's fuselage and fuel was directed into it from the fuel tanks and was eventually dispersed over the countryside. On their arrival they were given a brand new Short Sterling straight from the factory. The aircraft was LJ 938 'G' and was to be air tested and fuel consumption tested and fitted out for 'special duties', i.e. 'supply dropping' for SOE type operations. The air tests where successfully carried out between the 14th June and the 27th June, all proved satisfactory, especially the fuel consumption tests. They were then informed that they were to fly the aircraft to Rabat Sale in French Morocco and then on to Blida in French Algeria where they would join 624 Squadron. On the 29th June 1944, Cecil and his fellow crew members took off from Melton Mobray in their Short Stirling (LJ 938) 'G' and set course on the first leg of their journey to St Mawgan in Cornwall, arriving their 1hr.15mins later. They took off from St Mawgan at 0015 hrs on the 3rd July and followed the sea route off the coast of Spain which they could just about make out in the darkness. Just off Gibraltar Cecil requested a QDM and after almost seven hours flying they landed safely on the heavy wire mesh which had been placed on top of the sand at Rabat Sale to form a runway. When they arrived over Rabat the Skipper found difficulty in locating the runway because of the sand mixing with the wire mesh. Some crews found it nearly impossible to land at Blida and some were killed trying. They spent the night at Rabat Sale and took off the next morning on 5th July setting a course for Maison Blanche in Algeria, arriving there 3hrs.10mins later.

No 624 squadron was formed at Blida in September 1943 and its task was dropping SOE agents and supplies to the underground forces in Corsica, Yugoslavia, Southern France, Czechoslovakia, Northern Italy, Albania and Greece.

On the 24th July 1944 Cecil and his crew took off at 0745 hrs in Sterling 'K' to carry out supply dropping tests and flew a cross-country exercise to the Balearic Islands. Flying time was 3hrs.20mins. On the 31st July 1944 they set off on their first operation with the squadron dropping supplies to the French Resistance in southern France. They carried out a further five of these types of operations mostly at night during August. All of the supply material was carried inside the aircraft's fuselage which the Mid-Upper Gunner and Cecil pushed out through a trap door in the floor at a height of 400ft. Each package had a small parachute on top which was attached to a rail running down the length of the fuselage by a nylon cord, which disconnected from the package on being dropped. The nylon cords had to be retrieved back into the aircraft before the trap doors could be closed and after which Cecil would have informed his base at Blida that the operation had been a success.

His logbook shows that on the 6th August 1944 while dropping supplies at low level, their port inner engine was damaged by flak , but they managed to get to base safely. The Short Stirling had one particular drawback, and that was the undercarriage. It was operated electrically and sometimes failed to work. If this happened the undercarriage had to be retracted manually by turning hand wheels which where located on either side of the fuselage. It required 365 turns of each wheel to raise or lower the undercarriage. Thankfully this operation only happened once to Cecil.

Cecil and his crew had completed six operations with the squadron when word came through that it was being disbanded. His two Air Gunners who were Canadian were ordered to the Far East and the aircraft flew back to the UK with only one Pilot, Wireless Operator and Navigator. On the 16th November 1944 they left Maison Blanche in Sterling LK175 'R' taking a direct route across France to Melton Mobray. As they crossed the coast of northern France, Cecil received a radio message ordering them to land at Homesly South as there was fog at Melton Mobray. The fog was so bad they had to stay at Homsley South for the next five days waiting for it to lift. The total flying time from Maison Blanche to Melton Mobray was 7hrs.25mins. Cecil told me that he had enjoyed many a pint in the local pub during those five days which was called 'The Cat and The Fiddle'.

Story about the three crew members left behind at Blida

As Cecil and the crew were about to leave North Africa, they got a shock when told that their Bomb-Aimer (Bill Flanagan) and their two Gunners (Jimmy Huck and Freddie Blofeld) were required in the Far East to fight against the Japanese. When Cecil arrived back in the UK he kicked up a terrible stink about their three crew members being left behind in north Africa and in particular Jimmy Hucks who had joined up with the Navigator (both Canadians). They eventually got Jimmy Huck back and suspected it was because he was a Canadian and the 'powers that be' did not want to create a 'sticky' situation. The other two members who were left behind joined another crew and continued to operate in the Mediterranean Area. Cecil's crew got a new Bomb-Aimer (Sergeant Heppenstall) and a Rear Gunner (E Bestwick).

In 1992 Cecil went to stay with Freddie Blofield at his home at Gerards Cross in London and when he arrived he discovered that Freddie had married a very charming French girl whom he had met while serving in Algiers. Sadly Freddie died in 1994.

On his arrival back at Melton Mobray, Cecil and the crew were given some leave, and on their return were informed that they were being posted to No 5 Lancaster Finishing School at Syerston in Nottinghamshire. They spent the next two days converting onto the Lancaster. They completed their conversion course on 17th March 1945 (St Patrick's Day) and on the 18th were posted to No 61 Squadron at Skellingthorpe in Lincolnshire. Nine days later on the 27th they flew their first operation with the squadron to Farge in Germany in Lancaster Mk111 (QR-'Y').

61 Squadron was formed in 1937 as a bomber squadron with No 5 Group and it took part in many important raids including the first bombing on a German land target (Hornum), the first large bombing raid on the German mainland (Munchen-Gladbach) and the first bombing raid on Berlin and Peenemunde, and many more.

Cecil's fellow crew members were:

Captain	Warrant Officer Soar
Flight Engineer	Flight Sergeant Rees
Navigator	Warrant Officer McLean
Air Bomber	Sergeant Heppenstall
Wireless Operator	Flight Sergeant Keys
Mid-Upper Gunner	Sergeant Beswick
Rear Gunner	Flight Sergeant Huck

Their next operation was on the 4th April 1945 to Nordhausen in Germany and on the 9th April they visited Hamburg. This particular operation to Hamburg was an interesting one for Cecil to say he least. They took off from Skellingthorpe at 1430 hrs in Lancaster (QR-'Y') to bomb the oil storage tanks and submarine pens at Hamburg. They had just arrived over the target and there was Lancasters all over the place. Heavy flak had damaged Cecil's aircraft on the run in to the target and injured the Bomb-Aimer. He said, "You got used to the flak, if it did not hit you, you would ignore it, but you always wondered when you were going to be hit by it." Coming nearer to the target, Cecil got up to look out the astro dome to keep an eye out for enemy fighters, especially Me262s. Right at that moment the Rear Gunner shouted, "I see one a long way out." Cecil did not pay a lot of attention to it, and the next thing he heard was the rattle of the guns coming from his own Lancaster. The Lancaster behind them was hit by the Me262 and went straight down in a ball of flames. Cecil heard the whoosh of the Me262 pass overhead as close as a few feet, travelling at about 600mph. He found out later that the Lancasters crew which was shot down behind them (RF121), were on their last operation. The Pilot of the stricken aircraft was an Australian with an all Australian crew from 61 squadron.

With the war now over, and bomb stocks still very high, Cecil and his crew made several trips over the North Sea on 7th, 8th, 9th and 12th June 1945 were they jettisoned tons of unwanted bombs and ammunition.

Operation Dodge, bringing the Prisoners of War home

They carried their first Operation Dodge on the 12th May 1945. This was to be the first of many transporting the Prisoners of War home from Europe. This particular trip was to pick up POWs in Brussels and bring them back to Dunsfold in the UK. Their Lancaster carried 20 POWs on each trip, they all had to sit on the floor of the aircraft, and many of them had been in the struggle from the toe of Italy to the north of Italy. Cecil would keep them informed of their position and progress, and they always cheered when he told them that the English coast was in sight. He would hold his map up to them every so often and point out their position.

Cecil's logbook records that on the 24th June 1945 he and his crew went on a Cooks Tour of some of the bombed areas in Europe. They took off at 1100 hrs in Lancaster (OR-'Y') and set a course for the Dutch coast and flew low over Holland, Belgium and Germany gazing in amazement at the devastation caused by five years of allied bombing. On the 25th June 1945 Cecil flew his last operation of the war to Flensburg in Denmark, his logbook records that this was to, "Test the enemy radar system." On the 4th and 6th August they flew from Sturgate to Pomigliano and returned to Glatton in North Hants with POWs and again on the 12th, 13th and 15th August 1945. They carried out a further five Operation Dodge trips on the 18th, 21st and 26th November 1945.

Cecil carried out his last Operation Dodge to Italy on the 12th December 1945 and has an interesting story to it.

On the morning of the 12th December 1945, Cecil's Skipper (F/O Lovell DFM) took off from Carnaby at

0803 hrs in Lancaster (QR-'O') and set a course for Pomigliano in Italy. It took just over six hours to reach their destination, and when they did arrive they were met with gale force winds and driving snow. Just after landing in Pomiglianao they were sent to a hotel to await further orders as the weather by now had got much worse and the airfield was closed. Some of the crews had already been told that they may not get back to UK for at least two weeks, and were asked by a senior officer would any of them like to spend Christmas in Rome as it could be arranged. Cecil's crew quickly volunteered, and were soon on their way to Rome. They were billeted in the athletes dressing room of great Italian sports stadium for one week. The dressing room had been 'kitted out' especially for them and was very comfortable. A party and Christmas dinner was arranged for them on Christmas Day and everyone had a wonderful time. They did a lot of sight seeing in Rome, visiting many of its beautiful buildings, including the Vatican.

They were informed on the 1st January that the weather was clearing and the airfield was now opened. On the 2nd January Flying Officer Lovell took his Lancaster for a 45 minute air test, returning the next day to Glatton with their POWs.

Unauthorised Cargo!

At the end of January 1946, 61 Squadron was moved from Sturgate to Waddington. Most of the crews in the squadron owned their own bicycles and were told to leave them behind at Sturgate. They decided on a bold and furtive plan which resulted in loading their bicycles into the 'crew wagon' just before leaving for the dispersal, and hoping that no 'bod' at flying control would notice anything unusual as they transferred the lot into (QR-'W'). As they roared down the runway Cecil glanced back over the Lancasters main spar, and what a sight for sore eyes. There were kit-bags, suitcases, all sorts of 'odds and ends' and of course the 'seven bicycles' all in a heap. On their arrival at the dispersal at Waddington the crew carried out the unloading even more furtively, hoping that the 'bods' in Waddington Flying Control would think that the 61 Squadron aircrew always moved at such breakneck speed to clear their aircraft.

On the 6th February 1946 Cecil flew his last flight with his Skipper, Flight Lieutenant Lovell Lancaster and crew in Lancaster (QR-'N'). Cecil had by now served four years and 32 days in the Royal Air Force, completed 26 operations and had flown a total of 410hrs.45mins. It was therefore decided on the 13th June 1946 that he was to be de-mobbed. He was sent to Personnel Despatch Centre in London where he received his civilian suit, hat and gratuity. He returned to Northern Ireland with his English born wife where they lived and worked on the family farm in Armagh. Cecil eventually left the farm and got his own home and decided to seek employment with the then Ulster Transport Authority (green buses). He later gained employment as a grounds man in Theipval Military Barracks in Lisburn. This type of work was nothing new to him as he was used doing it on his family farm. Cecil's wife died in 1975, and three years later he decided to retire when the barracks was closed down. He has five daughters and one son and is now at the ripe young age of 89 and is looking for a 'rich widow' to take care of him.

Cecil joined the Royal Air Force Association (Armagh Branch) in 1948 when he was employed with the Ulster Transport Authority and later the Lisburn Branch where he is still a very active member. He remembers well the very first night he attended the Lisburn Branch and saw only five members, and asked, "My goodness is this all you have?" Cecil was asked by one of the members, "Would you like a job?" and he asked, "What sort of a Job?" and before he sat down he had been elected Chairman. He was also made Wings Appeal Officer, and worked extremely hard along with the Lord Mayor of Lisburn to raise funds. The branch now has between twenty to thirty members attending each meeting. Cecil has also held the post of Standard Bearer for Northern Ireland for two years and still at the age of 89 carries the Branch Flag when required. He still keeps in touch with his Skipper Pilot Officer Soar and sends him a copy of the Intercom magazine when he can.

Author's note

On the 4th/5th May 1996 I had the honour to be invited to the Royal Air Force College at Cranwell as the guest of Air Vice Marshal Tony Staple and his wife, along with Cecil, Bert Roberts and David McCausland (all members of the Aircrew Association Northern Ireland Branch). On our arrival at Cranwell, Air Vice Marshall Staples had kindly laid on an hours flight for us all in the Bulldog Trainer. I flew along side Cecil in echelon and watched him break off with his Pilot to carry out a series of aerobatics. Cecil's Pilot was Flight Lieutenant Hamilton and the aircraft was Bulldog XX538. "A day I shall never forget."

FLIGHT LIEUTENANT
ROBERT MICHAEL KILDEA
ROYAL AIR FORCE NO. 118092
PILOT
NO. 246 SQUADRON (LIBERATORS)

Robert Michael Kildea was born in Belfast on the 7th March 1918 and was educated at Hughes Academy in the East of the city. On leaving school he was employed with the Northern Ireland Education Department as an accounts clerk.

He joined the Royal Air Force Volunteer Reserve in Belfast on the 23rd March 1939 and commenced his flying training with 24 Elementary and Reserve Flying Training School at Sydenham in April. His made his first air experience flight on the 30th April 1939 in a Tiger Moth coded N6460, his instructor was Flight Sergeant Lake. He carried on with his flying training with Flight Sergeant Lake through May, June, July and August and was called to full time service with the outbreak of War in September 1939. On the 11th December 1939 he was posted to No 4 Squadron, 5 ITW at Hastings on the south coast of England where he was to commence his basic training.

He completed his basic training on the 10th June 1940 and was posted to No 4 EFTS at Brough to start his elementary flying training on B 2s. His first flight on this type was on the morning of the 11th June 1940 under the instruction of a Flight Lieutenant Steele. On the morning of the 24th June he had two flights with Flight Lieutenant Steele and at 1345 hrs he took to the air for the first time on his own. His elementary flying training finished on the 22nd May and he was assessed as being an 'average' Pilot.

On the 25th May he was posted to No 10 EFTS at Yatesbury near Calne where he was to commence a pre fighter course on Tiger Moths for one month and then on to No 8 Flying Training School at Montrose in Scotland where he completed a four week course on single engined Masters. At the end of the fighter course an entry in his logbook shows that he was 'not suitable to fighter aircraft' and was recommended for 'twins'. This decision had nothing to do with his flying ability but was deemed necessary because of his large stature. On the 16th September 1940 he was posted to the Advanced Training Squadron, No 10 FTS at Ternhill to start training on Avro Ansons. His first flight in the Anson was on the 18th

September on the instruction of a Flying Officer Bamber. On September 26th at 1550 hrs he was given his solo test by Squadron Leader Beck and soloed 30 minutes later. He qualified to wear his Wings on the 5th December 1940 and promoted to Flight Sergeant. On the 10th December 1940 his log book shows that he was posted to 86 Squadron at Gosport for six weeks although his log book does not show any evidence of flying here.

86 Squadron had just been reformed at Gosport on the 6th December for service with coastal command and was equipped with Bristol Blenheims 1Vs.

On the 15th January 1941 he was then posted to No 3 School of Ground Reconnaissance at Blackpool where he completed a Staff Pilot's course. On the 1st January 1942 he had a 72% pass and was assessed as 'above the average' as a Pilot. The chief instructor also wrote in his logbook, "A keen hardworking NCO who would have benefited by a longer period of instruction." On the 4th March Flight Sergeant Kildea was posted to No 4 COTU at Stranraer in Scotland where he was to convert onto Short Sunderlands. The OTU moved to Invergordon on the 14th April 1941. He finished the course on the 13th May and awaited his next posting to an operational squadron.

On the 13th May 1942 Flight Sergeant Kildea was posted to No 201 Squadron that was based at Lough Erne in County Fermanagh, Northern Ireland. He became 2nd Pilot to Pilot Officer Traill. The squadron was equipped with the Short Sunderland Mk 11 and its main task was anti-submarine patrols. The squadron moved to Pembroke Dock in June 1942. His logbook shows that he carried out his first operational patrol from Pembroke Dock on the 18th June. This was a 12hr.45mins anti-submarine patrol escorting Convoy H/G 84. On July 1st he carried out a nine hour anti-submarine patrol escorting Convoy SL.11 3F. On the 7th July 1942 he was off back to the coastal OTU at Stranraer and Invergordon where he was to complete a captain's course on Sunderlands and Londons. At the end of the course he was now assessed as 'above the average' as a Flying Boat Pilot.

On the 30th September 1942 he was posted to 246 Squadron on the Isle of Islay in Scotland. The squadron was formed at Bowmore in Scotland on the 1st September 1942 as a general reconnaissance Flying Boat Unit and was equipped with the Short Sunderland 11 and 111s. Flight Sergeant Kildea was now in command of his own aircraft. He carried out flight tests on Sunderland DV 979 on the 1st, 2nd and third of November. He flew anti-submarine patrols in DV 979 until the 15th December when an entry in his logbook shows that, "DV979 crashed and written off by Captain Lever."

His logbook shows that he was detached to 15 Group Headquarters at Liverpool from the 22nd November 1942 for one week returning to 246 on the 29th. On the 30th December 1942 he was posted to No 12 School of Technical Training for one week. He continued with anti-submarine patrols with 246 squadron until the 30th March 1943 when he was given two weeks leave. On his return from leave on the 16th May he was informed that he was being posted to No 86 Squadron that was based at Aldergrove in Northern Ireland and was equipped with the Consolidated Liberator Mk111A. He carried out a five week conversion course onto Liberators at No 1 Coastal Operational Training Unit at Beaulieu in Hants between the 21st June and the 30th July 1943 returning to 86 Squadron on the 2nd August. Flying Officer Kildea and his crew had carried out just three, thirteen hour long anti-submarine operations over the Atlantic from Aldergrove when tragedy struck them while returning from an anti submarine patrol on the 27th August 1943.

That fateful day

Flying Officer Kildea and his crew had taken off from Aldergrove on the 27th August 1943 in Liberator BZ802 'V'. Their task was to carry out a anti-U-boat patrol in the Bay of Biscay area. It must be said that the weather on their way home to Aldergrove was atrocious. It appears that Flying Officer Kildea had left his seat and handed over control of the aircraft to his 2nd in command Flying Officer Roberts and went to assist his Navigator. Unfortunately the Liberator crashed a short time later in bad weather near the summit of Cahan Mountain that overlooked the town of Castletown Bere in County Cork, Southern Ireland. The entire crew perished that night. The large four engined bomber came down in soft bog on the side of Cahan mountain, she bounced twice and came to rest some 100 yards further on. About one mile away from the crash site a local farmer. Mr Neilly Harrington had heard the plane fly low overhead and the loud explosion a short time later. He and several friends immediately went to see if they could help in any way. It took them at least half an hour to locate the crash as the weather was extremely bad and torrential rain had added to their difficult task.

The first thing they came upon was the giant skid mark of the aircraft that left a furrow in the ground over 100 yards long. A little further on they found one of the aircraft's wings which had broken away in the impact and then they found the aircraft's fuselage. They found two of the crew some distance away and on examination were found to be dead. They had either crawled from the wreck or had been thrown clear after the impact. Neither of them had anything visibly wrong, but had obviously suffered terrible internal injuries. A voice from the plane shouted,"Help me Paddy, get me out of here." It was the voice of Flying Officer Kildea, who although barely alive and was trapped by the body of the Bomb Aimer was able to shout for help for him and his comrades. The Bomb Aimer had been thrown back into the Navigator's seat where Flying Officer Kildea had been sitting. By now the local Priest had arrived, his name was Father Morgan and although he did not know the religious denomination of the dead he decided to administer the last rights to the six of them. Fearing that Flying Officer Kildea was also close to death he managed to crawl into the aircraft to where he managed to cut a hole in the Pilots shoe and administer the Holy Oils to his heel. Flying Officer Kildea died before he could be taken from the aircraft.

The names of the crew were:

Flying Officer Roberts from London
Flight Sergeant Edward Wells from London
Geoffrey Plume from Bishops Stanford
Sergeant John Rippon from Newcastle-upon-Tyne
Clifford Cropper (NAV) from London
Walter Harris from London

Flying Officer Kildea's Liberator had been modified and fitted with the secret anti-surface-vessel radar (ASV) and although ASV aids had come into service in 1941. Great care was to be taken by the Squadron Commander who arrived at the crash site and had changed into civilian clothing. He managed to destroy the Liberator without any problems. Another Ulsterman who was attached to the squadron was Flight Lieutenant Dickson. He was sent down to Eire to receive the crew's remains and here is his story of what happened. "During those days it was so sensitive to fly the bodies of the seven airmen out from Dublin, it was decided to bring them by road to Sligo and then on to Bundoran near the Border. All seven coffins were draped with the Irish Tri-Colour. I received the bodies at the pre-arranged time at precisely 2.00am. I commanded the detachment of Royal Air Force personnel who were to form a guard of honour and receive the bodies at Belleek. The convoy arrived from Eire and travelled 600 yards into the north and then turned around to head back home again. The Eire soldiers were immaculately dressed, hand picked, complete with shiny helmets and fixed bayonets, lined up on one side of the road and the RAF personnel on the opposite side to form a joint guard of honour to honour the dead. The Tri-Colours were removed and replaced by

Union Jacks and the coffins were carried between the two lines to a waiting RAF lorry. The captain in charge of the Eire soldiers then invited me to inspect his men, which I did, and then returned the compliment to him. The village pub was closed, and being the senior British officer I had it opened and we drank each other's health and enjoyed the hospitality of each other for a few hours. We all shook hands and said our goodbyes, the Eire soldiers headed back to Finner Camp and we set off for Castle Archdale to refuel our lorries before travelling on to Aldergrove. Flying Officer Kildeas body was later buried in Dundonald Cemetery just outside Belfast."

Local people at Castletown Bere kept the memory of the seven airmen sacred and had donated money to build a permanent memorial to the crew. At exactly 0730 hrs on Saturday the 27th August 1983, 50 years to the day when the aircraft crashed a beautiful commemorative plague was unveiled by Flying Officer Kildea's son Michael and Grandson. No advanced details of the ceremony were given to the outside world in case of opposition from unfriendly sources. Villagers from Castletown Bere climbed the 1,300ft mountain along with other relatives of the crew. One man at the ceremony, Mr Victor Sullivan was a witness to the fatal crash of the Liberator BZ802 V'. Although only a school boy at the time remembers the thunder of its engines passing low over his head before it crashed, just 700ft from safety.

WING COMMANDER
JOHN IGNATIUS KILMARTIN, DFC OBE
ROYAL AIR FORCE NO. 39793
BATTLE OF BRITAIN PILOT
NO. 43, 602, 128, 313, AND 504 SQUADRONS

John Ignatius (Killy) was born in Dundalk, Eire, in July 1913 and was the son of a forester and one of eight children. His father died when he was nine years old and he went to Australia under a scheme called the 'Big Brother'. He worked on a cattle ranch for a while in New South Wales and then went to Shanghai in China, where he lived with an aunt for two years and worked as a clerk in the accounts department of the Shanghai gas department.

In his spare time he was also a professional Jockey. Reading a local paper one evening he saw an advertisement for short service commission applicants in the Royal Air Force. He applied right away and received word about three months later. He returned to the UK in 1936 and was accepted as aircrew and was taught how to fly at a civilian school in Perthshire in Scotland.

In June 1937 he completed his flying training at No 6 Flying Training School at Netheravon and then joined 43 (F) Squadron at Tangmere in January 1938. He was promoted to Pilot Officer in April 1938.

At the outbreak of war he had been appointed adjutant but decided to join No 1 Squadron in France at the start of November 1939. He became involved in several of the squadrons early actions, claiming a Dornier destroyed on the 23rd and in April 1940 claimed a Bf109. On the 20th April he claimed a Ju 88 and a He111, and on May 10th he shared a Dornier 17. On the 11th May he destroyed two Bf110s and on the 12th May claimed a Bf 109. On the 14th May he claimed a further two Bf 109s and on the 15th another Bf110. On the 16th May 1940 he claimed another Bf110 and a further two Bf110s on the 17th along with a He111 damaged.

At the request of the commanding officer, the exhausted pilots of No 1 Squadron were withdrawn to England and were to be replaced by new men. At the end of May 1940 he returned to the UK and was posted to No 5 Operational Training Unit where he remained until August 1940. In September 1940 he returned to 43 Squadron at Tangmere as a Flight Commander and on September 6th he destroyed a Bf110 and another on the

7th. He was awarded the Distinguished Flying Cross on 8th October, and promoted to Flight Lieutenant in November 1940. In April 1941 he was given command of 602 Squadron which was based in Ayr in Scotland for a short period, and in May was sent to help form 313 Squadron, the third Czech fighter squadron until August 1942. In June he was posted out to west Africa where he took command of 128 Squadron at Hastings in Sierra Leone until August 1941. He returned to the UK in December that year and was posted to 504 Squadron at Middle Wallop and was promoted to Squadron Leader. In January 1943 he took command of 504 Squadron and was promoted to Wing Commander and led the Hornchurch Wing during May. Later that year he returned to No 5 OTU as an instructor, and then on to Headquarters 84 Group, in the new 2nd Tactical Air Force as Wing Commander Operations.

In 1944 he was given command of 136 Wing which was equipped with the Hawker Typhoon and took the unit to Normandy after the invasion. In January 1945 he was made an OBE and in June was sent out to Burma as Wing Leader, 910 Wing on Thunderbolts. He was later sent to Indonesia for a period, after which he commanded Medan Airfield.

He returned to the UK and posted to the Empire Flying School at Hullavington, then out to Iraq to reform 249 Squadron at Habbaniyah with Tempest V1s. He again returned to the UK where he attended the staff college at Bracknell, and was then posted to the Air Ministry as Deputy Chief of Air Staff Training. After that he became Wing Commander Admin at Wunstof, and was then seconded to NATO, Southern Europe Headquarters, on the intelligence staff in Naples for two years. He returned to the UK once again and became Wing Commander Ops at Turnhouse in the Fighter Command Caledonian Sector. His last posting in the Royal Air Force was to Borgentreich in Germany to command and control a reporting Station.

He retired from the Royal Air Force in 1958 and settled down in Devon, where he ran a chicken farm for fifteen years.

AIR MARSHAL
SIR JAMES MacCONNELL KILPATRICK, KBE CB LLD
MB BCH DPH
ROYAL AIR FORCE

James MacConnell Kilpatrick was born in Belfast on the 1st March 1902 and was educated at the Royal Belfast Academical Institution and Queens University, Belfast. He graduated in 1924 and in the following year, and was commissioned in the Royal Air Force and so began a career which, by the breadth and variation of experience that it embraced, fitted him admirably for the highest position in his service.

Following a couple of years spent as a Station or Squadron Medical Officer at various units at home and in India he began, in 1927 a long period of almost four years at the Princess Mary's Royal Air Force Hospital at Halton, where he developed his interest in pathology and public health. In 1931 he was awarded the Arnott Memorial Gold Medal for his work at Halton during an outbreak of cerebrospinal meningitis.

Three of his appointments were concerned with research and after service in Iraq he spent a year (1936) at the RAF Institute of Pathology and Tropical Medicine, Halton. In the two years up to the outbreak of war he was at the Chemical Defence Experimental Establishment at Porton. In 1939 he gained staff experience in the Air Ministry MA4 and later had a wartime tour in west Africa as principal medical officer. As a Group Captain he commanded RAF hospitals at Church Village and Rauceby before commencing in August 1945, the course at the RAF Staff College at Bracknell, which he completed with distinction.

He attained air rank as Director of Hygiene and Research in 1947, at a time of the most active growth of the research programme in aviation medicine at Farnborough. In 1950 he was appointed Deputy Director General. Appointed OBE in 1946 and CB in 1952. He was Knighted in 1953 and became Honorary Physician to the King in 1951 and to the Queen from 1952. He then became Director General of RAF medical services a post which he held until his retirement in 1957. He was a tall lean debonair gentleman with a moustache and he had a very friendly manner. He became Dean of the London School of Hygiene and Tropical Medicine and died suddenly in London on the 4th April 1960.

FLIGHT LIEUTENANT
WILLIAM JAMES LAWSON
ROYAL AIR FORCE NO. 144677
NAVIGATOR
NO. 265 SQUADRON

William James Lawson was born in 73 Mount Street in Belfast on the 2nd February 1923 and was educated at Mount Pottinger Primary School and later at Ardmore College, where he sat and passed his Civil Service exam. His parents later moved to the little seaside town of Cloughy, Ardkeen in County Down.

Jim, as he liked to be called joined the Northern Ireland Civil Service on the 13th September 1939 and was appointed to the post of Assistant Paper Keeper in the Estate Duty Office on the 18th September 1939 (Jim Mally was in the same office, read his story). On the 10th June 1941 Jim and his good friend Jim Ferguson, went along to the Royal Air Force Recruiting Centre at 71 Clifton Street and volunteered their services in RAF. They both were accepted for consideration as Flight Mechanics (FM).

Jim's parents were shocked to say the least when he came home and informed them what he had done; so when he told them that he had volunteered for aircrew duties and there was a long waiting list so he probably would probably be put on six months deferred service. He remembers his mother saying that hopefully the war would be over by then. With his parents blessing he went back to the recruiting office the next day and volunteered for aircrew. The change of heart by his parents was a result of German bombing on their city. Jim and his father had watched the Luftwaffe fly over Portavogie in County Down and drop their bombs on Belfast and then on their way to work two days later saw the damage and carnage that they carried out. Jim thought that he would prefer to be bombing the Germans than to be at the receiving end.

On the 1st July 1941, Jim received a letter from the recruiting office asking him to report there on the 5th July at 0900 hrs for attestation in the RAFVR. Jim reported as requested and was duly accepted and was informed that he would be leaving for England that night. He returned home and told his parents of this short notice, packed his bag and boarded the Heysham boat that night. On his arrival next morning at Heysham he was told to make his way to the RAF Receiving Depot at Padgate. During the next few days he was interviewed and medically examined and was told that he would be accepted as either a Pilot or Observer.

At that particular time the RAF was in desperation for Observers, Navigators, Bomb-Aimers and Air Gunners and although Jim would have much rather been a Pilot he accepted their decision to become an Observer/Navigator. He was assured that if he did not make the grade as an Observer he would be accepted as a Pilot. After being accepted as an Observer with a rate of pay of 2 shillings per day 10p Aircraftman AC2 Lawson was sent back home to Cloughy on the 9th July 1941 having been placed on the deferred service list. He was now in the RAFVR on deferred service without pay and was given a silver RAFVR lapel badge which he proudly wore until he was called up for service on Monday 13th October 1941.

If you have been accepted for training as Pilot or Observer you will, normally, first of all be placed on deferred service. This means that, although accepted for service in the Royal Air Force, you will remain in civil life until such times as you are called up for crew training, but as you have been attested, or enlisted, and have been given a Royal Air Force number, you are an aircraftman (AC2), and therefore are no longer free to join the Army or Navy, or the Royal Air Force in any other capacity than that for which you have now been accepted. His service number was 1482481 which remained with him until he received his commission on the 17th April 1943 when it changed to 144677. In early October 1941 Jim received a letter informing him that he was being recalled to service and for him to apply to the RAF Movement Control Officer at the Northern Ireland District Headquarters in Merville, Whitehouse, where he would receive a travel warrant and reserve passage to England. He also received an official' note telling him, "You are notified that you are not permitted either to keep or drive a motor car or motor cycle during your initial training. You should therefore not take a motor car or motorcycle with you on rejoining."

On Monday 13th October 1941 AC2 Lawson reported to the Aircrew Reception Centre (ACRC) at St Johns Wood near Regents Park in London where he joined hundreds of other hopeful young aircrew, all eagerly awaiting their chance to get into the air. After a few hours he was shown his bare billet. His home for the next few weeks was to be in luxury flats which were called Benlick Close. Pre-war these would have cost to rent £1,000 per annum and as Jim only earned £1-7-6 per week in the Civil Service, he never imagined that anyone could ever afford such luxury. They were billeted ten to a room in camp beds, and although they did see into the bathrooms and kitchens were never allowed the luxury of using them.

He spent six weeks at the Aaircrew Reception Centre, where he was initiated into the RAF lifestyle and was kitted out with his uniform and given a thorough medical examination which included a host of inoculations that was to cover him for overseas service. Here he was also introduced to the rudiments of RAF discipline, learning the art of square-bashing, by marching for miles up and down Avenue Road and marching about one mile three times a day to Regents Park Zoo for his meals. Once a month he would be marched to Lords Cricket Ground for 'pay-parade' and here he was given the princely sum of 17 Shillings per fortnight, after deductions of various kinds. Jim was delighted with his pay as he never had so much money, being used to two shillings and sixpence per week pocket money. Now he had eight shillings and sixpence to spend per week and this seemed like a fortune. He soon learned how to find his way around London on the tube (Swiss Cottage was the nearest to his billet) and he was amazed how far the tube would take him for sixpence (less than 2p). Apart from his visit to Padgate, Jim had never been outside Northern Ireland before and to able to visit Buckingham Palace, the Houses of Parliament, St Pauls Cathedral, West Minister Abbey, Piccadilly, Hyde Park and Madam Tussauds, etc, this had been quite an experience for him.

In November 1941 Jim was posted to the famous Battle of Britain Fighter Station at Kenley near London for his pre-initial training course. Kenley at that time had two Hurricane squadrons stationed there and as it was mild weather during that November, the pilots still sat outside the operations room in their wicker chairs waiting for the bell to ring, when they would race to their aircraft and take off to engage the Luftwaffe. Jim told me, "After an hour or so, the fighters would return and I was always excited and delighted to see some of them completing a 'victory roll' which meant that they had shot down an enemy aircraft." Being Irish himself, his favourite pilot was the famous Paddy Finucane (killed July 15th 1942).

It was Christmas day 1941 and as was with tradition in the RAF it was the officers turn to serve Christmas dinner to airmen. Although Jim did get a menu from that day

which had been signed by many of 'The Few', unfortunately it has been lost through time. At Kenley they were taken for square bashing and physical training by an NCO who came originally from one of the Guards Regiments. The standards he set were very high and Jim remembers having to parade in the snow at 0700 hrs, dressed only in a vest and shorts.

In mid-January 1942 Jim was given two weeks home leave and was pleased to show off his new uniform with his cadet white flash on his cap. On returning from leave he reported back to the ACRC in London where he was informed that he was too billeted in the Viceroy Court (another block of luxury flats) and after spending a week there he was transferred to Babbacombe in Torquay, Devon to start his initial training course on Navigation. The course consisted of him being trained how to use a navigation computer, a Mercators projection map, astro navigation (using a Sextant), aircraft instruments, compasses, time patrols and the mysterious art of dead reckoning and general Air Force disciplines. The course and the end of April 1942 and he was given a few days leave. On return from leave Jim was informed that he had passed all subjects and was promoted to Leading Aircraft Man (LAC) which meant a rise in pay from two shillings per day to four shillings and sixpence per day.

His next posting was in May 1942 which took him to the Elementary Air Navigation School (EANS) at Eastbourne where he was billeted in the Imperial Hotel on the sea front. It was not unusual in those days to have German Me109s fly over and machine gun the sea front from time to time. At Eastbourne Jim completed a two month Advanced Navigation and Armaments course and on completion of the course he was given four days embarkation leave, after which was he ordered to report to Weeton transit camp to prepare for overseas service. On the 28th September 1942, Jim, along with about 2,000 others boarded a troop ship, destination, unknown. For two days the ship sailed north toward the Hebrides, and then sailed south and anchored in Bangor Bay, County Down, Northern Ireland, where it joined the main convoy. The convoy lay off Bangor until Oct 4th until other troop and Merchant ships, Frigates, Destroyers, and Cruisers joined them. Jim could clearly see the Main Street in Bangor and Donaghadee, the cars, buses and people. it was heartbreaking for him as he was so close to but yet so far away from home. It would only have taken him half an hour to reach home and see his parents, if only he could manage somehow to get ashore. He realised that was impossible, as no one could tell when the convoy would sail. The large convoy set sail on the 4th October, again heading north, and once out of sight of land it turned west. Jim had a good idea now that he was heading for Canada or South Africa. The convoy sailed on a north, north westerly course for about one week and then turned south for South Africa. The convoy sailed on for a few days and again changed course and headed due east and by now the climate was tropical. Quite a lot of the RAF personnel who were not issued with tropical gear did suffer from severe sunburn. On the 15th October a Catalina flying boat flew overhead and escorted the convoy to Freetown in west Africa, arriving there the next day. Jim was delighted to see land again as the conditions on the ship had been very crowded. Their sleeping quarters were very cramped, so much so, they had to sleep on hammocks which were slung over the mess tables. They were all soon allowed up on deck where they were could see ships of all types, Royal Navy cruisers, destroyers, troop ships and merchant ships all around them as far as the eye could see. It was exciting to call at a foreign port and in no time at all Jim's ship was surrounded with 'bum' boats selling everything from fruit to local souvenirs. A few of the natives were allowed on board, and they did the bargaining, they pulled up their goods in a basket by rope from canoes. One of the natives who Jim talked to explained that he had nine wives and 17 children to support. This impressed him at the time, but not on reflection. The ship was being refuelled and her stores replenished getting ready for the next leg of the journey to Cape Town and Durban. The ship set sail and arrived in Cape Town on the morning of November 2nd where it stayed for a few hours. Cape Town was a memorable sight for Jim with Table Mountain and the cloud, known locally as the 'Table Cloth', which hovered over its flat top.

The ship arrived in Durban on the 5th November, this also was a memorable sight for Jim and the troops, for as they entered the harbour, were greeted with beautiful voice of the 'Lady in White' singing one of her songs. She always made a point of greeting all the troop ships to Durban Harbour. Jim disembarked the ship with the rest of his friends and had to spend the next few nights under canvas (six to a tent). His first night in a tent was a memorable one as he found a scorpion under his bed. Jim was soon informed that he was going by train to a place called East London on the south coast where he would receive his next posting. The journey was to take him via, Peter Maritzburg, Lady Smith, Bloanfontein, Spring Fanteur and Queens Town. He stayed in East London for a few days waiting for his posting to come through which it did and informed him that he going Queens Town.

Some of his friends were posted to other Air Navigation schools at Grahamstown and Outshoun. The journey to Queens Town by train did not take very long. Jim arrived at No 47 Air Navigation School in Queenstown on the 2nd December 1942. Everyone was very friendly showing him the ropes and he soon settled in. His Air Observer's course started on the 14th December with classroom lectures and then on the 21st December he had his first flight in an Anson with his Pilot Lieutenant van Aardt. A few days previous one of the school's Ansons had crashed killing the Pilot, Wireless Operator and three pupils. That same day Jim and his classmates were hurriedly taught how to slow march, so as they could form a funeral party the next day. The

navigation lasted for four months, flying in Ansons and Oxfords and when the course finished on the 27th March 1943 he had accumulated 73 hours flying by day and 18 hours by night. The night flying part of the course was carried out at an airfield called Aliwal North. He spent the first week of April at an Air Gunnery and Bombing School in Port Alfred and on the 10th April he learned that 21 out of the 30 who attended the Navigation course had failed. This made Jim very nervous, however when the big day came for the results to be announced he was delighted when he was told that he had passed with an average of 80% and was assessed as 'above the average' in the class. He was awarded his Observers Brevet and promoted to the rank of Sergeant and his Instructor told him that he had been recommended for a commission. If this recommendation was accepted by the Air Ministry it would be back dated to the 17th April, the day after his passing out parade. Jim was now fully qualified as an Observer which meant he had been trained as a Navigator, Bomb-Aimer and Air Gunner. This was to be one of the last Observer courses as later cadets were trained only for one of these classifications.

Because Jim had been assessed as above the average it was decided he should be sent on a General Reconnaissance Course that was to be held at the South African Air Force Station at George where he would receive specialist training in navigation and if successful would be posted to a coastal command station. The standards set at this particular school were very high, as most of the flying was carried out over the sea, where there was no a landmark or wireless beacons to help. After a stop at Port Elizabeth, Jim arrived at George on April 20th where he started a six week course at No 61 Air School. Some of the exercises that he carried out during the course were DR navigation, line ahead patrols, cross over patrols, square searches (for use when escorting convoys), this all proved vital when navigating a flying boat over the sea.

Jim carried out his first operational convoy patrol while at the school on the 29th May in an Anson. His Pilot was a Lieutenant Flesch. Confirmation of his commission came through on Wednesday 2nd June and it was back dated to April 17th. He was promoted to Pilot Officer and was given a £30 allowance to buy all of his officer's requirements. At the end of the course he was again assessed as 'above the average' with a pass mark of 87%. He left George on the 7th June 1943 and headed back to Durban, via Bloem Fontein and Lady Smith arriving in Durban on the 10th June. Upon his arrival he was informed that he had been appointed Officer Commanding No 2 Squadron. For the next two weeks Jim had a good time touring in and around Durban. Durban is a beautiful city and it has a replica of the Belfast City Hall. He learned to water-ski, watched lots of pictures on the 'Bioscopes' and managed to buy some of his new officers uniform. He met a Dutch sailor one evening at the Cinema and in conversation, discovered that he had been on one of the escort ships in Jim's convoy. The Dutch sailor had been torpedoed two days later, 100 miles of the coast of Durban.

On the 24th June Jim received notice to board the HMT Sibajak (a Dutch vessel) which was to take him to the Middle East. Shortly after boarding the vessel he met a Wren whose name was Couser and who came from Sydenham Drive in Belfast Northern Ireland (what a small world). The trip from Durban to Port said in Egypt took two weeks and two days with one stop at Aden on the 6th July. The troopship was excellent and as he was now an officer travelled 1st Class. He had a 'Crossing the Line' ceremony and some concert parties while on board, the temperature in the Red Sea was 120 degrees 'C'. The ship arrived at Port Said in Egypt on Saturday 10th July where Jim was informed to proceed to No 21 Personnel Despatch Centre which was at Kasfareet in the desert near the Suez Canal. Jim said it was a dreadful place. The accommodation was made of cement blocks and inside was completely bare, no beds and only four rough blankets lying on the floor, one of which they had to sleep on and the others they put over them as it got extremely cold in the desert at night. Jim was held at Kasfereet for 11 weeks awaiting his posting to a squadron. The worst 11 weeks so far in the Royal Air Force. Here he met two fellow Irishmen, a Flight Lieutenant AS Majury who was a Medical Officer from Antrim town and a Pilot Officer Waddell from Belfast. On the 26th September he finally left Kasfereet and headed for Jerusalem, and why to this day is still a mystery to him. On the way he passed through Ismalia, Kantara, Gaza and Lydda.

Jerusalem was a much better posting where he spent the next nine days and during that time he visited the old part of the city, the Mount of Olives, the Holy Seplechure and even managed to get a girlfriend whose name was Ralhaeli. On the 5th October, Jim was informed that he was being posted to East Africa, and on the 25th October he flew from Cairo to Nairobi in a Lockheed Lodestar, stopping off at Wadi Halfa and night stopping at Khartoum. The next morning the aircraft was refuelled at Malakal and flew on to Juba and Kisumu before landing in Nairobi. This was RAF Station Eastleigh. Eastleigh had been a peace time RAF Station and was the best Jim had ever visited. The officer's mess was superb, the accommodation was excellent and Jim had his own 'Batman' to do all his daily chores. He started lectures and did a few hours on a Link Trainer, this was to teach him how to land and fly an aircraft in an emergency.

On Sunday 29th November he left Eastleigh for Mombasa where he joined 209 Squadron. This was a Flying Boat Conversion Unit (FBCU) for the new Catalina squadrons forming in the area. and at long last he was about to join an operational squadron. This was the units 4th course, which lasted for two weeks, starting on the 7th December and on the 11th December, Jim had his first flight in a Consolidated Catalina. The course consisted of how to swing a compass, signal by Aldis lamp, semaphore, align a bomb-sight, take bearings from a loop aerial, swing the loop aerial for deviations, practice astro navigation and learning the mysteries of radar. "209 Squadron was the squadron which spotted the Bismarck."

He then left Mombasa on the 24th January on board a BOAC Empire Flying boat which was to take him to Diego Suarez in Madagascar where he joined 265 Squadron. Diego Suarez was a small settlement on the northern tip of Madagascar. There was no town as such then and the officer's accommodation was made of bamboo canes and palm leaves. Jim spent his 21st birthday at Diego Suarez. Just after he had arrived at Diego he was told that he would be Duty Captain until the 20th February when he would meet his crew and start full time operations. For some reason, the same day he was granted two weeks leave and managed to hitch a lift to Nairobi and back. This was to be a memorable two weeks leave as the aircraft, a Catalina, piloted by Flying Officer Joplin developed engine trouble and they had to land on an uninhabited coral reef, called Aldabra. The aircraft had been flying from Diego to Mombasa. The Navigator on the aircraft suggested that Jim do the navigating in view of the fact that he was off on two weeks leave, Jim readily agreed to do so. Some two to three hours on course to Mombasa, one the Catalina's engines failed and the skipper asked Jim for a course to the nearest landfall. This did not take Jim very long and soon he gave him a course to Aldabra Island which was shown on the chart as little more than a dot and was marked 'uninhabited'. Jim had flown close to it before and remembered it as a coral reef with a small island. It was their only hope as they were unable to maintain height and the sea was too rough to ditch the plane. They decided to jettison everything they could lay their hands on, including depth charges, machine guns, radar sets, etc. After a hour and a half or so of skilful flying by the Skipper, Flying Officer Joplin, they arrived at the coral reef with just 200 feet on the altimeter.

Aldabra turned out to be an Atoll, a elliptical coral reef surrounding a lagoon with a small island on the eastern side. Having no time to spare they crossed their fingers and the Skipper managed a good landing in the middle of the lagoon. There was a strong current running through the lagoon and as they couldn't taxi on one engine, soon found themselves drifting towards the coral reef. Luck was with them, and they managed to get front and rear anchors to hold before they drifted onto the dangerous reef. The Wireless Operator had managed to make contact with his base, and advised them that they intended attempting to land at or near Aldabra Island. They felt that if they could keep the aircraft off the corals, they could eventually be rescued. After they had made the anchors as secure as they could, they went out onto the wings to survey their new surroundings and to their amazement, saw a large wooden boat being rowed towards them (help could not have arrived that quickly). As it came closer to the aircraft, they could see it had six natives on board and not knowing if they friend or foe (cannibals), they drew there revolvers and awaited their arrival. One of natives, a huge man, was standing up on the stern of the boat, and shouted to them in French. The Skipper and several of the car's crew were Canadians and could speak French fluently and were able to converse with the natives. Jim and the crew were to learn that this man who was a Creole and his five companions where from the Gomoros Islands. They had been dropped off at Aldabra island by a ship en-route to India, so that they could catch the island's tortoises. (Aldabra Island is reputed to have the world's largest tortoise).

The ship was to call for them again on its return voyage in six weeks, but as more than six months had elapsed, they feared that their ship had been sunk, but were delighted to see the RAF crew because they had given up hope of ever getting home again. They gave Jim and the crew fresh water which they had found on the island and some fresh fish which they cooked on an open fire that night. Next day a Catalina 'A' of 209 Squadron, captained by Flight Lieutenant Temple Murray arrived overhead. The Wireless Operator was able to contact it and relate their problem. Temple Murray decided to land in the lagoon and give them some supplies and gave Jim a lift back to Mombasa. He landed all right, but was unable to moor up alongside because of the strong current. It was decided that he would taxi past them, and as they waited in the natives boat, he would trail a long rope from the port blister (the Catalina machine gun positions in the rear of the aircraft and used for entry and exit) and as he passed them they were to row like hell and try and catch the rope. On the fourth attempt they managed to catch the rope and were pulled alongside the Catalina as it taxied along. They and their supplies were transferred post haste and they then made a precarious take off for Diego Suarez, where they spent the night before leaving the next morning for Mombasa.

Jim never met up with Flying Officer Joplin or any other members of that crew, but he was reliably informed that they had to spend two weeks waiting for a ship to be dispatched from Mombasa with a new engine, which was eventually fitted under very difficult conditions. Jim's leave finished on the 13th March and on his return to Diego he met his new crew who he was to spend the rest of his operational tour with. They turned out to be a super bunch and soon a wonderful team spirit developed.

The crew

Captain	Flying Officer Smith
Second Pilot	Flight Sergeant Norton
	(later killed with Jack Loch)
W/Op/Air Gunners	Warrant Officer Brown
	Flight Sergeant Hughes
	Sergeant May
	Sergeant Smith
Flight Engineers	Sergeant Graham
	Sergeant Palmer

On the 14th March 1944 Jim and his crew in Catalina F.P.260 carried out their first anti-submarine patrol which lasted for 15hrs.35mins, 4hrs.30mins by day and 11hrs.5mins by night. 16 hours was the norm for these anti-submarine patrols. In six days Jim and the crew flew over 66 hours carrying out anti-submarine patrols and convoy escorts. When you add in, about two hours for briefing before going out on patrol, getting to your aircraft by motor launch, preparing your flight plan on board before taking off and then another two hours when you returned to be debriefed by the intelligence officer, something to eat, you were pretty exhausted as there was only one Navigator on the Catalina while all the other members of the crew were duplicated. The reason for only having one Navigator was because of the nature of his job which is to supply the Pilot with courses to fly, he had to carry out wind checks every half hour, (this means altering course three times and taking drifts on each course). Taking star shots with a sextant as often as you can (three two-minute shots of different stars, one to port, one to starboard, one ahead and one to starboard again) to obtain a fix, i.e. to fix your position. All stars are in a different position (angle) from every place on earth. By measuring the angle of the star and noting the exact time (to a second), the Navigator can then work out a position line on a map. By taking altitudes of three stars you can work out from logarithm tables, three position lines which should intersect at a point and this is your position. When Jim was operating in the Indian Ocean in 1944, there were no radio aids at all from which to get bearings, so all navigation was done by dead reckoning. So it would be unfair to ask another man to take over your estimated position, thus one Navigator has to be responsible from take off to landing.

When Jim's aircraft was escorting convoys, the Navigator had to plot a cross over patrol or a 'Box in line ahead' patrol, ahead of the convoy keeping the same distance ahead of it all the time. He had to maintain wireless silence, so when he found the convoy, he communicated to it by Aldis lamp and it would give its course and speed. It was every Navigator's ambition to get through his tour of operations without having to send a "not met" signal to base.

On one occasion Jim received an estimated position of a convoy but on arrival over the area there was no sign of it. So for a hour or so they carried out a 'square search' but still could not find it. He reluctantly gave the wireless operator the "not met" message to send to base. After a short delay base came back with a new position for the convoy, which was about 150 miles from where it should have been. They eventually found it. and were relieved, so much so, they forgot to fire the colours of the day from the Very Pistol. The Navy could be very trigger happy, and no one could blame them, so when a strange aircraft approached without identifying itself, they would shoot it down and ask questions later. Fortunately, when the Navy did open fire on them the shell exploded a short distance from the aircraft, they could feel the blast, so they very quickly fired the colours of the day before the Navy had time to fire off another shot. Jim readily admits the hectic schedule of operational flying did not continue during all of his tour. He was never at 'panic stations' and life was much more leisurely and there was lots of time between trips. He carried out anti-submarine patrols when each aircraft was despatched to a designated area to search for submarines and parallel track searches when five or six aircraft would fly on the same course but were approximately 20 miles separating each of them. This meant taking off from the same base at the same time, e.g. Diego Suarez, Mauritius, Seychelles, etc., were bases all over the Indian Ocean. Mombasa (Kenya), Dar-es-Salem (Tanganyika), Diego Suaraz (Madagascar), St Lucia (Zulu Land), Durban (South Africa), Port Louis (Mauritius), Victoria (Seychelles) and moorings at some of the smaller islands like, Lindi, Panla, Zanzibar which were between Madagascar and Kenya. In general, life could be pretty boring, flying 15 to 20 hours at a time over the sea and coming back with nothing to report. The weather was still their greatest enemy as they had to take off and land in all weathers and the sea could be a most uneven surface, not only could there be enormous waves, there could be enormous swells which presented the Pilots with a great number of problems. When taking off, if you did not have enough airspeed when you got to the top of the swell, the aircraft dropped like a brick into the trough, with such a bang that some of the rivets would pop out and started leaks. If the aircraft wasn't straight into wind, it could get below your tail and turn you over, and this problem did lose the squadron some aircraft.

It could be very frustrating getting back from a long trip and landing in a heavy sea and then have to taxi round for half a hour or more trying to catch your moorings. When one did eventually get tied up it could sometimes be so rough that the dinghies could not come alongside to get the crews ashore for ages. On one occasion, Jim and his crew were sent out to plot the course and the whereabouts of an anti-cyclone. When they found it, they had a headwind which was stronger than their airspeed. However those frustrations were compensated for by landing at places like the Seychelles, Mauritius and Durban. where they usually had a few days to relax between operations. By the end of 1944 most of the submarine activity in the Indian Ocean had ceased. Jim had accumulated 318 operational hours in Catalinas and had carried out 23 operations with the Squadron. The last one being an anti-submarine sweep on September 13th 1944. His last flight with Flight Lieutenant Smith and his crew was on the 24th November 1944 and his last flight with the squadron was on the 19th December 1944 with Flight Lieutenant Pinkard from the Seychelles to Diego. He was assessed as 'above the average' by the commanding officer when he finally left the squadron at the end of December 1944.

His next posting was an East African Communication Flight at RAF Eastleigh in Nairobi. The Com Flight was equipped with Dakotas and Lockheed Hudsons and Ropides. Their job was to fly supplies and personnel throughout the East African Command to Kenya, Tanganyika, North Rhodesia, Uganda, Somalia, Madagascar and Zanzibar. On his arrival at the EACF at the beginning of January 1945, Jim was appointed as Navigator to the Air Officer Commanding's aircraft which was a specially prepared Lockheed Hudson (FW579). It was minus the usual camouflage and was finished in aircraft aluminium for the AOC Air Vice Marshal Sir Brian Baker and all the other VIPs who might be in the area and who would require transport. These VIPs included the Commander-in-Chief General Anderson and the Station Naval Commander. The aircraft had three crew members, the Pilot was Flight Lieutenant Jimmy Harrop, Warrant Officer Cooper was the Wireless Operator and Jim himself was the Navigator. Being one of the AOC's crew had its benefits, where ever they went with him they would also received the VIP treatment.

The British High Commissioner of Madagascar put them up in his official residence and his beautiful French secretary even offered Jim accommodation in her apartment (perk of the job). Being the sweet innocent man that he was (ahem), he politely refused her offer and the Wireless Operator never forgave him for spoiling his chances.

As the AOC only flew a few times a month, Jim was also appointed Adjutant of all the communication flights and as such was responsible for all administration and discipline of the flight and when this was not to demanding, he would go on Dakota flights and see all over the command. Air Headquarters was in Cairo, Egypt, this allowed Jim to make several flights up the Nile to Cairo when the AOC had to visit there and these entailed stops at Juba, Malakal, Khartoum and Wadi Halfa, (all in the Sudan or on the Bank of the Nile) before landing in Cairo. They never landed at Luxor or Aswan, but often flew over them. He also had flights to the Belgian Congo and Aden. Jim was also the Station Entertainments Officer and was responsible for all dinner dances and parties in the officer's mess where the high society of Kenya were often entertained. In the summer of 1945 they sometimes forgot that there was a war on. The war in Europe had ended in June and they were expecting a posting to the Far East to fight the Japanese, and so decided to make the best of things while they lasted. In Mid-August Jim was on a flight from Nairobi to Tanganyika and Lusaka when the Wireless Operator passed him a message, stating that the Americans had dropped an atomic bomb on Japan. He had never heard of an atomic bomb until then, but it soon meant the end of the war in the Far East. As those places where then only small landing strips with a few ground crews, they had little or no celebrations, and by the time they got back to base the excitement had died down. Jim did have to organise a Victory dinner dance in the officer's mess where everyone let their hair down and had a hell of a good time.

Being 'tea total', Jim always found it difficult to enjoy these wild occasions, but he does remember getting into the spirit of things when he made himself sick by taking the flowers out of a vase and drinking the water. It was only a few weeks after this that he passed into one of the worst period of his service career. In mid-September 1945 he started falling about and passing out with severe stomach pains, and had to be admitted to the 87th General Hospital in Nairobi where he was diagnosed as having amoebic dysentery and a duodenal ulcer. Amoebic dysentery is mainly a tropical parasite disease and the infection is spread by food or water which has been contaminated by flies carrying the germ from human faeces.

The symptoms are abdominal cramps, diarrhoea with blood and mucus, etc. The amoebic germ attacks the intestines (eat holes in them) and if the infection spreads to the liver it will produce abscesses which can prove fatal. Treatment was extremely harsh for this condition in 1945, there was no antibiotic, so each day for two weeks Jim was given an enema every morning and then a tube with a funnel on the end was entered into his rectum and a yellow nicotine like substance was then poured into the funnel and when it had flooded his intestines the tube was removed. His bed had been raised on blocks at the bottom and he had to lie motionless for 12 hours at a time, before the liquid was allowed to run out. During this period he was not allowed to eat for six weeks and lived on milk only.

At the end of the two weeks, Jim was tested to see if the amoebic germ had been cleared, unfortunately the results were negative. This meant that he had to go through another two weeks treatment. The second course was successful but by then his was a physical wreck. His duodenal ulcer was now very painful, and the harsh treatment that he had received for one month for the amoebic dysentery had made it worse. His weight was now done to 100lbs. After another two weeks on milk and milk foods, Jim health and weight began to improve. Fortunately, at that time, Jim was very friendly with an auxiliary nurse whose name was Evanne. Her father had been a Colonel in the Bengal Lancers in India and had retired to a 12,000 acre Pyrethrum Farm at Mau Summit in Kenya. This was the Kenya Highlands which was over 100 miles north of Nairobi and she very kindly arranged with the permission of her parents for Jim to convalesce there.

Colonel and Mrs Knaggs had a beautiful colonial home with lots of horses and ponies, and as Evanne had managed to get some home leave to coincide with his, they spent some lovely times riding around the far. Jim was off-duty for almost three months hend because of his medical condition, was grounded and so became an Air Traffic Controller in Nairobi for the rest of his service in East Africa. Although he did enjoy this particular job at RAF Eastleigh and Kenya, he had now been overseas for more than three years and his thoughts of home were now beginning to fill his mind. He had missed so much the excitement of flying and seeing new places in this vast country. So when Squadron Leader Bogle, who was a close friend, suggested they buy a car between them, Jim readily agreed. They soon found a good second hand car which was a Morris 8, four seater open tourer and Jim still remembers the cars registration no. G260. This enabled Jim to get out and about more a meet people. Unfortunately Squadron Leader Bogle was posted out, so Jim bought his share of the Morris 8 and now had the car to himself.

Jim was offered a home posting in March 1946 and was delighted but at the same time would miss the friends he made in Nairobi. He left Mombasa on the morning of the 4th March in a BOAC 'C' Class Short flying boat. The Skipper, Captain Anderson set a course for Cairo in Egypt. Jim said the journey was a beautiful one, it took him to Kisumu, Port Bell, Laropi, Malakal and then landing on the Nile at Khortoum. Then on to W Halfa, Luxor and finally arriving in Cairo on the 6th March. He spent the next few days at a transit camp on the Suez Canal, before boarding the Liner SS Almanzora for Toulon in France. From Toulon he was trained to Dieppe passing through Paris on the way. The final stage was on the ferry to Newhaven and the sight of the White Cliffs of Dover at Beachy Head had brought tears to Jim's eyes. There were so many times when he wondered if he would ever see home again and here he was, almost there. From Newhaven he boarded the train for London and on his arrival was told to report to the Air Ministry where he would be informed of his next posting. He was immediately interviewed by a Flight Lieutenant Observer like himself, who advised Jim to report to some 'God forsaken' station somewhere in England. Jim was having none of this and said, "Have a heart; can't you give me a posting in Northern Ireland? I have not been home in over three and a half years." The Flight Lieutenant lifted his phone and spoke to Air Headquarters in Northern Ireland, who said they would be happy to take Jim, and he was soon on his way. He will never forget boarding the Liverpool boat and hearing the babble of all the Northern Ireland folk. After three weeks embarkation leave, he was posted to Long Kesh near Lisburn. It was in the process of being closed down and nobody seemed to know what to do with Jim. The Commanding Officer finally decided that he should be the Fire Safety Officer. The fire section had by now been closed, there was no staff and only two Karrier fire engines. Jim was soon amusing himself driving around the station. As Fire Safety Officer he was also responsible for Maghaberry RAF Station, which was close by. So when he felt competent enough at driving the fire engine, he decided to venture out on the Main Road and pay a visit to Maghaberry.

This was all great fun, but it only lasted for two weeks as he received notice that he was being posted to RAF Aldergrove as adjutant of 518 (Meteorology) Squadron which flew Halifaxes out over the Atlantic daily, to find out barometric pressures, wind speeds, temperatures, etc, at various heights from 50 feet to 20,000 feet. These were then relayed to the met office who then formulated the next day's weather forecast. Once he was settled in to the routine, Jim arranged that he could take up residence at home and travel back and forward to Aldergrove each day. He realised that he was due any day now for demobilisation, and decided to go back to Stormont to inquire if they had any promotion organised for him. He was told that his RAF service did not entitle him to promotion and that he would have to start where he left off.

By this time his colleagues who had entered the Civil Service the same time as him, but remained civilians, had got two or three promotions. Jim complained to the principal establishment officer, that he thought this was most unfair and told him that he was now in administration in charge of a squadron, which had the strength of 300 men and women. The Principal Officer agreed with Jim, that it was unfair, as the same thing had happened to him when he returned from the 1941/18 War and said, "If I had to make the same decision again, I would have still come back to the Civil Service." Jim applied to the RAF for an 18 month extension, which was granted. He then decided that he must get his 'Fit for Flying' category back again, before deciding what he was going to do in the future. This, and the relaxed life, he was now enjoying prompted him to continue service in the Royal Air Force.

The only event of note Jim said, "As adjutant of 518 Squadron, I was involved with its disbandment and the re-forming of it as No 202 Squadron, which was an old Catalina squadron and now in service as a helicopter squadron." On the 19th February 1948, word came through that he was to be de-mobbed at RAF Weeton, with his effective day of release as the 27th May 1948. His service life had come to end after almost seven years. He had completed 1,055 flying hours in Aver Anion, Airspeed Oxford, Lockheed Lodestar, Consolidated Catalina, Short Sunderland, and DH Raphide Dakota and Lockheed Hudson aircraft

In March 1948 he became a self employed manufacturer's agent and retired in 1985. He is a member of the Aircrew Association, Northern Ireland Branch.

WING COMMANDER
CHARLES WILLIAM LINDSAY, AFC
ROYAL AIR FORCE NO. 70402
PILOT
NO. 502 ULSTER SQUADRON

Wing Commander Lindsay was born in Strokestown, near Moville, in County Rosscommom and was educated at the Royal Belfast Acacemical Institution and was a keen rugby player at the school. On leaving school in 1929, he joined the Belfast Banking Company and was employed in it's Portadown and Antrim branches.His first love was aviation and wanted to fly so he joined the Royal Air Force Volunteer Reserve in the late 1920s.

He applied and was commissioned into 502 'Ulster' Special Reserve Squadron in 1929 as a Special Reserve Pilot and obtained his Wings a short time later. For the first ten years of it's existence 502 Squadron was equipped with, Vickers Vimy and Virginias, Handley Page Hyderabads and in 1935 received a few Westland Wallace and Wapitis which were later replaced by Hawker Harts and Hinds. Charles flew in all of these types.

At the end of 1938 the Royal Air Force Volunteer Reserve was formed in Belfast and carried out their flying training with 24 Elementary & Reserve Flying Training School at Sydenham just outside Belfast. Wing Commander Lindsay (then Flight Lieutenant) was seconded along with Flight Lieutenant Sloan (Chief Flying Instructor) and Sergeant Lake to take over the school as instructors to train the new Volunteer Reserve pilots. The school in 1939 was equipped with Hawker Hinds and Tiger Moths. Shortly after the outbreak of war Wing Commander Lindsay was mobilised and posted to RAF Upavon near Salisbury in Southern England where he was to become a Bomber Instructor. In April 1941 he was then posted to the RAF College at Cranwell again as a Bomber Instructor until 1942 and later to RAF Church Lawford as Chief Flying Instructor

until the end of 1943. On the 13th March 1942 he was awarded the Air Force Cross.

Squadron Leader NH Corry, DFC AE told me a story about how he and Wing Commander Lindsay 'borrowed' an Oxford on the 16th March 1943 to fly to Sydenham in Northern Ireland to watch an Inst rugby match, flying back to Church Lawford on the 18th.

In January 1944 he was posted to America to join No 5 The British Forces Training Services at Clewiston, and became the schools Commanding Officer. He remained at Clewiston until the end of 1945 when he returned to the UK. He was then posted to the Air Ministry in Whitehall until he was demobbed in 1946. On returning home to Northern Ireland he became the Chief Flying Instructor at Shorts and later he became Officer in Charge of Flying, and Chief Air Traffic Controller, finally retiring in 1970.

On his retirement Wing Commander Lindsay moved to Carrickfergus and purchased a petrol station on the Doagh Road, Newtownabbey. He also took up oil painting which his brothers told me he was very good at. Wing Commander Lindsay, AFC died at the age of 67 at Carrickfergus and is survived by his wife, daughter and two brothers. His wife is one of the Robinson family of Robinson Cleavers, a beautiful store in Belfast, and which sadly no longer exists.

SQUADRON LEADER
THOMAS JAMES LONG, DFC & BAR
ROYAL AIR FORCE NO. 133584
PILOT
NO. 37& 608 SQUADRONS
PATHFINDER FORCE

Tom Long was born in Belfast on the 28th November 1918 and was educated at Methody College. Before deciding to join the RAFVR, he went to the local Territorial Army recruitment office and asked there for some information. He declined this as there were only units of the Search Lights and Ack Ack.

Tom was indebted to another Ulsterman Charlie McDonald (later to become Wing Commander, DSO and DFC) because when Tom first saw the advertisement in the local paper for the RAFVR in early 1939, he applied to join. He was called for an interview in April 1939 and a medical in May. The Medical Officer failed him for one month as his pulse was too high and he had a touch of conjunctivitis in one eye. In June he was called back for re-examination. Tom had been on holiday in the Isle of Man so another appointment was made for him in July. When he arrived, there was no medical test, but an air display instead so it was August before he had his medical. While waiting for the medical he met Charlie McDonald who had been recalled from the Ministry of Labour. Tom had had his pulse rate checked in the waiting room and it was still high, and it was when he was talking to Charlie about a bicycle and in the middle of the conversation he took hold of Tom's wrist and told him that his pulse was now normal and he was accepted.

He joined the RAFVR in Belfast with 25 other bods in August 1939 and this was to be the last intake before the outbreak of war. He was issued with a kit bag which had a blue band around it and inside was a full flying kit, all brand new. Before being mobilised on the 1st September 1939 he attended a few lectures at the RAFVR Headquarters Office in Saxone House in Royal Avenue.

Tom remembers well being assembled in Saxone House on Sunday 3rd September 1939 listening to the voice of Chamberlain informing the people that war had been declared. It was immediately decided by the VR boys that their mess funds would be spent on a farewell luncheon in the Grand Central Hotel. During the luncheon Wing Commander Gauntlet the VR Commanding Officer

(now well oiled) stood up and addressed the boys and said, "Ulster has its own bomber squadron and why not it's own fighter squadron. Its Motto should be 'Ruthless, Relentless and Remorseless' and on the squadron crest should be the Red Hand of Ulster, winged and armed." Tom said, "When the party was over he went outside into Royal Avenue to find that the heavens had opened, and it was pouring down with rain." He remembers walking along Donegall Place and there wasn't a soul to be seen, the whole town was deserted. It was either Queens Arcade or Riddels Arcade that had an expanding gateway across the front and he remembers seeing a poster of the Belfast Telegraph stuck on the spikes of the railings. He pulled it off and kept it as a souvenir. From then on it was just a matter of reporting daily to Saxone House for duty. They were issued with respirators.

As Tom was employed with Corporation at this time it was the company's policy to make up your Air Force pay. Some people were luckier than others as they were paid both by their employers and the RAF. It made little difference to Tom as he got more pay with VR than he did with the Corporation. He received 16 shillings and sixpence per day and on his first pay parade he received £11. He also received an extra one shilling and sixpence per day for the days that he spent in civilian clothes after he was mobilised (for fair wear and tear).

As Tom and the other 25 who joined along with him were the last entry and had no flying experience, they were the first to be posted to England. The arrived at an Initial Training Wing at St Lenards on Sea to commence their basic training. The last person to be sworn into the RAFVR in Belfast before the outbreak of war was Leslie Sharp. His father was a Romanian Jew and there had been some legal problems receiving permission to allow him to join. (The story goes that the VR commander Wing Commander Gauntlet on the morning they were mobilised reportedly said, "Sharp I am waiting no longer, hold up your right hand," and Leslie was sworn in.) As Tom was in the last intake with the VR and had little or no flying experience it was decided to post them off first.

They arrived at St Lenards-on-Sea and were billeted in the 14 storey Marine Hotel. Tom said it looked like a ship built out of concrete. Some of the rooms contained five beds while others had four and some only two. They were soon told to pick a room and a bed. Tom and Leslie Sharp were on the fourth floor of the fourteen storey building. The rooms were empty except for a bare bed, (no bedding at all). They dumped their suitcases on the beds and went on parade. They were taken down into the basement of the hotel and were issued with two canvas bags. One large one and one small one. They were then taken into another room where there was a heap of straw and were told to fill the two bags up with the straw. The large one was known as a 'polyass' (mattress) and the smaller one which was cylindrical in shape was the pillow and was as rough as sandpaper. There were no sheets issued just a few blankets.

In each 'block' were four squadrons and each squadron had four 'Flights'. Each Flight had approximately 50 bods, so there were at least 1,000 bods in the apartments at any time. Tom and Leslie were in 'D' Flight along with another Ulsterman Ken Inskip who was detailed as the Flight's Commander. Ken had previously been in the army and was responsible for drilling the Flight. There was to Piers on the sea front, one was at Hastings and the other at St Lenards-on-Sea. They both had been taken over by the RAF for lectures. On one of the piers was a huge ballroom where they held lectures for the whole squadron on armament and navigation and the signals lectures were held in a local church hall.

Tom told me, "Every time I watch the TV series 'Dads Army', 'Menace on the Beach' it reminds me of my time at St Lenards-on-Sea with the mine pickets."

He remembers his very first lecture was given by a 1st Class Warrant Officer (in those days there were two classes of Warrant Officer). He lectured them on various ranks within the RAF and the respect that you should pay each one. "For instance," he said, "the Warrant Officer 2nd Class had a brass coat of arms on his sleeve where as the 1st Class Warrant Officer had a cloth coat of arms sewn onto his sleeve and they both wore the same shirts and uniforms as officers. They were to be highly respected but were not saluted." He also remembers while on parade one day the instructor had given them 'right dress' and then took himself off somewhere. Tom had been standing with his right arm up for quite causing him to faint. He was taken to the MO and given the rest of the day off. Tom was also given lectures on the 'Kings Regulations' and he remembers being told that while it

was an offence to be drunk and unfit for duty, you did not have to be disorderly (that was for civilians). Another thing which that was forbidden was the keeping of a diary or owning a camera. Air Commodore Critchley (was Brigadier Critchley) was on a visit to the ITW at St Lenards-on-Sea one evening when he asked to inspect the sentries. Tom had been on guard duty at the link trainer school down on the sea front when the Air Commodore stopped and asked him. "What are you doing in the Air Force?" Tom replied that he was a Pilot under-training. The Air Commodore said, "Surely Pilot's under-training are Sergeants?" Tom said, "Yes Sir, I am a Sergeant but there wasn't enough sergeant stripes to go round at the time. I was given one pair but I am wearing them under my Greatcoat." This was Tom's first encounter with a 'Brass Hat'. The Warrant Officer who had been lecturing them had been in Belfast at one time when he was in the Navy, (all of those people who had been in charge of the RAFVR had been themselves Reservists). He had been entertained in the City Hall in Belfast which he remembered was a magnificent building and what impressed him was that the entire ships crew were treated to a meal in the City Hall as everywhere else they had visited, officers only were treated.

They course at the ITW was only supposed to last for eight weeks but as the winter of 1938/39 had been a particularly severe one they were still there at Christmas. When they were being issued with their Christmas leave passes, Herbert Hanny who was from Bangor in County Down (and who had nice but cheeky manner) and could get away with it, was in the squadron office when his leave came through. They were all granted seven days leave but he pointed out that the English chaps will get a full seven days and I will only get five as it takes one day to get home by boat and a day to get back. The Warrant Officer told Hannay to leave it with him and he would see what he could do. The result was that the Ulster boys got two days 'travelling time' and that was established from then on for anyone travelling to and from Northern Ireland. (So it was Hannay from Bangor who had the 'cheek' to speak up in the squadron office who got this.) They had to remain at the St Lenards-on-Sea ITW until April and one of the good things about it was it gave the Royal Air Force time to install the 'link trainers'. These were visual link trainers as links were designed for blind flying. The link trainers were set up in a circular rooms with a panorama view around the walls. The scenery on the walls was varied as part it you did not have a horizon. This meant that the bods on the ITW course received link training before they went on Elementary Flying Training. In April 1940, nineteen of the original Ulstermen were posted to White Waltham where they were to start their Elementary Flying.

Tom told me when he was at White Waltham a Wellington landed, (probably someone coming for lunch). This was the biggest aircraft that he had seen and well remembers talking to the Wimpeys Rear

Gunner who was minding the aircraft while the officers were away in the mess. The rear gunner was an LAC and had a 'brass winged bullet' on his sleeve. Tom thought to himself, now that's the aircraft I want to fly. In April 1941, Tom was posted out to the Middle East. He flew out to Egypt with new Wellington 1Cs but on his arrival these were taken for other duties and he went to a Middle East 'pool' to await a posting. After a week or so he was posted out Greece (Menidi and Paramythia) where he joined 37 Squadron. The squadron was equipped with the Vickers Wellington. When they had to leave Greece they went to Egypt operating from Cairo West, Abu Suier and El -Daba.

The invasion of Crete had started and he was sent there on the first night. He told me that there were no maps of Crete available, they did not know how high the mountains were, and his instructions were 'avoid them'. "It was pitch black that night and we were supposed to attack Milme airfield and really we had as much chance of finding the airfield as finding a needle in a haystack." Tom explained to me, "When you were posted out to the Middle East, this usually meant a five year posting. The flying time to Egypt was about six hours but it took your documents six months to follow you." He had finished his tour with 37 Squadron and was wondering what would happen to him (some fellows were sent up to desert airfields to be Airfield Controllers and the odd one was lucky enough to be sent down to South Africa on Flying Boats. Tom however was posted back to the UK because of the expansion of the Operational Training Units (OTU) where they needed people with operational experience. He got down as far as Durban where he tried to hitch a lift on the liner Stratheden but was 'turfed off'. He eventually came back on a 9,000 ton cargo boat called the Empire Pride. Because she could reach a speed of 20 knots she was allowed to travel back on her own unescorted. He arrived back in the UK in January 1942, still a Sergeant and discovered his contemporaries were now Flight Sergeants. The papers that were to notify Tom of his promotion had taken six months to reach him. In July 1942 he received notification that he had been promoted to Flight Sergeant and 'mentioned in Despatches' for Distinguished Service.

His pay was back dated for fifteen months. He remembers well going into a post office to deposit all his back pay when the little old post mistress (probably about forty) asked him, "Where did you get all this, did you rob a bank?" Tom replied, "No mam, it was a post office." His Flight Sergeants Crown had just arrived but he never got time to wear it as he received another warrant advising him that he was now a Warrant Officer 1 and again received six months back pay. He had just been measured for his Warrant Officers uniform but before he could wear it, his commission had come through.

He had been commissioned for three months which you had to do on probation when he was promoted to Flight Lieutenant. So he had risen from Sergeant to Flight Lieutenant in a very short space of time. Tom had been an instructor at the OTU for two and a half years and he told me that if you were any use at all as an instructor it was virtually impossible to get away from it. He thought after two and a half years he had done enough. It was now 1944, so he applied to the unit's Commanding Officer requesting a transfer back onto operations. The Commanding Officer sent for Tom and said, "You have served us well here, we would like to keep you, but I can't very well stand in your way. I will release you just as soon as a replacement can be found to take your place."

Tom's replacement came in two weeks, another Flight Lieutenant. Tom met up with him for a chat and he told Tom that he had just come from a 'dirty' Squadron. Tom asked him, "What was a dirty squadron?" He explained to Tom that a Mosquito could climb so high and so fast that if a weather front was between them and Germany, they could climb over it, when the 'heavies' would have to go through it, (making them subject to icing and lightning etc.). "If the weather was bad we could be there and back when the 'heavies' would only have arrived over the target. The result was that we could operate in all sorts of 'dirty' weather, and that is how we got the name 'dirty' squadron."

When Tom's posting came through, he was sent to No 608 Squadron which had just been reformed at Downham Market and was to become part of No 8 Group's Pathfinder Force Light Night Striking Force. The squadron was equipped initially with Mk.XXs Mosquitoes between August 1944 and April 1945, Mk XXVs between October 1944 and April 1945 and Mk XVIs between March and August 1945. The squadron flew 1,726 operations between 5th August 1944 and 3rd May 1945, mostly against principal German industrial centres and ports, including Berlin, Frankfurt, Hanover, Essen, Stuttgart, Nuremburg, Hamburg, Emden and Kiel.

It was decided at a high level in Bomber Command to extend the light night striking force because they were finding that a Mosquito crew of two could carry a 4,000lb bomb and was far more economical than a Lancaster battling for hours and they could also do the job in half the time with fewer casualties.

Tom's story

"The Light Night Striking Force was part of 8 Group Pathfinder Force and was a different type of squadron to others. There were squadrons of Oboe markers who had the very latest equipment and could mark targets accurately. They were used mainly for marking targets for the heavies (Lancaster, Halifax and Stirlings) or for the light night striking force. Outside their range you would have to rely on H2s and Marker squadrons. They could turn out 120 aircraft on any one night, each aircraft could carry nearly two tons of high explosives and this was considered 'a very good raid'. "I carried out two daylight raids with the squadron the rest were all at night. The first daylight was when the Allied forces were crossing the

Rhine at a place called Wessel. The 2nd Tactical Air Force boys were strafing some 30,000 Germans when fog came down and they could not see. Our squadron was called in to bomb the Germans through the fog using Oboe. The second daylight raid was picking out the few remaining oil refineries still operating at Duisberg.

"On another raid I was flying a reserve aircraft as mine was in for servicing. The reserve aircraft was 'J' for Johnny. Just after take off the revs on the starboard engine went right off the clock. The whine coming from the engine was deafening as the prop had 'run away'. I managed to feather the prop right away and went haring across fields and hedges. I decided to open the throttles on the starboard engine again and climbed to 300ft and feather it again. I landed safely with a full load of fuel and bombs. I taxied up alongside another reserve aircraft, my Navigator and I gathered up all our bits and pieces and scrambled into the second aircraft. The Commanding Officer came on the scene to see what was going on but this time we had started both Merlins and the Commanding Officer gave us the thumbs up. I took off and caught up with the rest of the squadron and successfully marked the target and returned safely. On my return the ground crew told me that they had watched my take off over the hedges at the end of the runway trailing smoke. They all put their hands over their ears and dived for cover awaiting a loud explosion.

"Some nights we would have gone out to bomb Berlin, other nights we would go out 'spoofing'. Spoofing was when we would go out with the main force. I would be carrying bombs and target indicators, my Navigator would have a great bag of 'window' which he would let go like mad with the main force and then we would branch off to our target. When we would arrive over the target I would drop a target indicator, do a circuit and then bomb the marker and head for home. Meanwhile the main force would be off somewhere else doing another spoof raid.

"Another type of raid that I would do was a 'window opener', in other words if Cologne was the target for the main force that night. I would fly over the target dropping window and under the blanket of window the Pathfinders would go in and drop blind markers and visual markers and blind illuminators and visual illuminators and so on. All that would go on under the cover of window. Then the main force target indicators would go down and I would bomb on them. I would have to hang around making sure the target was hit and then head off for home.

"On a raid to Schwibrucken one night I was the first aircraft over the target. I had gone on in alone 'windowing'. I then had to go in and bomb on the target indicators and circle the target for 20 minutes observing what was developing and then fly off home with the report (special duties) on the operation.

"As the war went on more and more we were being used for battering Berlin. They stopped sending the heavies to Berlin because they could turn out 120 Mosquitoes a night. I visited Berlin 24 times. When I used to go home on leave, people in the street knew I was in Bomber Command and always asked the question 'Have you ever been to Berlin?' I would reply, 'No I have never been to Berlin'. I made my first trip to Berlin on October 6th 1944 and from that day to this no one has asked me have you ever been to Berlin."

The 16th April 1945 was the day the last raid of the war and that was the last time Tom flew a Mosquito. On one of the last three heavy raids to Keil one of Tom's Flight Commanders was missing. Tom had met him at the Hastings ITW in September 1939. His surname was Few. Tom said, "You had the 'First of the Few' and when I had completed my last raid to Berlin I was given some end of tour leave. When I returned the war was over and I met Charlie Lockier in the mess and asked him what had been happening when I was away. 'Well.' he said, 'We have had the 'Last of the Few'."

One of Tom's friends was an Oboe marker, his name was Robert Anthony Maurice Palmer and had been on the same Wellington conversion course with Tom back in 1940. He had been the Pilot of a Lancaster that had been fitted with Oboe and was acting as lead aircraft in a daylight formation raid at the end of the war when German fighters where no longer considered a threat. On his run in to mark the target he was hit by flak. the Lancaster was on fire, but he bravely continued his run in to mark the target. Enemy aircraft now attacked his aircraft in force. He was determined to complete his run and provide an accurate and easily seen aiming point for the other bombers. His aircraft was last seen spiralling down in flames and all onboard were killed. Such as the strength of the opposition that night, half of his formation failed to return. He was awarded the Victoria Cross for his bravery.

Pathfinder Bennett was reported to have said, "There would be no live Victoria Cross holders in 8 Group Path Finder Force."

Tom told me of a terrible accident one night involving a Wellington which had stalled above the airfield (it had been aborting a landing). The Pilot was trying a go around again and he was a small and lightly made up fellow. The Wellington controls needed tremendous pressure on the stick when the flaps are down. The aircraft crashed onto the runway with a terrible explosion. Tom was in the mess at the time and had hurried out to see what had happened. He was running across to the crashed Wellington with the Commanding Officer when he found a body about 100 yards from the aircraft, it was the bomb aimed. Tom stopped with him but the commanding officer said, "Leave him Tom, he is dead." They both ran on to the burning aircraft with the crew still inside. The nose of the Wellington had been wiped away and the Pilot was still strapped to his seat which was attached to the bulkhead, and all he had to do was pull the pin and jump down. The fellow who was beside him was not strapped in and was found over a hundred yards away. The Navigator was trapped but the fire crews managed to get him out alive. The Wireless Operator and Rear Gunner were both killed as the Wellington's fuselage had folded inwards on impact.

Tom was awarded the Distinguished Flying Cross on 16th February 1945 for completing 50 operations and a bar to the DFC on 17th July 1945 for completing 87 operations. He was also put forward for a Distinguished Flying Medal in 1941 but got a 'Mention in Despatches' instead for Distinguished Service.

His father was recommended for the Distinguished Conduct Medal in July 1916. When he had got to safety himself, he discovered that an officer from his company was missing. He went out again under fire into no man's land and found the officer seriously injured. He managed to carry him back under heavy shell and machine gun fire to his own lines. Unfortunately the officer died. Now as the officer was the one who recorded the award of the DCM to Mr Long, it was not honoured from a dying man.

When he was demobbed from the RAF he returned home to Northern Ireland and went to Queens University were he studied teacher training. Then began a career as a teacher which he finished as the principal of Whiteabbey Primary School. Tom is a member of the Air Crew Association Northern Ireland Branch.

SERGEANT
JH LOWRY
ROYAL AIR FORCE NO. 1027413
AIR GUNNER
NO. 60 OTU

KILLED IN ACTION 14TH JANUARY 1942

Sergeant John Havergal Lowry, son of William and Ellen Lowry was born in Rosetta Parade in Belfast on August 18th 1921 and was educated at Ravenscroft Public Elementary School and later at Bennett College in England. Before joining the Royal Air Force, he was employed in his fathers shoe and leather business.

Harvey as liked to be called by his friends joined the RAF in Belfast in mid 1940 and was selected to train as an air gunner. He was posted to No 10 Air Gunnery School at Castle Kennedy near Stranraer in Scotland. The school opened in 1941 and was first occupied by the Central Gunnery School, although most of his air gunnery training had to be carried out at nearby West Freugh because of water logging. No 10 AGS was formed there in 1941 and was equipped with Boulton Paul Defiants and Westland Lysanders. Harvey would have preferred to have been in bombers but as his eyesight was excellent at night he was singled out for night fighters. But he was very happy to have the honour anyway. He successfully passed the Gunnery course and was awarded his AG Brevet. Harvey often prayed in his turret at night for guidance to he who ruled the skies. In late 1941 Harvey was posted to No 60 Operational Training Unit at East Fortune near Haddington in Scotland to start his operational training on Defiants and Bristol Blenheims.

On the night of 14th January 1941, Harvey and his pilot Sergeant Drinkwater were carrying out high altitude tests in their aircraft when they were lost over the sea. They reported thick cloud, and were told by wireless to keep below it. The last time they spoke was when they were ten miles from the aerodrome. It was suggested then that their aircraft probably crashed into the sea at the mouth of the Firth of Fourth. Harvey is remembered on the Runnymede Memorial.

Sergeant Lowry's father received a letter three days after his death and it reads:

Royal Air Force Station
East Fortune
East Lothian
Scotland

17th January 1941

Dear Mt Lowry,

As your late son's Commanding Officer I write to you to try and express some of the sympathy we feel here for you in your losses. As I expect you know, your son with his Pilot, Sergeant Drinkwater were nearing the end of their training here which they had carried out with great success and I feel certain that they would have made a most active pair if they could have reached an Operations Squadrons.

On the night in question they were to have carried out an altitude climb but as they reported a thick layer of cloud they were told by wireless to keep below it and near the aerodrome. They were in constant conversation with our control by wireless and we know that they were just over the coast and within 10 miles of the aerodrome when they last spoke to us. They were then asked a question which they did not answer so I think we can be fairly certain of the time of the mishap, whatever it was. We have been able to find no trace of them or the aircraft so I think it is safe to presume that they went into the sea at the mouth of the Firth of Forth. As to the cause of the accident, we know nothing, but had it been engine failure I feel certain that they would have told us by wireless of it, and I think that there is not much doubt that your son's Pilot lost his sense of horizon in the darkness, and thus lost control of the aeroplane which must have dived into the sea.

Sergeant Drinkwater's next of kin is his mother, Mrs M Drinkwater, 127 Harding Bldv, Toronto, and Ontario, Canada. I thought you might like to write to her. As she lives in Canada, I am forbidden myself by regulations to write to her.

If there is anything further I can do for you or you would like to know, please do not hesitate in telling me. Your son's effects are returned by us to the

Permanent Committee of Adjustment who will wind up his estate and communicate direct with you.

Signed
Group Captain, Commanding RAF Station
East Fortune

FLYING OFFICER
EDWARD LUFF
ROYAL AIR FORCE NO. 47914
WIRELESS OPERATOR/AIR GUNNER
NO. 156 SQUADRON
PATHFINDER FORCE

KILLED IN ACTION 5TH MARCH 1943

Edward Luff was born in Belfast in 1917 and was educated at St Mary's Church of Ireland Primary School on the Crumlin Road. He joined the Royal Air Force in 1941 and later completed his Wireless Operator's training at the Royal Air Force College, Cranwell in Lincolnshire. On completion of his training, he was posted to No 156 Squadron at Warboys in Huntingdonshire. Edward took off on his 50th operation, on the 5th March 1943, his aircraft failed to return.

Brief history of 156 Squadron

No 156 Squadron was formed in October 1918 in England, and for some reason was disbanded a few weeks later. It was reformed in February 1942 at Alconbury as a medium bomber squadron where it was equipped with the Vickers Wellington Mk1C's, and attached to No 3 Group. When the Pathfinder Force was formed in August 1942, 156 Squadron was one of the four squadrons selected to form the ember of the new force.

The squadron remained as part of the Pathfinder Force until the end of the war, first flying Wellingtons and then the Avro Lancaster. When it finished operations at the end of the war the squadron marked the dropping zones at Rotterdam and The Hague for the bombers engaged in dropping food supplies to the starving Dutch people. It also was involved in the repatriation of British ex-Prisoners of war back to the UK. No 156 Squadron was finally disbanded in September 1945.

The following are copies of four of Pilot Officer Luff's operations taken from the squadron's operational record book.

February 14th 1943   Lancaster W.4854. Target Milan. Take off 1915 hrs. Landed 0255 hrs.

Crew
Squadron Leader SG Hookway
Flight Sergeant FW Hart
Flying Officer E Luff
Sergeant EP Alsop
Flying Officer RD Turk
Sergeant WH Clark
Sergeant D Heap

Details of Flight

Target Milan. Bright moon and good visibility. Primary target attacked at 2239 hrs from 10,000ft, visually by light of fires. Built up area and park clearly identified. Bombs were not seen to explode but believed to have fallen in built up area around aiming point, where many fires were seen spreading. Own illuminator flares were not dropped, as moonlight was sufficient. Moderate flak with about 40 S/L's (search lights) around the town. One photo attempted. Bomb load: 1 x 4 flares red, 2 x T.I red, 1 x 4, 000HC, 9 x 4 flares white.

February 28th 1943 Lancaster LM304. Target St Nazaire. Take off 1835. Landed 2345 hrs

Crew
Squadron Leader SG Hookway, DFC
Flight Sergeant FW Hart, DFM
Flying Officer E Luff
Sergeant EB Alsop
Flying Officer RD Turk
Sergeant WH Clark
Sergeant D Heap, DFM

Details of flight

Target St Nazaire. Ran up to target in nil cloud, bomb sight U/S. Bombed at 2111 hrs from 11,000ft on green T.I's. 4,000lb bomb burst in centre of green T.I's and another seen to burst on aiming point. Moderate heavy and a little light flak. Smoke screen seen in operation. About 15 to 20 S/L's (search lights) in cone at Wannes at

2058 hrs. Dummy seen in operation at Lannion. One photo attempted. Bomb load 4 x T.I. green, 1 x 4,000lb, 8 x 90 incendiaries.

March 3rd 1943   Lancaster LM304. Target Hamburg. Take off 1940 hrs. Landed 2400 hrs.

Crew
Squadron Leader SG Hookway, DFC
Squadron Leader JR White
Flight Sergeant FW Hart, DFM
Flying Officer E Luff
Sergeant EB Alsop
Flying Officer RD Turk
Sergeant WH Clark
Sergeant D Heap, DFM

Details of flight

Target Hamburg. Nil cloud, good visibility. Pinpointed river on run in and T.I. red, and bombed target at 2116 hrs from 18,000ft. Bombs and T.I green fell alongside red T.I's already on the ground. Good fires were seen when our aircraft was 48/50 miles away, and glow still seen as aircraft crossed the coast. Some heavy and slight light flak in target area. Over Dremer.orde ???? (this word was very faint on ORB) at 2125 hrs an aircraft seen alight in the air and crashed to the ground. One photo attempted. Bomb load 2 x T.I. white, 1 x T.I. yellow, 2 x T.I. green, 1X 4,000, 48 x 30 incendiaries.

On the 5th March 1943 Lancaster Serial No LM304, Code GT-J took off from RAF Station Warboys at 1908 hrs. Its target was the Krupps Work in the City of Essen. It failed to return. 442 aircraft from Bomber Command took off that night, 56 failed to return.

The crew of Lancaster GT-J were
Squadron Leader SG Hookway, DFC
Sergeant EB Alsop
Pilot Officer FW Hart, DFM
Flying Officer RD Turk
Flying Officer E Luff
Sergeant D Heap, DFM
Sergeant WH Clark

Flying Officer Luff's aircraft failed to return from this operation. Nothing was heard from it after take off. Its bomb load was 1 x T.I yellow, 2 x T.I. green, 1 x 4,000 HC, 9 x 8 x 30 incendiaries.

His aircraft crashed near Monchengladbach where all of the crew were laid to rest in the Stadfriehof. Their graves are now in Rheinberg War Cemetery. Grave 2.D.C.

FLIGHT LIEUTENANT
WILFRED RONALD MAITLAND, DFC
ROYAL AIR FORCE NO. 111680
NAVIGATOR
NO. 57 AND 156 SQUADRONS
KILLED IN ACTION 30TH MAY 1942

Wilfred Ronald Maitland was born in Dundrum, County Down, in 1920 and was educated at the Blue Coat School in Dublin and his higher education was completed at Campbell College in Belfast. He later moved to Tynan in County Armagh. On leaving Campbell, he joined the Royal Air Force in 1939/40 and served as a Sergeant Navigator before being commissioned.

Flight Lieutenant Maitland was awarded the Distinguished Flying Cross on the 17th May 1942 and his Citation reads:

> This officer has completed 32 operations with 57 Squadron before joining No 156 squadron, with which he acted as Bombing Leader for a period of six months. At all times he pressed home his attacks with great vigour and set a very high example to the navigators under his Instruction. His sorties included attacks on most of the important enemy targets.

Flight Lieutenant Maitland's last operation of the war was with 156 Squadron on the 30th May 1942. He was Navigator on Wellington Mk111, Serial No X3706, Code GT-C. Their target was the Gnome & Rhone factory in France. Unfortunately the records show that little damage was done to the factory that night. Their Wellington took off from Alconbury at 0027 hrs on the 30th May and crashed at Dugny on the northern outskirts of Paris, and some 6 km north West of Bobigny. Flight Lieutenant Maitland and the crew were all killed and were initially buried at Dugny, but after the had war ended, their remains were re-interred in Viroflay New Communal Cemetery.

The Crew
Wing Commander PGR Heath
Sergeant WG Thompson
Flight Lieutenant WR Maitland
Sergeant DKN Scott
Sergeant FG Brown
Flight Lieutenant PA Dalton

SQUADRON LEADER
JAMES YOUNG MALLEY, DSO* DFC*
ROYAL AIR FORCE NO. 88695
MASTER BOMBER AND MASTER NAVIGATOR
NO. 139, 149,160 AND 178 SQUADRONS

Squadron Leader James Mally, known to all as Jim, was born in 1917 in the County Tyrone Village of Auchnacloy, which was situated close to the border county of Monaghan in the Irish Republic.

He was educated, and boarded, at the Royal School in Dungannon, situated some 15 miles along winding country lanes from his home village. Ever the keen sports enthusiast, he played for the firsts in both rugby and cricket. Jim had planned to take a Law Degree but never resumed his studies. His academic record is not known and he left school in 1935 to join the Civil Service as a State Duty Officer. It is understood that this is what would today be termed a Customs Officer. With the return of peace, and subsequent to his distinguished Wartime service with the Royal Air Force, he rejoined the civil service in 1947, and rose to a senior post with the responsibility of training others. He remained in this post until 1959 when he was appointed Principal Secretary to the Northern Ireland Prime Minister Terence O'Neill a post he held until 1970. Jim was also a trustee of the Ulster American Folk Park in County Tyrone and was on the Council of the Churchill Trust from 1974 -1991. He was honoured to be awarded a Churchill Fellowship becoming only the third recipient after Dick Pim and Terence O'Neill. In 1985 Jim was appointed Deputy Lieutenant of Belfast.

On his retirement from the Churchill Trust, Jim was invited to attend the Guildhall in London, where Her Majesty the Queen, President of the Trust, presented him with a painting of Sir Winston Churchill.

The war years

Jim joined the Royal Air Force Volunteer Reserve as an Air Observer at the Clifton Street recruiting centre, Belfast on the Wednesday 3rd January 1940. At the age of 22 he made his way to the receiving centre at Cardington before undergoing square bashing rigors at Morecambe, en route to Initial Training at No 5 Initial Training Wing at Hastings, which was later moved to Torquay. This

initial training lasted between January 1940 until June 1940. Towards the end of June 1940 Jim was posted to No 11 Air Observers and Navigators School at Hamble to commence his navigational training. Hamble was equipped with the Avro Anson where Jim had his first air experience flight on Friday 5th July in Anson N9735 under the watchful eye of a Pilot Officer Mack.

On Tuesday 9th July 1940 his navigational training started in earnest when on the this day he took to the air in Anson N5379 and his instructor for the course was to be a Flight Lieutenant Rose. Training towards first Navigator continued through the summer and into early autumn when the school had moved to Watchfield, where Jim passed out successfully with a 79% rating in early October.

It is interesting to note that Jim arrived at Hamble in the last days of June ready to commence his course. At the same time another subject of this book, Ray Esler, ended his training at Hamble. The two would become leading Navigators and would parallel each other in the following years. Both served with No 149 Squadron at Mildenhall and, in the three months whilst stationed there together, would fly some of the same raids. Later both would also join Pathfinding Mosquito Squadrons and serve from airfields almost side by side.

Jim was then posted to No 8 Bombing and Gunnery School at Evanton where he made his first flight on Saturday 12th October, flying in Harrow 6947 as a first Navigator to Sergeant Morrison. He familiarised himself with the area prior to commencing bomb aiming training on Wednesday 23rd October, under a Sergeant Ball in Fairey Battle 5218. The course proceeded through until December, the only item of note in Jim's log being the number of pilots with unpronounceable Polish names (try Krzvrick, Kontowtt, and Prsylylak over the intercom). His gunnery course ended with a 70% pass and the comment, 'intelligent but inclined to be slow practically.' 70% also being obtained on the bombing course with the comment, 'average knowledge and very keen worker.'

With the basics now completed Jim found himself on the last lap before going operational when he was posted to No 15 Operational Training Unit at Harwell in December.

He was given some leave and on returning to Harwell he flew 10 times as second Navigator in an Anson Between the 4th and 15th February 1941. On Friday 21st February he flew with Squadron Leader Grant as First Navigator. For the rest of his service career he would never relinquish that position and, in the 127 operations that were to follow, would also fly as Squadron Navigation Officer, Squadron Operations Officer and Master Bomber. On Friday 14th March 1941 Jim had his last Anson flight prior to experiencing his first flight in a Wellington, R1010 that was Captained by a Sergeant Penekett for a three-hour air firing practice.

He continued through until the 20th of t he month when he had his second flight, again in R1010, with the then Pilot Officer Foreman, with whom he would carry our 29 of his 34 operations with No 149 Squadron. Towards the end of March, Jim was posted to the East Anglian base of Mildenhall, where he flew his first operation on Monday 7th April, a 'Nickel' raid to Northern France in Wellington 1325 that was captained by Flight Lieutenant Gilbert. His logbook shows the route taken was, Base to Beachy Head, Le Touquet, Oeinze, Dammartin, Buchy, Fe Camp, Shoreham, and Base. Their flight time was 4hrs.30mins.

It could have been this flight was made from 15 OTU, Wellington R1325 being used throughout March during Jim's operational training. Although it may have been temporary transferred to 149 Squadron, neither it or Flight Lieutenant Gilbert are referred to again.

No. 149 Squadron, Royal Flying Corps, was formed at Yapton in Sussex on Sunday 3rd March 1918 as a night bomber squadron and three months later went to France equipped with FE 2b's. After the Armistice No 149 was the FE Squadron chosen to accompany the Army of occupation into Germany. It returned to the UK in March 1919, and was later disbanded at Tallaght, County Dublin, Ireland the following August. The Squadron reformed at RAF Station Mildenhall in 1937 equipped with Heyfords and early in 1939 received its Wellingtons. In the Monday 4th September 1939 the squadron shared with No 9 Squadron the distinction of making the RAF's second bombing raid of the war. The squadron played a prominent part in the war carrying out an early offensive against Germany, Italy and enemy occupied territory. It took part in the first 1,000 bomber raid, and the raid against the German V-weapons experimental station at Peenemunde. In April 1945 it dropped food to the starving people of Holland and after Germany had surrendered, ferried many ex-POW's back to the UK from Europe.

Jim's first true operation with his new squadron was to Breat on Sunday 23rd February to attack the Scharnhorst and Gneisenau in the harbour. The aircraft was Captained by the officer commanding 'A' Flight Squadron Leader James, thereafter Jim flew mostly with Pilot Officer Foreman for the rest of his time with the squadron. The crew came from different places, one Irish, one Welsh, on Scottish and two English men, (the Captain Doug Foreman and the Rear Gunner were the two English men) and as a crew they were very happy and close friends. The aircraft that was used on the Brest raid was in fact Wellington R1343 that was 'F' for Freddie, the one used to make the popular wartime film "Target for Tonight". Jim told me that he had heard years later on the radio that 'F' for Freddie had gone to an honourable retirement. The 'honourable retirement' he said, was that 'F' for Freddie crash landed into a bombing range just seven or eight miles away from Mildenhall when we were held up coming back from Brest and was completely written off.

(It is unfortunate that Jim does not go into any detail in his log. The majority of these raids were to the very heart of Germany to the usual well defended targets and it is almost certain that not all were without some sort of problem.)

Of note in this apparently unremarkable period were three flights that would prove the endurance of the Wimpy. Two were to Stettin, or to correct Szczecin, in Poland. Each of these exceeded nine hours and the third was to Genoa and exceeded ten hours. In September 1941 Jim qualified as an astro navigator.

Jim had Completed 35 operations with 149 Squadron before his last flight that was to Berlin on the Friday/Saturday 7th/8th November 1941 with newly promoted Flight Lieutenant Foreman.

The sortie to Berlin took 7hrs.35mins and in what appears to be a horrendous night, Jim notes in his log that half of the attacking force of 74 bombers were lost. Other targets visited during his time with 149 Squadron were Hamburg, Ruhr, Cologne, Keil, Bremen, Dusseldorf, Karlsrule, Frankfurt, Hanover, Mannheim, Stettin, and Genoa.

Jim left RAF Midlenhall in early November at the end of his first tour and was awarded the first of his two DFC's on the 21st of the Month. His next posting was as Instructor, initially with No 40 Squadron at Alconbury for one month and then on to 15 OTU at Mount Farm and latterly at Harwell, where, on the Sunday 30th May 1942 he took part in a raid that would shape the bombing offensive for the rest of the war, and indeed for many years to come. This was the first of the 1,000 bomber raids, Cologne being the target. Two days later on the first day of June saw the second such raid. In both cases Jim was in Wellington 1023 with Flight Lieutenant Kelly to Cologne and Flight Lieutenant Sanderson to Essen. Although history judges the Cologne raid as a failure in terms of it's stated aim - the total destruction of a major city - the damage inflicted was considerable.

More importantly was the aim of Air Chief Marshall 'Bomber Harris', the head of Bomber Command. He fervently believed that strategic bombing was the way forward for this crews and, with the benefit of hindsight, it is difficult to argue that he was wrong. The story of the 1,000 bomber raid on Cologne is well documented and details the colossal effort which went into the raid which put up 1,046 assorted aircraft from no less that 37 squadrons and 15 operation training units, jointly operating from over 50 RAF station. Each crew briefing in dozens of locations throughout the country ended with a personal message from Harris as follows:

"The force of which you form a part tonight is at least twice the size and has more than four times the carrying capacity of the largest air force ever before concentrated on one objective. You have an opportunity, therefore, to strike a blow at the enemy which will resound, not only throughout Germany, but throughout the world. In your hands lie the means of destroying a major part of the resources by which the enemy's war effort is maintained. It depends, however, upon each individual crew, whether full concentration is achieved. Press home your attack to your precise objective with the utmost determination and resolution in the foreknowledge that, if you individually succeed, the most shattering and devastating blow will have been delivered against the very vitals of the enemy. Let him have it, right on the chin."

Immediately after the raid on Essen Jim was posted to 1653 Conversion Unit at Burn where he was to convert to the B-24 Consolidated Liberator bomber. It is very possible that this conversion actually commenced at Harwell as Jim's log shows him arriving at Burn on the 14th June, as Navigator to Squadron Leader S Clark, the officer commanding 'A; Flight, 1653 CU. For the rest of his brief stay at Burn he was teamed up with Pilot Officer Tannahill, with whom he would fly operationally on many occasions. The pair arrived at 1445 Conversion Unit that was based at Lyneham, early July 1943 to prepare for the long overseas haul to St Jean in Palestine to join 159 Squadron, and later to 160 Squadron.

No 159 Squadron was formed at Molesworth in Huntingdonshire on Friday 2nd January 1942, as a Liberator heavy - bomber unit for eventual transfer to the Middle East. Operating against targets in North Africa, Sicily, Southern Greece and the Mediterranean Sea. In November 1942 the Squadron began operations against the Japanese in Burma were it stayed until VJ Day.

They left Lyneham at 0800 hrs on the morning of Monday 15th July in Liberator MK11 and set course for Palestine arriving the next day. The journey that was to take them to St Jean in Palestine was flown operationally via Gibraltar and Fayid (Egypt}, the trip taking 22 flying hours. At 1500 hrs on Wednesday 17th July, Jim and Flying Officer Tannahill took off from their base in Liberator AL548 for their first sortie to Crete, flying time 8hrs.50mins. On July 29th. August 2nd, 6th and 9th they visited Tobruk and bombed the hell out of Field Marshal Rommels' Afrika Corps.

In the course of his 38 operations tour with 159 Squadron, Jim flew mainly with Tannahill and as well as Crete and Tobruk visited Benghazi, shipping strike at Suda Bay, Maleme. Tripoli, Naples, Sousse, Tunis, Heraklion, and Messina.

Jim was transferred to 178 Squadron that was based at Ghemines in February 1943 and carried out his last operation with the squadron on Wednesday 16th June with a raid to Bari in Liberator AL636 'F' which was Captained by Squadron Leader Pearson. On his transfer to 178 Squadron, he was appointed Squadron Navigation Officer and then Squadron Operations Officer. In this period he saw less of Tannihill, usually flying with either the Commanding Officer or a Flight Commander in the lead aircraft. In mid-March he was assessed by the Commanding Officer, Wing Commander McNair, with whom he had flown, as 'above the average as Navigator and Bomb Aimer' and 'a good squadron Navigation Officer'.

On leaving the squadron in mid-June the new Commanding Officer, Wing Commander McKay with whom he also had flown, assessed him as 'above the average as Navigator and Bomb Aimer' and 'handled squadron Navigation and Operations Officer duties in a most efficient manner'.

Since leaving the UK the previous July, Jim had added 38 operations to complete his second tour and take his total to 74. On Friday 23rd July 1943 he was awarded a well earned Bar to his DFC. Having survived this considerable number of very varied operations he must surely have enjoyed the sheer luxury of the trip back to the UK. Travelling first class in a BOAC Empire Flying Boat that was complete with beds. However, with a route that took him from Cairo to Khartoum to Stanleyville to Leopoldville to Lagos to Bathurst and to Lisbon, and which lasted for 61 flying hours over eight days. He was probable thankful for the comfort. Even the final leg from Lisbon to Bristol must have seemed like an uncomfortable seven hours in a lowly DC3. After a months well earned leave, Jim was promoted to Squadron Leader and took up his next posting as an instructor in charge of navigational training at 83 Operational Training Unit at Childs Ercall, known to most as RAF Peplow, near the Shropshire market town of Whitchurch. Here he was to 'fly a desk', probably screened, in his more management based role and flew on only eight occasions in the period of his posting from July 1943 to august 1944 (Twice in a Martinet with a Wing Commander Davis to Cottesmore and back and six times in a Wellington carrying out x-country and a few air tests).

As a Navigator of immense experience his value to the unit was doubtless considerable but, like many of this time, he wanted to go back onto operations. He had a hankering for the Pathfinder Force and the Mosquito, and whilst he had acquired the experience that was a prerequisite for this job, he failed his medical. I do not know why Jim failed the medical and declined to ask him but I do know that he appealed against the decision in August 1944. When he was recalled to the medical board for his appeal, the Medical Officer in charge was an Air Commodore O'Malley. He said, well I should not pass you, but I am not going to fail you.

He arrived at a Bomber Development Unit at Newmarket on Saturday 5th August where he was to complete a weeklong course learning the H2S radar system flying in an old friend the Wellington. He arrived at 1655 Mosquito Development Unit at Warboys around the 20th August and on the 23rd, 24th and 26th flew x-country exercises in an oxford with a Flight Lieutenant Glensor. His first flight in a Mosquito took place on Saturday 2nd September at 1105 hrs. The Captain of the aircraft was a Flight Lieutenant Letford.

They flew together again on the 3rd, 5th, 6th, 7th and 10th September carrying out x-country and night flying exercises before they joined 139 Squadron.

139 Squadron was formed at Villaveria, Italy in July 1918, as a fighter-reconnaissance squadron and was equipped with Bristol Fighters. It was disbanded in 1919 and reformed in 1936 at Wyton with Hawker Hinds during the early years of the war, a Jamaican newspaper The Daily Gleaner started a fund to buy bombers for Britain. The money Jamaica subscribed was the foundation of the Bombers for Britain fund, to which many other Colonies and Dominions subsequently contributed. Jamaica herself contributed enough money to buy twelve Blenheims by 1942 and in recognition of this service it was decided to name 139 (Jamaica) Squadron. In 1942/43 the squadron was re-equipped with Mosquitoes and in the summer of 1943 changed over to night raiding and joined the Pathfinder Force. The squadron was one of the units at the forefront of Pathfinder operations, paving the way for the main force. In concept, the act of Pathfinding, or to be more accurate, target marking is carried out today with the highly sophisticated laser marking techniques that are now available. Although 50 odd years apart in technological terms, both require the same of the marking aircraft, i.e., the accurate illuminating of the target.

Jim and Flight Lieutenant Letford arrived at the squadron early in September 1944 and flew together on their first raid that was on Thursday 14th September. Their target was Berlin. They took off at 2100 hrs in Mosquito XD-B and set course for the German capital, their flight time there and back would be 4hrs.50mins. Jim only flew one operation with Flight Lieutenant Letford who then failed to appear again in Jim's log. What happened to him is not known but, commencing on the 18th September, Jim first flew with Flight Lieutenant Willie Wilson. It is quite remarkable to note that in his entire time flying with the squadron, through to June 1945, Jim never flew with any other pilot, either operationally or otherwise.

"Berlin was a city which Jim would visit no less than 25 times operationally with this unit, 15 of those visits would be done consecutively."

Jim continued with the squadron to complete 53 operations. The last 12 of these operations he carried out as Master Bomber. The Master Bomber was the first over the target, and last to leave. Jim's very last operation with the squadron was on St George's Day Monday 23rd April 1945 with Flight Lieutenant Wilson to Keil.

Logbook entries of interest

Sept 30th 1944	Hamburg. *This operation was to bomb the flak batteries that were situated on top of huge above ground multi-storey concrete air-raid shelter that was close to the town centre.*
April 20th 1945	Berlin. *This was the last RAF raid on the German capital as the Russians were about to enter the city. A Mosquito from 109 squadron claimed the last bomb at (4,000lb Cookie) at 2.14 am.*
April 23rd 1945	Kiel. *Last Operational Flight with the squadron.*
May 28th 1945	Cooks Tour. *with Flight Lieutenant Wilson in XD-Q flying time 4hrs.15mins.*
June 8th 1945	Last Flight *with Flight Lieutenant Wilson and 139 Squadron (XD-G).*

Jim told me, "towards the end of my fourth tour we were marking so accurately that the whole of the mission, and there could be up to 100 Mosquitoes following you - would get there at the right time."

He also said, "I flew 53 missions on my last tour. They were all fairly well the same, though we did take a hiding once or twice. One was on a night when we had flown ten nights in a row and heading for a world record and our Commanding Officer was very keen for us to go on. We shouldn't have taken off on the eleventh night at all because the forecast was damn bad. It was low cloud all over England, and when we got back and found it like this, we had to go down to the south of England to find a station that could let us land. We lost three crews, and about five aircraft out of the ten. I was damn luck to survive, because we came through at about 300 feet underneath the clouds, and found ourselves clean over the runway. It made me very angry, because it was unnecessary and we all could have been killed."

With a total of 131 operations carried out over enemy territory I believe this to be the highest recorded in the entirety of the war for any member of bomber command aircrew. Jim moved with the squadron to Catterick in July 1945, and was awarded a well-earned Distinguished Service Order on 26th October, which he received from His Majesty King George IV at Buckingham Palace.

PILOT OFFICER
JOHN ARTHUR MARTIN, DFC
ROYAL AIR FORCE NO. 1112748
FLIGHT ENGINEER
NO. 620 & 115 SQUADRONS

John Alfred Martin was born in the beautiful village of Glynn, which is situated about two miles from the town of Larne, in County Antrim. He was educated at Glynn Primary School until the age of fourteen and on leaving school he was employed with the Shell Oil Company.

In October 1940 he went along to the RAF Recruiting Office, Clifton Street in Belfast, and joined as a Flight Engineer. No sooner had he signed on the dotted line, he was on board the next available boat to Liverpool and on his arrival was told to report to the receiving centre at Padgate for a further medical and form signing. In early 1941 he was transferred to RAF Ford on the south coast of England, where like many trainees was given some 'simple' tasks, like cleaning aircraft spark plugs. The Germans bombed the station relentlessly day and night, and after one such raid, John met six civilians from Northern Ireland who were working at Ford repairing battle damaged Havoc's and Blenheims. During another raid the civilians (including the six Northern Ireland lads) rushed to the safety of an air raid shelter, tragically it received a direct hit and all inside were killed. In the middle of 1942 John was transferred to RAF Watton, and much to his disgust was given the same menial job of cleaning aircraft spark plugs. He spent the next three months at Watton, and reckoned he was the best spark plug cleaner in the RAF. At the end of 1942 he was posted to No 90 Squadron at West Raynam to start his flight engineers training on B-17's.

No 90 Squadron had been selected to receive the first Boeing B-17 Flying Fortress's from America, and its role was to bomb Germany from a high level by day. The squadron flew its first operation of the war to Wilhelmshaven on the 8th July 1941, attacking the city from 30,000ft.

John explained, "The training which I and others received was totally inadequate for the job. On one occasion during a ground run, one of the B-17's engines suddenly burst into flames, which spread very quickly to the wing leading edge rubber de-icing boot. Within minutes the entire aircraft was engulfed in flames, with 50 calibre bullets exploding in all directions. The aircraft was a total write-off. The cause of the fire was that the engine fuel mixture had been set too rich. Soon after this unfortunate accident it was decided that the crews needed a lot more technical training on the B-17. It was soon arranged that they were to be sent to Burton Wood, which was an American maintenance base where they received a two month intensive course. After John had completed his training he returned to 90 Squadron where he learned that most of the squadrons Fortresses had either been lost or shot down. The squadron was disbanded in February 1942, but reformed again in November as a heavy bomber squadron, equipped with Short Stirling M1's and 111's.

John's next posting was to No 1651 Stirling Conversion Unit at Waterbeach, where he again found himself being given menial tasks like fitting undercarriage covers to the wheels of Stirlings to protect them from oil contamination which leaked constantly from its Hercules engines. It was at Waterbeach that John witnessed a tragic accident, when he watched two Stirlings collide taking off in different directions. The crews onboard both aircraft were killed. John till this day still thinks about the accident and can't understand why two aircraft were allowed to take-off at the same time coming towards each other.

After waiting for two years his patience finally paid off when he was posted to RAF Innsworth Lane where he was to start his Flight Engineers course. The training lasted for three months, and when it was finished he was transferred to Stormy Down where he completed a three month Air Gunners course. He was then awarded his Flight Engineers Brevet, and promoted to Sergeant. John didn't have much luck while at Waterbeach as he was given fourteen days in the guard room for taxiing a Stirling tail into a hangar wall, and on another occasion he was given a further fourteen days for wearing a civilian scarf in Cambridge (nabbed by American MP's).

John was then posted to a conversion unit at RAF Stradishal where he met up with his new crewmembers:

Pilot Officer FC McDonald (Pilot) later Squadron Leader, DFC*.
Pilot Officer GG Murray (2nd Pilot)
Pilot Officer PS Hobbs (Navigator)
Flight Sergeant HW Hill (Bombardier)
Sergeant J Hargraves (Mid Upper Gunner)
Sergeant D Canning (Rear Gunner)

When all of their training was completed John and his crew were posted to No 620 Squadron at Chedburgh to start operational flying. The squadron was equipped with Short Stirling Mk 111's, and was commanded by Wing Commander DH Lee, DFC.

Brief history of 620 squadron

The squadron was formed at Chedburgh in June 1943 as a heavy bomber squadron in 3 Group and was equipped with the Short Stirling. It transferred to 38 Group where it joined Transport Command. It bombed many targets in France, Germany, and Italy, and in 1944 began supply drops to SOE and Marquis personnel. The squadron also dropped the 6th Airborne Division at Caen, and just after D-Day towed fully loaded Horsa Gliders to France. In September 1944 it was heavily involved in re-supplying the harassed forces, losing five crews in the process. The squadron then began flying low-level operations, towing gliders into Italy and Holland, and also took part in the Rhine crossing. In May 1945 the squadron converted onto the Handley Page Halifax, and with the war almost over began flights into Czechoslovakia, Egypt, Italy, and in 1946 began searches for illegal ships trying to get into Palestine.

On one occasion when John and the crew had returned from a mine laying operation to the Frisian Islands, they were being de-briefed and for some reason they got the feeling that the Intelligence Officer did not believe that they had carried out the operation. On their next trip that was to Hamburg, a very bad electrical storm had blown up just as they were approaching the enemy coast. The Skipper, Squadron Leader MacDonald informed the crew that he was returning to base because of the bad weather. No sooner had he said it, when the Rear Gunner, 'crackled' in, "Skipper, that might not be a good idea because after the mine laying incident it is possible that the crew might be accused of LMF (lack of moral fibre)." The skipper reluctantly agreed as the whole crew agreed to carry on to the target. The journey was horrendous, something John will never forget. However they did arrive over the target, which they successfully bombed, and with a sigh of relief the Navigator set a course for home. The return trip back through the storm wasn't any easier. When they landed back at base the operations officer asked, "Where the hell have you been?" Everyone else abandoned the operation, and returned to base due to the bad weather." *(LMF I don't think so.)*

The following information has been taken from the squadrons ORB's. On the 2nd August 1943, John's aircraft, code EF433 took off at 2312 hours. Their target was Hamburg. Nine aircraft were detailed for the attack. Their bomb load consisted of 30lb and 4lb incendiaries. Very severe icing conditions were encountered, and only two of the aircraft reached the target. On the 12th August 1943 John and his crew were detailed to attack targets around Turin with a bomb load of 1,000lb and 500lb bombs and incendiaries of 30lb and 4lbs. They took off in EF433 at 2140 hours and successfully attacked the target. On the outward-bound journey the Rear Gunner, Sergeant Miller shot down an attacking Focke Wulf 190. The crew returned safely to base at 0505 hours.

The following is the combat report made by the Rear Gunner.

"On the night of the 12th/13th August 1943 our aircraft Stirling Mk111, EE951 'B' outward bound to Turin sighted one of our aircraft engaged in combat upon port beam, at position 4856N 0031E, 2309 hrs, heading 142 degrees M, height 10,000ft, IAS 158mph.

"At 2309 hrs Rear Gunner Sergeant GF Millar, opened fire at closing fighter believed to be Focke Wulf 190 at 600 yards with a four second burst, the enemy aircraft immediately caught fire coming towards our own aircraft. The Pilot, Flight Lieutenant Sheppard saw the enemy aircraft and immediately dived to port. The Rear Gunner fired two more three-second bursts and the enemy aircraft went into a spin. It was seen to hit the ground, and explode, by the Flight Engineer, Mid-Upper and Rear Gunner. The weather: Three quarter moon, clear skies above, no flak or searchlights. 'Enemy aircraft claimed destroyed'.

"On the 17th/18th August EE945 Gunners were again in action. They took off at 2055 hrs along with five other 90 Squadron aircraft. Their target was the experimental rocket facility at Peenemunde. Their bomb load was made up with 30lb and 4lb incendiaries. On returning from the raid their aircraft was attacked by a Dornier 217. After a short battle the Sterlings Gunners shot the Dornier down. They landed safely back at base at 23.30 Hours. 'Enemy aircraft claimed destroyed'."

On the 31st August 1943, John's aircraft along with six others from the squadron were detailed to bomb the city of Berlin. They took off at 2020 hrs in Stirling EF117 with a bomb of 2,000lb and 500lbs and incendiaries of 30lb and 4lb. They bombed the target successfully and landed back at base at 2310 hrs. On the 22nd September 1943, John's aircraft along with thirteen others took off at 1840 hrs to bomb the city of Hanover. Their aircraft's code was EF 433, and their bomb load was made up with 2,000lb and 1,000lb, and 500lb bombs, and incendiaries of 30lb and 4lb. They successfully bombed their primary target, and on their return were diverted to another airfield, as during their absence base had been rendered unserviceable for landing by enemy bombs. They landed at 0120 hrs

A couple of John's stories

During an air test on a brand new Short Stirling, John found a lunch box, a riveter's hammer, and an Ireland Saturday Night, (Belfast local newspaper). Left by a Shorts worker no doubt; John said the sanny's weren't very tasty but he enjoyed reading the Ireland Saturday Night.

Another favourite pastime of John's and the Skipper was when they were carrying out air tests, or cross country exercise over the Norfolk Broads; they would fly low and try to blow over the small yachts. The Rear Gunner would keep a 'tally' of the sinkings and inform the Skipper. So anyone reading this story, and who had a boat sunk by a four-engined bomber on the Norfolk broads anytime between 1943 and 1944, let me know and I will send you the culprit's address.

During his tour with 620 Squadron, John met a fellow Ulsterman from Bangor in the County of Down. His name was Sergeant R Mailey and he to was also a Flight Engineer on Stirlings. He was new to the station, so John took him under his wing, and showed him the 'ropes'. Just before Sergeant Mailey's first operation, John was with him going over the various tasks that would be required of him. The time came for him to be bussed out to his aircraft, which was waiting on a hard stand near the perimeter fence. Sergeant Mailey and his crew were going on a mine laying operation. John waved goodbye to his friend and stood and waited as its four Hercules engines roared into life. He watched the mighty aircraft taxiing to the end of the runway, turn, and start its take off run. Just as the aircraft got into the air, John watched in horror as the mines on board blew up killing all seven crewmembers. He said, "It was like confetti raining down at a wedding, and something I shall never forget."

On the final approach to bomb Munchen Gladbach the Skipper noticed that there was heavy flak all along the right hand side of the city. So he told the crew that he was going to bomb from the left. Just as they reached the aiming point, the aircraft was caught in a 'cone' of searchlights, all hell let loose. Jerry was throwing everything at them, including the kitchen sink. The Skipper immediately took evasive action, diving and climbing the aircraft to try and escape the cone. Luck was with them once more they had escaped the murderous flak.

With his first tour of operations completed, John was promoted to Flight Sergeant and given some well-earned leave. On his return from leave he and the crew were informed that that they were being posted to No 3 Lancaster Finishing School at RAF Feltwell where they would convert onto the Lancaster. The training lasted for two months. On completion of the course, and for some unknown reason he found himself posted back to 1652

Conversion Unit at Ratton Common as a Flight Engineer Instructor on Stirlings. Instructing definitely did not appeal to him, so he put in a request right away, asking to be allowed back onto operations. After a few days he was informed that his request had been granted, and that he was to report to No 115 Squadron at Witchford to start his second tour. John went on to complete another 26 operations with the squadron.

The following are a few of the targets John had 'dropped in on' during his two tours: Hamburg (four times in one week); Turin; Pennemunde; Berlin; Nurnberg (120 aircraft were lost that night); Manheim; Gilsen Kirchen; Muchen Gladbach; Munich; Momdane; Neuss; and the Frisian Island. John finished his second tour in March 1945, and on the 10th April he was awarded the Distinguished Flying Medal.

The Citation reads:

Flight Sergeant Martin has carried out a considerable number of sorties as a flight engineer of a multi-engined bomber. He started flying operations during the summer of 1943 and made four raids on Hamburg in nine days, when the city was being heavily bombed. Later in the Autumn he attacked many major German targets ranging from Berlin to Nuremberg and the Ruhr. On the 17th August 1943, his aircraft was attacked by a Dornier 17, which was shot down by his Air Gunners. Flight Sergeant Martin returned to operations in December 1944 and has taken part in day and night attacks on the Ruhr and enemy railway yards. On the 22nd February 1945 he was among the leading aircraft of a raid in bleak weather conditions over Osterfield. The flak was extremely accurate and the majority of the aircraft were severely damaged. Throughout his operational career, Flight Sergeant Martin has displayed great courage and devotion to duty, which is worthy of official recognition.

Wing Commander, Commanding
N0. 115 Squadron

Covering remarks made by Air Commodore Commanding:

Strongly recommended. Flight Sergeant Martin has operated with great determination against many heavily defended targets.

Air Commodore, Commanding
20th April 1945. No33 Base, RAF Waterbeach

Covering remarks by Air Officer Commanding:

Recommended for the award of the Distinguished Flying Medal.

Air Vice Marshal Commanding
No 3 Group. Royal Air Force

John had in fact been commissioned to the rank of Pilot Officer on 18th March 1945; therefore the award of DFM was substituted by Distinguished Flying Cross. During May 1945, John was posted to No 51 Squadron at Leconfield in Yorkshire. The squadron had just been transferred from bomber command to transport command and was ferrying troops and freight between the UK, India and Singapore. One particular trip that John wont forget was when his aircraft had been transporting fifty regular army personnel from the UK to India. The Stirling had landed at Castel Benito in North Africa for re-fuelling and maintenance for the final leg of its journey to India. The aircraft took off that afternoon, and during the climb out of Castel Benito, John discovered that the handle which operated the trim tabs had broken. He informed the Skipper and advised him to return to the airfield and have it repaired. It took all of the next day to fix the broken trim handle and re-rig it. They took off again that night, and on the initial climb out the port engine caught fire. John had great difficulty feathering it, so again they had to return to the airfield. The engine was replaced the following day and after a number of engine runs and adjustments, the aircraft was declared serviceable. They took off again and set course for India, but it wasn't 'third time lucky'. For some unknown reason when the Stirling got to 200ft all four

engines stopped, the crippled Stirling dropped like a stone and ploughed into the runway. The 'landing' was so severe it broke the Stirlings back in three places. The crew and its 'cargo' abandoned the aircraft as quickly as possible because it was full of fuel and could catch fire at any minute. Sadly four of the soldiers were killed.

The squadron was eventually re-equipped with the Avro York during 1946, and John continued flying in them as Flight Engineer until he was de-mobbed in 1947.

He subsequently returned home to Northern Ireland where he re-joined the Shell Oil Company, finally retiring in 1989 after 42 years service as the company's industrial marketing manager. John is now enjoying retirement and living in a beautiful bungalow overlooking Larne Harbour. You will know John's bungalow if you ever are passing as it has the name 'Leconfield' fixed in wrought iron on its gates. John is a dedicated member of the Royal Air Force Association (Larne Branch) and the Air Crew Association (Northern Ireland Branch).

FLIGHT LIEUTENANT
ALFRED MARTIN, DFC
ROYAL AIR FORCE NO.120240
NAVIGATOR
NO. 102 (CEYLON) SQUADRON

Flight Lieutenant Alfred Martin, DFC was born in 1920 in Sicily Park just of the upper Lisburn Road in Belfast. He began his education at Malone Elementary School and continued his further education at Friends School in Lisburn and graduated with a senior certificate. He decided at that time that he would like to make a career for himself in the insurance business and was successful in obtaining a position with the Liverpool & London Globe Insurance Co. in Belfast.

With the first Munich crisis and the sabre rattling by the Nazi's in Berlin, Alfred decided to join the RAFVR. Unfortunately his parents thought otherwise and said no to this. Not to be outdone by his parents decision Alfred went along to the recruiting office in Belfast and joined the Royal Engineers Branch (Antrim Fortress Company) of the Territorial Army. After a few weeks training he became a Sapper (Private).

With the war now coming ever closer to our shores he found himself called to full time service on the 26th August 1939 and told to report to Kilroot anti-aircraft emplacement (the emplacements are still visible to this day). His duties there were to man the batteries of searchlights that were to illuminate the sky in search of hostile aircraft. He also was operated from anti-aircraft sites at Magilligan and Greys Point.

During that period the RAFVR was looking for people and on hearing this Alfred decided this was his big chance. In April 1941 he went along to the Clifton Street Recruiting Centre where he and fifty other people applied to join the forces, only four of these were accepted and he was one of the luck applicants. He signed on as aircrew to become a Navigator/Observer.

Like many Northern Ireland folk during those times he went to the Belfast docks and boarded a ship that would take him to Liverpool to join the war. On his arrival at Liverpool he was trained down to Stratford-Upon-Avon and reported to the Shakespeare Hotel, which had been taken over as a Royal Air Force Reception Centre. It was here that he started his initial training that included medicals, square bashing and being issued with his uniform and kit. On completion of his initial training Alfred was posted to No 10 Operational Training Unit (OTU) at Scarborough where he was to embark on his navigational training, which would also take in bombing and gunnery exercises. The course commenced in the middle of April. The course ran for six weeks, finishing in May 1941.

With his basic navigation course completed he was told that he was going to Canada for his advanced navigation training. He was then told to report to the Liverpool docks were he boarded the passenger ship the Ulster Monarch which was sailing for what Alfred thought was Canada. For some unknown reason, which never has been fully explained, the Ulster Monarch docked in Reykjavik in Iceland for sixteen days. No one minded this at all as the weather in Reykjavik was beautiful and they were able to bathe in the hot Icelandic springs. Once again they boarded the ship and thought they were headed for Canada, but not so, the ship was heading back to Glasgow in Scotland were it joined a large convoy that was bound for Halifax in Nova Scotia, Canada (such was the MOD organisation in 1941). On his arrival in Halifax Alfred was trained down to Charlottetown on Prince Edward Island were he began his six week advanced navigational course. In January 1942 he was posted to Picton in Ontario to complete a bombing course that was carried out in Fairey Battles again the course lasted for six weeks. At the end of the training in Canada Alfred was awarded his 'O' Brevet and received his commission and promoted to the rank of Pilot Officer. It was now back to the UK.

After a few days leave in Picton he travelled back by train to Halifax in Nova Scotia were he boarded the SS

Bayano which was a 5,000-ton banana boat owned by Fyffe's. The trip from Canada took a long and dangerous sixteen days as the U-boat menace was at its height during these months. However the ship arrived safely at Liverpool where Alfred boarded a train that would take down to Bournmouth on the south coast of England. On his arrival he was to report to the aircrew reception centre where he spent a few days being briefed and getting to know some new people there. It wasn't long before he was posted to No 10 Advanced Flying Unit at Wigtown near Dumfries in Scotland. The unit was equipped with Fairey Bothas. During his training at Wigtown he managed to obtain a couple of trips home to Belfast via RAF Aldergrove. Alf happened to mention to me that he remembered very well that the Aldergrove runway was anything but level (60 years on Alfy and its still the same).

Alfred finished his advanced training in June 1942 and was posted to an operational training unit at Oxford. On his arrival he was transferred to one of Oxfords satellite airfields that was near Abbingdon where he was to train on Whitley's and meet his new crew. Alfred had his first mishap in an aircraft when his pilot landed his Whitley short of the runway at Charterhall. The aircraft was a totally destroyed and luckily the only one hurt was the Pilot who sustained a broken wrist. On returning to Oxford Alfred and his crew (minus the Pilot) were informed that they would be taking part in the first 1,000 bomber raid on Cologne and Essen. This was not entirely unusual, even though they were still under training every available aircraft had to be in the sky for that raid. Having successfully completed all his operational training Alfred and his crew were posted to No 102 (Ceylon) Squadron, which was based at Pocklington near Hull and equipped with Handley Page Halifaxs.

"102 Squadrons name will always be associated with the name Group Captain GL Cheshire, VC when on the night of the 12th/13th November 1940, Pilot Officer (as he was then) was captain of Whitley V P5005 'N' was detailed to attack an oil refinery at Wesseling, not far from Cologne. On his arrival over the target he found it covered in thick cloud, his radio had gone U/S so he decoded to bomb the railway marshalling yards at Cologne instead. As he approached the target his aircraft was rocked by a series of violent explosions. His cockpit was covered with smoke and fumes and the fuselage that had a large gaping hole in it and was also on fire. He decided to dive the aircraft to around 2,000ft, which extinguished the fire, and he managed to bring the Whitley and the crew safely back to base after being in the air for almost nine hours. Pilot Officer Cheshire was awarded an immediate DSO for this heroic act."

Alfred flew twelve operations with 102 Squadron, attacking targets such as Lorreen, St Nazaire, Essen, Hamburg, Berlin, Turin, Milan, and Stuttgart.

Unfortunately he and his crew did not return from their raid on the Skoda works at Pilsen in Czechoslovakia on the 16th April 1943. On their return journey over Belgium at 0400 hrs their aircraft was attacked by an enemy fighter, severely damaged with the port wing on fire, the port throttles and elevator control U/S, the captain gave the order for all to, "Bale out," and "abandon ship." The aircraft went into a spin and crashed below them. Alfred landed safely near the French village of Eppe-Sauvage. He managed to evade capture which was made possible with the help to a lot of brave French people who had not only risked their lives for him and his crew but for many others who had come before and after them.

The crew were

Flying Officer Welsh (the Skipper). He hitchhiked and walked and arrived back in the UK on June 22nd.
Flying Officer Bolton was OK.
Flying Officer Martin was OK.
Sergeant Laws was OK.
Sergeant Neill was wounded and became a POW.
Flight Sergeant Knight POW.
Pilot Officer Williams (reported killed).

On his safe return to England Alfred was promoted to Flight Lieutenant and was immediately awarded the Distinguished Flying Cross on the 6th July 1943.

Copy of Flight Lieutenant Alfred Martin's DFC Citation:

> Flying Officer Martin was the Bomb Aimer of an aircraft of 102 Squadron, which was detailed to attack Pilsen on the 16th April 1943. On the return flight over Belgium an enemy fighter shot down the aircraft and the order was given to bale out. Flying Officer Martin landed near Eppe Sauvage on the French side of the frontier with Belgium. He evaded capture and eventually arrived back safely in this country. For the courage and determination shown by this Officer I strongly recommend the award of the DFC.
>
> Signed CN CARR
> Air Vice Marshal,
> Air Officer Commanding,
> No 4 Group,
> Royal Air Force.
> 6th July 1943

Alfred sadly found himself being taken off operational flying duties. The reason for this action was, if he was shot down again over enemy territory he may be made to give the names of the people who had helped him to escape and therefore jeopardise any further escape attempts.

After a well deserved rest and becoming a bit fed up with doing very little Alfred applied for a staff navigational course. He was accepted and was posted to the RAF Station at Bishops Court in his home land of Northern Ireland. When he completed the course he found himself on a boat again this time it was bound for No 31 Air Navigation School in Port Albert, near London Ontario, Canada where he became an Instructor on Avro Ansons.

From Port Albert he was posted to No 7 Air Navigation School at Portage La Prairie, Manitoba, some 50 miles west of Winnipeg again as a Gunnery and Navigational Instructor in Ansons. Portage La Prairie l was a Standard British Commonwealth Air Training Plan School with eighteen acres of buildings and a triangle of runways. They were originally gravel and later concrete, each 3,000ft long. It had two site hangars 112ft by 160ft and two double hangars, measuring 224ft by 160ft. Alfred finally returned to the UK just after VJ Day in August 1945 and was eventually released from the RAF in December 1945.

On his return to Northern Ireland he was lucky enough to get his old job back with the Liverpool and London Globe Insurance Company. He remained with the company for one year and then decided to return to Canada to start a new life with his wife and family. Alfred lived in Canada from 1947 until 1968 when he returned to Northern Ireland and purchased a wholesale toys and fancy goods company, which had been owned by the Batty Brothers.

During this period in Canada Alfred thought it would be a good idea to start a Canadian branch of the Royal Air Force Escaping Society where he had the honour of being its first Chairman. Viscount Portal of Hungerford, KG GCB OM DSO MC founded the original RAF Escaping Society in London in 1945. Its members are made up from airmen who escaped from enemy held territory during World War II. In most cases the success of the escape was due to assistance by patriots in the occupied countries. During the period 1939-45 almost 3,000 British and Commonwealth airmen were returned to Allied territory. The object of the society is to remember those brave people who helped their members escape and to provide some financial aid to helpers who may still be suffering the results of imprisonment and torture at the hands of the enemy, or who are now aged and infirm.

Alfred Martin is still a very active member of the RAF Escaping Society and a founder member and President of the Aircrew Association (Northern Ireland Branch).

ARTHUR JAMES MAULTSAID
ROYAL AIR FORCE
RADIO OPERATOR

Arthur Maultsaid was born in Ravenhill Avenue on the 7th January 1923 and because of an illness in his childhood was unable to start primary school until he was six years old. When he did eventually start school he was firstly educated in Euston Street Primary School in Redcar Street of the Woodstock Road. He still remembers every teachers name, Mrs Buchanan who took the senior infants and Miss Holden who took the juniors an not forgetting the Headmistress, Miss Todd.

Arthur tells me that he got expelled from Euston St school because someone had hit his older sister. Although Arthur wasn't very big, he nearly knocked the stuffing out of the bully. Arthur was sent for by Miss Holden who told him to hold out his hand to be caned. Just as she brought the cane down Arthur moved his hand inwards causing Miss Holden to loss her balance and fall. So at the ripe old age of seven Arthur was expelled and his education was off to a good start. At that time schools were extremely hard to get into and the nearest one to Arthur was Harding Memorial that was on the Cregagh Road. Mr. Richard Taylor was the head master and another teacher called Arthur Lowry both knew about Arthur's record at Euston Street. Unfortunately they both refused to allow him into the school

As it happened Arthur had an aunt and uncle who were headmaster and headmistress of a Protestant school in Keady in County Armagh for forty years. They had a close friend, a Mr Dean who was the headmaster of Rossetta Elementary School in Belfast and spoke to him on Arthur's behalf He had no hesitation on taking him on. So Arthur started Rossetta at the age of seven and remained there until he was thirteen years old. He did extremely well at Rossetta, eventually winning a scholarship which took him to the Belfast Technical College and incidentally it was the first Scholarship that Rossetta had won.

When he left school he was employed for one year by Arthur McAuley estate agent and although he was doing well the war had started and he didn't really have any love for the business so he decided to join the Royal Air Force much to both his parents annoyance. In January 1941 and

at the age of 18 he went along to Clifton St Recruiting Centre and joined up. It wasn't long before he went to Padgate Receiving Centre near Liverpool where he received his RAF Number and signed the relevant documents. From Padgate he was posted down to Blackpool for basic training and to be kitted out. He also learnt the art of Morse code while he was at Blackpool.

When he applied to join the RAF he requested to be trained as a Wireless Operator Air Gunner but in fact had been selected to become a Pilot. Although Arthur didn't have a Grammar school education he did have the leaving certificate from Rossetta Elementary, which showed Honours in Geometry and Algebra. Arthur was delighted about this, but un fortunately just after he was accepted for aircrew he as struck down with scarlet fever which was a reoccurrence of what happened in his youth, and because of this he was told that he could not now become aircrew. Arthur was exceptionally good at Morse code and was proficient now in doing 25 words a minute, so in the meantime it was decided to make him a Morse code instructor at the Blackpool Winter Gardens.

Arthur's explanation of the old saying, "Gone for a Burton."

When you start doing the Morse code course you would try and achieve four to five words a minute and when you did you would sit a test. The test would be carried out in a classroom which was situated above Burton the Tailors on Blackpool sea front.

25 blokes would be marched in to do the test and if you did not pass you would automatically be taken off

the course. So if a friend asked where's so and so I haven't seen him for a while, the answer would be, "Oh he's gone for a Burton."

His explanation of old saying, "You have had it."

This saying we think evolved from the Armed Forces uniform stores.

When you join up you are taken to the uniform store and you would be issued with everything that you are entitled to and would come out of the stores with a mountain of equipment. Which would include helmet, boots, blankets, weebing, tunic and trousers, shirt, tie, etc. and a kit bag. You would then be taken back to your billets and empty all your equipment out of your kitbag on to your bed and check it.

You may have found that you are missing a tie, so off you go back to the stores and explain that you never received a tie. Now the store man would check down his list and say, "You have had it mate."

Eventually Arthur was posted to Compton Basset in Wiltshire to learn about the different types of radio transmitter and receiver's and when he eventually finished the course he was now a fully-fledged Radio Operator. He was posted to Isla in Scotland where one of the early warning radar stations had been set up and was still on the secret list. This station was know as Station 58, 60 Group. RAF Station Salito Bay. Arthur was based at Salito Bay for one year. He explained to me that there was two types of radar station; One which covered the ground which was called CHL (Chain Home Low). This would cover the sea. Isla radar station covered the whole of the North Channel right across to Ballycastle in County Antrim and Londonderry and most of the north approach area where the shipping Convoys would pass through. The larger of the two radar stations was know as Chain Home and had two 600ft masts erected vertically with a large curtain array between them. It sent out a signal that stretched 180 miles out west of Donegall. Arthur's job on Isla was amongst other things to sit and watch his radar screen for unidentified aircraft. The Germans would send Focke Wulf Condors from Norway right down to the Bay of Biscay and back again to spy on Allied convoys that would be forming up to go to various destinations. So it was Arthur's job to try and locate these aircraft until it was within reach of fighter squadrons in Ballykelly and Aldergrove who would go out and try and destroy them.

90% of all the information which he got would be sent to the Fighter Command operations room at Stormont Buildings in Belfast. The receiving aerial for Stormont was situated on the top of Ballmiscaw Hill.

While Arthur was based at Isla he was involved with the tragic loss of Amy Johnston who was a pioneering aviator of that time. Amy Johnson was a ferry pilot flying new aircraft from America in hops to Canada, Iceland and Scotland. This particular time Amy was leading 12 Lightning (P-38) type aircraft and she was the only one in the flight who could navigate so the were all following her.

The aircraft weight was kept down to a minimum and her aircraft was the only one to carry radio and navigational aids. All of the available space on board the aircraft was taken up by extra fuel tanks. This particular night the weather was atrocious, (high winds and an electric storm) and unfortunately Amy Johnson lost her way and they all perished. Arthur had watched her for quite a while on his radar screen and relayed calls to Stormont regarding her approximate position. He lost contact with her about 30 miles off the coast of Donegall. Years later when Arthur worked for the RNLI in Northern Ireland, he spoke to a man from Southern Ireland who remembers the same night very well as he worked secretly for the RAF Rescue Service and was called out to see if he could find any trace of survivors.

Story about Isla

A large freighter had run aground on rocks in bad weather just below the radar station, so on Arthur's first day off he decided to explore the stricken ship as the word had got about that it was full of goodies. When he arrived down at the ship he discovered that the breeches buoy was still attached. He managed to get into this and pull himself up onto the stern and clamber onboard. The sea was still very rough and the freighter was continually moving and eventually caused the breeches buoy lines to snap. Arthur was trapped; he headed for the radio room, as his main purpose was to try and get the Marconi Morse code tapper. On his way he discovered millions of pounds in Iraqi gold Dinar coins, lots of whiskey and boxes of BSA air rifles and ammunition. He tried for two days without success to get off the ship and was now worrying about being missed back at camp. He found a Carley float and managed to launch it not before taking off his uniform and boots which he tied around his neck. I must add at this point Arthur had a suitcase full of goodies which he had lashed to the Carley float. He wrapped his uniform up in an old oilskin and tied it to the float also. He slipped into the icy cold water and eventually got to the shore and still does not know to this day how he did. In the panic to get to the shore he had to let go the Carley float but managed to grab his uniform. Somehow he managed to climb the 60ft up the cliff and when he got to the top he found his bicycle, which he had left hidden and rode the two mile back to camp barefoot.

He arrived at the camp gate in the middle of the night, he was black having been covered from head to foot in oil from the ship. Everyone seemed to be asleep except for an RAF special policeman who was sitting in a small hut half asleep with his feet up against a coke fire. Arthur lifted a blanket and wrapped it around himself and on hearing the noise the policeman whose name was Corporal Pearce woke with a start and fell backwards drawing his revolver. He thought he had seen a large seal and was ready to shoot, Arthur shouted to him, "Its me Corporal, Arthur Maultsaid." Corporal Pearce said, "Where to hell have you been? Everyone has been looking for you." To cut a long story short, the result of this was Arthur was in sickbay for four days trying to get the oil of him. The only way to get it off was by using butter; he must have stunk to high doe.

When he was feeling better the Commanding Officer came down to see him to ask what had happened and were did he disappear to. Arthur said that he had fallen and couldn't remember anything. The CO left a special policeman Paddy Leach who was a friend of Arthur to stay and try and find out what happened to him. It was decided between the both of them that he would tell a little white lie and that was that he was walking along the cliff and his hat fell off and had blown down into the sea and he had gone down to fetch it. On the way down he stumbled and fell unconscious into the oily sea. He remembers wakening up and managed to climb up the cliff and cycling back to camp.

This explanation had to be written on a form 664 so as to allow him to get a new uniform kit otherwise he would have to pay for it himself. The Commanding Officer also had to countersign the demand. Arthur remembers losing all his goodies from the ship but did bury a few rolls of gold Dinars on the beach close to the ship. Perhaps they are still there today. Other people he can remember at Isla were 'Pop' who was 44 years old, an old man in comparison to most of the lads. Now Pop was a little overweight, and there was a WAAF who worked in the cookhouse and was a skinny wee waif. One night someone managed to 'obtain' a rather large keg of beer which was about 6f high and 4ft wide. It was decided to have a beer-drinking contest to see who could drink the most pints. Everyone thought that pop would win hands down, but not so, the little cookhouse waif left them all 'standing'. She won the competition hands down.

Isla had been a research station before the war and during that time there had been a man called Scott Taggart who designed radios. If you were a radio buff at that time and purchased the radio magazine Wireless World you would see ST 100's advertised. The ST stood for Scott Taggart 100 circuit. What you would do was go down to your local radio shop and by the parts to make up the ST100 and then you would advance to the ST200, ST300 ST400 and 600 ending up with a radiogram. Isla radio and radar station was involved at that time with the highly secret Ultra and Decca operation, Scott Taggart was one of the people along with 'other' in upgrading the station at Isla.

Arthur was promoted to LAC and had decided that he would like to be a Wireless Operator Mechanic Wombs with a reference from his Commanding Officer and Scott Taggart who had took Arthur under his wing he was posted to the wireless college at RAF Cranwell. This was now the end off 1942, the WOM course lasted for six months, which he passed, and his marks were 'exceptional'. So much so that they were the highest yet for this course and he was selected to become an instructor at Cranwell. Arthur had to attend a three month instructor's course to learn how to teach pupils and again at the end of this course he got 'As' in all his subjects. Something he is proud of to this day. It was practice, if a lot of Irish lads came down to Cranwell to learn to be WOM's they would automatically go to Arthur's class and he could guarantee by the time he had finished with them he wouldn't have one further training (FT) or cease training (CT).

Arthur learnt a lot himself while he was at Cranwell, so much so he was able to get a Radar Instructor's qualification put on his license. It is said that he was a good instructor, the best at that time, but he hated doing it. Other instructor's that he worked with at Cranwell were Wilson Little (Ulsterman), Pipperiski (Polish), Bolton (Cockney) before the war he was a Hoover salesman, 'King' Dickie Cooper and Percy West who was a math's genius. From time to time Arthur would be detached from Cranwell for weeks at a time, sent to various stations to teach refresher courses. One such course was to Mountbatten where they flew Short Sunderlands other stations were Colerne, Straddishall, Pocklington and many others. These refresher courses were designed to help WOM's who had been on a operational squadron a long time and who were receiving new aircraft with new w equipment which they knew very little about.

Arthur by now was getting a little tired of teaching and the only way to get out of Training Command was to apply for a overseas posting. This he did and at the end of 1943 he was off to Burma.

He Left Cranwell in December 1943 and went by train to Morcombe to be kitted out with his tropical kit. From Morcombe he was trained to Greenock in Scotland where he boarded the P&O ship Orantis. The ship sailed for India the next day and the crossing took nearly three months not caused by bad weather but because they had to dodge so many U-boats.

It was a long and boring trip with ten bods in a normally two-berth cabin taking turns at eight-hour shifts to get some sleep, fed twice a day and nothing much else to do. However on board the Orantis was a French Canadian who spent his time teaching everyone the words of Alluvetta in any language.

So when the ship sailed into Bombay harbour the whole ships company was on deck singing Alluvetta, That must have been something to hear. From Bombay they were trained to Whoril and then on to Puna and on his arrival Arthur was sent down with some bods to Belgorm that was an RAF station. There he was taught to drive heavy trucks and the art of jungle penetration which was getting him ready to go into Burma. The jungle training lasted for about three months, the first week consisted of how to make a mobile camp complete with kitchen and latrines, route marches were carried out twice a day two mile for the first week increasing to five miles the second week then ten miles the next with a full kit on your back and so on until you were proficient at doing 35 miles. Each week you were given a rigorous medical to make sure that you had no problems.

Arthur was one of the few bods who was able to stick the 35 mile hikes, he was 9st 10lbs fit as a fiddle and enjoyed walking. Coming near to the end of the course he was given the opportunity to learn how to drive a very large truck which was made by General Motors in America. This turned out to be a self-contained mobile radio unit with its own transmitter in a trailer hooked up behind. The whole unit weighed about 30 tons. At the end of this gruelling course, depending on how you had done you would be graded into one of five groups: Static; mobile; static/mobile; mobile/assault; and assault. Arthur was picked for the top assault group.

He was put into a group called the Advanced Landing Ground Unit. (ALGU) Number 915 ALGU. Soon Arthur and his team were flown by Dakota into Burma to start operations against the Japanese taking over an airstrip which had just been built by the army. His group consisted of 40 bods and Arthur was the senior NCO having been promoted to Corporal. Flying Officer MacKenzie was the units commanding officer and the unit in which they worked under was called Forward Area Maintenance Organization (FAMO). Arthur and his team were the communication team for FAMO. FAMO was responsible for supplying the army with whatever equipment was needed to do their job.

There were four or five Dakotas on hand which were piloted by Royal Canadian Air Force pilots and they called themselves Cannooks Unlimited. These aircraft were used to move Arthur and his team along with the heavy equipment up to forward landing strips if and when they were needed. Sometimes Arthur and his crew may have to be flown up by Auster to the forward landing group in hurry to get a communication link set up quickly.

Their equipment consisted of two large transmitters (Mobile units) and two large generators with Ford 10 engines to power 7kva ac mains and 2 RCA RA 88 receivers and 20 operators to man them. Also required in the team was two Wireless Operator Mechanics WOMs; Arthur was one and the other was a chap called Davy. Arthur and Davy ran the complete technical side of the operation. On their arrival at the forward landing ground they would install the mobile radio units, assemble the radio masts and set up the VHF frequencies for the aircraft. This allowed the pilots to speak directly to headquarters back at Calcutta. Also in the team they had a cypher officer and a signals officer, the cypher officer whose surname was Luney's, job was to decode the messages and the signals officer sent them out. The mobile receivers were set up at one end of the runway and the transmitter set up at the other end with a telephone link up between them. The generators were in constant use 24 hrs a day. Nearly every day the army would come out of the jungle and onto the strip and give Arthur a list of equipment that would be needed for the

next few days, this request would be in code and handed to the cypher officer. Arthur would then contact FAMO with the request and it would be flown into the ALG as soon as possible.

Ronnie MacKenzie who was the Signals Officer was an old hand at the job and in his training days not only learnt radio but he also learnt about airframe. When he did his airframe exam the pass out test was to make a chair out of a few bits of canvas, wire and string, and this had to be made in such a way that when it unfolded it would spring out into a chair, Now this was a piece of airframe ingenuity, it had to be strong enough to take a mans weight, and it was also Ronnie's pride and joy. Once a week by foul means or other a large keg of rum (five gallons) would find its way into the camp to be shared out amongst its members and sometimes it could be two kegs. On one of these particular days one of the airmen called Taff who didn't come from Ireland got himself drunk. Ronnie used to sit in the evenings relaxing on his pride and joy watching the sun setting. This particular evening the slightly intoxicated Taff asked Arthur for a pair of snips, he quietly crept up to were Ronnie was dozing on his chair and cut one of the supporting wires. The chair collapsed and bits of it flew everywhere. Ronnie was furious and nobody ever told him that it was sabotaged and he always thought that it just broke. After the war Ronnie became the signals officer in charge of Changi in Malaya. Arthur told me that most of the ALG's had been wiped out by the Japanese by the end of the war.

The Commanding Officer of 915 ALGU was a Wing Commander Bryant Fenn who had been one of the original Pathfinder Pilots in Mosquito's and as he was finished his tours he was posted to Burma, and in fact ended up as Mountbattens personnel pilot after the war.

His base was at Headquarters Calcutta.

True story about Wing Commander Fenn

This story begins as Arthur and his team arrived at the advanced landing ground, when one of them spotted a Mosquito sitting at the end of the runway like a brand new pin just waiting for take off. There was no one near it, so Arthur radioed back to HQ in Calcutta informing them of the situation. So the next thing he knew was the CO arriving by Auster. He stepped out of the aircraft and asked to be shown the Mosquito. The unit had its own Fitter who looked after the generators and vehicles the CO asked for him and headed down to the Mosquito. Now the Fitter had never seen a Rolls Royce Merlin before never mind worked on one but he did his best giving the engines and the airframe the once over. They eventually came to the conclusion that the aircraft was fit to fly except for one thing, the Mossie didn't have any fuel on board, perhaps that is why she landed there in the first place or someone had siphoned it out. The only petrol that the unit had was 40 octane, which the generator and vehicles used; the Mosquito required at least 100 octane. So nothing would do ,the

CO gave the order to fill her up as much 40 octane as could be spared. The CO somehow eventually managed to get the Mosquito started and taxied it up and down the runway several times the two Merlins belching black smoke.

After a while Wing Commander Fenn said we will go, taking a fitter and a Radio Operator with him. The Mosquito struggled into the air with the black smoke trailing behind her and we believe that she landed safely at a place called Matila.

Story about a Priest and security

One night a native came into Arthur's tent and scared the living daylights out of him, chanting, "Mass. Mass. Mass."

"You have three Catholics in your camp, Mass, Mass." Arthur shouted at him, "Mass, what do you mean Mass, we are in the middle of a bloody jungle?"

It transpired that there was a Catholic priest nearby and he knew that there was some of his flock in the camp. Arthur remembers two of their names, O'Driscal and Mike Keenan.

Now this advanced landing unit was supposed to be a highly secret organization and here's a jungle native asking for these three Catholics by name to take them to Mass which the priest was giving the following Sunday. The same native came back to Arthur one week later and asked him again in broken English, "can you fix radio for me?" Arthur replied "Yes, what kind of radio?" What had happened was the Japanese had confiscated all the local domestic radios and cut the short wave end out of them so the locals could only listen to Tokyo Rose broadcasting her propaganda. The native wanted to know could Arthur make the short wave work again, this to him was a dawdle. The native went a way and came back with a box full of radio's which were mostly American made. The story behind these radio's was, when the Japanese arrived in the area they blew up all the oil wells so as the allies couldn't use them.

There were also diamond mines in the area that the Japanese knew nothing about, so all the locals moved down into the mines with all their belongings until the war was over. One of the inhabitants who lived down the mines was a doctor from Portadown in County Armagh and his friend was none other than the Catholic priest. At this time Arthur could not remember the doctor's name. Originally the miners had their workshop above the ground where they would cut and polish the precious stones, now they were below ground all self contained complete with there own generator. Arthur had no problem fixing their radios and when he did he took the chance to visit the mine. In return for fixing the radio's he was given a handful of small rubies by the doctor from Portadown. What happened to them is a secret.

The war was coming to an end, so the unit was ordered to leave Magwi and go to Mingladon which was a large airfield outside Rangoon. At that time there were still a few Japanese fighting in different areas, so Arthur and his crew were on stand by to fly out at a minutes notice. They were there for two days when he remembers that three white coloured aircraft landed carrying a high-ranking delegation of Japanese from Siam. The last of the Atomic bombs had been dropped and the Japanese had asked for a 'truce'. Arthur was now given his instructions; when the three white aircraft took off again with the Japanese delegation, they were to follow them in the Dakota's complete with their mobile equipment. They followed the three aircraft and crossed into Siam landing at Donwang airfield, this was one of the biggest of the Japanese military airfields and pre-war it belonged to the Dutch KLM airline. When they landed at Donwang they immediately set up their radio station along the edge of the tarmac runway, the Japanese soldier's looked on mystified, (no one had told them of the truce). The British POWs were still being made to work, but it didn't take them long to find out what was going on. It wasn't long until Arthur and the crew had the mobile radio station up and working, Arthur told me that what had happened was that Mountbatten had got him and his unit to go into Donwang against the regulations of the truce. When they did arrive the Siamese underground had organized with POW's who had managed to break out of camps to try and get them back to the allies.

Arthur's job was to set up communication between Donwang and Rangoon to get the POW's out as soon as possible. They would be the link between the incoming aircraft and the ground. Every single aircraft that could fly and take passengers was ordered to fly to Donwang to pick up POW's. Arthur sent back word to headquarters at Rangoon that they were ready and to send as many aircraft as they possibly could. He said some of the men were in a terrible state. I don't need to say any more on that subject. Arthur took it upon himself to get the POWs into groups of 25 and line them up along the edge of the runway to await being picked up by the incoming aircraft. All of a sudden the sky was full of transport aircraft waiting to land and it wasn't long till Arthur and his crew had them working like a conveyor belt. They worked night and day continually for 14 days. Every conceivable type of aircraft landed at Donwang to take the POWs out and back to Rangoon. This evacuation was taking place under truce conditions, what an operation!

Arthur and his crew remained in Siam until August 1946. The Siamese government did award Arthur and his crew three medals but they were not recognized by the MOD, who eventually awarded them the Pacific Clasp.

Lord Louis Mountbatten sent Arthur a personnel letter of thanks and I quote its contents below.

To:1035403 Corporal Maultsaid A.

From: The Supreme Allied Commander South East Asia Command.

Your devotion to duty has resulted in your name being brought to my notice. I would like to thank you for your valuable services and to express my appreciation for the fine example you have set.

Signed
Louis Mountbatten

This letter was a marvellous reference for Arthur in years to come when he applied for employment.

Arthur returned home to the UK in August 1946 to be demobbed. He returned home to Northern Ireland and started a retail radio and television business. He also worked for various organizations fixing their transmitter receiver radio's one of which was The Royal Navy Lifeboat Institute. Arthur is retired now and lives with a friend on the Upper Newtownards Road.

FLIGHT SERGEANT
JOHN McADAM
BATTLE OF BRITAIN PILOT
ROYAL AIR FORCE NO. 748076
FIGHTER PILOT
NO. 41 SQUADRON, HORNCHURCH

Sergeant John 'Johnny' McAdam was born in Gillingham, Kent on the 21st March 1919 of Ulster parentage. His father had been a captain in the 'Black Watch' during the First World War and had been awarded the Military Cross. His father and mother who Johnny was extremely close to returned to Northern Ireland and took up residence in a beautiful house that had been given the name 'York Villa' in Cable Road, Whitehead. Captain McAdam became an official in the Ministry of Agriculture and for many years was Hon. Secretary of Whitehead Golf Club and during the season 1939-1940 was made Captain.

Sergeant John McAdam was educated at Whitehead Public Elementary School and studied for his higher education at the Belfast Royal Academical Institution (INST). He was a student of Engineering at Queens University Belfast but had to give this up due to him being called to full time service with the Royal Air Force Volunteer Reserve.

As a young lad John was intrigued with flying kites, this is were he possibly got his love for aircraft. A very close friend of his Squadron Leader NH Corry, DFC AE told me of how Johnny broke his arm jumping from his 1st floor bedroom window using his father's umbrella as a 'parachute'. Johnny was an ardent member of the 1st Whitehead Scout Group, a keen radio enthusiast, adored yachting and sailed a Waverly at the County Antrim Yacht Club in his spare time. John with his love of aviation decided to enlist in the RAFVR in Belfast on the 28th April 1939 as an AC2 (Under Training Pilot) and on the 29th April he was promoted to Sergeant and started his flying career in Tiger Moths at 24 E&RFTS at Sydenham. With the outbreak of war on the 3rd September 1939 of he and 190 other members of the RAFVR were called to full time service.

On the 30th October 1939 John along with three other Ulster VR (Johnny McCann, Winder McConnell and Jimmy McCausland) were posted to No 4 ITW at Bexhill on the south coast of England between Hastings and Eastbourne. As Sergeant Johnny Mc Adam was killed

in action on the 20th February 1941 and his flying logbook is missing and there is an 'official' version of his short career in the RAF. I would like to tell you Johnny's own account of what happened as I am honoured to have copies of personal letters that he sent home to his parents during those two years and I am indebted to his sister for allowing me to use them for his memoirs.

On completion of his initial training Johnny was posted to No6 SFTS at RAF Little Rissington on the 9th December 1939 where he started his flying training on Harvards.

The following are copies of the three letters that Johnny sent to his dad from Little Rissington.

Rissington
Thursday
25th January 1940.

Dear Dad

Many thanks for your letter which arrived this afternoon. It would seem that a letter that I wrote to Mum over a week ago and which contained all the details of my accident has not arrived. In case you have not got the story yet, here are the rough facts. About a fortnight ago I was doing some solo night flying in a Harvard. We were to fly to a place about 30 miles away and return to Oxford. There were three of us, the leading plane having an Instructor on board. We took off independently and had arranged to join formation in the air. I was the last one up and I joined formation with the other two before I raised my 'undercart'. As soon as I got to my station I pulled the lever to raise the wheels, but it wouldn't come. In a Harvard there is an arrangement whereby the operating lever has to be lifted radially outwards before pulling it back. This is so it will not become confused with the flap lever beside it. The lever is held in a slot and has to be lifted out against a spring. Well, apparently something had gone wrong with the spring and stuck it became, it wouldn't lift out of its slot and therefore could not be pushed backwards. Now for formation flying at a speed of 215mph and with the wheels down a Harvard wont go more than about 150mph. The result was that in about a minute or so the other two in front were about two mile ahead. After about another two minutes the lights of the planes in front disappeared, so I thought that I had better get back to the aerodrome alone.

You can imagine my feelings when I realised that the lights on the aerodrome had been extinguished. I was in the tightest spot of my career so far, I couldn't see a single thing, not even a light on the ground, not even a moon, at least not for another three hours. I tried to keep calm and collected but began to fear that somebody else was going to do the collecting. I was not quite decided what to do. That was putting it mildly. I undid my straps, opened the hood, throttled back and had a look overboard. I still could not see a thing. I had to decide what I was going to do and pretty quickly. Regulations say that you have got to head the machine for open country, switch off and bale out. However these regulations are not made by people when they are actually in the position concerned. I weighed up the whole thing in my mind and decided that if I still had the wheels down and full use of my engine I should be able to make some sort of a landing. After a bit however I thought that the idea of trying to land a two and three quarter ton piece of machinery moving at a landing speed of 85-95mph in a 'black out' might not work in practice. So I opened the throttle again and decided to gain a bit of height and reconsider the question of baling out. Well to be perfectly honest the only reason that I didn't jump was that I was just to scared to do so. The idea of landing on overhead high tension cable wires or a lake or a river or even a town didn't appeal to me. I decided to follow the originally set out in the hope of meeting the other two coming back. I had another go at the undercart but it was to no avail. I pulled at the lever until I was blue in the face and still it would not come.

In the end I pulled so hard that I pulled my wrist out of joint and that more or less finished things. I was by this time both a physical and nervous wreck. I managed to fly back and forwards along the course until I found a red railway signal lamp. I knew that if I kept to the South of that railway I would meet the other two coming back. Inside another two or three minutes I was saved.

The other two had missed me and were flying up and down the course looking for me. When I got back to the aerodrome I had a job putting the flap lever down but I made a reasonable landing. Well that's the story with all the details. It was found afterwards that a small stone had got jammed in the spring, preventing it from being compressed. The handle of the lever was bent one quarter out of alignment due to the pressure I had exerted on it. The lever is a half-inch diameter tube. I sounded the MO about the probability of a weeks leave but he wanted to keep an eye on me himself. My arm is practically OK now except for a slight pain when I twist my wrist. I didn't tell mum any details until after I was on the mend, I just mentioned that I had hurt my hand. Actually I didn't feel any pain until I was on the ground although I knew that something had gone wrong. However alls well that ends well and so fourth but I wouldn't take the proverbial pension to do it again. There is a bit of anxiety felt now for two of our boys who went up about four hours ago to do what is called a 'War Load Climb', i.e. climb to 25,000ft with 800lbs of sand in bags. They left the ground at about 2.30pm and it is now about 6.25pm and pitch dark. The endurance of the plane is about three hours, perhaps even less when continuing climbing. However they may have landed in some field in day light miles from anywhere and have not got in touch with the aerodrome yet. They are in an Anson which is quite a hefty machine to force land. However there is a full moon so they could even land at night. All the fields are covered in snow, which stands out well in moon light.

You were asking about 'patrols'. The only duty like that which we do is to report any suspicious planes we see and stand by when a general alarm is given. However we would only be used as a last resort, I am not a first line pilot yet. We do a lot of cross country, forced landing practice, practical navigation and so on, also lectures three times a week. At the rate at which we are going now it will be another two an a half to three months before I collect enough lectures and exams to get my Wings. We don't stand a chance of getting commissions until we are all Sergeant Pilots in No 17 Squadron. I feel quite satisfied at the moment. Re the saving money. I am quite willing to wager that I saved more in the time since Christmas than you did. By tomorrow (pay-day) Lloyds Bank will have £16-10-0 of mine. We get paid whether we are snowed up or in hospital. Of course I have included in that amount the money I brought back after Christmas. The only trouble is that when I draw any money my signature never seems to agree with the specimen. Will write again over the weekend. My congratulations on the promotion.

Yours John.

Little Risington
Sunday.

Dear dad,

You will find enclosed some pictures of my particular machine. In the two pictures of the instrument panel, several instruments are not shown as they are below the level; seen in the photograph, IE magnetic compass, fuel gauge etc. In the photo which was taken from the back of the cockpit (showing the windscreen) you can see the propeller blade on the right hand side. The small oval dark thing at the top of the picture is a darkened glass shade which prevents glare from spoiling your aim (lights in front). Of the two uppermost dials the one on the left is the fuel-air ratio. This instrument is used continuously because the air gets thinner as altitude increases. On the right top is an instrument with three needles. The upper gives oil temperature and the lower to give petrol and oil pressures. These two needles can just be seen at the top of the page scale photograph. Directly below this is the 'rate of climb' indicator, and below that is the 'turn and bank' indicator for blind flying. Below that are two gauges, the right hand one giving 'gun air pressure' in the gun firing pneumatic system. The left one gives the suction which works the instruments using gyroscopes.

On the extreme right of the large scale photo the upper dial is the supercharge (called manifold pressure) gauge and the lower one gives RPM. On the extreme left the upper dial gives the cylinder head temperature in 0C and below that is the carburettor temperature in 0C. Below the fuel-air ratio dial is the air speed indicator. Below that is the altimeter which actually has three hands concentric with one another like a clock. As the hands are all in line with one another you can only see the largest one. Below the altimeter are two small instruments, the left one being a clock and the right one giving outside temperature. The dial in the bottom left hand corner is the ammeter, serving the same purpose as on a car. The central ring is the control column with the trigger button on top. In the bottom right hand corner are the eight bomb selector switches. The bombs are of course only small ones for dive-bombing. The two central dials are the artificial horizon (using a gyroscope) and a gyrocompass also using a gyro. Along the bottom edge of the large-scale photograph is a row of various switches such as navigation lights, fuel gauge lights etc. The fuel gauges are down on the floor of the cockpit. The ignition switch is about half way up the left hand edge of the large-scale photograph. The little white spot just below the ammeter is the automatic horn cut out. Normally if the throttle was pulled back a certain distance the horn would sound if the undercarriage was not lowered. In certain aerobatics it is necessary to close the throttle and to stop the horn from blowing this button is pushed. To the right and left of this button are two knobs which are dimmers for the instrument lights. The two knobs above there are the gun sight light and the cockpit light. Just inside the right hand side of the cockpit can be seen the R/T control box and beside that the 'park brake'. This, when pulled, locks the fluid in the brake system and so locks the wheels. The photograph which seems to be composed of metal rods is a view of the left hand side of the cockpit. The two 'wheels' are the trimmers for the rudder and tail. TH means tail heavy. Just in front of these is the hand petrol pump. Above the pump are the throttle, mixture and airscrew pitch controls. (TM and P). Just over half way up the left hand side is the petrol tank selector. The undercart and flap selector handles are quite easily seen, the round handle being the undercarriage (marked LAND GEAR) handle. You can see the projection which prevents it from being pulled back until it is lifted. The rectangular handle (pointed directly at the camera) marked FLAP is the selector lever for the flaps. The knob marked PUSH (upside down) completes the operation after the levers have been selected. The hand hydraulic pump is used if the engine pump for these operations fails. The two selectors on the right hand top edge control the amount of distribution of suction to the gyro instruments. The knob and handle just below these control the heating of the carburettor. The dark object in the bottom right hand corner is my foot up against one of the rudder bars, and in the left bottom corner is the bucket seat, designed to receive a parachute. Well I think that is about all there is to say about the photographs.

I went down to Henley yesterday and shot up the boat race. I wasn't the only one because half the Air Force was there at the same time. I tried to take a photograph but I had to busy a time dodging other machines. I'm going to Cranwell tomorrow on a cross-country exercise about 300 miles return. I will give you my impressions of the trip tomorrow night.

Yours

John

PS These photos were taken with previous permission so you have no fears about them being illegal or secret.

What a wonderful and descriptive letter to his father. I am sure after he read it he knew as much about the Harvard cockpit as his son did.

Little Rissington
Sunday

Dear Dad

Many thanks for your letter and also the PTQ. (The PTQ was a students Magazine issued by Queens University students for 'Rag day'). Re the 'workshops of some kind' at Brooklands. If Mr Vickers or Mr Armstrong heard you talk of that factory in that manner I fear that you would have a libel suit against you. It us from these 'huts' as you call them that we get our Spitfires and Wellingtons. During the last two days or so, in fact during most of the week I have been sitting for exams. On Tuesday, Wednesday and Thursday I sat for the Second-Class Navigators Certificate and on Friday and Saturday I had a shot at the exam for a 'B' Licence. Neither of these things is necessary to me at the moment, but they are useful things to have when I am due for promotion. I don't fancy my chances for the 'B' licence but I think I have got through the navigators exam OK.

Our chances of getting into commissioned rank seem to be very slight at the present time. It appears that the air ministry prefer to give commissions to the fellows from the Colonies rather than those from the British Isles. Of the last two squads that left here, one yesterday and the other about a month ago there were 11 commissions given, 10 to Colonials and one the 'Honourable Anthony Duvivier'. The reason given is that there are far too many officers in the service as it is but the general opinion is that a Sergeant Pilot is a lot cheaper to keep than his commissioned counterpart. However I am probably talking through my hat.

Yours
John

Johnny completed his flying training at Little Rissington and on the 29th April 1940 and was awarded his Wings. On the 19th June 1940 he posted to No 6 OTU at Sutton Bridge where he commenced his operational training on Spitfires.

Three days later he was posted to 41 (F) Squadron at Catterick. On the 22nd June 1940 Johnny Joined 41 Fighter Squadron at Catterick . The squadron had seen its first action on the 17th December 1939 when Flight Lieutenant Webster in K9991 attacked a He 115 near

Whitby without success. 41 Squadron's first victory came on the 3rd April when Flight Lieutenant Ryder shot down a He111 off Whitby. When Johnny arrived at 41 Squadron in June little did he know three weeks later he would be fighting in the Battle of Britain.

The following are copies of letters which Sergeant John McAdam Johnny wrote to his mother and father from Hornchurch between the 22nd June 1940 and the 20th February 1941. They tell his own story.

Hornchurch
Sunday
September 1940

Dear Pop,

I am sorry for not writing before but as you know yourself the air has been pretty 'thick' round here for the last week. Yesterday of course was the big day for me, I sent a telegram in case the Air Ministry had thought I was missing and had informed you. The story is rather a long one but here goes. We came down here on Tuesday at very short notice and inside two days we lost the Commanding Officer (Squadron Leader Hood) and Flight Lieutenant Webster of whom you must have heard me speak. His total 'bag' was somewhere in the twenties before they got him. He got the DFC when I was home last

Authors note

On the 5th September 1940 Flight Lieutenant John Terrance Webster's Spitfire, R6635 collided with that flown by the Commanding Officer Squadron Leader Hood, whilst they were engaged in combat over the Thames Estuary. Flight Lieutenant Webster baled out, but was dead when he reached the ground. He was awarded the DFC on the 30th August 1940 (Squadron Leader Hood also died). His total was 11 and two shared destroyed and two unconfirmed destroyed and three damaged. One of his claims was a BF109E of Stab/JG51 that was flown by Major Werner Molders. His aircraft crash-landed on a beach in France. Molders was wounded.

Soon after that other pilots of ours were missing. Wallins in hospital, Sergeant Barr 'Lefty' just a bundle of nerves. Bannion's crashed twice, actually both times he got away by simply force landing as he was not on fire, merely a dead engine. Lovell baled out, Lock (my Co Pilot at Rissington) shot in the leg, Cory shot in the arm and three places in the legs. Stewart falling into the sea, and Ryan crashing on landing. Today I learn that Scott and Ford have both gone down in flames and Bannions has crashed again. As far as I can remember that is the sum total of our activities for yesterday's performance. Yesterday as you know was the big day for the Air Force. We had been up four or five times in the morning to tame some recco machines. But I was not happy because my engine was running very roughly. I still had the old 'Floater' EB-F.

Anyway the main raid came over and up we went. I got left behind in the main chase and so I climbed up to about 20,000ft and saw below me a ME109. From the way he went down I presume he never knew what hit him. *(Johnny's first kill)*. Then I saw another of our squadron on its own and we flew parallel about 100 yards apart watching each other's tails. We flew over the centre of the city miles above the balloons when I saw a lot of AA fire to the east of us and in a second or two I saw 500 bombers with a strong fighter escort above them. I told my companion I was going over to investigate, if he would watch my tail. Climbing up very carefully I saw that there were many separate squadrons at different levels. I choose a squadron which was about 35 or 40 strong and in line astern. I dived on the tail of the last one, he burst into flames and I followed him down and when I was sure he was gone *(2nd kill)* I zoomed up into a loop and dived down on the next one in line of the squadron *(third kill)*. By this time my machine was like a sieve, oil and glycol (used instead of cooling water) pouring out. However I got the one I aimed at and as I followed him down the rest of the squadron opened fire on me with a nice line of cross-fire, in addition to which I had a few 110's, 1109's and 113's chasing me. All my ammunition was gone and the plane was hardly moving. I thanked my lucky stars I had practiced my aerobatics to perfection. I did a loop, rolled of the top of it, looped again until I shook all of them off. All this time the glycol was spewing out of the nose of the plane and finally the radiator temperature dropped back to zero. The oil temperature went up and up and finally off the clock. Then of course a 109 had to come down and play with me so I had to do something to discourage him. I pulled the 'stick' straight back and put full right rudder on, and of course the plane spun.

I let it spin about three times and then pulled out very carefully because the machine was full of holes and was not so strong. The manoeuvre did not shake the 109 off and he came at me again. I trimmed the plane for a right hand gliding turn, lowered my seat, pulled my knees up and my head down to take full advantage of the armour plating behind me. I heard about 10 or 12 bullets hitting the plating and then miracle No 1 occurred. Sergeant Darling who was the 'companion' over the city came along to refuel and rearm and with his last burst hit the Me109 for a six, and I continued on my way. The engine by this time had run out of glycol and finally got red hot and seized (i.e. just stopped). The oil had sprayed onto the hot engine and it burst into flames, I looked around for a place to land but all I could see was houses. I was going to jump for it but I did not have enough height left. At last I found a field and glided towards it in a sideslip to keep the flames away from the cockpit. I tried to lower the flaps and slow down. When I thought I was about 40 feet up (I could not see anything because of the flames and smoke) I pulled the stick right back, hit the ground tail first and pancaked onto the ground. I went through a couple of walls and a few trees, cart wheeled over twice and finally came to rest upside down with me inside unhurt. (This was miracle No 2). It was getting rather hot inside and I was unable to get out. I was just going to 'shoot' myself to get it over with when a man came along with an axe and split the side of the cockpit open and pulled me out. I was taken to a house and of course was the centre of attraction for miles around. At last a policeman came along and fixed me up with transport to the aerodrome and that was more or less that. I have a few scrapes and bruises, nothing broken and am OK except I have been grounded for 24 hrs provisionally but otherwise feel quite fit.

Yours John

PS I wrangled a new uniform and flying kit out of this performance. *(A week later Johnny had to bale out over the sea.)*

This action actually took place on September 7th at Leonard Drive, Drakes Farm, Rayleigh after combat over Hornchurch in Spitfire EB-F code P9430. Johnny had shot down and destroyed a Dornier 17 (I wonder is the civilian still around).

Hornchurch
Saturday 1940

Dear Pop,

Very little activity to report except that I was hit on the head with a piece of a exploded AA shell. Luckily I had my 'Tin Hat' on so I am still alive. The hat however is rather the worse for wear and my spine feels as if somebody has tied a knot in it. There is a bright side to the story. I have a new tin hat now, and what's more, this one fits.

I don't think I told you but I have a motorbike here for getting from A to B. However the Squadron Leader isn't quite sure if he approves of pilots having motorbikes. Apparently if we brake our necks we may as well do it in action.

Authors Note: I think this next paragraph of his letter is so funny but so typical of those terrible days.

By the way, the following was the conversation heard on the R/T on Wednesday during a dog fight.

Spitfire Pilot 'A, "You B......D, You've shot me."

Spitfire Pilot 'B', (with a super Oxford Accent):- "Awfully sorry."

Yours
John

PS. I was thinking perhaps if I was home you could do a few sketches for me of things I remember. In conjunction with my logbook they would be quite useful after the war.

On the 23rd September 1940 Johnny was shot down during a squadron patrol off Dover, in Spitfire N 3118. He managed to bale out and was rescued from the sea and admitted to Dover Hospital.

Hornchurch
Friday
1940

Dear Mum

Many thanks for your letter. There were a few pieces cut out but I managed to get some sense out of it. Things have been rather quiet around here except for the fact that I shot another Me109 down on Wednesday. It was our big day because we met a squadron of eight Gerry's and eight of us got one each. I expect that they are still waiting for them in France to come back.

I see Norman Browne is still on the party racket but I am rather surprised to see as many as 24 at one party. The picture home must have suffered that night. Talking of parties reminds me that we had one on Wednesday night. It was in celebration of our big day and also in a small way for me as that day I had shot down my '5th Gerry'. However there are plenty left and I am going to try and get ten before we leave Hornchurch which may be in the near future.

I have been systematically refusing leave for the last month in the hope that I might get some round about Christmas. Please excuse this scribble but I am rather pushed for time.

Love John

Hornchurch
Tuesday
October 1940

Dear Mum and Dad,

It might interest you to know that I have done it again. On Saturday night last, on taking off with the rest of the squadron for a patrol, the 'thing' nearly shook to pieces and then the engine went on fire and seized. By this time I was at about 100ft up and on the momentum I was able to climb to about 500ft. All I could see around me was houses everywhere in all directions. Then I saw a park full of kids about 100 yards long (the park not the kids) just below me. I did the most vicious sideslip ever done in a Spitfire and slowed down to about 100mph and looked to see if the kids had taken the hint. Well you know what kids are, they just stand and gape.

So to cut a long story short, I ended up in someone's front garden. Having cut my wings off by going through in between a couple of houses. The only casualties were a dog and a couple of chickens. The aeroplane of course was a complete write off, except for the wireless set which I quickly transported to a place of safety. I drank the traditional cup of tea, refused dozens of cigarettes and offers of drinks and signed a couple of hundred autograph books. The Home Guard did not quite save me from having my jacket torn to pieces by souvenir collectors. The greatest surprise has yet to come. The crowd passed round a hat and collected £1-3-8 for me to buy a new Spitfire with. They are a bit short but every little helps. My Flight Commander suggested that I send it to the Telegraph, which I decided to do.

Yesterday the first of the fan mail arrived, 21 requests for autographs, 26 for souvenirs and 31 for both. The question of autographs was simple enough but the providing of 57 souvenirs was a problem. In the end I got permission to cut up part of one of the wings and everybody seemed satisfied. Here is an extract from one of the letters and one of the few which did not end up with a request. "I do wish to congratulate you on your skilful piloting, your lucky escape and the cheerful way you took it." I like the last line. I bet most people would be cheerful in my case. The writer (a girl) probably thought I was shot down. However I arrived back at the aerodrome festooned with belts of machine gun ammunition and with the wireless set on my shoulder. When I saw the MO he just said, "You again," and offered me a weeks leave. I was soft enough not to take it as we are rather short of experienced (ahem) pilots. However I took Sunday, Monday and Tuesday off to get things squared up.

It was now Wednesday because I had to leave the letter until today to get it finished. Many thanks for the biscuits, which are very much appreciated. Please do not send me anything else because I have not opened the tin I took away with me yet.

Love John

These next two letters were sent to another researcher who was investigating that particular crash at Hornchurch and 41 Squadron personnel. "It shows the quality of the man that Sergeant Johnny McAdam was."

Mrs A Green
43 Malvern Road
Hornchurch
Essex
RM11 1BG.

Dear Sir

Regarding our 'Hero', yes I can tell you every detail regarding this brave young man. I was 29 at the time and am still living in the same house, a minute away from where he crashed. It was Number 91 Globe Road, it is a big bungalow and is still the same, though the lady who lived there died a few years ago.

He came over our houses, very low and making an awful noise, we all knew he was going to crash. He headed for the park, and as you say, he would not land owing to the children playing so he went through the back garden to the bungalow, not touching the bungalow itself, but the garage at the side of the garden of it and the garden of the house at the other side. When he got out of his plane, do you know what he did, he calmly got his comb out and combed his hair. That always sticks in my mind, and if I remember rightly he had very fair hair, what nerve that man had, so brave we all cheered him and clapped him and then some one said we ought to have a collection for him, we all run home and got some money and put it in his helmet. He did not want to take it and kept saying no, no. But we all insisted, I can see him laughing now, he had a bright smile and if I remember rightly he was around 5ft 3 or 4 or round about that and medium build. I phoned my son and he remembers him taking the bullets out of the wing at the plane. My son was five years old at the time and my niece who also lived in Malvern Street did get his autograph, but over the years has lost it. She was 14 years old on the 14th October, two days after and remembers him well.

We are all so very sorry to hear that he was killed, we always wondered if he was still alive, I pass the bungalow several times a week and have thought of him often. Who would have thought when I was 29 that in 48 years time I would be writing about this brave young pilot

Yours Sincerely
Mrs A Green

Mrs NE Brazear
Hornchurch
Essex

Dear Sir,

Thank you for your letter, and photocopy of the crashed Spitfire at No 91 Globe Road. We live at No 90 Globe Road which is opposite. These are the facts as I recall them:- John McAdam crash landed when I was 14 and still at school. Our house was in direct line with take off from Horn church Aerodrome, (all grass), and when we heard the Spits and Hurricanes taking off, we used to be on the alert because we knew bandits were over the English Channel and on their way to us. On the day John crashed, we heard what sounded like an aircraft engine in distress and then an almighty crashing and banging. Our thoughts were immediately, one of theirs or ours. My mother and I rushed to the front door, just as John was climbing out of his Spitfire and went to his assistance with other neighbours. He shouted to us in no uncertain terms to stand clear as there was a risk of fire and the Spit was fully armed. Even after the shock of crashing his first concern was for the safety was of others. He worked on the plane for some minutes and then reappeared with bandoliers of ammo around his neck and body, he put them down and went back to the plane several times to make it safe.

Only then did he accept a cup of tea from a neighbour. Everybody was excited and asked John what happened and how he came to land by the bungalow. He said he thought he could manage a wheels down landing on the park, but when he saw the children playing on the swings and roundabouts, had to take avoiding action and crash through the side of the bungalow. To all of us, Sergeant John McAdam was a hero and a brilliant pilot. The gap between the bungalow and the house in Hillcrest Road is still only about 80 feet and yet he managed to steer the stricken aircraft clear of the children playing in the park and into the gap. Had he demolished the block of houses opposite the bungalow, which were all occupied and the loss of life would have been considerable. Eventually help arrived from Hornchurch Aerodrome and we only saw John once more when he came to view the scene with an officer.

Mrs NE Brazear

The next two letters letter which Johnny wrote to his parents were sent sometime during December 1940 or January 1941.

Hornchurch
Friday

Dear Pop

Many thanks for your letter. This is going to be a lot of scribble but I find that I have a spare moment, and I thought a line home might meet with approval. You probably know already (from mum) about our encounter with eight Me109s. eight came and eight stayed. Everyone of our Flight (B), the CO and the boss of (A) Flight got one. We had a terrific party that night. It might possibly interest you to know that I have now got 'five down' now and still going strong. I am scared to take a day off in case I miss anything because suddenly Me109's are few and far between. Perhaps you remember Locke, the fellow who was my co-pilot at Rissington. Well he has just came to a sticky end, multiple fractures in both legs and left arm and is generally knocked about. His flying days are over but his bag was 23 destroyed and seven probably destroyed.

He just got the DSO and he has already got a DFC and Bar. He forgot that Me110's always fly in pairs and he attacked the wrong one, shot it down and was watching it when about a dozen cannon shells hit him.

Yours
John

Hornchurch
Sunday

Dear Pop

I received your letter card, for which many thanks. Nothing very much has happened during the past week except that I am now nearly always a section leader and on Thursday I was Leader of 'R' Flight. Actually Thursday was another big day. On that day we were re-equipped with Spitfire 11's and I celebrated by making a Me109 swim home. He made a lovely splash about seven or eight miles from Dungeness. This, by the way with only three guns working, the other froze up owing to a break in the heater piping conducting hot air from the radiator. Another thing is that I nearly went to Egypt. Early in the week the CO asked for four volunteers to fly Hurricanes in the Middle East. My pal here said that he would go if I would go so they put the names in a hat and drew four out. My pal of course was one of the lucky ones and I was not. However it's all in the luck of the game.

Yours John

This may have been the last correspondence between Johnny and his parents before he died.

Sadly on the 20th February 1941while flying his Spitfire P 7302. Sergeant Johnny McAdam was shot down and killed in a snowstorm over Dover by Major Werner Molders. The time was 1600 hrs. (Sergeant Johnny McAdam was Molder's 100th victim.) His aircraft crashed near the Duke of York Military School at Dover in the Parish of Guston near the Swing Gate Inn.

Sergeant John McAdam baled out of his stricken Spitfire and landed in the sea of Dover. He managed to swim to a Rescue Boy, but when he was picked up by the Air Sea Rescue people he was dead. When his body was brought back to the squadron after it was picked up by the Air Sea Rescue it was found that his back was riddled with cannon rounds. This was confirmed to me by his armourer a Mr Ron Marshall who was there when they brought his body back to Hornchurch. Mr Marshall is also an Ulsterman and still lives in the outskirts of Belfast.

Sergeant John McAdam is buried quite close to me in Islandmagee Cemetery in Islandmagee which I visit it quite often, especially on Remembrance Sunday when I place a Poppy on his grave.

Sergeant Mc Adam's Flight Commander on that fateful day was a Pilot Officer Brown, later to become Squadron Leader MP Brown, AFC, and who wrote to me on the 10th December 2001 with his own personal account of what happened on the 20th February 1941.

On the 20th February 1941, I was leading a patrol of six Spitfires at 25,000 ft over the Dungeness area. The controller reported that there were Bandits in our vicinity at 6,000ft - some 19,000ft below us. We were concentrating on sighting them below to take advantage of height for our attack. Our top cover Spitfire reported that he had engine trouble and left to return to base. After two or three minutes I checked the sky above and saw a group of Me109's diving down on us from 3 o'clock. I shouted a warning and led the flight into a steep climbing turn to meet them head on. As I pulled hard into the climb there was loud banging noise in the rear fuselage and I thought I had been hit by cannon fire. In fact my aircraft had gone into an uncontrolled high-speed stall and I blacked out. When I came to I was in a steep spin. I recovered control and then climbed up to join the action again. As I climbed I saw a pilot on a parachute above me. I circled close to him and recognised that it was Sergeant Mc Adam. He was not conscious and white smoke was coming from a hole in the middle front of his Sidcot Flying Suit. There were no Me109's in sight. I stayed with him until he landed in the sea off Dover. While I continued to circle to guide the rescue boat, I was attacked and fired at by 109's, which then flew back to France. Sergeant McAdam must have been killed immediately by an incendiary shell which entered the back of his body.

He could not have been hit in the back when in the cockpit as he would have been protected by armour plating and fuselage, nor in the action baling out. He must have been fired on after he baled out and had pulled the ripcord. Who was responsible for this ?

Major Molders, the famous German ace, was credited with the shooting down of Sergeant John Mc Adam. Our own Spitfires were not fitted with cannons. It has been proposed by post war writers that Sergeant John McAdam was killed accidentally by enemy fire that was meant for me when I was circling him. The suggestion that Molders or one of his flight shot a pilot hanging on his parachute by mistake when he was aiming at a circling Spitfire is beyond belief. Sergeant McAdam had been shot before I climbed up to him and there were no Me109's in sight. When circling, my aircraft was always at right angles to the parachute and never in a direct line of sight. Sergeant Angus had also been shot down over the sea, again credited to Molders, but was not found and reported missing.

A sad day for the Squadron.

Squadron Leader MP Brown, AFC

Sergeant Johnny McAdam was killed on the 20th February 1941 at 1600 hrs. On the 21st February 1941 at 6.45pm a Post Office Telegram arrived at the family home in Whitehead (and I quote) "Request instructions for funeral No 748076 Sergeant J McAdam. Reply to Adjutant of RAF Station Hornchurch. Aeronautics Hornchurch."

The next day the 22nd February 1941 another Post Office Telegram arrived at the family home at 7.10am (and I quote) "Regret to inform you your son 748076 Sergeant John McAdam killed 20.2.41. Letter follows. Records Telex Ruislip."

This must have been a very emotional and traumatic time for his parents especially when they had received these two telegrams. Sergeant John McAdams father received this telegram from the Record Office in Ruislip on the 22nd February 1941.

Dear Sir.

It is my painful duty to confirm my telegram of yesterday's date in which you were notified of the death of your son, No 748076 Sergeant John McAdam of No 41 Squadron, Royal Air Force, who was killed in action during and engagement with enemy aircraft over the English Channel on the 20th February 1941.

The Air Council desire me, in conveying this information to you, to express their sympathy and deep regret at your son's death in his Country's Service.

I am,
Dear Sir,
Your Obedient Servant

Letter sent to Mr McAdam On the 6th March 1941 from the Commanding Officer of 41 Squadron.

RAF Catterick

Dear Mr McAdam,

Both you and 41 Squadron have suffered a severe loss by the death of your son. 'Macs' name had become almost proverbial for the manner in which he returned to duty after experiences which would have cracked up most people. No pilot in the squadron was keener or more devoted to duty and it is with deep regret that I send the sympathy of the squadron to you and his relatives.

Yours Sincerely
DO Findlay (Squadron Leader)
A Friends Appreciation of Sergeant J. McAdam.
"Cleanest, straightest fellow"

At the evening service in Whitehead Presbyterian Church on Sunday, The Rev. WFS Stewart, MA paid a touching tribute to the memory of Sergeant-Pilot McAdam, who had been brought up in connection with that congregation. Their thoughts turned in sympathy to the bereaved family in their hour of deep sorrow.

One of his closest friends writes this appreciation: "The whitest man I ever met was 'Johnny Mac' as we used to call him at Inst. The war meant an end of his engineering career, but he took it, philosophically, looking forward instead of back. Johnny, in the old First Whitehead Scout Troop, at Inst., at Queens and afterwards was the cleanest, straightest fellow I have ever met. 'Old fashioned,' they used to call him affectionately in Whitehead, but there was nothing 'old Fashioned' about Johnny the radio enthusiast, Johnny the yachtsman, sailing a Waverly at the County Antrim Yacht Club. Johnny the fair-haired lad in Airman's uniform, who thrilled his townsfolk with his flying, these are the memories that I and all his close friends will recall in the years to come. We who loved him are infinitely the poorer because 'One of our fighters has failed to return'."

A tribute paid by another close friend: "Small in stature, but a giant when it came to courage."

"All Whitehead mourned that day."

Extract taken from a letter by Squadron Leader George Herman Bannions, DFC who was a friend of Sergeant John McAdams. "Sergeant John McAdam was a young and very gallant young man to whom we should pay a Special Tribute. I certainly do."

John McAdam loved his mother and father dearly, so much so he had the name 'Pop' painted on the exit door of the cockpit on one of his Spitfire's and under the exhaust stubs of another. On hearing the news of her son's death. John's mother died one week later of a 'broken heart'. John's sister, Mrs Henshaw joined the WAAF's in 1940 when she was seventeen and a half and was posted to RAF Aldergrove as a Meteorologist where she remained until she was demobbed in 1946. Without her kindness and generosity in memory of her brother, this book would not have been published. Mrs Henshaw still lives next door to the family home in Cable Road, Whitehead, County Antrim.

FLIGHT LIEUTENANT
JSV McALLISTER, OBE DFC DFM
BAGR PHD
RAF NO. 1073644
NAVIGATOR

Flight Lieutenant JSV McAllister, known to all as Victor, was born in Historic Carrickfergus, on the shores of Belfast Lough on the 7th November 1918, and apart from his wartime service, lived there until his death in 1994. His primary education was at Joymount Public Elementary School, from where he won a scholarship to the Royal Belfast Academical Institution, which is known locally as Inst.

Following the Senior Certificate examinations in 1935 he won a further scholarship to attend Greenmount Agricultural College in Antrim where he obtained top marks in his year, taking first prize in Agricultural Science. Another Scholarship, from the Ministry of Agriculture took him to Queens University in Belfast to study Agriculture.

At the conclusion of his educational years he had completed his Bachelor of Arts and obtained his Doctorate. At 22 years of age Victor was not simply an academic but was also active in the Boy Scout movement with whom, as a member of the 1st Carrickfergus Troop, he obtained his Kings Badge in 1933. A keen sports enthusiast, he also played tennis, badminton and golf although rugby was his favourite, having played in every match for the Ulster Juniors in the seasons of 1937/38 and 1938/39. An accomplished academic and sportsman, Victor was without side and something of a perfectionist and would approach every situation with an inbuilt determination to do well. He was not an overly gregarious person, preferring to become voluble only when he knew precisely what he was talking about. By his own frank admission he did not have the personality to become a trailblazer in the services and would never rise, or be inspired to rise to a high rank. Victor did however have an inner strength and resolve which would carry him through the worst that the North African, the Mediterranean, and the European theatres of war could provide, as a DFM and two DFC's would subsequently attest.

By the time his graduation results were due in June 1940, Victor had already decided to volunteer for Army Service, his preference being a light armoured unit such as

the North Irish Horse. At that time the normal route for Graduate Enlistment was via the Joint Recruiting Board within Queens University. However, upon making his application he was informed that no recruits were needed until after the summer and he was advised to apply again at that time. In the interim, spent making use of his education in potato inspection for the Ministry of Agriculture, he reapplied in September to be told once more again there were no vacancies.

He enquired where he could join up immediately and was advised to try the Royal Air Force recruiting office in Belfast.

Thus started an association with flying which would not only lead to a distinguished spell in night flying but which would last well beyond the years of the Second World War. At the end of October 1940, Victor set off for Padgate, near Liverpool, with a number of other recruits. There the induction unit for Ulstermen was based and, after the medical and aptitude tests, he was kitted out and sent to West Kirby, near Birkenhead, for the dreaded square bashing and injections. Following basic training he was posted to Swanton Morley which was a new station, having opened in mid-September, with its first squadron arriving on the 1st November when 105 Squadron arrived from Watton with their Blenheim 1V's. Whilst there Victor experienced the actions of several Luftwaffe bombing raids, generally by single opportunist aircraft during daylight hours, and mainly on those which hampered the airfield defences. On the 27th of February, a Ju88 got a little carried away and bombed from too low an altitude resulting in its bombs not fusing and remaining intact and bouncing along the ground. Flight

Lieutenant Charlton, the station Armament Officer, defused these next morning. (Flight Lieutenant Charlton eventually dealt with over 200 unexploded bombs in the East Anglian area and was later honoured with the award of the George Cross.)

In early March the flying training system was ready and Victor was duly posted to No 5 Aircrew Reception Centre at Stratford-upon-Avon. Here, in addition to the routine square bashing and physical training, he was introduced to Morse code and the use of wireless telegraphy. Two weeks later he was sent to the Initial Training Wing at Aberystwyth for six weeks of intensive ground training following which the rest of his intake were given one weeks leave. Unfortunately Victor missed out, his leave being withheld due to the difficulty of travelling to and from Ulster at that time. The next stop was five days at Wilmslow in Cheshire where he was provided with a grey flannel civilian suit and a suitcase, which could only suggest the next of training would entail a journey, possibly overseas. Sure enough the young trainees then proceeded to Glasgow and on to Greenock for boarding the Union Castle vessel Windsor Castle for the six day crossing to Halifax, Nova Scotia, accompanied by a US warship returning home for repairs. During the first half of the crossing they had three Destroyer escort's but for the remainder of the journey had to rely on their speed to avoid the dreaded U-Boats, which thankfully did not happen. *(The Windsor Castle, 119,141 tons was subsequently sunk off Algiers on the 23rd March 1943.)*

Miami University-Florida

After the excitement of their safe arrival at Halifax, they faced a gruelling three days train journey before arriving in Toronto and the No 1 Manning depot at the Exhibition Centre. Six weeks were spent in this location and Victor remembers that the Canadians were warm and friendly people and extremely hospitable to the RAF. Then, on the 1st July, it was off to the sunnier climate of Florida for a twelve week Navigators Course at Miami University. Administered by Pan American Airways and using the Consolidated Commodore Flying Boats and a Vought Sikorsky Clipper, the University provided conditions far removed from those in Operational Flights, although Victor later considered that the Navigation and Meteorology courses were at least an equal of anything in the RAF at that time.

Victor's first flight in the Commodore Flying Boat was on the 2nd September which Captained by a Captain Roberts. He continued the course in Commodore's Nc 667, 668, and 669, eventually logging 46 hours tuition time and successfully completing the course on the 15th October. He was awarded an 'exceptional' rating having achieved an average 91.75% over the four disciplines of the course. The return journey home to the UK was of contrasts, commencing with the luxury of the air-conditioned stainless steel coaches of the Silver Bullet train to New York, and then onwards to the poor conditions of the partially completed transit camp at Moncton, New Brunswick. One week later it was back to Nova Scotia to embark from Halifax on the return journey to the Clyde. The journey home taking ten days in an unarmed Merchant Cruiser, with the sleeping quarters consisting of hammocks which had been hastily erected in the hold.

Bournemouth was the next destination, which was the receiving centre for all trained aircrew arriving from overseas, and it was here that Victor experienced a good example of the well known military phrase 'never volunteer for anything'. Shortly after arriving in Hampshire, a senior Air Ministry Officer arrived seeking people to train on 'radio locating' for night fighting. He explained that apart from the interesting nature of the work there were other possible benefits - small crews and good aircraft, probably Beaufighters, but most importantly he promised that volunteers would get to an Operational Unit and onwards to an Operational Squadron early. Consequently half the course volunteered and was immediately given two weeks leave and the remainder went direct to an OTU. In early December following his two weeks leave, Victor reported to No 3 Radio School at Prestwick where he completed a three week introductory course on radar, and a night vision test for which he was given 'above the Average'. He was again sent home on leave, for seven weeks this time, to await a posting to an OTU as a Sergeant Observer/Radio Operator.

1073644 LAC J.S.V. McAllister obtained a course pass but in the assessment by the Chief Instructor was 'below average'. For a person who had previously excelled in the USA and who would become a highly decorated night flying -back seater, this to me appears a strange result. Victor finally arrived at 54 OTU that was based at Church Fenton near Leeds, at the end of February 1941. Here, the first job was to crew up with a pilot and he was to be fortunate to meet fellow Sergeant AJ 'Ginger' Owen. The two became firm friends from the off and were to remain together as formidable team for the remainder of the war. Their first flight together as a team was on the 7th March in Blenheim 8674 lasting 2hrs.15mins.

Before the end of the Observer (Radio) course in May, 54 OTU was moved to Charterhall near Berwick although the final stages were to be completed at Winfield which was a satellite for Charterhall. The course ended on the 20th May after 57 hours of flying training and an assessment of 'average' an improvement compared to Prestwick. Following a short leave, the team were posted to No 600 (City of London) Auxiliary Squadron which was based at Predannack on the Lizard Peninsula in Cornwall. At that time the squadron was equipped with Beaufighter MkV1f's with the Mk 1V Radar, it's main function being defence against hit and run day raiders as well as intercepting mine laying/bombing aircraft in the English and Bristol Channel Areas.

Whilst there was not much enemy activity in the area this was beneficial, enabling Ginger and Victor to gain valuable experience together with their Beaufighter A1 Radar combination. They carried out their first Operational Reconnaissance on the 12th July, a date of some significance to some Ulstermen. Early in September the squadron moved to Church Fenton, the pair arriving in the Beaufighter V1 on the 4th, and it became obvious that an overseas posting was on the cards when khaki dress order was issued. At this time Ginger's ability as a pilot was recognised as he was the newest and youngest pilot on the Squadron to have an aircraft, V8410-'R' allocated to him. The following two months were spent carrying out familiarisation flights and on one of these they managed to arrange a trip to Carrickfergus. Victor recalled with a wry grin that he thought it doubtful if anyone had ever flown as low over his hometown as they did on that October day. The total journey took almost seven hours and was the longest single flight they ever made in a Beaufighter.

Towards the end of October a seven day leave was organised prior to embarking on their overseas posting and Victor decided to head home as it may be his last chance for some time. However this was not to be as he was taken off the train, having been informed that all leave had been cancelled as the squadron had been put on 'standby'. Not untypical in those times, the actual move did not happen until the 14th November when the Squadron left Church Fenton for Portreath near Penzance. Three days later they were Operational, flying their Beaufighter to Gibraltar, the overnight stop en route to Blida, the main French Air Force base in Algeria, some 30 miles south of Algiers City. Here the Squadron was to provide initial night fighter cover for the city and it's environs. After almost three weeks moving round between bases at Blida, Maison Blanche (Algiers civil airport) and Bou Farik (a small race track), the squadron settled on the 7th of December at Maison Blanche, from where Victor and Ginger recorded their first kill on the night of the 21st. Flying Beaufighter 8406-'T' they shot down a Heinkel 111, but not without a problem or two when the chase did not go entirely according to plan. A first success will always be a bit special and will remain clearly in the mind. Victor recalls that in their over excitement probably caused them to overhaul their eventual victim much too quickly. Ginger throttled back hard and dropped the undercarriage when visual contact was established and it is not clear whether the undercarriage was damaged by this action or by return fire from their prey, but in the eventual landing the aircraft crashed and careered off the runway, hit a parked Spitfire ER860, then hit a concrete mixer and a tanker before coming to rest, courtesy of a large pile of stones.

Although the aircraft was written off in the incident, both individuals emerged uninjured from the wreck, save for Victor's somewhat damaged nose. On returning to the dispersal area following some temporary repairs by the Medical Officer, the ground crew presented him with the clock from his instrument panel.

Victor's Logbook entry for the 21st reads:

Dec 21st   22.50pm. Beau V1. Sgt Owen, Self 'Scramble'. First operational contact. Heinkel 111 destroyed + one Beau, one Spit, one Bowser, also confirmed.

Wing Commander CP Green, DSO DFC, who had recently arrived as the new CO of 600 squadron, must have wondered what he had taken on particularly as the pair chose to wreck a spare aircraft, their regular 'R' being on maintenance.

At that time in December 1942, the front line was east of Bone near the Tunisian Border. Here the Luftwaffe had daytime control of the skies with their Focke Wulf 190's and created problems for the allied forces. Conversely 600 Squadron came to the fore at night.

On Christmas Day Victor's logbook shows that he and Ginger were chasing a Ju88 around the sky for 23 minutes without success. The squadron were additionally tasked to undertake long range daylight escort patrols, mainly for the naval convoys, however, on December 27th, the pair were given the job of escorting three Dakotas from Algiers to Bone. From there next morning they were asked to return to Maison Blanche carrying a VIP and took off with Randolph Churchill standing behind Ginger, but engine trouble soon after take-off meant a return to Bone and a departure in the morning following repairs.

On the 9th January 1943, the squadron commenced the move east of the small civil airfield at Setif where they were to remain until late April, also providing detachments to other air strips in the area. Shortly after this move Ginger developed Malaria and they missed out on being part of a detachment to Casablanca to provide night protection for the important conference then taking place. Some sort of solace was taken though when Victor and Ginger destroyed another Henikel 111 on January 2nd. At around this time another Beaufighter Squadron, No 255 had been operating much closer to the front line and had suffered the loss of practically all of it's aircraft in a daylight attack by Focke Wulf 190's. Consequently 600 Squadron was tasked to provide the forward protection and operated two detachments from the forward landing fields. 'Paddington' and 'Tingley', the detachments arriving at dusk and returning to Setif at dawn.

('Paddington', 'Euston', 'Waterloo', 'Marlebone', 'Kings Cross', and 'Victoria' were the six constituent landing strips at the base of Souk-el-Khemis.)

At Paddington, in common with the majority of these wartime strips, the dispersal accommodation was basic in the extreme, comprising of a small railway shed which quickly became cramped and unbearably stuffy. However it was from this strip that the pair scored their next kill on the opening day of March when they took off at 1840 hrs in their Beaufighter 'G' making contact with and destroying a Piaggio 108.

Victor's Logbook shows that on the 11th March they returned to Base with a 'bent weapon'.

At Tingley, almost on the Mediterranean coast just west of Bone, the normal detachment was one crew only. Nights were bitterly cold and sleep in the single Marquee available for dispersal, was near to impossible with the continual croaking of the Bullfrogs in the adjoining marshes. Highly unpopular with everyone, the air strip did not even boast landing lights. The pair continued the daily grind throughout the spring and into the summer, continually moving around the various bases serviced by the squadron. The monotony was broken however, on May 14th when they made contact with their second Piaggio 108 and damaged it. In late June the dust of North Africa was exchanged for that of Malta, the squadron moving to Luga on the 25th, the George Cross Island being better placed to provide support for the imminent Invasion of Sicily, which was to be the prelude to the initial landings on Mainland Europe.

In July Victor was awarded the Distinguished Flying Medal (DFM) and Ginger was promoted to Flight Sergeant, and not to be outdone, Victor's promotion to Flight Sergeant in July, coincided with kill numbers four and five when on the 16th July they shot down and destroyed a Heinkel 111 and a Cantz 1007. They also damaged a Ju88 on the 19th March. Victor's logbook shows that on the 9th July the pair took of on Patrol at 2230 hrs in Beaufighter V1-'U' to cover the invasion of Sicily. Although a well-established base, and destined to become the main RAF Malta Station, Luga in June/July 1943 was not a pleasant place. The build up for the operations against Sicily meant that a substantial influx of Squadrons and No 600 and it's Beaufighters found itself sharing the facilities with three other similarly equipped units, together with Spitfire, Kittyhawk, Mosquito, Baltimore and Boston squadrons. In total some 15 RAF front-line units were Malta based for the involvement in the offensive against the Island and it is not difficult to imagine the scene as several thousand personnel went about their duties in conditions designed for a few hundreds.

Mercifully such experiences were relatively short lived and on the 26th July the squadron moved to their first Sicilian base at Cassibile and from there carried out continual patrols throughout August helping to protect the newly taken territory. The pair's constant vigilance paid off, when on the 4th August they took of from base at 0355 hrs, and during their patrol shot down and destroyed another Ju88. They also provided support to the 8th Army for the Messina Strait crossing on the 2nd September and also took part covering the Salerno beach landings on the 9th. On the 17th September while on escort patrol they learnt that HMS Warspite had been damaged. The success of the landings meant another move for the squadron, this time to the Italian mainland at Monte Corvino Rovella with detachments being deployed as the invading forces moved inland. By the end

of that long important summer Victor had clocked up 189.50mins in 73 operational sorties, 72 of them with Ginger since their first on the opening day of July the previous year. As a team they had destroyed six and damaged two enemy aircraft, commencing with their inaugural kill in the previous December from Maison Blanche and concluding with the last on the 4th August when operating from Sicily. They also had played their part in the vital landings on Sicily, Messina and Salerno and had been in the vanguard of the RAF's move into the newly occupied territories.

By mid October Victor and Ginger had endured the alien climate of North Africa and the Mediterranean for almost a year. They had also endured the poor conditions and continual movements inherent in this theatre of war. As example, none is better than the period from their arrival in Blida in mid November to the move to the move to Malta the following June. In this 27 week period, excluding 5/6 weeks leave, the pair had made no fewer than 63 changes of location within the various detachments, seldom did they manage more than a few consecutive nights in one place before moving on, often for a single night before moving on again. In such trying conditions the four straight weeks on Malta must have been uncommonly welcome, despite the island being a hive of activity. By mid October the pair had completed a long Tour and had earned a rest, both looking forward to return home and a stint on the training of others.

On the 20th October they started their journey back to the UK, arriving in Tunis the next day. Here they enjoyed two week's rest and relaxation before joining a C.53 USAAF transport on the 5th November that would tale them to Prestwick. Travelling via Algiers, Oran, and Marrakesh. They arrived at Prestwick on the 10th November, the final stage in a C 54, taking a non-stop twelve hours. Whilst with the Squadron Victor had flown in the Beaufighter primarily with Ginger, a total of 282 times including their 73 logged operations. Of the remainder many were training or positioning flights, the majority of which were within the various theatres of war from Algeria into Malta and on the Sicily and the Italian mainland.

On leaving 600 Squadron, now as pilot Officer, Victor's assessment by Wing Commander Green was 'above the average' - with the additional comment from the CO, "A very good Nav/Rad who has done well in this unit." The CO also notes Victor's kill record and the award of his DFM after his third victory.

After a brief visit to West Kirkby, at that time a transit camp, Victor took some home leave until the 7th December when he was posted to No 62 OTU at Ouston, near Newcastle, on an Instructor Training Course. From there it was to Cranfield, near Bedford on the 21st to join 51 OTU. By this time Ginger had been posted as an Instructor to Twinwood Farm, also on the other side of the City. Cranfield was a fully active station in a beautiful location and is better known today as the

Cranfield Institute of Technology, and in addition to Aeronautical Engineering it also encompassed the disciplines of Agricultural Engineering and Biotechnology. It also specialised in Soil Survey with which Victor was to become involved in his post-war days. It did have one other advantage in that it's proximity to London allowed many show business stars of the day to perform there with Joe Loss, Alistair Sim and Gertrude Lawrence amongst the visitors.

Posted to Cranfield on the 21st December, Victor arrived after the New Year and first flew in the familiar Beaufighter on the 13th January. His Instructor duties included much ground based tuition followed by specific testing in the Unit's aircraft and the time soon passed until it was time to return to the sharp end in July. In advance of this Victor, ever the prepared type, managed to combine his instructional duties with some personal practice on the AI radar set and he left the OTU in mid July with a further 'above the average' rating.

Victor soon learned that he was to be posted to 85 Squadron that was based at West Malling and equipped with Mosquito Aircraft. He also realised that they were operating with the Mk V111 AI radar and decided to try and acquire some knowledge of it and arranged to go for a one week's course with No 54 OTU at Charterhall, which had only the ground mock up. He found that he only needed three days to learn the new set up but when he arrived at West Malling in late July, he found that the squadron had now been upgraded to the Mk X system. In addition, their Mosquito aircraft also carried the GEE navigational equipment, Monica, the Mk 1V rearward looking radar. TypeU, UV, ident and type Z, IR ident. Whilst he got some practical training with the new equipment he found that the educational films of the time were extremely useful. The MkV111 and the Mk X sets used much smaller 10cm wavelength than their predecessors and they transmitted using scanners that enabled them to operate at lower levels and cover a greater range.

In early 1944 Ginger's brother Don was killed whilst flying as a navigator with 85 Squadron from West Malling, near Maidstone. The squadron had been quite famous during the First World war having had the distinction of being commanded in succession by two pilots who had both been awarded the Victoria Cross - Major WA Bishop (March-June 1918) and Major M Mannock (June-August 1918). In the Second World War it was also gaining quite a reputation and had, on the 16th May 1943, accounted for the first Focke Wulf 190 shot down at night. By January 1944 the squadron's scoreboard had reached 200 victories. From January 1943 to March 1944 it was commanded by Wing Commander John Cunningham who arranged for Ginger and Victor to join the squadron after their rest period although he would have moved on before the pair arrived in July.

The renowned 'Cats Eyes' Cunningham was one of the best known night flyers of the war. He would rise to Group captain and win three DSO's and two DFC's, and

an OBE followed later. Post war he achieved fame as Chief Test Pilot for DeHavilland and was involved with many of their aircraft including in 1949, the first flight of the Comet Jetliner, The world's first such aircraft.

On the 1st May, 85 Squadron had been transferred from 11 Group at West Malling to Swannington near Norwich. They joined 100 Group, Brother of Bomber Command, to carry out bomber support missions. On the 21st July the squadron were temporarily taken off this role and returned to West Malling to help counter the threat of the V1 bomb over London.

The Officer's mess at West Malling was Douce's manor, normally referred to as the Manor House, situated on a slight rise on the outskirts of the village. The lounge walls were covered in Mural's by David Langdon whilst the bar in the cellar was well known for the names of the Battle of Britain pilot's written on the smoked stained ceiling. Today the Manor House is owned by a major insurance company and, when the lounge had been changed, the cellar bar remains in its original condition.

From Cranfield Victor met up with his pal Ginger at Twinwoods and they paid a quick visit to 85 Squadron at West Malling using a Twinwood Mosquito, this was Victor's first experience of the 'Wooden Wonder'. Possibly quite unofficial, they returned the Mossie and made their way to their new unit in a more conventional manner. They joined the squadron In time to get a few familiarisation flights on the mosquito and it's equipment before flying their first two Night Patrol's on the 5th August when, on the latter they shot down their first V1 flying bomb. On their next patrol on the night of the 7th August, Ginger became delirious with a recurrence of his earlier malaria and was hospitalised before returning to flying duties in early September. In the interim Victor flew wit another Pilot, Warrant Officer Alderton, and although they downed another V1 on the 12th August, he always felt it would have been more if Ginger had been the Pilot.

In late August the squadron returned to Swannington, which was to the North of Norwich, with Ginger returning to flying duties on the 6th September. The pair then carried out nine cross country and night exercises to become more used to the radar and Gee equipment before their next patrol on the 13th, this was to be a patrol over the Rhur and Frankfurt.

(100 Group was tasked for a number of different roles and had a variety of aircraft with which to carry them out. 85 Squadron, together with 157 at Swannington, both carried out intruder and high level bomber escort roles, both of which required a high degree of navigational skill.)

September proved to be a 'profitable' month for the pair destroying two Me110's 20 miles West of Munster on the 17th September, one Me110 damaged 10 miles West of Gutersloh on the 23rd, and one Ju88 probably destroyed over Kaiserlautern on the 27th. On the last day of September they also carried out an intruder attack to Rhein/Main Aerodrome, flying time there and back was 4hrs.50mins.

October was a bit quieter for Victor and Ginger the month was spent carrying out night flying exercises except for the 5th when they carried out two patrols, one to Saarbruken on the 5th and the second to Aalburg on the 15th.

November was again a busy month, with a lot of activity over enemy territory. The pair took off at 1825 hrs on the 1st November and headed for Oberhausen, arriving just 20 miles east of Muhlhausen when they made contact with a Ju88 and destroyed it. They had a repeat performance on the night of the 4th when they attacked and destroyed a second Ju88 10 miles South East of Bielefield, and on the 11th November destroyed a Focke Wulf 190 30 miles South East of Hamburg. Victors log book shows for that attack on the 11th that they returned to Swannington with their port engine U/S.

December came in with a bang when on the 4th they attacked and shot down another Ju88 over the Krefeld area. The closing months of 1944 were spent by the deadly Duo almost entirely over Germany, mainly in the Ruhr valley, and the following log book extract gives an example of what happened when the opposing sides met. The Operation on the night of the 22nd/23rd had been in support of Bomber Command operations against Koblenz and Bingen. Ginger and Victor had departed Swannington at 1615 hrs. in Mosquito MkXXX 'D' Donald. The following is a verbatim reproduction of Ginger's statement from the Intruder Personal Contact report filed with the Intelligence Officer after the operation.

"On patrol 1801 hrs, reached a position 4920N 4910E at 1810 hrs. when an A1 contact was obtained at a height of 14,000 ft., range six miles, crossing port to starboard. Chased aircraft for nine minutes on a north-westerly vector, visual being obtain at 2,000ft, time 1819 hrs. Closing in to dead below, I identified aircraft as a Me110 and noticed also the 'Jerry' markings on the undersides of wings. Dropping back to 150 yards I gave a short burst dead astern. Several strikes were observed and pieces flew off port wing of enemy aircraft, which started a starboard tun. Giving another short burst at about 200 yds , the port engine caught fire and the enemy aircraft spiralled down out of control and in flames to the ground, where it exploded and continued burning near 4920N 0714E at 1821 hrs. Height was now 17,000ft. and a 'Monica' contact was obtained almost immediately. This we converted to an A1 contact, range 4,000ft, crossing starboard to port and slightly above. Closing to 1,200ft I obtained a visual on and aircraft and on closing further to dead below identified it as a JU88. German markings were noted also on this aircraft. Dropping back to 150 yards. dead astern I gave a medium burst from which the port engine of the enemy aircraft caught fire and debris was seen streaming back with small explosions following this display. The JU88 then spun into the ground, exploding with contact with the ground and burning for some minutes after, position being 4918N 0651E at 1825 hrs.

"Resuming patrol, a third contact was obtained at 1850hrs, height 9,000ft, position 1930N 0830E. The range was four miles ahead on, slightly above. We chased aircraft through a steady weaving track (port to starboard) on an average vector of 355 degrees. Closing to 2,000ft obtained visual of an aircraft above. Climbing and closing the range further the enemy aircraft was identified as a Jug. Enemy aircraft then seemed to take a little more violent action, but dropping back to 100 yards and slightly above I gave a short deflection burst. Chunks flew off port wing and other strikes were seen. Enemy aircraft then dived extremely steeply to port (almost in a vertical dive) with the port engine belching out smoke. Following down I had to break off at about 7,000ft owing to steepness of dive. Enemy aircraft continued diving and was lost through a slight haze at 2,5000ft. Orbiting round I observed an explosion on the ground four minutes later at a position 4914N 0745E that was the area of combat. Time 1905 hrs."

The pair landed back at 2038 having expended 260 rounds of mixed armour piercing and high explosive. The Intelligence Officer signed off their claim for three aircraft destroyed with the benefit of the cine camera gun films which exposed automatically.

On the 27th January 1945 Victor was awarded a Bar to his DFC won the previous November for the completion of an outstanding tour. By this time he had guided his Pilot Ginger Owen, to 16 destroyed, one probable, three damaged and the one Me110 later confirmed as 'shot up' on the ground. In addition he had recorded a V1 destroyed when flying with Warrant Officer Alderton in Ginger's absence. All had come during night flying Operations. Ginger Owen was heard to comment on several occasions that he could see no aircraft in the position indicated by Victor. He was also heard to comment that he rarely knew Victor to be wrong. On one such occasion he recalls Victor screaming at him to, "Press the tit - the bloody thing is right in front of us." He was right.

On the occasion of receiving both his DFC's, Victor received a Postgram from Air Chief Marshall 'Bomber' Harris, the Commander-in-Chief of Bomber Command. Dated the 19th of November 1944 and the 27th of January 1945, copies of these were supplied by Victor. He had been promoted to Flight Lieutenant in January and, on completion of a further Operational Tour in February, had received a AOC's Commendation from the AOC 100 Group.

AOC's Commendation on completion of Operational Tour.
F/Lt JSV McAllister, DFC* DFM
(148826) Navigator

'For Meritorious service and good airmanship, in that a full operational tour has been completed without having been involved in an accident or ever having an unnecessary cancellation or abandonment of an operational sortie.'

January was relatively quite for Victor and Ginger carrying out two patrols over Frankfurt on the 2nd and

6th. February was quite a busy month, patrolling over Mannheim, Frankfurt, Hanover,

Rhur area, Dresden, Magdeburg, and Mainz, there was little enemy activity, and both men were, by Bomber Command regulations, due for a rest. They were offered the choice of the normal six month break from operations in a spell as instructors or a six week leave period. Opting for the leave they both spent two weeks at Ballinlough Castle in the Eire County of West Meath, the home of Sir Hugh Nugeant who was in charge of the Motor Transport Section at Swannington. Also in February the pair, along with a dozen or so fellow squadron members, went to the Martin Baker factory at Denham to act as guinea pigs. Ejector seat trials were being conducted and the company needed to assess if the force of the explosive cartridge used to eject the pilot from the cockpit would cause any spinal damage.

James Martin, and Ulsterman, ensured that each participant had their photograph taken prior to the test both at the top and bottom of the test gantry before providing all concerned with a memorable lunch. Furthermore, he arranged an afternoon visit to the local film studios where John Mills was taking part in scenes from Great Expectations. On their return to flying duties on the 15th April, and with Ginger now a Squadron Leader and OC 'B' Flight, they found that enemy activity was greatly reduced and they made what was to be their final wartime sortie over Germany on the 2nd May. This was a detail to patrol the southern border of Germany on the lookout for escapees trying to fly out of the country, using German marked allied aircraft which had previously been captured.

At the time of VE Day Victor had completed 134 flights in the Mosquito with 85 Squadron, mainly with Ginger, and logged 47 Operational Patrols. The majority of the work had involved either fighter cover or area patrols in support of Bomber Command Operations to the well-known target areas including, Dresden, Frankfurt, the Rhur, etc. Such patrols took different forms and give an indication of the changes in tactics that were employed during the time of attachment to 100 Group from May 1994 - May 1945. As reflected in Victor's log from the commencement of his time with the unit, the first used was the anti-diver patrol against the V1 flying bomb followed by the intruder patrol where the Mossies would loiter around German Airfields. The last used was when the Mosquito's would mingle with the bomber stream on the lookout for enemy night fighters. The latter was not overly successful, the majority of the squadrons kills coming from the attention to enemy airfields.

In practice these would be determined by the target chosen by Bomber Command. As an example is Victor's sortie of the night of the 22nd December 1944 which reports he and Ginger patrolling south of Frankfurt.

The targets for that night were Koblenz and Bingen, north and north-west of Frankfurt respectively. In this case 85 Squadron had positioned over the airfields that would respond to this threat. As it happens this was to be

Victor's most successful night, guiding Ginger to three confirmed kills.

Shortly after VE Day, on the 17th May, the pair undertook what was for them an unusual sortie. Leaving Swannington at 1500 hrs in Mosquito 'W' they carried out air to ground firing practice and proceeded without a break on a navigational trip. Crossing to the Hague, they went on to Rotterdam, Aachen, the Ruhr Valley, the Mohne Dam, Dunkirk, and Calais arriving back at Swannington at 2045 hrs, 5hrs.50 mins later. The pair surely found this trip of great interest as it would have been the first time either of them had seen these places in daylight. To complete a full day, they departed again at 2250 hrs for a 1hr.50mins A1 training sortie, now quite at home in the darkness.

In late June the squadron was returned to Fighter Command and moved to Castle Camps near Saffron Walden. The entire squadron detached, on the 13th August to Bradwell Bay, west of Clacton, for an air firing course. In early October it again moved, this time to Tangmere, to become part of the peacetime 11 Group Night Fighter Force. A brief visit was made to Lubeck in northern Germany before returning to Tangmere with Victor and Ginger participating in all these moves.

Shortly after the arrival at Tangmere of Clement Atlee, the newly elected Labour Prime Minister, arrived back from the Conference with his advisers. They were joined by many other new Cabinet members and an impromptu reception took place. During this Ginger and Victor were cornered by Lord Stansgate, the Minister for Civil Aviation, who proceeded to tell them how keen his son was to get into the RAF and become a Pilot. In the event his son did join up and attained the rank of Squadron Leader during his National Service. In the period following VE Day the flying was understandably greatly reduced although it is noticeable from Victor's log book much emphasis was still placed on training with the use of radar and practice air to ground firing. In addition this time was spent on GCI practice, previously only mentioned in Victor's log back in July 1943.

Victor and Ginger continued flying together through the Autumn of 1945 and into the first New Year of peace since 1939, making their last flight together on the 11th March 1946 doing what they excelled at - night flying. Victor's logbook shows:

March 11   14.40. Mosquito 'C'. S/Ldr Owen,
             NFT. 1hr.45mins.
March 11   19.10. Mosquito 'C'. S/Ldr Owen
             GCT. 1hr.50mins.

His last flight now behind him, Victor went on official accumulated leave prior to retiring from the Service in June and used his travel warrant for his honeymoon. It is of great interest to note that together Ginger and Victor had the unique record of shooting down a single engined, a two engined, a three engined and a four engined aircraft plus a V1 ælying bomb.

It is also of interest to note an interesting coincidence in Victor's log. In December 1943 he completed his 73rd Operational Sortie with 600 Squadron. His accumulated operational hours were 189.50 and on the 2nd May 1945 he completed his 47th operational sortie with 85 Squadron. His accumulated operational hours were also 189.50.

Victor's wife Kay was a war time WAAF who, at the time of the V1 flying bomb raids in 1944, was attached as an MT driver to a unit of Balloon Command at Kidbroke. During one such raid a V1 came down at Kidbroke, resulting in many fatalities amongst the WAAF's. Kay was seriously wounded and, despite several operations, she would carry shrapnel in her arm for the rest of her life. Victor would later relate the tale stressing that the VI involved was not one which he and Ginger had brought down and that while Kay had suffered more than any other family member, he got some medals while all she got was him! After periods in hospital and subsequent convalescence, Kay was posted to RAF Swannington where she was very nearly unlucky again. Soon after her arrival a Mosquito burned after crash landing along side her as she rode her bicycle around the perimeter track.

A related story

The Mosquito Pilot died in the inferno but the Navigator, Robert (Bob) Wright, a 1930's Hollywood scriptwriter, was badly burned and was pulled out by one of his ground crew. Following extensive treatment and plastic surgery under Sir Archibald McIndoe at East Grinstead, he was home convalescing when a V2 Rocket crashed down 50 yards away and he ended up back in hospital. Bob Wright was personal aide to Air Chief Marshal Sir Hugh Dowding during the Battle of Britain and his successor Sir Sholto Douglas.

Throughout the Battle of Britain in those crucial months of 1940, Wright was at Dowding's side or guarding his office door. He controlled all the Fighter's Chief's paperwork and his incoming telephone calls. Years later Dowding decided to break his silence regarding his direction of the Battle of Britain and selected Wright as the medium. In the foreword to Wright's 1969 book, Dowding and the Battle of Britain, Dowding described his as, "Someone who I felt understood and shared, with discretion, my views on my career in the Royal Air Force."

Following the war, Wright devoted himself to seek to put right what he described as, "The grave injustice done to Lord Dowding in November 1940," when the victor of the Battle of Britain was virtually dismissed. Such was Dowding's regard for Wright that he commended him to Sholto Douglas whom Wright went on to serve at home and in the Middle East. Douglas quickly warmed to the much travelled Wright and described him as, "One independent of mind and with a rather prickly dislike of red tape," in tune with his own outlook. Despite getting to know him well he never did discover how Wright, despite being officially medically categorised as 'permanently unfit for flying', managed to wrangle himself into John 'Cat's Eyes' Cunningham's 604 Squadron in the Autumn of 1941. He went on to serve with another squadron covering the 'Torch' landings in North Africa.

Later Douglas ordered him back to his desk, but once again, probably with the help of Sir Keith Park, somehow managed to re-join Cunningham, now the Commanding Officer of 85 Squadron. Following recovery from his crash which could have killed Kay, he was ordered back to Douglas's side, to become once again his personal assistant, Douglas then being CinC Coastal Command. After the war Wright returned to his screenwriting role at Elstree Studio's and then established himself as an author. Firstly he collaborated with CF Rawnsey, who was John Cunningham's Navigator, in writing 'Night Fighter', the 1957 story of Rawnsley's outstanding night fighting partnership with Cunningham. Secondly, he then collaborated with the Marshal of the Royal Air Force, Lord Douglas of Kirkside, as Sholto Douglas had become, on two autobiographical volumes, 1963 & 1966, describing the great airman's service in both World Wars.

Kay and Victor were married in June 1946 and, not wanting to be out done, Kay also used her final travel warrant for the honeymoon. Following the war Victor continued with his agricultural career and this developed into research work. He became a senior Scientific Officer in the Department of Agriculture and also accepted a post in the Faculty of Agriculture for Northern Ireland. He helped to develop many of the concepts now in use worldwide and is probably best known for pioneering work on the treatment and risks attached to the handling and disposal of animal wastes. He was also involved in the early work relating to dusting of calcined magnesite on herbage and the use of fertiliser units for advisory work, nutrient balances, etc. He also resumed playing rugby on his return to Carrickfergus in 1946, going on to Captain the local side and later serving his club as Chairman, President and Trustee. He was elected one of the very few Honorary Member's of the British Society of Soil Science in 1980 and was Chairman of the Northern Ireland Section of the Society of Chemical Industry and a member of it's Council

When following his chosen career Victor also maintained an active interest in aviation related matters. He was involved with the cadet forces of the RAF and served for 23 years as a member of the Air Cadet Council. He was also on the Morris Committee for the reorganisation of the Air Training Corps. Queens University Belfast also benefited from his presence as member of the Military Education Committee, from which position he had great involvement with the University Air Squadron. For these and other services he was awarded an OBE in 1972. His activates also extended to ex-service organisations including Past President of the Queens University Services Club, Past President of the

Northern Ireland Area of the Royal Air Force Association and founder member and Past President of the Northern Ireland Branch of the Aircrew Association. He was also very proud of his 37 years working as a Wings Day organiser for the Carrickfergus Branch of RAFA.

Victor always remained in frequent contact with Ginger and the two couples enjoyed many a re-union over the years despite his failing health.

Some statistics of interest

Aircraft Destroyed	17
Aircraft Damaged	3
Aircraft Probable	1
Total	21

Flights in type:

Anson	5
Beaufighter	345
Blenheim	28
Commodore Flying Boat	14
Douglas C53	3
Douglas C54	1
DC3 Dakota	3
Goeland	1
Magister	1
Mosquito	218
Oxford	12
Wellington	9
Total	640

WARRANT OFFICER
WILLIAM ALFRED McALLISTER
ROYAL AIR FORCE NO. 1798821
REAR GUNNER
NO. 44 (RHODESIA) SQUADRON

William Alfred McAllister was born on the 1st August 1924, in the town of Aughlish in County Tyrone. After completing his education, he was employed with the Great Northern Railway.

On the 22nd July 1943 he joined the Royal Air Force at the Clifton Street Recruiting Centre in Belfast. He was then sent to Newtownards Airfield where he was set some Aptitude Tests. After passing these he was posted over to London where he attended the Air Crew Reception Centre at Vice Roy Court near Lords Cricket Grounds in London. On completion of the necessary interviews he was selected to become an Air Gunner. He was then transferred to a Initial Training Wing at Bridlington in Yorkshire to start his basic training. On completion of his basic training he was then posted to the Elementary Air Gunnery School at Bridgenorth in Shropshire where he was instructed on the use of the Frazer Nash and Boulton Paul hydraulic turrets, and how to maintain them.

His next posting was to the No 1 Air Gunnery School at Penbury in South Wales where he carried out his Flying Training in the Avro Anson. The training consisted of a cine gun camera mounted in the Anson. The idea was that the pupil would aim the camera at a drogue target which was being towed behind a Martinet, and when he returned to base the film would be analysed by experts to assess how the pupil had progressed. He was also taught Turret Manipulation which was very important as it allowed the pupil to get used to the smooth action of the hydraulically operated turrets. Having successfully completed these two courses, Alfred was awarded his Air Gunners Brevet and promoted to the rank of Sergeant.

His next posting was to an Operational Training Unit at Bruntingthorpe where he was introduced to his new crew, (minus the Flight Engineer who he met later).

The new crew

Flying Officer JHT Haworth	Pilot
Sergeant FM Seiler	Flight Engineer
Flight Sergeant S Walters, CGM	Bomb Aimer
Sergeant 'Dusty' Saunders	Navigator
Sergeant E Gardiner	Radio Operator
Sergeant T Mackay	Mid-Upper Gunner
Sergeant WA McAllister	Rear Gunner

Alfred carried out his operational training from Bruntingthorpe's Satellite airfield at Bitteswell, learning how to use the four Browning machine guns in air-to-air firing. Here the crew also carried out Cross-Country exercises, and during one such exercise their Wellington lost one of its engines. The Pilot, Flying Officer Hayworth, immediately sent out the emergency code 'Darky', and they were soon directed safely to a Polish Fighter Base on the South Coast of Wales. When the Wimpy landed at the airfield, they found it deserted. The Polish Pilots seemingly had had a very successful day and were 'sleeping it off' and were not amused when they were woke up out of their 'party' sleep.

In early 1944 Alfred and the crew were transferred to a Heavy Conversion Unit at Wigslet in Lincolnshire where they converted to the four engined Short Stirling, and it was here that they picked up their Flight Engineer. The training consisted entirely of high level bombing which was carried out at Wainfleet. They were then transferred to RAF Syreston in Nottingham which was a Lancaster Finishing School, here they then converted onto the Avro Lancaster. Having now completed all of the training which was required of them, they were posted to No 44 Squadron at Dunholme Lodge near Scampton to start operations.

Brief wartime history of No 44 (Rhodesia) Squadron

The squadron was formed at Hainault Farm in Essex in July 1917 as a Home Defence squadron. It was the first Squadron to have flown the Sopwith Camel on night operations. One of its early Commanding Officers was Major AT Harris later to become Marshal of the Royal Air Force. The squadron was disbanded in 1919 and reformed again at Wyton in March 1937 as a bomber squadron, equipped with the Hawker Hind. It moved later to Waddington and was re-equipped with Bristol Blenheims and Handley Page Hampdens. At the outbreak of war the squadron was commanded by Wing Commander JN Boothman of the Schneider Trophy fame. The squadron was given the name Rhodesia Squadron in recognition of that countries generous donations to the war effort. This was particularly appropriate as approximately one quarter of the squadrons personnel were Rhodesian. In 1942 the squadron converted to Avro Lancaster's. The squadron was quite unique as for a time it had on its strength two Victoria Cross holders, Wing Commander RAB Learoyd and Squadron Leader JD Nettleton. The squadron had visited many heavily protected targets including. U-Boat pens, Peenemunde, and V-1 launching sites in France. It's last operation of the war was to bomb the SS barracks at Berchtesgaden.

It wasn't long before Alfred and the crew were attacking targets at Le Harve (low level daylight attack on a Panzer Division), Darmstadt, Carlsruhe, Muchen Gladbach, Kaiser Laughtern, Munster, and took part in the 2nd large raid on Cologne.

Alfred's last raid of the war took place on the 1st November 1944 when his aircraft Lancaster, Serial No LM650, Code KM-R took off from Spilsby at 1802 hrs to attack the City of Homburg . When they were on their final bombing run to the target, they flew into murderous flak.

Lancaster KM-T was hit three times

The first hit blew the port outer engine out of the wing, and as the outer engines supplied the hydraulic power to the aircraft, this meant that all of the gun turrets were out of action. The second hit blasted the cockpit on the port side killing the Pilot Flying Officer Haworth instantly, causing him to slump over the controls. The stricken Lancaster was now losing height rapidly. The Flight Engineer Sergeant Seiler was also badly wounded. The third hit struck the underside of the Lancaster, causing red hot shrapnel to blast a hole in the Rear Gunners position, wounding Alfred in his face and leg. The quick thinking of the Bomb Aimer, Flight Sergeant Walters, had by now been able to remove the body of the dead Pilot from his seat, and managed to bring the badly damaged aircraft back under control. By this time the starboard outer had also stopped, and with all hydraulics gone this meant that the bomb doors could not be closed, leaving the crew in a much more precarious situation. Flight Sergeant Walters had a limited knowledge of how to fly the Lancaster as most Captains would instruct some of his crew the basics of flying just in case this sort of situation would happen. Flight Sergeant Walters set a course for Hastings, and once he was over the Channel he jettisoned the bomb load. When the aircraft was within

range of Hastings, and he knew his crew would be safe, he ordered them to bale out as his flying experience was limited, and he could not land the aircraft especially in its poor condition. The crew of KM-T baled out, near the village of Roberts Bridge which is about three miles north of the town of Battle. The aircraft came down minutes later at 1745 hrs near Battle, six miles North West of Hastings. Flying Officer Haworth died in his aircraft, and the Flight Engineer Sergeant Seiler was found close to the aircraft with his parachute fully opened, but had died of his internal injuries. The rest of the crew were relatively unhurt, except for Alfred who had sustained another leg injury, caused by landing in rough ground inside a quarry.

For his courageous actions, Flight Sergeant Walters was awarded the Conspicuous Gallantry Medal. Flying Officer Haworth, who was born in Southern Rhodesia was buried in Maidstone Cemetery, and Sergeant Seiler lies in Eastbourne (Langley) Cemetery.

Alfred was picked up by ambulance and taken to a Casualty Receiving Hospital at Hawkhurst. After his wounds were healed he was sent to convalesce at Eastbourne for a few months. In early 1945 he rejoined his squadron at Spilsby, but was very disappointed at what he found, as so many of his close friends had been lost, the squadron was devastated. Because of the nature of his injuries which he had sustained in the crash, Alfred was unable to return to his air crew duties, and was given a temporary assignment at Spilsby as Bombing Range Controller. After a few months he re-mustered as an Air Field Controller, now known as an Air Traffic Controller, and was posted to the Air Traffic Controller School at Watchfield where he carried out a twelve week course.

Between 1945 and 1971 he had 'Controlled' quite a few Stations including:

Inverness (Dalcross)	1945
Middle Wallop (Home of the Army Air Corps)	1945/46
West Africa (Takoradi, Gold Coast, now Ghana)	1947
Swanton Morley (trained on radar and became an Instructor)	1947/58
Hulavington (training Wireless Operators)	1958
Shawbury (School of ATC to be upgraded to Local Controller and promoted to Flight Sergeant)	1958
Ternhill (No 5 FTS Grade 'A' Station)	1958/60
Gutersloh (Germany, Air Identification Zone Protection)	1960/62
Odiham (Wessex Station) (Helicopters)	1962/65
Shawbury (Search and Radar Approach Course)	1965

One incident at Odiham which is worth mentioning was when a Wessex broke an undercarriage wheel off due to a heavy landing. The Pilot held the aircraft in the hover while the ground crew repaired it. The Wessex was refuelled from the ground until the job was completed, saving a very valuable helicopter.

He came home to Northern Ireland in 1965 where he became Air Traffic Controller at RAF Ballykelly in County Londonderry. Alfred finally retired from the RAF in February 1971 after completing 28 years in the Service. When he retired he received a letter from Air Marshal Sir Robert Craven, KBE CB DFC MBIM RAF, Commanding Officer Maritime Forces, and Commanding Officer No 18 Maritime Group. On leaving the RAF he was employed with the Civil Service finally retiring on the 1st August 1989.

PILOT OFFICER
GEORGE A McAULEY, DFC
ROYAL AIR FORCE NO. 124267
PILOT
NO. 218 (GOLD COAST) SQUADRON

KILLED IN ACTION 20TH AUGUST 1942.

George McAuley was born at Play Hill, Cairncastle, in Larne in 1921. He was educated at Larne Grammar School, keen to study medicine, and was joint Head Boy during the 1939-1940 Session. George excelled in school sports and was outstanding in Rugby, Running and Boxing.

He decided to put the idea of studying medicine on hold, to join the Royal Air Force Volunteer Reserve in the summer of 1940, serving as a Flight Sergeant prior to being Commissioned in 1942. His father had served in the Merchant Navy in both World Wars as a Chief Engineer and was torpedoed during both campaigns.

Pilot Officer George McAuley was nineteen years of age when he was awarded the Distinguished Flying Cross with effect from the 31st July 1942 and by then he had completed 31 Operations on Vickers Wellington's, and Short Stirlings.

The Citation for his DFC reads:

Pilot Officer McAuley (deceased) is a cool and courageous Pilot, and has shown resolution when placed in harassing circumstances in the face of the enemy. On one occasion, after bombing Saarbrucken from a low level, his aircraft was attacked by an enemy fighter, by cool and skilful flying tactics this officer enabled his gunners to destroy the attacker. Immediately afterwards another enemy aircraft attacked from dead astern a was driven off whilst Pilot Officer G McAuley's aircraft was unscathed. This Officer was responsible for the successful outcome of both these combats. He has set a fine example of courage, skill and devotion to duty.

On the 27th July 1943 his father, Mr WH McAuley received the following letter from the Air Ministry in London:

1. I am directed to inform you that the King has been graciously pleased to confer the Distinguished Flying Cross on your son, the late Pilot Officer G McAuley (124267) with effect from 31st July 1942, and I attach for your information details of the services for which the award was granted. The award will be notified in the London Gazette on Tuesday, 27th July, 1943.

2. If you should so desire, arrangements will be made for you, as the recorded next of kin, to attend at

Buckingham Palace to receive the decoration from His Majesty. It is not possible at this stage to give any indication of the date of the ceremony you would be required to attend, but reasonable notice would be given. One other person, a blood relative of the deceased officer would be able to attend with you.

3. If for any reason you should not wish to attend, the decoration would be forwarded to you by post.

4. Please be good enough to indicate your wishes as soon as convenient.

I am, Sir,
Your obedient Servant,
FL Sheppard.

Pilot Officer McAuley's Combat report for the night of July 29th/30th 1942: "The enemy aircraft approached from the starboard quarter and was first sighted by the rear gunner at a range of 400 yards. It was slightly below our own aircraft. The enemy aircraft (unidentified but believed to be a Ju88) crossed to dead astern and came in, commencing to fire at a range of 300-400 yards. The Rear Gunner immediately returned the fire, the enemy aircraft broke away to starboard, when the Mid-Upper Gunner fired a short burst. This attack was repeated a further couple of times, during the attacks our own aircraft was doing violent evasive action and losing height quickly. The enemy aircraft then attacked from 20 degrees port astern and both Rear and Mid-Upper Gunners fired short bursts. He broke away to starboard at about 200 yards range whereupon Rear and Mid-Upper Gunners fired long bursts. There was a large red flash and the enemy aircraft then went into a steep dive. Another Ju88 then came in from dead astern but did not open fire. The Rear Gunner put a long burst into him at 200-150 yards and the enemy aircraft broke away. Cloud cover was gained and nothing more was seen of this machine. The aim of the first aircraft was very poor, the nearest distance trace to our aircraft being some 50 yards. The first enemy aircraft almost certainly was destroyed but not seen to hit the ground as the Gunners were occupied with the Ju88."

The crew

Captain	Pilot Officer McAuley
Rear Gunner	Sergeant Parker
Mid-Upper Gunner	Sergeant Nettleton

Before he was killed, Pilot Officer McAuley had carried out 31 Operations over enemy territory. His first operation was on the 27th November 1941 in a Wellington of 218 Squadron, Serial No X978, Code HA-S. He was Second Pilot during this trip and his Captain was Sergeant Lamerson. They took off at 1710 hrs to attack their target which was Dusseldorf, they reached and successfully attacked the target and landed safely back at Marham, Norfolk at 2246 hrs.

He went on to attack targets in Lorient, Brest, Wilhelmshaven, Hamburg, Rostock, Cologne (1,000 bomber raid), Gennvilliers, Stuttgart, Essen (1,000 bomber raid), Bremen (1,000 bomber raid), Vegesack, Saarbrucken, Dusseldorf, Duisberg, Osnabruck, Mainz, Flensburg and many 'Mining Operations'.

On the 4th/5th May 1942

Sergeant McAuley took off from RAF Marham in Norfolk in Short Sterling Mk1 Serial No W7521, Code HA-U at 2210 hours to bomb the German city of Stuttgart.

The crew

Pilot	Sergeant George McAuley, 124267 RAFVR.
2nd Pilot	Pilot Officer Richards
Flight Engineer	Sergeant George Leonard Arthur Neale, 528927 RAF
Observer	Sergeant Stanley Edgar Stevens, 1270512 RAFVR
Wireless Operator	Sergeant Brian William Roberts, 1375123 RAFVR
Wireless Operator	Sergeant Stronnell
Air Gunner	Sergeant Albert Edward Burkitt, 900855 RAFVR
Air Gunner	Sergeant Eric Nettleton, 994389 RAFVR

After having successfully bombed the target, the port outer failed, much flak was then experienced from the French Coast and the aircraft was badly damaged. The aircraft crashed landed at Mulbarton, five miles SSW of Norwich when three engines failed due to an airlock in the petrol system. None of the crew were seriously hurt thanks to the skilful flying of Pilot Officer McAuley.

The aircraft

Type	Short Sterling Mk.1
RAF No.	W.7521.

Contractor	Austin Motors Ltd
Contract No.	B982939/39
Engines	Bristol Hercules Mk.X1
TOC	12.04.1942
Cat 'E' (FB/T961)	05.05.1942
SOC	05.05.1942

On the 2nd June 1942 Pilot Officer McAuley was involved in an accident when he had to 'belly-land' his Sterling, after returning from a 1,000 bomber raid to Essen and proves again what a professional and excellent Pilot he was.

The Accident Report reads: "On landing Pilot Officer McAuley undershot and hit a tree in the dispersal area, damaging the undercarriage and tail plane. He went around and made a belly landing. The Pilot may not be to blame as the aircraft had a violent shuddering take place after which the load was jettisoned and great difficulty was experienced to keep the nose up in flight. The accident may be attributed to one of the following, (1) Technical failure, or (2) A bad approach by a very young inexperienced pilot with only three engines, (3) A spanner was found jammed in the rear elevator control."

Pilot Officer McAuley's last operation

On the 20th/21st August 1942 Pilot Officer McAuley and his crew were tasked to carry out a 'Forget-Me Not' operation (mine laying) in Kiel Harbour. They took off from RAF Downham Market, Norfolk on Thursday 20th August 1942 in Short Sterling Mk.1 Serial Number W.7615, Code HA-M at 2046 hrs. The Navigator set a course for Kiel Harbour. At precisely 2025 hrs Pilot Officer McAuley's aircraft was hit by light flak from 1./lei Flak Abt 828. His aircraft crashed into the sea between Ero and Kappeln (Geel) in Denmark. All of the crew were killed. Pilot Officer McAuley is remembered on Runnymede Panel No 70, his Wireless Operator Sergeant Brian William Roberts of Dagenham in Essex (married to Irene Roberts) is remembered on Runnymede Panel 75, his Rear Gunner Sergeant Albert Edward Burkitt is remembered on Runnymede Panel 79 and his Flight Engineer Sergeant George Leonard Arthur Neale, age 28, of North Allington, Dorsetshire (married to Kathleen Neale), is remembered on Runnymede Panel 90. Flight Sergeant Stanley Edgar Stevens (Observer), RAF No. 1270512 RAFVR, age 21 of Portishead in Somerset. His body was washed ashore at Vemmingbund on the 21st September 1942. He is buried in the Allied Military Plot, Row 1.3 at Aabenraa cemetery in Denmark. The body of Sergeant Hiley Rhys Davies (Air Gunner), RAF No. 655121 RAF, age 22, of Cardiff. His body was found at Fugsbolle Sonderskov on the Island of Langeland on the 27th September 1942. His burial took place on October 1st 1942. The coffin was transported to Odense by train, the coffin was draped in a Union Jack while in the Chapel prior to burial. Sergeant Eric Nettleton's body (Wireless Operator), RAF No. 994389 RAFVR was found on the 10th September, and is buried in Grave 4. C.6 in Kiel War Cemetery, Germany.

On the 21st August 1942, Pilot Officer McAuley's father received a Post Office Telegram at 2.26pm. It read:

> Priority. Mr WH McAuley. Church Farm. Ballygally. Cairncastle. County Antrim. Northern Ireland.
>
> Deeply regret to inform you that your son 124267 P/O George McAuley was reported missing as a result of Air Operations 20/8/42. Letter follows, any further information received will be immediately communicated to you.
>
> OC 218 Squadron

On the 2nd January 1943 a letter was delivered to Pilot Officer McAuley's father from the Air Ministry, Casualty Branch, 77 Oxford Street in London. It read:

> Sir, I am directed to refer to a letter from the Department dated 8th September, and to inform you with regret that no news has been received of your son, Pilot Officer George McAuley, since he was reported missing on the night of 20th/21st August 1942. The detailed report from his Squadron contains no information beyond that already communicated to you. Telegrams since received from the International Red Cross Committee, quoting official German information, state that the bodies of Sergeant Nettleton, Sergeant Stevens and Sergeant Davies, members of your son's crew were recovered on 10th, 21st and 27th September. The place of recovery is not stated and no mention is made of your son or the three other members of his crew. In view of the time which has elapsed it is felt that there can now be little hope that your son is still alive, but action to presume his death will not be taken until at least six months from the date on which he was reported missing. Such action would then be for official purposes only, and a further letter would be addressed to you before it was taken. I am to express the Department's deep sympathy with you in your great anxiety, and to assure you that enquiries are continuing through the International Red Cross Committee and any news received later will be at once passed on to you.
>
> I am, Sir
> Your Obedient Servant
> RS Keene
> for Director of Personal Services

A further letter was received by Pilot Officer McAuley's father from the War Organisation of the British Red Cross and Order of St John of Jerusalem Wounded, Missing and Relatives Department) 7 Belgrave Square, London SW1:

> Dear Mr McAuley,
>
> Although we are still, unhappily, without any news of your son, Pilot Officer G McAuley No 124267, we are writing to tell you we have now received, through the International Red Cross Committee, a further report about Sergeant Davies who was flying in the same aircraft. This report from the German Authorities, states that Sergeant Davies body was recovered from the shore and laid to rest in the Cemetery at Odense, which is in the North East of the Island of Funen, Denmark, thus indicating in what locality the disaster had occurred. We believe that you would wish to have this statement in your possession. We are so very sorry that we are unable to help you more and would like to offer you our very deepest sympathy in the cruel anxiety and sorry which you have been called upon to bear.
>
> Yours Sincerely,.....

A final letter was received by Pilot Officer McAuley's father from the Air Ministry on the 13th December 1946. It reads:

> Dear Mr McAuley,
>
> It is with deep regret I have to refer to the loss of your son the late Pilot Officer George McAuley, Royal Air Force but it is felt you would wish to be informed of the contents of a report received from the Royal Air Force Missing Research and enquiry Service, Denmark. Investigations carried out to ascertain the fate of your son and his comrades have brought to light news that the Stirling was lost at sea near Flensburg bay, east coast of Denmark on the border of the German province of Schleswig-Holstein, and it is feared that all members of the crew perished in the aircraft.
>
> The graves of Flight Sergeant Stevens, Sergeant Davies and Sergeant Nettleton have been located, their bodies having been washed ashore on various dates, on the coast of Denmark and Germany. Exhaustive enquiries have failed to produce evidence of the recovery of your son or the remaining members of the crew and it may, unhappily, prove that nothing further will become known. You may rest assured that enquiries are continuing over a very wide area, and the Missing Research teams are examining all graves of Allied fallen. In the case of those buried as unknown exhumation is undertaken in the hope of establishing identity and should any news of your son be received you will immediately be informed.

GROUP CAPTAIN
VHA McBRATNEY, AFC
PILOT

Vincent Herbert Alexander McBratney was born on the 15th of July 1913 at the family home in Blackabey in the district of Adare in County Limerick, at that time a part of the Ireland prior to the political divide. His father, known as 'Pappa Mac', was Alexander, a schoolteacher, and his mother was Jane Amelia, formerly Campbell. He also had one sister, Peggy.

In 1920/1 the family moved to the Ulster County of Donegal. It is thought that the move was due to the impending partition of Ireland which many thought would see the nine existing, and original, Ulster counties from the new Northern Ireland. However, Donegal, Monaghan and Cavan were not included in the 'new' Ulster and the family moved again in 1922/3, crossing the border to the small market town of Magherafelt in the Northern Irish county of Londonderry.

Pappa Mac continued to teach and played the organ in local churches, including the one from which he and Jane would subsequently be buried. As a result of his place of birth, the young Vincent was a British Subject as opposed to a British Citizen, as would become clear many years later when he and his wife applied for passports (see later).

Known to most as Mac, little is known of his formative years and his story commences with his arrival at the Royal Belfast Academically Institution - Inst to locals - after a period of secondary education at the Rainey Endowed School in Magherafelt. It is thought that he was obliged to leave Rainey after a serious altercation with a teacher, an early sign of the trait which would become more apparent as the years passed - Mac had a fiery temper when riled, nor did he suffer fools gladly.

At Inst from 1930/32, Mac stayed in digs in Belfast, travelling home to Magherafelt most weekends. He made his mark at school, using his impressive physical presence to good effect although his 13 stone and six foot plus frame would sometimes present a problem in the rugger scrum. He rowed in the Firsts in 1931 under the captaincy of Dennis Badger and assumed the captaincy himself the following year, guiding the school to a

successful season. A school prefect, he also played for the 1st Fifteen in teams which included future British Lions Sam Walker and Harry McKibbin.

The pre-war years

It is known that his first flight with the RAF was an 'unofficial' air experience flight with Charles Lindsay from Aldergrove. arranged by Lindsay, and Instructor, and sanctioned by the authorities as Mac was on the point of joining the service as a regular. Mac's logbooks and other written records provide the basis for his story which commences in the early thirties. The story is told around a long, long letter which Mac wrote in 1991 and which recalled almost his entire career. The letter is used almost in full and is shown in bold print, interspersed with the further detail from his log books, etc.

"In this narrative I can only record brief notes of all my service career - minus the mass of facts and detail otherwise I would end up with a book, because I had a massive flying career - both in time and variation, and served in, or travelled in, many parts of the globe, sometimes in very odd circumstances."

NO 5 FTS, Sealand

Mac was stationed at the training school from the first day of September 1933 until the last day of August the following year. Evident from his log is the more relaxed flying training programme, normal at this time, as compared to the build up that would become the case in the later thirties.

With No 6 Flight he commenced his elementary training and first flew on the 20th September in Avro 504N, K1046, with Sergeant Barretto. Solo flight followed in due course on the 4th November in Avro 504N, J8740. Of interest in the early period are the practice landings at strips which are unheard of now; Turtons Field and Boweres Field being examples. Elementary training ended with a final Avro flight on the 9th of February, by which time Mac accumulated 69 hours flying and was assessed as 'average'.

Following leave Mac commenced intermediate training on the Avro Tutor, first flying on the 18th of March in K3264 with the OC No 6 Flight, Flying Officer Parker. He flew a further five times with Sergeant Barretto before this Tutor solo on the 26th. After just two more Tutor flights on the 27th, Mac commenced advanced training, now with No 8 Flight, in the AW Atlas on the 4th of April, in K1477 with Flying Officer Vintras. On the 10th he had a Flight Commanders Test with the OC No 8 Flight, Flight Lieutenant Wright, before his first Atlas solo immediately afterwards.

In his final month at Sealand Mac had his Flight Commanders Test on the 14th followed by his CFI Test on the 22nd and the CFS Test on the 23rd. He had his last flight with the unit on the 27th and emerged with another 'average' assessment from CFI, Squadron Leader John Oliver, and an accumulated time of 146 hours.

Training Squadron & No 201 Sqn, Calshot

"Early on in 1935, I completed the specialist Flying Boat Pilots Course at RAF Base Caslhot, near Southampton, and soon afterward served in Egypt during the Ethiopian/Italian war, which included flying visits to Gibraltar, Malta, Cyprus, North African coastal ports and Aden in the Gulf. It was at this early stage I came to abhor the Arab animal." After leave Mac reported to Calshot on the 2nd of September 1934, to commence the Flying Boat Pilots Course, joining A Flight of the Seaplane Training Squadron and having his first two flights in the rare Sea Tutor, K3376, under Flying Officer Humphries on the 9th and 12th.

Later the same day he had a chick flight with the OC A Flight, Flight Lieutenant Chignell, immediately before his first Sea Tutor solo. Training with A Flight and the Sea Tutor continued until early January when he had his first flight in a Fairy Seal (floatplane) on the 3rd, going solo the same day. Some weeks previously, on the 23rd of October, he had had his first taste of a real flying boat with a one hour flight as a passenger in a Southampton.

On the 15th January he joined B Flight and had his first experience of the Saro Cloud, a 70 minute local affair in K2895 under Flight Lieutenant Chadwick, OC B Flight. He went solo on type on the 24th and thereafter flew as First or Second Pilot, taking turns with his fellow trainees. It is also noticeable in Mac's log that, in the this period, as much flying was logged as 'passenger' as was actually flying as he and his fellow trainees took practice turns at operating the navigational, photographic and signalling equipment. Such practice exercises frequently used the busy waters of the Solent with the 'interception'

of vessels like the Majestic and Titanic's sister, the Olympic together with units of the Home Fleet. On the 19th of March Mac joined C Flight and had his first go at the wheel of a Southampton, S1228, under the guidance of the OC C Flight, Flight Lieutenant Darbyshire. A second flight followed the same day and, upon return, Mac went up for this first Southampton sole - all ten minutes of it! A fourth flight on the same day completed his introduction to the type and it was to be exactly one week before he flew in it again, but this would be one which would stretch the boundaries of coincidence. On the morning of the 26th he took off with F/L Darbyshire for a 'forced landing on one engine' practice sortie. After lunch Mac went up himself and suffered a real starboard engine problem and had to force land!

On the 2nd of May Mac commenced a 14 day cruise along with the Seaplane Training Squadron CO, Squadron Leader McFarlane. Departing Calshot they travelled the entire eastern coastline of England and Scotland, and onwards to the Shetalnd and Orkney Islands, Fair Isle, Northern Ireland and Wales. In all, over 42 hours of flying time was squeezed into this period which included a forced landing at Aberdeen when the starboard engine started to fail. Mac's last flight with the Training Squadron came on the 30th May and he left with an 'above the average as pupil' assessment from Squadron Leader McFarlane and formally qualified as First Pilot (Day) on a type on the 7th of June. His accumulated flying hours now totalled 287.

Following a short leave Mac was not to be travelling far, remaining at Calshot with his posting to No 201 (FB) Squadron and had his first flight on the 25th of June in Southampton 9900.

Squadron duties at this time were fairly routine although for a 22 year old newly qualified Pilot they would hold a level of excitement. The following months saw Mac going through the normal squadron functions with several log entries providing a break from the norm.

15.7.35	Landing Dover Harbour (repeated several times)
7.9.35	Conveying the Captain of HMS Furious Calshot-Portland.
18.10.35	Intercepting SS Berengaria (formerly the Emporter of Germany - taken as compensation for the loss of the Lusitania)
22.10.35	Safety boat for FAA firing practice (repeated). Force landed 1800 hrs, starboard engine seized.
16.3.36	Exercise with Royal Sovereign. (RN Battleship of 1915 vintage, she was transferred to the Soviet Nay in 1944 and survived the war)
30.4.36	Automatic Control Test (This entry was Mac's first flight in the Saro London)

Now approaching the end of his time with 201, Mac had qualified as First Pilot (Night) on the 10th March and was assessed on the 25th by Squadron CO, Squadron Leader Breakey, as 'average' with the additional comment 'a good sound day and night pilot'.

His last flight with the squadron came on the 19th of May in a Saro London, taking his accumulated flying hours to 462, and he now prepared to join his new outfit at Felixstowe in preparation for the long haul out to Alexandria. Whilst with No 201 Squadron a fundamental change had taken place with the creation of Coastal Command as a separate entity within the RAF. Established on the 14th of July 1936, the first AOC-in-C was Air Marshall Sir Arthur Longmore*, KCB DSO, who took the new Command through the first 13 months of it's existence. (The name of Longmore appears later in this story and also in that of Squadron Leader SE Esler.)

No 230 Squadron, Felixstowe, Alexandria, Pembroke Dock 7 Singapore

"In 1936, October, I flew from England to Singapore in a formation of five flying boats via Marseilles, Malta, Egypt, Iraq, Basra, Karachi, Calcutta, Burma and finally Singapore. What a trip in those days! I spent the next three years in Singapore. During these years in the Far East we made flying visits to many places - to Calcutta, landing on the huge River Hooghly, to remote islands in the Indian Ocean, to many Malayan ports, to Mandalay in central Burma landing on the huge Irrawaddy River and from these further north to the boundary with China, and several visits to Borneo and Sarawak further east. All were of absorbing interest to we British young men and very educational."

(It is interesting to note Mac using the term 'We British', being a Limerick born man - but he did consider himself to be very much British.)

"The RAF view of Calcutta then was: The River Hooghly is the anus of India and Calcutta is 70 miles up it! I was to visit it again many years later during the fillings in 1949, horrible place.

"Our greatest effort was a four weeks Cruise, by four flying -boats, of the South China Sea. This took place 8th March - 9th April 1937. This included calls at Saigon (then French Indo China and new Vietnam), Hong Kong, Manila, British North Borneo, Sarawak (pronounced as 'Sara Wa'), Kuching the capital, and finally Singapore." Two very interesting points: "I was the first ever to take an RAF aircraft into Mandalay and in Kuching there lived the White Rajah, Sir Vyner Brook - an interesting British Colonial story. He was the last Rajah in Sarawak. He was a bit fed up with his two 'Princess' daughters - one married London dance bank leader Harry Roy and the other one an all-in wrestler."

(At the time, June 1936, the main part of the squadron was based in Egypt at Alexandria, Abourik and Lake Timsah.It is thought to be correct that Mac was sent to Felixstowe to join up with Squadron Leader Moulton-Barrett, who was collecting the new Singapore, K6912, for delivery to Egypt.)

Mac's first flight with his new squadron was also his first experience of the Singapore. This came on the 8th of June in an air test with Squadron Leader Moulton-Barrett in K6912, which the pair would remain with over the next few weeks and ultimately deliver to Egypt to join the main squadron. The following morning the pair carried out an air and w/t test followed by two sessions of 'dual instruction' for Mac. Later in the day, the fourth flight of the day, Mac went solo on type and qualified as First Pilot (Day). The pair continued flying together commencing on the 11th with four flights in and around Felixstowe carrying Naval Officers from the Naval Staff College. The next few days saw them testing the auto-pilot and they located to Plymouth on the 15th, still in K6912. On each of the next three days they further tested the auto-pilot and on the 19th, left on the first leg of the delivery flight to Alexandria, carrying the Squadron CO, Wing Commander W H Dunn, DSC. Leaving before dawn, the shared the controls on the 11+ hour leg direct to Lisbon. Two days later it was on the Gibraltar where engine problems kept them for four days before they left for Malta, ten hours away. Four days later they departed Malta for the final ten hours into Alexandria. In this tenday period they had flown a total of almost 38 hours to reach Egypt.

After one day's rest, Mac joined in with normal squadron activities for the first part of July with almost continual trips from Alexandria to Aborkir, some 25 minutes flying time further along the Egyptian coast. It was also during this period that he first encountered fellow Pilot Dennis Oliver, the two becoming great friends and sharing many experiences over the next few years before being posted together to the Central Flying School at Upavon.

At this time the whole squadron was preparing to return to the UK and it would appear the Mac had a couple of weeks local leave prior to the first day of August, when he was reunited with Squadron Leader Moulton-Barret. The carried out a few test flights in K4579 after it had had a new main-plane and engine fitted and they started the long haul back to the UK on the 4th, arriving at Pembroke Dock eight days and 38.5 flying hours later. The squadron now entered into a period of some weeks making preparations for the even longer haul out to Singapore, where it was to be based for a three year tour. After leave, and now a Flight Lieutenant, Mac returned to Pembroke Dock in early October and had his first flight in an old friend - K6912, which he had taken to Egypt in June and which he would now take on the first part of the trip to Seletar. The next few days were spent carefully checking out systems prior to departure on the 14th when he left as part of a five aircraft flight and, although running repairs meant some dropped out and re-joined, the flight arrived intact in Singapore 24 days later on the 6th November after 82+ hours airborne, Mac himself now in K6918 along with Wing Commander Dunn. Local leave was then taken and Mac first flew from Singapore on the second day of December on a 3.5 hour combined navigational exercise and sector patrol. Two days later he would link up again with Dennis Oliver and they would fly together many times over the next few years.

Logbook entries in this period provide some interesting and historical data.

16.12.36	Safety aircraft for No 36 Squadron, bombing. (No 36 Squadron were also at Seletar at this time)
4.1.37	Formation flying: Escort for AOC India.
8.1.37	Conveying AOC India to Mandalay and Calcutta. (The AOC India was Air Marshall Sir Ludlow-Hewitt who travelled with his local 'bearer' Mac and Dennis ferried them around for the next 6 days, firstly to the Irrawaddy River at Mandalay and onwards to Calcutta

(As a Major, Ludlow-Hewitt had been CO of No 15 Squadron back in 1915. As Air Chief Marshall Sir Edgar, he would be appointed AOC-in-C Bomber Command on the 12th of September this year. He was succeeded by Air Marshall Sir Charles Portal in April 1940.)

(Mac's notes show his arrival at Mandalay to be the first ever by an RAF aircraft.)

21.1.37	Aerial inspection of base defences (base being Seletar and the passenger being the then Air Commodore Tedder).
28.1.37	Live bombing - 4 x 250lb bombs dropped.
3.2.37	Escort for striking force: No's 100 and 84 squadrons. (No 100 Squadron were also at Seletar at this time but No 84 was in the Persian Gulf and records do not show a Far East detachment. However Mac kept a very accurate log and, in the absence of tracing any other squadron ending in the digit 4, it must be assumed that this is correct.) This was part of a large exercise with the RN and involved intercepting and shadowing by night and day, fleet elements.
23.2.37	Qualified 1st Pilot Night, Singapore MK 111
8.3.37	China Sea Cruise. (Commencing with a leg to Kam Rahn Bay, Saigon, in the French Indo China, and onwards to Kai Tak were they joined exercise simulating attacks on Kai Tak airfield and the RN Dockyard in Hong Kong. They returned to Singapore via the Philippines, Borneo and Sarawak. In total they were away for 33 days and spent almost 46 hours in the air.)
3.5.37	Formation flying - practice for Coronation Day.
7.5.37	Rehearsal for Coronation Flypast.
12.5.37	Taking part in Coronation celebrations.

Mac and Dennis took part in the celebrations at Kuala Selangor on the Malayan coast to the west of Kuala-Lumpur. They spent the afternoon of the 12th May carrying out four short local flights in which local residents were carried for air experience flights. These residents included local Malays together with Chinese and Indian natives. On one such flight on fewer than 19 people were carried aboard K6917. This break from the routines of squadron flying was probably welcomed by the crews who, even at this stage of the thirties, were aware that war was a real threat and who were getting used to a training schedule which was quite deliberate, as the continuing log entries show.

19.5.37	Exercise with HMS Diomede (this old cruiser, built in 1919, survived the war).
21.5.37	Oblique and vertical photography at Mersing + survey. (This flight to the eastern Malayan coast carried a Royal Engineers Captain and men and a boffin. It was one of a considerable number of photographic and defence survey patrols undertaken both before and after this date.)
21.7.37	Towing drogue for No 36 Squadron.
30.7.37	Light attacks on surface vessels (the above two flown by Mac in a Vildebeeste).
11.10.37	Exercise with HMS Dorsetshire and escort for No 100 (FB) Squadron. (HMS Dorsetshire, which had helped to deliver the final and fatal blow to the German battleship Bismarck, was sunk along with her consort, HMS Cornwall, in the Indian Ocean on the 5th April 1942 by Japanese bomber aircraft. Dorsetshire was commanded by Captain AWS Agar, VC DSO.)

From here until the turn of the year Mac's time was spent on bombing, photography and navigation practice sorties. In addition log book entries from November 1937 show the squadron changing name from No 230 (FB) to No 230 (GR).

13.1.38	China Sea exercise with HMS Eagle. (HMS Eagle, 23,000 ton aircraft carrier originally laid down in 1913 as the Chilean Dreadnought Almirante Cochrane. She was sunk by a German submarine in the Western Mediterranean on the 11th of August 1942.)
14.1.38	Photography for 100 Sqn torpedo drops.
26.1.38	Exercise with HMS Dorsetshire.
4.2.38	Interception and shadowing of HMS Dorsetshire.

Alington and myself standing on the cockpit seats with about half our lengths protruding up through the cockpit sliding roof hatch.

"Group Captain Dunn made a short introductory speech; the Air Marshall made a longer speech and the Sultan finished the proceedings with a short address in Malay and then pulled the cord and we were Flying Boat Perak! Lots of clapping followed. The next part of the event was to provide air experience in Perak for those who desired it. The Sultan declined; either due to his frail state or cold feet - I don't know; probably due to health reasons as he died two weeks later! However, the Sultana was very keen and was the first to board the aircraft. I recall that the Sultana was a small little individual dressed in flowing multi-coloured robes. She came alongside the main port-front entrance of the lower deck in a little dinghy and I helped here aboard. I noticed, with some surprise, that she was barefoot! She then climbed up the inside steps to the cockpit area where she stood beside me and held on to the back of my seat. She was obviously very thrilled with her first flight in an aircraft, especially in such a distinguished craft as Perka. The flight, like the others that followed was a short hop around the local area.

"With regard to the Lumat mooring and landing area; as I stated already, it was our favourite one for a variety of reasons from the operation and social points of view. to start with it was an excellent stretch of water at the estuary of the Lumat river, close to the town and coastline with adequate shelter from all directions in high wind conditions. Incidentally, we maintained similar 'advanced moorings' as they were termed, at various points around the coast of Malaya and in Sarawak and British North Borneo, and these were subject to regular flying boat visits from time to time.

"On the social side; Lumat is (or was) in the central part of a large rubber plantation area of Malaya. These plantations were owned, in the main by foreign concerns but almost exclusively managed by English Managers and the workers (or tapers) were in the main Indian Tamil coolies. the Manager was provided with a good residence and a vehicle and didn't have to work too hard! These were quite a few around Lumat and they ran a typical English Club in Lumat where they held their social functions - dances, dinners and the like. We had a set procedure when we decided to night-stop at Lumat. We flew circles around the town, starting at about 20 miles radius and decreasing it progressively until we ended up over Lumat.

"All the outer managers would then see or hear us and conclude' 'Oh there is a flying boat in tonight! We'll see them in the club.' We were then sure of having a party with some old friends. Another popular feature of our visit was - we brought copies of the Singapore Times and also, when we left we took their 'home' air mail for posting in Singapore, and if we were on our way home, and had some tinned foods left over, we would drop them off in the Club. Remember that, in those days, there was no internal air services and fairly slow overland rail transport!

"Needless to say, I was very proud of my charge Perak as was my crew. My Co-Pilot Alington was an ex Merchant Marine cadet and officer and was an excellent fellow and I took special interest in his Sunderland flying training. I was especially pleased to learn that he became a Wing Commander and that he survived the war, with distinction. Also poor Perak was shot down in the Mediterranean by the 'Wops' with the loss of all the crew as well at the aircraft."

"PS. Incredibly, no photographs of any kind were taken to record this event. Also any photographs I had of Sunderland flying were lost during the war."

CFS Upavon
No 8 FTS, Montrose
No 11 FTS, Shawbury

"I came to the UK on a troopship called Dunera on which I shared a cabin with my friend Dennis Oliver, arriving Southampton Jan 1939 and we both reported to the Central Flying School on Salisbury Plain, to complete the Flying Instructors Course after which we were both posted to Training Schools as Flying Instructors. This was the first time we had been separated in five years! I went to Montrose near Edinburgh and he went to a school near Oxford. We had no control over these postings. We were both Teachers in 1939 when war was declared. We had also both been promoted to Squadron Leaders and were both Chief Flying Instructors at different Training Schools - me being sent to Shawbury near Shrewsbury."

(To avoid confusion Mac was posted to Montrose as OC B Flight, his first CFI post coming with his next posting to Shawbury.)

"We had our last meeting in May 1940. I had flown down to his station for lunch visit and chat. When I said cheerio and hopped into my aircraft to fly back to Shawbury I wouldn't know we'd never meet again. He was killed by a 'Hun' bomb on the ground - having successfully baled out of his aircraft at night only a week before. Such is fate, or luck, or something.

"In early 1940 I was a very young Squadron Leader and my appointment was as CFI at No 11 FTS at Shawbury. In accordance with standard procedure I had to test every pupil, at the end of his final term, and pass him as fit for service flying duties. One morning as I sat in the instructor's seat, a pupil climbed into the front, the normal pilots seat, did up his straps and connected his speaking tube. I immediately recognised an Instonian scarf protruding above his flying suit and I said:

'Name?'
The reply via the tube, 'Corry Sur!'
'Where are you from?'
'Belfast Sur'
'Did you go to Inst?'
'Yes Sur, I was there the same time as you Sur'.
'I can assure you Corry, it wont do you any good'."

And so two Inst ex-pupils met, Sergeant Corry and Squadron Leader McBratney, in an RAF aircraft.

(Corry is Noel, later Squadron Leader. The above incident actually occurred during an aerobatics dual with Mac. In his own story, Noel tells the tale of a further 'scarf' encounter during his subsequent CFI test.)

"I should have mentioned that while at Montrose I had more than my share of luck! I was on fire in the air and was too low to jump! I ended in a field of curley kale, upside down, under a burning aircraft. Somehow I got out and, somehow, got about 100 feet away when it blew up! I was fit and back on flying in three months! Luck indeed!"

Mac's posting to CFS at Upavon was to C Flight, for the Flying Instructors No 57 Course, commencing on the 23rd of January 1939. His first flight came on that day in Hart K5856 as a passenger to Flying Officer Garvin. He proceeded through the course on Tutor, Anson, Fury and Oxford aircraft, the seven week flying element ending 91 flights later with his CFI test on the 14th March. At this stage two points are evident. Firstly that the effort is now being put into training for the impending war, at this stage less than six months sway and secondly, that Mac (and Dennis) was one of those well experienced 'above average' Pilots who could be relied upon, and who were earmarked for the all important FI and CFI roles in the near future. Many regular officers like him were being posted in to CFS at this time, officers who would go on to higher levels as the war progressed. However, a glance at Mac's subsequent career progression following his time at CFS begs a question.

Here we have a regular officer who has served over six years. He had been entrusted with some very senior passengers, including royalty and has obviously been well thought of by his superiors. Having had continually good assessments over the past few years it was probably a disappointment to Mac to receive and 'average' assessment from CFS. Doubtless he would have expected better even though he would have known, and accepted, that the standards at CFS were uncommonly high. This same assessment was to be repeated at his next three postings at Montrose, Shawbury and Silloth before he emerged from Catfoss with an exceptional assessment. this would seem a strange progression particularly when it is considered that Mac's first posing out of CFS was to Montrose as Flight Commander, to Shawbury with promotion as Squadron Commander and Chief Flying Instructor at an important new unit before taking up, with the promotion, two squadron commands, one of which was so important that it carried Winston Churchill's personal backing and for which Mac received the Air Force Cross. To move a career officer upwards in this way is to confirm one who is going places, as was true of Mac, but to do so for a string of average assessments does not tally. Given his refusal to suffer fools gladly, it is possible that his no-nonsense approach upset some of the unit commanders who had decided on the average ratings - such unfortunate occurrences were not unknowns whether occasioned by

envy or otherwise - but that his masters knew what they were dealing with and understood how he could seem in others eye. With goodbyes to his pal Dennis he was now posted to the oldest military airfield in Scotland, to the Intermediate Training Squadron of No 8 FTS at Montrose as OC C Flight and went aloft with his first pupil, Pilot Officer Dawbarn, in Oxford L4640 on the 28th March. The training regime continued day in and day out, rising in frequency as the outbreak of war approached. An analysis of Mac's time at Montrose gives an indication of the training effort being put in. In his 105 flying days he took no less than 367 pupil flights. given that he was on instructor in isolation it can be imagined the total which would accrue if all the various training units were taken into consideration. In addition, this was 1939 and the scale of training would increase many times over in the next couple of years.

Had his time at Montrose not been rudely interrupted by a serious incident, leading to a near three month lay off, his total would have almost doubled, However fate has a habit of interrupting without warning and for Mac that intrusion arrived on the 4th June.

On that day he concluded a two day visit to Abbotsinch, near Glasgow, Whether this was a wangled or official trip is not known but in any event he had managed to spend time with his wife Patricia, who accompanied him to the airfield to see him off. Patricia waved her goodbyes as she watched him take off in Hart K5005. She also witnessed the crash which followed almost immediately. Her feelings at that moment, and during the inevitable period of uncertainty afterwards, can only be imagined.

Mac's logbook , not completed by him, simply records:

4.6.39   Caught fire at 100 feet on take off: force landed in field: aircraft burned out.

In typically laconic parlance, it is note recorded that the burning plane landed upside down after clipping the perimeter fence on the way in. Mac suffered neck and shoulder injuries in escaping the wreck and would, in later days, suffer stiffness during cold weather as a result of these injuries. Although he would experience his fair share of forced landings during his subsequent career, this would be the only major incident in all his years of flying and would lead to his comment; "the only time I ever wanted to use a parachute I was too low to use it!" It is fair to assume that a couple of additional words were included when he first stated this. Mac did not fly again until the 26th of August and it is poignant to note that he was obviously unavailable to sign off his log at the end of June, nor to complete the entry for the fateful 4th of June. Both were completed in his absence by Pilot Officer Dawbarn, who had been his first pupil at Montrose some months earlier. Fit again, Mac took up the reins in late August and continued through the autumn. It is noticeable in his log that this period was one of much increased training activity, war now having been declared, and the numbers of Acting Pilot Officers passing through his hands was very high.

Little happened to break the routine of training in this period except for one incident which took place on the 20th of September. His log entry shows a one hour night sortie 'search for reported enemy aircraft'. As he was flying an unarmed Oxford it is not quite clear what he intended should he have come across such an animal! His last flight at Montrose came on the 22nd December and he bade goodbye to Scotland, by his own admission not his favourite place on earth. With the war now entering the new year, pilots with experience were in great demand for both operational and training duties. Many pilots like Mac, a regular, found themselves forming the nucleus of the training and station command posts. Accordingly he now found himself promoted to Squadron Leader and given command of No 2 Squadron at No 11 FTS, Shawbury. He was also appointed CFI for No 11, both appointments being effective on New Years Day 1940. After a brief leave over the Christmas period he arrived at Shawbury where his first three flights, commencing on the 8th of January, were local familiarisation sorties in Oxford and Hart aircraft. His first pupil flight seven days later was an aerobatics dual with one Sergeant Corry a fellow ex-Instonian. As Squadron Leader Noel Corry, DFC AE, Noel went on to serve with both Fighter and Bomber Commands and has his own chapter in this book.

Whilst at Shawbury Mac would also experience two types for the first time - the Battle and Spitfire, although his flying time was now reduced in comparison to previously as he took on the administration of the squadron. He undertook the CFI Tests, which would be one of his prime responsibilities, along with much aircraft testing and advanced training. it is noticeable in his log how the Pilots Under Training have changed as the numbers of Sergeants, probably VR, now outnumber the trainee officers. Mac's last flight at Shawbury came on the first anniversary of his dreadful crash, and he was posted to No 1 OTU at Silloth to form a new unit but, as a footnote to his time at Shawbury, we return to his old pal from Singapore days, Dennis Oliver, as Mac would now have another reason to remember the 4th of June. It is not known if they had any get together in the period since parting company after CFS some 15 months earlier, but Mac notes in his letter their last get together in May 1940; when he flew down to see Dennis near Oxford, "For a lunch visit and a chat." In fact this came on the fateful 4th of June and was Mac's last flight from Shawbury. He flew a Battle to Little Rissington, collected CFI Dennis and hopped on to Kidlington. Lunch and chat over, Mac returned to Shawbury not knowing he would never see Dennis again. He was killed some weeks later during a German air raid.

No 1 OTU, Silloth/Prestwick
No 2 OTU, Catfoss

"After Shawbury I had an unsettled spell of moving about forming new units and then moving on to the next one - a sort of 'former' and 'teacher'. This phase included a new unit at a station in East Yorkshire flying Blenheims and Beaufighters." Mac's actual position at Silloth is not clear but it is known that he was, in his own words, "A sort of former and teacher." He records that he moved from one posting to another forming new units. At Silloth, on the coast of what was then Cumberland, he set up the flying wing and would appear, from log entries, to have been 'in charge'. This was a new unit and it is probable that he set things up prior to handing over to a more senior officer when a certain stage in growth was reached. In any event he first flew from Silloth on the 11th of June in a Blenheim, his first flight in the type and would later add three more firsts whilst on station at Silloth - the Botha, Hurricane and Hudson, In addition, considering he was a 'boat' man,. his efforts were now tending towards fighter work, quite unusual for Coastal Command.

He also took advanced training and carried out many inter-station flights, mainly to and from Kirkbride. On the 3rd of September he moved on to Prestwick to set up a Blenheim Flight detachment of the OTU and spent the next six weeks shuttling between various stations before taking up his next posting as CFI, Fighters, at Catfoss, near Hull, effective on the 19th of October, although his log from September shows all his Blenheim flying time under No 2 OTU had a Blenheim detachment at Prestwick at this time but do note show No 2 OTU at the same base. The three Blenheim IV's used in this period were all Catfoss bound aircraft so it is possible that Mac was carrying out preliminary work, prior to the formation of No 2 Catfoss in October. In any event Mac arrived from Prestwick on the 27th of October and operated for the first time the next day on a dusk patrol, carrying an air gunner, enemy aircraft being reported in the area and this was repeated several times whilst at Catfoss.

His duties here included the normal CFI Tests but he also did a considerable amount of advanced training using Blenheim and Oxford aircraft. The pilots who were about to go into operational squadrons were put through their paces and covered all the disciplines of attack, formation flying, cloud flying, etc. etc. Mac also gave personal instruction to new instructors arriving on the unit prior to taking up their duties and was generally very busy, carrying out dozens of visits to many operational stations for reasons which are unclear although it is possible that these visits were connected with his desire for knowledge. Perhaps by visiting such stations he gained a better understanding which was used in his training regime. During May he was promoted Wing Commander, although there was to be no change in his duties for the remaining time at Catfoss and he made his last flight for the OTU on the 27th of June, prior to moving on to squadron command at Stranraer from the first day of July. His assessment of June 1941 from the Group Captain commanding Catfoss was his first 'exceptional', in this case as a Fighter Pilot.

A notable date in this period is the 4th of July 1940, the date of the marriage of Mac and Patricia. Known as Paddy, Patricia Miller was from Belfast and was educated at the city's Methody College. At the time of their wedding Paddy was completing a cordon bleu course at Glasgow Domestic College or, as she called it, Glasgow Dough School. Naturally both would have liked to have been married back home in Ireland but time off could not be arranged, apparently due to the attitude of Mac's Commanding Officer who would not allow more than one day off although, as Mac's log shows a gap from the 1st day of June until the 7th of July, he was maybe able to wangle something. In the event they were married at Kilmalcolm in Scotland and would remain happily together for over 55 years, sharing many of Mac's postings in various locations. At this time we come to a period in Mac's career when things are about to change again. In 1938 he concluded a five-year period as a flying-boat man who had seen considerable experience in the Far East. Then, due to greatly changing circumstances, he underwent a change of path and became a member of the all important training staff. For 2.5 years he trained new aircrew and rose to Chief Flying Instructor and Wing Commander, forming new units along the way and emerged as an exceptional Fighter Pilot. Now he was to swap the versatile Blenheim for the ungainly Catalina and undertake his first operational squadron command. some things however did not change - his straightforward approach and his ability to teach others and organise units, and he would us this to good effect over the next few years.

No 413 Squadron RCAS, Stranraer

"Then from there (believe it or not) I was posted to Stranraer as CO of a Canadian Squadron - flying boats again! These were American Catalina flying boats, MOST unexciting. Further, I had to form the unit from 'scratch' and collect the new aircraft. Fortunately for me, they posted in a new CO - a Canadian Wing Commander, who got himself and all his crew killed on the Squadron's first war sortie." After the experiences of the past year or so Stranraer must have come as a shock. Mac was to literally form the squadron from nothing, even to the extent of having to and collect it's first aircraft.

An extract from CATS, a Canadian newssheet which records memoirs of No 413 Squadron says, from a 1990 interview with Mac in his Adelaide Hills Home: "He arrived at Loch Ryan and Stranraer with a Sergeant as his only staff. There were no aircraft, no aircrew and on ground personnel."

The story of RAF Stranraer is best told by Mac himself from a letter of 1985:

"I assumed command of this Canadian squadron on 1 July 1941, at Stranraer and actually arrived on that date.

There were no aircraft and no squadron personnel and the RAF 'Station' consisted of a series of requisitioned buildings and hotels throughout the town with one prefabricated RAF building for the squadron, right on the main street, overlooking the waters edge. There were a number (small) of USN(AF) personnel awaiting our arrival - three officers and three petty-officer technical maintenance crew. The officers were:

Lieut George Hughes
Ensign 'Smithy' Smith
Ensign Emmet Hogan
Ensign D Eldred - late arrival

All the above were pilots and their designation, at that time, was 'Neutral Observer' and they were officially attached to the US Navy Air Attaché Office in London. While they had no official status or executive authority with me, it was agreed by Coastal Command HQ with the US authorities that they would 'help' where possible with the crew conversion and maintenance of aircraft - in summary, with the training of RAF personnel. they were an excellent group of people and this unusual arrangement worked beautifully. Hughes and Eldred were particularly outstanding officers.

"The whole exercise was a Coastal Command 'first', an experiment no less, in that the flying personnel came to 413 Squadron as complete ex-Blenheim crews with an operational tour under their belts - several with decorations and this transfer to 'boats' was regarded as something of a rest! I, myself, had come straight off Beaufighters and Blenheims in Yorkshire but I already had five years 'boating' experience, pre-war, and was an ex-CFS instructor.

"On 4 July we collected our first Catalina from Greenock. Myself with Hughes, Smith and three USN maintenance crew, were picked up at Stranraer by another Catalina from the Greenock Maintenance Unit. Flown by a Flying Officer Hanbury, and taken to Greenock where we collected the Squadron's first aircraft and made the first flight, ever, in a number 413 Squadron RCAF aircraft. The flight was, simply, Greenock-Stranraer, and the aircraft was Z2141. Hughes flew as Captain as, at that time, I had never handled a Catalina.

"It was really quite a historic day for Hughes and myself because it was:

1) My wedding anniversary - our first!
2) American Independence Day
3) 413 Squadron's first flight day
4) Hughes first flight as Captain, (neutral/observer) in an RAF aircraft during wartime in the UK.

"By the second week in July we had three aircraft and sufficient crews and maintenance personnel to commence training in the flying boat Art. There also arrived a new Station Commander - Wing Commander 'Laddie' Cliff, a very experienced flying-boat Pilot and an extremely nice guy. We were greatly helped by his presence at Stranraer. The training of land crews to the flying-boats role could be summed up as teaching Pilots seamanship/water handling and teaching Navigators the requirements of long-range navigation. Both the above items were, of course, foreign to Blenheim crews previously employed on short jaunts across the North Sea. so, we virtually set up a classroom school for Navigators and this was run by a newly arrived Canadian navigation specialist F/Lt Gordon. Like any other 'school' records, some couldn't make the grade and were replaced. In the event, Hughes and Smith initially did all the dual instruction from pilots and I carried out all the check tests prior to sending a Pilot off solo, which meant Captain with crew. Thus we had two opinions as to whether a Pilot was solo proficient or not.

"Flying facilities at Stranraer then were non-existent by latter day standards. there was no such thing as Air Traffic Control, no Met Section, no slipway for beaching aircraft and only the bare minimum of marine craft to carry out ferry and safety duties. Additionally, in spite of being located in relatively sheltered waters in Loch Ryan, the flying-boat moorings were exposed in gale wind conditions and there had been cases of flying-boats being lost, or sinking, at their moorings. About the second week in July my deputy and Flight Commander arrived and this was a great help. He was a Squadron Leader called Ware. I believe his first name was Moses. He had a university degree, was very efficient, a hard worker and was experienced as a Pilot. He was RAF not Canadian, survived the war and settled afterward in Bermuda. I have not seen him since. Notwithstanding deficiencies and some difficulties, our conversion programme progressed to plan, and by the end of July we had a few of our ex-Blenheim pilots flying as Catalina captains. Most of them liked the change but on or two did not and were posted by request. On taking command of No 413, I fully undertook that my appointment was for the conversion period only and that, in due course RCAF officers and other ranks would be posted in to take over."

Mac's log shows that W8419, ex No 119 Squadron, remained with 413 and Z2141 was used by him to qualify on type under Lieutenant Hughes, later to become a USN Admiral. Mac used 2141 to visit Lough Erne, carrying additional crew to fly an additional aircraft into Stranraer. the return flight from Lough Erne was via Bormore where more crew were collected. Between the two ferry flights the squadron ended up with five aircraft by late July, being the two above plus AH566 & W8434. The first aircraft in place, Mac then worked to bring the crews up to standard although his time at Stranraer was brought to an abrupt end when he was posted to command No 120 Squadron at Nutts Corner in Northern Ireland. It is thought likely that Mac had been originally intended to go to Nutts Corner sooner but was diverted to Stranraer to cover until the Canadian CO arrived. Conversely, it is equally likely that given the Coastal Command desire to try forming 413 with ex-Blenheim aircrew, that Mac's move was quite deliberate given his experience on the type from OTU.

Mac's successor, Wing Commander Briese was quickly followed in to Stranraer by two Squadron Leaders. All were Canadians and formed the senior part of the squadron. Mac recalled Briese as being a very nice guy, somewhat older than himself, and the two spent some days together prior to Mac's departure.

In the event Briese, along with his aircrew leaders and the two Squadron Leaders, were lost on a reconnaissance trip to Norway and Mac wrote more than once on this subject. He remembers discussing such sorties with Briese, the two being aware that the Luftwaffe was strong in the area, presenting a dangerous threat to slow flying reconnaissance aircraft. As a result the area was to be avoided unless in conditions of heavy cloud or poor weather. Mac was unable to understand how such a trip could be sanctioned, particularly when carrying the most important squadron officers. He described this loss as, "Very sad and unnecessary."

He was also saddened twofold when he later learned of the loss of ensign Eldred, killed in a night flying accident at Loch Ryan. In his own words, "This upset me greatly as I had formed a particular liking for Eldred." Unfortunately the accident also killed the pupil undergoing night flying training, Flying Officer Fowler. A holder of the DFC, Fowler had received all his conversion training up to solo from Mac. Mac's last flight for the Catalina Squadron came on the 9th of August and he spent a few days at Silloth, West Freugh and Catfoss before arriving at the new Nutts Corner airfield on the 23rd. His accumulated flying hours were almost 1,900.

No 120 Squadron Nutts Corner/Ballykelly

"I should have added that by then somewhere along the line, I was a Wing Commander myself. From Stranraer I was posted to form and Command what was to become the famous No 120 Squadron which was the very first RAF Squadron equipped with the big four engine Liberator. Our base was Nutts Corner, Northern Ireland. Most new crews were all experienced operational aircrews and therefore my initial job was to convert the Pilots to the new type of aircraft with tricycle under-carriage, and the use of four engines. My Liberators, with their very long endurance, and therefore range, were wanted everywhere. I had in Iceland, Gibraltar and Northern Scotland at the same time. I was happy to be allowed to retain command for almost a year and then I was posted to West Indies."

Named after a local farm/junction, Nutts Corner was a product of the immense drive to establish airfields in Northern Ireland quickly in order that Coastal Command could be better placed to meet the U-Boat threat. The site was only selected during the summer of 1940 and construction commenced some weeks later, was accorded the highest priority. Although not fully complete, the new station opened on the 2nd June 1941, the same day that No 120 Squadron was re-formed. Not initially popular with aircrews, the runways were too short and the taxiways too narrow and allowed no room for error. Given the boggy ground on which the airfield was constructed any failure to negotiate the taxiway properly would result in a marooned Liberator. On more than one occasion this would lead to incoming aircraft being diverted. Mac first flew with 120 Squadron in Liberator AM914 on the 24th August and spent the next few weeks assessing his crews in readiness for going operational. Although the majority of the crews were experienced operationally all were new to the Liberator. On the 20th September Mac had the honour of leading off the squadron's first operational sortie, an ASV sweep out to 22W. Accompanied by Jack Harrison, who would take over the squadron the following year, and Eric Estler he took AM924 away a few minutes before the legendary Terry Bulloch.

As Mac records, this flight established three notable firsts. It was the first operational flight for 120 Squdron, the first Liberator and the first from Nutts Corner Airfield. He did not fly operationally again for some months, being entirely involved in setting up this new unit, which would become the number one in Coastal Command. It is probably true that he was not encouraged to fly operationally as the effort was being put into bringing the Liberators into service was considerable. It was also political and involved Churchill, an ardent supported of the new unit, and accordingly it would be less than desirable to lose the CO. In the event he did two further operations in April 1942, both Convoy Escorts. Mac worked tirelessly to establish the new unit and carried out many flights checking out his crews for bombing, air firing, night flying, etc. He visited many airfields including Limavady, which the squadron would frequently use as a diversionary field. Prestwick, where the various modification and updates were applied. St Angelo, Stornoway, Mullaghmore, Ballykelly, Speke, Skitten, Tain, Sealand and Northolt were all visited and would play their part in the development of the squadron in one way or another.

His last job for the squadron was to oversee the move to Ballykelly and to hand over to his successor, Wing Commander Jack Harrison, DFC, before taking up his next posting in the warmer climates of the West Indies. No 120 Squadron had many fine pilots, at the time amongst the best available, and they undoubtedly took full benefit from a master motivators like Mac who by sheer hard work provided the example and inspiration which would put the squadron in a strong position. given the success which the squadron achieved, both during his time and later a lot of credit must go to Mac for laying such sound foundations. Certainly the powers that be must have recognised his efforts as he was awarded the Air Force Cross. At 29 years of age and having a wealth of experience from his various postings and 2,000+ flying hours, Mac was to become a 'former' again as Commanding Officer of the Flying Wing at the brand new Coastal Command training base of Nassau.

No111 (C) Nassau, Bahamas

Mac's next posting was to Nassau, Bahamas, to form a new unit at anew RAF station, the airfield and buildings being built by Americans under the 'lest-lend' agreement between USA and Britain. "I was the Commanding Officer of the Flying Wing and we were operating Liberators and the American B25 'Mitchell'. By then the USA had joined the allies at war.

"You probably know that the Governor of the Bahamas during the 40's was the ex-King of England, the Duke of Windsor. Well, when the new airfield was completed the local Government decided to call it Windsor Field (field being the American for an aerodrome) presumable in honour of his nibs the Duke. Well they organised a big opening ceremony with American, British and local Bahamian big shots present. I took a special part in the do. I carried out the inaugural landing in a Mitchell B25 with the Duke of Windsor in the co-pilots seat That was quite a one off historic event.

"With prior permission from the RAF Delegation in Washington DC I visited, by air Cuba and Jamaica, I actually flew the first ever RAF aircraft into Havana and later, on another flight into Kingston, Jamaica. Cuba was a friendly country, not communistic in those days pro USA, pro British and run by sugar millionaire's, these flights were what was called 'Showing the Flag' Britain was some country in those days. Yes Some Country. With regard to this West Indies duty, I could write a book alone on the Windsor's and the Sir Harry Oakes murder. This is still recorded as an unsolved murder crime. However about a dozen RAF Officers (then) could have spelled out a name. I knew him well."

Having been accompanied by Paddy both at Stranraer and back home in Ireland, Mac was to be disappointed that she would not be able to accompany him to the Caribbean. Unfortunately the U-Boats which he sought to conquer with 120 squadron made travel too risky, Paddy's planned journey was cancelled and she ended up staying with her mother in Ireland for the duration of Mac's overseas posting. Accordingly Mac left the UK aboard the rapid Queen Mary on the 11th August and arrived in the Bahamas via New York nine days later. Little is known of his first three months in Nassau, his log recording, "Certified no flying during months of August, September and October 1942 while waiting formation of station and arrival of aircraft from USA."

His logbook commences again on the 14th November with his first flight at the unit in Grumman Goose FP497, with Lieutenant Pike, RN followed by the first B25 Mitchell flight on the 25th. By this time the unit would appear to have been ready to operate and Mac spent the next few days checking out his senior Instructors and familiarising them with the local terrain.

Little is known of this unit but it would appear to have been given some priority as the Senior Instructors were initially all Squadron Leaders, probably using the posting as a lead into returning to the UK with the new aircraft.

Several interesting log entries from this period tell their own story.

19.12.42	In Mitchell FK167. Searching for missing US Nave aircraft, Andros area.
29/12/42	In Mitchell FK163. To satellite aerodrome for 'first landing' ceremony.
29/12/42	In Mitchell FK171. satellite to main aerodrome (both flights carrying HRH The Duke of Windsor, the Governor of the Bahamas for the occasion of naming Windsor Field).

These two flights constitute a story best told by Mac himself in a letter of May 1994.

"It will be noted that I used two different aircraft in this occasion. The reason, well I said to my Flight Commander I want to reserve aircraft to tag along behind me, just in case, and this it did. Well during the landing ceremony one of my ground crew came up to me and said 'Sir, you've got a hydraulic oil leak in the starboard undercarriage, we have to class your aircraft unserviceable.' so I said, 'Right, start up my reserve aircraft,' and nobody noticed the changeover except the Duke, he asked me why we came back in a different aircraft and I told him."

10/1/43	In Mitchell FK180. Nassau to Jamaica, A/C U/S on arrival. (This is thought to be the first RAF flight in the island - as referred to in Mac's text.)
19/1/43	In Mitchell FR384. Air sea rescue, search for missing US Army aircraft reported down in sea in Crooked Passage area, nothing sighted.
30/1/43	In Liberator 111 FL994. Local survey Bahamas (carrying Sir Cosmo Parkinson).
10/2/43	In Mitchell FR372. Dropping food and water to aircrew of wrecked US aircraft on Andros.
16/2/43	In Mitchell FR382. To Havana and San Antonio, Cuba (thought to be the first RAF flight into Cuba also referred to in Mac's text).

Regular testing and inter-island flying was the routine from then until leaving the unit in March. The final flight came on the 26th with a Liberator sortie into Windsor Field and Mac left the unit with an 'exceptional' rating from Group Captain Waite, Commanding Officer RAF Nassau.

RCAF Dorval/RAF Delegation Washington

"Early in 1943 I finished my West Indies tour and I was scheduled to return to the UK and of course to another job. But first there was another diversion, I was waiting in New York, in a hotel at RAF expense, for a troopship home, the troopship being one of the 'Queens' which was transporting thousands of US troops for the

build-up for the invasion of Europe against the Nazi's. I was advised (ordered more likely) to proceed to Montreal to carry out the Pilot conversion of the Pilots of No 10 squadron RCAF onto Liberators, with which they were about to be re-equipped. This annoyed me as it was still winter in Canada and I had just left the warm climate of the Bahamas. However, this chore was done in about a month and I came back to New York to board my trooper which was the Queen Elizabeth with twenty thousand American troops plus McBratney, all bound for the Scottish Clyde, two meals a day, breakfast and dinner and six bodies in a small cabin."

The ship sailed alone with no anti-submarine escort relying on its 28 knots speed and continual zigzag turns every few minutes. This increased the total journey time to 7.5 days (normal 4.5 for 'Queen's').

Next stop was an unscheduled two weeks at No 10 Squadron RCAF at Dorval where the Royal Air Force Flying College was established. Mac's experience on the Liberator was to be used to train No 10 crews who were re-equipping with the type in order to close the 'Atlantic Gap' very familiar to Mac after his time with No 120 squadron. No 10 Squadron RCAF were already experienced in U-Boat work and were familiar with the conditions in the North Atlantic off Newfoundland but they did not possess aircraft with enough range. At this time Liberators were not in good supply outside America and had not been used from the Canadian side of the Atlantic to help close the gap. Under a deal between the RAF and the US Government, the next allocation of Liberators for the RAF was waived providing it was given to the RCAF. Records show that No 10 Squadron received the first of these aircraft on St George Day 1943 although the serials of the aircraft used by Mac would suggest they may have arrived sooner.

Accordingly Mac was diverted from his journey back to the UK and attached to the Canadians at Dorval flying first on the 7th of April in Liberator BZ723. he only completed four flights, the last three days later, before heading homewards. It would seem a long way to go to make four flights, two of which were with a fellow Wing Commander called Ennis, so maybe Ennis felt confident enough to continue or, more likely another officer was posted in to relieve Mac. In any event he left Dorval and arrived in Washington, where he spent two weeks with the RAF Delegation before boarding the Queen Elizabeth for the journey home. (Dorval was later the base for No's231 and 243 Squadrons.)

HQ No 15 Liverpool

"Back home in the UK I had to take my turn in a staff job. First I spent a month's leave in a rented home by the sea in Portstewart with my wife (plus one). Then I was informed I was to report to the joint RN/RAF Combined Headquarters in Liverpool. This joint HQ combined two large staffs those of the C-in-C Western Approaches RN and No 15 Group RAF. What I was not told was that I was about to become an operator in the Allies most secret intelligence organisation. So secret that the world couldn't be told about it until 30 years after the war was won - 1975. It was referred to as 'Ultra'. Because of my undertaking (termed OATH) I couldn't even tell my wife. She first learned about it in 1975 when I told her here in Adelaide. It had one other devastating effect on my flying career - I was never allowed to fly on operations again, in other words there must be no risk of my being captured. So that, from summer 1943 I had the equivalent of a 'super safe' life insurance. Even after the war and my retirement from the RAF, I could not travel in a foreign country without prior Government permission, I was forbidden to accept employment with any foreign organisation and I had to report my place of domicile on 1st January every year and, of course, any change in it. Notwithstanding it was all of absorbing interest. I was angry at being trapped without having been given a choice in the matter. Here again a book length novel would be appropriate."

In his own text Mac refers to his having to take his turn at a staff job and examining his record to date, it is quite remarkable that he did not have to undertake this sooner. As the sort of person who would much prefer being at the sharp end, there is little doubt that a posting to Group would have appealed little to Mac however, in the event, he did find this period of great interest. Exactly what Mac did in this period working with the Ultra Team is not clear. In the 12 months with No 15 Group he flew less than 100 hours primarily around the airfields in No 15 Group and including Castle Archdale and Aldergrove where he would meet up again with two of his old units No's 201 and 120 Squadrons. He also visited his old base at Nutts Corner and the American unit at Toome. Many of these flights would involve carrying senior officers e.g. Air Vice Marshall Slatter, the AOC-in C No 15 Group and it is thought likely that Mac was hand-carrying the valuable Ultra information directly to the operating squadrons. In so doing he played his part in arguably the best kept secret of the entire war, the breaking of the German Enigma codes by the boffins at Bletchley Park, but therein lies a story which could not be told here and which is the subject of several books.

Mac is clear on how he unexpectedly enjoyed this key posting, not least because of the quality of the personnel involved at Derby House in Liverpool. This was the site of the joint RN/RAF Headquarters and to where the decoded submarine signals form Bletchley Park would come via the Admiralty. Derby House was under the command of Admiral Sir Max Horton, a legendary man who had been a successful WW I Submarine Commander. On the 13th of September 1914 he sank the German cruiser Hela and recorded the first ever sinking of an enemy ship by a British submarine. It is unfortunate that more details of Mac's duties are not known, for example, who did he take the information to at each squadron and how did they use it so as not to give the

game away? Research continues and will hopefully lead to an addition to Mac's story in Volume II. On one occasion the 18th January 1944, he hitched a ride from Ballykelly to his old base at Silloth in a Liberator with a Pilot who must have been quite familiar. No doubt he and Eric Esler (see separate chapter) had plenty to talk about and judging by the logged time, must have taken the long way round to catch up on their news. His Ultra time ended in late June 1944 and he moved on to the Army Staff College at Camberley.

Staff College Camberley No 132 OTU East Fortune

"After this job I was selected to attend Staff College Camberley. This was the Army Staff Course. I was one of three RAF Officers. strange to relate, I enjoyed it. Most of the directing staff were ex-eight army from the desert battle and we had 'star' visiting lectures including Month and Mountbatten. About this time I was promoted to Group Captain and posted to RAF station East Fortune, in Scotland, as Station Commander. It was the base of an Operation Training Unit flying Mosquito and Beaufighter aircraft.

"Scotland is a funny place, populated by funny people whom I never understood, and who used funny speech. I recall earlier when war broke out, the locals at Montrose objected to the heathen RAF flying on the Sabbath, and also I was booked by a cop in Perth for blowing my car horn at midnight on a Sunday. Strange people indeed. I think the Hun must have thought so too because all was silent, boring and dull at East Fortune, in East Lothian. Whilst there, peace broke out again. In consequence we all were reduced to our peace-time rank pre-war, plus promotion to a new peace-time rank, and I became a Wing Commander again."

In 1941 Mac returned to 'boats' after a spell on land based aircraft which ended with his assessment as an exceptional Fighter Pilot at Catloss, primarily on Blenheims. Now he was to make a further return, this time back to the faster twin-engine aircraft in the shape of the venerable Mosquito and with promotion to Group Captain following his Staff Course, was appointed Station Commander at No 132 OTU at East Fortune which, although never a front line station, did have a claim to a unique piece of aviation history. With an important strategic position at the foot of the Firth of Forth, East Fortune had been opened as an Royal naval Air Station in 1916 and, until the spring of 1918, operated airships as an in-shore screen for the Rosyth based battle Cruiser Squadron. In July 1919 it made history as a departure point for airship R.34 which, some 100+ hours later, arrived off New York to complete the first ever east-west Atlantic crossing. Another piece of east Fortune's past would not have been lost on Mac when he recalled his first squadron posting back in 1934, to No 201 Training Squadron at Calshot. 201 originated at East Fortune, having been established for torpedo training in 1918, shortly after the station was taken over by the RAF on the day of its creation, the 1st April 1918. Following the end of WWI, the RAF closed the station and, following disposal, the accommodation on the north side of the airfield was converted into a sanatorium. After the outbreak of WWII the site was requisitioned as a satellite for nearby Drem and, in June 1941, 60 OTU moved in from Leconfield to continue night-fighter training before being transferred to Coastal Command, re-designated 132 OTU, in November 1942. It then took on the new role of strike training. Mac first flew with his new OTU on the 7th of December 1944 in a Mosquito, a type new to him and, although he would also experience several other firsts including the Buckmaster, Beaufort, Auster and Dominee, it was the Mossie which would from the Backbone of the unit with 30+ on strength towards the end of Mac's posting a year later. Mac makes clear in his notes that he did not like either Scotland or it's inhabitants and that he did not particularly enjoy this posting. As a Group Captain he would have to come to terms with a severe reduction in his flying hours which stood at 2240+ at the commencement of this posting. One year later when he moved on this had only increased by less than 60 although, typical of Mac, he did assess his instructors personally. Also at this time he met up with Lloyd Wiggins then a Wing Commander, and the two became firm friends, later meeting up when both had moved down under. They enjoyed a continuing friendship for over 35 years, a time span which took Mac and Paddy past their 50th wedding anniversary at which Lloyd had the honour of giving the speech. His last flight at East fortune came just before Christmas 1945 with a Beaufighter flight to Lossiemouth and Wick and he departed for his next posting to HQ Coastal Command at Northwood. With the end of the war came many changes in the services, not least the RAF, where much rationalisation began under the new Labour government. As a result Mac was returned to his pre-war rank plus promotion and found himself one stripe less at Wing Commander level again.

No 230 Squadron Calshot

Mac also completed a staff tour at HQ Coastal Command in the London area and later Commander No 230 (Sunderland) Sqn at Calshot, near Southampton. The post-war RAF was a poor shadow of its war-time image. Most of the talent and civilian conscripts left to resume, or commence, civilian careers and there remained the few 'regulars' who survived, and a fair amount of rubbish collected during the war. "The 230 Squadron I took over was a product of this lot."

Now at October 1946, Mac was already seriously disillusioned with 'his' RAF. At 33 years of age and with 13 years regular service he was about to take command of another squadron. He had seen every aspect of service during a period of Hugh change which had seen the services generally rise to the challenge presented by the war.

The war over, he realised that the talent which had won it was largely gone, either dead or to rejoin civilian life.

Joining No 230 Squadron, back again at Calshot having just re-located from Castle Archdale, he was not happy at what he found. In his own words. "...There remained the few regulars who survived and a fair amount of rubbish collected during the war. The 230 Squadron I took over was a product of this lot." In his notes he does not mention anything further about his time at Calshot, almost as if it is of no significance to him. In addition, in going to Calshot he was also coming together with his old No 201 Squadron who, together with his 230, formed the Sunderland Wing. No 201 did have happy memories for him but at this juncture id did not seem to make any difference. The rot may have started during his staff stint at HQ Coastal Command where he would have been in a position to see just how the situation really was. In the event Mac arrived at Calshot in late September and started familiarisation flights in the Sunderland Mk V on the 3rd October. Thereafter it was a case of peacetime routines and little flying.

On the 1st of February 1947 he flew Sunderland NJ264, complete with 11 crew and six press photographers, to provide the initial escort to HMS Vanguard which was carrying the Royal Family to South Africa. The only other flight of any significance in the remainder of his period at Calshot came in early June. This was a five day mini-cruise which visited Belfast and Wig Bay, Stranraer, via Alness, Stornoway and Loch Boisdale.

In a decision that he would begin to regret in the months to come, Mac retired from the service, at his own request, in October 1947. However at the time he felt unhappy with the post-war situation within the RAF and decided to take a civilian position.

Air Survey Company, London Short Brothers & Harland, Rochester

"After this I did quite a bit of flying between UK and India on transport work. I also flew into Baghdad and Tehran and Cairo. Then I spent months in India on special high-altitude photographic work (for mapping purposes) using specially equipped aircraft. This included Burma, operating from Chittagong and living under canvas (no comfortable hotels in existence) I was in Calcutta and Decca in 1949 during the Hindu/Moslem killings when the Viceroy, Mountbatten, stayed on his royal backside in Govt. House and did nothing (except perhaps side with the Hindus)! This also included the night Ghandi was assassinated."

A strange tale from this period: "I was flown out (from the UK) by civil air line (BOAC) to Jakarta, Indonesia, to do a special job. I lived in the Quanta's Airways staff quarters in Jakarta, and the job I had to do necessitated that I acquire an Indonesian Civil Pilots Licence. To get this I had to have the sponsor of a locally established authority and the local British Consul didn't qualify, so my sponsor was the head of the 'Dutch Shell' oil organisation in Indonesia. The party I was supposed to meet was an American (it gets more mysterious by the minute!) and he had an aircraft I was to fly! However he never turned up as he bent the aircraft in the mountains, and BOAC flew me home again. I now have a document, signed by the Indonesian Minister of Air, which states that VHA McBratney is authorised to fly Indonesian registered aircraft within the dates (given) within the state of Indonesia. This document is the source of much comment and is certainly a 'one-off' bit of history.

"During that visit, which included Easter 1951, and which I spent in the mountains at Bandung with the British Consul and Air Attaché, I came to appreciate the origin of the term 'Dutch Treat'. As a race they are as mean as charity! There were two odd incidents worth mentioning, but first the background. The political atmosphere in the country was unstable and dangerous as the Dutch East Indies had become Indonesia and the Dutch were in the process of getting out (reluctantly). In consequence there was a strong anit 'white' nature atmosphere, and I had been warned by the British Consul not to walk alone on the city streets - but of course I did! One morning in the city centre while walking and window gazing, I suddenly became aware that I was being 'got-at' by a group of local Indonesian youths. this took the form of walking across my path and causing me to trip; first from one side and then the other side. I recall I went into a large cafe when I saw a police officer sitting alone at a table. Having ascertained he spoke English he was Eurasian half-caste) and that I could sit down, I told him what was happening and asked what it was all about. He said, 'Well, they think your are Dutch and they want you to hit one of them and then they will all attack you.' I asked if he could do anything and he said no just sit down here for a while and they will get bored and then move off. And thus it was! I learned afterwards that if I'd been alone in a rickshaw I would not have been molested because a native was pulling the rickshaw and earning money from me. I got a nice old 'strip' from the Consul.

"The second incident concerned the road journey back from Bandung to Jakarta at Easter. there was a fairly large group of us, American, British and some Dutch, all in convoy for security reasons; it was a 150 mile road journey, and it was late at night. Our convoy was halted about the half-way mark by Indonesian Military and told we would have to sit until it was declared safe to proceed. Apparently there was shooting action going on some miles ahead between the military and a group of insurgents who called themselves, 'The Heavenly Host'. These were the remnants of a Dutch Army Brigade who refused to acknowledge their new Indonesian masters and continued the old (now ceased) local war. They were led by an ex-Brigadier (Dutch Army) called Kurt Westerling. We all sat along the roadside for about three hours and, finally were allowed to proceed. I recall having a long chat with an American woman who said, 'I can't work out how a

British Air Force officer can find himself in this present situation.' I confess, the same thought passed through my mind - but I couldn't tell her!

"For the historical record, Westerling finally became a refugee in Europe. Bandung was an interesting spot. One still came across the odd Japanese ex-army deserter - always easily recognisable by his dress, his slant eyes and his bandy legs."

Civilian life, and the fairly hectic schedule required from his new employers, was probably the antidote required for Mac at this stage. Despite the fact that he loved the RAF he must have felt compelled to make the move and, from his correspondence and log. it would appear that he enjoyed civilian life. Coming into contact with some well know filers probably helped, along with the varied duties which the coming months would bring.

His civilian flying with the Air survey Company commenced on the 12th December 1947 when he collected DH Dove, VT-CKE, from Hatfield for local trials at the ASC base at White Waltham before delivery to India. On the 15th of January, following 'deinsectation' at London Airport, he departed the UK for the series of hops to Calcutta, arriving some 44 flying hours later on the 24th. At this stage memories of his time in the area in the middle thirties, with No 230 Squadron, must have been prominent in his mind. With no explanation for the gap, he next flies a month later from Dum Dum Calcutta) in a Leopard Moth. The same day he is back in VT-CKE preparing for the 26th of February departure to Allahabad carrying the Prime Minister of Bengal, Dr Roy and party, bringing them back to Dum Dum five days later. The next week was spent in Dominee aircraft carrying out extensive aerial surveys of the Don Valley in India. This ended on the 13th of March and, again without explanation, Mac next appears back at White Waltham on the 6th of April.

The next flight of significance is a seemingly innocuous entry for the 24th which records a 30 minute local flight in a Firefly Trainer. Under 'Captain' is the entry 'Mr Twiss & self'. Twiss being Peter, ex-navy and double DSC holder who would go on to a distinguished career with Fairey, including the March 1956 Fairey Delta 2 flight which was the first in excess of 1,000mph. At the time Peter Twiss was the number two to Fairey CTP Gordon Slade.

Mac and Peter would come together several time in the coming months, White Waltham being on of Fairey's flying test grounds, and he would to on to visit other at Heston and Ringway, very often ferrying Fairey spares or personnel. However the main function of air survey was the prime job and Mac spent most of his time on this, interspersed with interesting diversions.

Included in these were the test climb in Dakota AKNM to 26,500 feet from Prestwick, photographing Lords cricket ground from 6,000 feet, taking Gordon Slade and his wife to the Channel Islands and taking his wife Paddy and daughter Susan on a one day trip from base. In what must have been a hectic schedule their route was base, Ringway, Sydenham, Eglinton, Sydenham Base.

A rapid Rapide tour! On the 13th of September he delivered Gordon Slade and Peter Twiss to Farnborough, probably to participate in the SBAC show. In October 1948 he met us again with Dakota AKNM to start a relationship which would take him through until March 1950 and involve 120+ flights and thousands of miles. In November he took 'NM to Blackcushe to collect Tipsy (named after it's designer Mr E O Tips) OO-ULA for freighting to Belgium, delivering it to Avions at Gosselies.

Ever the teacher, Mac used 'NM to give dual instruction to several pilots, including a 30 minute session in early December - 'check out Mr Twiss' It is difficult to see why Peter Twiss needed checking out on a Dak.

The early part of 1949 was spent preparing 'NM for a spell in India and, after obtaining it's C of A, Mac carried out full load take-off checks before positioning to Blackbushe on the 21st of January for customs clearance en route from Rome. Carrying a crew of three and three passengers they arrived in Calcutta five days later after 35 flying hours and staging through Cyprus, Casrah, m Sharjah and working across India from the west. Working again from Dum Dum it was back to survey work and it now became clear why 'NM had been checked at altitude previously as many of the surveys carried out were from great height. Surveys were carried out of Nepal, Burma, and the Ganges as well as areas of Pakistan. On one flight, ex-Dum Dum on the 26th of February, the survey of the Ganges was completed but a problem existed on their return to base. Mac's log entry reads, "Communist riots at Dum Dum during this flight. Airport raided and guards murdered. Our hangar set on fire. Had to orbit airfield for 40 minutes on return." Mac and 'NM departed India for home on the 7th of April arriving back at White Waltham on the 11th.

After leave he was back in 'NM on the 4th of May carrying Gordon Slade for an oil filter test repeated six days later carrying Jimmy Matthew's, another of Fairey's test pilots. In between Mac had completed his 200th flight for ASC, taking a Rapide to Boscombe Down. On the 23rd he was with Gordon Slade in a Percival Q6 for IF practice followed the next day with two jaunts with Peter Twiss in a Fulmar to Hamble and back. For the next few weeks he was back in teacher mode giving AGH and IF practice to several filers and carrying out tests of instruments, engines and cameras. These were carried out in a variety of aircraft including Anion, Oxford, 'NUM, Rapped, Auster, Primer and Fulmar. In late July it was back to Gosselies in 'NM again freighting a Tipsy before another teaching and testing period which took him up to the next overseas trip. Again using 'NM Mac departed on the 12th of October and arrived in Calcutta five days later after staging through Marseilles, Bari, Nicosia, Baghdad, Tehran and western India. Later in the month it was back to survey work and this lasted until the year end, by which time 'NM was now based in Karachi.

Now into the new decade, the Standard Vacuum oil company chartered 'NM for 11 days to carry out a geologic survey of India and Pakistan. This ended back at Dum Dum on the 27th and Mac returned to company survey work until mid February when he commenced his last job for ASC - ferrying 'NM back to White Walthan. It is no known why Mac decided to leave ASC at this time nor is it known what he did between his last flight on the 3rd March and his first flight for Shorts at Rochester on the 22nd of January the following year. In the event he joined Shorts for barely four months before re-joining the RAF in June. It is possible that he was on a fixed contract with ASC although it would seem unlikely that they would have no flying for him for almost ten months. Perhaps Shorts was simply a stop gap until re-joining the service, the processing of his application maybe being slow? There are several questions here but equally there are several educated guesses which can be made. Mac was probably welcomed back into uniform as his posting to Bircham Newton and Northwood would suggest. His reinstatement in his former rank of Wing Commander is also a pointer.

Whatever the case his time at Rochester was fairly unremarkable save for meeting some more test pilots including Brooke-Smith, the Shorts CTP, and demonstrations for Shell, along with Flight and Aeroplane magazines.

His civilian career ended with such a Sealand demonstration on the 30th May 1951.

OATS Bircham Newton HQCC Northwood Armed Forces Staff College Norfolk, Va US Naval Station Oceana Norfolk, Va

"After this in 1951, I was back at Command HQ on a staff job for over two years, as Operations Officer for the command. This included the birth of NATO - an interesting period as our service had a NATO function as well as a national one. I also got quite a bit of flying of aircraft. This included visits to France, Norway, Gibraltar, Malta and Iceland - where the Americans had a NATO base. In 1952 I was very fortunate in being selected to go to the USA for a three year posting. This started with my attending the American Armed Forces Staff College at Norfolk, Virginia, where students included American Navy, Army and Air Force and Marines plus a single representative from foreign countries - like myself. Then followed a two year exchange (for me) tour with the US Navy Air Force - also operating from Norfolk, Virginia. I flew all over the US eastern states with the Yanks - including Bermuda and Canada: went to sea in a submarine and learned to fly their 'lighter-than-air' craft, a big sausage-like bag filled with helium with a cabin (called 'car') and two engines attached. Ridiculous creations.

"The joy of the American posting was enhanced by the fact that my wife and three children were with me. The kids went to US schools. My American tour terminated around May 1956 and we drove up to New York in my big Mercury car which I was freighting, home to UK with me on the good ship New Amsterdam which sailed from New Jersey to Amsterdam via Southampton. Driving under the Hudson River via the tunnel and being projected into the New York tea-time traffic rush in order to get out to our destination on Long Island was an experience for my beyond description. Perhaps this traffic joke will convey some idea: Question, what is a split second? Answer, the time in New York traffic between the lights going green and a blast on the horn of the guy behind you."

At his own request, Mac was re-instated in the RAF as a Wing Commander, with effect from the 4th of June 1951. On that day he commenced his second RAF stint at Bricham Newton at the Officers Advanced Training School for a short course before being posted to Coastal Command Headquarters at Northwood, as Operations Officer, termed Air 1, and first flew in his new position on the 2nd August. This was from Bovingdon, the airfield serving Northwood and was a Proctor flight to and form Rochester, possibly to visit Shorts. Still under 40 years of age and with 3,000 flying hours to his credit Mac would have considered rightly that he had much to offer and it is likely that the RAF he found was not the one he had left four years previously. This, and being at the heart of operations in the tip HQ, would have appealed to his desire to get things done, and done well. At this stage of the early fifties Coastal Command was still a sizeable force with several front line squadrons of Shackleton and Sunderland aircraft and their respective OCU's. Stations which would have been very familiar to Mac still operated including Aldergrove, Ballykelly Calshot and Pembroke Dock and he would visit several of these in the coming months along with others in the command including Topcliffe, St Mawgan, St Eval and Roborough - a list including many which he would have carried Ultra information to during 1943/4.

Although the full detail of his time at Northwood is not known, it can be seen from his log that he was heavily involved with, as mentioned in his text, the early days of NATO. This required several flights to numerous European destinations, many carrying Air Vice-Marshall Nicholetts and this accounted for much of Mac's time in his first year back in uniform (as Wing Commander, Nicholetts had commanded No 228 Squadron from November 1939/May 1941).

In May 1952 he was in Norway along with senior representatives from the US Navy and Marines and Norwegian Air Force. This trip was from his old Calshot base and used a No 230 Squadron Mk 1V Sunderland, PP117 and was followed by a second visit in July using a Hastings. In early October he made what was to be the first of many flights in the Shackleton, on this occasion as a passenger in VP256, departing Ballykelly for the 20 hour trip to Nova Scotia before switching to Lancaster A-FA for the onward trip to Newfoundland. A few days later he ended up at Dorval, the base where he helped train Canadian pilots some nine years earlier.

The turn of 1953 saw Mac in Gibraltar although there is no indication as to how he got there. The return to Bovingdon at the end of January was his one and only flight in a Lincoln and was via Shawbury, another of his old bases, due to engine trouble. A month of non-flying then preceded a Dakota trip to Iceland and then it was back to Bovingdon and into a long series of IF practice flights leading up to Ground Controlled Approach practice at Lyneham. Mac's last flight with HQ came on the 1st of December and he left Coastal Command Headquarters in January 1954 having been posted to the US for a three year tour.

His first destination in America was the Armed Forces Staff College at Norfolk, Virginia. Here, at the Naval Air Station, he joined with many peers for world-wide air forces although it is not known exactly the content of the course. During the three months here he flew on nine occasions, all in a Beechcraft SNB-5, the US Navy version of the Ceech Model 18. Following a gap, possible for leave whilst settling his young family he was posted, remaining at Norfolk, and joined the Staff of the Commander-Air-Force, Atlantic Fleet, and USN. Arriving in July 1954, Mac spent the next year in his staff role, possibly as RAF liaison officer, travelling throughout the eastern seaboard of the USA in execution of his duties. Frequently this included the company of US Admirals and visiting Washington.

He also flew in some quite diverse types including his first in an airship in January 1955, a two hour trip as passenger in a ZSG-4 and ended his first stint at the Command in the following August assisting with a hurricane evacuation at Pensacola. Then following a brief stay at the US Naval Air Station at Oceana attending the NO 8A Instrument Flight Course, all flights being in SNB-5 aircraft, before returning to the Command in the latter part of 1955. Routine staff duties then took his through until the following June when he was posted to command, now a Group Captain again, the ASWDU unit at St Mawgan in Cornwall.

Mac left the US in late June and took over command at St Mawgan on the 23rd of July.

ASWDU, St Mawgan

"On our return to the homeland my new RAF appointment took me to St Mawgan in Cornwall. I was given command of special one-off flying unit called 'The Air/Sea Warfare Development Unit'. Our job was the testing, proving and using of new airborne weapons, both electronic and explosive and the preparation of the user's handling notes. I held the job for slightly over two years. It was my last flying appointment in the RAF, and a very interesting one. I did one more job in a Group Headquarters in Plymouth, as Officer in Charge of Administration and then I resigned from the Royal Air Force, at my own request, as a Group Captain and continued to regret that decision ever since! My departure date was 15 July 1959."

His family settled, the first flight with ASWDU came four days after his arrival in Shackleton VP282, the first of three flights to get his hand in again. These were his first flights at the controls of a 'Growler', flown in the co-pilot seat and although he would fly many times on forthcoming trials work, it would be another three month before he would qualify on type due to the initial workload at St Mawgan. Command of a specialist unit and it's inherent administrative burden seem to have been overcome to an extent as Mac's log shows him maintaining a healthy number of flying hours in the coming months. He took part in many of the trials with RN submarines Trenchant and Artful and surface vessels Sturdy Whirlwind and Maidstone and the US nuclear submarine Nautilus. Included in these trials was that of Rinaldo along with HMS Sturdy off Gibraltar in November 1956 which entailed leaving St Mawgan for the 'Rock' with a total of 20 people aboard Shackleton VP285. As 285 was used for all subsequent Rinaldo work it must be assumed that it was fitted out as a trial platform. Mac Himself comments that this posting was a very interesting one and it can be seen from his log entries that the variety of tasks undertaken was wide. Included were shadowing Russian ships in the Channel, although how this came under his control at St Mawgan is difficult to see, and dropping a torpedo from a Shackleton at Culdrose. He also provided a platform for the photography by Flight magazine of a No 228 Squadron Shackleton off Lanes End.

His log also shows the ever increasing dependence on the various automated systems then being trailed and introduced for the RAF. It also demonstrates the endurance of the venerable Shackleton with one exercise out to 38 West entailing a 19 hours sortie. This was undertaken in the trials MK 1 VP 285 which he later delivered in January 1958, to No 41 MU at Aldergrove, returning in MK 11 WG553.

He visited many stations at home and abroad including the remaining Coastal Command stations in his native Ulster and in Malta, where he met up again with Air Marshall Nicholetts, now AOC Malta. The most obvious feature of his logbook in this period is his hands on involvement in all aspects of the unit's work. Typical of the man he had always been one for the direct approach, including checking out his aircrews personally and he made on exception here. It would be unusual for a Group Captain/Unit Commander to fly so much - Mac flew in excess of 500 hours in just under two years - and it is fair assumption that his hands on and direct approach is what was deemed as necessary for this unit.

His last official flight in Cornwall came on the 4th of June when he took charge of one last training sortie and it is probable that he knew at this time it would be his last at the sharp end of a major unit as, at the age of 46 his flying days were surely numbered. No doubt he did his usual good job at St Mawgan but, in June 1958 it was time to move on and he found himself back in a staff job

and posted to Coastal Command HQ at Mountbatten in Plymouth. Ending his flying career with a final training flight was a nice tough and possible quite deliberate because there is little doubt that Mac was a teacher par excellence. He did manage on last flight before leaving the unit and this came at the end of June, after he had relinquished command. In what was probably an indulgence, ranking having some privilege, he took a Shackleton up for a jaunt around the local area. It could just be a coincidence that the aircraft used was VP 282, the same as on his first flight with the unit almost two years previously but, knowing something of the man, it was more likely anything but. At Plymouth he was to become Officer in Charge of Administration and it is note hard to imagine how he felt. Whilst his various postings over the years had inevitably involved an amount of the dreaded paperwork, he had always managed to either minimise it or find a willing helper. Now he was to be surrounded by paper and he did not like it. After only a year at Montbatten Mac resigned his beloved service and in his own words, "...continued to regret that decision ever since."

The posting to an admin position undoubtedly held little appeal for a man of Mac's calibre and achievement. However, he surely realised that he had had some excellent postings over the years and that to spend what would probably have been around two years in such a job may not have been too bad. Conversely he may have privately questioned why he had ended up pushing paper. His open admission that he regretted leaving the service 'ever since' could suggest that he was too impulsive in leaving and perhaps should have waited longer. Also relevant was his dislike for Australia, to where he moved his family after leaving the service. This unhappiness, for whatever reason likely increased his regret. What caused this dislike for Australia is not known but it comes across clearly in his various communications over the years and is further evidence by this desire no to be buried down under.

Mac's last log entry comes on his 19th wedding anniversary, the 4th of July 1959, with a flight which took his total to 4,052 hours in his 26 years of service. In Anson VP532 two young lads named John and Peter had a 35 minute flight around Roborough near Plymouth. Under the command of Group Captain VHA McBratney, AFC, they thoroughly enjoyed their first ever flight. Particularly as the Pilot was their Dad.

And so ended the flying career of Mac McBratney, spanning the years from 1933-1959 and encompassing the myriad changes of that period. Were he alive today he would doubtless admit that the move to Australia was good for his family, his sons John and Peter and his daughter Susan doing well and integrating into the evolving nation as their own families developed. Despite his own dislike for the nation, which it is believed was shared by Paddy albeit to a lesser extent, he contented himself with his own work as his family extended. However, his regret at leaving the service never waned and it is quite possible that this was the prime cause for his growing dislike of Australia. Had he remained at Mountbatten and completed the admin posting he would, in all likelihood, have moved on the either station command or a senior training position and ultimately reached Marshall rank. He would have known this as he would have known that his unwanted move into admin was not a signal from he superiors. Under these circumstances his premature resignation could only lead to regret.

The later years

"Looking back over the years, I feel I have had my share of luck and fortune and have experienced a wonderful career. After all, I might have stayed in Ulster, like a lot of my school contemporaries and become a banker, clerk, school teacher, a parson or a doctor - or even a crooked lawyer - all nice safe, duff careers! No! never; not for me. I have never had a civil career in the UK, I came right out here after my civil retirement. In terms of material gain and success, I was again fortunate, but I never liked it nor have I ever liked the country or the people. I'm now retired again and have few friends. I am what some people term a 'loner' but indulge two hobbies actively at an advanced level. Amateur Radio and Photography I've been in both since my early teens. I have world coverage daily, on my radio and operate my own photographic dark-room. I even work two hams in NI. One in the Cavehill Road and on in Bangor."

Mac sailed to Australia in the Autumn of 1959 and arrived Melbourne just before Christmas. In his own words this was a spec visit to check things out. He travelled alone leaving Paddy, Peter and Susan in their village home near Plymouth. His eldest son John was apprenticed to Smiths Instruments in Watford and remained there in digs. On registering with the Government Employment Agency in Melbourne, Mac was informed that his lack of qualifications would mean that the best he could hope for would be a trainee clerk position with some large company. This response can only be taken to mean that Mac had decided to have nothing to do with aviation for which he was eminently qualified. From a letter of Peter's he says, "Father had little to do with the RAF or any retired RAF or RAAF organisations after he left the air force. I am not sure why but he actively discouraged contact. I think it was a way of saying he had left that very satisfying left behind for a new one in Australia and no amount of contact would bring it back."

Mac's reaction at being offered a clerk's position can only be imagined, as can his response to the unfortunate person who informed him, but a quitter he never was and soon things were looking up. Whether by design or accident, Mac attended a social function and met the General Manager of a large steel company. Within a few days a job was offered and it can only be assumed that the General Manager had some connection with the services or was very astute. Either way Mac was offered the position of State Manager responsible for setting up a new factory in Adelaide for the production of steel roof decking. With memories of his past, Mac was once again a former and teacher and was to use his experience in establishing units. A good job now sorted, Mac arranged for his family to travel out from the UK and, around May/June 1960, Paddy and Co became £10 Poms and set sail for the antipodes. There they all settled down in their new Adelaide home and started the next stage of their lives. Mac remained with his new employers, doing well for the rest of his working life, retiring at the age of 63 in the middle seventies by which time John, Peter and Susan had all flown the nest. He and Paddy then moved out to a new home in the Adelaide Hills where he was able to devote more time to his various hobbies of pigeon breeding and racing and photography and he took up with ham radio, all of which he carried out with his customary keenness and success.

Shortly after his retirement Mac was to be pleasantly surprised by an arrangement made by his youngest son. Perusing the local newspaper, Peter read with interest that the 1977 competition for the Fincastle Trophy (for submarine hunting) was to be held at RAAF Edinburgh, situated less than 15 miles from Adelaide. Competed for by Commonwealth nations such as Canada and Australia, the UK was to be represented by a Nimrod of non other than No 120 Squadron. Knowing of his Father's history with the Squadron, Peter decided to do something out of character and, despite being aware of Mac's views towards things aviation, he started the ball rolling with a view to organising a re-union between the two parties. He contacted the CO of the Squadron detachment Group Captain John Pack, and explained that the first CO of the unit was now living in Adelaide and would it be possible to visit? John Pack agreed to call back and did so two days later, obviously having checked Mac out, inviting father and son, Son being a chip off the old block also asked if his son could come! And so on the Sunday following the competition, three generations of McBratney turned up at RAAF Edinburgh and were met with No 120 Squadron treatment at its best.

In honour of the first CO, the visiting aircrew and their Nimrod were on parade and, although Peter cannot remember the outcome of the trophy competition, he does remember Mac being taken in hand by John Pack and they toured the Nimrod and spent some time in the cockpit. "I watched and enjoyed seeing Father's face come alive with the memories of sitting in the seat up front."

Afterwards they all adjourned to the mess and Peter recalls how difficult it was to tear themselves away at the conclusion of the visit. He also remembers how from that time onwards, Mac took more interest in contact with others from the RAF and how he assisted a number of people who were researching his period of service. That he enjoyed this surprise and that it opened a new avenue for his knowledge is not in doubt and yet he remained, by his own admission a bit of a loner! He did have some very good friends, including Lloyd Wiggins from East Fortune days, but seemed to take more pleasure from his hobbies than from anything else, other than his family. Immediately following this enjoyable outing another matter of significantly less enjoyment came to a conclusion, but this was one which gave Mac great irritation.

He had always held a British passport but, in 1977 and probably in advance of one of his trips back to the UK, he applied for a new single family passport which would cover both he and Paddy. He was less than pleased to receive a short reply from an underling at the British High Commission in Canberra informing him that as he was a British Subject as opposed to Paddy being a British Citizen, it would not be possible to issue a joint passport. To be so told that he was of lesser status than Paddy did not go down too well and caused him to comment, "After a lifetime of service to King and country, I am still only a second class Englishman."

Whilst the regulations regarding citizenship which were applicable in 1977/78 were there to be enforced, it seems a poor show that a man who had given so much in his career should be treated in such a way. After all, this was a man who had been entrusted with details of the Enigma/Ultra secret during the Second World War and who, as a result, was under a strict duty to remain tight lipped. This duty also precluded him from taking employment with any foreign organisation and he was additionally required to notify the authorities of his address each January until the expiry of a ten year period in 1975. Given the importance attached to this secret by the British Government, and as he had been resident in Australia for 17 years by this time, it is inconceivable that the High Commission in Canberra did not know who he was. Little wonder Mac was so irritated.

As he entered his final years his health began to fail and his hobbies waned, with the exception of his ham radio time which, in Peter's words occupied him day and night right up to a few months before he died. It was amazing to see how many people across the world he contacted, including a few old RAF members. Father preferred Morse code to voice and could still send at 25 words a minute when he stopped! Included in his contacts was his eldest son John who lived in another state. They were in the habit of making contact each Sunday. Mac died peacefully at his Australian home on the 9th of January 1996 in his 83rd year. The details of his final months were not known, despite correspondence, and it was not until the February that the facts were known when his son Peter wrote.

I had been in correspondence with Mac for some time and it is known that he derived a lot of pleasure from this contact. In the words of retired RAF Officer Frank Davison, who retired to Australia in 1965, "Mac often mentioned his contact with you and showed me the many cuttings you sent. The service was always

Mac's main interest in life." Frank Davison met Mac in 1965 and they established a friendship which lasted until Mac's death.

In my letter of November 1995, I invited Mac to a No 120 Squadron function to be held at Kinloss in April 1996. In the words of his son Peter, "There was nothing he would have liked better and he spoke of the possibility with some considerable enthusiasm. His illness was of concern to him and a number of times he expressed the wish to recover sufficiently to travel." Mac had suffered a fall at his remote home earlier in 1995 and it would appear that this was the last in a line of health problems.

Again from son Peter: "When Father broke his hip he finally agreed to move from the relative isolation of the Adelaide Hills. This last illness coincided with their move to the new house near us, the doctor and a lot of their friends in the city. We moved Mother to the new house a few days before Father came out of hospital. That was on the 8th of December. They spent Christmas in the new place together with my sister Susan, who came over from Melbourne. In the new year we were all quite sure that the move had been the right one. Father looked and sounded much brighter. He was even walking around a bit and getting used to the idea that they were only 2km or three minutes from us and we could walk up the road to see them. On January 9th Father and Mother had been to the doctor for a routine check in the morning. The doctor told me that he thought that Father was progressing well and they had shared a joke or two and a cup of coffee. After lunch Father went off for a sleep and did not wake. Mother did not want to have a funeral as such and wanted to keep the memorial service simple and to only invite those friends who were closest. The service was on Friday the 12th January, Lloyd Wiggins giving a kind an caring address, and Father was cremated afterwards wearing his RAF uniform."

In 1998 I was asked by Mac's family in Australia and sister Peggy, still living in Belfast, if I would possible for me to help to organise a burial service for Mac in Northern Ireland. Their parents lay together in their adopted home town of Magherafelt in County Londonderry. As a result Mac was buried with full military honours by his beloved Royal Air Force on the 25th September. In attendance were his wife, his son Peter, sister Peggy and her son and representatives from many of the squadrons and units with which he had been associated.

Group Captain VHA Mac Mc Bratney, AFC RAF (retd) had come home.

During one of my last conversations with Group Captain McBratney, he mentioned to me that one of the last things that he would like to do was to walk down past the 'Rainey' in Magherafelt. I had arrived early at the church carrying with me the Group Captains ashes, and I remembered his final request. So I looked at my watch, picked up the bag containing his ashes, said nothing to no one, got up and walked down past the Rainey. I was very proud that day."

Record of Service

No 5 FTS Sealand, 1.9.38/31.8.34
AB & C Flts Training Squadron
RAF Calshot, 1.9.34/6.6.35
No 230 (FB) Squadron, Felixstowe & Pembroke Dock
Seletar, 6.11.36/5.12.38
CFS Upavon, 23.1.39/23.3.39
No 8 FTS Montrose, Flt CO 24.3.39/31.12.39
No 11 FTS Shawbury Sqn, CO/CFI 1.1.40/10.6.40
No 1 OTU Silloth CFI, 10.6.40/3.9.4 (detachment
Prestwick) 4.9.40/19.10.40
No 2 OTU Catfoss, CFI 19.10.40.30.6.41
No 413 Squadron RCAF Co Stranraer, 1.7.41/22.8.41
No 120 Sqn Nutts Corner, etc. CO
23.8.41/10.8.42
HMT Queen Mary (Transit), 11.8.42/18.8.42
No 111 OTU Nassau, CFI 20.8.42/30.3.43
RAFFC Dorval CFI Montreal, 5.4.43/19.4.43
RAF Delegation Washington, 20.4.43/4.5.43
HMT Queen Elizabeth (Transit), 5.5.43/11.5.43
No 1 PDC West Kirkby, 12.5.43/6.6.43
HQ No 15 Group Staff Officer Liverpool, 6.6.43/June 44
Staff College Camberley, July/Nov 1944
No 132 OTU East Fortune Station, CO Dec 1944/
Oct 1946
HQ Coastal Command Northwood
No 230 Sqn Calshot Sqn, CO
Retired RAF, 3.10.47
Air Survey Company
Shorts
HQCC Operations Officer - Air, 1 March 1951/
Jan 1954
Armed Forces Staff College Norfolk Virginia, 20.1.54
US Naval Station Oceana Staff Officer, Aug 1955
ASWDU CO
HQ Coastal Command QIC Admin Plymouth
Retired, RAF 19.7.59

Flights in type

ANSON	155
ATLAS	92
AUSTER	14
AVRO 504	123
BATTLE	39
BEAUFIGHTER	5
BEAUFORT	17
BLENHEIM	228
BOTHA	61
BUCKMASTER	2
BULLDOG	1
CATALINA	18
CONSOLIDATED P2Y	7
CONVAIR (?)	1
DEFIANT	1
DH 86	1
DOMINEE	25
DOUGLAS DC3	129
D'LAS R4D-8 (US NAVY SUPER DC3)	17
D'LAS R5D (US NAVY DC4)	1
DOVE	32
DEVON	1
FAIREY JUNIOR (BELGIAN)	4
FAIREY PRIMER	2
FIREFLY	3
FORTRESS B 17	2
FULMAR	7
FURY	
GLADIATOR	1
GRUMMAN GOOSE	1
GRUMMAN MALLARD	1
HALIFAX	1
HART	1
HASTINGS	3
HORNET MOTH	15
HSS-1 HELICOPTER	1
HUDSON	2
HURRICANE	8
LANCASTER	2
LEOPARD MOTH	1
LIBERATOR B24	87
LINCOLN	1
MAGISTER	12
MARTIN P-5M MARLIN	4
MARTIN PBM-3 MARINER	8
MARTINET	2
MASTER	1
MENTOR	2
MITCHELL B25	71
MOSQUITO	14
MOTH MINOR	4
OXFORD	606
PERCIVAL Q6	2
PROCTOR	3
RAPIDE	45
SARO CLOUD	38
SARO LONDON	10
SEA OTTER	6
SEA TUTOR	20
SEAL (FAIREY)	4
SEALAND	19
SHACKLETON	138
SINGAPORE	300
SND-5-BEECHCRAFT	83
SOUTHAMPTON	130
SPITFIRE	2

STINSON	2	VILDEBEESTE	23
SUNDERLAND	59	WALRUS	6
TIGER MOTH	41	WELLINGTON	1
TUTOR	74	ZSG-3 (AIRSHIP)	4
VARSITY	38	**TOTAL FLIGHTS**	**2885**

WARRANT OFFICER
CORBET MICHAEL McBRIDE
NAVIGATOR
NO. 520 SQUADRON

Corbet Michael McBride was born in Downpatrick on the 27th July 1923 and was educated at Down High School. On leaving school he was employed for three years as an Apprentice Pharmacist.

Corbet joined the Royal Air Force at the Clifton Street Recruiting Office in Belfast on the 1st July 1941. On completing the usual forms and medical he was sent home for six months until there was a training course available for him. On the 9th February he was posted to the Padgate Receiving Centre, where he received his medical and signed the necessary forms. From Padgate he was then transferred to the No 1 Aircrew Reception Centre at Lords Cricket Ground in London where he was selected for aircrew training and kitted out with his new uniform etc. From the Air Crew Reception Centre he was then posted to No 1 Initial Training Wing at Newquay to start his basic training (square bashing and rifle drill).

On completion of his basic training he was then transferred to Clyffe Pipard to start his Pilot Training. The airfield at that time was just a grass field. He flew the Miles Magister for three weeks and after accumulating 12 hours on the type, but unfortunately during one of his landings, managed to 'wipe' off the undercarriage of a Master and after an inquiry he had to settle for a Navigators position. He was then posted to a Holding Unit at Heaton Park in Manchester, and then on to a Hotel in Hastings which had just been bombed by a couple of Focke Wulf 190's. Because of the damage done to the hotel he was moved to another in Harrogate. On the 2nd November 1942 he boarded the Queen Elizabeth which was to take him to Canada for further training.

He arrived in New York harbour four days later and was immediately trained to an Air Crew Distribution Centre in Moncton near Ontario, Canada. From Moncton he posted to the No 32 Bomb and Gunnery School at Picton where he completed a three month Gunnery and basic Navigational training on Avro Anson's, and Bristol Bolingbrokes,(Canadian version of the Blenheim). He was then transferred to the No 5 Air

Navigation School at Ancieinne Lorette in Quebec where he successfully completed a five month advanced navigation course. Corbet's passing out parade was held up for a short while due to him bursting his ear drums during training. The passing out ceremony finally took place in September 1943 was attended by Queen Julianna of Holland as there was a large contingent of Dutch crews attending that particular course.

In October 1943 he was posted to Summer Side on Prince Edward Island where he was to complete specialised Navigation Training over the sea. The course lasted for one month and in December 1943 he was flown to No 111 Operational Training Unit in Nassau in the Bahamas to complete his operational training on B-25 Mitchel's and B-24 Liberators, and meet his new fellow crew members.

The new crew were:

Pilot	Paul Fisher
2nd Pilot	Stanley Lawson
Wireless/Operator (3)	Peter Waller, Arthur New, Dave Clout
Wireless/Mechanic	Arthur Polland (Polly)
Flight Engineer	R.Dunningham (Dunny)

After completing their operational training Corbet and his crew were transferred back up to Moncton in Ontario, Canada to await transport to take them home to the UK. They waited a few days before boarding the Empress of Scotland, which would take them to Liverpool. The ship was packed to capacity, with Army, Naval and RAF personnel, so over crowded it meant that the RAAF personnel were fed twice a day, at 7.00am and 7.00pm. The return trip took twelve days this time as the Empress was not as fast as the Queen Elizabeth. On their arrival at Liverpool Corbet and his crew were immediately trained down to Harrogate for a few days and then on to a Heavy Conversion Unit at Long Town for two weeks of conversion training onto the four engined Handley Page Halifax heavy bomber. During their Conversion training Corbett and the crew were posted to a Heavy Conversion Unit at Royal Air Force Station at Aldergrove in Northern Ireland. This suited Corbet to a 'T' as he was able to sneak home to Downpatrick and see his parents from time to time. The training at Aldergrove lasted for six weeks and during that time a Halifax took off from Aldergrove on a training flight and crashed on a site which now is the Antrim Forum.

On completion of the training, Corbet and the crew were posted out to Gibralter where they joined No 520 Squadron which was equipped with Handley Page Mk V Halifax's. Most of Corbet and his operations were Met Flights. He remained in Gibralter until 1946 and during his tour Corbet was 'Mentioned in Dispatches'.

Brief history of 520 Squadron

520 squadron was formed out of No 1402 met flight in Gibralter in September 1943 and served as Gibraltar's Met Flight until it was disbanded in April 1946. The squadron also had a few Martinets which it used for target-towing. The squadron's main equipment were a Lockheed Hudson Mk111, Handley Page Halifax's Mk 111A, one Hawker Hurricane Mk11c, one Supermarine Spitfire MkVB, and a few Vickers Warwick's.

When the squadron disbanded in 1946 Corbet and his crew were posted back to the UK. After a few days the crew were split up and Corbet was posted to Thorney Island near Portsmouth and then up to RAF Lossimouth which at that time had a Navigational School, and their he was appointed as Screen Navigator on Halifax's. After a brief period at Lossimouth he was transferred to Fyffe where he completed an Instructors Course on Navigational Training. He was then posted to Hallness near Invergordon where he instructed on the Short Sunderlands and was finally released from the Royal Air Force in August 1946. He returned home where he took up employment within the Civil Service until retired in May 1984.

FLIGHT LIEUTENANT
REGINALD GEORGE McCADDEN, DFC
RAF NO. 129577
NAVIGATOR
NO. 76 SQUADRON

Reginald George McCadden was born in Dundee, Scotland on the 10th March 1914. His parents were both Ulster Folk who were living in Scotland at the time of his birth, as his father was a Sub-Mariner in the Royal Navy and had been awarded the Distinguished Service Medal for his part in the sinking of a German submarine in 1916. Reg's grandfather had also served in the Royal Navy.

The McCadden family came home to Northern Ireland shortly after the end of the First World War and settled in Rossetta just of the Ormeau Road. Reg was educated at St Mary Magdalene Primary School, Rossetta Public Elementary, and the Belfast College of Technology. He then graduated to Queens University were he started studying for a BSc in Commerce, which he had to finish after the war as he had decided to enlist in one of the Services.

During those early school years he was an all round sports enthusiast, especially so in football and had played for Cliftonville in the amateur league. He was also appointed to the Belfast Education Office in Victoria Street for nine years. Reg's thoughts of aviation go back until he was three years old, and living in Scotland when he remembers watching the German Zeppelin's bombing Edinburgh. Coming from a family with a naval background he decided to follow in his grandfather and father's footsteps. In 1940 he went along to the Clifton Street Recruiting Office and joined the Royal Navy. He was duly accepted and set sail for Portland Harbour in May 1940, and after he had completed his training he was posted to His Majesties Anti-Aircraft Vessel Foyle Bank, and it was not long until he got his first taste of action.

HMAV Foyle Bank had been built at Harland and Wolfe shipyard in Belfast and was completed in 1930 as a merchant Ship but had been converted to an anti-aircraft vessel in 1939. Her sister ship the Lagan Bank was also built in Belfast in the 1930's. Reg's position on the Foyle Bank was Ammunition Officer and he was responsible for making sure that the ships guns had their required quota of ammunition from the magazine. The ship had a crew of 300 men of which 40 were from Northern Ireland. On the 4th July 1940 while it was moored at Portsmouth, the Foyle bank was attacked by 26 German Stuka dive Bombers. The ship had received a sustained attack for 18 minutes by the dive bombers, the crew had fought back courageously but the ship had received 22 direct hits which had now crippled her, and sadly she sank to the bottom of Portsmouth harbour. When the attack was over 176 brave men had lost their lives and out of the 40 Ulstermen who had fought so gallantly only eight came home. Reg himself was badly wounded in the ankle, his best friend George Polley from Hay Park Street off the Ormeau Road, and who had been standing beside him during the murderous attack, had disappeared in one of the explosions and was never seen again.

Leading Seaman Jack Mantle who was grievously wounded during the attack was posthumously awarded the country's highest honour, the Victoria Cross, for his heroic action in staying at, and operating the starboard 2 pounder Pom Pom guns manually as the electrically operated mechanism had been damaged and put out of action. He continued to fire the gun until he himself was killed. Soon after this traumatic incident Reg decided the Navy was not for him, and returned home to Northern Ireland. He thought very carefully about what he was going to do next as he was still keen to help the war effort. In January 1941 Reg for a second time visited the Recruiting Office in Clifton Street and joined the Royal Air Force, and was accepted as Aircrew. At the end of January 1941 he was posted to the Imperial Hotel at Stratford-upon-Avon, not to learn Shakespeare but where he donned his new RAF uniform and learned about the art of square-bashing. After completing the square-bashing course he was posted to the Initial Training Wing at Scarborough, and while he was there he was selected for the squadron's football team.

On completing his Initial Training, Reg was sent to America to start his aircrew training. In April 1941 he set sail from the Clyde in Scotland on board the Liner Britannic (the sister ship of the ill-fated Titanic) that would arrive in Nova Scotia a week later. The Britannic was escorted by HMS Rodney and four Tribal Class Destroyers. Not long into their journey, HMS Rodney and three of the Destroyers left the Britannic to engage the German Battleship Bismarck, which they sank on 27th May 1941.

On arrival in Nova Scotia, Reg was put on a train to Toronto where he was interviewed by the Stars newspaper reporter, as somehow word had been received in Toronto that the liner had been chased by the Bismarck. It was not long before he boarded another train that was south bound for the Americas to a little town near Albany Georgia. Reg had arrived in the Americas wearing his smart grey suit and not his RAF uniform, as America had not yet entered the war. Reg was told to report to the Graham Aviation Company where he would join course No 42C. The course was operated by the US Army Air Force Air Force Primary Training School at Southern Field, Georgia. Here he would start his flying career under the Arnold scheme and little did he know at that time that not only was Graham Aviation going to play a part in his life but play a very special part in mine sixty years late.

When he arrived at the airfield he was met by Mr John Graham Senior, who himself was an Ulsterman, born in Bangor County Down, and had immigrated to America with his family in the early 1900's.

A brief history of Graham Aviation

In 1936 William J Graham buys Pittsburgh-Butler Airport and forms Graham Aviation. 1940-44: Graham Aviation begins a Civil Pilot Training Program at eight locations in conjunction with nine western Pennsylvania colleges. 1941-44: Graham Aviation operates a US Army Air Force Primary Pilot Training School at Southern Field, Americus, GA 1944: William J Graham purchases Pittsburgh Institute of Aeronautics and makes Graham Aviation a division of PIA, PIA moves to Allegheny County Airport. 1946: Graham operates Johnstown Municipal and Cumberland (MD) Airport. 1951: Graham Aviation receives a contract from the US Air Force for operating of Greenville (MS) AFB for Primary Pilot Training. 1953: Graham Aviation transfers USAF operation to Marianna, Florida. 1961: Graham Aviation receives USAF contracts for support services at Williams AFB, Arizona and Moody, AFB GA. 1963 Graham contracts with NASA for facilities Operation and maintenance at NASA's Manned Spacecraft Centre at Huston Texas. 1960: John Graham II (Jack) operates Ft

Lauderdale Executive Airport, Florida. 1968-69: Jack Graham receives contract for flight screening of US student pilots, Craig, AFB Al. 1989-2003. PIA is recognised as one of the largest and best aviation maintenance facilities in the USA.

The course Commanding Officer was a strict West Point trained soldier called Lieutenant Knight. He tried to unsuccessfully to apply the Army Air Corps discipline to the RAF recruits. Reg commenced his flying training on the Boeing Stearman DT17's, and completed 70 hours on this type. He found the climate at the base most uncomfortable, always hot and very humid, making it quite difficult to sleep at night. Because of this William John Graham (Senior) arranged for Reg to complete a further 30 hours training at Butler Field Pennsylvania where the climate was much cooler. Reg told me that without Mr John Graham's help and hospitality he may not have finished the course.

After successfully completing his Primary Training he departed Southern Field and went to Macon Field in Georgia where he completed a further 70 hours in the Vultee dive bomber. His next move was to Dothan Field Air Force base in Alabama to start his Advanced flying in Harvard's. It was during the final stage of this training at night when he had an unfortunate accident that was to put pay to him receiving his Wing.

Reg explains about the accident

"On one of my night solo flights in the Harvard, I had completed the usual number of circuit and bump exercises. During my final approach I selected 'Undercarriage Down', all my cockpit indications showed normal, but unfortunately the aircraft belly landed with the wheels 'up'." By this time Reg had over 200 hours flying experience under his belt, and just weeks before this mishap, Wing Commander Hogan (later Air Vice Marshal Hogan, DFC CB) who at that time was posted to America to supervise the training of all RAF pilots at US Flying Schools had asked Reg personally if he would like to stay on at Dothan Field and become a flying instructor. Unfortunately the outcome of the subsequent inquiry found Reg to blame for the accident, and within two weeks he was informed that he was being posted back via Moncton, Ontario, to Trenton Royal Canadian Air Force Base in Toronto where he was to be interviewed by a Selection Board. The chairman of the Board was quite prepared to overrule the decision that had been made in the Americas and offered Reg a new flying course. Reg was bitterly disappointed at having been turned down for his Wings, and politely refused, but asked if he could be considered for navigational duties.

His request was granted and he was posted to No 4 Air Observers School in Ontario Canada to start his Navigation Course on Avro Ansons. Reg successfully completed the course on the 28th August 1942 and was immediate awarded his commission and promoted to the rank of Pilot Officer. Having now completed his training he was posted back to the UK in September 1942 onboard the liner Stirling Castle. The liner docked in Portsmouth a few weeks later. Reg was given 14 days leave which he took advantage of to come home and get married. On returning from leave he was posted to No 44 Air Observers Advanced Navigational School at RAF Station Bibbington. The school was equipped with Avro Ansons, and the course lasted for three weeks. Reg passed the course with flying colours and the Chief Instructor wrote a comment in his Log Book stating, "A keen and willing worker."

It was now the end of November 1942, Reg was transferred to No 20 Operational Training Unit (OUT) at Lossiemouth in Scotland for Operational Training in Wellingtons. Here he met his new crew who were:

Pilot	Sergeant George Dunn
Bomb Aimer	Andy Maitland
Air Gunner	Pilot Officer Joe Scrivenor
Wireless Operator	Jock Todd (from Montrose in Scotland)
Rear Gunner	Dixie Dean (Canadian)

The Station Navigational at that time was another fellow Ulsterman Squadron Leader Ray Esler, DSO DFC*. On the 5th January 1943 Reg and his new crew took off on their first flight in a Wellington from the airfield at Elgin (Elgin was a Satellite airfield for Lossiemouth). Most of their training consisted of cross-country, live bombing (250lb), infra red and air to air firing. During the course Reg and his crew carried out twenty training flights in the Wellington and by the end of the course had accumulated 36hrs.50mins (day flying) and 41hrs.10mins (night flying). On one training flight Reg and the crew had to bale out of Wellington 'E' code 2713 after the port outer failed. Both he and the crew all landed safely at Aughter Mochty near Cupar in Fyfe. (The pilot of the Wellington elected to stay with his aircraft and managed to keep control until he landed safely at leuchars.) Having to bale out of his aircraft automatically qualified Reg to become a member of the elite 'Caterpillar Club'. On landing, Reg gathered up his parachute and walked to a main road where he managed to hale a local buss which took him to the town's police station. The Station Bobby made Reg a welcome cup of tea, and telephoned RAF Leuchars to let them know where Reg was. Very soon after an RAF driver turned up and drove him back to Elgin.

The Station Navigational Officer Squadron Leader Esler was able to 'wrangle' a few days 'survival' leave for Reg at the end of the course. The night before he went on leave he learned that a brand new Avro Lancaster was to land at Leuchars the next morning en-route to RAF Aldergrove. So he thought his luck was in or was it? The next morning he reported to the Station Flight Office were he met the ATA Pilot of the Lancaster. The Pilot briefed Reg in what to do should an emergency arise

during the short flight to Aldergrove. Just before take-off, the Pilot informed Reg that he had just been told to go to Kirkbride where he was to pick up another passenger. The weather at Kirkbride was extremely misty, and was causing the Lancaster Pilot some problems. He had tried to make an approach to the airfield three times, and on the fourth the mighty Lancaster ran off the end of the runway and got bogged down up to her 'uxters'. Reg decided it would be much safer if he headed for the Stranraer boat and luckily enough he managed to get the last sailing that day to Larne.

On his return to Lossiemouth from leave, Reg and his crew were informed that they were being posted to the 1663 Heavy Conversion Unit (HCU) at RAF Rufforth in Yorkshire. Here they met their new Flight Engineer as they were starting a conversion course unto the Handley Page Halifax. The course lasted for almost six weeks and was completed on the 2nd May 1943. Having now finished all their training Reg and his crew were posted to No 4 Group where they joined no 76 Squadron at Linton-on-Ouse which was close to Home-on-Spalding Moor.

Brief history of 76 Squadron

76 Squadron was initially formed at Rippon in Yorkshire in September 1916 as a Home Defence Unit, and was disbanded in June 1919 at Tadcaster. It was reformed in April 1937 at RAF Finningley in Yorkshire as a Heavy Bomber Unit, equipped with Wellesleys, but was re-equipped with Handley Page Hampdens and Avro Ansons a short time later. The squadron took up the role of Group Training Unit. At the outbreak of war the squadron bombed targets in industrial centres, railway gun batterises, oil and petrol installations and channel ports. It made three heroic attacks on the Tirpitz in Trondheim during March and April 1942 and on the night of 10th/11th April 1942 made history by dropping the first 8,000lb bomb on Essen. From 1942 until April 1943 the squadron was commanded by Wing Commander GL Cheshire, VC DSO DFC. When Cheshire left the squadron on being posted to Marston Moor as the Station Commander, No 76 Squadron's diarist wrote,"What our squadron has lost, Marston Moor will gain. It was under the character and personal supervision of Group captain Cheshire that the squadron became what it is today. One of the finest in Bomber Command."

The months of May and June were certainly very busy ones for Reg and his crew. The had visited some of the most heavily defended targets in Germany (Dortmund, Dusseldorf, Essen, Wuppertal, and Krefeld, to name but a few). On the Wuppertal raid on the night of 29th May, 37 aircraft failed to return. On the night of 17th/18th August 1943 Reg and his crew took off to bomb the Peenemunde Rocket Research Plant on the Baltic Coast were the V-2 rockets were being built and tested. Their aircraft was Halifax 'G' code LK903. This was the first raid to Peenemunde, and was an unique operation that the RAF had launched to destroy a secret research establishment located at the remote place in Germany which was the embryo of the space age and employed some of the most brilliant scientists in the world. These scientists were building a rocket which Hitler planned to build in large numbers to destroy London and beyond. This was the first night that the Germans used their new 'Schrage Musik' weapons ; these were twin upward firing cannons fitted in the cockpit of Me110's. Two of these 110's found the bomber stream on the way home from Peenemunde and are believed to have shot down at least six of the bombers. Altogether 46 aircraft failed to return from that raid.

As Reg was explaining to me how his aircraft was one of the first over the target, and wakened the Germans up. I noticed a little tear in his eye when he said how lucky he and his crew had been. He still felt guilty for the 46 other crews who were not so lucky. The flight time for the raid was 7hrs.40mins.

On the 23rd August 1943 Reg and his crew along with 700 other aircraft from various squadrons bombed Berlin (58 aircraft failed to return). Reg wrote in his log book, "The Reich capital received a nice 'pranging'." Other targets visited by Reg were: Gelsenkirchen; Bochum; Cologne; Aachen; Montbeliard; Hamburg; Mannheim; Milan; Montlucon; Munich; Mondane; and Leverkausen. His last operation of the war was on the 3rd/4th October 1943 to bomb the city of Kassel. Their flight time was 6hrs.35mins.

Reg and his crew had now completed 27 Operations and it was time for a well earned rest. In May 1944 he was posted to the Central Navigational School at RAF Shawbury where he completed an Instructors course, and in August 1944 he was posted to No 1652 Heavy Conversion Unit at Marston Moor as a Navigational Instructor. His first four flights as an instructor were carried out in an Oxford with Group Captain Delap, DFC as Pilot (another Irishman who had sunk the first German U-boat of the war U-31 with Bomber Command on the 11th March 1940). They flew from Marston Moor to Aldergrove to Sydenham to Aldergrove and back to Marston Moor (was this a 'jolly'?). On the 28th June 1945 Reg transferred to No 1660 Conversion Unit at Swinderby as Navigational Instructor on Lancasters. His log book records that on the 7th July 1945 he was acting as navigator on Lancaster TV-'0' when he returned to Germany for the first time since October 1943. His Pilot was Squadron Leader Belasco. They were on a 'Cooks Tour' to Germany with staff officers from RAF Cranwell: They took off from Swinderby at 1345 hrs and Reg set a course for Germany. They flew over Halcheren Island, Krefield, Essen, Duisberg, Dusseldorf, Cologne, Aachen, Antwerp, Cap Grisnex, Folkstone, Westmalling, Brentwood, and landed back at base 5hrs.20mins later. On the 20th July he flew as Navigator to Wing Commander Lyster, DSO DFC AFC in Lancaster TV-'0' on a trip to 17 OUT at Silverstone.

In August 1945 he moved to 7 Group Headquarters at St Vincent's in Grantham were he made two flights in a Proctor and Dominee as a passenger. In September 1945 he was again on the move to No 12 Parachute and Glider School at RAF Shawbury instructing in Halifax's. His last flight with the RAF was on the 4th October 1945 in a Boeing as a passenger on a 51 Squadron, Special Communication Squadron demonstration flight. The war in Europe and the Far East was now at an end. Reg had now flown a total of 716hrs.40mins with the RAF. He was awarded the Distinguished Flying Cross on the 7th December 1943. It wasn't until the 31st November 1945 that he was able to attend Buckingham Palace to receive it, the same day that Group Captain Leonard Cheshire received his Victoria Cross.

Reg was released from the RAF in December 1945 and on his return to Northern Ireland he went back to Queens University and finished his BSc in Commerce and graduated in June 1947. Shortly after graduating he was employed with the New Forge Canning Company as Factory Manager, and became personnel Assistant to Mr R Clements for the next twelve years, eventually becoming a Company Director himself. In 1960 Reg decided to attend the Administrative Staff College in Henley along with sixty others from all over the world where he completed a course for senior Executives on Business Practices.

Reg finally retired from the Company after twenty eight years service in 1964. Reg was also Chairman of the Trustee savings bank 1978-1983, President of the Rotary Club (Belfast) 1968-1969, Captain of Shandon Golf Club, Life Member of the Royal Air Forces Association, and founder member of the Aircrew Association (Northern Ireland Branch).

When I had the pleasure of meeting Reg in 1993 he was not enjoying good health, but him and I did enjoy a few of his Gin and Tonics. He and his wife were lovely people and made me very welcome. We became very good friends over the next few months. During one of my many visits, Reg produced a little piece of paper from his wallet which was wrapped up into neat squares. He had kept this since 1941, and written on it was the name and address of his Flying Instructor Mr Martin Gracey at Southern Field Georgia. Reg said it might be out of date, but of some use to me and my research. I decided there and then that I would try a find his instructor. To cut a long story short and after a lot of letter writing and telephone calls I found Martin Gracey in New Port News in Virginia. I wrote to him several times explaining about Reg and low and behold, he sent me a photograph of himself and Reg beside their aircraft. I flew out to meet Martin and his wife in 1994, Reg unfortunately was unable to travel with me because of his health. While I was there, Martin arranged for me to have lunch with Four Star General Jon Micjael Loh at the Air Combat Command Headquarters, Langley

Air Force base in Virginia. General Loh was the Supreme Commander of the United States Air Combat Command. A day in my life that I shall never forget. In 1996, Martin flew over to Northern Ireland to meet up with his pupil who he not seen for fifty one years. Reg's health was failing by now and he was in hospital. The two pals had a great chat reminiscing over old times. Sadly Reg died shortly after this.

While I was out visiting Martin in Virginia, we flew up to Pittsburgh to PIA where he introduced me the son of the late Jack Graham (Jack Graham the Third). Jack and I still remain close friends to this day.

FLIGHT SERGEANT
DAVID EDWIN McCAUSLAND
ROYAL AIR FORCE NO. 1900638
AIR GUNNER
NO. 21 SQUADRON SOUTH AFRICAN AIR FORCE

David Edwin McCausland was born on the 2nd September 1925 in Beragh County Tyrone and was educated at the Omagh Technical College. David's family went to Alexandria in Egypt in 1933 (his father was in the Army and this was the beginning of a six year tour). From 1933 to 1935 David, was educated in Egypt and from 1935 to 1937 he was at school in Hong Kong and Kowloon. From 1937 to 1939 he finished his overseas education at Rawalpindi in India.

On return to the UK David completed his education at Omagh Technical College. During this time he joined the Air Training Corps.

On leaving Omagh Technical College in 1943 he made his way to Newtownards town hall to be tested for the Royal Air Force and aircrew. After successfully completing the test on the 21st September 1943 he was sent to Clifton Street Recruiting Centre where he joined up. On the 28th September 1943 David was posted to Padgate to begin his six weeks basic training and then on to the Aircrew Receiving Centre in London for two weeks induction training. After his training he was selected as an Air Gunner.

On the 7th December 1943 he was posted to No 20 Initial Training Wing (ITW) at RAF Usworth and then on to RAF Bridgnorth Elementary Air Gunnery School for basic air gunnery training and aircraft recognition etc. He successfully completed all his basic training by April 1944. During his short stay at RAF Usworth a Halifax Bomber had crashed close by. David, along with another airman was detailed to guard it. As the Halifax had come down in a hay field they found a nice warm haystack that was close to the wreckage and decided to make themselves comfortable. Unfortunately the two being so comfortable fell asleep only to be awakened by the approach of their Squadron Commander who would not have been amused.

In April 1944 Dave was posted close to home at No 12 Air Gunnery School at Bishopscourt in County Down where he was to start his Air Gunner Training. This posting was unusual as it was not the norm to send Northern Ireland people back home for training. The

school was equipped with the Avro Anson for gunnery training. Dave's first flight was on the 28th May 1944; take off was at 0810 hrs with his pilot Sergeant Bogie in Anson LT575. His training consisted of chasing a Martinet aircraft that was towing a Drogue, which Dave was to shoot at (not the Martinet).

He successfully completed his gunnery training on the 30th June 1944; the Chief Instructor Wing Commander PH Agnew remarks that he entered in Dave's log were 'a good practical Air Gunner'. On completion of his air gunnery course Dave was expecting some well earned leave home, instead he was sent off with forty others to Scotland to board the Union Castle Liner Capetown Castle that had been turned into a troopship. On their first day at sea they were told that they would be transferring to the South African Air Force that was extremely short of Wireless Operators and Air Gunners.

In August 1944 Dave was posted to No 70 Operational Training Unit Middle East Forces at Shandur on the Great Bitter Lakes where he would start Air Gunnery Training on Martin Marauders.

Dave was allocated to the top turret position of the Marauder that was very cramped. The turret was fitted with two .5 Browning machine-guns. There was complete rotation of the turret through 360 degrees that could fire right up and round; and down to a certain degree and you sat on an armoured seat that was pulled up beneath you. The Martin (B-26) Marauder was a heavily armed high performance aircraft and had a tricycle undercarriage. Armament consisted of a nose and tail 0.50in machine guns plus two 0.50s mounted in the dorsal turret and four fixed guns two on the side of the aircraft and two on each wing. It was powered by two 1,800hp R-2800 Double Wasp radials that allowed the aircraft to achieve speeds of 315mph and a max height of 25,000ft and a range of 1,000miles. The Marauder's nickname was 'The Widow Maker' as it had a very high take off and landing speed and high wing characteristics which made it a very difficult aircraft to fly, resulting in a lot of casualties during training. The RAF were only equipped with two Marauder squadrons and the South African Air Force equipped with five. Dave's first flight in a Marauder was on the 28th August for conversion and gunnery training.

The training lasted for six weeks and he finished the course on the 11th October with a note in his log book gunnery assessment signed by the Chief Gunnery Leader, "Should do well on ops." With all of his gunnery training completed Dave was ready for an operational squadron and it was not long until he boarded a Dakota on the 20th October 1944 that was to take him to Bari in Southern Italy via Algiers, Benghazi and Castel Benito. He arrived in Bari where he joined 21 Squadron South African Air Force, Desert Air Force.

The squadron then moved to Jesi in Northern Italy in December 1944 where he teamed up with his new crew. On the 28th December and at the ripe old age of eighteen and nine months he carried out his first operation to bomb the Rail Bridges at Zidani Most in Yugoslavia. The trip had been pretty uneventful but the next one was not to be so easy. Dave's next operation was to Undine in Northern Italy and the target was the marshalling yards. The Marauders were escorted by eight of P-47 Thunderbolts. When they arrived over the target they were greeted by a massive hail of flak, this was extremely heavy as the Germans were waiting for them. Dave's aircraft was hit many times and on arrival back at base looked more like a colander. The fitters counted over 400 holes in the aircraft. While over the target Dave felt a large thump from under his seat and thought no more of it as they were eager to get out of the area as soon as possible. When he landed back at base he retrieved his parachute and discovered a large hole had been blasted right through it. (*Dave still has a piece of the same parachute to this day, in fact his wife Dorothy wore a piece of it on their wedding day.*)

On at least two operations into Yugoslavia they were carrying 'extraneous bods' who the crew were not allowed to speak to. Dave later found out that they were in fact SOE. During that raid one of Dave's close friends whom he joined up with, Johnny Hipwell was flying in an aircraft about a 'box' away from him. Dave watched in horror as Johnny's Marauder took a direct hit and was blown out of the sky and unfortunately took two other Marauders with it (there was not a single aircraft that came back from that raid without a hole in it). Three Marauders and one Thunderbolt failed to return from Udine with a loss of eighteen crewmembers).

In January 1944 Italy had a particularly severe winter and it was one morning during this time Dave's Marauder was being prepared for take off that the unthinkable happened. Everyone had spent the cold winter morning scraping ice and snow of their aircraft. Without any warning a Marauder from 30 Squadron that had just taken off, exploded in a fireball and crashed onto a taxi track, hitting three other aircraft waiting to take off. They all exploded, debris was thrown for thousands of yards. Eighteen aircraft were destroyed twenty-two aircrew and four ground crew were killed. Dave and his crew had another lucky escape when they bombed an ammunition dump at Malcontenta in Northern Italy. They approached the target at 10,000ft it had received several direct hits, moments later the explosions and flames were rising 5,000ft above them. His aircraft was thrown all over the sky with the force of the explosion.

On another raid when flying in a formation of twelve aircraft, Dave suddenly saw eleven aircraft going away from him. In fact it was his own aircraft falling away from the others as it had been hit by flak in the starboard engine and was loosing height rapidly. As the Marauder was electrically powered, including the guns, the skipper ordered that the crew were not to operate anything electrically as he had to conserve all the power that he had left to fly the aircraft. This made the Marauder extremely vulnerable to attack but thankfully two Spitfires came to escort them back to base. All the way back they were losing height and receiving a lot of light flak from below, suddenly they were hit in the port engine. As they were off the coast, just south of Venice and getting ready to abandon the aircraft the Skipper spotted an airfield in the distance. He decided to head for it and carry out an emergency landing, not knowing if it was still in enemy hands. Good luck was still with them, they touched down and all scrambled out safely just before the Marauder blew up. The airstrip that they had landed on had only been captured a few days earlier by the advancing Allied Forces. During his year in Italy Dave visited targets such as Zidani Most (bridges in Yugoslavia), Udine (marshalling yards in Italy), Goriza (marshalling yards in Italy), Torre-Di-Zuind (factory in N. Italy), Arsie (road bridge N. Italy), Conegliano (marshalling yards N. Italy), Monfalcone (shipping), Gemona (marshalling yards N. Italy), Casarsa, Pontebba, Gemona (marshalling yards), Pontebba, Gemona, Biauzzo, Dubova and Zalog (Yugoslavia), St Veit (Austria), Malcontenta, Lake Comachio, Port Garibaldi, 29th Panzer Division (near Argenta), Imola, San Lorenzo, and Trieste (harbour).

Dave and the crew lived in very crude and cramped conditions mostly in tents that had no beds. He slept for three months on two blankets on top of a sheet of corrugated iron. When they came back from a raid they had no pubs to go into ("like the lads back home"), had no leave breaks and worked 24 hours a day.

Dave's log shows an entry for the 17th April 1945: "Skipper, 2nd Pilot and Navigator. (operational tour expired grounded today)."

Log entry for the 14th June 1945: "Fly-past for the 6th South African review."

Log entry for the 23rd June 1945: "Rehearsal Fly-past."

Log entry for the 28th June 1945: "Fly-past. Salute taken by Field Marshall Alexander, Air Vice Marshal Foster, and All Units of DAF (represented)."

Dave spent a year in the Italian campaign and had started his second tour of duty when he was twenty. Out of forty friends who came with him to Italy only thirteen came back to the UK In all he had carried out 37 operations with 21 Squadron South African Air Force and 189 hours flying. His last Operation Flight in a Marauder was on the 24th April 1945 to Trieste Harbour. His last flight in a Marauder was on the 17th July when transiting from Rivolto to Capidochino.

Dachau

At the end of the war and on his way home Dave passed through Dachau Concentration Camp. He told me that he still remembers the horrors that he saw to this day. The camp was so silent not a sign of a living animal or bird just an air of complete doom. He watched as mass graves were dug to bury the hundreds of bodies that had not been incinerated and said that it was so hard to take in how one human being could do that to another. He also remarked to me, "In retrospect, what was unique about the Italian Campaign was the many different forces that were working and fighting together. Indians, Brazilians, New Zealanders, Goums from N. Africa, Americans, Jews, all in the 8th Army. On my squadron the ground crew were both black and white. It was really amazing." Dave told me that he is particularly proud of his period with the South African Air Force. He told me that, "It is a great eye opener for people to go to Undine Cemetery and see the last resting place of nineteen and twenty year olds," including the grave of John Hipwell David's first friend in the Royal Air Force. From all four corners of the world they fought side by side and died side by side. It makes you wonder where we go wrong today. In December 1946 Dave arrived back at North Weald in the UK and finally released from the Royal Air Force on the 11th July 1947.

Civilian life

Following his RAF service David was commissioned in the Auxiliary Air Force as a Fighter Controller with 3502 Ulster Fighter Control Unit. He served some eight years and was honoured with the Air Efficiency Award for this work. He joined the ranks of the Northern Ireland Civil Service, starting as a clerk. During his career he became Private Secretary to the Minister of Agriculture Mr Harry West. Dave was also Press Officer and Head of The Information Division and finally retired from the Civil Service in March 1986.

After he retired from the Civil Service Dave took on the job of Consultant to the Food Industry and Co-ordinator on the Northern Ireland input into Food and Farming Year and subsequently was involved with the Belfast 1991 program, including 'The Tall Ships' visit to the Province. Dave was a founder member of the Northern Ireland Branch of the Air Crew Association. He was the Chairman 1987/88 and the PRO for the Branch since it was founded in 1983. Since leaving the Royal Air Force he has continued his interest in the Royal Air Force Association and Royal Air Force Benevolent Fund. He also takes great pride in being a Life Member of the South African Air Force, Aircrew Association and the Marauder Historical Society.

WARRANT OFFICER
WILLIAM McCLINTOCK
ROYAL AIR FORCE NO. 1795177
NAVIGATOR

William McClintock was born in Cullybackey, County Antrim, on 13th October 1923 and was educated at Buick Memorial Primary School and Ballymena Technical College. On leaving college, he was employed with the local firm Frazer and Haughton Ltd, for two years before joining the Royal Air Force.

He was demobbed from the RAF in July 1950, and in August of that year joined the Imperial Civil Service, and was employed there for twenty seven years before accepting early retirement in 1977.

Most of William's working life was spent in Northern Ireland except for a three-year spell at the Consulate in Istanbul, Turkey, and a number of shorter terms at the Embassy in Teheran, Persia. On accepting early retirement at the age of fifty-four he decided to advance his education and obtained six 'O' Levels attending night classes at Castlereagh College of Further Education. He then took up employment with the Probation Office, when the Community Service Scheme was introduced in Northern Ireland. Later he accepted employment with Castlereagh College and remained there until retirement. His hobbies are bowling, fishing, membership of the Royal Air Force Association (Carrickfergus Branch), Aircrew Association (Northern Ireland Branch), Mosquito Aircrew Association and 684/31 Squadron Association.

Royal Air Force career

William joined the Royal air Force at Clifton Street Belfast on his eighteenth birthday 13th October 1941, and was called for service on 3rd December 1941.

He volunteered for aircrew duties but was astonished to learn that there was a nine-month deferment and immediately signed on as a Ground Wireless Operator. He was then posted to Padgate in Lancashire on 4th December 1941 where he spent one week being kitted out and receiving inoculations, etc. On or about the 11th December, he was posted to Blackpool to begin Wireless Training. This part of the course dealt mainly with learning the Morse code and drill. Having joined the Air Training Corps in 1940 he was partly trained in Morse

and passed the weekly tests with ease not realising that this could have a significant bearing in his grading at a later date. The course had been a mixture of Ground and Aircrew Wireless Operators. Volunteers were requested for aircrew and the majority of the course volunteered, unfortunately only three applicants were successful in the selection board and William was passed as, "Fit Pilot, unfit Navigator." One of the other successful candidates was another Ulsterman named Arnold Exeley who also qualified as a Pilot in South Africa and was killed later in action in North Africa. A week later William was taken off the course and was transferred to the Air Receiving Centre at Lords Cricket Ground in London. He was billeted at a large block of flats that were called Viceroy Court which overlooked Regents Park.

In March 1942 William was posted along with twenty five other cadets to RAF Finningley, this was a real surprise as all of the ITW's were at various seaside resorts around the country, St Andrews, Scarborough, Torquay, etc. This small group had a squadron leader in charge, Flying Officer as the Navigation Instructor, and the remaining instructors were drawn from the instructors on the Operational Training Unit (OTU), which at that time were converting crews to Wellington aircraft.

The first and second one thousand bomber raids were carried out during William's spell at Finningley and he watched as many of his instructors took part on these epic raids.

On completion of the course he was promoted to Leading Aircraftsman (LAC) and his pay was increased to 7 shillings and sixpence per day (37 1/2 new pence). He was then posted to Brighton and was billeted in the Grand Hotel to await the next stage of training. By this time the Pilots, Navigators, Bomb Aimers Scheme had been introduced, this was to overcome the fact that the majority of cadets preferred to be Pilots. In October William was posted to Scone in Perth for his ten hours flying in Tiger Moths for assessment. On completion of the course in early November he was sent home on leave to await his next posting.

Eventually a letter arrived mid December instructing him to report on the 1st January 1943 to Heaton Park Manchester. Here aircrew were assembled in large numbers to be informed which category they had been graded. Naturally the scheme was devised to obtain the necessary numbers of Navigators and Bomb Aimers, many were disappointed. William was one of about thirty Cadets who were graded as Navigator/Wireless Operators, this group being specially trained to fly in Beaufighter and Mosquito aircraft.

This unfortunately meant another delay with an eighteen week Wireless Operators Course at No 1 Radio School RAF Cranwell which was equipped with Proctor and Dominee aircraft. During his training at Cranwell William got his first glimpse of the new jet aircraft which was of course the very secret Gloster Whittle. He wondered at that time how could this aircraft possibly fly without propellers. Bill successfully completed the course in July, and after a spell of leave returned to Heaton Park and eventually he was trained up to Greenock in Scotland were he boarded the old four funnelled liner Aquatania and sailed for New York, the journey taking seven days. These large liners that included the 'Queens' were able to sail across the Atlantic unescorted as they could reach speeds in excess of 20 knots. They would change course every two minutes as it was estimated that 'U' boats took three to four minutes to line up a torpedo attack.

About 300 cadets were on board and the food was excellent, everything that was severely rationed at home was available on board. They arrived in New York in the midst of a heavy fog. Sailing up the Hudson he could see this bank of fog ahead which blanketed out the Statue of Liberty and the famous skyline. The next stage of his journey was by rail from New York to Moncton Nova Scotia which was the aircrew receiving centre for all cadets arriving and leaving Canada. From Moncton he was posted to No 33 Air Navigation School (ANS) at Mount Hope Hamilton, Ontario where he completed a 22 week course on both navigation and wireless. The course finished by late February 1944. Just before the course ended, six volunteers were asked for to attend and Operational Training Unit (OTU) at Greenwood, Nova Scotia on Mosquito aircraft. William quickly volunteered and was accepted, but unfortunately on the day before graduation a number of the course decided to say goodbye to their girlfriends in Hamilton. This was discovered and as a result, those who had volunteered for Greenwood were removed and instead were posted to complete the course at No 1 School of General Reconnaissance at Summerside, Prince Edward Island. Of the six volunteers who had gone to Greenwood five

were killed in action during the following six months. On completion of the navigation course there was automatic promotion to Sergeant and an increase in pay of 12 shillings and sixpence (62/1/2) per day.

A further move back to Moncton, then on to Summerside at Prince Edward Island where the six week course started in March 1944. This was an extremely concentrated course and prepared Navigators to fly on long trips over the sea, often without good navigation aids. One of the subjects on the course was ship recognition, this entailed the student being able to recognise every type of the worlds fighting ships. Also the type and tonnage of all Merchant Ships. When the course ended William came 3rd out of a class of 26, and was considered a 'specialist' in reconnaissance and graded 'above average'.

In late April he returned to Moncton and then on to Halifax Nova Scotia to board the Liner Empress of Scotland that had been previously named the Empress of Japan, for the journey back again unescorted to Liverpool. The journey was very uncomfortable due to overcrowding. The Liner was designed to carry 1,100 passengers pre-war, but it was estimated to be carrying around 7,000. On arrival in Liverpool he boarded a train for Harrogate that was the receiving centre for all categories of aircrew returning to the UK. Again there was a large build up people and Bill knew that there was going to be a long delay in getting to an OTU. He decided to volunteer for Bomber Command but as he was a general reconnaissance trained Navigator, the request was turned down. William waited around Harrogate for three months and was sent to various training centres throughout the UK for experience on Tiger Moths. It was while on one of these courses at Scone near Perth in Scotland that he met Pilot Officer Rawcliffe whom he was later to crew up with at No 8 Operational Training Unit.

Eventually in February 1945, after wasting nine months at Harrogate he was posted to No 3 School of General Reconnaissance at Squires Gate in Blackpool, the course lasting six weeks combining for the first time both navigation and wireless. On completion of this course William was graded as 'above the average'.

On the 23rd March 1945 William was posted to No 8 OTU at Haverford in west Wales, where he was selected for photographic reconnaissance, flying Mosquito aircraft. The course also involved him having to complete a 3 x 2 hrs in a decompression chamber which simulated a height of 35,000ft, to make sure he was suitable for high altitude flying. Halfway through the course another delay, when the OTU transferred to Mount Farm near Oxford. On one of the training flights with his Pilot, Flying Officer Rawcliffe, while taking off the booster on the port engine burst and he lost control, causing him to swing off the runway heading straight for a fire tender. When he was about 100ft away from it Flying Officer Rawcliffe pulled back hard on the control column, the Mosquito rose to approximately 50ft narrowly missing the fire tender, stalled and crashed nose into the ground, both escaped unhurt although the Mosquito was a total write off. On successfully completing the OTU course William was graded as 'good average'.

684 Squadron, Alipore, Calcutta, South East Asia

William and Flying Officer Rawcliffe were posted to join 684 Squadron which was based at Alipore in Calcutta India, but first they were transferred to No 309 ferry Unit at RAF Benson to collect a Mark XXX1V Mosquito Reg No RG253 and prepared for the long journey to India which would take two weeks and 27hrs.15mins flying hours to reach Calcutta. By this time the bomb had been dropped and with the surrender of the Japanese, the trip to India was leisurely, stopping over for sight seeing. They left RAF Benson on the 18th September 1945, their route was to take them via St Mawgan in Cornwall for overseas briefing, then on to Istres (France), Luqa (Malta) Cairo West (Egypt), Habbanyia (Iraq), Bahrain (Persian Gulf), Karachi (India), arriving at Alipore Calcutta on the 4th October 1945 at 1300 hrs.

A post war survey programme had been approved for the squadron and it was decided to close Alipore down. The ground staff was already on the long journey by ship around the coast of Malaya and on to Saigon in French Indo China. On 19th October the last six of the squadron's aircraft left for Saigon in very poor weather conditions, one crew disappeared and was never found, and two other aircraft crashed one being the Squadron Commander who came down in Burma. When William and the other crews met their Commanding Officer, Wing Commander Lowry, DFC*, they soon settled and were very surprised to find so many Japanese manning every position around the camp. By this time the locals realised that the British Forces were holding until the French Army arrived and the camp was being attacked every night. Shortly after this Wing Commander Lowry left Saigon to visit the squadron detachment which was on the Cocas Islands, unfortunately the plane disappeared during this flight. Squadron Leader Newman then took command of the squadron. The Japanese were still heavily armed and carried out the majority of the defensive duties until the arrival of the French Army and Air Force in mid November. In early January the squadron moved to Bangkok (Siam) where it continued its aerial survey work of North Vietnam. Siam was virtually untouched during the war and as the basic food, which was rice, was in short supply, necessitating weekly rice surveys to be carried out to enable ample supplies to be sent to the starving population of South East Asia.

The squadron had now acquired a reputation for aerial survey work.

By July 1946 the squadron that meanwhile had been renumbered 81 Squadron moved to Seletar, Singapore and a detachment was sent to Batavia (Indonesia) where a survey of the Island was completed in six weeks. On return to Singapore detachments were sent out to Labuan (North Borneo), Mingladon (Burma), Delhi (India), and further surveys or 'special duties' were carried out. On completion of his tour with 81 Squadron in February 1948 he was graded as a PR Navigator 'exceptional'. William then volunteered to crew a surplus Dakota KN 150 back to RAF Lyneham in the UK along with its Pilot, Wing Commander McConnell, DSO, DFC*, who had flown Beaufighters and Mosquitoes over the North Sea against the Germans. The route back to the UK was similar to his outward journey, finally arriving back Lyneham, on the 11th March 1948 to clear customs. William arranged to meet Wing Commander McConnell four days later when he was getting his leave fixed up at the Air Ministry in London. Wing Commander McConnell asked William where the nearest airfield was to his home, he replied, "Aldergrove." Wing Commander McConnell was ferrying the Dakota to Carlisle, so he and William flew the aircraft to Aldergrove on the 11th March where he let William out, and took off on his own again heading for Carlisle.

On completion of his leave William was posted to 120 Squadron at Leuchars flying in Avro Lancasters carrying out local photography and air sea rescue duties. During the summer of that year William found himself being posted to St Eval in Cornwall as a Navigator Instructor at an Air Training Corps (ATC) summer camp which catered for up to 600 cadets per week. On his return to Leuchars, William asked for a refresher course at 236 Operational Training Unit (OTU) at Kinloss and went there in early October. On completion of the course in January 1949, he was posted with his new crew to 203/36 Squadron that was based at St Eval. This squadron as well as Air Sea Rescue duties, carried out long range meteorological trips out into the Atlantic. A special bonus was that every third weather trip, they landed at Gibraltar and completed a further Met trip on the return journey. Naturally these visits were very popular and always finished with a battle of wits with the customs authorities.

William remained as Navigator with the Squadron until his release in July 1950 and the final entry by his commanding officer in his logbook reads, "Above the Average," and "An Outstanding Navigator and a most willing and conscientious worker."

During his flying career in the Royal Air Force he visited a total of fifty five Aerodromes and accumulated a total of 1427 hours flying and flew in the following aircraft: Proctor; Dominie; Anson; Oxford; Mosquito Mks V1, 1X, X1X, XV1, and XXX1V; Sentinal; Tiger Moth; Dakota; Harvard; Sea Otter; Sunderland, Lancaster; Wellington; and Beaufighter.

PILOT OFFICER
G MARSHAL McCOMBE
ROYAL AIR FORCE NO. 104492
NO. 78 SQUADRON

Marshal McCombe was educated at the Belfast Royal Academical Institution from 1928 until 1934. He was brilliant wing three quarter and a record long jumper in 1933. Once joining the Royal Air Force and on completion of his flying training, he was posted to no 78 Squadron at Croft, County Durham.

On the night of the 7th November 1941 Pilot Officer McCombe took off with his crew from Croft in Whitley Serial No Z6948 Code EY-F at 2231 hrs. Their target was Berlin. At 0630 hrs on the 8th November his aircraft was shot down by a German night fighter and crashed between Oudemirdum and Nijemirdum (Friesland) some 20 Kilometres south west of Sneek in Holland. All hands were killed. The Pilot of the Night Fighter was Oberlieutenant Ludvig Becker of the 4./NJGI. Pilot Officer McCombe is buried with three other members of the crew in Nijemirdum General Cemetery.

The crew of Whitley Z6948, EY-F:

Pilot Officer GM McCombe
Sergeant JW Bell is buried in Lemmer General Cemetery
Sergeant GT Webb
Sergeant D Cameron
Sergeant R Boucher

SQUADRON LEADER
WILLIAM WINDER McCONNELL, DFC*
BATTLE OF BRITAIN PILOT
ROYAL AIR FORCE NO. 81643
FIGHTER PILOT
NO. 245, 32, 607, 249, 1, 174 SQUADRON

Squadron Leader William Winder McConnell was born in Belfast on the 9th June 1917 and was educated at Malone Public Elementary School, the Belfast College of Technology and Graduated from Queens University with a BSc in Commerce. On graduating from Queens, Winder was employed with the Northern Ireland Electricity Department as a clerk.

Ever since Winder was a small boy he wanted to fly and had his first flight at Newtownards Airport in 1936. Three years later on the 2nd February 1939 he joined the Royal Air Force Volunteer Reserve (24 Elementary and Reserve Flying Training School) which was based at Sydenham Airport, the headquarters being located at Saxone House in Royal Avenue.

Winder completed his training on Tigermoths at 24 E&RFTS around May 1939 and with the outbreak of war in September 1939 he was called to full time service. On the 29th October 1939 Winder was posted to No 4 Initial Training Wing at Bexhill-on-Sea where he completed the usual square bashing and aircrew selection exams. His initial training finished on the 9th December and was posted to No 6 Service Flying Training School at Little Rissington that was equipped with Harvards. While he was training at Little Rissington he lost a very dear friend (Ulsterman) Herbie MaGarry when he failed to return in his Harvard during a training flight. Winder successfully completed his flying training at No 6 SFTS on the 18th June 1940 and was promoted to the rank of Sergeant.

On the 18th June 1940 Winder was promoted to Pilot Officer and posted to No 245 Squadron that had detachment based at Hawkinge. The squadron had been equipped with the Fairy Battle up until March 1940 when it was re-equipped with Hawker Hurricane 1s. On the 1st June 1940 the squadron destroyed four BF 109's and damaged two with the loss of two Pilots. Winder started training on the Hurricane's right away and was posted with the squadron when it moved to Royal Air Force Aldergrove in Northern Ireland on the 6th July 1940 the squadron's task was to protect the city of Belfast against

the Luftwaffe. Winder carried out mostly night fighter patrols over Belfast and around the coast of Northern Ireland looking for Focke Wulf Condor reconnaissance aircraft that were shadowing Convoys arriving from Canada and America.

(On the 13th May 1941 245 Squadrons Commanding Officer shot down and destroyed a Dornier 17 near the Maidens in the Irish Sea. This was the CO's 13th Kill since the war had started.)

No 32 (F) and 607(F) Squadron
Winder was posted to No 32 (F) Squadron at Acklington from the 19th September 1940 for five days and then joined No 607 (F) Squadron 11 Group at Tangmere on the 25th September 1940.

He moved to the squadron in September at the height of the Battle of Britain and it here Winder had his first encounter with the enemy. On the 1st October 1940 while on a Channel patrol he met twenty Me110's and twenty Me109's. He singled out one of the 109's and while attacking it head on it shot at him with its cannons leaving a large hole in his wing that you could drop a football through.

On the 14th October 1940 he was posted to No 249 (F) Squadron that was based at North Weald. (On the 16th August 1940 Flight Lieutenant JB Nicholson, in Hurricane P3576, gained the only Fighter Command Victoria Cross by staying with his burning aircraft when he attacked a BF110. 249 Squadron gave a brilliant account of itself during the Battle of Britain). On the 28th October 1940 he and another Pilot Flight Lieutenant 'Butch Barton' shared in destroying a Ju88. On the 29th while taking off from base Winder was jumped by a Me109 but escaped unhurt.

While patrolling near Dover on the 10th January Winder was attacked by a BF 109 and was badly wounded in the leg by its cannon fire. He decided to bale out and on landing broke his leg, while his Hurricane smashed into the face of the Dover cliffs. Wing Commander Victor Beamish who was the squadron's Commanding Officer and a fellow Irishman, shot down the BF109 that had attacked Winder.

The events that led up to that unlucky morning are as follows in Winders own words:

"The squadron was scrambled and I went to my aircraft Hurricane GN-N only to find another Pilot sitting in the cockpit and who refused to get out. I hastily returned to Operations to find out what was going on, I was told that there had been a mix up and was allocated another aircraft GN-Y. By the time I had got airborne the rest of the squadron had disappeared. It was while I was looking for them that I was pounced by the 109 and hit in the leg by its cannon fire. I baled out and was picked up later having sustained a broken leg."

Pilot Officer McConnell was in hospital from the 10th January until the middle of May 1941 and when he had recovered sufficiently enough he was transferred to the Imperial Hotel at Torquay to convalesce.

On the 23rd May 1941 after he had fully recovered he was posted to No 1 Squadron at Redhill where he became an instructor on Turbanlight training. This occupation he thoroughly detested. On the 8th June 1941 he was promoted to Flying Officer. On the 28th March 1942 he received very welcome news when he was told that he had been posted to 174 (FB) Squadron then forming at Manston as a Flight Commander. He was promoted to Flight Lieutenant on the 18th June 1942. The squadron was equipped with Hawker Hurricane 11B's and was used as a fighter bomber unit. The squadron was used for bombing attacks on shipping and airfields and on the 29th June damaged a 4,000 ton ship that had to be beached. The squadron suffered heavy casualties during Operation Jubilee (Dieppe) when it lost five of its Pilots including its free French Commanding Officer Squadron Leader Fayolle.

After the death of the Commanding Officer Winder was promoted to Squadron Leader and given Command of 174 Squadron. Winder was awarded the Distinguished Flying Cross on the 30th June 1942 after the Dieppe raid and added a Bar to the DFC on the 22nd September 1942. The squadron was re-equipped with Hawker Typhoon 1B's in April 1943 as the Hurricanes were becoming vulnerable for attack operations over Europe. On the 14th July 1943 Winder led the first typhoon attack on Poix Airfield and continued operating with the squadron until February 1944 when he was shot down over Europe in his Typhoon. He managed to bale out but on landing he was captured by the Germans and interned in Stalag Luft 111 until he was released on the 8th June (VE Day) 1945. On his return to the UK on the 9th June he was posted to No 106 Personnel Reception Centre at Cosford to be debriefed. On the 9th June he was posted to No 112 Personnel Reception Centre at Church Fenton to await his appointment. On the 10th October 1945 Winder was posted to No 2 Flying Training School at Yatesbury on an Instructors course. He had only completed three trips on a Tiger Moth when he was informed that he was being released from the Royal Air Force. By the end of the war Winder had completed 220 operational hours and 150 sorties.

The aircraft types which he flew during his RAF career were the Tiger Moth, Hawker Hind, Hawker Hurricane 1 & 11B, Miles Magister, Miles Master, Supermarine Spitfire VB and the Hawker Typhoon.

Aer Lingus, Dublin

Winder reluctantly left the RAF on the 25th February 1946 and returned to Northern Ireland taking up his post again with the Northern Ireland Electricity Department. He dearly wanted back to flying so applied to Aer Lingus in Dublin for a flying position and was accepted on the 1st October 1946. He remained with Aer Lingus until the 31st December 1976 when he was almost sixty, flying DC3's, Viscounts, Fokker F27's and Bristol Freighters. He still wanted to fly and managed to get a position with Zambian Airlines flying Boeing 707's until his license ran out on 9th June 1977 when he became sixty. His first flight in an aircraft was almost 41 years earlier at Newtownards airport. Winder was a very keen member of the Aircrew Association in Dublin. Sadly he died at his home in Dublin on the 13th October 1998.

WING COMMANDER
WILLIAM EARNEST McCREA, DFC
ROYAL AIR FORCE NO. 146428
PILOT
NO. 57 SQUADRON

Wing Commander McCrea, son of an auctioneer, was born in Ramelton County Donegall on 3rd April 1921, and was educated at Foyle College in Londonderry and later at Queens University in Belfast. During the next three years at Queens he started a basic Arts degree and later changed to History with Chemistry and Mathematics.

Towards the end of 1940 he met Wing Commander Miles Villiers Delap (another Ramelton man) who was the Commanding Officer of the University Air Squadron and had been awarded the DFC on 2nd March 1940 for the sinking of the first German U-(U31) by Coastal Command. This was possibly the first DFC to be awarded to an Irishman during the Second World War. Wing Commander Delap had been flying Blenheims with 82 Squadron against the German breakthrough 1n 1940 and had been badly injured when baling out of his damaged aircraft. After a chat with Wing Commander Delap he decided to join the squadrons first course and then enlisted into the RAF in August1941. Mac reported to the Air Crew Receiving Centre in London and as he had successfully completed his ITW training with the air squadron his first posting was to the USA to train as a pilot under the 'Arnold' training Scheme. His sea journey across the Atlantic was in the Highland Princess, a converted meat ship which had been on the Argentine run. All of her refrigerated equipment had been removed and hammocks installed. The crossing took six days, experiencing severe Atlantic gales and the musty smell of meat which lingered throughout the ship. After docking Mac was transferred to Moncton in Nova Scotia where they were issued with ill fitting grey suits which they had to wear whilst training in the United States. At that time America had not entered the war so they were not allowed to wear uniform.

Mac's first posting on 5th November was to the Aircrew Primary Flying School in Americus Georgia which lasted until 10th January 1942. Here they trained under the Army (West Point) system of merits and demerits which included square meals, etc., and many other unnecessary and niggling impositions. The course included a number from Queens Air Squadron and a number of policemen who had recently been allowed to volunteer for aircrew duties. Naturally the cadets did not take kindly to this form of discipline but had to accept it otherwise they would fail the course. During a visit to the cinema, the film was stopped and an announcement made that the Japanese had bombed Pearl Harbour, the audience responded by standing and singing "God Bless America". Now that America was at war the cadets were allowed to wear their uniform. On successfully completing the course he transferred to the Basic Flying Training School at Machon Georgia, flying in Vultee BT17s. The course lasted nine weeks and he then was posted to the Advanced Flying School at Dothan Alabama flying in Harvards. He completed the course in May 1942 and was awarded his wings. Mac then returned to the UK via Moncton Canada and was transferred to a holding unit in Bournemouth to await his next stage of training.

In July 1942 Mac was posted to No 3 AFU at RAF Long Newton and South Cerney flying in Oxford aircraft. Here he found that the training in the UK was vastly different from that which he had experienced in America. The runways were lit up with 'Goose' flares, and it was a very attractive way of flying. Here at No 3 AFU Mac experienced his first of many slices of luck when the instructor came into the crew room and said to the trainee sitting beside him saying, "Ill take you first." Within half an hour they were both killed in a crash. The course was completed on 18th August 1942 when he was transferred to 18 OTU at RAF Luffenham. No 18 OTU was equipped with the Vickers Wellington aircraft. On the 27th September Mac took off on a night flying cross-country exercise and on their return to base were on the circuit for landing the port engine went on fire. The staff Pilot took control and tried to make an emergency landing, unfortunately the bomb dump got in the way and the aircraft crashed, fortunately the crew escaped with nothing more than superficial injuries and were badly shaken. On the 27th December Mac was posted to 1660 HCU at RAF Swinderby and there was a delay before the training in Lancasters was due to commence. During this delay he received instruction on the Avro Manchester. On his final trip in a Manchester, Mac was landing at Wickenby a station not far from Swinderby, the aircraft suddenly slewed off the runway and became bogged down, stopping operations for the night. Later the Station Commanding Officer arrived armed with six spades and ordered the crew to dig it out which they duly did. Mac successfully completed the OTU course and was transferred to No 57 Squadron at Scampton. He had his first flight in a Lancaster (W4232B) on 7th February 1943. His first operation was to Lorient on 13th February and the aircraft returned early due to mechanical trouble. On the 19th February 1943 Mac flew his first complete operation to Wilhelmshaven as Second Pilot. Mac went on to complete 29 Operations with the squadron between 4th February 1943 and 30th October 1943 which I have listed below.

Operations

Scampton 6th February 1943 to 29th August 1943.
East Kirkby 29th August 1943 to 20th October 1943.

February 13th	Lorient (early return)
February 19th	Wilhelmshaven (Second Pilot)
February 27th	Mining - East Frisian Islands
February 28th	St Nazaire Submarine Pens
March 22nd	St Nazaire Submarine Pens
March 29th	Berlin
April 3rd	Essen
April 9th	Duisberg (early return)
April 10th	Frankfurt (on three engines)
April 28th	Lubeck Bay Mining
April 30th	Essen
May 4th	Dortmund (see newspaper cutting)
May 12th	Duisburg
May 13th	Pilsen
May 23rd	Dortmund
May 25th	Dusseldorf
May 27th	Essen
May 29th	Wuppertal (abandoned before take-off)
July 8th	Cologne
July 9th	Gelsenkichen (early return)
July 24th	Hamburg
July 25th	Essen (early return)
July 27th	Hamburg
July 29th	Hamburg
August 2nd	Hamburg (fire storm)
August 27th	Nurenburg
August 31st	Berlin
September 3rd	Berlin
September 6th	Munich
October 5th	Frankfurt
October 6th	Stuttgart
October 8th	Hannover
October 18th	Hannover

Mac's experiences in three of these raids, Frankfurt, Dortmund and Hamburg are highlighted in the enclosed press reports. He was awarded the Distinguished Flying Cross on 29th October 1943. The Citation states:

> This Officer has completed many successful operations, including such targets as Berlin, Hamburg and many Industrial centres in the Ruhr. He has displayed great skill and leadership and his efforts throughout have been featured by determination of a high standard. One night in September when returning from an attack on a target in the Rhur his aircraft was intercepted by a fighter. A prolonged combat ensued but coolly and skilfully Pilot Officer McCrea finally succeeded in out-manoeuvring his adversary, the bomber sustained much damage but the pilot flew it back to base. He displayed great courage and resolution in trying circumstances.

Story of Dortmund raid, 4th May 1943

Mac's aircraft was attacked by a German night fighter within sight of the fires of Dortmund, his Lancaster received three bursts of cannon fire from astern, and the Rear Gunner was wounded. The crew heard bullets ripping through the aircraft, which stalled and went out of control. Mac (then Sergeant) went on his knees under the control column, and by a tremendous effort brought the aircraft out of the stall, but he found he could not hold it by himself. At that moment he took the decision to jettison his bomb load. The elevator trimming tab cable had been cut, the port aileron badly holed, and the hydraulics damaged. *(When the cannon shell severed the elevator trim control cable, it had the effect of trimming the elevator fully back and put the aircraft into a stall.)* Even the help of the Flight Engineer was not enough, and the Bomb Aimer had also to come to their assistance. The Rear Gunner had been severely wounded in the stomach and in the arm, but refused to leave his turret until the Lancaster was well out to sea. The first Mac knew of his 'trouble' was when he told him over the intercom, that he thought he had stopped something. He had to handle the turret with his left hand only, and when at last he agreed to the Mid-Upper Gunner going to his aid the turret doors had jammed, and the Mid-Upper Gunner had to use an axe to cut them off. Thinking it would be impossible to make a landing, Mac ordered the crew to stand by to bale out. Then he found that the Rear Gunner was so badly wounded that he could not have made it. The Flight Engineer, therefore, left him for a minute to see if he could do anything about the elevator rim tab. By manipulating the broken cable he managed to take the strain from the control column for a while, and by using the emergency system they got the undercarriage down and landed without further harm. This was the first major attack on the city of Dortmund with 596 aircraft taking part. Dortmund had an important railway junction and was the centre of the steel, coal and synthetic oil industries of the Ruhr. Thirty one aircraft failed to return and seven others crashed in bad weather returning to their bases. 4,000lb and 8,000lb bombs were dropped every minute on Dortmund that night as well as tens of thousands of incendiaries. On landing Mac rang up control and told them that he had been wounded onboard, the ambulance came haring out to the Lancaster. Mac turned the aircraft off into an intersection, cut the engines and electrics. The 'meat wagon' came to the back door of the aircraft and one of the medical Corporals tried to manoeuvre the injured gunner out of the door, and Mac can remember that the other Medic grabbed him by the feet and pulled hard. The poor gunner obviously in great pain let out a terrible scream as his stomach was wide open and the Navigator who was Burmese hit the medic quite hard. The medic then turned on the Navigator shouting at the top of his voice, "I will see you court marshalled for striking an NCO." (Luckily nothing ever came of the incident.) The next day Bill went to inspect his aircraft and found that the bomb bays had been wrecked by the night fighters cannon shells. It was just a mass of metal. The ground staff had counted over 75 bullet holes apart from the cannon shell damage. Every propeller blade was holed, all 12 of them. In the end the aircraft had to be scrapped.

Story of Frankfurt raid, 10th April 1943

On April 10th 1943 Mac and his crew took off for operations over Frankfurt. They had just made their operational height over the base when he lost his starboard outer engine. Mac told me, "If you lost the port inner, that was serious as it operated the hydraulics for the rear turret and as the starboard engine wasn't so serious." So he took the decision after consultation with his crew that he would carry on to the target which now he says on reflection it was, "One step short of madness, you were young and you did those sort of things in those days." They flew all the way to Frankfurt and back on three engines. They arrived over the target 30 minutes late. Mac said it was quiet, no night fighters, no flak. It seemed like everyone had gone home. On the way home they were loosing valuable time and the Navigator finally said, "I haven't got a clue where we are, but I think we are over the channel." By that time the sun was coming up, and Mac can remember flying on top of a blanket of cloud, so he decided to drop down and see if he could see a cast line. As soon as he broke cloud he was blasted by flak and immediately came back into cloud. He waited another half hour and dropped down again and eventually got a

fix over the south coast of England. They had gone miles off course. It was almost daylight when they got back to Scampton and landed on three engines. They went straight to the crew room for a well earned breakfast only to find the ground crews were knocking the locks of their lockers as they had already been 'written off'.

On one occasion when Mac returned from leave he was asked to report to his Commanding Officer. On his arrival there he was introduced to Wing Commander Guy Gibson, who informed Mac that he forming a 617 Squadron and was searching for experienced Pilots and their crews. At that time Mac had the rank of Sergeant and was unable to join Gibson's new squadron as he was in the process of changing Navigators. So Mac was very close to becoming a Dambuster Pilot.

Meeting Bomber Harris

Some time later Pilots from all the squadrons in the area were told to assemble for a meeting. The Base commander entered and introduced Air Chief Marshal 'Bomber' Harris. He spoke for about fifteen minutes and praised them and their crews for the excellent job that they were doing. Mac recalls him saying, "I can't promise you anything but look left and right at the chaps sitting beside you, in six months time only one of you will be there. If you are an NCO, you will be commissioned, if you are commissioned you will be two ranks higher, that at least is something to look forward to." They all stood up as the ACM Harris walked down the centre towards the door, spontaneously the Pilots clapped, stamped their feet and cheered. As he reached the door it seemed as if he was going to say something, he came to attention, saluted, and walked out. This was a very moving for them all. Mac said, "He was sometimes portrayed as a callous chap, but he did care."

I should like to say at this point while interviewing Wing Commander McCrea he was quite emotional, hence the impact that the memories of Harris still had on him.

A short time after this, the squadron had a Royal occasion when the King and Queen came down to Scampton to meet the Dambusters and 57 Squadron. Mac had the honour of being introduced to both of them. His Aunt who lived in London wrote to him as she had recognised him on the news reel, talking to the King and Queen.

Mac also recalls amusing and serious interludes, around the middle of 1943. The Germans had introduced a 'Master Search Light' that was directed by radar. Mac's nickname for them was 'Blue Masters', as they appeared as blue light in the ground, and fixed on the aircraft without warning. After a few operations, Pilots became 'air wise' so you waited on 'Joe', the unfortunate Pilot who was unlucky enough to get coned. This usually had disastrous results, this enabled the other aircraft to fly around the cone of search lights.

Mac recalls that on an operation to Duisburg, he was 'Joe', a very hair raising experience, he recalls that he eventually got out of it by twisting, turning and stalling, losing about 3,000ft. Mac never flew straight and level once he crossed the enemy coast, he always corkscrewed and changed height continually. When Mac returned from this raid in the early hours, although extremely tired, he decided to visit his girlfriend in Lincoln. Informing his friends of his address in Lincoln, set off on his motorbike around 0400 hrs. He would not elaborate on what happened during the next four to five hours.

Later an airman who had cycled all the way from Scampton arrived and knocked on the door with the news, "Sergeant McCrea, you are on Ops tonight, briefing at 1500 hrs." Mac arrived back in time for the briefing, looked at the map and nearly passed out, the target was the Skoda works at Pilsen in Czechoslovakia, a seven and a half hour trip. He was tired before the raid, when he returned he was utterly exhausted and slept for twenty four hours. A raid to Wuppertal was the next operation, the crews had been fed a lot of duff information regarding the targets in Wuppertal and were unhappy about this. They were told the targets would be railway stations, factories, and military installations, etc. Mac said we knew in our hearts it was a direct attack on the homes of the Ruhr workers. Mac remembers well the 'ripple' which went around the briefing room, the crews started to stamp their feet in disgust. The Commanding Officer was very annoyed about this and told them to shut up and said, "You will go were you are told to go." So that was the end of it. Prior to this operation, Mac was carrying out the usual air test on his Lancaster and during the flight he put her to full throttle, suddenly he felt a severe pain in his ear, he landed and was taken straight to hospital. It was six weeks before he had recovered and able to resume operations again. His next trip was to Cologne and Gelsenkirchen.

The Hamburg raids, July 24th, 27th, 29th and 2nd August 1943

Mac took part in all four of the heavy raids on Hamburg which was attacked by American bombers during daylight and the Royal Air Force by night. Mac recalls that in the first raid on 24th July 'Window' was used for the first time, which completely confused the German night fighters and there was no opposition whatsoever over the target. The second raid on the 27th was the night of the fire storm. He saw the fire well before he reached the target. He remembers turning his aircraft to beam to get a look at the fires, because he could not see them as he was going home, something Mac has never forgotten. On the third trip to Hamburg on the 29th, Mac said that he could see the fires from miles out. Mac's aircraft was in the third wave and was briefed for Z+45. He queried the timing as other waves of 57 Squadron were briefed Z+5 and Z+10, but Z+45 was confirmed by the briefing officer. When Mac arrived over the target, there was little or no activity, search lights or night fighters and he saw one Lancaster had been shot down.

On their return they were informed that a mistake had been made, the correct time should have been Z+15. The error had been discovered after they had taken off, but were allowed to carry on. The squadron lost three aircraft because of bad briefing.

On the 4th raid on the 2nd August they experienced severe icing and were not sure if they hit the target. Icing was smashing on to the fuselage and the St Elmo's Fire was everywhere, from prop tip to prop tip and even arcing across the control column.

Mac and his crew bombed Nureburg on the 27th August and Berlin on the 31st August. On the 3rd September 1943 the operation was Mac's last trip to Berlin and one which he is not particularly proud of. Over the target he was attacked by a fighter which fired at his aircraft several times, he managed to shake it off loosing 2,000ft in the process. He asked his Navigator for a course back to base which he put on his compass and started for home. After about ten minutes he noticed that there was no ground activity, continued flying and after another ten minutes he looked out the port window and saw the aurora borealis, and exclaimed in a loud voice, "Oh my God, what have I done, we are on our way to Russia." Mac said, "Sorry lads, I have made a mistake and set a reciprocal course and we have lost half an hour." Mac asked his Navigator for a course north and skirted around Berlin and came back an hour late behind the main bomber stream.

Later the Flight Engineer informed Mac that the fuel situation was critical. Mac said they had to keep going, the alternative was to come down in enemy territory or in the sea, the chose the latter. A close check was kept on the fuel and the Navigator was able to get an accurate fix, they were heading for Yorkshire and would land at the first airfield they see. They crossed the coast and spotted an airfield and landed. Mac remembers that it was a Canadian bomber station and the Station Commander an Air Commodore coming out to meet him and dishing out big cigars to everyone. The next morning after getting 200 gallons of fuel, they set off for East Kirky flying at tree top height, they had not a care in the world that morning and low flying rejuvenated their spirits after the activities of the previous night. A few miles from the base they ascended to 1,000ft and received permission to land. On the circuit the port outer engine cut, and just as he got into the Funnel the starboard engine cut, as he was coming over the perimeter fence the third engine cut, he made a perfect landing and as he pulled off the runway the fourth engine died. The Flight Engineer had not selected the proper tanks, they had been flying on the almost empty ones. The 'Chiefy' arrived, Mac told him of the mistake, and asked him, "Could you fix us up with a tow." They were towed back onto dispersal and nothing more was said or recorded about the incident. An entry in Mac's logbook records that he landed on one engine, few people have managed to do this. Mac's next trip was to Munich on 6th

December, Frankfurt on 5th October and Stuttgart on the 6th October.

His penultimate operation was to Hanover on 8th October was one which he will always remember, and during this experienced the worst twenty minutes of his career. He was flying in a 'borrowed' aircraft and on approaching the target he noticed an aircraft some fifty yards to port had a fire on his starboard engine. As Mac got closer to the aircraft he could see by its letters that it was a 50 Squadron aircraft 'VN'. There seemed to be no chance for the Pilot, yet he still seemed to be determined to continue on to the target. Mac was getting closer, and just before the target, the aircraft exploded in a ball of flames and went down. Fortunately Mac's aircraft escaped unscathed, Mac has always remembered this. Ten days later he flew his last operation again was to Hanover.

Late in September the squadron had moved from Scampton to East Kirkby and Mac told his crew that he was going to see how high his aircraft Lancaster EB944 could reach. Eventually he reached 29,000ft, and told his crew you have just been up as high as Mt Everest. Usually in the raids Mac was always in the first wave to reach base. He recalls that once when using his experience he was ready to press his R/T button when he heard an Australian voice call up, "This is 'S' for Sugar," and was given permission to land, and Mac was given the second landing spot. He asked his Rear Gunner where 'Sugar' was, and the reply came back, "Miles away." Mac had to go round again and eventually saw the Australian enter the funnel, where he was jumped by an intruder. Mac could only watch as the tracer rounds hit the Australians aircraft, it went down in flames with its Rear Gunner still shooting at the intruder until the aircraft exploded on the ground. Mac switched off his landing lights and headed for Nottingham to escape the intruder, he stayed away for forty minutes before returning and landing safely. Mac said that there was a lot of intruders at that time.

Mac finished operations on the 18th October 1943 with a total of 1025hrs.35mins flying time and flew had flown in the following aircraft: PT17's; Vultee 13A; Harvard; Oxford; Wellington Mk 1C/111; Manchester; Lancaster MK1/111; Martinet; Hurricane; and Master.

His crew members in Lancaster ED 944 were:

Sergeant Glencross
Sergeant Guy
Sergeant Coxall
Sergeant Adams
Sergeant Adams
Sergeant Allen
Pilot Officer Sherrett

He finished the war as a Flight Lieutenant, promoted to Squadron Leader in 1954 and Wing Commander in 1964. Mac was rested from operations and posted to No17 OTU at Silverstone in North Hants as an Instructor on the 30th October 1943 flying Wellingtons which he did not like at all. Here he met his wife Glynns where she was serving in the WAAF on Christmas Eve, and married her shortly after D-Day. He remained there until 12th December 1943 when the OTU moved to Turn Weston and was stationed there until 1st November 1944. During his spell at OTU he admits to 'bending' one or two Wimpys. His next posting was to No 3 FIS at Ludgate Bottom on 8th November 1944 and completed the course on 13th December 1944. He was then posted to the Bomber Command Instructors School (BICS) at Finningley and remained there until 3rd March 1945 and then on 13th September 1945 he was posted to 90 Maintenance Unit at Warton. Here he was hospitalised, suffering from Asthma attacks and was invalided out of the RAF in September 1945.

Mac returned home to Northern Ireland with his wife Glynns and rejoined Queens University, completing a pass Degree and Honours Degree in 1948. He rejoined the RAF again in 1948 with the Education Branch at South Cerney, hoping to be able to get flying again, but unfortunately he had lost his hearing in his right ear, and never flew again. He served at the Initial Training School at South Cerney as Chief Ground Instructor, This was just the same as the old ITW's during the war, where the short service aircrew joined up and did their ground training. He also had three spells at the Air Ministry in London in the resettlement department. His duties were to help air and ground crews resettle into civilian life. Mac's last position in the Royal Air Force was at the Staff College at Bracknall, involved with the training of foreign aircrew and he retired with the rank of Wing Commander in May 1972. Mac is still is in contact with his Mid-Upper Gunner Chris Allen who rang him up after an interval of forty five years, and said, "Do you remember a certain week-end in London in 1943?"

Mac is an enthusiastic golfer representing Ulster and played in the Irish Championships at Ross's Point in 1965, and reached the semi-finals. At the age of 44 he was selected to play for Ireland (oldest player to play for Ireland) in the European Championships in June 1965, when Ireland won the Championship. After three years representing Ireland he retired from competitive golf. On leaving the RAF he joined the Halton Heath Golf Club which was opened by the News of the World. When this was taken over by Rupert Murdock he quickly sold it to the members. At that time Mac became secretary and held the position for another 16 years. He finally retired in 1988 and still plays a good game of golf, is a member of the Bomber Command Association.

SERGEANT
GA McGARVEY
ROYAL AIR FORCE NO. 969452
GUNNER
NO. 455 SQUADRON, ROYAL AUSTRALIAN AIR FORCE

The information that I have on Sergeant GA McGarvey is very limited. He was educated at the Belfast Royal Academical Institution in Belfast 1933/39. He joined the Royal Air Force when war broke out.

On completion of his Gunnery Training he was posted to No 455 Squadron which was based at Swinderby in Lincolnshire. Sergeant McGarvey was killed on the 7th November 1941 taking part in a 'Rover' patrol towards Koln. Sergeant MA Jenkins, the Skipper of the Hampden, Serial No AE243, Code UB-B took of from Swinderby at 1830 hrs and were shot down somewhere over Belgium. All are buried in Heverlee War Cemetery, Belgium.

The crew of Hampden UB-B:

Sergeant MA Jenkins
Sergeant DR Rawlings
Sergeant GA McGarvey
Flight Sergeant Morris

WING COMMANDER
HUNTER McGIFFIN, OBE AE
PILOT
NO. 502 (ULSTER) SQUADRON
ROYAL AUXILIARY AIR FORCE

Wing Commander Hunter McGiffin was born in Northern Ireland and educated at Campbell College. He had two great passions, one was motor racing and the other flying and he excelled at both.

As a member of the Ulster Automobile Club Hunter took part in the Class 'A' Trials in the Circuit of Ireland Rally in 1937 where he finished 2nd, racing alongside fellow Ulstermen and 'flyers' Wing Commander Terry McComb, Squadron Leader Jack Harrison and Wing Commander Ken Mac Kenzie. In 1963-64 he drove in the Circuit of Ireland in the Touring Class with his son driving a Sunbeam Rapier and received Finishing Awards in both years.

Hunter's flying career started on Sunday 14th February 1937 when he received a phone call from his good friend Jack Harrison, telling him that he was visiting RAF Station Aldergrove just after lunch where he knew one or two of the chaps in 502 Squadron and would he like to look around. Hunter eagerly agreed and, on their arrival at the squadron he met fellow Campbellians George Gardiner, Brian and Terry Corry. Hunter also met the squadron commanding officer Wing Commander JC Russell, DSO who asked him would he like a flight in a Westland Wallace. (This was not the first time that Hunter had taken to the air as he had had a flight with the squadron in October 1936 during an air display.)

Hunter joined 502 (Ulster) Squadron on receiving his commission on the 1st July 1937 and learned to fly in the squadron's Avro 504 N's and soloed after just three flights on the 20th July. His instructor was a Squadron Leader Tom Blithe (later badly burned during the Battle of Britain when the fuel tank of his Hurricane blew up and ,he was one of the first McIndoe 'Guinea Pigs'). Most of Hunter's aviation was carried out at weekends although some flying was allowed during week-days. Between 1937 and 1939 Hunter flew the squadron's Hawker Hind, Hart and Avro Anson's. In August 1939, Hunter, would fly a Hawker Demon from Sydenham at night for the search light and anti-aircraft gun batteries to practice on (he was

the target). His course would take him up to Coleraine then down the Antrim coast to Aldergrove and back to Sydenham and for his trouble he was paid 30 shillings for each night flight (a tidy sum in those days). When war came on the 3rd September he was called to full time service and spent the first year of the war flying convoy escorts and anti-submarine patrols over the Atlantic and around the Isle of Man in Avro Ansons. These patrols were usually of about 4hrs.30mins duration. In August 1940, Flight Lieutenant Hunter McGiffin, Flight Lieutenant Brian Corry and Sergeant Patterson were sent to Abbingdon in England where they were instructed on how to fly the Armstrong Whitworth Whitley. Hunter's duel instruction on the Whitley was only 1hr.30 min and he was then told to instruct B Corry and Sergeant Patterson on how to fly it. It is a well documented fact that one of the stations Flight Commander, a Flight Lieutenant Tomlin, did in fact land his Whitley in Germany on the 16th March 1940 and on realising his mistake took off again landing in France 30 minutes later.

On the way to Abbingdon, Hunter and Brian Corry decided to stay the night at the Regent Palace Hotel in London and shortly after they had arrived the Germans bombed the hell out of the nearby area. The next morning was a Sunday and before driving to Abbingdon they decided to view the destruction and aftermath of the night before.

At that time the new very secret ASV (Air to Surface Vessel) radar equipment was just being installed in Coastal Command's aircraft and as Hunter was the only qualified Whitley Pilot he was selected to go to West Freugh in Scotland to pick up the Whitley which had been fitted with the new secret radar equipment. He and his crew were then sent to RAF St Athan in Wales where they attended a course on how to use the ASV with the 'boffins' until mid-December returning to Aldergrove with the aircraft on the 22nd just in time for Christmas.(Hunter mentioned to me that it was possible that his aircraft was the very first one to be fitted with the new radar.) Flight Lieutenant Terence Corry was the first in the squadron to find a U-boat using the new ASV. A logbook entry for December shows that he had been assessed as 'above the average' as a Pilot. On the 27th January 1941 the squadron moved to Limavady and soon saw action when on February 10th, Flying Officer JA Walker, while escorting convoy WS 6, depth charged and severely damaged the German U-boat, U-93 some 300 miles west-north-west of Ireland.

Hunter was married on the 24th April 1941 and spent his honeymoon in Portstewart on the north coast of County Antrim. He and his good lady celebrated their 59th Wedding Anniversary this year but sadly he died a few months later. Hunter continued flying the Whitley on anti-submarine patrols through to October 1941.

A related story

Bismarck, the notorious German battleship which had sunk HMS Hood, the world's biggest battle cruiser on the 24th May 1941, with the loss of 1,416 souls (only three survived) was spotted coming out of Norway. 502 Squadron was immediately put on standby to attack her and it's Whitleys were armed with armour piercing bombs. Six crews were on permanent standby, they slept on camp beds in an old school at the edge of Limavady airfield. Eventually the word came through that the Bismarck had gone off into the Atlantic and everyone was stood down. Having been confined for such a long time Hunter said, "Right lads, we are all off into Londonderry and we will meet in the Melville Hotel for drink." (At that time it was even possible to get the odd 'steak' in Londonderry as it was close to the Southern Border.) Having had their fill of food and drink they all drove back to Limavady around midnight. At that time Hunter was living out in a greengrocers house and he remembers very well climbing into bed at one o'clock in the morning (bleutered) and at seven minutes past one the phone rang and he was instructed to report to the operations room right away. The rest of the crews had just arrived before him still quite worse the wear for drink. The intelligence people had information that the Bismarck had left Norway and was heading for France and that Hunter and the other crews had to fly their aircraft immediately to St Eval in Cornwall. They took off at 0300 hrs on the morning of the 27th May and set course for St Eval, arriving there three hours later, hoping to find and sink the Bismarck. When they landed at St Eval they went to the operations room only to be told that the Navy had the Bismarck cornered and they would not be needed. They climbed back on board their Whitleys and returned to Limavady. As we all know now the Royal Navy 'avenged' the sinking of the Hood at 1036 hrs on the morning of the 27th May when HMS King George V, HMS Rodney and HMS Dorsetshire sank the Bismarck. On the 29th May 1941 Hunter felt very honoured when he was selected to escort the King George V and eight other destroyers into Glasgow after the sinking. The flying time for the escort was seven hours, three hours by day and four hours at night.

Humorous story

Flying around the Donegal coast during a sortie, Hunter spotted a coaster that had run aground. He informed his crew that he was going to have some fun and carry out a 'practice dive-bombing' of the coaster with smoke-floats, one of which landed right on the deck of the coaster. The next thing Hunter heard was his Rear Gunner requesting him to turn the aircraft around so he could see what was happening. The crew spotted three or four blokes abandoning ship as they flew over it, Hunter reckoned it was bods stealing the ships cargo and who scarpered when they thought it was being bombed.

On July 22nd Hunter was posted to Aberdeen where he completed a 'blind approach' course and on returning to his squadron at the end of June he was again assessed as 'above the average' as a Pilot.

During the first week in October 1941 the Commanding Officer sent for Hunter and told him that he had worked extremely hard for the squadron and it was time for a rest. He had by now completed over 1,276 flying hours.

Hunter flew to Hooton Park and then continued on to Derby House which was the headquarters of the North West Approaches, were he met his old friend Flight Lieutenant George Gardiner who had been posted to there as a Controller. George offered Hunter the choice of two jobs, one was he could be an Instructor at an OTU on Whitleys or he could become an Instructor at No 3 (P) Advanced Flying Unit (AFU) at South Cerney. He had no hesitation on picking South Cerney. On the 18th October he attended a two month instructors course at the Central Flying School at Upavon near Salisbury. The course was pretty intense which he passed with an exceptionally high pass mark and, became a fully qualified Pilot and Beam Approach Instructor on the 14th December 1941. He arrived at No 3 (P) Advanced Flying Unit on the 16th December to take up his position and met the schools Chief Flying Instructor 'Speedy' Holmes who was one of the great and very well known old Sussex cricketer. The aircraft which he instructed on were Blackburn Bothas, Air Speed Oxford, Avro Anson, Bristol Blenheim, Miles Master and Magister, M18's and Tiger Moths. Hunter managed to get into a flight that had a Flight Commander and his assistant. He said that these two chaps were real hard cases when it came to instructing, and as they both were ex-Halton apprentices and who had risen from the ranks, knew all the tricks of the trade.

Just before Christmas Hunter was relaxing in the officer's mess at lunch time reading the promotions page of an RAF magazine, when he suddenly spotted that he had been promoted to Squadron Leader (first he heard of it). He went along to see the station Adjutant who rang Group Headquarters and they confirmed this as being right. George Ward from Castle Ward in Bangor County Down, Northern Ireland, had been a Squadron Commander at No 3 AFU and had just to be posted to another station. Hunter was asked by the station Adjutant would he like to take over his duties and to continue training the squadron.

On the 24th February 1943 Hunter attended a three month Advanced Instructors Course at the Empire Central Flying School at Hullavington and on completion of this particular course he was now qualified to inspect any of the bomber squadrons around the country. On the 3rd and 4th April 1943 four of them went up to check on a bomber squadron that was operating out of Linton-on-Ouse in Yorkshire. On their arrival they asked if they could go on one of the next operations. The squadron in particular was No 78 and it was tasked for a raid that night to Essen. Hunter got kitted out with flying gear and they took off in a Halifax and set a course for their objective.

When they arrived over the target it was very hairy, the sky was full of flak. A Halifax that was just in front of them was hit by the flak, it blew up and just disintegrated. The Bomb Aimer dropped his bombs and they set a course for home. On the way back over Holland, Hunter asked the Captain would he like a break and took over. Just as he was settling down to fly the Halifax the Rear Gunner shouted into the intercom, "Skipper, 'corkscrew', 'corkscrew' port, we are being attacked by a German night fighter." Luckily, Hunter being an experienced Bomber Pilot reacted right away and turned the Halifax immediately to the left, losing 500ft in a very short space of time. The German night fighter was lost as they entered cloud. Sadly one of the Instructors who took part on the raid to Essen did not return and it was left to Hunter to inform the Commanding Officer at Hullavington of the loss. Hunter was informed by a rather irate and annoyed CO, that in the first place they should never have been allowed to take part on an operation and that each one of them involved would receive a 'rocket' in due course.

One week later the crew that Hunter had flown with on the raid to Essen were shot down during attacking the Skoda arms works at Pilsen in Czechoslovakia. The Captain and Rear Gunner were killed and the rest of the crew were POWs. Back at No 3 AFU Hunter was now Officer Commanding Training and Assistant Chief Flying Instructor, teaching bods on how to become flying instructors.

On the 8th May 1944 he was posted to No 6 Advanced Flying Unit at Windrush were he became the station commander where he remained until the 23rd April 1945. Windrush was a small station with about 500 people in total and 100 of them were WAAFs (lucky WAAFs).

The air officer commanding the group contacted Hunter and said, "Hopefully we are coming to the end of the war and, it is quite possible that your station will be closing. If you like you can stay on there as Wing Commander, but there is a position for you as OC Flying at No 7 Air Navigation in Bishops Court, Northern Ireland. The only problem will be that you will have to drop down a rank to Squadron Leader." Hunter had no hesitation in accepting this posting as it would mean that he could see his wife and family every day. Hunter became OC Flying at Bishops Court in April 1945 and remained there until April 1946.

Bishops Court story, 'Cooks Tour'

In July 1945 the Chief Flying Instructor at Bishops Court, Hunter, and two others decided to go on a 'Cooks Tour' of Germany. They flew down to the USAAF base at Amber's Field on the east coast of England in an Avro Anson, refuelled and then set a course for Eindhoven in the Netherlands. Just as Hunter landed, one of the Ansons tyres burst on hitting a piece of metal on the runway. They tried in vane to get a replacement tyre locally and found themselves stranded in Eindhoven for three days. Finally, Hunter decided to position the Anson as close as he could to the control tower and asked his Wireless Operator to remove the trailing aerial and try and hook it up to the aerial on top of the tower. This he managed to do and was able to contact Bishops Court direct and informed them of their predicament. The ground crew soon had a replacement wheel and tyre flown out to Eindhoven, allowing Hunter and his party to take off again, setting course for Muchen-Gladbach, Cologne, Dusseldorf, Essen, Duisberg and finally back to Bishops Court Hunters tour finally finished at No 7 Air Navigational School in April 1946 and he left the Royal Air Force. But not for long.

The reformed 502 (Ulster) Squadron

In June 1946 it was decided to re-form the Auxiliary Air Force and 502 (Ulster) Squadron. Shortly after leaving the Royal Air Force Hunter was approached by Jack Shillington who was then the Secretary of the Territorial Army and Royal Air Force Association in Northern Ireland. He told Hunter that he would like to set up a meeting with him and Lord Londonderry at Mount Stewart for a chat regarding 502 Squadron and would he like to go.

Hunter, eager to get back into the air, accepted and after the meeting had agreed to reform the squadron and become its new Commanding Officer. Hunter was immediately re-commissioned for five years and with the job came a beautiful house on the Malone Road in Belfast, which he used as the squadrons headquarters. Hunter set about recruiting air and ground crews, of which there was no shortage of volunteers. He was given a 'Regular' Adjutant, clerk (who was later killed on a test pilots course when his aircraft collided with another aircraft) and assistant and between them they gradually built up the squadron from scratch.

The first two aircraft to arrive at the newly reformed squadron were a Harvard and an Oxford and on the 18th December 1946, the squadron received its first Canadian built Mk.B.25 Mosquito and became a Light Bomber Unit. In December 1947 the squadron converted to the night-fighter role and was re-equipped with Mosquito NF.30's. Hunter also flew the Spitfire F 22's with the squadron and just before it received the DH Vampires he decided to leave the RAF. This was mainly due to family business pressures. In 1973 Hunter was awarded an OBE by the Queen at Buckingham Palace. This award was made to him in recognition of his outstanding work with the Territorial and Royal Air Force Associations. Lord Antrim was Chairman of the Association at that time and Hunter Vice Chairman. He was asked to take on the role of Chairman but had to decline again due to pressure of running the family business.

Sadly Wing Commander W Hunter McGiffin, OBE AE, died in the autumn 2000.

List of aircraft types that Wing Commander McGiffin flew during his Air Force career: Avro 504N; Avro Tutor; Avro Cadet; Avro Anson; Hawker Hart; Airspeed Oxford; Miles Master; Percivil Proctor; Miles Magister; Tiger Moth; Miles M18 and M28; Hotspur Glider; Auster; Harvard; Hawker Hind; Hawker Demon; Armstrong Whitworth Whitley; Vickers Armstrong Wellington; Blackburn Botha; Bristol Blenheim; Bristol Beaufighter; Hawker Hurricane; Hawker Typhoon; Mustang; Supermarine Spitfire Mk1-11a and 22's; and the De Havilland Mosquito.

FLIGHT LIEUTENANT
CHARLES McKAY
ROYAL AIR FORCE NO. 571983
AIRCRAFT FITTER/AIR GUNNER/PILOT
NO. 502 (ULSTER) SQUADRON

Flight Lieutenant Charles McKay, or Chas as he liked to be called by his friends, was born in Islandmagee on the 31st December 1921. Islandmagee is situated between Carrickfergus and Larne in County Antrim. He was educated at Kilcoan Primary School on the island and then on to Carrickfergus Model Primary, finishing his education at the Royal Belfast Academical Institution (Inst).

His primary ambition was to become a veterinary surgeon but as he did not have the necessary qualifications for this he decided to join the Royal Air Force and become a Fitter. He applied to join the RAF around the end of July 1937 and was accepted one month later in August. On the 31st August 1937 he was posted to the No 1 School of Technical Training at RAF Halton where he joined No 1 (A) Wing (A.37 Entry).

On completion of his apprenticeship on the 9th December 1939 he received a very satisfactory report in his mathematics, science, drawing, general studies, technical, discipline, PT and drill and athletics and was posted back to Northern Ireland were he joined 502 (Ulster) Squadron at RAF Aldergrove. He served as an Fitter/Air Gunner with 502 Squadron at Aldergrove and was on detachment with the squadron when it moved to Limavady, St Eval and Homslet South between the 9th December 1939 and the 1st March 1943. In early March 1943 Chas decided that he wanted to become aircrew, so he applied and was sent to aircrew reception centre where he was accepted as a Pilot. He completed his initial training by early May 1944 and on the 9th May he arrived in Canada to join No 25 EFTS in Assiniboia in Saskatchewan. His elementary training started on the 9th May in a Cornell monoplane trainer. The flight was for him to gain air experience and familiarisation of the cockpit. His training continued on the Cornell through to the 16th of May when he flew his first solo. The course finished on the 14th July 1944 and his proficiency as a pilot was assessed as 'high average'. In mid July Chas was posted to a Bombing and Gunnery School at Picton that is on Prince Edward Island near Toronto. The course lasted for thirteen weeks.

On the 22nd October 1944 Chas was posted to No 16 SFTS at Haggersville near Hamilton Ontario. He embarked on his service training on Harvards on the 26th October and soloed on the type on the 13th November. He continued training on the Harvard until the 16th March 1945 when he was awarded his well deserved Wings by Prince Bernhardt of the Netherlands. The reason for this was there had been a large contingent of Dutch Pilots on his course. He was assessed as 'average' as Student Pilot and 'average' as a Pilot Navigator. On the 26th March 1945 Chas boarded a train that took him to Moncton and boarded a ship that brought him back to Harrogate in England. On his arrival back in the UK Chas was posted to No 18 EFTS at Fairoaks for ten days training on DH 82A's (Tiger Moths). He completed one through to 25 flying exercises during the course, this was just to get him used to the RAF's way of flying. At the end of the course Chas was promoted to Flight Sergeant. On the 1st October 1945 Chas was posted to No 3 PAFU at South Cerney where he started his advanced flying training on 'twins'. Between the 12th October and the 15th November he was instructed on the Link Trainer and had his first flight in the Oxford on the 16th October and soloed on the type three days later. On the 24th November 1945 he was posted to No 1547 BAT Flight at Watchfield for a few days training on Beam Approaches.

In January 1946 Chas was posted to No 10 Staff Air Navigation School at Swanton Morely where he attended a Pilot Navigational Instructors course and then on to No 6 Flying Training School at Little Rissington on the 22nd July 1948 where he received his instructors certificate and became a Staff Pilot Instructor on Ansons and Harvard, Prentice, Spitfire, Mosquito, Lancasters and Vampires. He had his first flight in a Spitfire MK X1V on the 23rd September 1948, his first flight in a Mosquito on the 15th December 1948 and his first flight in a Jet which was a Vampire solo on the 3rd December 1948 (quite an achievement for someone who was an aircraft Fitter some eight years earlier). On the 4th January 1949 Chas was posted from Little Rissington to No 4 SFTS at Ternhill where he instructed on Harvard, Prentice and Wellingtons until the 8th November 1950 when he was again transferred. His flying logbooks shows that he was assessed as 'above the average' as a Pilot.

Chas moved on to No 101 FRS at Finningley in at the end of November 1950 where he instructed on Wellingtons until the middle of February 1952. On the 7th December he visited Aldergrove in Wellington NC 920 (NF) with Sergeant Smith and two passengers, returning to base the same day. In the middle of February 1952 Chas was transferred to 215 AFS at Finningley where he was to gain experience on Meteor V11's. Had his first flight in a Meteor along with his instructor on the 14th February 1952 and soled on the type five days later. Some of his other duties allowed him to take part in Battle of Britain displays at various RAF Stations around the UK. He must have had a slight mishap on the 20th June as his log shows DNCO (crash landing) and was flying again on the 23rd. He became an instructor on Meteor's at Finningley until the 8th January 1953. His logbook assessment shows him to be 'above the average' as a Jet Pilot.

On the 4th February 1953 Chas was posted to No 98 Squadron at Fassberg in Germany as an Instructor. The squadron had become a fighter/ground attack squadron and was equipped with Vampire FB5's and Meteor 7.s and Venoms. With these types of aircraft the squadron worked up into rocketing in addition to the fighter task and continued serving as an integral part of the 2nd Tactical Air Force in Germany. On June the 2nd his log shows that he took part in the Coronation Flypast over Hamburg. Most of his log entries show that his duties were gunnery exercises, (Fassberg range, Cine gun tail chase, air to ground firing, sight test and battle formations). On the 2nd December 1954 Flight Sergeant McKay was assessed as 'above the average' as Pilot, 'average' as a Pilot Navigator, 'average' in air-to-air firing, 'above the average' in air-to-ground firing and 'master green' rating in instrument flying.

On his return to the UK on March 17th (St Patrick's Day) he received his permanent commission and promoted to Pilot Officer. He was posted to 253 Squadron at Waterbeach as an instructor. 253 Squadron had been reformed on the 17th March 1955 as a Night Fighter Squadron and was equipped with Venom NF.2A 'N'. On the 7th August 1955 he was once again on the move to No 228 OCU at Leeming as an Instructor on Meteors, Venoms and Vampires. His log book shows on the 2nd February 1957, that he was 'above the average' as a Pilot, 'above the average' as a Pilot/Navigator and as an Air Gunner he was 'exceptional'.

Chas returned to 253 Squadron on the 29th October 1955 where he continued instructing and flying in formation at 25,000ft, 35,000ft, 40,000ft, 42,000ft and 44,000ft up until the 1st February 1958 when he developed a medical problem as his flying log shows: "Pilot Officer McKay is filling a Ground Appointment with a limited medical category. He is limited to Dual Flying only," and was signed by Flight Lieutenant Bennett, Officer Commanding, Fighter Squadrons Support Section. RAF Aldergrove. Chas was posted back to Northern Ireland on the 9th September 1957 where he joined Fighter Commands Liaison Unit at RAF Aldergrove. With his flying now being curtailed his logbook shows that he flew seven times during October and only twice in November and December. On October 30th he flew a Chipmunk around for some local flying with a Sergeant Davies as his Second Pilot and the next day flew an Auster with Sergeant Davies again some local flying. On the 28th Of November it was back into the seat of the Vampire that he flew only four times during November and December. In July 1958 Chas was posted to No 4 School of Recruit Training where he embarked on a Fighter Controllers Course and qualified as Fighter Controller in January 1961 and was promoted to Flying Officer and became Fighter Controller at RAF Boulmer.

Here he controlled Javelins, Hunters, Meteors and Canberras. His Log shows that he posted to the Middle East for a week in October 1960 as Chief Fighter Controller for Exercise Jessie and in August 1961 he was Controller of an exercise that required the careful controlling of aircraft taking part in 110 runs at varying fighter target speeds at RAF Boulmer on Supersonic Overlay trials. He was detached to Cyprus (Nicosia) during the first in September 1961 and in May 1962 was promoted to Flight Lieutenant and posted to Madalena in Malta as Fighter Controller. The aircraft types that he controlled here were, Canberra, Hunter, Javelin, Devon, Venom, Valiant, Beverly, Britannia, Lightning, Sea Venom, Sea Hawk, Shackelton, Crusader and VC10s. Most of the controlling exercises were carried around Luqa, Germany, Gibraltar, France, Cyprus, El Adem, Spain and Wheelus Field.

Flight Lieutenant McKay was very keen to get back into flying so he applied and was accepted for some medical tests. His log shows that on the 7th July 1965 he completed a High Altitude Decompression Test at RAF Cranwell. The results were 'satisfactory'. In July 1965 Chas was sent to the School of Refresher Training and took to the air again on the 15th July in a Jet Provost as Second Pilot to a Flight Sergeant Waring. On the 27th July he was back in the Captain's seat. On the 19th August he took to the air in a Varsity as Co-Pilot to a Flight Lieutenant Thompson and on the 26th August he took command of the aircraft himself. In September 1965 Chas was posted to the No 2 Air Navigational School at Gaydon where he again to up the duty of Flying Instructor on Varsitys. He continued as an instructor with the school until April 1968 when he made his last flight with the Royal Air Force on the 30th April 1968 in Varsity WL632.

Flight Lieutenant Chas McKay left the Royal Air Force in May 1968 after thirty one years and having amassed 3,000 flying hours as a 1st Pilot and 4,100 flying hours as a dual Pilot in 20 different types of aircraft. These included: DH.82 A; Cornell; Harvard; Oxford; Anson; Prentice; Spitfire; Mosquito; Lancaster; Vampire; Balliol; Wellington; Meteor; Venom; Chipmunk; and Auster.

On the 14th June 1968 Flight Lieutenant C McKay received the following letter from the Secretary of State:

The Secretary of State for Defence has it in Command from her Majesty the Queen to convey to you on leaving the Active List of the Royal Air Force her thanks for your long and invaluable Services.

May I take this opportunity of wishing you all good fortune in the future.

Signed: Merlyn Rees

On Leaving the Royal Air Force Chas became the fire prevention officer to the Eastern Health Board that took in hospitals and old peoples residences, finally retiring in 1983. Sadly Chas died in Islandmagee on the 5th December 1989 and is survived by his wife Erika and son Robert who still live in the family home on the Lower Road Islandmagee.

SERGEANT
PATRICK McKENNY
ROYAL AIR FORCE NO 1014144
PILOT
NO. 114 (HONG KONG) SQUADRON
WEST RAYHAM

Patrick McKenny was born in Dromore, County Tyrone, in 1919, and was educated at the Christian Brother's School in Omagh. He left Dromore in the 1930's to take up employment with the firm of Mycocks in Manchester, England.

He left Mycocks to join the Royal Air Force as a Pilot and unfortunately I have little information regarding where or when he completed his Pilot training, before he joined 114 Squadron at West Rayham.

Sergeant Patrick McKenny's last operation with 114 Squadron was on the 24th/25th April 1942. He took off from West Rayham in Norfolk with his crew, Sergeant J McIntyre and Sergeant J Lewis at 2215 hrs on 24th April 1942 in Bristol Blenheim Mk 1V (V5458) RT-O. Their operation that night was an intruder over Leeuwarden airfield in northern Holland. They were lost without trace and all of them are remembered on Panel 88 of the Runnymede Memorial. Sergeant McKenny and his crew are also honoured in No 2 Group Bomber Command's Roll of Honour.

SERGEANT
ROBERT CHARLES McLAREN
ROYAL AIR FORCE NO. 1515312
NAVIGATOR
NO. 626 SQUADRON

KILLED IN ACTION 14TH JANUARY 1944

Robert Charles McLaren was born in Ballykeel, Sixmilecross, in the County of Tyrone in 1924. He was the youngest son of Mr Thomas James McLaren and Mrs Emma McLaren. He was educated at Ballykeel Primary School, and in 1940 he joined Queens University in Belfast, where he studied Medicine. He joined the Air Squadron at Queens and was called to full-time service in May 1942.

On completion of a medical and air crew selection board, he was assigned the job of Navigator. He was then posted to an initial training wing for basic training and then on to a navigation school for his basic and advanced navigation training. In April 1943 he was promoted to the rank of Sergeant and in December 1943 was posted to No 626 Squadron at Wickonby in Lincolnshire. The squadron was equipped with the four engined Avro Lancaster Mk I and 111's, and its motto was, "To Strive and Not to Yield."

Sadly on the 15th January 1944 Sergeant McLaren's father received a letter from 626 Squadrons Commanding Officer, which informed him that his son had been reported missing. The Commanding Officer also said, "Sergeant McLaren had during his short time with us made many friends and he will be sadly missed. Personally I had every confidence in his courage and ability. All ranks here wish to join with me in offering their deepest sympathies to you in your great anxiety." On the 14th January 1944 Sergeant McLaren and the crew of Lancaster Serial No. ME576. Code UM-A2 took off from Wickonby at 1645 hrs. Their target was the city of Braunschweig (Brunswick). It is known only that their Lancaster crashed near Halberstadt where all were initially buried. In 1945 their remains were exhumed and re-interred in the British Military War Cemetery in Berlin.

The crew of Lancaster UM-A2 were:

Flight Sergeant KN Elkington
Sergeant BG Martin
Sergeant RC McLaren
Flight Sergeant AM Goodall RCAF

Sergeant LJ Pasfield
Sergeant MA Brooks
Sergeant AA Johnson

The Squadron
The squadron was formed at Wickonby in Lincolnshire on the 7th November 1943 and formed part of No 1 Group's Heavy Bomber Ranks. It took part in many of the attacks on enemy targets, and after its final raid, helped to drop food to the starving Dutch people, and later took part in the re-patriation of British Prisoners of War, and bringing home troops from Italy. The squadron was disbanded in October 1945.

The operation
This was to be the first major raid of the war to Brunswick. Almost 500 Lancaster's took part in the attack, 38 of them did not return. Eleven of the aircraft were Pathfinders. It is known that many German night fighters entered the bomber stream soon after they had crossed the German frontier near Bremen. Two other Irish men lost their lives that night on the same raid. Flying Officer G Colbert, DFC, from Sixmilecross (156 Squadron), and Flight Sergeant Samuel Brown Stevenson, DFM, from Fahan in County Donegal (No 97 Squadron). On the 13th June 1944 Mr Thomas McLaren received a letter from the War Organisation's British Red Cross Society and Order of St John of Jerusalem Wounded Missing and Relatives Department, which said that there was still no news of their son. However, the letter also said that the International Red Cross had received a report that five airmen, who were flying in the same aircraft, had been buried by the Germans at

Halberstadt, which was 32 miles south-east of Brunswick. It was not until October, 1948, that the McLaren family were able to discover where their son 'might' be buried, thanks due to a 'Silver Cigarette Case'.

A letter from the Air Ministry dated October 27th that year, said, that in one of the graves at Halberstadt, a silver cigarette case marked with the initials 'C McC' had been found. Sergeant McLaren's mother remembered that her son had been given a present of a silver cigarette case by his girlfriend, and decided to contact Sir Ronald Ross of Dunmoyle to see if they could find the girl who lived in Londonderry. Thankfully the girl was found and she confirmed that she had given Charles the case but did not know at that time that his surname was spelt with an 'L' and not a 'C'. This information was forwarded to the Air Ministry, and in March 1949 Mr McLaren received a letter which said it could now confirm that his son was buried in Halberstadt Cemetery. The cigarette case was eventually sent back to the family and is now in the possession of Sergeant McLaren's brother, Lexie. Sergeant McLaren's brother Lexie, his wife Ida, and their grand-daughter Ruth visited his grave in Charlottenburg in 1993.

FLIGHT LIEUTENANT
RICHARD WORTLEY McLERNON, DFC
PILOT
NO. 571 PATHFINDER FORCE SQUADRON

Flight Lieutenant Richard McLernon was born in Belfast in 1921 and was educated at the Royal Belfast Academical Institute.

Following the outbreak of war he decided to join the Royal Air Force, so in February 1941 he went to the recruiting office at Clifton Street to offer his services as aircrew. He was accepted and soon boarded the Liverpool boat and the next stop was Padgate Receiving Centre. He arrived at Padgate on the 20th February 1941 and after being sworn in, signing the necessary documents he went to Number 1 Receiving Wing at Babbacombe where he was accepted as aircrew.

On the 29th March 1941 he was posted to Number 8 Initial Training Wing (ITW) at Newquay to start his basic training, square bashing, etc. Having completed his basic training he was then posted to Number 4 Personnel Dispatch Centre at West Kirby on the 29th May to await an overseas posting. Thirteen days later on the 12th June he boarded HMS California which was an armed Merchant Cruiser and sailed for Canada.

The California had a gross weight of 16,792 tons and her top speed was 16 knots and her main armament was eight six-inch guns. The ship arrived at Halifax Nova Scotia towards the end of June, it wasn't long before Richard boarded a train which was to take him to No 32 Elementary Flying Training School at Swift Current in Saskatoon changing trains at Montreal on the way. He arrived at Swift Current at the latter end of June with other RAF personnel at it wasn't long before they settled into their new surroundings.

His first air experience flight at Swift Current was in a Tiger Moth on the 14th July 1941 under the instruction of Pilot Officer Vokes. Pilot Officer Bradbury took over on the 23rd July teaching him the art of basic flying. His big day came on the 1st August when he had just completed 9hrs.30mins training, Flight Lieutenant Bullmore who was one of the school's senior flying instructors took him up for a test flight to see if he was ready to fly solo. They landed and Flight Lieutenant

Bullmore gave Richard the thumbs up and off he went on his own, his first solo.

He continued his flying training at Swift Current until the end of August and his first assessment of ability as a pilot was 'average' and signed in his flying log by the Station Commanding Officer Wing Commander FB Burton on the 2nd September 1941. A few days later he was posted to number 34 Service Flying Training School (SFTS) in Alberta where he started training on twin engined Oxfords. His first flight in an Oxford was on the 6th September under the instruction of Flight Lieutenant Price. He continued training on the Oxford until the 30th September when he did a solo test with Flight Lieutenant Hunter and flew solo himself the same day. LAC McLernon finished the course at the end of November having accumulated 138hrs.45mins flying training and was awarded his wings on the 28th November 1941 and was assessed in his logbook as 'average' Pilot/Navigator by the school's Commanding Officer.

On the 1st December 1941 he went by train to Number 3 'Y' at Debert for a week and then on to Number 3 'Y' at Halifax Nova Scotia waiting for a week for a ship to take him back to the UK.

On the 13th December he boarded HMS Letitia which headed out onto the Atlantic and sailed for England. This wasn't the first time he had come into contact with the Letitia, when he was ten years old she ran aground at Groomsport near Bangor in County Down and he went down to see it with his parents.

He arrived back in England towards the end of December and on Boxing Day was posted to Number 3 Personnel Reception Centre (PRC) at Bournemouth and on the 8th February he was posted to 1520 Beam approach training flight at Holme-on-Spalding Moor. This was a short course lasting two weeks finishing on the 22nd February. On the 22nd February he was posted to

Number 11 Advanced Flying Unit at Shawbury to become an Instructor teaching navigation. When the instructors course finished on the 26th May he was posted to Number 5 Air Observers School (AOS) at Jurby in the Isle of Man to train Navigators. The Navigation Training was carried out in Blenheims and a lot of the time over his homeland Northern Ireland, a couple of typical training routes over Northern Ireland were Base to Kesh, Ballymena, Dungannon, Newry, Downpatrick, and Base. Base to Kesh, Antrim, Portrush, Newry, Downpatrick, and Base.

On the 13th July he was posted even closer to home at Number 7 Air Observers School at Bishops Court in County Down which was only a stone's throw from his home. This time the training was carried out in Avro Ansons and again a lot of the training took place over Northern Ireland. It was about this time that he put in a request to his Commanding Officer that he would like to join an operational squadron, his request was granted and he was put on the operational list. He continued instructing with the school until his posting came through for OTU training in January 1944. Before leaving Bishops Court his logbook shows that he was assessed as 'above the average' as a Staff Pilot and 'above the average" as a Pilot Navigator/Navigator. In February 1944 he was posted to Number 26 Operational Training Unit at Little Horwood in Bucks to start training on Wellingtons. During his training he completed some decompression tests and his log book shows:

This is to certify that Pilot Officer McLernon-Pilot-26 OTU has been subjected to Decompression Chamber Tests in view of selection for High Altitude Flying Tests carried out in accordance with H.Q.92 Group letter 92G/S1/24/MED Dated 6.5.43. (App: B S88423 Dated 6.4.43.Total for Complete Tests:- 4 Hours at 37,000 feet.

Found fit for high altitude flying

Signed CF Down F/O
Medical Officer
IC SSQ 26 OTU RAF

He completed the course by the middle of March and his log book assessment for the 18th March shows that he was 'above the average' as a Pilot on Wellington 3 and 5's.

On the 20th March 1944 he was posted to 1665 Mosquito Training Unit which was based at Warboys. His first flight in a Mosquito with the unit was on the 21st March under the instruction of Flight Lieutenant Hatton, he flew with him on the 23rd and on the 26th flew a solo test with Flight Lieutenant Broom, later to become Air Marshal Sir Ivor Broom, KCB CBE DSO DFC ** AFC. Pilot Officer McLernon continued training in the Mosquito with 1665 Unit until the 10th May 1944 and was assessed as 'average' as a Mosquito Pilot. With all his operational training completed he was now ready to join an operational squadron and he didn't have long to wait. On the same day that he finished his training he was

posted to 571 Squadron which was based at Downham Market in Norfolk.

571 Squadron was formed at Downham Market in Norfolk, as a light bomber unit of Number 8 Pathfinder Force(PFF) group's Light Night Striking Force and was equipped with the Mosquito MKXV1. A detachment at Gravely received the first aircraft and began operations from there on the 12th/13th April. The squadron moved from Downham Market to Oakington near Cambridge in the middle of April 1944 and remained there until after VE Day. 571 Squadron was mainly engaged in the bombing of German industrial targets and in particular Berlin. The squadron's main armament was the 4,000lb 'Cookies' and during march 1945, visited Berlin on no less than 22 nights, The squadron was also involved in mine-laying against the Dortmund Ems Canal and the first daylight attack on the synthetic oil plant at Duisberg. Each 571 Squadron Mosquito was fitted with the Navigational Aid Gee and Loran . The Gee type that was used was the Gee RF 25 set or the later version the RF27 set for long range navigation. This device was designed to receive radar signals from three fixed transmitters stationed in the UK and after October 1944 from three fixed stations which were established in France and were known as the Rheims Chain.

Loran was also a long range navigational aid and it's aim was to improve navigational accuracy beyond the range of Gee. Loran was a result of joint US and British Scientific development and was originally developed to aid aircrew flying over the ocean. On the 10th of May 1944 Pilot Officer McLernon met his Navigator Pilot Officer Deacon who was to remain with him until he left the squadron in January 1945. They flew together as a team on the morning of the 10th May 1944 and later that day flew on their first operation with the squadron which was to Ludwigshaven. The attacking Mosquito force varied between 27 and 30 aircraft. Ludwigshaven was visited no less than nine times in May.

Their next operation was on the 14th May to Cologne and on the 16th May paid their first visit to Berlin. They visited Cologne again on the 19th and Berlin for the second time on the 22nd. On the 21st May they visited Hanover and Berlin again on the 23rd and the 27th. They visited Ludwigshaven for a second time on the 29th May. On the 30th May they were tasked to attack and bomb Leberkusen, their Mosquito ML 941 was armed with a 4,000lb 'Cookie'. Pilot Officer McLernon and his Navigator Pilot Officer Deacon took off from Oakingdon at 23.06 and headed for the enemy coast. Pilot Officer Stan Deacon however developed problems following the siphoning of fuel from the drop tanks. They had just reached 28,000 feet and crossed the enemy coast when the starboard engine began to cut out. Vapour locks had built up in the fuel system. They tried unsuccessfully to correct this problem but with the engine faltering continually they decided to abort the primary target and head instead for Dusseldorf. In clear conditions they began to approach the city, where the defences, now they had been alerted soon sent up many searchlight beams in their direction. The flak commander however, knowing that only one aircraft was involved did not bother to fire. Pilot Officer Deacon identified the bend in the River Rhine and then at 0027 hrs over the centre of the city he released the 'cookie' and landed back at Oakingdon one hour later. They had completed tenoperations over enemy territory during May:

Visiting Berlin on four occasions;
Visiting Cologne on two occasions;
Visiting Ludwigshaven on two occasions;
Visiting Hanover on one occasion; and
Visiting Dusseldorf on one occasion.

June 1944

June was the month in which the Allies launched their invasion of Europe and Bomber Command's war efforts were directed in support of this invasion in Normandy. It was also the month that 571 achieved the status of a two flight squadron. The squadron flew 21 out of the 30 nights in June and dispatched some 216 sorties in total. 195 reached their primary targets 18 their secondary, whilst three were aborted. On the 28th June the entire squadron was directed by the Master Bomber to bomb Metz rather than Saarbrucken which was the designated primary target. In June 1944 Pilot Officer McLernon and Pilot Officer Deacon carried out seven operations visiting Berlin three times and Leverkusen/Osnabruck/Homberg and Saarbrucken once.

July 1944

In July they carried out eight operations against Buer-Sholven, Homberg, Berlin, Hamburg, and Frankfurt. On the 16th July in ML120 crashed whilst landing following a raid on Homberg. The aircraft was a write off. In this incident Pilot Officer McLernon made a normal landing but as the aircraft settled the undercarriage began to collapse. Immediately he opened up the throttles in an attempt to take off again but unfortunately there was not quick enough response from the engines and the aircraft pancaked onto the runway. The accident was caused by a faulty selection box and no fault was attributed to the Pilot. The highlight of the month was undoubtedly the visit of HRH King George V1, Queen Elizabeth and HRH Princess Elizabeth on the 5th July. Pilot Officer McLernon recalls that prior to the visit a trial parade was held under the 'eyes' of the station Warrant Officer. The visit lasted about one hour.

Their attack on the 4th July to Sholven Buer was on an oil plant in the Ruhr and they visited Berlin again on the 18th/23rd and 24th July. Their last operation in July was on the 28th to Frankfurt.

August 1944

In August they carried out nine operations against Hanover, Berlin, Mannheim, Cologne, Hamburg and Frankfurt. On the 13th August the squadron dispatched nine aircraft to form part of a 30 strong Mossie attack on Hanover. Flying Officer McLernon recalls flying over the Dutch coast in MM121, they saw two large explosions in the vicinity of The Hague. These may have been V1's as no major Bomber Command attacks were directed to that area. Their route took them near Munster and Osnabruck flak defences and several crews were coned and fired on. The Hanover defences were caught out that night as the opposition was weak the operation was a complete success and all the crews were back at base by 0200 hrs. They attacked Berlin on the 14th, 16thand 25th, Mannheim on the 17th and27th. Their last operation of the month was to Frankfurt on the 30th. One brilliant raid carried out by 571 Squadron was to mine the Dortmund Ems Canal on the 9th-10th of August. The Dortmund Ems Canal was opened in 1889, and was 168 miles long, being part of the Mitteland canal system. It was 125ft wide, 16ft deep and had a flat bottom section of some 59ft.

Barges of up to 600 tons moved raw materials and manufactured goods along it between the Rhur area of Dortmund and the sea. By 1944 the traffic was measured in millions of tons, much of it being strategic war production material. The object of the operation was to disrupt the flow of traffic along the canal at some suitable point where mine laying was feasible. The strategic planners decided that six mile straight stretch of the canal near the Rhine north of Munster was a suitable place. The weapon used was the A MK 1V mine commonly known as the 1,500lb A MK 1-1v mine which was a cylindrical container120 inches long and 18 inches in diameter. It could be triggered by either an acoustic or magnetic emission from a ship or by incorporating a time delay. The mine itself was composed of either 750lb of Amatol or 775lbs of Minol explosive.

The crews used a five to six mile stretch of the old Bedford River which was largely unobstructed and without any farms near to it. Crews would climb to a height of about 25,000ft over the fens and then the Navigator guided the Pilot onto the correct approach path. When about 12 miles from the dykes the Pilot put the nose down and the Mossie went into a dive at 260 knots. When the aircraft was done to about 10,000ft the flaps were lowered and the bomb door opened to slow the dive to about 200 knots . The final approach was made at about 200ft and the Mossie was guided to an imaginary AP on the dyke by the Navigator. 16 aircraft were detailed for the mining operation, ten of which came from 571 squadron The mining operation to the Dortmund Ems canal on the 9th/10th August was a complete success. Everyone made it back safely to Oakington, with the 'Brooms' landing first at 0418 hrs

At debriefing back at Oakington, AVM Bennet was on hand to learn of the outcome of the operation and to congratulate the returning crews after their novel attack. The outcome seemed to be seven out of ten mines hit the target for 571 Squadron, with one probable and no losses.

I would like to say a few words about Air Marshal Sir Ivor Broom and his Navigator:

Sir Ivor enlisted in the RAFVR in 1939 leaving behind his job in the Inland Revenue Service in Ipswich. After training as a Pilot he was posted to 114 Squadron flying Blenheim Mk 1v's. He completed 12 operations before he was posted to Malta. He served with distinction in 105 and 107 squadrons between July and September 1941 and completed a further 33 operations The island was at this time under intense enemy bombardment from the air and at one point he found himself in command of 107 Squadron as a Sergeant Pilot, all the commissioned pilots having been killed, or posted missing. He was commissioned Pilot Officer on the spot and eventually posted back to the UK and eventually finished up as an Instructor on 1655 Mosquito Training Unit (MTU). It was at 1655 MTU that he met his Navigator Tommy Broom who had earlier crashed in Belgium. He had escaped back to England through the Resistance Escape Network and following a commission was posted to 1655 MTU as Chief Ground Instructor. On 571 Squadron they flew together in MM 118 coded 'R' for Romeo, the aircraft having two crossed broomsticks painted on the fuselage below the cockpit, and beneath it the inscription "The Flying Brooms". On the 8th August they were both granted immediate awards, Tommy the DFC and Sir Ivor a Bar to his DFC.

Sir Ivor Broom is now Sir Ivor Broom, KCB CBE DSO DFC ** AFC and Tommy added a Bar to his DFC for his efforts in bombing a railway tunnel on the 1st January 1945.

September 1944

In September Flight Lieutenant McLernon carried out six operations they visited Bremen on the 1st and 17th. Hanover on the 5th and 18th to Frankfurt on the 12th and 15th to Keil, and Berlin also on the 18th. In October they carried out ten operations, visiting: Brunswick on the 2nd; 'Gardening' on the 5th; Berlin on the 11th and 27th; Cologne on the 13th and 28th; Hamburg on the 15th and 23rd; and Wiesbaden on the 23rd. Berlin was bombed on the 27th, this was the largest Mosquito attack on the capital to date. It was bombed in two waves by a force of 60 Mosquitoes on the 27th, 571 despatched four aircraft to support the first wave and eight on the second. The marking was carried out by 139 squadron aircraft equipped with H2S under the direction of a Master Bomber. There was a great deal of cirrus cloud about, with 10/10ths cover at times between 20-29,000ft, and beneath this there was a layer of alto stratus cloud between 15-19,000ft. As a consequence crews had difficulty in locating the Rms en-route to the target. The crews judged because of the bad weather it was not worth the effort.

Pilot Officer McLernon had a minor mishap on the afternoon of the 28th before the operation actually started. At about 1530 hrs crews were completing their night flying tests to ensure that the aircraft and its equipment was fully functional, when MM121 was pranged. What happened was Pilot Officer McLernon was taxing along the perimeter to the main runway when the aircraft's brakes failed to hold and the aircraft swung off the strip onto the grass and into a ditch. The starboard undercarriage leg collapsed and the tail swung into a stationary bowser. The aircraft was taken away to the workshops for repair and it never flew operationally again.

October 5th Operation to mine the Kiel Canal

The Kiel Canal owed its existence to 19th century German aspirations to become a significant naval power like Britain. It was constructed to allow naval vessel passage between the North Sea and the Baltic Sea without the need to pass through the straits between Norway and Denmark. The Kaiser Wilhelm, or Keil canal, opened in 1895 and was some 61 miles long, flowing at sea level through the state of Schleswig Holstien. The canal gave access from the naval town of Keil with its dockyards, construction yards, arsenals and engineering works to the German inland ports. By 1944 the canal was 335ft wide with a flat bottom section of 144ft and with a depth of 36ft. The port of Keil had by 1944 a population of 250,000 people and from it German Naval vessels, including submarines sailed forth to attack Allied shipping. Millions of tons of war materials were transported through the canal every year.

It was decided to disrupt the movement of material and vessels by mining the canal. For this operation to be successful a fairly straight section of waterway had to be attacked otherwise it would be impossible to drop the mines accurately into the canal. The code name for the operation was Operation Lettuce and it was scheduled for the night of the 5/6th of October, with nine Mosquitoes of Number 8 Group detailed to mine the canal using the tactics as those used against the Dortmund Ems Canal.

571 Squadron's contribution to this operation was to be 4 crews. The Battle orders for the 5th October 1944 was:

ML 942 'D'	W/C RJ Gosnell S/L RY Ashley 2043-2341 hrs
PF 387 'F'	F/L CC Margerison F/L RJ Clark 2044-2358 hrs
MM 118 'M'	S/L RJ Greenleaf P/O KR Rendell 2045-0022 hrs
MM 121 'T'	F/O RW McLernon F/O S Deacon 2046-0013 hrs

The weather was perfect, with the moon fully out, giving perfect visibility for the night bombing operation, they could see Heligoland Island clearly below. This was their turning point for the Danish coast. Over the mainland they flew between Heide and Meldorf, and at the appropriate descent point put on full flaps, opened the bomb doors and dived to 1,000ft to look for the red spot markers on the ground. These had fallen accurately about one mile south of the village of Offenbuttel which was to the west of the canal. From this point they turned onto a course of 090 degrees true and held it until the canal appeared ahead. Then they turned over it and flew down to 200ft on the final bombing run. There was a thin ground mist hanging on the floor of the valley at about 50ft but with little or no wind there was no problems with drift. Flying Officer McLernon dropped his 1,500lb naval mine almost at the junction of the canal with the Gieslau Canal.

The canal was protected by a string of flak towers all of which were ready and waiting. Flight Lieutenant Chris Margerison and Flight Lieutenant Bob Clark in PF 387 remembers his final run along the canal. He comments: "After dropping the mine the guns were throwing up so much 'rice' at us, that I flew down below the tree level. The trees were over the wings! Bob yelled, 'What's the matter Chris? Watch out for those wires.' There was no way I was going to start to climb." Squadron Leader Johnny Greenleaf and Pilot Officer Rendell began their approach and although they 'gardened' without any problems, as they climbed away from the canal their aircraft was hit by cannon fire. A 37mm shell fragment hit the aircraft shattering the Perspex canopy flinging plastic fragments into the Pilot's face. The shell struck him on the left arm and then hit the Navigator in the head killing him instantly. Squadron Leader Greenleaf's oxygen mask was torn from his face and his injury and the blast had left him momentarily dazed. The air was rushing in through all the holes in the canopy and the fuselage, its blast icy. Glancing over to the Navigators position where Kenneth Rendell should have been sitting he saw the body of his Navigator slumped on the cockpit floor. One glance was sufficient to confirm that he was dead. The aircraft responded to the controls despite the damage, and using his emergency route card which he had stuffed down his boot he set a course for the English coast which he reached some 40 minutes later. He immediately recognised the area and turned towards Woodbridge and made an emergency landing there at 0020 hrs. The ambulance took him to hospital for treatment, but for him there was to be no more operational flying, just a long stay in hospital.

For his heroic efforts in bringing home his aircraft and navigator he was granted the immediate award of the DSO, though many of his friends believed he should have received the VC.

Flying Officer Richard Wortley McLernon was awarded the Distinguished Flying Cross on the 19th October 1944. His last operation with 571 Squadron was on the 28th October 1944 ,his task was to attack and bomb Cologne.

733 aircraft attacked Cologne that night, the force was made up of 428 Lancasters, 286 Halifaxs, 19 Mosquitoes. Four Halifax and three Lancaster's were lost. He had by now carried out 50 operations over enemy territory all of which bar two his aircraft carried the 4,000lb 'Cookie' bomb. In January 1945 the number of operational sorties dispatched by the squadron dropped dramatically. The prime reason for this was the bad weather conditions during the month, a combination of fog and low cloud. There were however two other contributory factors, firstly the loss of three aircraft and one damaged, and secondly the loss of aircrew through postings. For the first time since its inception, no new aircrew personnel were posted into the squadron during the month. Pilot Officer McLernon and Flying Officer Deacon's tour of duty was now expired, and it was here that they parted company each being posted to separate OTU's.

Pilot Officer McLernon was promoted to Flight Lieutenant and posted to number 16 Operational Training Unit as an Instructor. He arrived at the unit on the 7th January 1945 and started flying Mosquito Mk 3's on the 16th January. On the 21st February he was detached to Number 3 Flying Instructors School 77 Course where he completed his Instructor's Course .The course finished on the 7th April and he was assessed as an 'average' Flying Instructor and awarded the Category 'C' in his logbook. He returned to 16 OTU at Upper Heyford to take up the job of instructing on Mosquitoes and on the 14th July was detached to Bomber Command Instructor's School at Finningley for an advanced instructors course (which finished on my birthday the 21st August 1945). He was assessed at the end of this fiveweek course as 'average' as a Pilot Instructor and returned to 16 OTU at Upper Heyford. He was now a fully fledged Instructor and hated it, he continued instructing with the unit until the 26th April when he had his final flight in a Mosquito.

His last log entry shows:

April 3rd   Mosquito Mk 3 No 'L' Self & F/O
              Woirin Ex 3

On his demobilization in May 1946 his logbook shows that he was assessed as 'above the average' as a Mosquito Pilot and it was signed by Squadron Leader JR Goodman for the chief instructor No 16 OTU. On his demob Flight Lieutenant McLernon had completed 50 Operations flown a total of 1732hrs.15mins in Tiger Moth, Oxford, Anson, Blenheim, Wellington and all Mk's of Mosquito up Mk16. He returned to Northern Ireland and rejoined the Civil Service's Education Branch and finally retired in 1985 and is a member of the Aircrew Association Northern Ireland Branch.

WING COMMANDER
KENNETH WILLIAM MacKENZIE, DFC
AFC AE FIME
ROYAL AIR FORCE NO. 84017.
BATTLE OF BRITAIN PILOT
NO. 43, 247 & 501 SQUADRONS

Wing Commander Kenneth William MacKenzie was born in Belfast in on 8th June 1916 and was educated at South Down Preparatory College, in Eastbourne England and then at Methody College Belfast. Ken's father Dr WR MacKenzie was an eminent surgeon at the Samaritans Hospital on the Lisburn Road for many years and later Consultant to the Royal Ulster Constabulary in Enniskillen.

He was also a surgeon in the Royal Army Medical Corps during the First Word War and held the rank of Captain. His mother was a Matron during the First World War in England on the south coast, and later became a County Officer in the St John's Ambulance in Enniskillen during the Second World War. In 1950 she received an MBE and went on to become a Justice of the Peace.

Ken played a lot of rugby at Methody, and also enjoyed some success in athletics. Making model-flying aircraft became a craze for Ken, making them accurate even to the smallest detail. He made models both big and small with some of the miniatures being fashioned to scale in compressed paper and wood. Ken also made model ships to scale and won many prizes for his work. He was also mechanically minded as well as air-minded, and had a gift for tuning car engines, some of the successes won by Ulster racing drivers were directly due to his genius in this direction. It was in 1934 when Alan Cobham, as he was then visited the Sydenham area on the outskirts of Belfast with his famous Flying Circus. This was quite a historical event for Belfast, as the area used was destined to become Belfast's first Civilian Airport that was situated at the head of Belfast Lough and close to the plane makers Short and Harlands.

Ken decided to invest seven shillings and sixpence (old money) on a short flight in one of the Circus' Avro 504 aircraft and from the moment he landed he decided that flying was what he wanted to do. On leaving Methody College he started an Engineering Apprenticeship at Harland and Wolf before going on to Queens University to study for an Engineering Degree, and wondering if by combining both air and ground interests could be

envisaged. There was little thought of war at that time, although Germanys re-arming programme was well publicised. In 1935 Ken was overjoyed to hear that Airwork Limited were opening up what was to become the Northern Ireland Aero Club at Newtownards airport which was situated at the head of Strangford Lough, and the western boundary on the famous Comber Straight, part of the Ulster TT Race Course. With the approval and support of his parents, Ken became one of the club's founder members and still to this day come September he presents the Civilian Wings to the clubs new Pilots. Ken commenced flying as soon as possible with the club. The clubs Chief Flying Instructor (CFI) at that time was a Mr Bryant, who was ex Royal Air Force, and who brought the RAF high standards into the Civilian Club Program and sequences.

The new club also enjoyed the Patronage of Lord Londonderry who was the Secretary of State for Air and who's estates covered most of the local area. Some of the Londonderry family also became members and learnt to fly there. The club was equipped with Avro Cadets, which were powered by a 25 Horse Power Siddeley Lynx engine. These aircraft were similar in general specification and performance to the Avro Tutors that were being used by the RAF for elementary instruction. Ken flew solo in six and a half hours and thereafter enjoyed days and weekends of intensive training and instruction in all the facts of elementary flying training, navigation, X country and aerobatics eventually obtaining his 'A' license. This early training played a very important part later in his Air Force career. Ken also enjoyed spending time in the club's hangar with the aircraft Fitters learning their practices and maintenance schedules from them, and always listening and learning 'when allowed'. The CFI encouraged Ken to perfect his aerobatic skills and turned a blind eye to his blatant showing off over Bangor Bay at weekends. The CFI knew that Ken was a born aviator and encouraged him to work towards his assistant instructors license.

Ken was now studying hard at Queens University for his Engineering degree, and was a member of the Universities Officer Training Corps (OTC) Royal Corps of Signals. The Civil Air Guard training was well underway in England and the RAF Volunteer Reserve Schools well into their stride, whilst the Auxiliary Squadrons were expanding and being re-equipped with modern aircraft. With War clouds gathering over the country, Ken decided to join 502 (Ulster) Squadron Auxiliary Air Force squadron that was stationed at RAF Aldergrove, and close to the shores of Lough Neagh. This seemed a good idea at the time though the prospect of flying a lumbering great Handley page Heyford bomber did not appeal to him as he felt he would be more suited to fighters. Ken filled in the appropriate application form and sent it along with a brief CV and waited for an interview. He also had a love for fast cars, his first one was a Wolseley Hornet Swallow (two seater), which cost him £20. After a year he exchanged it for a 1934 MG 'PA' that had belonged to Terry McCombe, later (Wing Commander McCombe). Ken loved this car and had it tuned to perfection, so well tuned that he came in third in a race at Phoenix Park in Dublin.

It was not long before Ken received his appointment for 502 Squadron Auxiliary Air Force and duly reported to the Adjutants office at RAF Aldergrove. Having had two years University OTC Training, Ken had a sound grounding in discipline, but also had a fair share of an Ulsterman's distrust and tolerance of 'Bull'.

Therefore, his first 'rub' with the regular Air Force in the shape of this tubby, unfit little Squadron Leader interviewing officer did not go down too well. His manner, facetious questions, lack of knowledge and contempt for civilians and general attitude put Ken off right away. So much so, Ken thanked him for his trouble and wasting his time and left the Adjutant spluttering with rage. The Royal Air Force Reserve had just opened an office in Belfast City centre in Royal Avenue above the Saxone shoe shop. They also started a flying school at Sydenham, which was now fully established as an airfield in the form of No 24 Elementary and Reserve Flying Training School. The school was run by Short Brothers and Harland whose shipyards and administration buildings were adjacent on the road to the airfield. Ken decided to try there, so he joined the RAFVR in early 1939 and having already had some basic flying experience stood by him. The schools Chief Flying Instructor was a Flight Lieutenant D Sloan who had been seconded from the RAF. He was assisted by Flight Sergeant W Lake, both of whom were qualified RAF Flying Instructors and ex Central Flying School (CFS) and last but not least Flight Lieutenant George Lindsay (later awarded the Air Force Cross) who was transferred from Aldergrove.

Ken started his flying training in Tiger Moths and soon graduated onto Hawker variants, Hind (dual), Audax and Harts. All entrants into the RAFVR were initially Sergeants and this status was resented as they were absorbed into the Regular Air Force Units.

The RAFVR was conceived for a rapid expansion the Pilot and Navigator establishment that was necessary for the upcoming emergency. The lads in the VR at Sydenham were a mixed bunch of individuals, coming from all walks of life and social backgrounds, with one common factor, a keenness to fly, either because of their love for flying, or because of the threat of war and a desire to get into it early. Most of them were either professionally qualified, training to be, or in jobs already and not dependent upon the RAFVR for salary. Ken had now planned to make flying his career and combine it with engineering were possible either as a civilian or in the RAF. War was now certain and everyone looked forward to it, just as they would a rugger match without any thought for political or national implications. At Sydenham, under Flight Lieutenant David Sloan and his team of Flying Instructors, moral was high, attendance intensive and the instruction could not be faulted. David Sloan was the typical RAF type, extrovert, with a ginger mustache, ruddy complexion and infectious manner, and a very easy going attitude, but suffered fools with a quiet discipline. Flight Sergeant William Lake, was a likable, sardonic and vastly experienced NCO of the best possible type. Their team was a marvelous combination to handle the mixed bag of Ulstermen. The town centre instructors were either seconded RAF of retired RAF.

The servicing crews at 24 E& RFTS were mainly local or Short and Harland engineers with a couple of Ex RAF retired senior NCO's who had years of experience on the Hawker variants and Rolls Royce engines. Ken's respect for the ground crews was born at 24 E&RFTS and has never wavered, he told me that their efficiency and dedication was enhanced by their sense of humor and was found nowhere else. Ken's previous flying experience on Avro cadets and having obtained his 'A' License stood by him in good steed. So much so, when he had his first air experience flight in a Tiger Moth in the VR on 17th March (St Patrick's Day) with Flight Sergeant Lake he was able to fly solo the same day and it wasn't long before he graduated onto the Hawker variants. He resigned from the Northern Ireland Aero Club and the OTC at Queens University and gave up any ideas to become an assistant instructor at Newtownards to concentrate on the VR. In this way he was lucky and able to get in many hours concentrated training that included x-country flights to Scotland and England. The VR pay kept him in pocket money and helped to pay the running costs of his little MG 'PA'.

24 E&RFTS received several more Hawker variants over the months and were mostly ex North West Frontier aircraft. Whilst testing one of these aircraft Ken found the

aileron controls sloppy and landed to have them looked at by the Ground Engineers. They opened up the instection panels in the fabric on the wings and were swamped in a cascade of table tennis balls. The wings were so full of them that Ken and his pals sold them to the local sport shops in Belfast. Apparently what had happened was, being ex Indian aircraft they had been put in for buoyancy should they have to ditch on the flight back to the United Kingdom. On the 31st July 1939 the Sydenham airfield was to be officially opened by the then Secretary of State for Air Captain HH Balfour. Ken was picked to give an aerobatic display in the Hawker Hart and later was presented by Captain Balfour with the Short and Harland Cup, "For the best all round trainee," and was thrilled to have this honour bestowed on him. Ken never saw the Cup again as he was called to full time service, and thought it was lost forever but luckily I discovered it in 1997 in a cardboard box at Queens University Air Squadron were it had lain for almost sixty years. Ken made a sentimental journey home that year to take possession once more of his prize which was presented to him by and old friend, Lady Mairi Bury at Newtownards Flying Club. In 2002 Ken decided to present the Cup to the Northern Ireland Wing of the Air Training Corps, to be presented each year to the best cadet. In August 1939 the VR were mobilised, the dogs of war had been released on the continent, but war had not yet been declared. Ken had to report daily to the VR Headquarters in Royal Avenue, Belfast and flying at Sydenham had virtually stopped. They were soon informed that their aircraft were to be flown to England and dispersed around various service flying training schools. On September 3rd, came the declaration of war. The VR boys still had some money left in their kitty, so they arranged a farewell luncheon in the Grand Central Hotel in Royal Avenue. Appropriate speeches were made, barrels of 'Liffy water' (Guinness) with a sprinkling of Old Bushmills whiskey. This was to be last time that some of them would see each other for six years. It was not until late December 1939 when Ken's posting eventually came through to proceed to No 3 Initial Training Wing (ITW) at Hastings in East Sussex, England. He arrived at No 3 ITW that was based in the Marine Court Hotel in Hastings on the 28th December 1939 together with several hundred others. The place was a shambles, bare, dirty, and badly lit. They had to march everywhere, and had to queue for long periods for toilets, bathroom and food. They were drilled up and down the promenade day in and day out, took part in PT, lectures, and played a lot of rugby and squash. Ken was made a Squad Commander in charge of about 60 men, everyone by now was being fed up waiting for postings to a Service Flying Training School (SFTS). At last in February his prayer was answered, but not as he had hoped to an SFTS for advanced flying but to an Elementary Flying Training School (EFTS). On the 22nd February Ken was posted to No 5 EFTS at Hanworth on the Great West Road outside London. Hanworth was first associated with aviation during the First World War and it was here that Ken was first introduced to the Miles Master that was an all wooden aircraft. He was assessed at the end of the course as 'above the average' as a Pilot. The highlight of the course came on the last day when a student skidded into a line of packed Magisters, and managed to write off about seven of them. From Hanworth Ken was posted to No 3 Service Flying Training School (SFTS) at South Cerney, for advanced flying, arriving there on 25th May. Now this was more to Ken's liking. The weather was exceptionally good and Ken hoped for a quick refresher course and then off to a squadron. On finishing the course he was again assessed as 'above the average' and recommended for Spitfires and Hurricanes, Ken was delighted. Before leaving South Cerney however, as he was returning to the mess on his 250cc OK Supreme motorcycle and turning onto the mess drive he forgot about the large roundabout in front of the main entrance and rode straight through the rose bed leaving a trail of broken rose bushes and trees behind him and coming off his bike at the far side covered in thorns. His next day was spent replanting and digging the rose bed over and losing a day's leave. Before his next posting Ken returned home to Northern Ireland for four days leave. On returning from leave and now resplendent in his Pilot Officer's uniform Ken was informed that he had been posted to No 6 OTU at Sutton Bridge. He arrived at the OTU on 30th August where he met several instructors who had already seen action in France. The next day Ken was introduced to the Hawker Hurricane. This introduction was brief and to the point, a short cockpit check on the operation of the undercarriage and flaps and a quick flight in a Harvard with an instructor called Flying Officer Jackman. After two short flights in the Harvard Ken went solo on the Hurricane, he said it was glorious, here was an aircraft that could be danced in the air. It was responsive, strong, stable, and forgiving except for spinning, which required considerable height in hand for recovery. The operational training was intensive; formation height climbs, aerobatics, and experimenting with the tightest possible turn 'greying out', recovering and sustaining the turns until blacking out. Learning to tighten the stomach muscles and flying the Hurricane to it's limit.

On September 21st 1940, with the Battle of Britain into its third phase Ken was posted to No 43 Fighter Squadron, the famous 'Fighting Cocks'. The squadron had been withdrawn after a mauling at Tangmere and was moved to Ushworth, there Ken teamed up with Flight Lieutenant Frank Carey, DFC & Bar, DFM who was a very experienced pre-war Fighter Pilot. Squadron Leader TFD Morgan, DFC was the Commanding Officer. He had just taken over from Squadron Leader CB Hull who was lost together with Dick Reynolds an ex Hawker test pilot from Tangmere on September 7th. Squadron Leader Hull had just taken over from another Ulsterman Wing

Commander JVC Badger, DFC who had been shot down during the battle and died of his wounds later. The squadron was shattered, but not down hearted, the 'vets' such as Frank Carey, Jim Hallowes, Killy Kilmartin, (native of Dundalk), welcomed Ken into the squadron.

Ken flew seventeen sorties in five days with the squadron, mostly led by Frank Carey. These were long-range local reconnaissance and sector exercises, landing late in the evening to be refueled and sent off on an operational patrol returning to base, as it was getting dark. On the 28th September while on a dusk patrol, Ken was vectored onto a HE111 over Newcastle. Visibility was poor with broken cloud but the German aircraft was visible between the layers. Ken got to about 400 yards from him and made a quick burst as it crossed from right to left. No strikes were seen and it disappeared into the murk. The next day 27th September Ken was told to report to No 501 Squadron Aux Air Force 'County of Gloucester' which was based at Kenley in Surrey. He was thrilled to bits at this news as he was now able to get into the thick of the Battle. Ken had made his farewells to 43 Squadron and thanked them all for their help. The short intensive time spent with them had given him confidence in his aircraft and himself.

501 squadron was commanded by Squadron Leader HAV Hogan, a very senior Squadron Leader who was efficient, cool, and above all a good Pilot whom the squadron had considerable respect as a leader. 501 squadron had already seen considerable action with the Advanced Air Striking Force (AASF) in France during the German advance and had only got out at the last moment via the Channel Islands. The squadron had an impressive record and high score and still had many 'old hands' such as Ginger Lacy, Daff Dorn and Hawkeye Lee, etc. The Battle was entering the final stage. Three months had passed since the beginning and although Fighter Command had taken a heavy toll, lost many aircraft and men. The Luftwaffe had also lost 1,700 aircraft. When Ken arrived at Kenley in late September the night Blitz had started in earnest to pound cities. Kenley had been peacetime RAF Station with permanent buildings. Ken was immediately welcomed by the Squadron Commander and his staff and informed about the Luftwaffe's previous exploits. Kenley had been attacked on a couple of occasions and the damage was extensive and visible.

On October 1st Ken was told to carry out a sector recce his call sign was (Mandril Squadron), he got to know the controllers well and be vectored around at low, medium, and high altitudes to keep a look out for bandits. Ken was allocated Hurricane SD-X, NoV6799 that was just out of servicing and went over it with the Fitters and Armourers just to get the feel of it. On the 2nd October he took SD-X for a short air test and on his return pronounced her a worthy steed. Ken now knew that he had joined a formidable band of warriors; the ground crews were real characters in their own right and were the backbone of the squadron.

October 4th brought Ken's first fully operational flight with 501, first flying as Blue 2 in a flight of four on a recce sortie, which unfortunately produced nothing. Upon returning to base he would land, taxi in, get out and inspect his aircraft, report to the Intelligence Officer and report any technical defects to the ground crews. On October 4th they were scrambled for a second time around 1100 hrs, the weather was still mist and rain with drifting cloud layers and enemy activity was fighter-bombers and Me109's. Ken went after a Ju88 that was over Kent and in the vicinity of Folkstone. Suddenly he spotted the 88 coming towards him, he shouted, "Tally Ho," and called attack. He eased SD-X to full power, boost and revs up, gyro sights on, and guns to fire. Ken expected the 88 to attack head on but at the last minute he turned, allowing Ken to deliver a full deflection shot from the stern quarter. Ken followed him round with a beam attack, cutting off the corner in a very tight turn with a closing speed of about 80 to 100 knots. He opened fire at about 80 yards with a log burst into the 88's port engine, smoke and flames came from the damaged engine and some bits also fell of it. The bomber's Rear Gunner then had Ken in his sights and opened fire hitting his port wing, but stopped abruptly as though he had been wounded. The 88 ran for cloud cover with his port engine belching smoke but no longer on fire. Ken attacked again but lost him in cloud, he broke off the attack as visibility was now down to 100 yards and made his way back to Kenley, which he found with considerable difficulty by following the Purley Way (main road). Ken was tickled pink, his second operation with the squadron and one JU88 claimed damaged. That evening Ken celebrated, and woke the next morning at six o'clock with a somewhat sore head.

The one that didn't get away

The morning of the 7th October 1940 had just dawned; the weather was fine, visibility good and some showers forecast for later. The squadron had been brought to readiness early and had been scrambled around 1100 hrs against a large force of enemy aircraft, but no 'trade' was spotted. The squadron landed back at base after a long 1hr.30min sortie and after a rapid refuel to standby' they were scrambled again. Control had informed the squadron that 150-plus bandits had been spotted in waves coming from Calais and heading for Dover at different flight levels. Squadron Leader Hogan was leading the patrol, Ken was flying along side him at a height of 20,000ft over Sevenoaks when he spotted two Me109's flying in front and below them, going south-east exactly as informed by control.

The two Me109's split up as Ken and Squadron Leader Hogan dived to attack them. In the ensuing dog fight Ken was attacked but got clear and chased another Me109 into clouds. He broke cloud at about 6,500ft, being pretty sure that the Me109 would come out on a reciprocal course. He did in fact come out at right angles then turned towards the sea, Ken with a superb height advantage did a half roll after him giving his Hurricane everything it had. Closing fast from astern, Ken opened up hitting the Me109 in the radiator and under the engine from 150 yards, he slowed rapidly, loosing height and ditched in the sea of Hythe. He watched the aircraft sink slowly and the Pilot get out. This particular aircraft was the subject of a dramatic recovery 35 years later by the enthusiasts of the Brenzett Aeronautical Museum. With considerable activity still going on above him, Ken quickly climbed to 23,000ft and decided to patrol between Folkstone and Dover. Suddenly he spotted eight Me109's coming across the coast at about 1,000ft above him, with enough speed in hand he pulled up into a loop under them and he was so close he was able to give one a quick burst in the belly from about 200 yards and seeing many hits entering the radiator and cockpit area. The Me109 took evasive action and half rolled into a dive with glycol streaming from his radiator, Ken was not far behind him ready for the Coups de Gras. They were passing Folkstone harbour when Ken closed right up within 100 yards, he opened fire, but nothing happened, he was out of ammunition and soon he would be out of fuel. Ken was determined that this was one German who wasn't going to get away. Ken approached the 109 from the left, and could see it's Pilot peering at him, the German thought he was almost home but Ken had other ideas for him. He lowered his undercarriage thinking to knock the Germans tail off with it but the drag only slowed him down. Ken decided to edge alongside the Me109 with meticulous care he positioned his wingtip about ten feet above the Me's tail. Then against all the rules and all his instincts he thrust his control column hard over smacking the wing of his Hurricane down onto the Me109's port tail plane breaking it off. Ken also lost at least four feet from his own wing tip, fortunately the tip snapped off cleanly without interfering with the aileron. The 109 crashed into the sea and partially sank without any sign of its Pilot getting out. Out of the empty sky came two more Me109'3 with guns blazing, no doubt looking for revenge for their comrade. Ken knew he was a sitting duck, out of ammo he shot down to sea level with the 109's in hot pursuit, thankfully they both were poor shots although he was hit in the radiator and the armour plate behind his seat.

Ken approached Folkstone and the pair of 109's broke off, he managed to gain enough height to avoid the Dover cliffs and crash-landed his Hurricane with its wheels up close to a gun site on a hill just north of Folkstone and close to Hawkinge aerodrome. In the forced landing, Ken had foolishly undone his cockpit harness ready for a quick exit, this was a grave mistake, as on landing he was thrown violently forward into the gun sight, splitting his jaw and smashing some of his front teeth. In a short while he was picked up in an Army car and taken to a naval sick quarters in the harbour area and examined by a naval doctor. Ken's jaw was cut open across his mouth and found that he could put his tongue through it.

The sequel to this episode was to come in 1948 when Ken was posted to the Air Staff Headquarters at Fighter Command, when he was moving furniture into a new house at Northwood, which he had just purchased. Ken was in uniform and watching the Pickford's removal men hard at work when one of them came over to his wife and asked her, "Did he ever land a Hurricane on its belly near Folkstone during the Battle of Britain?" "Yes," she replied, 'why do you ask?" "Well," he said, "I was the one who went to help him out of his aircraft after he crashed and as we approached him he was already out of it and he pulled us down onto the grass, as he thought the aircraft might catch fire and explode." It's a small world.

Baled out

On the 25th October 1940 the squadron was back to strength and the weather was fine. The squadron had been in readiness from 0730 hrs as large formations of enemy aircraft were reported to be boiling up. After lunch Ken had been scrambled and was flying Hurricane V 6806 above Kent at 28,000ft and had been vectored onto a large formation of Me109's, which were at different levels. Crossing over a small formation with a good height advantage, the Commanding Officer gave Ken the order to attack with his section. Ken immediately called to his section, "Bandits below at two o'clock. Attack. Attack. Go." He half rolled down to start his attack, and as his port wing came up there was an almighty bang, another aircraft had hit him taking his port wing of at the root. Ken's 'Red 2' a Czech Pilot Officer V Goth had well and truly clobbered him. The impact was like hitting a brick wall, his aircraft flicked over and over, juddering and shaking as the engine raced at full speed as his throttle had been jammed. In a few minutes the engine had torn itself out of its mountings, Ken jettisoned the hood and baled out, deciding to delay opening his parachute until he reached 16,000ft. He drifted down gently, and landed safely in a small hayrick close to a fruit farm near Goudhurst in Kent, where he was met by the inevitable, "Yes?" A farmer with a pitchfork. When the farmer realised who Ken was he took him back to his farm and gave him a cup of tea. Ken asked politely, could he use the telephone to contact Kenley so as they could pick him up, the farmer replied, certainly, just as long as you pay for it.

Battle of Britain tapestry

The beautifully worked lace curtain is five yards long and sixty-five inches wide. It took two years to design and produce and depicts scenes witnessed during the bombing of London during the Battle of Britain. One of the scenes that it depicts is that of Wing Commander Ken Mackenzie severing the tail of the German Me109 with his own wing tip. The tapestry was on display just after the war ended at Parliament Buildings Northern Ireland, before it was exhibited in provincial towns.

His aircraft

Regarding his aircraft, so much has been written about the Spitfire and Hurricane. Ken flew both these magnificent chariots and liked both of them but preferred the Hurricane for its ruggedness, stability and light controls with viceless flying characteristics. It could take anything that you could give it and out turn anything flying at the time; well flown the Hurricane was a match for anything. The Messerschmitt BF109E that he was competing with was, he considered overrated but better armed, even after the Luftwaffe seemed to abandon the cannon firing through the centre of the propeller boss. The 109 was undoubtedly heavy and its elevator controls were vicious in a fast steep dive and had a tendency to flick approaching a stall.

His armament: Ken considered the armament of the Hurricane inadequate in hitting power and range.

His training: His training proved satisfactory in all respects, except in Gunnery, but in many instances determination was lacking and knowledge of just how much the aeroplane could take, or the pilot gave it when flown to its limit.

Pilots and Squadrons

Some or both were in the forefront at all times, squadrons because they were well led and had an elite who scored the most and lasted the longest. 501 was luckily, one of the 'Few' and ended up with one of the highest scores as a squadron. Pilots: some squadron had a few 'killers', 501 had its generous share of these but many lacked the killer instinct that was essential for success in any sport, or war where physical and mental skills are combined to survive.

The Battle of Britain was now over, Ken had enjoyed it and was still alive, what else mattered. By the end of the Battle of Britain 501 squadron score stood at 149 German aircraft destroyed. In December 1940 Ken was promoted to Deputy Flight Commander. The squadron then returned to it's home base of Filton in 10 Group. 501 Squadron came to Ballyhalbert in Northern Ireland with a detachment to Eglington in October 1942 for a well-earned rest. It was joined by three more Ulstermen, Flight Lieutenant Cecil Austin from Londonderry, and Sergeant William Polley from Lisburn and Warrant Officer Lockington 'Lockie' Lilburn from Belfast.

247 Squadron Predannack (Night Fighters)

After a spot of leave Ken was posted to 247 squadron at Predannack on the Lizard, the most southerly airfield in England. It had been constructed upon marshy ground on the Moorland overlooking Mullion and Kynance Coves. The newly built runway was concrete and proud to the ground, so woe betide anyone running off it into the marshy surrounds. Accommodation was in nissen huts, wooden offices and a small hangar or two. Officers were billeted in the Mullion Cove Hotel. Ken arrived at 247 on the 19th June 1941, the squadron was unique in it was the very last squadron in England to be equipped with and use the Gloster Gladiator. The squadron was commanded by Squadron Leader PG St G O'Brian, a quiet spoken Canadian who had joined the RAF. The Flight Commanders were Flight Lieutenant DG (Splinters) Smallwood and Johnny Carver. The squadron had been re-equipped with Hurricane Mk2 C's and B's. The Mk2 B's were fitted with additional underwing fuel tanks and were armed with 12 x. 303 calibre machine guns, while the Mk2 C's had a normal tankage fitted but carried some of the first 20mm cannon, two in each wing. The aircraft was painted black for camouflage in the night role and fitted with shields over the stub exhausts, this stopped the glare from the hot exhausts and reduced the blinding effect of back pressure with violent flame and sparks when throttling back on landing. Operations from Predannack were usually over the UK during night attacks on harbours and cities, convoy patrols round the coast and into the Bristol Channel. When there was little local activity, Ken would carry out night and dusk intruder attacks into France. These attacks were code named 'Mandolins'. During his initial flying with 247 Squadron in June 1941, Ken was averaging two sorties a day, or night but 'no trade'. He was made Training Officer and Deputy Flight Commander. July took on a more serious look with much more intensive training patrols and 'firing in' the cannons. On the 7th July Ken was scrambled to cover a convoy in the entrance of the Bristol Channel at 8,000ft. Arriving on station he overshot the convoy that was reported approaching Lundy Island. Orbiting Barnstable Bay, Ken was informed by sector to watch out for a bandit approaching from the north at 7,000ft. He decided to climb to 9,000ft to height in hand but saw nothing.

Control gave him another plot coming in from the north, same height as before. Ken spotted him and immediately informed sector and kept the bandit in sight and identified it as a Ju88 that was doing about 260 knots in a shallow dive towards Falmouth. Closing up on him within 800 yards and now about 1,500ft, at 200 yards he gave him a burst below and astern but lost sight of him momentarily but sighted him again at about 100 yard's range. This time he gave the 88 a long raking burst from below and astern. There was no result and Ken throttled back for a third attack. Suddenly the 88 burst into a sheet of flame and blew up, causing Ken to take immediate avoiding action, he pulled the Hurricane up steeply and away to his left and as he did so his windscreen was spattered with oil and debris.

He informed sector of this, and returned to base, landing in good weather, jubilant, his first kill at night.

On the 13th September 1941 he shot down and destroyed a Heinkel 111 and by the 29th September he had completed 14 operations with 247 Squadron.

That fateful operation

September 29th 1941 was one of those days, Ken had been briefed to attack Lannion airfield in Brittany. He took off at dusk from Predannack to follow a first strike by Whirlwind Fighters of 263 Squadron. It was with mixed feelings when they took in four Hurricane Mk2c's as they were convinced that there were few, if any good targets at Lannion at that time. After take off they dipped down onto the sea from Predannack to cross the Channel at 200ft in order to get under the German Radar. Cruising at a speed of 230 knots, the weather was hazy with some high stratus cloud. The sea looked dark and as usual cold and uninviting but calm. Ken looked across at the other aircraft and said they all looked like crows. They crossed the French coast passing Les Triege Islands to the east. Ken selected full power, checked all instruments, switched on their Gyro Gun Sights, set guns to fire and pulled up to 600ft for his diving attack on Lannion. Flying in line abreast and 200 yards apart, he dived to attack at 100ft and as he dived the flak defences opened up immediately with intense and accurate fire from all sides of the airfield and outside it. Visibility was very poor. With his number 2 Ken weaved and fired at buildings and dispersal's, he managed to silence a gun post about half a mile from the north of the Aerodrome. The flak was coming up by now in a constant stream and getting more accurate missing Ken by a few feet. Red 1 and 2, and Blue 2 had pulled away, but Ken was determined to have a last attack on his way out to the coast. By now the sky was alive with flak and he was sweating like a pig. He managed to silence one more flak post but was 'coned' by the rest as he passed to the south of the airfield. He was now down to 50ft to try and upset their aiming. But he was too late, he felt the bullets hitting the front of his Hurricane, radiator fluid and engine oil came across his windscreen. He immediately pulled up to gain height and nurse his damaged engine. His aircraft was in a bad way, engine was running rough, oil fumes were coming into the cockpit, and power was falling off. He eased back on the boost and revs as the engine temp gauges rapidly rose to danger levels.

It was now clear to Ken that he was not going to make it back to base, so would he bale out or ditch the aircraft in the sea. He had already baled out once and did not like the prospect of doing it again. Suddenly the Merlin seized and the prop stopped. The sea below him was rising rapidly and as he glided down he hastily jettisoned the cockpit hood. He was about five miles from the coast and six feet up from the sea, he stalled the aircraft and she struck immediately. The aircraft slowed rapidly and pitched forward violently, water and spray everywhere. He quickly vacated the aircraft and this was his last recollection until he wakened up floating around in his 'K' type dinghy. Ken now admitted to himself, "I'm right up the creek." It was a desolate feeling in that dinghy, 120 miles of formidable sea to base and England. It was around 2100 hrs, by this time the sea was calm, light wind and a friendly moon. The visibility was one mile or so with the French coast outlined in silhouette. He had no accurate idea of his position but thought he was in Lannion bay.

Prisoner of War

He decided to paddle for home, eventually he fell asleep and when he awoke he found himself being prodded by a rifle of a Kriegs Marine, one of several who stood around him with guns at the ready. They were surprised to find a British Pilot as nothing was known to them about an aircraft ditching and apparently they had been summoned by some local lighthouse keeper, who had seen Ken's boat approaching the island and thought it was a Frenchman making for England. After some Ersatz coffee Ken was taken aboard the German patrol boat, plus his dinghy. The patrol boat set sail and about half an hour later stopped at the fishing village of Rampol. Ken was to remain there until someone picked him up. He had not long to wait for his escort who drove him to Lannion in a Luftwaffe staff car and on his arrival he was surprised to be taken to the officer's mess were he was met by an elderly Luftwaffe Colonel and given a slap up lunch, with a delicious steak. His first night in captivity was spent in cold, bare cell in the guardroom at Lannion and was not a pleasant one. A hard wooden bed without a mattress, one chair, a toilet bucket and one blanket with a straw filled pillow. Concrete walls about 10ft x 6ft with a small window on top. He was now feeling a bit sorry for himself. "The luck of the Irish," he said to himself.

Soon he was entrained from Morlaix Station in a second-class carriage, accompanied by a middle-aged guard. They set off via Paris for Germany, and when they arrived at Le Mans Ken's guard bought him some peaches and grapes from a station vendor. Ken said, the strange thing was, "The presence of a British prisoner of war went completely unnoticed. Arriving at the terminus in Paris, it was like a Bank Holiday, massive crowds everywhere." In the mayhem Ken slipped away from his middle-aged guard, and just as he thought he had got away with it, he heard someone shout behind him, "Halt!" He looked around to see the Hauptmann and some individuals pointing guns at him. Caught again. He was taken to the station police headquarters and handed over to them and later was put on a small truck and delivered to the Gare-du-Nord.

Dulag Luft

His next stop was Frankfurt-am-Main where he was handed over to the station police and placed in the hands of two Luftwaffe NCO's and driven to Dulag Luft which was the Luftwaffe Reception Centre for Royal Air Force and Fleet Air Arm prisoners. There he was quizzed quite stiffly by their Reception Centre Committee. He was next taken to Lubeck on the Baltic and on arrival was marched some distance to a large camp that turned out to be the most miserable, inadequate, and badly staffed camp possible. It consisted of wooden huts with the usual double barbed wire fencing around the perimeter with the internal trip wire over which one did not venture without the risk of being shot by guards. Lookout towers were situated at strategic points along the wire fencing. Accommodation was primitive and the atmosphere was spiritless especially amongst the Army prisoners, most of whom had been taken at Dunkirk. The food was near starvation diet that consisted of four or five potatoes in some weak soup, four slices of bread, butter and jam, Ersatz coffee, saccharine and a small ration of sugar. The camp guards were a scruffy and arrogant lot. It was now October 1941 and on the Baltic coast it was getting cold, especially at night, but the days were generally fine and sunny. Soon Ken was told to get ready as he was going to be moved to a camp at Wurburg which was near Kassel. He was marched down to the railway station where he boarded a train that was a heavily guarded passenger train with guards sitting on the carriage roofs.

Oflag 63, Warburg

On his arrival at Warburg (Oflag 63) he was kept outside the camp for several hours. Once inside, he soon settled in. It was a large camp covering an extensive area, without trees of course and the surrounds well cleared of 'obstructions' that could provide cover. There was ample room for a sports ground and gardens, and the Dining Hall was adjacent to the cook house. The barrack blocks were quite far apart so the each became a sort of separate entity, split into rooms taking 18 to 20 people. With a small room at one end for two only, the Commanding Officer and his Adjutant, opposite which was the latrine, a room with several large buckets only. The accommodation was crowded and each inmate stored his small cache of belongings on, or below his bunk in a locker. The camp had a large but very mixed crowd of prisoners. British Army, RAF, Navy, FAA, and some Indian Army Officers. Committees were set up to organise and co-ordinate various activities. The winter of 1941 was particularly severe, the cold was intense and at night they were more or less locked in with closed windows and the Fug with red hot coke stone, was terrible, only to be relieved in the morning by a short sharp run and rolling naked in the snow. The three services maintained a dignified individuality and identity, but co-operated where necessary. The Navy and FAA, in Ken's block were a bit stand-offish and aloof. The Indian officers lived almost separately but were a wonderful and friendly crowd. On parade they were always the smartest turned out, and were a well-decorated lot, from the First World War. When Ken was invited to take tea with them it always began with a silent Toast to the King and Emperor, most impressive, with all standing to attention. At Warburg, Ken received his first Red Cross Parcel, these were issued individually. Towards the end of 1941 Ken heard that they were going to be segregated into separate camps for each Service. Administered and guarded by similar German Services and that RAF prisoners at Warburg were going to Schubin in Poland, which was not far from Danzig. This move was welcomed by all, as the chances of escaping, possibly to Sweden looked promising.

Schubin Offlag XXB

They were moved from Warburg to Schubin in well-guarded cattle trucks. Schubin was some 70-miles from Danzig, and near a village and railway station.

On their arrival at Schubin they had a long weary march the camp. It was totally different from Warburg and Lubeck. They had been expected to be arriving in a Luftwaffe controlled camp as previously informed, but no, it was another Wehrmacht administered camp. So much for the segregation under similar Services. There were the usual perimeter fences and watch towers, some of which had British Bren guns, which had been captured in France. There was quite a large mansion house that had been an orphanage. They marched in and paraded inside the wire and reported to the Senior British Officer who was Wing Commander Hetty Hyde. It was obvious the place was uninhabitable, it was filthy everywhere; broken furniture, beds crawling with bugs, dirty straw filled mattresses. The floors were covered in garbage and the smell and stench of stale urine was terrible. The Senior British Officer (SBO) inspected it all himself with his staff and ordered them to remain outside while he went and seen the Camp Kommandant who was a stiff Prussian Officer much older with an artificial leg and an arrogant manner. After a while the Kommandant had gratuitously agreed that the accommodation was uninhabitable and brought in Polish labour the next day to clean it up. The mood in the camp was dangerous from the start and morale was low, but everyone did their best to settle in. The communal lavatory was a long 40 seater, straddling a foul smelling pit that was periodically emptied by a 'Honey Wagon', which was a horse drawn wooden tanker with an antiquated hand pump to fill it with. The washhouses were bare, concrete walls that were also filthy. The whole thing was not encouraging. Soon after they arrived, tragedy struck when a chap, who was in rather a depressed state decided to walk straight to the perimeter wire and commenced climbing it. Immediately several fluent German speakers contacted the watch towers and told the guards that he was a 'krank', sick and to let them go over and bring him back. However a foot guard outside refused to listen, panicked and shot him at point blank range.

By this time a hostile crowd had gathered and the situation was getting ugly. There was nearly a mutiny as he lay on the ground and no one near him. Extra guards with machine guns were brought in whilst he was removed, only to die later. The atmosphere between the POW's and the Germans worsened and the SBO's liaison with the Kommandant deteriorated through no fault of his own. Escape tunnelling was intensified, with five going at the one time, it was, "All systems go." The winter of 1942 was intensively cold, so much so the Fug in the barrack blocks actually froze to the inside of the windows and walls. The SBO was informed that the camp was being evacuated and they were going to be moved once more in the spring, March was talked about on the grapevine, so it was decided that a maximum effort was to be made for people to escape before the move. They did and thirty-three souls got clean away, although none of these reached home, some of them were free for up to two weeks. The escape involved over 4,000 German troops being brought into the area to assist 1,000 or more German police, and home guards in searching for the escapes. In the meantime, as the panic and usual reprisals and chaos subsided they learnt that the Kommandant and the Abwehr Officer had been suspended and new ones appointed. Rittmeister Reimer was made Security Officer, who was a decent cheery fellow, and who carried out his duties effectively but reasonably. At the end of April 1942 the whole camp was paraded and informed that they were to prepare for another move, this time to Sagan, Stalag Luft 111. Ken had been a prisoner for one year and seven months, been in four different camps and had worked on three tunnels, two ladder jobs, the second time in a minor role of construction only. He had settled into the Kriegie (prisoner) life, made a lot of friends and remained solidly independent. Letters and parcels which came from England relieved some of the boredom and monotony. He had many projects in hand, together with sport and reading kept him well occupied. Therefore at that particular time he more or less resigned himself to assisting whatever way he could, but was indifferent to actually escaping. At Warburg he had, like many others, constructed himself a box in which he kept his personal effects. This was made, not with the usual false bottom, but with a false back, with a row of sharp nails protruding inside to deter the 'ferrets' from measuring the dimensions with their hands and arms. With a spare 2 x 24 x 18 inches available, the false back was used to carry all sorts of 'goodies'; master maps, tools, compasses, camera and radio components. The false back in Ken's box was never found, it had survived Warburg and Schubin and now had arrived safely at Sagan.

Sagan Stalag Luft 111

Arriving at Sagan was an experience in itself. Here was a large purpose built, escape proof, Prisoner of War camp, administered and run for the Royal Air Force by their opposite numbers the Luftwaffe. Stalag Luft 111 was located about 80 miles south east of Berlin, with a convenient railway station nearby at Sagan. Ken could see and hear the RAF bombing raids on Berlin, and later on when the RAF used the 'Block Buster' bombs, he could feel the actual detonations. The north compound was new and almost a model POW camp, this part was occupied by about 250 prisoners, some of whom had initially volunteered to go across to help get the camp ready. These stalwarts had already made plans for tunnelling and when finally transferred from the east compound, soon got at least three tunnels going. Unfortunately when Ken and his friends arrived at Luft 111 they were split up between the north and the east compounds. Ken went to the east compound, this was an intensive area, well clear of trees. Large and well-

separated barrack blocks raised on short stilts to enable, "Ferrets to crawl under and search for dispersed sand."

On his arrival, Ken had established a half 'Ulster Room'; although not quite enough for a rugby team. The food was good, with Canadian and Argentine bulk issue parcels, augmenting the standard English parcels. Moral rose despite the poor escaping prospects. Relations with the camp guards, ferrets and admin personnel were on a more common ground. Both being Air Force and additionally the war was not looking good for Germany, so many were looking out towards their own interests. At this camp of course you have undoubtedly have heard of the famous 'Wooden Horse' that was conceived by Williams, Condor and Phillpot. The story is too well known to be repeated, being so well presented in William's book and the subsequent film. Ken did actually help with the design of the Horse, but had no other involvement. At the time the Wooden Horse was going well, Ken displaced a cartilage in his right knee in a big way which was caused by playing rugby in a combined, Aussie and New Zealand team versus the rest. Despite the Medical Officer's attempt to straighten the leg by, "Jumping on it," he could not straighten out. He decided to send Ken under guard by train to Obermassfeld Hospital which was near Meinigen to have it operated on. Ken was taken to Sagan station in a lot of pain and boarded the train for the journey which took him via Leipzig, where he had an hours wait for the connection to Meinigen. Sitting with the guard in the middle of the centre platform in Leipzig station, Ken marvelled at the wonderful expanse of curved glass roofing above him. Not a crack or broken pane to be seen! Yet according to the news item a day or so before, the RAF had bombed Leipzig station. They boarded the train for Meinigen, via Arnstadt and Erfurt and eventually arrived at Obermassfeld Hospital, which was an experience in itself. It was staffed by German and British doctors and medical orderlies, the latter taken from France and Dunkirk. Ken was soon operated on by an eminent London orthopedic surgeon who did a wonderful job. He was kept at the hospital for a month or so to recuperate and get the leg back too normal, and while doing so and for the first time met some American Aircrew. It seemed their daylight raids, as expected were taking a heavy toll, the 'Waist and Dorsal' Gunners were the main casualties. Returning to Sagan and the east compound he was informed that the three 'Wooden Horse Men' had all got out and all three had made it. With Christmas 1943 approaching, there were many stills at work making home brewed raisin hooch, hopefully ready in time for the Camp Christmas pantomime. The winter of 1943 was extremely hard, snow on the ground that restricted movement and inhibited 'activities' which required the camouflage of the dirty surface sand now hidden. Spring came quietly in 1944, Ken along with a large contingent from the north compound were taken to a new camp just north of Stalag Luft 111, but which was still in sight of

Sagan. A few months after settling in, Ken heard about the terrible cold-blooded shootings of some fifty of the escapees out of 83 who had got out of the tunnel Harry in the north compound in March. It was from the camp he saw his first jet aircraft, which was an Me262, he had previously heard the new noise but was never able to spot what was making it. It caused considerable speculation and conjecture and soon became quite commonplace.

He also witnessed a deep penetration daylight raid by American Flying Fortresses when a wide spread formation of twenty of them appeared well to the west of the camp flying at about 18,000ft.

He watched the flak burst amongst them and several being shot down and heard later that they had been attacking a BMW engine factory. It had reminded Ken of his first escort mission to Cherbourg in 1941; it seemed a long time ago. In October Ken was surprised and delighted to be told that he was included in the next batch of POW's to be repatriated. This was the outcome of some collaboration with the Medical Officer, him putting on an act, but it worked. He soon left, meeting up with several batches of prisoners from other compounds and camps; Army, Navy, Allied officers, old prisoners, wounded men, and several very sad cases of depression. Ken arrived in Sweden in a matter of days and was looked after very well; the food was good and too much of it. After a few days he embarked along with the other POW's onto the SS Drotling, arriving at Liverpool on the 10th October 1944.

He was taken to a nearby medical centre where he was given a full medical examination, interrogated for a short time and sent home on three weeks leave. "It was quite a home coming."

Back to flying

Ken soon arrived home to see his parents and friends, and to collect his 1939 Austin 8. When his leave was finished it was back to England to contact some old friends at Headquarters Fighter Command at Bentley Priory. Ken was eventually offered a post as an Instructor on Spitfires at Command Communications Squadron which was based at Bovington where they had some spare Spitfires. It was not long until Ken was flying again, and it was great to back in the air again. He managed to get a few hours in at Bovington before being posted to No 53 OTU at Kirton-on-Lindsay in December 1944. This was a Spitfire Operational training Unit (OTU) and near Scunthorpe with Hibaldston as its satellite nearby. The OTU was equipped with Spitfire MkV's, Master Mk2's and Martinets. The Master and Martinets were new to Ken, they were made of an all-wooden construction and fitted with Bristol Mercury V111 or Xv Super Charged air cooled engines. Ken was made Flying Wing Adjutant and it was not long until he got into the swing of things. The winter of 1944 was another hard one and particularly in Lincolnshire, flying was reduced in consequence. After three months with the OTU, Ken was posted to the Central Gunnery School at Catfoss to become a qualified

Pilot Attack Instructor. He met many of his old Fighter Command friends here. After passing out as a Pilot Attack Instructor he returned to join the Gunnery Squadron at Hibaldston that was equipped with Master's for dual instruction and Spitfire's for practice dog fights. The war was coming to a close and the need for replacements diminished. It was at Kirton-on-Lindsay and Hibaldston that Ken for the first time experienced the 'new look' Royal Air Force with nearly as many girls servicing the aircraft as men, it took some time getting used to them.

In very high wind conditions when operating Spitfires it was necessary to find some means of keeping its tail on the ground when taxing down wind. This sometime was achieved by one or two of the ground crews sitting or hanging on the tail plane either facing the front or the back of the aircraft. Reaching the take off point, the Pilot would stop, wait and see the ground crew 'ballast' visibly off and clear before opening up to take off. One morning a WAAF ground crew was bent over the tail of a spitfire facing backwards, upon reaching the takeoff point the Pilot forgot about her, and despite the tail heaviness he should have experienced, opened up and took off with the WAAF tightly stuck to the leading edge of the tail plane by the air stream on her back. Now this was noticed by all on the ground, flying control was informed immediately. The Pilot was contacted and told to do a quick, quiet, slow decent and landed with WAAF still in place.

She nonchalantly got off the tail and was picked up by a waiting ambulance and brought back to dispersal and seemed none the worse for her ordeal. She asked for a cigarette, then it suddenly struck her and said, "Oh my God," and fainted.

This incident hit the headlines of the daily newspapers the next day.

VE Day, and RAF Keevil

The news was good; May 8th and VE Day came with suitable celebrations on the station and in Scunthorpe. No 53 OTU was closed and on the 17th June Ken was posted to No 61 Fighter OTU at Keevil as a Flight Commander. 61 OTU was equipped with the North American Mustang (P51). The P51 was built to a British specification and fitted with a Packard built Rolls Royce Engine. At that time was offered a permanent commission, and asked if he would like the opportunity to complete his Engineering Degree at the Air Force's expense. Keevil had been a wartime station and the Mustangs were being replaced once again by Spitfires. Before the Mustangs left Keevil Ken decided to find out how far one of them could be flown with all long-range tanks fitted. Carrying some food and a Thermos in the roomy cockpit which had arm rests fitted to the Pilot's seat and other amenities not associated with British aircraft. Ken took off to fly the length and breadth of England, Ireland, Scotland, and Wales for some six hours. The Packard Merlin never missed a beat, but Ken became quite exhausted sitting in the one position for so long.

At Keevil Ken was selected for two very worthwhile courses becoming a Qualified Flying Instructor (QFI). Having completed the course, he was posted to the Empire Flying School at Hullavington where the new concept of instrument flying and instrument rating scheme was being taught.

Here he had a wide selection of aircraft to fly which included Spitfire, Harvard, Meteor, B Buckmaster, Lancaster, Oxford and Vampire. It was an intensive course, but rewarding and Ken was passed out as an instrument rating examiner and he returned to Keevil, as Squadron Commander. On the 16th October 1947 the Squadron moved to RAF Chivenor which was near Barnstable in north Devon to be equipped with the superb Spitfire Mk XX1 and MkXX11 which were fitted with the two stage Rolls Royce Griffin engine and a large five bladed prop. Ken said she was magnificent to fly and handle. They were now designated No 203 Advanced Flying School (AFS), but in reality still an OTU Unit.

Headquarters Fighter Command

In February 1949 Ken was posted to the air staff at Headquarters Fighter Command at Bentley Priory. It's Commander-in Chief being Air Marshal Sir Basil Embrey. From the Senior Air Staff Officer, Air Vice Marshal David Atcherly down to the most junior Flight Lieutenant was a galaxy of the most highly decorated, energetic Fighter Pilots and Navigators one could hope to gather in one setting; each a character in his own right. Day and night fighters, what a team to join.

With food rationing still in force, Ken would organise a source of supply of legs of ham and crates of eggs from his friends in Northern Ireland who were food wholesalers. Now to collect these, Ken would arrange a weekend 'training and liaison' visit to RAF Aldergrove in an Oxford or Anson to bring back the 'goodies' to England. At Fighter Command headquarters, Ken was responsible for the day to day running of the Day Fighter OTU's.

RAF Stradishall

After a tour of two years during which he was lucky enough to be selected for the Fighter Command rugby team, he was promoted to Wing Commander and posted to No 226 OTU at RAF Stradishall near Cambridge. He took over as Officer Commanding the Flying Wing and Chief Instructor on Meteor 7's and 8's, P.R.Mk9's with Martlets as target towers. The latter being later replaced with Mosquito's suitably modified by Marshals of Cambridge. At Stradishall Ken produced about 30 Pilots per month and two or four fighter recco Pilots as required. Paddy Barthropp was Officer Commanding Flying at Waterbeach that was just north of Stradishall and had custody of Hurricane Mk2 LF-363. In 1952 he decided to bring the fighter over to Stradishall for Ken to fly, but no violent manoeuvres were allowed. Ken was delighted at having this chance to fly his 'favourite' chariot one more time. LF-363 is now one of the two

remaining. Hurricanes from the Battle of Britain memorial Flight 34 years later. Towards the end of Ken's tour at RAF Stradishall, the Group Air Officer in Charge, Air Vice Marshal Richard Atcherly carried out his last AOC's inspection of the station, after all the ceremonies he said to Ken, "Mac, you are one of the best officer commanding's a flying I ever had, but you will never get on unless you are blunt and more tolerant." He never did either of them. At the end of his tour however, Ken was awarded the Air Force Cross and again assessed as 'exceptional' as a Pilot and Instructor.

Headquarters Middle East Air Force

Towards the end of August 1953 Ken was posted to Headquarters Middle East Command at Ismalia in the Canal Zone, Egypt, on the air staff as Wing Commander Operational Training. His command territory from Ismalia extended to Cyprus, Iraq, Sharjah, Muscat and over to East Africa. He had detachments at various other locations, including training teams with local Nationals and airfields at Amman and Mafrag in Jordan. Ken found this posting very exciting and interesting, never having been to the Middle East before, he took every opportunity to fly around his 'manor', so to speak. In November 1954 they had to evacuate the Canal Zone and hand it back to Egypt necessitating his headquarters be transferred to Nicosia Airport in Cyprus. Life in Cyprus was idyllic, peaceful and friendly, Ken mixed with the Greek and Turkish Cypriot alike. He enjoyed the excellent swimming, picnicing facilities. Unfortunately these ideal settings soon vanished as the island erupted in turmoil, though the early stages of the EOKA campaign did not affect him to badly, except that he had to carry a side arm again. Ken left Cyprus and Headquarters Middle East Command some months before the Suez Crisis in March 1958. Before leaving he had the honour of flying the first aircraft into the new airfield at Akrotira; a Communications Squadron Pembroke from Nicosia which was carrying members of the press.

Air Ministry

On his return to England at the end of March 1956 Ken was posted to the Air Ministry, soon to become the Ministry of Defence (AIR) and confined to a desk. He was in charge of the operational training in bomber and coastal commands making frequent visits to their stations. By now Ken had several thousand flying hours on many types of aircraft, and without loosing any more lives, he reckoned he still had a few to go. The MOD (Air) in 1956 still had a Communication Squadron at Whitewaltham near Reading, commanded by an old friend of Ken's. So he made good use of it. The most attractive aircraft they had was the Balliol and this type of aircraft had been introduced into the RAF as an advanced Trainer, The Balliol was powered by a Rolls Royce Merlin, it was a noisy rattly but very robust aircraft. As we know Ken was a great motorcar enthusiast and had purchased an ELVA Mk2, which was powered by a Coventry Climax 1100cc engine. He competed in quite a lot of races with this car and during his career he became the first chairman of the newly founded RAF Motor Sports Association.

Headquarters, Persian Gulf

In November 1963 Ken was posted to as Wing Commander Admin Headquarters Persian Gulf in Bahrain with Air Commodore Geoffrey Millington as Commander. Ken knew Bahrain from his earlier tour in the Middle East and looked forward very much to this posting. The evening he arrived at Muharraq he was invited to an Army cocktail party at their mess in Manama. Here he met the British Head of Customs, Lionel Irvine who was from Belfast and an old school pal. He also met the Commandant of the Bahrain police who had been the Head Constable at Enniskillen and knew his mother and father very well (small world). In Bahrain they enjoyed a peaceful life with it's Ruler and his people, being made welcome everywhere he went. The RAF presence was considerable, and also a strong Military and Naval presence with their headquarters at Jufair. His tour was now overshadowed by the knowledge that the UK Labour Government, in their churlish wisdom were thinking about withdrawing the British presence from the Gulf (as they did with disastrous results). When this decision was put to the Gulf States, it caused great concern amongst them, because as long as Britain policed the area, in their opinion there would be peace and stability, and where these exist there is trade and prosperity.

Kenya

After the Gulf Ken was posted to Eastleigh at Nairobi in Kenya as Officer Commanding Royal Air Force and during his tour in Nairobi, there had been considerable operational activity in the remote and arid areas on the Somali and Ethiopian borders against the Shifta gangs where he was supporting the Kenya Army and police. This gave Ken the opportunity to do quite a lot of flying in the Dehavilland Beavers and Scottish twin Pioneers. Both were short take off and landing (STOL) aircraft and great to fly on recco's, supply and casualty evacuation flights. Kenya was a wonderful country and Ken loved it and resolved to go back sometime, little did he know what was ahead.

Maintenance Command Andover

From Nairobi Ken was posted back to Maintenance Command at Andover and despite being promised a good posting and promotion by the AOC including Johnny Johnson for all the work Ken had done for him but this did not materialise. At Andover, the only saving grace for Ken was having the command communication flight on the airfield next door to the headquarters.

When Ian Smith declared UDI in Rhodesia, Ken was posted with an RAF detachment to Lusaka in Zambia, with Jimmy James as his AOC.

Lusaka, Zambia

Using a squadron of Gloster Javelins and Mobile Radar, their job was to watch the Rhodesian Air Force whilst our Transport Command Britannia's ferried oil in from Nairobi, and there was never a dull moment. While he was in Zambia, the new RAF Commander of the Zambian Air Force and their Defence Secretary asked Ken if he would consider taking over as Commander, as their President wanted to have his own Air Force and would shortly be recruiting to that end. This would mean retiring from the Royal Air Force prematurely, which at this stage he was not adverse at doing as he felt he had reached a dead end. Further more he had had his first brush with the unions and civilian's who were now manning 60% of the units command. What he had seen and been introduced to in their manning, working hours restrictive practices and inefficiencies, not only in the civilian establishments either, had blunted his already waning enthusiasm and respect for the service and Government, he was serving and had loved.

Zambian Air Force & Air Kenya Ltd

After several months, whilst waiting for his retirement to come through, Ken invested in some property in Kenya and became Chief of Staff of the Zambian Air Force. As his tour was finishing Ken was asked to take over as Managing Director of a large civilian light aircraft charter company. This was based at Nairobi, Malindi, Mombasa, and Nanyuk. The aircraft were a mixture of Piper, Cessna, Beech, and several hired during the peak periods, including an Islander. The pilots were a mixture of local ex patriots and RAF. The appointment was a new challenge and enjoyable to start with until the 'Bag of Worms' emerged. (Read Ken's Book, "Hurricane Combat.")

Aviation Consultant

At this particular time, Ken had several requests to represent various overseas companies who had interests in East Africa. So he decided to set up as an Aviation Consultant. Then on the 1st April 1973 Ken decided to call it a day. His Irish luck was holding good and maybe one more 'life' left. Over 4,000 hours flying in some sixty different types of aircraft. Eight or is it nine 'lives' lost, but not one engine or major failure throughout his flying career, in war and peace and all kinds of weather. Visiting many countries, meeting many wonderful people and flying and valued aircraft. Some good, some bad, especially the superb Hawker Hurricane in combat. Ken had an exciting life, with no regrets, none the worse for it and still one life remaining.

My wife Pat and I have had the honour to become close friends with Ken and his wife Margaret, a friendship we both treasure to this day. Ken and Margaret live in retirement now in Lutterworth, England and I am sure if any 'Ulster folk' are passing their door they would be very welcome to call for a 'wee cup of tea'.

For the record

Aircraft destroyed or damaged (1940-1941):

4th Oct	Ju88	Damaged
5th Oct	Bf 109E	Destroyed
7th Oct	Bf 109E	Destroyed
7th Oct	Bf 109E	Destroyed
25th Oct	Bf 109E	Destroyed
25th Oct	Bf 109E	Destroyed
25th Oct	Bf 109E	Damaged
27th Oct	Bf 109E	Destroyed
29th Oct	Bf 109E	Destroyed
30th Oct	Bf 109E	Destroyed
9th Nov	Bf 109E	Damaged
14th Nov	Bf 109E	Damaged
15th Nov	Bf 109E	Destroyed
15th Nov	Bf 109E	Damaged
23rd Nov	Ju88	Destroyed
28th Nov	Bf 109E	Destroyed

Assessments

1938-39 as a Pilot - above average
1940 as a Pilot - above average
1948 as a Pilot and Instructor - above average
1950 as a Pilot and Instructor - exceptional
1953 as a Pilot and Instructor - exceptional

Aircraft flown

Avro Cadet	Hs 748
Avro Tutor	Hunter 6
Avro Anson 1 to 30	Islander
Audax	Magister
Aztec	Master 1,2, & 3.
Balliol	Martinet
Beagle Twin	Mustang
Beagle Pup	Monospar
Beaver	Mosquito 6
Buckmaster	Meteor 4,7,8, & 14.
Beech Baron 55 & 58	Moth
Beech Bonanza	Navajo
Beech King Air	Oxford
Beverly 2nd Pilot	Proctor
Caribou	Prentice
Cherokee 6/260; 6/300; 140	Percival Q6
Commanche 180; 250.	Pioneer Twin
Commanche Twin	Pembroke
Devon	Spitfire 1, 2, 5, 9, 14, 16,
Dominee	21 & 22
Dakota	Sneca
Harvard	Skyvan
Hurricane 1; 2; B; C.	Skyservant
Hart	Vampire
Hind	Venom

Royal Air Force Courses Completed:

Pilot Attack Instructors, Catfoss
Flying Instructors School, Lulsgate Bottom
Empire Flying School, Hullavington
Officers Administration School, Digby
Offensive Support, Old Sarum
Air Defence, Old Sarum
Transport Support, Old Sarum
Amphibious Warfare, Fremington
Royal Air Force Qualifications
QFI, PAI, IRE
Lancaster Civilian Qualifications
Instructor on Single engine/multi-engined aircraft

Ken is also Vice President of the Newtownards Flying Club and once a year travels from Cyprus to present the students who have qualified for their Private Pilots Licence (PPL}with their Wings and also presents 'The Student of the Year Shield' to the best all round student. He is also:-

President of the 501 Squadron Association;
President of the Hurricane Society;
Patron of the Gloucester Aviation Society;
Chairman of the Cyprus Aircrew Association;
1st Chairman of the Royal air Force Association; and
Past Secretary of the Battle of Britain Association.

Ken has recently had street named after him by Harborough District Council (Ken MacKenzie Close).

FLIGHT SERGEANT
ROBERT ANGUS MOORE
ROYAL AIR FORCE NO. 1074933
WIRELESS OPERATOR/AIR GUNNER
NO. 297 SQUADRON

KILLED IN ACTION 23RD AUGUST 1943

Robert Angus Moore was born in Bangor, County Down, on the 24th August 1919. He was educated at Bangor Grammar School were he excelled at sports. He was Lieutenant of the 1st Bangor Church Boys Brigade, and would have made Captain had he returned from the war. He was employed in the Civil Service (Ordnance Survey) Department in Ormeau Avenue, Belfast.

On joining the RAF he was posted to an initial training wing at Blackpool where he would have carried out his basic training, and then on to a Wireless and Gunnery School for his Wireless and Gunnery Training. On successfully completing his training, he was posted to No 297 Squadron which at that time was based at Brize Norton. It is known that he had carried out at least 44 operations before he was killed, and had been involved in a previous crash possibly in a Whitley when it ran out of fuel and crashed in France. He was reported missing for three days, but had managed to evade capture and got back to the UK.

Fight Sergeant Moore and the crew of his Albemarle may have been shot down by two enemy aircraft that were seen in the area. His aircraft is known to have crashed into the sea of the north east coast of Spain.

The crew

Pilot	Berty Curtiss
Navigator	Bruce Bowden
Wireless Operator	Robert Angus Moore
Rear Gunner	Nicky Nun

Flight Sergeant Robert Angus Moore and his crew are remembered on the Runnymede Memorial.

SERGEANT
VICTOR ALEXANDER CHESTNUT MUSSEN
ROYAL AIR FORCE NO. 1672363
PILOT
NO. 502 (ULSTER) AUXILIARY AIR FORCE

Victor Alexander Chestnut Mussen was born in Dunmurry on the 27th December 1923 and was educated at Inchmarlo Prep School and later at the Royal Belfast Academical Institution. On leaving Inst he was employed with his father who was a Wine and Spirit Merchant and who also owned two public houses in Dunmurry.

Victor volunteered to join the Royal Air Force on the 1st April 1941 at the age of 17 years and 3 months but was not accepted until 10th January 1942. He then proceeded to the Padgate Receiving Centre in England for attestation. It was here that the medical officer discovered a small but significant problem with his eyesight and that was serious enough to rule him out of becoming a Pilot. He was however offered the position of Wireless Operator which he accepted and was posted to an initial training wing at Blackpool for basic training and to start his Wireless Operators Training. From Blackpool he was posted to Compton Bassett where he completed an Advanced Wireless Course. On successfully passing his wireless training he was then transferred to the Airborne Forces Experimental Establishment at RAF Sherburn-in-Elmet which at that time was 'top secret'. The AFEE was equipped with Whitley, Hudson, Halifax, Albemarle, Stirling, Lancaster and Wellington aircraft. These were used for the testing of Hengist, Waco, Horsa, Hotspur, Hamilcar, Hadrian gliders and troop dropping. Victor flew in all the types mentioned and he was also responsible for the maintenance of all the aircraft and glider radio's. His first flight with the AFEE was on the 20th November 1942 in a Whitley (EB356). He took off at 1400 hrs with his Pilot Flying Officer Roscoe, DFC towing a Hengist Glider for 45 minutes. Most of the AFEE Pilots were experienced and many had already completed one tour of operations.

Near disaster in an Albermarle

The Albemarle was not a particular favourite with the Pilots at the AFEE for towing the heavy gliders. It was originally conceived as a fast bomber but it served exclusively as a glider tug and troop dropping. Victor was sitting comfortably in an armchair in the mess one Sunday afternoon, thinking that he had finished duty for the day when a call came through from operations requesting that he report back to dispersal. The 'boffins' had waited weeks to carry out 'special' test on a fully loaded Horsa Glider which was to be towed by a fully loaded Albermarle and the main requirement of the test was, there must be 'nil' wind. The time was 1800 hours and nil wind. Victor climbed into his Radio Operators seat closely followed by a 'boffin' who had brought along with him a 'magic box' which he plugged into the aircraft systems. The magic box turned out to be for measuring temperatures in different parts of the aircraft as it was towing the glider. The Pilot started up the Albermarles twin Bristol Hercules engines and taxied out to the main runway and took off, or as Victor laughingly said, "Staggered off." The Albermarle just managed to get airborne before it ran out of runway, but was unable to gain any height and hanging at about 50ft. The Skipper looked back at the Horsa glider and to his horror saw that it was flying at a very acute nose up attitude, almost stalling and ready to fall out of the sky. He knew that if he released the glider all on board would surely be killed.

Luckily the terrain around Sherburn was extremely flat, allowing the Skipper to fly a long flat turn back to the airfield. The Pilot continued the turn and was lining the struggling Albemarle up for the main runway and noticed that the altimeter showed that they were almost down to zero feet. So low in fact, as they crossed over a road near the perimeter fence, Victor saw a little girl on a bike probably on her way to Sunday school and he could see that she was carrying a bible. He thought to himself, "God, is this an omen?" The Pilot skilfully landed the

Albermarle and released the Horsa Glider much to the relief to all concerned. Victor's last flight with AFEE was on the morning of the 6th June 1943 in a Halifax (W7719) towing a Hamilcar for 1hr10mins. His Skipper was Flight Lieutenant Fink.

He was then posted to the station headquarters at RAF Newton for a three month course on wireless procedures. It was during this course that he discovered that sitting at his wireless set for long periods during the night and everyone chain smoking around him with boredom he was unable to open his eyes one morning. The medical officer rushed him to Nottingham Infirmary where they carried out some tests. They treated his eyes for three months and after the treatment was finished he was given a routine 'night vision' test by the MO. The result of the test was that Victor could now see things better than other people could at night, his eyesight were so exceptional that he was given an ordinary eye test and discovered that his eyes were now perfect. "It was like a miracle," Victor said. He immediately decided to re-muster as a Pilot and applied to the aircrew selection board. His application was approved by the end of December.

Victor was posted to No 6 Initial Training Wing at Aberystwyth in Wales and then to Grading School at No 23 Elementary Flying Training School at Clyff Pypard. His first air experience flight was on the 5th January 1944 in a Tiger Moth with his instructor, Flight Lieutenant Young. He continued training in the Tiger Moth until the 30th January and flew solo after eight hours tuition. Victor was then selected for a pilot's course and was transferred to the Aircrew Dispatch Centre at Heaton Park in Manchester to await a course. On the 16th March he was posted up to Scotland where he joined the No 14 (Pilot) Advanced Flying Unit at Banff and completed 7hrs.35mins training on the Units twin engined Oxfords.

He returned to the Aircrew Dispatch Centre at Heaton Park at the end of April 1944 and on the 13th July was transferred to Hornchurch where he hoped he would be starting some serious flying. He was soon informed that this was only an 'emergency posting' to help boost the local civilian morale and to help counteract the damage resulting from the V1 and V2 attacks that were now coming daily from France. They arrived at Hornchuch in 'tipper' lorries and were soon sent into the local town where they viewed at first hand the devastation of these powerful weapons. They helped the local people as best they could by putting tarpaulins over the roofs of damaged houses, clearing rubble and generally assisting where it was most needed. They did have people from the Ministry of Works who were attached to the RAF advising them on what to do and how to do it. At the beginning of October he was sent back to Heaton Park and informed that there was now a flying course available for him in Canada. He set sail for Canada on board the Liner Mauritania on the 20th October and arrived in Moncton three weeks later. He was then trained down to Miami in Oklahoma via Chicago and Kansas City to start his primary flying

training on PT19's at the No 3 British Flying Training School. Victor's first flight in the PT19 was on the 26th January 1945, taking off at 1339 hrs with his civilian instructor Mr FP Davis. The flight lasted for 50 minutes. His first solo in the PT19 was on the 6th February and he was tested on the 'link trainer' from time to time by Mr Argodale and Mr W Smith. Victor completed his primary training on the 28th March and was assessed by the schools Chief Flying Instructor as 'proficient'.

Having successfully completed his primary training his next step was advanced training and this was carried out in the AT6A (Harvard). His first flight in the Harvard was on the 9th April along with his Instructor Mr Weblemoe. His other instructors on this advanced course were, Mr Quisenberry, Mr Smith (Link), Mr Trawick, Mr Argodale, Mr Simpson, Mr Morgenstern, Mr Shortess, Mr CJB Murdoch, Mr Grantham-Jones and Flight Lieutenant Deuntzer. Victor soloed on the AT6A on the 17th April and went on to successfully finish the very intense seven month course which involved passing no less than 30 different exercises and was awarded his Wings at the end of August 1945. During his training in Canada the war in Europe had ended but the conflict in Japan was still raging. He received lectures on Japan and the Pacific and was told that he would not be going back to the UK but would travel direct to the Pacific. By the time he finished his course at the end of August the atomic bombs had been dropped on Hiroshima and Nagasaki and Japan had surrendered. He was trained back to New York where he boarded the Queen Elizabeth and arrived back in the UK on the 4th September 1945. On his arrival he was transferred to the No 7 Personnel Dispatch Centre (PDC) at Harrogate to await further orders. At that time it was possible for anyone who had volunteered in 1940 to receive a discharge from the Royal Air Force. Now that the war was over Victor saw no reason for him to remain and at this point decided to apply for his discharge.

He was then transferred firstly to Eastchurch on the 25th October and then on to Witchford on the 30th and finally discharged from Hednesford on the 12th December 1945. He officially left the Royal Air Force on the 14th February 1946 when his demob leave ended. Victor returned home to Northern Ireland and continued working for his father in the Wine and Spirit trade and helping out with the two public houses in Dunmurry.

502 (Ulster) Squadron, Royal Auxiliary Air Force, RAF Aldergrove

In June 1947 Victor decided to join the newly reformed 502 (Ulster) Auxiliary Air Force Squadron at RAF Aldergrove. The squadron at that time was commanded by another Ulsterman Wing Commander Hunter McGiffin (see his story) and was equipped with Oxfords, Harvards and Mosquito Mk.B.25's. Victors first refresher flight with the squadron was on the 15th June 1947 in an Oxford (3398) with Flight Lieutenant McDermott, the flight lasting 50 minutes. On the 6th

July he flew the Oxford solo and an hour later flew it again with Pilot Officer Miskimmen and Warrant Officer Gant *(Gant was later killed when his Spitfire crashed near Bandbridge in County Down in April 1950).*

On the 21st September 1947 Victor had his first flight in a Mosquito T111 (349) with Warrant Officer Gant (Green Ticket Exercise). He flew the Mosquito again on the 9th November with Flight Lieutenant McDermott and again on the 7th, 14th and 21st December with Flight Lieutenant Guy Clark. On the 15th February he flew solo in Mosquito (349) for 1hr.15mins carrying out gliding and climbing turns, take off into wind, and approach and landing exercises. Most of the squadron's flying was carried out at weekends and comprised of taking Air Training Corps Cadets and 3502 Squadron personnel on air experience flights, instrument flying, navigational exercises around Northern Ireland and England and height climbs to 25,000 and 30,000ft. On the 22nd July 1948 he carried out a navigation exercise with Corporal Stewart from Aldergrove to Westkappelle, Koblenz, Dortmund, Westkappelle and back to Aldergrove. The flight time was 3hrs15mins. His last flight in the Mosquito (937) was on the 3rd October 1948.

On one occasion when he was on final approach to land at Aldergrove in a Mosquito, his cockpit suddenly filled with what Victor thought was smoke but turned out to be engine coolant vapour. He was completely blinded by this and the only thing he could do was to stick his head out of the cockpit window and try and land the aircraft safely. This he managed to do and after the Mosquito was inspected it was found that a jubilee clip had came loose on a coolant pipe. On October 3rd, 7th, 24th and 31st Victor concentrated flying the Harvard, this was in preparation of the squadron being re-equipped with the Spitfire Mk22's. His first solo flight in the Mk22 was on the 31st October 1948 and lasted for 30 minutes. His logbook shows that on the 10th September 1949 he flew a 'shadow' exercise with HMS Implacable in Spitfire 605 and on the 17th September took part in the Battle of Britain display at Aldergrove in Spitfire 373. He also took part in the formation fly past for Her Majesty at Balmoral on the 15th July 1950 and the Sydenham display on the 26th August.

In 1950 Wing Commander Hunter McGiffin decided to retire from the RAFVR, and so, handed over command, this time to a regular officer, Squadron Leader DFB Sheen, an Australian who had won the DFC and Bar during the Battle of Britain.

19th November 1950: A tragedy hits 502 Squadron

Victor explained to me, "We flew the Spitfire in those days in a formation of four when we carried out a particular type of fast climb through dense cloud. This was called a 'battle climb' and the idea was to spiral up through the clouds to 30,000ft as fast as you could in formations of four at one minute intervals and once we 'usually' cleared the cloud we would reform on each other." On this particular occasion, the 19th November 1950, while carrying out this exercise the cloud ceiling did not clear at 30,000ft. So the leader of the formation, when he got to 30,000ft remembering that the Mk22 could not go much higher informed the others that they would have to come down through the cloud again. So you can guess the confusion that this was about to cause as everyone was in this thick cloud at approximately one minute intervals apart. After a period of time some of the aircraft were still on their way up while others were on their down. "At one stage I saw a Spitfire go right over my cockpit hood, no more that 20 feet away.

"Shortly after I landed I was informed that my good friend, Warrant Officer Gant had crashed near Bandbridge and was killed. Flying Officer Bill Polly (from Lisburn) who was also on the same exercise with Bob Johnson, decided to stick together and headed east out over the sea and then let down until they cleared the cloud and got their bearings. The first airfield they came across was Newtownards and as they both were running short on fuel decided to land. Unfortunately in doing so Bill's aircraft went up on its nose and was slightly damaged. "That left Bob Mooney and myself, we decided to contact Aldergrove and ask for assistance. They gave us a course which brought us in around the back of Lough Neagh, close to Toome airfield in County Londonderry. By now our 'low fuel' red light was flashing, so Bob Mooney made the decision to land at the airfield. I decided to carry on to RAF Aldergrove informing the tower on the way of my low fuel situation and requesting permission to land straight in without having to carry out a circuit.

"I landed safely, but while I was taxiing round to the dispersal point the Griffin suddenly gave a loud splutter and stopped, out of fuel. I had the sad duty of informing Warrant Officer Ronnie Gant's wife that he had been killed in a flying accident."

Victor's first flight in a jet

In March 1951, the squadron was re-equipped with De Havilland Vampire FB.5s and in preparation of his first flight in a Jet aircraft, Victor was given two familiarisation flights in a Meteor (734) on March 1st with a Flying Officer Griffin. An hour later he climbed into the cockpit of a Vampire (838) for the first time and flew it solo for 35 minutes. Again most of the exercises that were carried out in the Vampire were 30,000ft speed Rrns, squadron formations (3, 4, 6 and 9 Ship), high level QGH, aerobatics, snake climb 35,000ft battle formation, anti-aircraft flag firing and taking part in Battle of Britain displays. On the 30th September 1951 he took part in exercise 'Pinnacle' flying Vampire 296 and managed to intercept five B29s. Victor decided to leave 502 Squadron in 1952 as his father had died and he had to take over the running of the family business. His last flight in a Vampire was on the 19th January when he flew to Hooton Park where his aircraft went U/S and his last flight with the squadron was the next day when he was returned to Aldergrove in a Harvard flown by Flight Lieutenant Fox. Victor continued to run his father's two public houses in Dunmurry until 1969 when he decided to sell them to the Croft Inn Group. He remained with the Croft Inns as an Administration Manager for the next 17 years. The Croft Inns were eventually taken over by the Guinness Company and they re-employed Victor as a consultant for two years. and he finally retired in 1988, and lives with his wife in Millisle, County Down.

When Victor left the Royal Air Force in January 1951 he accumulated 700 hours flying time in the following aircraft types: Armstrong Whitworth Whitley and Albemarle; Lockeed Hudson; Handley Page Halifax; Short Stirling; Avro Lancaster; Vickers Wellington; Tiger Moth; Airspeed Oxford; Cornell PT19; Harvard AT6A; Horsa Glider; DeHavilland Mosquito; Supermarine Spitfire Mk22; Gloster Meteor; DeHavilland Vampire; and Balliol.

The following information I thought would be of interest especially to 502 (Ulster) Squadron buffs as it was taken from Victor's flying log book.

Aircraft types and serial numbers

Airspeed Oxford	3398, NM294, 791,
Mosquito	349, 982, 306, 352 (U), 282, 242, 937, 298, 595, 524.
Harvard 11B	155, 222, 249, 707, 717, 767.
Spitfire Mk22	373, 388, 402, 483, 488, 493, 499, 561, 566, 567, 605, 620, 670.
Meteor	594, 734, 774, 594.
Vampire	91, WA 292, 294, 296, 297, 304, 309, 384, 392, 567, 527, 838.

Aircrew names mentioned in his log book

Squadron Leader Hunter McGiffin, Flight Lieutenant PAC McDermott, Warrant Officer Gant, Flying Officer Cole-Baker, Flight Lieutenant Guy Clark, Pilot Officer Miskimmen, Flight Lieutenant Gray, Warrant Officer Lewis, Flight Lieutenant Corkin, AC Moore, Sergeant Morrison, AC Eaton, Corporal Cooper, Corporal Irwin, AC Parsons, AC Patterson, P11 Seaton, P11 Cambell, Flying Officer Bowden, R McIlmail, C Doak, AC Derrick, Corporal Darra, AC Twiss, Corporal Wafer, Corporal Robinson, AC McMullan, AC McHugh, Flying Officer Mail, Corporal Edwards, Corporal Stewart, AC Wasson, Corporal Geddis, P11 Hanna, Corporal Rogers, AC Harbinson, AC Collins, LAC Karmody, Sergeant Joyce, S Durant, Flight Lieutenant Burgess, P11 Gardiner, Flight Lieutenant McDonald, McCandless, Flying Officer Polley, Corporal Geddis, Corporal Dickey, Flight Lieutenant Fox, Flight Lieutenant Callaghan, Flying Officer Griffin, Flight Lieutenant Bushen, O/C Riley, Pilot Officer Harbinson, Corporal Shaughnessy, Flight Lieutenant Mooney, Pilot Officer McPherson, Flight Lieutenant Saker, Pilot Officer Milner.

FLYING OFFICER
VICTOR STEPHEN NEILL
ROYAL AIR FORCE NO. 745252
PILOT
NO. 611 SQUADRON

KILLED IN ACTION 4TH MAY 1943

Victor Stephen Neill, the youngest son of Mr Samuel James and Mrs Sarah Jane Neill, was born in Belfast on the 4th June 1919. He was educated at Fane Street Public School from 1931 until 1936, and completed his higher education at the Oranges Civil Service Academy from 1936, where he spent the next year and finished his studies at the Belfast College of Technology in 1939. On leaving the Civil Service Academy in 1937, he was employed as a Clerk with the Belfast Corporation Transport Department in Sandy Row.

Victor like a lot of young people at that time had a passion for flying and decided to join the RAFVR in Belfast on 10th March 1939. He learned how to fly the Tiger Moth and Hawker Hind aircraft at the 24 Elementary and Reserve Flying Training School at Sydenham. 24 E & R FTS was established by Short Bros and Harland on the 1st January 1939 at the Belfast Airport and was used exclusively for the training of RAF Reserve Pilots under the command of Wing Commander Gauntlet. The schools Chief Flying Instructor was Flight Lieutenant D Sloan, another Ulsterman who had been seconded from 502 Ulster Squadron. Ground lectures were held at the RAFVR Centre above the Saxone shoe shop in Donegall Place, Belfast. Victor successfully completed the flying course and flew solo sometime during May 1939.

With the outbreak of war AC 2 Neill was called to full-time service and on 12th December 1939 he was posted to No 59 Initial Training Wing at St Lenards-on-Sea to start his basic training. He spent the next six months at the ITW learning the art of square bashing, physical training and how to salute, etc. He was promoted to Sergeant on the 19th April 1940, and on the 1st July 1940 was sent to the No 50 GR Pool ??? where he spent the next two months awaiting a posting to start his flying training. He received his posting on the 31st August and transferred to No 15 STFS where he successfully completed his service flying training and was awarded his Wings on the 13th November 1940. On the 2nd

November 1940 Victor was posted to No 55 OTU to commence his operational training on Hawker Hurricanes, and on the 17th June 1941 he was assigned to No 245 Squadron at RAF Aldergrove in Northern Ireland. This posting was extremely handy for Victor as it was only 15 miles away from his home in Belfast, which he visited as often as he could between sorties. At that particular time 245 Squadron was allocated for the defence of Belfast when it was flying 'fighter nights' over the City. Victor was transferred from 245 squadron to 1423 Flight on the 25th August 1941 were he spent the next eight months, and on the 31 December 1941 he was promoted to Flight Sergeant.

On the 2nd of April 1942 he was posted to 611 Squadron which was based at Drem in Scotland. The squadron at that time had been 'retired' to Scotland after having a hectic previous year, and its task at Drem was to carry out convoy patrols and the odd scramble. Victor was one of 611 Squadrons new pilots, as most of its more experienced ones had been posted overseas in March. The new pilots had to work extremely hard training on the new Mk 1X's over the next three months and in June the squadron returned south to join 11 Group at Kenley. The squadron had now started to be re-equipped with the Mk Vb Spitfires and was carrying out intensive 'Sweeps' and 'Rhubarbs' into France. In July 1942 the squadron moved to Biggin Hill where it was kept busy for the next ten months. Biggin Hill at that time was commanded by that legendary pilot Group Captain Adolf Gysbert (Sailor)

Malan, DSO & Bar, DFC & Bar who during his career shot down and destroyed 34 enemy aircraft and damaged at least 16 more.

Victor received his commission on the 22nd June 1942,and promoted to Pilot Officer and six months later climbed the ladder to Flying Officer.

Victor's demise

On Tuesday 4th May 1943 Victor took off from his Base RAF Station Manston, East Kent, in his Spitfire 'LF' (Low altitude Fighter) Mk1X Serial No (EN567) at 17.45 hours on a 611 Squadron sortie to escort bombers to Antwerp. He was flying as Red 2 to the Wing Commander Flying. At approximately 1840 hrs Victor and his squadron were attacked by Luftwaffe Interceptors when about ten miles west of Antwerp at a altitude of 23,000ft. In the ensuing melee, none of 611 squadrons pilots noticed what had happened to Victor, but Flight Sergeant Due did happen to observe a Spitfire in distress, the machine was spinning down, and apparently, no effort was made by it's pilot to bale out. Flight Sergeant Due followed the stricken Spitfire down to 5,000ft. No R/T communication was received by anyone from Victor, which may suggest that he had been previously incapacitated or that his radio had sustained some damage. It was generally concluded that it was Spitfire EN567 that was seen spinning down. Victor failed to return to Manston that day, and like so many others, neither his body or his aircraft have ever been found. He was 24 years of age. During one of Victor's home leaves he visited his former colleagues in the Belfast Corporation Transport Department in Sandy Row and when the question of a mascot for his aeroplane arose he was presented with a large copy of the Belfast Coat-of-Arms which he had transferred onto his Spitfire when he returned to base. The motto on the Coat-of-Arms reads "Good Value for Money". A Transport official said, "Every time Victor's fighter goes into action, the Belfast Coat-of-Arms goes into action also." Victor's mother Mrs Sarah Jane Neill, a well known figure in the Belfast Savings Group, and Honorary Secretary of the Adelaide Avenue Branch, which in December 1942 raised the sum of £2,368 for Wings for Victory Day, and that eventually topped over £5000.

Flying Officer Victor Stephen Neill is remembered on the Runnymede Memorial.

WARRANT OFFICER
JOHN KENNEDY PARKINSON
ROYAL AIR FORCE NO. 1796365
AIR GUNNER
ROYAL AIR FORCE BOMBER COMMAND

John Kennedy Parkinson was born in Downpatrick County Down on the 28th September 1922 and was educated at Ballygally Primary and Down Royal. On leaving Down Royal, he was employed at a solicitors officer in Belfast. John decided to join the Royal Air Force in April 1943 and was soon posted to the ACRC in London.

After completing the selection board it was decided that he was to become an Air Gunner and was posted to the Initial Training Wing at Bridlington on the 27th June 1943 to start his basic training. On the 13th July 1943 he commenced his Air Gunnery training at RAF Pembrey in Wales on Bristol Blenheims. This training continued through to the 7th August where he successfully passed the course and was promoted to the rank of Warrant Officer. The chief examiner remarked in his logbook, "A hard worker who will pull his weight in Aircrew."

On the 10th August 1943 John was posted to No 20 OTU which at that time was based at Lossiemouth in Scotland to commence his operational training on Wellingtons. His operational training continued through to 13th September. It was during this period that John now acquired a lucky mascot which was hung up in his turret and went with him on every flight. It took the form of a little sailor doll and was no more than two inches long and he called it Sinbad. His wife still has Sinbad and no doubt it will be passed on her Grandchildren.

Note: On the 17th August John's log was signed by the Officer Commanding 'C' Flight 220 OTU, Acting Squadron Leader IW Bazalgette, DFC. On the 17th August exactly two years later he was to be posthumously awarded the Victoria Cross for his gallantry during a daylight raid on Trossy St Maximin on the 4th August 1944. His courage and devotion was beyond praise.

On completion of his OTU training John was posted to 1658 HCU at Riccall where he met his crew and start his conversion training onto the Handley Page Halifax as a Mid Upper Gunner. His first flight recorded in his logbook was on the 8th October in Halifax Code ZD-E. The conversion training was completed on the 30th

November 1943. With all his training now finished Warrant Officer Parkinson joined 158 Squadron on the 1st December 1943. The Squadron was based at RAF Lissett in Yorkshire and had just converted from Wellingtons onto Halifax's and continued with them until the end of the war. Lissett was a satellite airfield to Driffield. 158 Squadron had an interesting wartime career in as much as it took part in the first 1,000 bombing raid and also played an active part in the mine laying campaign. Among its Halifax's were two particularly distinguished specimens, the first was Halifax Mk 111 coded LV907 F-Freddy or Friday the 13th as it was affectionately named and the second was LV917 C-Clueless. Both of these aircraft joined the squadron in March 1944 and between then and VE-Day flew 128 and 100 operational sorties respectively. Both participated on the squadrons final wartime operation which was to Wangerooge on the 25th April 1945.

John's first flight with the squadron was on the 4th December and this was to be a local exercise getting the crew familiar with the area. These and other types of local exercises continued until the 20th January 1944 when he flew on his first operation which was to Berlin. Unfortunately his aircraft had to return to base early due to the port outer engine being U/S. On January 23rd John and his crew flew from Lissett to RAF Leconfield and were transferred to the newly formed 640 Squadron. 640 Squadron was formed at Leconfield in Yorkshire on the 7th January 1944 as a heavy bomber unit made up from 'C' Flight of 158 Squadron at Lissett. The squadron flew its first two missions from Lissett but all subsequent missions from Leconfield. Between January 1944 and April 1945 the squadron won the No 4 Group (Bombing)

Cup Trophy no less than five times. A record unequalled. John's second operation on the 15th February was again to Berlin, and while over the target he was wounded in the head by heavy flak. Towards the end of 1944 John had completed 34 operations (this was no mean feat).

Targets visited

Berlin, Stuttgart, Frankfurt, Villeneuve, Torgnier, Trappes, (Maisy, D-Day), Ottignes, Mantes Gassicourt, Morsalines, Hasselt, Boulogne, Siracourt, Evrecy, Dise Mont, Dumlegur, Caen, Ferm Du Forrestei, Wanne Eickle, Foret De Nieppe, and Chappelle Notre Dam. His last operational trip was to Foret Du Nieppe on the 5th July 1945 and his total flying hours with the squadron was 35hrs.30mins (day) and 123hrs.21mins (night). As Warrant Officer Parkinson had passed away I have no way of verifying my next statement and that is I think because of his exhausting operational career he may have been stood down from his squadron and posted to 1658 Heavy Conversion Unit as an Instructor until the 330th September 1945.

John's logbook shows that on the 1st November 1944 he was posted home to Northern Ireland were he joined No 12 AGS at Bishopscourt near Downpatrick as an Air Gunner Instructor on Avro Ansons and Wellingtons. Here he remained until the 1st May 1945 when he was on the move again to No 5 Air Navigation and Bombery School in Jurby on the Isle of Man. His logbook also records that he started instructing at Jurby on Wellingtons on the 15th May 1945 until the 31st May 1945 when his logbook shows that his last official instructional flight was indeed on that day in Wellington Code LP907. John did not enter dates for his last log entries but it shows that he attended No 3 Aircrew Holding Unit (ACHU) at Penrhos, ACAC ??? at Catterick, No 4 Maintenance Unit (MU) at New Market. No 12 School of Technical Training (S of TT). Sometime during 1946 John was posted overseas to Palestine and became Lord Tedder's personal driver and helped with the casualties after the bombing of the King David Hotel in Jerusalem.

His total flying hours in Blenheims, Wellingtons, Halifax and Anson types was 217hrs.13mins (day) and 152hrs.42mins (night)

John left the Royal Air Force in 1947 and returned to Northern Ireland where he joined the Civil Service and became Deputy Principal in the personnel department. He retired from the Civil Service in 1982 and died in 1994.

FLIGHT LIEUTENANT
WILLIAM FRANCIS POLLEY
ROYAL AIR FORCE NO. 1481712
ROYAL AIR FORCE FIGHTER COMMAND

Flight Lieutenant Bill Polley was born on the 29th of April 1921 in the County Down village of Cloughy, situated a few miles south of the fishing village of Portavogie, on the eastern shore of the picturesque Ards Peninsula. He was educated at Regents House Grammar in Newtownards, where he gained his senior certificate in 1940. He had previously applied to join the Royal Air Force in 1938 but was advised that his junior certificate was insufficient and that he should continue his education until gaining his senior.

That now done, Bill found himself doubting his desire to join the Royal Air Force and, probably as a result of the influence of his ex-Royal Navy uncle, decided to join the 'Sailors'. The Caledonian Wireless College in Belfast's Ann Street accepted Bill's application in early 1940 and he started his six-month course on wireless telegraphy and the maintenance of shipboard communication equipment. Having successfully completed the course towards the end of 1940, the Royal Navy recruiting office was the next stop. Unfortunately he was advised that no vacancies existed at that time and it was suggested he tried the Royal Air Force. Disappointed, Bill visited Clifton Street recruiting centre and volunteered for the RAF. He was accepted for service but, like so many of his fellow countrymen at that time, was told to go home and await his call up. Six months later his orders arrived and Bill was soon en route to the Lancashire depot where most Ulstermen first found themselves after call up.

Padgate and the No 3 Receiving Centre was the first stop, arriving on the 29th June 1941, one of 65 recruits from Ulster of whom 30 plus applied for aircrew. Including Bill only six were accepted. Now Aircraftsman 2nd Class WF Polley was then London bound to the Aircrew Reception Centre at Regents Park, arriving on the 8th July. For two weeks lectures were interspersed with square bashing in Regents Park and during this time Bill recalls living in a flat in Bentinet Close for two weeks, recalled because of the scarcity of creature comforts which did not even stretch to a bed, he had to lie on and MOD issue 'biscuit' (type of mattress). On the 23rd July it was northwards to Scotland and the Initial Training Wing at St Andrews to prepare for his elementary training. Bill was then posted to No 18 EFTS at Fairoaks in Surrey on the 18th October to start his flying training. This commenced on the 20th October in Tiger Moth N9449, under the instruction of Pilot Officer Sunderland, but was abruptly ceased seven days and four flights later when he was sent to Heaton Park in Manchester to await transportation to Canada en-route to the United States of America for further flying training. (This would seem a curious way to start a pilot's training, and it can only be assumed that the initial flying was by way of an assessment before further training was judged prudent.) Bill arrived at Heaton Park on the 5th November, where he waited two weeks for a ship which would take him to Canada. On November 21st he boarded the vessel Pasteur and arrived in Halifax, Nova Scotia, 12 days later.

On his arrival in Halifax, he swapped the ship for a train, and travelled to the No 31 Personnel Despatch Centre at Moncton in the Canadian province of New Brunswick, where he spent two weeks awaiting his onward transport to the warmer climates of Maxwell Field, Alabama. Bill arrived at the Aircrew Reception Centre at Maxwell Field, Alabama on the 18th of December and found himself once again suffering the same basics as had been the case at Regents Park in London. Thankfully this time the lectures and square bashing were short lived and he was onward again ten days into 1942, this time further south to Arcadia in Florida. Bill arrived at the civilian Riddle Aeronautics Institute at Carlstorm Field in Florida on January 11th 1942. The school was situated to the north of Fort Myers in the southern part of Florida. After a gap of almost three months took to the air again on the 13th January, this time in the very different Boeing Stearman (PT17c) under the instruction of a Mr Taylor, who stayed with Bill until his primary training finished.

12 days later he went solo and continued through the course until late March, successfully negotiating his 20, 40 and 60-hour checks before taking his final check flight with the chief flying instructor for the US Army, RM Fahringer (Bills total flying hours were now 60hrs.05mins.)

With his primary training completed Bill was back to Gunter Field, Alabama to commence his basic flying training. The school was equipped with the Vultee Bt13 for this task and he was now being trained by the United States Army Air Force facility, which had Royal Air Force instructors on its staff. One of these instructors, Pilot Officer ACmJonas, was to be Bill's principal tutor for this stage of his training. Bill's first flight in the Vultee came on the last day of March with Pilot Officer Jonas, and his solo on the type followed eight days later. Basic training continued into May, and the interim check stages being again passed without any problems, and it is interesting to note the American terminology for some of the flying exercises, 'Lazy eights', 'Chandelles', 'Pylon eights', 'Immelman turns' being a few examples. Towards the end of Bill's basic training at Gunter Field a very serious incident occurred which resulted in serious casualties and damage to the unit's aircraft.

On the 20th May, 36 Vultee's left Gunter Field for a cross country day and night exercise. One of each group of six aircraft carried an instructor and the plan was to fly sectors from Gunter to Crestview, Mobile, Crestview, and Gunter. On their arrival at Mobile they had to land due to very poor weather, planning to continue when it had passed. In the event it did not clear until late in the day and, given the all clear by the Met Office, the flight back to Gunter Field was planned, entailing a night arrival at their base. At the commencement of the exercise Bill had only six hours of night flying to his credit and it is likely that the other trainees had more or less the same. Under these circumstances the six instructors in charge of the exercises must have been confident in both the Met Office all clear, and in their ability to get their aircraft and pupils safely back to Gunter Field. Accordingly all 36 Vultees departed Mobile but the weather closed in again after dark and in the ensuing conditions tragedy struck. Out of 36 departing Vultees only six arrived safely at Gunter Field, excluding Bill. 16 made night-forced landings, 14 crashed, three of the pilots baling out. Unfortunately seven other pilots were not so lucky and were killed including, as Bill remembers, Leading Aircraftman Stanley Peattie, another Ulsterman who burned to death when trapped in his aircraft. It is not known how many British or Commonwealth pilots were amongst the trainees.

Bill was lucky when he spotted the beacon of a disused airfield in the distance and force landed safely on an overgrown runway. Given the conditions, nobody was around so he walked the few miles towards the local town of Greenville where he found a hotel. From there he rang Greenville Field to find they had posted him missing. They told him to remain where he was until the morning and he recalls being able to do some shopping in Greenville until his lift arrived later in the day. Bill was almost at the end of his time at Gunter Field and had his last flight there only eight days after the terrible events of the night of the 20th of May, it being noticeable that some 16 flights were carried out in this period, commencing as soon as he arrived back at base. It would appear that the instructors, quite rightly, had got the trainees back into the air before they could dwell on the tragedy.

With a total flying time of some 140 hours, (73 on Vultees) Bill finished at Gunter Field, his log being signed by the Squadron Commander Captain JO Gault.

It was then on to the next stage of flying training at the Advanced Flying School at Craig Field which was located on the Alabama river at Selma, some 130 miles south of the state capital, Birmingham. As was the case at Gunter Field, the Advanced Flying School was also a United States Army Air Force facility employing Royal Air Force personnel amongst it's instructors, this time flying Harvards (At-6As) and it was one of these, a Flying Officer DR Stephens, a Flight Commander, who took Bill for his first flight on the 5th June, his solo following three flights later. On the 18th July he commenced a gunnery course at Elgin Field and his log notes his score as, "Highest on record in course." Back at Craig Field Bill had finished his training with a final flight on the last day of July and his logbook was signed off by the squadron Commanding Officer, 1st Lieutenant Elmer E Taggart. Having now successfully passed all of his Pilot's exams Bill was awarded his Silver Wings, promoted to Sergeant and prepared to make the long journey back to the UK Unfortunately, Bill was also all too near another tragedy that would happen a few weeks after leaving Alabama in early August.

No 31 Personnel Despatch Centre Moncton
SS Awatea
No 1Y Depot Halifax Nova Scotia
HMT Queen Mary

Three days after leaving Alabama Bill was back at the Moncton Despatch Centre to await transport home. This took a number of days many of which were used for sightseeing locally, until the 20th August, when he departed for Halifax to board the SS Awatea for the trip home. He and some 300 other returning aircrew sailed on board the vessel on the 22nd August, part of a convoy bound for Liverpool, but they were destined to run into trouble. A few hours out of Halifax the marauding U-boats struck the convoy and the Awatea was suddenly involved in a collision. A United States escort ship the

Ingram had turned across her bows so closely that a collision was inevitable. She was rammed by the much heavier merchantman, cut in two, both pieces of the Ingram sank immediately with all lives lost. Bill notes in his log, "Saved by the American Corvette Ingram." It sank with 59 personnel. It was a terrible loss of life, the actions of the corvette were questioned, the aircrew onboard their merchantman wondering how such a tragedy could have happened. Perhaps in the heat and confusion of battle a manoeuvre had been attempted which had been cut to fine or, as many believed was the case, the US Skipper had sighted a torpedo and deliberately placed his ship between it and the valuable merchant ship. Whatever the reason the aircrew onboard the Awatea were truly thankful for the sacrifice of the American sailors. A case of the few saving the many.

(The USS Ingraham was in fact a destroyer of the Benson Class, of some 2,400 Tons, mounting 5-inch guns and carrying some 208 crew. The Awatea herself was badly damaged and was forced to return to Halifax where she disembarked her 'cargo', whilst the remainder of the convoy continued on towards England.)

And so, only two days after leaving Nova Scotia, Bill found himself back again and had to wait a further eleven days before boarding a train bound for New York and the fast transport, the Queen Mary. Boarding the Queen Mary early on the 5th September and setting sail the same evening, they arrived in Southampton five days later and reported to the Aircrew Receiving Centre at Bournemouth on the 11th. Here he passed the time for the next two weeks with lectures whilst waiting news of his next destination. This was to be at the Advanced Flying Unit at Ternhill in Shropshire where he spent just under two weeks flying Miles Magisters in order to familiarise himself with the British as opposed to the American instrumentation. He also spent some eight hours on the Link Trainer, being assessed as 'average' for the instrument flying requirements. It is also interesting to note that the certificate which is attached to Bill's flying logbook which all pilots were required to sign prior to their first solo on type. This was routine but the additional clause required them to acknowledge that under no circumstances would solo low flying be attempted. Perhaps a reference to the number of accidents that were hitherto commonplace with young pilots eager to show their abilities. After spending six weeks lecturing at Calveley, Bill emerged from Ternhill in early December 1942 with an 'average' assessment with the additional comment, "Quite a steady Pilot - aerobatics improving but need practice." Having commenced his Pilot Training back in October of the previous year. Bill was now ready to take the next step towards becoming operational. Accordingly he now found himself posted to an Operation Training Unit prior to joining a squadron. Commonly referred to as Royal Air Force Stroud, Aston Down in Gloucestershire was the location of No 52 Operational Training Unit. Bill

arrived there on the 7th December, first flying with Flight Lieutenant Hopkins, who was officer commanding 'B' Squadron in a Miles Magister on the 11th, and experiencing a Mk11 Spitfire M7910 for the first time four days later.

He remembered well the contrast to the types flown in training, the power and acceleration being quite astonishing, "If you could pull yourself off the back of the seat." Spitfire familiarisation continued through until February 1943, including much air firing practice, something which Bill seemed particularly good at, emerging with an 'above the average' assessment from the Officer Commanding, Air Firing Squadron.

Overall his assessment from the Chief Flying Instructor of No 52 OTU, Squadron Leader CGH Crusoe, was 'average' and Bill left Aston Down as a qualified Sergeant Pilot complete with his Wings.

No 501 Squadron 'County of Gloucester' Royal Auxiliary Air Force, Ballyhalbert, County Down Northern Ireland

With the motto "Fear Nothing" the squadron had been known as 'City of Bristol' until May 1930, when it changed to 'County of Gloucester'.

At the time of Bill's posting to 'A' Flight, the squadron was based in his homeland of Ballyhalbert on the Ards Peninsula, County Down, having been involved in the war from the outset with its Hurricanes, including two months in France before it surrendered. It also covered the retreating British Expeditionary Force from its base in St Helier and served with 11 Group in the Battle of Britain, claiming 149 enemy aircraft destroyed. In April 1941 501 took over No 66 Squadron's Spitfires and took on convoy patrols and escort work before moving to cover Bomber Command sorties. In October 1942 it was 'retired' to Ulster where it replaced 504 Squadron, where it undertook what was considered as mundane and boring shipping patrols. Bill joined the squadron during this period, arriving on the 17th of February 1943 and first flying the nest day with Flight Lieutenant Scorer on two local familiarisation sorties before going aloft in his first operational SpitfireVB AR295.

The posting back home suited Bill, he was a short distance from his home in Cloughy and his local knowledge was useful to the squadron and made life a little easier at Ballyhalbert through his contacts. A farming cousin of Bill's ensured a continuous supply of fresh farm eggs, and knowledge of local dance halls provided useful information for the other crew members. Bill also caused a few problems for the golfers as he enjoyed beating up the local golf course on more than one occasion. It was known for the local golfer's to shout out when they saw a Spitfire coming over, "Look out, here comes that 'edgit' Polley again." Ballyhalbert was not an ideal station for fighters and was not in good condition, like many World War II airfields it had been built in a hurry and suffered accordingly, not helped by the location on the low lying peninsula with its constant exposure to the worst of the weather, whatever its direction. It has to be acknowledged that Northern Ireland did not possess many sites that were suitable for airfields and several of those constructed during the early war period suffered from weather and/or drainage problems. Accordingly the buildings soon deteriorated and so was the case with Ballyhalbert, where internal walls would be running with water on more occasions than was comfortable. The poor position and weather conditions also took their toll on the pilots with several losses in accidents on or around the airfield. On 17th February 1943 Sergeant Stanley, flying Spitfire AB960 SD-X was killed when he flew into the hills near the Mourne Mountains about 40 miles west of the base near Ballynahinch. His body was recovered from Slieve Greeba later that day. Flying Officer Woodshend flying Spitfire BL615 collided with Pilot Officer Powierza during a dogfight practice. Flying Officer Woodshend was killed when his parachute became entangled around the tail of his Spitfire which then dived vertically onto the beach at Cloughy, Bill's hometown. Pilot Officer Powierza was able to regain control of his aircraft and return to base.

On the 4th April 1943 Sergeants Nichol (BL688 SD-H) and Patterson (P8741 SD-J) collided during Squadron formation near Portaferry, Co Down. Patterson was killed and Nicol crash-landed at Ballyhalbert. Such were the conditions suffered by both ground and aircrew, not only in Ireland. Like crews the world over, they accepted their lot and made the best of it.

(Not too many Ulstermen served in 501 Squadron during the war, Bill being unable to recall any during his time and he would not have known Ken MacKenzie, later Wing Commander, DFC AFC AE. Ken did a wonderful job in the squadrons Hurricanes during and after the Battle of Britain (see his own chapter) and not forgetting Warrant Officer Lockington Lilburn who joined the squadron on the 3rd December 1942 another of the original RAFVR pilots trained at 24 E&RFTS at Sydenham before the outbreak of war, and Flight Lieutenant Cecil Austin.)

Bill continued working up throughout March and April as the squadron prepared to return to the mainland after it's rest period.

Flying almost daily and often multi-tasked, he went through the practising of formation flying, dog-fights, air-to-air and air-to-ground gunnery, Balbo, Rhubarb, Cine-Gun and Affiliation with other squadrons including Tomahawks and Sunderland's, etc, no doubt learning from the more experienced pilots on the unit. Such training was repetitive and not without losses, as was the case during a 'Balbo' exercise on the 12th of April when Bill's notes in his log, "Pete Rogerson killed." The squadron was informed that it was moving shortly back to the mainland, but not before what Bill recalls was, "A tremendous party," leaving Ballyhalbert. On the last day of April 1943 Bill took of from Ballyhalbert for the last time in his Spitfire MkVb BM641 and arrived at High Ercal 1hr.15mins later, after refuelling

he took off and set coarse for Westhampnett, the home of 83 Operational Training Unit. Bill was to remain with the squadron for the rest of the war, moving with them many times over the next two years until the end of hostilities.

Westhampnett was his first taste of a 'true' operational base and, after two days of squadron exercises, carried out his first convoy patrol on the 3rd of May in Spitfire Vb BL778. For the next two weeks it was escorting bombers to their target and convoy work. During this period he encountered Bf109's and FW 190's on a regular basis but for some reason they did not want to get involved. He did eight further sorties coupled with continual practice including squadron and wing formations, an indication of the tactics employed by the Tangmere Wing, to whom the squadron was attached. On the 17th May the squadron moved to Martlesham Heath for ten days of air-to-air firing practice during which Bill maintained his excellent firing record, shooting the end off the drogue three times. From here they also mounted further patrols before returning briefly to Westhampnett en-route a short stay at Woodvale. The reason the squadron was sent up to Woodvale was, Martlesham Heath had been attacked by FW190's on May 2nd and in doing so caused considerable damage to the airfield. This news was not well received at 11 Group Headquarters, so the squadron was sent up to Woodvale for some special training. After less than a week they moved again to Westhampett for ten days before locating permanently at Hawkinge on the 21st of June just prior to Bill's commission to Pilot Officer. On the 21st June, 501 Squadron flew up to its old Battle of Britain base at Hawkinge to replace No 91 Squadron who had been actively engaged on 'Jim Crow' patrols which entailed flying up and down the home coastline, seeking enemy raiders as they crossed the coast.

At around this time the squadron added the Spitfire Mk 1X to its inventory, although Bill did not fly this type until December when his log shows a Mk 1Xa, a type that he was to fly frequently, remaining with the Mk Vb until the Hawker Tempest arrived. Now settled again, the squadron returned to intensive patrols and sweep sorties over the next few months. Flying many hundred of sorties in the period through until moving on to Southend on the 21st of January 1944, a month in which Bill passed the 500 hour mark and, on the 7th, was promoted to Flying Officer. The move to Southend was to be brief and used for Cine and air-to-air firing practice and the squadron returned to Hawkinge on the 1st February and remained until the end of April.

Some Log entries for this period of interest:

| 1st February 1944 | To Bradwell Bay. Did a sweep and collected some eggs. |
| 13th February 1944 | To Bradwell Bay. Did a recce into Headquarters and got seven eggs confirmed. *(A strange pair of entries.)* |

14th February 1944   Calibration to 23,000ft.
                     Bloody Cold!

Bills log shows several such Tests for calibration or height purposes, 33,000ft being recorded on one occasion.

Once again it was the same routine covering convoys, shipping and escorting various bombers, the time mainly in support of operations against the French coastline in preparation for the forthcoming invasion. A move to Friston on the 30th April made the flight to the landing beaches a little shorter and the period through until D-Day was spent providing escorts to the bombers that were hammering the inland railways and communications generally. At Friston they joined forces with No 350 (Belgian) Squadron who had the same task.

Some Log entries of interest

5th May 1944	Testing 45 gallon drop tank. OK good manoeuvrability.
24th May 1944	In Tiger Moth from base to Hawkinge, taking Benny to his mistress.
29th June 1944	*(On cine gun test)* Chased a buzz bomb. Tempest beat me.

D-Day 6th June 1944

It is officially recorded that Bills Spitfire Mk 2b SD-F was the very first aircraft over the beaches on the 6th June along with his good friend Flying Officer Bennet.

Bill made three sorties on the 6th June 1944, the first was a shipping recce to Cherbourg, the second was a sweep over the invasion coast, and the third was a low level cover over the beaches. In the next few weeks his log shows him visiting many places that became well known as result of the invasion, including Caen, Bayeaux, Carentan, Barfleur, and Arras. A brief move to Tangmere on the 2nd July allowed a long patrol over Caen the following day, returning once again to Westhampett on the 4th.

Two Log entries of interest:

July 14th 1944	Convoy Patrol, Pilot Officer Andrews killed yesterday. Willis shot down (landed France) North of Caen.
July 17th 1944	Escort Mitchell's to St Malo, Landed on American Station in France. Engine failed at 14,000ft behind German Lines. Hit by flak.

On July 18th 1944, a pair of Hawker Tempest Mk.Vs flew into Westhampnett, they caused quite a stir amongst the pilots and ground crews. At that time the Tempest was the fastest fighter in service anywhere in the world, with a top speed of 427mph, derived from it's 2,180 hp Napier Sabre engine to combat the V1s. Conversion to the tempest was now the order of the day and this was achieved very quickly according to Bills log. He first flew the Tempest V on the 20th July 1944, a brief 10 minute local before adding another two spitfire escorts on the 22nd/23rd. The 26th saw him get another two flights in the new mount, a total of 75 minutes. The next day he made his final two Spitfire flights, one an air test and the last a 'fighter sweep' over Paris. He would not fly the Spitfire again during the rest of his time with 501 and became a Tempest pilot from the 28th onwards, making his first flight in anger the following week.

Several historical accounts refer to No 501 squadron moving to Manston on the 2nd August to begin conversion to the tempest. Bill's log clearly shows that he first flew the new aircraft on the 20th July 1944 while still at West Hampnett.

(The Hawker tempest, derived from the Typhoon, which entered service with the RAF in April 1944 and was one of the fastest of all World War II fighters, to the extent that they were able to claim the destruction of 20 Jet powered Me262s whilst with the 2nd TAF in Europe. They will be remembered for their dramatic tank and train busting roles but had the majority of their successes when deployed against the flying bombs. In just under three months from June 1944, they destroyed more than one third of the entire RAF total over 1,750 such bombs. In later versions they would be the RAF's last single seat piston engined fighter-bomber and would remain in RAF service until 1951.)

The squadron moved to Manston in Kent on the 2nd August, and on the 5th Bill made his first 'anti-diver' patrol in Tempest EJ585 SD-A, shooting one down near Ashford in Kent opening the squadrons score sheet. He quickly went on to shoot down another which he shared with Flight Sergeant Ryman.

Bill later recalled:

"Very often we were to close to our targets (V1s) before we got the opportunity to open fire, and the biggest danger was getting an 'airburst' from one of the exploding V1s. On one such occasion I was chasing a Doodle Bug to quickly and I knew that was overhauling the beast to quickly and that I was also extremely close to some armoured balloons. I fired a long burst and pulled up steeply to starboard, almost directly above the V1 just as it exploded. The blast caught my left wing and tumbled my aircraft into a series of snap rolls. After what seemed to be an eternity the aircraft regained some stability, and as my gyros had tumbled it was many ageing moments before I realised that I was upside down."

This short passage by Bill will highlight some of the problems that were faced by the Fighter Pilots when engaging a V1.

"The V1s had a few 'nick names', (Doodle Bug), (Buzz Bomb) but the proper name for it was Fieseler F1 103 Flying Bomb. Each one carried a warhead containing 1,870lbs of high explosive, and this would produce a huge amount of debris if exploded in mid-air, and fatal damage to aircraft that came to close.

"The V1 was so big a threat at that time, the Prime Minister himself said that the squadron was to consider itself expendable. The Secretary of State for Air informed the pilots himself that they were prepared to sacrifice the lives of several pilots for every V1 shot down."

The other aspect that was highlighted by Bill was the conflict with 'other elements' of the home defensive scheme. "In the early days of the V-weapon campaign the squadrons of 150 Wing complained of being fired on by our own anti-aircraft guns, while the gunners complained that the fighters had strayed into their gun zones."

No doubt both were correct.

Log entries on interest:

August 5th 1944	Tempest SD-A. 'Anti-diver patrol'. Destroyed one Doodle Bug near Ashford and one shared with Flt/Sgt Ryman.
August 18th 1944	Tempest SD-Z. 'Anti-diver patrol'. One Doodle Bug destroyed, blew up.
August 26th 1944	Tempest SD-H. 'Anti-diver patrol'. Destroyed one Doodle Bug, blew up. Refuelled & rearmed at Newchurch. Fired at three others, got hits on two, no claims.
August 28th 1944	Tempest SD-Z. 'Anti-diver patrol'. One Buzz Bomb destroyed.

On the 23rd September 501 Squadron was again on the move, this time to Bradwell Bay in Essex, close to the Southend to enable night patrols to be maintained against the flying bombs coming across the east and south coast. 501 Squadron became 'specialists' in the anti flying-bomb patrols and, in the second week of August, went 'night operational'. Bill made his first night patrol on the 16th, adding a further 11 before the end of the month. September started the same way and, after a quickly taken leave, Bill rejoined at Manston ready for the move to Bradwell Bay on the 23rd.

Log entries of interest:

September 23rd	Flight Sergeant Bonham crashed.
September 29th	Tempest SD-F 'anti-diver patrol'. Got two Buzz Bombs. Paddy Farraday crashed and killed.
October 3rd	Squadron Leader Joe Berry killed, *(at that time he was the top scoring V1 Ace. 61 destroyed).*
October 12th	Tempest SD-C 'anti-diver patrol'. Chased two Buzz Bombs, boys got there before me.
October 24th	Tempest SD-C 'anti-diver patrol'. Flak destroyed four.

By October 1944 most of the V1 launching sites in the Pas-de-Calis had been captured by the advancing Allies.

The Luftwaffe's answer was to resort to its original intention of air launching the V1's from Bomber Units based in central Holland. From November 1944, although the flying bombs were still coming over the English coast in quantity, the radar gun sight fitted to the anti-aircraft guns enabled them to take a useful toll. As the Allies advanced into Europe and eventually over ran the V1 Launching Sites, the squadrons contacts gradually diminished.

The only contact Bill had during November 1944 was on the 9th. Logbook extract for the 9th November 1944:

Tempest MkV 'Anti-diver patrol'. Chased one- 10 took over.

The patrols continued with much night flying training in between, a pattern that was followed until the end of the war. The squadron moved once again on the 3rd of March this time to Hunsdon in Hertfordshire, continuing the same pattern, the need for patrols diminishing as VE Day approached. The invasion forces now capturing most of the occupied Europe and over-running the flying bomb launch sites, in addition the anti-aircraft guns located around southern England were making use of radar sighting and were imposing a good toll of incoming bombs. Bills last contact with the flying bombs came on the 8th March 1945, the anti-aircraft guns beating him to the draw and at the end of the month the squadron started a move back to a day fighter role. However enemy activity was by then almost non-existent and the squadron's purpose was no longer there. Accordingly 501 Squadron 'County of Gloucester' Royal Auxiliary Air Force was disbanded just ahead of VE-day, on the 21st April, although it did reform just over one year later using Spitfire LF16e's before being re-equipped with the Vampire. Bill's last flight with 501 Squadron came the day before the unit's disbandment, his 152nd Tempest flight, and one of the last the squadron flew in the war years. With the end of 501 Squadron, Bill moved on to a new Unit. He had been with 501 Squadron since being posted to Ballyhalbert in February 1943 and had clocked up in excess of 500 flights in their Spitfire and Tempest aircraft. He had experienced practically every aspect of a fighter's role in both day and night techniques, and was a very experienced pilot with much yet to offer in the Royal Air Force.

No 165 (Ceylon) squadron at Royal Air Force Bentwaters in Suffolk was the next stop and gave Bill his first experience of the excellent (P-51) Mustang, although he would only make a handful of flights in this type before reverting to the more familiar Spitfire, in this case the Mk1Xe. 165 Squadron had been formed in the spring of 1942 and had a very similar history to 501 Squadron in terms of tasks. In August 1942 it had been involved in the ill-fated Dieppe operation, which had cost the lives of so many Canadians, providing cover for Royal Navy warships. It then undertook shipping and escort work and moved briefly on to anti-diver patrols before reverting back to escort duties. January 1945 saw a conversion to the P-51 Mustang and escort activity for Bomber Command then followed until March, when it provided cover for the Rhine Crossing. It's last operation came with the Guernsey landings and, like 501 Squadron, its role then disappeared. It remained in existence through until September 1946 when it was disbanded and renumbered as 66 Squadron.

At the time of Bill's joining the squadron, flying was drastically reduced and was limited to brief training flights and air-tests. VE-day occurred only a few days after his arrival and, like his previous unit, 165 Squadron no longer had a specific purpose. The 28th May 1945 saw Bill taking to the air for the first time with his new unit. Flying with 'B' Flight, he flew the Mustang for the first time, switching to the Spitfire at the end of the month.

Log entries of interest:

28th April 1945	Mustang Mk 111. SD-Y Familiarisation and local.
14th May 1945	Auster Mk1. 'Sk' Flying Officer Bennet and self to Hunsdon.
14th May 1945	Auster Mk1 'Sk' Self and Flying Officer Bennet to Base.

RAF Bentwaters was vacated by the squadron at the end of May 1945 and moved up to Aberdeens Dyce Airfield in readiness to move to Vaernes in Norway.

Following some leave, Bill arrived at Dyce in time for the move to Sumburgh, where three days were spent prior to moving on to Vaernes, the airfield serving Trondheim.

8th June 1945	Spitfire 1Xe SD-Q Self. Air test.
17th June 1945	Spitfire 1Xe SD-Q Self. Dyce to Sumburgh.
20th June 1945	Spitfire 1Xe SD-Q Self. Sumburgh to Vaernes, Norway.

Now with 'A' Flight, Bill made the 2hrs.30mins flight in his Spitfire 1Xe, arriving at the Norwegian airfield on the 20th June, in what must have been a low fuel state after this length of flight in a short range Spitfire.

Vaernes was the location for both a large German garrison numbering several thousand and an Allied Prisoner of War camp where some 400 Naval personnel were interned. The squadron was part of the token force that was to take over from the Germans pending the arrival of the Allied land forces in sufficient numbers to take full control of the facility. In the interim, as Bill remembered, the 10,000 Germans remained in 'charge' of the camp to the extent that a German Colonel was allowed to retain his gun. The Germans also manned the front gate of the camp compound and had still retained the use of their staff cars, while the Royal Air Force officers had to walk. Bill also recalled buying cigarettes (legitimately sponsored) from Gallaghers at the rate of £1 per 1,000 and using these to make trades with the German prisoners and also remembered the German stores of thousands of barrels of wine and brandy in the

surrounding caves and, although it is unclear what happened to these, an educated guess could get close. Flying time did not amount to much during June and July, their prime task was seemingly preparation for the formation Flypast at Oslo on the 23rd July to mark the Norwegian Flag day, an occasion which may have marked the final liberation of the Norwegians as by this time the main land forces had arrived to replace the Germans. Bill was promoted to Flight Lieutenant in early July, and made his last flight in a 165 Squadron Spitfire SD-M on the 3rd August 1945. On the 5th August he was made Air Priority Officer at Oslo to arranging trips to Europe for high ranking officers, VIPs, and those requiring to travel on sick leave. On the 7th August 1945 he returned from Oslo as a passenger in a Mosquito. This took him up to the 24th November when he returned to the UK in a Dakota and went on indefinite accumulated leave.

His last log entry reads as follows:

24th November 1945	Dakota. H-B. Flying Officer An Other. Self. Oslo-Hunsdon. England. (This seems to be my last trip - & what a bloody aircraft to finish up in !!)

Goodbye, dear old Norway

On his return from Norway Bill was posted home to Northern Ireland, arriving on the 3rd December just in time to spend Christmas in Cloughy with his family. Bill's record of service shows him returning to duty on the 8th February 1946 when he was posted down to Castle Archdale near Enniskillen to take up the post of Commanding Officer whilst he waited for his release date from the Royal Air Force. Bill was released from the service on the 26th June 1946, although his last official day in the Royal Air Force was in early September. On demob, he completed a teacher training course at Larkfield Training College and took up his first post as Principal of Legacurry Primary School in 1948 and continued his career by taking an MA Degree at Trinity College in Dublin and eventually became Principal of Ballymocash and Largymore Schools, in the Lisburn Area. He finally retired from teaching in 1984.

In the interim period Bill joined 502 (Ulster) Royal Auxiliary Air Force Squadron in January 1950 as a part time pilot flying at weekends and during the school holidays. The squadron had up until that time had been commanded by Squadron Leader Hunter McGiffin an Ulsterman from Bangor County Down. He had handed over command to a regular officer, Squadron Leader DFB Sheen, an Australian who had won the DFC and Bar in the Battle of Britain. Bill was commissioned in the rank of Flying Officer for five years active and five years reserve service and looked forward very much to be sitting in the 'driving seat' of a Spitfire once again. On the 26th February 1950 Bill took to the air once more in one of the Squadrons Harvard trainers, under the instruction of

Flight Lieutenant McDonald, and soloed just 1hr.30mins later. He continued training exercises on the Harvard through onto the 14th May when he took to the air again in a Spitfire F.22 code 'V'. On the 19th November 1950 Bill had a lucky escape when he and some others were taking part in a flight formation exercise. This exercise involved climbing in formation of fours, spiralling up through cloud to 30,000feet and reforming with the squadron above the cloud. The aircraft were all spaced at one minute intervals, on this occasion the cloud did not clear at 30,000ft. The Flight Leader realising this, informed the others to drop down again. This caused big problems as some of the squadrons aircraft were still on the way up, at one stage another pilot Victor Mussen saw a Spitfire fly right over his cockpit no more than 20 feet away. Bill decided to drop down and head east out to sea to get his bearings. The first airfield he saw was Newtownards which he headed for as his fuel state was now critical. Unfortunately on landing Bill's Spitfire went up on its nose. (Read Victor Mussen's story for more detail on this story.)

502 Squadron deserted its F.22 Spitfires for DH FB.5 and FB.9s between 1951 and 1957, and so on the 11th March Pilot Officer Bill Polley entered the jet age when he flew a FB.5 Vampire with Flight Lieutenant D Baker for the first time which he continued to fly until December 1952, when he decided to quit flying on the birth of his first child. Bill transferred to Air Traffic Control in December 1952 and was promoted to Flight Lieutenant in

1954 and had his active service extended for one year at the end of his five year period. In February 1955 he returned to general duties in a ground position. In 1956 Bill was called up with the squadron during the Suez crisis and had to obtain a 'special leave of absence' from teaching during that four-month period. He obtained a further one-year extension of service until March 1958. However, in March 1957, No 502 Squadron was disbanded and Bill was transferred into Reserve relinquishing his commission at the end of his Royal Air Force career in January 1960. Bill became a member of the Ulster Defence Regiment in the 1970s rising to the rank of Major, finally retiring from the Regiment in June 1978. He proudly wore his RAF Wings on his army uniform.

Flight Lieutenant William Francis Polly joined the Royal Air Force on 29th June 1941, and left in January 1960, between those dates he had carried out 227 War time operations, (181 in Spitfires and 46 in Tempests) and had flown in 15 different types of aircraft including: Avro Anson; Auster; BT-13 Vultee; DC3 Dakota; Harvard; Hawker Hurricane; Miles Master; DH Mosquito; North American (P51) Mustang; Oxford; PT-17 Stearman; Spitfire Mks 1, 11, VB, 1X and F22s; Hawker Tempest; Tiger Moth; and DH Vampire. He had accumulated 1045hrs.30mins flying time.

Bill was founder member of the Aircrew Association Northern Ireland Branch, he unfortunately died four years ago after a short illness.

FLYING OFFICER
WILLIAM ANDREW POWER
ROYAL AIR FORCE NO. 1061443
WIRELESS OPERATOR/AIR GUNNER
NO. 40, 77 AND 24 SQUADRONS

William Andrew Power was born in Newry in the County of Armagh on the 23rd January 1919 and was educated at the Newry Model and Newry Technicnical College where he obtained a junior certificate. Bill joined the Royal Air Force in late 1939 as Wireless Operator/Air Gunner, but it wasn't until the 28th August 1940 that he was posted to Blackpool to start his initial training.

On the 23rd November Aircraftsman William Power was posted to the No 2 Signals & Wireless School at Yatesbury where he was to embark on his wireless career in the RAF. The school was equipped with Dominie and Percival Proctors. His first flight was on the 1st January 1941 in a Dominie Mk1 R9548 that was captained by a 'Mr Taylor'. The types of exercises that he carried out during the course were, Harwell boxes, D/F loop, daily inspections, fault finding, signals and code tuning and cross country flying. He successfully completed the course by the end of August 1941. Bill was then posted to No 2 Air Gunnery School at Dalcross on the 29th August to commence his air gunnery training on Boulton Paul Defiants. He finished the course at the end of August with a pass mark of 69% and was assessed as an 'average Gunner' by the school's Chief Instructor (Wing Commander Lewis). After have passed both the radio and gunnery courses AC2 William Andrew Power received his Wireless Operator/Air Gunners Brevet and was promoted to Sergeant. Having now completed all his training Bill was posted to No 15 OTU at Harwell where he commenced operational flying training on Wellingtons and Avro Ansons. The course commenced on the 22nd October 1941 and finished five months later on the 31st March 1942.

On the 22nd March Bill and his crew were told to report the Overseas Aircraft Delivery Unit at Harwell where they were informed that they were being posted overseas to join No 2 Mets and Middle East Forces at Shaloufa in the Middle East. They were to flight test a Wellington Code Z 8513 at the OADU and deliver it to a squadron in Malta on their way to the Middle East. The

flight-testing lasted for five days and consisted of fuel consumption tests, guns and turret tests and A & E Tests and was soon ready for its trip to Gibraltar. The Wellington Z8513, captained by Pilot Officer Smith and his crew took off from Harwell on the morning of 28th March and landed two hours later at Portreath in Cornwall. Bill's logbook shows that they stayed in Portreath until the 2nd April when they took off and set a course for Gibraltar arriving there eight hours later. They stayed in Malta until the 4th April when they took off once more arriving in Malta 5hrs.30mins later. On the 6th April they left Malta in another Wellington DV505 and headed for El- Lyum.

On the 27th April Bills log shows that he and the crew had their first flight at No 2 Multi Engine Training Squadron on the morning of 27th April in Wellington Z8765 which was captained by a new Pilot Sergeant Shard. They flew three training exercises between Shalufa to Lydda, Lydda to Habbaniya, Habbaniya to Lydda and Lydda to Shaloufa. Bill and Sergeant Shard were then posted to commence operations with No 40 Squadron at Shaloufa. No 40 Squadron was RFC was formed at Gosport in Hampshire on the 26th February 1916, and from August 1916 until the Armistice served on the Western Front as a Fighter Squadron. It was disbanded in 1919 and reformed as a bomber squadron in 1931 and during the Second World War was equipped with Blenheims and Wellingtons operating from bases in England, The Middle East, bombing targets in North Africa, Sicily, Sardinia, Rhodes, Crete, Greece, Pantellaria, Lampedusa, Italy and the Balkans with Liberators. The squadron also took part in the Berlin Air

Lift in 1947. Bill completed his first operation with the squadron to Benghazi on the 24th June 1942 with Sergeant Shard and the crew. Their flying time for this operation was 7hrs.50mins.

Field Marshall Rommel had launched his offensive in North Africa on the 26th May 1942 which totally surprised the Allies, but more than one third of the German tanks were lost on that first day. By the 1st June Allied Air Forces began to bomb Rommel's beleaguered Afrika Corps. The rest of June Bill and the crew spent bombing and strafing enemy transports, landing grounds and mechanised units in Abar-El-Sakkuti, Charring Cross, Fuka and El-Daba. By the middle of June Rommel's army had captured Tobruk. Bill's log entries for July shows that the squadron concentrated all their efforts on Tobruk, bombing its harbour, shipping and petrol installations on the 11th, 13th, 15th, 18th, 25th, 29th and 31st July. By the middle of July Rommel's advance had been halted at El Alamein and Field Marshal Bernard Law Montgomery had taken over command of the British Eighth Army.

August: There was to be no let up for Rommel and his Afrika Corps as Bill and the crew again bombed Tobruk on the 2nd, 5th, 7th, 9th, 11th, 13th, 16th, 19th, 29th and 31st August.

September: Again they bombed and laid mines in Tobruk Harbour on the 2nd, 3rd, 6th, 10th, 18th, 21st, 24th and 27th September. Towards the end of September 1942 Monty had launched his offensive against Rommel and the Afrika Corps and by November 3rd they were in retreat. Tobruk and El Alamein fell in November. The operation on the 29th September which was to lay mines in Tobruk Harbour was to be Bill's last with the squadron. By the end of September 1942 Bill had completed 39 operations with 40 Squadron (in all but two of these ops he was the Front Air Gunner) and it was now time for a break for him and the crew. He was posted back to the UK on the 5th October 1942 and was given some well-earned home leave. After returning from leave in February 1943 Bill was posted to No 19 OTU that was based at Kinloss in Scotland where he became a Wireless Operator Instructor, instructing on Whitley's and Avro Anson's. At the end of December 1942 Bill had had enough of instructing and requested to be allowed back onto operations. His request was granted and at the beginning of February 1943 he was posted to 1663 Heavy Conversion Unit at Rufforth where he completed a six week conversion course onto Halifax V's and met his new captain (Flight Sergeant Sykes) and crew. Bill joined 77 Squadron at Elvington near the end of February 1943. The squadron was formed at Edinburgh in October 1916 and it's role was defending the city against enemy airships, working along side the Forth Garrison batteries in case of enemy landings. The squadron was disbanded in 1919 and reformed again in June 1937 at Finningley in Yorkshire as a Bomber Unit. At the outbreak of war it was equipped with Whitleys, later becoming equipped with Handley

Page Halifax B11. One of its better known operations of the war was in September/October 1944 when it helped to fly half a million gallons of much needed petrol to an airfield in Brussels for the Second Army which then was so desperately short of fuel for its lorries and tanks. In May 1945 the squadron was transferred to Transport Command where it took part in the Berlin Air Lift and was subsequently disbanded in 1963.

Bill made his first X-country flight with Flight Sergeant Sykes on the 31st March at 1900 hrs in Halifax KN-X. His first operational flight was on night of the 9th April 1944. They took off at 2100 hrs in Halifax KN-A to bomb the Lille-Delivrance goods station. 239 aircraft took part in that raid from various squadrons and only one Lancaster was lost. Their next raid was on the following night, again take off time was 2100 hrs and the target was the railway yards at Tergnier. 157 Halifaxes of 4 Group and 10 Pathfinder Mosquitoes took part in this raid. 10 Halifaxes failed to return. They laid mines off Heliogoland on the 12th April, and off Malmo on the 18th. They bombed the marshalling yards at Ottignies on the 20th April (196 Aircraft took part on this raid and all returned safely) and bombed the railway yards at Laon on the 22nd.

Bill's luck was about to change

On the night of the 23rd April Bill and the crew took off from Elvington at 2105 hrs in Halifax KN-P LW270 on a mine laying operation and set a course for the coast of Denmark. The aircraft was carrying four mines and the target was 54o 48'N/12o42'E and KN-P had flown 133 hours. While over Denmark they were attacked by Bf110's at 13,500ft. Their port engine and wing caught fire and they were loosing height rapidly. The Captain, Flight Sergeant Sykes gave the order to bale out of the crippled Halifax. One chute failed to open. Four of the crew managed to escape back to Sweden, sadly three were killed. KN-G crashed at Hjaelm which is about six miles North West of Nykobing in Denmark.

The names of the Crew are as follows:

Flight Sergeant PDSykes	Pilot. Killed. Buried in Svino Cemetery.
Flying Officer JH Murray	Navigator. Escaped.
Sergeant F. Haynes	Air Bomber. Escaped.
Flight Sergeant WA Power.	Wireless Op/Air Gunner. Escaped.
Sergeant G Jones	Flight Engineer. Killed. Buried in Svino Cemetery.
Sergeant WH Loverock	Mid Upper Gunner. Killed. Buried in Svino Cemetery.
Sergeant JJ Harrison	Rear Air Gunner. Escaped.

Bill's escape story

Bill had landed safely on a deserted beach and it wasn't long before he met one of the local residents. Bill explained who he was and showed him his silk escape map and asked where he was, by this time he was feeling pretty miserable and wondering about what had happened to the rest of his crew. He had just sat down on the sand to gather his wits about him when suddenly a German fighter appeared out of nowhere and flew low up the beach towards him and flew low right over his head. Just as he was about to head inland the local whom he had just met returned and now realising that Bill was British eagerly embraced him and told him to hide in a haystack. He returned after darkness with beer and some bread. The next night under the cover of darkness Bill was taken to a Doctor IB Hansons house. On entering he was delighted to see his Navigator was alive and well. It was not long before a meeting was set up with the local Resistance who were to provide them with bicycles and money for their escape home. Another one of Bill's crew arrived at Dr Hanson's that evening. They stayed at Dr Hanson's for four nights, being well fed and able to take a bath. Under the circumstances they were treated very well. Soon they were informed by the local Resistance that they were to cycle to the local railway station where the were to board a train that would take them to Copenhagen and that they would be accompanied by one of their members for the entire journey. They had just boarded the train at Copenhagen when a troop of German Soldiers who were going on leave got on. The Resistance chap thought it would be a good idea if they all split up and were given Danish newspapers to read. By the time they arrived at Copenhagen, they were all very tired and frightened. They left the train and were taken to a flat that was above a stationary shop. Here they were met by a Danish Fireman in uniform, who gave them all a terrible fright as they thought it was an SS officer waiting to arrest them. Bill and the other two-crew members stayed at the flat for about four days, cooking their own meals and talking to no one. Soon they were taken down to the docks under the cover of darkness by taxi to a club. There they met some more escapees, "Jewish people who had fled Germany."

Sometime later they were taken down to a small harbour where they boarded a barge, unfortunately the local resistance people had been tipped off that night that the Germans were searching all barges leaving the harbour. So it was decided to wait until the following night and they hid between the docks until it was safe to carry on with their journey to Malmo in Sweden. On their arrival in Sweden they were immediately arrested by the Swedish Police (this was the first time that Bill had ever seen the inside of a prison cell). Bill was interrogated by the police but only gave his name, rank and serial number and demanded to see the British Consul who duly arrived and had them released into his custody. They were taken to his residence and given some money to buy some new clothes (the old ones were sent back through channels to the Danish Resistance to help future escapees).

They left Malmo by train for Stockholm and on their arrival were taken to a large shop to buy some proper clothes. As Bill was an extremely big man he found it difficult to find an overcoat that would fit him and had to settle for a Swedish Air Force officers great coat. Two days later on the 8th May 1944 they were taken to the airport and to Bill's surprise he spotted four Mosquito's sitting on the Tarmac. They all belonged to the British Overseas Airways Corporation (another story) and who had the contract to bring ball bearings out of Sweden to help the war effort. Bill and the crew were told to climb into the bomb bays of the Mosquito's and hold on. The registration of Bill's particular aircraft was G-CGGC and was piloted by a Captain Brown. The flight time from Stockholm to Leuchars in Scotland was 2hrs.55mins.

Bill wrote an entry in his flying log that reads, "Fastest time to date for escape from Denmark. Thanks to Doctor I Hanson and the numerous friends in the Danish underground movement who helped at great danger to their own lives."

On his arrival back in the UK Bill was taken down to London where he was debriefed and sent home on leave for six weeks. On his return from leave in August 1944 Bill was posted to 24 Squadron at Hendon for VIP duties, flying in Avro Anson, Flamingo, Domine and Dakota's as a Wireless Operator. The squadrons had become a Short Range VIP unit, returning many important people and Royalty to their liberated countries. In October 1945 the squadron was occupied ferrying important dignitaries back and forward to the Nuremburg Trials. One of Bill's more famous trips was Operation Arganaut on the 18th January 1945 when he escorted 'The Big Three' (Churchill, Roosevelt and Stalin) where they all met at Satchi for a conference on board Bill's Dakota FL584. Bills logbook shows that Operation Arganaut to Russia started on the 19th January 1945 and finished on the 1st February 1945. The total flying time for this operation was 39hrs.05mins.

Bill remarked to me that he remembers the trips to Satchi very well, "It was a terrible place and you were always up to your knees in mud."

Some of his other VIP Duties were:

Bringing the King and Queen to Long Kesh (not long ago was the notorious Maze Prison) on the 17th July 1945 onboard Dakota KG770. Bill told me that when they arrived overhead Long Kesh the pilot told him that he may have some bother landing due to cross winds. The Queen Mother noticing this left her seat and asked the Captain, "Which bounce do you think we will land on."

Bill flew Sir Hartley Shawcross who was a senior Judge at the Neremburg War Trials on the 9th July 1945 and again on the 28th July in Dakota KN282. Bill was also personal Wireless Operator to Lieutenant General Sir Titchard Mc Creery who was General Officer Commanding the British Forces in Austria. On one such trip while taking the General back to Vienna they broke the Hendon to Vienna record taking a total 3hrs.25mins. Some of Bill's VIP duties took him to France, Belgium,

Germany, Italy, Austria, Reykjavik, Capodichino, Malta, North Africa and Greece. In April 1947 Bill was posted to an Air Sea Rescue flight at Kinloss in Scotland as a Wireless Operator in Ansons. On one of his more memorable trips his Pilot flew so low over the sea, he actually bounced the Anson over the waves causing damage to the aircraft including losing Bill's trailing aerial who injured himself on the 1154 and 1155 radio sets.

When he completed he last trip with the RAF in 1947 he had accumulated 1881hrs.30mins in Domine, Anson, Halifax, Lancaster, Proctor, Wellington, Flamingo, Martinet, Defiant, Whitley and Dakota's.

Bill was released from the RAF in 1947 and returned home to take up civilian employment. He is a member of the Air Crew Association Northern Ireland Branch, The Royal Air Force Association and the Royal British Legion.

FLIGHT SERGEANT
JACK DONNELLEY PRINGLE
ROYAL AIR FORCE NO. 1485878
PILOT
NO. 263 SQUADRON

KILLED IN ACTION 28TH MAY 1944

Jack Donnelley Pringle, son of Mr Robert Samuel Pringle and Mrs Margaret Pringle, was born in Chichester Avenue in Belfast on the 12th May 1923. He was educated at the Royal Belfast Acedemical Institute (Inst) from the 1st September 1936 until the 22nd June 1939. The family later moved to a house named, 'Pat-a-ra' on the Carnmoney Road near Glengormley and worshipped in St Peters Church on the Antrim Road.

Jack was a studious lad and took his junior certificate, which was equivalent to the school leaving certificate. His brother attended the Belfast Mercantile College, now known as the Belfast High School and joined the Merchant Navy where he served during the Second World War. Jacks father who was a cashier at the Belfast Co-op had suffered a severe stroke, which had left him in poor health for some time. This unfortunately meant that Jack had to leave school at the age of sixteen to find employment. Jack's father died at the age of forty-nine in 1941, leaving Jack, the eldest of three children, and the sole breadwinner of the Pringle family. On leaving Inst he was employed as a general clerk until he applied to join the Royal Air Force on the 26th July 1941. Jack was accepted into the RAF on the 28th July 1941, and travelled to England the next day by boat. On his arrival in England he was then trained down to London where he attended an aircrew selection board at the No 3 Aircrew Reception Centre in London and was accepted as aircrew (Fighter Pilot). The following week LAC Pringle was posted to No 17 Initial Training Wing to start his basic training. On the 8th April 1942 he was sent to the No 51 Group (Pool) to await his posting to start his flying training.

At the end of April he went to Canada where he trained under the Arnold Scheme and promoted to Sergeant. He arrived in Moncton Ontario on 11th June 1942 and was sent to the No 31 RAF Personnel Despatch Centre. Four weeks later he boarded a train which would take him over the border into America where he would start his Pilot Training at Cochrane and Napier Fields in Alabama. Jack successfully completed his Pilot Training and was awarded his Wings on the 27th February 1943 with an 'above the

average' assessment. His instructors were so impressed with his flying he was invited to stay on at Napier Field as an instructor but he declined the offer. In January 1943 he was trained back up to the No 7 Personnel Reception Centre in Moncton, Ontario, Canada, where he waited until May for a boat to take him back to the UK. On his return to England he was posted to the No 5 Advanced Flying Unit where he trained on the Hawker Hurricane, and on the 27th July transferred to No 59 Operational Training Unit again flying Hurricanes. Jack was promoted to Flight Sergeant on the 27th February 1943. His record of service shows that on the 20th October 1943 he was posted to 193 Squadron which at that time was stationed at Harrowbeer near Plymouth in southern England and equipped with the Hawker Typhoon 1b's. 193 Squadron was formed at Harrowbeer in December 1942 as a fighter/ground attack squadron. When it was formed it had no aircraft of its own and so its pilots were detached to 257 and 266 Squadrons for training on the Typhoon On the 13th December Jack was advised that he was being posted to No 263 Squadron at Harrowbeer, taking up his post on the morning of 5th January 1944.

In May 1944 Jack was given two weeks compassionate leave to visit his mother who had been admitted to hospital where she was to have a major operation. This visit coincided with his 21st birthday. Jack returned to his squadron on the 26th May and two days later he was killed. On the evening before his death, he had joined some of his friends in the mess who were having a sing-song. Jack had a lovely singing voice, and was asked him to sing The Rose of Tralee. For some unknown reason he told his colleagues that he felt it would be unlucky for him to sing that particular song. His friends gave him a bit of banter, and managed to persuade him to sing the song. The next day, 28th May 1944, Jack along with a number of others were detailed for bombing practice. The squadron was being prepared for D-Day which was just six days away, and it was felt that bombing E-boats rather than attacking them with rockets would be more effective.

Flight Sergeant Pringle and Flight Sergeant Dunlop were tasked to practice in Lyme bay, a mission time of no more than 30 minutes. Others in the squadron who were off duty were attending nearby Yelverton Church. Pilots who flew from Harrobeer already knew that the church was only slightly off set from the end of the main runway, and indeed when the airfield was constructed it was intended for use by the American Air Force. But in spite of its proximity, and the fact most of the two story buildings in and around the tiny village of Yelverton had been reduced to single story, the Americans still refused to use it. Flight Sergeant Dunlop was the first to take off with Jack following closely behind. His wheels now retracted and aircraft trimmed he looked round to see if Jack was tucked in behind his wing and saw that he was a lot lower than he should have been. He then observed that Jack was looking down into his cockpit, and it was obvious to him that his aircraft was not gaining height. Suddenly there was a thump when Jack's Typhoon struck one of the towers on the church, tearing away one of its undercarriage legs. If he had been just two feet higher he would have cleared the obstruction. Jack fought bravely to prevent his aircraft careering into the village. It impacted the ground, some 500 yards after hitting the church tower, somersaulted several times near to a farm and exploded into pieces killing Jack.

Flight Sergeant Iain Dunlop later said, "I knew Jack was in serious difficulties when he was looking down into his cockpit during his last moments, he must have been trying to establish a reason for the sudden loss of power from his Napier Sabre engine."

An eyewitness who had attended Jack's memorial service afterwards spoke of the sound of the Typhoon's engine screaming just before impact. Flight Sergeant Dunlop remembered that just a few days earlier, several of the squadrons Typhoons had had their three bladed propellers replaced by four bladed ones, and some of the pilots had experienced engine over-runs and seizures with the four bladed propeller. The Typhoons required fine pitch for take off and problems had taken place during pre-flight run-ups. Jack's aircraft was one of those fitted with the four bladed propellers, and it is now certain that he, too, had experienced an over-revving engine.

The final epitaph to Jack Pringle came from his mother who wrote a poem to her dead son. It read:

You sailed on Friday evening
You waved your cap to me
I think I see you still
So young, so gay, so free
And the memory of that evening
Will ever stay with me.

An appeal through the columns of the RAF News in 1996, requesting information about the tragic death of a wartime Typhoon Pilot (Jack Pringle) brought about the full story at a memorial service to him in Devon.

Ken Rimell, founder member of the Typhoon and Tempest Association at the Museum of D-day Aviation at Shoreham Airport in West Sussex, read the newspaper appeal and contacted Jack's relatives. As a result, the family were to learn at first hand about Jack's final moments. The Typhoon and Tempest Association managed to track down the Pilot Flight Sergeant Iain Dunlop who now resides in Malahide, County Dublin, Ireland, and who was flying along side Jack when the accident happened, asking him to attend the Memorial Service. Ken decided that it would be fitting to hold the Memorial Service to Jack in Yelverton Parish Church where the tragic accident had happened 58 years before.

On Sunday the 18th May 1997 the Memorial Service was held in Yelverton Parish Church where a new flag staff and plaque were dedicated during the service to commemorate the life of Flight Sergeant JD Pringle of 263 Squadron. The service was attended by Jack's sister Pat, (who was 10 years old when her brother was killed), her husband Dr Jim Purser, Flight Sergeant Iain Dunlop, and members of the Royal British Legion. The Royal British Legion provided the plaque which now is placed on the door of the tower which Jack's aircraft struck, and Colonel and Mrs Betty Middleton were the prime movers in paying for the flag staff. Mrs Middleton was 17 years old at the time of the accident, and she recalled, "It was a lovely Sunday morning in May and the Church was completely packed with servicemen. I heard this most ghastly noise, a screaming and screeching, and realised that one of the planes had just taken off and something was going to happen. He hit the tower and the coving stones tumbled down the roof into the grounds." The church was packed with Sunday worshippers who sang Jack's favourite song, The Rose of Tralee, and who mourned the loss of the young pilot. Jack was the second Ulsterman to have been killed with 263 Squadron. Pilot Officer Vivien Lester Currie was killed when returning from a ground strafing raid in France on the 23rd July 1942.

FLYING OFFICER
GEORGE PURDAN
OBSERVER/NAVIGATOR
NO. 644 (SPECIAL DUTIES) SQUADRON
TARRANT RUSHTON

George Purdan was born in Larne County Antrim on the 20th June 1923 and commenced his primary school education at Oriel Collegiate School in Larne, completing his higher education at Larne Grammar School. George, like so many others in this book, had a long time passion to join the Royal Air Force and to fly. So he decided to join the Queens University Air Squadron in 1941 where he successfully completed the No 3 course.

On joining the Royal Air Force George travelled by ship from Belfast to Liverpool and onwards by train to Brighton to the aircrew reception centre. It was here that he completed the necessary forms and documentation to become aircrew. George was then posted to the Elementary Flying Training School (EFTS) at Cambridge for a thirteen-week elementary course flying Tiger Moths. At the end of the course he was graded as a Navigator. (In late 1941 some of the brighter pupils lost out on being accepted as Pilots because the Air Force was extremely short of Navigators and Radio Operators.) After completing his elementary training George was informed that he was being posted to Herton Park in Manchester where he was kitted out for an overseas posting to South Africa. On receiving his tropical kit at Herton Park he was trained down to Southampton and boarded a troopship. The ship set sail in early December bound for South Africa arriving in Durban six weeks later. On his arrival in Durban George was trained to No 44 Air School for navigational training (Grahamstown was nicknamed 'City of the Saints').

He commenced his navigational training on the 28th January 1943 in an Anson that was piloted by a Lieutenant Thomsen. The flying time for his first exercise was 3hrs.20 mins. The course lasted for five months and at the end George had completed a total of 90hrs.05mins flying time and was awarded his 'O' Brevet on the 8th May 1943 (the 'O' Brevet was changed to the 'N' Brevet when he returned to England). George said goodbye to his South African friends on the 11th May 1943 and set sail that evening for Gurnet in

Scotland, the return trip taking only three weeks. When the ship was safely out to sea a friend gave George two letters from well wisher's in Durban. The letters turned out to be Birthday cards from two very close friends that he had stayed with in Durban as the both knew that George would be at sea for his birthday.

On his arrival back in the UK He was instructed to proceed to Harrogate and then on to No 2 (O) Advanced Flying Unit at Milldam to start his advanced navigational course in Avro Ansons. George told me very funny story that happened to him when he was waiting at Harrogate. He was seconded to the Coldstream Guards Infantry Division for three weeks and was instructed on the Sherman tank and bren gun carrier. Having completing the course he was posted to No 81 Operational Training Unit at Sleap in Tilstock near Shrewsbury where he commenced operational nav training in Whitleys and Stirlings. This was somewhat of a specialised course as the aircraft that he was flying in was also glider towing and 'can dropping'. Now that he had completed all the necessary training that was required of him George and his new crew were posted to 644 Squadron at Tarrant Rushton which was near to Blanford in Dorset. 644 Squadron was formed at Tarrant Rushton on February 1944 from 298 Squadron personnel and equipped with the four engined MkV Halifax bomber. It began to drop supplies to Special Operation Executive (SOE) forces in France, Belgium and Germany on the 30th March1944 and had completed forty such trips by the end of April 1944. On the 5th June 1944 twenty aircraft took off from Tarrant Rushton towing two Hamilcar and fifteen Horsa Gliders across the

English Channel. This as you may well know was Operation Tonga. When the mother aircraft returned to Tarrant Rushton they were immediately refuelled fifteen taking off again towing fifteen Horsa Gliders across the Channel to landing sites already occupied. All the gliders landed safely despite heavy flak. On the 31st August the squadron had it's first operational loss when Flying Officer W Calverly and his crew failed to return.

September 1944 brought Operation Market Garden that was the Arnheim assault and on the first day September 17th the squadron towed fourteen Horsa Gliders and seven Hamilcars. On the 19th September a similar operation took ten Horsa's and one Hamilcar to Arnheim. George was very much involved with the training of the glider pilots for Market Garden.

He also took part in many operations supplying equipment and arms to the SOE. His log book records:

April 19th 1944   Halifax V11 Code 'S' Operation SOE.

April 21st 1944   Halifax V11 Code 'S' Operation SOE.

April 22nd 1944   Halifax V11 Code 'S' Operation SOE.

This type of operation to the SOE meant that the aircraft and crew had to fly below 1,000ft (George told me this was the norm most times to come into the drop zone at 300ft). Other operations which George carried out:

Operation Can Drop	Dropping Supplies to the Allies and SOE.
Operation Mush	Mass glider practices for the Arnheim assault.
Operation Moses, Bob, Bruce, Shaffle, Curb and Crop 17	Were all supply dropping to the Norwegian Underground Forces.

Another very interesting operation mentioned in George's logbook is Operation Longstick. This operation was carried out on the 13th March 1945 and involved dropping 48 parachutists from the 3rd and 4th Air Landing Anti-Tank Batteries, Royal Artillery and the 6th Airborne Division. The crews assembled on the Tarrant Rushton runway and the intention was to drop a 6 pounder anti-tank gun, a jeep and eight men from each Halifax. The aircraft being drawn from both 644 and 292 Squadrons at Netheravon before the American General Brereton. There is a very amusing side to this story (although the chap that was involved did not see the funny side of it at the time). All the aircraft had been parked on the perimeter track awaiting take off, the crew were nervously sitting about waiting for the order to put on their chutes and board the aircraft. When along came a very senior RAF officer in a pick-up truck, it stopped beside one of the Halifaxes; he stepped out and stood under the port

wing and was looking closely at the 6 pounder anti-tank gun that was protruding below the bomb bay. All of a sudden there was an almighty crash when all the underwing and bomb bay stores fell unto the ground narrowly missing this senior officer who by this time had turned white with fear then red with rage. What had happened was an 'Erk' had been in the cockpit and was testing the switchery when he inadvertently tripped the Jettison switch for the anti-tank gun and the underwing stores. The senior officer turned towards the rear door of the aircraft, out of which slid a figure in RAF overalls. I am sure all can guess what happened next, the very senior officer was heard to say to the Erk, "You Stupid F....r !" and beckoned him in a voice that any RSM would have been proud off to come closer. The Erk took some time to react as he was looking with horror at the shambles that he had just caused, but he eventually turned to the senior officer and said, "Sorry Sir. Testing the switches, Sir. Tripped the jettison switch, Sir." The Senior Officer merely pointed into the distance and said, "Guardroom at the double."

George's logbook shows that on the 6th June 1944 (D-Day) he carried out Operation Mallard, this was dropping supplies to the Allies in France and on the 13th June 1944 he carried out Operation Sunflower again dropping supplies to the advancing armies. On the 16th of August 1944 and the 9th September 1944 George and the crew carried two very 'special' operations code named Kipling. This involved dropping SAS personnel into France and Belgium complete with their jeep and full equipment. On the 24th March 1945 George and the crew carried out an operation code named Varsity, this was the mass glider lift for supporting the main assault for the Rhine Crossing, an operation that he remembers very well.

One of the last 'special' operations that George and his crew carried out with the squadron was code named Operation Doomsday, this involved dropping the 6th Airborne Division into Denmark for its repatriation. In all he carried out four of these operations starting 10th, 12th, 18th and 19th March 1945. His last two trips with 644 Squadron was to fly to Brussels to bring back POW's.

With the war now over George left 644 Squadron and was posted to 299 Squadron at Shepherds Grove, arriving there on the 10th December 1945 (this was his last flight in a Halifax). His duties were mostly mail runs to France, Belgium and Germany. His last flying job with the RAF was when he routed brand new Short Stirlings from the Shorts factory in Belfast to Maghaberry to be scrapped.

It was now the middle of 1946, George and his crew had split up and talk of demob was being muttered. He applied for the job of Sports Officer at RAF Station Dishford and after sitting an exam he was accepted were he remained until he was de-mobbed a few months later in August 1946.

He returned home to Northern Ireland and took up his place in the family business in Larne.

WARRANT OFFICER
DAVID RUSSELL
ROYAL AIR FORCE NO. 947592
WIRELESS OPERATOR/AIR GUNNER

I was conceived after WW1, when my father was still listed as ex-soldier. He'd been a sapper. The Battle of Cambrai had left him with a shortened right arm, the hand and forearm of which were set like concrete. He was a strong disciplinarian - timed his wallops with great precision. My head and neck are still a bit off the plumb. He became a most uncivil civil servant.

My mother was gentler, could use a sewing machine as if she'd invented it and was a gifted pianist. Mrs Beeton learned cooking from her. The old treadle Singer gave up the ghost after she'd stitched, gratis, for every importunate housewife in the district. Her small fingers exercised the keys of pianos, organs, harmoniums and even accordions in the Methodist and Episcopalian churches, in the Elim Tabernacle and the Mustardseed Mission, and, since she was wholly ecumenical, in the Catholic church halls.

I was born on 16th March 1920. In Mrs Connolly's kitchen. I was in a hurry and my mother didn't have time to finish her cup of tea and take me home. I caught polio when I was two. I spared myself the curse of a calliper on my left leg by kicking up a hell of a row when I saw the thing in the hands of the doctor. I exercised my new teeth on the arm of the nurse whose job it was to save the doc from pain around the genitals. The consultant's gloomy prognosis of potential permanent lameness turned out to be a rumour. Instead of hopping around like a juvenile John Silver I managed to cram so much physical enjoyment into the days of my youth that when I was saying goodbye to my mum in November '39 she complained that she hadn't seen me since I was five.

When I was seven I fell out of a tree from an altitude of fifteen feet, but Joey Adams broke my fall; he wasn't well afterwards. At the age of eight I nearly drowned when Eddie Boyce and I tried to navigate a tin bath across the Forth River. Life has always been hectic. Even now, in advanced old age, things happen. Last Monday, for instance, I saw a small boy fall off his bike, on Wednesday the bin men came, and, just yesterday Mrs Baxter, next door, put up a new set of curtains.

Back in 1927, Miss Caldwell, my teacher at Forth River PES, presented me with the only academic prize I ever won - a book called 'Scamp and I', all about a fox terrier dog. I didn't read it because the Hotspur was better. I'm discounting 'Play up, Swifts!' here, the prize I got for Sunday School attendance, because I mitched most of the time and used my penny collection to buy a poke of brandy balls in Mrs Crossley's parlour-shop. I got 'Play up, Swifts!' because my Uncle Willie was the Sunday school superintendent and was dead scared of my mother.

Except for periods of sleep I spent my boyhood in Woodvale Cricket Club, where I found touch-rugby, soccer, rounders and cricket more absorbing that the Latin and Maths I suffered at the Royal Belfast Academical Institution, where I pursued an undistinguished academic career from '31 to '39. I can't remember anything about what Julius Caesar got up to in Gaul, but I have vivid memories of 'Churchy-One-Over' on the backfield. I became a damned good swimmer only because my bosom pal, Stanley Thompson, could do the crawl when he was seven. I hated him. When the pair of us were ten, standing with chattering teeth after a freezing swim at Ballyholme, we both caught a lightning glimpse of the uncovered treasures of a seventeen-year-old girl as her robe fell open when drying herself. We solemnly concluded that the poor girl was deformed. Innocence! My God, they're at it these days in the long grass before they hit nine!

I learned all I ever needed to know about matters of the flesh in the school scout troop. Probably the most dangerous book I read at the time was Lord Baden-Powell's 'Scouting for Boys', because the qualms of conscience I suffered over the wicked thoughts I got about

Olive McKelvey drove me to become a born-again Christian. For three weeks.

I pass my Senior Certificate exam, against odds, in 1938 and crowned my academic career by being elevated to the captaincy of the First Eleven in 1939. This entitled me to an embossed badge on my blazer; I learned to walk like a crab.

Since my father was a civil servant, he envisaged a career for me as Permanent Secretary at the Ministry of Finance, but after seeing Errol Flynn in 'The Dawn Patrol' I decided to go to Clifton Street rather than Stormont.

The RAF doctors at Cardington who conducted my medical were myopic and passed me fit for flying duties, even thought I was three days into a virulent bout of 'flu and had a temperature of a hundred and three. It appeared that the selection board were looking particularly for Observers, but since I often got lost on my way to the loo and, anyway, didn't fancy the flying asshole brevet, I became a Wop/AG. During my viva voce, when I was on the point of flaking out, one of my inquisitors, a Group Captain, said, "What's the log of a million?" In my fevered condition I replied that if he ever found out I'd be pleased if he'd let me know.

I did a sixteen-week wireless course at Prestwick and failed to understand a damned word of it. The chief instructor, a latter day Oscar Wilde, told me I wasn't a 'signal' success. Gawid!

By the end of my gunnery training at Dumfries I'd come to the conclusion that I wasn't going to prove a menace to the Luftwaffe. My first lesson was conducted by Sergeant Bert Smith, a fellow Ulsterman who later distinguished himself as an outstanding airman and with whom, after almost sixty years, I am still in touch. Having stripped a Browning for our edification, Bert came to the nub of his lecture. He removed the little sticks of cordite from a .303 round and placed several of them in the bowl of his pipe, inverted it and applied a match underneath. This resulted in a mini-explosion. The accumulated gunge erupted from the stem, leaving his pipe as clean as a whistle. This is one part of my RAF education that I'll never forget; all I remember about Browning guns is that they had breech-blocks and cooling jackets, smelt awful when fired and made an irritating noise when you pressed the trigger.

I wanted to go on Blenheims because I'd be the only gunner aboard and therefore responsible for protecting the other two guys in the crew, God help them. So off I went to OUT at Bicester. An unsuspecting Canadian, a big farmer from Manitoba, called Butch, took me on as guardian of the turret and we selected Johnny from the bunch of sprog observers in the sergeants' mess, on the basis that he might be a good navigator because he had a broken nose and played rugby.

The first advice I got when we joined 21 Squadron at Watton, Norfolk, came from a home-baked navigator from Holywood- "Enjoy yerself, son, while ye can," he said, "Ye've got two weeks!" Low-level attacks in daylight on shipping were a sure method of depriving a poor bloke of his allotted three score years and ten- the mortality rate was like a cricket score. Our hair-raising practice flights at zero feet provided me with the happiest moments in my flying career, but when I met the real McCoy off the Dutch coast and realised the flak ships were spitting at me in a most ill mannered way, I wanted to become a GD clerk. Doug Cooper, from Strabane, led that raid, leaving me with the impression that our masters at the air ministry had either decided that the Irish were expendable, or simply the best spearheads in the business. Doug was later shot down and helped build the wooden horse at Stalagluft Three. I met him again forty years later when I joined the Aircrew Association here. He gives me lifts to our meetings and drives his car as if he's on a nine pounds booster aboard a Blenheim being chased by ME 109's.

The few sorties I and my gallant crew performed with twenty-one from Watton and Lossiemouth made not the slightest dent in the German war effort. We were probably saved from premature violent death by being posted to the Middle East, to 84 Squadron at Mosul in Iraq. Our subsequent operations from El Adem and Gambut in the Libyan Desert held fewer hazards- this time no low-level stuff- there were even occasions when we had the luxury of fighter protection. We found that the best way to ensure survival was to operate with the Free French Squadron, whose Gallic insouciance led them to ignore every tenet of aerial discipline; they continually strayed out of formation and became sitting ducks for the ME's.

It was at Gambut that I witnessed possibly the daftest of all flying accidents, an occurrence that defied imagination, again involving the French- three bombed-up Blenheims warming up at one end of the runway, three at the other, all six simultaneously releasing their brakes and roaring forward. Their terminal velocity left no hope of achieving take-off speed before the inevitable head on collision in the middle of the airstrip. I suppose the names of the victims were recorded on War memorials somewhere in France under the legend "Mort pour la Patrie" and we can only hope that their loved ones never learned of the circumstances of their deaths.

Probably the greatest risk I took in the Western Desert was the night the three of us climbed aboard our aircraft at dispersal to listen to the wireless on the old R1082. Butch and Johnny, up front, put on their flying helmets, while their AG crammed himself way back in the turret to search for frequencies for the Forces' Programme. Up came Ann Shelton singing about her reluctance to set the world on fire, the announcer read out messages to homesick squaddies serving '... somewhere in the Middle East'. Atmospherics played old harry with good reception, so that if you turned down the volume and faded the music you could ham the BBC accent and sound among the crackles just like the bloke back in London. The message Butch got was, "Are you listening, Sergeant Lloyd Butcher? There's a greeting here from your girlfriend Bubbles!"

The aircraft begins to rock as the big fellow bounces in his bucket seat- "Oh my gracious God almighty, I got a message, Johnny! I got a message, Dave!" From the turret comes, "Bubbles still loves you, Lloyd. She misses you badly. She's taking good care of the horse and Patch and she hopes you're wrapping up warm and not forgetting to write often. And now that you're far away in a strange country, she says, for Christ's sake stay there!"

Butch doesn't at first jump to the situation, because the radio apparatus in the plane is as much a mystery to him as it is to his W.op/AG. Johnny's quicker and is suffering a sudden burst of incontinence up front. The bellow of rage resulting from sudden understanding sends the perpetrator on a mile dash to the safety of the admin. Tent.

The cramped turret of a Blenheim was a lethal place to be, even in peacetime, particularly if the pilot ever decided to violently wallop the controls around. At such a time the fellow in the turret rattled around like a marble in a tin box. On our next trip Butch fully got his own back on the 'lil Irish bastard'. That chastened lad had to report to the MO seeking sticking plaster.

In retrospect, our tour of ops in the desert was a mere curtain raiser for what came next, when, after the Japanese attack on Pearl Harbour and the sinking of the 'Prince of Wales' and 'Repulse', we were hurriedly dispatched Far East.

Butch decided he'd had enough of the Middle East and got himself posted back to Bubbles. He was later killed in a flying accident, probably exploring things at zero feet. Thus pilotless, our crew proceeded to become rudderless- Johnny was commandeered by another skipper with the rank of Pilot Officer and a public-school accent.

Eighty-four got a new C.O. for our big adventure- Wing Commander Johnny Jeudwine. He became very famous later, but I had nothing to do with that. - He craved a Wop/AG and I was it; I felt sorry for him. Our navigator was Geoff Palmer, a small self-effacing young fellow, not very robust, but with loads of guts.

Who were these Jap's anyway? All they had was a tin navy, their army rode bikes like donkeys and their air force, manned by pilots legs were too short to reach the rudder pedals and who were colour-blind and wore poached egg glasses because of the rice, had advanced little from days of Orville and Wilbur. That's what our RAF gaffers told us; my mother used to tell us all about Rumplestiltskin and Gargantua.

We started on the long journey from Heliopolis in Eqypt full of heady confidence. Where the hell was Singapore? Up to the right of Burma? Where the hell was Burma anyway? And Malaya? Wasn't India somewhere along the way? Each plane carried two ground staff, poor lads sitting for long hours in claustrophobic misery, in the dark, amidships. We flew a leg here, a leg there, slept hungry and exhausted wherever we could lay our heads- Columbus' matelots probably had a better appreciation of their destination than ordinary joe's like me. Our

initial euphoria gradually began to drain as we approached the black cloud of despair that hung over an area of the world that stretched from the east coast of India right to the Marshall Islands in the far Pacific. Gloom and despondency met us at every place we landed. The farther we flew from Egypt the more depressing things became. Our landing at Karachi provided us with an insight into the obsolescence of the Raj, for it was there that we were confronted by a bevy of awful English memsahibs, all so patronisingly upper class, so brassy, so affected, so dismissive of anyone below the rank of Squadron Leader that we found ourselves taking the mick out of them. When Geoff told them the meaning of 'Semper in Excritu' emblazoned on the fuselage, they melted away. Our pilot shrugged apologetically as they spirited away from him for recherché tiffin, while we hunkered under the starboard wing with our chapattis and mugs of char.

I began to feel sorry for our boss early on in our relationship. Here was the commander of a bunch of very young men, all as aggressively intentioned as himself, yet at every point where we touched down we seemed to be an embarrassment too the resident personnel. Our first port of call in Burma, when we eventually reached that neck of the woods, was a pattern for all subsequent arrivals. We landed on an apparently deserted airfield. There wasn't a single airman to greet us, at least not until we pulled off the runway and could be identified as friendly aircraft. We climbed out. Several ground staff emerged sheepishly from the rubber, whence they'd betaken themselves in alarm when they'd heard the roar of our engines.

The Blenheim in it's war paint intrigued them. The characteristic roar of our number two coming in to land sent them scurrying back to the cover of the jungle. The potent, mythical reputation of the Japanese had penetrated as far as this outpost of the Empire. We were stunned by the revelation, but very soon came to accept that as far as our compatriots were concerned out here in the tropics, the British bulldog had developed hard pad.

The Wingco emerged from a hastily convened confab in the ops room and said "I don't think we're very popular here, gents. Something tells me that our hosts are concerned that the presence of our aircraft will attract the attention of the Jap air force."

Whereas Geoff and I volubly expressed our disgust, our boss philosophically shrugged his shoulders and prepared for the next leg of our flight toward Singapore.

Defeatism, a word I'd heretofore never heard, became a sorry reality during the remainder of 84's debacle in the Far East. All the doubts that developed during our unhappy introduction to this theatre of operations were reinforced with chastening clarity when we landed in Malaya. Geoff and I accompanied our captain into the station ops room. A sleek, immaculate, suntanned Group Captain, complete with fly swat, enquired in an abstract way who the hell we were. His attention was concentrated more on an equally sartorial Squadron Leader engaged on a telephone call. The three of us were tired, unshaven, scruffy and needing something to eat. Hunger had become a feature of our lives from the moment we'd left Egypt- was it four days before? Jeudwine could reply, the Squadron Leader turned from the phone, "Kuantan's bought it Ronnie," he said "The place is infested. They need assistance."

The Group Captain didn't appear perturbed about the plight of the people of Kuantan, "Oh, the navy'll get them out, old boy." He said.

I found myself thinking that this man and his companion resented the advent of a trio of blokes from another world, fellows who'd already had their baptism of trouble much earlier on and were here now, representing an implicit criticism of the soft, well upholstered, sun warmed existence of people, who up to that date, had never heard a shot fired in anger. I just couldn't assimilate how a Wing Commander heading a squadron that could potentially play an effective role when established at a suitable base could be treated with an offhandedness that almost amounted to disdain. Now, so many years afterwards, I sometimes wonder what happened to those two insensitive bastards.

The next couple of months were spent in a struggle to untangle some logic from the predicament we found ourselves in. If there was an overall plan of defence, or even a scheme for organised retreat we never heard of either. We weren't, after all, to fly into our initial destination, Singapore, "England's impregnable bastion" in the Far East. Instead we were diverted to Sumatra. "Where's Sumatra, Geoff?" "Somewhere around, Dave."

We landed on a wet airstrip in the middle of a wet jungle with wet trees washing the Blenheim as we taxied. We were met by a fat guy in jungle green. "Jesus!" I say, "He's speaking German!"

"He's Dutch!" the Wingco explains.

In Sumatra we found the Dutch not only unprepared for the coming of the Japs, but quite unequipped to deal with the arrival of a few friendly bombers manned by guys without a single white flag in their kit. Having landed at the asshole of nowhere at one end of this island, all we could find was a motoring map to get us to the other. This was quite a challenge for Geoff, left on his tod to usher over the jungle without mishap as far as Palembang down in the south. His Wop/Ag had a redundant wireless, since there wasn't a single Grace Darling down below to lend a helping hand to lost airmen.

Even though we were close to the equator, our reception at Palembang was less than lukewarm- no Dutch treat in store here. Once precariously established, we managed to mount raids against the yellow invader, using adapted antique Dutch bombs.

We did targets in Thailand and Malaya and Burma, persuaded not so much by zeros as by hunger and lack of sleep and bedevilled by persistent rumour. That lonely man, Wing Commander Jeudwine, never once departed

from his mood of quiet confidence; the rest of us borrowed our attitude from him. The abandoned girl's school we'd made our home in became overcrowded with service personnel on the run from places in the hands of the Japs. After a long, tiring sortie you often found your precious mattress already occupied, so you kipped down on the hard veranda, throwing missiles at the gibbering, sleep-destroying monkeys in the surrounding rubber and cursing the clouds of mosquitoes that were a torment throughout the night.

When things became unbearable, the Wingco found time to befriend a receptive English rubber planter with a spacious tropical villa. The few aircrews who'd contrived to survive the long flight from Egypt found themselves living there for a short time in unwonted comfort and with full bellies. We should by now have had twenty-four aircraft, but I don't think we ever mustered more than ten, of which six might at any given time be fit to mount an operation. Despite the improvement in our domestic situation, Geoff treated me to a bleak summary of our position, "We're up shit creek, Paddy, me lad! Singapore's buggered, the little yellow men have grabbed Hong Kong and the Philippines and the Solomons. They're swarming around Celebes and New Ireland and Ambon and Bali and Lombok and Timor and Borneo and the Moluccas! If we don't push the buggers back here in Sumatra, they're going at such a rate of knots they'll finish up on the Old Kent Road having a barney with the Germans as to whether Hitler or Hirohito takes over in Buckingham Palace!"

I was depressed for a while, until a bit of comic relief was awarded us by an Air Vice marshal who suddenly dropped in to show the flag. This fellow completely misread the men he was addressing, "There'll be no retreat! We'll fight to the last man! Look, use your initiative! There's a dozen of ways to skin a cat. Just think, if you tie six empty beer bottles together and drop them on the enemy the noise they make can be terrifying! Aggression! Aggression! Aggression! Any Questions?"

The AVM wasn't pleased when Shorty Cameron, one of our Aussie navigators, raised his hand, "Sir, excuse me, sir" said, "but suppose, sir, the Jap ack-ack boys hit our bomb load, sir, will the bottles not break, sir?"

Wing Commander Jeudwine studied his feet and his shoulders shook. I learned later that the AVM, loath to be the last man, got himself to Australia before the island folded.

The most illustrative manifestation of the shambles we'd flown into was revealed when we crossed from Palembang to Sembawang aerodrome at Singapore with the purpose of performing a few ops on places farther north now occupied by the enemy.

It was a large well established airbase, yet we were received by a mere handful of apprehensive tenants who vanished into the blue once they'd established our credentials. The entire station had decamped to the safety of the surrounding trees in anticipation of one of their regular Jap air raids. We sat in splendid isolation on the steps of a veranda the whole afternoon, watching in complete safety an air attack on the centre of Singapore. Sembawang itself had been attacked on other occasions, yet the bomb holes had never been filled in, a situation so completely different from all our previous experience and further confirmation of the craven inertia that had spread like a disease in this part of the world. Little wonder that the Japanese treated their captives with such contempt when the surrender took place.

There were two dromes at Palembang, P1 and P2. We were based at P1. Sumatra was next on the Jap agenda, so we weren't surprised when they hit P2. We saw their Para boys floating in the sky as we flew from P1 to bomb their invasion fleet, then strafe their barges and riverboats as they came up the Moesi River. When we returned to P1, the residents there, except for our loyal ground crews and spare flying personnel, had all fled in complete disarray, leaving behind their possessions. The members of Eight-four were left in sole ownership of the airfield. We'd earlier found a couple of serviceable short nosed Blenheims left there by their crews. Jeudwine brought them into active service for low level attacks along the teeming river.

We spent one more eerie night on that forsaken airfield, wandering round the deserted billets littered with discarded kit; the place was like part of a ghost town. Word came through that the Jap Paras had taken P2 and that the south of the island was in a state of complete chaos. Our role in this corner of the East Indies had come to an ignominious end. We packed our ground lads and loose aircrew colleagues into our knackered aircraft and took off for Java. At least one of our crowded Blenheims failed to reach its destination; we watched it plunge into the thick jungle below and knew that the war was over to the poor confused souls inside.

The main airport at Batavia was crammed with civilians looking for a means of evacuation to Australia. Lockeed Lodestars were taking off loaded to the gunwales; we'd arrived once more into the midst of demoralisation. And of course the airport authorities wanted to ditch us on the spot; it was as if we were suffering from foul pest. The writing on the wall was now so legible that only a drunken blinkered optimist could imagine that there was a pup's chance of amelioration in the plight of the people here. At this stage all of us were exhausted, yet angry and frustrated because we could find no local support for our intention to have a go, even without the aid of empty beer bottles.

Since we were regarded as leprous at Batavia, the Wingco foraged around, making phone calls and buttonholing Dutch officers, until he found a base near the north coast at Kalidjati. By another ironic twist of fate we found ourselves billeted and fed in the exclusive tropical mansion of Mr Jackson, a leading planter. Mr Jackson did the sensible thing he quickly packed and went off to seek escape from the island. Leaving us in possession of his home. Two of us found ourselves

guardians of the keys to the wine cellar and were told off by our boss for getting plastered and mincing around wearing Mr Jackson's best duds. We managed to have a somewhat desperate singsong to the accompaniment of the big Bechstein Grand amid the potted palms on the wide, tiled veranda before Jeudwine, craving action, prodded us out to the drome four miles away. He was adept at commandeering transport.

For several days we managed to ply the trade we'd studied, bombing our earlier domicile in Sumatra, having a go at the Palembang oil wells, looking for shops, digging out targets, losing another valuable aircraft to Jap fighters.

Our sojourn in paradise was a transitory interlude in our Far East adventure – the idyll was rudely shattered by the arrival of the Japanese invasion fleet only a few miles north of us, with nothing between it and the drome save a handful of startled Dutch home guards. The Wingco committed everything he could muster into a last ditch attempt to salvage some honour from a situation that no divine intervention could free us from. The invading enemy vanguards were already on their way without opposition toward our base.

It was dark as we scrambled aboard. We reached our target in no time at all. I recall Jap fighters in the murk with arclamps in their noses, ill-directed flak from the ships, a couple of short trips back to the airfield for reloading, then the final flight of my wartime career in the beloved Blenheim. Three enemy tanks emerged prematurely from the rubber at the end of the runway as we taxied to a standstill. No fuel left, no means of opposing the attackers. Jeudwine threw a port flare into the cockpit and we took to our heels. Once again our squadron friends had not deserted us. They'd assembled an odd array of transport at a safe location to evacuate the scene. The few equipped with weapons were putting up sufficient resistance to facilitate our departure.

Bandoeng next in the centre of the island. We were overcrowded in our beat up truck, but came across a harassed Dutchman seeking to get rid of six brand new Chevrolets for free and tanked up. Five of us took possession of a smart red saloon. Our Chauffeur was Doug Argent, one of our navigators. He survived the war to later become the director of 'Steptoe', 'Fawlty Towers' and 'Till Death'. On our way to Bandoeng we picked up a lone Englishwoman walking along the road wearing a flimsy print dress and a pair of white high-heeled shoes. She was carrying a little wirehaired fox terrier and had no luggage. She was making for the same destination as ourselves, two hundred miles away.

Bandoeng was hiving with lost souls - people who'd got out of Singapore. Australian servicemen, Dutch home guards, Javanese and Ambonese auxiliaries, thousands of RAF ground staff recently shunted off ships, antiaircraft troops without guns, shore based sailors, homeless Europeans. We found accommodation for a short spell at the airport there. Orders came from somewhere that we were to change our vocation.

Henceforth we were to be guerrillas, fighting hit-and-run campaigns in the jungle. I was given a Lee Enfield rifle and a bag of ammo which I immediately expended when waves of Jap Zeros and Army Ninety-Sevens screamed in for low-level target practice. It was at the edge of the runway that I made a new friend, an Aussie air gunner called Phil Corney. He too had a WW1 rifle. We popped off in a futile way at the attackers, laughing at our own impotence and shouting abuse at the great hulk of a soldier, a real macho character who was imploring us between chattering teeth to join him in his slit trench, where we wouldn't draw attention to ourselves.

We didn't, after all, become guerrillas. New orders came that all trained airmen and key personnel were to get themselves to Tjilatjap, a port on the south coast for evacuation by ship to Australia. Back aboard our Chevs, our superannuated bus, our trucks, our motorbikes for the long trip to the coast and our inevitable welcome. Waves of twenty-seven Betties saluted our arrival, wiping out the docks and the godowns and the port installations without let or hindrance. The series of large bamboo army barracks, each with its long sleeping platforms, were every one deserted, but crammed with abandoned equipment, suitcases, kitbags, backpacks, wallets of photographs, letters from home, a hopeless jumble indicating a hasty, panic-stricken flight. We weren't surprised, we'd seen it before. Apart from ourselves there seemed to be no people in Tjilatjap, not even a sign of a native.

We took cover in the rubber when the next wave of bombers arrived. The port was in flames, the trees were on fire, the billets were burning, we were in the midst of disaster. "Don't know who they're bothering," Phil said, "They're only wrecking their own property! Don't they know we're buggered?"

It soon became obvious that no relief-ship would ever hazard approaching the place. When the thunder ceased we went down to see the destruction at the docks. Debris and wreckage floated on the calm surface of the estuary, the river reflecting the flames rising from the adjoining buildings. Jeudwine assembled us in reasonable order on the dockside, "Right," he said, and even now he was still in complete command of himself, "Your duty is clear, Wreck everything you can lay hands on, set fire to the oil storage tanks, leave nothing useful to the bastards. After you've done that, go and find any method of extricating yourself from this mess. It's every man for himself now!"

"Every man for himself!" I'd read such words in the 'Modern Boy' and 'Chums Annual' but had never thought I'd ever have to apply them to myself. I formed a mental picture of this wee man from Belfast having to do a commando job to save his bacon and just couldn't believe he'd be up to it. I therefore shadowed my boss for the next few hours in the hope that he'd let me tag along on whatever venture he decided to embark upon. Tjilatjap was a furnace. We roved about in an orgy of destruction that was strangely enjoyable, a kind of therapy that softened the anger and frustration that had affected us for

so long. It seemed a sin to push all those new American cars into the estuary, but contrition didn't last long when Phil found a crate of Bob Daniels which we'd no intention of destroying.

We performed our scorched earth policy unsteadily until exhausted, then devoted our efforts to find a means of escape. Someone discovered a modern ocean-going tug at the far end of the dock, a vessel capable of accommodating at least forty refugees, provided they slept back to back. But to continue our long run of foul luck, its Dutch owners had immobilised it and it had to be abandoned.

Reduced now to desperate measures, we sorted out two lifeboats from the detritus that littered the estuary. These and a small flat-bottomed river launch were to be our means of escape. We were to become sailors; we were going to Australia!

Although Eighty-Four had ceased to have any fighting potential, it's aircraft gone and its complement of tradesmen scattered all over the island, having been decanted from a ship almost into Japanese hands, its commander still contrived to maintain his dignity and authority. Some drifted off in search of an independent means of getting away from the beleaguered Indies, the majority elected to take their chances with the Wingco. We foraged for fresh water and portable food, biscuits mostly. Cartons of canned beer were added to our supplies.

I can still conjure up a picture of those two old lifeboats low in the water, overloaded with passengers foolishly equipped with kitbags, backpacks and suitcases. One man even carried a portable radio! Jeudwine gave orders to jettison the lot, except for the bare essentials.

The river estuary was wide and the sea a long distance from our point of departure. Three of our number manned the little launch attached by a rope to the first boat, it being similarly attached to the second. The launch, under full power, laboured in great distress to fulfil its function of towing us toward the ocean. We were bound for Oz! The only person who appeared to consider the voyage capable of achievement was Wing Commander Jeudwine – the rest of us said, "Baa!"

It soon became apparent that the three men aboard the launch were in great difficulty, having been breathing in fumes from the stricken engine. The tow rope had to be cut and the trip rescued. We were just abreast of an island in the mouth of the estuary and since the second lifeboat was leaking like a sieve, the CO shouted orders for both to put in to the shore. Both craft were to be emptied and everyone was to assemble on the beach of the island. It was quite clear that lifeboat number two was useless. Jeudwine was quick to face reality. In his usual calm way he outlined his plan. One lifeboat with a greatly reduced crew, the second being abandoned, might be able to reach Australia. He'd take only those with a knowledge of sailing, preferably Australians; the remainder would stay on the island with an equitable share of the provisions. If others found a method of getting away they should be victualled as far as possible and take their chance. In an estimated time of perhaps six weeks he'd return by flying boat to rescue those remaining.

In our innocence Geoff and I thought we were bound to accompany our skipper on his voyage - after all, we'd been with him throughout everything. He took us aside and asked if we knew anything about seamanship. Cursing my Methodist upbringing and recalling my tin-bath argosy with Eddie Boyce, I replied that I didn't; Geoff was equally honest. I was heartbroken at our rejection, even though I knew he was right to leave us behind, the trip was risky enough without a couple of useless dependents clinging to his coat tails.

I spent the rest of the evening swimming to and from the anchored lifeboat, ferrying stuff from the beach. On my final swim I awarded myself the privilege of carrying my pilot's kit. The elected crew, twelve in number, were all aboard as Jeudwine and I trod water beside the boat, both pretending not to weep as we shook hands in farewell. Sitting in the stern, Phil held up the bottle of Veuve Cliquot we'd bought together in Bandoeng, intending to share it when our relief ship landed us in Australia.

"I'll keep it for when we get together again, Irish," he said.

That was the last I ever saw of either Wing Commander John Jeudwine or Sergeant Phil Corney.

Three days later we spotted another lifeboat drifting seawards on the current of the river. It was a beat up old vessel- no self respecting professional sailor would have contemplated stepping aboard her, but eight of us claimed our share of the provisions and set off on the bosom of the wide Indian Ocean under a ragged sail and a cracked mast, eight ignorant sergeants fortified by the experience of once having sailed celluloid ducks at home on bath night.

Our intention was to hug the Java coast until we could purloin a more suitable craft, after which we'd steer eastward toward Sumbawa, Flores and Timor. If we branched southeast at Timor we'd in a couple of months perhaps, collide with Australia - we couldn't miss it, it was a big country.

Ten days later, having been baling continuously, we capsized in mountainous breakers, but close enough to reach the beach without loss, although the swirling undertow had stripped most of our clothing from us. We'd left forty-odd refugees back on the little island and knew that Java was already in Jap hands, and, soon, so were we.

For those who know nothing about Bushido, I pause at this juncture to submit a little vignette that may illuminate a facet of oriental culture not seen nowadays:

His name's Yamaguchi, or Kobiashi, or Morioka, it doesn't matter. He's more coffee coloured than yellow, He's a gocho, a corporal. His boyhood hero was Ghengis Khan. He's not nice. He got his second stripe for proficiency with the bayonet at the Rape of Nanking and he's zenophobic about white men. His voice isn't musical.

Maybe he's had a failed marriage or a rectal fissure, for he certainly isn't in the best of moods.

He draws the eight scarecrows up in a line facing him. He's got a chorus of clones with him.

"You, Blanda-ka?" he screeches. (The Suffix "ka" indicates a question)

They say, "Eh?"

He wallops them.

"You, Blanda-ka?" he yells again.

They say "Eh?" again.

He thumps them again, So do his mates. They appear to relish the exercise.

"I think the little bastard wants to know if we're Dutch, "Willie suggests,

"Blanda's the Malay word for Hollander."

(Willies's an educated Aussie, he knows the Binomial Theorem and three soliloquies from "Hamlet")

"No," they say.

"You, Ingirris-ka?"

"Not English - Australian, " Willie replies, pointing to himself, Gordy, Slim and Danny.

"Canadian," says Lloyd.

"English," says Davy, "Ireland,"

"Irelando-ka?" says the Nip. Actually he doesn't say it, he's a rough lad, he spits it.

"Yes," says Davy.

The gocho pulls Davy from the line, possibly because Davy's smaller than Lloyd. The boys call Lloyd 'Elevated Arse".

The gocho studies Davy. Davy has no trousers.

"You, heytai-ka?" bellows the corporal.

Davy says, "Eh?

The gocho thumps Davy.

"Heytai! Heytai" he screams, putting his rifle on his shoulder and miming a bloke on the march.

Willie clarifies, "Tojo wants to know if you're a squaddie, Paddy"

"No," says Davy, shaking his head vigorously. Maybe being a heytai isn't a good thing.

The Jap undulates his hand to indicate waves, "Youi, Kaigun-ka?" he demands.

"No," says Davy.

Tojo stiffens, his eyes become slits, his face turns red, then black and he screws it up like Fumanchu having a bad time on the loo. Davy doesn't like his tone when he lacerates his vocal chords.

"You, Hikoki-ka!" His voice turns falsetto, due to over-emphasis. He points to the sky.

Davy's a mug, "Yes," he responds, wishing he'd joined the Girl Guides.

Five times they pick themselves up from the sand, knowing there'll probably not be a sixth, because the gocho and his boys are tired now and they're close to the equator.

Lloyd climbs groggily to his feet, "Jesus H Keerist!" he gasps, "mebbe the lil' bastard wuz downstairs when we strafed their friggin invasion barges!"

It should be noted that in anticipation of further such interviews, Davy re-mustered to Cook, Lloyd to Headquarters Clerk and the four Aussies blandly asserted their attachments to the RAAF Equipment Branch. The two English guys both became Instrument Mechanics.

It should be further noted that not all Japanese invaders behaved like this particular gocho. Some were quite generous and were wont to offer you a revolver to commit suicide because you turned chicken under fire. Most of them were sharp witted, although there was the odd country bumpkin whose lift didn't go up to the top – like the fellow we saw trying to mend a bicycle puncture with a needle and thread and the one who belted Lloyd because he couldn't transfer the tick from a tin alarm clock into the watch he'd liberated from Slim.

As a piece of useless information, it should be recorded that the Japs didn't actually commit 'harakiri' when they decided to join their Shinto gods – they committed 'seppuku'. Harakiri was the method. 'Hara means stomach, 'kiri' means cut. They used to like squatting on the ground, shoving in the knife and depositing their guts in a wee bowl before they died. Wasn't that ducky?

Willie blamed the English for our predicament. Joe and Eric came in for a lot of stick. "Eh, say, cheps," Willie says, " Where's your jolly old Pommie Empire these days? What's happened to all the pink on the map? The yellow hordes are on their way, don't you know? Tojo and his oppos are gonna knock your District Officer outta his charpoy' eh what? They're gonna be playing polo on the howdah along with Gungo Din and making a Khyber Pass at all the English roses in the bungalows. Meh God, cheps, Tommy Atkins has made a pig's arse outta Malaya and Singapore and Borneo, same as he did at Gallipoli where meh old pater said goodbye to his left leg!"

Flushed with their unexpectedly easy victories all over the Far East, the Japs at first behaved like Sunday school graduates, even inviting the vanquished to play them at baseball. And since the Dutchmen in the camp were old flabby colonials, our lifeboat crew went out to confront the enemy on the sports field. We were eejits, we beat them. The Nips of course are a courteous race, magnanimous in victory, sporting in defeat. They gave us a few hearty thumps on the back. With their rifle butts. The short honeymoon was over.

A week later they caught three Dutchmen coming back over the fence at midnight, having been visiting their wives a stone's throw away from the camp. Sergeant Major Nakamura took great pains arranging the prisoners on the soccer field in staggered ranks on three sides of a square. There were six hundred of us and he was determined that no one should miss any detail of the show. The fourth side of the square was unoccupied, except for the heaped soil by the three graves.

Kees van Vlierden, our camp interpreter, begged us young airmen not to create a scene when the men were shot. Kees' face was badly bruised, because he had dared to plead with the camp commandant all night not to carry out the sentence. "Gentlemen," he said, "the mood has changed, there'll be no more baseball. The Japanese never threaten lightly and they've already indicated that they will tolerate no demonstration when they shoot these men."

I prefer not to go into the details - just to say that the commandant had no intention of using a firing squad when he could give an opportunity for three very young unblooded recruits to get some buckshee bayonet practice. It wasn't pretty.

There was a typically oriental cynical aftermath to the execution - next morning the Jap Sergeant Major marched smartly on to the soccer pitch and placed a bunch of flowers on each grave, bowed in that stiff military way of theirs and departed.

"What a lovely lad!" Joe Morley remarked, "The knightly spirit of Bushido hasn't gone for a Burton after all!" I've still got a mental picture of the commandant calmly supervising the murder, one hand in the pocket of his jodhpurs, the fingers of the other holding a tortoiseshell cigarette-holder which he flourished like an actor in a drawing room comedy.

Having had our short experience as guerrillas, then as mariners, we now became coolies. We filled in bomb holes under the equatorial sun and built runways and starved and cheated and stole, all the time forming bonds that could never have been formed in different circumstances. Now and then we got an unexpected bonus - like the day the Nips sent us out on a working party to a big warehouse chock full of scotch, rum, gin, brandy, liqueurs and wine. Since the Japs had forsworn drink in their promotion of their 'Greater East Asia Co-Prosperity Sphere', our job was to commit the sacrilege of destroying every bottle in the place. Our careful Dutch colleagues wet themselves as we filled our water bottles with cocktails of every drink we found and stuffed contraband in our breeches' pockets and under our tropical straw hats. Our small British contingent staggered back to camp under great duress and suffered the violent inquest at the guardroom with insulated stoicism.

After a couple of months the Japs moved us to the big POW camp at Bandoeng. As we came to a halt inside the gates I was accosted by one of the inmates there, "Jesus, Paddy! You're dead! You got drowned at Tjilatjap!" It was one of my old squadron muckers. Archie Wakefield; we'd left him back at the island. He explained that they'd found my playbook and wallet in six feet of water after we'd set sail for Australia, so I must have gone to Davy Jones's locker. All my old colleagues were established here at Bandoeng. We celebrated our reunion without even a biscuit or a sip of beer.

The POW's had been collecting books outside the camp when out on working parties and because I hadn't failed my Senior Certificate and was therefore highly educated I was appointed Librarian. Colonel Laurens Van der Post came in on my first morning and asked if I'd any westerns. He only read cowboy books because he'd never done his Senior Certificate. I gave him all the advice he needed; I therefore became his guru long before he became Prince Charles's. Zane Grey was his favourite author.

The job didn't last long. The Japs crammed five hundred of us aboard a ship bound for the Japanese mainland via Singapore. We were three weeks at Changi blatantly ostracised by the resident POW's there, because they'd now become highly organised and didn't want a bunch of itinerant scarecrows to rock the boat. What stuck in our craw was the fact that among the many British officers there we discovered a number of ex-rubber planters and colonial civilians who'd been given courtesy commissions before the fall of Singapore. This gave them a POW status denied to the 84 Squadron aircrews, who'd been through shit, but who'd never been able to apply for officer status either in Libya or the Far East. Although we were only temporary guests at Changi we still had to sweat as daily labourers while these people relaxed on deckchairs outside the bungalows in the officers lines.

Our cruise liner bound for Nippon was called the 'Mata Maru', an old rusted bucket built on the Clyde in 1913. They put us in among the rats in the hold and kept us battened down there for nearly a month. We sweated back-to-back, playing 'I Spy' and holding spelling bees and wondering en route when the Yanks would put a torpedo into us. We landed at Moji on Honshiu in midwinter in the few ragged tropical duds we possessed. Our contingent of skeletal British ambassadors caused derision on the sixteen-hour journey from Moji to Wakayama.

I became a barrack honcho there. If Heinz had fifty-seven different varieties I copped for nine more, numbering among them on Chinese, called Sam Wee, re-christened 'Wee Wee', two New Zealand fighter pilots, a couple of Canadians, a vagrant from Glasgow, a university don and four survivors of the 'Prince of Wales' who'd done three weeks in an open boat and finished up with eight left out of twenty-four.

The first instruction I received from Flash Harry, our camp commandant, was "You must teach all Blitish sojah notta go mad!" I didn't succeed. I didn't like being a honcho. Honcho-ship entitled the holder of the honour to a gratuitous drubbing from any Jap who felt like a bit of exercise. All our orders and numbering had to be done in the Japanese language and since several of our inmates were innumerate, even in the King's English, the honcho was often called to account because of their deficiencies in a foreign tongue. "Koo-me-goo-me-migi-mas-susume!" means "Right wheel, quick march!" - it's still fresh in my memory.

Our menu was skinny. The subject of grub became an all-pervading obsession twenty-four hours a day. Tommy Fisher, from Ballinamallard, was our camp cook. He worked miracles with the loaves and fishes, except that he hadn't a slice of nutty crust and never saw a single sardine. Rice and weevils were our staple diet. We had two resident RAF medics, Bob Wilson from Greenisland and Harry Knox from the Cliftonville Road. Both were appalled when they discovered that we were frying our rice in lathe oil; it tasted awful, but we regarded it as a nostrum for beri beri and 'happy feet'.

Having worked as a labourers for a spell in a factory at Wakayama, we ended up at a mining camp in the mountains at Ikuno. At the time I turned the scales at just under seven stones, yet, like the rest of the boys, managed to do a daily ten-hour shift in the malevolent copper mine two miles from the camp. There was at least a modicum of saving grace in working at Ikuno - the Nip guards were wary of the numerous cave-ins down below and elected to stay on the surface while their Korean colleagues took over the job of supervising us. Most of them were pigs.

The prisoners worked in pairs. Down in the pitch darkness of number 17 level I had the distinction of digging copper ore with one, Taff Greenman, a Welsh con man, an AC plonk with a propensity for covert sabotage and inspired thievery. Our boss was a cross-eyed oriental called Pissyfriss Wilfred; he lived in a state of intellectual twilight. We stole his grub and knocked his tobacco and put pit props across the lines when he wasn't looking, so that full buggies ended up buried in the sides of the tunnel. When he sought our help to correct the derailment, we let him use his crowbar to do all the heavy pushing and heaving, while we grunted and panted dramatically, determined not to expend a single calorie in support. When Pissyfriss hid his baccy we scraped hairy tree-bark from the pit props and smoked it in our pipes. The Japs gave us cotton bags full of rice husks to rest our heads on after lights out; Taff and I smoked our pillows.

Taff was repulsive. He had a pair of opaque glasses with lenses as thick as bottle-bottoms. They were scuffed and skew-whiff, held together with bits of string. He always said that when he came out of the opticians he went and got his ears insured. Some Nip back in Java had thumped him and he'd lost most of his false teeth, but still had the rest of his denture. He found an ex-dental mechanic in Barrack Six, an inventive bloke who fixed him up with a set of aluminium molars that sounded like castanets. His field-grey leer would have put children to flight. He got himself a day off once by rubbing salt in his eyes until he looked like a character out of science fiction. He was a great companion, because he had a brain like a trap and could remember every detail of HG Wells' 'History of the World'. He also had an extensive repertoire of naughty songs which had delivered all on one note. I was never bored, even though he coast me several black eyes and an occasional split lip.

Taff and I were supposed to fill six buggies before 'lunch'. We usually did three and philosophically accepted the nastiness that followed. We discovered early on that when you threw a load of pit props into the buggy, then covered them with copper ore the job became less onerous. We also found that the biggest rocks blasted down by the shot-firers took a much shorter time to complete the load, provided you had the strength to lift them over the side. I didn't have the strength - I got a boulder half over the side and my tummy muscles collapsed. When I saw the blood spattering the rock I found I'd lost the end of the middle finger of my left hand. Taff ran off to interrupt Pissyfriss' siesta in his cubbyhole near the mine cage. The only way to impress a Jap that you were sick was to bleed like a stuck pig. Pissyfriss fetched Snoopy from upstairs. The guard's nickname was apt. Whatever had hit him in China had knocked his head off the plumb, so that he appeared to be ever trying to look up ladies' skirts.

Snoopy plotted an erratic course as he prodded me the two miles back to camp. I left a trail of blood so that the working party could find their way home. I was warmly received by Doc Knox, whose only anaesthetic was the Rubayat of Omar Khayyam. He used a scalpel for every ailment from carbuncles to pleurisy, but delegated common boils to his orderly, Crippin. Knox always prefaced his use of the knife with a selection of quotes, such as "Come fill the cup….(slash) and in the fire of spring…(gasp)..the winter garment of repentance fling!" He was a great guy, much respected by his patients. I didn't enjoy his ministrations on this occasion, but he fixed me up, even to the extent of climbing on to the low roof of his surgery' and coming back with a thin strip of lead which he bent over my finger to keep it isolated during working hours. Four hours later Taff arrived breathless at my bed space, "Here it is, Paddy!" he said, "Found it in among the ore! Come on – Knox'll sew it back on!". Our medic shook his head sadly, "Too late," he said. I took the spare piece of my anatomy to the cookhouse and asked Tommy to make soup.

Knox managed to get me a day off work. I spent it in the empty billet, feeling sorry for myself and trying to read pages 51 to 100 of "Murder at the Opera", knowing that pages 101 to 150 were elsewhere in the camp. In any case some clever bloke would tell me who done it long before I could find pages 251 to 300.

During our time in Japan we managed to keep informed about what was happening in the wide world outside. You could judiciously select a dim Nip and do a bit of pumping in wonky Japanese and pidgin English. We purloined newspapers and learned a lot from the campaign maps they featured. We didn't even need to do this when Germany capitulated because our hosts celebrated the event by beating hell out of us. We know the Yanks were island-hopping closer and closer to Japan and that the yellow men were being stuffed in Burma and , since their navy had taken an awful pasting, their imports had dwindled to a trickle. So had our grub. The guards kept reminding us that we were for the chop when the Yanks invaded, so it became a question whether we'd expire from starvation before this could happen. The atom bomb saved our bacon. We canonised Robert Oppenheimer.

The British aircraft carrier 'Implacable' landed us at Vancouver. Thinking that we'd go crazy now that we were free, the Canadians put us under guard right from the gangplank to the special train that was to take us right across the country to Nova Scotia, a five-day trip. Despite close supervision, dozens of liberated POW's escaped on the way and ended up having a ball in Hollywood and Acapulco. How the hell Monty Montgomery got himself to Australia without calling with his missus in Preston will forever be a mystery.

I was a right jackass. I jumped off the train when it stopped to take on water at North Bay, Ontario. I called to surprise Aunt Minnie and Uncle Joe, not knowing that Aunt Minnie was a religious maniac. She kept me prisoner for four whole days. Stuffing me with food and forcing me to drink gallons of milk, while she kept poor old Joe in a corner because he had dared to buy me a beer when we were out for a walk. She was built like a second-row forward, trotted out more Biblical quotations than Billy Graham and kept putting half nelsons on me and kissing me on the cheek; her lips were like a vacuum cleaner. She hadn't signed the Geneva Convention. I finally walked out like Captain Oates and gave myself up at the local office of the Military Police.

Civilian life has been tame. I'm so damned respectable now that I express shock at the humping scenes in TV plays and never give a second look at girls wearing short skirts. I suppose I'm neuter gender. I've tried to sanitize my vocabulary during peacetime, because I used to use language that you'd only hear nowadays in the playground of an infant school.

I took up teaching after the war and graduated in languages at Trinity College Dublin - extern. Finding a modest job as a school principal after many years in the classroom turned out to be a difficult proposition, because preferment invariably went to applicants with strong church connections.

A Boys Brigade captain stood a better chance than a Chindits major. My regimented exposure to Methodism during my youth and the discovery of so many hypocrites masquerading as Christians in the congregation drove me on to the golf course on the Sabbath. "My God! He must be an atheist!".

I've written three novels in retirement, the sort that once you put them down you can't pick them up again; they're hidden from the family. Despite my failure as a modern day Charles Dickens, I find little to complain about. After all, poor Geoff died of Beri Beri, dysentery and starvation in Wakayama and I lost a host of friends who'd have made a rich contribution to life if they'd lived. Johnny Jeudwine made Australia in forty-six days. True to his word he risked a return by Submarine to rescue his comrades, but they were already in the bag. After a tremendous flying career he was killed in '45, testing a Typhoon. Phil Corney died in Perth before he hit forty.

A week after I got home from Aunt Minnie's I bumped into that flabby git, Willie W,. in Royal Avenue, on his way home from flying a desk in his doting uncle's insurance brokerage.

"Oh?" he squeaked, " So we're back again, are we? You've had a right cushy old time in the Raff, eh, Davy?"

I told him it was better than working.

FLIGHT LIEUTENANT
ARTHUR RUSK
PILOT
COASTAL COMMAND

Arthur Rusk was born in Belfast on the 22nd March and was educated at the Belfast Royal Academy. He joined the RAFVR in Belfast in August 1939 and carried out his basic flying at the 24 Elementary and Reserve Flying Training School at Sydenham. With war being declared in September 1939 he was called to full time service.

He was then posted to an Initial Training Wing at St Lenards-on-Sea where he carried out his basic training, square-bashing, rifle drill. etc.

On completion of his basic training he was posted to Coastal Command and based at St Eval in Cornwall and it was during an operation from there that he was credited with sinking a German U-boat. Later on he was posted over-seas to India where he flew Lockheed Hudsons, and was mentioned in despatches. After the war he flew for Ulster Aviation, and was the pilot of a Miles Aerovan which overturned in high winds, killing one of Lord Londonderry's prize bulls. (The tail boom of the Aerovan is still being used today as a wind sock at the Newtownards Airfield). Arthur left Ulster Aviation to take up employment with British Caledonian Airlines, and eventually became one of their senior captains. While working with BCAL he was seconded to Rolls Royce for a time as a sales representative selling BAC 111's to South America, and was also involved in taking their VIP's on 'special trips'. He later left British Caledonian Airlines and was employed with Laker Airways, and sometime after that joined the aviation firm of Hunting were he was involved in an aerial survey of Fiji.

SERGEANT
PATRICK MORRIS RUSK
ROYAL AIR FORCE NO. 1062426
FIGHTER PILOT
NO. 222 (NATAL) SQUADRON

Patrick Maurice Rusk, Pat as he liked to called by his friends, was born in Belfast on the 12th June 1922 and was educated at the Belfast Royal Academy. Pat excelled in all sports but especially at Rugby playing for the school's First XV.

Sergeant Pat Rusk was killed in January 1942 and as his logbook is missing I am relating this story to the readers using extracts taken from Pat's own private diary for which I am indebted to his sister-in-law Mrs Betty Rusk.

Patrick Maurice Rusk joined the RAF at the age of 18 in September 1940 and in January 1941 was posted to an initial training wing near Plymouth where he completed his basic training. His diary shows that during his basic training he attended a navigation course and passed the exam with an 89%, and 94% (armaments), 83% (airmanship), 90% (aircraft recognition). Cadet Rusk was then posted to No 15 Service Flying Training School, near Hull in February 1941and started his flying training in Tiger Moths. He had his first air experience flight in a Tiger Moth on March 1st with his instructor Flight Lieutenant Dodwell, learning how to fly straight and level, and getting used to the controls. He flew the Tiger Moth solo on March 18th after 6hrs.15mins instruction and completed the course on April 24th.

On March 20th 1941 he watched as a Whitley land down wind, and crash into one of the schools Tiger Moths carrying into the next field. On the 25th April 1941 he was given ten days home returning on the 3rd May. He managed to get the 5.50pm train from Selby which took him to Stranraer via York-Newcastle and Carlisle. He then boarded the 0630 hrs Stranraer to Larne boat at a cost of £3. Pat spent the next ten days with his family and visited some of his friends. On the Saturday 3rd May his leave was finished and said his goodbyes to his family and made his way down to the Heysham boat in Belfast only to be told that it was full and to try again tomorrow. He decided not to waste the night so he went to the Floral Hall where he met Maybeth McMullan from Carrickfergus and they danced the night away. It had just gone past midnight, Sunday 4th May and unknown to Pat or his partner,

Belfast was about to have its 2nd German air raid. Pats Diary: "The time was now 12.15am and I heard the terrific nose of sirens and bombs going off. The anti-aircraft guns didn't stop until 4.00 am. I went down town with a friend and saw the biggest fires I had ever seen in my life, buildings falling and unexploded bombs going off at Sydenham." He decided to make his way to Larne by train as the whole of the Belfast Dock area had been badly damaged by the Luftwaffe. He managed to get the Larne-Stranraer boat and arrived back on station at 0300 hrs.

Pat was then posted to RAF Kidlington on May 6th and on his arrival was very disappointed to see the twin engined Airspeed Oxfords sitting on the Apron as he had hoped to go on to fighters. He went to see the Squadron Commander and put his case to him but unfortunately his request was turned down so he unpacked his kit and resigned himself to fly Oxfords. The Oxford made its first flight back in 19th June 1937 and was built in large numbers to train RAF Pilots, Air Gunners, Bomb Aimers, Camera Operators, Navigators and Radio Operators. The Oxford had dual controls making it suitable as twin engined trainer and its power plant were two Pratt & Whitney R-985-AN6 Wasp Junior radial piston engines. 8,585 Airspeed Oxfords were built. Pat's first flight in the Oxford was on May 8th 1941 with his instructor Flight Lieutenant Powell and lasted 30 minutes, and flew it solo on May 11th. His training continued with lectures and Link training and continuous flying both day and night. On Friday 27th June Pat sat his Wings exam and had a flying test on 28th June with the Chief Flying Instructor. He received his results on Friday 4th June and had passed all the exams with a 81.7% pass mark and was placed 11th overall on the course. Pat was awarded his Wings during the 1st week in July and on Friday 11th July he was given ten days home leave. He got into Belfast at 11.30am on July 12th and went straight home to meet his parents. On July 17th the weather was beautiful so he took his mother to Portrush to see an old friend, when he got back home a telegram had arrived from 15 SFTS informing him that he was to report to No 57 Operational Training Unit at Hawarden on July 20th. On Friday, July18th he decided to go to the Capitol Cinema on the Antrim Road to see the movie 'Down went M'Ginty' and in the evening he went to the Floral Hall at Bellevue, (quoting in his diary) "Very poor show of girls."

On Saturday morning he went down into Belfast to organise his travel warrant back to the mainland that night. He said his goodbyes once more to his family and friends and boarded the Heysham boat that night arriving there early next morning. He was then trained down to Hawarden, travelling all day arriving there that evening, and to his great surprise and delight found the airfield covered with Spitfires. He was going to be a fighter pilot after all. On Tucsday 22nd July he flew in a Miles Master with the units Chief Flying Instructor, Squadron Leader Dishworth for 1hr.15mins. The Miles Master was first delivered to the RAF in the mid-1930's, and was the first of its high performance monoplanes trainers. The reason it was used at Hawarden and many other OTU's was that it had similar handling characteristics to those of the Hurricane and Spitfire.

Pat's diary shows that he flew the Spitfire (PW-L) for the first time on July 31st. He took the aircraft to 3,000ft where he tried to carry out a roll, unfortunately in doing so put the Spitfire into an inverted spin but managed to dive out of it. He pulled back on the stick to hard, causing the aircraft to go into a very high-speed stall, which he corrected and landed very shaken. On August 12th,13th,14th 1941, Pat flew (PW-N) and (PW-S), carrying out formation flying, dog-fight practice, Cine gun and air to air firing. On Sunday 17th his diary shows that he hit the Spitfire propeller low-flying on the sands of the River Dee (whoops). On Thursday 28th Carter hit Pat in mid-air, his elevator touched his navigation light. Pat's engine gave out at 1,300ft, and for some reason roared back into life again at 500ft at full throttle and he landed safely. On Saturday 30th August he was posted up to Drem in Scotland near Edinburgh for some advanced practice flying. Pat's diary shows that he flew home to Northern Ireland on 4th September in a 'Maggie', he was very nervous as he had to cross the sea in 10/10 cloud. He eventually came out of the cloud over Maghermourne and headed for Aldergrove and then down to Sydenham where he parked the aircraft for the night. It was great to be home and he went to the Floral Hall that night with some friends. The next day he left Sydenham at lunch time in terrible weather, flying over Bangor at zero ft and headed out to sea, flying all the way back to Drem at 500ft. In September he had his firsts scramble, "Terrific fun, but didn't see the 'brat', but according to operations he was very close."

On Friday September 19th, Pat received the news that he had been waiting for. He was being posted to No 222 Squadron in 11 Group at Manston. He left Drem that

night and caught the 22.00pm London bound train from Edinburgh, arriving in London at 0930 hrs the next morning. He took another train to Manston, arriving there at 1900 hrs only to find that the squadron had moved to North Weald. The station Adjutant arranged a new travel warrant for Pat and he left for London on the 2 o'clock train arriving there at tea-time. Pat decided to stay overnight in a bed & breakfast and woke around 9.00am and had to rush to Victoria railway Station by 9.30am. He arrived at North Weald at lunch time. No 222 Squadron was formed the same day as the RAF was, 1st April 1918 and was equipped with Sopwith Camels. It was disbanded in February 1919, and reformed as a fighter squadron at Duxford in October 1939. It served with distinction throughout the Battle of Britain and the Second World War, and was finally disbanded at Leuchars in Scotland in November 1957. In August 1941 the squadron was equipped with Spitfire MkVb's.

Pat carried out his first sortie with the Squadron on September 30th. This was a 'Rhubarb' operation to Dunkirk (a 'Rhubarb' sortie was a small-scale fighter or fighter-bomber attacks on ground targets of opportunity).

Between September 30th 1941 and January 1942 Pat had carried out almost fifty different types of sorties to the Continent. These included many sweeps into France. convoy patrols, and Rhubarbs.

Pats Diary shows that on October 2nd he flew a sweep to Berck-Sur-Mer, "Lots of 109's, Yanks got five."

Oct 3rd	Sweep to Ostend/Newport. Blenheims wrote off a power station- all aircraft returned.
Oct 13th	Sweep to Mazingarbe, lots of flak at coast and 109's inside. Ferraby shot up but OK. 18 Blenheims bombed railway. Returned with only 10 gallons of petrol left.
Oct 18th	Rhubarb to Furnes, flew 200 yards from beach, past within 30 yards of Dunkirk Lighthouse, attacked Furnee Aerodrome at 500ft & beat up its hangars.
Oct 21st	Sweep to St Omer, 109's flew right under us (all painted black).
Oct 26th	Sweep up the French Coast from Le Touquet to Gravelines, had a collision with Pilot Officer Saunders in cloud on way back! His elevator hit my wing.
Nov 1st	Squadron and Eagles escorted Hurricane bombers to Neuve Chapelle. Flew at 500ft all the way, bombers were a great success in hitting factory.
Nov 7th	Rhubarb to Berck-sur-Mer to attack an alcohol distillery with Blue section. (Pat was Blue (2). He shot at a factory, army camp, and a large building on the coast, and saw a 'dummy' airfield with false 109's parked.)

Nov 12th   Diversion Sweep to Dunkirk. *(Pat was Red (2) to Flight Lieutenant Davies. He saw thousands of aircraft over the Channel at the same time.)*

Dec 12th   Rhubarb to Gris-nes in France, went down on Drome to attack 3 Ju87's (probably dummies), pulled out far to late and nearly pranged in a wood. IFF set blew up and had to pull of the hood.

On Christmas Eve Pat's diary shows that he was on pay parade and received £5.14shillings. On Christmas day he carried out some low flying and had his turkey dinner at 1630 hrs. (marvellous trifle) and to bed at 2300 hrs.

On December 30th Pat was given five days leave. Little did he or his parents know that this would be the last time that he would see his family and Ulster's shores. Pat managed to catch the 12.29pm train from North Weald to Heysham and once on board he was allocated a cabin. The boat docked in Belfast the next morning at 10.30am, it was a bit late because of the thick fog on the way over. He spent the next few days meeting with some friends, and going to the Embassy Club in the evenings. All too quickly his leave had expired and it was time to head back to North Weald, boarding the Heysham boat in Belfast on January 5th and arriving back at North Weald the following day at 1600 hrs. His diary shows that his new Spitfire 'Y' had arrived while he was on leave and he flew it for the first time on January 11th, when he took part in a Rhubarb to Griz Nez, but had to return to base due to a snow blizzard, and nearly 'pranged' into the London Balloon Barrage. On January 21st he carried out a Rhubarb to Berck, where he beat up some factories and a goods train, and on January 22nd he carried out two convoy patrols. On January 27th Pat had just taken delivery of another new Spitfire and was returning from a sweep over France. As he approached Dover he dived down low, and in doing so, his wing or wings separated from the Spitfire. The aircraft crashed and Pat was killed. Sergeant Patrick Morris Rusk is buried in Drumbo Cemetery a few miles outside Belfast.

SERGEANT
WALTER FREDERICK RUSK
ROYAL AIR FORCE NO. 966122
PILOT
NO. 7 SFTS

KILLED ON ACTIVE SERVICE 8TH OCTOBER 1940

'The Blond Bombshell'

Walter F Rusk the son of Mr WP Rusk a Belfast businessman, was born in Belfast on July 11th 1910, and soon after in his young life the Rusk family moved to Whitehead. Walter was educated at Larne Grammar School where he excelled in many sports. He had however, a zealousness for speed, as did his brother John. Both had a passion for cars but their overriding ultimate in speed was in motorcycles.

Walter was also an extremely good photographer, and was very proud of his small collection of good quality cameras. On leaving school he was employed for a while selling petrol at a garage that was owned by McMullans of Belfast. In 1928 Walter decided to leave Northern Ireland and headed for Australia where he worked for three years on his Uncle's Ranch. Motor cycles were still his first love and it was here that he learnt the hard lesson of racing, riding on the rough tracks and roads of Australia. But it wasn't long before homesickness got to him and he returned home to Northern Ireland where he took up Motor Cycle racing with his younger brother John.

The motorcycling career of Walter F Rusk, 1926-1940

1926: In 1926 Walter was riding a five year old 490cc Norton when he won the 62 mile motorcycle race at Temple. His average speed was 57.55mph. He won the event by over six minutes from SJ McBride who was from Ballyhackamore and riding a 249cc S.G.S at an average speed of 52.32mph. The third placed rider was EG Lammey from Moneymore riding a 348cc AJS.

1931: Walter started road racing in 1931 along side his brother John, in a sport that was to make him a hero of thousands. He rode his first road race on June 24th, 1931 at the Enniskillen 100, riding a 1926, 490cc Norton. Unfortunately after just three laps he had to retire after 'frying' his clutch. In July 1931 he entered for the Temple 60 which was held at the Temple Race course again riding a 1926 490cc Norton. He went on to win the 62 mile race and set a new lap record of 58mph. On

August 8th he raced at Ballydrain coming off at Ballydrain Corner and on September 5th rode in his first Ulster Grand Prix on a 500cc AJS, setting a new lap record on the 2nd Lap of 87.54mph. On the 3rd Lap the bike dropped a valve and he had to retire. Chambers a well known motorcycle dealer (Donegall Pass) at that time had the AJS especially sent over from the factory for Walter to ride. Later in the race Stanley Woods eventually set a record of 89.67mph. He then raced in the last race of the season in Belfast with his brother John in the Carrowdore 100 on September 26th. Walter was riding the works 500cc AJS when he came off during the 1st Lap. Sadly his brother John also came off during the first lap and was killed. He was 24 years of age. This was a terrible tragedy for Walter and his family.

1932: Walter decided that he would continue racing in memory of his brother John, and started to show his true potential in 1932 when he rode in his first North West 200 race, riding in the 350cc Class. He came second to his very great friend Walter Handley after a very close and exciting race. It was at the Ulster Grand Prix on September 2nd when he finally made his mark when he was riding Walter Handley's 250cc Rudge. The Clady course was 20.5 miles long and over ten laps. Walter took the lead from Ted Mellors (Imperial Factory Team) on the 5th Lap, and on the 8th lap had to retire with valve trouble.

1933: Walter's first race of the 1933 season was the North West 200. He retired during the 4th lap riding a 493cc Sunbeam 95. On May 6th he rode the 493cc Sunbeam 95 in the Leinster 200 again having to retire early. On May 31st he rode in the Cookstown 100 riding the 493cc Sunbeam. He lost a foot-rest during the race but carried on coming in 6th overall with the fastest lap of 67.38mph. 1933 also saw him make his debut at the Isle of Man TT again riding the 493cc Sunbeam. This race was just a learning curve for Walter. On June 28th he had the fastest lap (71.65mph) on his Sunbeam at the Enniskillen 100 but had top retire during the race. On August 12th he was invited to ride a Works Norton in the Ulster Grand Prix and came a close second to another 'Ulster Great' Stanley Woods and just missed the lap record of 89.56mph.

Remember this is 1933. Walter was enjoying one of his 'gentle' cruises around the Isle of Man course, and zooming through the peaceful main street of Kirkmichael at over 80mph was stopped by the local Bobby for being a shade too hectic, so soon after his dinner. The constable raised a restraining hand, and Walter stopped just in front of him. The local Bobby was pleasant but firm and snipped the rubber band off his little black note book with a grim smile.

Summonses were issued very quickly on the Island at that time, and the next day Walter appeared before the Magistrates, charged with (these words were taken from the original Summons): "You are hereby commanded to summon Walter Frederick Rusk C/O 'Granville' Loch Promenade Douglas. At the High Bailiffs Court to be holden in the Court House, in the Town hall of Douglas, on Friday next 9th June 1933 at 10.30 o'clock in the fore noon to answer suit of Thomas Cringle, Inspector of Police, Plaintiff who Charges that the said Defendant Walter Frederick Rusk, the person driving a light 'locomotive' to whit motorcycle CZ.2204 did on the 31st May 1933 in a public highway to whit Bray Hill in the town of Douglas unlawfully fail and neglect to carry a bell or other instrument to give audible and sufficient warning of the approach or position of the 'light locomotive' afore said by sounding such Bell or other Instrument." Contrary to the Statute in that case made and provided Highway Act of 1927, given at Douglas, the 5th day of June 1933. The idea of a bell on a racing bike is rather quaint, but mark the sequel to this story. The stern Manx Justice's were appalled at such behaviour in their fair domain, inflicted the fearsome fine of 2 shillings and sixpence (12pP) with the positively crippling Court Costs of 2 shillings and eight pence (16p). I am credibly informed by a family member that Walter had to borrow the odd two pence.

From then on Walter was always in the Newspapers with headlines: "Walter Rusk known as the crazy young Devil from Ireland, nicknamed 'The Blond Bombshell', who is always so cheerful, sings and whistles all day"; "Ulsterman in famous team, leaps to motorcycle fame, regarded as a fine and natural rider, Ulster Grand Prix 1933"; "Unknown rider leaps to fame in Grand Prix"; "Belfast man shines in 'Nortons' private war"; "Belfast mans brilliant riding"; "Belfast man's brilliant victory in Northwest 200"; "Rusk smashes all lap times at Ulster Grand Prix 18th August 1934"; and "Rusk breaks World Records 18th August 1934".

1934: His first race of 1934 was at the Leinster 200 when had to retire during lap 14 riding his 493cc Sunbeam. On May 12th he had his first win in the North West 200 riding a works factory built 350cc Velocette with a fastest lap and a class record of 73.66mph. On May 23rd he came 1st in the Cookstown 100 and set a new lap record. It was then across to the Isle of Man TT, riding in both the Junior and Senior races on Velocettes. He came 7th in the junior race and then came his moment of triumph when he stood on the rostrum at the visitors ceremony by finishing in 3rd place in the senior race on the 500cc factory built 'Dog Kennel' Velocette. On June 23rd he entered the Dutch TT where he raced Guthbert Emery's 350 and 500cc Factory built Velocette's. Walter finished 2nd in the 350 race and had to retire in lap one with a, "Broken top fork spindle," in the 500. On July 1st Walter road a factory built 500cc Norton in the German Grand Prix. Walter was not officially entered, but as Jimmy Guthrie had dropped the 500 Norton in Holland, sustaining a broken arm and concussion, Joe Craig hired Walter to ride the Norton. Walter had to retire on the 3rd lap but not before setting a new lap record in the second lap. July 7th and 8th saw him racing both the Norton 350 and 500cc machines in the Swiss Grand Prix. He came 3rd in the 350cc race and retired in lap 31 of the 500cc race, again not before setting a new lap record during lap 30.

The following week on July 15th he was again in action in the Belgium Grand Prix riding the 350cc Works Velocette, and had to retire during lap 8 with a broken fork spring (after setting the fastest lap). In August it was back to Northern Ireland when he raced a Works 500cc Velocette in the Ulster Grand Prix and won the race. It was during this race that Walter broke the 90mph barrier, on the 3rd lap Walter even had to stop at Muckamore to change a defective spark plug during the race, but with great determination and skill increased his speed every lap until he reached the staggering 92.13mph lap record. (This was the year that Walter, because of his thick blond hair inherited the nick- name, the 'Blond Bombshell'.) On September 2nd he came 2nd in the Swedish Grand Prix riding a works 500cc Velocette, and on September 8th came 2nd in both the 350cc and 500cc races riding works Velocette.

1935: In 1935 he was 'invited' back to join the Works Norton team, and on May 11th he won the 350cc race at the North West 200 for a second time on a Works Norton again taking the lap and class record (76.22mph). On May 11th Walter came 2nd in the Isle of Man Junior race on a Works Norton and 3rd in the senior race again on the Works Norton. On June 30th he won the 350 race in the Swiss Grand Prix on the Works Norton and came 2nd in the 500 race again riding the Works Norton (410 miles in the one day). On July 6th he won the 350 race in the Dutch Brand Prix again on the Works Norton, and also won the German Grand Prix on July 14th riding the Works Norton. On July 21st he came 2nd in the Belgian Grand Prix, riding the 500cc Works Norton, and on

August 24th riding the same machine at the Ulster Grand Prix, came off during the 2nd Lap.

1936-1937: In early spring 1936 Walter had been returning to Whitehead from a day out in Portrush riding his Norton 'Inter'. As he approached Larne on the coast road a dog ran out in front of him, he managed to miss it, but in doing so, he hit the sea wall and fractured his left arm. Had it not been for his good riding ability in an emergency, he might have been seriously injured or killed. Walter was still conscious at the time, and was taken by a passing car to the Larne District Hospital where his fracture was set immediately by Dr Crawford Blair of Larne. A relative of the famous rider thought it would not be long before Walter would be in the riding seat again. How wrong he was. Walter's arm was not healing in the way that it should, and in July was informed by the doctor that the bone between his shoulder and elbow would not join. So it was decided to take a section of bone from his shin and graft it into his arm to help keep the bones in place while the fracture was healing. This was a new and daring operation for that period, and was carried out by a Mr MST Irwin. Walter himself said at the time, " I am allowing six weeks for the bones to heal, three weeks more to tone up my muscles, and then its time to practice for the Isle of Man." This injury was so severe it put him out of racing for almost two years, and it is well known in the motorcycle fraternity of that time that Walter 'did race' while his arm was still in a 'L' shape plaster, having a friend tie his hand to the left hand grip so he could operate the clutch. On another occasion Walter had shot himself in the foot after climbing over a fence when his shot-gun went off. His doctor said he would never race again, but he was back racing on his bike a week later with his foot in plaster and there is a photograph to prove it.

1938: Walter is back. Walter returned to racing in 1938 and his first race of the season was at the Isle of Man TT when he rode a 250cc OK Supreme, but had to retire during the 3rd lap due to a split fuel tank. On June 22nd he came off his 250cc OK Supreme during the Enniskillen 100 race and was taken to hospital, but he was allowed out the next day. On August 7th he was back with the Norton Team riding the 350cc Works Norton in the German Grand Prix, unfortunately he came off during lap 10. On August 19th he came 2nd in the Ulster Grand Prix riding the 350cc Works Norton. This was another of the many great battles between Walter and Mellors.

1939: Walter started the 1939 season by racing a Ron Harris 350cc 'Kit' Velocette in the North West 200 in May (Norton had pulled out of racing in 1939). He came off during lap 15 at the Shell Hill Bridge when leading Jimmy Little and sustained minor facial cuts. Walter was joint 350cc fastest lap with Jimmy Little.

Walter again rode the 350cc Ron Harris Velocette in the Junior race at the Isle of Man TT and came 20th. He would ride the new Works V4 Water Cooled, Super Charged AJS in the Senior, and finished the race in 11th

place. August 19th was to be Walter's finest hour when racing in the Ulster Grand Prix. He rode the 499cc Super Charged AJS to exactly 100mph, making him the first rider ever in history to lap a British Road Race Course at over 100mph. The line up for the 1939 Ulster Grand Prix was a formidable one despite the absence of the Works Nortons and Velocettes (they had pulled out of racing due to the threat of a world war). Walter took the lead right from the very start of the race. From Aldergrove he accelerated to Muckamore, then along the straight to Clady, and he was first past the stands with an amazing speed of 96.85mph, and completed the second lap in 12mins.20secs, which gave him a speed of 99.93 mph, just two seconds outside the magic 100mph. On his third lap Walter had broken the 100mph barrier, giving the Ulster Grand Prix the title of 'Fastest Grand Prix in the World'. During the 4th lap disaster struck the 'Blond Bombshell' when the right fork link broke. During practice Walter had asked his mechanic, Ginger Matthew's who was former AJS employee to increase the boost of the supercharger. This could only be done by fitting a smaller sprocket to the blower which was mounted in front of the engine and driven by a chain from the engine main shaft. Matthew's told Walter, "I'm not giving you any more power, you're lapping at 99.6 at the present, and you'll blow the effing thing up." Matthews said, "I didn't give him anymore power and he still lapped at over 100mph."

There is a true story about what actually happened the night before the race when Walter met two friends at the Chambers Garage in Belfast, Terry Hill and David Woods who was the foreman of the Chambers Garage. Walter explained to them that his mechanic Ginger Mathews would not increase the boost for fear of blowing up the engine, and asked them if they would help. David Woods told Walter to wait until everyone had left the garage and returned letting themselves in with his own keys. He changed the sprocket on the blower, and the next day Walter went out and broke the 100mph barrier, thanks to his friends who I know he had many. The 'star' of the Sammy Miller Motorcycle Museum in Birmingham is the ex Walter Rusk Liquid Cooled V-Four, 499cc Super Charged AJS. For achieving this 100 mph record, Walter was awarded a gold medallion which was presented to him by the Motor Cycle Union of Ireland on the 21st August 1939.

Walter's short RAF career

Just after war was declared in 1939 Walter decided to join the RAF and become a Fighter Pilot and was a promising pupil right from the start. He was posted to start his flying training at No 7 Elementary Flying Training School at Peterborough and went solo after just 4hrs.30mins instruction. He was awarded his Wings in August 1940 with a pass mark for the course was 78%. Sadly a short time later, on the morning of October 6th 1940, Walter was killed along with his instructor when their Miles Magister crashed during a training exercise. His father rushed to his bedside but unfortunately by the time he got there, Walter had passed away. It was a sad end for one of Ulster's best loved motorcycle racers, and he would be sadly missed by all who knew and loved him. As far as we know, Walter and his instructor were following the course of a river when the Magisters engine stopped causing the aircraft to stall, and being so low, they could do nothing to recover it. The Pilot died instantly, and Walter died in hospital two days later.

A last letter home

On the 14th September 1940 Walter had been on weekend leave with a friend in London and had witnessed his first dog-fight. On his return to camp he wrote a letter to his parents relating to them what had happened during his weekend leave in London:

Dear Mum and Dad,

Today I saw first of all, about 25 of our planes chasing 25 of theirs away from the city centre, they caught up with them just as they disappeared behind the clouds.

To make up for this an hour later, there was a marvellous dog-fight just above the Strand at about 10,000ft, two enemy bombers with a swarm of about 20 fighters around them. It was impossible to tell whether they were 'ours' or 'theirs'. However after about one to two minutes, the big bomber got it, and started spinning to the ground. Twas a wonderful view we got, the pilot had baled out or rather one of the crew, I don't know which and then as it came screaming down in spinning circles the bombs appeared to go off for it disintegrated at about 3,000ft, and still falling straight for the Strand it came down in about three large pieces. The wind caught these and blew them over and they landed in Victoria Station.

I with a friend got a car and raced round and found the whole tail plane with the fins and tail wheel landed on top of a three storey house. They let me up to examine it, since they thought I was an official, as I was there so soon. I got a bit for a souvenir, and I was tempted to take the little plate on the tail with the name Dornier, Year of Manufacture and No etc, but I thought the Air Ministry could learn more from that so I left it.

Walter

Walter at the time of his death was thought to be one of the most promising motorcycle riders in the world, if not, indeed the best. He had been competing in racing for over seven years, during which he had set many new world records, had numerous spills, and sometimes missing death by inches. It was indeed feared at one time after his accident in early 1936 that he would never ride again, at least by everyone except Walter himself. He never for a moment thought that his racing career was finished. His dogged persistence was such that it was just as if it was his will power, and that alone which eventually mended the broken bone. His Ulster Grand Prix ride in August 1939 will go down in history, as he was the first rider ever to lap the famous Clady circuit at over 100mph. One of Walters closest friends, Squadron Leader NH Corry, DFC AE told me that Walter had been courting his sister Vera in the 30's and that he knew him to be one of nature's gentlemen. He raced not to win but for the thrill of it, win or lose it did not matter to Walter, and to this day many of his friends still speak affectionately of him as he was one of the grandest sportsmen motorcycling has ever known. Sergeant Walter Frederick Rusk was interred at Eastfield Cemetery in Peterborough aged 29 years.

Shortly after Walters untimely death, Mr JE Little and his brother decided that it would be a fitting tribute to Walter if they had a 'Walter Rusk Memorial Trophy' made in his honour. In fact three were created in his memory. The first one would be awarded for the best performance in International Road Racing by an Irish rider (I believe another late and great Ulster rider Joey Dunlop held this trophy for years right up until he was killed in 1999). The second trophy was awarded for the best performance in Irish Races by an Irish rider, and the third trophy (won 12 successive years by Sammy Miller) is the award of the Ards Motor Cycle Club, and is the premier award for the clubs Boxing Day trial.

SERGEANT
ROBERT SCOTT, VC
LEADING AIRCRAFTSMAN
NO. 4535

Robert Scott was born on the 4th June 1874 of Ulster parents who had just recently left town land of Ballinran near Kilkeel County Down to settle in Haslingden in Lancashire. As a boy he had worked in one of the towns cotton mills and the age of twenty sought a more active life and joined the 1st Battalion of the Manchester Regiment in 1895 with his elder brother.

After completing his basic training he saw some service in England but it was not long until he boarded the Troopship SS Goth and sailed south to Africa where the Boer War had already started. It was not long however until this quiet shy unassuming modest man would be awarded the highest military honour that their country could bestow on him the Victoria Cross.

How Robert Scott won his Victoria Cross

On the 5th January 1900, Private Robert Scott, accompanied by fifteen other soldiers from the Manchester regiment took up their positions in a Sangar on a hill near Ladysmith, known to the British Army as Wagon Hill and Caesar's Camp. They knew that the Boers were about to launch a determined attack on the town and their Sangar was directly in the firing line. Spasmodic outbursts of gun fire shattered the silence while Scott and his companions prepared their positions. By midnight all was silent, but it was an eerie silence. The soldiers knew that the enemy was preparing for the attack. Slowly the hours dragged by, punctuated only by the occasional whiz of a bullet from the Boer lines. By one o'clock in the morning the attack had started in earnest. The whole hillside was swarming with Boers, bullets flew through the night air as they made a determined effort to overcome the position. One by one the soldiers fell as the Boers bullets found their marks. Within a matter of hours the strength of the party had been reduced to half, and before dawn fourteen of the sixteen were dead.

Private Scott and Private James Pitt were left alone to hold off the Boers attack

A bullet had nicked Scott's right ear, but he pulled his Balaclava helmet over his head, donned his tin hat and picked up his rifle and returned fire. As the hours dragged slowly by the sun beat relentlessly on the outpost. Fourteen corpses lay where they had fallen. Noon passed and still there was no sign of assistance. One more attack and the battle may be won. They could not hope to hold out much longer as there was no food and even worse no water. They would soon be forced to give in but not as long as they were able to lift their rifles. The Boers would not give up either, they were determined that Ladysmith should fall that day and would not let a couple of men stand in their way. Bullet after bullet pinged the stones all around these two brave men, the battle for Ladysmith was all but over. Two gallant men who had been cut off from the main force could not hold out much longer.

Hold out they did, counter attack at Caesar's Camp

The sound of rifle fire from the rear caused the two gallant men to look around and wonder of wonders they were saved from certain death. Reinforcements had arrived. The position had been held and what happened in the next few minutes could not be recalled by the two survivors. The Boers had been driven off, another attack repelled and Ladysmith had been saved. Private Scott and Pitt had no Captain to lead them and no Colonel to give them commands, but they knew they had their duty to do. For their Gallantry Lance Corporal Scott and Private J Pitts were awarded the Victoria Cross on the 6th January 1900 in the Field of Battle. Later he said that it was the proudest moment in his whole life when he was presented with the Victoria Cross by Field Marshal Lord Kitchener at a special venue in Victoria South Africa in 1901.

Lance Corporal Robert Scott's Victoria Cross Citation

Scott R and Pitts J during an attack on Caesars Camp in Natal on the 6th January 1900, these two men occupied a Sanger on the left of which all their men had been shot down and positions occupied by Boers. They held their post for fifteen hours without food or water, all the time coming under extremely heavy fire. Keeping up their fire and a smart outlook even though the Boers occupied some Sangers on their immediate left rear. Private Scott was wounded.

When he returned home in October 1902 at the end of his Service, he received a heroes welcome. Corporal Scott, VC was met by the Mayor, the Corporation Brass Band and many representatives of every organisation in the town. Civilian life did not suit such a man and within two years he had left his job in Manchester and rejoined his old regiment. On April 1st 1907 he was promoted to Sergeant as he had now married Miss Alice Grimshaw, a native of his home town. The Vicar of the Parish Church, the Reverend Lewis Robbs declined to accept the usual fee remarking that such an honour could fall to very few clergymen.

Sergeant Scott served right through the First World War as a Quarter Master during which he was awarded the Meritorious Service Medal. He was on active service throughout the war being posted with his wife and daughter Ellen to Cleethorpes. The German Zeppelins made the coast a very dangerous place, so much so wife and daughter were sent home to Ireland. In 1923 Regimental Quarter Master Sergeant (RQMS) left the Army once again and came to Northern Ireland with his wife where they settled in Ballinran near Kilkeel County Down where he served for a brief period with the Royal Irish Constabulary. When the war clouds settled over the country once more in 1939 Sergeant Scott tried to join his old Regiment 'The Manchester's' and serve his country once more. As he was now sixty five years young and in spite of his service record had to be turned down. Such a man took it unkindly to be unable to get into the service. Not to be outdone Sergeant Scott, VC decided to write to an 'old friend' Sir Winston Churchill (whom he had served with in South Africa) asking him for his help. His old Friend did not let him down, he wrote a letter to the powers that be in Northern Ireland requesting that Sergeant Scott be given every assistance in seeking a position within the 'establishment'.

In 1942 a glimmer of hope arose when he learnt that the Royal Air Force needed men over the age of forty. Soon Sergeant Scott was knocking at the door of the RAF Recruiting Office at Clifton Street in Belfast. He was somewhat disappointed when he was placed in medical grade three and was offered clerical duties. This was better than nothing and he served there until the end of hostilities and was the very first person to be demobilised at Victoria Barracks. (During his service

with the RAF he was transferred for a short time to Southampton area when it was being so heavily attacked by the German V1s.) While serving in Southampton and in the sergeants mess one evening he met one of the few Ladysmith veterans, a Colonel Hardcastle (a young officer at the time of the battle but still remembered him). One of the honours that was accorded to this gallant soldier while serving with the RAF was when he was invited to, "Take the Salute," at a march past of his old Regiment the Manchester's. During the celebrations to mark the Centenary of the Victoria Cross he was entertained by some of the worlds most select clubs and societies. At a dinner for the holders of the VC he was entertained by the Prince of Wales at the Royal Gallery of the House of Lords. During his retirement he was a distinguished guest at many functions and at the Bi-Centenary of the "Blood Suckers", his old Regiment he was presented to the Queen Mother.

This gallant shy individual had now served in three major wars and a lifetime of service had ended for Leading Aircraftsman Robert Scott, VC. The year was now 1945 and at the ripe young age of seventy one he returned to his home at the foot of the Mourne Mountains (Bigniand). He attended two Coronations, one in 1937 and one in 1953. He took his place in the ranks of the Victoria Cross holders and on both occasions was presented to the Monarch. He was President of the Belfast Branch of the South African War Veterans, A Life Member of the Royal Air Force Association, a Life Member and Vice President of the Kilkeel Branch British Legion and always maintained close touch with all his friends.

The Last Post

Sadly in February 1961, at the age of eighty seven, and the oldest Victoria Cross holder during the three World Wars, Sergeant Robert Scott, VC died and on the 23rd February 1961 he was buried with full military honours in Kilkeel Church Yard. The funeral was attended by representatives of the Kings Regiment, former members of The Manchester Regiment also attended to honour the man who gave the Regiment its first Victoria Cross. The General Officer Commanding Northern Ireland was also represented as were members of the Kilkeel Branch of the British Legion who formed a guard of honour. Sergeant Scott's scarlet tunic of the Manchester Regiment, his medals gained in three Wars and his regimental badge lay on the draped coffin. The next Sunday, just sixty five years after the gallant stand on the hill near Ladysmith (South Africa), the Regiment that has Ladysmith among it's Battle Honours will pay tribute to the memory of Sergeant Scott, VC. The Regiment had it's barracks in England named Ladysmith Barracks after the battle and awards of Private Robert Scott and Private J Pitts. Thirty six years after his death Sergeant Robert Scott was honoured by his home town in a special ceremony. Haslingdens Army Cadets and the Kings and Manchester Regiments Association attended the unveiling of a Memorial plaque outside his birthplace in Peel Street.

Sergeant Scott's Victoria Cross and other medals are now on display in Ashton-Under-Line town Hall. Sergeant Robert Scott's awards are:

Victoria Cross;
Queens South African Medal with three Bars;
Kings South African Medal with two Bars;
War Medal;
Coronation Medal 1937;
Coronation Medal 1953;
Long Service Medal; and
Meturious Service Medal.

FLIGHT SERGEANT
EDMUND VERNER SHAW
ROYAL AIR FORCE NO. 748518
PILOT
NO. 218 AND 70 SQUADRON

KILLED IN ACTION 21ST MAY 1942

Edmund Verner Shaw was born in Church View Holywood in the County of Down in September 1919. He was educated at a public elementary school in Holywood and then Strandtown Public Elementary, finishing his education at the Royal Belfast Academical Institution, where he studied for five years. On leaving school, he was employed as a clerk with the Belfast Steamship Company from 1937 to 1939.

Edmund Shaw joined the Royal Air Force Volunteer Reserve in May 1939 and started his basic flying training course at 24 Elementary and Reserve Flying Training School at Sydenham soon after.

His first and only flight at Sydenham was an air experience flight with Sergeant Lightbody in Tigermoth N6745 on the 5th August 1938. The flight lasted 15 minutes. His logbook was counter signed by Flight Lieutenant Sloan who was the Chief Flying Instructor at the school. When war was declared in September 1939 he was called to full time service. On the 3rd December 1939 he was posted to No 5 ITW at Hastings on the south coast of England to start his six month basic training course. He was then posted to No 13 EFTS at White Waltham to commence his elementary flying in Tiger Moths. His first flight with the school was on the 15th May 1940 in Tiger Moth K4260 with his instructor Flight Lieutenant Valance. On May 31st he soloed in Tiger Moth N6796 after 7hrs.10mins tuition. He took the aircraft up again that same day and carried out some taking off into wind, powered approaches, gliding turns and landing exercises. The course finished having now completed 56hrs. 05mins instructional flying on the 29th June 1940 and he was assessed as an 'average' Pilot.

On the 29th June 1940 Edmund was posted to No 10 SFTS at Ternhill where he was to start training in twin engined aircraft. The service school was equipped with the Avro Anson which he first flew on the 2nd July 1940 under the instruction of a Sergeant Cockburn.

They flew the aircraft three times that day getting him used to the cockpit layout and gaining some air experience in the Anson. He soloed in the Anson on the 11th July

after nine hours tuition and finished the course on the 12th October with an 'average' pass. He was awarded his Wings and promoted to Sergeant. Having completed his flying training Edmund was posted to No15 OTU at Harwell on the 15th October. The Unit was located between Oxford and Reading and was equipped with Wellingtons. His first flight in a Wimpy was on October 28th with Pilot Officer Clarke as his instructor and on the 9th October carried out his first solo. His operational training continued through to the middle of December and by this time he had accumulated 235 hours and promoted to Flight Sergeant. The type of training that he carried out at the OTU was air firing, low level bombing, circuits and landings, line over-lap and instrument flying.

Flight Sergeant Edmund Verner Shaw was now completely trained and ready for an operational squadron. On the 14th December 1940 he was posted to 218 (Gold Coast) Squadron that was based at Marham near Kings Lynn. He spent the next two days meeting up with his new crew. 218 Squadron was equipped with the Mk 1C Wellington which was a long range version of the aircraft. The squadron's targets during the war was of the widest variety, ranging from industrial centres, railway installations, V-weapons sites, gun batteries, to Channel ports and petrol storage sites. Some of the squadrons honours included a Victoria Cross that was awarded posthumously to Flight Sergeant AL Aaron for his, "Most conspicuous bravery during a raid on the 12th/13th August."

Flight Sergeant Shaw's first flight with his new crew was on the 17th December 1940 when they carried out a X-County exercise at 15,000ft using oxygen. His first operational was on the 22nd December 1940 to bomb the docks at Calais. The aircraft Wellington R1008 was under the command of Squadron Leader Ault who was the officer commanding 'C' Flight and Edmund was his Second Pilot. They took off at 1750 hrs and set course for the French sea port of Calais which they successfully attacked returning to Marham 3hrs.30mins later. He carried out a second operation with Squadron Leader Ault to Boulogne on the 29th December 1940. On December 31st he took over command of Wellington T.2801 when he flew a 1hr.40mins local Flying and W/T exercise.

On the 1st January 1941 he met his new Captain Flying Officer Anstey. They flew together on the 3rd January on an operational test in Wellington R1210. His fellow crew members were Sergeants Jackson, Thomas, Rose and Robinson.

Subsequent Operations with 218 Squadron.

January 4th	Duisberg.
January 9th	Rotterdam.
February 7th	Boulogne.
February 10th	Hanover (industrial target).

On evening of February 11th 1941 Flying Officer Anstey took off from Marham in Wellington R1210 'O', their target was the City of Bremen. Flight Sergeant Shaw was the 2nd Pilot. Sergeant Jackson (Observer), Sergeant Thomas (Wireless Operator), Sergeant Robinson (Front Gunner) and Sergeant Stephen (Rear Gunner). When they reached their target they found it covered with 10/10th cloud. They concentrated their attack on the searchlights and anti-aircraft emplacements. A few fires were observed through the clouds. On their return to base the wireless failed and over England unexpected fog had descended over most of the RAF bases. On their return from Bremen they were fired on by some of the local London anti-aircraft gun crews. They flew north trying in vain to find Marham in the fog, visibility was down to four miles and eventually they ran out of fuel over Cumberland. At precisely 0215 hrs, Flying Officer Anstey gave the order to abandon the aircraft when they were just north of Tebray, all the crew landed safely, the Wellington crashed and was written off.

(79 Hampdens, Wellingtons and Whitleys took part on that raid to Bremen and all the aircraft returned safely to England. However due to the fog and low cloud 11 Wellingtons, seven Whitleys and four Hampdens crashed at various locations around the country. Most of the crews parachuted to safety but five aircrew were killed.)

Flight Sergeant Shaw must have been slightly injured when he parachuted from his aircraft as his flying log shows that he spent the next week in a hospital in Prestwick. He returned to flying on the 8th March carrying out a local flying and M/F calibration exercise with Flying Officer Anstey and the crew in Wellington R1496. His log shows that on the 10th March 1941 he

was assessed as 'average' as a Pilot-Navigator by the squadron Commanding Officer who also added that Flight Sergeant Shaw will become above average with a little more experience. Their eighth and final operation with 218 Squadron was on March 30th when they took off in Wellington R.1594 'S and were to attack the Scharnhorst and Gneisenau that lay in Brest Harbour. No hits were reported on either ships. The trip lasted for 5hrs.05mins.

At the beginning of April 1941 Flight Sergeant Shaw and the crew were informed that they were being transferred to 70 Squadron that was based in Kabrit in Egypt.

On the 2nd April they were posted to No 3 GPRTF at Stradishall and the next day flew Wellington T.2616 on a fuel consumption test in preparation for their journey to Egypt. They took off from Stradishall at 2020 hrs on April 6th and set a course for France and then Malta, landing there 8hrs.30mins later. They had a three day break in Malta before taking off again at 2320 hrs on the 9th April. They set a course for Abu Sueir in North Africa arriving there seven hours later. According to Edmunds logbook they left T.2616 at Abu Sueir and were taken overland by transport to Kabrit (LG 104). Kabrit airfield was situated on the shores of the Great Bitter Lake in Egypt. His next log entry shows that on the 20th April Flying Officer Anstey and his crew took off from Kabrit in Wellington N.2739 at 1420 hrs in the afternoon and set course for Fuka in Egypt arriving there two hours later where they joined 70 Squadron. No 70 Squadron had been based in Egypt since the outbreak of war and was equipped with Vickers Valentias but in 1940 was re-equipped with the Vickers Wellington Mk 1C's. Flight Sergeant Shaw and his crew carried out their first operation with 70 Squadron in the early hours of the 21st April, taking off at 0210 hrs in Wellington N.2739 to attack German military transport west of Fort Capuzzo. On the 23rd April they bombed Benghazi and again on the 24th April. The squadron bombed Benghazi harbour so many times during the next few months it was dubbed the 'mail run'. Flight Sergeant Shaw and his crew flew the 'mail run' fifteen times.

These operations against Benghazi are commemorated in the famous 70 Squadron song, 'The Mail Run Melody' and is sung to the tune of 'Clementine'. Here a few of its verses:

Down the flights each ruddy morning
Same old notice on the flight board
Same old notice on the flight board
Maximum effort guess where to.

Chorus.....

Seventy Squadron, Seventy Squadron
Though we say it with a sigh
We must do the ruddy Mail Run
Every night until we die.

Chorus....

Take off from the Western Desert
Fuka, 60 or 90 (Sixty or Oh-nine)
Same old Wimpy, same old aircrew
Same old target, same old time.

Chorus....

Have you lost us , Navigator?
Come up here and have a look
Someone's shot our starboard wing off
We're all right then, that's Tobruk.

On May 1st 1941 they were sent on detachment to Shaibah in Iraq. On May 2nd they bombed enemy troops and gun emplacements at Habbaniyah. Their aircraft was hit by flak and had to force land at Habbaniyah where the Wellington was shelled and burnt out. All of the crew were safe they left Habbaniyah the next day and flew back to base as passengers in another Wellington via Shaibah and Lydda, arriving back at Kabrit on the 4th May. On May 28th took off to bomb an enemy aerodrome at Scarpanto but when they were one hundred miles from the target they lost the port engine and had to jettison their bomb load and all loose material, to maintain height on one engine (they returned to base safely).

On June 21st they attacked Benghazi harbour and managed to sink a 3,000 ton steamer.

Other operations carried out by Flying Officer Anstey and Flight Sergeant Shaw were to: Beirut (docks); Eleusis (Athens aerodrome); Bardia (military transports); Corinth Canal; Berka (aerodrome); Martuba (aerodrome); Maleme (aerodrome); Piraeus (oil refinery); Dernia (stores); Dropped supplies to Imperial Forces at Mt Olympus (Greece); and Gazala (landing ground).

Flight Sergeant Shaw's last operation with 70 squadron was on the 7th December 1941 but they had to return to base as the port engine went u/s. Between the 16th April 1941 and the 14th January 1942 he had completed 41 Operations with the Squadron (which included fifteen 'mail runs' to Benghazi). Flight Sergeant Shaw was now due a well earned rest from operations and he soon learned that he was being posted back to the UK where he was to join 21 OTU.

Back to the UK

He said his goodbyes to Flying Officer Anstey and the crew on the 14th January 1942 and made his way overland to the ME Pool at Genifa where he had to wait almost a month for transport to take him back to the UK. He eventually boarded a Pan American Douglas DC-3 which took him to Lagos in Nigeria, via Heliopolis (Cairo), Wadi Seidna (Khartoum), El Fasher (Sudan), Maudugari (Nigeria), Kano (Nigeria) and finally at Lagos on February 19th. He was billeted at the Royal Hotel in Lagos from the 19th February until the 1st March when he boarded the MS Battory which sailed that night for the UK arriving there on the 21st March. On his arrival back in the UK Flight Sergeant Shaw was posted to the 1653 Conversion Unit at Polebrook where he completed a conversion course unto Liberators. His first flight in the Liberator (AL 581) was on the 12th April with Pilot Officer Tuckwell and Flight Lieutenant Dyers at the helm. On April 17th Flight Sergeant Shaw took the controls of AL522 for a 1hr.20mins flight (Flight Sergeant Russel was his Second Pilot) and he flew (AL585) the next day again as captain with Pilot Officer Muirhead as his number two. He completed the Liberator conversion course on April 20th and was posted to 20 Operational Training Unit as an instructor on Avro Ansons. He started flying with the OTU on the 25th April. Sadly on May 21st he had just finished a cross-country exercise in Anson N5259 with his pupils and while coming into land, the aircraft hit Pylon Cables. The aircraft crashed and all on board were killed. Flight Sergeant Shaw had completed a total of 47 operations, 833 flying hours in Tiger Moth, Avro Anson Wellington and Liberators.

Flight Sergeant EV Shaw is buried in Dundonald Cemetery, Northern Ireland.

Authors note

On the very last page of Flight Sergeant Shaw's logbook I found a beautiful little 1942 Calendar which his mother had sent him for Christmas. It was still open at May.

On the inside of the Calendar there is a beautiful verse which simply reads:

We can always cheer up
We can always be gay
As long as life gives us
A friend on the way.
From Mother, to Edmund.

FLIGHT LIEUTENANT
WILLIAM SHIMMONS, AE
ROYAL AIR FORCE VOLUNTEER RESERVE
FIGHTER PILOT
NO. 79, 87 AND 247 SQUADRONS

Bill Shimmons was born on the 24th February 1914. On leaving school, he was employed in the engineering department of the General Post Office in Belfast. From a very early age Bill was keen on all types of aircraft books, going to see Cobbams flying circus and air displays in the province. The very first air display that he attended was held in Dunmurry, and he had to walk all the way from his home in the Stranmillis Road to Dunmurry to see the show.

In 1938 the Royal Air Force Volunteer Reserve had advertised in Northern Ireland for aircrew, and so he applied to join as a Pilot, but before he could be accepted he had to obtain permission from his employer. His request was turned down as he was employed in a 'reserved occupation'. Bill was very disappointed, so much so he asked his father who was then Manager of the Employment Exchange in Corporation Street, Belfast for advice on this matter. His father immediately arranged an interview with a Mr Polkinghorne who was another official at the Ministry of Labour and was told once again that permission to join the RAFVR was refused. Bill was not satisfied with this and told the official that he was going to join the RAF with or without his permission. Bill met Mr Polkinghorne after the war when he moved down to Donaghadee, and he said, how he always remembered the outcome of that meeting when Bill told him how determined he was to join the RAFVR and left the room. A few weeks later Bill was informed by his employer that their policy had changed and that he was free to join the RAFVR if he still so desired. Bill submitted his application form immediately, as it was now January 1939, and the age limit for pilots was 25. Bill would have been 25 on the 24th February 1939, so he hadn't much time left.

He was soon informed that he had been accepted for pilot training with the RAFVR subject to him passing a medical. One of the things that Bill was going to be asked to do during the medical was to balance a 6 inch nail on a flat piece of wood and raise it above his head with either hand. He practised this for several days prior to the

medical until, he was proficient at it. He was also told that he had to practice holding his breath for two and half minutes. When he eventually got to the medical the 6 inch nail had a head of one and a half inches in diameter and he only had to hold his breath for one minute. This after all his practising was no problem to him and he successfully passed the medical and enlisted into the Royal Air Force Volunteer Reserve in Belfast in January 1939. After completing some basic training at 24 E & RFTS at Sydenham, he was offered a five week flying course at Brough in Yorkshire, starting in May 1939. He now had to apply for some 'special' leave from his employer which they granted. He arrived at Brough on the 1st May 1939 and had his first air experience flight the next day in a Blackburn B2 aircraft G-ACBJ. (The Blackburn B2 was quite similar to the Tiger Moth.) The flight lasted for 25 minutes, and his instructor was Flying Officer Corfe.

Bill completed his first solo flight after eight hours instruction in a B2 on the 10th May (G-ACEN). His solo flight lasted for 25minutes.

Bill's first engine failure
Everything went well on the course except for one episode, when he was flying solo on June 1st on a cross-country exercise. He was flying G-ACLC, and was approximately 30 miles from base, when suddenly at a height of 2,000ft his engine stopped. He immediately looked around for a suitable field to make an emergency landing. Having selected a suitable place he landed and did so and very successfully. He got out of his aircraft as soon as it had come to a complete stop, and a farmer who

had been watching came over to see if Bill was all right. The farmer invited Bill into his house and gave him a very welcome cup of tea. Bill then asked if he could use his telephone to ring his base at Brough to tell them what had happened. He was put through to his instructor Pilot Officer Corfe, who flew down straight away with an Engine Fitter, but he was unable to fix the fault with the aircraft. Flying Officer Corfe decided the best thing to do was to fly Bill back in his own aircraft and leave the Fitter to guard the u/s aircraft, and arrange to take it back to Brough later by road.

This was Bill's first experience of an engine failure and unfortunately was not to be his last.

Bill successfully completed the course on the 24th June 1939 and was assessed as having 'average' proficiency as Pilot. During the course he had completed 25hrs.25mins (Dual) and 25hrs (Solo) and five hours in the Link Trainer. Registrations of other Blackburn B2's at Brough were: G-ACBJ; G-ACEN; L-6891; G-AEBG; G-ACBH; G-ACBK; G-ACBM; G-ACLD; G-ACLC; and L-6893. After completing the flying course, Bill returned to Northern Ireland to his civilian occupation. War was declared on the 3rd September 1939, and like the other 200 Royal Air Force Reservists in Northern Ireland he was called to full time service. He was instructed to report to the RAFVR headquarters in Donegal Place, which at that time was situated above the Saxone shoe shop. Bill was sent home that evening and told to report there again the following week.

At the end of September 1939 Bill was posted along with about ten others to an initial training wing at Hastings on the south coast of England, where he attended aeronautical lectures, drill practice, and square bashing. Bill especially enjoyed taking part in the sport activities as he had played rugby for the YMCA, soccer for Coleraine and had just signed for Cliftonville for the season 1939. (Bill reckoned that this war was going to be very enjoyable for him.) He played a number of matches for 11 group, and as a matter of interest, Peter Doherty the Northern Ireland international was also playing on the same team. Bill knew this would not last too long as he had 50 hours flying experience under his belt, and pilots were in great demand at that time. He was right, at the end of April he was posted to No 7 EFTS which was based at Desford near Leicester where he began his elementary flying training on Tiger Moths. All of his Northern Ireland friends were left at Hastings and he did not meet up with any of them again until the end of the war (most of them had been killed by the end of 1941). His flying training on Tiger Moths commenced on the 1st May 1940 and he soloed on the type on the 17th May, and successfully completed the course on the 28th June 1940. He was again assessed as an 'average' Pilot and had now accumulated 105 flying hours.

Bill's next posting was to No 12 SFTS at Grantham, arriving there on the 1st July 1940. Here he commenced training on Fairey Battles. His first air experience flight in

the Battle was on the 3rd July, and his instructor was a Flight Lieutenant D Smith. After just four hours instruction he completed his first solo on the type, and after seven hours completed his first nightime solo. Bill continued training in the Fairey Battle until the end of September 1940.

On September 10th he experienced his second engine failure.

On the morning of the 10th September 1940, Bill had been taken up for a test flight with his instructor, Flight Lieutenant Gatescole in Fairey Battle Code 6768. They had been airborne for about 20 minutes with Bill at the controls, when without warning the Battle's engine seized. Flight Lieutenant Gatescole immediately took control of the aircraft and selected a suitable field where he made an excellent 'wheels up' landing. Bill unfortunately had received injuries to both his legs and a deep gash to his head, and was detained in sick quarters for a week. Bill's father was informed that his son had been injured on 'active service'.

Bill was awarded his Wings on the 12th August 1940 and when the course was completed at the end of September, his pass mark for the course was 80.9%. He was now assessed as being 'above the average' as a Pilot.

On the 1st October 1940 he was posted to No 56 OTU at Sutton Bridge where he was to commence his operational training on Hawker Hurricane fighters. On the 1st October Bill was commissioned to the rank of Pilot Officer. On the 4th and 5th October he had ninety minutes dual training in a Harvard, and on the 7th flew his first solo in a Hawker Hurricane, Code L2052. Over the next two weeks he carried out many fighter exercises which included formation flying, target practice, flying in cloud, and practice dog fighting. On the 10th October Bill was tasked to carry out an exercise which he completed successfully. On his approach to the airfield he selected undercarriage 'down' for landing, but nothing happened, the undercarriage had failed to come down. He quickly tried to contact Flying Control but without success. It was now late in the afternoon and was getting dark. Bill had never flown a Hurricane before at night and decided something had to be done 'toute suite'. He tried again to lower the undercarriage with the 'Down' select button, and finally tried to lower it using the undercarriage emergency hand pump, but it was no use. Bill now realised that he had no alternative but to make a 'wheels up' landing and hope for the best. He landed the Hurricane with some minor damage to the aircraft and he sustained some injuries to his head. This meant spending one week in sick quarters. His father was informed a second time that his son was again injured on active service. Bill completed his operational training on the 7th December 1940. Having now completed all of his flying training, Bill was posted to his first operational squadron, which was No 79 squadron and based at Biggin Hill. The squadron was equipped with Hurricane Mk 1's. and was under the command of Squadron Leader Hayworth who took Bill up on his first day with the squadron as his No 2 for some practice dog fighting, fighter tactics, and close formation flying. (Bill was flying Hurricane 2671).

Brief history of 79 Squadron

79 Squadron was formed in August 1918 as a training squadron and was equipped with Sopwith Camel Dolphins. The squadron moved to France in March 1918 and had its first kill on the 22nd March. The squadron served with distinction during the First World War destroying at least sixty four enemy aircraft, eight kite balloons, but at a cost of losing may of its fine pilots. The squadron was disbanded in 1919 and reformed again in March 1937 at Biggin Hill as an interceptor squadron equipped with Gloucester Gauntlets and in November 1938 Hurricane 1's, and assigned with the defence of Greater London.

It was sent to France for ten days May 1940 where it successfully destroyed 25 enemy aircraft in this short space of time, on returning to Biggin Hill it became heavily involved in the Battle of Britain, and in May 1942 was ordered overseas to India, mainly taking part in 'Rhubarbs'. In September 1944 the squadron was re-equipped with the Republican Thunderbolt and was a great success against the Japanese. The squadron was disbanded in December 1945 and reformed in November 1951 in Buckeburg, Germany, where it remained for the next ten years as part of the 2nd Tactical Air Force flying Gloucester Meteor's and Supermarine Swifts. The squadron was finally disbanded in 1961.

The next day Bill and Squadron Leader Heyworth took off again and headed for the Channel to carry out some more practice flying. During the exercise they were informed over the R/T to be on the look out for two Me109's in their area. They did make contact with the two bandits who were heading towards Letouquet in France, but were able to get close enough to identify the two aircraft as being ME 109's. They headed for the cover of cloud and disappeared before they had a chance to attack them. (Bill received a congratulations from the CO as this officially was his first combat operation with the squadron.) On the 9th December 1940 Bill was scrambled and took off in 3771 in a section of three Hurricanes, with a report of six Me 109's in their area. They made contact with the 109's at 10,000ft, opened fire immediately but they were too far away from them to inflict any damage (one was claimed damaged). On hearing their fire the enemy quickly headed towards France and the safety of their own airfields. On landing back at Biggin Hill, Bill and the other pilots were told to pack their kit immediately as the squadron was being moved to Pembrey in South Wales. On his arrival at Pembrey on the morning of the 10th December, Bill was introduced to a pilot called, 'Leader the Football Coupon Man'. He and Bill became very close friends.

On Christmas day Bill and 'Leader' took off for some practice formation flying, Bill was the leader. As it was

Christmas day Bill decided that the two of them would 'shoot up' the officers mess where the Christmas dinner was being served. This they did and upon landing were informed to report to the Commanding Officer. They got a right rollicking from him, and he did remark to them on their way out, "By the way your formation flying was excellent." Bill's friend Leader was later killed in action. On January 10th 1941 the squadron was scrambled, Bill was No 2 to Squadron Leader Heyworth. They had a report that a lone Junkers 88 was approaching their location at 20,000ft. The squadron climbed in formation to intercept the bandit and made contact at 28,000ft, only to discover that the Junkers was a Beaufighter. Bill's logbook reads, "Returned to Base disappointed." There was very little activity during January 1941, and most of their flying was night flying practice and practice fighter attacks during the day. Bill's night flying was assessed in January as 'above the average', and he was posted to No 87 Squadron at Charmy Down near Bath. 87 Squadron at that time was engaged in mostly night fighting activities, and was commanded by Squadron Leader I Gleed. Bill's Flight Commander was a New Zealander called Derek Ward, and his No 2 was Roland Beaumont. Bill admits that he felt a bit awed as Gleed, Ward, Beaumont, and Sergeant Badger carried out aerobatic displays before the war.

Brief history of 87 Squadron

87 Squadron was formed in September 1917 and was equipped with the Sopwith Dolphin. In April 1918 moved to France. It returned to England and was disbanded at Ternhill in June 1919. It was reformed in March 1937 at Tangmere and was equipped with Hawker Furies, and three months later moved to Debden and was re-equipped with the Gloster Gladiator. The following year it received the Hawker Hurricane Mk 1's and went to France for a second time as part of the British Expeditionary Force, where it saw a lot of action. The squadron returned to England at the end of May 1940 at continued operating to the end of the war. During that time it operated from Church Fenton, Colerne, Charmy Down. The squadron then moved to North Africa in December 1942 where it carried out mostly convoy work. In April 1943 the squadron was re-equipped with the Supermarine Spitfire MkVb, Vc, V 111, and 1X. The squadron moved to Italy in December 1943 where it remained until September 1945 carrying out escort flights for Dakota's and 'Cab Rank' duties for the 5th Army. The squadron was disbanded at the end of December 1946. It was re-formed as a night-fighter squadron at Wahn in Germany in January 1952, where it served in the 2nd Tactical Air Force. It was finally disbanded at Bruggen in January 1961.

Bill's third engine failure

For the next three months all of their flying duties were night patrols, co-operation night flying activities and some formation practice during the day. Although one exception was on the 23rd February when returning from a search light co-operation exercise and flying over his base at 2,000ft, Bill's engine spluttered and stopped, but thankfully he was able to make a successful landing. After his aircraft was examined it was discovered that his fuel had been contaminated with water. On the 6th February Bill's logbook shows that he took off on a patrol in Hurricane Y7011 to Exeter, as enemy aircraft had been reported. Nothing was seen so he returned to base. On the 21st February 1941 the squadron was on a fighter night patrol over London when it was being heavily bombed. All of the pilots were given a different height to fly at, Bill was at 17,000ft. He said, "It looked like all of London was on fire, I was able to see the Dome of St Pauls Cathedral quite clearly towering through the black smoke." After orbiting for about 30 minutes he made contact with a Heinkel 111, and opened fire, which was returned before he lost sight of it. Fifteen minutes later he intercepted another Heinkel 111 and again attacked. The Heinkel pilot immediately took evasive action by going into a steep dive, closely followed by Bill. He looked at his petrol gauges and they were showing almost empty and decided to return to Charmy Down for refuelling. He set a course for base, and shortly after this he discovered that his radio was u/s. His fuel was now dangerously low, and fortunately he spotted Andover RAF Station where some night flying was taking place. Andover's runway lights were on so he decided to make a quick landing. He rang Charmy Down and informed them what had happened and that he was safe. Bill was given accommodation for the night, and returned early the following morning to his base. When 87 Squadron moved to Charmy Down as a night fighter squadron they were 'adopted' by the Christopher Hotel in Bath. Most of the pilots spent their off duty time there yarning and having the 'odd' beer in the hotels large lounge. Every time the squadron shot down a German aircraft the proprietor would open a bottle of champagne, and a good time was had by all. The pilots signed their names on the lounge ceiling, and some of those included Ian Gleed, Derek Ward, Rodney Ratner, Roland Beaumont, S badger, and D Watson. All of these pilots had been in France.

While touring in the South of England in the early 1990's Bill and his wife decided to call at the Christopher Hotel, and to Bill's surprise and disappointment found that the hotel had been completely refurbished and all of the signatures had been painted over. The owner was very apologetic.

Only two night patrols were carried out in April. On the 11th May 1941 the squadron was ordered to Portland Bill as 50 plus enemy aircraft were reported to be approaching the coast. When they reached the area the aircraft had apparently returned to France. In late May Squadron Leader Gleed had all the pilots practice short take-off's and landings using only a quarter of the runway. This went on for the next two weeks, and the reason for it was, the squadron was being transferred to the Scilly Isles

where the runway was extremely short. A lot of enemy aircraft activity had being reported by coast guards and lighthouse keepers. Squadron Leader Gleed made a few enquiries and was told that was impossible for Hurricanes to take off or land on such a short airfield as it was only just over 400 yards long. Squadron Leader Gleed informed group that his 'boys' could take off and land anywhere. The C/O decide to fly over to St Mary's in the Scilly Isles and see for himself. He carried out a few landings and take-offs just to prove that it could be done. The next day a detachment of Hurricanes of which Bill was one, flew over to the Scilly Isles and landed safely. It did take a lot of concentration as the pilots had to more or less climb a cliff face just above stalling speed so as they could touch down at the beginning of the runway with full brakes on. They soon settled down in one of the towns hotels and were made very welcome by the locals.

On the 2nd June 1941 Bill was assessed as 'above the average' as a Pilot, 'average' in Air Gunnery and 'average' in Bombing.

In the first two weeks of June six enemy aircraft had been shot down and destroyed by the squadron, including two Dorniers, two Focke Wulf Condors, one Junkers 88, and one Heinkel 111. 87 Squadrons crew were always at instant readiness and this meant sitting in their cockpits with a telephone resting on top of their aircrafts exhaust stubs which was connected to the lighthouse and coast guard. They had to start up their engines every half hour to keep them warm. The weather was perfect and it was quite enjoyable soaking up the sun. If the lighthouse keeper or the coast guard spotted anything their signal would be to fire a red flare, and off they would go. On the 8th July D Ward and Bill having been on duty for some four hours, and the evening was getting dark, they decided to call it a day. As they were taxiing up to park their aircraft at dispersal, a position that was about half way up the airfield, suddenly they heard a soft bang as a red flare was fired from the lighthouse. Without hesitation both pilots opened full throttle and took off across the airfield which was about half the normal take off space. Within ten minutes they had intercepted a Dornier, when they got within range they both opened fire. It went down in flames, they had got her. They followed the Dornier down until it hit the water and watched as some of its crew clambered into their dinghy. Bill checked later and discovered that Dornier's crew had been picked up by the RAF's air sea rescue boat. On the 31st July Bill's logbook shows that their task for that morning was a full Squadron 'battle climb' to 30,000ft, led by Squadron Leader Gleed. They took off and entered cloud at 2,000ft and emerged at 20,000ft and all returned to base 'alone'.

Bill's log shows that on the 24th August he had his first flight in a Spitfire P8098 for 40 minutes.

Bill also carried out a few Havoc Co-operation flights. The Havoc's were fitted with a very powerful search light in the nose which enabled it to light up the land or sea at night. They were also fitted with the new A1 radar which enabled it to pick up enemy aircraft at night.

Bill became very friendly with one of the Havoc's pilot, a Flying Officer French. It was good practice for night formation flying but light was not a great success. On one occasion using the search light and the A1 radar they did make contact with the enemy, but once the light was switched on, the enemy saw it and took evasive action and contact was lost. The squadron remained in the Scilly Isles until October 1941 carrying out mostly interception patrols.

On the night of the 2nd/3rd October 1941 the squadron was ordered up on a night fighter patrol over the city of Bristol which was being heavily bombed. Bill was flying at a height of 17,000ft and after a time he spotted an aircraft and made an approach onto it. The aircraft turned north and he followed it, and closed in. When Bill got close enough he identified the aircraft as a Heinkel 111. He closed in on the enemy and was now 400 yards or so from it, and opened fire with a two second burst, fire was returned from the Heinkel and it went into a steep dive, but Bill lost sight of him. (A Heinkel 111 was reported to have crashed into the Bristol Channel by the Observer Corps at the exact same time Bill had made contact with his. He now claimed the aircraft destroyed.)

Bill's fourth engine failure

Bill had now been airborne for 1hour.20mins, so he decided to return to base for re-arming and re-fuelling. After flying on for a further fifteen minutes the engine, without any warning stopped, and he began to glide. He immediately contacted his base on the R/T and was told to keep transmitting until they were able to get a fix on him. This he did and was informed by control that he was twelve miles north of his base. By now he was down to a height of 14,500ft remembering what he was taught at OTU, he knew that for every mile he glided the Hurricane, he would lose 1,000ft, and so decided to try and make it back to base. When he was at 7,000ft he saw a flashing beacon in the distance and recognised it as Charmy Down, which he estimated to be at least 12 to 14 miles away. He knew now that he had no chance of making the airfield, so he decided to bale out. He radioed base and told them his position and what he was going to do. They replied, "OK", and wished him the best of luck. He settled down and composed himself, he trimmed the Hurricane as best he could to fly straight and level, disconnected his oxygen, radio and seat harness. He then released the side panel, climbed out onto the wing and jumped. Unfortunately as Bill jumped the slip-stream caught him and blew him to the rear of the aircraft where he hit the tail plane a violent blow with his left side. The next thing he remembered was being caught up on the aircraft's tail wheel and his parachute harness being tangled around it. He suddenly thought to himself, "This is it, my times up."

Because of the dreadful knock which he had received to his side he was now in great pain and felt himself losing consciousness. He had to act quickly, and decided

that he had nothing to lose, and pulled the ripcord of his parachute. Everything then went black, and the next thing that he remembered was wakening up just as he hit the ground. When he had sufficiently steadied himself up he made his way to the nearest house. The occupants helped Bill into the house, and he asked if he could use their telephone to contact his base. A short time later a crew arrived which took him back to Bath and into a military hospital. After a thorough examination he was told that he had six broken ribs, and that his left leg was almost severed below the knee. He spent the next three weeks in the hospital, and the following six weeks convalescing, and was passed medically fit for operational flying.

Squadron Leader Ian Richard Gleed, DSO DFC C de G (Belgium) C de G (France) was shot down and killed by Lieutenant Reinert of JG77 on April 16th 1943.

Flight Lieutenant Derek Ward, DFC & Bar was shot down and killed by Oberleutnant HJ Marseille on 17th June 1942.

On his return to the squadron, Bill was promoted to Flight Lieutenant, and was immediately posted to 247 Squadron which was based at Predannack in Cornwall. Bill was disappointed having to leave 87 Squadron as he had spent ten very happy months there and had made many good friends.

Brief history of 247 Squadron

The squadron was formed as part of a coastal unit during the First World War forming part of the seaplane and flying boat base at Felixstowe and was disbanded in 1919. It was reformed again at Roborough in August 1940, and was equipped with the Gloster Gladiator's and was part of the Sumburgh Fighter Flight defending the Shetlands. While there it destroyed two enemy aircraft. In August 1940 the squadron moved to St Eval in Cornwall for the protection of the south coast cities and towns. In June 1941 the squadron was again on the move to Predannack. It's Gladiators had now been replaced with the Hurricane Mk 1's and it was carrying out 'Intruders' and 'Rhubarbs' into occupied France. In January 1943 the squadron was re-equipped with Hawker Typhoon 1b's. The Typhoons were to carry out Intruders and attack the V1 Rocket sites in France. The squadron moved to Coulombes in France just after D-Day, and was involved with the army attacking any targets that was requested by them. The squadron moved into Germany in 1944 where it remained until August 1945 when it returned to the UK. The squadron was re-equipped with the Hawker Tempest and then became the first unit to fly the DH Vampire in 1946. In May 1951 it received the Gloster Meteor F8, and four years later the Hawker Hunter F1, F4, and F6. The squadron was disbanded at RAF Odiham 1957.

Bill joined 247 Squadron at Predannack as 'A' Flight commander on the 23rd November 1941. The squadron at that time was commanded by a Canadian, Squadron

Leader Peter St G O'Brian. For the first two months Bill was carrying out various tasks, which included convoy patrols and Havoc co-operation flights.

A lot of scrambles to Lands End were encountered by the squadron between November and the end of February 1942, which were all false alarms. On March 1st 1942, 'A' Flight was posted to Exeter for further training, which included dawn patrols, checking the Black Out in Plymouth, practice search lights, formation flying, fighter tactics, and convoy patrols.

On the 3rd May 1942 it had been reported to the Commanding Officer that an enemy raid was expected on Exeter, and so he organised night flights with six Hurricanes to patrol the city (thankfully these reports proved to be unfounded).

On June 2nd Bill took off on an Intruder to Lannion Airfield near Caen in Northern France in Hurricane ZY-N, having to cross the Channel flying at sea level to avoid the German radar. When he reached the French coast he started to climb, and turned his petrol indicator to 'Gravity Feed', suddenly, without warning, as he approached 1,000ft the Merlin cut out, and he started to glide. Bill had to make a decision very quickly. He decided, as he was so low that he would try and make a 'wheels up' landing on the beach. When he reached 500ft he remembered that he had turned the petrol to 'Gravity Feed', so he very quickly reached down and turned it to on again, the mighty Merlin spluttered back into life. Bill decided to continue on to Lannion, on his arrival there was nothing to be seen but low cloud, and decided to return back to base.

On his way back he spotted a German ammunition train, and was determined to attack it. He swooped down low and give the train a long burst of cannon, he pulled up steeply and when he looked back the engine had stopped and he could see a lot of steam coming from the engine's smoke stack.

On June 8th 1942, Bill decided that he would have another go at Lannion Airfield. The flight went well and when he reached Lannion he saw some Me109's on the ground. He dived down and opened fire with long bursts from his cannons. Unfortunately in doing so he awakened the German flak gunners, (just like Wing Commander Ken MacKenzie the year before). Bill thought that the best thing for him to do was to get the hell out of there and return to base. This operation lasted for 2hrs.25mins. In the middle of June 'B' Flight now joined them at Exeter. The squadron continued with convoy, dusk patrols, and the odd scramble at night. On June 17th Bill went on an Intruder to Vannes in France, when he reached there the cloud base was down to below 800ft, and returned to base. Bill took off on a dusk patrol on the 22nd July and quickly made contact with a Heinkel 111, but lost it soon after it disappeared into cloud. His next Intruder patrol was to St Brieu near Rennes in France on the 27th August, his logbook shows that when he arrived over the target he was illuminated by a search light. He

was a height of 3,000ft and opened fire as he flew down the beam. The light went out as he pulled up at 200ft. On returning to base he used up his remaining ammunition on an Army Camp which he knew was at Yffiniac in Northern France.

During September he carried out a few Havoc co-operation flights, and some practice formation flying at 20,000ft. On the 25th September the squadron moved to High Ercal in Shropshire where it began flying 'Roadstead' operations (attacks on enemy coastal shipping). Things were pretty quiet now through to February 1943. In January 1943 the squadron began be re-equipped with the new Mk1b Hawker Typhoons. All of January and February was spent training on the new aircraft, Bill was very impressed with the Typhoon's performance. His first flight in the M1b Typhoon was on the 13th January 1943 when he took ZY-E up for a 15 minute air experience flight. Bill continued training on the Typhoon until the 16th February 1943. In early March it was decided that Bill, now having completed three operational tours in fighter, was to be taken off operational flying and given a rest. He fought this decision rigorously but to no avail.

In early March 1943 Bill joined No 56 Operational Training Unit at Teal near Dundee. On his arrival he was given the position of Chief Flying Instructor at its satellite station at Friockheim Angus. His responsibility was to train new pilots who were coming mostly from Canadian training schools. The majority of these pilots were Canadian and very keen to learn how to fly, and get into the action. Bill had been the CFI with the OTU for three months, when on the 28th May 1943 he was leading a section of three Hurricanes on a battle formation take-off. Just as he was approaching 200ft his engine failed, and as he was too low to return to the airfield he made a brave attempt at a 'wheels up' landing in the nearest field. Everything went well until the touch down point where there was a mound of earth about two feet high running from one end of the field to the other. The mound caught his radiator and flicked the Hurricane onto its back, and by good luck it didn't catch fire.

A young farm labourer had witnessed the crash and rushed over to help Bill out of the wrecked Hurricane. He firstly had to tunnel through the earth to reach the cockpit and then carefully pulled Bill free. Bill knew at that point that he was badly hurt as he couldn't move his legs, and was in great pain. The farm labourer then rushed back to call for help. An ambulance arrived soon after and rushed Bill to Stracathro Military Hospital where he lay unconscious for three weeks. Bill remained dangerously ill for the next four weeks, having sustained a fractured spine, double head fracture, fractured jaw, broken leg, and broken ribs. Bill's back was set in plaster which stayed on for the next six months, he said it was pure agony. After the six months he was taken by bus to a rehabilitation hospital at Loughborough College where he remained for the next seven months. He was then given two months leave, and on his return was sent to have a medical examination. After the medical the board stated that Bill was medically unfit for any further flying, and was graded A4-B4. As you can imagine Bill was devastated by this news, however he realised that there was nothing that he could do about it, and decided to get on with his life whatever it brought for him.

Bill was posted back to Northern Ireland where he was put in charge of all Air Sea Rescue Units in the province. He was based at Stormont Buildings in Belfast, after spending a few months there he was offered a flying control course. After successfully completing the course he was posted back to Northern Ireland where he became Flying Control Officer at Ballyhalbert in County Down, Aldergrove, and finished the war as senior Flying Control Officer at Long Kesh airfield near Lisburn. Just after his de-mobilisation in 1946, Bill received a letter from the Irvine Parachute Company to say that he had qualified as a member of the Caterpillar Club after his sortie over Bristol when he had to bale out of his Hurricane. He was asked by the company if he could send them some details of that night which he did and duly received his gold 'Caterpillar' badge and membership card.

The parachute that Bill was wearing that day was designed by Leslie Leroy Irvine, who was a parachute pioneer and stuntman in the United States of America. Irvine decided to immigrate to England in 1926 where he set up his parachute factory in Letchworth in Hertfordshire. His invention saved the lives of thousands of aircrew during the war.

One of Bill's sons, Roland Shimmons followed in his fathers footsteps and joined the RAF as a Fighter Pilot, rising to the rank of Wing Commander. He joined that elite bunch of pilots in the Battle of Britain Memorial Flight. So it must be quite unique for father and son to have flown the Hawker Hurricane in the RAF. Bill told me that he remembers the day very well when his son Roland rang him and said, "Hey Dad, guess what I was flying today, yes a Hurricane." Bill was a very proud man that day. Bill Shimmons and his lovely wife Grace were an extremely quiet and private couple, and lived on the Killaughey Road in Donaghadee, County Down, within a few yards of the local cricket club, of which he was a founder member. Bill and his wife Grace, sadly are now both dead. It was a privilege for me to have been invited into their home to chat about Bill's RAF career.

I am still in touch with his son Roland who is now a senior member of the Air Accident Investigation Board.

FLIGHT LIEUTENANT
JOHN SIMPSON
ROYAL AIR FORCE NO. 117426
PILOT
NO. 12 SQUADRON

PRISONER OF WAR STALAG LUFT III, SAGAN

John Simpson was born in Dungannon on January 3rd 1923 and was educated at Dungannon Royal School. He left school in July 1940 and was employed in his father's newspaper business, the Tyrone Printing Company Ltd. The company was responsible for the publication of one of the town's weekly news papers the Tyrone Courier.

John enjoyed sports at school and was vice captain of the school's rugby team and when they had just got into the final of the Medallion Shield, he was taken to hospital with appendicitis, needless to say they lost the Medallion Final. He was also a very good cricketer, and scored a hat trick of three wickets with three consecutive balls against Portora Royal School. John's father died while he was a Prisoner of War, and this meant that his mother had to take charge of the family business and hold it together until he came home.

Sometime during the Autumn of 1940, John travelled to Belfast where he met an RAF recruiting officer who talked him into joining as aircrew. He went to the Clifton Street Recruiting Office where he attended a medical which he passed, except for his eyesight which was not 100%. Because of this the medical officer offered him a ground crew position which he politely refused. The medical officer then decided to take a second look at John's eyes and passed him with the bare minimum. Like so many hopefuls before and after him he boarded the Heysham boat in Belfast which was to take him to the Padgate Receiving Centre. On his arrival he was given another medical including an eye test. John asked the doctor if he could put the eye test off until the next day as he had a terrible headache that had been brought on by the rough sea crossing. The doctor refused his request and carried on with the examination. On completion of the medical he informed John that his eyesight was just outside the border line, but because his headache may have had something to do with it, he would pass him. John was hoping that he would be sent home on deferred leave for a while, but this was not to be as his services were required right away. He did however receive ten days leave which enabled him to come home and say his goodbyes to his parents.

Then it was back to Padgate where he received his new uniform and kit, and then was trained down to an initial training wing at Brighton for his basic training. The local hotels and bed and breakfast houses welcomed this as the 'Erks' had to be billeted there and the MOD footed the bill. With the basic's now out of the way John was posted with five other bods to the Royal Air Force College at Cranwell. He thought to himself at the time this move was pretty swift as he knew that Cranwell had a flying training school there. John was going to be very disappointed, because on his arrival at Cranwell he was informed by the Orderly Sergeant that he was being sent to the gas centre. The other five bods were sent to various units such as the fire station, officers mess and motor transport section.

John passed the next few months at the gas centre, and every Saturday morning they had a practice gas attack warning. The Sergeant in charge seemed to like the way John spoke as he could understand him, so he gave him the job of sitting in the back of the gas van, swinging a large wooden rattle around, blowing a whistle, and shouting into a microphone, "Gas attack, gas attack. Wear your gas mask." as they drove round the station. If the Sergeant spotted anyone not wearing their mask he would put them on a charge. The Station Commander, Air Commodore Probin came to inspect the gas centre one Saturday morning, as he wanted to see how the set up worked for himself. So he drove his car around complete with its pennant behind John's van while he was speaking his bits into the microphone and swinging his rattle. Two days later on the Monday morning, word came through that AC2 Simpson was required at headquarters, no one knew what he had done, right, wrong or otherwise. He duly arrived at the station headquarters and was marched into the station commanders office, who asked him what was he was doing working in the gas centre. John was about to say, "Now that's a good question," but decided that might not be a good idea. He explained to the Air Commodore that he had volunteered for aircrew duties and was told at the recruiting office that he would be needed urgently. John thought that something had gone wrong somewhere along the lines of communication. The Air Commodore seemed very interested and asked John to leave it with him and he would look into the matter right a way.

The Air Commodore had been true to his word, and a few days later word came through that John was being posted to an initial training wing at Leuchars in Scotland. An army NCO had been brought in specially to drill the trainees in the art of square bashing and rifle drill. John said, what they had done at Brighton was nothing in comparison to what this guy dished out as they had to march at a much faster rate and for longer.

John said that in those days at Leuchars one could go and stand at the end of the runway, and literally thumb a lift from an aircraft which was about to take off on a training exercise. At that particular time there had been a Dutch squadron training in Lockheed Hudsons and were only too willing to give anyone a lift. So off John went one day and stood at the end of the runway with his thumb stuck high in the air, and sure enough a Hudson came towards him and stopped, the door opened and he hopped in and was told to sit on a bed. This was John's first ever flight in an aircraft. He listened as the aircraft's engines roared at full throttle and started off down the runway. The next thing he knew, he was airborne and flying at 3,000ft. After about half an hour the aircraft went into an almost vertical dive with its Pratt and Whitney engines screaming. John by this time had started to panic and all of a sudden the Hudson began to level out with a tremendous racket coming from the back of the aircraft. The racket came from the Rear Gunner as he opened up testing his machine guns. John was by now in a state of fright, but was confident that the Pilot knew what he was doing. What actually happened that day was that an outline of a ship had been painted somewhere on the ground and the Dutch crew were practising bombing it and the Rear Gunner had opened up with his guns blazing as the aircraft pulled out of its dive. This manoeuvre was carried out four times during the exercise and when the Hudson returned to Leuchars and John got out, he found that his legs were a bit 'wobbly'. This as he said, "Was a good Baptism for me."

John finished his initial training at RAF Leuchars and was given two weeks leave and on his return was told to report to the Air Crew Receiving Centre in Regents Park, London. He spent his two weeks leave with his family in Dungannon and when it finished returned to Larne to board the boat. When he arrived at the terminal he was informed by an official that the boat was full and he would have to wait until the next day for a sailing. His travel warrant was stamped, "Unable to sail," and he went home again and returned the next day. On his arrival at the Air Crew Receiving Centre, he presented himself to the senior NCO, who immediately put him on a charge because he was a day late. John objected strongly, which did him no good. He was billeted near to St Johns Wood and remembers well that he wanted to go out for a walk. He decided to go along to the NCO anchorage who informed John that as he was still on a charge, and was confined to his billet. John was cross, and said the NC,O "You mean to tell me that this is English Justice." The NCO must have taken cold feet at this outburst, and decided to let John out for his walk. The next morning John was marched in front of the Commanding Officer by a Warrant Officer to answer to the charge of being late for duty. The officer asked John what excuse did he have, if any.

John explained that he had turned up for the boat on time, only to be told that he could not get on it as it was full and that his travel warrant had been stamped to that effect. He noticed the officer looking over his shoulder and talking to the Warrant Officer in a low voice. The officer remarked, "As this airman has had his travel warrant stamped by the transport authorities in Northern Ireland, I am going to dismiss this case." The Warrant Officer jumped briskly to attention and shouted, "Yes Sa, Very good Sa." So John was dismissed with a clean record, which was very important as it so happened later on. After completing the various tests at the ACRC in Regents Park, John was selected to become a Pilot and was delighted. He was then posted to No 14 EFTS at Fairoaks where he learned to fly in Tiger Moths. He had his first air experience flight in the Tiger Moth (T5749) on July 10th with his instructor Pilot Officer Baker. He completed the EFTS course on October 24th 1941. At the end of October 1941 John was then posted to No 2 SFTS at Brize Norton where he was to start his training on twin engined Oxfords. He had his first flight in the Oxford on October 28th with his instructor Flying Officer Green and flew solo for the first time on December 7th. Half way through the course John was moved to RAF Lyneham near Brize Norton where he joined the No 2 SFTS and finished the course at the end of March 1942. He was then posted to the No 2 Advanced Flying Unit at Wing near Leighton Buzzard where he completed his flying training on Oxfords and was awarded his Wings.

While John was training at Lyneham, he was transferred to a blind approach training school at Ipswich. During this course a tailor from Austin Reeds visited the station and selected six of the aircrew trainees including John and told them that the company would like to make their officers uniforms. They all duly informed the tailor that they had not yet received or might not want their commissions. The tailor said, "OK, if you don't need the uniform, then you won't have to pay for it." The next day one of the six went flying and landed his Oxford with its 'wheels up'. Austin Reed lost out on him as he did not get his commission. John at that time was in two minds whether or not to take his commission, so he wrote to his father in Dungannon, suggesting that he might not accept it as he was worried about having to take another medical. His father wrote back and told him not to be silly, "You've earned it so take it, as it will make a tremendous difference to the comfort of your service career." John received his commission in April 1942 and promoted to Pilot Officer. He went for his medical and passed it with flying colours, except for his eyesight and they refused to accept him in any shape or form as aircrew. He asked to see the Chief Medical Officer who told him that he was sorry but there was nothing that he could do under the circumstances. John was very disappointed and pointed out to the medical officer, that he was to receive his Wings in two days time and that I am not here to see whether or not I am fit to fly. I am here on commission.

The chief medical officer sat up and said to John, "You mean to tell me that you have already finished your flying training?" "Yes sir," John replied, "and with respect, regardless of what you do now, I will get my Wings before your report goes through." The medical officer sat back in his chair, rubbing his chin, deep in thought and said to John, "All right, I will pass you fit, but I would advise you to wear goggles from now on, and I will write a note to that effect in your record." John told him that he had never had any problems with his eyes during all of his training. The medical officer gave him a glare and said sarcastically, "I am writing on your report that I have advised that you wear flying goggles at all times." John never wore goggles from that day until he left the RAF.

John's next posting was to the No 1527 Beam approach training flight at Ipswich where he spent the next five days on Oxfords learning Beam approaches. He had by now accumulated 173 flying training hours. He was then posted to No 26 Operational Training Unit at Wing which was a few miles north east of Oxford to start his operational training on Wellingtons. Here he met his new crew, they were a mixture from all over the place. His Navigator was Scottish, his Wireless Operator and Air Gunners were both Canadians, and his Front Gunner was a Londoner. They had their first flight as a crew on June 23rd 1942 in Wellington (908). The instructor for this flight was a Flight Sergeant Lewis and on 28th June John took command of the aircraft. Their operational training continued through to the 18th August when they were given some well earned leave. On returning from leave in the middle of September 1942, John and his crew were informed that they had been posted to No 12 Squadron at Binbrook which had a grass airfield and was equipped with Wellingtons. Early on the morning of 16th September they took off for a 'dual' flight with a Sergeant Pearce, and later that evening John and his crew took off on their first operation which was to bomb the Krupps Factories in Essen, Germany. As this was his first operation John flew as Second 'Dickie' Pilot to a Pilot

Officer Morton. One of the aircraft that was lost that night crashed into the Krupps Factory with a full load of incendiaries onboard. John and his crew returned safely.

John had now been given command of his own aircraft, and on September 30th 1942 laid mines of Texel in the Frisians in Wellington (960M). On the 5th October they bombed the city of Aachen along with 257 other aircraft. John was again 2nd 'Dickie' Pilot to a Sergeant Bayley. Halfway to Aachen Sergeant Bayley took ill and asked John to take over the aircraft which he did and continued on to Aachen. The weather had been bad over Aachen and the Pathfinders were unable to mark the target properly but the force was able to carry out their attack and managed to damage or destroy 22 industrial buildings that night. On their return from Aachen John told one of his crew to waken Sergeant Bayley to ask him if he wanted to land the aircraft as he was still Skipper. He said, "No, Just you carry on." After three weeks at Binbrook, John and his crew moved with the squadron to a brand new airfield at Wickenby, and were the first operational crew to land there. He remembers when he was a few miles from the airfield, he was informed by ground control to fly 221 degrees, and as the airfield came into sight he saw the new runway and it looked like it stretched from Yorkshire to London.

Operation number four was to bomb the town of Osnabruck on October 6th 1942. This was carried out successfully and on their return the crews were informed that the squadron was being re-equipped with the new four engined Lancasters. Some of the squadron's Wellingtons had been already flown to various OTUs and maintenance units around the country, and were awaiting delivery of the new Lancaster replacements. A signal came through from group on the 7th October that nine aircraft from 12 Squadron would be required the following night to lay mines at St Nazaire. Group was informed that 12 Squadron had been stood down awaiting their new aircraft. Group asked how many aircraft do you have at this present moment, and were told, three! One of which was John's aircraft (780W). The Commanding Officer agreed to let his three remaining aircraft and their crews go on this raid. Barely enough fuel was found that would take them to St Nazaire but the crews were told to land at Boscombe Down on their return journey as they would not have enough fuel to reach Wickonby. (Word got about that the aircrews were having to empty their cigarette lighters.)

On October 8th John his crew and the two other 12 squadron aircraft took off that night and set course for St Nazaire harbour to lay their mines. They had reached the target without any problems and were returning home when they were attacked by very accurate German flak batteries and shot down over Lorion in France. The mines had to be laid at 800ft, and because they had to conserve what petrol they had left to get back to Boscombe Down had to fly low level across France. John's aircraft was hit in the port engine which put paid to his instruments, and the ailerons had also been damaged by the flak. His aircraft was now losing height fast, and it was too low for the crew to bale out, and their was nothing he could do about it. He decided to switch on his belly lights and see where he was, and out of the gloom in front of him he spotted a few houses and beyond them some large fields. So he decided to ditch in one of them, as this may be the only chance of saving his crew.

He immediately informed his crew of his intentions and told them to prepare for a crash landing. The aircraft came to a grinding halt in the field, and John climbed out through the escape hatch on the roof and made his way along the fuselage to the rear of the Wellington, where most of his crew were getting out. He counted the crew as they came out and found that Temple the Rear Gunner was missing. John went back into the aircraft and found him lying semi-conscious over the main spar. What had happened was, his turret had sustained a hit from the flak and part of it had been blown away along with its guns. The Rear Gunner had managed to climb into the fuselage while John was crash landing and the impact had thrown him hard against the spar and caught him in the stomach. John had a look at him and found that he was also badly wounded. He managed to drag him out of the aircraft and shouted to the rest of his crew to get away from the aircraft. John made his way back into the stricken Wellington to retrieve the explosives and destroy it before the Germans came. He primed the incendiaries and knew that there was a fifteen second delay before they would burst into flames. He vacated the aircraft and waited, but nothing happened. He waited a further fifteen minutes and still nothing happened. He was sure that he had primed the explosives correctly, and he remembers going back into his aircraft for a second time to recheck the explosives. He was standing at the Wireless Operators position at the time, when he thought to himself, I must get my hat and reached up and took it. When he came out of the aircraft he met his crew all with their hands up in the air, being shouted at by a nervous German soldier. The German was excited, waving his gun in the air, forcing them all to march down a road till they came to a railway station. Soon a car arrived, and we got into it. A guard shouted something in German. We did not understand. He then said in French, "Seulmenent les blessie." John understood this to mean, "Only the wounded," and told the crew, except Temple to get out. John's French came in handy again on the long train journey to Germany. None of the guards spoke English and none of John's crew spoke German. John tried French and one guard understood. From that on English was translated to French and then into German and vice versa for German to English. By the time the train journey had ended, they had become quite good at it. They carefully helped the wounded Air Gunner into the back of the car, and the rest of the them walked about half a mile to the nearest German headquarters.

Prisoner of War, Stalag Luft III, Sagan

After being interrogated at various locations they were eventually taken to Stalag Luft III Prisoner of War Camp at Sagan which was at that time located 90 miles east of Berlin and in Germany. It has since been renamed Zagan and is now in Poland. Here John and his crew were to remain for the next thirty months. The Germans had purpose built Stalag Luft III to house all captured Allied aircrews. In October 1942, John was located in the east compound of the camp. There were two compounds at that time, one for officers and the central compound was for the NCO's. The Germans had underestimated how many POW's they were going to acquire and had to build another compound which became known as the north compound. The east compound had eight barrack blocks and the north had eighteen. The whole of the east compound was eventually moved to the north compound in April 1943. The Germans thought that it would be a good idea to do this as they could search the prisoners and their huts more easily, taking them from one compound to another. John went on to tell me about his time in Stalag Luft III. He said that it was remarkable what people were able to make and 'acquire' in the camp. Nails that had been pulled out of the walls, angle brackets taken off the corners of the wooden huts were used as 'prangers' (hammers). They were able to make hack-saw blades combs and many other useful bits of equipment. They had some of the best forgers in the country who could make them German documents, and tailors who could turn RAF uniforms into double breasted suits.

The east compound was then used to house the now famous 'Wooden Horse' project and the east compound housed the 'Tom', 'Dick', and 'Harry' tunnels and they were the camps biggest claim to fame. John told me that he had read an article in a newspaper recently about the fifty Prisoner's of War that escaped from Stalag Luft III and who were machine gunned to death by the Germans. This John said, "Was definitely not true. They were all individually shot as they were caught, on the direct orders of Adolf Hitler." After the massacre, the senior British RAF officer Group Captain Massey was summoned to the camp Commandants office for a meeting. (The camp Commandant seemingly was a good and fair officer.) He stood up and read out a letter which he had in front of him. He said that the men were shot while trying to escape. (I found even now that John was still quite moved talking about this.)

Group Captain Massey then asked the Commandant, "How many were wounded?" His answer was, "I am sorry but I am not permitted to say anything other than read this notice to you." It was obvious to Group Captain Massey that there was no wounded and all had been murdered. The lucky ones were the ones who got back to camp. From that time on in the camp, no POW's were allowed to attempt to escape. There were two senior British officers in Stalag Luft III, Group Captain Massey was one of them and the other was an Australian Group

Captain. Massey had hurt his ankle badly after he had landed by parachute, and could be seen walking around the camp wearing one flying boot and a shoe on the other. During 'Appel' (roll call) the Group Captain never had to attend parade. He would walk round the perimeter circuit by himself, this was a privilege afforded to him by the camp Commandant. One day a new guard who was on duty in one of the towers opened fire just in front of the Group Captain, probably thinking that he was about to hop over the fence, he never stopped or stumbled and just kept walking.

Christmas time, Stalag Luft III

During Christmas at the camp some of the prisoners managed to save up some raisins, which they had got in their Red Cross parcels. These were turned into a 'special brew', and drunk on Christmas morning. The prisoners also put on special plays at Christmas time in their huts which were converted to a makeshift theatre. The theatre held about 250 people and the seats were made from plywood from the Red Cross parcels. This wood was not normally given to the prisoners, as they could use it for all sorts of things, i.e. supports for the escaping tunnels. A special case had been made for the theatre and was eventually accepted by the Germans. Plays and reviews would be performed in the theatre all year round, and sometimes as many as six were produced in the year.

Some crews who had been shot down, had arrived in the camp with tickets in their pockets for a Show in the West End of London for, 'French Without Tears'. As it so happened the prisoners were putting on 'French Without Tears' that week, and their tickets were honoured in the camp.

At one of the concerts given by the POW's, there was a review written by a prisoner called 'French Mullan', he was an Irishman and the RAF had been his permanent career. The German staff had been invited to his review and were seated in the front row. One of the actors who was a comedian, referred to Stalag Luft III as this part of the British occupied Germany. Unfortunately one of the German officers was quite fluent in English and knew exactly what was being said. He immediately jumped up from his seat, and raised merry hell and closed the theatre that night. The Germans stopped the review as they would not tolerate anything that they thought was mocking them or their country.

'Tom', 'Dick' and 'Harry'

John did manage to get involved in this project and was prepared to do anything to help the escaping committee with their project. John said, "A lot of the prisoners did not want anything to do with escaping, but they did have to supply some of their bed-boards to shore up the tunnel." John had been friendly with one of the Canadians in hut 104 where one of the tunnel entrances went down at least forty feet. He would call round from time to time and help him extract the soil from the

tunnel. The Canadian was responsible for carrying the soil manually up the 40ft and asked John if a pulley wheel could be made to make his job easier.

John said that he would have a go at making one but this was not a success, so the Canadian had to revert back to his muscle power. John had been down the tunnels on many occasions, but never was allowed to dig. His job was to operate the air pump and help get rid of the sand. This was done by making bags out of any material that they could get their hands on. Two bags were joined together with a strap about four feet long and was put around your neck with the bags down the inside of your trousers. With both hands in your pockets you would hold a pin which when pulled would release a little flap on each bag, and you would just wander around the camp dispersing the sand and rubbing it in with your feet, as seen in the film 'The Great Escape'.

The cricket team

The camp had their own cricket teams, and John played for the 'Ireland' team. It was an earth wicket as there was no grass in the compound at all. John did not have enough Irishmen to make a team so he improvised with a few Canadians. They were able to beat the Welsh and Scottish teams on many occasions but were no match for England and Australia. The wicket was constantly watered and rolled to keep it in good condition as the spin bowlers found it hard to make the ball spin early. There was never any bother in obtaining cricket balls as they were sent through the Red Cross parcels.

The golf team

The golf team on the other hand were not so well equipped as they had only one mid-iron golf club and a home-made ball which burst after about six hits, and had to be continually sewn up.

The Americans managed to get their hands on a baseball bat and would organise tournaments among the eighteen huts.

The famous mouse trap

John had been having some problems with the local mice population and decided it was time to do something about it. Their food was stored in a cupboard that was attached to the wall and all their tinned food was punctured by the Germans so that it could not be stored for any length of time. mouse droppings were continually being found in the larder every morning. He could hear the mice when they came out at night scraping away in the cupboard. John was determined to make a mouse trap and get rid of the little pests. So he decided to have a word in the ear of one of the German 'Feltwebels', and told him that he was going to make a, "Mouse kriegskerfangen ein maken," this was John's way of telling the German, "A mouse prisoner machine." The German was only too willing to help John make his 'mouse kriegskerfangen'. John's fellow room mates laughed at this idea, but he was determined and eventually made a successful mouse trap, and I will try and explain how it was built. It was two inches square and about two feet long and solid at one end. At the other end he hinged a piece of timber with cardboard and using elastic bands set the trap protruding from the shelf with bait in the box. When the mouse walked into the end of the box it would over balance and fall off the shelf. The trap itself was tied with a piece of string anchored to the wall which meant it did not hit the floor. The mouse was still alive inside the trap, and the problem was, who was going to kill the mouse. A chap called 'Dicky Turner said brazenly, "You catch it, and I will kill it."

So when the time came to try out the deadly invention, just before lights out, John set the trap and got into bed. The lights went out, and within thirty seconds the trap fell and all his mates laughed. John got out of bed and shook the trap and sure enough, he had caught his first mouse. He turned to Dicky and said, "There you are Dicky, its all yours." All the room mates started cheering and chanting, "Come on Dicky, a bargain is a bargain." So he took the mouse trap away and it wasn't long before he was back and said, "How do you kill a mouse?" John caught three more that night. So famous did his mouse trap become 'abroad' that it was borrowed from compound to compound and by the time John was repatriated he had dispatched many a 'Krout Mouse'. The prisoners had been moved out of Stalag Luft III in January 1945, when the Russians were knocking on their door. They were marched out of camp at night in the middle of winter, ending up in Tarmstadt Naval Base which is in the north of Germany. They were put into lice infested huts and remained there for two or three months, and later forced to march eastwards and were never in huts or barracks again. The German guards had laid down their weapons and fled. They slept in fields for a while and eventually came to a huge estate where they found themselves a warm hayloft to sleep in. One of the prisoners found a motor car and managed to get it going, so John and he headed towards the allied lines. Driving around in the car John spotted some signs on the road

that he recognised, so they followed them and eventually came to the headquarters of the Fife and Forfar Regiment. John had met them a few years earlier when they were stationed in Dungannon and some of them did remember being based there, and were able to talk about mutual friends to John. John had his car filled with fuel and set off along with another friend whom he had met, his name was Squadron Leader Grant. They eventually arrived at Celle Air Force Base in France, and were later flown to Eindhoven in Holland where they boarded a Lancaster which took them to Brize Norton. The pilot of the Lancaster allowed John to fly his aircraft part of the way home. When John was training at Brize Norton a few years earlier, it was just a grass air-strip with a few Nissan huts and now it was a huge base complete with a concrete runway.

John was demobbed from the Royal Air Force in January 1946. He returned home to Dungannon in Northern Ireland to help his mother run the family business.

In 1980/81 the Royal Air Force News published some photographs of a crashed Wellington and its crew. These photographs had been taken by a German Naval officer who had been stationed at Lorion. The Naval officer whose flak unit had claimed the shooting down of the Wellington returned to Germany at the end of the war. When he died his widow decided to sell the house, and when she was clearing out the attic in 1980 she found the photographs. Thankfully, the widow realised that they may be of interest to someone and sent them to the Royal Air Force. They knew that the aircraft was a 12 Squadron Wellington by the code (BJ780) and registration (PH) which could be clearly seen in the photographs. The morning John's copy of the RAF News arrived at his home, he also received three phone calls from eager colleagues who had seen it before him.

John is a member of the Aircrew Association (Northern Ireland Branch), and the Royal Air Forces Association (Carrickfergus Branch). He is now retired and living with his good wife in Islandmagee County Antrim, Northern Ireland.

SERGEANT
VICTOR HALL SKILLEN
ROYAL AIR FORCE NO. 745460
BATTLE OF BRITAIN PILOT
NO. 23 SQUADRON

KILLED IN ACTION 11TH MARCH 1941

Victor Hall Skillen was born in Holywood County Down in 1917 and was educated at Sullivan Upper School on the Belfast Road, Holywood. Victor did exceptionally well while at school and was very keen on sports, playing for the schools 1st XV during the season 1934-1935.

Victor had a great enthusiasm for flying and joined the Royal Air Force Volunteer Reserve in Belfast in 1939. He learnt his flying skills at the 24 Elementary & Reserve Flying School at Sydenham during that period. At the outbreak of war he was called to full time service and sent to England where he would receive his advanced flying before being posted to an operational squadron.

After successfully completed all his operational flying training, Victor was posted to No 29 Squadron at Digby. The squadron at that time was equipped with the Bristol Beaufighter Mk1f's. On Saturday 21st September 1940, Sergeant Victor Skillen and his Navigator Aircraftman DW Isherwood were returning to base from an evening patrol (2105 hrs), in their Blenheim L1507, when it hit a flood light while landing at Ternhill. They were both unhurt and their aircraft was repairable. Sergeant Victor Skillen was killed on the 11th March along with his navigator Sergeant DW Isherwood while flying their Blenheim on an night intruder patrol over France on 11th March 1941.

WING COMMANDER
ROBERT CECIL SMYLIE, DFC DFC (USA) DFM AE
RAFVR NO, 749511
AIR OBSERVER/NAVIGATOR

Wing Commander Robert Cecil Smylie was born in Belfast on 28th June 1911 and died suddenly at his home in Bangor, County Down, on the 3rd April 1980, at the age of 68. He was known as a cheerful and courteous person. He was cremated at Belfast's Roselawn Cemetery after a funeral service on Easter Monday 1980. Officiating at the Service was the Reverend Malcolm Redman, who was a friend of Cecil's, the pair having gone to school together. In his address the Reverend Redman paid tribute to Cecil's outstanding service in both the war and to his local community.

Cecil's flying career was one of great achievement and it is unfortunate that he was unable to personally contribute to this book. As a result some detail is not known. However, with material kindly supplied by his son Peter and one or two other sources a record of his service has been assembled. This comprises a record of his postings, flights and operations together with several examples in part or whole, taken from letters or articles. He was educated at Glenola College in Bangor and Methody College in Belfast, and was a great lover of sports and represented Northern Ireland in athletics from 1932-34. He excelled in the javelin and discus, ran 100 yards in 10.2 seconds, the 200 in 20.4 seconds and managed 21 feet in the long jump and was a member of the Ulsterville HAAC and played rugby for Bangor and Malone Rugby Clubs. When he left college he was employed for a time in Riddel's, of Donegall Place Belfast, and was in the sales section of the Bangor gas department, before becoming a commercial traveller. Cecil married Donaghadee girl Rebecca (Ruby) Cunningham on the 14th December 1937 and their first daughter, Patricia was born in May 1939, followed by Valerie in July 1941 and son Peter in July 1943.

He joined the RAFVR in May 1939 as a Leading Aircraftsman and was mobilised at the outbreak of war in September 1939. After induction at Padgate and basic training he was posted to No 1 Air Observers and Navigation School at Prestwick near Ayr in Scotland, which was equipped with Fokker and Anson type aircraft.

On the 3rd January 1940, 749511 LAC Smylie had his first local flight in Fokker G-AFZR under the instruction of Flight Sergeant Palethorpe. He records this aircraft as a Fokker 30 seater, although the exact type is not known. Most of his training flights took him from Prestwick to, Stranraer, Lockerbie, Kirkpatrick, Glenluce, Dumfries, Carlisle, Ronaldsway and Blackpool. He finished his training on the 1st May 1940 after completing 65 hours of flying tuition. It is interesting to note the high standards applied in that the course certificate shows him attaining 1046 marks out of a possible 1300, or 80.5%, and being assessed only as 'average'. However when examining the elements relating purely to navigation, in which he would later surpass when he obtained a top mark of 99.2%.

On the 1st May Cecil was posted to No 9 Bombing and Gunnery School at Penrhos in North Wales, which was equipped with Fairy Battles. He first flew on 9th May in Battle 5259 and trained on this type along with the Hawker Demon and passed out on the 28th June with an assessments of, "Above the average, reliable and should do well for the bombing course and will make a good gunner for the gunnery segment." He was also awarded his 'O' Brevet and promoted to the rank of Sergeant. Having now completed his navigation and gunnery training he was posted to No 10 Operational Training Unit (OTU) at Abingdon near Oxford on the 30th June to commence an eight week, navigation, bombing and gunnery course the flying training being carried out in Ansons. He first flew with the OTU on 15th July in Anson N3306 under the watchful eye of Pilot Officer Outram. One week of this course was spent at Jurby flying in Whitleys and carrying out live bombing and air firing. The week with the Whitley was to be an indication of his next destination.

Cecil passed out from Abingdon on the 1st September with what, in terms of this book, appear to be a unique assessment.

Navigation	Above the average.
Bombing	Above the average.
Gunnery	Above the average.

It was probably at this stage that he was earmarked for greater things. Certainly his progress in the next few months was rapid commencing with his posting as a new sergeant to his first operational squadron. With the official motto, "Swift and Sure," and the unofficial WW2 name of 'York's Own Squadron', this 4 Group unit, which was then based at Dishforth near Rippon, had achieved several notable 'firsts'.

The first 'Nickle' raid over Germany on the first night of the war, 3/4th September 1939, along with Whitleys of No 58 Squadron. This was also the first occasion that RAF aircraft entered German airspace during the war.

The first attack on a land target - Hornum on the island of Sylt on 19th March 1940.

The first big attack on the German mainland - Munchengladbach on the 11th May 1940.

The first big attack on Italy, to the Fiat works in Turin, on 11th June 1940.

The first area bombing attack on the German industrial centre at Mannheim on the 16th December 1940.

The squadron also participated in two notable parachute drops, Operation Colossus on 10th February 1941 to destroy an aqueduct in Southern Italy, and on 27th February 1942, in Operation Biting, to capture a complete 'Wurzburg' radar station near Le Havre. The latter raid partly was delivered courtesy of Wing Commander PC Pickard, at that time the squadron commanding officer. He was also known at the time for the documentary 'Target for Tonight' that featured Wellington 'F' for Freddie and later achieved fame as the leader of the daring Mosquito raid on Amiens Prison. Cecil joined the squadron on 2nd September 1940, and carried out his first operational flight as First Navigator on the 4th, a long 10hour trip to Berlin and back in Whitley V-N1414.

Flying with 'B' Flight, his pilot was Squadron Leader JB Tait OC 'B' Flight who, in July 1944, would succeed VC holder Wing Commander Leonard Cheshire as commanding officer of No 617 'Dam Duster' Squadron. Before his next operation on the 14th, he had formally qualified as Sergeant Observer Navigator and between then and the end of his first tour almost exactly one year later on the 8th September, he completed a further 28 operations to destinations including Keil, Leipzig, Turin,

Bremen, Cologne, Antwerp, Zeebrugge, Boulogne, Berlin, Duisberg, St Nazaire, Brest and Wilhelmshaven. Cecil's flying log also records him being under dual tuition as a Co-Pilot on several occasions commencing on the 6th September 1940, four days after his arrival on the squadron. Such entries continue throughout his time with 51 Squadron and total 30 hrs including night flights. On the 8th August 1941 his last 51 Squadron operation to Keil, his log shows that he was 2nd Pilot/ Bomb Aimer with 3.5 hours at the controls. This dual training continues to the end of his log and can only be seen as being unofficial, although it must have been with 'approval'. Between the 2nd and 22nd of February 1941 he was posted to Manby at the No 1 Advanced Air Navigation School and returned to the squadron as a fully qualified Bombing Leader having completed the Bombing Leaders course. He received his commission at the end of June 1941, and promoted to Acting Pilot Officer, and then became Squadron Navigation Officer, and Squadron Bombing Leader on the 1st July.

With one exception, the raid on Keil in early August, Cecil was not operational during the rest of his time with 51 Squadron, being tour expired and probably screened from operations. As well as flying with Squadron Leader Tait, he also flew on operations with Sergeant Wilson, Sergeant Bulpitt, Pilot Officer Reardon, Flying Officer Hawley, Wing Commander Wilson, Sergeant Cole, Squadron Leader Putt, and Wing Commander Burnett.

On the 22nd August 1941 Cecil was awarded a well-deserved Distinguished Flying Medal. The citation reads:

> This Officer has displayed courage and initiative as a bomb-aimer throughout many bombing raids on enemy territory. Since January 1941, he has been Flight Commander, and has shown exceptional qualities of leadership, resourcefulness and organising ability. His unit has always been well trained and disciplined, and has participated in raids on Berlin, Kiel, Cologne, Hamburg and Lorient, and many other targets.

He remained with the squadron until the 11th October 1941, having been promoted to Flight Lieutenant on 1st September, his final log entry being signed by Wing Commander Pickard. There is little doubt that Cecil made his mark within 4 Group during this period with 51 Squadron and that he was on the list to join the very good team at Heslington Hall. A footnote to Cecil's time with 51 Squadron is a copy of a telegram dated April 5th 1941. This was from him to his wife Ruby, at that time staying at her parent's home in Donaghadee. "Safe on ground - very fit, Love Cecil." Study of his log would suggest no reason for this message unless Ruby had heard something on the BBC that gave cause for concern. More likely is that because Cecil did not tell his wife that he was on operations, as is known from various correspondences, and that she somehow learned of his activities either through a newspaper or somebody home on leave.

Having finished a tour with an operational squadron, Cecil was rested and posted to No 19 Operational Training Unit at Kinloss in Scotland as Bombing Leader. He took up the new post on 11th October. He instructed on Ansons and Whitleys, and his log shows that he also kept his hand in 'training as a pilot'. The posting to Kinloss lasted for twelve weeks. On the 2nd January 1942 he was posted to headquarters 4 Group at Hoslington Hall as bombing leader for one year, where he was involved with crew training probably in a planning or strategy role.

No operations are recorded for this period and very little flying, in fact only eight flights in one year with a total of ten hours in all that I have listed below:

24th Jan	Magister W/Co Buchanan Map Reading York-Leeming.
24th Jan	Magister W/Co Buchanan Leeming-Dalton (forced landing).
26th Feb	Whitley V F/Sgt Cussens Photographing anti-aircraft and search light defences and testing 'monocular' attachment to 'automatic bomb sight'.
25th Apl	Tiger Moth S/Ldr Lawerence York-Croft-York.
2nd Jul	Halifax W/Co J Marks Map reading Linton-Radlett.
2nd Jul	Halifax W/Co J. Marks Map reading Radlett-Linton (2nd Pilot Air Vice Marshall Carr).
30th Jul	Tiger Moth W/Co Merritt Linton-Leeming-Skipton-York.
2nd Oct	Anson Sgt Lockwood, Abingdon-York.

Cecil made a big impact on at Group Headquarters, where the standards were very high. The group was widely acknowledged to have turned out many of best crews in bomber command. Cecil's later return to the group, organised by the AOC, justified his worth.

158 Squadron, Rufforth

Promotion to Squadron Leader followed on the 1st January 1943 at the end of his headquarters stint, and just before his return to operations with 158 Squadron at Rufforth where he was appointed Flight Commander of 'C' Flight.

Brief history of 158 Squadron

The squadron was formed in September 1918, and disbanded two months later without becoming operational. It was reformed in February 1942 at Driffield as a bomber squadron in 4 Group, and during the rest of the war took part in many major raids over Europe, including the first 1,000 bomber raid. The squadron was initially equipped with Wellingtons, and converted to Halifaxes in the summer of 1942. Among its Halifaxes were two particularly distinguished specimens, the first was LV907 'F-Freddie', or Friday the 13th, as it was named,

and the second was LV917 'Clueless', which was successively designated 'T-Tare', 'H-Harry' and 'C-Charlie'. Both of these aircraft joined the squadron in March 1944, and flew on the squadron's final wartime operation, which was an attack on Wangerooge on the 25th April 1945. Cecil went on to complete 12 operations with the squadron the first being to Lorient with Flight Lieutenant Viney (pilot) on the 14th January 1943. He also visited Hamburg, Cologne, Wilhelmshaven, Dortmund, Duisberg, Le Creusot, and Gelsenkirken. The Le Creusot raid on the 19th June was the heaviest raid of the war so far, and was made up of 290 aircraft from 3, 4, and 8 Groups. 181 Halifaxes, 107 Stirlings, and 2 Lancasters, their target was the Schneider armaments factory at the Breuil steelworks (two Halifaxes were lost). The squadron moved to Lissett sometime during March.

Cecil was awarded the Distinguished Flying Cross on 13th August 1943, after completing his second tour of operations. His logbook shows that his last flight with 158 Squadron was with Pilot Officer Cameron in a Halifax on the 29th August, two days before he left the squadron to take up his next posting at the RAF Staff College to attend the 10th War Course.

An article from an unknown internal source on leaving 158 Squadron

158 Squadron lost one of its most colourful personalities last week when Squadron Leader 'Paddy' Smylie, DFC DFM, was posted to the RAF Staff College. He has gone for training, which will give him the strength to bear the additional weight of rings, which will surely climb towards his elbow in the near future. 'Paddy' Smylie was 'C' Flight Commander and in that capacity set a standard his successor will find difficult to maintain. It was a standard inspired by his own capacity for hard work and perhaps even more by his personality and courage. He worked hard and played hard. He was straight and firm but always fair, and from the newest AC2 on his section to the Wing Commander he was regarded and approached as a friend. His record of service is one of which he may be justly proud. From an AC2 in the RAFVR in May 1939 he graduated via the Prestwick Navigation School, the Penhros Gunnery and Bombing Course, and Abingdon OTU to 51 Squadron at Dishforth. Those were the days when Whitleys were our main striking force, when the squadron had to struggle to put up six or seven and when 40 or 50 on any target was a 'powerful force'. It took him just over a year to complete his first tour but at the end of that time he had 34 trips in his log and the DFM on his chest. He took his commission in June 1941 and was made Flight Lieutenant in September 1941. He came to 158 in January of this year after three months as Chief Bombing Leader at Kinloss and twelve months as Bombing Leader at 4 Group. In January 158 were struggling hard at Rufforth. They were grim days and the magnificent spirit of this Irishman was badly needed. It was the teething time of the Halifax - when it was a struggle to get four out of twelve off the deck. But from its tough beginning 158 won its way from the bottom to the top of Bomber Command's list of successful squadrons. "It was the Spirit of the Squadron that did it," Squadron Leader Smylie

declared this week. "And no matter how bad things are from time to time," he added, "that Spirit will carry on in 158." Well, no one should know better for no one contributed more to the building and moulding of that spirit. We extend our good wishes to Squadron Leader Smylie, and wish him good luck in his new sphere. He told us that if he doesn't like his new job he is coming back for a third tour. Our hope is that he comes back to 158.

Also of interest at this time

A letter to Cecil from the AOC 4 Group reads as follows:

Headquarters
No 4 Group
RAF
York
27th August 1943.

Dear Smylie,

I was very pleased to see you last night before you left us for the 'Brains Trust' and I feel that I cannot let you go, even temporarily, from the Group without thanking you for all you have done both at this headquarters and 158 Squadron.

Believe me, when I say that I will watch your career with the greatest of interest and when you have completed your Staff College Course I will make every endeavour to have you back in No 4 Group. As you know, as the Bases form there is quite an interesting job on the base headquarters for a Wing Commander and I hope that you will come back and fill one of them. Let me know later the exact date that you will finish in order that I can put in a claim for your services.

Thank you again for all you have done.

Yours Sincerely
CR Carr
Air Marshal

Air Marshall Carr was on General Eisenhower's air staff at Station Headquarters Allied Expeditionary Force. SHAEF.

Eric Waller sent this letter to Cecil:

RAF Base
Driffield.

My Dear Smylie,

I'm so sorry I didn't see you before you left Lissett to say my 'au revoir'.

I know you will enjoy the staff course and hope you will find it of value. Have you any definite ideas about what you want to do after the course? Would you like to come back to me as Wing Commander Air at base headquarters? It will be an interesting job building up the new squadrons etc, and I would like to have you back again if it could be arranged. By the way I don't think I congratulated you on your DFC, I'm very glad about it.

Let me know sometime how you are getting on and also what you think about the W/Co Air job.

Best of luck
Yours ever
Eric Waller (Walker)

With such eminent officers seeking his services, Cecil did return to 4 Group headquarters as a Staff Officer, Operations and Tactics Controller from the 1st December 1943 to the 11th of April the following year. He was promoted to Wing Commander on the 15th April 1944 immediately after his arrival at headquarters 44 (Bomber Base) at Holme on Spalding Moor, where he was appointed Air 1, and remained until the following March.

Cecil was awarded the DFC upon completing his second tour with 158 Squadron and was also awarded the United States of America DFC on the 1st December 1943, although the Citation is dated November 1944. The Citation reads as follows:

For extraordinary achievement while participating in many attacks on some of the most heavily defended targets in Germany. At all times Wing Commander Smylie has displayed outstanding qualities of leadership and devotion to duty. His courage and skill reflect highest credit upon himself and the Armed Forces of his country.

Signed
By Command of Lt General Spaatz
EP Curtis
Brigadier General USA
Chief of Air Staff

Authors note

I received the following information from a most reliable source.

Cecil was seconded to the United States Army Air Force for a period to instruct their bomber crews in the art of bomb aiming using the British bombsights as it was regarded as being more accurate than its American equivalent. To do this task properly he had to fly on operations with the B-17 crews. On the way back from one such operation at night, the aircraft was badly damaged by flak. The Pilot and Co-Pilot were wounded, two engines had packed up and they had lost indication on all of the cockpit instruments. Cecil with all his courage and vast knowledge of navigation was able to guide the stricken Fortress home (without instruments).

It is known from his record of service that he flew operationally with the USAF in Fortresses on eleven occasions.

Cecil received a letter from Air Marshal Carr on the 29th June 1945 and it reads as follows:

Air Staff
SHAEF

Dear Paddy,

Thank you very much for your Air Mail letter. You seem to be leading the simple life with a vengeance. As you will see by the address I am now Deputy Commander of Air Staff to General Eisenhower. The powers that be have promoted me to Air Marshal. It is a most interesting job, but ends shortly as the Supreme Command is packing up in a couple of weeks.

I have however, another good appointment awaiting me in August and I am looking forward to a good leave. I was very pleased I left No 4 Group when I did, when it was on the crest of a wave. My wife and I visited York a month ago, but things were not the same. Jimmy Clapperton was still there and most of the old hands.

I have just come back from a lovely trip by air, Copenhagen, Stockholm, and Oslo. Magnificent food, drink and women. Here we are in Frankfurt, or rather what was Frankfurt as Bomber Command have destroyed practically everything. I have been to most of the big cities in Germany and how the Huns took it I don't know. I also went to the Bertchesgaden, which was also ruined.

I much appreciate your thought in writing and hope we may meet again. The best of luck to you.

Yours Sincerely
CR Carr

It was now approaching the end of hostilities, Cecil left 44 Base and headed for Air Headquarters West Africa, 114 Transport Wing which was based at Accra. The trip to Accra from Hurn took 24hrs.45mins in a Halifax. His Pilot was Pilot Officer Leicester, while Cecil acted as 2nd Pilot, along with Pilot Officer Humphreys, who was a back up. They left Hurn on the morning of the 17th July, the journey took them via, Lisbon, Rabat, Freetown, landing at Accra two days later. They flew from Accra to Takoradi on the 23rd July 1945, and it is here unfortunately that Cecil's log ends (there seem to be some pages missing). I think it is possible that this comfortable posting was a thank you from his superiors and were probably to oversee the return of peacetime conditions and the run down of the RAF in the region.

Cecil was 'Mentioned in Despatches' on the 23rd June 1945, during his time at Accra.

He was demobbed from the Royal Air Force in November 1945 and returned home to Northern Ireland where he became General Manager of Carrocon Products Ltd of Carrowdore in County Down. It is thought that he may have been a sales representative for this company at the outbreak of war. He entered into community life by serving on Bangor Council and took an active part in the Freemasonry Order including the Masonic schools. He also served as Governor of Bangor Grammar School. Whilst taking part in these activities with his usual relish, he would have been the first to admit that his main interest was in the welfare of Ex-Servicemen and their dependants Over the years he helped many through the Officer's Association, Royal Air Force Association, and the Royal British Legion. His sudden death at an early age came as a blow to all his family and his considerable circle of friends and acquaintances. Cecil was one of those highly likeable achievers who gave so much during the war years and afterwards, but did not live the life that he could have reasonably expected.

Some details of Wing Commander Smylie's service in the Royal Air Force.

Aircraft types flown:

Anson	Halifax
Battle	Harvard
B-17 Flying Fortress	Magister
Dakota	Tigermoth
Demon	Whitle
Fokker	

Total Flying Hours: Day 650
                    Night 307
Total Operational Bomber Sorties: 51
Awarded DFM June 1941
Awarded DFC August 1943
Awarded DFC (US) December 1943
Mentioned in Despatches June 1945

SQUADRON LEADER
JAMES BRAIDWOOD STARK, DFC
ROYAL AIR FORCE NO. 134754
PILOT
NO. 58 & 298 SQUADRONS

Squadron Leader James Braidwood Stark although born in Glasgow on the 14th December 1915 moved with his parents to Bangor in the County of Down, Northern Ireland, on the 116th June 1926. He was educated at the Albert Road Primary School in Glasgow and on arrival in Bangor attended the National School in Main Street and completed his education at Bangor Grammar School.

On leaving school he was employed with the Law, Union and Rock Insurance Company. While his parents were away on holiday he tried to enlist in the Navy and on his arrival at HMS Caroline he was informed by the Chief Petty Officer that they were full up.

Not to be outdone and determined to join up he went along to Queens University OTC but again was told that they were not accepting any recruits. So what was left for James? Yes, the good old Royal Air Force. The next day he went along to the RAF recruiting office in Clifton Street and was accepted as aircrew and was informed that he would be graded accordingly. He had hoped to become a tail gunner.

His first posting was to Padgate Receiving Centre in Cheshire where he passed his medical and was sworn in. He was then sent back home to Northern Ireland and was told that he would be sent for in due course.

James was called up on the 29th July 1940 and was posted to a receiving centre at Babbacombe for two weeks training and then on to an initial training wing at Abberystwyth. Here he received his uniform, various vaccinations, etc. and in order to help the effects of the medication to wear off more quickly he was given endless hours of drill instruction and PT. On September 27th he was posted to No 12 EFTS at Prestwick in Scotland to start his elementary flying training in Tiger Moths. Jim remarked, "The greatest aircraft God ever created."

On the 29th September 1940 James had his very first air experience flight in a Tiger Moth T 7085 with his instructor Flying Officer Maynard. The training continued which consisted of, the effect of controls' taxiing, straight and level flying, clombing and stalls. On the 21st October

after completing 11 hours instruction he flew the aircraft solo. (His instructor jokingly told him, "All right Stark, you can go up now on your own and break your own bloody neck.") The training continued until the end of October when he was posted to a Service Flying Training School for twin engined training. He arrived at No 6 SFTS at Little Risington in the Cotswolds at the beginning of November 1940 to commence training on twin engined Avro Ansons. His first 'short' flight (ten minutes) in the Anson was on the 7th November in N5293 and his instructor was a Flight Lieutenant Chesterman. The course was initially only supposed to finish after eight weeks but due to the very bad weather it lasted for four months. It was at No 6 SFTS that James encountered the word 'censorship'. When writing a letter to his mother he discovered that there wasn't much left of his original letter by the time she received it. So he used to end all his letters by writing at the end, "Hell roast the bloody spy that censors this letter." The Avro Anson was to the young pilots a pretty ancient aircraft as it had been built in peacetime but it did the job that was required of it. As the course was behind schedule the pupils flew day and night (weather permitting) to catch up. James finished the course on March 26th and was awarded his flying badge. His total flying hours to date was now 123hr.20mins and he was given some home leave.

On his return from leave he was informed that he was being posted to No 19 OTU at Kinloss in Scotland to start his operational training in Whitleys. His first flight in a Whitley was on the 29th April 1941. The aircraft K9047 was piloted by Sergeant Boothby and lasted for 1hr.15mins and it was not long before James took over the controls. James told me that the Whitley was nicknames 'The Flying Coffin' because of its shape and not because of any bad flying characteristics. The days by now were often longer and the weather much better allowing plenty of flying. On the 9th May he flew his first night flight in Whitley L9037 and finished the course by the 15th June and was now ready for his operational squadron. James was posted to No 58 Squadron at Linton-on-Ouse and arrived there on the 20th June 1941.

58 Squadron was formed at Cramlington in Northumberland in January 1916 as a home defence squadron equipped with FE 2b's. In the summer of 1919 it moved to Egypt and re-equipped with Vickers Vimy Bombers. In 1925 Squadron Leader AT Harris (later to become Marshal of the Royal Air Force) took command of the squadron which by then was flying Vickers Virginia's. At the outbreak of the Second World War the squadron was based at Linton-on-Ouse and equipped with Whitleys. The squadron's targets ranged from airfields, road and rail, industrial centres to channel ports and oil installations. In April 1942 the squadron was transferred to Coastal Command where for the remainder of the war it carried out general reconnaissance duties. The squadron was disbanded a few weeks after VE Day.

At this point Jim was transferred to 35 Squadron for a while still based at Linton-on-Ouse. Before James could become Captain of his own aircraft he was required to complete a certain number of operational flights as a Second Pilot and so spent the last few days in June and all of July being trained for Captain by Squadron Leader Leonard Cheshire and Squadron Leader Willie Tait. His first operational trip was on the night of the 26th June in Halifax L9500 to Keil. The aircraft was Captained by Flight Lieutenant Elliot. His second operation was again to Keil but this time in daylight. The aircraft was captained by Squadron Leader Willie Tait. He flew nine times as Second Pilot to Tait during his '2nd Dickie' training. Operations 3, 4 and 5 were to Magdeburg, Frankfurt and Leuna.

Operation No 6 was a very different and important one. They took off and flew to La Rochelle to bomb the German battle cruiser Scharnhorst.

The following is Jim's own account of the attack on the Scharnhorst

"We stayed overnight on the 23rd at a station called Stanton Harcourt in Oxfordshire. The aircraft was bombed up and we took off and set course for Exeter where we met another squadron and together in a loose formation we crossed the English coast and flew south giving Brest a wide berth. Of course on our arrival which was heralded well in advance, units of the German Luftwaffe were waiting for us (mainly Me 109's). It was a beautiful day and from my grandstand view in the 'Astro Dome' I could see a magnificent blue sky that was filled with Me109's. My job was 'fire control', in short I had to scan the skies for enemy fighters and shout instructions for the gunners to where the attack was developing from. Our gunner shot down one Me109 and badly damaged another one, at least smoke was pouring from it when I saw it go down. We dropped our bombs on the German cruiser and paired off back to England very 'shaken'. The squadron casualties were very high that night. The Halifaxes met fierce fighter opposition and a lot of flak, five direct hits were seen to hit the Scharnhorst, three of these were armour piercing bombs that passed right through the ship. Five of the Halifaxes were lost and all of the remainder were damaged but the raid put the cruiser out of action for a further four months."

It was while serving with 35 Squadron that James encountered his first crash. "On the 17th July 1941 we took off with Squadron Leader 'Willie' Tait in Halifax L9495 with a VIP on board (Commander in Chief of Bomber Command). We flew him from our base to Middleton St George and on our return Tait very kindly let me fly the aircraft and of course he took over for the landing. In changing seats with him, I did not bother to put up the 2nd 'Dickie' seat and strap myself in. We made the approach and were committed to the landing, when suddenly in front of us there was a magnificent display of pyrotechnics from the control tower. One of our aircraft's main undercarriage legs had not come down and the aircraft crashed and slid unto the runway. We all made a hasty exit from the aircraft."

On July 30th he returned to 58 Squadron and was now a fully qualified captain. He completed a few 'nursery' trips to Antwerp, Calais, and Dunkirk and then onto bigger targets in the Whitley. His next five operations were to Dunkirk, Hamburg, Krefeld, Ostend and Antwerp. Operation No 12 was on the 1st November 1941 to attack harbour targets at Keil. Two Whitleys failed to return from the raid. On the 2nd November Jim was posted to No1 Beam Approach Training (BAT) Flight at Abbingdon where he was to train on Whitley 111's. When he completed the training two weeks later he was posted to No 76 Squadron where he completed a Halifax conversion course before returning to his own squadron. On his return to 58 Squadron, something happened that was to alter his operational career. 58 Squadron complete with it's Whitleys were transferred to Coastal Command. On Wednesday 8th April 1942 the squadron flew south to its new base at St Eval in Cornwall and its new task was to sink U-boats. His first operation from St Eval was on the 28th April in Whitley Z9142 but unfortunately as they were just 45 minutes into the operation they had to return to base due to an oil leak in one of the engines.

On May 2nd James sighted his first U-boat but it dived and got away. The squadron moved to Stornaway in Scotland in August 11942 and carried out anti-submarine patrols as far as Iceland and the Norwegian coast. Then on December 8th the squadron moved to RAF Lyneham and took off again the next day for Holmsley South. The squadron was now being re-equipped with Halifaxes. From January 18th until the end of February 1943 the crews trained hard and soon got the feel of the new aircraft. They flew back to St Eval at the end of the month to resume anti-submarine and convoy patrols.

May 1943: 'The month the German Navy lost 41 U-boats'

Operation No 52. **"One to Remember".**

The sinking of U-boat U528, a Type 1XC/40 which was commanded by Oberleutnant zur See Georg von Rabenau. The Halifax crew were:

Pilot	Pilot Officer JB Stark
2nd Pilot	Pilot Officer HW Burroughs
Navigator	Warrant Officer GA Roy, RNZAF
1st WOP/AG	Flight Sergeant ED Jones
Bomb Aimer	Pilot Officer GP Ruickbie
Engineer	Sergeant J Young
Air Gunner	Sergeant JE Abbey, RCAF
2nd WOP/AG	Flight Sergeant K Hopper

James own words regarding the sinking of U 528:

"We took off around 0300 hrs on the morning of the 11th May in Halifax 'D' HR942 and rendezvoused with convoy OS 47 about 0600 hrs which was located in the North Atlantic south west of Ireland. As I approached the convoy I fired off the colours of the day to identify myself. I flew up the centre of the convoy and received a signal by Aldis lamp from the Commodore of the convoy. The signal read 'Cobra'. This indicated to me what type of search we had to carry out. All the searches had code names of snakes, and 'Cobra' meant a square search around the convoy. At approximately 0930 hrs we sighted a U-boat, but it submerged before we could attack it. I flew back to inform the Commodore's ship to advise him about the danger and then returned to the previous position where I had sighted the U-boat. On my arrival I saw a fully surfaced U-boat in position 4655/1444 which I attacked from the port bow. The depth charges straddled the boat and its stern lifted out of the water and rolled before disappearing. A large piece of debris was thrown into the air by what seemed to be a secondary explosion and then the U-boat went down for a second time. Only the bow of the boat could be seen at this time. I saw an oil patch on the surface of the sea, approximately 100 yards across and having seen nothing more I returned to the convoy to report. The escort vessels HMS Mignonette and Fleetwood continued the attack on the damaged U-boat forcing it to the surface."

The escort vessels picked up 15 survivors. Major credit was given was given to James and his crew for destroying U528 and he was awarded the Distinguished Flying Cross for his efforts.

58 Squadron went on to sink five more U-boats and shared in the destruction two others. On the 14th May 1943 Jim had completed 53 operations and was rewarded with a well-earned rest.

His next posting was to Holmsley South MU near Bournemouth on the south coast of England where he was given the position of test pilot. The job entailed flight testing the Halifaxes that had been serviced, repaired and rebuilt at the MU. On the 1st July 1943 James was posted to No 1 OTU at Thornaby (Coastal) as an instructor on Halifaxes. This posting lasted until the middle of October when he was posted to 1674 Heavy Conversion Unit at Longtown converting twin engined pilots unto the Halifax. By the end of November 1943 James had accumulated 902 flying hours and was assessed as 'above average' as an Instructor Pilot by the officer commanding 1674 HCU.

On the 25th November 1943 James was informed that he was to be posted on a Flying Instructors Course that was held at No 3FIS at Lulsgate Bottom near Bristol. This news cheered him up to no end because he realised that if the Air Ministry had sent him on this course it would by all accounts mean that he would be posted back onto an operational squadron. James knew that the Air Ministry had a knack of spending a vast amount of money teaching people skills they would never use. The school was equipped with Oxfords and he had an excellent time there as there was plenty of flying and it was Christmas. At the beginning of January 1944 and after successfully passing the instructors course he was assessed as 'average' as a Pilot and 'average' as a Flying Instructor. At the beginning of January he returned to the conversion unit fully convinced that he would be sent to an operational squadron. How wrong could he be, all through January February and the greater part of March he toiled away converting twin engined pilots onto Halifaxes. At the end of March 1944 he was again assessed as 'above the Average' as an Instructor Pilot. On the 25th March he received the news that he had been waiting for and this was to inform him that he was to be posted back onto an operational squadron. He was elated at this news.

On the 27th March James was posted to 298 Squadron at Tarrant Rushton that was near the town of Blandford in Dorset.

298 Squadron was formed at Thruxton on the 24th August 1942 and for some unknown reason was disbanded again in October 1942. It did not reform again until November 1943 at Tarrant Rushton and was equipped with Halifax V's from 'A' Flight of 295 Squadron. The squadron missions were to tow Hamilcar and Horsa Gliders for the Normandy Landings in June 1944. It also carried out Operations Coup de Main, Tonga and Mallard. These were code names for dropping Jeeps by parachute from extremely low levels (500ft in some cases) with SAS and SOE personnel on board. It was also was heavily involved in Operation Varsity (Rhine crossing). The squadron was disbanded in December 1946. He was quite happy to fly the Halifax again, but the task he was about to undertake was something he had not experienced with Coastal Command. His primary duty was to train the glider pilots how to fly their gliders and then tow them and their equipment across to Europe. In short they were the air arm of the airborne

divisions. There were approximately 12 airfields in that part of the country involved in glider towing operations.

"When I arrived on squadron my main task was to train the glider pilots how to fly them and most days I would spend three hours at a time in the air with them. I would taxi onto the runway in front of the glider and stop, the ground crews would attach the towrope to my aircraft and I would take off hoping that the glider would get airborne behind me. On the down wind leg the glider pilot would release his craft from the towrope and glide down and land. I would then fly to a prescribed place and drop the towrope and land. I would taxi back onto the runway in front of another glider and the whole process would be gone through again and so on for the next three hours." In April James carried out a lot of night exercises, towing gliders around the south of England and letting them land at other airfields getting them used for the Arnheim drop and D-Day. He also was involved in the dropping of 'dummy' parachutists, these exercises were valuable for future use against the Germans. James logbook shows that on April 2nd in Halifax KK he carried out 'dummy dropping' and on April 9th and 11th carried out 'parachute dropping'. James told me, "We did have a 'side line' and that was to drop SOE people and their supplies into France to assist the French Resistance."

Preparation for D-Day

During the second week in May a 24 hour curfew was put on the whole station and that meant all leave was cancelled on till further notice. All operational flying was stopped but the night exercises intensified. Everyone was flying four hours on particular exercises and other were mostly glider towing. On the 14th May 1944 all aircrew were summoned to the main briefing room and informed that as from tomorrow detailed briefing for a future important operation would begin. They were shown a rota, whereby three crews at a time were to report to the 'special' hut that had been set aside for the job in hand. James and his crew reported as instructed at 1000 hrs the next day and when they entered this special hut they were duly impressed with what they saw. Laid out on the floor was a complete detailed model of the beach head or that part which they were going to. On a table at the side of the room was what we nowadays consider to be a TV set. It was however a simulator and when the intelligence officer who was briefing them switched it on it showed a simulation of an aircraft. Just as if they were flying it over the beach head. Then when the film was finished the officer moved the switch to a different position, this time it showed the same scene, except there was a filter on it which gave the impression of them flying the aircraft by moon light. James and the crew were told to study the beach head model and the simulator very carefully for the next half hour, after which three more crews would take it over. This was the first of many trips, which James and his crew paid to that 'special' hut.

As well as endless briefings, they also had to carry on with their day to day work flying circuits and bumps for the benefit of the glider pilots. They had visits from time to time from VIP's and the first to arrive was Air Vice Marshal Leigh-Mallory who was Air Officer Commanding (AOC) and he explained to the crews of the task ahead of them and what an important job they were going to do. The next VIP to visit was Field Marshal Montgomery, Commander of the British Land Forces. At the end of May all the crews were summoned to the briefing room and this time all the senior officers of the station were there, i.e., the station commander, squadron and flight commanders and with them was General Eisenhower.

Sunday June 4th: 'S' for sugar, the aircraft which James and his crew were going to fly was towed out of its hangar after having just completed a 300 hour inspection. James and his crew were about to give it an air test that included testing the wireless, guns, navigation, hydraulics, instruments and engines. After the test was completed James and his crew spent the rest of the day in the briefing room with the rest of the pilots. Further information was being continually put upon the briefing board and now the final arrangements were about to be posted up.

Monday June 5th: All of Sunday morning was spent loading up the gliders and then towing them out to be positioned on the runway. Then in late afternoon the pilots and engineers taxied their aircraft out and placed them in the appointed positions at the side of the runway. That being done James and the crew returned to camp for their final briefing.

D-Day June 6th, 1944: At 0130 hrs on the morning of the 6th June 1944 James and his crew were driven out to their aircraft Halifax 'S' for sugar where they hung around awaiting orders. In the distance they could see the glider pilots, soldiers and gun crews approaching their aircraft. They all stood around talking to each other, then their commanding officers arrived in jeeps and started blowing whistles, this was the signal to board their aircraft and start engines. The leading aircraft which was on the runway ahead of the leading glider moved off and the 2nd aircraft took its place and so on until the whole two squadrons with their gliders were airborne. They flew a few mile in a south westerly direction and then the formation in line astern slowly turned and flew along the south coast of England until the got to the Isle of Wight when they turned to starboard and set course for France. The Channel was decidedly choppy and was filled with craft of all shapes and sizes. They were rapidly approaching the beach head and all that time James was talking to the glider pilot, keeping him posted as to exactly where they were, etc. It was just beginning to get light when they crossed the French coast and there was plenty of 'opposition' (heavy machine-gun fire). James could now see the landing zone ahead of him for the gliders and he called to the glider pilot, "Can you see the landing zone in front of you?" He replied, "Yes." James told him to go when he was ready, then he felt the familiar surge forward as the glider let go. The Tail Gunner informed James that the glider had gone so he throttled back and then turned to port and headed up the French coast to Le Havre where he released the tow rope and set course for home. Back at Tarrant Rushton the briefing room was in turmoil, with flight commanders checking on casualties, engineering officers trying to find out the state of the aircraft, intelligence officers endeavouring to get information from aircrews and war correspondents shoving microphones in your face attempting to get a story. James' big concern was the state of his squadron as there was to be a second 'lift' that afternoon in which he was not taking part as his aircraft and crew were OK. However if there were any others damaged or missing he would be called upon to replace them. Fortunately there had been no casualties or aircraft missing or damaged and at approximately 1930 hrs that evening the second 'lift' took off with far fewer aircraft that the mornings show. The main reason for this was that the greater part of the diversion had been carried out that morning. James and the crew were very disappointed that they could not take part on the 2nd lift as they would have been able to see the dropping zones in daylight. However they did get an opportunity to see it on D-Day plus five when they took off on Sunday 11th June along with six other aircraft and set course for Caen in France. On this particular occasion they were not towing gliders but had a jeep and a 25-pounder in the bomb bay. They were to drop the jeep and 25-pounder by parachute to the 6th Airborne Division who by this time was in a fairly bad was since the Germans Panzers had closed in on them.

James explains:

"With the Jeep and 25 Pounder in the bomb bay of the Halifax it meant that the bomb doors were held open with part of the load protruding beneath the aircraft. This gave the Halifax the aerodynamic capability of a pregnant hippo. All six aircraft reached the dropping zone safely, released their load and returned to Tarrant Rushton. That was to be the last trip that James and his crew were involved in with the Invasion."

On one occasion while towing a glider James and the crew just managed to avert a disaster when he had just taken off from Tarrant Rushton. The glider pilot was far too high above the Halifax (should have been below) causing the aircraft to violently nose down and heading for the runway. Luckily James being a proficient pilot knew exactly what had happened and was able to correct this (the tow rope for towing a glider was over 100 yards long). On the 4th July 1944 he took a war correspondent on a trip and on the 3rd, 7th, 15th and 28th July he returned to France only this time he was dropping supplies to the French Resistance. August 1944 operations were primarily dropping SOE and SAS personnel into France from a height of 500 feet. These people were to operate behind the enemy lines. On the 17th and 18th September 1944 he and the crew carried out Operation Market Garden. This operation involved towing Hamilcar and Horsa gliders full of troops and their equipment into Holland.

James's account of the Arnheim operations

"On the 17th and 18th September 1944 the battle for Arnheim had started. By noon over one thousand troop carriers and 500 gliders were heading for Holland. I along with my crew with a Hamilcar on tow crossed the English coast at about 5,000ft. We crossed the Dutch coast just north of Amsterdam and then set a course for Arnheim. The dropping zones were at least eight miles from the bridge and this certainly contributed to the 'final disaster'. On the 17th we took off from Tarrant Rushton along with nineteen other aircraft towing seven Hamilcars and thirteen Horsa Gliders and eight of each the following day. On the 19th we 'delivered' ten Horsa Gliders complete with their personnel and equipment safely to their dropping zones."

From October until January 1945 the squadron returned to dropping SOE and SAS type operations.

The Rhine crossing

On the 24th March James and the squadron took part in the epic Operation Varsity towing six Horsa and twenty five Hamilcar Gliders for the crossing of the Rhine. Over 21,000 airborne infantry were dropped that day north west of Wesel and who quickly overcame enemy resistance and linked up with Montgomery and Pattons main force. (One Halifax was shot down over the target.)

After the Rhine Crossing operation James and his crew returned to dropping supplies to agents in Europe.

It was now the middle of April 1945 and James had completed a total of 82 operations and 1351 flying hours. "It was now time for another well earned rest."

At the end of May 1945 he was posted to the School of Air Support (Transport Supply Wing) at Old Sarum near Salisbury as an Instructor. Here he flew Tiger Moths, Proctors and Ansons. He also lectured on airborne operations and helped to organise air displays and the end of each course. Having failed to obtain a permanent commission on medical grounds, James was demobbed from the Royal Air Force in February 1947.

He returned to Northern Ireland to take up his pre-war post with Law, Union and Rock Insurance Company, now the Royal Insurance Company until he finally retired. At the end of my interviews with this charming man he laughingly told me that he reckons that France's dairy market suffered a great deal during the war because of all the cows that had been killed by his stray bombs. James still lives in Bangor in the County of Down in Northern Ireland and is a member of the Air crew Association.

LIEUTENANT
ROBERT STERLING, DFC
PILOT/OBSERVER
ROYAL FLYING CORPS
NO. 6 SQUADRON

Lieutenant Robert Stirling was born on the Ballygomartin Road in Belfast in 1893 and was educated at the Boys Model School. On leaving school, he became an apprentice architect with the ship building firm of Workman and Clark and later worked for a chemist in Royal Avenue, Belfast, who was renowned for selling 'Irish Violet' perfume that came in a green bottle and laced with a green ribbon. Robert was also a member of the 'C' Specials in Belfast.

Like many young men of that period, he had a great desire to fly and so on the 30th March 1917, aged 24 joined the Royal Flying Corps. He was immediately posted to Reading where he was to start his basic training and become a Pilot. On completion of his four months basic training. In July Cadet Stirling was then posted to No 49 Training Squadron at Spittle Gate to start his flying training on Maurice Farman Short Horn aircraft. His first flight in an aircraft was on the 14th August 1917 when he took to the air in a Maurice Farman, code A7077 with his Pilot Lieutenant Evans. They flew at a height of 500ft for 15 minutes and during the flight he was given control of the aircraft. Cadet Stirling's total flying time for week ending 28th August 1917 was 15 minutes 'dual'. Cadet Stirling flew the Farman twice on August 30th and five times on the 31st, taking control of the aircraft from his Pilot Sergeant Darrell on each occasion. Each flight lasted no more than 20 minutes flying at a varying heights of 300, 400, 500 and 700feet.

No 49 Training Squadron moved to Doncaster on the 12th September 1917 and during that month cadet Sterling flew the Farnham 16 times, carrying out landings and engine cuts with his instructors Sergeant Darrell and Flight Sergeant Guyatt. During the month of October he carried out practice landings in fog, learning how to correct 'one wing low' and flying straight and level.

On the 12th October Cadet Stirlings big day had arrived when his instructor Flight Sergeant Guyatt informed him that he was going to fly the aircraft solo. Having completed a total of eight hours flying instruction, Cadet Stirling climbed into the cockpit of his

Maurice Farman Shorthorn aircraft, code 7093, at 0720 hrs and took off. Unfortunately after being in the air for just five minutes he crashed his 'machine' trying to escape an embankment (this was his first 'prang'). Luck was not with Cadet Stirling again on the morning of 21st October 1917 when he flew his second solo. He took off with his instructor, Lieutenant Round at 0715 hrs for a 15 minute lesson that went well, landed and let his instructor out and took off at 0735 hrs in the Maurice Farman, code 2192. Five minutes later he landed the aircraft rather heavily, breaking both of the aircraft's landing wires. The first two weeks in November were spent flying with his instructors Flight Sergeant Guyatt and Lieutenant Round and on the 17th November he completed two satisfactory 15 minute solo flights reaching a height of 600 ft. According to his flying logbook his 5th solo on the 19th was, "Rather bumpy."

On the 8th December 1917 he was posted to No 20 Training School at Harlaxton flying only three times during that month, and I assume it was because of bad weather as his flying log shows in the remark column (very cold). At the end of December 1917 he had flown a total of 9hrs.50mins (dual) and 2hrs.5mins (solo). No flying was recorded during the month of January. Cadet Stirling next took to the air on the 4th February 1918 when he flew a DH6 for the first time. He took off at 4.40pm with his instructor Lieutenant Arbothnot for a ten minute 'very bumpy' air experience flight. He flew the DH6 again on the 6th February 1918 with his instructor to a height of 1,200ft and reported again that the weather was very bumpy. He flew again on the 25th/27th and 28th carrying out gliding turns, flying straight and level and practised landings. Cadet Stirlings first solo in the DH6 was at 1740 hrs on the 8th March 1918 and on the 9th he had to force land the aircraft. His logbook shows that on the 12th March he took off at 0715 hrs with his instructor Lieutenant Arbothnot in DH6 2807 and carried out 20 side slip landings (14 in Drome area) and (six at Ponton) and 18 cross wind side slip landings (12 in Drome Area) and (six at Ponton).

On the 21st March 1918, Cadet Stirling had his first flight in an RE8 with Lieutenant Arbothnot and flew it solo the next day. Cadet Stirling was presented with his Wings on the 23rd March 1918 after completing 25 hours instruction. While flying RE8 solo on the 24th March his logbook shows that he got lost and had to make a forced landing at Stoned in Cambridgeshire. After making a few enquiries as to where he was, he took off again and landed safely back at Harlaxton. On the 30th March he flew to Cranwell and back in an RE8 at a height of 4,000ft. His next posting was to No 50 Training Squadron on the 4th May 1918. The squadron was equipped with the BE 2E and his training on this type consisted of turns and landings, dropping bombs, aerial gunnery and formation flying. On the 13th May 1918 Cadet Stirling was posted to No 64 Training Squadron at Harlaxton where he carried out bombing techniques. On the 31st may his logbook shows that he, "landed rather heavily", in an R.E8, breaking the aircraft's centre section, and on the 6th June 1918 he flew an R.E8 from Cranwell to Ponton. On the 15th June 1918 he was posted to an Army co-op station at Winchester where he attended a two week training course on how to co-operate with the army on the ground.

France

In the middle of July 1918, and now a fully trained airman Lt Robert Stirling was posted to Abeele in France where he joined No 6 squadron. Shortly after his arrival Lt Stirling wrote off two of the squadrons RE 8's, the first on the 22nd July and the second on the 24th July. I am reliably informed by a family member that the next day 25th July went something like this. Lt R Sterling was summoned to the Commanding Officer's office where he was told to sit down. The CO informed him that since starting his flying career on the 14th August 1917, he had damaged or destroyed no less than 12 aircraft. The CO told him that this was even quicker that the enemy was destroying them and it could no longer be tolerated. He went on to say, however, you are an extremely good aviator and have decided not to take you off flying duties. Therefore, as and from 23rd August you will be appointed (Observer Officer) flying.

On the 31st July 1918, the squadron had moved to the advanced aerodrome at Amien, where Lt Robert Sterling took to the air for the first time as an Observer. He took off at 1700 hrs in an R.E8 with his Pilot Lt Owen and flew to a height of 2,500ft to familiarise himself with the local landmarks over Amien.

The following are log entries taken from Lt Sterlings flying logbook, from August 1918.

August 8th	Flying R.E8. Encountered heavy machine gun fire from the ground at Le Quesnal. Height 2,000ft.
August 12th	Flying R.E8, 11.40am. Dropped five bombs over Franear & L Reion. Height 3,300ft.
August 21st	Flying R.E8, 11.40am. Dropped six bombs on Favrevil Height 9,000ft.
August 23rd	Flying R.E8, 7.15pm. Dropped six bombs on Bapaume & fired 60 rounds. Height 2,300ft.
August 24th	Flying R.28, 4.45pm. Five Huns fired at us while over Groisilles & then ran like the Devil. Height 2,300ft.
August 24th	Flying R.E8, 10.55am. Had to land at La Bellerve due to failing light & returned to Aux-Le-Chateau at 10.55 hrs the next morning.
August 25th	Flying R.E8, 6.50am. While on Line Reconn, saw four Huns shoot down one of our aircraft. Height 3,000ft.
Sept 2nd	Flying R.E8, 6.50am. While on Line Recon, felt sick in the air over Vitry. Height 2,000ft.
Sept 2nd	Flying R.E8, 3.30pm. Took off again & dropped ammunition to troops near Dury. Height 2,000ft.
Sept 3rd	Flying R.E8, 3.25pm. Dropped ammunition to troops near Boville and dropped two bombs on Namel. Height 800-2,000ft.
Sept 5th	Flying R.E8, 5.45am. Attacked anti-aircraft battery at Marquoin and had the pleasure of seeing it silenced. Machine badly cut with 'Archie' (anti-aircraft fire). Fired 20 rounds. Height 800-2,300ft.
Sept 9th	Flying R.E8, 8.45am. Dropped four bombs dropped on cross roads at Marquion. Fired 350 rounds, pilot fired 450 rounds into trenches west of road north of Marquion. Height 800-2,000ft.
Sept 19th	Flying R.E8, 5.30am. Dropped four bombs & machine gunned trenches near Bois-de-Ecluse. Machine shot through longeron and main spar.. Height 2,000ft.
Sept 23rd	Flying R.E8, 8.40am. Dropping messages to 3rd cavalry Division & reporting on Drome at Cherienne. Height 1,000ft.

Story of an Ireland Saturday Night

Lt Sterlings mother sent her son a copy of the Ireland Saturday Night newspaper when she could, to keep him up to date with the local news and sport. On the 26th September 1918 Lt Sterling was informed that his brother was in trenches near the town of Bapaume. He had a talk with his pilot and they agreed to try and locate his brother. His logbook entry for this amazing adventure shows, "26th September 1918. Take off 1.00pm in R.E8 4930 with Lt Owen (Pilot)." They set a course for Cambrai and flew at a height of 3,000ft. The Remarks column reads:

"Line Recon. Dropped ISN to Billy at Bapaume. *(How's that for brotherly love.)*

All the following ops were carried out in R.E8's with his pilot Lt Owen:

Sept 29th	6.25am. Dropped 2x40lb Phos bombs as smoke screen to cover our 'Fan'. Height 3,000ft.
Sept 3oth	6.00pm. 'Dropped ammunition to our advancing troops digging into shell holes in of Joncourt, and dropped 4x25lb bombs and engaged Huns in trenches. 22 Huns in open. DHT ?? Going east from Gunere, good results CLB call answered by SE5 straffing the Hun trenches. Height 500-2,000ft.

On the 1st October 1918 Lt Robert Sterling and his Pilot 2nd Lt James Owen MM were awarded the Distinguished Flying Cross in recognition of gallantry in flying operations against the enemy by the King. Their Citation reads:

On 1st October, when on patrol, these officers displayed marked gallantry and endurance. Flying at altitudes from 500 to 1,000 feet for three hours, they successfully located the enemy defence lines. Frequently attacked by machine-gun fire from the ground, they never refused to engage. Having obtained the formation required, they attacked enemy transport that was crowded along a certain road, continuing the attack as far as 7,000 yards behind the enemy lines

Oct 2nd	3.40pm. Crashed.
Oct 3rd	4.10pm. Attacked and harassed by 'loco' enemy machines. Foggy. Cavalry getting ready to go into action. Height 500-2,000ft
Oct 4th	4.10pm. Dropped four bombs on Geneve 'Damps' Sniper caught us with four shots. Height 200-500ft.

Oct 6th	10.40am. Dropped four bombs on East of Brancourt. Shot Huns in the open. Landed at new drome. Height 1,000-2,000ft.
Oct 7th	12.40pm. Dropped four bombs in trenches south of Brancourt. Shot Huns in Ponchaux. Chased a two-seater. Height 500-2,000ft.
Oct 8th	9.25am. Dropped four bombs on Hun transport east of Fresnoy. Contact with FAN, so as to give line to Cavalry.
Oct 8th	15.35pm. 3 Division asked us to make a recon of Jerazn. Dropped four bombs on Huns in trenches and had a dust with a machine gun. Height 800-3,300ft.
Oct 9th	11.30am. Two reconn flights for 3 Division at Busigny. Huns demoralised and retreating from Reumont. Fired 500 rounds & dropped four bombs. Height 200-2,000ft.
Oct 11th	05.45am. Cavalry contact, Placing line 2 000 yds north and 2,000 yds south of Le Cateau. Height 500-1,000ft.
Oct 13th	08.50am. Engaged Huns defending Molain with machine guns and bombs. Height 400-1,000ft.
Oct 14th	09.50am. Four bombs dropped on Pommerevil. Archie active. Height 6,500ft.
Oct 16th	13.10 pm. Foggy all day, change to new drome. Height 600ft.
Oct 18th	13.30pm. Air Patrol on Hun trenches, going through wood. Height 4,000-6,000ft.
Oct 23rd	11.40am. Dropped four bombs on Preux. Height 1,000ft.
Oct 24th	06.30am. Thick fog. Patrol impossible. Height 1,000ft.

The Great War ended on the 11th November 1918.

Nov 16th	12.00pm. First move to Germany. Gondrecourt. Height 3,000ft.
December 8th,10th & 22nd	Formation Reconns.

Lt Sterlings logbook shows that on the 31st December 1918 he flew with his Pilot Lt Owen to Le Flaches to visit his brother Billy. (This was to be his last flight with Lt Owen). Lt Sterlings last operational flight in France was on the 13th February, when he and his Pilot Lt Willis went 'hedge hopping' around Namur and Dinant at a height of 20ft.

His total observing time was now 122hrs.45mins.

Mesopotamia

The post-war distribution of the Ottoman Empire gave Britain control of many parts of the Middle East. Most of which were potentially unpredictable, especially as their native leaders had not been consulted. The Turks had faced revolts in many of the Arab provinces, now the British faced the same difficulties. No 6 Squadron arrived in Basrah in June 1919, equipped with R.E8's to quell Sheik Mahud's rebellion. They had to operate from various landing grounds and very often these were in rough and rugged areas. The rebellion was easily contained and it was not long before the Sheik was imprisoned. Most of the operations No 6 Squadron carried out were to support isolated garrisons in remote areas that were easy targets for the rebel tribesmen. Lt R Sterling, DFC arrived in Mesopotamia in July 1919 with the squadron, which was now officially a bomber squadron. Its duty was policing the areas in Mesopotamia and later in Palestine. His first flight in Mesopotamia was in the afternoon of 26th July 1919 when he set course in the R.E8 for Basra with his Pilot Lt Frith (he remarked in his logbook that it was 'very hot'). His next flight was on the 18th September air testing an R.E8 over Baghdad at 400ft. On the 1st, 2nd & 3rd Oct he began bombing practice, and on the 15th Oct flew to Baghdad visit Allen in hospital (possibly a crew member from the squadron). On 26th Oct, he and his Pilot set out to escort a Vickers aircraft, which was taking photographs of 'Hit & Baghdad'. The Vickers had to make a force landing in the desert. Lt Sterling and his Pilot landed alongside the Vickers, removed the camera and returned it to base. On 10th December 1919 he took off at 0920 hrs from Baghdad and set course for Hillah to take photographs. His logbook shows: "Force landed in desert and had to walk six miles in boiling sun to get to railway line. Ten rolls of film OK." On the 11th December 1919 he took off at 0845 hrs and set course for the airfield at Abu Kamal in response to a message for assistance. After landing at Abu Kamal they took off again at 1330 hrs and headed for Deir es Zor. On their arrival they flew around the airdrome and found it in flames, an Arab flag was flying and they were immediately fired upon from troops on horse back. At 1015 hrs on the 12th December, they took off and set course again for Deir es Zor where they landed. They interviewed a Captain Boyse, who had come out under Arab escort and took a message back to base from him. On the 13th December they took off for a third visit to Deir es Zor. They also carried out a recon of the Abu Kamal district from a height of 300ft. They watched thousands of Arabs approaching, came back and

gave the information to the authorities in Baghdad. On 16th December they took off at 0745 hrs and bombed Abu Kamal from 6,000ft, later landing at hit owing to low cloud cover, eventually returning to Baghdad at 1130 hrs. January 1920, a new year, and things were quiet for the first three weeks. On the 20th January they took off at 0815 hrs and set course over the mountains to Bushere airfield. On the 23rd January they took off from Bushere to bomb and machine gun Lhumbeh, during this operation they received some rifle fire from the ground. On the 31st January 1920, they took off at 0845 hrs and set course with 2x112lb bombs to bomb the town of Brit. On the 6th March 1920, they took off on their last operation and while flying over the target (Kalmeh), they encountered heavy rifle fire. Their wing and fuselage were hit in several places. Things were very quiet between the 10th March and the middle of May. On the 18th May 1920, Lt Sterling and his Pilot escorted the Shah from Lawrence to Bushere. During his tour in Baghdad, Lt Sterling became air adviser to Sheik Fisal. This conflict was now coming to an end for Lt Sterling and on the 8th July 1920, he was handed a hand written letter by one of his staff, which simply said:

> To Flying Officer Sterling
> 'C' Flight
> Bushere
> 8-7-XX
>
> Sir,
>
> Please accept our best wishes as a small token of respect from all the men of 'C' Flight. We wish you the best of luck and every success for the future.

The letter was signed by 21 of his fellow aviators. (I am not absolutely sure when Lt Sterlings rank changed to Flying Officer.)

Flying Officer R Sterling's last flight was in a Bristol Fighter when he flew to Hillah and on to Baghdad. "Then Home." On his return home to Northern Ireland Lt Sterling joined the Northern Ireland Civil Service as a Principal Officer in the department of finance. The government at that time did not treat their ex-servicemen very well and promotion for them within the establishment was hard to get. Lt Sterling was a man who never took no for an answer, he had been through two wars and was not prepared to take this lying down. He was extremely well liked by his staff and decided to speak to his superiors about their grievances. He told them that unless these matters were put right, he was prepared to go to the press and inform them how ex-servicemen were being treated so disgracefully by the government.

Home Guard

Shortly after war had been declared in September 1939, Lt Sterling decided to join the Ulster Home Guard and became a Sergeant cook. He was affectionately known to his friends as 'Sergeant Snowball'. On one occasion he was attending a camp in the Mourne Mountains, with men from the two city battalions of the Ulster Home Guard, and who were living under strict military conditions.

The following is taken from a local newspaper

There, men whose wives have trouble bundling them out for business at 8.30am are daily on breakfast parade at 7.30. There, men who might complain if their slippers weren't duly warmed for their return from the office are sleeping on boards and straw paliasses as if they had never heard of spring mattresses. There, heads of city firms and civil service departments are being hewers of wood and drawers of water, doing everything, in fact, that the army does for itself.

A DFC Cook.

In a place of such surprises it was with no astonishment I saw a principal officer of the civil service, holder of the DFC, won as a fighter pilot in the last war. Flying Officer Robert Sterling was preparing dinner for hundreds of men as if born into the business. This man, still simply a 'Volunteer', notwithstanding his record is one of eight men who attended a course at the Army catering school so the battalion could become the only one in Ulster with its own cooks. Just after leaving the Royal Flying Corps he attended his doctor complaining about severe chest pains. The doctor told him that he had a heart condition and had about six months to live. 'He outlived his doctor'.

Somme Medal

Lt Sterling was also awarded the Somme Medal. Although he was in France too late for the Somme Battle he had flown over it on several occasions on active service. Because of this the French government decided to award it to him. He had also received two commissions in the forces; one with the Army prior to 1st April 1918 and one with the Royal Air Force after it was formed on 1st April 1918. When he was re-mustered from Pilot to Observer he would flip the lid of his tunic pocket up were he had his wings sewn onto it. His Observer's Brevet was just above it.

The Observers Brevet was known as the 'Flying Arsehole'. He was also an expert in stripping down a Lewis Gun.

"A very nice Parade," said Her Majesty

There was an unbounded enthusiasm in the Balmoral show grounds when the Queen and Duke of Edinburgh inspected 3,000 ex-service men and 1500 ex-service women and 500 war invalids.

Among their ranks were two very proud veterans, Flying Officer Robert Sterling, RFC RAF and his son Flight Lieutenant RA Sterling. Flying Officer Sterlings medal ribbons drew the attention of the Duke of Edinburgh and he stopped and spoke to both of them.

After the inspection Her Majesty was heard to say, "A very nice Parade."

Shortly before Flying Officer Sterling, DFC died, his son Robert decided to take him on an Ulsterbus trip to the continent. They spent three days in Paris and later drove up and visited the Somme battlefields and passed through areas that his father had flown over during the First World War.

"I Remember"

The following is a memory of Robert Sterling written in his own words.

"My first memory goes back sixty-eight years when I first went to school at the age of four. I was dressed in a pair of pink wool combinations, thick hand knit black wool stockings that came well up my thighs, a pair of corsets with thick elastic which connected with buttons on my stockings and held them up, a petticoat, a frock and a pair of boots. I was a little boy and this was the style for boys of that age and that time. My other memories are many and it would be impossible to express them in eight hundred words so I will limit myself to a memory concerning mainly one person. He was a young man, a few years older than myself and we used to play in fields off the Ballygomartin Road, Belfast, and now occupied by the Woodvale Cricket Club and partly by Corporation houses.

"He had made a large kite known as a 'Bender'. In the centre was an upright stick and at the top a split cane joined by string and the whole covered with Irish Linen and balanced by paper tails. When the kite was flown he joined it to a long board on four wheels. He put me on the board and the kite pulled me right down the field. The young man was shy, but once a few tough boys had come up from the Shankill Road to Woodvale Park and started to do a thing that one never sees now but was fairly common then. They had caught a frog and intended to insert a straw in its hind portion and blow it up till it would burst. He went over and spoke to them and gave them a lecture on kindness to animals and persuaded them to give up the idea of killing the frog. Although shy, this young man had 'guts'. Time passed and he went to University and qualified as a doctor. Instead of going in to practice he joined the medical service of the Indian Army. A few years later the First World war broke out and when it had been in progress a few years, the great news came that the young man had been awarded the Victoria Cross for bravery in Mesopotamia.

"His name was Jack Sinton.

"Meanwhile I had joined the Royal Flying Corps and later in France I was given an immediate award of the Distinguished Flying Cross. Later the fighting finished and we were forward with the Army of occupation, when on the border of Belgium and Germany heavy rain started and we pegged our aeroplanes to the ground with long metal corkscrews. It rained so long that when it ceased it was not possible to make the aeroplane serviceable again. We were then posted to Mesopotamia and a fresh lot of aeroplanes sent out to be re-built at Basra. During 1920 I was posted to a detached flight at Bushire on the Persian Gulf and whilst there we entertained a lot and had many foreign persons to dinner. One night I was sitting next to one of two Russian brothers called Kharnoff who had been in business in Odessa until the revolution in 1917 when they came and started business in Persia. In order to make conversation I asked him did he know my uncle called Robert Herd who taught languages in Odessa and held the honorary rank of Colonel in the Imperial Russian Army. He looked blank but when I remembered that in some text books on the Russian language my uncle had written, his name had become 'Gurd'. When I mentioned this he said he knew him, but I got a great surprise when he asked me did I know Jack Sinton. Over thirty years later I was on parade with the British Legion in Balmoral show grounds, Belfast and Prince Philip kindly spoke to me. About five lines behind me I noticed Jack Sinton, who was now Brigadier General JA Sinton, VC OBE and I said to my eldest son, who was also with me on parade, would he like to hear a good story.

"When the parade was at ease I took him to the Brigadier and asked him had he a good memory, he said he had. I asked him could he cast his mind back half a century, he said he could, I asked him did he remember flying a kite attached to a board with four wheels and putting a little boy on it when the kite pulled the board down the field, he said he did. Well I said, 'I am that little boy.' He smiled and asked me did I remember when he tied the kite to his bicycle and it pulled him over the hedge. I said I wasn't there at that particular incident. I then told him how when dining in Southern Persia in 1920, a Russian called Kharnoff had asked me did I know Jack Sinton. He smiled and said he remembered Kharnoff. He then noticed the Burma Star amongst my son's medal and asked him had he been down the Arakan and my son said, 'Yes.' Just then the parade was getting ready to be called to attention and when he was saying, 'So long,' he said, 'I would like to see you again,' but this was not to be. He died shortly afterwards."

Flying Officer Robert Sterling died in 1968.

LIEUTENANT
WILLIAM ALEXANDER DAVID STERLING, KMN
ROYAL INTELLIGENCE CORPS

William Sterling was born in Belfast and was educated at the Royal Belfast Academical Institution. He was going on to Queens University to study Civil Engineering, but decided to join the Army instead. Because of his great knowledge in languages he joined the Royal Intelligence Corps in 1943.

After some very intensive training in England, he received his commission and was posted out to the Far East, where he operated from India, Hong Kong, Singapore and Rangoon. He left the Intelligence Corps in 1947 and decided to return to Northern Ireland and take up his place at Queens University and became a Civil Engineer. Due to the nature of his wartime duties in the army, I have no further information on this part of his career. In order to get the responsibility and type of work that he wanted, he had to return to the Far East and was employed in Qualalumpur in Malaya for the

Tunku Abdul Ramin. The Tunku Abdul Ramin was the head of Malaya at the time of the Malayan independence celebrations.

William was awarded the KMN (equivalent of the OBE) by the Tunku Abdul Ramin for designing and building the major flyover in Qualalumpur for the independence celebrations. He then came back to the UK and took up a post with a multi-national Firm in London, travelled the world, and became an expert on building aircraft runways to handle jet aircraft. He died in later years after a Kidney operation.

FLIGHT LIEUTENANT
ROBERT A STERLING
ROYAL AIR FORCE NO. 1138730
AIR OBSERVER/NAVIGATOR
NO. 27 SQUADRON

Robert A Sterling was born on the Woodvale in Belfast on the 18th January 1923 and was educated at the oldest school in Belfast, Fourth River Primary. After completing his primary education, he went on to the Royal Belfast Academical Institution where he obtained a Senior certificate.

His mother was born in Scotland of a Polish mother and a west of Ireland father. They both married in Northern Ireland when her family moved here before the First World War. His mother had been reared in the Catholic tradition in Scotland and found it very difficult to relate to the Irish brand of Catholicism that prevailed in Belfast at that time. His father came from a Presbyterian background and their friendship from the very beginning came in for strong criticism from both churches. This made his father move to England where he joined the Royal Flying Corps in 1917. He went on to produce two daughters and three sons and outlived the doctors who had written him off. Bob as he likes to called by his friends, was the original seven stone weakling at school, he did not take part in any of the school sports as wasn't very strong. His mother often said that he did not have a very strong grip of the earth. Bob was very keen on jazz music and still has a good ear for it today.

Among his other many interests was the cinema and in his regular visits the news reels showed the alarming growth of the Nazi dictatorship and their growing belief that might was right. Like many at that time he saw the steady growth of Nazism through Austria, the Nuremberg Rallies, Czechoslovakia, the Sudeten and the rape of Ethiopia by the Italian fascists. One of the most depressing sights that he remembered about that time, was that of the Ethiopian Emperor, Haile Selassie, the 'Lion of Judah' standing in front of the League of Nations in Switzerland pleading for help and getting a stony faced response. He remembers the famous footage of Mussolini's son-in-law who was the King of Umberto, flying over Ethiopia in an open cockpit with a white scarf around his neck, flying in the wind with a huge smile on his face. He was actually strafing the Ethiopians who were herders of sheep. Bob could see well this terrible war machine building up, Adolf Hitler, Goebels and Hermann Goering who had prostituted an honourable career which he had built up during the First World War and to a lesser extent China's and Japan's role in the Far East. He remembers well his father who had obtained a DFC in the First World War saying, "This was the war to end all wars," and the Prime Minister Neville Chamberlain coming back from his famous visit with Adolf Hitler waving his piece of paper, "Peace in our time."

This all took place in September 1939 and Bob was very keen to join the Royal Air Force, but still had another year to complete at school in order to sit his Senior Certificate. This was one of the longest years in his life, particularly as his cousin Camac had joined the RAFVR prior to the outbreak of war and was now flying with Bomber Command, Bob went through the agony of Dunkirk, The Battle of Britain and the death of Camac in July 1940 who was killed over Belgium before he was eligible to join.

In January 1941 Bob joined the RAF at the recruiting office in Clifton Street, Belfast. This was a tremendous opportunity for him as he was not a robust person at that time and he was concerned that he might not pass the medical. After passing the medical, he was posted across on what was called the 'Irish Party' as 60% of the entrants came from Southern Ireland. Bob set sail on the Heysham boat and arrived at the receiving centre At Padgate near Warrington. When they arrived at Padgate they could not understand why they were being rushed through, and there was always someone in front of them shouting, "Make way for the Irish Party. Make way for the Irish

Party." They found out afterwards that the previous Irish contingent had gone into Warrington, got drunk and fought the bit out with the locals. That's the reason they wanted rid of them as soon as possible.

Robert passed all the tests that was required of him, including the dreaded 'Mercury' test where one was required to blow up a column of mercury in a glass tube with the aid of a rubber tube and a glass mouth piece, to a certain level and sustain it there for a minute. The mouthpiece was so designed so as one could not put their tongue over the mouthpiece and hold it, (cheat). Bob tried once and failed. He tried a second time and failed and the doctor said to him, Mr Sterling you are only allowed three attempts at this test. So compose yourself and have a final go. So he did, and by now was getting the hang of the mouth piece and was able to semi-cover it with his tongue and keep the mercury up for one minute (just).

Bob had now passed all the necessary tests and was selected for Pilot/Observer training. At the interview there was a very senior officer who Bob noticed was wearing a Victoria Cross ribbon on his tunic from the First World War. The officer quizzed Bob about his father who also was a Pilot/Observer in the First World War. Bob felt that the interview was going well, and was informed that he was being put forward for Pilot training. He hesitated for a moment and told the senior officer that he would rather be an Observer/Navigator, due to the previous history of his father wrecking 12 aircraft and his cousin Camac being killed in 1940. After this Bob was sent home for a brief period and on his 18th birthday was called to report to an induction centre at Stratford-on-Avon. The induction centre was a pleasant place and here Bob received his new uniform, and had all the administrative data for his military service completed, all medical checks and jabs provided and of course where he learned to salute. One thing he does remember very well was the FFI inspection that translated means 'Free From Infection'. It was indeed this particular check that has given him a lasting memory of Stratford because it was carried out on the stage of the Shakespeare Memorial Theatre. It meant standing along with the other raw recruits at one side of the stage and on the word of command had to march smartly to the centre of the stage, drop your trousers so that a doctor could examine your genital area and when this was done, pull your trousers back up and march smartly off again. *(So Bob can honestly say that he has appeared on the stage of the Shakespeare Theatre and whatever battle was ahead of him his equipment was in perfect fettle for it.)*

He was then posted to the initial training wing at St Andrews in Scotland, another pleasant area. It was here that he was to learn the rudiments of becoming part of that greatest flying force in the world, the RAF. He was put through the paces of drill, historical background, military law and plenty of PE. What surprised Bob the most here was that around 70% of the course (some 50 of them) were Army. This was because the Air Force was

so short of people, they had trawled the Army and asked for volunteers to re-muster as aircrew and many took the opportunity to do so. Some of these people had already seen service in the Norwegian Campaign and Dunkirk. They were a right motley bunch, including one who went on to be a highly decorated Navigator on Beaufighters with a Strike Wing in the North Sea campaign, winning two DFC's. His name was Robert Irving and had been the music master at Winchester College and was called up. For some unknown reason he had been sent to an obscure gun site emplacement in east Anglia, and when he was offered the opportunity to join the RAF he jumped at it. After the war he became the Director of the New York Ballet Company in America.

Bob said, that the army were a tremendous bunch of lads, and who already knew a lot of the ropes and were very good at looking after one another in the service life. As Bob was the youngest of the motley crew the army took him in hand and taught him everything they knew. It was here at St Andrews that the decision was taken as to what sort of Navigators/Wireless Operators they were going to be. In Bob's case he had been selected for the new Beaufighter aircraft that were being used for anti-shipping strikes in Coastal Command. Out of all Bob's course only one had to drop out. He had been a Sergeant in the Scots Guards and because he could not stand the 'lack' of discipline he decided to leave. When he finished the course at St Andrews, Bob was a lot fitter and now an AC2.

Bob's next posting was to the No 1 Signals School at RAF Cranwell in November 1941, where he was to undergo a full Wireless Operators and Navigation course in addition to the Coastal Command School of General Reconnaissance and hopefully at the end of it become fledged Wireless Operator/Navigator.

He told me that the course was quite an experience. He had his first flight in a De Havilland Dominie on the 26th November 1941, but the bulk of his training took place on Percival Proctors and Avro Ansons. These were light aircraft that did not take kindly to turbulence. At the beginning of the course Bob found communicating through the Morse code very difficult and sometimes sheer agony, but learned to forget about it as dots and dashes and listen to its musical cadence and rhythm it started to make sense.

He found that people with a musical ability managed it quicker. By the 1st December his instructor had assessed him as 'moderate', then 'satisfactory', and later to 'average' with a few 'above the average's thrown in for good measure. At the end of the course his instructor wrote in his logbook, "Above the average," and a "Good operator," and achieved a receiving speed of 25 words a minute.

Time then to move on to the real meat of his training, the navigation course. Bob was posted to No 6 Air Observers Navigation Course at Staverton, which was situated between Gloucester and Cheltenham on the 20th December 1941, and had his first flight on the 24th December 1941 in an Avro Anson. It was Christmas Eve and the weather was bitterly cold. He was billeted in a Nissan hut that had two coke fed stoves and which contributed little heat. It was so cold that he slept in his flying gear and studied in either the NAAFI or at a local pub called the Bat 'e' Ball. The Anson was a well-tried sturdy aircraft, and one of Bob's first duties when they got airborne was to wind up the undercarriage (it was not automatic) and this operation took 120 turns of the winch. The course was very intensive and took in subjects of dead reckoning navigation, compasses, meteorology, maps and charts, instruments, reconnaissance, photography and practical work. The course lasted for just over three months and he was assessed as 'average'. Of the 52 trainees who completed the course, nine were commissioned as Pilot Officers and Bob was fortunate to be one of them at the age of 19. The remainder were promoted to Sergeant.

Bob was then sent home on some leave and in his case to be re-kitted. He acquired his uniform in Austin Reeds in Belfast, and as he was leaving the shop in his brand new uniform with his civilian clothing under both his arms a Warrant Officer entered (who knew from experience that Bob was a 'sprog'), and saluted the dashing new Pilot Officer smartly, and all Bob was able to do was nod in the general direction in some embarrassment. Bob was then posted to No 3 School of General Reconnaissance at Squires Gate, Lytham, St Annes near Blackpool on the 27th April 1942. It was here that he would polish up his skills for the low level flying and anti-shipping attacks that he would be carrying out in the new Beaufighters. Here he learned the skills of astro navigation, dead reckoning over the sea, harbour reconnaissance and aerial photography. Most of his instructors had already completed operational tours in Coastal Command. Bob set out on his first flight on the 2nd May 1942 with several other trainee Navigators, the aircraft was a Blackburn Botha, about which he knew little or nothing, but those deficiencies he was about to discover. However the bus taking them to the aircraft was an old one with sliding doors and on the way out had to make a sharp turn, causing the doors to slid open and a member of his party, a Pilot Officer Browne was thrown out and landed on his head. As a result of this he was concussed and had to be taken to hospital, and they continued with the exercise.

There were five of them on board the Botha, the Pilot was a Pilot Officer Appleford and Bob was designated as the 2nd Navigator. They took off and set a course for the Isle of Man, which was to be the focal point of the navigational exercise, and as they got close. Bob noticed a substantial oil leak coming from the starboard engine. He tapped the Pilot on the shoulder and pointed this out to him, the Pilot immediately saw the problem and shouted that he wanted a course back to base and that he was going to shut down the engine. He advised the rest of the crew that they should prepare for a possible crash landing in the sea. Bob then discovered that the Botha could not maintain height on one engine as it was underpowered,

and it was for this reason (and some others) that it had been withdrawn from operational service. They started to lose height quickly, and on the way back they passed over a convoy heading south down the Irish sea. The Pilot shouted for someone to fire the Verey Pistol. However the crew were unable to find the red cartridge which indicated a distress and informed the Pilot, his reply to this was. "Fire whatever the hell was there." This they did and watched as the convoy spread out below. It was only when the got back and checked the colour codes that they discovered that a particular cartridge meant, "Scatter - There is an enemy submarine in your area." Bob was sure they had knocked several years off the lives of those members of the convoy.

They continued on, losing altitude all the time, until the Blackpool tower came into view. It was a beautiful day and the crew could see the people playing on the beach and it looked as if they might make it, but the Pilot decided it would be too risky and decided to land the aircraft 1/4 mile offshore. They all had been knocked to the floor of the aircraft by the impact and the next thing Bob knew was that he was being used as a stepping stone by some of the others trying to get the upper hatch opened. They all managed to get out through the hatch and discovered that the plane had settled on a sand bank, and although it was below the water the wings were only about a foot under the water. The Pilot had been knocked unconscious by the impact and two of the others had tried to get him ashore. However the strength of the ebb tide prevented them from doing so and they had to let him go. (The Pilot was later picked up by the Lifeboat.) Bob found the dinghy release handle and pulled it but nothing happened. As Bob was a non-swimmer, he decided to inflate his Mae West and head for the shore which he could see in the distance. Fortunately a policeman who was on patrol on the beach and saw Bob, stripped to his long johns, swam out and brought him safely to shore. Bob remembers the people on the beach smiled and applauded this brave airman. He looked around but could see no one else from the crew, and was taken to a local hotel where he had a warm bath and a change of clothing. While he was lying on the bed contemplating these events, the door burst open and the Chief Ground Instructor, who happened to be an Ulsterman came in accompanied by his wife and asked, "Where the bloody hell have you been, everybody including the lifeboat has been looking for you?" Despite Bob's protestations that he was all right the CGI insisted that he had to be medically checked for any other effects, particularly shock, so he drove Bob back to the sick quarters where the others were assembled in various stages of shock with blankets around them and supping hot sweet tea. One was reading a soaking wet birthday card and muttering through his chattering teeth, "Some bloody fine birthday this turned out to be."

Fortunately the doctor was also an Ulsterman who had attended the same school as Bob's cousin Camic Sterling, assured Bob that he was all right to go back to his billet on the understanding that if he felt ill to let him know. Later in the evening Bob went down to the local pub where the plane could be clearly seen out of the window as the tide had receded and when he was asked by the locals did he know anything about it, he admitted that he did. After that the complimentary drinks came rolling up and he eventually retired back to camp in a fairly happy state. However he felt worse for wear, the next morning rising with a massive hangover (delayed shock), and apart from missing that days flying he had no further ill effects. Bob was later told that the Chief Instructor was almost apoplectic that any member of Coastal Command could not swim, rendering necessary swimming instruction to be introduced at the local baths on later courses.

Bob finished the course on the 30th May 1942. The Chief Instructor's remarks in his logbook reads, "Pilot Officer Sterling crash landed on his first air exercise, but only missed one subsequent trip. Very keen and should be an asset to his squadron with experience," signed, Squadron Leader W Stacey. Bob still had one further course to complete before he could be considered for an operational squadron, and that was to take place at No 2 Operational Training Unit at Catfoss in Yorkshire, arriving there on the 1st July 1942, Bob joined 'C' Flight where he continued training in navigation, coding, meteorology, ship recognition, reconnaissance, aircraft recognition and signals, all extremely important in the type of operations which he was about to carry out.

However one of the most important part of this course was to bring together the Navigators and the Pilots who had been trained specifically to fly Beaufighters on Coastal Command operations and train them as crews flying together. Bob said, "On reflection it was very much like a marriage bureau because it was left very much to the individuals to choose their flying partner. Authority did not dictate that 'X' should fly with 'Y' and it merely rubber stamped the decisions made during the course." Bob had already survived one crash, so was fairly cautious about choosing a Pilot, and it was here that he first met David Innes an Australian who was trained in Canada, and who was to become his Pilot for most of his remaining flying career. Bob knew that he and Dave were going to have to work very hard together at becoming a team, because in the coming months and possibly years they would have to depend so much on each other. As they both hit it off, Bob agreed, and never had cause to regret it, and indeed the two have remained life long friends ever since. In early July they joined 'Y' Flight and had their first flight in a Beaufighter together on 27th. Bob completed the course on the 25th August 1942, some nine months after his first flight at Cranwell, and as a result of their co-operation Bob had obtained the highest marks of all his training experience and obtained an 'above the average' assessment as a Wireless Operator/Navigator and was recommended for specialist training in navigation.

Bob and his Pilot were informed that they were destined for the Middle East with a strong possibility of being posted to Malta where they would be joining an anti-shipping squadron. Malta at that time was then in a state of siege as the convoys trying to reach the island were being hammered by the Axis forces. They were immediately sent on embarkation leave, kitted out with their tropical gear and dispatched to Greenock in Scotland. After they were joined by what seemed hundreds of service personnel they set sail for Africa. However when he awoke the next morning and went up on deck, he was astonished to find that they were anchored in Bangor Bay, Northern Ireland and he could pick out all of the local landmarks. After a few days the convoy was completed and they set off around the north coast of Ireland and into the Atlantic. Bob has little recollection of that journey, except that the cramped conditions made life very difficult and despite the fact that strenuous efforts were being made to keep them occupied there really was not a great deal to do. There had been a lot of card playing and gambling which seemed to be the main preoccupation of the many commonwealth personnel they had on board. In due course they arrived at Freetown in West Africa and disembarked to join a smaller ship which was to take them to Takoradi, again in West Africa. At Takoradi they joined an even smaller ship called the Hi-Lee which had a Chinese crew and Scandinavian Officers. Live pigs were kept in cages on deck and when required the cook would emerge with one of the largest cooking knives Bob had ever seen. The cook would then put a sack over the pig's head, and slit its throat. Naturally the pig did not take kindly to this and the whole ceremony was accompanied by squeals and yells of encouragement from the rest of the crew. The ship was infested with giant beetles and Bob was glad when they reached Lagos. Not surprisingly he was taken to hospital were he remained for a couple of days with a stomach bug. After Bob left hospital, he and his pilot were taken back to the docks where they boarded a BOAC Flying Boat that was to fly them to Cairo in Egypt. The flying boat was a Caledonia Class, Registration G-ADHM. Now this was really luxurious travel, they flew across Africa, over the Belgian Congo and up into Cairo. Their journey took them via Libreville, Leopoldville, Coquichatville, Stanleyville, Laropi, Malakal, Khartoum, Wadi Halfa and Cairo. The trip took 14 days and 33 hours flying and they were entertained by the local population at the various night stops, particularly in the Belgian Congo were they saw the local sights and sampled the lethal Congo Beer. Congo Beer was made from onions and had a deceptively light taste just like lemonade but left you with a hell of a hangover.

They arrived in Cairo on 7th November 1942 and were stationed at Almaza. Here they had to wait two weeks on another aircraft coming to take them onto Khartoum and finally Malta. In the intervening period they sampled the local sights of Cairo including the

Pyramids. They even managed to get into a King's tomb, climbing up a rickety old wooden stairway, and in the main chamber of the tomb there was an old Egyptian fortune-teller. They tossed him some coins to see who would be the fortunate one to have his fortune told and Bob lost. The old fortune-teller firstly lit a magnesium flare which cast a blue light around the walls, and he drew some symbols in the sand. He told Bob that he was about to undergo great danger but would survive and would in later life return to Egypt (The first bit was certainly true but not so the second).

However their 'holiday' came to an end on the 23rd November when an aircraft eventually arrived to take them to Khartoum. They took off at 0630 hrs and arrived in Khartoum six hours later. On their arrival they were informed that instead of going to Malta they would pick up their own aircraft and fly it instead to India where they were to help reform 27 Squadron which had been wiped out in the Japanese advance through Java. Bob and Dave picked up their aircraft, a Mk V1 Beaufighter (V1 T5266) at Khartoum but were delayed by the aircraft swinging on landing after an air test and they had to wait until it was repaired. They took off from Khartoum on the 9th December 1942, and eventually reached Kanchapara near Calcutta on 12th January 1943, after a further delay at Karachi due to aircraft trouble. The flight out to India took them via Khartoum (Wadi-Seidna), Aden (Sheik Othman), Salalah, Masira, Karachi, Jodapur, and Allahabad and then into Armada Road where the squadron formed up.

27 Squadron and Wing Commander EJB Nicolson, VC and DFC

"The Whispering Death"

No 27 Squadron badge incorporates an elephant and their motto is "Quam Cellerrime Ad Astra (With All Speed To The Stars)". The squadron adopted the elephant for it's badge during the first world war in order to perpetuate the memory of its first aircraft, the Martinsyde Elephant which the squadron flew in France. No 27 Squadron was formed in Hounslow Middlesex in November 1915, and in March 1916 went to France equipped with the Martinsyde Scouts. The squadron played a very important part in the development of all weather flying and high altitude reconnaissance. The squadron returned to England in January 1920, and in the following April No99 Squadron in India was re-designated to 27 Squadron. Based on the Indis River and equipped with DH9 A's the squadron found itself involved in operations with the tribal troubles of the northwest frontier and again in 1928 during the Afghan troubles. In 1939 it became a Ferry Training Unit (FTU) at Risalpur and in 1941 when the Japanese attacked in the Far East, the squadron was flying Blenheims in Malaya as a Night Fighter Unit. After a short spell of fighting the squadron was almost annihilated, but was reformed in 1942 and became the first squadron to fly the new

Beaufighters, named the 'Whispering Death' by the Japanese. During the war in the Far East it inflicted heavy losses on enemy rail, river, road transport, Troops and installations. In 1943, 27 Squadron had two commanding officers, one was Wing Commander EG Nicolson, VC, who won the DFC during his tour with 27 Squadron, and the second was Wing Commander HC Daish. No 27 Squadron was disbanded in 1946.

It was during his tour in Calcutta that Bob witnessed the affect of the Japanese capture of Burma, (which was the traditional rice producer for India) on the people of Bengal (now Bangladesh). Deprived of food they uprooted themselves and went to Calcutta to live on the streets in hope that they would find food. However as food particularly rice, was scarce they were the last in line, and they died in their thousands. Bob witnessed this himself on the Hooghly Bridge and at Chowringee. More people died in the Bengal famine of 1942 than the total Allied deaths in World War II. Pilot Officer DT Innes RAAF and Pilot Officer RA Sterling, officially took up their posting with the squadron on 27th January 1943, and they knew that the task of taking on the might of the Japanese forces was a daunting one. There were many problems getting the aircraft serviceable, this was mainly with the ammunition belting, (the aircraft cannons were jamming frequently, causing premature explosions in the breeches) and the supply of spares. The actual operational flying was very strenuous as they had to cross mountain ranges between India and Burma, climbing to 10,000ft and then rapidly dropping down to ground level to attack their targets in the river valleys, railways and roads. Operating at low level, meant that if anything happened, one had less than a fifty-fifty chance of getting back to base.

They environment was hostile, the weather was very hot and sticky giving rise to skin complaints such as 'prickly heat' which on occasions could cover the whole body and lead to boils and other types of sores. Various forms of fever were also prevalent, malaria, dengue, sandfly and occasionally blackwater, and dysentery was also a frequent 'visitor'. Once, Bob was stricken down with a fairly severe fever and had to be admitted to hospital. The actual fever was never diagnosed despite several copious blood samples taken but it was put down to suspected malaria. On the 2nd February, Bob and Pilot Officer Innes commenced training on low level attacks, cannon tests and air to ground firing. This was getting them ready for the job in hand. The squadron then moved to Agartala airfield in the Bengal to start operations. One week later they flew their first their first operation against the enemy. It was at 0900 hrs on the morning of the 16th February 1944 when they took off in their MkV1 Beaufighter (EL364) on an offensive sweep on Japanese transport (traffic on railway and aerodromes at Shewbo). They flew in very low and encountered lots of Japanese small fire. The flight time for their first op was 4hrs.10mins.

The following operations were taken from Bob's logbook

18th March 1943: Beau 'T' EL364. to Ramu and Toungoo. Their targets were not sighted but they did manage to 'prang' two steam engines and damage some factories. (Eight Beaufighters took part in this raid.)

26th March 1943: They attacked Toungoo Airfield and damaged and possibly destroyed one T.45. This operation was a particularly hectic one as they were attacked by two Japanese Fighters and lost their No 1 who was Squadron Leader Stratham, (He is buried in Rangoon). Bob's aircraft was hit coming out of the attack, and he thought he had been hit in the leg as he felt warm liquid running down his leg. His first thought was that it was blood, but in fact it was water that was leaking from a small container which was close to his leg and had been hit by small arms fire. (Three Beaufighters took part in this raid.)

4th May 1943: Bob and Dave took off along with another Beaufighter and two Hurricanes to strafe Railways and Factories at Yev-Budalin including its aerodrome.

14th May 1943: Again they took off in pairs to shoot up and patrol South Rampee Islands near Akyab and the Kaladan River to Paletwa. Sampans damaged.

25th June 1943: Took off for Chittagong to strafe concentration of enemy barges.

18th July 1943: Attacked Railway at Legyi to Monyua. Damaged eight engines and two barges.

20th August 1943: Attacked rail and road targets east of Thazi. One water tower and two three-ton lorries damaged.

9th October 1943: Six Beaufighters took off to strafe enemy huts at Hata in Myitha Valley.

17th October 1943: Took off for R Chindwin-Kalewa-Pakokka. Attacked and damaged 280ft steamers and one barge.

21st Nov 1943: Attacked and damaged four locomotives and four light tanks at Railway Thazi and Kyaukse.

2nd Dec 1943: Took off to attack Irrawaddy-Prome-Henzada and Rail to Kyawgin Destroyed one 60ft steamer, damaged one 50ft steamer, one launch, two train ferries, two barges, six sampans, one factory, two water tanks. Fired 994 Rounds of cannon.

16th Dec 1943: Attacked Japanese Communications at Melun-Ketpan-Tauwqui-Gwa Bay-Ramree Island. Damaged one bridge and two ferries. Bullet exploded behind Navigator and punctured water bottle.

Bob and his Pilot Flight Lieutenant Innes carried out their last operation with the squadron was on the 7th March 1944 when they attacked the railway at Monywa-Saigang and Schwebo. At the end of their tour they had carried out 35 of these dangerous low-level attacks on Japanese targets, leading 29 of them. When on operations in Burma Bob and his Pilot always carried a belt of silver coins around their waist and always wore army boots and never flying boots. This was in case they were shot down and captured by the Japanese. They also carried a pistol for this reason. "If you could not stick the pressure, you would shoot yourself. War was a very serious business."

The Squadron Commander Wing Commander James Brindley Nicolson, VC DFC wrote the following remarks in Bob's flying logbook:

Assessment and Ability as Navigator/Wireless Operator: 'Above the average' at Low Level.

Remarks:
A very sound young Navigator has been strongly recommended for a Pilot's course. He and his Pilot have one of the most successful crews on this unit. Thoroughly keen and a first class operational type.

Signed
James B Nicolson
Wing Commander

Wing Commander JB Nicolson had strongly recommended Bob and Dave for the award of the Distinguished Flying Cross, but for one reason or another they were never gazetted. Bob knows from correspondence that Dave had with Nicolson that he was very unhappy with the outcome and tried to have it reviewed but was unsuccessful.

Bob and Dave's end of tour leave was spent in Darjeeling, here they met up with some Americans and were looking forward to a fairly hectic celebration of the completion of their tour of operations. However fate decreed otherwise as Bob was stricken down with a severe fever and had to be admitted to hospital. The actual fever was never diagnosed despite several copious blood samples being taken but put down to suspected malaria. Dave had gone back to the squadron by himself to gather up their belongings and arrange their next posting. He found that Bob had been recommended to go into Burma with the Chindits as an RAF Liaison Officer to arrange supply drops, but when Dave pointed out that Bob was a non-swimmer this was withdrawn, and they were both posted to No 22 Ferry Unit. Bob and Dave tried very hard to stay with the squadron when it moved to Cholavaram, but much to their annoyance this was not to be and they were posted to No 22 Ferry Control that was based at Allahabad in central India. When they left the squadron, out of the original thirty-six aircrew, they were down to eight. Here Bob spent the next year and a half ferrying all types of aircraft with a wide variety of pilots all over the sub-continent. He said it was a 'gypsy' like existence taking strange aircraft to any number of destinations, however his flying experience grew enormously in this period. Most of the flying was long distance with overnight stops and there could be large variations in the weather. One of the more serious hazards involved the cloud conditions caused by the heat and the most dangerous was the cumulo-nimbus cloud. There had been some cases of aircraft actually breaking up in these clouds. Bob and his Pilot always carried a very 'special' little set of documents with them everywhere they flew. These stated that holders of the documents had to be returned to their units after having delivered an aircraft with all possible speed, and everyone had to assist them from the most senior officer to the lowest rank. This included free messing and free transport and sent back with all possible haste, as their duties required them back at base as soon as possible.

There were a number of 'highlights' that happened to Bob and Dave during their tour in India. The first was in June 1944 just before Dave returned to Australia, when he and Bob were asked to undertake a Court of Inquiry into an accident which happened when a 15cwt lorry taking ground crew back to lunch overturned, killing one person and injuring several others. It apparently was due to the governor on the vehicle which restricted the speed at which it could travel becoming stuck and the driver was unable to control it on the turn causing it to overturn. As most of those involved were no longer at Allahabad they were provided with the use of a light aircraft so that they could fly to the various locations and take statements. When they interviewed the driver, an Indian, in hospital, a they asked him why he hadn't tried to immobilise the vehicle by switching off the engine or use the gears, he told them that it would have been of no use because his horoscope for that day was bad.

The next 'highlight' led to another visit to the hospital when he woke up one morning and was violently ill and had a dull ache in his right side. He was driven to an army hospital in the middle of Allahabad, a somewhat ancient building and prepared for an operation. He was met by an Australian who was a Fellow of the Royal College of Surgeons, and after examination, informed Bob that he had an acute appendicitis. The doctor told Bob that he was delighted that he had come to see him as he had not carried out any surgery for the previous six months apart from a circumcision. The anaesthetist, who was a lady army doctor told Bob that the anaesthetic would be ether, and when he was taken into the operating theatre she told him to be good and take deep breaths. This he did until he was nearly early under, when he said to himself, "Why should I be good?" and started to struggle a bit. However she managed to hold the mask over his mouth long enough for him to go under. After the operation when she came to see him and he apologised to her for his behaviour, but she was kind enough to tell him not to worry and to bring his own anaesthetic the next time preferably, "A bottle of Gin."

A more serious 'highlight' was Bob's second crash, when his pilot a Warrant Officer Jones was killed and Bob was seriously injured. The aircraft was only 10 minutes into its flight.

Bob tells the story in his own words

"It was on the morning of the 9th May 1945 when the crash occurred. Warrant Officer Jones and myself were shelled to take a Beaufighter (NE818) to a forward squadron in the Arakan. We had stayed overnight in Calcutta and took off at 0900 hrs from Dum-Dum on what promised to be a normal trip but when we reached about 700ft and I was releasing my seat belt the aircraft almost over turned and when it regained normal level I asked Jonah what was wrong and he told me that the port engine had packed up. As we were fully loaded with fuel and ammunition for operational flying this was serious and I asked him where he was proposing to put down as the conventional wisdom in this situation was to put down somewhere straight ahead. He said that he was going to try and get back on the circuit and land at Dum-Dum. This was unusual to say the least but Jonah was a first class Pilot who had been an instructor and I was confident of his judgement. I strapped myself in and braced myself in case of a crash as Jonah managed to gain sufficient height to regain the circuit and line up with the runway. I thought we were going to make it. However just as we were almost at the aerodrome Jonah shouted, 'Christ, Paddy, there is a Dakota of the Chinese Airways Corporation on the runway,' and was taking off in front of him. *(These were the US Pilots who flew the 'hump' from Calcutta to Chungking.)* He yelled that he was about to try and go round again.

"We were now very low and managed to skim over the hangars at the end of the runway but unfortunately we hit the trees on the perimeter and hit the ground twice. Despite being strapped in I found myself out side, standing upright, and could not hear a thing, with no sign of the aircraft or Jonah. I realised then that I was seriously hurt, and I have very little recollection of what ensued as I was lapsing in and out of consciousness.

"I vaguely remember the ambulance ride into the Army hospital in Calcutta with its sirens screeching. I remember being in an old ward which was dark. The corridor outside I could see was lit up and a nurse was playing a Bing Crosby record 'Silent Night, Holy Night', I thought, 'Christ I've made it.' I can't remember much after that."

A Wing Commander investigator came in to talk to Bob about he crash and at the end of the chat said to Bob, "You are a very lucky sod to be alive, because there is nothing bigger than a three foot square piece of metal left from your Beaufighter." Bob explains, "Apparently I had multiple injuries with my right arm broke, an injured back and damaged vertebra where I had gone through my strap and had other major injuries. Because of the heat they were loath to put me in plaster of paris in case of it causing suppuration and instead kept me sedated to cut down movement. I tried to find out what had happened to Jonah but was fobbed of for about ten days until they told me that he had been killed. He too had been thrown out and had been found wrapped round a tree having been killed instantly. He is buried in a war cemetery in Calcutta. On that very same day, 2nd May 1945, his friend and Commanding Officer from 27 Squadron, Wing Commander Nicolson, VC DFC, was killed not far from were Bob had his accident after the Liberator in which he was flying as an observer caught fire and also crashed."

Another coincidence that happened on the 2nd May, was when another of Bob's friends, a Flight Lieutenant Franklin, who was then No 224 Group Navigation Officer was drowned while swimming at Akayab not far from where Wing Commander Nicolson and Bob had their accidents. Smithy (alias Squadron Leader Lewis G Smith, DFC,DFM) his old Commanding Officer visited Bob in hospital several times and had decided that the best way to speed up his recuperation was to bring him back to Allahabad, which he did. He also managed to get Bob a medical assessment that would allow him to fly an ancient Liberator back to England as Navigator and despite the fact that he was still in bandages the doctors gave him one (admittedly, the lowest one). He took off for England in the Liberator (KH348) leaving Jodhpur at 1025 hrs on the morning of the 28th June 1495. Because of his excitement and anticipation after being away from home for three years, the old Liberator seemed incredibly slow, compelling them to make stops at Karachi, Bahrain, Habbinyah, Cairo, Castel Benito, Elmas and eventually arriving at Holmesley South in the south of England five days and 30hrs.30 mins flying time later on the 3rd July. Bob had not warned his family that he was coming home in case some hitch would occur which would cause some disappointment, and his arrival did cause a little consternation to say the least. During his leave period the Japanese had surrendered and Bob naturally thought that he would not be required to return as he had almost completed his tour. The government however had different ideas as they wanted to keep as many troops in India because of possible trouble arising from the impending independence of India and Pakistan, and were actually sending more troops out there and so Bob was ordered back to India.

He set off from St Mawgan on the 26th August 1945 in a Liberator (KN390) and eventually arrived in Allahabad on the 2nd September where he joined No 36 SP Squadron. Here he flew in Dakotas and Expediters until his last trip, which was on the 12th December 1945 when he flew with a Flight Lieutenant G Taylor from Raipur to Base on a 'Grog Lift'. It had been a memorable trip but it had unsettled him. The war was over and although he still wanted to fly and had been promised a Pilot's course, several matters were exercising his judgement. Firstly was the question of his physical fitness. The last three years with fevers and a crash had taken its toll and he no longer was as fit as he had been and the thought of a desk job depressed him. It was about this time an event occurred which shook the station and the Station Commander to their foundations and that was when a group of RAF nurses arrived to take over the former Army hospital in Allahabad. The Group Captain had never had women on the station in his entire career and soon non-fraternisation arrangements were made to ensure that the socially starved RAF bods were kept apart from the 'new' intake. This went on for a few days when the nurses, who also found the rules restrictive,

introduced a rule themselves that an invitation from them would suffice for access and this changed things completely. Normal fraternisation and co-operation took place and within six months several permanent liaisons were formed which led to marriages. Bob paid tribute to the nurses who carried out such wonderful work in the most difficult circumstances. They operated close to the battle front in such places as Imphal and the Arakan. Some were captured by the Japanese and treated abominably by them. But nothing deterred them and they brought a sense of normality into some of the most distressing situations and they will always remain high in the affections of servicemen.

With the end of the war, thoughts returned to him about what he was going to do when he returned home to Northern Ireland and the concentration on service life diminished. As his demobilisation date approached he was torn by doubts about whether to stay or leave but his mind was finally made up when he thought about the difficulties that would arise when trying to lead a normal life within the confines of service life. Bob therefore decided to leave the Royal Air Force having completed four years and 550 flying hours and he knew that he would miss it. He told me, "There is a freedom about flying which cannot be experienced anywhere else especially in those days. The life is akin to the gypsy existence which had a latent appeal to all of us, the desire to get away from it all and problems which on the ground loom large are minuscule from the air." He left Allahabad to travel by rail to Bombay where he was to embark for the journey home. His great friend 'Smithy' had to drive him to the station as everything was at a standstill because the RAF strike which took place in protest about slow repatriation by the government. He never saw Smithy again although they did exchange correspondence on their return. Smithy graduated as an electrical engineer and returned to the Middle East to work and Bob never heard from him again. Bob said that Smithy had impinged largely on his life. Bob does not remember very much about the voyage back to the UK except that one of the army personnel was stricken down with smallpox and while the ship raced to get him to Aden he died before their arrival and was buried at sea. They entire ships company had to be revaccinated and were monitored on their return to the UK. They entered Liverpool flying the 'Yellow Jack' flag and as outsiders were a little cautious about coming amongst them the customs check was the fastest you have ever seen. Cases were chalked with great speed and they could have taken all the rubies of the east through without hindrance. Bob said, "It is difficult to know what to say about his experience in India. It was a culture shock as one could not be indifferent to it. It either repelled you or fascinated you. It was difficult to come to terms with a situation where the vast majority lived in abject poverty and were more than grateful to perform services for a mere pittance. There was a colossal gap between rich and poor and while one could only marvel at palaces and trappings of the Princes, it was difficult to fully appraise them in the light of a comparison with the hovels in which most of the population lived." Bob overheard one army chap on board the ship remark as they left Bombay, "If that's the biggest jewel in the Empire's crown give me the slums of brum."

And yet Bob said that despite all this many of the people one met were wonderful. One couldn't have served beside better soldiers than the Sikhs and Gurkhas, and in general most of the population lived their lives with a fantastic acceptance that as there was little they could do about it, they might as well get on with it in whatever circumstances arose. It was of no surprise to Bob to learn that despite all the advances that have been made in the west in the standards of living, technology and the arts, India remains much the same as when he was there over 50 years ago. And so after some leave he was eventually demobilised on the 9th June 1946 at a bleak, wind swept God forsaken spot in the middle of nowhere called Hednesford, where he was given a demob suit and gratuity and left to get on with the rest of his life as best he could. Bob found it extremely difficult to come to terms with the process of peace and reconciliation with the former enemy states in the interest of peace and commerce. He was also disappointed how quickly the sacrifice of so many appeared forgotten in the rush for normality and any rewards were so meagre and grudgingly given.

Bob returned to his home to Northern Ireland in June 1946, and because of his harrowing encounters in the Far East and being mentally drained, he found that when he did get home, he just could not get interested in anything. He definitely did not want to go back and study at university for four years as he had already had six years in the war. Bob could not think of anything else, and sometimes he and his friend Dave Russell would meet and walk round Belfast trying to decide on their future. Bob's father was now becoming worried about his son and told him that his brother was going back to Queens University to study Civil Engineering and his pal Dave Russell is going into teaching along with Bob's younger brother. He advised his son to try and get into the Northern Ireland Civil Service until he got himself sorted out. This Bob did and was accepted as a temporary clerk. He later went on into agriculture and was responsible for the buying of cattle in Northern Ireland and paying the farmers as at that time no one else could buy them. He then went into education and was responsible for school planning, building departments, scholarships and teacher training.

A story regarding Bob's time in 'scholarships'

A new grant aided project had just come out which was called State Exhibition and these were for the top 25 pupils who had achieved the Senior Certificate exam (science and literature, etc.). The grants were worth £80 per year. Bob's secretary came into his office one day and said that there was a 'wee boy' out side who wished to see him. Bob asked her to 'wheel him in', he asked the little lad what it was about, and he replied, "The State Exhibition grant." The boy had dark hair and was wearing an Inst blazer and he had won one of these State Exhibitions grants having attained top marks in his Senior Certificate. His mother was a widow and he wanted to know how the money was going to be paid. Bob told him that it would be paid in instalments of two £30 and one £20. After talking to the 'wee boy' for a while, he discovered that his name was Kenneth Percy Bloomfield, Now Sir Kenneth Bloomfield. They still laugh about it today when they meet.

From education he went back into agriculture and was responsible for marketing and later moved into commerce and became a buyer for the industrial development board, which involved buying land. This would be done either by agreement or Bob had the power to take it. He had purchased more land in his first year than had been bought in the previous four years, producing 7,000 jobs a year. Bob was then given the chance of a post at the New York office, but due to another commitment at home his missed the job. He was then asked to go to the Ulster Office in London, which he accepted and became the UK representative for Northern Ireland endeavouring to attract industry to the province. Bob returned to Northern Ireland as a new organisation was being set up called the commissioner for complaints and he was given the job of Principal Officer. He retired from the civil service in the 1980's. He still loves jazz music and is a member of the Aircrew Association.

PILOT OFFICER
RC STERLING
ROYAL AIR FORCE NO. 77981
BOMB AIMER/NAVIGATOR/OBSERVER

KILLED IN ACTION 23RD JULY 1940

Pilot Officer Cemic Sterling, son of Mr & Mrs David C Sterling was born in Belfast on 7th March 1918 and was educated at Dale Holme Private School on the Ballygomartin Road, and later at Royal Belfast Academical Institution where he completed his Junior Certificate. Cemic was very shy but hard working pupil. He played rugby for Inst and was a popular member at Woodvale Cricket and Towns Club.

On leaving school he was employed at the Belfast Harbour Office and was a member of the Royal Air Force Volunteer Reserve. With the outbreak of war he was called to full time service and applied for Pilot training, but unfortunately did not make the grade and was selected for a Navigator/Bomb Aimer course.

After completing his initial training Cemic was posted to No1 Air Observers Navigation School (AONS) at Prestwick on 30th July 1939 to start his navigation training in civilian Fokker aircraft and Avro Anson's. On 13th October 1939 Cemic had his first air experience flight in Fokker G-APZR to Carlisle-Stranraer and back to Prestwick. Flying time 30 minutes. His navigation training continued through until the 10th January 1940 when he passed the course and was assessed as 'above the average'. His total flying time now was 53hrs.50 mins.

Prestwick story

This story was told to me by Bert Smith a very close friend of Cemic's. It was Christmas time in Prestwick when half a dozen of them went for a walk to try and get rid of the heaviness which food and drink brings to one. They ended up at the bridge at Brig-a-Doon. It was covered in hard crisp snow and as they walked across it, it crackled under foot. They all stood on the bridge for a while and one of them said, "We will all make a promise to meet hear after the war to remember this day." By the end of July Cemic was the only one left alive out of the six. Having successfully completed the course at Prestwick he was then posted to No 7 Bombing and Gunnery School at Newton Down near Nottingham on 16th January 1940 to commence his bombing and gunnery

course in Fairey Battles, Westland Wallace and Whitley's. He took off with his instructor Sergeant Joce at 0920 hrs on the 18th for a 50 minute flight in Battle 5001. This flight was uneventful but the second, two hours later with Pilot Officer Stanton in Battle 5021 crash landed due to its undercarriage not coming down. He completed the course on the 15th March 1940 and was awarded his Navigators Brevet and received his commission. Cemic was now Pilot Officer Sterling. Having been fully trained in the art of navigation and bomb aiming Cemic was posted to No 15 OTU at Harwell just south of Oxford. Here he converted onto Wellingtons and had his first flight in a Wimpy on 8th April when he was Assistant Navigator. The course was very intense carrying out long cross-country exercises practically every day and night from 27th March until the course finished on 1st June 1940. On the 2nd June Cemic joined an Armament Flight at Harwell were again the training was very intense carrying out navigation, high level bombing and air firing every day for the next ten days.

On the 10th May 1940 they took off from base at 1025 hrs and shortly afterwards the Skipper encountered a defect with his Wellington (L4231) necessitating him to land at RAF Aldergrove in Northern Ireland. The exact log entry for the 10th shows, "Base to Aldergrove - Landed Aldergrove for repairs and crashed on test."

As Aldergrove was quite near to Cemic's home he asked permission from his Captain, Pilot Officer Clarke to visit his parents. The Skipper inquired from the ground crew how long did they think the repairs would take and was told about two days. The Skipper told Cemic off you go but you had better report back here each day just in case. Cemic scrounged a lift down to Ardoyne and walked through Twadell Avenue where he met his sister Betty. Cemic was able to spend the next four days with his family. He was recalled to Aldergrove on the 14th May and on leaving told his parents that he would ask his Pilot to circle the family home, this his Skipper did and Cemics family was out to watch, little knowing this was to be the last time they would see their son and brother alive.

His total flying hours were now 128hrs.50mins day and 28hrs.35mins night.

Cemic and his new crew Pilot Officer Barrett, Flying Officer Gardiner and Pilot Officer Benny were posted to 149 Squadron at Mildenhall in Suffolk on the 18th June 1940. Their first flight with the squadron was on 20th May 1940 when they took off at 1200 hrs in Wellington R.3163 on a flight test, which lasted for 30 minutes.

149 Squadron was formed at Mildenhall in 1937 as a Night Bomber Unit, and at that time was equipped with Handley Page Heyfords. The squadron was re-equipped with Wellingtons in early 1939, and on 4th September 1939, shared the distinction with No 9 Squadron in making the 2nd bombing raid of the war when they attacked German warships at Brunsbuttel. The squadron played an important part in the early offensive against Germany, Italy and other occupied enemy territory, and took part in the first 1,000 bomber raids. It also took part in the Battle of Hamburg and the famous raid against the German V-weapons experimental station at Peenemunde. Towards the end of the war it dropped food to the starving people of Holland and ferried Prisoners of War back to England from Europe. Among its many decorations won by its members was a Victoria Cross awarded posthumously to Flight Sergeant RH Middleton, RAAF, for his part in a raid on Turin on the night of 28th/29th November 1942. The squadron was disbanded at Gutersloh in Germany in August 1956.

Between 30th June and 29th June 1940 Cemic and his crew carried out air firing-high level bombing-ZZ landings and cross-country pin point exercises.

1st Operation: On the 29th May 1940 Pilot Officer Sterling and his crew took off from Mildenhall at 2155 hrs in Wellington R3613 on their first operation, which was to bomb the enemy lines of communication in Belgium. Flight time 3hrs.25mins.

Pilot Officer Sterling and his crew were sent with a detachment from 149 Squadron to Salon in the south of France on the 15th June 1940 to serve with the Advanced Air Striking Force.

2nd Operation: On the 16th June 1940 they took off at 0610 hrs to bomb Genoa, they saw the target ten miles away but when they arrived over the target they encountered a thunderstorm and returned to Salon with their bombs. Flight time 4hrs.10mins

3rd Operation: On the 17th June 1940 Cemic and his crew took off for home along with the detachment leaving Salon at 1100 hrs. Their route back to the UK took them

via Arles, Castres, Bordeaux, Nantes, St Cast-Bath and Banbury. Flight time 6hrs.25mins.

On the 20th and 21st June they carried out some air tests and air firing over the Wash.

4th Operation: Their fourth operation was on the 25th June to Hamburg to bomb the search lights and anti-aircraft emplacements with 4x250lb bombs and incendiaries. Take off time was 2215 hrs and the flight time was 5hrs.20mins.

5th Operation: Cemic was appointed Squadron Bombing Leader and now took over the role of Nav/Bomb Aimer on each trip.

Their 5th operation was on the 27th June, when they took off at 2235 hrs to bomb the Focke-Wolfe Aircraft Works at Bremen with 8x250lb bombs. They encountered slight anti-aircraft opposition over the target. Flight time was 5hrs.20mins.

6th Operation: On the 29th June 1940 Cemic and his crew took off at 1125 hrs to bomb Germany. His logbook entry reads, "Operations against the enemy, brightening up the Black Forest." Five containers of 25lb incendiaries and 1x250lb light cased bomb. Flight time 6.00hrs.

7th Operation: logbook reads, "21st July 1940, Take off time 2202 hrs (Wellington T2459). Operations against the enemy *(target not mentioned)*. Flight time 6hrs.15mins.

8th and final Operation: They had set out from base at 2115 hrs on the 23rd July 1940, "Operations against the enemy." When over the North Sea they were attacked by two enemy night fighters, one of them was shot down and the second, minutes later met the same fate. It was during this engagement that Cemic received a fatal bullet wound to the back of his neck and died a short time afterwards. He was the only member of the crew who had been injured in the attack. The final entry in his logbook shows, and was probably entered by his Pilot Officer Barrett, "Returned owing to casualty to P/O/ Sterling. Flight time two hours.

Cemic's total flying hours when he was killed was 220hrs.20 mins day and 60hrs.30mins night.

Pilot Officer Sterling's body was returned to his home on the Ballygomartin Road in Northern Ireland and he is buried in Dondonald Cemetery. It was one of the few cases when a coffin was able to be opened when it came home.

The day after Cemic was killed his Commanding Officer Wing Commander Whitley sent a moving letter to Cemic's mother, and it reads:

Royal Air Force
Mildenhall
Bury St. Edmunds
24.7.40

Dear Mrs Sterling,

It is with very deep regret that I have to inform you of the death of your son. Please accept the deepest sympathy of myself and that of all the officers and men of No 149 Squadron in your bereavement.

Your son was a most efficient young officer and full of courage and tremendously keen on his job. To give you some idea of what I thought about him, I selected him amongst all the other observers, some of whom had been here a great deal longer than he had, to become my Squadron Bombing Leader.

He was so popular with his brother officers and we feel his loss most deeply. He had set out on a bombing raid against the enemy on the evening of the 23rd. when over the North Sea they were attacked by two enemy fighters. One of them was shot down and it is believed that the other one met the same fate. It was during the engagement that he received fatal injuries from which he died a short time afterwards. He suffered no pain and he was unconscious from the start.

Please let me know if there is any further information I can give you or any way in which I can be of assistance to you, and I shall be only too pleased to help.

Yours Sincerely
(Signed) JR Whitley
Wing Commander
Commanding 149 Squadron

Woodvale Cricket and Tennis Club cancelled their Saturday match as a mark of respect to a dear friend.

When Cemic was in France he wrote a letter home to his best friend Bert Smith, "I find France quite hectic, and very demanding on my health. I am keen to do well in the Royal Air Force. Thought about nothing else."

FLIGHT SERGEANT
SAMUEL BROWN STEVENSON, DFM
ROYAL AIR FORCE NO. 1980507
NAVIGATOR
NO. 97 (STRAITS SETTLEMENTS) SQUADRON

KILLED IN ACTION 14TH JANUARY 1944

Samuel Brown Stevenson, or 'Brownie' as he was known to his friends, was born in Fahan, County Donegal during 1921, and was the son of Mr SB and Helen Stevenson The family later moved to Knockbreda Park in Belfast.

Samuel was educated at Rossetta Public Elementary School from 1931 until 1934. His higher education was carried out at the Belfast Royal Academical Institute from 1934 until 1939.

Samuel enjoyed sports at Inst excelling at Rugby and Crick, winning the schools Captain Medallion 1936/37 and during the 1938/39 season was captain of the 2nd fifteen and was occasionally asked to play for the 1st's. He also became one of the school's prefects and was also a very keen Youth hosteler, and hill walker, climbing the Mourne Mountains on many occasions. He also enjoyed badminton and tennis and became a member of the Local Defence Force before the war broke out.

Samuel was the nephew of Mr JF Stevenson, who was the Managing Director of Messrs Victor H Robb & Company Ltd, Automobile Engineers of Chichester Street in Belfast. Samuel was also employed with the company until he joined the Royal Air Force at the outbreak of war.

After completing his navigation and flying training he was posted to No 97 Squadron at Bourn. Samuel had completed over 30 operations with 97 Squadron, when sadly on the 14th January 1944 he and most of his crew were killed when a German night fighter shot down their Lancaster Serial No ND421 code OF-S and they crashed on the island of Texel just of the Netherlands coast. Samuel and his crew took off at 1646 hrs from RAF Bourn on a Pathfinder mission to 'Mark' the town of Braunschweig (Brunswick) in Germany. Their bodies were recovered from the wreckage and were laid to rest on the 16th January in Den Burg General Cemetery. The others who died were later washed onto the island, and buried beside their comrades. Flight Sergeant AC East and Flying Officer RR Brown survived the crash and were later captured and became Prisoner's of War.

167 other airmen and soldiers are laid to rest alongside Samuel and his comrades.

496 Lancaster's and two Halifax's took off on that operation. 38 of the Lancaster's were lost, eleven of them were Pathfinders.

The crew of Lancaster ND421 OF-S:

Flight Lieutenant KM Steven, DFC	Killed
Flight Sergeant AC East	Prisoner of War
Flight Sergeant SB Stevenson, DFM	Killed
Flying Officer RR Brown	Prisoner of War
Flight Sergeant WC Gadsbey	Killed
Warrant Officer CJ Skinner	Killed
Sergeant LNJ Laver	Killed

Flight Sergeant Samuel Brown Stevenson was posthumously awarded the Distinguished Flying Medal on the 15th February 1944 for completing many successful operations against the enemy in which he displayed high skill and devotion to duty.

Short history of 97 Pathfinder Squadron
97 Squadron was formed originally at Waddington in Lincolnshire on the 1st December 1917, and served in France equipped with the Handley Page 0/400's in a night bombing role. It was later re-equipped with DH 10's and served in India, operating from Waziristan and flew the first air-mail services from Bombay to Karachi. In 1939 it became a Group Pool Squadron, and in May 1940 became a heavy bomber squadron equipped with Whitley's. In February 1941 the squadron was re-equipped with the Avro Manchester. In June and July 1942 the squadron took part in the 1,000 bomber raids on Cologne, Essen and Bremen. In 1943 it became part of No 8 Pathfinder Group and became a Marker Squadron. In June 1943 it successfully marked the Zeppelin Works at Fredrichshafen and the Italian naval base at Spezia. In 1946 the squadron was re-equipped with the new Avro Lincoln and was finally disbanded in 1955.

FLYING OFFICER
CHARLES FULLERTON STEWART, DFM
ROYAL AIR FORCE NO. 169048
REAR GUNNER
NO. 35 AND 582 (PATHFINDER) SQUADRON

KILLED IN ACTION 29TH AUGUST 1944

Charles Fullerton Stewart, son of William and Sarah Black Stewart, was born in 1923 in Daisy Hill, Clogher in County Fermanagh, and was educated at Elm Park School in Armagh and at St Columba's College in Dublin. His father Major Stewart won the Military Cross during the First World War. Charles became a member of the Home Guard before joining the Royal Air Force in September 1940.

In October 1940 he was posted to the receiving centre at Padgate and then on to an initial training. On completion of his basic training he was then posted to No 8 Air Gunnery School in Scotland where he attended a gunnery course and then went on to an Operational Training Unit. Sometime during 1941 Charles was promoted to Flight Sergeant and posted to No 35 (Madras Presidency) Squadron which was based at Gravely in Huntingdonshire.

In 1941 the squadron was equipped with Handley Page Halifax's, and in July 1941 made its first raid on Berlin. Two Halifax's were despatched, and the pilot of the only one known to have reached and bombed the target, was Flying Officer GL Cheshire, now Group Captain GL Cheshire, VC DSO DFC. No 35 Squadron continued to play a major part in historical bomber command raids, i.e. Le Creusot on 19th/20th June 1943 and Peenemunde on 17th/18th August 1943 and many others. When the Pathfinder Force was formed in August 1942, and No 35 Squadron was one of five squadrons selected to form the nucleus of the force. The first Pathfinder Force attack was against Flensburg on August 18th/19th 1942, and in March 1943 the squadron Halifax's backed by Mosquito's bombed the city of Essen using the target-finding aid 'Oboe'.

Flight Sergeant Stewart was awarded the DFM on May 14th 1943 for gallantry and devotion to duty, and when he was home on leave, was honoured by the people from his home town of Clogher, when over 150 people attended the protestant hall and presented him with a suitably inscribed Gold wrist watch, which he was wearing when he was killed in August 1944. His father Major Stewart, MC and his mother were also present at the presentation. On October 17th 1943 Flight Sergeant Charles Fullerton

Stewart was awarded the Pathfinder Force Badge by the Air Officer Commanding, Pathfinder Force Group Captain DCT Bennett.

In April 1944 Charles Fullerton Stewart was promoted to Flying Officer and posted to No 582 Squadron at Little Staughton near St Neots. The squadron was equipped with Avro Lancaster B1's and 111's and it formed part of the Pathfinder Force (No 8 Group) and during the period April 1944 to April 1945 flew 2,157 sorties against the enemy, dropping over 8,100 tons of bombs. A Victoria Cross was awarded posthumously to Captain EE Swales, South African Air Force for his conspicuous bravery during a raid on Pforzheim on February 23rd/24th 1945. It is worth mentioning that the squadron was also awarded four Distinguished Service Orders, sixty nine Distinguished Flying Crosses and twenty Bars to the DFC and twenty nine Distinguished Flying Medals.

Sadly Flying Officer Charles Fullerton Stewart DFM was killed on an operation to Stettin on 29th August 1944 aged 22. Their aircraft coded '60-'E' (PB202) took off from Little Staughton at 2110 hrs setting a course for Stettin in Poland. It crashed at Vorupor about 19 kilometres west of Thisted. All of the crew are buried in Norre Vorupor Northern Cemetery in Denmark. (Coll. Grave 4. 126).

Flying Officer Charles Fullerton's crew were as follows:

Squadron Leader AL Farrington
Flying Officer GR Bradley, DFM
Flying Officer AC Strout, RCAF
Flying Officer LV Tyndale, RCAF.
Warrant Officer H Silverwood, DFM
Flight Sergeant DEJ Stevens
Flying Officer CF Stewart, DFM

Flying Officer Bradley's first tour had been with 35 Squadron along with Flying Officer Stewart, DFM, Warrant Officer Silverwood had flown in Whitleys with 77 Squadron. Squadron Leader Farringdon was an Australian from Balgowials, Sydney, who had joined the regular Royal Air Force on a short stay service commission in the late 1930's. His brother Hugh Stewart lives in Fivemiletown, County Fermanagh.

THE MARQUESS OF LONDONDERRY, KG MVO

Charles Henry Vane-Tempest-Stewart, Seventh Marquess of Londonderry was born in London on 13th May 1878. He was educated at Eton College and Sandhurst Military College, served in the Royal Horse Guards throughout the First World War and was ADC to Lt. General Sir William Pulteney. He became second in command of his regiment, and was twice mentioned in despatches. Lord Londonderry first came into aviation in 1919 when Churchill made him Under Secretary of State for Air.

In 1920-21 he was made Finance Member of the Air Ministry, being responsible for the demobilisation and reorganisation of the RAF in peacetime, and stabilising what remained.

From 1921 to 1926 he became Leader of the Senate and Minister of Education in Northern Ireland, but returned to England as First Commissioner of Works 1928-29. On November 5th 1931 he was appointed Secretary of State for Air in Mr Ramsey MacDonald's Government, and was responsible for the RAF's number of squadrons and aircraft. From then on he fought strenuously for the re-arming and enlargement of the RAF. He was fully aware at that time to the danger to his country of cutting down the Air Force while other countries were expanding theirs, namely Russia, Germany, and Italy. Lord Londonderry fought hard and alone for the continued existence of the RAF as a military weapon.

As Secretary of State for Air, his first inspection of the RAF, (January 1933) proved a most useful experience. Passing through Italy he met and talked to Mussolini and General Balbo (the Italian Air Minister). Of General Balbo he said that he was quite a striking individual, and had a zest for showmanship. General Balbo had sent a special aircraft to meet Lord Londonderry in Brindisa, which would fly him across the Apennines into Rome Aerodrome. On July 5th 1933 General Balbo, General Pellegrini and General Cagno were guests of Lord and Lady Londonderry at Mount Stewart. They had arrived earlier on Lough Foyle with their armada of twenty-four flying boats enroute to Newfoundland and America.

On February 27th 1933 Lord Londonderry entertained the Duke of York (King George VI) to dinner at Londonderry House, the Heads of the of the RAF and Higher Officials of the Air Ministry. The King always showed a great personal interest in the new Air Force. In December 1933 Lord Londonderry decided to make a second tour of the outlying stations, taking a 16,000-mile flight to India. He left Croydon for Cairo on 13th December 1933, and after a stay in Egypt flew onto Assovan and Wadi Halfa arriving there on 27th December, eventually arriving in Calcutta a few days later. While in Calcutta he stayed with Lord and Lady Willingdon, and visited Peshanar and Quetta on the Frontier.

In September 1934, the Prince of Wales flew to RAF Cranwell to open the new buildings of the RAF. In introducing His Royal Highness, Lord Londonderry referred to the college as the very heart from which the RAF derived its strength and virility. In 1935 Prime Minister Stanley Baldwin made Lord Londonderry Lord Privy Seal and added, "You can remain Leader of the House of Lords for as long you wish." Lord Londonderry's wife, Lady Edith was very much against him accepting this post as she felt it was merely another stage in the plot to push him out of government altogether. However he was persuaded by some of his more intimate political friends to accept the appointment as this would mean that he would remain in the cabinet, and take an 'official' interest in the Air Ministry. On November 7th Lord Londonderry went to Buckingham Palace to deliver up his seals of office and relinquished his post of Lord Privy Seal and the Leader of the House of Lords.

Lord Londonderry later said, "It was with no small personal gratification that, there were no fewer that 70,000 applications and enquiries from men anxious to obtain information as to the terms of enlistment in the RAF. The enthusiasm of 1935, which led to the training of so many airmen, made a not inconsiderable contribution to the defeat of Goering's Luftwaffe in the Battle of Britain in the late summer and early autumn of 1940."

At that time he could have resigned and many in the cabinet would have been relieved as they thought the RAF as a nuisance. However, he decided to stay as he was determined not to abandon his colleagues in the Air Ministry who looked upon him to maintain the fight for the RAF. He had the full confidence of the Air Staff and the RAF. The Prime Minister at that time wrote Lord Londonderry a letter saying, "We all owe you a great deal for your handling of Air Force questions in the House of Lords." After he left the Air Ministry he returned to Northern Ireland were he became Chairman of the Civil Air Guard and played a prominent part in helping the formation of the Air Training Corps in Northern Ireland, eventually becoming its Regional Commandant. He relinquished this position in May 1946.

In 1932 a 50 acre portion of Lord Londonderry's estate which was turned into an airfield was opened on Friday 31st August 1934. The Newtownards Municipal Civil Airport was born. The facilities included a hangar, clubhouse and Air Work Ltd of Heston was contracted to run the airfield. The Duke of Abercorn was invited to make the opening speech. He admired Lord Londonderry very much, but he hated flying and said, "I hope the only time I fly is when I am going to heaven." Dr D'Arcy, Primate of all Ireland gave the Episcopal blessing. The first aircraft which Lord Londonderry flew at Newtownards was an Avro Cadet, and after breaking a bottle of champagne over it, his wife Lady Edith, named it 'Finian the White'. The airfield was one of the first eight civil aeronautical ground radio centres in the British Isles. Having this facility at Newtownards now meant that weather reports and information regarding aircraft movements would be available for the first time. It also meant that the station would be in direct communication with other civil airfields and would also provide wireless directional guidance for aircraft crossing the Irish Sea. At least 15,000 people attended the opening ceremony and short flying display. The flying display was opened by Flight Lieutenant RWE Byrant, the Chief Flying Instructor and Manager of the Aerodrome, who gave a spectactular flying display in Lord Londonderry's newly christened Avro Cadet, 'Finian the White'. A Klemm 'Swallow' was put through its paces by Mr Collins, shortly followed by an Avro Commodore flown by Mr Alan Muntz. Next on the program was an Airspeed Courier flown by Lieutenant Tillard, of RK Dundas Ltd. Mr RAC Brie stole the show with his outstanding display in the Avro Tutor. The show was closed by a single chequered Hawker Fury from 43

(F) Squadron. *(I wonder could the Pilot have been a young Pilot Officer JVC Badger?)*

In March 1935 Lord Londonderry made plans to visit Adolf Hitler in Germany in the interest of peace. He was very well aware of the mass production of the German factories, and that they would very soon be producing the aircraft for the biggest air force in the world. However it was not until 29th January 1936 that was he able to leave for Germany. He was accompanied by his wife, Lady Edith and youngest daughter Lady Mairi. Goring had kindly placed his own private aircraft, a Ju52 at Lord Londonderry's disposal. His visit was entirely private and unofficial, and he was received with the utmost consideration and courtesy. Of Hitler, Lord Londonderry said, "At the beginning of the first of two interviews in February 1936, Hitler was extremely embarrassed and awkward; I even had to take the lead in sitting down, a lead which he followed with gratitude." During his visit he also met Joachim von Ribbentropp (the German Foreign Minister), Field–Marshall Herman Goring (Head of the Luftwaffe and Lord Londonderry's opposite number in the German Government), Dr Joseph Goebbels (the German Propaganda Minister) and General Udet, one of Germany's most famous flying aces. Lord Londonderry returned from Germany far from satisfied, but was confident that there was still time to come to an understanding with Hitler. He said that it was obvious to him that Germany was seeking the friendship of England and hoping that they could reach bilateral agreements on many issues. On September 31st he decided to go again to Germany by air, this time he stayed in Dass, which is about 150 miles from Berlin as he felt it was now even more imperative than ever to reach an understanding with Germany before it was too late.

Lord Londonderry was an excellent pilot himself and had his own grass airstrip just below the Temple in Mount Stewart. He had previously flown many aircraft types but never by himself. So at the age of 54 he decided to qualify as a Pilot. He owned an Avro Cadet, Hornet Moth and a two seater Percival Q6. One of his friends Lord Guinness put him in touch with Captain Valentine Baker (the second partner of Martin Baker ejector seats), who taught him to fly at Heston Aerodrome. Captain Baker had his own methods of teaching and new pupil how to fly. He would deliberately distract their attention while in the air, and immediately invert the aircraft. Then he would shout, "What the hell are you going to do about it?" He also taught Lord Londonderry's daughter Lady Mairi to fly at Heston when she was 11 years of age.

Lady Mairi said laughingly, "I had completed 60 hours dual with him, and that must be a record." Lady Mairi also excelled as an aeroplane model maker and has a wonderful collection consisting of over 200 aircraft.

In 1936 Lord Londonderry was made Honory Air Commodore of 502 (Ulster) Squadron and it is known that he flew with the squadron many times unofficially on operations during the Second World War.

In 1936 Lord Londonderry caused a little bit of a stir when he invited Hitler's Foreign Minister Herr Joachim von Ribbentropp over to Mount Stewart. Ribbentropp's swastika adorned Ju 52 landed at Newtownards airfield in May for a two-day visit. This was the only time a Nazi aircraft ever landed on Northern Ireland's soil. His visit was very much misinterpreted by many, as Lord Londonderry was only trying to seek friendly relations with the Germans. Ribbentropp was no friend of Lord Londonderry. A strong guard of Ulster 'B' Specials were thrown around the aircraft until it left.

Lady Mairi told me that during Ribbentropp's short stay her father had organised for the three Auxiliary Air Squadrons to visit Aldergrove, 602 City of Glasgow, 603 City of Edinburgh and 607 City of Durham. 602 Squadron brought along six of its Hawker Harts and its Commanding Officer, Squadron Leader the Marquess of Clydesdale. *(In April 1933 a page in aviation history was written when Squadron Leader the Marquess of Clydesdale became one of the first men to fly over Mount Everest in a Westland Wallace.)* 603 Squadron's Commanding Officer Squadron Leader Lord GN Douglas-Hamilton attended with some of his new Hawker Harts, and 607 Squadron with eight of its Westland Wapiti's. 607 Squadron's Commanding Officer was Squadron Leader WL Runciman.

On the Saturday, her mother, Lady Edith, had organised a wonderful luncheon party in honour of his visit. The Commanding Officers and Pilots from the three Auxiliary were invited, and seemingly Von Ribbentropp was very impressed with this. He asked, "Does this happen very often?" Lady Edith, quick as flash declared, "Oh yes, and practically every weekend." Of course she was only joking, as she too wanted to impress.

Because Lord Londonderry tried to bring England and Germany closer together and so avoid the catastrophe of war, many people have asserted that he was in favour of dictatorship. They couldn't have been further from the truth. He greatly opposed Communism and Fascism and Nazism. His own personal view had been that we should have tried to get hold of the Germans when they were weak and practically defenceless and mould them into shape, and he recognised that we did not handle Hitler firmly enough in the early stages.

In 1947 while piloting a Glider from Newtownards airfield, Lord Londonderry suffered terrible back injuries when the towrope of the glider broke. The aircraft stalled causing it to crash into the ground. Lady Mairi said, "This really was the beginning of the end for my father, as he suffered a series of strokes after the accident." Lord Londonderry died in February 1949 and is buried in a beautiful part of Mount St known as Tir-Nan-Og. His wife, Lady Edith designed his burial tomb.

I would like very much to thank Lady Mairi Bury for inviting me into her home and relating her father's story to me. I believe the Aviation fraternity in Northern Ireland owes a great deal to her father; no one took a greater interest in aviation in this country in its embryo stage than he did.

WARRANT OFFICER
ALFRED CUMMINGS STOREY
ROYAL AIR FORCE NO. 1086889
ROYAL AIR FORCE BOMBER COMMAND
WIRELESS OPERATOR/AIR GUNNER

Warrant Officer AC Storey was born in Belfast on the 3rd of January 1922 and was educated at Euston Street Public Elementary School. On leaving school he was employed on a relative's farm in County Antrim.

In December 1940 Alfred decided that farming was not for him and went along to the Clifton Street Recruiting Centre to join the RAF. He remembers well when he was a boy in the early 1930's a German Zeppelin airship flying low over Clandeboy Street of Templemore Avenue in Belfast and ever since then had his heart set in joining the Air Force. On the 3rd January that was his 19th birthday he was accepted into the RAF and was posted across to Padgate Receiving Centre. On his arrival he was told that he was to go back home for three months that was due to the extremely bad weather that had caused most of the training schools to close.

It was not long before he received word to report back to Blackpool where he was to receive his basic training, square bashing on the sea front. He remembers being on the beach one morning when a Blackburn Botha and a Boulton Paul Defiant flew very low over them. The Defiant passed close to the Botha and while doing so cut it's tail plane off. The Defiant crashed into the ground and the Botha exploded into the railway station, the death toll was 20 including four civilians. When his basic training was completed Alfred was posted to the No 2 Signals School at Yatesbury to start his wireless training. Yatesbury was the station headquarters for 25 Group and something like 25 other signal stations under its wing. Syroncestor was the main control centre and Yatesbury was No 2. The course concentrated on radio theory and Alf very quickly became proficient in sending and receiving Morse Code achieving a speed of eighteen words a minute plus and mastered the 11082/83 transmitter receiving set. Once these speeds in Morse had been achieved he commenced flying training in Dominie aircraft carrying out exercises such as receiver tuning, DF loops, verification, homing and controlled approaches through cloud. The training course lasted for one month,

he successfully completed on the 24th September 1942 and he was then posted to No 1 Air Gunnery School at Pembrey. Alfred arrived at No 1 AGS Pembrey on the 30th October 1942 to commence his air gunnery course flying in Blenheims. He completed the course successfully on the 6th November 1942 and was promoted to the rank of sergeant. His pass mark was 83% and was assessed in his logbook as, "A very good gunner." He was then transferred to South Kensington Science Museum where he completed a two week course on the 'theory of radar'.

In December 1942 Alf was posted to No 3 Radio School at Prestwick in Scotland were he was to complete his training as a Radio Operator in Coastal Command. The training lasted for two weeks and was carried out in Blackburn Bothas. Just as he was leaving he heard that the school was being moved down to Hooton Park. His next posting was in February 1943 to No 3 OTU (Coastal) at RAF Station Cranwell where he was to commence his operational training flying in Avro Ansons and Wellingtons. He completed the course towards the end of April and along with his new crew were transferred to 172 Squadron at RAF Chivenor in early May and informed that they were being posted overseas. At that time RAF Chivenor was a holding unit for RAF crews who were transferring overseas.

In June 1942 Alf and his crew were sent to RAF Station Lyneham to pick up a brand new Wellington that was heavily loaded with stores and spare parts for the journey overseas. Unfortunately on take-off one of the Wellingtons engines cut causing the aircraft to swing of the runway finally coming to rest just a few feet from a hangar. The aircraft was soon repaired allowing them to return to Chivenor. On the 12th July they took off for Blida (Algeria) via Port Lyautey (French Morroco), Ras-El-Ma where they refuelled for the final stage to Blida and joined 36 Squadron in late July 1943. During the first few weeks in the squadron the crew were kept busy instructing other crews in the use of 'Leigh Lights'. In August they commenced anti-submarine and convoy patrols, which they continued, on these duties until May 1944. The squadron was tasked with maritime reconnaissance and searching for U-boats and later covered convoys in the Anzio landings. In May 1943 the squadron successfully led the Royal Navy to three U-boats, which were eventually sunk.

By this time the squadron were flying six different versions of the Wellington, Mk1C, V111, X, X1, X11 and X111s. As the year progressed the squadron diversified into supply dropping and reconnaissance for 'human torpedoes'. On completion of his tour with the squadron Alf had flown 296hrs.20mins by day and 337hrs.40mins by night. In March 1944 he was promoted to the rank of Flight Sergeant.

On 13th July 1944 Alf was posted down to No 66 Air School at Youngs Field which was near Cape Town in South Africa where he was to become a Staff Wireless Operator Instructor instructing new aircrew. The journey down to South Africa was to take him via Castel Benito, Benina, Cairo West, Almaza, Wadi Halfa, Makakal (Kenya), Juba, Kisumo, Tabora (Tanganyika) Tabora, Ndola, Bullawayo and finally Pretoria. The journey took fifteen days and thirty fours hours flying time. He remained there until the 13th 1945 when he was posted to No 44 Air School at Grahamston South Africa where he continued as an instructor until June 1946.

In June 1946 Alf returned to the UK for demobilisation and returned home to Northern Ireland. He decided to join the Merchant Navy and attended a radio school on the Lisburn Road Belfast and obtained his 'ticket'. On completion of the course he was very disappointed to find out that there were no vacancies. He applied for a position with the Government Communication Headquarters (GCHQ) and was accepted and after training at Bletchley Park returned to work in Northern Ireland. GCHQ had an operation near to Gilnahirk on the outskirts of Belfast. Alf's job was the interception and monitoring signals coming from Eastern Europe. He enjoyed the work tremendously as the job involved him working on his own and in his own style. He remained there until the local station closed in July 1978, he took early retirement and joined the Police Authority in a position that he was already very proficient (Message Switching System) and remained there until his retirement in 1987.

On leaving the Royal Air Force Alf had accumulated a total of 1070hrs.20mins flying time and had flown in Proctor, Dominie, Blenheim, Botha, Anson, Wellington and Dakota's. He is now an active member of the local branch of the Air Crew Association.

SQUADRON LEADER
GEORGE ANTHONY TAYLOR
ROYAL AIR FORCE VOLUNTEER RESERVE NO. 748609
PILOT AND INSTRUCTOR
NO. 266 SQUADRON

Shortly after I started to interview Anthony he took ill and died, and soon after that his wife also passed away. So the following story is based on the brief time that I was able to speak to him. Anthony Taylor, or Tony as he liked to be called, was born in Belfast on the 7th August 1916, and was educated at the Christian Brothers School in Belfast and later at St Malachy's College on the Antrim Road.

Tony sent me a letter a few days before he died. entitled 'Memories of Tony Taylor', and I think it is best if I relate it to you word for word.

Memories of Tony Taylor

"In June 1939 I decided to join the Belfast Branch of Royal Air Force Volunteer Reserve (RAFVR). It was number 24 Elementary and Reserve Flying Training School and flying was done at Sydenham, now called Belfast City Airport.

"I was due to complete my five year apprenticeship in pharmacy in September 1939, having passed my Part One examination in May. I had the opportunity to spend the winter at day classes for Part Two at the Belfast School of Technology. In 1940 I could spend two weeks locums at various seaside resorts in Northern Ireland earning some money. My boss in the pharmacy knew the right people in both these activities. I joined the RAFVR in June 1939 and during my summer holidays that year did some Tiger Moth flying at Sydenham, also there were lectures held at the RAFVR Headquarters in Donegall Place above the Saxone Shoe Shop. We seemed to be playing darts most of the time when at the aerodrome. Later Royal Air Force (RAF) members from Belfast will be shaken when they know the day we joined was with the rank of Leading Aircraft Men, so that if necessary they could be reduced to that rank at once if punishment became necessary. The following day we were promoted to Sergeant, temporarily but very definitely, paid ten shillings and six pence per day. Alternate Fridays we collected nine pounds ten shillings. Dole money in those days was ten shillings per week, yes per week. So we were rich. The 1st September

arrived with our call up papers. These didn't surprise me because we'd had a year of uncertainty with Neville Chamberlain rushing backwards and forwards waving bits of paper about. On Sunday the 3rd September 1939 we gathered (about sixty of us) in the town centre and heard Mr Chamberlain's declaration of war. This did bring us down to earth and thoughts of real war began to worry us. There were words of 'death' and 'wounded' within six months and some very worried people. For people like myself there was the option of staying in the RAF at that moment, or having the call up deferred and being allowed to continue with my studies. I stayed in lucky me. Somebody raised a suggestion about mess funds, a decision was made to spend our funds on lunch in the Grand Central Hotel. I didn't know we had any funds and Sunday was always a miserable day in Northern Ireland in those times and of course there was nowhere else available.

"At lunch I found myself at a table with David Mills, Louis Arneill and Tom Wilson. A round of drinks was ordered (four large brandies), cost ten shillings, by Tom Wilson, who was a real 'Jack-the-Lad' (though nobody had heard the phrase in those days). Another lot was given to the waiter (before the meal), I bought four cigars (ten shillings) and four more brandies were bought. I wasn't sure what to do with the drinks. I was twenty-three years of age and a teetotaller. I was used to being in pubs, because my golfing partner was a drinking man, also many ladies asked the chemist to collect a half bottle for them, for delivery with their medicines. Afterwards I spent a couple of hours walking up and down Royal Avenue trying to sober up. We got our uniforms but still continued to wear our civvies. In between lectures we were free to lounge about, (there were no flying instructors as they had been recalled to their units). We (us four) supplemented our pay by going to the 'dogs' at Dunmore or Celtic Park two or three times a week, and listening to whispers such as the third dog in the fourth race. Some Fridays two or three car loads of us would go to a Chalet south of Newcastle on the Mourne Mountains, where food such as beans or egg on toast was available. We called in at the Donard Hotel for a beer where a poker school would operate from Friday night to Monday morning when we would return to Belfast and have a shave in McMullens barber shop in the Classic Cinema. Our main eating house was the Abercorn (strictly male). On the 29th November 1939 we donned our uniforms and departed Belfast via Larne, Stranraer to Hastings (there were twenty-five of us for drill and lectures)..

"Here are the names I remember: Red Thompson; Tom Davidson; Tom Wilson; Fred Conway; Louis Arneil; Sam Millar; David Mills; Sam Keenan; Tom Condy; Jack Brown; Jack McWaters; Tom Kennedy; Eric Hill; Marcus Beattie; Bill Shimmons; Bill Menary; and Dougie Neal.

"We arrived in Hastings. The Commanding Officer was a Squadron Leader AHH Gillingan, ex Royal Naval Air Service and one of the famous Sussex cricketing family. His number two was Flight Lieutenant Fitz Clarence Langford.

"There were twenty five Irish, twenty five Scots, and six lads from Stoke on the top floor of our hotel, The Alexander. The first three floors were taken up by English lads and the basement was the bar. The other instructors around included Wally Hammond, Leonard Crawley, Don Masbill, Eddie Phillips, Len Harvey and his trainer Snowy Buckingham. It was to be a two month course but we had the bad winter of 1939/40 held up flying training so we did the course a second time, and even a third time and by then we were good (even though I say it myself). Finally came the big day, Red Thompson, Tom Wilson, and I packed our gear and departed Hastings on 27th May 1940 to go to Cambridge (Marshalls Airfield). One special thing about Hastings. On Sunday nights we went to the Whiterock Pavilion to its weekly concert. On Sunday night 17th March 1940 we had a special 'Irish Night' and there, the three of us met three Auxiliary Transport Service (ATS) girls, one of whom has now celebrated fifty two years of married life with me. We did our flying training at Cambridge in Tiger Moths, then on to Sealand for service training on Master 1's. On 17th June 1972, after 17,901 hours and 10 minutes of flying time, I quit."

Here Tony's letter ends.

I spoke to his wife who was able to tell me that he joined 266 Squadron (Spitfires) although he did not fly operationally with the squadron. He then went to RAF Cranwell where he became an Instructor on Oxfords. Then on to Shawbury instructing on Oxfords.

He was then posted out to South Africa as an Instructor on Oxfords, but returned to the UK as the ship that was carrying the Oxfords was sunk by a German U-boat. He was then posted to Brize Norton instructing on 'Horsa Gliders' and finally to Transport Command in Canada.

After the war he joined British Eagle Airlines and retired in 1972.

FLYING OFFICER
WILLIAM HERBERT ROBERT SMITH
ROYAL AIR FORCE NO. 758003
NO. 220 SQUADRON (COASTAL COMMAND)

KILLED IN ACTION 19TH OCTOBER 1941

Flight Sergeant WHR Smith was the son of Mr Charles B Smith of Rossetta Avenue in Belfast. He was born on 15th January 1921, and was educated at Belfast Royal Academical Institute from 1930 until 1933 and Methody College from 1933 until 1937.

He joined the Royal Air Force in 1939/40 and after completing his flying training, joined 200 Squadron which was based at Wick in Scotland, and equipped with the Lockheed Hudson. His aircraft was shot down and he was killed along with his crew somewhere over Norway. He is remembered on the Runnymede Memorial.

SERGEANT
WALTER THOMPSON
ROYAL AIR FORCE NO. 1066764
PILOT
NO. 75, 218 AND 156 SQUADRONS

Walter Thompson was born in Ballymena, County Antrim on 22nd November 1921, the son of Mr John G. and Mrs Thompson who lived in Mount Street in the town. The youngest of a family of seven, he had three brothers (George, Harry and Jim) and three sisters (Hester, Maud and Ethel). His mother died when he was five years of age.

Walter received his early education at Ballymena Primary School, known then as Ballymena Model School, and at thirteen years of age, he progressed to Ballymena Academy. When he was fifteen years of age the family moved to Hillmount Gardens in Finaghy, and, for his final years of grammar school education, Walter attended Methodist College (1937-40). After leaving college in June 1940, Walter joined up to serve his country, and on the 31st August, he enlisted in the Royal Air Force Volunteer Reserve. During the following eleven months he received his initial training and flying instruction to enable him to become a Pilot in Bomber Command. Then between August and November 1941, he was attached to No 21 Operational Training Unit at Moreton in the Marsh, Gloucestershire where he completed his training to prepare him for operational service.

After brief postings to squadrons 218 and 75, Sergeant Pilot Walter Thompson, affectionately known to his colleagues as 'Tommy', was transferred to the newly formed 156 Squadron on March 1st 1942. At that time the squadron was based at Alconbury in Cambridgeshire and was equipped with the Vickers Wellington twin engined bomber, which had an operational a crew of five. On operations during March and April, Walter was 2nd Pilot and then, in early May, he was assigned his own aircraft. As Captain he took part in bombing missions to various targets in France and Germany and, notably he participated in the first and second 1,000 bomber raids on Cologne on 30th/31st May and on Essen on 1st/2nd June respectively.

Having successfully completed 22 sorties, Walter's final mission commenced when he took off, at 2257 hours on the 5th June 1942, in Wellington Mk1C, Serial No DV812, Code GT-?. The members of his crew were Sergeants T Whelan, W Pereira, JC Mason and SA Marr, some of whom had flown with Walter on previous missions. Their target for the attack was Essen, an important industrial city in the Ruhr and location of the giant Krupps armament factory. The squadron's operational record for that evening reports, "Nothing was heard of this aircraft after time of take off." Wellington DV812 failed to return, Walter and the members of his crew were classified as 'missing'. Later this changed to 'killed in action'. En route to the target Walter's aircraft was attacked and shot down by a German night-fighter over Ijsselmeer, formerly known as the Zuider Zee, in the Netherlands. The Pilot of the night fighter, a Dornier 215B, was Hauptmann (Flight Lieutenant) Helmut Lent. Lent, 11./NJG2 became one of the Luftwaffe's leading night fighter aces with 102 kills to his credit and rose to the rank of Oberst, (Group Captain). He was killed in a flying accident in October 1944. The Wellington which had been piloted by Walter crashed into the sea south of Hoorn at 0037 hrs. Some days later the bodies of Walter and two of his crew, Sergeant's Pereira and Marr, were washed ashore. The bodies of Sergeant's Whelan and Mason however, were never found and are remembered on the Runnymede Memorial.

One hundred and eighty aircraft took off that night to bomb Essen, twelve did not return.

Walter is buried at Bergen General Cemetery near Alkmaar and, alongside him lays his comrade Sergeant Marr, his Rear Gunner. Walter's supreme sacrifice is acknowledged locally on War Memorials at Methodist College, Ballymena Academy, Lowe Memorial Presbyterian Church Belfast, and in the Book of Remembrance in St Anne's Cathedral. Belfast.

SQUADRON LEADER
ROBERT WILLIAMSON TURKINGTON, DSO DFC*
ROYAL AIR FORCE NO. 117519
PILOT
NO. 72, 601 AND 241 SQUADRONS

Robert Williamson Turkington was born on the 13th June 1920, of Ulster parentage in the town of Mhow Bandicui which is in Central India. His father was a railway engineer working for the Indian railways. His parents returned home to Northern Ireland when he was very young and settled in their home town of Lurgan in County Armagh. Robert was educated at the Lurgan College where he became head boy and when he left college he decided on an aviation career with Short Brothers in Belfast.

On the 5th November 1940 he went along to the Royal Air Force Recruiting Centre in Clifton Street and volunteered his services as a Pilot.

As Squadron Leader Turkingtons flying logbook is sadly lost I can only give you the information regarding his RAF Career from his record of service and my own research.

On the 5th October 1940 AC2 Turkington was posted to No 3 Reception Centre at Padgate. From Padgate he went to Calshot and then on the 4th January 1941 to No 9 AW. A week later he went No 10 Initial Training Wing. On completion of his initial training he was promoted to LAC and posted overseas to America to train as a Pilot under the Arnold Scheme. He arrived in America on the 16th May 1941 and on the 30th May arrived at a personnel transit centre where he remained until the 9th June. LAC Robert Turkington carried out his pilot training at Arcadia, Gunther Field, Elgin Field and Craig Field. He successfully completed the pilots course at Craig Field on the 18th December 1941 and was presented with his 'Silver' Pilots Wings and promoted to Flight Sergeant.

On the 6th January 1942 he left 31 Personnel Dispatch Centre at Moncton Ontario Canada and arrived back in the UK 18 days later. On his arrival back in the UK he spent almost four months awaiting a posting to No 5 (P) Advanced Flying Unit. From No 5 AFU he went to No 52 Operational Training Unit. On the 14th July 1942 Robert Turkington was promoted to Flying Officer and posted to No 43 (F) Squadron at Tangmere. On the 24th October 1942 he moved with the squadron overseas to North Africa were he joined the eastern Air Command where he

remained for one year. It was with 43 Squadron that he first engaged in combat when on the 10th November 1943 he shot down and destroyed a JU88. He went on to shoot down a further ten enemy aircraft with the squadron. On the 26th October he joined the 324 Wing Training Flight Mediterranean and Middle East Forces until the 12th March 1944 and promoted to Flight Lieutenant. He then joined 72 Squadron at Lago in Southern Italy flying Spitfire 1X and Vc's operationally. In Italy he achieved considerable success in 'slimming' down the enemies numbers.

On the 24th June 1944 he was posted to No 241 Squadron that was now based at Tortoretto in Italy as 'D' Flight Commander again operating in Spitfire 1X and V111's. The squadron by this time was now operating with the American 57th Bomb Wing helping to find shipping targets for them. On the 29th July 1944 his record of service now shows that he was promoted to Squadron Leader and posted to 601 Squadron at Perugia as its Commanding Officer. He remained with 610 Squadron until the 1st February 1945 when he was posted to RHQ Desert Air Force where he liased with the 8th Air Force until the 2nd June 1945 when he returned to 241 Squadron at Treviso as it's Commanding Officer. It is a well documented fact that when Squadron Leader Turkington was awarded the DSO on the 20th April 1945 and was summoned to receive the award at Buckingham Palace. He respectfully wrote a letter to the King explaining that as his squadron was about to be disbanded and that he would like to remain here with his staff and would it be possible to have his DSO sent to him.

Sadly on the 29th July 1945 the day 241 Squadron was disbanded at Treviso in Italy, Squadron Leader Robert Willaimson Turkington, DSO DFC and Bar had just taken off in the last Spitfire to leave when it exploded in mid-air, crashing down on the runway.

Having a full load of fuel his aircraft burnt so intensely it was late in the afternoon before his body could be recovered. (It was rumoured at the time that his aircraft had been sabotaged.)

The official report of the crash is as follows:

Squadron Leader Turkington took off in Spitfire MK 423 on a cross country flight to Naples. His engine was heard to cut-out and he immediately turned to starboard in an attempt to return to the landing strip. The aircraft began to lose height and, suddenly, struck the ground with the nose and starboard wing. It then burst into flames. Flight Lieutenant Jones from 601 Squadron saw the incident from start to finish and stated that Squadron Leader Turkington probably died instantly. His body was recovered later that afternoon, after the heat had subsided.

Paddy' Turkington was one of the most popular men in the Royal Air Force. His officer commanding Group Captain Dundas was on leave at the time (OC 244 Wing) in Naples. He returned for the funeral which was held the following day in Mestre British Military Cemetery.

Squadron Leader Turkington was buried with full Military Honours at Mestre British Military Cemetery in Italy on the 30th July 1945.

On the 18th October 1944 a letter arrived at his mother's house in Lurgan from the town clerks office. It reads as follows:

Dear Mrs Turkington,

At a recent meeting of the Lurgan Urban District Council reference was made to the high honour conferred on your son, Squadron Leader RW.Turkington, on his award of a bar to DFC, and on his promotion to Squadron Leader, for gallantry and distinguished services with the RAF, and I was directed to ask you to be good enough to convey to him the Council's hearty congratulations and best wishes for a safe and speedy return to Civil life.

The Council and the citizens of Lurgan are very proud indeed of the magnificent services being rendered by our young men in the present world conflict and sincerely hope that their efforts will not be in vain.

Yours Sincerely
WR Gracey
Town Clerk

The Turkington family dedicated a beautiful stain glass window in his memory in the Bann Foot Methodist Church. Just before Squadron Leader Turkington's mother died she made it known to the family that she would like to be buried wearing her sons Silver Pilots Wings. Her wishes were carried out. (Mrs Mary Amelia Turkington Died on the 18th December 1962.)

Squadron Leader Robert Williamson Turkington DSO DFC and Bar

His record of Awards:

18th December 1941	Awarded his Flying Badge 'USA Silver Wings'.
25th January 1944	Awarded the Distinguished Flying Cross.
22nd September 1944	Awarded a Bar to the Distinguished Flying Cross.
20th April 1945	Awarded the Distinguished Service Order.

Squadron Leader Turkington had flown 677 operational hours when his first tour ended in January 1944 and completed his second tour on the 24th January 1945. His citation for his DSO reads:

This officer has set a fine example of skill, determination and devotion to duty. He has completed a large number of sorties and much of the success achieved by the squadron can be attributed to this officer's efficiency and resolution. During a sortie in July he destroyed and probably damaged a second aircraft, although only one cannon was functioning in his aircraft. Squadron Leader Turkington is a gallant and inspiring Flight Commander.

Squadron Leader Robert Williamson Turkington, DSO DFC and Bar, his record of enemy aircraft damaged and destroyed:

1943	43 (F) Squadron 'The Fighting Cocks'
10th Nov	Shot down and destroyed a JU88 near Algiers.
27th March	Damaged a He111 off the coast over a convoy.
27th March	Shot down and destroyed a S-79.
13th May	Damaged a RE2001 off the North African Coast.
18th July	Damaged a Bf109 near Syracuse, Augusta.
2nd Nov	Shot down and destroyed a Bf109 over Velmonte.
6th Nov	Shot down and destroyed a Bf109 over Volturno.
10th Nov	Shot down and destroyed a BF109 over Volturno.
11th Nov	Shot down and destroyed a Ju88 over Volturno.
26th Nov	Shot down and destroyed a Ju88 over Capua.
15th Dec	Damaged a FW190 near Cassino.
1944	**241 Squadron**
19th July	Shot down and destroyed a Bf109 near Ancona.
21st July	Shot down and destroyed (2) Bf109s near Ancona.
29th July	Shot down and destroyed (2) Bf109s near Falcona.

What a very sad end for such a gallant Airman.

Authors note

I think it very fitting that I should end this story by adding the poem which Squadron Leader Noel H Corry, DFC AE wrote for this book.

The Royal Air Force Volunteer Reserve

"Young Men, Little more than school boys,
Jousting with the Luftwaffe in the sky
To determine whose turn it is to die, to-day.

If its mine, I'll not have seen the wily one
That came at me from out the sun
And set my world alight.

And then, how shall I fare ?
I trust that you, so very far below,
Will never get to know the way of it".

SQUADRON LEADER
JAMES BROWN WARWICK, DFC
ROYAL AIR FORCE NO. 156612
NO. 49 SQUADRON & 54 BASE CONINGSBY

Squadron Leader James Brown Warwick, DFC was born in Belfast in 1921 at 986 Crumlin Road Ligonel, the house itself is called 'Avonlea' and his sister Elly still lives there today. I had the pleasure of meeting Elly a few years ago and talking to her about her brother's life, and career in the RAF and the events leading up to his untimely death.

Jim was educated at the Boys Model School which at that time was on the Cliftonville Road and at the Oranges Civil Service Academy near Queens University in Belfast. At the age of seventeen he moved to London in late 1938 and in December of the same year joined the Imperial Civil Service and worked in the offices of the Air Ministry in Berkeley Square House. While he was employed at the Air Ministry he met another Ulsterman Mr Tony Smith who has helped me greatly with this story as he kept a day by day diary of those particular days. On the 13th September 1939, ten days after the outbreak of war Jim and Tony left Kings Cross railway station in a special train which took them to Harrogate, to which nearly all the occupants of the Berkeley Square Office had been evacuated, for an indefinite period to escape the expected bombing of London.

When they arrived at Harrogate station they joined a queue and were eventually given a street map and a document which required a Mr Stockman to provide them with bed and breakfast, evening meal and full board at the weekends for 21 shillings a week (£1.10p). It was a cosy three bedroom council house and was home not only to Mr & Mrs Stockman but also their son and daughter. Jim and Tony were left in no doubt that there was one double bed between them. They soon found out that 'doubling up' was the norm and they stayed with the Stockman family until the end of January, by which time they had started earning some overtime and each of them found much better accommodation. The expression 'good friends' had an entirely innocent meaning in those days and before Jim and Tony went their separate ways they spent all their time together at the cinema, theatre, pubs and cycling long distances all over West Riding at the

weekends and even enrolled at the same dancing school. Tony explained that their extravagant lifestyle was financed by the allowances they received for occasionally staying in the office overnight for duty as fire picket or air raid warden and first aid duty.

After Dunkirk, the production departments of the Air Ministry were hived off to become the Ministry of Aircraft Production and at the end of July 1940 the Minister, Lord Beaverbrook decided that they were to return to London, where Jim and Tony worked at ICI House which was on the embankment, near Lambeth Bridge. The Ministry also occupied the adjoining Thames House which had three floors underground, and when the bombing started, rooms in the lowest floor were turned into offices and bedrooms for the Cabinet Ministers and sleeping accommodation for those who were taking turns on duty as firemen, air raid wardens or first aid workers.

Jim met an English girl in 1940, fell in love and got engaged to her on the 27th February 1941, and had a wonderful engagement party for all his friends. Tony remembers well the 17th March 1941 (St Patrick's Day when the Permanent Secretary (Sir Archibald Rowlands) entertained all the ARP workers to sherry in the Minister's conference room and Jim dispensed sprigs of shamrock to everyone including Rowlands. Jim joined the Royal Air Force soon after this, and Tony met him on the 26th December 1941 just before he was being posted to Canada to start his navigational training. From Canada he was posted down to Florida for six months for advanced navigational training.

On his return from Florida he was posted to 1661 Conversion Unit and on the 29th April 1943 he was posted to 49 Squadron which was based at Fiskerton in

Lincolnshire and was equipped with the Avro Lancaster B1's and 3's. Jim completed two operational tours with 49 Squadron.

Here is a list of some of his operations with 49 Squadron:

Date	Target	Remarks
13.6.43	Bocham	Navigation excellent.
15.6.43	Oberhausen	'SBC' Hung up. B/A injured, rear turret fuselage, port tail plane, Perspex above B/A position, and starboard inner engine cowling damaged by fighter. Attack by Me110, aircraft successfully engaged the enemy and saw the port engine burst into flames, side slip and disappeared into cloud below.
13.7.43	Turin	
25.7.43	Hamburg	
26.7.43	Essen	Early return, port Outer and port inner both failed.
28.7.43	Hamburg	
30.7 43	Hamburg	
04.8.43		Promoted to Pilot Officer.
10.8.43	Mannheim	
11.8.43	Nuremberg	
16.8.43	Milan	
18.8.43	Peenemunde	

Authors note on this epic raid

596 aircraft: 324 Lancasters; 218 Halifaxes; and 54 Sterlings made up this special raid which Bomber Command was ordered to carry out against the German research establishment on the Baltic coast where V-2 Rockets were being built and tested. The Pathfinders found Peenemunde without difficulty in the moonlight and the Master Bomber controlled the raid successfully throughout. 560 aircraft dropped nearly 1,800 tons of bombs; 85% of the tonnage was high explosive. The raid set back the V-2 experimental programme by at least two months and reduced the scale of the eventual rocket attack.

Bomber command lost 40 aircraft: 23 Lancasters; 15 Halifaxes; and 2 Stirlings and this was the first night on which the Germans used their new 'Schrage Musik' weapons; these were twin upward firing cannons fitted in the cockpit of Me110's. It is believed that they shot down six of the bombers.

31.8.43	Munchen Gladbach	
01.9.43	Berlin	
04.9.43	Berlin	
07.9.43	Munich	
3.9.43	Hannover	
8.9.43	Hannover	Shot up many night fighter interceptions.
2.10.43	Hegan	
3.10.43	Munich	

5.10.43	Frankfurt	
19.10.43	Hannover	
1.10.43	Leipzig	Early return, crew turned back at Standel with one engine failed and another failing.
19.11.43	Berlin	Navigation excellent. The turrets froze up.
4.11.43	Berlin	Early return. Mid upper turret completely iced up, rear turret 'sluggish' because of icing.

Having completed two tours of operations Jim was posted to Number 1485 Bombing and Gunnery Flight at Bardney on the 14th January 1944, and on the 4th February 1944 he was promoted to Flight Lieutenant. On the 5th February 1944 he was posted to 1661 Heavy Conversion Unit for instructional duties and on the 15th he was awarded the Distinguished Flying Cross (DFC) and promoted to the rank of Squadron Leader.

On the 25th August 1944 Jim was posted to 54 Base at Coningsby for Station Navigational Officer, this meant that he was now "screened off operational duties".

That fateful day and night

Wing Commander Guy Penrose Gibson, VC DSO* DFC* was very discontent with being grounded and in desperation, he turned to the one man above all others whom he felt would understand and he was, 'Bomber Harris'. It was Harris who had been his Group Commander on his first tour of operations, so it was Harris he would go to, to plea to be put back on operations. Harris quite wrongly according to his own admission gave into Gibson's request, yet perhaps the time had come when even such a powerful character as Harris could no longer deny Gibbon his destiny.

So Harris reluctantly agreed that Gibson should fly one more mission, but he gave strict instructions that the target selected for him must be close to Allied lines and not deep into enemy territory. So with this in view Gibson was posted to the Master Bomber team at 54 Base at Coningsby on the 4th August 1944 as Operations Officer.

The raid that was eventually chosen for Gibbon was Munched Gladbach and the adjacent town of Rhedyt which was close to the German border and he was to lead this raid as Master Bomber.

Authors note

It is at this point, before I go any further with this story, that I must point out that there have been many theories about what happened to Wing Commander Guy Gibson and Jim Warwick that fateful night. So what you are about to read has been personally researched by myself.

The aircraft which was chosen for Gibson was to be a Mosquito AZ-E Code KB 267 of 627 Squadron which was based at Woodhall Spa. The raid was to mark and bomb two very important rail lines, one coming from

Aachen to the southwest and the second one coming from Cologne. The two lines met at Rhedyt before running a further two miles north to Munchen Gladbach where they connected with the main route from the Ruhr into Holland. The aiming points were chosen and a force of 220 Lancasters and apportioned equally between them, nine Mosquitoes would mark the targets. Three for aiming points and a tenth, which would be flown by Gibson as the Master Bomber. Blue, red and green markers were to be used by the Mosquito Pathfinders (Gibson was red).

Sometime during the 19th Wing Commander Gibson was told that his Navigator who was picked to go with him was 'not available'. On hearing this he was furious and immediately went to the officer's mess where he met Jim Warwick. How Jim was recruited by Gibson for this operation I do not know. Was it an invitation, nor indeed if it was an invitation. Gibson had no proper authority over any individual aircrew at Coningsby or Woodhall Spa, but as BASO he was Jim's immediate superior. The distinction between an officer's wish and a direct order can be very slender.

Squadron Leader Jim Warwick informed the Wing Commander that he had never flown in a Mosquito before and that he was the Station Navigation Officer and therefore was non-operational. Whatever words were said next between the two officers I do not know except to say that Jim Warwick had to fly with Gibson that night.

(I would like to point out at this time again, that Jim Warwick had never flown in a Mosquito before and Gibson had only flown one for 11hrs.30mins and only in daylight.)

Author's Note:

I have spoken to Warrant Officer Alan B Webb who was the 627 Squadron Engineering Officer on the 19th and who was personally involved with this operation and he kindly gave me these words on what happened.

"I was given the task by Wing Commander Gibson to take Squadron Leader Jim Warwick, DFC out to their aircraft and to give him some instruction on the Mosquito cockpit. I had only met Jim Warwick for about ten minutes and did my best to show around the cockpit and helped him on with his kit. My most vivid memory of him was that he looked like a school boy and as I was 24 at that time he looked to young to be in the Royal Air Force. I remember thinking, "I hope these two know what they are doing with my Mosquito." Jim Warwick told me that he had never seen a Mosquito before never mind flying in one. Perhaps I did not give him adequate instruction, I don't know, but suddenly, I was rudely thrown out of the aircraft by Gibson and Warrant Officers in those days did not argue with bad tempered Wing Commanders.

"Wing Commander Gibson gave brakes 'off' at 1940 hrs and took off for his target and that was the last I saw of both of them. En-route to the target the weather was atrocious, the Lancasters and Mosquitoes encountered electrical storms and thunder clouds which set up terrible turbulence causing the Lancasters to be thrown about all over the sky, causing many of the crews to keep their navigation lights on to avoid collisions.

Flight Lieutenant George Laing, DFC
97 Path Finder Force

On arriving over the target they found it was shrouded in mist and only a church steeple was visible from above. After the first markers were dropped, Wing Commander Gibson dropped into the mist to check where they had fallen, and not being completely satisfied asked for a second lot of markers to be dropped. This was done and for a second time Gibson dropped into the mist to check were they had fallen, but during that time contact was lost. It is not known whether he hit power lines or a rooftop but whatever was the cause of loss of radio contact his aircraft was still able to fly. Whether it was damage sustained here which caused the eventual crash or flak on the way home we shall never know. Twenty minutes after the first markers were dropped on the targets, the last bombs went down on Mucnchen Gladbach and Rheydt. The operation had been a success and the order was given to return home.

But tragedy was about to strike these two brave pilots, while returning home and over the town of Steenbergen, between 0030 hrs and 0045 hrs both engines of their aircraft stopped (according to a Dutch farmer who witnessed the incident). The aircraft crashed into a field near the sea wall. On hearing the loud explosion many of the people of Steenbergen rushed to the scene to see if they could help, but they could do nothing as the Mosquito had nose dived at about 400mph and buried itself 20 feet into the ground. What was left of Wing Commander Gibson was found in the cockpit area of his aircraft while Squadron Leader Warwicks remains were found some 500 yards away close to a farm house gate. Both bodies had been terribly mutilated and were in an unrecognisable state, so much so that the only identification was an identity disc marked JB Warwick and an envelope in one of his tunic pockets addressed to Squadron Leader JB Warwick, DFC Royal Air Force Coningsby. The only clue to the identity of the second member was a tiny white tab sewn onto a charred sock which was written the name Gibson. Their remains were carefully gathered together and placed in single coffin and all their documents which were found in the aircraft where safely hidden in Steenbergen town hall.

The Deputy Lord Mayor of Steenbergen was a very loyal Dutchman and knew the feelings of the towns people towards the Nazis and he decided to give the two heroes a ceremonial burial with a cortege led by the civil defence in uniform. But the local German Commandant on hearing of this plan, next morning ordered the immediate burial of the two airmen. This did not prevent the people of Steenbergen honouring the two crewmen of the Mosquito with a worthy burial. The coffin was placed in funeral car and covered with the flag of the Netherlands and the cortege was followed by the deputy Lord Mayor, a pastor, and a Roman Catholic priest. Wing Commander Guy Penrose Gibson, VC DSO* DFC* and Squadron Leader James Brown Warwick, DFC were buried in the local Roman Catholic Cemetery at Bergen-up-Zoom. Much to the annoyance of the German troops watching, many of the villagers attended the funeral of the two brave aircrew whose lives had been given in the cause of their liberation.

A single white cross marked the joint grave and on it were stencilled the words, 'Squadron Leader JB Warwick DFC. 156612' and underneath were four words, 'and Guy Gibson RAF'.

At the base of the cross two small conifers had been planted and it wasn't until months later, and after Steenbergen had been liberated that the Missing Research and Enquiry Units had confirmed that the unknown airman was none other than Wing Commander Guy Penrose Gibson, VC DSO* DFC*.

Guy Gibson and Jim Warwicks crash has prompted almost as much speculation as the death of Glen Miller and Rudolf Hess. Some theories being muted were sabotage, pilot error, that they were shot down by light flak on the way home. Much later Bomber Harris said; "I believe I know the truth. I'm afraid his Mosquito broke up." In the eyes of many this was an accident waiting to happen. The operation had been organised in a hurry and Gibson and Warwick had been ill prepared. They were flying in an unfamiliar aircraft, more over Jim Warwick as he had never seen a Mosquito before never mind having flown in one and had not flown operationally for months. Both of them were undertaking complicated duties for which they had not rehearsed. The most likely theory for the accident which I have taken from Alan B Webb's book 'At First Sight' and is a factual and anecdotal account of 627 Squadron is that the fuel transfer cocks in a Mosquito were behind the pilots seat and therefore had to be operated by the Navigator in a proper sequence. That night coming back it was dark and remember Jim had had only ten minutes instruction on the cockpit layout by Alan Webb, it is probable that the fuel transfer cocks were mistakenly operated in the wrong sequence causing the aircraft's engines to be starved of fuel. Seemingly the grave lay unattended, overgrown and neglected during the 1960's, until Jan and Connie Van-Den Driesshen came across the grave of these two brave warriors. Ever since then they have cleaned it, and have looked after it at their own expense and they have travelled the 50 mile round trip from their home in Rotterdam once a fortnight for 30 years to look after the grave.

Memorial Service at Steenbergen 19th September 1974

The Royal Air Force Association held a Memorial Service in Steenbergern on the 19th September 1974 to commemorate the 30th Anniversary of the death of Wing Commander Guy Penrose Gibson and Squadron Leader James Brown Warwick.

In attendance were Air Marshal Sir Harold Martin, KCB DSO DFC AFC RAF and also Air Chief Marshal Sir Agustus Walker, GCB CBE DSO AFC MA RAF (Ret).

The Service was conducted by the Reverend AF Vickers, BA DIP TH RAF and also in attendance were the band of the Royal Air Force in Germany and was conducted by Squadron Leader JW Martindale, LRAM ARCM RAF, Director of Music RAF Germany.

The Royal Air Force staged a memorable flypast in honour of the two distinguished flyers and this consisted of the Battle of Britain Memorial Flight Lancaster, an Avro Vulcan from 617 Squadron and a Harvard. A bronze plaque was mounted on the wall at the entrance of the cemetery in memory of Wing Commander Gibson and Squadron Leader James Warwick. Jim's sister Elly was also in attendance at the service and thought it was a very fitting tribute to her brother. When the ceremony was over at the cemetery, the people of Steenbergen also honoured the two airmen by naming two streets after them, one called Warrick Straat and the other Gibson Straat. Both streets are close to where their aircraft crashed. For some reason unknown to me the crash site of Wing Commander Gibson's Mosquito was excavated on the 11th and 12th December 1986, although I think the reason may have been that there was going to be large commercial premises built on top of it. I am in no doubt however that this excavation was done officially with the knowledge of the Air Historical Branch and the British Embassy in The Hague as I have a copy of a letter which was sent to the Historical Branch after the excavation.

The letter reads as follows:

BRITISH EMBASSY
Lange Voorhout 10
2514 Ed The Hague
Tel : 070-645800 Ext 141
14th January 1986

Air Commodore HA Probert, MBE MA RAF (RETD)
Head of the Air Historical Branch (RAF)
Ministry of Defence
Lacon House
Theobalds Road
London WC 1X 8RY

Dear ....,

The purpose of this letter is just to confirm the telephone call which Gerrie Zwanenburg made to you before Christmas. The excavation of the Mosquito took place on the 11th and 12th December and I attended on both these days. It had disintegrated on impact and there had been a very fierce fire. Parts of the cockpit instruments were found as well as one landing wheel and a shattered engine at a depth of about three metres. There was no trace of either aircrew or their clothing.

I hope that we can now consider the matter finally closed.

Yours Sincerely,
....

Propellor memorial

A local Resistance member Albert Postma, had long pondered as to the manner of a more fitting tribute to the two airmen in particular and the Royal Air Force in general for its part in World War Two.

Albert's dream came to fruition on the 7th May 1990 when former members of 106 and 617 Squadron, Path Finderforce and other units of Bomber Command, relatives of Guy Gibson and Jim Warwick. Members of the Royal Netherlands Air Force and many other dignitaries witnessed the joint unveiling of the Memorial by Group Captain Leonard Cheshire, VC DSO DFC and Mr G Van Wijk (Burgomaster of Steenbergen) escorted by Albert Postma, D Jordan, DFM and D Richards both members of 106 Squadron.

The memorial consists of a two metre column of red granite, into opposite sides of the base are inset the squadron crests of 106 and 617 Squadron and fronted by a dedicatory plaque.

The top of the column is surmounted by a propeller of a Lancaster R5697 which was also shot down on the 21st December 1942 on the outskirts of Amsterdam whilst operating with 106 Squadron Syerston when Guy Gibson was the Squadron Commander.

Many organisations and individuals in Holland gave of their time, financial and other support, including a 25,000 Guilder donation from the township of Steenbergen.

Royal Mail Leicester honours Dambusters
9th November 1995

The Royal Mail Leicester has paid tribute to the Dambusters of the RAF's 617 Squadron and the Dutch people by donating a post box to the Cemetery in memory of Wing Commander Guy Gibson and Squadron Leader Jim Warwick. The post box has been specially adapted to house a Book of Remembrance for use by the hundreds of well wishers who make the pilgrimage to Steenbergen every year to pay tribute to the two Airmen. The idea came from a local resident of Hinckley Mr John Reed who approached the Royal Mail in Leicester. John wanted to provide a place for a Book of Remembrance, which would bring a part of England's heritage to Holland to thank the people for looking after these graves.

Nick Edwards, the Royal Mail's area manager for Leicester said: "We are delighted to have been asked to help find a suitable place for a Book of Remembrance for these important graves. The post box was delivered by managers from Royal Mail Leicester and was installed in the cemetery wall at Steenbergen, Holland where the grave has been tended for thirty years by local people Jan and Connie Van-den-Driesschen." Nick Edward also said, "Post boxes are for sending messages and by sending this box to the people of Holland, we are passing on a message of thanks to the Dutch, reminding them that these heroes of World War two will never be forgotten."

There are 30,000 Allied Airmen who were killed during World War two buried in Cemeteries around Holland and looked after by Dutch people.

SQUADRON LEADER
ERIC WATSON
ROYAL AIR FORCE NO. 163102
PILOT
NO. 70, 37, 40, SQUADRONS

From Avro tutor to Tornado

Squadron Leader Eric Watson was born in Aughavilly in the County of Armagh, on the 11th February 1922, and was educated at Aughavilly Public Elementary School. His teacher was a Miss Georgina Baird who was the mother of Mr John Taylor MP. He continued his higher education at the Armagh Royal just before joining the Royal Air Force in 1941.

Eric was 'bitten' by the aviation bug five years earlier, in 1936, when he and his cousin Cecil Keys cycled to RAF Aldergrove on Empire air day. Eric joined the Air Training Corps on the same day, and was taken for an air experience flight with the Station Commander in an Avro 504 N Tutor biplane. He enlisted into the RAFVR through the Air Training Corps in September 1941, and then became a member of the Queens University Air Squadron until he was called to full-time service on the 9th September 1942.

He was sent to the aircrew reception centre in London where he was accepted as aircrew and then told to report to Woolworth's Department Store where he would be kitted out. The MOD had taken over the whole of Woolworth's top floor and used it as a uniform store. Eric was issued with all his aircrew clothing which include a hot weather Topee. He was then posted to an ITW at Blackpool where he completed his basic training. He was billeted out with some of the local landladies, and remembers quite a few humorous stories about them, which he refuses to allow me to print.

On the 13th January 1943, Eric boarded the Liner, Dominion Monarch at Liverpool. He recalls, marching through the streets of Liverpool complete with his kit-bag on his shoulder and wearing his Topee on his head, and a local remarking, "Eh, poor buggers, they're off to Iceland." To him the Topee was a bluff.

Tuesday January 19th: Eric's position on board ship was well forward at 'B' deck, on mess 20, and he soon found a hammock to sleep on.

Wednesday January 20th: The liner sailed from Prince's Wharf in Liverpool at 1015 hrs, and proceeded in convoy. Eric went up on deck, and sighted the Isle of Man at 1500 hrs, Eire at 1630 hrs, and then the County Down coast of Northern Ireland around 1730 hrs.

Thursday 21st January 1943: The coast of Scotland came into view at 0830 hrs, and their was quite a lot of people onboard being sea-sick, which was probably increased by the gunnery practice. The ship dropped anchor off Greenock sometime during the night, and Eric remembers one chap in particular whose home was in sight of the ship, leaning on the rails with tears running down both cheeks.

Friday 22nd January 1943: It was a bitter cold day and the ship was still at anchor. There was not very much to do onboard other than the daily parade at 1030 hrs and the usual emergency boat drills every four hours or so.

Saturday and Sunday 23rd & 24th January 1943: The ship was still at anchor on Saturday, and at 1245 hrs on Sunday the Captain gave the order to weigh anchor, and they sailed from the Clyde at 0115 hrs. As dawn broke the County Antrim Coast was now in view, and the ship entered the Channel between the northern coast of Northern Ireland and Rathlin Island. The Antrim coast remained in view until 0530 hrs, and the sea was getting rougher now as they were in the Atlantic Ocean.

Monday 25th January 1943: The ship ran into a severe Atlantic gale around 1100 hrs, making everyone onboard very ill. The waves were higher than the ship itself, and looked like hills and valleys. Eric said if only the British Isles knew what the Merchant Seamen went through, they would not waste a scrap of food.

Tuesday 26th January 1943: The gale had now subsided, although the sea was still quite turbulent but thankfully getting calmer by the day. A Flying Fortress (B17)p flew low over the ship, no doubt 'shadowing' the convoy for U-boats. The ship was now in the Gap, a dangerous and unprotected area where U-boats would lie and wait for convoys. This necessitated the convoy to make a special zig zag manoeuvre to avoid the threat.

Thursday 28th January 1943: Group Captain's and Officer Commanding's Inspection.

Friday 29th January 1943: The heat was now increasing above and below decks. The ship was having concert tonight with the help of some of the personnel onboard.

Saturday 30th January 1943: Eric had to gargle twice daily with Potassium Permanganate against a particular infection which had broken out on the ship.

Sunday 31st January 1943: A Church service was held today in brilliant sunshine and Eric watched his first flying fish shooting out of the water, it skimmed along one foot above the water for about 30 feet and then disappeared below the waves.

Monday 1st February 1943: He saw the first sign of land at midday, and was told that the ship had been ordered to turn back. It thankfully had been a bluff because of the U-boat menace, which was waging at that time against the convoys. The convoy had a number of escorts, one of which was the aircraft carrier, HMS Argus and she was equipped with Fairey Swordfish Aircraft. Eric recalls on one particular day when a gale was blowing and the Swordfish were coming into land on the carrier, and were just hovering stationary a few feet above the carrier's deck, then would suddenly drop onto it. Seven weeks and five days later they arrived at Dacca in India for re-fuelling, and then sailed on down to Freetown in Sierra Leone, West Africa, and then over the equator where he had the usual service being shaved by Neptune. They eventually arrived in Capetown, South Africa where they spent one day taking on water, fuel and provisions. Their next port of call was Port Elizabeth, before sailing south for the next fourteen days; so far south in fact, they were in amongst huge icebergs. The ship then did a u-turn and headed north again finally docking in Durban. Yes, the famous 'White Lady' was standing at the end of the pier waiting to greet them, and singing her heart out. It had been a long hard journey on the boat, which had taken all of eight weeks with over 7,000 men accommodated in the hold of a refrigerator ship. The personnel were allowed off the ship in relays, and once off, there was a fleet of cars laid on to pick them up and take them to a Woolworth's restaurant where they were to be fed and cleaned up. Eric counted what cash he had left, and decided to order a big steak. When he had finished his meal he called for the waitress and asked for the bill, she said, "There is no charge, as the gentleman sitting over in the corner has paid all the bills." Eric received this type of hospitality no matter where he went.

He was then taken to an ITW at Carewood where he spent the next four months carrying out his basic training. On completion of this he was trained up the Johannesburg and then on to Bulawayo in Rhodesia.

On August 14th 1943 Cadet Eric Watson had arrived at No 27 EFTS at Induna in Southern Rhodesia where he was to start his flying training. The school was equipped with the Tiger Moth, and he had his first air experience flight in Moth (5432) on the 17th August. His instructor was an ex-Battle of Britain Pilot, Warrant Officer Wolstenholme. On the morning of the 11th September 1943 he had his first solo test with Flying Officer Law, 30 minutes later he flew his first solo. He successfully completed the elementary course on the 14th October 1943, having accumulated 73hrs.25mins on Tiger Moths. The EFTS Commanding Officer assessed him, "Ability as Pilot, made a poor start but has made fair progress. Ability as Pilot Navigator, compass courses fair. Map reading good."

The next phase of his flying training took place at No 21 SFTS at Kumalo in Southern Rhodesia. The school was equipped with the Airspeed Oxford. Eric's first flight in the Oxford was on the 23rd November 1943, and his instructor was Warrant Officer Luck. On the 29th October he flew Oxford (V3179) solo for fifteen minutes. When he needed to fly the aircraft on instruments only he had another instructor, a Cadet Frank Ridley, who Eric was to meet again years later at an AOC inspection at RAF Aldergrove. Eric completed the SFTS course on the 21st April 1944 and was awarded his Wings by Group Captain Judges who was an Australian. He was now assessed as having 'average' ability as a Pilot, and 'average' ability as a Pilot Navigator. He now embarked on a journey by train, which would eventually take him to an aircrew reception centre in Cairo, Egypt. En-route through Northern Rhodesia (Zambia) they took the opportunity to play a few games of rugby against any of the local schools that were willing to take them on. Most of the locals were big lads, all over six foot in height and just as wide. Eric said that he and the lads were lucky to get through some of the games without getting hurt.

When they reached the Congo the train ran out of rails, and they then had to board trucks that were to be their means of transport for the next 500 'bumpy' miles to reach the RAF Station at Broken Hill. They then crossed the Congo River on a huge Raft which was powered by a tractor engine, and on again by truck, arriving at Albertville on Lake Tanzania. This was a huge lake that took at least two days to cross and to reach the RAF Station at Kisumu in Kenya, which is just about slap bang on the equator. They spent a few days at Kisumu and then continued their journey northwards passing through Uganda, Ethiopia, Sudan, and finally reaching the No 5 Aircrew Reception Centre in Cairo. After this long and really unnecessary trip it wasn't surprising that Eric was struck down with malaria. Thankfully he fully recovered from the fever, and it never bothered him again during his

RAF career. From Cairo, Eric was transferred to the No 3 Aircrew Reception Centre in Jerusalem and then on the No 77 OTU at Quastina which was just south of Tel Aviv. On the 15th June 1944 he arrived at the No 77 Operational Training Unit which was just south of the city of Tel Aviv in Palestine. Here he was to start his operational training on the Vickers Wellington. Quastina was the main base for operations against Crete and all round that area. After spending the first two weeks in the class room he had his first flight in a Wellington on the 1st August. His instructor for the flight was a Pilot Officer Appleton. Ten days later Eric flew the aircraft himself, and completed his OTU training on the 15th October 1944. He had now accumulated 348hrs.15mins instructional flying, and was assessed as 'proficient' as a Medium Bomber Pilot by the Unit's Flight Commander. On the 21st October he was posted to the No 3 Base Personnel Depot in Naples, Italy, where he remained for the next two weeks awaiting his posting to an operational squadron. The journey from Quastina to the BPC in Naples took him up through Algiers in North Africa and across to Sicily, and then up to Naples in Italy and eventually arriving at No 70 Squadron in Foggia on the 6th November 1944. Eric carried out 18 operations with the squadron and most of them were to Yugoslavia, dropping supplies to the Partisans at Tuzla. He also carried out operations against the Germans when they came through northern Greece, Albania, into Yugoslavia. By the time the Germans reached Trieste there was very few of them left. 70 Squadron had done a magnificent job in knocking out bridge's and railway lines halting the German retreat.

On the 19th November his logbook shows that after successfully bombing a rail and road bridge at Podgoria at low level, he had to pull the aircraft up through the 'Gate', and when they got back to base his aircraft had received 65 major holes in it which was caused by the intense German flak over the target. Every one of the aircrafts petrol tanks had been holed, but it was the 'self sealing system' that had saved their bacon. Eric was also engaged in dropping supplies near to the Russian lines in east Yugoslavia, and had bombed the Casara rail bridge in Italy several times, and the motor transport concentrations at Matesevo and Klopot. On the 13th/14th December 1944, flying his Wellington 'Z' MF423 and carrying troops to Athens he had to force land near Araxos, having to destroy his aircraft on the ground in case it was captured.

The names of his fellow crew members at 70 Squadron were: Flying Officer Boyde; Pilot Officer Clarke; Sergeant Macpherson; Sergeant Hawes; Sergeant Long; Sergeant Ross; Sergeant Conroy; Sergeant Griffin; and Sergeant Parry.

70 Squadron had its own squadron song and it came about when in 1940 it had bombed shipping in Benghazi harbour so many times it was dubbed the 'Mail Run' and the squadron song was given the name, 'The Mail Run

Melody', and it was sung to the tune of Clementine and it went like this:

Down the flights each ruddy morning
same old notice on the flight board
Same old notice on the flight board
Maximum effort guess where to.

Chorus

Seventy Squadron, Seventy Squadron
Though we say it with a sigh
We must do the ruddy Mail Run
Every night until we die.

Take off from the Western Desert
Fuka, 60 or 09 (Sixty or Oh-nine)
Same old Wimpy, same old aircrew
Same old target, same old time.

Chorus again....

In January 1945 Eric and his crew were transferred to No 37 Squadron still at Tortorella in Italy. Here they converted onto the mighty four engined Consolidated Liberator Bomber. Eric and his crew had their first familiarisation flight on the Liberator on the 28th January 1944, and after four more flights he took the controls himself. Eric and his crew carried out 17 operations with the squadron and their first operation was to drop supplies to the Yugoslav Troops near Ballingclay on the 14th February. On the 17th he bombed the dock installations at Trieste in NE Italy. He bombed the marshalling yards in Padua, Verona and Gemona, the Naval Yards at Pola. On the 15th March 1945 he was assessed as 'above the average' as a Heavy Bomber Pilot by the commanding officer of 70 Squadron.

On the 11th March 1945 Eric was transferred to No 40 Squadron at Foggia in Italy as Training Officer and Deputy Flight Commander, where he assisted new pilots to convert onto the Liberator. He also flew on operations with the squadron, the first on the 20th and 21st March to the marshalling yards at Pragersko and Novoska. On the 24th and 31st March he bombed the marshalling yards at Dobova in Yugoslavia and the marshalling yards at Graz in Austria. On April 2nd he attacked and bombed the marshalling yards at Trento in the Brenner Pass in Italy and on the 4th bombed the marshalling yards at Brescia in North Italy.

On April 19th he flew his last operation of the war, which was to bomb the troop concentrations and ammunition dumps at Malabergo in advance of the 8th Army in Italy. Eric's logbook shows that on the 8th May 1945 he transported 1,000 gallons of MT Petrol in 200 cans to Rivolto in Northern Italy. He had now completed 33 operations and had accumulated 549 flying hours. On the 16th May 1945 Eric transported 25 ex Prisoners of War from Pomiglianao in Italy to Westcott in England for repatriation, and another 25 on the 25th May 1945 to Oakley in England. On the 3rd June he repatriated 25 French ex-concentration camp internees from Zemun in Belgrade to Istres in France, and another 25 on the 12th May 1945.

On the 6th October 1945 he was transferred to the No 2 OATS in Malta where he completed a four week commando course. On completion of this course he was sent back to 40 Squadron which had moved to Abu Suir in Egypt. It was now August 1945, and the squadron had now converted to the long-range Lancasters of Tiger Force for the final attack on Japan, which were to be based in Burma. However Tiger Force was not required as the Japanese had surrendered. Eric left 40 Squadron on the 25th January 1946 to take command of No 205 Group Headquarters at Fanara on the Great Bitter Lakes in Egypt. At the end of April 1946 he was informed that his tour in the Middle East had now expired, and that he was being posted back to the UK. Getting back to the UK at that time wasn't all that easy, so he decided to make his way to the No 21 Personnel Transit Centre which was right in the middle of the desert to await an aircraft to get back to England. He waited for the next ten days and no sign of an aircraft. He was by now hot and bothered and totally fed up, so he decided to telephone an 'old friend' ('Square McKee'), who was the AOC of flying training command. He asked Eric what was the problem and how could he help. Eric explained that he was trying to get home for the past ten days and was stuck at this transit camp in the middle of the desert, miles from nowhere. The AOC told Eric to wait and he would see what he could arrange.

True to his word he rang back and told Eric that he had been speaking to the station Senior Air Staff Officer (SASO) who was a Group Captain Laird, and that he had arranged transportation that would take him to Fayid. When he arrived a few days later at Fayid, he was surprised when he was met by his Rear Gunner and Bomb Aimer. He asked, "What the hell is going on?" His Rear Gunner told him that he was to fly a Lancaster back to the UK and that he and the Bomb Aimer were to accompany him. When Eric saw the Lancaster, he found it in a terrible state, filthy and leaking oil from every orifice. Eric managed to get the four Merlins going, but because of the Lancasters poor state he thought it would be better if he flew it over land to Sicily and then north up to Italy, landing at Castel-Benito for re-fuelling. He took off again and set course for the UK landing a few hours later at Black Bushe.

After being debriefed, Eric was given two weeks leave and returned home to Northern Ireland to see his family. On his return from leave he was posted to RAF Station Snaith, which was an aircrew holding unit. He remained here for almost six weeks, and was then posted to a Dakota Squadron at RAF Full Sutton, dropping hay to starving cattle on the moors during that dreadful winter of 1946. In October 1946 the Unit moved to RAF Wymeswold. This was to be Eric's last flying assignment

with the Royal Air Force as he was soon to be demobbed. However 'civvy street' held no appeal for Eric, so he rejoined the RAF in September 1947 on a permanent commission and so followed a new life on the ground.

On rejoining the RAF in September 1947 he was posted to the Headquarters Maintenance Command where he became Aide-de-Camp (ADC) to the Air Officer Commanding No 46 Group, and remained here until June 1952. On the 12th June 1952 he was posted overseas where he commanded the RAF element at the Supreme Headquarters Allied Powers Europe in Paris. Here he acted as Aide-de-Camp to General Gunther who was the Supreme Commander of SHAPE. Four years later, Eric returned to the UK where he worked on the development services for the Blood Hound Missile's. He also worked as Planning Officer in the Headquarters of Signal Command, and with the Inspectorate of Recruiting in London. In 1964 he was posted overseas again to Changi in Singapore, where he worked in the intelligence branch of the Commander-in-Chief's Staff. During the 'confrontation' with Indonesia, he was seconded onto the staff of an American General in the South East Asia Treaty Organisation (SEATO) in Bangkok, Thailand.

RAF Debden and its closure

He then returned to the UK once more and was posted to RAF Waddington in Lincolnshire with the Vulcan Force as station administration officer.

His last command was at RAF Debden where he had been Officer Commanding Administration of the school before taking over the station. It was decided by the powers that be to close RAF Debden, and to mark the closure of this famous war-time Battle of Britain Station, a special ceremony was laid on, with special guests attending. The Guest of Honour was none other that Group Captain Douglas Robert Stewart Bader, DSO & Bar DFC & Bar CBE KBE. Also in attendance were fourteen Four Star Generals from the United States Air Force, who had either served with the famous Eagle Squadrons or been on operations when America joined the conflict. There were also many senior, serving and retired RAF officers who had served on the station during the Second World War.

Some of his last postings included, spells as admin officer with the famous Red Arrows Squadron at the Central Flying School in Little Rissington, and the RAF Police Training School. His final posting before he retired was to Strike Command, when the RAF was about to be re-equipped with the Tornado and Nimrod in the Early Warning Role. Eric became the Project Officer for all supporting services for these aircraft. Eric was now fifty five years of age and still a young man, and was invited to stay on for a further five years to oversee the Tornado's introduction complete. On his 60th birthday he was finally 'eased' from behind his desk at Headquarters Strike Command, having completed forty two years in the finest Air Force in the world, and it was with considerable pride that he received the Queens Commendation for his work and Loyal Service.

Eric had served for 42 years with the Royal Air Force and had completed 30 war-time operations. He had flown a total of 706hrs.10mins in Tiger Moths, Airspeed Oxfords, Vickers Wellingtons, Consolidated Liberators, Lockheed Lodestars, Avro Lancasters and Dakotas.

SERGEANT
THOMAS RONALD AUGUSTA WEST
ROYAL AIR FORCE NO. 1110187
PILOT
NO. 76 SQUADRON

KILLED IN ACTION 2ND JUNE 1942

Thomas Ronald Augusta West was born in 1914, in the town land of Crock na Crieve, Ballinamallard, in County Fermanagh and was educated at Pretora College in Enniskillen. He later studied at the Green Mount Agricultural College in Antrim as his full time employment was working as a farmer.

Thomas joined the Royal Air Force in Belfast sometime between the end of 1939 and the beginning of 1940 he was sent to Canada where he completed his flying training. On completion of his training he was promoted to Sergeant and was awarded his Wings. On his return from Canada towards the end of 1941 he was posted along with his new crew to 76 Squadron which was based at Middleton St. George in County Durham. The squadron at that time was equipped with the Handley Page Halifax.

Short history of 76 Squadron
76 squadron was formed at Rippon in Yorkshire in September 1916 as a Home Defence Squadron. The squadron was disbanded at Tadcaster in June 1919, and reformed at Finningley in April 1937 equipped with the Vickers Wellesley. In 1939 it was re-equipped with the Avro Anson and Handley Page Hampdens and in September 1939 the squadron moved to Upper Heyford where it became the second squadron in the RAF to be equipped with the Handley Page Halifax. The squadron started operations on the 12th/13th June 1941, and two of its better known raids were the attacks on the Tirpitz in Trondheim Fiord and the V2 rocket secret installation site at Peenemunde. From August 1942 until April 1943 the squadron was commanded by Wing Commander GL Cheshire, later to become Group Captain GL Cheshire, VC DSO DFC RAF (retd). When he left the squadron in April 1943 to be posted to Marston Moor one of it's officers wrote in the squadron diary, "What the squadron has lost, Marston Moor will gain." 76 Squadron was disbanded in May 1945. Sergeant West and his crew had completed seven operations over enemy territory before he was killed on an operation to bomb the Krupps Steel

Works in Essen. Sergeant West's first operation of the war was to Dunkirk on 27th/28th April 1942. Two crews were briefed to attack the docks at Dunkirk. They took off from Middleton St George at 2202 hrs in Halifax R9456 (MP-F) on the 27th and arrived over the target at 0022 hrs at 13,700ft. There was no cloud and a bright moon was shining, heavy flak was being fired at the two Halifaxes from all angles, but no damage was done to his aircraft and he returned to base safely at 0154 hrs.

The crew of R9456, (MP-F) were:

Sergeant West
Sergeant Miles
Sergeant Reilly
Sergeant Thompson
Sergeant Van Schank
Sergeant Morton

The second aircraft, W1017 (MP-T) was not so lucky. It was Captained by Sergeant Morris and while he was taking evasive action from the flak over Dunkirk, he lost control and the aircraft crashed. Sergeant PC Morris, Sergeant GA Simpson, Sergeant J Potts and Flight Sergeant G Sanderson were all killed and are buried in Dunkirk Town Cemetery. Pilot Officer WA Trickett RAAF, Pilot Officer WA Shiells, and Sergeant JW Brown were taken prisoner by the Germans.

Sergeant West's second operation was to Hamburg on the 3rd/4th may 1942 in Halifax R9456 (MP-F). They took of from Middleton St George at 2300 hrs on the 3rd May. Seven crews were briefed for this operation and all the aircraft took off. Most of the crews were able to pinpoint themselves close to the target Area, but 10/10th cloud over the Area made it impossible to identify the primary target. Bombs were dropped on ETA (estimated time of arrival) and in one case on a concentration of flak in the target area. Results could not be ascertained owing to the thick cloud. Heavy opposition from flak and searchlights were encountered at the mouth of the Elbe on the way in, but very little over the actual target area. Night-fighters were active however. Visibility above the clouds was very good and several of the crews saw fighters in the vicinity of the target. These were successfully avoided by the crews and no combat was reported. One aircraft R9451 (MP-H) failed to return. It was piloted by a Sergeant JB Williams and his crew when it crashed at Ottensen, 3km SSW of Buxtehude. Sergeant Williams whose parents lived in Vacoas on the island of Mauritius, is buried in Hamburg Cemetery. The rest of those who died have no known graves. Sergeants CR Fox and NH Leeman were taken prisoner by the Germans.

The bomb load for this particular raid was 7 x 4,000lb HE bombs and 2500 x 4lb incendiaries.

The crew of R9456 (MP-F) were:

Sergeant TRA West
Sergeant Willmott
Pilot Officer EA White, RCAF
Sergeant W Charlesworthy
Sergeant JA Oldfield
Sergeant HD Jones
Sergeant Davison

Sergeant West and his crew landed safely at Middleton St George at 0531 hrs.

Sergeant West's third operation was to Stuttgart on the 5th/6th May 1942. Six aircraft from the squadron were allocated for the attack on the Stuttgart docks area, but only five took off, one having to be cancelled owing to technical trouble. The aircraft (MP-C) had to return early with the port outer engine U/S, after jettisoning its bombs in position 51.05N, 02.15E. The remaining four aircraft encountered good weather and successfully reached the target area.

Sergeant West and his crew took off from Middleton St George at 2157 hrs on the 5th May 1942 in Halifax R9456 (MP-F) at 2157 hrs. They obtained good pinpoints en route, but, however at this point, conditions were not so good as a ground haze extended to a considerable height. This obscured the primary target to some extent and only Sergeant West and the crew of (MP-B) were able to positively identify it. They made their attack at 0125 hrs from about 13,000ft. The first load of Incendiaries from (MP-B) were seen burning in a field approximately one and a half miles North East of the aiming point. The second lot were believed to have been dropped in a built up area around the aiming point and a fire giving off a very red glow was started. Sergeant West's incendiaries are believed to have fallen east of the target. No bursts were observed, but fires were seen to start shortly afterwards. Big fires were also reported to the

south east of the target area, by his crew, and on return, saw fires and explosions in approximately position 49.41N, 03.40E at 0257 hrs. The crews of (MP-Y) and (MP-S) did not see the primary target. Bombs from (MP-Y) were released on ETA on a concentration of flak and searchlights. No definite results could be observed by Sergeant West and his crew. Those from (MP-S) are believed to have fallen in a built up area of the target and started a fire with a red blaze. Several other fires, some of which could be seen for 36 miles were burning fiercely in the same area. All of 76 Squadrons aircraft returned safely to base around 0600 hrs.

The bomb load for this operation was 12 x 500 HE bombs and 3240 x 4 and 240 x 30lb incendiaries.

Sergeant West's fourth operation was to St Nazaire on the 22nd/23rd May 1942. Five of 76 Squadrons aircraft were allocated for this operation. He took off from Middleton St George in Halifax W1064 (MP-J) at 2341 hrs. He had a new aircraft and a new crew for this operation who were:

Sergeant P Wright
Sergeant Painter
Pilot Officer Crane
Sergeant WJ Norfolk
Pilot Officer WB Mulligan, RNZAF
Sergeant Killner

This attack on St Nazaire was completely foiled by poor weather conditions, and a heavy ground haze persisted and 8/10 to 10/10th cloud prevented the crews from identifying the target. In each of the five cases the bomb load had to be jettisoned. The outward and return journey proved uneventful for each aircraft, with the exception of aircraft (MP-B) which was piloted by Pilot Officer Norfolk and who had sighted a night-fighter. An Me109 came into attack 'B' from the starboard side, but evasive action was taken by the Captain by diving towards the enemy aircraft, which banked away steeply and passed over 30 yards above the aircraft. The aircraft 'B' was travelling north at the time of the attack (0350 hrs). The night-fighter came from the north east and then departed south east. All of 76 squadrons aircraft arrived safely back at base around 0600 hrs.

The bomb-load for each aircraft was 12 x 500lb bombs with the exception of (MP-J) which carried 11 x 500lb

Sergeant West's fifth operation was to bomb the Gnome et Rhone Works in Paris/Gennevilliers. Sergeant West and his crew took off from Middleton St George at 2358 hrs on the 29th May 1942 in Halifax (MP-J). Seven crews from 76 Squadron were briefed for an attack on the Gnome et Rhone Works in Paris/Gennevilliers. The route he took was via Peterborough, Abingdon, Worthing, St Valery-en-Caux to the target. The weather conditions were moderate. 6/10 to 7/10th cloud was encountered at 6,000 to 7,000ft on the outward trip, but a clear patch over the target area and excellent visibility enabled the crews to obtain pinpoints on the river and docks in the area. Aircraft 'M', 'S', 'Y', 'O', and 'C' were able to identify and attack the primary targets between 0255 hrs and 0310 hrs from heights varying from 4,000ft to 9,000ft. One burst from 'M' was observed as a direct hit on a railway line in the vicinity of the target. Bursts from 'S' and 'C' were seen to be very close to the target. No bursts were observed by the crews of 'Y' and 'O', but both were confident they found the target, search-light glare prevented actual pinpointing of the target. Bomb bursts were observed in the target area. Two aircraft were 'coned' by search-lights which were very active in the target area. Six of the squadron's aircraft landed safely at base on return, including Sergeant West and his crew. Their time of landing is recorded as 0616 hrs. The bomb load for this operation was 14 x 400lb GP bombs.

The aircraft 'G' which was Captained by Pilot Officer Anderson was hit by flak and crashed over the target area. Pilot Officer Anderson and his crew were all killed and are buried in Viroflay New Communal Cemetery in France. His crew were:

Pilot Officer NH Bowack
Flight Sergeant D A Miner
Sergeant W Brown
Sergeant T R Marshall
Sergeant J Nicol
Sergeant M S D Corker

Sergeant West's sixth operation was to Cologne on the 30th/31st May 1942. This was the first of the 1,000 bomber raids on selected targets in Germany, making it the greatest air operation ever carried out. Air Chief Marshal Sir Arthur T 'Bomber' Harris had picked Hamburg for the first 1,000 bomber raid, but as the weather over Germany was unfavourable for the next few days, he decided to send the bombers to his second choice, which was Cologne. 1,047 aircraft were despatched that night and this number was made up of as follows:

1 Group	156 Wellingtons
3 Group	134 Wellingtons, 88 Stirlings
4 Group	131 Halifaxes, 9 Wellingtons, 7 Whitleys
5 Group	73 Lancasters, 46 Manchesters, 34 Hampdens
91 (OTU) Group	236 Wellingtons, 21 Whitleys
92 (OTU) Group	63 Wellingtons, 45 Hampdens
Flying Training Command	4 Wellingtons

Aircraft Totals: 602 Wellingtons; 131 Halifaxes; 88 Stirlings; 79 Hampdens; 73 Lancasters; 46 Manchesters; and 28 Whitleys. The total tonnage of the bombs dropped on Cologne was 1,455 tons, two thirds of this tonnage was incendiaries, and approximately 868 aircraft bombed the main target.

Sergeant West and his crew took off from Middleton St George at 2349 hrs in Halifax R9387 (MP-Z).

Twenty-one crews from 76 Squadron took part on this raid, including two from a conversion flight, and were detailed to attack the German city of Cologne. The route Sergeant West took was from base to Spalding, Southwold, Ouddorp, and Cologne. Owing to a layer of icing conditions at 10,000ft, all aircraft climbed rapidly to 15,000ft and proceeded to the target at this altitude. The average outside temperature was minus 20 degrees centigrade. On arriving at the target, very slight cloud was found, with perfect visibility, although dense smoke rising to 2,000ft from the already burning city prevented pinpointing the actual aiming point. The city itself was clearly identified. All attacks were definitely made on the target area. Owing to the intensity of fires already burning, it was difficult to observe individual bursts and stick incendiaries, but their bombs certainly added to the general conflagration and enlarged the area of destruction. On returning, the glow of the fires could be seen clearly up to 100 miles away. The opposition encountered both in crossing the coast and the heavily defended belt on route was intense at first, but over the target area itself, both searchlights and flak appeared to have already been largely put out of action by previous attacks. Searchlights, however, from the neighbouring districts were still very active. Aircraft 'C' was hit by heavy flak, but fortunately without serious results. No night-fighters were sighted by any of 76 Squadron's aircraft, but several aircraft were seen shot down in flames both on the outward and return journeys. Whether enemy, or friendly fire is not known. There were only two failures from this operation; both jettisoned their bombs in the sea. Flight Sergeant Clack had to return early with oil trouble in his port outer engine, and Sergeant Bingham had problems with the top hatch of his aircraft which flew open and could not be closed.

The RAF casualties were extremely high, 41 aircraft were lost. 29 Wellingtons, four Manchesters, three Halifaxes, two Stirlings, one Hampden, one Lancaster, and one Whitley.

Flying Officer LT Manser from 50 Squadron was awarded the Victoria Cross that night when flying his Avro Manchester on the approach to Cologne, he was caught in a searchlight cone and his aircraft was badly damaged by flak. Pilot Officer Manser held his aircraft steady until his bomb load was released and, despite further damage was able to set a course for home although he and his crew could have safely baled out after leaving the target area. But the Manchester steadily lost height and, when it became obvious that there was no hope of reaching his base, Pilot Officer Manser ordered his crew to bale out. In holding his aircraft steady for the last man to leave, Pilot Officer Manser lost the opportunity to save himself and was killed. He is buried at Heverele War

Cemetery in Belgium. On the evening of the 1st June 1942 Sergeant West and his crew took off as part of the second one thousand bomber raid from Middleton St George. Their target was the Krupps Works in Essen, and they were completely innocent of the fact that this was to be their last raid.

They took off in Halifax W1064 (MP-J) at 2306 hrs from Middleton St George and set their course for Essen in Germany. Twenty four crews were briefed to attack the Krupps Works in the centre of Essen. The total bomb load for 76 Squadrons aircraft was, 62 x 1000lb HE bombs, 16000 x 4lb and 484 x 30 lb incendiaries. A concentration of aircraft from all units made the attack on the city. They followed twenty Wellingtons into the target who were to pinpoint their position and release flares only, so that the entire target area would be lit up for the fire raisers. Crews of aircraft, 'E', 'M', 'A', 'C', 'U', 'T', and 'R' were selected as 'markers', for their particular skills of the 'TR' operations. They were briefed to attack the precise aiming point that was a large shed right in the middle of the Krupps works. The aircraft were to be on the target between 0052 hrs and 0105 hrs and to release their bombs from 16,000ft. The remaining aircraft were detailed to attack from 14,500ft to 15,000ft between 0105 hrs and 0125 hrs. Once again intruder aircraft from Fighter Command were detailed to attack Luftwaffe aerodromes near the route. On the outward flight all aircraft had to fly between two layers of cloud, but the lower layer broke up somewhat near the Dutch coast and except for a thin layer of low cloud over the target, with some breaks, visibility was good. On arrival of the squadrons marker forces, flares were generally found to be west of the aiming point, but precise pinpoints close to and some distance to the east of the target were obtained and bombs dropped definitely on the target. Fires were seen, one or two of which appeared to be 'dummies' over a wide area. In the distance, the red embers of Cologne were clearly seen by most crews. Opposition from flak and searchlights was considerably less that usual in this area, and the searchlight belt itself which was crossed on the route out and back appeared to be non existent. No night fighters were encountered by any of the crews over the target, but one Rear Gunner reported seeing two single engined aircraft (unidentified) near the target. One of them was seen to be hit by flak, explode and fall in flames. Twenty of the squadron's aircraft landed back at base safely. Sergeant West and his crew had successfully bombed their objective and were returning home when the starboard inner engine began to vibrate and within a short time the unit seized. Their aircraft was then attacked by a German night fighter which was piloted by Oberleutnant Heinrich Prinz zu Sayn-Wittgenstein, 111./NJG2. Sergeant West's Halifax staggered and shook from the blows of the exploding cannon shells. In the seconds that followed four of his crew leapt free from the stricken aircraft. Unfortunately Sergeant West and Sergeant Thompson, were not amongst them. Sergeant West's aircraft crashed

at 0145 hrs between Bossut and Grez-Doiceau (Brabant), 15 km South of Leuven, Belgium. Those who died were Sergeant TRA West and Sergeant JR Thompson (Mid-Upper Gunner) and are buried in Heverlee war cemetery in Belgium.

"Sergeant West and Sergeant Thompson (Rear Gunner) were buried by the Germans on a Luftwaffe airfield so as not to allow the civilian population of the occupied country to decorate the airmen's graves." Sergeant's WJ Norfolk and Wright evaded capture under the protective shield of the famous 'Comet Escape Line' over the Pyrenees to Gibraltar. It is known that Sergeant Norfolk evaded the search parties for weeks and eventually received help from the village of Gottechain, and by July he was in Brussels. Pilot Officer WB Mulligan, RNZAF and Sergeant JA Oldfield spent the rest of the war in a German Prisoner of War Camp No (357). The Essen raid had marked the squadrons first 'home-runs' of the war.

On the 14th September 1942 Sergeant WJ Norfolk, now safely home in England wrote a letter to Sergeant West's sister from his home in Elm Field Road, Cleethorpes:

My Dear Mrs West,

It is with regret that I have to write and tell you that your brother Sergeant Ronnie West was killed in action at about 2am on the morning of the 2nd June 1942. I had known your brother for just a month and he was a great friend of mine. I was his engineer and had accompanied him on four trips. On our fourth trip we were returning home when we were attacked by a night fighter. Our aircraft caught fire and your brother gave instructions for us to bale out. As Engineer it was my duty under such circumstances to give the Pilot his parachute and clip it on for him, this I did before clipping on my own. Mr Wright's son was the first to go out followed by the Wireless Operator. The last I saw of your brother, he was sitting in his Pilot's seat holding the aircraft steady with his feet swung round ready to follow me out. Exactly what happened after that is not known, but a few days after that I was given the numbers of the two British Airmen who were buried in the village of Bossut-Gres-Doiceau and your brothers number was one of them. Further information, I haven't got.

Please accept my deepest sympathy on your sad loss.

Yours sincerely
Bill WJ Norfolk

On the 29th June 1947 Bill, now Flight Lieutenant Norfolk wrote a second letter to Sergeant West's sister from the RAF Delegation in Brussels, Belgium.

Dear Miss West,

Three weeks ago I was posted from the Ministry to the Delegation, unfortunately my stay in Belgium will not be long as everything is closing down just as quickly as things can be done, and I expect to leave towards the end of the month (July).

One of the first things that I did on arriving here was to go to the cemetery where your brother was buried to get some photographs for you. As you may already know, your brother's grave has been moved into a large British Military Cemetery. When the Germans originally buried English airmen they usually positioned their graves so that the civilians of the Occupied Country couldn't decorate the graves with flowers, and Ron was eventually buried on a German airfield. Now, the Ministry Research Branch are establishing the identities of all airmen, and re-interring them in large cemeteries, in Heverlee near Louvain, there are 800 graves, most of them English airmen, and as you will see from the enclosed photographs Ron is lying next to his Mid-Upper Gunner Sergeant Thompson. I am enclosing the negatives, as I have copies of the photos. Perhaps,

you have the address of Sergeant Thompson's next of kin, and I wonder if you would mind sending these on to his people, the photo of his grave. I must confess that I have never written to his people, and in my travels up and down I didn't know where to post it.

I hope that your sister and family are very well, also your mother and father. Kind regards and best wishes.

Yours Sincerely
Bill

We Shall Remember Them.

FLIGHT SERGEANT
GEORGE WILSON
ROYAL AIR FORCE NO. 522964
AIR GUNNER
NO. 156 SQUADRON

George Wilson was born in 48 Frederick St, Newtownards on the 2nd August 1916. Flight Sergeant Wilson was a Rear Gunner on board Lancaster JA681 GT- of 156 Squadron, then based at Warboys in Huntingdonshire.

The crew of JA681 was:

Flying Officer MD Shanahan, RAAF	Captain
Flight Lieutenant HM Stafford, RAAF	Navigator
Warrant Officer JC Collins, RAAF	Wireless Operator
Sergeant T Hoyle, RAF	Flight Engineer
Sergeant NH Denyer, RAAF	Bomb Aimer
Flight Sergeant G Wilson, RAF	**Air Gunner**
Warrant Officer DL Dodds, RAAF	Air Gunner

(Warrant Officer Collins from Western Australia was a champion surfer.)

Flight Sergeant Wilson's aircraft took off from its base at 1948 hrs on the 3rd September 1943, to attack Berlin. Nothing was heard from the aircraft after take off. There has never been any trace of a crash site or any graves associated with JA681, it is assumed that all were lost and like many other Royal Air Force aircraft crashed into the sea, and was lost with all of its crew. As Sergeant George Wilson has no known grave, his name along with the rest of his crew are commemorated on the Air Forces Memorial at Runnymede near Windsor. (Sergeant G Wilson on Panel No 140). This Memorial is dedicated to all Royal Air Force and Allied airmen who lost their lives whilst flying with the RAF in North West and Central Europe

Berlin 3/4th September 1943

On the night of the 3rd/4th September 1943 316 Lancasters and four Mosquitoes took off from various RAF Stations in England to bomb Germany's capital Berlin. The Mosquitoes were to act as 'spoof' markers just outside Berlin to attract German night fighters away from the main force. 22 Lancasters were lost during the raid, almost 7% of the Lancaster force.

130 aircrew were killed, 110 were taken Prisoners of War and two were interned in Sweden and one managed to get back to England. 965 tons of bombs, 583 high explosives and 382 incendiaries were dropped on Berlin that night.

Short History of 156 Squadron, Pathfinder Squadron

156 Squadron was formed in October 1918 and was disbanded in November of the same year without having become operational. It was reformed in February 1942 at Alconbury in Huntingdonshire, and was equipped with the Vickers Wellington and operated with No 3 Group. When the Pathfinder Force was formed in August 1942, 156 squadron was selected to form the nucleus of the new force. During its operational career it dropped over 16,000 tons of bombs and lost 45 Wellingtons and 117 Lancasters.

When 156 Squadron had finished operations, it marked the dropping zones at Rotterdam and The Hague for the bombers to drop food supplies to the starving Dutch people and also brought back ex Prisoners of War from Belgium and Italy to England. When the squadron was disbanded in September 1945 its crews had been awarded 22 Distinguished Service Orders and one Bar to the DSO, 296 Distinguished Flying Cross's and 22 Bars to the DFC's, five Conspicuous Gallantry Medals (Flying), 110 Distinguished Flying Medals, and one Bar to the DFM and one British Empire Medal.

SERGEANT
SAMUEL WILSON
ROYAL AIR FORCE NO. 947285
AIR GUNNER
NO. 203 SQUADRON

Samuel Wilson was born in Ballymoney, County Antrim, on February 22nd 1917, and was educated at the Vow National School. On leaving school he entered employment with the Home and Colonial grocery chain, and in 1939 he was promoted to the position of charge hand of their Bradbury Place store in Belfast. He volunteered for the Royal Air Force on the outbreak of war in 1939 and graduated on the 148th Course of basic training at RAF Uxbridge in August 1940.

He was then transferred to guard a dummy airdrome at Balfen, near Beccles, which was bombed twice during his time there. From there he was posted to an Air Gunnery School at Driffield in Yorkshire for gunnery training. After surviving the heavy bombing of Driffield he was posted to South Africa where he completed an air gunnery course in Capetown. In mid 1941 Sergeant Wilson was posted to No 203 Squadron in Kabrit, Egypt, where the squadron was equipped with the Bristol Blenheim Mk 1V's. In April 1941 the squadron was sent to Crete, where for a week, it helped to protect the evacuation of troops out of Greece. The squadron had a difficult time in Crete, losing eight of its fourteen aircraft. Sometime during the desert battle Sergeant Wilson had to bale out of his Blenheim over Tobruk, and was captured by the Italians. He was released the next day when his captors surrendered to the Australians.

Between February 1942 and October 1943 the squadron was equipped with various types of aircraft, i.e. Lockheed Hudson 11/111's, Martin Maryland 11's, Martin Baltimore 1,11,111 & 111a's, carrying out anti-shipping and convoy escort patrols. In 1943 the squadron was re-equipped with Vickers Wellington X111's and transferred to India where it carried out anti-shipping sorties. Sergeant Wilson was a Rear Gunner on these Wellingtons and was credited with three kills. two Fiat MC200's and one Me 109F, plus quite a few 'half' kills. Sergeant Wilson was later seconded to the United States Air Force in Tunisia where he became a Gunner on Liberators. When he asked the Squadron Commanding Officer at what angle do the bombardment squadron harmonise their guns, he was told, "Hell son, we don't 'harmonise' our guns we just fill the sky full of lead." Shortly after that, 203 Squadron ended up escorting three surviving American aircraft home from their first operation. Next day they asked the RAF for guidance on gun harmonising and formation defence. Sergeant Wilson was shot down a second time off the coast of Italy when they were carrying out a shipping strike. He sustained a broken leg and shrapnel wounds, and managed to survive three days in a survival raft. He was eventually picked up by an Air Sea Rescue squadron from Malta and then hospitalised in Palestine.

Once he had recovered from his wounds he was posted back to the United Kingdom and then to RAF Annaloo in County Londonderry in 1945.

This was a very handy posting for him as it was less that thirty miles from his home. Sergeant Wilson was demobbed in early 1946. He then returned to the grocery trade, and in 1967 opened his own supermarket.

Sadly he died of a heart attack on 28th September 1980 and is buried in Drumreagh Presbyterian Burying Ground.

PILOT OFFICER
JOHN DAVID WRIGHT
ROYAL AIR FORCE NO. 65591
PILOT
NO. 7 SQUADRON

KILLED IN ACTION 25TH AUGUST 1941

John David Wright was born in 1919, and was the son of Robert and Jane Wright of Hillcrest, The Square, Hillsborough, County Down, and he was educated at Friends School in Lisburn. His contemporaries recall that he excelled in every sport. He played cricket for his school, and was a member of the Downshire team which won the Football Cup in 1939.

He was also a founder member of Downshire Tennis Club and played for Dromore Rugby Club in the year when they won both the Harden Cup and the Towns Cup. He sang in the choir of Hillsborough Parish Church and was a member of the church youth club.

When he had finished his education he was employed in the Northern Ireland Ministry of Commerce. In June 1940 he decided to join the Royal Air Force and volunteered as aircrew. He left home on the 24th June and sailed to England that night, arriving the next day at RAF Padgate, near Warrington. Later in 1940 he was in a group of aircrew trainees who were photographed at St John's College in Cambridge, which probably was used as an initial training wing.

David's 1941 diary reveals that from January 1st until 30th April he was attending lectures and receiving flying instruction at RAF Kidlington, near Oxford.

His diary shows that he clearly revelled in the art of flying:

January 1st   Flew first solo in Oxford. Two very good landings.

January 11th   Had great time this morning low flying. Had controls and thoroughly enjoyed hopping trees, etc. at about 160/180mph. Instructor pleased but warned me against low flying solo.

January 16th   Had a great time doing steep or climbing turns at 10,000ft. Dived with engines off from 6,000ft and, with difficulty, pulled out at 1,000ft. Felt reckless after that little thrill but restrained myself.

March 4th   Had some take-offs under hood. Night flying after ten o'clock. Really enjoyed it and made three good landings. In bed at 2.00am.

April 10th   Did my Pilots badge test in the afternoon. Good show. Went up above the clouds and had great fun playing in their valleys.

April 19th   In evening went to Woodsock with JS to arrange for course celebration.

April 21st   Solo formation and Chief Flying Instructors Test.

April 24th   Evening course 'do'.

April 25th   Rose feeling none to good. Flew for an hour at 11.00am. In good form. Did 300 on the clock.

April 30th   Went to Flight for last time.

On the completion of his flying training David was given ten days leave and returned home to Hillsborough on 3rd May 1941 to spend some time with his parents and friends.

In a letter from Kiddlington on 18th April 1941 John had written to his mother that he had passed his Wings exam, ("I should have told you this some time ago but forgot. We are not, however, allowed to wear our wings until we leave this station.")

But, although there is mention of an armaments exam, there is no reference in the diary to any exam results or Wings Parade or the notification that he was to be commissioned.

David was still at home on May 10th but there is no further diary entries until July 8th, when he wrote, "Little flying in afternoon." On July 9th he wrote, "Finished off

Flying," and on July 11th, "Terrific rush getting clearance chits signed. Stan arranged for us to get down by ATA transport. Arrived at Prestwick 4.30 pm and at Stranraer at 7.30 for 2 am boat," all of which, and the, "Kitbag arrived from Lossie," on 8th August suggest that after his previous home visit he had gone direct to RAF Lossiemouth, which at that time accommodated No 20 Operational Training Unit for night bomber training on Wellingtons and Ansons. Under the plan 'Banquet' the unit would have had a defensive role in the event of an invasion of Scotland.

On 16th July 1941 he joined No 7 Squadron at Oakington, near Cambridge. No 7 Squadron was formed at Farnborough in Hampshire in may 1914, under Major JM Salmond (later Marshal of the Royal Air Force, Sir John Salmond). The squadron took part in the Battles of Loos, the Somme and Arras flying RE 8's. It was disbanded at Farnborough in September 1919. In June 1923 it was reformed at Bircham Newton as a heavy bomber unit and when the Second World War broke out it was training crews to operational standard at Doncaster. More than 580 decorations were awarded to No 7 Squadron during the Second World War. After the war it was equipped with the Vickers valiant, the first of the four-jet V-bombers. In July 1941 David's diary shows that he was posted to Wyton, near Huntingdon, where he spent a week flying Wellingtons and practising night landings on the 'Link Trainer'.

He returned to Oakington on 28th July and had his first experience of landing a Short Stirling. After only two more circuits on 29th July, when he achieved, "A perfect three pointer," and twenty minutes of low flying practice on 2nd August, he wrote, "In evening I got a chance to go to Berlin. Had a great trip and encountered quite a lot of flak on the way over. Terrific searchlights in Berlin. Had no oxygen during the whole flight, although at 20,000ft for two hours." The flight lasted seven hours and the Captain was Flying Officer Blunden. On 5th August he recorded, "Flew in morning with Blacklock; now in his crew. In afternoon went to intelligence block. Had trip to Karlsruhe. Arrived there about 0030 hrs after a quiet trip but some slight opposition and held in searchlight for half a minute. 1st back." That flight, with Blacklock as captain, lasted 5hrs.35mins. On 7th August, again with Blacklock on a flight lasting 3hrs.50mins, "Went to Essen (Krupps). Had a good trip across. Wizard night. Followed by enemy aircraft but they did not attack."

In the early hours on 12th August David was suffering severe stomach pain and was seen by a doctor, who suspected appendicitis. Although he felt fit again about three days later, he was not permitted to fly again until the 18th August, when he was first pilot during a 2hrs.35mins, "Height test and George bombing procedure. Indulged in a little low-flying and got some twigs in the cowling of the starboard inner engine." On 19th August, "Ops night with Blunden to Kiel. Not very exciting. Did not see target and returned with load." The

duration of that operation was not recorded in his diary.

The final entry in David's diary was for August 21st: "Left 1200 to go to Lossie. Artificial horizon went u/s in cloud and engines cut but finally arrived OK." In a letter to his mother on 23rd August 1941 he wrote: "I flew up to Lossiemouth with my crew a few days ago and caused quite a stir, as it was the first time the type of plane I fly (Short Stirling) had landed there. I met most of my old friends and spent a very pleasant hour with them." On 26th August 1941 his parents received a telegram from the Commanding Officer at Oakington; "Deeply regret to inform you that your son Pilot Officer JD Wright 89594 missing from air operation on 25th/26th stop letter follows stop any further information received will be immediately communicated to you." They heard nothing further for some five months until, in January 1942, the Air Ministry notified them that the Red Cross Society had learned from Sergeant DA Lloyd, the Wireless Operator, who was a prisoner of war in Germany,

David's parents were informed that their son's plane had crashed and that he and the other five crew members had been killed and were buried at Trier in Germany, close to the border with Luxembourg.

Their first letter that Mr and Mrs Wright wrote to Mrs Dorothy Lloyd, his wife, was necessarily sent to the Air Ministry for forwarding but thereafter they corresponded directly with her and with the mother of the First Pilot, Kenneth Blunden, and they sent food and cigarettes to Sergeant Lloyd. With remarkable compassion, they refrained from seeking his account of how their son had died, believing that a response to such a request might bring retribution upon him. Sixteen months later after suffering a stroke, Mr Wright died on 6th June 1944 (D-Day), the very day on which Allied land forces gained a foothold in France. Mrs Wright died in March 1947 and thus neither she nor her husband ever knew exactly where their son was buried or the state of his grave, and it is by no means certain that she ever knew how her son died.

In early 1947, Mrs Blunden contacted the clergyman at Aach near Trier, who expressed his sympathy at her loss of her only son and added, "At the funeral of the airmen, I prayed at the graves for them and also for their relatives and loved ones..... I can assure you that the grave has been kept nice all the year round and covered with flowers. I myself and a Fraulein Anna Borne have seen to this and I believe we have kept the grave as you would have wished it. I have had a worthy oak cross put on the grave together with a shield engraved with the names of the six airmen. The crash happened as follows; on the night of August 25th/26th, 1941, there was a terrible storm and many aircraft were heard flying over Trier, mostly very low. Suddenly I heard a terrible crash and I saw from my bedroom window a large fire burning in the direction of Trier. An aircraft had tried to land by the Sievericher Hof, a large farm 1km from Aach in the direction of Trier and had caught the corner of the roof of a barn about 30ft high and had exploded. One of the crew baled out and landed safely. He came through the wood in the rain and spent the night in a house named Erlehof. The next morning he surrendered and went safely to a POW camp. The other airmen in the crashing aircraft must have been killed instantaneously and the next day they were all buried in Aach. Later we received the names of the airmen from Berlin."

In October 1947 Anna Borne wrote to the Blundens. "In 1941, shortly after the accident, I willingly undertook the care of the grave and from then on without interruption have personally looked after and put flowers on it, in the thought that the dead who rest here are our loved ones, for whom you are unable to perform this office yourselves. Today I have placed fresh flowers on the grave for All Souls Day. Rest assured that your dear son's grave is not forgotten. I have often wished that the relatives could see it. Foreign soldiers rest here with our own dear dead ones under the shadow of our little church, where there is no longer enmity but only rest and peace." In December 1947, Mrs Blunden sent copies of those letters to Mrs Wright, being unaware that it was too late for them to give her comfort, and wrote, "It makes one feel that amongst the many cruel Germans there remain a few who have hearts of gold."

Soon afterwards, Anna wrote to the Wright family observing that, "They rest here in our churchyard in the midst of our own beloved dead without being in any way distinguished from them." In April 1948, Anna wrote to David's sister Dorothy: "Now we have since yesterday the new currency and we have to wait and see how things will be. For the time being we are and will remain poor people and the innocents all have to suffer too for what in those times our fanatical leaders have brought about."

In September 1948, the Air Ministry confirmed what the Wright family had already heard from a distressed Anna. The remains of the six airmen had been removed from Aach and re-interred in the British War Cemetery at Rheinberg, 11 miles North west of Duisburg (Plot 8, Row F, Grave 6/9). As well as on their grave at Rheinberg, the names of the gallant crew appear in the No 7 Squadron Roll of Honour at Longstanton Church (near Oakington) which also has a stained glass window depicting the history of the squadron.

On a Sunday evening in March 1933, Mr & Mrs Lloyd were watching 'Songs of Praise' which was broadcast from Hillsborough Parish Church and Mrs Lloyd was prompted to write to the Rector: "Denis and I would be so grateful if you could possibly give us some information about a Pilot Officer David Wright's family in Hillsborough who was a member of my husband's crew of a Stirling Bomber when they were shot down over Germany in August 1941. Mr & Mrs Wright wrote to me when Denis was a prisoner of war and asked if, when he returned home, we could visit them to give details of what happened on that fateful night; but Denis was in such a poor state of health that we felt it was not possible but we always regretted that we did not go, mainly of course for

them and their family's sake. If you could possibly find out if there are any relatives of this sad family still alive, it would give us so much pleasure if it were possible to get in touch with them after all these years."

David's sister Dorothy visited the Lloyds and returned with a copy of 'RAF Bomber Command 1939-1945' by Peter Hancock, who knew the Blunden family well. With acknowledgements to No 7 Squadron Association and to the squadron's operation records now in the Public Record Office, he reveals that on the 25th August 1941 six aircraft were despatched to bomb Karlsruhe. According to the squadron records, "The weather was bad and several of the aircraft encountered electrical storms. Two were forced to abandon and jettison bombs. Flying Officer KO Blunden possibly encountered similar conditions and failed to return. Two reached and bombed the target, another bombed an aerodrome."

He reveals also that in May 1945 Denis Lloyd wrote to the Blundens: "I have just arrived home safely and in fairly good health and am glad to be able at last to give you full details of the accident that cost you so dearly. I'm afraid I cannot give you any definite reason as to why the accident happened and for security reasons I could not write the full story in Germany. Owing to the loss of our own aircraft while we were on leave, Wing Commander Graham gave us an old plane out of a training flight which had been previously relegated owing to its general behaviour and age; if there had been any serious defects, of course Mr Blunden would have refused to fly in it, but it was mainly a succession of small things that went wrong with it and consequently, right or wrongly, we had no confidence in the aircraft. Due to several minor defects, we took off much later than the other planes that night for a raid on Karlsrhue; I remember that as we left the Ground Engineer had a few bad moments with the fuel supply, while I had some trouble with the electrical equipment.

"Once in the air, however, everything seemed all right and Mr Blunden never hesitated about carrying on. I think we must have been flying for about two hours (we had taken off at 2045 hrs) when the trouble started. I had spent most of the time using the radio equipment and consequently I wasn't connected to the rest of the crew by telephone, if anything unusual had been happening I wasn't aware of it, as is so often the case with the Radio Operator. Owing to violent static, I realised we were approaching a severe thunderstorm and for the next few minutes I was very busy preparing all my equipment to meet it. By the time I was able to switch over to the intercom to speak to Mr Blunden, the aircraft was tossing about in an alarming manner. The first thing I heard was Mr Brew, our Rear Gunner, telling Mr Blunden that our navigation lights were on and that 'They' were still firing at us, presumably he meant flak. I could not and still do not understand why the lights were on but most probably it was the storm that upset the electrical equipment. Mr Blunden didn't answer for a time and the aircraft continue to pitch. Suddenly he called up and told us to get ready to bale out. I picked up my parachute and started to make my way to the hatch at the rear of the plane. Almost immediately, I was thrown flat on the floor and I think the aircraft must have gone into a spin, as I could not move at all owing to the pressure exerted by centrifugal force. After what seemed to be an eternity, I found that by making a great effort I could slowly crawl towards the rear. Mr Blunden had probably got the plane out of the spin but we were still diving very steeply. When I eventually reached the escape hatch, I could discern in the dim light that the Perspex glass had all gone and that the wooden cover of the hatch was swinging open in the slipstream. The rear turret appeared to be empty and, assuming that Mr Drew had already left the aircraft via the hatch, I managed to get my chute on after a great deal of effort and struggled out feet first. I pulled the ripcord immediately as I realised that, after diving for so long, we must be very near the ground; the chute opened all right and almost immediately I saw the aircraft directly below me, for the navigation lights were still on. The next moment it hit the ground and burst into flames. Of course I expected that at least part of the crew would have had time to escapee, especially from the front hatch, and consequently did not believe the Germans at Trier when they told me that the bodies of the other six crew members had been recovered from the wreckage.

"When not one of them arrived at Dulag Luft, however, I took the risk of giving them the name and rank of Mr Blunden and the rest of the crew. The Germans assured me that the grave would be marked and I know that at that time they buried British airmen with full military honours. I'm sorry I was never able to obtain any information about this however, and all I could do was to give all the details to our own Red Cross authorities when I arrived at Stalag V111B. The day I arrived in England, I made out a full report of the disaster and said that the probable cause of loss was ice, for several other of our aircraft had trouble with it in the same storm, as I later learned from later prisoners from the squadron; I gave as the secondary cause the condition of the aircraft, with the possibility that we were hit by flak, which could account for the broken glass of the escape hatch. The only consolation I can offer you, Mrs Blunden, is that Kenneth did not suffer in any way.

The aircraft was not on fire in the air and, during the dive, everything was too unreal to experience horror or fear, and he had never known the latter."

The Crew killed:

Captain/Pilot	Flying Officer Kenneth Oswald Blunden aged 23 RAFVR
2nd Pilot	Pilot Officer John David Wright aged 24 RAFVR
Rear Gunner	Pilot Officer Edgar Frederick Drew aged 27 RAF
Navigator	Sergeant John Duncan Edworthy aged 26 RCAF
Flight Engineer	Sergeant George Nicholson aged 27 RAF
Front Gunner	Sergeant William Everitt Allan aged 24 RCAF

Survivor:

Wireless Operator	Sergeant Denis A Lloyd, RAFVR

The Aircraft and its operational record
Short Stirling N6020 (MG-B), taken on charge at Wyton on 29th April 1941, and taken into No 7 Squadron Service on May 5th 1941.

15th May 1941	Berlin.
23rd May 1941	Cologne. Bomb distributor, port undercarriage and intercom failures; receiver u/s; bombed Manstede.
7th June 1941	Brest.
9th June 1941	Off Dunkirk, damaged by enemy action.
10th June 1941	Emden. Damaged by enemy action.
26th June 1941	Keil. Did not locate target, bad visibility.
28th June 1941	Bremen.
29th June 1941	Hamburg. Extensive flak holes; bomb doors damaged.
5th Aug 1941	Karlsruhe.
19th Aug 1941	Kiel.
25th Aug 1941	Karlsruhe. (Kenneth Blundens 26th Operation, and David Wrights 5th) Failed to return.

SQUADRON LEADER
WILLIAM HERBERT WRIGHT
ROYAL AIR FORCE NO. 976233
PILOT
NO. 134 SQUADRON MIDDLE EAST

William Herbert Wright was born in Ravenhill Park in Belfast on the 5th July 1921 and was educated at Rossetta Public Elementary School and at Methodist College until 1937. He continued his higher education at Altmore College, which was primarily to help with his forthcoming civil service exams.

In February 1939 he moved to London where he became a junior clerk with the Ministry of Labour, helping with the massive state of unemployment, which was sweeping the country at that time. He remained in this department until the outbreak of war, and then became involved with the registering of people first of all for national service and later conscription. As soon as recruiting opened in London he and two colleagues decided to join the RAF, and were accepted as ACHGD(Aircraft Hands General Duties). "In other words," Bill said, "the lowest form of animal life, no trade, and the rate of pay was two shillings (10p) per day at that time rising to two shillings and sixpence (12p) per day in 1940." Bill was a little fortunate in that being an established civil servant his balance of civil pay was made up, so in other words he was earning just as much in the RAF as was in civilian life. But compared to and ordinary ACHGD on RAF pay only, he was somewhat of a wealthy man. The ACHGD's were receiving 14 shillings per week where as Bill was getting £2 per week and was able to buy a Morris Minor car which cost him the princely sum of £8. It was a fabric bodied Morris Minor with a gravity fed petrol tank and he ran his beloved Minor on the meagre petrol ration of the day, which was supplemented by the siphoning of waste pipes from the petrol bowsers on the station. (Basic petrol rationing was two gallons per month).

There was a supplementary petrol ration given to business people and this special ration would be also given on compassionate grounds, such as persons who may have had an invalid in the family. Eventually even the basic rationing soon disappeared during the war, which caused the price of cars to drop dramatically. One of the chaps who he had joined the RAF with was posted to another station and he never saw him again. But his particular friend who

was called Temple and got the nick name 'Shirley Temple' were together for quite a while and they eventually were able to re-muster to aircrew. Temple re-mustered as an Air Gunner, and during his gunnery training was asked to make a trip on a bomber whose gunner had taken ill. Sadly he did not return from that raid.

Bill had all sorts of jobs as an ACHGD which included humping large bags of coal. This did not last to long as he dropped one on his foot, injuring his big toe He was then put onto light duties, which allowed him to wear plimsolls instead of the regulation boots. The light duties consisted of the cleaning out of latrines. Bill was informed by another colleague who he was working with, that as he was engaged in carrying out sanitary duties he was entitled to an extra three pence a day sanitary duty pay. He informed his Senior NCO that this had not been taken into account when calculating his pay, and was told to make application for this three pence extra a day which he had not received. The Accountancy Department claimed that there was no such a payment and subsequently Bill and his mate (Tommy Thomas) were taken off sanitary duties and transferred to the cookhouse, where they learnt to peel potatoes, and wash pots and pans. They heard later that they had been replaced by two civilians who had taken over the sanitary duties.

So after a few weeks in the cookhouse Bill was posted to RAF Filton, which was part of Flying Training Command and No 6 Service Flying Training School and was equipped with the North American (AT6) Harvard for training fighter pilots, and Avro Ansons for bomber pilots. Bill was still not however allowed anywhere near an aircraft. The day before he arrived at Filton the station had been visited by the Luftwaffe during the day, and one of his first tasks there was to assist in the clearing of the air raid shelters over at the Bristol Aviation Company. One of the company's shelters had received a direct hit, and Bill's job was to help with the removal of the bodies, and he remembers it was very distressing time for him.

From Filton he was posted to RAF Colerne which was still under construction, no roads, toilets, cook houses, etc., and the first thing he was issued with was a pair of wellington boots which were to allow him to wade through the ankle deep mud. His barracks had no plumbing, and so had to go onto the local town by truck for a bath once a week whether he needed it or not.

Bill was asked if he would volunteer for a 'secret' job, and remembers well a friend telling him, "Never volunteer for anything in the RAF." He decided to stick his neck out and volunteered, and this turned out to be a detachment with himself and a few others to a small village called Doltings which was close by Shetland Mallon in Somerset. When they arrived in Dalton they were taken to a direction finding tower that had been built in the middle of a large field. Inside the tower there were three Wireless Operators and three Radio Telephonists and some permanent guards. As the nearest RAF station was miles away he had to be billeted out in the local pub where he stayed for quite happily for the next few weeks.

They were supposed to work two hours on and four hours off, right throughout the day and night. However by mutual agreement it was decided to work twenty-four hours on and forty-eight hours off. This they did and it turned out very well. It meant that when Bill had his two days off he would hitch a lift up to London and see a show, and then spend the night at the YMCA hostel, and get back the next day. One day as he was walking around the field he had a brilliant idea which he thought would help supplement his beer money, and this was, he would set snares in the gaps of hedges to catch rabbits. He would wait sometimes for two days and then go out and collect any which had been caught, and give one to his landlady, and take the rest down to the local butcher and sell them for two shillings and sixpence each. Bill said that he could have spent the rest of the war there rightly, but unfortunately all good things sometimes come to an end. When his tour of duty had finished at the direction finding tower he returned to RAF Colerne. On his arrival back he was sent for by the Station Commander who told him that he had been promoted to Leading Aircraftsman and had been accepted for Pilot Training, and to report immediately to the initial training wing at Babbicombe to start his initial training. He felt a bit of a 'top knob' now, as it had taken nearly eighteen months for him to get to Pilot Training.

He spent the usual time at ITW learning how to march, salute, navigation, signals, Morse code, hygiene and sanitation and all sorts of things. When he finished the course he was told that he would be going overseas to start his flying training, and was sent by train up to West Kirkby to await his posting and as usual for those days he had to wait around for a few weeks before his draught

came through. He was standing on parade with about fifty others when a Flight Sergeant called them to attention. He told them that he was going to call out their names one by one in alphabetical order, and when they heard theirs being called, they were to answer with their number, fall out and go to the other side of the parade ground. The Flight Sergeant went through the very long list of names and when he eventually finished, Bill's name had not been called. He was standing on his own in the middle of the parade ground. The Flight Sergeant marched smartly over to him and asked Bill for his name and number. He went through his list again and said, "Sorry mate, your name is not on my list." This was a bitter blow for Bill having to watch all his mates being marched off to be kitted out for South Africa.

The Flight Sergeant went away and came back a few minutes later to Bill and told him that all he could do was to report on parade every morning until his name was called, and if anyone reported sick or was missing for any reason he could take their place. This of course never happened as all these new recruits were a fit bunch of lads. After about a fortnight reporting every morning, and in between times picking up waste paper around the station and drinking gallons of YMCA tea, Bill decided to go to the orderly room as he was very frustrated and asked, "Am I going to finish the war here standing at the back of a parade ground."

The Flight Sergeant in charge decided to refer back to the original list and check again for Bills name and said, "No, you are definitely not on this list." Then, he turned the page over, and of course going in alphabetical order, he found the name Wright on the back of the paper, and the Flight Sergeant hadn't noticed it. It was decided that the best and quickest thing to do was to send Bill to Torquay where he would be made up into another draught, and by this time it was May 1941. The weather was beautiful, and there was nothing that Bill could do, and just had to wait until another course had finished. He was by now in the Royal Air Force eighteen months.

When the course that he had been waiting on finished had completed he was posted along with them to a personnel dispatch centre at Wymslow which was just outside Manchester. He remained here for a brief period, and then one evening he was told to pack his kit bag, and get ready for an early departure the following morning. He was shown how to mark his kit bag as this was very important, and still remembers the marking that he had put on his. He had to paint the letters, EATS (Empire Air Training Scheme), LEAK (code name for Liverpool. Port of embarkation), and the letter 'R', which stood for the good ship Roua Heena. The Roua Heena had been a peacetime refrigerator vessel and had now been converted into a troop-ship.

He was given a full days ration, and then trained up to Liverpool. The Roua Heena sailed for Canada early in June, taking eleven days to reach its destination. The weather en-route was diabolical, high winds and rough seas threw the ship about like a cork in the bath. Then on one fine misty morning as they steamed very slowly through the fog they heard the sound of a 'Whoop, whoop, whoop'. Cutting through the fog was a Canadian corvette which had come out to meet them, and as the mist lifted he saw for the first time the coast of Nova Scotia. The Roua Heena docked in Halifax harbour around 1500 hrs and of course another air force 'cock up' was about to happen. Bill and the others were told to prepare themselves for disembarkation, and to put on their full webb kit, and then report to their respective mess tables and wait for further orders. They waited from 1500 hrs until around midnight until someone came along with tea and sandwiches. They sat up all night, and around 8 o'clock the next morning they were told that they could leave the ship. Bill was relieved of all of his English money and given a receipt for this, and on reaching the quay side at Halifax was given ten Canadian Dollars. It was also a great relief to be able to get rid of his gas mask as they hopefully would not be needed in Canada.

Bill was taken by truck to a train station where he boarded a train which he said looked as if it came from the World War One era as it had hard and uncomfortable wooden seats. The train started to pull out of the station, and Bill still did not know where his next destination would be. He had not been travelling for very long when an NCO came to inform him that if he wanted any breakfast, to go to the rear of the train. Most of the guys were quite tired and decided to skip breakfast, but Bill and a few others decided to investigate. This is one of Bill's very clear memories, as he reached the rear of the train, stepping out of a very uncomfortable 1914/18 coach into what was could only be called a 'fairy land'. The dining car was 1st Class and a coloured gentleman in a white jacket showed them to a table which was decorated with a white table cloth and shining cutlery.

Now Bill wasn't a porridge eater, but when he was served this particular bowl of porridge which was laced with sugar, cold milk, bacon and eggs and probably the best cup of coffee he had ever tasted, he just could not resist it. The train made its first 'watering hole stop' at a place called Troural. On the opposite platform there were a large group of middle-aged ladies who Bill gathered might have belonged to our equivalent of our WDS. The ladies had been expecting a troop train going in the other direction, and were there to greet it. Having now seen Bill's train, all the ladies came across to his side of the station and distributed oranges, chocolate and all sorts of goodies, which he had not seen under rationing back in the UK. That had been a very nice welcome to Canada. The train was very slow and stopped at various little stations as they made their way through Canada. The only sour note that he had about Canada was when the train stopped in the province of Quebec at a place called Campbell Town. The train had stopped for about twenty minutes to take on more water, and the boys were

stretching their legs walking up and down the platform. Bill said, "It was a place we found less than welcome, the locals did not speak to us, unless they were spoken to in French, and even then they were still pretty cool with the RAF lads." One of Bill's Canadian friends explained to him later that the were French Canadians, and that their war finished in 1940, and so they were not very interested anymore (but this had been the exception).

The next morning they arrived in Quebec City where they had a brief stop and then travelled on to Toronto, where they were conveyed by truck to the Exhibition Grounds, which would be equivalent of our Balmoral show grounds. Bill and the lads were disappointed when the found out that they were to be accommodated in a large exhibition hall which was labelled 'Swine'. However they were told that they would just have to make the best of it, and that evening their first meal made up for it as the Canadian Air Force cook give them a meal fit for a king.

Bill and his friends were allowed into Toronto for an hour or so each day but were told not to stray to far. Bill had always fancied 'coffee and doughnuts', so he looked around for a suitable cafe and had the biggest doughnut he had ever seen. He also bought a packet of Life Savers which were a small sweet with a hole in the centre, not unlike our Polo mints. They hung around the Manning Depot for about a week, and during this short spell in Toronto Bill and some of the lads were asked to carry out some special duties at military funerals, and were asked to form the Guard of Honour and form part of the gun salute. These were funerals of servicemen who had been killed while on training duties.

Then on a beautiful Sunday morning they were eventually moved out and trained down to St Catherine's Flying Training School Ltd in Ontario, which was about twelve miles from the Niagara Falls. This was to be Bill's first introduction to proper flying.

It was now July 1941, and St Catherine's was a delightful place. Every Sunday after lunch they were taken for a swim on Lake Ontario. The weather was very hot, and it wasn't uncommon to have 102 degrees in the shade. The food was magnificent, and this may have contributed to a lot of air sickness as the British lads were not used to this, due to the food rationing back home. The morning came when Bill was shown out to his aircraft which was called a Fleet Finch. The aircraft he was expecting to fly was the Tiger Moth. The Fleet Finch was similar to the Tiger Moth except it was powered by a radial engine and had an enclosed cockpit, tail wheel and brakes which made it much easier to handle on the ground than a Tiger Moth. Otherwise a similar aircraft to fly and had the same characteristics as the Tiger Moth.

On the 22nd July 1941, Bill was introduced to his instructor Mr Patterson. He was a civilian instructor and employed by the Royal Canadian Air Force. Bill's first flight was an air experience flight, getting him familiarised with aircraft's controls and engine procedures. The flight lasted for one hour which took him up to the Niagara Falls. They were not allowed to fly over the river as it bordered with America which at that time was still a neutral country. This part of Canada is known as the garden of Canada as it is covered in peach trees. The local farmers in a sort of a patriotic fervour would deliver a basket of fresh peaches to the mess for the pupils every morning. A little anecdote regarding the peaches: One morning Bill was going up with his instructor and asked him, "What are we going to be doing today, sir?" The instructor replied, "Well Bill, whatever it is, it wont be to far from Base as I have just had a feed of your peaches, and I want to remain in gliding distance from the loo." Bill's training progressed through July and August, and on the 13th August his big day came when Mr Patterson told him, "OK Bill, she's all yours." Bill flew solo after ten hours tuition for about 30 minutes and when he landed he still felt that he was still at 5,000ft.

The big worry in all of the pupil's minds was of course would they ever be competent to fly solo. It was generally expected of them to fly solo within eight hours of starting the course. When Bill was coming up to the eight hour mark he was far away from being competent in going solo. He could fly the aircraft, take offs were no problem, but the difficulty was landing it. One of his colleagues had the appropriate name of 'Angel', and unfortunately, Angel never did make it. He got to the stage of his first solo, and took off , but then panicked and couldn't land. Basically he was too short in stature to be a pilot as he would have slide down in the seat to reach the rudder pedals, this meant he could not see out, and if he reached up to see out his feet left the rudder pedals. Eventually two instructors took off and formatted on him and led him into land. That unfortunately was his first and last solo, and he was posted to a Navigation School. Bill finished the course at St Catherine's in the middle of September with 66hrs.25 mins to his credit.

On the 25th September 1941, Bill was posted the No 2 SFTS at Uplands in Ottawa. RAF Uplands was a civilian airfield and the Canadian Air Force had taken over half of it which they used for the training of service pilots in the Harvard (AT6). Bill's first flight in the Harvard was on the 28th September 1941 with his instructor Pilot Officer Sproule. He flew the aircraft solo on the 6th October 1941. Again he went through the process of learning a new cockpit, and getting used to an aircraft whose wheels retracted, and most importantly of all, "Remembering to put them down again." The course went fairly uneventfully for Bill, the night flying part of the course was not his favourite but he managed it all the same.

By now he was in the depths of the Canadian winter, it was extremely cold and the runways were covered in snow which the RCAF made no attempt to clear. They just brought in huge rollers which packed it down. They marked the runway on either side with miniature Christmas trees which peeped through the snow. It was now December 7th, the course was almost finished and the news had just come through on the wireless that the

Japanese had bombed Pearl Harbour. America was now in the war (great to have an ally).

The 19th December was Wings Day at Uplands when all the trainees who had successfully passed the course were presented with their Wings and it was quite an elaborate ceremony. Some of Bill's pals came over from St Catherine's to congratulate him and wish him well for the future. During the Wings ceremony Bill was also presented with his Sergeants stripes which he had promptly sewn on to his uniform.

No sooner had he had them sewn on when he was told to remove them as word had come through that he had been commissioned. This had been the first time that he had received information that he had been promoted in writing and he still can remember the official wording of the telegram. It stated:

976233 LAC Wright, discharged from the RAF with effect from 2359 hrs, 18/12/41, grants a commission as rank of Pilot Officer RAF with effect from 0000 hrs 19th December 1941.

Bill was granted some leave which he decided to spend with some friends over at St Catherine's, who wanted to entertain him over the Christmas period. Some of whom he remains friends with to this day. On Christmas morning Bill went for a walk into the town of St Catherine's, and as he was walking along, if one car stopped a dozen stopped and asked Bill if he would like to spend Christmas them and their family. Bill said that the hospitality that was shown to him by many Canadians was tremendous and it was only marred by the incident with the French Canadians. After Christmas, Bill was told to report back to the Halifax 'Y' depot, which was the centre for embarkation to the UK. He had to make his way there by the 30th December. He spent New Years Eve in Halifax, and much to his dismay discovered that the Canadian authorities did not want a lot of 'rowdy drunks' roaming around Halifax, so it was decided to close all pubs, bars, and liquor establishments over the New Year period.

A few days later Bill left Halifax on which he said could only be described as a 'tub'. A little vessel called the Beaver Hill which had previously been a cargo ship, and what had been part of the Canadian Pacific Fleet. As soon as it left port a senior Naval Officer informed the crew that the ship was carrying a large cargo of high explosives. They set sail from Halifax in diabolical weather, and the Beaver Hill was struggling to keep up with the rest of the convoy. Not only were the seas extremely rough, it was very cold and the spray from the sea was freezing on the rigging of the ship to an extent that the ship was starting to become top heavy. The ship was rolling quite heavily in the rough seas, and it sometimes felt to Bill that it may not recover from some of the rolls, and sink.

Crew members were sent up in that freezing weather armed with axes to chop the ice away from the rigging and masts. The sea crossing was perilously slow, taking sixteen days to cross the Atlantic, and one of the most welcome sights towards the end of his journey was seeing the coast of Donegal as they sailed round the north coast of Ireland. The ships captain announced to all that he had been advised that the Germans had just mined the Mersey estuary and he could not dock in Liverpool immediately, but would be putting into Belfast instead. This news of course delighted Bill as he hoped that he might be able to nip home and see his family.

He spoke to his Commanding Officer about getting ashore, but he told Bill, "Not a chance." No one was allowed of the ship, but he did compromise, and said, "We might be able to get a phone call through to your folks and they could come down to the ship and meet you." However it was not be, as they sailed down Belfast Lough and were just passing Carrickfergus, a signal came through to the captain telling him that the Mersey had now been 'swept' and he could proceed to Liverpool.

The ship arrived late in the evening; everyone disembarked and boarded a train that took them down to Bournemouth, which had a reception centre for aircrew coming from various parts of the Commonwealth. Bill spent the next fortnight at the centre, doing very little, and then was told that he was going to Blackpool where he was to board another ship that was to take him to another unknown destination overseas. Bill tried to point out to his superiors that he was due some embarkation leave, and that he was particularly keen to get home and see his family and girlfriend. He was told that he should have arranged this before leaving Bournemouth, but he could have a 48 hour pass. (A 48 hour pass did allow English chaps to get home.) Bill was desperate and decided to take a chance and came home using his logbook. When he got to Heysham the customs officials (even though he was sailing from one part of the UK to another) searched his kit and told him that he could not take his logbook with him. Bill protested strongly about his treatment, but nevertheless they took it from him, and gave him a receipt. It was almost a year later when serving in the Middle East that he got it back again which was very awkward. He arrived home and got engaged which he had hoped to do. He then planned to go back, and ask for compassionate leave to get married. When he did arrive back in Blackpool he discovered that he was already late for his ship. All his friends had been recalled from their 48-hour pass, and as Bill was in Northern Ireland he could not be contacted. Bill was told that he had one hour in which to board his ship otherwise he would be Court Marshalled for missing his overseas posting, and he reckoned that he was about to embark on a very long engagement, and he was right as it was four years before he would see his future wife again.

Posted overseas

Bill found his ship and boarded her, not feeling very happy, but it was better than the last two ships he was on.

The ship was called the Arundel Castle, which had been one of the Union Castle Fleet that had been on the South African run before the war.

The ship was very crowded, and as regards the sleeping arrangements it was six bods to a two berth cabin. The catering on the ship was excellent as the ships cooks were endeavouring to keep with its pre-war standards. The officers were fed along with the 1st class passengers, they had the same choice of menu, with wine at every meal. The drink on board the ship was extremely cheap, for example a Gin and Tonic was the equivalent of about two new pence, and Bill can remember one of the lads having his 21st Birthday party on board, starting with a bottle of champagne for breakfast costing 15 shillings (75p). They eventually arrived in the port of Freetown in West Africa, and were not allowed ashore, nor were they allowed to sleep on deck because the mosquitoes were quite bad in that area. The ship again set sail, this time setting a course for Cape Town in South Africa and when the arrived the locals greeted them right royally, just the same as the Canadians had done. On leaving the ship they were put into army trucks and taken to a camp which was about ten miles outside Cape Town. The camp was called Retreat, and halfway between Cape Town and Retreat was a delightful seaside resort. Apart from being under canvas it was really quite comfortable. Bill remained in Cape Town for the next two weeks, and once again he boarded another luxury Liner called The New Amsterdam which was a Dutch ship as the name implies. The New Amsterdam had apparently completed only one Atlantic crossing as a passenger vessel. It had sailed from Amsterdam to New York and during that time Holland has been invaded by the Germans. The liner was then turned into a troop ship, which in this configuration was capable of carrying up to 3,000 troops. The only difficulty was that it was a problem carrying enough water for so many people on long journeys.

The ship sailed up the Red Sea, and through the Suez canal and headed for Kasafareet in Egypt where the ship spent a few hours, taking on fresh water and stores. At this particular time the war in the desert was not going well for the Allies, Rommel was pushing hard for El Alamein. There were hundreds of pilots in Bill's group but none of them had an aeroplane to fly. So it was decided to train them south from Cairo to El Shalal were they boarded a riverboat that would take them down to the Sudanese border where they boarded a train for Khartoum. On arriving at Khartoum Bill and the lads were taken out to a deserted airfield which was called Gordons Tree. It had been used during the Eritriean Campaign. Here, they 'kicked' their heels for a while and were eventually sent back to Cairo. After a few weeks in Cairo Bill was posted to an aircraft delivery unit, where he became a Ferry Pilot. He said would have been a lovely war for him if only he had been able to stay there. He was quartered in a beautiful house boat which was moored on the river Nile in Cairo and he was treated like a lord.

His duties there involved being flown by Dakota from Cairo to Takor-Radi in West Africa where he would pick up Spitfire, Hurricane or Tomahawk and fly it back in easy stages, first to Khartoum, and then on to Cairo. When he returned to Cairo and if he had no further flying duties the rest of the day was his own. But as he said himself, "All good things must come to an end." In November 1942 he found himself being posted to the Sudan again, this was a torturous journey by train and riverboat to an obscure place called Carthago which was in the Red Sea hills, south west of Port Sudan. He joined the No 71 Operational Training Unit where he obtained a 100% pass in his Hurricane exam and was given an 'average' assessment as a Fighter Pilot, Bombing and Gunnery. Bill started his operational training on Harvards, Hurricanes and Tomahawks on the 3rd November 1942 and finished the course in December 1942.

On completing the OTU course he was posted back to Cairo where he became operations officer to the Bomber Wing for a brief period and then posted to his first operation squadron.

Bill joined 134 Squadron at Shandur in the Middle East on the 26th January 1943. The squadron at that time was equipped with the Hawker Hurricane Mk 11b's.

No 134 Squadron was formed in July 1941, and twelve days later embarked on Aircraft carrier HMS Argus bound for Russia as part of the 151 Wing. On arriving in Venga the squadron was involved in bomber escort duties to protect Soviet bombers. The squadron later began training Soviet pilots and their Hurricanes were eventually handed over to the Russians. The squadron then moved back to the UK (minus its aircraft) where it was re-equipped with Spitfires and was operational again by February 1942 when it moved to Eglington in Northern Ireland. Two months later the squadron moved to Egypt arriving in Palestine in June where it became a non-flying unit until January 1943 again becoming operational as a fighter unit. Here it carried out convoy escort patrols and also attacked enemy tanks with firebombs. The first half of 1944 saw the squadron heavily involved with the 'Cab Rank' duties with the army.

Bill's first flight in one of the squadrons Hurricanes 11b's was on the 27th January 1943, and his first operational flight was on the 28th January to carry out a sector recce over the Shandur area. On the 4th February 1943 he flew up to landing ground 121 at Sidi-Barani which was under the command of Group Captain Stan Turner, DFC and Bar and DFM and who was a distinguished Battle of Britain Pilot. He then returned to the squadron where he carried out escorting patrols on convoys that were coming out of Alexandria and Malta. He didn't see much action here as the convoys in this area weren't often attacked, but he did manage a few chases against PR Ju88's which would come over.

The Ju88's had been stripped down to allow them to achieve very high altitudes. The Mk 11b Hurricane's however found it difficult to reach them. Subsequently the squadron was equipped with a few Spitfires that could get up to the altitude to attack the Ju88's. The squadron began to move up the desert in various stages to Kilo 8 (Cairo), BV (Amud), Bersis and El Quassasin.

Operation Thesis

On July 23rd the squadron took part in Operation Thesis which was to attack and destroy buildings and personnel in Crete. Flying Officer Manser force landed, Sergeant Horsley was missing, Flying Officer Lowen and Bill were wounded by flak. The story behind Operation Thesis was apparently that the Commando's had landed in Crete and had done quite a bit of damage on the ground before they left. The Germans were convinced that the locals, the Cretians had helped the Commando's so they shot dead 100 hostages. This incensed everyone so greatly that the AOC decided that a massive raid on the Germans was in order. Three squadrons of Hurricanes were ordered to attack the western side of the island and three squadrons including 134 were to attack the centre of the island, and another three were to attack the eastern end. A total of nine squadrons were involved each mounting nine aircraft. They were to be led into the target by Maryland bombers because the attack was to be made at very low level all the way so as not to be detected by the German radar. The fighter pilots navigation was not great at low level over the sea, so they were extremely glad of the Maryland's to show them the way. Bill told me, "There is an odd 'quirk' to this story, 134 Squadron was to fly from its own airfield to join 123 Squadron and the Royal Herleric Squadron. The Greek Squadron was ordered to take off and meet near Tobruk. When they flew down to meet up with the other squadrons, the Commanding Officer, a man called Hawkeye Leigh informed them that they would be taking off at first light. Therefore they would not need a breakfast. But that he would arrange a super breakfast for them all when they returned from the operation, and was able to arrange to have extra cooks sent over from Cairo."

Bill had a dream on the eve of the raid and that was, Hawkeye Leigh and himself would be delayed and late in getting back from the raid, all the breakfasts had been eaten and nothing left for them. In the morning when he went to the mess for a mug of tea, Bill told Hawkeye of his dream. He just laughed and said, "Paddy, you and I will be at the top table at the big breakfast." It transpired Hawkeye Leigh was shot down, and Bill was wounded. So the dream did come true after all. The incident of his own wounding was also interesting as it was the element of chance. Bill had found a target which was an ammunition dump and an Army barracks that was also close by. As Bill was busily strafing the target, he heard a loud bang.

He was right down at zero feet, and at the time didn't realise that both he and his aircraft had been hit. Prior to take off the crews were given instructions in case they had to force land in Crete, and if they did, they should get away from the place which they had been strafing and not land beside the troops which they had just been 'hammering' (naturally enough.) So Bill called up his leader on the R/T and said, "It's Paddy and I've been hit. I am braking off the attack now." He did a very sharp turn, and in doing so had noticed a lot of his blood around his instrument panel, and suddenly realised that he had been hit. A short time after his wounds began to hurt. He had received some shrapnel in his left hand, a large piece was buried in his left leg, and another small piece in his chest.

He decided to head for home, the aircraft was continuing to fly the way he wanted it to, and he wasn't prepared to go anywhere else on his own. He made the decision to head south for Africa again. Somewhere along the way he realised that he was losing a lot of blood, and was worried that he might pass out, and that he would die. He remembered being told at the briefing that there would be Air Sea Rescue vessels that would position themselves at various intervals along the coast. He thought if he could spot one of these boats he would bale out over it, and be picked up. He flew on for while looking for an ASR boat but did not see one . The longer he flew, the more he thought, "I was hit from below, and I am sitting on my parachute, and it may be damaged," so he ruled out the idea of baling out.

He decided to fly on and eventually made back to base, to make matters worse he had to land in a storm. The 'meat wagons' rushed out as soon as he landed and rushed him into a casualty clearing unit. While he was being attended to by the doctors the rest of the squadron had arrived back from the operation. Bill's immediate leader who was called, Slim Wolf Reese, a very experienced, and a very stout pilot, and who had been slightly ahead of Bill and to his right during the operation, came into see how he was. He said to Bill, "Paddy about the same time that you were hit, a bullet came through my cockpit, it just went in one side and out the other. When I landed I took a piece of string and stretched it between the entrance hole and the exit hole, and it would have gone straight though my head, but for the fact I was looking over my shoulder to see what had happened to you." The casualty station was only equipped for emergency first aid, and two days later Bill was air evacuated by Dakota back to Cairo and taken to a proper hospital where he was operated on immediately to remove the various pieces of shrapnel from his hand, leg and chest. The largest wound was on his left leg.

One of Bill's colleagues, a Canadian, Johnny Long, had also been wounded in the raid. They lost another two pilots, one had been shot down and killed, and the second had been taken prisoner. Out of the nine aircraft four were lost which was a very high percentage. Johnny Long and Bill were in the Cairo hospital for almost three weeks, going through various operations to have the shrapnel bits removed. Then they were declared 'walking wounded' by the doctor and allowed out of hospital in the afternoons. About this time they heard a rumour that their squadron was about to be re-equipped with new aeroplanes and change it's command. Bill had come to the conclusion that they were going to get Spitfires and going to Italy, because just after the Crete raid, Mussolini had 'resigned'. On the 17th August he was discharged from the hospital and flew back to Cairo in a Dakota and re-joined the squadron where they heard the news that Italy had surrendered. The squadron flew back to the canal zone and traded in their Hurricane 11b's for 11c's which was the four cannon version, and flew them on a series of hops out to India. Their route took them via El Quasassin, Cairo West, Lydda, Habbaniya, Shaibah, Bahrein (Muharrag Island), Sharja, Karachi (Mauripur Road), Jodphur, Delhi, Allahabad, Dum Dum and finally landing at Comilla to join the war in Burma. Although the Hurricanes were fitted with long range tanks it still took them a few days to complete the journey.

It was now December 1943

The squadron remained at Comilla for a brief period before moving down to East Bengal. They started operations right away, and most of the sorties were strafing Japanese supply vessels on the rivers, escorting supply bombers (Liberators), attacking ammo dumps, convoy patrols, escorting high speed launches and the occasional midnight Rhubarb. Very little in the way of air-to-air combat took place. When they carried out a Rhubarb (small scale fighter or fighter bomber attacks on ground targets of opportunity) it had to be a moonlit night. They would take off in half hour intervals so as not to get in each others way and were not given any specific targets. They were just told were the bomb line was, and anything on the far side of the bomb line was a legitimate target. They used the rivers to help navigate and if they spotted sampans or camp fires they would attack. They were also involved in 'Cab Rank' duties, this was in close support of the Army. What happened was, the aircraft and their crews were always at the ready, waiting until the Army would call for their support. The intelligence people would brief the crews to what the army required and the Hurricanes would go in and strafe the enemy positions. This went on until eventually the monsoons came along and halted flying. The squadron was then re-equipped with the P-47 (Jug) Thunderbolt, an aircraft that Bill was not particularly fond of. It was now December 1945, and Bill had completed two tours with the squadron and it was time for a rest. He was posted to Bangalore where he flew a desk for a while, which drove him potty. He applied to rejoin his squadron but his request was turned down. He was asked if there was anything else that he might like to do, would he like to go home, which he did not agree with. So it was decided to send him back to the Middle East where he joined No 73 Operational Training Unit at Fayid in Egypt where he became an Instructor on Hurricane 11's Thunderbolts, Fairchild. Ansons and Harvards. In January 1945 Bill was posted to Shaluffa where he joined No 11 FIC to become an Instructor on Harvards. On completion of the course Bill was awarded a category QSE and then returned to No 73 OTU at Fayid where he became the assistant chief flying instructor, and when the chief was later posted Bill became the CFI.

In August 1945 both wars had come to an end. Bill was asked by the Unit's Commanding Officer to fly his Thunderbolt in a battle formation over the cities of Cairo and Alexandria to remember the war dead. On the 26th September 1945 he was assessed as 'above the average' as a Flying Instructor.

Bill's Commanding Officer told him that Shaluffa was about to be taken over by the South African Air Force and as he had completed over four years in the Middle East it was time for him to go home. On the 20th October he boarded a Wellington at Shaluffa which was to fly back to the UK, via Kilo 40 (landing ground), El-Adam (Tobruk), Luqa (Malta), Marseille (France) and St Mawgan in Wales. On landing at Marseille they ran into a spot of trouble when their aircraft burst a main wheel. The Skipper of the Wellington who was a Group Captain called for the Engineering Officer for assistance. He came out and explained that he was sorry but did not have any spare wheels as he had just installed the last one on to a Vickers Wellesley. He then told the Group Captain that it would be at least a week before he received any spares. The Group Captain informed the engineer that he was heading back to the UK 'today', and would he kindly remove a serviceable wheel of the Wellesley and fit it to his Wellington. The Engineering Officer didn't argue and they were soon on their way again. Just as they were approaching the English coast a Controller contacted the captain and informed him that he would have to divert to Blackbushe as Wales was covered in fog. On landing, the aircraft and parachutes were handed over, and on entering the de-briefing room, Bill was informed that he was to report to the Air Ministry in London. On arriving at the

Ministry he was advised that he could go on indefinite leave due to his length of service overseas. That was fine with Bill as he wanted to get home as soon as possible and get married. He made the long journey by train to Stranraer and then across by boat to Larne and the train again down to York Street station and home. The family were all glad to see him return safe and sound, especially his fiancée. In November 1945 he was called to RAF Aldergrove which at that time had a holding unit for people like himself who were waiting on either to be de-mobbed, or a posting. He explained to the Officer in Charge that he had just made arrangements to be married and would it be possible to have a two-week pass. The OIC told Bill that was no problem, and that he would organise it right away for him. Soon after he was married Bill was sent to Long Kesh, just outside Lisburn where he was de-mobbed. He was then sent to Victoria Barracks in Belfast where he received his de-mob suit, hat and shoes. He was once again a civilian. Bill had accumulated over 680 flying hours in the RAF on nine different types of aircraft which included the Fleet Finch, North American Harvard, Hawker Hurricane, Tomahawk, Supermarine Spitfire, Thunderbolt, Fairchild Argus, Miles Martinet, Vickers Wellington and h ad visited at least 70 different airfields. He had decided that he did not want to return to the civil service, which had been he pre-war occupation. The money wasn't much good and the prospect for promotion was limited. Bill's father at that time had his own manufacturing business in Belfast, and as he was coming up to retirement age, offered the business to Bill. He accepted and successfully ran the company until he retired himself.

Bill is a life member of the Royal Air Force Association and was chairman of the Belfast Branch in Clifton Street, and was also a member of the RAFA Northern Ireland Council. He is a member of the Air Crew Association (Northern Ireland Branch) and the Burma Star Association.

SQUADRON LEADER
ROBERT RONALD WRIGHT, DFC AE
ROYAL AIR FORCE NO. 69514
BATTLE OF BRITAIN PILOT
NO. 248 AND 235 (F) SQUADRON

Robert Ronald Wright was born in Belfast on the 10th April 1917 and was educated at the Belfast Academical Institution. Ronnie was 'Larmor' House member at Inst, he enjoyed all aspects of sport, playing Scrum half at 2nd/3rd levels and won his rowing colours with the 1st 1V and also took part in golf match against the staff.

He also excelled at acting, so much so he performed on stage in Archie Douglas's 'Taming of the Shrew' and in Jamison's 'Macbeth'. On leaving Inst in 1934 he was employed with W&T Avery Ltd the scale manufacturers.

Ronnie like so many other young people of that time had a passion to fly an aeroplane and, in January 1939 he joined the Royal Air Force Volunteer Reserve in Belfast. He began his flying career at 24 Elementary and Reserve Flying Training School at Sydenham and on the morning of the 5th February when he had a 30 minute air experience flight in a Tiger Moth (N6461) with Flight Lieutenant David Sloan, the School's Chief Flying Instructor. He also had instruction from the schools two other instructors, Flight Lieutenant Charles Lindsay (later awarded the AFC), Flight Sergeant Peter Lake Sergeant Winder and Pilot Officer Cannam. Having completed 11hrs.5mins instruction, Ronnie soloed at 1635 hrs in the afternoon of the 27th February in Tiger Moth (N 6460) after having his final lesson from Flight Lieutenant Sloan a few minutes earlier. Whilst at Sydenam he flew the schools Hawker Audax (K3691) and Hawker Hind (K6818).

Sergeant Ronnie Wright had completed 77hrs.50 mins flying time at Sydenham when he was called to full time service on the 1st September just before war was declared. On the 6th November 1939 the Chief Flying Instructor Flight Lieutenant Sloan assessed Ronnie as 'above the average' as a Pilot. On the 10th November 1939, Ronnie was posted to No 1 Initial Training Wing at Cambridge to begin his basic training, which he completed by the 26th December. The next day he went to No 9 Service Flying Training School at Hullavington that was equipped with Hawker Harts and Hawker Audax's.

His first flight at the SFTS was on the 4th January 1940 in Hawker Hart (K6512) under the instruction of a Flight Lieutenant Sindall. He successfully finished the course on the 8th June and was again assessed as 'above the average' as a Pilot by the officer commanding. On the 10th June 1940 he was posted to No 5 Operation Training Unit at Aston Down where he had hoped to start flying Spitfires, but he was to be disappointed as he had been selected to fly Blenheims. His first flight in the Blenheim was on the 10th June and his instructor was a Flight Lieutenant Smith. Two days later he soloed in Blenheim L6652 and on the 22nd June completed the course with an assessment of 'average' as a Fighter Pilot and had accumulated 217 flying hours. He was posted to his first operational squadron at 248 Squadron at Dyce in Scotland on the 23rd June 1940.

The squadron was originally formed at Horsea in August 1918 from the seaplane flight which had been operative since 1917 that was based there. The squadron was disbanded in March 1919 with a record of six U-boats sighted, attacking four of them and sinking one. It also was credited with attacking one Zeppelin.

The squadron was reformed at Hendon in October 1939 as a twin engine fighter squadron and was equipped with Bristol Blenheims. The squadrons first operations were flown from Dyce in Scotland on defence sorties and later on reconnaissance patrols around Norway and the Dutch coast. In January 1941 it was re-equipped with Beaufighters which it used on mine searches and convoy patrols. In January 1944 the squadron was re-equipped with the Mosquito and joined the famous Banff Strike Wing concentrating on shipping strike along the Norwegian coast where it remained until the 1st October 1946.

On the 2nd August 1940 the squadron moved to Sumburgh. He carried out his first operation with the squadron on the 9th September 1940 in Blenheim (L9450) with fellow crewmembers, Sergeant Watts and Sergeant Yates. Ronnie had flown with the squadron throughout the Battle of Britain, carrying out long-range sorties to Norway, seeking out the expected German Naval Fleet. Some of these long-range sorties were to Trondheim Fjord, Statlandet and Bergen.

His logbook shows that on November 4th while carrying out a night flying practice exercise his engines cut and he had to crash land. On November 23rd he attacked the German wireless station at Allesund (Norway).

When I had the pleasure to interview Ronnie at his home in Old Bosham in Chichester, he told me this very funny story that happened to him during this period.

"I was on a night patrol when control vectored me onto an unidentified aircraft. When I reached the aircraft its navigation lights were switched off and due to the weather conditions it was practically impossible to identify the aircraft type. However I did make several attempts to contact the aircraft but to no avail. So I contacted control and told them I was going try and shoot it down. I got off a few long bursts at it when it disappeared into cloud and that was the last I saw of it. A week later I was summoned to an inquiry in London and on my arrival I was ushered to a small ante room where I was surprised to meet my very close friend, Wesley Snoddon, with whom I had joined the VR with in Belfast 1939.

"I was very glad to see someone from home and after we had our chat, I asked him, 'What on earth are you doing here?' he replied, 'Well about a week ago I was on exercise in my Whitley and got lost in bad weather, when some silly bugger, shot me down. I know now it was one of our own aircraft that was involved and that's why I am here for the inquiry.' Well, I laughed my leg off and told Wesley, 'I'm the silly bugger that shot you down'."

Sadly Sergeant Wesley Snoddon was killed along with his crew on the night of 13th March 1941. His was flying in an Whitley N1493 of 77 Squadron, the aircraft had taken off from Topcliffe at 1937 hrs and it's target was Hamburg. It was last heard calling for assistance at 2353 hrs, after which the aircraft and it's crew disappeared without trace. All are commemorated on the Runnymede Memorial.

In January 1941 Ronnie received his commission and promoted to Pilot Officer. On the 6th February the squadron moved back to Dyce for three weeks, and then on to Wick at the beginning of March, returning to Dyce again on the 15th June.

Extracts from his log continued:

March 1st	Blenheim 'A'
	Chased a Ju88.
May 10th	Blenheim 'J'
	Attacked & damaged FW Condor.

June 1st	Blenheim 'A'
	Reccon for the 'Bismarck'.
June 11th	Blenheim 'D'
	Chased Ju88.
June 12th	Blenheim 'G'
	Search for Lutzow, attacked by Me109.

On the 14th June the squadron moved south to Bircham Newton where it carried out mostly anti E-boat patrols.

June 17th	Blenheim 'P'
	Anti E-boat Patrol to Imuiden.
June 25th	Blenheim 'P'
	Anti E-boat Patrol.

In July 1941 the squadron began to re-equip with Bristol Beaufighters carrying out mine searches and convoy close escort patrols. On the 22nd August it took part in its first Beaufighter shipping strike on armed trawlers and 'R' boats. Ronnie had his first 30 minute air experience flight on the Beaufighter with Flight Lieutenant McHardy on the 10th July and flew it solo a few hours later. The squadron moved to Detling on the 21st August to escort a convoy and then across to Aldergrove in Northern Ireland on the 26th for three days escorting a convoy on its way from America and possibly a chance to visit his folks. The squadron moved again on the 29th to Carew Cheriton in Wales to escort another convoy and then during the month of September moved to Bircham Newton. Kemble and Port Reath. On October 1st 1941 the squadron flew out to Malta via Gibraltar, to give protection to a convoy. During his sector from Malta to Gibraltar, Ronnie was attacked by three Italian Macci 200's but managed to outrun them. When they arrived at Gibraltar the convoy had already left and were instructed to Fly on to Fayum, in Egypt via Idku (Idku was a landing ground on the northern coast of Africa).

On their arrival at Fayum the squadron were informed by the senior officer in Egypt that they were not needed only their aircraft. They returned to the UK by sea via Kaasferit, Durban, Capetown and New York. They spent four days in New York taking in some of the sights and on the 20th January departed the 'Big Apple' on board the first ship to take American troops for service in Britain. Ronnie rejoined 248 Squadron on the 1st February 1942 at Bircham Newton and on the 8th was promoted to Flying Officer. (February, March April and May saw the squadron alternate between Bircham Newton, Dyce, Wick, Sumburgh and Predannack airfields.)

Log extracts for April and May 1942:

April 1st	Beau (G)
	While escorting escaping Norwegian
	Ships, attacked and damaged a He111
	(probable).
April 6th	Beau (C)
	Escorted to Commandos St Nazaire
	(providing cover for a secret force
	attacking St Nazaire).

April 18th	Beau (G)
	Escort to home Fleet, the battleship King George 'V' HMS Victorious, one Cruiser and ten DRS.
April 21st	Beau (G)
	Recce to Bergen and Haugusund, Convoy found. Lots of flak.

At the end of April 1942 Ronnie had completed his first tour of operations with having carried out 89 sorties. On May 21st Ronnie was posted to the Central Flying School at Upavon where he was to complete an instructors course at No 7 Flying Instructors School on Oxfords. At the end of the four week course he was assessed as 'average' as an Instructor.

On completion of the instructors course he was posted to No 2(C) OTU at Catfoss where he instructed on Martinets, Blenheims and Beaufighters until the 28th July 1943. (Ronnie was promoted to Flight Lieutenant on the 8th January 1943.) His log entry for the 25th July 1943 shows that the Chief Instructor assessed his as 'above the average' as a Pilot Instructor and 'above the average' as an Air Gunnery Instructor. On the 28th July 1943 he was posted back onto an operations, joining 235 Squadron at Leuchars in Scotland.

Short history of 235 Squadron

The squadron was formed in August 1918 as a Royal Navy Coastal Station at Newlyn in Cornwall. The base was used for Short float planes and anti-submarine patrols. It was disbanded in February 1919 and reformed at Manston in October 1939 as a Fighter Squadron and was equipped with Fairey Battles and Blenheims. In December 1940 the squadron was re-equipped with Beaufighters and in June 1943 was re-equipped again with Mosquito's and became part of the anti-shipping Banff Strike Wing in Scotland. The squadron was disbanded in July 1945.

He spent all of August converting onto the rocket firing Beaufighters and on September 8th carried out his first operation with the squadron.

Log extracts for Sept, Oct, Nov and December 1943:

Sept 21st	Beau (B)
	Fighter patrol sighted six FW 190's.
Sept 8th	Beau (B)
	Fighter protection for ASR Halifax's.
Oct 2nd	Beau (B)
	A/A patrol with cruiser Bermuda.
	(The squadron was now carrying out anti-aircraft patrols in the Biscay area under the direction of HMS Bermuda.)

Oct 14th, 15th, 20th and 24th Fighter patrols.

Ronnie carried out his 100th operation with the squadron on the 10th December when he was on a fighter patrol of the Spanish coast. He attacked one JU88 and two fishing boats (three Spaniards were killed, they reported having been attacked by a Ju88).

Dec 24th	Beau (N)
	Shipping Recco, two blockade runners and eight destroyers found. The Sunderland which was shadowing them was shot down by accurate flak. Bill Moore was shot down 30 minutes before we reached scene whilst attacking HE177. Enemy destroyed by McCormack, Bills No 2.
Dec 28th	Beau (C)
	Fighter escort to two cruisers which had just sunk three German destroyers, three Narvik Class sighted fleeing for home.
Dec 31st	Beau (D)
	Compass U/S and lost, homed by Scillies who picked us up on RDF heading for Brest.

I found this note attached to Ronnie's logbook for December:

To:- All 19 Group Stations & Squadrons.

From 19 Group

Personal from AOC to Station and Squadron Commanders

As a result of operations during the first few days one valuable enemy blockade runner was sunk by an aircraft and two Narvik and one Elbing destroyers were sunk and others damaged by HM Ships. This highly successful operation largely made possible by the consistent accuracy of positions given in sighting reports, and the excellent procedure in shadowing and homing.

Well done all aircrews and maintenance personnel.

Signed OCG

The squadron moved to St Angelo near Enniskillen, County Fermanagh in Northern Ireland on the 27th January 1944.

Log Extract for the 16th February 1944:

| Feb 16th | Beau (D) |
| | One JU 290 destroyed. Homed in by HMS Biter, was vectored for 40 minutes before making contact. Fired 120 rounds at the Hun. (Lt Pape and Lt Bergman and eight crew were clueless (enemy crew). |

On the 14th April 1944 Ronnie was awarded a well earned Distinguished Flying Cross and, on the 15th received a Postagram from Air Officer Commanding 19 Group: "Heartiest congratulations from the AOC and all at No 19 Group on your award of the DFC."

| April 27th | Beau (D) |
| | Strike. (anti flak) against force in Lorient Channel. Only two trawlers and many fishing boats seen. |

His log also shows another entry for the 27th, "Intercepted off Concarneau by Spits. Scared Stiff."

The squadron started to convert to the Mosquito MkV1 during the middle of May 1944.

Ronnie received his first flight in the Mosquito on the 20th May with a Flying Officer Martlet at the controls. He flew the aircraft solo the next day along with Pilot Officer Ross, DFC.

D-Day 6th June 1944

Log extracts for June 1944: June 6th was to be Ronnie's 115 Sortie.

June 6th	Beau (L) Self & F/Off Ross DFC Fighter Patrol. Ushant- Ile De Sein. Six enemy ships and three minesweepers seen flak from shore & ships.
June 9th	Beau (L) Self & F/Off Ross DFC Fighter patrol. Ushant. Saw one Mosquito in distress. Escorted it to Predanack and resumed patrol. One Ju88 destroyed (60 rounds).

(The Ju88 was later confirmed as an Irish Zenith from Rennes. One body baled out, 'chute' did not open.)

June 15th	Beau (L) Self & F/Off Ross DFC Fighter patrol Ushant. Sighted one U/Boat periscope depth. (U-Boat had just sunk a frigate.)
June 16th	Mos (B3) Self & F/Off Ross DFC Cannon test. 'Clot' left Pitot Head cover on.
June 30th	Mos (D) Self & F/Off Ross DFC Strike of 21 Mosquitoes & 12 Beaus. Against four 'M' Class mine sweepers in Concarnau. Good prang.

(One Mosquito was lost during this strike [Pilot Officer Tonge] and two damaged. One 'M' Class mine sweeper sunk and 100 German casualties.)

Log extracts for July and August 1944:

July 9th	Mos (G) Self & F/Off Ross DFC Strike with 18 Mosquitoes. Anti-flak four TTA's damaged of St Nazaire. Inaccurate flak from shore batteries.

("Two ships later learnt sunk, four aircraft damaged, two returned on one engine and 'Baby' Nunn Belly landed for the 3rd time.")

The squadron's commanding officer Wing Commander JV Yonge shot down two Dornier 217's on July 21st.

Aug 12th	Mos (D) self & F/Sgt Hosier Strike at Gironde. Cancelled due to VHF 'D' caused force to return.
Aug 15th	Mos (M) self & W/Off Ganner Coastal Recco, Ushante-Gironde. Minesweeper in Benoet.

Aug 25th	Mos (H) self & F/Off Barber Armed Recco, Ushante-Gironde, 12 A/C 1 'M' Class minesweeper in Benodet. Leader decided not worth it.

On the 14th September 1944 the squadron moved north to Scotland where it joined the famous anti-shipping 'Banff Strike Wing' with 144 and 404 Squadrons. Their job was now to strike at anything that came out of Norway, anti-shipping and anti-submarine strikes. The 'Wing' consisted of Beaufighters of 144 and 404 Squadrons and Mosquitoes of 235 Squadron and a Strike Wing comprising 248 and 333 (Norwegian) Squadron. The Beaufighters moved to Dallachy in October 1944. The Wing was led by Group Captain Max Aitken and at one time his six squadron commanders were made up of an Englishman, an Australian, a New Zealander, a Norwegian, a Frenchman and an Irishman. (Such was the ferocity of the aircrew losses that four were killed on operations.)

Log extracts for September, Banff Strike Wing:

Sept 28th	Mos (A) Self & F/Off Ross DFC Strike at Stavanger-Kristiansand with 36 Aircraft. Target found. Not a gun fired.

Ronnie's 130 operation was on the 30th September with F/Lt Ross, DFC (just promoted) on an armed recco with 43 aircraft to Utero-Statlandet. Nothing seen and not a gun fired. On the 2nd October they received word that there was German shipping in Sogne Fjord, Leval and Statlandet. one MV of 2,000 ton, one TTP at Sogne Fjord, two TTA's at Laval and one Barge at Statlandet. "Strike Force arrived 1hr.40mins later but targets had flown." Ronnie's last operation of the war was his 132nd and also the completion of his second tour. He took off from Banff on October 10th with Flight Lieutenant Ross, DFC In Mosquito (K) and headed for a AV Sweep around Otero-Kristansand. 18 Aircraft took part and nothing was seen except some flak from Lister, Mandel and Kristansand. Ronnie added, "Much twitch, one hour on coast and Lister very cross." His last flight with the squadron was on the 17th October when he took part in a press-demonstration with Flying Officer Lowe.

On the 18th October 1944 the Squadron Commander Wing Commander JV Yonge wrote in Ronnie's logbook that he was "above the average' as a GR Pilot and 'above the average' as an Air Gunner.

On completion of his second tour, Ronnie was posted to the Station Headquarters at Banff. His duty there was to fly air and ground crews between Banff, Dallachy and Leuchars in an Oxford.

On the 24th October 1944 he was then posted south to the Station Headquarters at Langham were he became Operations Controller until the 4th December 1944. His only log entry for this posting was on November 18th when he flew in a Fleet Air Arm Baracuda with a Lt Clarke on a one hour local flight.

On the 4th December Ronnie was promoted to Squadron Leader and posted to the Station Headquarters at Ballykelly in Northern Ireland again as Operations Controller flying around in Oxfords until the beginning of February 1945. His last flight with Royal Air Force as Captain was on the 24th January 1945 in an Oxford, his No 2 was a Flight Lieutenant Irvine, DFC (flying time 2hrs.05mins). On the 6th February 1945 he was posted overseas to Air Headquarters in Freetown West Africa as Operations Controller where he spent the next three months. During the 1st week in May he was again on the move and was to be his last posting, this time as Officer Commanding RAF Port Etienne in Mauratania. The posting at Port Etienne was completed on the 11th November 1945 and he was finally released from the Royal Air Force on the 5th December 1945. Ronnie returned to his previous employer Avery's where he remained until his retirement in 1982.

I had the pleasure and honour to meet Ronnie and his lovely wife a few years before he died. They both made me extremely welcome and during my visit he came down stairs wearing his war-time RAF uniform, still fitting him like the day he was measured for it.

Sadly Ronnie died on the 18th August 1997.

A summary of his operations from August 1940 until October 1944

Total sorties on 1st tour	89
Total hours on 1st tour	307hrs.40mins
Total sorties on 2nd tour	43
Total hours on 2nd tour	197.00hrs
Total sorties	132
Total operational hours	504hrs.40mins
Total logged flying hours	1251hrs.45mins

Types of aircraft flown during his RAF career:.

Tiger Moth
Hawker Hart, Hind and Audax
Bristol Blenheim Mk1 and 1V
Bisley
Oxford
Beaufighter Mk1 and V1
Martinet
Spitfire
Beaufort
Mosquito Mk V1

Awards:

The Distinguished Flying Cross
The Air Efficiency Award

FLIGHT SERGEANT
WILLIAM LEWIS JOHNSTON YOUNG
ROYAL AIR FORCE NO. 1058075
BOMBER PILOT
NO. 106 SQUADRON

William Lewis Johnston Young was born in Blacksessiagh in Omagh, County Tyrone, on the 13th July 1918 and was baptised on 16th October 1918 at Ballynahatty by the Rev George Browne. He was educated at Ballynahatty Presbyterian Church School and the Masonic Boy's School in Dublin where he played cricket for the Leinster Boys Cricket Team.

His advanced education was carried out Lurgan College where he excelled in Rugby playing for the 1st XV, finally joining Queens University Belfast where he received his Degree in Applied Science and Technology in 1937.

William joined the Royal Air Force in Clifton Street on the 6th July 1940 and became AC 2 WLJ Young. On the 26th October he was promoted to LAC and posted to No 10 Elementary Flying Training School at Weston Super Mare to commence his elementary flying. His first 35 minute air experience flight was on October 28th 1940 in a Tiger Moth (N6788) under the instruction of Flying Officer Weston. He went solo on the 1st December after 12hrs.30mins tuition. He successfully completed the course on the 10th January 1941 with an assessment of 'above the average' after flying 20 hours solo.

Cadet Young's next posting was to No 2 Service Flying Training School (FTS) at Brize Norton where he was to train on the Twin Engined Airspeed Oxford. His first flight in the Oxford was on the 17th January 1941 under the instruction of Flying Officer Filleul. William flew the Oxford solo on the 14th February and continued his training until the 6th May 1941 when he was awarded his Wings and promoted to Sergeant. The schools Commanding Officer Wing Commander Larkin gave William an assessment of 'below the average' and added that he was slow to learn but tries hard. (I doubt the CO must have got out of the wrong side of the bed that morning). On completion of his flying training William was posted to the No 2 School of Navigation on the 5th May where he completed a five week Advanced Navigation Course.

His next posting was to No 14 Operational Training Unit (OTU) at Cottesmore where he was to commence operational training on Avro Ansons and Handley Page Hampdens. His first flight in the Hampden was on the 9th August with Flying Officer Petty and went solo the next day. Most of William's training on the Hampden consisted of high and low level bombing and air firing. He also received instruction on how to abandon the Hampden and know how to use the dinghy. He had by now completed 209hrs.30mins flying training. He finished his OTU training on the 17th September with an assessment of 'average' as a Medium Bomber Pilot, 'above the average' in Bombing and 'average' in Air Gunnery. Having completed all his basic, elementary and operational training Sergeant William Young was posted to his first operational squadron. This was 106 (B) Squadron which was based at RAF Conningsby.

Short history of 106 (B) Squadron

The squadron was formed initially at Andover in Hampshire in September 1917 and from May onwards served in Ireland as an Army co-operation unit. It was disbanded in 1919 and reformed in June 1938 as a bomber squadron. At the outbreak of the Second World War the squadron was equipped with the Handley Page Hampdens. It soon re-equipped with the Manchester's and in the summer of 1942 it converted to the Avro Lancaster and took part in the 1,000 bomber raids on Cologne, Essen and Bremen. Wing Commander Guy Penrose Gibson was the squadron's Commanding Officer at that time. The squadron also took part in the first 'Shuttle Bombing' raids on Friedrichshafen and

Spezia and in 1944 bombed the coastal gun battery at St Pierre and the V-1 storage sites at St Leu d'Esserent. In 1945 it took part in the Rhine crossing and in April 1945 carried out its last operation, which was to bomb the oil refinery at Vallo in Norway. During the war the squadron carried out nearly 6,000 sorties and dropped almost 18,000 tons of bombs and mines. The squadron was disbanded in February 1946. A Victoria Cross was awarded to Sergeant NC Jackson for conspicuous bravery during an attack on Schweinfurt on the 26th/27th April 1944.

William joined 106 Squadron at Conningsby towards the end of September 1941 and had his first flight with the squadron on the 30th September in a Hampden (AE317). This was a night flying exercise with Sergeant Davies and Sergeant Hunter.

On October 10th he carried out his first operation with Sergeant Davies and Hunter, which was to bomb the Krupps Works at Essen in Hampden (AE317). The flight time was 7hrs.10mins.

Other log entries 1941

Oct 12th	Hampden (AE317) Operation to bomb a Chemical factory at Huls 6hrs.00mins.
Oct 20th	Hampden (AD785) Operation to bomb the city of Bremen 8hrs.40 mins.
Oct 23rd	Hampden (P4329) Operation to bomb the Deutsche Werke U-Boat yard and Naval base at Kiel 7hrs.10mins.
Oct 26th	Hampden (P4323) Operation to bomb the city of Hamburg. 8hrs.30mins.
Oct 31st	Hampden (P4323) Operation to bomb the city of Hamburg. 8hrs.20mins.
Nov 4th	Hampden (AD749) Operation to bomb Keil Harbour. 7hrs.20mins.
Nov 7th	Hampden (P4323) Operation mine laying near Oslo. 6hrs.10mins.

The next month was spent carrying out crew training:

Dec 23rd	Hampden (AT123) Opertation mine laying in the Frisians. 7hrs.10mins.
Dec 28th	Hampden (AT123) Operation to bomb the chemical works at Huls. 7hrs.

1942

Jan 9th	Hampden (AE261) Operation to Bomb Brest. 6hrs.
Jan 15th	Hampden (AE186) Operation to the city of Hamburg. 7hrs.20mins.
Feb. 11th	Hampden (AE186) Operation to bomb the city of Mannheim. 7hrs.40mins
Feb 27th	Hampden (AT190) Operation to bomb the Floating Dock in Keil Harbour. A direct hit was seen hitting the bows of the Gneisenau rendering it useless for the end of the war.
Mar 3rd	Hampden (AD749) Operation to bomb the Renault Factory in the town of Boulogne-Billancourt just west of the centre of Paris. 5hrs.15mins
Mar 9th	Hampden (AT191) Operation to bomb the city of Essen. 6hrs. Last op in a Hampden.

The squadron was now being re-equipped with the new Avro Manchester and for the next month William and his crew spent all their spare time training on the new aircraft.

William's first operation on the Manchester:

April 13th	Manchester (7643) Operation to bomb Essen. 5hrs.20mins.
April 15th	Manchester (7463) Operation to bomb Dortmund. 6hrs.30mins.
April 22nd	Manchester (7348) Operation ?????????. 6hrs.
April 25th	Manchester (7376) Operation to bomb the Heinkel Factory at Rostock.
April 26th	Manchester (7398) Operation to bomb Rostock. 8hrs.10mins
April 28th	Manchester (7498) Operation (possibly Cologne or Kiel). 7hrs.45mins.

Flight Sergeant WLJ Young missing presumed dead

On the night of the 2nd/3rd May William took off in his Manchester to lay mines in Kiel bay and failed to return. It is now known that his aircraft (L7399) ZN-XXP came down in a field at Lilholdt near Skrydstrup in Norway. Five of the crew were killed including, Flight Sergeant WLJ Young, Sergeants Graham Wale, AC Bryce, H MaClean and RG Davies. All of who are buried in a collective grave in Aabenraa Cemetery Denmark. There were two survivors, Sergeant Hanks and Sergeant Kendall. Flight Sergeant Young had completed a total of 464 flying hours inTigermoth, Oxford, Avro Anson, Handley Page Hampdens and the Avro Manchester. On the 6th May 1942 a letter arrived at William's home, it was addressed to his mother who was married to a Captain Rev WL Cochrane of Waringstown.

No 106 Squadron
Royal Air Force
Conningsby
6th May 1942

Dear Mrs Cochrane

I am writing to express my sympathy in the anxiety you must be feeling on receiving the news that your son is missing.

He was captain of an aircraft, which left here on the night 2nd/3rd May 1942 to lay mines in enemy waters, and I regret that he did not return. No messages were received from the aircraft after leaving here, and we are, therefore, entirely without knowledge as to what happened, and we can but hope that the aircraft force landed, or that the crew baled out and are quite safe although prisoners of war.

Any news of the crew will come from the International Red Cross Society, who will immediately inform the Air Ministry, but a letter to the following address would, I am sure, meet with sympathetic assistance:- Wounded, Missing and Relatives, Dept., British Red Cross Society, 7 Belgrave Sq, London, SWW 1.

Your son had served with my Squadron for eight months, and had won for himself a reputation as first class pilot. He had taken part in 22 raids on enemy territory performing his difficult and dangerous duties with the greatest skill and courage. I thought very highly of him, and had in fact recently strongly recommended him for a commission. He was extremely popular with the flying colleagues and ground crews, and we are all sorry at his loss. Personal effects will be forwarded to the Central Depository, Colnbrook, by whom they cannot be released until compliance with the regulations required by the Regimental Debts Act. Regarding this, the Committee will communicate with you direct.

Once, again, both personally and on behalf of the Squadron, I offer my very sincere deep sympathy and hope that soon there will be good news.

Signed
Wing Commander, Commanding
No 106 Squadron
Royal Air Force
Wing Commander Guy Penrose Gibson

William's mother was a very quiet person and, this was not the first or the last tragedy to befall her. She had lost her brother at Dunkirk. Her husband Lyons, was a Padre in the Black Watch, her eldest son, John, in the North Irish Horse (Tanks), her second son William, a Pilot in the RAF and her daughter, Esther, in the Womens Volunteer Service in London - and this a country without conscription.

The 'saga' of Flight Sergeant Youngs logbook

Approximately ten years ago I was given a logbook by my very good friend Jack Woods who had received it from a young boy whose father was a builder. His father had been renovating an old house in the seaside town of Bangor, County Down and had just demolished an old meter box cupboard in one of the rooms. He noticed some old newspapers lying at the bottom of the cupboard, he lifted them and dumped them into a skip outside. Luckily just as he threw them into the skip, a book fell out of the middle of the newspapers onto the footpath and he noticed the words Royal Air Force written on it. The father brought it home and gave it to his son. The young lad did not have clue what it was and gave it to Jack to give to someone who would be interested in it. I, being an aviation historian knew right away what it was and decided to do some research and try and find the family. I put advertisements in various newspapers but without success. My next step was to write to the 106 Squadron Association and ask if they had any knowledge of Flight Sergeant WLJ Young or his family. They were most helpful over the next few weeks with information regarding Flight Sergeant Young but no leads to his family. Then, bingo, out of the blue, the secretary found a letter from F/Sgt Youngs nephew who had written to the association regarding his uncle years ago.

I now had a contact name and address to write to. I wrote to his nephew Bill (JWO Young who lives in Midhurst West Sussex) and told him the tale regarding the logbook and that I would like to return it to the family. Bill wrote back and told me that his father, Flight Sergeant Young's brother was still living in Belfast and that he would fly over and meet me at the earliest convenience. This he did and we all met in his father's house where I was delighted to hand over the logbook to Mr Young (Senior). I found this to be a very emotional time for Mr Young as he was very close to his brother.

A few weeks later I was asked back to the Young's house and when I arrived, Mr Young Senior handed me his brother's logbook and said, "John you are a very honest fellow, the family and I have decided to let you keep the logbook and find a good home for it in the future."

I must be honest and say, I left that house a little tearful but a very proud man. I decided in April 2003 that I would donate Flight Sergeant Youngs flying logbook to the 106 Squadron Association's Museum at Metheringham Airfield in Lincoln.